C000268731

Goodword ENGLISH-ARABIC Dictionary

Goodword ENGLISH-ARABIC Dictionary

Mohd Harun Rashid

GOODWORD

First published 2006
Reprinted 2011

Goodword Books
1, Nizamuddin West Market, New Delhi-110 013
email: info@goodwordbooks.com
Printed in India

see our complete catalogue at
www.goodwordbooks.com
www.goodword.net

Introduction

This English-Arabic dictionary, containing more than twenty thousand words and phrases, has been prepared with a view to fulfilling the needs of students and research workers in the field of Arabic language and literature.

In order to reduce the dictionary to a convenient size, all Arabic words and phrases have been given in their most condensed forms and all slang and obsolete words have been discarded. Foreign words have been given in both their Arabicized and non-Arabicized forms and English words are repeated in several places to indicate their usage as different parts of speech, e.g., noun, verb, adjective, adverb, etc.. For instance, the word 'tone' means لهجة or نغمة when it occurs as a noun in the sentence, but when it occurs as a verb, it has the meaning of نغم or تناغم. The noun has thus been distinguished from the verb, etc., so as to prevent users of the dictionary from making mistakes which could arise from the transliteration pattern. In many places, however, we have not repeated the word, but have used commas to distinguish the verbal meaning from the nominal, adjectival or adverbial.

Vowel signs, which are not in use in English, do however play an important role in the pronunciation of Arabic words. Without them, it is very difficult for a foreign learner, particularly a beginner, to pronounce words correctly. Keeping this fact in view, we have done our best to indicate the pronunciation of Arabic words with the help of an excellent system of transliteration based on principles laid down by Abdullah Yusuf Ali, a reputed translator of the Quran into English. Wherever possible, the transliteration pattern corresponds with the international system of phonetics, so that it may be easily understood.

All these features make this dictionary one of the most useful and reliable works of reference for learners and we hope it will meet the needs of all those who have been in quest of just such a dictionary.

The following are the transliteration symbols:

ā, ī, ū: the short line above these letters denote prolongation as in ناصر (nāṣir) نصير (naṣīr) and منصور (manṣūr).

’ A quotation mark above the letter indicates hamza (ء).

‘ A quotation mark above the letter indicates ‘ain (ع) which is a strong guttural sound.

ḍ for ض (ḍad). It is an emphatically palatal d.

dh for ذ (dhāl). It is like d with a slight difference. It is voiced interdental fricative, as th in this.

gh for غ (ghain). It is pronounced as a guttural g.

ḥ for ح (ḥā). It is a guttural h.

kh for خ (khā). It is an emphatic sound of کھ.

ṣ for ص (ṣād). It is pronounced as a strong s.

sh for ش (shīn) as in shoe in English.

ṭ for ط (ṭā). It is strongly articulated palatal t.

th for ث (thā) as in thin.

ẓ for ظ (ẓā). It is an emphatic sound of z.

Abbreviation and other symbols used in the dictionary:

abbr	abbreviation
artic	article
adj	adjective
adv	adverb
aux v	auxiliary verb
conj	conjunction
eg	for example
etc	et cetera
interj	interjection
pl	plural
prep	preposition
pron	pronoun
sing	singular
v	verb

New Delhi

Oct. 2005

Mohd. Harun Rashid

A

a (artic)	واحد، حرف تنكير	*wāḥid, ḥarfu tankīr*
aback (adv)	إلى الخلف،إلى الوراء	*ilal khalf, ilal warā'*
abandon (v)	هجر، تخلى	*hajara, takhallā*
abandoned (adj)	مهجور، متروك	*mahjūr, matrūk*
abandonment (n)	هجر، تخلٍّ	*hajr , takhallin*
abase (v)	أذل، أخزى	*adhalla, akhzā*
abasement (n)	ذلة، تحقير	*dhillah, taḥqīr*
abash (v)	أخجل، أخزى	*akhjala, akhzā*
abashed (adj)	مخجول	*makhjūl*
abate (v)	خفض، ضعف	*khaffaḍa, ḍa'ufa*
abatement (n)	تخفيض، خمود	*takhfīḍ, khumūd*
abbreviate (v)	اختصر، أوجز	*ikhtaṣara, aujaza*
abbreviated (adj)	مختصر، موجز	*mukhtaṣar, mūjaz*
abbreviation (n)	اختصار، إيجاز	*ikhtiṣār, ījāz*
abdicate (v)	تنازل عن، تخلى عن	*tanāzala 'an, takhallā 'an*
abdication (n)	اعتزال، تنازل	*i'tizāl, tanāzul*
abdomen (n)	بطن، جوف	*baṭn, jauf*
abdominal (adj)	بطني	*baṭnī*
abduct (v)	اختطف، خطف	*ikhtaṭafa, khaṭafa*
abduction (n)	خطف، اختطاف	*khaṭf, ikhtiṭāf*
abductor (n)	مختطف، خاطف	*mukhtaṭif, khāṭif*
abed (adj)	في الفراش	*fil firāsh*
abhor (v)	اشمئز، مقت	*ishma'azza, maqata*
abhorrence (n)	اشمئزاز، كره	*ishmi'zāz, kurh*
abhorrent (adj)	مشمئز، ماقت	*mushma'izz, māqit*
abide (v)	بقي	*baqiya*

abiding (adj)	باقٍ، دائم	*bāqin, dā'im*
ability (n)	مقدرة، موهبة	*maqdarah, mauhabah*
abject (adj)	مقنط، دنيء، خسيس	*muqniṭ, danī', khasīs*
ablaze (adj)	متوهج، ملتهب	*mutawahhij, multahib*
able (adj)	قابل، قادر	*qābil, qādir*
abloom (adj)	مزهر	*muzhir*
ablutions (n)	وضوء، غسل	*wuḍū', ghasl*
ably (adv)	بمقدرة، ببراعة	*bi maqdarah, bi barā'ah*
abnegation (n)	إنكار النفس	*inkārun nafs*
abnormal (adj)	غير سوي، غير طبيعي	*ghair sawī, ghair ṭabī'ī*
abnormality (n)	شذوذ، شيء شاذ	*shudhūdh, shay' shādhdh*
aboard (adv)	في القطار أو الطائرة	*fil qiṭār awiṭ ṭā'irah*
abode (n)	مسكن، مقر	*maskan, maqarr*
abolish (v)	أبطل، ألغى	*abṭala, alghā*
abolition (n)	إبطال، إلغاء	*ibṭāl, ilghā'*
abominable (adj)	بغيض، شنيع	*baghīḍ, shanī'*
abominate (v)	أبغض، كره	*abghaḍa, kariha*
abomination (n)	بغض شديد، كره	*bughḍ shadīd, kurh*
abort (v)	أجهض، أسقط	*ajhaḍa, asqaṭa*
abortion (n)	إسقاط، إجهاض	*isqāṭ, ijhāḍ*
abortive (adj)	عقيم،خائب	*'aqīm, khā'ib*
abound (v)	غزر، وفر	*ghazura, wafara*
about (adv)	حول، نحو	*ḥaula, naḥwa*
about (prep)	عن	*'an*
above (adv)	فوق، آنفا	*fauqa, ānifā*
above (adj)	سابق، متقدم	*sābiq, mutaqaddim*
above (prep)	فوق، وراء	*fauqa, warā'a*
above-mentioned(adj)	مذكور آنفا	*madhkur ānifā*

abrasive (adj)	كاشط، ساحج	*kāshiṭ, sāḥij*
abreast (adv)	جنبا إلى جنب	*jamban ilā jambin*
abridge (v)	اختصر، قصر	*ikhtaṣara, qaṣṣara*
abridged (adj)	مختصر، موجز	*mukhtaṣar, mūjaz*
abridgment, -gement	اختصار، خلاصة	*ikhtiṣār, khulāṣah*
abroad (adv)	خارج البيت	*khārijal bait*
abrogate (v)	أبطل، ألغى	*abṭala, alghā*
abrogation (n)	إلغاء، إبطال	*ilghā', ibṭāl*
abrupt (adj)	مفاجىء، غير متوقع	*mufāji', ghair mutawaqqa'*
abruptly (adv)	فجاءةً، بغتةً	*fujā'atan, baghtatan*
abruptness (n)	فجاءة، فظاظة	*fujā'ah, faẓāẓah*
abscond (v)	فر، توارى	*farra, tawārā*
absence (n)	غياب، انعدام	*ghiyāb, in'idām*
absent (adj)	غائب، غير موجود	*ghā'ib, ghair maujūd*
absentee (n)	غائب، متغيب	*ghā'ib, mutaghayyib*
absent-minded (adj)	ذاهل، غافل	*dhāhil, ghāfil*
absolute (adj)	مطلق، ثابت، كلي	*muṭlaq, thābit, kullī*
absolutely (adv)	مطلقاً، حتماً	*mutalaqan, ḥatman*
absolution (n)	غفران، تبرئة	*ghufrān, tabri'ah*
absolutism (n)	استبداد، حكم مطلق	*istibdād, ḥukm muṭlaq*
absolve (v)	غفر، سامح	*ghafara, sāmaḥa*
absorb (v)	امتص، استغرق	*imtaṣṣa, istaghraqa*
absorbed (adj)	ممتص، مستغرق	*mumtaṣṣ, mustaghriq*
absorbing (adj)	مستغرق، ممتع	*mustaghriq, mumti'*
absorption (n)	استغراق، امتصاص	*istighrāq, imtiṣāṣ*
absorptive (adj)	ممتص	*mumtaṣṣ*
abstain (v)	أمسك، امتنع	*amsaka, imtana'a*
abstention (n)	إمساك، انقطاع	*imsāk, inqiṭā'*

abstinence (n)	امتناع، إمساك	*imtinā', imsāk*
abstruct (v)	لخص، جرد	*lakhkhaṣa, jarrada*
abstruct (n)	خلاصة، تجريد	*khulāṣah, tajrīd*
abstruct (adj)	تجريدي، عويص	*tajrīdī, 'awīṣ*
abstructed (adj)	ذاهل، شارد العقل	*dhāhil, shāridul 'aql*
abstruction (n)	تعبير تجريدي	*ta'bīr tajrīdī*
abstruse (adj)	مبهم، غير واضح	*mubham, ghair wāḍiḥ*
absurd (adj)	سخيف، مضحك	*sakhīf, muḍḥik*
absurdity (n)	سخف، بطلان	*sukhf, buṭlān*
absurdly (adv)	بكيفية سخيفة	*bi kaifiyyah sakhīfah*
abundance (n)	غزارة، وفرة	*ghazārah, wafrah*
abundant (adj)	غزير، وافر	*ghazīr, wāfir*
abundantly (adv)	بوفرة، بغزارة	*bi wafrah, bi ghazārah*
abuse (v)	أساء استعمال شيء	*asā'a istimāl shay'*
abuse (n)	شتم، إساءة استعمال	*shatm, isā'atu isti'māl*
abusive (adj)	مؤذٍ، فاسد، فاضح	*mu'dhin, fāsid, fāḍiḥ*
academic (adj)	أكاديمي	*akādīmī*
academy (n)	أكاديميا، مجمع علماء	*akādīmā, majma'u 'ulamā*
accede (v)	وافق، تبوأ	*wāfaqa, tabawwa'a*
accelerate (v)	عجل، سرع	*'ajjala, sarra'a*
acceleration (n)	تعجيل، تسريع	*ta'jīl, tasrī'*
accelerator (n)	مسرّع، معجل	*musarri', mu'ajjil*
accent (n)	نبرة الصوت	*nabratuṣ ṣaut*
accept (v)	اقتنع، قبل	*iqtana'a, qabila*
acceptable (adj)	مقبول، مرضٍ	*maqbūl, murḍin*
acceptance (n)	قبول، تسليم	*qabūl, taslīm*
accepted (adj)	مقبول	*maqbūl*
access (n)	وصول،وسيلة الوصول	*wuṣūl, wasīlatul wuṣūl*

accessibility (n)	سهولة الحصول	*suhūlatul ḥuṣūl*
accessible (adj)	ممكن الوصول	*mumkinul wuṣūl*
accession (n)	وصول، بلوغ، زيادة	*wuṣūl, bulūgh, ziyādah*
accessory (adj)	إضافي، ثانوي	*iḍāfī, thānawī*
accident (n)	حادث، عرض	*ḥādith, 'araḍ*
accidental (adj)	اتفاقي، عرضي	*ittifāqī, 'araḍī*
accidentally (adv)	مصادفةً، عرضاً	*muṣādafatan, 'araḍan*
acclaim (v)	هلل، هتف	*hallala, hatafa*
acclaim (n)	هتاف الاستحسان	*hutāful istiḥsān*
acclamation (n)	هتاف، تهليل	*hutāf, tahlīl*
accommodate (v)	زوّد، كيّف	*zawwada, kayyafa*
accomodation (n)	مسكن، مقر	*maskan, maqarr*
accommodations (n)	لوازم المعيشة	*lawāzimul ma'īshah*
accompaniment (n)	مصاحبة، مرافقة	*muṣāḥabah, murāfaqah*
accompany (v)	صاحب، رافق	*ṣāḥaba, rāfaqa*
accomplice (n)	شريك في جناية	*sharīk fī jināyah*
accomplish (v)	أتم، أنجز	*atamma, anjaza*
accomplished (adj)	بارع، مصقول	*bāri', maṣqūl*
accomplishment (n)	إتمام، نيل	*itmām, nail*
accord (n)	صلح، اتفاق	*ṣulḥ, ittifāq*
accord (v)	لاءم، اتفق	*lā'ama, ittafaqa*
accordance (n)	مطابقة، موافقة	*muṭābaqah, muwāfaqah*
accordingly (adv)	وفقا لذلك	*wafqan li dhālik*
according to (prep)	وفقاً لـ، طبقاً لـ	*wafqan li, ṭibqan li*
account (n)	محاسبة، حساب	*muḥāsabah, ḥisāb*
account (v)	حاسب، أحصى	*ḥāsaba , aḥṣā*
accountable (adj)	مسؤول، محاسب	*mas'ūl, muḥāsab*

accountancy (n)	علم المحاسبة، محاسبة	*'ilmul muḥāsabah, muḥāsabah*
accountant (n)	محاسب،كاتب حسابات	*muḥāsib, kātibu ḥisābāt*
account book (n)	دفتر حساب	*daftaru ḥisāb*
accumulate (v)	تراكم، تجمع	*tarākama, tajamma'a*
accumulation (n)	تراكم، تكدس	*tarākum, takaddus*
accuracy (n)	صحة ، دقة	*ṣiḥḥah, diqqah*
accurate (adj)	صحيح، مضبوط	*ṣaḥīḥ, maḍbūṭ*
accurately (adv)	بدقة، بالضبط	*bi diqqah, biḍ ḍabṭ*
accursed (adj)	ملعون، لعين	*mal'ūn, la'īn*
accusation (n)	اتهام، تهمة	*ittihām, tuhmah*
accusatory (adj)	اتهامي	*ittihāmī*
accuse (v)	اتهم ، ادعى	*ittahama, idda'ā*
accused (adj)	متهم، مدعى عليه	*muttaham, mudda'ā 'alaih*
accustom (v)	عوّد، مرن	*'awwada, marrana*
accustomed (adj)	معتاد، متعود	*mu'tād, muta'awwid*
ache (n)	وجع، ألم	*waj', alam*
ache (v)	وجع، آلم	*waja'a, ālama*
achieve (v)	أحرز، أنجز	*aḥraza, anjaza*
achievement (n)	إحراز، إنجاز	*iḥrāz, injāz*
acid (n/adj)	حمض ، حامض	*ḥamḍ, ḥāmiḍ*
acidic (adj)	حامض، حمضي	*ḥāmiḍ, ḥamḍī*
acidify (v)	حمّض، حمض	*ḥammaḍa, ḥamuḍa*
acidity (n)	حمضيّة، حموضة	*ḥamḍiyyah, ḥumūḍah*
acid test (n)	امتحان حاسم	*imtiḥān ḥāsim*
acidulous (adj)	قليل الحموضة، مز	*qalīlul ḥumūḍah, muzz*
acknowledge (v)	اعترف، سلم	*i'tarafa, sallama*

acknowledged (adj)	معترف به	*mu'taraf bih*
acknowledgement (n)	اعتراف، تشكر	*i'tirāf, tashakkur*
acme (n)	ذروة ، رأس	*dhirwah, ra's*
acquaint (v)	أطلع، أخبر	*aṭla'a, akhbara*
acquaintance (n)	اطلاع، معرفة	*iṭṭilā', ma'rifah*
acquainted (adj)	مطّلع، عالم به	*muṭṭali', 'ālim bih*
acquiescence (n)	قبول، إذعان	*qabūl, idh'ān*
acquire (v)	أحرز، اكتسب	*aḥraza, iktasaba*
acquired (adj)	مكتسب، مقتبس	*muktasab, muqtabas*
acquisition (n)	اكتساب، إحراز	*iktisāb, iḥrāz*
acquisitive (adj)	مولع بالاكتساب، اكتسابي	*mūla' bil iktisāb, iktisābī*
acquit (v)	برأ، أحل	*barra'a, aḥalla*
acquittal (n)	تبرئة، إطلاق، براءة	*tabri'ah, iṭlāq, barā'ah*
acre (n)	أكر، مقياس للمساحة	*akar, miqyās lil masāḥah*
acrimonious (adj)	لاذع، قاسٍ	*lādhi', qāsin*
acrimony (n)	حدة، حرافة	*ḥiddah, ḥarāfah*
acrobat (n)	بهلوان	*bahlawān*
acrobatic (adj)	بهلواني	*bahlawānī*
acrobatics (n)	حركات بهلوانية	*ḥarakāt bahlawāniyyah*
across (adv/prep)	عبر، على	*'abra, 'alā*
act (v)	عمل، مثل	*'amila, maththala*
act (n)	عمل، تمثيل	*'amal, tamthīl*
acting (n)	فن التمثيل المسرحي	*fannut tamthīl al masraḥī*
action (n)	عمل، فعل، سلسلة الأحداث	*'amal, fi'l, silsilatul aḥdāth*
activate (v)	نشّط، أعدّ	*nashshaṭa, a'adda*
activation (n)	تنشيط ، تحريض	*tanshīṭ, taḥrīḍ*

active (adj)	نشيط، فعلي، فعال	*nashīṭ, fi'lī, fa''āl*
actively (adv)	بنشاط، بهمة	*bi nashāṭ, bi himmah*
activity (n)	نشاط، كد، فعالية	*nashāṭ, kadd, fa''āliyyah*
actor (n)	فاعل، ممثل	*fā'il, mumaththil*
actress (n)	فاعلة، ممثلة	*fā'ilah, mumaththilah*
actual (adj)	واقعي، فعلي، حقيقي	*wāqi'ī, fi'lī, ḥaqīqī*
actuality (n)	حقيقة، أمر واقع	*ḥaqīqah, amr wāqi'*
actualize (v)	حقق، تحقق	*ḥaqqaqa, taḥaqqaqa*
actually (adv)	في الواقع، في الحقيقة	*fil wāqi', fil ḥaqīqah*
actuate (v)	شغل، حرك	*shaghghala, ḥarraka*
acuity (n)	حدة، مضاء	*ḥiddah, maḍā'*
acumen (n)	فطنة، براعة	*fiṭnah, barā'ah*
acute (adj)	حاد، حاذق	*ḥādd, ḥādhiq*
acuteness (n)	حذق، حدة	*ḥidhq, ḥiddah*
adage (n)	مثل سائر	*mathal sā'ir*
adamant (adj)	قاسي القلب، صلب	*qāsiyul qalb, ṣulb*
adapt (v)	هايأ، تلاءم	*hāya'a, talā'ama*
adaptable (adj)	قابل للتهايؤ	*qābil lit tahāyu'*
adaptation (n)	مهايأة، تكيف	*muhāya'ah, takayyuf*
add (v)	أضاف، ضم	*aḍāfa, ḍamma*
addict (n)	منصب، مدمن	*munṣabb, mudmin*
addicted (adj)	مدمن، منعكف على	*mudmin, mun'akif 'alā*
addiction (n)	إدمان، انعكاف	*idmān, in'ikāf*
addition (n)	إضافة، زيادة	*iḍāfah, ziādah*
additional (adj)	إضافي، زائد	*iḍāfī, zā'id*
address (v)	خاطب، وجّه	*khāṭaba, wajjaha*
address (n)	عنوان، خطاب	*'unwān, khiṭāb*

addressee (n)	مرسل إليه، مخاطب	*mursal ilaih, mukhāṭab*
adept (adj)	خبير، ماهر، متضلع	*khabīr, māhir, mutaḍalli'*
adequacy (n)	كفاية، وفاء، سداد	*kifāyah, wafā', sadād*
adequate (adj)	كاف، واف، مطابق	*kāfin, wāfin, muṭābiq*
adequately (adv)	بكفاية، بسداد	*bi kifāyah, bi sadād*
adhere (v)	التصق، شايع	*iltaṣaqa, shāya'a*
adherence (n)	مشايعة، تماسك، التصاق	*mushāya'ah, tamāsuk, iltiṣāq*
adherent (n)	مشايع، نصير	*mushāyi', naṣīr*
adhesion (n)	التصاق، تماسك	*iltiṣāq, tamāsuk*
adhesive (adj)	دبق، لزج	*dabiq, lazij*
adhesive (n)	مادة دبقة	*māddah dabiqah*
adieu (interj)	وداعًا	*wadā'an*
adjacent (adj)	مجاور، متاخم	*mujāwir, mutākhim*
adjectival (adj)	نعتي ، وصفي	*na'tī, waṣfī*
adjective (n)	نعت ، وصف	*na't, waṣf*
adjoin (v)	جاور، حاذى	*jāwar, ḥādhā*
adjoining (adj)	مجاور، محاذٍ	*mujāwir, muḥādhin*
adjourn (v)	أجل، انفض	*ajjala, infaḍḍa*
adjournment (n)	تأجيل،انفضاض،إرجاء	*ta'jīl, infiḍāḍ, irjā'*
adjudge (v)	قضى، أصدر حكما	*qaḍā, aṣdara ḥukman*
adjunct (n)	ملحق، مضاف	*mulḥaq, muḍāf*
adjunction (n)	إلحاق، ضم	*ilḥāq, ḍamm*
adjure (v)	استحلف، ناشد	*istaḥlafa, nāshada*
adjust (v)	كيف، نظم، عدل	*kayyafa, naẓẓama, 'addala*
adjustable (adj)	ممكن تعديله	*mumkin ta'dīluh*
adjustment (n)	نظم، ضبط، توافق	*naẓm, ḍabṭ, tawāfuq*

admeasure (v)	قاس، حدد	*qāsa, ḥaddada*
admeasurement (n)	قياس، تحديد الحصة	*qiyās, taḥdīdul ḥiṣṣah*
administer (n)	دبر، أدار	*dabbara, adāra*
administration (n)	إدارة، حكومة	*idārah, ḥukūmah*
administrative (adj)	إداري، حكومي	*idārī, ḥukūmī*
administrator (n)	مدير، مدبر	*mudīr, mudabbir*
admirable (adj)	رائع، ممتاز، بديع	*rā'i', mumtāz, badī'*
admirably (adv)	بكيفية بديعة	*bi kaifiyyah badī'ah*
admiral (n)	أمير البحر	*amīrul baḥr*
admiration (n)	إعجاب، استحسان	*i'jāb, istiḥsān*
admire (v)	يُعجب بـــ، استحسن	*yu'jab bi, istaḥsana*
admissible (adj)	جدير بالقبول، مقبول	*jadīr bil qabūl, maqbūl*
admission (n)	قبول، تسليم	*qabūl, taslīm*
admit (v)	سلم، قبل	*sallama, qabila*
admittance (n)	دخول، قبول	*dukhūl, qabūl*
admitted (adj)	معترف به	*mu'taraf bih*
admonish (v)	ذكر، عاتب	*dhakkara, 'ātaba*
admonishment= admonition		
admonition (n)	تذكير، عتاب	*tadhkīr, 'itab*
adolescence (n)	مناهزة البلوغ، مراهقة	*munāhazatul bulūgh, murāhaqah*
adolescent (adj)	مراهق، يافع	*murāhiq, yāfi'*
adopt (v)	تبنى، اتخذ	*tabannā, ittakhadha*
adopted (adj)	متبنى	*mutabannā*
adoption (n)	تبنٍّ، اتخاذ	*tabannin, ittikhādh*
adorable (adj)	جدير بالتوقير	*jadīr bit tauqīr*
adoration (n)	توقير، افتنان، تكريم	*tauqīr, iftinān, takrīm*

adore (v)	هام، وقر	*hāma, waqqara*
adorn (v)	رصع، زين	*raṣṣa'a, zayyana*
adornment (n)	تزيين ، زينة	*tazyīn, zīnah*
adulation (n)	تمليق، مداهنة	*tamlīq, mudāhanah*
adult (n/adj)	بالغ، مراهق	*bāligh, murāhiq*
adulterate (v)	مذق، زغل، زيف	*madhaqa, zaghala, zayyafa*
adulteration (n)	مذق، غش	*madhq, ghishsh*
adulterer (n)	زاني، فاسق	*zānī, fāsiq*
adulteress (n)	زانية، عاهرة	*zāniyah, 'āhirah*
adulterous (n)	مختص بالزنا	*mukhtaṣṣ biz zinā*
adultery (n)	زنا، فسق	*zinā, fisq*
adulthood (n)	سن البلوغ، سن الرشد	*sinnul bulūgh, sinnur rushd*
advance (v)	قدّم، تقدّم	*qaddama, taqaddama*
advance (n)	تقدم، ترقٍّ	*taqaddum, taraqqin*
advanced (adj)	مقدم، متقدم	*muqaddam, mutaqaddim*
advancement (n)	تقدم، ترقية	*taqaddum, tarqiyah*
advantage (n)	فائدة، مصلحة	*fā'idah, maṣlaḥah*
advantageous (adj)	مفيد، ملائم	*mufīd, mulā'im*
advent (n)	ورود، مجيء، إتيان	*wurūd, majī', ityān*
adventure (n)	مغامرة، مخاطرة	*mughāmarah, mukhāṭarah*
adventurer (n)	مغامر، مجازف	*mughāmir, mujāzif*
adventuress (n)	مغامرة ، مخاطرة	*mughāmirah, mukhāṭirah*
adventurous (adj)	مغامر، خطر، مقحام	*mughāmir, khaṭir, miqḥām*
adverb (n)	ظرف	*ẓarf*

adverbial (adj)	ظرفي، تمييزي	*ẓarfī, tamyīzī*
adversary (n)	خصم، غريم	*khaṣm, gharīm*
adverse (adj)	معاكس، مناوئ	*mu'ākis, munāwi'*
adversity (n)	ضرّاء ، ضيقة	*ḍarrā', ḍīqah*
advertise (v)	أعلن، أعلم	*a'lana, a'lama*
advertisement (n)	إعلان، نشرة	*i'lān, nashrah*
advertiser (n)	معلن	*mu'lin*
advice (n)	نصيحة، إعلام	*naṣīḥah, i'lām*
advisable (adj)	مستصوب، ملائم	*mustaṣwab, mulā'im*
advise (v)	نصح، أوصى	*naṣaḥa, auṣā*
adviser (advisor) (n)	ناصح، مشير	*nāṣiḥ, mushīr*
advisory (adj)	استشاري ، شوري	*istishārī, shūrī*
advocacy (n)	دفاع، تأييد، محاماة	*difā', ta'yīd, muḥāmāt*
advocate (v)	دافع، أيد	*dāfa'a, ayyada*
advocate (n)	محامي، مؤيّد	*muḥāmī, mu'ayyid*
aegis (n)	حماية	*ḥimāyah*
aerial (adj)	هوائي، جوي	*hawā'ī, jawwī*
aerial (n)	هوائي، آرية	*hawā'ī, āryah*
aerodrome (n)	مطار	*maṭār*
aerogramme (n)	رسالة جوية	*risālah jawwiyyah*
Aeronautic, -al (adj)	مختص بالطيران	*mukhtaṣṣ biṭ ṭayarān*
aeroplane (n)	طائرة، طيارة	*ṭā'irah, ṭayyārah*
aesthete (esthete) (n)	محبّ الجمال	*muḥibbul jamāl*
aesthetic (adj)	جمالي، ذوقي	*jamālī, dhauqī*
afar (adv)	بعيدًا	*ba'īdan*
affable (adj)	أنيس، لطيف	*anīs, laṭīf*
affair (n)	أمر، شأن	*amr, sha'n*
affect (n)	عاطفة، شعور	*'āṭifah, shu'ūr*

affect (v)	أثر، أولع، تكلف	*aththara, aula'a, takallafa*
affectation (n)	تكلف، تظاهر	*takalluf, taẓāhur*
affected (adj)	متأثر، مصاب، متكلف	*muta'aththir, muṣāb, mutakallaf*
affecting (adj)	مؤثر، محرك العواطف	*mu'aththir, muḥarrikul 'awāṭif*
affection (n)	عاطفة، تأثير، حب	*'āṭifah, ta'thīr, ḥubb*
affectionate (adj)	حنون، ودود	*ḥanūn, wadūd*
affective (adj)	مؤثر، عاطفي	*mu'aththir, 'āṭifī*
affidavit (n)	شهادة بقسم	*shahādah bi qasam*
affiliate (v)	ضم، انضم	*ḍamma, inḍamma*
affiliated (adj)	منضم، مدمج	*munḍamm, mudmaj*
affiliation (n)	انضمام، إدماج	*inḍimām, idmāj*
affinity (n)	صلة، انجذاب، قرابة	*ṣilah, injidhāb, qarābah*
affirm (v)	أثبت، أكد	*athbata, akkada*
affirmation (n)	إثبات، توكيد	*ithbāt, taukīd*
affirmative (adj/n)	إيجابي ، إيجاب	*ījābī, ījāb*
affix (v)	ألحق، أضاف	*alḥaqa, aḍāfa*
affix (n)	ملحق، إضافة	*mulḥaq, iḍāfah*
afflict (v)	ابتلى ، آلم	*ibtalā, ālama*
affliction (n)	بلاء، ألم	*balā', alam*
affluence (n)	وفرة، غنىً، سعة	*wafrah, ghinān, sa'ah*
affluent (adj)	وافر، غني، غزير	*wāfir, ghanī, ghazīr*
afford (v)	تحمّل، استطاع	*taḥammala, istaṭā'a*
affordable (adj)	قابل للتحمل	*qābil lit taḥammul*
afforest (v)	شجّر	*shajjara*
afforestation (n)	تشجير	*tashjīr*
affray (n)	شجار، شغب	*shijār, shaghab*

affrong (v/n)	أهان، إهانة	*ahāna, ihānah*
afield (adv)	خارج الوطن	*khārijal waṭan*
aflame (adj)	مشتعل، ملتهب	*mushta'il, multahib*
afloat (adj)	طافٍ، شائع	*ṭāfin, shā'i'*
afraid (adj)	خائف، مرتعب	*khā'if, murta'ib*
afresh (adv)	من جديد	*min jadīd*
after (adv)	في ما بعد	*fī mā ba'd*
after (prep)	بعد، خلف	*ba'da, khalfa*
afterbirth (n)	مشيمة، حبل سري	*mashīmah, ḥabl surrī*
aftercare (n)	عناية	*'ināyah*
after-effect (n)	عقبول	*'uqbūl*
afterlife (n)	حياة بعد الموت	*ḥayāt ba'dal maut*
aftermath (n)	عقبول، نتيجة	*'uqbūl, natījah*
afternoon (n)	بعد الظهر	*ba'daẓ ẓuhr*
afterward (adv)	في ما بعد، بعد ذلك	*fī mā ba'd, ba'da dhālik*
afterworld (n)	آخرة	*ākhirah*
again (adv)	مرةً ثانيةً	*marratan thāniah*
against (prep)	تجاه، ضد	*tujāha, ḍidda*
age (n)	عمر، عصر	*'umr, 'aṣr*
age (v)	كبر، هرم	*kabura, harima*
aged (adj)	هرم، مسن	*harim, musinn*
ageless (adj)	دائم الشباب، أبدي	*dā'imush shabāb, abadī*
agency (n)	وكالة، مكتب تجاري	*wakālah, maktab tijārī*
agenda (n)	جدول أعمال	*jadwalu a'māl*
agent (n)	وكيل، عامل	*wakīl, 'āmil*
age-old (adj)	قديم جدا	*qadīm jiddā*
aggravate (v)	فاقم ، هول	*fāqama, hawwala*

aggravation (n)	مفاقمة، إثارة	*mufāqamah, ithārah*
aggregate (adj/n)	كلي، مجموع	*kullī, majmū'*
aggregate (v)	جمع، تجمع	*jamma'a, tajamma'a*
aggregation (n)	مجموعة	*majmū'ah*
aggression (n)	تعدٍّ، اعتداء	*ta'addin, i'tidā'*
aggressive (adj)	مناضل، اعتدائي	*munāḍil, i'tidā'ī*
aggressor (n)	معتدي، باغي	*mu'tadī, bāghī*
aggrieve (v)	أحزن، آلم	*aḥzana, ālama*
aggrieved (adj)	محزون، مضطهد	*maḥzūn, muḍṭahad*
agile (adj)	رشيق، سريع الحركة	*rashīq, sarī'ul ḥarakah*
agitate (v)	هيج، هزز	*hayyaja, hazzaza*
agitation (n)	إثارة، اهتياج	*ithārah, ihtiyāj*
agitator (n)	مهيج، مقلق	*muhayyij, muqliq*
aglow (adj)	متقد، متوهج	*muttaqid, mutawahhij*
ago (adv)	مذ، منذ	*mudh, mundhu*
agonize,-ise (v)	عذب، ألم	*'adhdhaba, allama*
agonized (adj)	في عذاب شديد	*fī 'adhāb shadīd*
agony (n)	ألم شديد، نزع	*alam shadīd, naz'*
agrarian (adj)	زراعي، حقلي	*zirā'ī, ḥaqlī*
agree (v)	وافق، اتفق	*wāfaqa, ittafaqa*
agreeable (adj)	مقبول، سار	*maqbūl, sārr*
agreed (adj)	متفق عليه	*muttafaq 'alaih*
agreement (n)	معاهدة، اتفاق	*mu'āhadah, ittifāq*
agricultural (adj)	زراعي	*zirā'ī*
agriculture (n)	زراعة، فلاحة	*zirā'ah, filāḥah*
aground (adj)	على الأرض	*'alal arḍ*
ah (interj)	آه	*āh*
ahead (adv)	إلى الأمام	*ilal amām*

aid (v)	عاون، ساعد	*'āwana, sā'ada*
aid (n)	عون، مساعدة	*'aun, musā'adah*
aide (n)	معاون	*mu'āwin*
ail (v)	أوجع، توجع	*auja'a, tawajja'a*
ailment (n)	مرض، قلق	*maraḍ, qalaq*
aim (v)	طمح، اعتزم	*ṭamaḥa, i'tazama*
aim (n)	مطمح،هدف،غرض	*maṭmaḥ, hadaf, gharaḍ*
aimless (adj)	بلا هدف	*bilā hadaf*
air (n)	هواء، جو، نغمة	*hawā', jaww, naghmah*
airbase (n)	قاعدة جوية	*qā'idah jawwiyyah*
airborne (adj)	منقول بالطائرة	*manqūl biṭ ṭā'irah*
air-brake (n)	مكبح هوائي	*mikbaḥ hawā'ī*
air-conditioned (adj)	مكيّف الهواء	*makayyaful hawā'*
air-conditioner (n)	مكيّف	*makayyif*
air-conditioning (n)	تكييف الهواء	*takyīful hawā'*
aircraft (n)	سفينة هواء، طائرة	*safīnatu hawā', ṭā'irah*
aircraft-carrier (n)	حاملة طائرات	*ḥāmilatu ṭā'irāt*
aircrew (n)	ركب جوي	*rakb jawwī*
airfield (n)	مهبط، مطار	*mahbiṭ, maṭār*
air force (n)	سلاح الطيران	*silāḥuṭ ṭayarān*
air hostess (n)	مضيفة هواء	*muḍīfatu hawā'*
airily (adv)	بابتهاج، بخفة	*bibtihāj, bi khiffah*
airiness (n)	ابتهاج، بشاشة	*ibtihāj, bashāshah*
air line (n)	خط جوي	*khaṭṭ jawwī*
airmail (n)	بريد جوي	*barīd jawwī*
airplane (n)	طائرة، طيارة	*ṭā'irah, ṭayyārah*
airport (n)	مطار	*maṭār*
air proof (n)	صامد للهواء	*ṣāmid lil hawā'*

airway (n)	خط جوي	*khaṭṭ jawwī*
airy (adj)	هوائي، جوي	*hawā'ī, jawwī*
akin (adj)	مماثل، مجانس	*mumāthil, mujānis*
alarm (v)	أنذر، نبه	*andhara, nabbaha*
alarm (n)	إنذار، ذعر	*indhār, dhu'r*
alarm clock	ساعة منبهة	*sā'ah munabbihah*
alarming (n)	منبه، مقلق	*munabbih, muqliq*
alas (interj)	واحسرتاه	*wāḥasratāh*
album (n)	ألبوم	*albūm*
alcohol (n)	كحول، روح الخمر	*kuḥūl, rūḥul khamr*
alcoholic (adj)	كحولي	*kuḥūlī*
alert (adj)	يقظ، نشيط	*yaqiẓ, nashīṭ*
alert (v)	نبه، حذر	*nabbaha, ḥadhdhara*
alien (adj/n)	أجنبي، مغاير	*ajnabī, mughāyir*
alienate (v)	حوّل، نفر	*ḥawwala, naffara*
alienation (n)	تحويل، تغريب	*taḥwīl, taghrīb*
alight (adj)	مشتعل، مضطرم	*mushta'il, muḍṭarim*
alight (v)	حط، انحط	*ḥaṭṭa, inḥaṭṭa*
align (v)	نظم، رصف	*naẓẓama, raṣafa*
alignment (n)	رصف، تخطيط	*raṣf, takhṭīṭ*
alike (adj)	متماثل، متشابه	*mutamāthil, mutashābih*
alive (adj)	حي، ناشط	*ḥayy, nāshiṭ*
all (adj/adv)	جميع، جميعًا	*jamī', jamī'an*
Allah (n)	الله	*allāh*
all-around (adj)	عام، شامل	*'āmm, shāmil*
allegation (n)	ادعاء، زعم	*iddi'ā', za'am*
allege (v)	ادعى، زعم	*idda'ā, za'ama*
alleged (adj)	مزعوم	*maz'ūm*

allegiance (n)	ولاء، وفاء	*walā', wafā'*
allegory (n)	استعارة، مجاز	*isti'ārah, majāz*
allergy (n)	تجاوب	*tajāwub*
alliance (n)	اتحاد، حلف	*ittiḥad, ḥilf*
allied (adj)	متحد، متحالف	*muttaḥid, mutaḥālif*
allocate (v)	وزع، حصص	*wazza'a, ḥaṣṣaṣa*
allopathic (adj)	الوباثي	*alūbāthī*
allopathy (n)	ألوباثيا، علاج الداء بضده	*alūbāthiyā, 'ilajud dā' bi ḍiddih*
allot (v)	حصص، خصص	*ḥaṣṣaṣa, khaṣṣaṣa*
allotment (n)	تخصيص، حصّة	*takhṣīṣ, ḥiṣṣah*
allottee (n)	محصّص له	*muḥaṣṣaṣ lahū*
allow (v)	سمح، سلم	*samaḥa, sallama*
allowable (adj)	مسموح به، جائز	*masmūḥ bih, jā'iz*
allowance (n)	حصّة، إباحة	*ḥiṣṣah, ibāḥah*
all right (adj/adv)	حسن، حسنًا	*ḥasan, ḥasanan*
allure (v/n)	أغرى، إغراء	*aghrā, ighrā'*
alluring (adj)	مغري، فاتن	*mughrī, fātin*
allusion (n)	تلميح، تورية	*talmīḥ, tauriyah*
allusive (adj)	تلميحي، إلماعي	*talmīḥī, ilmā'ī*
ally (v)	حالف، صاهر	*ḥālafa, ṣāhara*
ally (n)	حليف، نصير	*ḥalīf, naṣīr*
almighty (n)	كلي القدرة، قدير	*kulliyyul qudrah, qadīr*
almond (n)	لوز	*lauz*
almost (adv)	تقريباً، غالباً	*taqrīban, ghāliban*
alms (n)	صدقة، زكاة	*ṣadaqah, zakāt*
alone (adj)	وحده، متوحد	*waḥdah, mutawaḥḥid*
alone (adv)	بمفرده، وحده	*bi mufradih, waḥdah*

along (adv/prep)	بجانب، برفقته	*bi jānib, bi rifqatihi*
alongside (adv/prep)	بمقربة، بجانب	*bi maqrabah, bi jānib*
aloof (adj)	بعيد، عن بعد	*ba'īd, 'an bu'd*
aloud (adv)	بصوت عال	*bi ṣaut 'ālin*
alphabet (n)	حروف أبجدية	*ḥurūf abjadiyyah*
alphabetical (adj)	أبجدي	*abjadī*
alphabetically (adv)	أبجديًا	*abjadiyyan*
already (adv)	سابقًا، قبل الآن	*sābiqan, qablal ān*
alright= all right		
also (adv)	أيضًا، كذلك	*aiḍan, kadhālik*
alter (v)	بدّل، تبدّل	*baddala, tabaddala*
alterable (adj)	متبدّل، متغير	*mutabaddil, mutaghayyir*
alteration (n)	تبديل، تبدّل، تغير	*tabdīl, tabaddul, taghayyur*
altercation (n)	مشاجرة، خصام	*mushājarah, khiṣām*
alternate (v)	ناوب، تناوب	*nāwaba, tanāwaba*
alternate (adj)	متبادل، متناوب	*mutabādil, mutanāwib*
alternative (n/adj)	خيار، خياري	*khiyār, khiyārī*
alternatively (adv)	بالتناوب، بالتبادل	*bil tanāwub, bit tabādul*
although (conj)	مع أن	*ma'a anna*
altitude (n)	علو، ارتفاع	*'uluww, irtifā'*
altogether (adv)	تمامًا، جميعًا	*tamāman, jamī'an*
aluminiu (aluminum)	معدن الالومنيوم	*ma'dinul alūminyūm*
always (adv)	دائمًا، أبدًا	*dā'iman, abadan*
am (v)	أكون	*akūn*
amalgam (n)	مزيج، اندماج	*mazīj, indimāj*
amalgamate (v)	دمج، التحم	*damaja, iltaḥama*
amalgamation (n)	دمج، اندماج	*damj, indimāj*

amass (v)	جمع، كدّس	*jama'a, kaddasa*
amateur (n)	هاوي، غير محترف	*hāwī, ghair muḥtarif*
amaze (v)	أذهل ، أدهش	*adhhala, adhasha*
amazed (adj)	مدهوش	*madhūsh*
amazement (n)	دهشة، انذهال	*dahshah, indhihāl*
amazing (adj)	مدهش، مذهل	*mudhish, mudhhil*
ambassador (n)	سفير	*safīr*
ambiguity (n)	غموض، التباس	*ghumūḍ, iltibās*
ambiguous (adj)	غامض، ملتبس	*ghāmiḍ, multabis*
ambiguously (adv)	بإبهام، بغموض	*bi ibhām, bi ghumūḍ*
ambition (n)	مطمح، طموح	*maṭmaḥ, ṭumūḥ*
ambitious (adj)	طموح، طماح	*ṭamūḥ, ṭammāḥ*
ambulance (n)	سيارة إسعاف	*sayyāratu is'āf*
ambush (n)	كمين،مكمن،مرصاد	*kamīn, makman, mirṣād*
ambush (v)	هاجم من مكمن، ترصد	*hājama min makman, taraṣṣada*
amend (v)	أصلح، عدل	*aṣlaḥa, 'addala*
amendable (adj)	قابل للتنقيح	*qābil lit tanqīḥ*
amendment (n)	تنقيح، إصلاح	*tanqīḥ, iṣlāḥ*
amends (n)	تعويض، مجازاة	*ta'wīḍ, mujāzāt*
amenity (n)	لطافة، نعمة	*laṭāfah, ni'mah*
amiability (n)	أنس، ود	*uns, wudd*
amiable (adj)	أنيس، لطيف، ظريف	*anīs, laṭīf, ẓarīf*
amicable (adj)	حبي، سلمي	*ḥubbī, silmī*
amicably (adv)	سلميًا، وديًّا	*silmiyyan, wuddiyyan*
amid (amidst) (prep)	بين، في وسط	*baina, fī wasaṭ*
amiss (adj)	خاطئ	*khāṭi'*
amity (n)	صداقة، مودة	*ṣadāqah, mawaddah*

ammunition (n)	ذخيرة حربية	*dhakhīrah ḥarbiyyah*
amnesty (n)	عفو عام	*'afw 'āmm*
amoeba (n)	أميبة	*amībah*
among (prep)	وسط، بين	*wasaṭ, baina*
amongst (prep)	وسط، فيما بين	*wasaṭ, fīmā baina*
amoral (adj)	فاقدالصفات الأخلاقية	*fāqiduṣ ṣifāt al akhlāqiyyah*
amorous (adj)	مفطورعلى الحب،حبي	*mafṭūr 'alal ḥubb, ḥubbī*
amount (n)	مبلغ، مجموع	*mablagh, majmū'*
ample (adj)	متسع، وافر	*muttassi', wāfir*
ampleness (n)	وفرة، اتساع	*wafrah, ittisā'*
amplification (n)	توسيع،تضخيم،إسهاب	*tausī', taḍkhīm, ishāb*
amplify (v)	وسّع، ضخّم	*wassa'a, ḍakhkhama*
amplitude (n)	سعة، مدى	*sa'ah, madā*
amuse (v)	سلى، ألهى	*sallā, alhā*
amusement (n)	تسلية،لهو	*tasliyah, lahw*
amusing (adj)	مضحك، مسلٍ	*muḍḥik, musallin*
an (artic)	واحد، أداة تنكير	*wāḥid, adātu tankīr*
anal (adj)	شرجي، إستي	*sharajī, istī*
analogic (adj)	تشابهي، قياسي	*tashābuhī, qiyāsī*
analogous (adj)	متشابه	*mutashābih*
analogue (n)	مماثل، نظير	*mumāthil, naẓīr*
analogy (n)	قياس التمثيل	*qiyāsut tamthīl*
analysis (n)	تحليل، تجزية	*taḥlīl, tajziyah*
analyst (n)	محلل، معرب	*muḥallil, mu'rib*
analytic-al (adj)	تحليلي، إعرابي	*taḥlīlī, i'rābī*
analyze,-ise (v)	حلل، أعرب	*ḥallala, a'raba*
anarchic-al (adj)	فوضوي	*fauḍawī*

anarchism (n)	فوضوية	*fauḍawiyyah*
anarchist (n)	فوضوي	*fauḍawī*
anarchy (n)	فوضى، فوضوية	*fauḍā, fauḍawiyyah*
anatomical (adj)	تشريحي، تحليلي	*tashrīḥī, taḥlīlī*
anatomy (n)	علم التشريح	*'ilmut tashrīḥ*
ancestor (n)	سلف، جد أعلى	*salaf, jadd a'lā*
ancestral (adj)	سلفي، مختلص بالسلف	*salafī, mukhtaṣṣ bis salaf*
ancestry (n)	سلسلة النسب،أسلاف	*silsilatun nasab, aslāf*
anchor (n)	مرساة	*mirsāt*
anchor (v)	رسا، أرسى	*rasā, arsā*
anchorage (n)	إرساء، مرسى	*irsā', marsā*
ancient (adj)	قديم، عتيق	*qadīm, 'atīq*
and (conj)	و، حرف العطف	*waw, ḥarful 'aṭf*
anecdotal (adj)	قصصي	*qaṣaṣī*
anecdote (n)	حكاية، قصة، نادرة	*ḥikāyah, qiṣṣah, nādirah*
anew (adv)	من جديد	*min jadīd*
angel (n)	ملك، ملاك	*malak, malāk*
angelic (adj)	ملكي، سماوي	*malakī, samāwī*
anger (n/v)	غضب، أغضب	*ghaḍab, aghḍaba*
angle (n)	زاوية، صنارة	*zāwiyah, ṣinnārah*
angle (v)	صنر، صاد بالصنارة	*ṣannara, ṣāda biṣ ṣinnārah*
angrily (adv)	بغضب، غاضبًا	*bi ghaḍab, ghāḍiban*
angry (adj)	غاضب، ساخط	*ghāḍib, sākhiṭ*
anguish (n/v)	كرب، ألم، ضيق	*karb, alam, ḍīq*
anguished (adj)	مصاب بكرب	*muṣāb bi karb*
angular (adj)	زاوي، ذو زوايا	*zāwī, dhū zawāyā*
animal (n/adj)	حيوان، حيواني	*ḥaiwān, ḥaiwānī*

animate (v)	أحيا، نشط	*aḥyā, nashshaṭa*
animated (adj)	حي، متحرك	*ḥayy, mutaḥarrik*
animating (adj)	محيي، منشّط	*muḥyī, munashshiṭ*
animation (n)	إحياء، انتعاش	*iḥyā', inti'āsh*
animosity (n)	عداء، بغض	*'idā', bughḍ*
ankle (n)	رسغ	*rusgh*
anklet (n)	خلخال	*khalkhāl*
annals (n)	حوليات، أخبار تاريخية	*ḥauliyyāt, akhbār tārīkhiyyah*
annex (v)	أضاف، ألحق	*aḍāfa, alḥaqa*
annexation (n)	إلحاق، ضم	*ilḥāq, ḍamm*
annexe (annex) (n)	ملحق، ذيل	*mulḥaq, dhail*
annihilate (v)	محق، أباد	*maḥaqa, abāda*
annihilation (n)	محق، إبادة	*maḥq, ibādah*
anniversary (n)	ذكرى سنوية	*dhikrā sanawiyyah*
annotate (v)	حشى، شرح	*ḥashshā, sharaḥa*
annotation (n)	تحشية، تعليق	*taḥshiyah, ta'līq*
announce (v)	أعلن، أذاع	*a'lana, adhā'a*
announcement (n)	إعلان، إذاعة	*i'lān, idhā'ah*
announcer (n)	معلن، مذيع	*mu'lin, mudhī'*
annoy (v)	أغضب، ضايق	*aghḍaba, ḍāyaqa*
annoyance (n)	إزعاج، زعل	*iz'āj, za'al*
annoying (adj)	مزعج، مضجر	*muz'ij, muḍjir*
annual (adj)	سنوي، حولي	*sanawī, ḥawlī*
annually (adv)	سنويًا	*sanawiyyan*
anonymous (adj)	غفل من الاسم	*ghufl minal ism*
another (adj)	آخر، ثانٍ	*ākhar, thānin*
answer (n/v)	جواب، أجاب	*jawāb, ajāba*

answerable (adj)	مسؤول، مطالب	*mas'ūl, muṭālab*
ant (n)	نملة	*namlah*
antagonism (n)	خصومة، عداء	*khuṣūmah, 'idā'*
antagonist (n)	خصم، مقاوم	*khaṣm, muqāwim*
antagonistic (adj)	مخاصم، عدائي	*mukhāṣim, 'idā'ī*
antagonize,-ise (v)	خاصم، قاوم	*khāṣama, qāwama*
antecede (v)	سبق، تقدم	*sabaqa, taqaddama*
antecedence (n)	تقدّم، أسبقية	*taqaddum, asbaqiyyah*
antecedent (adj/n)	سابق، سابقة	*sābiq, sābiqah*
antelope (n)	ظبي	*ẓaby*
anterior (adj)	أمامي، متقدم	*amāmī, mutaqaddim*
anteriority (n)	أمامية	*amāmiyyah*
anthem (n)	نشيد، ترنيمة	*nashīd, tarnīmah*
anthology (n)	مقتطفات أدبية	*muqtaṭafāt adabiyyah*
anthropologist (n)	أنثروبولوجي	*anthurūbūlūjī*
anthropology (n)	أنثروبولوجيا، علم الانسان	*anthurūbūlūjiyā, 'ilmul insān*
anti (n)	مقاوم	*muqāwim*
antiacid (n)	مقاوم للأحماض	*muqāwim lil aḥmāḍ*
anti-aircraft (n/adj)	مضاد للطائرات	*muḍādd liṭ ṭā'irāt*
antibiotic (adj)	مضاد للجراثيم	*muḍādd lil jarāthīm*
anticipate (v)	توقع، انتظر	*tawaqqa'a, intaẓara*
anticipation (n)	توقع، حدس	*tawaqqu', ḥads*
anticipatory (adj)	توقعي، انتظاري	*tawaqqu'ī, intiẓārī*
anticlimax (n)	هبوط مفاجئ	*hubūṭ mufāji'*
anticyclone (n)	إعصار مضاد	*i'ṣār muḍādd*
antidote (n)	ترياق	*tiryāq*
antifertility (adj)	مانع للحمل	*māni' lil ḥaml*

antipathetic (adj)	منفر، كريه	*munaffir, karīh*
antipathy (n)	كراهيّة، تنافر	*karāhiyyah, tanāfur*
antiquity (n)	آثار عصور قديمة	*āthāru 'uṣūr qadīmah*
antiseptic (adj/n)	مانع للعفونة	*māni' lil 'ufūnah*
antisocial (adj)	معادٍ للمجتمع	*mu'ādin lil mujtama'*
antithesis (n)	تضاد، تباين	*taḍādd, tabāyun*
antithetic-al (adj)	تضادي، تناقضي	*taḍāddī, tanāquḍī*
antonym (n)	مطابقة	*muṭabiqah*
anxiety (n)	قلق، جزع	*qalaq, jaza'*
anxious (adj)	قلق، متلهف	*qaliq, mutalahhif*
anxiously (adv)	بقلق، برغبة	*bi qalaq, bi raghbah*
any (adj/pron)	أي، أي شخص	*ayy, ayyu shakhṣ*
anybody (pron)	أي إنسان	*ayyu insān*
anyhow (adv)	بأية حال	*bi ayyati ḥāl*
anymore (adv)	بعد الآن	*ba'dal ān*
anyone (pron)	أي شخص	*ayyu shakhṣ*
anything (pron)	أي شيء	*ayyu shay'*
anyway (adv)	على كل حال	*'alā kulli ḥāl*
anywhere (adv)	في أي مكان	*fī ayyi makān*
apart (adv)	بمعزل، على حدة	*bi ma'zil, 'alā ḥidah*
apart from (prep)	بصرف النظر عن	*bi ṣarfin naẓar 'an*
apartment (n)	شقة	*shaqqah*
apathetic (adj)	فاتر الشعور	*fātirush shu'ūr*
apathy (n)	فتور الشعور، بلادة	*futūrush shu'ūr, balādah*
ape (n)	قرد	*qird*
apex (n)	قمّة، قلة	*qimmah, qullah*

aphorism (n)	حكمة، مثل حكيم	*ḥikmah, mathal ḥakīm*
aphrodisiac (n/adj)	مثير للشهوة الجنسية	*muthīr lish shahwah al jinsiyyah*
apologetic (adj)	اعتذاري، تبريري	*i'tidhārī, tabrīrī*
apologist (n)	مدافع	*mudāfi'*
apologize,-ise (v)	اعتذر، استسمح	*i'tadhara, istasmaḥa*
apology (n)	اعتذار، دفاع	*i'tidhār, difā'*
apostle (n)	رسول، حواري	*rasūl, ḥawārī*
apostolic (adj)	رسولي	*rasūlī*
apostrophe (n)	فاصلة عليا	*fāṣilah 'ulyā*
appal (v)	أرعب، روع	*ar'aba, rawwa'a*
appalling (adj)	موعب، مروع	*mur'ib, murawwi'*
apparatus (n)	جهاز، عدة	*jihāz, 'uddah*
apparel (n)	ملابس، كساء	*malābis, kisā'*
apparent (adj)	واضح، ظاهر	*wāḍiḥ, ẓāhir*
apparently (adv)	بوضوح، ظاهراً	*bi wuḍūḥ, ẓāhiran*
appeal (n)	استغاثة، إغراء	*istighāthah, ighrā'*
appeal (v)	استغاث، أعجب	*istaghātha, a'jaba*
appealing (adj)	مغري، فاتن	*mughrī, fātin*
appear (v)	ظهر، بان، بدا	*ẓahara, bāna, badā*
appearance (n)	ظهور، مظهر، مثول	*ẓuhūr, maẓhar, muthūl*
appease (v)	أشبع، هدأ	*ashba'a, hadda'a*
appeasement (n)	تسكين، تهدئة	*taskīn, tahdi'ah*
appellant (adj)	مستأنف	*musta'nif*
appellation (n)	لقب	*laqab*
append (v)	ألحق، ذيل	*alḥaqa, dhayyala*
appendage (n)	ملحق، ذيل	*mulḥaq, dhail*
appendix (n)	زائدة، ملحق	*zā'idah, mulḥaq*

appetite (n)	شهيّة، شهوة	*shahiyyah, shahwah*
appetizer (n)	طعام مشهي	*ṭa'ām mushahhī*
appetizing (adj)	مشهي، مشحذ	*mushahhi, mushaḥhidh*
applaud (v)	صفق، هلل	*ṣaffaqa, hallala*
applause (n)	تصفيق الاستحسان	*taṣfīqul istiḥsān*
apple (n)	تفاح	*tuffāḥ*
applicable (adj)	قابل للإستعمال	*qābil lil isti'māl*
applicant (n)	طالب الوظيفة، مقدم الطلب	*ṭālibul waẓīfah, muqaddimuṭ ṭalab*
application (n)	طلب، استعمال	*ṭalab, isti'māl*
applied (adj)	مستعمل، تطبيقي	*musta'mal, taṭbīqī*
apply (v)	يقدم طلبًا، استعمل	*yuqaddimu ṭalaban, ista'mala*
appoint (v)	حدد، عين	*ḥaddada, 'ayyana*
appointment (n)	تعيين، وظيفة	*ta'yīn, waẓīfah*
apportion (v)	وزع، قسم	*wazza'a, qassama*
apportionment (n)	توزيع، وزيعة	*tauzī', wazī'ah*
apposite (adj)	ملائم، مناسب	*mulā'im, munāsib*
apposition (n)	إضافة، عطف بيان	*iḍāfah, 'aṭfu bayān*
appraisal (n)	تسعير، تثمين	*tas'īr, tathmīn*
appraise (v)	خمن، ثمن	*khammana, thammana*
appreciable (adj)	ممكن إدراكه	*mumkin idrākuhu*
appreciate (v)	قدر قيمة الشيء	*qaddara qīmatash shay'*
appreciation (n)	إيجاب، إدراك	*ījāb, idrāk*
appreciative (adj)	تعبيري، استحساني	*ta'bīrī, istiḥsānī*
apprehend (v)	قبض على، فهم	*qabaḍa 'alā, fahima*
apprehensible (adj)	ممكن فهمه	*mumkin fahmuh*

apprehension (n)	فهم، إدراك	*fahm, idrāk*
apprehensive (adj)	خائف، سريع الفهم	*khā'if, sarī'ul fahm*
apprentice (n)	متمهن، ممرّن	*mutamahhin, mumarran*
apprenticeship (n)	تمهن، تدريب	*tamahhun, tadrīb*
apprise (v)	أخبر، أعلم	*akhbara, a'lama*
approach (n)	طريق، اقتراب	*ṭarīq, iqtirāb*
approach (v)	اقترب، دنا	*iqtaraba, danā*
approachable (adj)	ممكن الوصول	*mumkinul wuṣūl*
appropriate (adj)	ملائم، مناسب	*mulā'im, munāsib*
appropriately (adv)	بنوع مناسب	*bi nau' munāsib*
appropriateness (n)	ملاءمة، مناسبة	*mulā'amah, munāsabah*
approval (n)	موافقة، تصديق	*muwāfaqah, taṣdīq*
approve (v)	وافق، استصوب	*wāfaqa, istaṣwaba*
approved (adj)	موافق عليه	*muwāfaq 'alaih*
approximate (adj)	متقارب، يقارب	*mutaqārib, yuqārib*
approximately (adj)	على وجه التقريب	*'alā wajhit taqrīb*
apricot (n)	مشمش	*mishmish*
April (n)	أبريل، نيسان	*abrīl, nīsān*
apron (n)	مئزر، وزرة	*mi'zar, wazrah*
apt (adj)	جدير، مناسب	*jadīr, munāsib*
aptly (adv)	بكفاءة، بجدارة	*bi kafā'ah, bi jadārah*
aptness (n)	جدارة، مقدرة	*jadārah, maqdarah*
aptitude (n)	استعداد، أهلية	*isti'dād, ahliyyah*
Arab (n/adj)	عربي	*'arabī*
Arabian (adj)	عربي	*'arabī*
Arabic (adj)	عربي، عربية	*'arabī, 'arabiyyah*
arbiter (n)	حكم، فيصل	*ḥakam, faiṣal*
arbiterage (n)	عملية راحلة	*'amaliyyah rāḥilah*

arbitrary (adj)	تحكمي، جائر	*taḥakkumī, jā'ir*
arbitrate (v)	حكم، توسط	*ḥakkama, tawassaṭa*
arbitration (n)	تحكيم	*taḥkīm*
arbitrator (n)	محكم، قاضي عرفي	*muḥakkam, qāḍī 'urfī*
arch (n)	قوس، قنطرة	*qaus, qanṭarah*
archeological (adj)	آثاري	*āthārī*
archeologist (n)	عالم بالآثار	*'ālim bil āthār*
archeology (n)	علم الآثار القديمة	*'ilmul āthār al qadīmah*
archbishop (n)	رئيس الأساقفة	*ra'īsul asāqifah*
arched (adj)	ذو قناطر، مقنطر	*dhū qanāṭir, muqanṭar*
archer (n)	نبال، رامي	*nabbāl, rāmī*
archery (n)	رماية	*rimāyah*
architect (n)	مهندس معماري	*muhandis mi'mārī*
architectural (adj)	معماري، بنائي	*mi'mārī, binā'ī*
architecture (n)	فن العمارة	*fannul 'imārah*
archly (adv)	بمكر	*bi makr*
archness (n)	مكر، خبث	*makr, khubth*
ardent (adj)	متحمّس، متقد	*mutaḥammis, muttaqid*
ardently (adv)	بحماسة، بغيرة	*bi ḥamāsah, bi ghairah*
ardour (ardor) (n)	حماسة، غيرة	*ḥamāsah, ghairah*
arduous (adj)	شاق، قاسٍ	*shāqq, qāsin*
are (v)	يكونون	*yakunūn*
area (n)	منطقة، دائرة	*minṭaqah, dā'irah*
arena (n)	ميدان المصارعات	*maidānul muṣāra'āt*
argue (v)	جادل، تنازع، باحث	*jādala, tanāza'a, bāḥatha*
argument (n)	مناظرة، مناقشة	*munāẓarah, munāqashah*
argumentative (adj)	جدلي	*jadalī*

aright (adv)	باستقامة، بالضبط	*bistiqāmah, biḍ ḍabṭ*
arise (v)	نهض، استيقظ	*nahaḍa, istaiqaẓa*
aristocracy (n)	أرستقراطية، طبقة الأشراف	*aristuqarāṭiyyah, ṭabaqatul ashrāf*
aristocrat (n)	ارستوقراطي	*aristūqarāṭī*
aristocratic (adj)	أرستوقراطي	*aristūqarāṭī*
arithmetic (n)	علم الحساب	*'ilmul ḥisāb*
arithmetic-al (adj)	حسابي	*ḥisābī*
arithmetician (n)	ماهر في الحساب	*māhir fil ḥisāb*
ark (n)	فلك	*fulk*
arm (n)	ذراع، سلاح	*dhirā', silāḥ*
arm (v)	سلح، درع	*sallaḥa, darra'a*
armament (n)	قوات حربية	*quwwāt ḥarbiyyah*
armẹd (adj)	مزوّد بالسلاح	*muzawwad bis silāḥ*
armed forces (n)	قوات مسلحة	*quwwāt musallaḥah*
armful (n)	ملء الذراع	*mil'udh dhirā'*
armless (adj)	بدون سلاح	*bidūn silāḥ*
armour (armor) (n)	درع	*dir'*
armoured (adj)	مدرّع، مصفح	*mudarra', muṣaffaḥ*
armoury, armory (n)	مصنع الأسلحة	*maṣna'ul asliḥah*
armpit (n)	إبط	*ibṭ*
arms (n)	أسلحة	*asliḥah*
army (n)	جيش، جند	*jaish, jund*
around (adv)	حول، حوالي	*ḥaula, ḥiwālai*
arouse (v)	أيقظ، هيّج	*aiqaẓa, hayyaja*
arrange (v)	نظم، رتب	*naẓẓama, rattaba*
arrangement (n)	نظام، ترتيب	*niẓām, tartīb*
array (v)	نظم، كسا، رتب	*naẓẓama, kasā, rattaba*

arrears (n)	متأخرات	*muta'khkhirāt*
arrest (n/v)	اعتقال، اعتقل	*i'tiqāl, i'taqala*
arrival (n)	وصول، قدوم	*wuṣūl, qudūm*
arrive (v)	وصل، قدم	*waṣala, qadima*
arrogance (n)	تكبر، عجرفة	*takabbur, 'ajrafah*
arrogant (adj)	متكبر، متعجرف	*mutakabbir, muta'ajrif*
arrogantly (adv)	بعجرفة، بتكبر	*bi 'ajrafah, bi takabbur*
arrow (n)	سهم	*sahm*
arsenal (n)	دار الأسلحة	*dārul asliḥah*
arson (n)	إحراق الممتلكات	*iḥrāqul mumtalakāt*
art (n)	فن، طريقة، حيلة	*fann, ṭarīqah, ḥīlah*
artery (n)	شريان، طريق رئيسة	*shiryān, ṭarīq ra'īsah*
artful (adj)	داهية، بارع	*dāhiyah, bāri'*
article (n)	مقالة، شيء	*maqālah, shay'*
articulate (adj)	واضح	*wāḍiḥ*
articulate (v)	وضح، بين	*waḍḍaḥa, bayyana*
artifice (n)	خداع، حيلة	*khidā', ḥīlah*
artificial (adj)	اصطناعي،غير طبيعي	*iṣṭinā'ī, ghair ṭabī'ī*
artificiality (n)	اصطناعية، تكلف	*iṣṭinā'iyyah, takalluf*
artificially (adv)	بتكلف، بتصنع	*bi takalluf, bi taṣannu'*
artillery (n)	مدفعية	*midfa'iyyah*
artisan (n)	صانع ماهر	*ṣāni' māhir*
artist (n)	ماهر بالغناء والتمثيل	*māhir bil ghinā wat tamthīl*
artiste (n)	مغني، راقص	*mughannī, rāqiṣ*
artistic (adj)	فني	*fannī*
artistry (n)	مهارة فنية	*mahārah fanniyyah*

as (pron)	الذي، التي	*alladhī, allatī*
as (conj)	كأن، مثل، بحيث	*ka'anna, mithl, biḥaithu*
as (adv/prep)	مثلاً، ك	*mathalan, ka*
ascend (v)	صعد، ارتفع	*ṣa'ida, irtafa'a*
ascendancy (-dency)	سطوة، نفوذ	*saṭwah, nufūdh*
ascendant, -dent (n)	صاعد، سائد	*ṣā'id, sā'id*
ascending (adj)	صاعد، طالع	*ṣā'id, ṭāli'*
ascent (n)	صعود، ارتقاء	*ṣu'ūd, irtiqā'*
ascertain (v)	حقق، تحقق	*ḥaqqaqa, taḥaqqaqa*
ascetic (n/adj)	زاهد، زهدي	*zāhid, zuhdī*
asceticism (n)	تنسك، زهد	*tanassuk, zuhd*
ascribe (v)	نسب إلى	*nasaba ilā*
ascription (n)	نسبة ، عزو	*nisbah, 'azw*
asexual (adj)	عديم الجنس	*'adīmul jins*
ash (n/v)	رماد، زهرة الغابة	*ramād, zuhratul ghābah*
ashamed (adj)	خجلان، مستح	*khajlān, mustaḥin*
ashore (adv)	على الشاطئ	*'alash shāṭi'*
Asia (n)	آسية	*āsiah*
Asian (adj)	آسيوي	*āsīwī*
aside (adv)	جانبًا، على جنب	*jāniban, 'alā jamb*
ask (v)	سأل، طلب	*sa'ala, ṭalaba*
asleep (adj)	نائم، راقد	*nā'im, rāqid*
aslope (adj/adv)	منحدر، بانحدار	*munḥadir, binḥidār*
asocial (adj)	لا اجتماعي	*lā ijtimā'ī*
aspect (n)	وجه، هيئة	*wajh, hai'ah*
aspiration (n)	طموح، تنفس	*ṭumūḥ, tanaffus*
aspiratory (adj)	تنفسي	*tanaffusī*

aspire (v)	طمح، ابتغى	*ṭamaḥa, ibtaghā*
ass (n)	حمار، شخص أبله	*ḥimār, shakhṣ ablah*
assail (v)	أغار، هاجم	*aghāra, hājama*
assailant (n)	مغير، مهاجم	*mughīr, muhājim*
assassin (n)	قاتل، سفاح	*qātil, saffāḥ*
assassinate (v)	اغتال، ذبح	*ightāla, dhabaḥa*
assassination (n)	اغتيال، قتل	*ightiyāl, qatl*
assault (v)	هاجم، اغتصب	*hājama, ightaṣaba*
assault (n)	هجوم، اغتصاب	*hujūm, ightiṣāb*
assemble (v)	اجتمع، احتشد	*ijtama'a, iḥtashada*
assembly (n)	اجتماع، جمعية	*ijtimā', jam'iyyah*
assent (n/v)	موافقة، وافق	*muwāfaqah, wāfaqa*
assert (v)	جزم، أكد	*jazama, akkada*
assertion (n)	جزم، تأكيد	*jazm, ta'kīd*
assertive (adj)	جازم، قطعي	*jāzim, qaṭ'ī*
assess (v)	خمن، عين	*khammana, 'ayyana*
assessment (n)	تخمين، تعيين	*takhmīn, ta'yīn*
asset (n)	شيء ثمين	*shay' thamīn*
assiduous (adj)	مجتهد، مواظب	*mujtahid, muwāẓib*
assign (v)	تخلى، عين	*takhallā, 'ayyana*
assignment (n)	تعيين، واجب	*ta'yīn, wājib*
assimilate (v)	استوعب، شبه	*istau'aba, shabbaha*
assimilation (n)	استيعاب، امتصاص	*istī'āb, imtiṣāṣ*
assist (v)	عاون، ساعد	*'āwana, sā'ada*
assistance (n)	مساعدة، معاونة	*musā'adah, mu'āwanah*

associate (v)	زامل، شارك	*zāmala, shāraka*
association (n)	جمعية، مزاملة، صلة	*jam'iyyah, muzāmalah, ṣilah*
assort (v)	نسّق، رتب	*nassaqa, rattaba*
assorted (adj)	منسّق، متنوع	*munassaq, mutanawwi'*
assortment (n)	تنسيق، تشكيلة	*tansīq, tashkīlah*
assume (v)	افترض، اتخذ	*iftaraḍa, ittakhadha*
assumed (adj)	مفروض، مزعوم	*mafrūḍ, maz'ūm*
assumption (n)	افتراض، اتخاذ	*iftirāḍ, ittikhādh*
assurance (n)	توكيد، ثقة	*taukīd, thiqah*
assure (v)	أكد، أثبت	*akkada, athbata*
assured (adj)	واثق، مضمون	*wāthiq, maḍmūn*
assuredly (adv)	يقينًا، حقًا	*yaqīnan, ḥaqqan*
astonish (v)	أدهش، حير	*adhasha, ḥayyara*
astonished (adj)	في دهشة، متحير	*fī dahshah, mutaḥayyir*
astonishment (n)	دهشة، ذهول	*dahshah, dhuhūl*
astray (adj)	ضال، تائه	*ḍāll, tā'ih*
astrologer (n)	منجم، يازرجي	*munajjim, yāzirjī*
astrology (n)	علم التنجيم	*'ilmut tanjīm*
astronomy (n)	علم الفلك	*'ilmul falak*
asunder (adv)	إربًا	*iraban*
asylum (n)	مأوى، ملجأ	*ma'wā, malja'*
asymmetric (adj)	غير متناسق	*ghair mutanāsiq*
at (prep)	على، في، إلى	*'alā, fī, ilā*
atheism (n)	إلحاد، كفر	*ilḥād, kufr*
atheist (n)	ملحد، كافر	*mulḥid, kāfir*
atheistic (adj)	إلحادي، كفري	*ilḥādī, kufrī*
athlete (n)	رياضي، قوي الجسم	*riyāḍī, qawiyyul jism*

athletic (adj)	رياضي، نشيط	*riyāḍī, nashīṭ*
athletics (n)	ألعاب رياضية	*al'āb riyāḍiyyah*
Atlantic (n)	محيط أطلنسي	*muḥīṭ aṭlansī*
atmosphere (n)	جو، هواء	*jaww, hawā'*
atom (n)	ذرّة، أطمة	*dharrah, aṭamah*
atomic (adj)	ذرّي، أطمي	*dharrī, aṭamī*
atone (v)	عوض، كفر	*'awwaḍa, kaffara*
atonement (n)	كفارة، تعويض	*kaffārah, ta'wīḍ*
atop (prep)	في أعلى	*fī a'lā*
atrocious (adj)	شنيع، فظيع	*shanī', faẓī'*
atrocity (n)	شناعة، فظاعة	*shanā'ah, faẓā'ah*
attach (v)	ألصق، لحق، ضم	*alṣaqa, laḥiqa, ḍamma*
attachment (n)	مصاحبة، صداقة، اتصال	*muṣāḥabah, ṣadāqah, ittiṣāl*
attack (n)	مهاجمة، هجوم	*muhājamah, hujūm*
attack (v)	هاجم، أغار	*hājama, aghāra*
attain (v)	نال، بلغ	*nāla, balagha*
attainable (adj)	ممكن المنال	*mumkinul manāl*
attainment (n)	إحراز، بلوغ	*iḥrāz, bulūgh*
attempt (n/v)	محاولة، حاول	*muḥāwalah, ḥāwala*
attend (v)	حضر، لازم	*ḥaḍara, lāzama*
attendance (n)	حضور، خدمة	*ḥuḍūr, khidmah*
attendant (n)	خادم، مصاحب	*khādim , muṣāḥib*
attention (n)	اهتمام، عناية	*ihtimām, 'ināyah*
attentive (adj)	يقظ، منتبه	*yaqiẓ, muntabih*
attentively (adv)	بانتباه، بتيقظ	*bintibāh, bi tayaqquẓ*
attest (v)	صدق، قرر	*ṣaddaqa, qarrara*
attestation (n)	تصديق، شهادة	*taṣdīq, shahādah*

attitude (n)	موقف، وضع	*mauqif, waḍ'*
attorney (n)	محامي، وكيل مفوض	*muḥāmī, wakīl mufawwaḍ*
attract (v)	جذب، لفت	*jadhaba, lafata*
attraction (n)	جذب، إغراء	*jadhb, ighrā'*
attractive (adj)	جذاب، ساحر	*jadhdhāb, sāḥir*
attribute (n)	صفة، سجية، خاصة	*ṣifah, sajiyyah, khāṣṣah*
attribute (v)	نسب، عزا إلى	*nasaba, 'azā ilā*
attribution (n)	عزو، نسبة	*'azw, nisbah*
attributive (adj)	عزوي، وصفي	*'azwī, waṣfī*
attune (v)	ناغم، دوزن	*nāghama, dawzana*
atypical (adj)	غير سوي	*ghair sawī*
auction (n)	مزاد، حراج	*mazād, ḥarāj*
auctioneer (n)	دلال، بائع بالمزاد	*dallāl, bā'i' bil mazād*
audibility (n)	مسموعية، إمكان السمع	*masmū'iyyah, imkānus sam'*
audible (adj)	ممكن سماعه، مسموع	*mumkin simā'uh, masmū'*
audience (n)	مستمعون، جلسة	*mustami'ūn, jalsah*
audio (adj)	سمعي، سماعي	*sam'ī, samā'ī*
audit (n)	فحص الحسابات	*faḥṣul ḥisābāt*
audition (n)	استماع، تجربة أداء	*istimā', tajribatu adā'*
auditor (n)	مستمع، فاحص	*mustami', fāḥiṣ*
auditorium (n)	قاعة الاستماع	*qā'atul istimā'*
augment (n/v)	زيادة، زاد	*ziyādah, zāda*
augmentation (n)	زيادة، ازدياد	*ziyādah, izdiyād*
august (adj)	جليل، مهيب	*jalīl, muhīb*
August (n)	أغسطس، آب	*ughusṭus, āb*
aunt (n)	عمة، خالة	*'ammah, khālah*

auspicious (adj)	سعيد، موفق	*sa'īd, muwaffaq*
austere (adj)	قاسٍ، صارم	*qāsin, ṣārim*
austerity (n)	قسوة، صرامة	*qaswah, ṣarāmah*
authentic (adj)	موثوق به	*mauthūq bih*
authenticate (v)	وثق، صدق	*waththaqa, ṣaddaqa*
authenticity (n)	موثوقية، صحة	*mauthūqiyyah, ṣiḥḥah*
author (n)	مؤلف، مصنف	*mu'allif, muṣannif*
authoress (n)	مؤلفة، مصنفة	*mu'allifah, muṣannifah*
authority (n)	سلطة، شهادة	*sulṭah, shahādah*
authorization (n)	تفويض، ترخيص	*tafwīḍ, tarkhīṣ*
authorize,-ise (v)	فوّض، رخّص	*fawwaḍa, rakhkhaṣa*
authorized,-ised(adj)	مفوّض، مجاز	*mufawwaḍ, mujāz*
autobiographer (n)	مترجم لنفسه	*mutarjim li nafsih*
autobiographic (adj)	متعلق بالسيرة الذاتية	*muta'alliq bis sīratidh dhātiyyah*
autobiography (n)	سيرة ذاتية	*sīrah dhātiyyah*
autocracy (n)	أوتوقراطية، حكم مطلق	*ūtūqarāṭiyyah, ḥukm muṭlaq*
autocrat (n)	حاكم مطلق	*ḥākim muṭlaq*
autocratic (adj)	أوتوقراطي،استبدادي	*ūtūqarāṭī, istibdādī*
autograph (n)	مخطوطة أصلية	*mukhṭūṭah aṣliyyah*
automatic (adj)	أوتوماتيكي، ذاتي الحركة	*ūtūmātīkī, dhātiyyul ḥarakah*
automatically (adv)	أوتوماتيكيًّا، تلقائيًّا	*ūtūmātīkiyyan, tilqā'iyyan*
autonomous (adj)	استقلالي، مستقل	*istiqlālī, mustaqill*
autonomy (n)	استقلال، حكم ذاتي	*istiqlāl, ḥukm dhātī*
autumn (n)	خريف	*kharīf*
autumnal (adj)	خريفي	*kharīfī*

auxiliary (adj)	مساعد، إضافي	*musā'id, iḍāfī*
avail (v)	أفاد، استفاد	*afāda, istafāda*
avail (n)	فائدة، نفع	*fā'idah, naf'*
availability (n)	تيسر، انتفاع	*tayassur, intifā'*
available (adj)	متيسر، مستفاد	*mutayassir, mustafād*
avarice (n)	طمع، جشع	*ṭama', jasha'*
avaricious (adj)	جشع، طماع	*jashi', ṭammā'*
avenge (v)	انتقم، أخذ بالثأر	*intaqama, akhadha bith tha'r*
avenger (n)	منتقم، آخذ بالثأر	*muntaqim, ākhidh bith tha'r*
avenue (n)	سبيل، طريق	*sabīl, ṭarīq*
average (adj/n)	متوسّط، نسبة	*mutawassiṭ, nisbah*
averse (v)	كره، امتنع	*kariha, imtana'a*
aversion (n)	كراهة، نفور	*karāhah, nufūr*
avert (v)	حوّل، منع	*ḥawwala, mana'a*
aviation (n)	طيران، ركوب الهواء	*ṭayarān, rukūbul hawā'*
aviator (n)	طيّار	*ṭayyār*
avoid (v)	أبطل، تجنب	*abṭala, tajannaba*
avoidable (adj)	ممكن اجتنابه	*mumkin ijtinābuh*
avoidance (n)	إبطال، اجتناب	*ibṭāl, ijtināb*
await (v)	انتظر، ترقب	*intaẓara, taraqqaba*
awake (v)	أيقظ، استيقظ	*aiqaẓa, istaiqaẓa*
awake (adj)	يقظان، مستيقظ	*yaqẓān, mustaiqiẓ*
awaken (v)	أيقظ، نبه	*aiqaẓa, nabbaha*
awakening (n/adj)	يقظة، موقظ	*yaqẓah, mūqiẓ*
award (n)	جائزة، مكافأة	*jā'izah, mukāfa'ah*
award (v)	منح، أعطى	*manaḥa, a'ṭā*

aware (adj)	مطلع، دارٍ به	*muṭṭali', dārin bih*
awareness (n)	اطلاع، إدارك	*iṭṭilā', idrāk*
awash (adj)	مغمور بالماء	*maghmūr bil mā'*
away (adj/adv)	بعيد، غائب، بعيدًا	*ba'īd, ghā'ib, ba'īdan*
awe (n)	هيبة، رعب	*haibah, ru'b*
awesome (adj)	مرعب، مهيب	*mur'ib, muhīb*
awful (adj)	مرعب، مروع	*mur'ib, murawwi'*
awfully (adv)	برعب، للغاية	*bi ru'b, lil ghāyah*
awhile (adv)	لحظةً، لوقت ما	*laḥẓatan, li waqtim mā*
awkward (adj)	سمج، غير ملائم	*samij, ghair mulā'im*
awkwardly (adv)	بسماجة، بخرق	*bi samājah, bi khurq*
awkwardness (n)	سماجة، خرق	*samājah, khurq*
awl (n)	مثقاب، مخراز	*mithqāb, mikhrāz*
axe (ax) (n)	فأس، بلطة	*fa's, balṭah*
axis (n)	محور، مدار	*miḥwar, madār*
ay (aye) (adv)	دائمًا، أبدًا	*dā'iman, abadan*
ay (aye) (interj)	نعم، بلى	*na'am, balā*

B

BA	بكالوريوس في الفنون	*bukālūriūs fil funūn*
babble (n/v)	ثرثرة، ثرثر	*thartharah, tharthara*
babe (n)	رضيع، طفل	*raḍī', ṭifl*
baby (n)	طفل، رضيع	*ṭifl, raḍī'*
baby farm (n)	محضن	*maḥḍan*
babyhood (n)	طفولة، طفولية	*ṭufūlah, ṭufūliyyah*
babyish (adj)	طفلي، طفولي	*ṭiflī, ṭufūlī*
bachelor (n)	أعزب، عزب	*a'zab, 'azab*
bachelorhood (n)	عزوبة، عزبة	*'uzūbah, 'uzbah*

back (v/n)	ظهّر، ظهر	*ẓahhara, ẓahr*
back (adj/adv)	خلفي، إلى الخلف	*khalfī, ilal khalf*
backache (n)	وجع الظهر	*waj'uẓ ẓahr*
backbite (v)	اغتاب، وشى	*ightāba, washā*
backbiter (n)	مغتاب، واشٍ	*mughtāb, wāshin*
backbiting (n)	اغتياب، نميمة	*ightiyāb, namīmah*
backbone (n)	أساس، سلسلة فقرية	*asās, silsilah faqriyyah*
backdate (v)	أرّخ بتاريخ سابق	*arrakha bi tārīkh sābiq*
backdoor (n)	باب خلفي	*bāb khalfī*
backed (adj)	مؤيّد، معضد	*mu'ayyad, mu'aḍḍad*
background (n)	خلفية، منظر خلفي	*khalfiyyah, manẓar khalfī*
backing (n)	ظهارة، عون	*ẓihārah, 'aun*
backlog (n)	ركام من أعمال	*rukām min a'māl*
backside (n)	مؤخر، خلف	*mu'akhkhar, khalf*
backstage (adv)	خلف الستارة	*khalfas sitārah*
backstairs (n)	سلم خلفي	*sullam khalfī*
backstreet (n)	شارع خلفي	*shāri' khalfī*
backtrack (v)	غير الموقف	*ghayyaral mauqif*
backward (adj/adv)	متخلف، إلى التخلف	*mutakhallif, ilat takhalluf*
backwardness (n)	تخلّف، ارتجاع	*takhalluf, irtijā'*
backwards (adv)	إلى الخلف	*ilal khalf*
backyard (n)	فناء خلفي	*finā' khalfī*
bacteria (n)	بكتيريا، جراثيم	*baktīriyā, jarāthīm*
bacterial (adj)	جرثومي، بكتيري	*jurthūmī, baktīrī*
bad (adj)	سيئ، رديء	*sayyi', radī'*
bad (adv)	بطريقة سيئة	*bi ṭarīqah sayyi'ah*

badminton (n)	بدمنتن	*badmintun*
baffle (v)	حيّر، أربك	*ḥayyara, arbaka*
bafflement (n)	إرباك، حيرة	*irbāk, ḥairah*
baffling (adj)	محيّر، مربك	*muḥayyir, murbik*
bag (n)	كيس، حقيبة	*kīs, ḥaqībah*
baggage (n)	أمتعة السفر	*amti'atus safar*
bail (n/v)	كفالة، كفل	*kafālah, kafala*
bailable (adj)	ممكن الكفالة	*mumkinul kafālah*
bailment (n)	إطلاق بكفالة	*iṭlāq bi kafalah*
bailor (n)	مودع، كفيل	*mūdi', kafīl*
bailsman (n)	كافل، ضامن	*kāfil, ḍāmin*
bait (n/v)	طعم، زوّد بطعم	*ṭu'm, zawwada bi ṭu'm*
bake (v)	خبز، شوى	*khabaza, shawā*
baker (n)	خبّاز، فران	*khabbāz, farrān*
bakery (n)	مخبز، فرن	*makhbaz, furn*
baking (n)	خبز، خبزة	*khabz, khabzah*
baking powder (n)	ذرورالخبز	*dharūrul khabz*
baking soda (n)	صودا الخبز	*ṣūdal khabz*
balance (n)	ميزان، توازن، رصيد	*mīzān, tawāzun, raṣīd*
balance (v)	وازن، عدّل	*wāzana, 'addala*
balanced (adj)	متوازن	*mutawāzin*
balancer (n)	موازن، بهلوان	*muwāzin, bahlawān*
balance sheet (n)	ميزانية	*mīzāniyyah*
balcony (n)	شرفة، بلكون	*shurfah, balkūn*
bald (n/v)	أصلع، صلع	*aṣla', ṣala'a*
ball (n)	كرة، حفلة راقصة	*kurah, ḥaflah rāqiṣah*
ball (v)	كور، تكور	*kawwara, takawwara*
ballad (n)	قصيدة قصصية	*qaṣīdah qaṣaṣiyyah*

ballet (n)	رقص مسرحي	*raqṣ masraḥī*
ballestic (adj)	بالستي، قذفي	*bālistī, qadhafī*
ballestic missile (n)	قذيفة بالستية	*qadhīfah bālistiyyah*
balloon (n)	بالون، منطاد	*bālūn, munṭād*
ballot (n)	اقتراع سري	*iqtirā' sirrī*
ballot box (n)	صندوق الاقتراع	*ṣundūqul iqtirā'*
ballot paper (n)	ورقة الاقتراع	*waraqatul iqtirā'*
ballroom (n)	قاعة الرقص	*qā'atur raqṣ*
balm (n)	بلسم، مسكن للألم	*balsam, musakkin lil alam*
balmy (adj)	بلسمي، مسكن	*balsamī, musakkin*
bamboo (n)	خيزران	*khaizurān*
ban (n/v)	حظر، حظر	*ḥaẓr, haẓẓara*
banana (n)	موز، شجرة الموز	*mauz, shajaratul mauz*
band (n)	نطاق، فرقة، عصابة	*niṭāq, firqah, 'iṣābah*
band (v)	ربط، جمع	*rabaṭa, jama'a*
bandage (n)	عصابة،ضمادة	*'iṣābah, ḍimādah*
bandit (n)	قاطع الطريق	*qāṭi'uṭ ṭarīq*
bandmaster (n)	قائد فرقة موسيقية	*qā'idu firqah mausīqiyyah*
bandsman (n)	عضو فرقة موسيقية	*'uḍwu firqah mausīqiyah*
bandwagon (n)	عربة الموسيقي	*'arabatul mausīqī*
bang (n)	ضربة عنيفة	*ḍarbah 'anīfah*
bangle (n)	سوار، دملج	*siwār, dumluj*
banish (v)	طرد، نفى	*ṭarada, nafā*
banishment (n)	طرد، نفي	*ṭard, nafy*
bank (n)	مصرف، بنك، منحدر	*maṣraf, bank, munḥadir*

bank (v)	أودع في مصرف، تراكم	*awda'a fī maṣraf, tarākama*
bank account (n)	حساب في بنك	*ḥisāb fī bank*
bank bill (n)	حوالة مصرفية	*ḥawālah maṣrafiyyah*
bank book (n)	دفتر الحساب	*daftarul ḥisāb*
banker (n)	صاحب البنك	*ṣāḥibul bank*
banking (n)	صناعة مصرفية	*ṣinā'ah maṣrafiyyah*
banking house (n)	شركة مصرفية	*sharikah maṣrafiyyah*
banking money (n)	أوراق مالية	*aurāq māliyyah*
bank note (n)	ورقة مصرفية	*waraqah maṣrafiyyah*
bank rate (n)	سعر الخصم	*si'rul khaṣm*
bankrupt (n/v)	مفلس، فلس	*muflis, fallasa*
bankruptcy (n)	إفلاس، افتقار	*iflās, iftiqār*
banner (n)	علم، راية	*'alam, rāyah*
banquet (n)	مأدبة، وليمة	*ma'dubah, walīmah*
banyan (n)	أثأب	*ath'ab*
baptism (n)	معموديّة، تنصير	*ma'mūdiyyah, tanṣīr*
baptist (n)	معمّد، منصّر	*mu'ammid, munaṣṣir*
baptize,-ise (v)	عمّد، نصّر	*'ammada, naṣṣara*
bar (n)	مشرب، بار، حاجز	*mashrab, bār, ḥājiz*
bar (v)	سدّ، حظر	*sadda, ḥaẓẓara*
barbarian (n)	شخص همجي	*shakhṣ hamajī*
barbaric (adj)	همجي، بربري	*hamajī, barbarī*
barbarism (n)	همجيّة، توحش	*hamajiyyah, tawaḥḥush*
barbarity (n)	توحّش، همجية	*tawaḥḥush, hamajiyyah*
barbarous (adj)	وحشي، بربري	*waḥshī, barbarī*
barber (n)	حلاق، مزين	*ḥallāq, muzayyin*
bare (adj/v)	عارٍ، عرى	*'ārin, 'arrā*

barefooted (adj)	حافي القدمين	*ḥāfil qadamain*
bareheaded (adj)	حاسر الرأس	*ḥāsirur ra's*
barely (adv)	فقط، بالجهد	*faqaṭ, bil jahd*
bargain (n/v)	مقايضة، قايض	*muqāyaḍah, qāyaḍa*
bargaining (n)	صفقة، مقايضة	*ṣafqah, muqāyaḍah*
bark (n)	لحاء الشجر، نباح	*liḥā'ush shajar, nubāḥ*
bark (v)	نبح، كسا باللحاء	*nabaḥa, kasā bil liḥā'*
barker (n)	نبّاح	*nabbāḥ*
barley (n)	شعير	*sha'īr*
barley corn (n)	حبة شعير	*ḥabbatu sha'īr*
barmaid (n)	ساقية، خادمة الحانة	*sāqiyah, khādimatul ḥānah*
barman (n)	ساقي	*sāqī*
barn (n)	مخزن الحبوب	*makhzanul ḥubūb*
barrac (n)	ثكنة، قشلاق	*thuknah, qushlāq*
barrage (n)	سد من النيران	*sadd minan nīrān*
barred (adj)	ممنوع، مسدود	*mamnū', masdūd*
barrel (n)	برميل، أسطوانة	*barmīl, usṭuwānah*
barren (n)	عاقر، غير مثمر	*'āqir, ghair muthmir*
barricade (n/v)	حاجز، حجز	*ḥājiz, ḥajaza*
barrier (n)	عائق، حاجز	*'ā'iq, ḥājiz*
barring (prep)	ماعدا	*mā 'adā*
barrister (n)	محامٍ	*muḥāmin*
barter (n/v)	مقايضة، قايض	*muqāyaḍah, qāyaḍa*
base (n)	أساس، قاعدة	*asās, qā'idah*
base (adj)	دنيء، رديء	*danī', radī'*
baseball (n)	كرة القدم	*kuratul qadam*
base board (n)	لوح القاعدة	*lauḥul qā'idah*

baseless (adj)	لا أساس لــه	*lā asāsa lahu*
base line (n)	خط قاعدي	*khaṭṭ qā'idī*
basely (adv)	بحقارة، بخسة	*bi ḥaqārah, bi khissah*
basement (n)	دور تحتاني	*daur taḥtānī*
bash (n)	ضربة عنيفة	*ḍarbah 'anīfah*
bash (v)	ضرب بعنف	*ḍaraba bi 'unf*
bashful (adj)	خجول، حيي	*khajūl, ḥayī*
bashfully (adv)	بخجل، باستحياء	*bi khajal, bistiḥyā'*
bashfulness (n)	خجل، استحياء	*khajal, istiḥyā'*
basic (adj)	أساسي، قاعدي	*asāsī, qā'idī*
basically (adv)	أساسيًا	*asāsiyyan*
basin (n)	طست، حوض	*ṭast, ḥauḍ*
basis (n)	أساس، قاعدة	*asās, qā'idah*
basket (n)	سلة، سفط	*sallah, safaṭ*
basketball (n)	كرة السلة	*kuratus sallah*
bastard (adj)	نغل، رديء	*naghil, radī'*
bastardize,-ise (v)	نغل	*naghghala*
bastardy (n)	نغولة	*nughūlah*
bat (n)	مضرب، خفاش	*miḍrab, khuffāsh*
batch (n)	خبزة، دفعة	*khabzah, duf'ah*
bath (n)	غسل، استحمام	*ghasl, istiḥmām*
bath (v)	غسل، استحم	*ghasala, istaḥamma*
bathing (n)	اغتسال، سباحة	*ightisāl, sibāḥah*
bathing cap (n)	قلنسوة السباحة	*qalansuwatus sibāḥah*
bathing suit (n)	ثوب السباحة	*thaubus sibāḥah*
bathroom (n)	حمام، مرحاض	*ḥammām, mirḥāḍ*
bathtub (n)	حوض الاستحمام	*ḥauḍul istiḥmām*
batsman (n)	ضارب الكرة	*ḍāribul kurah*

battalion (n)	جماعة منظمة	*jamā'ah munaẓẓamah*
batter (v)	ضرب بشدة، هاجم بعنف	*ḍaraba bi shiddah, hājama bi 'unf*
battery (n)	سرية مدفعية، بطارية	*sariyyah midfa'iyyah, baṭṭāriyyah*
batting (n)	ضرب بالمضرب	*ḍarb bil miḍrab*
battle (n)	قتال، حرب، معركة	*qitāl, ḥarb, ma'rakah*
battle (v)	قاتل، حارب	*qātala, ḥāraba*
battle cruiser (n)	طرّاد	*ṭarrād*
battlefield (n)	ساحة القتال	*sāḥatul qitāl*
battleplane (n)	طائرة حربية	*ṭā'irah ḥarbiyyah*
battleship (n)	سفينة حربية	*safīnah ḥarbiyyah*
bauxite (n)	بوكسيت	*būksīt*
bawdry (n)	فسق، فجور	*fisq, fujūr*
bawdy (adj)	فاسق، فاجر	*fāsiq, fājir*
bawl (v)	صاح، زعق	*ṣāḥa, za'aqa*
bay (n)	خليج، نباح	*khalīj, nubāḥ*
bay (n/adj)	كمتة، كميت	*kumtah, kumait*
bazaar (n)	سوق	*sūq*
be (v)	كان، أصبح	*kāna, aṣbaḥa*
beach (n)	شاطئ رملي	*shāṭi' ramlī*
beachy (adj)	رملي، مرمل	*ramlī, murmil*
beacon (n)	مرشد، منارة للتحذير	*murshid, manārah lit taḥdhīr*
beacon (v)	هدى، أرشد	*hadā, arshada*
beak (n)	منقار، قمّة	*minqār, qimmah*
beaked (adj)	ذو منقار	*dhū minqār*
beaker (n)	كأس كبيرة	*ka's kabīrah*

beam (n)	شعاع، ابتسام	*shuʻāʻ, ibtisām*
beam (v)	أشع، ابتسم	*ashaʻʻa, ibtasama*
beamy (adj)	متلألئ، مشرق	*mutalaʼliʼ, mushriq*
bean (n)	لوبيا، حبّة	*lūbyā, ḥabbah*
beanfeast (n)	مأدبة سعيدة	*maʼdubah saʻīdah*
bear (n)	دبّ، شخص فظّ	*dubb, shakhṣ faẓẓ*
bear (v)	حمل، ولد	*ḥamala, walada*
bearable (adj)	محتمل، ممكن حمله	*muḥtamal, mumkin ḥamluh*
beard (n)	لحية، شوكة	*liḥyah, shaukah*
bearded (adj)	ذو لحية، ذو شوكة	*dhū liḥyah, dhū shaukah*
beardless (adj)	أمرد، بلا لحية	*amrad, bilā liḥyah*
bearer (n)	حامل، رسول	*ḥāmil, rasūl*
bearing (n)	احتمال، صلة، معنى	*iḥtimāl, ṣilah, maʻnā*
bearish (adj)	دبي، فظ	*dubbī, faẓẓ*
beast (n)	بهيمة، دابة	*bahīmah, dābbah*
beastly (adj)	بهيمي، بغيض	*bahīmī, baghīḍ*
beat (n)	ضربة، طريق معتادة	*ḍarbah, ṭarīq muʻtādah*
beaten (adj)	مضروب، مطروق	*maḍrūb, maṭrūq*
beatification (n)	تطويب، غبط	*taṭwīb, ghabṭ*
beatify (v)	طوّب، غبط	*ṭawwaba, ghabaṭa*
beatitude (n)	طوبى، سعادة	*ṭūbā, saʻādah*
beautician (n)	مجمّل، مزين	*mujammil, muzayyin*
beautification (n)	تجميل، تزيين	*tajmīl, tazyīn*
beautifier (n)	مجمّل، مزين	*mujammil, muzayyin*
beautiful (adj)	جميل، حسن	*jamīl, ḥasan*

beautify (v)	جمّل، حسّن	*jammala, ḥassana*
beauty (n)	جمال، حسن	*jamāl, ḥusn*
beauty parlour (n)	مؤسّسة تجميل	*mu'assasatu tajmīl*
beauty sleep (n)	نوم الحسن	*naumul ḥusn*
beauty spot (n)	شامة، خال	*shāmah, khāl*
because (conj)	لأن، بسبب	*li anna, bi sababi*
becharm (v)	فتن، سحر	*fatana, saḥara*
beckon (v)	أومأ، أشار	*auma'a, ashāra*
become (v)	أصبح، لاق	*aṣbaḥa, lāqa*
becoming (adj)	مناسب، لائق	*munāsib, lā'iq*
becomingly (adv)	بملاءمة، بلياقة	*bi mulā'amah, bi liyāqah*
bed (n)	فراش، سرير	*firāsh, sarīr*
bed (v)	نام، اضطجع	*nāma, iḍṭaja'a*
bed bug (n)	بقة الفراش	*baqqatul firāsh*
bedchamber (n)	غرفة النوم	*ghurfatun naum*
bedclothes (n)	شراشف	*sharāshif*
bedding (n)	فراش، شراشف	*firāsh, sharāshif*
bedeck (v)	زخرف، زيّن	*zakhrafa, zayyana*
bedevil (v)	فتن، أفسد	*fatana, afsada*
bedew (v)	بلّل، رطّب	*ballala, raṭṭaba*
bedfellow (n)	ضجيع،شريك الفراش	*ḍajī', sharīkul firāsh*
bedlam (n)	مجنون، جنون	*majnūn, junūn*
bedouin (n/adj)	بدوي	*badawī*
bedridden (adj)	طريح الفراش	*ṭarīḥul firāsh*
bedroom (n)	حجرة النوم	*ḥujratul naum*
bedspread (n)	غطاء السرير	*ghiṭā'us sarīr*
bedspring (n)	نابض السرير	*nābiḍus sarīr*

bedstead (n)	هيكل السرير	*haikalus sarīr*
bedtime (n)	وقت النوم	*waqtun naum*
bedward (adj)	نحو الفراش	*naḥwal firāsh*
bee (n)	نحلة، اجتماع الأصدقاء	*naḥlah, ijtimā'ul aṣdiqā'*
beef (n)	لحم البقر	*laḥmul baqar*
beefeater (n)	آكل لحم البقر	*ākilu laḥmil baqar*
beef tea (n)	مرق لحم البقر	*maraqu laḥmil baqar*
beefy (adj)	سمين، بدين	*samīṇ, badīn*
beehive (n)	خليّة نحل	*khaliyyatu naḥl*
beeline (n)	خط مباشر	*khaṭṭ mubāshir*
beer (n)	جعة، بيرة	*ji'ah, bīrah*
beerhouse (n)	حانة الجعة	*ḥānatul ji'ah*
beeswax (n)	شمع العسل	*sham'ul 'asal*
beet (n)	شمندر، بنجر	*shamandar, banjar*
beetroot (n)	جذر الشمندر	*jidhrush shamandar*
befall (v)	حدث، أصاب	*ḥadatha, aṣāba*
befit (v)	لاق، ناسب	*lāqa, nāsaba*
befitting (adj)	ملائم، مناسب	*mulā'im, munāsib*
befool (v)	ضحك على	*ḍaḥika 'ala*
before (adv/prep)	من قبل، أمام	*min qablu, amāma*
beforehand (adv)	مقدّمًا، قبلاً	*muqaddaman, qablan*
beforetime (adv)	سابقًا، في ما مضى	*sābiqan, fī mā maḍā*
befoul (v)	لوّث، وسّخ	*lawwatha, wassakha*
befriend (v)	صادق، أيد	*ṣādaqa, ayyada*
befuddled (adj)	مرتبك، سكران	*murtabik, sakrān*
beg (v)	تسوّل، التمس	*tasawwala, iltamasa*
beget (v)	ولد، أنجب	*wallada, anjaba*

beggar (n)	متسول، فقير	*mutasawwil, faqīr*
beggary (n)	فقر، فاقة، شحاذة	*faqr, fāqah, shiḥādhah*
begin (v)	بدأ، شرع	*bada'a, shara'a*
beginner (n)	مبتدئ، حديث	*mubtadi', ḥadīth*
beginning (n)	بداية، ابتداء	*bidāyah, ibtidā'*
begrudge (v)	حقد على	*ḥaqada 'alā*
beguile (v)	خدع، غش	*khada'a, ghashsha*
beguiling (adj)	خادع، مغرٍ	*khādi', mughrin*
behalf (n)	مصلحة، نيابة	*maṣlaḥah, niyābah*
behave (v)	سلك، سار	*salaka, sāra*
behaviour (n)	سلوك، سيرة	*sulūk, sīrah*
behead (v)	قطع الرأس، ضرب العنق	*qaṭa'ar ra's, ḍarabal 'unuq*
behest (n)	أمر، وصية	*amr, waṣiyyah*
behind (adv/prep)	إلى الوراء، وراء	*ilala warā', warā'a*
behindhand (adj)	متخلّف، متأخر	*mutakhallif, mut'akhkhir*
behold (v)	شاهد، لاحظ	*shāhada, lāḥaẓa*
behold (interj)	لاحظ، انظر	*lāḥiẓ, unẓur*
behove (v)	ينبغي، يلزم	*yambaghī, yalzim*
being (n)	كائن، كون	*kā'in, kaun*
bejewel (v)	زين بالجواهر	*ẓayyana bil jawāhir*
bejewelled (adj)	مزين بالجواهر	*muzayyan bil jawāhir*
belabour (v)	ضرب، نزل على	*ḍaraba, nazala 'alā*
belated (adj)	متأخر، مبطئ	*muta'akhkhir, mubṭi'*
beleaguer (v)	حاصر، طوق	*ḥāṣara, ṭawwaqa*
beleaguered (adj)	محاصر	*muḥāṣar*
belfry (n)	برج الجرس	*burjul jaras*

belie (v)	كذّب، ناقض	*kadhdhaba, nāqaḍa*
belief (n)	إيمان، عقيدة	*īmān, 'aqīdah*
believable (adj)	ممكن تصديقه	*mumkin taṣdīquh*
believe (v)	آمن، صدّق	*āmana, ṣaddaqa*
belittle (v)	صغر، استخف	*ṣaghghara, istakhaffa*
bell (n)	جرس، ناقوس	*jaras, nāqūs*
bellied (adj)	بطين، ذو بطن	*baṭīn, dhū baṭn*
belligerence (n)	قتال، خصام	*qitāl, khiṣām*
belligerent (adj)	محارب، مخاصم	*muḥārib, mukhāṣim*
bellow (n/v)	خوار، خار	*khuwār, khāra*
belly (n/v)	بطن، نفخ	*baṭn, nafakha*
bellyful (adj)	ملء البطن	*mil'ul baṭn*
belong (v)	انتمى، تعلق	*intamā, ta'allaqa*
belongings (n)	أمتعة، ممتلكات	*amti'ah, mumtalakāt*
beloved (adj)	محبوب، حبيب	*maḥbūb, ḥabīb*
below (prep/adv)	تحت، أدنى	*taḥta, adnā*
belt (n/v)	حزام، طوّق بحزام	*ḥizām, ṭawwaqa bi ḥizām*
bemoan (v)	تحسّر، ندب	*taḥassara, nadaba*
bemock (v)	سخر، هزأ	*sakhira, haza'a*
bemuse (v)	شده، أربك	*shadaha, arbaka*
bench (n)	مقعد، دكة	*maq'ad, dikkah*
bend (n)	حنية، التواء	*ḥanyah, iltiwā'*
bend (v)	حنى، وتر	*ḥanā, wattara*
beneath (adv/prep)	تحت، دون	*taḥta, dūna*
benedict (n)	متزوج بعد عزوبة طويلة	*matazawwij ba'da 'uzūbah ṭawīlah*
benediction (n)	بركة، تبرك	*barakah, tabarruk*

benefaction (n)	إحسان، صدقة	*iḥsān, ṣadaqah*
benefactor (n)	محسن، جواد	*muḥsin, jawwād*
benefactress (n)	محسنة، كريمة	*muḥsinah, karimah*
beneficence (n)	إحسان، جود	*iḥsān, jūd*
beneficent (adj)	محسن، مفيد	*muḥsin, mufīd*
beneficial (adj)	نافع، مفيد	*nāfi', mufīd*
beneficiary (n)	مستفيد، منتفع	*mustafīd, muntafi'*
benefit (n)	فائدة، نفع	*fā'idah, naf'*
benevolent (adj)	محسن، كريم	*muḥsin, karīm*
benight (v)	أظلم، دهم بظلام	*aẓlama, dahama bi ẓalām*
benighted (adj)	مظلم، جاهل	*muẓlim, jāhil*
benign (adj)	كريم، لطيف	*karīm, laṭīf*
benignant (adj)	رؤوف، نافع	*ra'ūf, nāfi'*
benignity (n)	لطف، رأفة	*luṭf, ra'fah*
benison (n)	بركة، هبة	*barakah, hibah*
bent (n)	ميل، انحناء	*mail, inḥinā'*
bent (adj)	منحنٍ، ميّال	*munḥanin, mayyāl*
benumb (v)	شل، خدر	*shalla, khaddara*
benzine (n)	بنـــزين	*binzīn*
bequeath (v)	ورّث بوصية	*warratha bi waṣiyyah*
bequest (n)	إرث بوصية	*irth bi waṣiyyah*
bereave (v)	سلب، حرم	*salaba, ḥarama*
bereft (adj)	محروم، معتوه	*maḥrūm, ma'tūh*
beriberi (n)	بري بري	*barībarī*
berlin (n)	برلينية	*barlīniyyah*
berry (n)	توت	*tūt*
berseem (n)	برسيم	*birsīm*

berth (n)	مضجع، وظيفة	*maḍja', waẓīfah*
beseech (v)	التمس، تضرع	*iltamasa, taḍarra'a*
beseem (v)	لاق، وافق	*lāqa, wāfaqa*
beset (v)	أحدق، حاصر	*aḥdaqa, ḥāṣara*
besetting (adj)	محدق، مزعج	*muḥdiq, muz'ij*
beside (prep)	بجانب، قرب	*bi jānib, qurba*
besides (prep/adv)	عدا، فوق ذلك	*'adā, fauqa dhālik*
besiege (v)	حاصر، اكتنف	*ḥāṣara, iktanafa*
besieger (n)	محاصر، مضايق	*muḥāṣir,, muḍāyiq*
besmear (v)	لطخ، لوّث	*laṭṭakha, lawwatha*
besmut (v)	لوث بالسخام	*lawwatha bis sukhām*
besom (n)	مكنسة، مقشة	*miknasah, miqashshah*
besot (v)	خبّل، أسكر	*khabbala, askara*
bespangle (v)	زين باللمع	*zayyana bil luma'*
bespatter (v)	وحل، لوث	*waḥḥala, lawwatha*
bespeak (v)	حجز، أوصى على	*ḥajaza, auṣā 'alā*
bespoke (adj)	موصًى عليه	*mūṣan 'alaih*
best (adj/adv)	أفضل، على أحسن وجه	*afḍal, 'alā aḥsani wajh*
bestial (adj)	وحشي، بهيمي	*waḥshī, bahīmī*
bestiality (n)	بهيمية، وحشية	*bahīmiyyah, waḥshiyyah*
bestir (v)	أثار، حث	*Athāra, ḥaththa*
bestow (v)	منح، وهب	*manaḥa, wahaba*
bestowal (n)	منحة، هبة	*Minḥah, hibah*
bet (n/v)	رهان، راهن	*rihān, rāhana*
bethel (n)	بقعة مقدسة	*Buq'ah muqaddasah*
bethink (v)	تأمّل، تذكر	*ta'ammala, tadhakkara*
betide (v)	حدث، وقع	*ḥadatha, waqa'a*
betoken (v)	دل على	*dalla 'alā*

betray (v)	خدع، غرر	*khada'a, gharrara*
betrayal (n)	خداع، غدر	*khidā', ghadr*
betroth (v)	خطب	*khaṭaba*
betrothal (n)	خطبة، خطوبة	*khiṭbah, khuṭūbah*
better (adj/adv)	أحسن، على نحو	*aḥsan, 'alā naḥwin*
	أحسن	*aḥsan*
betterment (n)	تحسين، تحسن	*taḥsīn, taḥassun*
betting (n)	رهان، مراهنة	*rihān, murāhanah*
bettor (n)	مراهن	*murāhin*
between (prep/adv)	بين، فيما بين	*baina, fīmā baina*
bevel (adj/v)	مائل، أمال	*mā'il, amāla*
bevelled (adj)	مشطوب، مائل	*mashṭūb, mā'il*
beverage (n)	شراب، مشروب	*sharāb, mashrūb*
bevy (n)	جماعة، سرب	*jamā'ah, sirb*
bewail (n)	ندب، نياحة	*nadb, niyāḥah*
bewailing (n/adj)	ندب، نادب	*nadb, nādib*
beware (v)	احترس، حذر	*iḥtarasa, ḥadhara*
bewilder (v)	حيّر، أربك	*ḥayyara, arbaka*
bewildered (adj)	منذهل، مرتبك	*mundhahil, murtabik*
bewildering (adj)	مذهل، مربك	*mudhhil, murbik*
bewilderment (n)	انذهال، ارتباك	*Indhihāl, irtibāk*
bewitch (v)	سحر، فتن	*saḥara, fatana*
bewitching (adj)	ساحر، فاتن	*sāḥir, fātin*
bewitchment (n)	سحر، افتتان	*siḥr, iftinān*
beyond (prep/adv)	وراء، أبعد	*warā', ab'ad*
biangular (adj)	ذو زاويتين	*dhū zāwiyatain*
biannual (adj)	نصف سنوي	*niṣfu sanawī*
biannually (adv)	مرتين في السنة	*marratain fis sanah*

bias (n/adj)	منحرف، مائل، تحيز	*munḥarif, mā'il, taḥayyuz*
biased (adj)	منحرف، متحيز	*munḥarif, mutaḥayyiz*
biaxial (adj)	ذو محورين	*dhū miḥwarain*
bibliographic (adj)	ببليوغرافي	*bibiliugharāfī*
bibliography (n)	ببليوغرافيا	*bibiliugharāfiyā*
bibiliophile (n)	محب الكتب	*muḥibbul kutub*
bicentenary (adj)	واقع كل مئتي سنة	*wāqi' kulla mi'atai sanah*
bicentric (adj)	ثنائي المركز	*thunā'iyyul markaz*
bicephalic (adj)	ذو رأسين	*dhū ra'sain*
biceps (n)	عضلة ذات الرأسين	*'aḍalah dhātur ra'sain*
bicloride (n)	ثاني كلوريد	*thānī kulūrīd*
bicromate (n)	ثاني كرومات	*thānī kurūmāt*
bicker (n/v)	تخاصم، تخاصم	*takhāṣum, takhāṣama*
bicycle (n)	دراجة	*darrājah*
bicyclist (n)	راكب الدراجة	*rākibud darrājah*
bid (v)	عرض سعراً، أمر	*'araḍa si'ran, amara*
bid (n)	أمر، عطاء، دعوة	*amr, 'aṭā', da'wah*
biddable (adj)	سهل الانقياد	*sahlul inqiyād*
bidder (n)	آمر، مزايد	*āmir, muzāyid*
bidding (n)	أمر، مزايدة	*amr, muzāyadah*
bide (v)	بقى، أقام في	*baqā, aqāma fī*
biennial (adj)	واقع كل سنتين	*wāqi' kulla sanatain*
biennium (n)	فترة سنتين	*fatratu sanatain*
bier (n)	نعش، تابوت	*na'sh, tābūt*
bifacial (adj)	ذو وجهين	*dhū wajhain*
biff (n/v)	ضربة، ضرب	*ḍarbah, ḍaraba*

bifurcate (v)	أقسم إلى شعبتين	*aqsama ilā shu'batain*
bifurcation (n)	تفريع، تشعيب	*Tafrī', tash'īb*
big (adj)	كبير، قوي، عظيم	*kabīr, qawī, 'aẓīm*
bigamist (n)	مضارّ	*muḍārr*
bigamous (adj)	متزوج على ضر	*mutazawwij 'alā ḍurr*
bigamy (n)	تزوج على ضر	*tazawwuj 'alā ḍurr*
bihead (n)	غرور	*Ghurūr*
biheaded (adj)	مغرور	*maghrūr*
bihearted (adj)	كريم، سخي	*karīm, sakhī*
big money (n)	أرباح طائلة	*arbāḥ ṭā'ilah*
bigmouthed (adj)	كبير الضخم	*kabīruḍ ḍakhm*
bigness (n)	كبر، عظم	*kibar, 'iẓam*
bigot (n)	متعصب، رفضي	*Muta'aṣṣib, rafaḍī*
bigoted (adj)	شديد التعصب	*shadīdut ta'aṣṣub*
bigotry (n)	تعصب أعمى	*ta'aṣṣub a'mā*
big shot (n)	شخص عظيم الشان	*shakhṣ 'aẓīmush shān*
big-ticket (adj)	غالٍ	*ghālin*
big top (n)	خيمة كبرى في سيرك	*khaima kubrā fī sīrk*
bijou (n)	جوهرة، حلية	*jauharah, ḥulyah*
bike (n/v)	دراجة، ركب الدراجة	*darrājah, rakibad darrājah*
biker (n)	راكب الدراجة	*rākibud darrājah*
bikini (n)	بيكيني، ثوب السباحة	*bīkīnī, thaubus sibāḥah*
bilabial (adj)	متعلق بكلتا الشفتين	*muta'alliq bi kiltash shafatain*
bilateral (adj)	ثنائي، من الجهتين	*Thunā'ī, minal jihatain*
bilberry (n)	عنب الدب	*'inabud dubb*

bile (n)	صفراء، مرارة	*ṣafrā', marārah*
bile duct (n)	قناة الصفراء	*qanātuṣ ṣafrā'*
bilestone (n)	حصاة صفراوية	*ḥaṣāt ṣafrāwiyyah*
bilge (n)	جوف المركب	*jauful markab*
bilge water (n)	ماء آسن	*mā' āsin*
bilharzia (n)	بلهرسية	*bilharsiyah*
bilingual (adj)	ثنائي اللغة	*thunā'iyyul lughah*
bilious (adj)	صفراوي	*ṣafrāwī*
biliteral (adj)	ثنائي الحروف	*thunā'iyyul ḥurūf*
bilk (n/v)	خداع، خدع	*khidā', khada'a*
bill (n)	منقار، فاتورة، قائمة	*minqār, fātūrah, qā'imah*
billboard (n)	لوحة إعلانات	*lauḥatu i'lānāt*
billfold (n)	محفظة جيب	*miḥfaẓatu jaib*
billhook (n)	منجل، سكين	*minjal, sikkīn*
billiards (n)	لعبة البليارد	*lu'batul bilyārd*
billing (n)	إعلان عن حفلة مسرحية	*i'lān 'an ḥaflah masraḥiyyah*
billion (n)	بليون	*balyūn*
billionaire (n)	بليوني	*balyūnī*
bill of credit	سند على الدولة	*sanad 'alad daulah*
bill of debt	سند، كمبيالة	*sanad, kambiyālah*
bill of divorce	ورقة الطلاق	*waraqatuṭ ṭalāq*
bill of exchange	تحويل	*taḥwīl*
bill of fare	قائمة الطعام	*qā'imatuṭ ṭa'ām*
bill of health	براءة الصحة	*barā'atuṣ siḥḥah*
bill of rights	ميثاق الحقوق	*mīthāqul ḥuqūq*
bill of sale	عقد البيع	*'aqdul bai'*

billow (n)	كتلة، موجة عظيمة	*kutlah, maujah 'aẓīmah*
billow (v)	تلاطم، انتفخ	*talāṭama, intafakha*
billowy (adj)	متلاطم، منتفخ	*mutalāṭim, muntafikh*
billsticker (n)	ملصق الإعلانات	*mulṣiqul i'lānāt*
billy (n)	غلاية، رفيق	*ghallāyah, rafīq*
billy goat (n)	ذكر الماعز	*dhakarul mā'iz*
bimonthly (adj/adv)	نصف شهري	*niṣfu shahrī*
binary (adj)	ثنائي، مثنى	*thunā'ī, muthannā*
bind (v)	ربط، حزم	*rabaṭa, ḥazama*
binder (n)	مجلّد، رباط	*mujallid, ribāṭ*
bindery (n)	معمل التجليد	*ma'malut tajlīd*
binding (n)	رباط، إيثاق	*ribāṭ, īthāq*
binocle (n)	منظار ثنائي	*minẓār thunā'ī*
binocular (adj)	ثنائي العينين	*thunā'iyyul 'ainain*
binomial (adj)	ذو اسمين	*dhū ismain*
bio	حياة	*ḥayāt*
biochemical (adj)	كيميائي حيوي	*kīmiyā'ī ḥayawī*
biochemist (n)	عالم بالكيمياء الحيوية	*'ālim bil kīmiyā' al ḥayawiyyah*
biochemistry (n)	كيمياء حيوية	*kīmiyā' ḥayawiyyah*
biographer (n)	مترجم حياة	*mutarjimu ḥayāh*
biographical (adj)	متعلق بسيرة	*muta'alliq bi sīrah*
biography (n)	سيرة، تاريخ حياة	*sīrah, tārīkhu ḥayāt*
biological (adj)	أحيائي، بيولوجي	*aḥyā'ī, buyūlūjī*
biological warfare	حرب بيولوجية	*ḥarb buyūlūjiyyah*
biology (n)	علم الأحياء، بيولوجيا	*'ilmul aḥyā', buyūlūjiyā*
biopsy (n)	دراسة النسيج	*dirāsatun nasīj*

bioscope (n)	مسلاط سينمائي	*mislāṭ sīnmā'ī*
bioscopy (n)	كشف حيوي	*kashf ḥayawī*
biosphere (n)	محيط حيوي	*muḥīṭ ḥayawī*
biosynthesis (n)	تخليق حيوي	*takhlīq ḥayawī*
biotechnology (n)	تكنولوجيا حيوية	*tiknūlūjiyā ḥayawiyyah*
biotic (adj)	حيوي، أحيائي	*ḥayawī, aḥyā'ī*
bipartisan (adj)	متعلق بحزبين	*muta'alliq bi ḥizbain*
bipartite (adj)	ذو قسمين، ثنائي	*dhū qismain, thunā'ī*
biplane (n)	ذات السطحين	*dhātus saṭḥain*
bipolar (adj)	ذو قطبين	*dhū quṭbain*
birch (n)	شجرة البتولا	*shajaratul batūlā*
bird (n)	طير، طائر	*ṭair, ṭā'ir*
birdbrain (n)	شخص أبله	*shakhṣ ablah*
birdcall (n)	صوت الطائر	*ṣautuṭ ṭā'ir*
birdie (n)	طويئر، طائر صغير	*ṭuwai'ir, ṭā'ir ṣaghīr*
birth (n)	ولادة، أصل	*wilādah, aṣl*
birth certificate	شهادة الميلاد	*shahādatul mīlād*
birth control	تحديد النسل	*taḥdīdun nasl*
birthday (n)	عيد الميلاد	*'īdul mīlād*
birthmark (n)	وحمة	*waḥmah*
birthmate (n)	لدة	*lidah*
birthplace (n)	مسقط الرأس	*masqaṭur ra's*
birthrate (n)	نسبة المواليد	*nisbatul mawālīd*
birthright (n)	حق المولد	*ḥaqqul maulid*
birth sin (n)	خطيئة أصلية	*khaṭī'ah aṣliyyah*
biscuit (n)	بسكويت	*biskwīt*
bisect (v)	نصّف، شطر	*naṣṣafa, shaṭara*
bisection (n)	شطر، تنصيف	*shaṭr, tanṣīf*

bisector (n)	منصف الزاوية	*munaṣṣifuz zāwiyah*
bisexual (n/adj)	خنثى، ثنائي الجنس	*khunthā, thunā'iyyul jins*
bishop (n)	أسقف، مطران	*usquf, muṭrān*
bishopric (n)	منصب الأسقف	*manṣabul usquf*
bison (n)	بيسون	*bīsūn*
bit (v)	شكم، كبح	*shakama, kabaḥa*
bit (n)	شكيمة، قضمة	*shakīmah, quḍmah*
bitch (n)	كلبة، أنثى الكلب	*kalbah, unthal kalb*
bite (v)	عض، قطع	*'aḍḍa, qaṭa'a*
bitewing (n)	رقيقة العض	*raqīqatul aḍḍ*
biting (adj)	شديد، قارص	*shadīd, qāriṣ*
bitter (adj)	مر، عنيف، قاسٍ	*murr, 'anīf, qāsin*
bitterly (adv)	بقسوة، بمرارة	*bi qaswah, bi marārah*
bittersweet (n/adj)	حلو مر	*ḥulw murr*
bitty (adj)	صغير، ضئيل	*ṣaghīr, ḍa'īl*
bitumen (n)	قار، بيتومين	*qārr, bītūmīn*
bituminous (adj)	بيتوميني، قاري	*bītūmīnī, qārrī*
bivalve (n/adj)	ذو مصراعين	*ḍhū miṣrā'ain*
bivouac (n)	إقامة مؤقتة	*iqāmah mu'aqqatah*
biweekly (adj)	نصف شهري	*niṣfu shahrī*
bizarre (adj)	شاذ، عجيب	*shādhdh, 'ajīb*
blab (v)	أفشى سرًا	*afshā sirran*
blabber (n/v)	ثرثرة، ثرثر	*thartharah, tharthara*
black (adj/n)	أسود، لون أسود	*aswad, laun aswād*
blackball (n)	كريّة سوداء	*kurayyah saudā'*
blackbelt (n)	منطقة سوداء	*minṭaqah saudā'*
blackberry (n)	ثمر العليق	*thamarul 'ullaiq*

blackbird (n)	شحرور، شحور	*shuḥrūr, shaḥwar*
blackboard (n)	سبورة، لوح أسود	*sabbūrah, lauḥ aswad*
black buck (n)	ظبي أسود	*ẓaby aswad*
blacken (v)	سوّد، فحم	*sawwada, faḥḥama*
black eye (n)	كدمة حول العين	*kadmah ḥaulal 'ain*
blackguard (n)	وغد، وبش	*waghd, wabash*
blackhead (n)	أسود الرأس	*aswadur ra's*
blackheart (n)	قلب أسود	*qalb aswad*
blackhearted (adj)	أسود القلب	*aswadul qalb*
blacking (n)	دهان أسود	*dihān aswad*
blackish (adj)	مسوّد	*musawwad*
black knot (n)	عقدة سوداء	*'uqdah saudā'*
blackleg (n)	ساق سوداء	*sāq saudā'*
blacklist (n)	لائحة سوداء	*lā'iḥah saudā'*
black magic (n)	سحر أسود	*siḥr aswad*
blackmail (n)	ابتزاز بالتهديد	*ibtizāz bit tahdīd*
black mark (n)	نقطة سوداء	*nuqṭah saudā'*
black market (n)	سوق سوداء	*sūq saudā'*
blackness (n)	سواد، دهمة	*sawād, dahmah*
blackout (n)	فترة التعتيم	*fatratut ta'tīm*
black sheep (n)	خروف أسود	*kharūf aswad*
blacksmith (n)	حداد	*ḥaddād*
blacktop (n)	زفت الطرق	*ziftuṭ ṭuruq*
black vomit (n)	قيئ أسود	*qai' aswad*
black widow	أرملة سوداء	*armalah saudā'*
bladder (n)	مثانة	*mathānah*
blade (n)	نصل، ورقة نبات	*naṣl, waraqatu nabāt*
blame (n/v)	ملامة، لام	*malāmah, lāma*

blamed (adj)	لعين، ملوم	*la'īn, malūm*
blameful (adj)	مستحق اللوم	*mustaḥiqqul laum*
blameless (adj)	بريء، بلا عيب	*barī', bilā 'aib*
blameworthy (adj)	مستحق للوم	*mustaḥiqq li laum*
blanch (v)	بيض، أبيض	*bayyaḍa, abyaḍa*
bland (adj)	لطيف، عليل	*laṭīf, 'alīl*
blandish (v)	تملق، داجن	*tamallaqa, dājana*
blank (n/adj)	فراغ، أبيض	*farāgh, abyaḍ*
blank (v)	محا، سد	*maḥā, sadda*
blank endorsement	تحويل الغفل	*taḥwīlul ghufl*
blanket (n)	بطانية، حرام	*baṭṭāniyyah, ḥirām*
blanket (v)	غطى بحرام	*ghaṭṭā bi ḥirām*
blare (v/n)	بوّق، بواق	*bawwaqa, buwāq*
blarney (n)	تملق، مداهنة	*tamalluq, mudāhanah*
blase (adj)	سئم من الملذات	*sa'im minal maladhdhāt*
blaspheme (v)	جدف، سب	*jaddafa, sabba*
blasphemous (adj)	مجدف، تجديفي	*mujaddif, tajdīfī*
blasphemy (n)	تجديف، سب	*tajdīf, sabb*
blast (n)	عصفة، نفخة، انفجار	*'aṣfah, nafkhah, infijār*
blast (v)	نسف، أذبل	*nasafa, adhbala*
blasted (adj)	ذابل، مدمر	*dhābil, mudammar*
blatant (adj)	صخاب، سمج	*ṣakhkhāb, samij*
blather (n)	كلام أحمق	*kalām aḥmaq*
blather (v)	تكلم بحماقة	*takallama bi ḥamāqah*
blaze (n)	لهيب، وهج، تأجج	*lahīb, wahj, ta'ajjuj*
blaze (v)	التهب، توهج	*iltahaba, tawahhaja*
blazer (n)	سترة فضفاضة، متوهج	*sutrah faḍfāḍah, mutawahhij*
blazing (adj)	متوهج، ملتهب	*mutawahhij, multahib*

blazon (n)	شعار النبالة	*shi'ārun nabālah*
blazonry (n)	زخرفة، شعار النبالة	*zakhrafah, shi'ārun nabālah*
bleach (n/v)	تبييض، بيّض	*tabyīḍ, bayyaḍa*
bleacher (n)	قصار الأقمشة	*qaṣṣārul aqmishah*
bleaching powder	مسحوق التقصير	*masḥūqut taqṣīr*
bleak (adj)	أجرد، كئيب	*ajrad, ka'īb*
blear (v)	أدمع، أعشى	*adma'a, a'shā*
blear (adj)	دامع، غائم	*dāmi', ghā'im*
blear-eyed (adj)	دامع العينين	*dāmi'ul 'ainain*
bleary (adj)	غائم، متعب	*ghā'im, mut'ab*
bleat (n/v)	ثغاء، ثغا	*thughā', thaghā*
bleed (v)	استنـزف، استدمى	*istanzafa, istadmā*
bleeding (n/adj)	نزف، دامٍ	*nazf, dāmin*
bleeding heart (n)	قلب دامي	*qalb dāmī*
blemish (v)	عاب، شوه	*'āba, shawwaha*
blemish (n)	عيب، وصمة	*'aib, waṣmah*
blench (v)	نكص، أبيض	*nakaṣa, abyaḍa*
blend (v/n)	مزج، مزيج	*mazaja, mazīj*
blender (n)	مولّف	*muwallif*
bless (v)	كرّس، أسعد، بارك	*karrasa, as'ada, bāraka*
blessed (adj)	سعيد، مقدس	*sa'īd, muqaddas*
blessing (n)	نعمة، بركة، عطية	*ni'mah, barakah, 'aṭiyyah*
blight (n)	تلف، فساد، آفة	*talaf, fasād, āfah*
blind (adj)	أعمى، ضرير	*a'mā, ḍarīr*
blindfold (v/n)	عصب العينين، عصابة	*'aṣabal 'ainain, 'iṣābah*

blindly (adv)	بتهور، بلا تبصر	*bi tahawwur, bilā tabaṣṣur*
blind man's buff	غميضة	*ghummaiḍah*
blindness (n)	عمًى، تهور	*'aman, tahawwur*
blind spot (n)	نقطة عمياء	*nuqṭah 'amyā'*
blind worm	عظاية عمياء	*'iẓāyah 'amyā'*
blink (v)	طرف، نظر، أومض	*ṭarafa, naẓara, aumaḍa*
blink (n)	لمحة، نظرة، وميض	*lamḥah, naẓrah, wamīḍ*
blinkard (n)	أعشى	*a'shā*
blinker (n)	ضوء وامض	*ḍau' wāmiḍ*
bliss (n)	منتهى السعادة	*muntahas sa'ādah*
blissful (adj)	سعيد، مغبوط	*sa'īd, maghbūṭ*
blister (n/v)	نفطة، نفط	*nafṭah, naffaṭa*
blister gas (n)	غاز منفط	*ghāz munaffiṭ*
blithe (adj)	مرح، مبتهج	*mariḥ, mubtahij*
blitz (n)	حرب خاطفة	*ḥarb khāṭifah*
blot (v)	انتفخ، دخّن	*intafakha, dakhkhana*
block (n)	عائق، سد	*'ā'iq, sadd*
block (v)	عاق، سد	*'āqa, sadda*
blockade (n/v)	حصار، حاصر	*ḥiṣār, ḥāṣara*
blockage (n)	سد، انسداد	*sadd, insidād*
blockbuster (n)	قنبلة شديدة الانفجار	*qumbulah shadīdatul infijār*
blockhead (n)	أحمق، أبله	*aḥmaq, ablah*
blood (n)	دم، قتل	*dam, qatl*
bloodbank (n)	بنك الدم	*bankud dam*
bloodbath (n)	حمّام الدم	*ḥammāmud dam*

blood count (n)	تعداد الدم	*ta'dādud dam*
bloodcurdling (adj)	مروّع، مفزع	*murawwi', mufzi'*
blooded (adj)	أصيل، صافي الدم	*aṣīl, ṣāfiyud dam*
blood group (n)	زمرة الدم	*zumratud dam*
bloodily (adv)	بقسوة، بوحشية	*bi qaswah, bi waḥshiyyah*
bloodless (adj)	فاقد الدم، أبيض	*fāqidud dam, abyaḍ*
bloodletting (n)	إراقة الدم	*irāqatud dam*
blood money (n)	ثمن الدم	*thamanud dam*
blood pressure (n)	ضغط الدم	*ḍaghṭud dam*
bloodred (adj)	قانٍ، أحمر كالدم	*qānin, aḥmar kad dam*
blood relation (n)	قرابة دم	*qarābatu damin*
bloodshed (n)	إراقة الدم	*irāqatud dam*
bloodstain (n)	لطخة الدماء	*laṭkhatud dimā'*
bloodstained (adj)	ملطخ بالدم	*mulaṭṭakh bid dam*
bloodstone (n)	حجر الدم	*ḥajarud dam*
bloodsucker (n)	علقة، دودة	*'alaqah, dūdah*
blood test (n)	فحص الدم	*faḥṣud dam*
bloodthirsty (adj)	سفاح، وحشي	*saffāḥ, waḥshī*
blood transfusion (n)	نقل الدم	*naqlud dam*
blood-type (n)	زمرة الدم	*zumratud dam*
blood vessel (n)	وعاء دموي	*wi'ā' damawī*
bloody (adj)	دموي، ملطخ بالدم	*damawī, mulaṭṭakh bid dam*
bloom (n/v)	إزهار، أزهر	*izhār, azhara*
blooming (adj)	مزهر، مزدهر	*muzhir, muzdahir*
blossom (n)	إزهار، تفتح	*izhār, tafattuḥ*
blossom (v)	أزهر، تطور	*azhara, taṭawwara*

blossomy (adj)	مزهر، مزدهر	*muzhir, muzdahir*
blot (n/v)	لطخة، لطّخ	*laṭkhah, laṭṭakha*
blotch (n/v)	لطخة، لطّخ	*laṭkhah, laṭṭakha*
blotter (n)	ورقة نشاف	*waraqatu nashshāf*
blotting paper (n)	ورق نشاف	*waraqu nashshāf*
blouse (n)	بلوزه	*bulūzah*
blow (n)	نفخ، عاصفة، ضربة	*nafkh, 'āṣifah, ḍarbah*
blow (v)	عصف، نفخ، انتفخ	*'aṣafa, nafakha, intafakha*
blower (n)	مروحة، متفاخر	*mirwaḥah, mutafākhir*
blowhard (n)	متفاخر، متبجح	*mutafākhir, mutabajjiḥ*
blown (adj)	منتفخ، متفتح	*muntafikh, mutafattiḥ*
blownup (n)	انفجار، هبة	*infijār, habbah*
blowy (adj)	عاصف، كثير الريح	*'āṣif, kathīrur rīḥ*
blubbery (adj)	منتفخ، سمين	*muntafikh, samīn*
blugeon (n/v)	هراوة، ضرب بالهراوة	*hirāwah, ḍaraba bil hirāwah*
blue (adj/v)	أزرق، زرق	*azraq, zarraqa*
blue baby (n)	وليد أزرق	*walīd azraq*
blueberry (n)	ثمر العنبية	*thamarul 'inabiyyah*
bluebird (n)	عصفور أزرق	*'uṣfūr azraq*
blue-black (adj)	أسود مزرق	*aswad muzarraq*
blue blood (n)	نبالة، أصل	*nabālah, aṣl*
blue-blooded (adj)	نبيل، كريم المحتد	*nabīl, karīmul maḥtid*
bluebonnet (n)	قلنسوة زرقاء	*qalansuwah zarqā'*
blue book (n)	كتاب أزرق	*kitāb azraq*
blue-chip (adj)	ناجح، مربح	*nājiḥ, murbiḥ*
blue devils (n)	حزن، قنوط	*ḥuzn, qunūṭ*

blue flag (n)	راية زرقاء	*rāyah zarqā'*
bluejack (n)	بلوط رمادي	*ballūṭ ramādī*
blueprint (n)	طبعة زرقاء	*ṭab'ah zarqā'*
blues (n)	كآبة، ضيق الخلق	*ka'ābah, ḍīqul khulq*
bluff (n/v)	خداع، خدع	*khidā', khada'a*
bluish (adj)	ضارب إلى الزرقاء	*ḍārib ilaz zarqā'*
blunder (n)	خطأ فاضح	*khaṭa' fāḍiḥ*
blunder (v)	أخطأ، غلط	*akhṭa'a, ghaliṭa*
blunt (adj)	عديم الحس، فظ	*'adīmul ḥiss, faẓẓ*
bluntly (adv)	بفظاظة، بخشونة	*bi faẓāẓah, bi khushūnah*
bluntness (n)	فظاظة، خشونة	*faẓāẓah, khushūnah*
blur (n)	لطخة، ضبابية، غير واضح	*laṭkhah, ḍabābiyyah, ghair wāḍiḥ*
blur (v)	لطخ، أعشى	*laṭṭakha, a'shā*
blurred (adj)	غير واضح	*ghair wāḍiḥ*
blush (v)	احمر، تورد	*iḥmarra, tawarrada*
blushful (adj)	متورد، خجول	*mutawarrid, khajūl*
blushing (adj)	خجل، متورد	*khajil, mutawarrid*
blushing (n)	احمرار الوجه	*iḥmirārul wajh*
bluster (v)	عصف، هدد	*'aṣafa, tahaddada*
bluster (n)	عاصفة، تهديد	*'āṣifah, tahdīd*
board (n)	لوح، مائدة، جانب	*lauḥ, mā'idah, jānib*
board (v)	ركب متن السفينة	*rakiba matnas safīnah*
boarder (n)	ثاوي، تلميذ داخلي	*thāwī, tilmīdh dākhilī*
boarding (n)	ثواء، ألواح خشبية	*thawā', alwāḥ khashabiyyah*
boardinghouse (n)	مثوى، نزل	*mathwā, nuzul*

boarding school	مدرسة داخلية	*madrasah dākhiliyyah*
boast (n/v)	تباه، تباهى	*tabāhin, tabāhā*
boaster (n)	متباه، متفاخر	*mutabāhin, mutafākhir*
boastful (adj)	متبجح، مفاخر	*mutabajjiḥ, mufākhir*
boat (n)	سفينة، مركب، زورق	*safīnah, markab, zauraq*
boating (n)	ركوب الزوارق	*rukūbuz zawāriq*
boatman (n)	نوتي، بحار	*nūtī, baḥḥār*
boat race (n)	سباق الزوارق	*sibāquz zawāriq*
bob (v)	هز، تمايل	*hazza, tamāyala*
bobby (n)	شرطي، بوليس	*shurṭī, būlīs*
bodied (adj)	ذو جسد	*dhū jasad*
bodiless (adj)	غير مادي، غير جسدي	*ghair māddī, ghair jasadī*
bodily (adj)	جسدي، مادي	*jasadī, māddī*
body (n)	جسم، شخص	*jism, shakhṣ*
bodyguard (n)	حرس، بطانة	*ḥaras, biṭānah*
boer (n/adj)	بويري	*buwairī*
bogey (n)	بعبع، شبح	*bu'bu', shabaḥ*
bogeyman (n)	بعبع	*bu'bu'*
boggle (v)	أجفل، تردّد	*ajfala, taraddada*
bogus (adj)	زائف، غير حقيقي	*zā'if, ghair ḥaqīqī*
boil (v/n)	غلى، غلي	*ghalā, ghaly*
boiler (n)	غلاية، مرجل	*ghallāyah, mirjal*
boiling (n/adj)	غلي، مهتاج	*ghaly, muhtāj*
boiling point (n)	نقطة الغليان	*nuqṭatul ghalayān*
boisterous (adj)	شديد، عاصف	*shadīd, 'āṣif*
bold (adj)	جسور، واضح	*jasūr, wāḍiḥ*

boldly (adv)	بجسارة، بإقدام	*bi jasārah, bi iqdām*
boldness (n)	جسارة، جراءة	*jasārah, jarā'ah*
bollard (n)	مربط الحبال	*marbiṭul ḥibāl*
bolster (n)	وسادة، مسند	*wisādah, misnad*
bolt (n/v)	رتاج، ثبت بالرتاج	*ritāj, thabbata bir ritāj*
bomb (n/v)	قنبلة، قذف بالقنابل	*qumbulah, qadhafa bil qanābil*
bombard (v)	قذف بالقنابل	*qadhafa bil qanābil*
bombardier (n)	قاذف، مدفعي	*qādhif, midfa'ī*
bombast (n)	كلام منمق	*kalām munammaq*
bombastic (adj)	منمق، مزوق	*munammaq, muzawwaq*
bomber (n)	قاذفة القنابل	*qādhifatul qanābil*
bombproof (adj)	صامد للقنابل	*ṣāmid lil qanābil*
bombshell (n)	قنبلة	*qumbulah*
bona fide (n)	صادق، أصلي	*ṣādiq, aṣlī*
bonanza (n)	كتلة ضخمة	*kutlah ḍakhmah*
bond (n)	قيد، ميثاق، رباط	*qaid, mīthāq, ribāṭ*
bond (v)	حجز، رهن	*ḥajaza, rahana*
bondage (n)	عبودية، استرقاق	*'ubūdiyyah, istirqāq*
bonded (adj)	محجوز، مضمون	*maḥjūz, maḍmūn*
bondmaid (n)	أمة، جارية	*amah, jāriyah*
bondman (n)	عبد، رقيق	*'abd, raqīq*
bone (n)	عظم	*'aẓm*
bone meal (n)	مسحوق العظام	*masḥūqul 'iẓām*
boner (n)	غلطة شنيعة	*ghalṭah shanī'ah*
bonesetter (n)	مجبر العظام	*mujabbirul 'iẓām*
bonfire (n)	مشعلة	*mash'alah*

bonnet (n)	قلنسوة نسوية	*qalansuwah niswiyyah*
bonny (adj)	جميل، رائع	*jamīl, rā'i'*
bonus (n)	شيء إضافي	*shay' iḍāfī*
bon voyage (n)	رحلة سعيدة	*riḥlah sa'īdah*
boo (n)	صوت ازدراء	*ṣautu izdirā'*
boob (n)	معتوه، مخبل	*ma'tūh, mukhabbal*
booby (n)	أبله، مغفل	*ablah, mughaffal*
book (n)	كتاب، دفتر، سجل	*kitāb, daftar, sijill*
book (v)	سجل، حجز	*sajjala, ḥajaza*
bookbinder (n)	مجلد الكتب	*mujallidul kutub*
bookbinding (n)	تجليد الكتب	*tajlīdul kutub*
bookcase (n)	خزانة كتب	*khizānatu kutub*
book end (n)	مسند الكتب	*misnadul kutub*
bookish (adj)	كتبي، مولع بالكتب	*kutubī, mūla' bil kutub*
bookkeeper (n)	كاتب الحسابات	*kātibul ḥisābāt*
booklet (n)	كتيب	*kutayyib*
book review (n)	مراجعة الكتاب	*murāja'atul kitāb*
bookseller (n)	بائع الكتب	*bā'i'ul kutub*
bookshop (n)	مكتبة	*maktabah*
bookstall (n)	كشك الكتب	*kushkul kutub*
bookstore (n)	مكتبة، مخزن كتب	*maktabah, makhzanu kutub*
bookworm (n)	عثة الكتب	*'uththatul kutub*
boom (n)	ذراع المرفاع، ذراع التطويل	*dhirā'ul mirfā', dhirā'ut taṭwīl*
boom (v)	دوى، اندفع، ازدهر	*dawwā, indafa'a, izdahara*
boomrang (n)	بمرنغ	*bamrangh*

boon (n)	نعمة، عطية، هدية	*ni'mah, 'aṭiyyah, hadyah*
boost (n)	تأييد، عون، تشجيع	*ta'yīd, 'aun, tashjī'*
boost (v)	رفع، أيد، قوى	*rafa'a, ayyada, qawwā*
booster (n)	مؤيد، معزز	*mu'ayyid, mu'azziz*
boot (n)	غنيمة، غطاء واقٍ	*ghanīmah, ghiṭā' wāqin*
booth (n)	كشك، سقيفة	*kushk, saqīfah*
booty (n)	غنيمة، كسب عظيم	*ghanīmah, kasb 'aẓīm*
booze (n)	شراب مسكر	*sharāb muskir*
boozy (adj)	سكير، ثمل	*sikkīr, thamil*
border (n)	حافة، حد، حاشية	*ḥāffah, ḥadd, ḥāshiyah*
borderer (n)	ساكن الحدود	*sākinul ḥudūd*
borderland (n)	منطقة حدود	*minṭaqatu ḥudūd*
border line (n)	حد، فاصل	*ḥadd, fāṣil*
bore (v)	أضجر، ثقب	*aḍjara, thaqaba*
bored (adj)	ضجر، برم	*ḍajir, barim*
boredom (n)	ضجر، برم	*ḍajar, baram*
borer (n)	ثقاب، مثقب	*thaqqāb, mithqab*
boric (adj)	بوريك	*būrīk*
boric acid (n)	حمض البوريك	*ḥamḍul būrīk*
boring (n/adj)	ثقب، مضجر	*thaqb, muḍjir*
born (adj)	مولود	*maulūd*
borough (n)	قصبة	*qaṣabah*
borrow (v)	استعار، أعار	*ista'āra, a'āra*
borrower (n)	مستعير، مقترض	*musta'īr, muqtariḍ*
borrowing (n)	استعار، اقتراض	*isti'ār, iqtirāḍ*
bosom (n)	صدر، حضن، قلب	*ṣadr, ḥiḍn, qalb*

bosom (v)	كتم، عانق	*katama, ʻānaqa*
bosom friend (n)	صديق حميم	*ṣadīq ḥamīm*
boss (n)	رئيس، مفوض	*ra'īs, mufawwaḍ*
botanic (adj)	نباتي	*nabātī*
botanist (adj)	عالم النبات	*ʻālimun nabāt*
botany (n)	علم النبات	*ʻilmun nabāt*
both (adj/pron)	كلا، كلتا	*kilā, kiltā*
both (conj)	معًا	*maʻan*
bother (v)	أربك، أزعج	*arbaka, azʻaja*
bothersome (adj)	مزعج، مزعل	*muzʻij, muzʻil*
bottle (n)	زجاجة، قربة	*zujājah, qirbah*
bottom (n)	أدنى، أسفل، قعر	*adnā, asfal, qaʻr*
bottomless (adj)	لا قعر له	*lā qaʻra lahu*
bottommost (adj)	أسفل، أعمق	*asfal, aʻmaq*
bough (n)	غصن، فرع	*ghuṣn, farʻ*
bounce (v)	وثب، ارتد	*wathaba, irtadda*
bounce (n)	وثبة، طرد	*wathbah, ṭard*
bouncer (n)	واثب، متبجح	*wāthib, mutabajjiḥ*
bouncily (adv)	بمرح، بحماسة	*bi maraḥ, bi ḥamāsah*
bouncing (adj)	قوي، نشيط	*qawī, nashīṭ*
bouncy (adj)	متحمس، مرن	*mutaḥammis, marin*
bound (adj)	مقيد، متجه	*muqayyad, muttajih*
bound (v)	قيد، حد	*qayyada, ḥadda*
bound (n)	قيد، حد، وثبة	*qaid, ḥadd, wathbah*
boundary (n)	تخم، حد	*takhm, ḥadd*
bounden (adj)	مدين، ملزم	*madīn, mulzim*
boundless (adj)	غير محدود	*ghair maḥdūd*
bounteous (adj)	كريم، سخي	*karīm, sakhī*

bountiful (adj)	جواد، كريم	*jawwād, karīm*
bounty (n)	سخاء، محصول	*sakhā', maḥṣūl*
bouqet (n)	باقة أزهار، صحبة	*bāqatu azhār, ṣuḥbah*
bourgeois (adj)	بورجوازي، طبقة متوسطة	*būrjawāzī, ṭabaqah mutawassiṭah*
bout (n)	فترة، مباراة، قتال	*fatrah, mubārāt, qitāl*
boutique (n)	دكان صغير	*dukkān ṣaghīr*
bow (v)	خضع، انحنى، حنى	*khaḍa'a, inḥanā, ḥanā*
bow (n)	انحناء، قوس	*inḥinā', qaus*
bowdlerize,-ise (v)	هذب كتاباً	*hadhdhaba kitāban*
bowels (n)	أمعاء، أحشاء	*am'ā', aḥshā'*
bower (n)	كوخ ريفي، تعريشة	*kūkh rīfi, ta'rīshah*
bowery (n)	ذو تعاريش	*dhū ta'ārīsh*
bowfin (n)	بوفن	*būfin*
bowl (n)	طاس، زبدية، لعبة البولنغ	*ṭās, zubdiyah, lu'batul būlingh*
bowl (v)	دحرج الكرة	*daḥrajal kurah*
bowlegged (adj)	متقوس الساقين	*mutaqawwisus sāqain*
bowler (n)	بولر، لاعب بالكرة	*būlar, lā'ib bil kurah*
bowling (n)	لعبة بولنغ	*lu'batu būlingh*
bowman (n)	رامي السهام	*rāmis sihām*
box (n)	صندوق، مقصورة، كشك	*ṣundūq, maqṣūrah, kushk*
boxcar (n)	شاحنة صندوقية	*shāḥinah ṣundūqiyyah*
boxer (n)	ملاكم، بكسر	*mulākim, baksar*
boxing (n)	صندقة، ملاكمة	*ṣandaqah, mulākamah*
box office (n)	شباك التذاكر	*shubbākut tadhākir*
boxwood (n)	خشب البقس	*khashabul baqs*

boxy (adj)	صندوقاني	*ṣundūqānī*
boy (n)	صبي، غلام	*ṣabī, ghulām*
boyfriend (n)	صديق، رفيق	*ṣadīq, rafīq*
boyhood (n)	صبا، صبوة	*ṣibā, ṣubuwwah*
boyish (adj)	صبياني	*ṣibyānī*
boy scout (n)	كشاف	*kashshāf*
brace (n)	دعامة،حمالة البنطلون	*di'āmah, ḥammālatul banṭlūn*
bracelet (n)	سوار، دملج	*siwār, dumluj*
bracken (n)	سرخس	*sarakhs*
bracket (n)	معقف، هلال، كتيفة	*mu'aqqaf, hilāl, katīfah*
bracket (v)	وضع بين هلالين	*waḍa'a baina hilālain*
brackish (adj)	مويلح	*muwailiḥ*
brae (n)	منحدر تل	*munḥadaru tall*
brag (n)	تباه، تفاخر	*tabāhin, tafākhur*
brag (v)	تباهى، تفاخر	*tabāhā, tafākhara*
braggart (n/adj)	متبجح، هجاص	*mutabajjiḥ, hajjāṣ*
braid (v)	ضفر، عقص	*ḍafara, 'aqaṣa*
braid (n)	جديلة، ضفيرة	*jadīlah, ḍafīrah*
braiding (n)	ضفر، أشرطة زينية	*ḍafr, ashriṭah zīniyyah*
brain (n)	دماغ، ذكاء	*dimāgh, dhakā'*
braincase (n)	قحف الدماغ	*qiḥfud dimāgh*
brainchild (n)	بنت الفكر	*bintul fikr*
brain fever (n)	حمى دماغية	*ḥummā dimāghiyyah*
brainless (adj)	متبلد الذهن	*mutaballidudh dhihn*
brainpower (n)	مقدرة عقلية	*maqdirah 'aqliyyah*
brainsick (adj)	معتوه، ضعيف الذاكرة	*ma'tūh, ḍa'īfudh dhākirah*
brainstorm (n)	فكرة بارعة	*fikrah bāri'ah*

brainwash (v)	غسل الدماغ	*ghasalad dimāgh*
brainwashing (n)	غسل الدماغ	*ghaslud dimāgh*
brain wave (n)	موجة دماغية	*maujah dimāghiyyah*
brainy (adj)	ذكي، سريع الفهم	*dhakī, sarī'ul fahm*
brake (n)	مكباح، فرملة	*mikbāḥ, farmalah*
brake (v)	كبح، فرمل	*kabaḥa, farmala*
brakeman (n)	كبّاح	*kabbāḥ*
braking power (n)	قدرة فرملية	*qudrah farmaliyyah*
bramble (n)	عليق	*'ullaiq*
brambly (adj)	عليقي	*'ullaiqī*
bran (n)	نخالة، ردة	*nukhālah, raddah*
branch (n)	غصن، فرع	*ghuṣn, far'*
branch (v)	تغصن، تفرع	*taghaṣṣana, tafarra'a*
brand (n)	علامة تجارية، جمرة	*'alāmah tijāriyyah, jamrah*
brandy (n)	شراب مسكر	*sharāb muskir*
brass (n)	نحاس أصفر، وقاحة	*nuḥās aṣfar, waqāḥah*
brass band (n)	فرقة نحاسية	*firqah nuḥāsiyyah*
brat (n)	طفل مزعج	*ṭifl muz'ij*
bravado (n)	تظاهر بالشجاعة	*taẓāhur bish shajā'ah*
brave (n/adj)	شجاع، رائع	*shujā', rā'i'*
bravery (n)	شجاعة، بسالة	*shajā'ah, basālah*
bravo (interj)	مرحى، بخ بخ	*marḥā, bakh bakh*
browl (n)	شجار، برولة	*shijār, barwalah*
brawl (v)	تشاجر، هدر	*tashājara, hadara*
brawn (n)	قوة عضلية	*quwwah 'aḍaliyyah*
brawny (adj)	قوي، قاسٍ، عضل	*qawī, qāsin, 'aḍil*
bray (v/n)	نهق، نهيق	*nahaqa, nahīq*

braze (v)	نحس، قسى	*naḥḥasa, qassā*
brazen (adj)	وقح، نحاسي	*waqiḥ, nuḥāsī*
brazier (n)	نحاس، مجمرة	*naḥḥās, majmarah*
breach (n)	خرق القانون، صدع، ثغرة	*kharqul qānūn, ṣad‘, thughrah*
breach (v)	خرق، نقض	*kharaqa, naqaḍa*
bread (n)	خبز، قوت	*khubz, qūt*
breadbasket (n)	سلة الخبز	*sallatul khubz*
breadfruit (n)	ثمرة الخبز	*thamratul khubz*
breadth (n)	عرض، اتساع	*‘arḍ, ittisā‘*
breadwinner (n)	معيل، عائل	*mu‘īl, ‘ā’il*
break (v)	كسر، نقض، انقطع	*kasara, naqaḍa, inqaṭa‘a*
break (n)	كسر، انقطاع	*kasr, inqiṭā‘*
breakable (adj)	قابل للكسر	*qābil lil kasr*
breakage (n)	كسر، حسم الكسر	*kasr, ḥasmul kasr*
breakaway (n)	انفصال، تحول	*infiṣāl, taḥawwul*
breakdown (n)	تعطل، انهيار	*ta‘aṭṭul, inhiyār*
breaker (n)	كسارة، ناقض	*kassārah, nāqiḍ*
breakfast (n)	فطور، صبحة	*fuṭūr, ṣubḥah*
breakout (n)	كسر الحصار للتحرر	*kasrul ḥiṣār lit taḥarrur*
breakthrough (n)	اختراق مفاجئ	*ikhtirāq mufāji’*
breakwater (n)	حائل الأمواج	*ḥā’ilul amwāj*
breast (n)	ثدي، صدر	*thady, ṣadr*
breastbone (n)	عظم الصدر	*‘aẓmuṣ ṣadr*
breastfeed (v)	أرضعت من الثدي	*arḍa‘at minath thady*
breastplate (n)	درع الصدر	*dir‘uṣ ṣadr*

breath (n)	نفس، تنفس، لحظة	*nafas, tanaffus, laḥẓah*
breather (n)	متنفس، استراحة	*mutanaffis, istirāḥah*
breathing (n)	تنفس، لحظة	*tanaffus, laḥẓah*
breathless (adj)	عديم النفس	*'adīmun nafas*
breathtaking (adj)	مثير، ملهث	*muthīr, mulhith*
breathy (adj)	أنفاسي	*anfāsī*
breech (n)	مؤخرة البندقية	*mu'akhkharatul bunduqiyyah*
breed (v)	ولد، سبب	*wallada, sabbaba*
breeder (n)	مسبب، محدث	*musabbib, muḥdith*
breeding (n)	توليد، تربية	*taulīd, tarbiyah*
breeze (n)	نسيم، سهولة	*nasīm, suhūlah*
breezily (adv)	بمرح، بابتهاج	*bi maraḥ, bibtihāj*
breezy (adj)	منسم، مبتهج	*munassim, mubtahij*
bretheren (n)	إخوان	*ikhwān*
brevity (n)	ايجاز، قصر	*ījāz, qiṣar*
brew (v)	خمر، أحدث	*khammara, aḥdatha*
brew (n)	شراب مخمر	*sharāb mukhammir*
brewage (n)	تخمير الجعة	*takhmīrul ji'ah*
brewer (n)	مخمر الجعة	*mukhammirul ji'ah*
brewery (n)	مصنع الجعة	*maṣna'ul ji'ah*
brewing (n)	تخمير الجعة	*takhmīrul ji'ah*
bribe (n/v)	رشوة، رشا	*rishwah, rashā*
bribee (n)	مرتشي، قابل الرشوة	*murtashī, qābilur rishwah*
briber (n)	راشي، مقدم الرشوة	*rāshī, muqaddimur rishwah*
bribery (n)	ارتشاء، رشوة	*irtishā', rishwah*

brick (n)	آجر، قرميد	*ājurr, qirmīd*
brickbat (n)	ملاحظة جارحة	*mulāḥaẓah jāriḥah*
bridal (adj)	زفافي، عرسي	*zifāfī, 'ursī*
bride (n)	عروس، عروسة	*'arūs, 'arūsah*
bridecake (n)	كعكة العرس	*ka'katul 'urs*
bridegroom (n)	عريس، عروس	*'arīs, 'arūs*
bridge (n/v)	جسر، جسر	*jisr, jassara*
bridgehead (n)	رأس الجسر	*ra'sul jisr*
bridle (n/v)	لجام، ألجم	*lijām, aljama*
brief (n)	وجيز، مختصر	*wajīz, mukhtaṣar*
brief (v)	أوجز، لخص	*aujaza, lakhkhaṣa*
briefcase (n)	محفظة جلدية	*miḥfaẓah jildiyyah*
briefly (adv)	باختصار، بإيجاز	*bikhtiṣār, bi ījāz*
brigade (n)	لواء، فرقة	*liwā', firqah*
brigadier (n)	عميد، قائد	*'amīd, qā'id*
brigadier general	قائد لواء	*qā'idu liwā'*
brigand (n)	لص، قاطع طريق	*liṣṣ, qāṭi'u ṭarīq*
bright (adj)	مشرق، زاهٍ، بارع	*mushriq, zāhin, bāri'*
bighten (v)	أشرق، ابتهج	*ashraqa, ibtahaja*
brilliancy (n)	تألق، ذكاء	*ta'alluq, dhakā'*
brilliant (adj)	لامع، رائع، ذكي	*lāmi', rā'i', dhakī*
brim (n)	طفح، حرف	*ṭafḥ, ḥarf*
brim (v)	طفح، أترع	*ṭafaḥa, atra'a*
brimful (adj)	طافح، مترع	*ṭāfiḥ, mutra'*
bring (v)	حمل، أورد	*ḥamala, aurada*
brink (n)	حرف، حافة	*ḥarf, ḥāffah*
briquette (n)	فحم حجري	*faḥm ḥajarī*
brisk (adj)	رشيق، سريع، ناشط	*rashīq, sarī', nāshiṭ*

bristle (n)	هلب، شعر خشن	*hulb, sha'r khashin*
bristly (adj)	هلبي، خشن	*hulbī, khashin*
British (n/adj)	بريطانية، بريطاني	*birīṭāniyah, birīṭānī*
Briton (n)	بريطوني	*birīṭūnī*
brittle (adj)	قصف، زائل	*qaṣif, zā'il*
brittleness (n)	قصافة، هشاشة	*qaṣāfah, hashāshah*
broach (n)	مبزل، مثقاب	*mibzal, mithqāb*
broach (v)	ثقب، افتتح	*thaqaba, iftataḥa*
broad (adj)	عريض، واسع	*'arīḍ, wāsi'*
broadcast (v)	نشر، أذاع	*nashara, adhā'a*
broadcasting (n)	إذاعة، نشر	*idhā'ah, nashr*
broaden (v)	وسع، اتسع	*wassa'a, ittasa'a*
broad jump (n)	قفز طويل	*qafz ṭawīl*
broadleaf (adj)	عريض الأوراق	*'arīḍul aurāq*
broad-minded (adj)	متحرر، واسع الصدر	*mutaḥarrir , wāsi'uṣ ṣadr*
broadness (n)	وسعة، عرض	*wus'ah, 'arḍ*
brocade (n)	قماش مقصب	*qumāsh muqaṣṣab*
brocade (v)	قصب،طرز	*qaṣṣaba, ṭarraza*
brocaded (adj)	مقصب، مطرز	*muqaṣṣab, muṭarraz*
brochure (n)	نبذة، كراسة	*nubdhah, kurrāsah*
broil (v)	شوى، سخن	*shawā, sakhkhana*
broil (n)	شواء، شجار	*shiwā', shijār*
broiler (n)	مشواة	*mishwāt*
broke (adj)	مفلس، عديم الفلوس	*muflis, 'adīmul fulūs*
broken (adj)	مكسور، مفلس	*maksūr, muflis*
broken-down (adj)	معطل، مفلس	*mu'aṭṭal, muflis*
broken-hearted (adj)	مسحوق الفؤاد	*masḥūqul fu'ād*

broker (n)	وسيط، تاجر	*wasīṭ, tājir*
brokerage (n)	سمسرة	*samsarah*
bronze (n)	برونز	*burūnz*
Bronze Age (n)	عصر البرونز	*'aṣrul burūnz*
bronzy (adj)	برونزي	*burūnzī*
brooch (n)	بروش، دبوس	*burūsh, dabbūs*
brood (n)	حضنة، فقسة	*ḥaḍnah, faqsah*
brood (v)	أطال التفكير، حضن	*aṭālat tafkīr, ḥaḍana*
broody (adj)	حضون، متفكر	*ḥaḍūn, mutafakkir*
brook (n)	غدير، جدول	*ghadīr, jadwal*
brook (v)	تحمل، أطاق	*taḥammala, aṭāqa*
broom (n)	مكنسة، رتم	*miknasah, ratam*
broth (n)	مرق، مسلوقة	*maraq, maslūqah*
brothel (n)	مأخور، مبغى	*ma'khūr, mabghā*
brother (n)	أخ، صديق	*akh, ṣadīq*
brotherhood (n)	أخوة، إخاء	*ukhuwwah, ikhā'*
brother-in-law (n)	أخو الزوج، أخو الزوجة	*akhuz zauj, akhuz zaujah*
brotherly (adj)	أخوي	*akhawī*
brow (n)	حاجب العين	*ḥājibul 'ain*
brown (adj)	أسمر	*asmar*
brownie (n)	كعكة جنية	*ka'kah jinniyyah*
brownish (adj)	مسمر	*musammar*
brownstone (n)	حجر أسمر	*ḥajar asmar*
bruise (v)	رض، خدش	*raḍḍa, khadasha*
bruiser (n)	رجل فظ	*rajul faẓẓ*
brunt (n)	وطأة عظمى	*waṭ'ah 'uẓmā*
brush (n)	فرشاة، أجمة	*furshāt, ajamah*

brush (v)	نظف بالفرشاة	*naẓẓafa bil furshāt*
brush-off (n)	رفض	*rafḍ*
brushwood (n)	أغصان مقطوعة	*aghṣān maqṭū'ah*
brusque (adj)	فظ، جافٍ	*faẓẓ, jāfin*
brusqueness (n)	فظاظة، خشونة	*faẓāẓah, khushūnah*
brutal (adj)	وحشي، مؤلم	*waḥshī, mu'lim*
brutally (adv)	بقسوة، بشراسة	*bi qaswah, bi sharāsah*
brutality (n)	وحشية، فظاظة	*waḥshiyyah, faẓāẓah*
brutalize,-ise (v)	وحش، توحش	*waḥḥasha, tawaḥḥasha*
brute (n)	شخص وحشي	*shakhṣ waḥshī*
brutish (adj)	بهيمي، وحشي	*bahīmī, waḥshī*
bubble (n)	فقاعة	*fuqqā'ah*
bubble gum (n)	علكة فقاعية	*'ilkah fuqqā'iyyah*
bubbler (n)	نبع فوار	*nab' fawwār*
bubbly (adj)	فوار، فقاعي	*fawwār, fuqqā'ī*
buck (n)	ذكر الظبي، رجل شاب	*dhakaruẓ ẓaby, rajul shābb*
bucket (n)	دلو، سطل	*dalw, saṭl*
bucket shop	مكتب المضاربة	*maktabul muḍārabah*
buckle (n)	إبزيم، بكلة	*ibzīm, buklah*
buckle (v)	ثبت بإبزيم	*thabbata bi ibzīm*
buckskin (n)	جلد الغزال	*jildul ghazāl*
buckwheat (n)	حنطة سوداء	*ḥinṭah saudā'*
bud (n/v)	برعم، تبرعم	*bur'um, tabar'ama*
Buddhism (n)	بوذية	*būdhiyyah*
Buddhist (n/adj)	بوذي	*būdhī*
budding (n/adj)	تبرعم، ناشيء	*tabar'um, nāshi'*

budge (v)	زحزح، تحرك	*zaḥzaḥa, taḥarraka*
budget (n)	ميزانية، مجموعة	*mīzāniyyah, majmū'ah*
budgetary (adj)	ميزاني	*mīzānī*
buff (n)	أصفر برتقالي، جلد	*aṣfar burtaqālī, jildul*
	الجاموس	*jāmūs*
buffalo (n)	جاموس، جاموسة	*jāmūs, jāmūsah*
buffer (n)	حاجز، صاقل، مصد	*ḥājiz, ṣāqil, miṣadd*
buffet (n)	صنوان السفرة،	*ṣinwanus sufrah,*
	مقصف	*maqṣaf*
buffoon (n)	مضحك، مسخة	*muḍaḥḥik, muskhah*
buffoonery (n)	تهريج، تضحيك	*tahrīj, taḍḥīk*
bug (n)	بق، مخبول	*baqq, makhbūl*
bugger (adj)	لوطي، تافه	*lūṭī, tāfih*
buggery (n)	لواطة، مضاجعة	*liwāṭah, muḍāja'atudh*
	الذكور	*dhukūr*
buggy (n)	بوجيه	*būjiyyah*
bugle (n)	بوق، نفير	*būq, nafīr*
bugler (n)	بواق، مبوق	*bawwāq, mubawwiq*
build (v)	بنى، أنشد	*banā, anshada*
builder (n)	باني، مشيد	*bānī, mushayyid*
building (n)	مبنى، بناء	*mabnā, binā*
buildup (n)	إنشاء، بناء	*inshā', binā'*
built-in (adj)	مبيت	*mubayyat*
built-up (adj)	مركب	*murakkab*
bulb (n)	مصباح كهربائي،	*miṣbāḥ kahrabā'ī,*
	بصلة	*baṣalah*
bulbar (adj)	بصلي	*baṣalī*
bulge (n)	تورم، انتفاخ	*tawarrum, intifākh*

bulge (v)	تورم، انتفخ	*tawarrama, intafakha*
bulgy (adj)	متورم، ناتئ	*mutawarrim, nāti'*
bulk (n)	حجم، معظم الشيء	*ḥajm, mu'ẓamush shay'*
bulkhead (n)	فاصل إنشائي	*fāṣil inshā'ī*
bulky (adj)	ضخم، كبير الحجم	*ḍakhm, kabīrul ḥajm*
bull (n/adj)	ثور، ثوري	*thaur, thaurī*
bulldog (n)	بلدغ	*buldugh*
bulldoze (v)	مهد، أرهب	*mahhada, arhaba*
bulldozer (n)	جرافة لشق الطرق	*jarrāfah li shaqqiṭ ṭuruq*
bullet (n)	رصاصة	*raṣāṣah*
bulletin (n)	نشرة مختصرة	*nashrah mukhtaṣarah*
bulletin board (n)	لوحة النشرات	*lauḥatun nashrāt*
bulletproof (adj)	صامد للرصاص	*ṣāmid lir raṣāṣ*
bullock (n)	عجل، ثور مخصي	*'ijl, thaur makhṣī*
bully (n/v)	متنمر، تنمر	*mutanammir, tanammara*
bumble (v)	طن، أز	*ṭanna, azza*
bump (v)	صرع، صدم	*ṣara'a, ṣadama*
bump (n)	ضربة، صدمة، نتوء	*ḍarbah, ṣadmah, nutū'*
bumper (n)	مصد، كأس مترعة	*miṣadd, ka's mutra'ah*
bumpkin (n)	شخص ريفي	*shakhṣ rīfī*
bumptious (adj)	مغرور، معجب بذاته	*maghrūr, mu'jab bi dhātih*
bumpy (adj)	وعر، متخبط	*wa'r, mutakhabbiṭ*
bunch (n)	باقة، حزمة	*bāqah, ḥuzmah*
bundle (n)	حزمة، رزمة	*ḥuzmah, rizmah*

bung (n)	سطام لثقب البرميل	*siṭām li thuqbil barmīl*
bung (v)	سد، كدم	*sadda, kadama*
bungalow (n)	بنغل، بيت أرضي	*banghal, bait arḍī*
bungle (v)	عمل بغير براعة	*'amila bighairi barā'ah*
bungler (n)	عامل غير بارع	*'āmil ghair bāri'*
bungling (adj)	غير بارع	*ghair bāri'*
bunk (n)	سرير مبيت	*sarīr mubayyat*
bunker (n)	غرفة محصنة، مستودع للفحم الحجري	*ghurfah muḥaṣṣanah, mustauda' lil faḥm al ḥajarī*
bunkhouse (n)	مبنى للعمال	*mabnā lil 'ummāl*
bunny (n)	أرنب	*arnab*
buoy (n/v)	طافية، طفا	*ṭāfiyah, ṭafā*
buoyancy (n)	طفو، مرح، بشر	*ṭufuww, maraḥ, bishr*
buoyant (adj)	مرح، مبتهج	*mariḥ, mubtahij*
burden (n)	حمل، عبء	*ḥiml, 'ib'*
burden (v)	أثقل، أرهق	*athqala, arhaqa*
burden of proof (n)	عبء الإثبات	*'ib'ul ithbāt*
burdensome (adj)	ثقيل، مرهق	*thaqīl, murhiq*
bureau (n)	منضدة، مكتب	*minḍadah, maktab*
bureaucracy (n)	دواوينية، بيروقراطية	*dawwāwīniyyah, bīrūqarāṭiyyah*
bureaucrat (n)	دواويني، بيروقراطي	*dawwāwīnī, bīrūqarāṭī*
bureaucratic (adj)	بيروقراطي	*bīrūqarāṭī*
burgeon (n/v)	برعم، تبرعم	*bur'um, tabar'ama*
burger (n)	برجر	*barjar*
burglar (n)	لص، سارق	*liṣṣ, sāriq*
burglary (n)	سطو، لصوصية	*saṭw, luṣūṣiyyah*

burial (n)	قبر، دفن	*qabr, dafn*
burial ground	مدفن، مقبرة	*madfan, maqbarah*
burier (n)	دافن	*dāfin*
burlap (n)	خيش	*khaish*
burlesque (n)	سخرية، هزل	*sukhriyyah, hazl*
burn (v)	احترق، اتقد	*iḥtaraqa, ittaqada*
burner (n)	مضرم، حارق	*maḍram, ḥāriq*
burning (adj)	مشتعل، متوهج	*mushta'il, mutawahhij*
burnish (v)	صقل، لمع	*ṣaqala, lamma'a*
burnt (adj)	محترق، محروق	*muḥtaraq, maḥrūq*
burp (v/n)	تجشأ، تجشؤ	*tajashsha'a, tajashshu'*
burrow (n)	جحر، وجار	*juḥr, wijār*
burry (adj)	خشن، شائك	*khashin, shā'ik*
bursar (n)	أمين الصندوق	*amīnṣ ṣundūq*
bursary (n)	خزانة المال	*khizānatul māl*
burst (v)	انفجر، تفطر	*infajara, tafaṭṭara*
bury (v)	دفن، أخفى	*dafana, akhfā*
burying (n)	دفن، قبر	*dafn, qabr*
burying ground	مدفن، مقبرة	*madfan, maqbarah*
bus (n)	أوتوبوس، حافلة	*ūtūbūs, ḥāfilah*
bush (n)	شجيرة كثيرة الأغصان	*shujairah kathīratul aghṣān*
bushy (adj)	ملتف الأشجار	*multafful ashjār*
busily (adv)	بانكباب، بنشاط	*binkibāb, bi nashāṭ*
business (n)	تجارة، مهنة، عمل	*tijārah, mihnah, 'amal*
businesslike (adj)	فعال، عملي	*fa''āl, 'amalī*
businessman (n)	رجل أعمال	*rajulu a'māl*
busk (v)	هيأ، أعد	*hayya'a, a'adda*

bust (v)	كسر، انفجر	*kasara, infajara*
buster (n)	عاصفة هوجاء	*'āṣifah haujā'*
bustle (n)	ضوضاء، نشاط صاخب	*ḍauḍā', nashāṭ ṣākhib*
busy (adj)	مشغول، ناشط	*mashghūl, nāshiṭ*
busy body (n)	فضولي، متشاغل	*fuḍūlī, mutashāghil*
but (conj/prep)	لكن، غير	*lākin, ghaira*
butane (n)	بيوتان	*biutān*
butcher (n)	جزار، قصاب	*jazzār, qaṣṣāb*
butcherly (adj)	وحشي، سفاك	*Waḥshī, saffāk*
butchery (n)	جزارة، سفك الدماء	*jizārah, safkud dimā'*
butler (n)	ساقي، خادم كبير	*sāqī, khādim kabīr*
butt (v)	نطح، ناكب	*naṭaḥa, nākaba*
butter (n)	زبدة، تملق	*zubdah, tamalluq*
butterfingered (adj)	رخو الأصابع	*rikhwul aṣābi'*
butterfly (n)	فراشة	*Farāshah*
buttermilk (n)	مخيض اللبن	*makhīḍul laban*
butternut (n)	جوز أرمد	*jauz armad*
buttery (adj)	مزبد، زبدي	*muzabbad, zubdī*
buttock (n)	ردف، عجز	*Ridf, 'ajuz*
button (n)	زر	*Zirr*
buy (v)	اشترى، ابتاع	*Ishtarā, ibtā'a*
buyer (n)	مشتري، مبتاعٍ	*mushtarī, mubtā'in*
buzz (v)	أز، غمغم	*azza, ghamghama*
buzz (n)	غمغمة، أزيز	*ghamghamah, azīz*
buzzard (n)	صقر	*ṣaqr*
buzzword (n)	كلمة طنانة	*kalimah ṭannānah*
by (prep)	بجانب، بواسطة	*bi jānib, bi wāsiṭah*
by (adv)	جانباً، قريباً	*jāniban, qarīban*

bye-bye (interj)	وداعاً	*wadā'an*
by-election (n)	انتخاب فرعي	*Intikhāb far'ī*
by-gone (adj)	ماضٍ، مهجور	*māḍin, mahjūr*
by-law (n)	قانون داخلي	*qānūn dākhilī*
by-line (n)	خط ثانوي	*khaṭṭ thānawī*
bypass (n)	ممر جانبي	*mamarr jānibī*
bypass (v)	تجنّب، أهمل	*tajannaba, ahmala*
by-product (n)	حصيلة ثانية	*ḥaṣīlah thāniyah*
bystreet (n)	شارع فرعي	*shāri' far'ī*
byway (n)	طريق فرعي	*ṭarīq far'ī*
byword (n)	مثل سائر	*Mathal sā'ir*
Byzantine (n/adj)	بيزنطي	*Bīzanṭī*

C

cab (n)	سيارة أجرة	*sayyāratu ujrah*
cabal (n)	عصبة سرية	*'uṣbah sirriyyah*
cabaret (n)	حانة، ملهى	*ḥānah, malhā*
cabbage (n)	كرنب، بنكنوت	*Kurnub, banknūt*
cabin (n)	قمرة، كوخ	*qamrah, kūkh*
cabin boy (n)	غلام السفينة	*ghulāmus safīnah*
cabin class (n)	درجة قمرية	*darajah qamriyyah*
cabinet (n)	مجلس الوزراء، دولاب	*majlisul wuzarā', dūlāb*
cable (n)	كبل، مرسة	*kabl, marasah*
caboodle (n)	جماعة، مجموعة	*jamā'ah, majmū'ah*
cachet (n)	ختم، طابع	*khatm, ṭāba'*
cackle (v)	ثرثر، أضحك	*tharthara, aḍḥaka*
cacophony (n)	تنافر النغمات	*tanāfurun naghmāt*
cactus (n)	صبار	*ṣabbār*

cadaver (n)	جثة، جيفة	*juththah, jīfah*
cadaverous (adj)	جيفي، كالميت	*jīfi, kal mait*
caddy (n)	كادي	*kādī*
cadence (n)	ايقاع الخطو	*īqā'ul khaṭw*
cadet (n)	طالب عسكري	*ṭālib 'askarī*
cadre (n)	إطار، كادر	*iṭār, kādar*
Caesar (n)	قيصر	*qaiṣar*
caesura (n)	وقف، انقطاع	*waqf, inqiṭā'*
cafe (n)	قهوة، مقهى	*qahwah, maqhā*
cafeteria (n)	قفطير، مطعم	*qafṭīr, maṭ'am*
cage (n)	قفس، تقفيصة	*qafas, taqfīṣah*
cage (adj)	حذر، محترس	*ḥadhir, muḥtaris*
caitiff (adj/n)	خسيس، حقير	*khasīs, ḥaqīr*
cajole (v)	تملق، داهن	*tamallaqa, dāhana*
cake (n)	كعكة، قطعة	*ka'kah, qiṭ'ah*
calamitous (adj)	فاجع، مشؤوم	*fāji', mash'ūm*
calamity (n)	كارثة، نكبة	*kārithah, nakbah*
calcify (v)	كلس، تكلس	*kallasa, takallasa*
calcium (n)	كلسيوم	*kalsiūm*
calculable (adj)	ممكن إحصاؤه	*mumkin iḥṣā'uh*
calculate (v)	حسب، أعد	*ḥasaba, a'adda*
calculated (adj)	محسوب، معد	*maḥsūb, mu'add*
calculating (adj)	حذر، حاسب	*ḥadhir, ḥāsib*
calculation (n)	حسبان، إحصاء	*ḥusbān, iḥṣā'*
calculator (n)	آلة حاسبة	*ālah ḥāsibah*
calculous (adj)	حصوي، متحجر	*ḥaṣawī, mutaḥajjir*
calculus (n)	حصاة	*ḥaṣāt*
caldron (n)	مرجل، قدر	*mirjal, qidr*

calender (n)	تقويم، لائحة	*taqwīm, lā'iḥah*
calender month (n)	شهر شمسي	*shahr shamsī*
calender year (n)	سنة شمسية	*sanah shamsiyyah*
calf (n)	عجل	*'ijl*
calfskin (n)	جلد العجل	*jildul 'ijl*
calibrate (v)	قوم، حدد	*qawwama, ḥaddada*
calibration (n)	تقويم، معايرة	*taqwīm, mu'āyarah*
caliph (n)	خليفة المسلمين	*khalīfatul muslimīn*
caliphate (n)	خلافة إسلامية	*khilāfah islāmiyyah*
call (v)	دعا، نادى، صوت	*da'ā, nādā, ṣawwata*
call (n)	نداء، زيارة قصيرة	*nidā', ziyārah qaṣīrah*
call boy (n)	خادم في فندق	*khādim fī funduq*
call girl (n)	بغي التلفون	*baghiyyut tilifūn*
call house (n)	مأخور، بيت الدعارة	*ma'khūr, baitud di'ārah*
caligrapher (n)	خطاط	*khaṭṭāṭ*
caligraphy (n)	خط، علم الخط	*khaṭṭ, 'ilmul khaṭṭ*
calling (n)	دعوة، دافع، حرفة	*da'wah, dāfi', ḥirfah*
calling card (n)	بطاقة زيارة	*biṭāqatu ziyārah*
callous (adj)	قاسي، جاسىء	*qāsī, jāsi'*
calm (adj/n)	هادئ، هدوء	*hādi', hudū'*
calmness (n)	سكون، هدوء	*sukūn, hudū'*
calorie (n)	كالوري، سعر	*kālūrī, si'r*
calumny (n)	افتراء، نميمة	*iftirā', namīmah*
Calvinism (n)	كالفينية	*kālfīniyyah*
Calvinist (n)	كالفيني	*kālfīnī*
cam (n)	حدبة، كامة	*ḥadabah, kāmah*
camaraderie (n)	صداقة حميمة	*ṣadāqah ḥamīmah*
camber (v/n)	حدب، احديداب	*ḥaddaba, iḥdīdāb*

camel (n)	جمل	*jamal*
camel's hair (n)	وبر الجمال	*wabarul jimal*
camera (n)	كاميرا، مصورة	*kāmīrā, muṣawwirah*
cameraman (n)	مصور	*muṣawwir*
camouflage (v)	موه، خدع	*mawwaha, khada'a*
camouflage (n)	تعمية، تستر عن العدو	*ta'miyah, tasattur 'anil 'aduww*
camp (n/v)	خيمة، خيم	*khaimah, khayyama*
campaign (n)	حملة سياسية	*ḥamlah siyāsiyyah*
campaign (v)	أدار حملةً	*Adāra ḥamlatan*
campfire (n)	نار المخيم	*nārul mukhayyam*
camphor (n)	كافور	*kāfūr*
campus (n)	حرم الجامعة	*ḥaramul jāmi'ah*
can (n)	كأس، علبة	*Ka's, 'ulbah*
can (v)	استطاع، أمكن	*istaṭā'a, amkana*
canal (n)	قناة، ترعة	*qanāt, tur'ah*
canalize,-ise (v)	شق قنوات	*shaqqa qanawāt*
canard (n)	إشاعة كاذبة	*ishā'ah kādhibah*
canary (n)	كناري	*kanārī*
cancan (n)	كنكان، رقصة رشيقة	*kankān, raqṣah rashīqah*
cancel (v)	أبطل، شطب	*abṭala, shaṭaba*
cancellation (n)	شطب، إبطال	*shaṭb, ibṭāl*
cancer (n)	سرطان، آفة مهلكة	*sarṭān, āfah muhlikah*
candid (adj)	صريح، نزيه	*ṣarīḥ, nazīh*
candidacy (n)	ترشح، ترشيح	*tarashshuḥ, tarshīḥ*
candidate (n)	مرشح	*murashshiḥ*
candidature=candidacy		
candle (n)	شمعة	*sham'ah*

candlelight (n)	ضوء الشمعة	*ḍau'ush sham'ah*
candlestick (n)	شمعدان	*sham'adān*
candlewick (n)	فتيل الشمعة	*fatīlush sham'ah*
candour (n)	صراحة، صدق	*ṣarāḥah, ṣidq*
candy (n)	حلوى، حلواء	*ḥalwā, ḥalwā'*
cane (n)	قصب،قصب السكر	*qaṣab, qaṣabus sukkar*
cane sugar (n)	سكر القصب	*sukkarul qaṣab*
canine (adj)	كلبي	*kalbī*
canister (n)	علبة صغيرة	*'ulbah ṣaghīrah*
canker (n)	قرحة أكالة	*qarḥah akkālah*
cankerworm (n)	قادحة، سوسة أكالة	*qādiḥah, sūsah akkālah*
canned (adj)	معلب، مسجل	*mu'allab, musajjal*
cannibal (adj)	إنسان متوحش	*insān mutawaḥḥish*
cannon (n)	مدفع، قديم	*midfa', qadīm*
cannonade (n)	رشق بالمدافع	*rashq bil madāfi'*
cannonball (n)	قنبلة، جلة	*qumbulah, jullah*
cannonry (n)	رشق بالمدافع	*rashq bil madāfi'*
canny (adj)	حكيم، بارع	*ḥakīm, bāri'*
canoe (v/n)	غدف الكنو،كنو	*ghaddafal kanw, kanw*
canon (n)	قانون، شريعة	*qānūn, sharī'ah*
canonical (adj)	قانوني،مقدس،مقبول	*qānūnī, muqaddas, maqbūl*
canonize,-ise (v)	طوّب، مجّد	*ṭawwaba, majjada*
canon law (n)	قانون كنسي	*qānūn kanasī*
canopy (n)	ظلة، غطاء زيني	*ẓullah, ghiṭā' zīnī*
cant (n)	رياء، نفاق	*riyā', nifāq*
canteen (n)	مطعم، مقصف	*maṭ'am, maqṣaf*
canter (v/n)	خب، خبب	*khabba, khabab*

canticle (n)	أنشودة، نشيد	*unshūdah, nashīd*
cantilever (n)	كابول	*kābūl*
cantilever bridge (n)	جسر كابولي	*jisr kābūlī*
canto (n)	نشيد، قصيدة	*nashīd, qaṣidah*
canton (n)	إقليم، قسم	*iqlīm, qism*
cantonment (n)	معسكر، مخيم	*mu'askar, mukhayyam*
cantor (n)	قائد جوقة الترتيل	*qā'idu jauqatit tartīl*
canvas (n)	خيمة، قماش القنب	*khaimah, qumāshul qunnab*
canvas (canvass) (v)	طوف، صوت	*ṭawwafa, ṣawwata*
canyon (n)	واد ضيق	*wādin ḍayyiq*
cap (n)	قلنسوة، غطاء، ذروة	*qalansuwah, ghiṭā', dhirwah*
cap (v)	غطى بقلنسوة	*ghaṭṭā bi qalansuwah*
capability (n)	قدرة، قابلية	*qudrah, qābiliyyah*
capable (adj)	قادر، قابل	*qādir, qābil*
capacious (adj)	واسع، فصيح	*wāsi', faṣīḥ*
capacity (n)	قدرة، أهلية	*qudrah, ahliyyah*
cape (n)	كاب، لفاع	*kāb, lifā'*
caper (v/n)	طفر، طفرة	*ṭafara, ṭafrah*
capillary (adj)	شعري	*sha'rī*
capillary action	فعل شعري	*fi'l sha'rī*
capital (n)	عاصمة، رأس مال	*'āṣimah, ra'smāl*
capitalism (n)	رأسمالية	*ra'smāliyyah*
capitalist (n)	رأسماليا	*ra'smāliyā*
capitalistic (adj)	رأسمالي	*ra'smālī*
capitalization (n)	تمويل	*tamwīl*
capitalize,-ise (v)	مول	*mawwala*

capital levy (n)	ضريبة الرساميل	*ḍaribatur rasāmīl*
capitation (n)	ضريبة الرؤوس	*ḍarībatur ru'ūs*
capitulate (v)	استسلم	*istaslama*
capitulation (n)	استسلام، معاهدة	*Istislām, mu'āhadah*
caprice (n)	نزوة، حولية	*nazwah, ḥuwwaliyah*
capricious (adj)	نزوي،متقلب الأطوار	*nazwī, mutaqallibul aṭwār*
Capricorn (n)	جدي	*Jady*
capsicum (n)	فلفل	*filfil*
capsize (v)	انقلب، قلب	*inqalaba, qallaba*
capsule (n)	كبسولة، كيس	*kabsūlah, kīs*
captain (n)	رئيس، قائد، نقيب	*ra'īs, qā'id, naqīb*
caption (n)	تعليق، عنوان	*ta'līq, 'unwān*
captivate (v)	فتن، أسر	*fatana, asara*
captivating (adj)	ساحر، فاتن	*sāḥir, fātin*
captive (adj)	أسير، مفتون	*asīr, maftūn*
captivity (n)	أسر، سبي	*asr, saby*
captor (n)	آسر، معتقل	*āsir, mu'taqil*
capture (v)	أسر، قبض على	*Asara, qabaḍa 'alā*
car (n)	سيارة، حافلة	*sayyārah, ḥāfilah*
carafe (n)	غرافة، دورق	*Gharrāfah, dauraq*
caramel (n)	كرميلة	*karamīlah*
caramelize,-ise (v)	كرمل	*karmala*
carat (n)	قيراط	*qīrāṭ*
caravan (n)	قافلة	*qāfilah*
carbohydrate (n)	كربوهيدريت	*karbūhaidirīt*
carbolic (adj)	حمض الكربوليك	*ḥamḍul karbūlīk*
carbon (n)	كربون	*karbūn*

carbonated (adj)	محول إلى كربونات	*muḥawwal ilā karbūnāt*
carbon copy (n)	نسخة كربونية	*nuskhah karbūniyyah*
carbon dioxide (n)	ثاني أكسيد الكربون	*thānī aksīd al karbūn*
carbonic (adj)	كربوني	*karbūnī*
carbonic acid (n)	حمض الكربونيك	*ḥamḍul karbūnīk*
carbonous (adj)	كربوني	*karbūnī*
carbon paper (n)	ورق الكربون	*waraqul karbūn*
card (n)	بطاقة، ورقة لعب	*biṭāqah, waraqatu la'ib*
cardboard (n)	كرتون	*kartūn*
cardiac (adj)	قلبي، فؤادى	*qalbī, fu'ādī*
cardinal (adj)	رئيسي، أساسي	*ra'īsī, asāsī*
cardinal number	عدد أصلي	*'adad aṣlī*
cardinal points	جهات أصلية	*jihāt aṣliyyah*
cardiologist (n)	عالم بالقلب	*'ālim bil qalb*
cardiology (n)	دراسة أمراض القلب	*dirāsatu amrāḍil qalb*
care (n)	رعاية، عناية	*ri'āyah, 'ināyah*
care (v)	اهتم، أعنى	*ihtamma, a'nā*
careen (v)	أمال المربك	*amālal markab*
career (n)	مهنة، سيرة	*mihnah, sīrah*
carefree (adj)	مبتهج، خلو من الهم	*mubtahij, khilwum minal hamm*
careful (adj)	يقظ، محترس	*yaqiẓ, muḥtaris*
carefully (adv)	باهتمام، بعناية	*biḥtimām, bi 'ināyah*
carefulness (n)	انتباه، عناية	*intibāh, 'ināyah*
careless (adj)	مهمل، طائش	*muhmil, ṭā'ish*
carelessly (adv)	بإهمال، بعدم اعتناء	*bi ihmāl, bi 'adami i'tinā'*

caress (n/v)	ملاطفة، لاطف	*mulāṭafah, lāṭafa*
caretaker (n)	ناظر، متولي	*nāẓir, mutawallī*
cargo (n)	حمولة، شحنة	*ḥamūlah, shaḥnah*
caricature (n)	كاريكاتورية، صورة هزلية	*kārīkātūriyyah, ṣūrah hazliyyah*
caricaturist (n)	رسام كاريكاتوري	*rassām kārīkātūrī*
carillon (n)	مصلصلة	*muṣalṣilah*
caring (adj)	حذر، مهتم	*ḥadhir, muhtamm*
carload (n)	حمولة الشاحنة	*ḥamūlatush shāḥinah*
carnage (n)	مذبحة، مجزرة	*madhbaḥah, majzarah*
carnal (adj)	جسدي، شهواني	*jasadī, shahwānī*
carnation (n)	لون قرنفلي	*laun qaranfulī*
carnival (n)	عيد المرفع	*'īdul marfa'*
carnivore (n)	حيوان لاحم	*ḥaiwān lāḥim*
carnivorous (adj)	لاحم، آكل اللحوم	*lāḥim, ākilul luḥūm*
carouse (n)	احتفال مخمور	*iḥtifāl makhmūr*
carpenter (n)	نجار	*najjār*
carpentry (n)	نجارة	*nijārah*
carpet (n)	سجادة، بساط	*sajjādah, bisāṭ*
carpet bag (n)	خرج السفر	*khurjus safar*
carpet bagger (n)	ذو الخرج	*dhul khurj*
carport (n)	سقيفة السيارة	*saqīfatus sayyārah*
carriage (n)	مركبة، حافلة	*markaba, ḥāfilah*
carrier (n)	ناقل، حمال	*nāqil, ḥammāl*
carrion (n)	جيفة، قذارة	*jīfah, qadhārah*
carrot (n)	جزر، جزرة	*jazar, jazarah*
carroty (adj)	جزري اللون	*jazariyyul laun*
carry (v)	نقل، حمل	*naqala, ḥamala*

cart (n)	كارة، عربة صغيرة	*kārrah, 'arabah ṣaghīrah*
cartage (n)	نقل بالكارة	*naql bil kārrah*
cartel (n)	كارتل، نقابة انتاجية	*kārtil, niqābah intājiyyah*
cartilage (n)	غضروف، قرقوش	*ghuḍrūf, qarqūsh*
cartload (n)	حمل كارة	*ḥimlu kārrah*
cartographer (n)	خرائطي	*kharā'iṭī*
cartography (n)	خرائطية	*kharā'iṭiyyah*
cartoon (n)	رسم كاريكاتوري	*rasm kārīkātūrī*
cartridge (n)	خرطوشة، لفيفة	*kharṭūshah, lafīfah*
carve (v)	نحت، نقش، قطع	*naḥata, naqasha, qaṭa'a*
carved (adj)	منقوش، منحوت	*manqūsh, manḥūt*
carving (n)	نقش، حفر	*naqsh, ḥafr*
cascade (n)	شلال صغير	*shallāl ṣaghīr*
case (n)	وضع، حال، قضية	*waḍ', ḥālah, qaḍiyyah*
casebook (n)	سجل القضايا	*sijillul qaḍāyā*
casement (n)	نافذة بابية	*nāfidhah bābiyyah*
casework (n)	تقصي السيرة	*taqaṣṣis sīrah*
cash (n)	نقد، أوراق مالية	*naqd, aurāq māliyyah*
cash (v)	صرف، دفع مبلغًا	*ṣarafa, dafa'a mablaghan*
cashbook (n)	دفتر الصندوق	*daftaruṣ ṣundūq*
cashier (n)	أمين الصندوق	*aminuṣ ṣundūq*
cash register (n)	مسجلة النقد	*musajjilatun naqd*
casing (n)	غطاء، إطار	*ghiṭā', iṭār*
casino (n)	كازينو، ملهى	*kāzīnū, malhā*
cask (n)	برميل خشبي	*barmīl khashabī*

casket (n)	علبة للجواهر	*'ulbah lil jawāhir*
cassette (n)	كاسيت	*kāsīt*
cast (v)	طرح، ألقى، أطلق	*ṭaraḥa, alqā, aṭlaqa*
castanet (n)	صنج	*ṣanj*
castaway (adj)	مطروح، منبوذ	*maṭrūḥ, mambūdh*
caste (n)	فرقة، طبقة	*firqah, ṭabaqah*
castigate (v)	أنب، عنف	*annaba, 'annafa*
castigation (n)	تأنيب، عقاب	*ta'nīb, 'iqāb*
casting (n)	مصبوب، مطروح	*maṣbūb, maṭrūḥ*
casting vote (n)	صوت مرجح	*ṣaut murajjaḥ*
cast iron (n)	حديد مسبوك	*ḥadīd masbūk*
castle (n)	قصر، قلعة	*qaṣr, qal'ah*
cast-off (adj)	مهمل، منبوذ	*muhmal, mambūdh*
castor (caster) (n)	قندس، كستور	*qundus, kastūr*
castrate (v)	خصى، شوه	*khaṣā, shawwaha*
castration (n)	خصي، تطويش	*khaṣy, taṭwīsh*
casual (adj)	عرضي، طارئ	*'araḍī, ṭāri'*
casually (adv)	عرضًا، مصادفةً	*'araḍan, muṣādafatan*
casualty (n)	كارثة، إصابة	*kārithah, iṣābah*
cat (n)	قط، هر	*qiṭṭ, hirr*
cataclysm (n)	جائحة، شغب	*jā'iḥah, shaghab*
catalogue (n)	قائمة، فهرس	*qā'imah, fihris*
catalysis (n)	حفز	*ḥafz*
catalyst (n)	حفاز	*ḥaffāz*
cataract (n)	شلال، سد	*shallāl, sudd*
catarrh (n)	نزلة، زكام	*nazlah, zukām*
catarrhal (adj)	نزلي، زكامي	*nazlī, zukāmī*
catastrophe (n)	كارثة، جائحة	*kārithah, jā'iḥah*

catastrophic (adj)	فاجع، مؤلم	*fāji', mu'lim*
catcall (n)	صيحة، شغب	*ṣaiḥah, shaghab*
catch (v)	أخذ، أمسك، قبض	*akhadha, amsaka, qabaḍa*
catching (adj)	معد، مغرٍ، فاتن	*mu'din, mughrin, fātin*
catchment area	مستجمع الأمطار	*mustajma'ul amṭār*
catchy (adj)	آسر، جذاب	*āsir, jazzāb*
catechism (n)	تعليم شفهي	*ta'līm shafahī*
categorical (adj)	صريح، مطلق	*ṣarīḥ, muṭlaq*
categorize,-ise (v)	صنف	*ṣannafa*
category (n)	صنف، طبقة	*ṣinf, ṭabaqah*
cater (v)	زود بالطعام	*zawwada biṭ ṭa'ām*
catering (n)	تزويد بالطعام	*tazwīd biṭ ṭa'ām*
caterpillar (n)	يسروع	*yusrū'*
caterwaul (n)	مواء الهر	*muwā'ul hirr*
catharsis (n)	تطهير العواطب، تنفيس	*taṭhīrul 'awāṭib, tanfīs*
cathartic (adj)	مسهل	*mushil*
cathedral (n)	كاتدرائية	*kātadrā'iyyah*
catheter (n)	قسطر	*qaṣṭar*
cathode (n)	كاتود، قنطرة	*kātūd, qanṭarah*
catholic (adj)	كاثوليكي، جامع	*kāthūlīkī, jāmi'*
catnap (n)	نوم خفيف	*naum khafīf*
cat's cradle (n)	سرير الهر	*sarīrul hirr*
cattle (n)	ماشية، بهائم	*māshiyah, bahā'im*
catty (n)	كاتي، قاسٍ	*kātī, qāsin*
catwalk (n)	ممر ضيق	*mamarr ḍayyiq*
caucus (n)	مؤتمر حزبي	*mu'tamar ḥizbī*

cauliflower (n)	قرنبيط	*qarnabīṭ*
causation (n)	تسبيب، سب	*tasbīb, sabb*
causative (adj)	سببي، مسبب	*sababī, musabbib*
cause (n)	سبب، علة	*sabab, 'illah*
cause (v)	سبب، أوجب	*sabbaba, aujaba*
causeless (adj)	بغير سبب	*bighairi sabab*
caustic (adj)	كاوٍ، ساخر	*kāwin, sākhir*
caustic soda (n)	الصودا الكاوية	*aṣ ṣūdā al kāwiyyah*
cauterize,-ise (v)	كوى، وسم	*kawā, wasama*
cautery (n)	كي، ميسم	*kai, mīsam*
caution (n)	حذر، احتراس	*ḥadhar, iḥtirās*
caution (v)	حذر، نبه	*ḥadhdhara, nabbaha*
cautionary (adj)	تحذيري، تنبيهي	*taḥdhīrī, tambīhī*
cautious (adj)	حذر، محترس	*ḥadhir, muḥtaris*
cautiously (adv)	بحذر، باحتراس	*bi ḥadhar, biḥtirās*
cavalier (adj)	متعجرف، محتال	*muta'ajrif, muḥtāl*
cavalry (n)	فرسان، سلاح الفرسان	*fursān, silāḥul fursān*
cavalryman (n)	فارس، خيال	*fāris, khayyāl*
cave (n/v)	كهف، جوف	*kahf, jawwafa*
cave dweller (n)	ساكن الكهوف	*sākinul kuhūf*
cave-in (n)	انهيار، انحطاط	*inhiyār, inḥiṭāṭ*
caveman (n)	انسان الكهوف	*insānul kuhūf*
cavern (n)	كهف كبير	*kahf kabīr*
cavernous (adj)	متكهف	*mutakahhif*
caviar (n)	كافيار	*kāfyār*
cavil (n)	اعتراض تافه	*i'tirāḍ tāfih*
cavity (n)	فجوة، حفرة	*fajwah, ḥufrah*

cavort (v)	طفر، وثب مرحًا	*ṭafara, wathaba marahan*
cease (v)	وقف، انقطع	*waqafa, inqaṭa'a*
cease (n)	وقف، انقطاع	*qaqf, inqiṭā'*
cease fire (n)	وقف إطلاق النار	*waqfu iṭlāqin nār*
ceaseless (adj)	متواصل، مستديم	*mutawāṣil, mustadīm*
cedar (n)	أرز، سدر	*arz, sidr*
cedar bird (n)	عصفور الأرز	*'uṣfūrul arz*
cede (v)	تخلى عن، تنازل	*takhallā 'an, tanāzala*
ceiling (n)	سقف، غماء	*saqf, ghimā'*
celebrant (n)	محتفل، مقيم الاحتفال	*muḥtafil, muqīmul iḥtifāl*
celebrate (v)	احتفل، مجد	*iḥtafala, majjada*
celebrated (adj)	شهير، معروف	*shahīr, ma'rūf*
celebration (n)	احتفال، تمجيد	*iḥtifāl, tamjīd*
celebrity (n)	شهرة، شخص مشهور	*shuhrah, shakhṣ mashhūr*
celestial (adj)	سماوي، إلهي	*samāwī, ilāhī*
celibate (n)	عزب، أعزب	*'azab, a'zab*
cell (n)	حجيرة، صومعة، خلية	*ḥujairah, ṣauma'ah, khaliyyah*
cellular (adj)	خلوي، مسامي	*khalawī, masāmī*
celluloid (n)	سليوليد	*saliulīd*
cellulose (n)	سلولوز	*salūlūz*
celsius (adj)	سلسيوسي	*salsiusī*
celt (n)	سلتي	*saltī*
celtic (adj)	سلتي	*saltī*
cement (n)	إسمنت، لصاق	*ismant, liṣāq*

cement (n)	مكن، ألصق	*makkana, alṣaqa*
cemetery (n)	مقبرة، مدفن	*maqbarah, madfan*
censor (n)	مراقب، ناقد معادي	*murāqib, nāqid mu'ādī*
censorious (n)	عياب، انتقادي	*'ayyāb, intiqādī*
censorship (n)	مراقبة المطبوعات	*murāqabatul maṭbū'āt*
censure (n)	نقد، لوم	*naqd, laum*
census (n)	إحصاء رسمي	*iḥṣā' rasmī*
cent (n)	سنت، مأة	*sant, mi'ah*
centenarian (n)	المئوي	*almi'awī*
centenary (n/adj)	ذكرى مئوية، مئوي	*dhikrā mi'awiyyah, mi'awī*
centennial (adj/n)	مئوي، قرني	*mi'awī, qarnī*
centi	مئة	*mi'ah*
centigrade (adj)	سنتيغرادي	*sintīgharādī*
centigram (n)	سنتيغرام	*sintīgharām*
centilitre (n)	سنتيلتر	*sintīlitr*
centimetre (n)	سنتيمتر	*sintīmitr*
central (adj)	مركزي، رئيسي	*markazī, ra'īsī*
central bank (n)	بنك مركزي	*bank markazī*
centralism (n)	مركزية، تركيز	*markaziyyah, tarkīz*
centralization (n)	مركزة، تمركز	*markazah, tamarkuz*
centralize,-ise (v)	مركز، تمركز	*markaza, tamarkaza*
central orbit (n)	مدار مركزي	*madār markazī*
centre (center) (n)	مركز، قلب	*markaz, qalb*
century (n)	قرن، مأة سنة	*qarn, mi'atu sanah*
ceramic (adj)	خزافي	*khazzāfī*
ceramist (n)	خزاف، فخار	*khazzāf, fakhkhār*
cerebral (adj)	دماغي، عقلي	*dimāghī, 'aqlī*

cerebrate (v)	فكر، تفكر	*fakkara, tafakkara*
cerebration (n)	تفكير، نشاط عقلي	*tafkīr, nashāṭ 'aqlī*
cerebrum (n)	مخ، مقدم الدماغ	*mukhkh, muqaddamud dimāgh*
cerement (n)	كفن	*kafan*
ceremonial (adj)	احتفالي، رسمي	*iḥtifālī, rasmī*
ceremonious (adj)	رسمي، مولع بالرسميات	*rasmī, mūla' bir rasmiyyāt*
ceremony (n)	احتفال، مراسم	*iḥtifāl, marāsim*
cerise (n)	أحمر كرزي	*aḥmar karazī*
certain (adj)	يقيني، معين، مؤكد	*yaqīnī, mu'ayyan, mu'akkad*
certainly (adv)	من غير ريب	*min ghair raib*
certainly (interj)	طبعًا، بالطبع	*ṭab'an, biṭ ṭab'*
certainty (n)	يقين، ثقة، حقيقة	*yaqīn, thiqah, ḥaqīqah*
certificate (n)	شهادة، سند	*shahādah, sanad*
certified (adj)	مصدق، موثق	*muṣaddaq, muwaththaq*
certified copy (n)	نسخة مصدقة	*nuskhah muṣaddaqah*
certify (v)	صدق، شهد	*saddaqa, shahidah*
certitude (n)	يقين، ثقة	*yaqīn, thiqah*
cervical (adj)	عنقي	*'unuqī*
cervix (n)	عنق، رقبة	*'unuq, raqabah*
cessation (n)	توقف، انقطاع	*tawaqqauf, inqiṭā'*
chaff (n)	عصافة، حثالة	*'uṣāfah, ḥuthālah*
chain (n)	سلسلة، قيد	*silsilah, qaid*
chain gang (n)	عصبة مسلسلة	*'usbah musalsalah*
chain letter (n)	رسالة مسلسلة	*risālah musalsalah*
chain reaction (n)	تفاعل متسلسل	*tafā'ul mutasalsil*

chain store (n)	مؤسسة سلسلية	*mu'assasah silsiliyyah*
chair (n)	كرسي، مقر السلطة	*kursī, maqarrus sulṭah*
chairman (n)	رئيس المجلس	*ra'īsul majlis*
chairwoman (n)	رئيسة المجلس	*ra'īsatul majlis*
chaise (n)	شيز، مركبة صغيرة	*shīz, markabah ṣaghīrah*
chaise longue	شيز لنغ	*shīz lungh*
chalet (n)	شاليه، كوخ	*shālīh, kūkh*
chalice (n)	كأس القربان	*ka'sul qurbān*
chalk (n)	طبشورة، حوارى	*tabshūrah, ḥawwārā*
chalk (v)	كتب بالطباشير	*kataba biṭ ṭabāshīr*
chalky (adj)	طباشيري	*ṭabāshīrī*
challenge (v)	تحدى، اعترض	*taḥaddā, i'tarada*
challenge (n)	تحدٍّ، اعتراض، اختبار	*taḥaddin, i'tirāḍ, ikhtibār*
chamber (n)	حجرة، مجلس، قاعة	*ḥujrah, majlis, qā'ah*
chamberlain (n)	أمين الخزانة، مهجعي	*amīnul khizānah, mahja'ī*
chambermaid (n)	خادمة، مهجعية	*khādimah, mahja'iyyah*
chamber of commerce	غرفة التجارة	*ghurfatut tijārah*
chameleon (n)	حرباء، شخص متقلب	*ḥirbā', shakhṣ mutaqallib*
champ (v)	عض، قضم	*'aḍḍa, qaḍama*
champ (n)	عض، قضم	*'aḍḍ, qaḍm*
champion (n)	بطل، نصير	*baṭal, naṣīr*
championship (n)	بطولة، نصرة	*buṭūlah, nuṣrah*
chance (n)	فرصة، احتمال	*furṣah, iḥtimāl*
chancellor (n)	رئيس الجامعة	*ra'īsul jāmi'ah*

chancy (adj)	محفوف بالمخاطر	*maḥfūf bil makhāṭir*
chandelier (n)	ثريا	*thurayyā*
chandler (n)	شماع	*shammā'*
change (v)	غير، بدل	*ghayyara, baddala*
change (n)	تبديل، تبدل	*tabdīl, tabaddul*
changeable (adj)	متقلب، ممكن تغييره	*mutaqallib, mumkin taghyīruh*
changeless (adj)	غير متبدل	*ghair mutabaddil*
changeling (n)	طفل استبدل بآخر	*ṭifl ustubdila bi ākhar*
changer (n)	صراف	*ṣarrāf*
channel (n)	سبيل المواصلات، مجرى قناة	*sabīlul muwāṣalāt, majrā qanāt*
chant (n)	أنشودة، أغنية	*unshūdah, ughniyyah*
chant (v)	أنشد، غنى	*anshada, ghannā*
chaos (n)	حالة التشوش	*ḥālatut tashawwush*
chaotic (adj)	مشوش، مهرجل	*mushawwish, muharjal*
chap (n)	فتى، غلام، زبون	*fatā, ghulām, zabūn*
chaparal (n)	دغل، أجمة	*daghal, ajamah*
chapel (n)	كنيسة صغيرة	*kanīsah ṣaghīrah*
chaplain (n)	قسيس ملحق بمؤسسة	*qissīs mulḥaq bi mu'assasah*
chapter (n)	فصل، باب	*faṣl, bāb*
char (v/n)	فحم، فحم	*faḥḥama, faḥm*
character (n)	خلق، ميزة، دور	*khuluq, mīzah, daur*
characteristic (n)	خصيصة، صفة مميزة	*khaṣīṣah, ṣifah mumayyazah*
characterization (n)	تصوير للخصائص	*taṣwīr lil khaṣā'iṣ*
characterize,-ise (v)	ميز، وصف، صور	*mayyaza, waṣafa, ṣawwara*
charade (n)	تمثيلية تحزيرية	*tamthīliyyha taḥzīriyyah*

charge (n)	حمل، شحنة، رعاية، تهمة	*ḥiml, shiḥnah, ri'āyah, tuhmah*
charge (n)	شاحن، فرس	*shāḥin, faras*
chariot (n)	معجلة، مركبة	*mu'ajjalah, markabah*
charioteer (n)	سائق المعجلة	*sā'iqul mu'ajjalah*
charisma (n)	قدرة خارقة، سحر	*qudrah khāriqah, siḥr*
charismatic (adj)	فاتن، ساحر	*fātin, sāḥir*
charitable (adj)	خيري، متصدق	*khairī, mutaṣaddiq*
charity (n)	إحسان، صدقة، مؤسسة خيرية	*iḥsān, ṣadaqah, mu'assasah khairiyyah*
charm (n)	سحر، جمال، فتنة	*siḥr, jamāl, fitnah*
charm (v)	رقى، فتن	*raqā, fatana*
charmer (n)	ساحر، فاتن	*sāḥir, fātin*
charnel house (n)	موضع جثث الموتى	*mauḍa'u juthathil mautā*
chart (n)	خريطة، جدول	*kharīṭah, jadwal*
charter (n)	شرعة، دستور، براءة	*shir'ah, dustūr, barā'ah*
chartered (adj)	قانوني	*qānūnī*
chartered accountant	محاسب قانوني	*muḥāsib qānūnī*
chartist (n)	خرائطي	*kharā'iṭī*
charwoman (n)	خادمة نهارية	*khādimah nahāriyyah*
chary (adj)	خجول، حذر	*khajūl, ḥadhir*
chase (v)	تعقب، تصيد	*ta'aqqaba, taṣayyada*
chase (n)	تعقب، صيد	*ta'aqqub, ṣaid*
chaser (n)	نوع من الشراب	*nau' minash sharāb*
chasm (n)	شق، فجوة	*shaqq, fajwah*
chaste (adj)	عفيف، محتشم	*'afīf, muḥtashim*
chasten (v)	أدّب، هذب	*addaba, hadhdhaba*

chasteness (n)	عفة، طهارة	*'iffah, ṭahārah*
chastise (v)	أدب، عاقب	*addaba, 'āqaba*
chastisement (n)	عقاب، تأديب	*'iqāb, ṭa'dīb*
chastity (n)	عفة، طهارة	*'iffah, ṭahārah*
chat (v/n)	تحادث، محادثة	*taḥādatha, muḥādathah*
chatlaine (n)	مشبك	*mishbak*
chattel (n)	متاع، عبد	*matā', 'abd*
chatter (v)	ثرثر، زقزق	*tharthara, zaqzaqa*
chatterbox (n)	ثرثار، مهذار	*tharthār, mihdhār*
chatty (adj)	حديث، هاذر	*ḥiddīth, hādhir*
chauvinism (n)	شوفينية	*shūfīniyyah*
chauvinist (n)	شوفيني	*shūfīnī*
chaw (v)	مضغ	*maḍagha*
cheap (adj)	رخيص، حقير	*rakhīṣ, ḥaqīr*
cheapen (v)	رخص، قلل الثمن	*rakhkhaṣa, qallalath thaman*
cheat (v)	خدع، غش	*khada'a, ghashsha*
cheat (n)	خداع، غش	*khidā', ghishsh*
check (v)	فحص، أوقف، وبخ	*faḥaṣa, auqafa, wabbakha*
check (n)	وقف، فحص، توبيخ	*waqf, faḥṣ, taubīkh*
checkbook (n)	دفتر شيكات	*daftaru shīkāt*
checked (adj)	ذو ترابيع	*dhū tarābī'*
checker (n)	رسم ذو ترابيع	*rasm dhū tarābī'*
checkered (adj)	ذو ترابيع	*dhū tarābī'*
checkpoint (n)	حاجز تفتيش	*ḥājizu taftīsh*
checkroom (n)	حجرة الإيداع	*ḥujratul īdā'*
check-up (n)	فحص	*faḥṣ*

cheek (n)	خد، وجنة	*khadd, wajnah*
cheekbone (n)	عظم وجني	*'aẓm wajnī*
cheeky (adj)	وقح، صفيق	*waqiḥ, ṣafīq*
cheer (n)	هتاف، ابتهاج	*hutāf, ibtihāj*
cheer (v)	ابتهج، هتف	*ibtahaja, hatafa*
cheerful (adj)	مبتهج، مرح	*mubtahij, mariḥ*
cheerfully (adv)	بمرح، بابتهاج	*bi maraḥ, bibtihāj*
cheerless (adj)	حزين، كئيب	*ḥazīn, ka'īb*
cheery (adj)	مبتهج، مرح، طروب	*mubtahij, mariḥ, ṭarūb*
cheese (n)	جبن، جبنة	*jubn, jubnah*
cheeseburger (n)	نوع من سندويشة	*nau' min sandwīshah*
cheesecake (n)	فطيرة الجبن	*faṭīratul jubn*
cheesecloth (n)	قماش جبني	*qumāsh jubnī*
cheesy (adj)	جبني، تافه	*jubnī, tāfih*
chef (n)	طاهي	*ṭāhī*
chemical (adj)	كيميائي	*kīmyā'ī*
chemical engineering	هندسة كيميائية	*handasah kīmyā'iyyah*
chemical warfare	حرب كيميائية	*ḥarb kīmyā'iyyah*
chemist (n)	كيميائي، صيدلي	*kīmyā'ī, ṣaidalī*
chemistry (n)	علم الكيمياء	*'ilmul kīmyā'*
chemotherapy (n)	معالجة بالموادالكيميائية	*mu'ālajah bil mawādd al kīmyā'iyyah*
cheniile (n)	شنيل	*shanīl*
cheque (n)	شيك	*shīk*
cherish (v)	أعز، حفظ	*a'azza, ḥafiẓa*
cherry (n/adj)	ثمر الكرز، كرزي	*thamarul karaz, karazī*
chervil (n)	سرفيل	*sarfīl*

chess (n)	شطرنج	*shaṭranj*
chessboard (n)	رقعة الشطرنج	*ruq'atush shaṭranj*
chessman (n)	حجر الشطرنج	*ḥajarush shaṭranj*
chest (n)	صدر، صندوق	*ṣadr, ṣundūq*
chestnut (n)	كستناء	*kastanā'*
chesty (adj)	مغرور	*maghrūr*
chew (v/n)	مضغ، مضغ	*maḍagha, maḍgh*
chewing gum	علكة	*'ilkah*
chic (n)	أنيق، شكل جميل	*anīq, shakl jamīl*
chicanery (n)	خداع، حيلة	*khidā', ḥīlah*
chick (n)	صغير الطير	*ṣaghīruṭ ṭair*
chicken (n)	دجاجة، لحم الدجاجة	*dajājah, laḥmud dajājah*
chicken feed (n)	مبلغ تافه	*mablagh tāfih*
chickenhearted (adj)	مخلوع الفؤاد	*makhlū'ul fu'ād*
chicken pox (n)	جديري	*judairī*
chide (v)	عنف، وبخ	*'annafa, wabbakha*
chief (n/adj)	رئيس، زعيم	*ra'īs, za'īm*
chief justice (n)	رئيس المحكمة العليا	*ra'īsul maḥkamah al 'ulyā*
chiefly (adv)	خصوصًا،على الخصوص	*khuṣūṣan, 'alal khuṣūṣ*
chief of staff	رئيس الأركان	*ra'īsul arkān*
chief of state	رئيس الدولة	*ra'īsud daulah*
chieftain (n)	رئيس القبيلة	*ra'īsul qabīlah*
chiffon (n)	شيفون	*shīfūn*
child (n)	طفل، غلام	*ṭifl, ghulām*
childbearing (n)	إنجاب الأولاد	*injābul aulād*
childbed (n)	مخاض، نفاس	*makhāḍ, nifās*

childbirth (n)	ولادة، وضع	*wilādah, waḍ'*
childhood (n)	طفولة	*ṭufūlah*
childish (adj)	طفلي، صبياني	*ṭiflī, ṣibyānī*
child labour (n)	تشغيل الأولاد	*tashghīlul aulād*
childless (adj)	أبتر، بلا أولاد	*abtar, bilā aulād*
childlike (adj)	طفلي، بريء	*ṭiflī, barī'*
chili (n)	فلفل	*filfil*
chill (n)	برد معتدل	*bard mu'tadil*
chilling (adj)	بارد، فاتر	*bārid, fātir*
chimney (n)	مستوقد، مدخنة	*mustauqad, midkhanah*
chimney cap (n)	غطاء المدخنة	*ghiṭā'ul midkhanah*
chimney corner (n)	زاوية المستوقد	*zāwiyatul mustauqad*
chimney piece (n)	رف المستوقد	*rafful mustauqad*
chimney pot (n)	قدر المدخنة	*qidrul midkhanah*
chimney sweeper (n)	منظف المداخن	*munaẓẓiful madākhin*
chimney swift (n)	سمامة المداخن	*samāmatul madākhin*
chimpanzee (n)	شيمبانزي	*shīmbānzī*
chin (n)	ذقن	*dhaqan*
Chinese (n/adj)	صيني	*ṣīnī*
Chinese wall (n)	سور صيني	*sūr ṣīnī*
chink (n)	شق، صلصلة	*shaqq, ṣalṣalah*
chink (v)	رن، صل	*ranna, ṣalla*
chintz (n)	قماش قطني مطبع	*qumāsh quṭnī muṭabba'*
chip (n)	رقاقة، قطعة	*ruqāqah, qiṭ'ah*
chip (v)	قطع، كسر، شظى	*qaṭṭa'a, kasara, shaẓẓā*
chipmunk (n)	صيدناني	*ṣaidnānī*
chipper (n)	مشظاة	*mishẓāt*

chipping (n)	رقاقة، شظية	*ruqāqah, shaẓiyyah*
chiropodist (n)	أقدامي	*aqdāmī*
chiropody (n)	أقدامية	*aqdāmiyah*
chirp (v/n)	سقسق، سقسقة	*saqsaqa, saqsaqah*
chirpy (adj)	مرح، مبتهج	*mariḥ, mubtahij*
chisel (n)	منحت، منقاش	*minḥat, minqāsh*
chiselled (adj)	منحوت بإزميل	*manḥūt bi izmīl*
chit (n)	مذكرة صغيرة	*mudhakkirah ṣaghīrah*
chitchat (n)	قيل وقال	*qīl wa qāl*
chivalrous (adj)	فروسي، بطلي	*furūsī, baṭalī*
chivalry (n)	فرسان، فروسية	*fursān, furūsiyyah*
chive (n)	ثوم معمر	*thaum mu'ammar*
chivy (v/n)	طارد، مطاردة	*ṭārada, muṭāradah*
chloric (adj)	كلوري	*kulūrī*
chloric acid (n)	حمض كلوري	*ḥamḍ kulūrī*
chloride (n)	كلوريد	*kulūrīd*
chlorine (n)	الكلورين	*alkulūrīn*
chloroform (n)	كلوروفورم	*kulūrūfūrm*
chocolate (n)	شوكولا	*shūkūlā*
choice (n)	خيار، اصطفاء	*khiyār, iṣṭifā'*
choir (n)	خورس، مجموعة	*khūras, majmū'ah*
choirboy (n)	غلام الخورس	*ghulāmul khūras*
choke (v)	أوقف، سد، خنق	*auqafa, sadda, khanaqa*
choke (n)	كبت، خنق، سد	*kabt, khanq, sadd*
cholera (n)	كوليرا، هيضة	*kūlīrā, haiḍah*
cholestrol (n)	كولستيرول	*kūlistīrūl*
choline (n)	الكولين	*alkūlīn*
choose (v)	اختار، فضل	*ikhtāra, faḍḍala*

chop (v)	قطع، فرم	*qaṭa'a, farama*
chop (n)	قطعة، شظية، ضربة	*qiṭ'ah, shaẓiyyah, ḍarbah*
chopper (n)	مفرمة، ساطور	*miframah, sāṭūr*
chopping (n/adj)	تقطيع، متحول	*taqṭī', mutaḥawwil*
chopping knife (n)	مفرمة، مخرطة	*miframah, mikhraṭah*
chopstics (n)	عودان	*'ūdān*
choral (adj)	كورسي، خورسي	*kaurasī, khaurasī*
chorale (n)	خورس، ترنيمة	*khauras, tarnīmah*
chord (n)	وتر، وتر الدائرة	*watar, watarud dā'irah*
chord (v)	ناغم، تناغم	*nāghama, tanāghama*
chore (n)	عمل روتيني	*'amal rūtīnī*
choreographer (n)	مدير الرقص	*mudīrur raqṣ*
choreography (n)	وضع الألحان الراقصة	*waḍ'ul alḥān ar rāqiṣah*
choric (adj)	كورسي، خورسي	*kaurasī, khaurasī*
chortle (v/n)	أضحك، ضحكة	*aḍḥaka, ḍaḥakah*
chorus (n)	كورس	*Kauras*
chorus girl (n)	فتاة الكورس	*fatātul kauras*
chosen (adj)	مختار، مصطفى	*mukhtār, muṣṭafā*
Christ (n)	مسيح، عيسى	*masīḥ, 'īsā*
christen (v)	عمد، سمى	*'ammada, sammā*
christendom (n)	نصرانية	*naṣrāniyyah*
christening (n)	حفلة التعميد	*ḥaflatut ta'mīd*
Christian (n/adj)	نصراني، مسيحي	*naṣrānī, masīḥī*
christianity (n)	نصرانية	*naṣrāniyyah*
Christmas (n)	عيد الميلاد	*'īdul milād*

Christmas Eve	عشية الميلاد	*'ashiyyatul mīlād*
chromatic (adj)	لوني، ملون	*launī, mulawwan*
chrome (n)	كروم	*kurūm*
chromic (adj)	كرومي	*kurūmī*
chromic acid (n)	حمض الكروميك	*ḥamḍul kurūmīk*
chromium (n)	كروم	*kurūm*
chromosomal (adj)	كروموسومي	*kurūmūsūmī*
chromosome (n)	كروموسوم، صبغي	*kurūmūsūm, ṣibghī*
chronic (adj)	مزمن، مدمن	*muzmin, mudmin*
chronicle (n/v)	تاريخ، أرخ	*tārīkh, arrakha*
chronological (adj)	كرونولوجي	*kurūnūlūjī*
chronologist (n)	عالم بالكرونولوجيا	*'ālim bil kurūnūlūjiyā*
chronology (n)	كرونولوجيا،علم التاريخ	*kurūnūlūjiyā, 'ilmut tārīkh*
chronometre (n)	كرونومتر	*kurūnūmitr*
chub (n)	شوب	*shaub*
chubby (adj)	لحيم، ربيل	*laḥīm, rabīl*
chuck (v)	قذف، طرح	*qadhafa, ṭaraḥa*
chuckle (v)	ضحك في خفوت	*ḍaḥika fi khufūt*
chuckle (n)	ضحكة خافتة	*ḍaḥakah khāfitah*
chum (n)	صديق حميم	*ṣadīq ḥamīm*
chummy (adj)	حميم، ودود	*ḥamīm, wadūd*
chump (n)	مغفل، أبله	*mughaffal, ablah*
chunk (n)	قطعة غليظة، مقدار وافر	*qiṭ'ah ghalīẓah, miqdār wāfir*
chunky (adj)	قصير، مكتنز	*qaṣīr, muktaniz*
church (n)	كنيسة	*kanīsah*
churchgoer (n)	إلف الكنيسة	*ilful kanīsah*

churchman (n)	كاهن،عضو الكنيسة	*kāhin, 'uḍwul kanīsah*
churchyard (n)	فناء الكنيسة	*finā'ul kanīsah*
churlish (adj)	فظ، غليظ	*fazẓ, ghalīẓ*
chute (n)	شلال، قناة	*shallāl, qanāt*
cider (n)	عصير التفاح	*'aṣīrut tuffāḥ*
cigar (n)	سيجار	*sījār*
cigarette (n)	سيجارة	*sījārah*
cinch (n)	شيء سهل	*shay' sahl*
cinder (n)	جمرة حارة، رماد	*jamrah ḥārrah, ramād*
cine (n)	فيلم سينمائي	*fīlm sīnmā'ī*
Cinema (n)	فيلم سينمائي، صالة سينما	*fīlm sīnmā'ī, ṣālatu sīnmā*
cinematic (adj)	سينمائي	*sīnmā'ī*
cinematograph (n)	فن سينمائي	*fann sīnmā'ī*
cinematographer (n)	مصور سينمائي	*muṣawwir sīnmā'ī*
cinematography (n)	فن التصوير السينمائي	*fannut taṣwīr as- sīnmā'ī*
cinnamon (n)	قرفة	*qirfah*
cipher (n)	كتابة رمزية، صفر	*kitābah ramziyyah, ṣifr*
circle (n)	دائرة، حلقة، مجموعة	*dā'irah, ḥalqah, majmū'ah*
circlet (n)	دائرة صغيرة	*dā'irah ṣaghīrah*
circuit (n)	دائرة، دورة	*dā'irah, daurah*
circuit (v)	دار، طاف	*dāra, ṭāfa*
circuit breaker (n)	قاطع الدائرة	*qāṭi'ud dā'irah*
circuitous (adj)	غير مباشر	*ghair mubāshir*
circuitry (n)	مجموعات الدارات الكهربائية	*majmū'ātud dārāt al kahrabā'iyyah*
circular (adj)	مستدير، دائري	*mustadīr, dā'irī*

circular (n)	رسالة سيارة	*risālah sayyārah*
circulate (v)	دار، انتشر	*dāra, intashara*
circulating (adj)	دائر، منتشر	*dā'ir, muntashir*
circulation (n)	دوران، تداول	*dawarān, tadāwul*
circumcise (v)	ختن، طهر	*khatana, ṭahhara*
circumcision (n)	ختان، تطهير روحي	*khitān, taṭhīr rūḥī*
circumference (n)	محيط الدائرة	*muḥīṭud dā'irah*
circumfluent (adj)	جارٍ، مطوق	*jārin, muṭawwiq*
circumlocution (n)	إسهاب، إطناب	*ishāb, iṭnāb*
circumnavigate (v)	باحر	*bāḥara*
circumscribe (v)	حدّد، طوق	*ḥaddada, ṭawwaqa*
circumscription (n)	حد، منطقة	*ḥadd, minṭaqah*
circumspect (adj)	حذر، محترس	*ḥadhir, muḥtaris*
circumstance (n)	ظرف، وضع، حالة	*ẓarf, waḍ', ḥālah*
circumstantial (adj)	ظرفي، عرضي	*ẓarfī, 'araḍī*
circumvent (v)	دار، طوق، خاتل	*dāra, ṭawwaqa, khātala*
circus (n)	سيرك	*sīrk*
cirrus (n)	طخاف، طخاء	*ṭakhāf, ṭakhā'*
citadel (n)	قلعة، حصن	*qal'ah, ḥiṣn*
citation (n)	استشهاد، ذكر	*istishhād, dhikr*
cite (v)	استشهد، أورد	*istashhada, aurada*
citizen (n)	مواطن، مديني	*muwāṭin, madīnī*
citizenship (n)	مواطنية	*muwāṭiniyyah*
city (n)	مدينة	*madīnah*
city editor	محرر الأنباء المحلية	*muḥarrirul ambā' al maḥalliyyah*
city state	دولة المدينة	*daulatul madīnah*
civic (adj)	مديني، مدني	*madīnī, madanī*

civil (adj)	مدني، متمدن، أهلي	*madanī, mutamaddin, ahlī*
civil defense	دفاع مدني	*difā' madanī*
civil disobedience	عصيان مدني	*'iṣyān madanī*
civil engineer	مهندس مدني	*muhandis madanī*
civil engineering	هندسة مدنية	*handasah madaniyyah*
civilian (adj)	مدني	*madanī*
civility (n)	لطف، كياسة	*luṭf, kiyāsah*
civilization (n)	حضارة، تمدن	*ḥaḍārah, tamaddun*
civilize,-ise (v)	حضر، ثقف	*ḥaḍḍara, thaqqafa*
civilized (adj)	متحضر، مهذب	*mutaḥaḍḍir, muhadhdhab*
civil law	قانون مدني	*qānūn madanī*
civil marriage	زواج مدني	*zawāj madanī*
civil rights	حقوق مدنية	*ḥuqūq madaniyyah*
civil servant	موظف مدني	*muwaẓẓaf mādanī*
civil service	إدارة مدنية	*idārah madaniyyah*
civil war	حرب أهلية	*ḥarb ahliyyah*
clad (adj)	مكسو، ملبوس	*maksuww, malbūs*
claim (v)	ادعى، طالب	*idda'ā, ṭālaba*
claimant (n)	مطالب، مدعي	*muṭālib, mudda'ī*
clamorous (adj)	مطالب صاخب	*muṭālib ṣākhib*
clamour (n)	صخب، مطالبة	*ṣakhab, muṭālabah*
clamp (n)	ملزم، مشد	*milzam , mishadd*
clan (n)	عشيرة، جماعة	*'ashīrah, jamā'ah*
clandestine (adj)	سري، خفي	*sirrī, khafī*
clang (v/n)	رن، رنين	*ranna, ranīn*
clank (n/v)	صليل، صلصل	*ṣalīl, ṣalṣala*

clap (v/n)	صفق، تصفيق	*ṣaffaqa, taṣfīq*
clapper (n)	لسان الجرس	*lisānul jaras*
claret (adj)	أحمر أرجواني داكن	*aḥmar urjuwānī dākin*
clarification (n)	توضيح، اتضاح	*tauḍīḥ, ittiḍāḥ*
clarify (v)	وضح، صفى	*waḍḍaḥa, ṣaffā*
clarinet (n)	كلارينت، مزمار	*kalārīnat, mizmār*
clarion (n)	بوق، صوت البوق	*būq, ṣautul būq*
clarity (n)	وضوح، جلاء	*wuḍūḥ, jalā'*
clash (v)	اصطدم، تعارض	*iṣṭadama, ta'āraḍa*
clash (n)	اصطدام، معركة	*iṣṭidām, ma'rakah*
clasp (n)	إبزيم، مشبك	*ibzīm, mishbak*
clasp (v)	شبك بإبزيم	*shabaka bi ibzīm*
class (n)	صف، درجة، صنف	*ṣaff, darajah, ṣinf*
class book (n)	دفتر الصف، كتاب الصف	*daftaruṣ ṣaff, kitābuṣ ṣaff*
classical (adj)	ممتاز، تقليدي، كلاسيكي	*mumtāz, taqlīdī, kalāsīkī*
classicism (n)	كلاسيكية	*kalāsīkiyyah*
classicist (n)	كلاسيكي	*kalāsīkī*
classifiable (adj)	قابل للتصنيف	*qābil lit taṣnīf*
classification (n)	تصنيف، تبويب	*taṣnīf, tabwīb*
classified (adj)	مبوبة	*mubawwabah*
calssify (v)	صنف، بوب	*ṣannafa, bawwaba*
classmate (n)	رفيق الصف	*rafīquṣ ṣaff*
classroom (n)	حجرة الدراسة	*ḥujratud dirāsah*
class struggle	صراع طبقي	*ṣirā' ṭabaqī*
classy (adj)	أنيق، ممتاز	*anīq, mumtāz*
clatter (v)	صلصل، ثرثر	*ṣalṣala, tharthara*

clatter (n)	قعقعة، فوضى	*qa'qa'ah, fauḍā*
clause (n)	جزء من جملة	*juz' min jumlah*
clavichord (n)	موترة المفاتيح	*muwattaratul mafātīḥ*
claw (n)	مخلب، خدش	*mikhlab, khadsh*
clawed (adj)	ذو مخالب	*dhū makhālib*
clay (n)	صلصال، وحل	*ṣalṣāl, waḥl*
clay pigeon (n)	حمامة طينية	*ḥāmāmah ṭīniyyah*
clean (adj)	نظيف، صافٍ، طاهر	*naẓīf, ṣāfin, ṭāhir*
clean-cut (adj)	واضح، بين	*wāḍiḥ, bayyin*
cleaner (n)	منظف	*munaẓẓif*
cleanliness (n)	نظافة، طهارة	*naẓāfah, ṭahārah*
cleanly (adj)	نظيف، مهندم	*naẓīf, muhandam*
cleanse (v)	نظف، طهر	*naẓẓafa, ṭahhara*
clean-shaven (adj)	حليق الشعر	*ḥalīqush sha'r*
clean-up (n)	تنظيف	*tanẓīf*
clear (adj)	واضح، صافٍ، بريء	*wāḍiḥ, ṣāfin, barī'*
clear (adv)	بوضوح، تماماً	*bi wuḍūḥ, tamāman*
clear (v)	برأ، نظف، وضح	*barra'a, naẓẓafa, waḍḍaḥa*
clearance (n)	مقاصة، تصريح، تصفية	*muqāṣṣah, taṣrīḥ, taṣfiah*
clear-cup (adj)	واضح، محدد	*wāḍiḥ, muḥaddad*
clear-headed (adj)	صافي الذهن	*ṣāfiyudh dhihn*
clearing (n)	أرض مقطوعة الشجر	*arḍ maqṭū'atush shajar*
clearing house (n)	دار المقاصة	*dārul muqāṣṣah*
clearly (adv)	بوضوح، بجلاء	*bi wuḍūḥ, bi jalā'*
clearness (n)	وضوح، جلاء	*wuḍūḥ, jalā'*
clear-sighted (adj)	جلي البصر	*jaliyyul baṣar*

cleat (n)	ممسك، حافظة النعل	*mimsak, ḥāfiẓatun na'l*
cleavage (n)	شق، اختراق	*shaqq, ikhtirāq*
cleaver (n)	ساطور الجزار	*sāṭūrul jazzār*
cleft (n/adj)	شق، مشقوق	*shaqq, mashqūq*
clemency (n)	اعتدال، رأفة	*i'tidāl, ra'fah*
clement (adj)	معتدل، رؤوف	*mu'tadil, ra'ūf*
clench (v)	أطبق، ثبت	*aṭbaqa, thabbata*
clergy (n)	اكليروس	*iklīrūs*
clergyman (n)	كاهن، قسيس	*kāhin, qissīs*
cleric (n/adj)	رجل دين، اكليريكي	*rajulu dīn, iklīrīkī*
clerical (n/adj)	كاهن، اكليريكي	*kāhin, iklīrīkī*
clerk (n)	كاتب، بائع	*kātib, bā'i'*
clever (adj)	حاذق، ذكي، رشيق	*ḥādhiq, dhakī, rashīq*
cleverly (adv)	ببراعة، بمهارة	*bi barā'ah, bi mahārah*
click (v)	طقطق، تلاءم	*ṭaqṭaqa, talā'ama*
click (n)	طقطقة، قرقعة	*ṭaqṭaqah, qarqa'ah*
client (n)	موكل، زبون	*muwakkil, zabūn*
cliff (n)	جرف	*juruf*
climate (n)	مناخ، طقس	*munākh, ṭaqs*
climatic (adj)	مناخي، جوي	*munākhī, jawwī*
climatology (n)	علم المناخ	*'ilmul munākh*
climax (n)	صورة معراجية، ذروة	*ṣūrah mi'rājiyyah, dhirwah*
climb (v)	تسلق، ارتفع	*tasallaqa, irtafa'a*
climber (n)	متسلق الجبال	*mutasalliqul jibāl*
clinch (v)	أمسك، حسم	*amsaka, ḥasama*
clincher (n)	حقيقة حاسمة	*ḥaqīqah ḥāsimah*
cline (n)	ميل، انحدار	*mail, inḥidār*

cling (v)	امتسك، التصق	*imtasaka, iltaṣaqa*
clinging (adj)	ضيقة	*ḍayyiqah*
clinic (n)	عيادة، مستوصف	*'iyādah, mustauṣaf*
clinical (adj)	سريري، تحليلي	*sarīrī, taḥlīlī*
clinician (n)	طبيب سريري	*ṭabīb sarīrī*
clink (v)	صلصل، خشخش	*ṣalṣala, khashkhasha*
clink (n)	صلصلة، خشخشة	*ṣalṣalah, khashkhashah*
clinker (n)	خبث المعادن	*khabathul ma'ādin*
clip (n)	مشبك، مشط	*mishbak, mushṭ*
clip (v)	ثبت بمشبك	*thabbata bi mishbak*
clipboard (n)	لوح مشبكي	*lauḥ mishbakī*
clipper (n)	مجز، مقلمة	*mijazz, muqallimah*
clipping (n)	قصاصة، قراضة	*quṣāṣah, qurāḍah*
clique (n)	زمرة، عصبة	*zumrah, 'uṣbah*
clitoris (n)	بظر	*baẓr*
cloak (n)	عباءة	*'abā'ah*
cloak-and-dagger	تجسسي	*tajassūsī*
clobber (v)	ضرب بقسوة	*ḍaraba bi qaswah*
clock (n)	ساعة كبيرة	*sā'ah kabīrah*
clod (n)	كتلة تراب	*kutlatu turāb*
clog (v)	عاق، سد	*'āqa, sadda*
clog (n)	عائق، سد، ثقل	*'ā'iq, sadd, thiql*
cloister (n)	موضع منعزل	*mauḍa' mun'azil*
cloistered (adj)	متوحد، منعزل	*mutawaḥḥid, mun'azil*
close (v)	أغلق، ختم، انسد	*aghlaqa, khatama, insadda*
close (adj)	قريب، حميم	*qarīb, ḥamīm*

closed (adj)	مغلق، مسدود	*mughlaq, masdūd*
closed chain (n)	سلسلة مقفلة	*silsilah muqaffalah*
closed shop (n)	مؤسسة مقفلة	*mu'assasah muqaffalah*
close-mouthed (adj)	قليل الكلام	*qalīlul kalām*
closet (n)	خزانة، حجرة صغيرة	*khizānah, ḥujrah ṣaghīrah*
close-up (n)	صورة فوتوغرافية	*ṣūrah fūtūgharāfiyyah*
closing (adj)	نهائي، ختامي	*nihā'ī, khitāmī*
closure (n)	إغلاق، نهاية	*ighlāq, nihāyah*
clot (n)	جلطة، كتلة	*jalṭah, kutlah*
clot (v)	تجلط، تكتل	*tajallaṭa, takattala*
cloth (n)	قماش، نسيج	*qumāsh, nasīj*
clothe (v)	كسا، ألبس	*kasā, albasa*
clothes (n)	ملابس	*malābis*
clothing (n)	ملابس، غطاء	*malābis, ghiṭā'*
cloud (n)	سحابة، حشد، شائبة	*saḥābah, ḥashd, shā'ibah*
cloud (v)	حجب، غشى	*ḥajaba, ghashshā*
cloudburst (n)	وابل، مطر غزير	*wābil, maṭar ghazīr*
cloudless (adj)	صافٍ، صاحٍ	*ṣāfin, ṣāḥin*
cloudy (adj)	غائم، غامض	*ghā'im, ghāmiḍ*
clout (n)	نفوذ، سلطة، ضربة	*nufūdh, sulṭah, ḍarbah*
clown (n)	مهرج، فظ	*muharrij, faẓẓ*
clownish (adj)	فظ، أخرق	*faẓẓ, akhraq*
club (n)	نادٍ، ملهى	*nādin, malhā*
clubhouse (n)	منتدى	*muntadā*
clubman (n)	عضو في نادٍ	*'uḍw fī nādin*

clue (n)	مفتاح، إشارة	*miftāḥ, ishārah*
clump (n)	مجموعة، كتلة	*majmū'ah, kutlah*
clumpy (adj)	أجمي	*ajamī*
clumsy (adj)	غير ملائم، غير مصقول	*ghair mulā'im, ghair maṣqūl*
cluster (n)	مجموعة، جماعة	*majmū'ah, jamā'ah*
clutch (v)	قبض بإحكام	*qabaḍa bi iḥkām*
clutch (n)	قابض، قبضة	*qābiḍ, qabḍah*
clutter (v)	ركم، كوم	*rakama, kawwama*
clutter (n)	ركام، كومة	*rukām, kaumah*
coach (n)	مدرب رياضي، حافلة	*mudarrib riyāḍī, ḥāfilah*
coach (v)	درب، درس	*darraba, darrasa*
coaching (n)	تدريب	*tadrīb*
coachman (n)	حوذي	*ḥūdhī*
coagulate (v)	خثر، جلط	*khaththara, jallaṭa*
coagulation (n)	تجليط، تخثير	*tajlīṭ, takhthīr*
coal (n)	فحم، جمرة	*faḥm, jamrah*
coalesce (v)	اندمج، التحم	*indamaja, iltaḥama*
coalfield (n)	حقل الفحم	*ḥaqlul faḥm*
coalition (n)	ائتلاف، اتحاد	*i'tilāf, ittiḥād*
coal mine (n)	منجم الفحم	*manjamul faḥm*
coarse (adj)	خشن، رديء، شديد	*khashin, radī', shadīd*
coarsen (v)	خشن، خشن	*khashuna, khashshana*
coast (n)	شاطئ، ساحل	*shāṭi', sāḥil*
coastal (adj)	ساحلي	*sāḥilī*
coast guard (n)	خفير السواحل	*khafīrus sawāḥil*
coat (n)	سترة، غطاء، فروة	*sutrah, ghiṭā', farwah*

coating (n)	غلاف، غطاء	*ghilāf, ghiṭā'*
co-author (n)	مؤلف مشارك	*mu'allif mushārik*
coax (v)	تملق، لاطف	*tamallaqa, lāṭafa*
coaxing (adj)	متملق	*mutamalliq*
cobble (v)	رقع الأحذية	*raqqa'al aḥdhiyah*
cobbler (n)	قبلر، مرقع الأحذية	*qablar, muraqqi'ul aḥdhiyah*
cobra (n)	أفعى سامة جدًا	*af'ā sāmmah jiddā*
cobweb (n)	بيت العنكبوت	*baitul 'ankabūt*
cochineal (n)	قرمز	*qirmiz*
cock (n)	ديك، ذكر الطائر	*dīk, dhakaruṭ ṭā'ir*
cockfight (n)	مصارعة الديك	*muṣāra'atud dīk*
cocktail (n)	كوكتيل، نوع من شراب	*kūktīl, nau' min sharāb*
cocky (adj)	مغرور، معجب بذاته	*maghrūr, mu'jab bi dhātih*
coconut (n)	جوزة الهند	*jauzatul hind*
coddle (v)	عامل برفق، دلل	*'āmala bi rifq, dallala*
code (n)	مدونة، دستور، شفرة	*madwanah, dustūr, shifrah*
codicil (n)	ملحق وصية	*mulḥaqu waṣiyyah*
codify (v)	نسق، نظم	*nassaqa, naẓẓama*
co-education (n)	تعليم مختلط	*ta'līm mukhtalaṭ*
co-educational (adj)	مختلط	*mukhtalaṭ*
coefficient (n)	معامل، درجة	*mu'āmil, darajah*
coerce (v)	أجبر، أكره	*ajbara, akraha*
coercion (n)	إجبار، قسر	*ijbār, qasr*
coercive (adj)	إكراهي، قسري	*ikrāhī, qasrī*

coexit (v)	تواجد، تعايش	*tawājada, ta'āyasha*
coexistence (n)	تواجد، تعايش	*tawājud, ta'āyush*
coffee (n)	قهوة	*qahwah*
coffee house	مقهى	*maqhā*
coffer (n)	صندوق، خزينة	*ṣundūq, khazīnah*
coffin (n)	تابوت	*tābūt*
cogent (adj)	قوي، مقنع	*qawī, muqni'*
cogitate (v)	دبر، تأمل	*dabbara, ta'mmala*
cogitation (n)	تأمل، تفكير	*ta'ammul, tafkīr*
cognate (adj)	شقيق، نسيب، قريب	*shaqīq, nasīb, qarīb*
cognation (n)	قرابة، نسابة	*qarābah, nasābah*
cognition (n)	معرفة، إدراك	*ma'rifah, idrāk*
cognizance (n)	علم، إدراك	*'ilm, idrāk*
cognizant (adj)	عالم، مطلع على	*'ālim, muṭṭali' 'alā*
cognize (v)	علم، أدرك	*'alima, adraka*
cohabit (v)	تعايش، عاشر	*ta'āyasha, 'āshara*
cohabitation (n)	تعايش، مساكنة	*ta'āyush, musākanah*
cohere (n)	التحم، اتحد	*iltaḥama, ittaḥada*
coherence (n)	تماسك، اتحاد	*tamāsuk, ittiḥād*
coherent (adj)	ملتحم، مترابط	*multaḥim, mutarābiṭ*
cohesion (n)	تماسك، التحام	*tamāsuk, iltiḥām*
cohesive (n)	ملصق، متماسك	*mulṣiq, mutamāsik*
cohort (n)	عصبة، جماعة	*'usbah, jamā'ah*
coil (n)	سلسلة، لفة	*silsilah, laffah*
coil (v)	لف، التف	*laffa, iltaffa*
coin (n)	عملة، وتد	*'umlah, watid*
coin (v)	سك، صاغ	*sakka, ṣāgha*
coinage (n)	سك، صياغة	*sakk, ṣiyāghah*

coincide (v)	تزامن، تطابق، توافق	*tazāmana, taṭābaqa, tawāfaqa*
coincidence (n)	تزامن، تطابق، توافق	*tazāmun, taṭābuq, tawāfuq*
coincident (adj)	متوافق، متزامن	*mutawāfiq, mutazāmin*
coir (n)	ليف جوز الهند	*līfu jawzil hind*
coitus (n)	جماع	*jimā'*
coitus interruptus	عزل	*'azl*
coke (n)	كوك	*kūk*
colander (n)	مصفاة	*miṣfāt*
cold (adj)	بارد، غير متحمس	*bārid, ghair mutaḥammis*
cold-blooded (adj)	متغيرالحرارة، وحشي	*mutaghayyirul ḥarārah, waḥshī*
cold-cream (n)	كريم بارد	*kirīm bārid*
cold frame (n)	وقاء بارد	*waqā' bārid*
cold-hearted (adj)	لا مبالٍ	*lā mubālin*
cold war (n)	حرب باردة	*ḥarb bāridah*
cold wave (n)	موجة باردة	*maujah bāridah*
colic (n/adj)	مغص، مغصي	*maghṣ, maghṣī*
collaborate (v)	اشترك، تعاون	*ishtaraka, ta'āwana*
collaboration (n)	اشتراك، تعاون	*ishtirāk, ta'āwun*
collapse (v)	انهار، أخفق	*inhāra, akhfaqa*
collapse (n)	انهيار، انهيار صحي	*inhiyār, inhiyār ṣiḥḥī*
collar (n)	قبة، قلادة، طوق	*qabbah, qalādah, ṭauq*
collate (v)	فحص، وازن	*faḥaṣa, wāzana*
collation (n)	فحص، موازنة	*faḥṣ, muwāzanah*
colleague (n)	زميل، رصيف	*zamīl, raṣīf*

collect (v)	جمع، اجتمع	*jamaʻa, ijtamaʻa*
collection (n)	جمع، مجموعة	*jamʻ, majmūʻah*
collective (adj)	جمعي، جماعي	*jamʻī, jamāʻī*
collective agreement	اتفاق جماعي	*ittifāq jamāʻī*
collective bargaining	مساومة جماعية	*musāwamah jamāʻiyyah*
collective farm	مزرعة تعاونية	*mazraʻah taʻāwuniyyah*
collective note	مذكرة جماعية	*mudhakkirah jamāʻiyyah*
collective noun	اسم جمعي	*ism jamʻī*
college (n)	كلية، جماعة	*kulliyyah, jamāʻah*
collegiate (adj)	ذو علاقة بكلية	*dhū ʻalāqah bi kulliyyah*
collide (v)	تصادم، تعارض	*taṣādama, taʻāraḍa*
collision (n)	تصادم، تعارض	*taṣādum, taʻāruḍ*
collocate (v)	نظم، رتب	*naẓẓama, rattaba*
collocation (n)	تنظيم، رصف	*tanẓīm, raṣf*
colloquial (adj)	عامي، محكي	*ʻāmī, maḥkī*
colloquy (n)	حديث، مكالمة	*ḥadīth, mukālamah*
collude (v)	تآمر، تواطأ	*taʼāmara, tawāṭaʼa*
collusion (n)	تواطؤ، مؤامرة	*tawāṭuʼ, muʼāmarah*
collusive (adj)	تآمري، تواطئي	*taʼāmurī, tawāṭuʼī*
colon (n)	قولون، نقطتان	*qūlūn, nuqṭatān*
colonel (n)	زعيم، كولونيل	*zaʻīm, kūlūnīl*
colonial (adj)	مستعمري،استعماري	*mustaʻmarī, istiʻmārī*
colonialism (n)	استعمارية	*istiʻmāriyyah*
colonist (n)	مستعمري	*mustaʻmarī*
colonize,-ise (v)	استعمر	*istaʻmara*
colony (n)	مستعمرة، جالية	*mustaʻmarah, jāliyah*

colossal (adj)	ضخم، هائل	*ḍakhm, hā'il*
colour (color) (n/v)	لون، لوّن	*laun, lawwana*
colourful (adj)	ملون	*mulawwan,*
colouring (n)	تلوين، تلون	*talwīn, talawwun*
colourist (n)	ملون، مدبج	*mulawwin, mudabbij*
column (n)	رتل، عمود	*ratal, 'amūd*
columnist (n)	صاحب العمود	*ṣāḥibul 'amūd*
coma (n)	سبات، إغماء	*subāt, ighmā'*
comatose (adj)	سباتي، نعسان	*subātī, na'sān*
comb (n)	مشط، عرف الديك	*mushṭ, 'urfud dīk*
comb (v)	مشط، نقب	*mashshaṭa, naqqaba*
combat (v)	صارع، قاتل	*ṣāra'a, qātala*
combat (n)	نزاع، قتال	*nizā', qitāl*
combatant (n)	مقاتل، محارب	*muqātil, muḥārib*
combative (adj)	مستعد للقتال	*musta'idd lil qitāl*
combination (n)	اتحاد، ائتلاف، ضم	*ittiḥād, i'tilāf, ḍamm*
combine (v)	ضم، وحد	*ḍamma, waḥḥada*
combust (v)	أحرق، احترق	*aḥraqa, iḥtaraqa*
combustion (n)	إحراق، احتراق، حريق	*iḥrāq, iḥtirāq, ḥarīq*
come (v)	جاء، أتى، وقع	*jā'a, atā, waqa'a*
come across	عبر، صادف	*'abara, ṣādafa*
come back	رجع، عاد	*raja'a, 'āda*
comeback (n)	استعادة	*isti'ādah*
comedian (n)	ممثل هزلي	*mumaththil hazlī*
comedic (adj)	كوميدي، هزلي	*kūmīdī, hazlī*
comedy (n)	كوميديا، حادثة	*kūmidiyā, ḥādithah*
	مضحكة	*muḍḥikah*
come in	دخل، حل	*dakhala, ḥalla*

comely (adj)	وسيم، جميل	*wasīm, jamīl*
come-on (n)	إغراء، إغواء	*ighrā', ighwā'*
comer (n)	قادم، وافد	*qādim, wāfid*
comet (n)	مذنب	*mudhannab*
comfort (n)	راحة، رفاهية	*rāḥah, rafāhiyyah*
comfort (v)	عزى، أراح	*'azzā, arāḥa*
comfortable (adj)	مريح، مشجع	*murīḥ, mushajji'*
comic (adj)	هزلي، مضحك	*hazlī, muḍḥik*
comma (n)	فاصلة، شولة	*fāṣilah, shaulah*
command (v)	أمر، قاد	*amara, qāda*
command (n)	أمر، قيادة، إشراف	*amr, qiyādah, ishrāf*
commandant (n)	آمر، قائد، حاكم	*āmir, qā'id, ḥākim*
commander (n)	آمر، قائد	*āmir, qā'id*
commander in chief	قاعد أعلى	*qā'id a'lā*
commandment (n)	أمر، وصية	*amr, waṣiyyah*
commando (n)	مغوار، مغاوير	*mighwār, maghāwīr*
commemorate (v)	أحيي ذكرى	*aḥyā dhikrā*
commemoration (n)	إحياء ذكرى	*iḥyā'u dhikrā*
commemoratory(adj)	تذكاري	*tidhkārī*
commence (v)	استهل، بدأ	*istahalla, bada'a*
commencement (n)	حفلة التخريج، بدء	*ḥaflatut takhrīj, bad'*
commend (v)	مدح، أودع	*madaḥa, auda'a*
commendation (n)	إطراء، إيداع	*iṭrā', īdā'*
commensurate (v)	تعادل، تكافأ	*ta'ādala, takāfa'a*
comment (n/v)	تعليق، علق	*ta'līq, 'allaqa*
commentary (n)	تعليق، تفسير	*ta'līq, tafsīr*
commentator (n)	مفسر، معلق	*mufassir, mu'alliq*
commerce (n)	تجارة، متجر	*tijārah, matjar*

commercial (adj)	تجاري، متجري	*tijārī, matjarī*
commercialism (n)	تجارية	*tijāriyyah*
commercialization (n)	تتجير	*tatjīr*
commercialize,-ise (v)	تجر	*tajjara*
commiserate (v)	آسى، عزى	*āsā, 'azzā*
commission (n)	وكالة، لجنة	*wakālah, lajnah*
commission (v)	فوض، كلف	*fawwaḍa, kallafa*
commissioned officer	ضابط مقلد	*ḍābiṭ muqallad*
commissioner (n)	مفوض، مندوب	*mufawwaḍ, mandūb*
commit (v)	ارتكب، حول، أودع	*irtakaba, ḥawwala, auda'a*
commitment (n)	ارتكاب، إيداع	*irtikāb, īdā'*
committal (n)	ارتكاب، تحويل	*irtikāb, taḥwīl*
committee (n)	لجنة، مجلس	*lajnah, majlis*
commode (n)	خزانة، منضدة	*khizānah, minḍadah*
commodious (adj)	ملائم، واسع	*mulā'im, wāsi'*
commodity (n)	سلعة، بضاعة	*sil'ah, biḍā'ah*
common (n)	عام، شائع، عادي	*'āmm, shā'i', 'ādī*
common law	قانون عادي	*qanūn 'ādī*
commonly (adv)	عادةً، عموماً	*'ādatan, 'umūman*
common noun	اسم نكرة	*ismu nakirah*
commonplace (n)	شيء عادي	*shay' 'ādī*
common room (n)	حجرة الاستراحة	*ḥujratul istirāḥah*
common sense (n)	فطرة سليمة	*fiṭrah salīmah*
commonwealth (n)	كومنولث، دولة	*kūmanwilth, daulah*
commotion (n)	اضطراب، ثورة	*iḍṭirāb, thaurah*
commercial (adj)	كوميوني، طائفي، اشتراكي	*kūmiunī, ṭā'ifī, ishtirākī*

communalism (n)	كوميونية، طائفية	*kūmiuniyyah, ṭā'ifiyyah*
commune (n)	مجموعة، جمعية	*majmū'ah, jam'iyyah*
communicant (adj)	مبلغ، ناقل	*muballigh, nāqil*
communicate (v)	بلغ، أفشى، أوصل	*ballagha, afshā, auṣala*
communication (n)	إبلاغ، إفشاء، اتصال	*iblāgh, ifshā', ittiṣāl*
communicative (adj)	صريح، موصل	*ṣarīḥ, muwaṣṣil*
communion (n)	مشاركة، طائفة	*mushārakah, ṭā'ifah*
communism (n)	شيوعية	*shuyū'iyyah*
communist (n)	شيوعي	*shuyū'ī*
community (n)	جماعة، جمهور، جالية	*jamā'ah, jumhūr, jāliyah*
community centre	مركز اجتماعي	*markaz ijtimā'ī*
commutation (n)	ركوب، تعديل، إبدال	*rukūb, ta'dīl, ibdāl*
commute (v)	ركب، عدل، أبدل	*rakiba, 'addala, adbala*
compact (adj)	متضام، مكتنز	*mutaḍāmm, muktaniz*
compact (v)	تدمج، تضام	*tadammaja, taḍāmma*
companion (n)	رفيق، دليل	*rafīq, dalīl*
companionship (n)	رفقة، عشرة	*rifqah, 'ishrah*
company (n)	رفاق، جماعة، شركة	*rifāq, jamā'ah, sharikah*
comparative (adj)	مقارن، نسبي	*muqārin, nisbī*
comparatively (adv)	نسبياً، بالنسبة	*nisbiyyan, bin nisbah*
compare (v)	وازن، ضاهى	*wāzana, ḍāhā*
comparision (n)	مقارنة، مضاهاة	*muqāranah, muḍāhāt*
compartment (n)	حجيرة، مقصورة	*ḥujairah, maqṣūrah*
compass (n)	نطاق، حد، بوصلة	*niṭāq, ḥadd, būṣlah*
compassion (n)	حنو، شفقة	*ḥunuww, shafaqah*
compassionate (adj)	شفوق، رحيم	*shafūq, raḥīm*
compel (v)	أجبر، أكره	*ajbara, akraha*
compelling (adj)	إجباري، إلزامي	*ijbārī, ilzāmī*

compensate (v)	عوض، كافأ	*'awwaḍa, kāfa'a*
compensation (n)	تعويض، مكافأة	*ta'wīḍ, mukāfa'ah*
compete (v)	تنافس، اشترك	*tanāfasa, ishtaraka*
competence (n)	كفاية، مقدرة، أهلية	*kifāyah, maqdarah, ahliyyah*
competency (n)	أهلية، مقدرة	*ahliyyah, maqdarah*
competent (n)	مؤهل، مقتدر	*mu'ahhal, muqtadir*
competition (n)	منافسة، مباراة	*munāfasah, mubārāt*
competitive (adj)	تنافسي، سباقي	*tanāfusī, sibāqī*
competitor (n)	منافس، مزاحم	*munāfis, muzāḥim*
compilation (n)	تأليف، جمع	*ta'līf, jam'*
compile (v)	ألف، جمع	*allafa, jama'a*
compiler (n)	مؤلف، جامع	*mu'allif, jāmi'*
complacence-cy (n)	رضاء، رغبة	*riḍā', raghbah*
complacent (adj)	راضٍ، راغب	*rāḍin, rāghib*
complain (v)	شكى، تشكى	*shakā, tashakkā*
complainant (n)	مدعي، شاك	*mudda'ī, shākin*
complaint (n)	شكوى، اتهام	*shakwā, ittihām*
complaisance (n)	كياسة، لطف	*kiyāsah, lutf*
complaisant (adj)	لطيف، كيس	*laṭīf, kayyis*
complement (n)	تكملة، ملحق	*takmilah, mulḥaq*
complementary (adj)	متتام	*mutatāmm*
complete (n)	تام، كامل	*tāmm, kāmil*
complete (v)	تمم، أكمل	*tammama, akmala*
completely (adj)	تماماً، كليةً	*tamāman, kulliyyatan*
completion (n)	إتمام، إكمال	*itmām, ikmāl*
complex (n)	مركب، معقد	*murakkab, mu'aqqad*
complexion (n)	بشرة، مظهر عام	*basharah, maẓhar 'āmm*

complexity (n)	تعقيد، تعقد	*ta'qīd, ta'aqqud*
compliance (n)	مطاوعة، إذعان	*muṭāwa'ah, idh'ān*
compliant (adj)	مطاوع، مذعن	*muṭāwi', mudh'in*
complicate (v)	عقد، صعب	*'aqqada, ṣa''aba*
complicated (adj)	معقد، صعب	*mu'aqqad, ṣa'b*
complication (n)	تعقيد، تعقد، ارتباك	*ta'qīd, ta'aqqud, irtibāk*
complicity (n)	اشتراك في جريمة	*ishtirāk fī jarīmah*
compliment (n)	مدح، إطراء	*madḥ, iṭrā'*
complimentary (adj)	مدحي، مجامل	*madḥī, mujāmil*
comply (v)	أطاع أذعن	*aṭā'a, adh'ana*
component (n)	مركب، جزء أساسي	*murakkab, juz' asāsī*
compose (v)	ركب، نضد	*rakkaba, naḍḍada*
composed (adj)	مركب، هادئ	*murakkab, hādi'*
composer (n)	مؤلف موسيقي	*mu'allif mausīqī*
composite (adj)	مركب، مؤلف	*murakkab, mu'allaf*
composition (n)	تركيب، تأليف	*tarkīb, ta'līf*
composure (n)	هدوء، رصانة	*hudū', raṣānah*
compound (adj/v)	مركب، ركب	*murakkab, rakkaba*
comprehend (v)	فهم، أدرك	*fahima, adraka*
comprehensible (adj)	ممكن إدراكه	*mumkin idrākuh*
comprehension (n)	فهم، إدراك	*fahm, idrāk*
comprehensive (adj)	شامل، جامع	*shāmil, jāmi'*
compress (v)	ركز، ضغط	*rakkaza, ḍaghaṭa*
compressible (adj)	قابل للانضغاط	*qābil lil inḍighāṭ*
compression (n)	ضغط،انضغاط،كبس	*ḍaghṭ, inḍighāṭ, kabs*
compressor (n)	ضاغطة، معصرة	*ḍāghiṭah, mi'ṣarah*
comprise (v)	تضمن، شمل	*taḍammana, shamila*
compromise (v)	سوى، وفق	*sawwā, waffaqa*

compromise (n)	حل موفق، صلح، تسوية	*ḥall muwaffaq, ṣulḥ, taswiyah*
compromising (adj)	مسوٍّ، موافق	*musawwin, muwāfiq*
compulsion (n)	إكراه، إجبار	*ikrāh, ijbār*
compulsive (adj)	مكره، ملزم	*mukrih, mulzim*
compulsory (adj)	إجباري، إلزامي	*ijbārī, ilzāmī*
compunction (n)	وخز الضمير	*wakhzuḍ ḍamīr*
computation (n)	حساب، تخمين	*ḥisāb, takhmīn*
compute (v)	حسب، أحصى	*ḥasaba, aḥṣā*
computer (n)	كمبيوتر، آلة حاسبة	*kambiutar, ālah ḥāsibah*
comrade (n)	رفيق، خدن	*rafīq, khidn*
concatenation (n)	سلسلة، تسلسل	*silsilah, tasalsul*
concave (v/n)	قعر، مقعر	*qa''ara, muqa''ar*
conceal (v)	كتم، أخفى	*katama, akhfā*
concealment (n)	كتمان، إخفاء	*kitmān, ikhfā'*
concede (v)	منح، سلم	*manaḥa, sallama*
conceit (n)	غرور، تصور، وهم	*ghurūr, taṣawwur, wahm*
conceited (adj)	مغرور، معجب بذاته	*maghrūr, mu'jab bi dhātih*
conceivable (adj)	ممكن تصوره	*mumkin taṣawwuruh*
conceive (v)	حمل، تصور، أدرك	*ḥamala, taṣawwara, adraka*
concentrate (v)	ركز، تركز	*rakkaza, tarakkaza*
concentrated (adj)	مركز، مكثف	*murakkaz, mukaththaf*
concentration (n)	تركيز، تركز	*tarkīz, tarakkuz*
concept (n)	فكرة، مفهوم، رأي	*fikrah, mafhūm, ra'y*
conception (n)	تصور، حمل، إدراك	*taṣawwur, ḥaml, idrāk*
conceptual (adj)	مفاهيمي	*mafāhīmī*
concern (n)	قلق، هم، شأن	*qalaq, hamm, sha'n*
concern (v)	أقلق، هم	*aqlaqa, hamma*

concerned (adj)	قلق، متورط	*qaliq, mutawarriṭ*
concerning (prep)	في ما يتعلق به	*fī mā yata'allaq bih*
concert (n)	حفلة موسيقية	*ḥaflah mausīqiyyah*
concerted (adj)	مدبر، متفق	*mudabbar, muttafaq*
concession (n)	تسليم، منح، امتياز	*taslīm, manḥ, imtiyāz*
concessionary (adj)	امتيازي، التزامي	*imtiyāzī, iltizāmī*
conciliate (v)	استرضى، وفق	*istarḍā, waffaqa*
conciliation (n)	استرضاء، مصالحة	*istirḍā', muṣālaḥah*
conciliatory (adj)	استرضائي، صلحي	*istirḍā'ī, ṣulḥī*
concise (adj)	موجز، مختصر	*mūjaz, mukhtaṣar*
conclave (n)	اجتماع سري	*ijtimā' sirrī*
conclude (v)	أنهى، استنتج	*anhā, istantaja*
conclusion (n)	خاتمة، استنتاج	*khātimah, istintāj*
conclusive (adj)	نهائي، حاسم	*nihā'ī, ḥāsim*
concord (n)	توافق، معاهدة	*tawāfuq, mu'āhadah*
concordance (n)	اتفاق، انسجام	*ittifāq, insijām*
concrete (adj)	صلب، عيني، ملموس	*ṣulb, 'ainī, malmūs*
concrete (v)	قسى، حجر	*qassā, ḥajjara*
concrete mixer	خلاطة الإسمنت	*khallaṭatul ismant*
concur (v)	اتفق، تزامن	*ittafaqa, tazāmana*
concurrence (n)	اتفاق الرأي، تعاون	*ittifāqur ra'y, ta'āwun*
concurrent (adj)	متزامن، مساعد	*mutazāmin, musā'id*
condemn (v)	أدان، شجب	*adāna, shajaba*
condemnation (n)	إدانة، شجب، لوم	*idānah, shajb, laum*
condensation (n)	تكثيف، تلخيص	*takthīf, talkhīṣ*
condense (v)	لخص، كثف	*lakhkhaṣa, kaththafa*
condensed (adj)	موجز، مكثف	*mūjaz, mukaththaf*
condensed milk	حليب مكثف	*ḥalīb mukaththaf*

condenser (n)	مكثف	*mukaththif*
condescend (v)	تنازل، تلطف	*tanāzala, talaṭṭafa*
condition (n)	حالة، منـــزلة، شرط	*ḥālah, manzilah, sharṭ*
conditional (adj)	مشروط، شرطي	*mashrūṭ, sharṭī*
conditioned (adj)	مكيف، مشروط	*mukayyaf, mashrūṭ*
conditioning (n)	إشراط، تكييف	*ishrāṭ, takyīf*
condolence (n)	مؤاساة، تعزية	*mu'āsāt, ta'ziyah*
conducive (adj)	مفضٍ إلى	*mufḍin ilā*
conduct (n)	سلوك، إدارة	*sulūk, idārah*
conduct (v)	هدى، أوصل، أدار	*hadā, auṣala, adāra*
conduction (n)	توصيل، تدبير	*tauṣīl, tadbīr*
conductive (adj)	موصل، توصيلي	*muwaṣṣil, tauṣīlī*
conductor (n)	هادي، قائد، موصل	*hādī, qā'id, muwaṣṣil*
cone (n)	كوز، مخروط	*kūz, makhrūṭ*
confection (n)	مربى، حلوى، معجون	*murabbā, ḥalwā, ma'jūn*
confectioner (n)	حلواني	*ḥalwānī*
confectionery (n)	دكان الحلواني	*dukkānul ḥalwānī*
confederacy (n)	تحالف، اتحاد	*taḥāluf, ittiḥād*
confederate (adj)	متحالف، متعاهد	*mutaḥālif, muta'āhid*
confederation (n)	اتحاد، ائتلاف	*ittiḥād, i'tilāf*
confer (v)	تباحث، منح	*tabāḥatha, manaḥa*
conference (n)	مؤتمر، تشاور	*mu'tamar, tashāwur*
conferment (n)	إنعام، منح	*in'ām, manḥ*
confess (v)	اعترف، أقر	*i'tarafa, aqarra*
confession (n)	اعتراف، عقيدة	*i'tirāf, 'aqīdah*
confidant (n)	صديق حميم، مؤتمن	*ṣadīq ḥamīm, mu'taman*
confide (v)	وثق، ائتمن	*wathaqa, i'tamana*
confidence (n)	ثقة، توكل	*thiqah, tawakkul*

confident (adj)	واثق، جريء	*wāthiq, jarī'*
confidential (adj)	خصوصي، حميمي	*khuṣūṣī, ḥamīmī*
confidentiality (n)	ثقة بالنفس	*thiqah bin nafs*
configuration (n)	شكل، ترتيب، وضع	*shakl, tartīb, waḍ'*
confine (n)	حدود، منطقة	*ḥudūd, minṭaqah*
confine (v)	قيد، حبس، حصر	*qayyada, ḥabasa, ḥaṣara*
confined (adj)	ضيق، محبوس	*ḍayyiq, maḥbūs*
confinement (n)	تقييد، ولادة	*taqyīd, wilādah*
confirm (v)	أكد، عزز	*akkada, 'azzaza*
confirmation (n)	تثبيت، تصديق	*tathbīt, taṣdīq*
confirmative (adj)	مؤكد، تأييدي	*mu'akkid, ta'yīdī*
confirmed (adj)	مصدق، مثبت	*muṣaddaq, muthabbat*
confiscate (v)	صادر الشيء	*ṣādarash shay'*
conflict (n)	نزاع، صراع، تعارض	*nizā', ṣirā', ta'āruḍ*
confluence (n)	مجمع، احتشاد	*majma', iḥtishād*
conform (v)	طابق، أطاع	*ṭābaqa, aṭā'a*
conformation (n)	تكييف، تعديل، انطباق	*takyīf, ta'dīl, inṭibāq*
conformity (n)	انطباق، مطابقة	*inṭibāq, muṭābaqah*
confound (v)	أربك، أخزى	*arbaka, akhzā*
confront (v)	واجه، قابل	*Wājaha, qābala*
confrontation (n)	مواجهة، تحدي	*muwājahah, taḥaddī*
confuse (v)	شوش، أربك	*shawwasha, arbaka*
confused (adj)	مشوش، مرتبك	*mushawwash, murtabik*
confusion (n)	تشوش، ارتباك	*tashawwush, irtibāk*
confute (v)	دحض، أفحم	*daḥaḍa, afḥama*
congeal (v)	جمد، خثر	*jammada, khaththara*
congenial (adj)	متجانس، ملائم	*mutajānis, mulā'im*
congenital (adj)	خلقي، فطري	*khilqī, fiṭrī*

congest (v)	زحم، ازدحم، ركم	*zaḥama, izdaḥama, rakama*
congested (adj)	مزدحم، مكتظ	*muzdaḥim, muktaẓẓ*
conglomerate (adj)	مختلط، معنقد	*mukhtaliṭ, mu'anqad*
conglomeration (n)	خليط، مجموعة	*khalīṭ, majmū'ah*
congratulate (adj)	هنأ	*hanna'a*
congratulation (n)	تهنئة، تهانٍ	*tahni'ah, tahānin*
congratulatory (adj)	تهنئي	*tahni'ī*
congregate (v)	اجتمع، احتشد	*ijtama'a, iḥtashada*
congregation (n)	جماعة، طائفة	*jamā'ah, ṭā'ifah*
congregational (adj)	جماعي، طائفي	*jamā'ī, ṭā'ifī*
congress (n)	اجتماع، مؤتمر	*ijtimā', mu'tamar*
congruent (adj)	منسجم، ملائم	*munsajim, mulā'im*
congruity (n)	تطابق، انسجام	*taṭābuq, insijām*
conjecture (n)	حدس، حزر	*ḥads, ḥazr*
conjoin (v)	ضم، اتحد	*ḍamma, ittaḥada*
conjugal (adj)	زوجي، زواجي	*zaujī, zawājī*
conjugate (v)	صرف، وحد	*ṣarrafa, waḥḥada*
conjugation (n)	تصريف، اقتران	*taṣrīf, iqtirān*
conjunction (n)	ضم،اتحاد،حرف عطف	*ḍamm, ittiḥād, ḥarfu 'atf*
conjuncture (n)	وضع، أزمة	*waḍ', azmah*
conjure (v)	سحر، استحضر	*saḥara, istaḥḍara*
connect (v)	ربط، اتصل	*rabaṭa, ittaṣala*
connected (adj)	مرتبط، مترابط	*murtabiṭ, mutarābiṭ*
connection (n)	ربط، علاقة، صلة	*rabṭ, 'alāqah, ṣilah*
connective (adj)	رابط، ضام	*rābiṭ, ḍāmm*
connivance (n)	تغاضٍ، تستر	*taghāḍin, tasattur*
connive (v)	تغاضى، تستر	*taghāḍā, tasattara*
connoisseur (n)	خبير، عليم	*khabīr, 'alīm*

connotation (n)	دلالة، تضمن	*dalālah, taḍammun*
connote (v)	تضمن، أفاد	*taḍammana, afāda*
conquer (v)	فتح، تغلب	*fataḥa, taghallaba*
conqueror (n)	فاتح، منتصر	*fātiḥ, muntaṣir*
conquest (n)	فتح، انتزاع	*fatḥ, intizā'*
conscience (n)	ضمير، عقل	*ḍamīr, 'aql*
conscientious (adj)	حي الضمير	*ḥayyuḍ ḍamīr*
conscious (adj)	شاعر، واعٍ، دارٍ	*shā'ir, wā'in, dārin*
consciousness (n)	شعور، وعي، صحو	*shu'ūr, wa'y, ṣaḥw*
conscript (v)	جند إلزاميًّا	*jannada ilzāmiyyan*
conscript (adj)	مجند إلزامي	*mujannad ilzāmī*
conscription (n)	تجنيد إلزامي	*tajnīd ilzāmī*
consecrate (v)	كرس، خصص	*karrasa, khaṣṣaṣa*
consecration (n)	تكريس، رسامة	*takrīs, risāmah*
consecutive (adj)	متعاقب، متتابع	*muta'āqib, mutatābi'*
consecutively (adj)	بالتتابع، على التوالي	*bit tatābu', 'alat tawālī*
consensual (adj)	رضائي	*riḍā'ī*
consensus (n)	إجماع، اتفاق	*ijmā', ittifāq*
consent (n)	موافقة، قبول	*muwāfaqah, qabūl*
consent (v)	وافق، قبل	*wāfaqa, qabila*
consequence (n)	نتيجة، عاقبة	*natījah, 'āqibah*
consequent (adj)	ناتج، لازم	*nātij, lāzim*
consequent (n)	نتيجة طبيعية، تالٍ	*natījah ṭabī'iyyah, tālin*
consequently (adv)	هكذا، بناءً على ذلك	*hākadhā, binā'an 'alā dhālik*
conservation (n)	صيانة، حفظ	*ṣiyānah, ḥifẓ*
conservative (n/adj)	محافظ على القديم	*muḥāfiẓ 'alal qadīm*
conservatory (n)	تحفظي، احتياطي	*taḥaffuẓī, iḥtiyāṭī*
conserve (v)	صان، حفظ	*ṣāna, ḥafiẓa*

consider (v)	فكر، تأمل	*fakkara, ta'ammala*
considerable (adj)	هام، كبير	*hamm, kabīr*
considerably (adv)	إلى حد بعيد	*ilā ḥaddin ba'īd*
considerate (adj)	مراعٍ لحقوق الآخرين	*murā'in li ḥuqūqil ākharīn*
consideration (n)	تفكير، اعتبار، رأي	*tafkīr, i'tibār, ra'y*
consign (v)	سلم، أفرد	*sallama, afrada*
consignment (n)	وديعة، بضاعة الأمانة، تفويض	*wadī'ah, biḍā'atul amānah, tafwīḍ*
consist (v)	تألف، انسجم	*ta'allafa, insajama*
consistency (n)	متانة، قوام	*matānah, qawām*
consistent (adj)	متين، ثابت	*matīn, thābit*
consolation (n)	تعزية، مؤاساة	*ta'ziyah, mu'āsāt*
console (v)	عزى، واسى	*'azzā, wāsā*
consolidate (v)	قوى، أدمج	*qawwā, admaja*
consolidated (adj)	مدمج، موحد	*mudmaj, muwaḥhad*
consolidation (n)	اندماج، ضم	*indimāj, ḍamm*
consonance (n)	انسجام، تناغم	*insijām, tanāghum*
consonant (n)	حرف ساكن، صوت ساكن	*ḥarf sākin, ṣaut sākin*
consort (n)	زوج، زوجة	*zauj, zaujah*
consortium (n)	اتحاد، جمعية	*ittiḥād, jam'iyyah*
conspicuous (adj)	واضح، بارز	*wāḍiḥ, bāriz*
conspiracy (n)	تآمر، مؤامرة	*ta'āmur, mu'āmarah*
conspirator (n)	متآمر	*muta'āmir*
conspire (v)	تآمر، تعاون	*ta'āmara, ta'āwana*
constable (n)	شرطي مسؤول	*shurṭī mas'ūl*
constancy (n)	ثبات، استقرار	*thabāt, istiqrār*
constant (adj)	مستقر، متواصل	*mustaqirr, mutawāṣil*
constantly (adv)	باستمرار، دائماً	*bistimrār, dā'iman*

constellation (n)	مجموعة نجوم، مجموعة متألقة	*majmū'atu nujūm, majmū'ah muta'alliqah*
constipation (n)	قبض، إمساك	*qabḍ, imsāk*
constituency (n)	دائرة انتخابية	*dā'irah intikhābiyyah*
constituent (n)	ناخب في دائرة انتخابية	*nākhib fī dā'irah intikhābiyyah*
constitute (v)	أنشأ، نصب	*ansha'a, naṣṣaba*
constitution (n)	دستور، قانون	*dustūr, qānūn*
constitutional (adj)	دستوري، أساسي	*dustūrī, asāsī*
constrain (v)	أجبر، قيد	*ajbara, qayyada*
constraint (n)	إكراه، إجبار، قسر	*ikrāh, ijbār, qasr*
constrict (v)	قلص، عصر	*qallaṣa, 'aṣara*
constricted (adj)	ضيق، محدود	*ḍayyiq, maḥdūd*
construct (v)	بنى، أنشأ، شيد	*banā, ansha'a, shayyada*
construction (n)	بناء، مبنى	*binā', mabnā*
constructive (adj)	بنائي، تشييدي	*binā'ī, tashyīdī*
construe (v)	أول، ترجم	*awwala, tarjama*
consul (n)	قنصل	*qunṣul*
consulate (n)	قنصلية	*qunṣuliyyah*
consult (v)	تشاور، استشار	*tashāwara, istashāra*
consultant (n)	مستشار، ناصح	*mustashār, nāṣiḥ*
consultation (n)	تشاور، نصيحة	*tashāwur, naṣīḥah*
consultative (adj)	استشاري، شوري	*istishārī, shūrī*
consume (v)	استنفد، استهلك	*istanfada, istahlaka*
consumer (n)	مستهلك، آكل	*mustahlik, ākil*
consummate (v/adj)	أكمل، كامل	*akmala, kāmil*
consumption (n)	استهلاك، ضنًى	*istihlāk, ḍanan*
contact (n)	اتصال، تلامس	*ittiṣāl, talāmus*

contact (v)	اتصل، راجع	*ittaṣala, rāja'a*
contagious (adj)	معدٍ، ناقل للعدوى	*mu'din, nāqil lil 'adwā*
contain (v)	اتسع، احتوى	*ittasa'a, iḥtawā*
container (n)	إناء، وعاء	*inā', wi'ā'*
contaminate (v)	لوث، شاب	*lawwatha, shāba*
contamination (n)	تلويث، تلوث	*talwīth, talawwuth*
contemplate (v)	تأمل، اعتزم	*ta'ammala, i'tazama*
contemplation (n)	تأمل، اعتزام	*ta'ammul, i'tizām*
contemporary (adj)	معاصر، حديث	*mu'āṣir, ḥadhīth*
contempt (n)	ازدراء، احتقار	*izdirā', iḥtiqār*
contemptuous (adj)	مزدرٍ، متكبر	*muzdarin, mutakabbir*
contend (v)	ناضل، تنافس	*nāḍala, tanāfasa*
content (adj)	مكتفٍ، مطمئن	*muktafin, muṭma'in*
content (n)	قناعة، اطمئنان، محتوى	*qanā'ah, iṭmi'nān, muḥtawā*
content (v)	أشبع، اكتفى	*ashba'a, iktafā*
contented (adj)	راضٍ، قانع	*rāḍin, qāni'*
contention (n)	نضال، تنافس	*niḍāl, tanāfus*
contentious (adj)	كثير الخصام	*kathīrul khiṣām*
contest (n)	نضال، منافسة	*niḍāl, munāfasah*
contest (v)	ناضل، نافس	*nāḍala, nāfasa*
context (n)	سياق، بيئة	*siyāq, bī'ah*
contexual (adj)	قريني	*qarīnī*
contiguous (adj)	مجاور، متماس	*mujāwir, mutamāss*
continent (n/adj)	قارة، عفيف	*qārrah, 'afīf*
continental (adj)	قاري، أوروبي	*qārrī, urūbī*
contingent (adj/n)	عارض، فرقة	*'āriḍ, firqah*
continual (adj)	متواصل، مستمر	*mutawāṣil, mustamirr*

continually (adv)	باستمرار، على الدوام	*bistimrār, 'alad dawām*
continuance (n)	بقاء، استمرارية	*baqā', istimrāriyyah*
continuation (n)	استمرار، استئناف	*istimrār, isti'nāf*
continue (v)	استمر، واصل	*istamarra, wāṣala*
continuity (n)	تواصل، استمرار	*tawāṣul, istimrār*
continuous (adj)	متواصل، مستمر	*mutawāṣil, mustamirr*
continuously (adv)	باستمرار، باتصال	*bistimrār, bittiṣāl*
contort (v)	لوى، ثنى	*lawā, thanā*
contortion (n)	لي، التواء، اعوجاج	*lai, iltiwā', i'wijāj*
contour (n)	كفاف، محيط	*kifāf, muḥīṭ*
contraband (n)	سلع مهربة	*sila' muharrabah*
contraception (n)	منع الحمل	*man'ul ḥaml*
contraceptive (adj/n)	مانع للحمل	*māni' lil ḥaml*
contract (n)	عقد، اتفاقية	*'aqd, ittifāqiyyah*
contract (v)	عقد، التقط	*'aqada, iltaqaṭa*
contradic (v)	كذب، ناقض	*kadhbhaba, nāqaḍa*
contradiction (n)	تكذيب، تناقض	*takdhīb, tanāquḍ*
contradictory (adj)	متناقض، متناف	*mutanāqiḍ, mutanāfin*
contrary (adj)	متضاد، متعارض	*mutaḍādd, muta'āriḍ*
contrary (n)	ضد، نقيض	*ḍidd, naqīḍ*
contrast (v)	تغاير، تضاد	*taghāyara, taḍādda*
contrast (n)	تغاير، تباين	*taghāyur, tabāyun*
contravene (v)	انتهك، نافى	*intahaka, nāfā*
contribute (v)	تبرع، أسهم	*tabarra'a, ashama*
contribution (n)	تبرع، مأثرة، خدمة	*tabarru', ma'tharah, khidmah*
contributor (n)	متبرع، مشارك	*mutabarri', mushārik*

contrivance (n)	اختراع، حيلة	*ikhtirā', ḥīlah*
contrive (v)	اخترع، احتال	*ikhtara'a, iḥtāla*
control (n)	ضبط، تحكم	*ḍabṭ, taḥakkum*
controller (n)	مراقب، ضابط	*murāqib, ḍābiṭ*
controversial (adj)	جدلي، خلافي	*jadalī, khilafī*
controversy (n)	جدل، نزاع	*jadal, nizā'*
controvert (v)	جادل، أنكر	*jādala, ankara*
convalescence (n)	نقاهة	*naqāhah*
convalescent (adj)	ناقه	*nāqih*
convection (n)	حمل حراري	*ḥaml ḥarārī*
convene (v)	دعا، اجتمع	*da'ā, ijtama'a*
convenience (n)	ملاءمة، راحة	*mulā'amah, rāḥah*
convenient (adj)	ملائم، مريح	*mulā'im, murīḥ*
convent (n)	دير، رهبنة	*dair, rahbanah*
convention (n)	مؤتمر، دعوة، اتفاقية	*mu'tamar, da'wah, ittifāqiyyah*
conventional (adj)	عادي، تقليدي	*'ādī, taqlīdī*
converge (v)	تقارب، تجمع	*taqāraba, tajamma'a*
convergence (n)	تقارب، نقطة الالتقاء	*taqārub, nuqṭatul iltiqā'*
conversant (adj)	مطلع، خبير	*muṭṭala', khabīr*
conversation (n)	محادثة، مداولة	*muḥādathah, mudāwalah*
conversational (adj)	تحادثي، تخاطبي	*taḥāduthī, takhāṭubī*
converse (v)	تحدث، تحادث	*taḥaddatha, taḥādatha*
converse (adj)	مضاد، مخالف	*muḍādd, mukhālif*
converse (n)	ضد، عكس	*ḍidd, 'aks*
conversion (n)	تحويل، تحول	*taḥwīl, taḥawwul*
convert (v)	حول، تحول	*ḥawwala, taḥawwala*

convert (n)	مهتدي إلى دين	*muhtadī ilā dīn*
convex (n/adj)	محدب، مسنم	*muḥaddab, musannam*
convey (v)	بلغ، نقل	*ballagha, naqala*
conveyance (n)	نقل، وسيلة نقل	*naql, wasīlatu naql*
convict (v/n)	أدان، مدان	*adāna, mudān*
conviction (n)	إدانة، إقناع	*idānah, iqnā'*
convince (v)	أقنع، أثبت على	*aqna'a, athbata 'alā*
convinced (adj)	مقتنع	*muqtani'*
convincing (adj)	مقنع	*muqni'*
convivial (adj)	مرح، مخمور	*mariḥ, makhmūr*
convocation (n)	اجتماع، مجمع	*ijtimā', majma'*
convoke (v)	دعا إلى الاجتماع	*da'ā ilal ijtimā'*
convolution (n)	التفاف، لفة	*iltifāf, laffah*
convoy (n)	مواكبة، مرافقة	*muwākabah, murāfaqah*
convulse (v)	زلزل، هز	*zalzala, hazza*
convulsion (n)	اضطراب عنيف	*iḍṭirāb 'anīf*
cook (v)	طبخ، طها	*ṭabakha, ṭahā*
cook (n)	طاهي، طباخ	*ṭāhī, ṭabbākh*
cool (adj)	هادئ، بارد معتدل	*hādi', bārid mu'tadil*
cool (v)	برد، سكن	*barrada, sakkana*
cooler (n)	مبرد، سجن	*mubarrid, sijn*
coolie (n)	حمال، شيال	*ḥammāl, shayyāl*
cooling (n)	تبريد، إبراد	*tabrīd, ibrād*
coop (n)	خم، مكان ضيق	*khumm, makān ḍayyiq*
cooper (n)	صانع البراميل	*ṣāni'ul barāmīl*
cooperate (v)	تعاون، عاون	*ta'āwana, 'āwana*
cooperation (n)	تعاون، معاونة	*ta'āwun, mu'āwanah*
cooperative (adj)	تعاوني، متعاون	*ta'āwunī, muta'āwin*

coordinate (v)	سوى، نسق، تساوى	*sawwā,nassaqa,tasāwā*
coordination (n)	تسوية، تنسيق	*taswiyah, tansīq*
cope (v)	تغلب على المشكلات	*taghallaba 'alal mushkilāt*
copious (adj)	غزير، وافر	*ghazīr, wāfir*
copiously (adv)	بوفرة، بغزارة	*bi wafrah, bi ghazārah*
copper (n/adj)	نحاس، نحاسي	*nuḥās, nuḥāsī*
coppersmith (n)	نحاس	*naḥḥās*
copula (n)	صلة، رابط	*ṣilah, rābiṭ*
copulate (v)	تسافد، جامع	*tasāfada, jāma'a*
copulation (n)	تسافد، جماع	*tasāfud, jimā'*
copy (n)	نسخة، نموذج، مخطوطة	*nuskhah, namūdhaj, makhṭūṭah*
copy (v)	نسخ، قلد	*nasakha, qallada*
copybook (n)	دفتر الخط	*daftarul khaṭṭ*
copying (n)	نسخ، تقليد	*naskh, taqlīd*
copyright (n)	حق النشر	*ḥaqqun nashr*
coral (n/adj)	مرجان،مرجاني اللون	*marjān, marjāniyyul laun*
cord (n)	حبل، وتر، نسيج	*ḥabl, watar, nasīj*
cordial (adj)	قلبي، عميق	*qalbī, 'amīq*
cordially (adv)	بحرارة، بمودة	*bi ḥarārah, bi mawaddah*
cordon (n)	نطاق من الشرطة	*niṭāq minash shurṭah*
core (n)	قلب، لب	*qalb, lubb*
cork (n)	فلين، فلينة	*fillīn, fillīnah*
corn (n)	حبة قمح أو ذرة	*ḥabbatu qamḥ au dhurah*
cornea (n)	قرنية العين	*qarniyatul 'ain*

corner (n)	حافة، زاوية، ناحية	*ḥāffah, zāwiyah, nāḥiyah*
cornerstone (n)	حجر الزاوية، أساس	*ḥajaruz zāwiyah, asās*
cornice (n)	افريز، طنف	*ifrīz, ṭunuf*
corona (n)	جزء ناتئ من طنف	*juz' nāti' min ṭunuf*
coronation (n)	حفلة التتويج	*ḥaflatut tatwīj*
coronet (n)	إكليل، تاج صغير	*iklīl, tāj ṣaghīr*
corporal (n)	رتبة عسكرية	*rutbah 'askariyyah*
corporation (n)	مجلس بلدي، شركة	*majlis baladī, sharikah*
corporeal (adj)	جسدي، مادي	*jasadī, māddī*
corpse (n)	جثة، جيفة	*juththah, jīfah*
corpulent (adj)	سمين، بدين	*samīn, badīn*
corpus (n)	مجموعة كاملة	*majmū'ah kāmilah*
correct (v)	صحح، أدب	*ṣaḥḥaḥa, aḍdaba*
correct (adj)	صحيح، مضبوط	*ṣaḥīḥ, maḍbūṭ*
correction (n)	تصحيح، تأديب	*taṣḥīḥ, ta'dīb*
correlate (v)	ارتبط، ربط	*irtabaṭa, rabaṭa*
correlation (n)	ربط، ارتباط	*rabṭ, irtibāṭ*
correspond (v)	تطابق، تراسل	*taṭābaqa, tarāsala*
correspondence (n)	تماثل، مراسلة	*tamāthul, murāsalah*
correspondent (adj/n)	مراسل، متراسل، مناسب	*murāsil, mutarāsil, munāsib*
corridor (n)	رواق، دهليز	*riwāq, dihlīz*
corrigendum (n)	جدول الخطأ	*jadwalul khaṭa'*
corroborate (v)	أيد، وثق	*ayyada, waththaqa*
corroboration (n)	تأييد، توثيق	*ta'yīd, tauthīq*
corrugate (v)	غضن، جعد	*ghaḍḍana, ja''da*
corrupt (v)	رشا، أفسد	*rashā, afsada*

corrupt (adj)	فاسد، عفن	*fāsid, 'afin*
corruption (n)	فساد، رشوة	*fasād, rishwah*
cosmetic (n)	مستحضر التجميل	*mustaḥḍarut tajmīl*
cosmic (adj)	كوني، واسع	*kaunī, wāsi'*
cosmology (n)	علم الكونيات	*'ilmul kauniyyāt*
cosmopolitan (adj)	كوزموبوليتاني، عالمي	*kūzmūbūlītānī, 'ālamī*
cosmos (n)	كون، نظام كوني	*kaun, niẓām kaunī*
cost (v)	كلف، قدر	*kallafa, qaddara*
cost (n)	ثمن، كلفة، نفقة	*thaman, kulfah, nafaqah*
costly (adj)	غالٍ، نفيس	*ghālin, nafīs*
costume (n)	زي، لباس	*ziyy, libās*
cot (n)	سرير طفل	*sarīru ṭifl*
coterie (n)	زمرة، حلقة	*zumrah, ḥalqah*
cottage (n)	كوخ، بيت صغير	*kūkh, bait ṣaghīr*
cotton (n)	قطن، قماش قطني	*quṭn, qumāsh quṭnī*
couch (n)	سرير، أريكة	*sarīr, arīkah*
couch (v)	طرز، سدد	*ṭarraza, saddada*
cough (n/v)	سعال، سعل	*su'āl, sa'ala*
council (n)	مجلس شورى، جمعية	*majlisu shūrā, jam'iyyah*
counsel (v)	نصح، أشار	*naṣaḥa, ashāra*
counsellor (n)	ناصح، محامي، مشير	*nāṣiḥ, muḥāmī, mushīr*
count (v)	عد، قدر، حسب	*'adda, qaddara, ḥasaba*
count (n)	عد، إحصاء	*'add, iḥṣā'*
countenance (n)	ملامح، وجه	*malāmiḥ, wajh*
counter (n)	نضد، ضد، شباك	*nuḍud, ḍidd, shubbāk*
counter (v)	قاوم، ضاد	*qāwama, ḍādda*
counter (adj)	مضاد، مقابل	*muḍādd, muqābil*

counteract (v)	ضاد، عادل	*ḍādda, ʻādala*
counter-attack (n)	هجوم معاكس	*hujūm muʻākis*
counter-claim (n)	دعوى مضادة	*daʻwā muḍāddah*
counterfeit (v/adj)	زيف، زائف	*zayyafa, zā'if*
counterpart (n)	نظير، نسخة مطابقة	*naẓīr, nuskhah muṭabaqah*
counterpoint (n)	طباق	*ṭibāq*
countess (n)	كونتس،زوجة الكونت	*kūntis, zaujatul kūnt*
countless (adj)	لا يعد، لا يحصى	*lā yuʻadd, lā yuḥṣā*
country (n)	بلد، دولة	*balad, daulah*
countryman (n)	ريفي، فلاح	*rīfī, fallāḥ*
countryside (n)	ريف	*rīf*
county (n)	كونتية، إقليم	*kūntiyyah, iqlīm*
coup (n)	انقلاب غير متوقع	*inqilāb ghair mutawaqqaʻ*
couple (n)	زوجان، زوج	*zaujān, zauj*
couple (v)	ربط، تزوج	*rabaṭa, tazawwaja*
couplet (n)	زوج، دوبيت	*zauj, dūbait*
coupon (n)	قسيمة، كوبون	*qasīmah, kūbūn*
courage (n)	شجاعة، جراءة	*shajāʻah, jarāʻah*
courageous (adj)	شجاع، جريء	*shujāʻ, jarī'*
courier (n)	رسول، ساعي	*rasūl, sāʻī*
course (n)	سبيل، غضون، مقرر تعليمي	*sabīl, ghuḍūn, muqarrar taʻlīmī*
court (n)	دار القضاء، ساحة	*dārul qaḍā', sāḥah*
court (v)	غازل، أغرى	*ghāzala, aghrā*
courteous (adj)	لطيف، أنيس	*laṭīf, anīs*
courtesy (n)	لطف، كرم، بشاشة	*luṭf, karam, bashāshah*

courtship (n)	تودد، مغازلة	*tawaddud, mughāzalah*
courtyard (n)	فناء، ساحة الدار	*finā', sāḥatud dār*
cousin (n)	ابن عم، بنت عم	*ibnu 'amm, bintu 'amm*
covenant (n)	ميثاق، عهد، عقد	*mīthāq, 'ahd, 'aqd*
cover (n)	غطاء، غلاف، حجاب	*ghiṭā', ghilāf, ḥijāb*
cover (v)	غطى، حجب، أخفى	*ghaṭṭā, ḥajaba, akhfā*
coverage (n)	تغطية	*taghṭiyah*
covert (adj)	سري، خفي	*sirrī, khafī*
covet (v)	اشتهى، طمع	*ishtahā, ṭami'a*
covetous (adj)	مشته، طماع	*mushtahin, ṭammā'*
cow (n/v)	بقرة، روع	*baqarah, rawwa'a*
coward (adj/n)	جبان، نذل	*jabān, nadhl*
cowardice (n)	جبن، نذالة	*jubn, nadhālah*
cowboy (n)	راعي البقر	*rā'il baqar*
cower (v)	انكمش مرتعداً	*inkamasha murta'idan*
cowhide (n)	جلد البقرة	*jildul baqarah*
cowman (n)	راعي البقر	*rā'il baqar*
coy (adj)	خجول، خفر، حيي	*khajūl, khafir, ḥayī*
cozy (cosy) (adj)	مريح و دافئ	*murīḥ wa dāfi'*
crab (n)	سرطان	*sarṭān*
crabbed (adj)	معقد، مبهم	*mu'aqqad, mubham*
crack (v)	انشق، انفلق	*inshaqqa, infalaqa*
crack (n)	انشقاق، طقطقة	*inshiqāq, ṭaqṭaqah*
crack-down (n)	اتخاذ إجراءات صارمة	*ittikhādhu ijrā'āt ṣārimah*
cracker (n)	مفرقعة نارية	*mufarqa'ah nāriyah*
crackers (adj)	معتوه، مخبول	*ma'tūh, makhbūl*
crackle (v)	طقطق، تفرقع	*ṭaqṭaqa, tafarqa'a*
cradle (n)	مهد، أرجوحة	*mahd, urjūḥah*

craft (n)	حرفة، مركب	*ḥirfah, markab*
craftsman (n)	حرفي، فنان	*ḥirafī, fannān*
cram (v)	كظ، أتخم	*kaẓẓa, atkhama*
cramp (n)	تشنج، كلاب	*tashannuj, kullāb*
crane (n)	غرنوق، رافعة	*ghurnūq, rāfi'ah*
crank (n)	كرنك، مهووس	*karank, mahwūs*
cranny (n)	شق، صدع	*shaqq, ṣad'*
craps (n)	كرابس	*karābs*
crash (v)	حطم، عطب	*ḥaṭṭama, 'aṭaba*
crash (n)	صوت التحطم، دهدهة	*ṣautut taḥaṭṭum, dahdahah*
crate (n)	قفص كبير	*qafaṣ kabīr*
crater (n)	فوهة البركان	*fūhatul burkān*
crave (v)	اشتهى، تاق	*ishtahā, tāqa*
craven (n)	شخص جبان	*shakhṣ jabān*
crawl (v/n)	دب، دبيب	*dabba, dabīb*
crayon (n)	كريون، قلم ملون	*karyūn, qalam malawwan*
craze (n)	خبل، جنون	*khabal, junūn*
crazy (adj)	مجنون، مخبل، واهن	*majnūn, mukhabbal, wāhin*
creak (v/n)	صر، صرير	*ṣarra, ṣarīr*
cream (n)	كريم، قشدة، زبدة	*kirīm, qishdah, zubdah*
crease (n)	خط، جعدة	*khaṭṭ, ja'dah*
create (v)	خلق، أبدع	*khalaqa, abda'a*
creation (n)	خلق، تخليق	*khalq, takhlīq*
creative (adj)	مبدع، إبداعي	*mubdi', ibdā'ī*
creator (n)	خالق، مبدع	*khāliq, mubdi'*
creature (n)	مخلوق، إنسان	*makhlūq, insān*

credence (n)	تصديق، اعتقاد	*taṣdīq, i'tiqād*
credentials (n)	أوراق اعتماد	*aurāqu I'timād*
credible (adj)	جدير بالثقة	*jadīr bith thiqah*
credit (n)	تصديق، ائتمان، دين	*taṣdīq, i'timān, dain*
creditable (adj)	جدير بالتصديق	*jadīr bit taṣdīq*
credulity (n)	سذاجة	*sadhājah*
credulous (adj)	ساذج، غر	*sādhij, ghirr*
creed (n)	عقيدة، اعتقاد	*'aqīdah, i'tiqād*
creek (n)	نهير، ممر ضيق	*nuhair, mamarr ḍayyiq*
creep (v)	زحف، دب	*zaḥafa, dabba*
creeper (n)	نبات معترش	*nabāt mu'tarish*
creepy (adj)	منمل، زاحف	*munmil, zāḥif*
cremate (v)	أحرق الجثة	*aḥraqal juththah*
cremation (n)	إحراق الجثث	*iḥrāqul juthath*
crescent (n/adj)	هلال، هلالي	*hilāl, hilālī*
crest (n)	عرف الديك، قمة، ذروة	*'urfud dīk, qimmah, dhirwah*
cretin (n)	معتل العقل	*mu'tallul 'aql*
crevice (n)	فلع، شق	*fal', shaqq*
crew (n)	عصبة، طاقم	*'uṣbah, ṭāqim*
crewel (n)	غزل صوفي	*ghazl ṣūfī*
crib (n)	مذود، مهد	*midhwad, mahd*
cricket (n)	كريكيت، جدجد	*kirīkīt, judjud*
crime (n)	جناية، جريمة	*jināyah, jarīmah*
criminal (n/adj)	مجرم، جنائي	*mujrim, jinā'ī*
crimp (v)	جعد، ثنى	*ja''ada, thanā*
crimson (n)	لون قرمزي	*laun qirmizī*
cringe (v)	انكمش، تذلل	*inkamasha, tadhallala*

crinkle (n)	جعدة، خشخشة	*j'dah, khashkhashah*
cripple (n)	أعرج، أشل	*a'raj, ashall*
crisis (n)	أزمة، بحران	*azmah, buḥrān*
crisp (adj)	قصم، مجعد	*qaṣim, muja''ad*
critorion (n)	ميزان، معيار	*mīzān, mi'yār*
critic (n)	ناقد، منتقد	*nāqid, muntaqid*
critical (adj)	حاسم، خطر، انتقادي	*ḥāsim, khaṭir, intiqādī*
criticise (v)	نقد، انتقد	*naqada, intaqada*
criticism (n)	نقد، انتقاد	*naqd, intiqād*
critique (n)	مقالة نقدية	*maqālah naqdiyyah*
croak (n/v)	نقيق، نق	*naqīq, naqqa*
crochet (n)	نسيج محبوك	*nasīj maḥbūk*
crockery (n)	آنية فخارية	*āniyah fakhkhāriyah*
crocodile (n)	تمساح	*timsāḥ*
croft (n)	مزرعة صغيرة	*mazra'ah ṣaghīrah*
crony (n)	صديق حميم، خليل	*ṣadīq ḥamīm, khalīl*
crook (n)	محتال، خطاف	*muḥtāl, khaṭṭāf*
crook (v)	التوى، حنى	*iltawā, ḥanā*
crop (n)	غلة، حصاد	*ghallah, ḥiṣād*
crop (v)	حصد، قص	*ḥaṣada, qaṣṣa*
croquette (n)	كروكيت	*kurūkīt*
cross (n)	صليب، محنة	*ṣalīb, miḥnah*
cross (v)	عبر، صالب، شطب	*'abara, ṣālaba, shaṭaba*
cross (adj)	معاكس، معارض	*mu'ākis, mu'āriḍ*
cross-eyed (adj)	أحول	*aḥwal*
crossfire (n)	نيران متقاطعة	*nīrān mutaqāṭi'ah*
crossing (n)	عبور، ممر	*'ubūr, mamarr*
crossroad (n)	طريق متقاطعة	*ṭarīq mutaqāṭi'ah*

cross-section (n)	مقطع مستعرض	*maqṭa‘ musta‘raḍ*
crosswind (n)	ريح متعامدة	*rīḥ muta‘āmidah*
crosswise (adv)	بالعرض	*bil ‘arḍ*
crossword puzzle	أحجية الكلمات المتقاطعة	*uḥjiyyatul kalimāt al mutaqāṭiyah*
crouch (v)	حنى، انحنى	*ḥanā, inḥanā*
croup (n)	كفل الفرس، خناق	*kafalul faras, khunāq*
crow (n)	غراب، صياح	*ghurāb, ṣiyāḥ*
crow (v)	صاح، تبجح	*ṣāḥa, tabajjaḥa*
crowbar (n)	عتلة، مخل	*‘atalah, mukhl*
crowd (n)	زمرة، حشد	*zumrah, ḥashd*
crowd (v)	احتشد، ملأ	*iḥtashada, mala’a*
crowded (adj)	مزدحم، مكتظ	*muzdaḥim, muktaẓẓ*
crown (n)	تاج، قمة	*tāj, qimmah*
crown (v)	توج، كلل	*tawwaja, kallala*
crucial (adj)	حاسم، عصيب	*ḥāsim, ‘aṣīb*
crucifix (n)	صليب، مصلوب	*ṣalīb, maṣlūb*
crucify (v)	صلب، عذب	*ṣalaba, ‘adhdhaba*
crude (adj)	فظ، جافٍ، غير مصقول	*faẓẓ, jāfin, ghair maṣqūl*
cruel (adj)	وحشي، قاسٍ	*waḥshī, qāsin*
cruelty (n)	وحشية، قسوة	*waḥshiyyah, qaswah*
cruise (n)	طافٍ في البحر	*ṭāfin fil baḥr*
cruiser (n)	مطوفة، طراد	*muṭawwafah, ṭarrād*
crumb (n)	كسرة، فتاتة	*kisrah, futātah*
crumble (v)	فتت، حطم	*fattata, ḥaṭṭama*
crumblings (n)	كسر، فتات	*kisar, futāt*
crumple (v)	جعد، تجعد	*ja‘‘ada, taja‘‘ada*

crunch (v)	طحن بالأسنان	*ṭaḥana bil asnān*
crusade (n)	حرب صليبية	*ḥarb ṣalībiyyah*
crush (n)	حشد، عصير	*ḥashd, ʻaṣīr*
crush (v)	عصر، حطم، شق	*ʻaṣara, ḥaṭama, shaqqa*
crust (n)	قشرة، غلاف	*qishrah, ghilāf*
crusty (adj)	قاسٍ، قشري	*qāsin, qishrī*
crutch (n)	عكاز، دعامة	*ʻukāz, diʻāmah*
cry (n)	صياح، بكاء	*ṣiyāḥ, bukā'*
cry (v)	صرخ، صاح، بكى	*ṣarakha, ṣāḥa, bakā*
crying (adj)	ملح، شنيع	*muliḥḥ, shanīʻ*
crystal (adj)	شفاف، بلوري	*shaffāf, ballūrī*
crystal (n)	بلور، شيء شفاف	*ballūr, shay' shaffāf*
crystalize,-ise (v)	بلور، تبلور	*balwara, tabalwara*
cub (n)	جرو الثعلب	*jarwuth thaʻlab*
cube (n)	مكعب	*mukaʻʻab*
cubic (adj)	مكعب	*mukaʻʻab*
cuckoo (n)	وقواق، وقوقة	*waqwāq, waqwaqah*
cucumber	قثاء، خيار	*qiththā', khiyār*
cud (n)	جرة، مضغة	*jirrah, muḍghah*
cuddle (v)	عانق، حضن	*ʻānaqa, ḥaḍana*
cudgle (n)	نبوت، هراوة	*nabbūt, hirāwah*
cue (n)	إلماع، إشارة	*ilmāʻ, ishārah*
cuff (n)	طرف الكم، صفعة	*ṭaraful kumm, ṣafʻah*
culminate (v)	أوج، تأوج	*awwaja, ta'awwaja*
culmination (n)	تأوج، ذروة	*ta'awwuj, dhirwah*
culpable (adj)	جدير باللوم، مدان	*jadīr bil laum, mudān*
culprit (n)	مجرم، متهم	*mujrim, muttaham*
cult (n)	طائفة دينية	*ṭā'ifah dīniyyah*

cultivation (n)	زراعة، تهذيب	*zirā'ah, tahdhīb*
cultural (adj)	ثقافي، مستولد	*thaqāfī, mustaulad*
culture (n)	ثقافة، تثقيف	*thaqāfah, tathqīf*
cultured (adj)	مثقف، مستولد	*muthaqqaf, mustaulad*
cumbersome (adj)	ثقيل، مزعج	*thaqīl, muz'ij*
cumulative (adj)	متراكم، تصاعدي	*mutarākim, taṣā'udī*
cumulus (n)	نغاض، ركام	*naghghāḍ, rukām*
cunning (adj)	ماكر، محتال	*mākir, muḥtāl*
cunning (n)	مكر، دهاء	*makr, dahā'*
cup (n)	فنجان، كأس	*finjān, ka's*
cupboard (n)	صوان، دولاب	*ṣuwān, dūlāb*
cupidity (n)	طمع، جشع	*ṭama', jasha'*
curate (n)	مساعد الخوري	*musā'idul khūrī*
curb (n/v)	شكيمة، شكم	*shakīmah, shakama*
curd (n)	خثارة اللبن	*khuthāratul laban*
curdle (v)	خثر، أفسد	*khaththara, afsada*
cure (v)	شفى، عالج	*shafā, 'ālaja*
cure (n)	معالجة، دواء	*mu'ālajah, dawā'*
curfew (n)	حظر التجول، ناقوس الغروب	*ḥaẓrut tajawwul, nāqūsul ghurūb*
curiosity (n)	حب الاستطلاع، طرفة	*ḥubbul istiṭlā', ṭurfah*
curious (adj)	محب الاستطلاع، طرف	*muḥibbul istiṭlā', ṭarif*
curl (v/n)	عقص، عقصة	*'aqaṣa, 'iqṣah*
curling (n)	كرلنغ	*karlingh*
currency (n)	عملة، تداول	*'umlah, tadāwul*
current (adj)	جارٍ، رائج	*jārin, rā'ij*
current account	حساب جاري	*ḥisāb jārī*
currently (adv)	في الوقت الحاضر	*fil waqtil ḥāḍir*

curriculum (n)	منهاج الدراسة	*minhājud dirāsah*
curriculum vitae	بيان السيرة	*bayānus sīrah*
curry (n)	بهار هندي	*bahār hindī*
curse (n/v)	لعنة، لعن	*la'nah, la'ina*
cursed (adj)	ملعون، بغيض	*mal'ūn, baghīḍ*
cursive (adj)	جارٍ، خط رقعة	*jārin, khaṭṭu ruq'ah*
curt (adj)	جافٍ، مختصر	*jāfin, mukhtaṣar*
curtail (v)	قصر، اختصر	*qaṣṣara, ikhtaṣara*
curtain (n)	ستارة، حجاب	*sitārah, ḥijāb*
curve (n)	انحناء، تقوس	*inḥinā', taqawwus*
curve (v)	حنى، قوس	*ḥanā, qawwasa*
cushion (n)	وسادة، بطانة، حافة	*wisādah, biṭānah, ḥāffah*
cushy (adj)	يسير، هين	*yasīr, hayyin*
custard (n)	قستر	*qastar*
custodian (n)	حارس، أمين	*ḥāris, amīn*
custody (n)	كفالة، حجز	*kafālah, ḥajz*
custom (n)	عادة، عرف	*'ādah, 'urf*
customary (adj)	عرفي، معتاد	*'urfī, mu'tād*
customer (n)	زبون، عميل	*zabūn, 'amīl*
customs (n)	رسوم جمركية	*rusūm jumrukiyyah*
cut (v)	قطع، قص	*qaṭa'a, qaṣṣa*
cut (n)	قطعة، حصة	*qiṭ'ah, ḥiṣṣah*
cute (adj)	حاد الذهن، ذكي	*ḥāddudh dhihn, dhakī*
cutlery (n)	سكاكين المائدة	*sakākīnul mā'idah*
cutter (n)	مقطع، قاطعة	*miqṭa', qāṭi'ah*
cutthroat (n/adj)	سفاح، قاسٍ	*saffāḥ, qāsin*
cutting (n/adj)	قطع، قاطع	*qaṭ', qāṭi'*

cycle (n)	مجموعة، سلسلة،	*majmū'ah, silsilah,*
	دراجة	*darrājah*
cyclone (n)	إعصار، زوبعة	*i'ṣār, zauba'ah*
cylinder (n)	أسطوانة، عمود	*usṭuwānah, 'amūd*
cylindrical (adj)	أسطواني	*usṭuwānī*
cymbal (n)	صنج	*ṣanj*
cynic (n/adj)	ساخر، متشائم	*sākhir, mutashā'im*
cypher= cipher		
cyst (n)	كييس، متانة	*kuyais, matānah*
cyto (n)	خلية، حشوة	*khaliyyah, ḥashwah*
czar (n)	امبراطور	*imbarāṭūr*

D

dab (v/n)	ربت، تربيتة	*rabbata, tarbītah*
dabble (v)	بلل، رش	*ballala, rashsha*
dad (n)	أب (بلغة الأطفال)	*ab (bi lughatil aṭfāl)*
daddy (n)	أب	*ab*
daemon = demon		
daffodil (n)	نرجس بري	*narjis barrī*
dagger (n)	خنجر، مدية	*khanjar, midyah*
daily (adj/adv)	يومي، كل يوم	*yaumī, kulla yaum*
dainty (adj)	لذيذ، نيق	*ladhīdh, nayyiq*
dairy (n)	ملبنة، مصنع لبن	*malbanah, maṣna'u laban*
dairymaid (n)	عاملة في ملبنة	*'āmilah fī malbanah*
dairyman (n)	عامل في ملبنة	*'āmil fī malbanah*
dais (n)	منصة ، مصطبة	*minaṣṣah, misṭabah*
daisy (n)	زهرة الربيع	*zahratur rabī'*

dale (n)	وادٍ، وهدة	*wādin, wahdah*
dalliance (n)	مداعبة، مغازلة	*mudā'abah, mughāzalah*
dally (v)	داعب، عبث	*dā'aba, 'abatha*
dam (n/v)	سد، سد	*sadd, sadda*
dam (n)	أم الحيوان	*ummul ḥaiwān*
damage (v)	ضر، آذى	*ḍarra, ādhā*
damage (n)	ضرر، تلف	*ḍarar, talaf*
damaging (adj)	مؤذٍ، ضار	*mu'dhin, ḍārr*
Damascus (n)	دمشق	*dimashq*
Dame (n)	امرأة، سيدة	*imra'ah, sayyidah*
damn (n/adj)	لعن، لعين	*la'n, la'īn*
damn (v)	أدان، أهلك	*adāna, ahlaka*
damnable (adj)	لعين، رديء	*la'īn, radī'*
damnation (n)	إدانة، لعنة	*idānah, la'nah*
damned (adj)	ملعون، مدان	*mal'ūn, mudān*
damp (n/adj)	رطوبة، رطب	*ruṭūbah, raṭb*
dampen (v)	رطب، بلل	*raṭṭaba, ballala*
damsel (n)	آنسة، عذراء	*ānisah, 'adhrā'*
dance (v/n)	رقص، رقص	*raqaṣa, raqṣ*
dancer (n)	راقص، راقصة	*rāqiṣ, raqiṣah*
dancing (n/adj)	رقص، راقص	*raqṣ, rāqiṣ*
dandy (adj)	شديد التأنق	*shadīdut ta'annuq*
danger (n)	خطر، مخاطرة	*khaṭar, mukhāṭarah*
dangerous (adj)	خطر، محفوف بالمخاطر	*khaṭir, maḥfūf bil makhāṭir*
dangerously (adv)	على نحو خطر	*'alā naḥw khaṭir*
dangle (v)	تدلى، استرخى	*tadallā, istarkhā*
dank (adj)	شديد الرطوبة	*shadīdur ruṭūbah*

dapper (adj)	خفيف، نشيط	*khafīf, nashīṭ*
dare (v)	جرأ، جسر	*jara'a, jasara*
dare (n)	جراءة، تحدٍّ	*jarā'ah, taḥaddin*
daredevil (n)	متهور، مقحام	*mutahawwir, miqḥām*
daring (n)	جسارة، جراءة	*jasārah, jarā'ah*
dark (n)	ظلام، جهل	*ẓalām, jahl*
dark (adj)	مظلم، داكن	*muẓlim, dākin*
darken (v)	أعتم، أظلم	*a'tama, aẓlama*
darkness (n)	ظلمة، ظلام، عتمة	*ẓulmah, ẓalām, 'atmah*
darling (n/adj)	حبيب، عزيز	*ḥabīb, 'azīz*
darn (n)	رفو، رتق	*rafw, ratq*
dart (n)	رمح خفيف، سهم	*rumḥ khafīf, sahm*
dash (v)	طرطش، خيب، صدم	*ṭarṭasha, khayyaba, ṣadama*
dash (n)	ضربة عنيفة، اندفاع	*ḍarbah 'anīfah, indifā'*
dashboard (n)	حاجبة	*ḥājibah*
dashing (adj)	جسور، مندفع، أنيق	*jasūr, mundafi', anīq*
data (n)	معلومات، حقائق	*ma'lūmāt, ḥaqā'iq*
date (n)	تاريخ، عصر، تمر	*tārīkh, 'aṣr, tamar*
date (v)	أرخ، حدد التاريخ	*arrakha, ḥaddadat tārīkh*
dated (adj)	مؤرخ	*mu'arrakh*
dateless (adj)	غير محدود	*ghair maḥdūd*
date-palm (n)	نخلة	*nakhlah*
daughter (n)	ابنة، بنت	*ibnah, bint*
daughter-in-law (n)	زوجة الابن	*zaujatul ibn*
daunt (v)	أرهب، روع	*arhaba, rawwa'a*
daunting (adj)	مروع، مرهب	*murawwi', murhib*

dawdle (v)	توانى، أضاع	*tawānā, aḍā'a*
dawn (n)	فجر، بزوغ	*fajr, buzūgh*
dawn (v)	بزغ، اتضح	*bazagha, ittaḍaḥa*
day (n)	يوم، عهد	*yaum, 'aḥd*
daybreak (n)	فجر، طلوع النهار	*fajr, ṭulū'un nahār*
day-dream (n)	حلم اليقظة	*ḥulmul yaqẓah*
daylight (n)	ضوء النهار	*ḍau'un nahār*
daylong (adv)	طوال النهار	*ṭiwālun nahār*
daytime (n)	نهار	*nahār*
daze (v)	بهر، دوخ	*bahara, dawwakha*
daze (n)	انبهار، دوخان	*imbihār, dawakhān*
dazzle (v)	التمع، بهر	*iltama'a, bahara*
dazzling (adj)	باهر، متألق	*bāhir, muta'alliq*
deacon (n)	شماس الكنيسة	*shammāsul kanīsah*
deaconess (n)	شماسة	*shammāsah*
dead (n/adj)	ميت، خامد، كاسد	*mait, khāmid, kāsid*
deaden (v)	أمات، أخفت	*amāta, akhfata*
dead letter (n)	حرف ميت	*ḥarf mait*
deadly (adj)	مميت، مهلك	*mumīt, muhlik*
deaf (adj)	أصم، أطرش	*aṣamm, aṭrash*
deafen (v)	أصم، طرش	*aṣamma, ṭarrasha*
deafening (adj)	مصم، مطرش	*muṣimm, muṭarrish*
deafness (n)	طرش، صمم	*ṭarash, ṣamam*
deal (v)	وزع، تعامل	*wazza'a, ta'āmala*
dealer (n)	تاجر، بائع	*tājir, bā'i'*
dealing (n)	معاملة، علاقات	*mu'āmalah, 'alāqāt*
dean (n)	عميد كلية	*'amīdu kulliyyah*
dear (n/adj)	عزيز، غالٍ	*'azīz, ghālin*

dearly (adv)	كثيراً، بثمن غالٍ	*kathīran, bi thaman ghālin*
dearth (n)	قلة، مجاعة	*qillah, majā'ah*
death (n)	موت، وفاة	*maut, wafāt*
deathbed (n)	فراش الاحتضار	*firāshul iḥtiḍār*
deathless (adj)	خالد، باقٍ	*khālid, bāqin*
deathly (adj)	مميت، مهلك	*mumīt, muhlik*
death rate	نسبة الوفيات	*nisbatul wafayāt*
death tax	ضريبة الإرث	*ḍarībatul irth*
death-trap (n)	شرك الموت	*sharakul maut*
debar (v)	منع، حظر	*mana'a, ḥaẓẓara*
debase (v)	انخفض، أذل	*inkhafaḍa, adhalla*
debate (v)	ناقش، حاج	*nāqasha, ḥājja*
debate (n)	مناقشة، مناظرة	*munāqashah, munāẓarah*
debauch (v)	أفسد، فسق	*afsada, fasaqa*
debauch (n)	فسق، فجور، دعارة	*fisq, fujūr, di'ārah*
debauchery (n)	فسوق، إغواء	*fusūq, ighwā'*
debilitate (v)	أضعف، أوهن	*aḍ'afa, auhana*
debility (n)	ضعف، وهن	*ḍa'f, wahn*
debit (n)	مدين، نفدة مسجلة	*madīn, nafdah musajjalah*
debonair (adj)	لطيف،ظريف، كيس	*laṭīf, ẓarīf, kayyis*
debris (n)	أطلال، أنقاض	*aṭlāl, anqāḍ*
debt (n)	دين، إثم	*dain, ithm*
debtor (n)	مدين، مديون	*madīn, madyūn*
debunk (v)	فضح الزيف	*faḍaḥaz zaif*
debut (n)	ظهور أول	*ẓuhūr awwal*

decade (n)	عقد، عشرة	*'aqd, 'asharah*
decadence (n)	انحطاط، تدهور	*inḥiṭāṭ, tadahwur*
decadent (adj)	متفسخ، متدهور	*mutafassikh, mutadahwir*
decamp (v)	ارتحل فجأةً	*irtaḥala faj'atan*
decant (v)	صفق، صب	*ṣafaqa, ṣabba*
decanter (n)	مصفق، قنينة	*miṣfaq, qinnīnah*
decay (v)	فسد، اضمحل	*fasada, iḍmaḥalla*
decay (n)	فساد، اضمحلال	*fasād, iḍmiḥlāl*
decease (n)	موت، وفاة	*maut, wafāt*
deceased (adj)	ميت، متوفى	*mait, mutawaffā*
deceit (n)	خداع، غش	*khidā', ghishsh*
deceitful (adj)	خادع، مخاتل	*khādi', mukhātil*
deceitfully (adv)	غدرًا، بخيانة	*ghadran, bi khiyānah*
deceitfulness (n)	خداع، ختل	*khidā', khatl*
deceive (v)	خدع، خاتل	*khada'a, khātala*
deceiver (n)	مخادع، مخاتل	*mukhādi', mukhātil*
decelerate (v)	بطأ، أنقص	*baṭṭa'a, anqaṣa*
December (n)	ديسمبر، كانون الأول	*dīsimbir, kānūnul awwal*
decency (n)	احتشام، لياقة	*iḥtishām, liyāqah*
decent (adj)	لطيف، لائق	*laṭīf, lā'iq*
decentralize,-ise (v)	أبطل المركزية	*abṭalal markaziyyah*
deception (n)	خدعة، خداع، غش	*khud'ah, khidā', ghishsh*
deceptive (adj)	خادع، مضلل	*khādi', muḍallil*
decide (v)	فصل، قرر	*faṣala, qarrara*
decided (adj)	محدد، مصمم	*muḥaddad, muṣammam*

decidedly (adv)	حتماً، تصميماً	*ḥatman, taṣmīman*
decimal (adj)	عشري	*'ushrī*
decimetre (n)	ديسمتر	*disimitr*
decipher (v)	حل الشفرة	*ḥallash shifrah*
decision (n)	فصل، عزم	*faṣl, 'azm*
decisive (adj)	فاصل، بات	*fāṣil, bātt*
deck (n)	ظهر المركب	*ẓahrul markab*
deck (v)	زين، زخرف	*zayyana, zakhrafa*
declaim (v)	خطب	*khaṭaba*
declamation (n)	خطاب، خطبة	*khiṭāb, khuṭbah*
declaration (n)	إعلان، تصريح، بيان	*i'lān, taṣrīḥ, bayān*
declare (v)	أعلن، صرح	*a'lana, ṣarraḥa*
declension (n)	تصريف الأسماء	*taṣrīful asmā'*
decline (v)	انخفض، ذبل، هبط	*inkhafaḍa, dhabala, habaṭa*
decline (n)	ذبول، انحطاط	*dhubūl, inḥiṭāṭ*
decode (v)	حل الشفرة	*ḥallash shifrah*
decompose (v)	فسد، انحل	*fasada, inḥalla*
decomposition (n)	حل، تحليل	*ḥall, taḥlīl*
decorate (v)	زخرف، زين	*zakhrafa, zayyana*
decoration (n)	زخرف، وسام	*zukhruf, wisām*
decorative (adj)	زخرفي، زيني	*zukhrufī, zīnī*
decorator (n)	مزخرف، مزوق	*muzakhrif, muzawwiq*
decorum (n)	ذوق، لياقة	*dhauq, liyāqah*
decoy (n)	شرك، مشرك	*sharak, musharrik*
decrease (v/n)	نقص، نقص	*naqaṣa, naqṣ*
decree (n)	مرسوم، حكم	*marsūm, ḥukm*
decree (v)	قضى، رسم	*qaḍā, rasama*

decrepit (n)	عاجز، مقعد	*'ājiz, muq'ad*
decry (n)	انتقد بقسوة، ندد	*intaqada bi qaswah, naddada*
dedicate (v)	كرس، خصص	*karrasa, khaṣṣaṣa*
dedicated (adj)	موقوف، مخصص	*mauqūf, mukhaṣṣaṣ*
dedication (n)	تكريس، وقف	*takrīs, waqf*
deduce (v)	استخرج، استدل	*istakhraja, istadalla*
deduct (v)	حسم، اقتطع	*ḥasama, iqtaṭa'a*
deduction (n)	حسم، اقتطاع	*ḥasm, iqtiṭā'*
deed (n)	عمل، صنيع	*'amal, ṣanī'*
deem (v)	اعتبر، اعتقد	*i'tabara, i'taqada*
deep (adj)	عميق، داكن، قعير	*'amīq, dākin, qa'īr*
deepen (v)	عمق، عمق	*'amuqa, 'ammaqa*
deeply (adv)	بعمق، بتعمق	*bi 'umq, bi ta'ammuq*
deer (n)	أيل، ظبي	*ayyil, ẓaby*
de-escalate (v)	خفف، خفض	*khaffafa, khaffaḍa*
deface (v)	شوه، محا	*shawwaha, maḥā*
de facto (adj/adv)	واقعي، في الواقع	*wāqi'ī, fil wāqi'*
defamation (n)	قذف، افتراء	*qadhf, iftirā'*
defame (v)	قذف، افترى	*qadhafa, iftarā*
default (n)	تخلف، إهمال	*takhalluf, ihmāl*
default (v)	تخلف، أهمل	*takhallafa, ahmala*
defaulter (n)	مختلس، متخلف	*mukhtalis, mutakhallif*
defeat (v/n)	هزم، هزيمة	*hazama, hazīmah*
defect (n)	عيب، خلل، قصور	*'aib, khalal, quṣūr*
defective (adj)	ناقص، معيوب	*nāqiṣ, ma'yūb*
defence (n)	حماية، دفاع	*ḥimāyah, difā'*
defend (v)	حمى، دافع	*ḥamā, dāfa'a*

defensible (adj)	ممكن الدفاع عنه	*mumkinud difā' 'anhu*
defensive (adj)	دفاعي، واقٍ	*difā'ī, wāqin*
defer (v)	أخر، أرجأ	*akhkhara, arja'a*
deference (n)	رعاية، إذعان	*ri'āyah, idh'ān*
defiance (n)	تحدٍ، ازدراء بالخطر	*taḥaddin, izdirā' bil khaṭar*
defiant (adj)	متحدٍّ، جريء	*mutaḥaddin, jarī'*
deficiency (n)	نقص، عجز، قصور	*naqṣ, 'ajz, quṣūr*
deficient (adj)	ناقص، عاجز	*nāqiṣ, 'ājiz*
deficit (n)	عجز، نقص	*'ajz, naqṣ*
defile (v)	دنس، لوث	*dannasa, lawwatha*
defilement (n)	تجنيس، تدنيس	*tajnīs, tadnīs*
define (v)	عرف، عين	*'arrafa, 'ayyana*
definite (adj)	واضح، معين	*wāḍiḥ, mu'ayyan*
definitely (adv)	قطعيًا، نهائيًا	*qaṭ'iyyan, nihā'iyyan*
definition (n)	تعريف، تعيين	*ta'rīf, ta'yīn*
definitive (adj)	حاسم، قطعي	*ḥāsim, qaṭ'ī*
deflate (v)	فرغ، ضائل	*farragha, ḍā'ala*
deflation (n)	انكماش، تفريغ	*inkimāsh, tafrīgh*
deflect (v)	أزاغ، عطف، مال	*azāgha, 'aṭafa, māla*
deflection (n)	إزاغة، انحراف	*izāghah, inḥirāf*
deform (v)	مسخ، شوه	*masakha, shawwaha*
deformation (n)	تشويه، مسخ	*tashwīh, maskh*
defraud (v)	خدع، احتال	*khada'a, iḥtāla*
defy (v)	تحدى، قاوم	*taḥaddā, qāwama*
degenerate (v)	تفسخ، انحط	*tafassakha, inḥaṭṭa*
degeneration (n)	تفسخ، انحطاط	*tafassukh, inḥiṭāṭ*
degradation (n)	إهانة، إخزاء	*ihānah, ikhzā'*

degrade (v)	أنزل الرتبة، أخزى	*anzalar rutbah, akhzā*
degrading (adj)	مخزٍ، مهين	*mukhzin, muhīn*
degree (n)	درجة، منـــزلة، شهادة	*darajah, manzilah, shahādah*
dehydrate (v)	زموه، جفف	*zamwaha, jaffafa*
dehydration (n)	زموهة، تجفيف	*zamwahah, tajfīf*
deify (v)	أله، عظم	*allaha, 'azzama*
deity (n)	اله، معبود	*ilāh, ma'būd*
dejected (adj)	مغتم، مكتئب	*mughtamm, mukta'ib*
dejection (n)	اكتئاب، تغوط	*ikti'āb, taghawwuṭ*
delay (v)	أجل، أخر	*ajjala, akhkhara*
delay (n)	تأخير، توانٍ	*ta'khīr, tawānin*
delectation (n)	بهجة، سرور	*bahjah, surūr*
delegate (n/v)	مندوب، انتدب	*mandūb, intadaba*
delegation (n)	وفد، ندب، بعثة	*wafd, nadb, ba'thah*
delete (v)	شطب، أزال	*shaṭaba, azāla*
deletion (n)	شطب، انشطاب	*shaṭb, inshiṭāb*
deliberate (adj)	متعمد، مدروس	*mata'ammid, madrūs*
deliberately (adv)	بتعمد، بتأنٍ	*bi ta'ammud, bi ta'annin*
deliberation (n)	تروٍ، تأنٍ	*tarawwin, ta'annin*
delicacy (n)	رقة، كياسة	*riqqah, kiyāsah*
delicate (adj)	شهي، ناعم، لطيف	*shahiyy, nā'im, laṭīf*
delicious (adj)	لذيذ، مبهج، شهي	*ladhīdh, mubhaj, shahī*
delight (n)	بهجة، سرور	*bahjah, surūr*
delight (v)	أبهج، ابتهج	*abhaja, ibtahaja*
delightful (adj)	مبهج، سار	*mubhij, sārr*
delightfully (adv)	بسرور، بابتهاج	*bi surūr, bibtihāj*

delineate (v)	صور، رسم	*ṣawwara, rasama*
delineation (n)	تصوير، وصف	*taṣwīr, waṣf*
delinquency (n)	إهمال، جنوحية	*ihmāl, junūḥiyyah*
delinquent (adj)	مهمل، جانح	*muhmil, jāniḥ*
deliver (v)	سلم، حول، أنقذ	*sallama, ḥawwala, anqadha*
deliverance (n)	حرية، إنقاذ	*ḥurriyyah, inqādh*
delivery (n)	تسليم، تحويل، خلاص	*taslīm, taḥwīl, khalāṣ*
delta (n)	مثلث، دلتا	*muthallath, diltā*
delude (v)	ضلل، خدع	*ḍallala, khadaʻa*
deluge (v)	غمر، فاض	*ghamara, fāḍa*
delusion (n)	ضلال، وهم	*ḍalāl, wahm*
delusive (adj)	مضلل، وهمي	*muḍallil, wahmī*
demand (n)	مطالبة، طلب	*muṭālabah, ṭalab*
demand (v)	طالب، تطلب	*ṭālaba, taṭallaba*
demean (v)	خفض، سلك	*khaffaḍa, salaka*
demeanour (n)	سلوك، تصرف	*sulūk, taṣarruf*
demented (adj)	مخبل، معتوه	*mukhabbal, maʻtūh*
demerit (n)	نقيصة، عيب	*naqīṣah, ʻaib*
demise (n)	موت، زوال	*maut, zawāl*
democracy (n)	ديموقراطية	*dīmūqarāṭiyyah*
democrat (n)	ديموقراطي	*dīmūqarāṭī*
democratic (adj)	ديموقراطي	*dīmūqarāṭī*
demolish (v)	دمر، هدم	*dammara, haddama*
demolition (n)	تدمير، تخريب	*tadmīr, takhrīb*
demon (n)	عفريت، جن	*ʻifrīt, jinn*
demonstrate (v)	أظهر، شرح	*aẓhara, sharaḥa*

demonstration (n)	إظهار، إثبات	*iẓhār, ithbāt*
demonstrative (adj)	إشاري، إثباتي	*ishārī, ithbātī*
demoralization (n)	فساد في الأخلاق	*fasād fil akhlāq*
demoralize,-ise (v)	أفسد الأخلاق	*afsadal akhlāq*
demote (v)	أنزل الرتبة	*anzalar rutbah*
demur (v)	اعترض، تردد	*i'taraḍa, taraddada*
den (n)	عرين، وكر	*'arīn, wakr*
denial (n)	رفض، إنكار	*rafḍ, inkar*
denigrate (v)	شوه السمعة	*shawwahas sum'ah*
denomination (n)	طائفة، فئة	*ṭā'ifah, fi'ah*
denominator (n)	مخرج الكسور	*makhrajul kusūr*
denote (v)	دل، أشار	*dalla, ashāra*
denouement (n)	حل العقدة، ختام	*ḥallul 'uqdah, khitām*
denounce (v)	اتهم، شجب	*ittahama, shajaba*
dense (adj)	كثيف، مزدحم	*kathīf, muzdaḥim*
density (n)	كثافة، غزارة	*kathāfah, ghazārah*
dent (n)	سن، شوكة	*sinn, shaukah*
dental (adj)	سني، أسناني	*sinnī, asnānī*
dentist (n)	طبيب الأسنان	*ṭabībul asnān*
denude (v)	عرى، جرد	*'arrā, jarrada*
denunciation (n)	شجب، اتهام	*shajb, ittihām*
deny (v)	رفض، جحد	*rafaḍa, jaḥada*
depart (v)	رحل، غادر	*raḥala, ghādara*
departed (adj)	ماضٍ، ميت	*māḍin, mait*
department (n)	شعبة، قسم	*sḥu'bah, qism*
departure (n)	رحيل، انطلاق	*raḥīl, inṭilāq*
depend (v)	اعتمد، توقف	*i'tamada, tawaqqafa*

dependable (adj)	جدير بالثقة	*jadīr bith thiqah*
dependant = dependent		
dependence (n)	توقف، اعتماد	*tawaqquf, i'timād*
dependency (n)	توقف، بلد تابع	*tawaqquf, balad tābi'*
dependent (adj)	متوقف، متدلٍّ	*mutawaqqif, mutadallin*
depict (v)	صور، وصف	*ṣawwara, waṣafa*
depiction (n)	تصوير، رسم	*taṣwīr, rasm*
deplete (v)	استنزف، فصد	*istanzafa, faṣada*
depletion (n)	استنزاف، فصد	*istinzāf, faṣd*
deplorable (adj)	بائس، حزين	*bā'is, ḥazīn*
deplore (v)	أسى، أرثى	*asā, arthā*
deploy (v)	نشر، انتشر	*nashara, intashara*
deployment (n)	نشر، انتشار	*nashr, intishār*
deport (v)	نفى، رحل	*nafā, raḥḥala*
deportation (n)	ترحيل، تغريب	*tarḥīl, taghrīb*
deportment (n)	مشية، سلوك	*mishyah, sulūk*
depose (v)	عزل، خلع	*'azala, khala'a*
deposit (n)	وديعة، تأمين	*wadī'ah, ta'mīn*
deposit (v)	أودع، أقر	*auda'a, aqarra*
deposition (n)	خلع، عزل	*khala', 'azl*
depositor (n)	مودع	*mūdi'*
depot (n)	مخزن، محطة	*makhzan, maḥaṭṭah*
deprave (v)	أفسد الأخلاق	*afsadal akhlāq*
depravity (n)	فساد، فسوق	*fasād, fusūq*
deprecate (v)	استنكر، استرحم	*istankara, istarḥama*
depreciate (v)	خفض القيمة	*khaffaḍal qīmah*
depredation (n)	سلب، نهب	*salb, nahb*
depress (v)	أحزن، كسد	*aḥzana, kassada*

depressed (adj)	حزين، كئيب	*ḥazīn, ka'īb*
depressing (adj)	محزن، مضايق	*muḥzin, muḍāyiq*
depression (n)	حزن، كآبة	*ḥuzn, ka'ābah*
deprivation (n)	حرمان، تجريد	*ḥirmān, tajrīd*
deprive (v)	حرم، جرد	*ḥarama, jarrada*
deprived (adj)	محروم، مجرد	*maḥrūm, mujarrad*
depth (n)	عمق، جوف	*'umq, jauf*
depute (v)	انتدب، ناب	*intadaba, nāba*
deputy (n)	نائب، مفوض	*nā'ib, mufawwaḍ*
derail (v)	خرج عن الخط	*kharaja 'anil khaṭṭ*
deranged (adj)	مخبل، مشوش	*mukhabbal, mushawwash*
derelict (adj)	مهجور، مهمل	*mahjūr, muhmal*
deride (v)	سخر، استهزأ	*sakhira, istahza'a*
derision (n)	سخرية، هزء	*sukhriyyah, huz'*
derivation (n)	اشتقاق، أصل	*ishtiqāq, aṣl*
derivative (adj)	مشتق، ثانوي	*mushtaqq, thānawī*
derive (v)	اشتق، استنتج	*ishtaqqa, istantaja*
derogatory (adj)	ازدرائي، حاط	*izdirā'ī, ḥāṭṭ*
derric (n)	مرفاع، دريك	*mirfā', dirīk*
descend (v)	هبط، نزل	*habaṭa, nazala*
descendent (adj/n)	هابط، سليل	*hābiṭ, salīl*
descent (n)	هبوط، أصل، نسب	*hubūṭ, aṣl, nasab*
describe (v)	وصف، رسم	*waṣafa, rasama*
description (n)	وصف، تصوير	*waṣf, taṣwīr*
descriptive (adj)	تصويري، وصفي	*taṣwīrī, waṣfī*
desecrate (v)	دنس، نجس	*dannasa, najjasa*
desert (n/adj)	صحراء، صحراوي	*ṣaḥrā', ṣaḥrāwī*

deserts (n)	أهلية، استحقاق	*ahliyyah, istiḥqāq*
deserve (v)	استحق، استأهل	*istaḥaqqa, ista'hala*
deserving (adj)	مستحق، لائق	*mustaḥiqq, lā'iq*
design (v)	رسم، خطط	*rasama, khaṭṭaṭa*
design (n)	رسم، تخطيط، خطة	*rasm, takhṭīṭ, khiṭṭah*
designate (v)	خصص، دل	*khaṣṣaṣa, dalla*
designation (n)	تعيين، دلالة	*ta'yīn, dalālah*
designer (n)	مصمم، مدبر	*muṣammim, mudabbir*
designing (n)	تخطيط، تصميم	*takhṭīṭ, taṣmīm*
desirable (adj)	مرغوب، جذاب	*marghūb, jadhdhāb*
desire (v)	رغب، تاق	*raghiba, tāqa*
desire (n)	رغبة، توق، أمنية	*raghbah, tauq, umniyyah*
desirous (adj)	راغب، تواق	*rāghib, tawwāq*
desist (v)	كف، انفك	*kaffa, infakka*
desk (n)	طاولة، منضدة	*ṭāwilah, minḍadah*
desolate (adj)	مهجور، بائس	*mahjūr, bā'is*
desolate (v)	خرب، تخلى	*kharraba, takhallā*
desolation (n)	أسىً، إقفار	*asan, iqfār*
despair (n)	يأس، قنوط	*ya's, qunūṭ*
despair (v)	قنط، يئس	*qanaṭa, ya'isa*
despairing (adj)	يائس، قانط	*yā'is, qāniṭ*
despatch=dispatch		
desperate (adj)	يائس، متهور	*yā'is, mutahawwir*
desperation (n)	يأس، قنوط	*ya's, qunūṭ*
despicable (n)	خسيس، حقير	*khasīs, ḥaqīr*
despise (v)	ازدرى، استخف	*izdarā, istakhaffa*
despite (prep)	على الرغم	*'alar raghm*

despoil (v)	سلب، نهب	*salaba, nahaba*
despondency (n)	قنوط، كآبة	*qunūṭ, ka'ābah*
despondent (adj)	قانط، مكتئب	*qāniṭ, mukta'ib*
despot (n)	حاكم مطلق، مستبد	*ḥākim muṭlaq, mustabidd*
dessert (n)	حلوى، عقبة	*ḥalwā, 'uqbah*
dessertspoon (n)	ملعقة العقبة	*mil'aqatul 'uqbah*
destabilize,-ise (v)	أفقد الاستقرار	*afqadal istiqrār*
destination (n)	غرض، مصير	*gharaḍ, maṣir*
destiny (n)	قدر، قسمة	*qadar, qismah*
destitute (adj)	معدم، محروم	*mu'dim, maḥrūm*
destitution (n)	إملاق، فقر	*imlāq, faqr*
destroy (v)	أتلف، دمر	*atlafa, dammara*
destruction (n)	تدمير، تخريب	*tadmīr, takhrīb*
destructive (adj)	متلف، مخرب	*mutlif, mukharrib*
detach (v)	فصل، فك	*faṣala, fakka*
detached (adj)	منفصل، مستقل	*munfaṣil, mustaqill*
detachment (n)	انفصال، كتيبة	*infiṣāl, katībah*
detail (n)	تفصيل، إسهاب	*tafṣīl, ishāb*
detail (v)	ذكر بالتفصيل	*dhakara bit tafṣīl*
detailed (adj)	مفصل، بالتفصيل	*mufaṣṣal, bit tafṣīl*
detain (v)	عاق، اعتقل	*'āqa, i'taqala*
detect (v)	اكتشف، استبان	*iktashafa, istabāna*
detection (n)	كشف، اكتشاف	*kashf, iktishāf*
detective (n)	كشاف، بصاص	*kashshāf, baṣṣāṣ*
detention (n)	اعتقال، احتجاز	*i'tiqāl, iḥtijāz*
deter (v)	أعاق، ردع	*a'āqa, rada'a*
detergent (n)	منظف، مسهل	*munaẓẓif, mushil*

deteriorate (v)	فسد، تلف	*fasada, talifa*
deterioration (n)	فساد، إفساد	*fasād, ifsād*
determination (n)	عزم، تصميم	*'azm, taṣmīm*
determine (v)	حدد، قرر	*ḥaddada, qarrara*
deterrent (n)	مانع، رادع	*māni', rādi'*
detest (v)	مقت، كره	*maqata, kariha*
detestation (n)	مقت، كره، بغض	*maqt, kurh, bughḍ*
dethrone (v)	خلع عن العرش	*khala'a 'anil 'arsh*
detonate (v)	تفجر، فرقع	*tafajjara, farqa'a*
detonation (n)	تفجير، انفجار	*tafjīr, infijār*
detract (v)	قلل، حط من القدر	*qallala, ḥatta minal qadr*
detriment (n)	ضرر، أذىً	*ḍarar, adhan*
devalue (v)	انخفض، خفض القيمة	*inkhafaḍa, khaffaḍal qīmah*
devastate (v)	دمر، خرب	*dammara, kharraba*
devastating (adj)	مدمر، مخرب	*mudammir, mukharrib*
devastation (n)	تخريب، دمار	*takhrīb, dimār*
develop (v)	نمى، تطور	*nammā, taṭawwara*
development (n)	تنمية، تطور	*tanmiyah, taṭawwur*
deviant (adj)	منحرف	*munḥarif*
deviate (v)	انحرف، زاغ	*inḥarafa, zāgha*
deviation (n)	انحراف، ضلة	*inḥirāf, ḍallah*
device (n)	أداة، مكيدة	*adāt, makīdah*
devil (n)	شيطان، شخص شرير	*shayṭān, shakhṣ shirrīr*
devilish (adj)	شيطاني، مفرط	*shayṭānī, mufriṭ*
devious (adj)	متمعج، ضال	*mutama''ij, ḍāll*
devise (v)	اخترع، دبر	*ikhtara'a, dabbara*

devoid (n)	خلو، عارٍ	*khilw, 'ārin*
devolution (n)	تفويض، أيلولة	*tafwīḍ, ailūlah*
devolve (v)	انتقل، حول	*intaqala, ḥawwala*
devote (v)	وقف، خصص	*waqafa, khaṣṣaṣa*
devoted (adj)	مخلص، مكرس	*mukhliṣ, mukarras*
devotee (n)	تابع متحمس، متعبد	*tābi' mutaḥammis, muta'abbid*
devotion (n)	تقوى، إخلاص	*taqwā, ikhlāṣ*
devotional (adj)	تعبدي	*ta'abbudī*
devout (adj)	خاشع، مخلص	*khāshi', mukhliṣ*
dew (n)	ندى، طراوة	*nadā, ṭarāwah*
dexterity (n)	حذق، براعة	*ḥidhq, barā'ah*
dextrous,dexterous (adj)	حاذق، بارع	*ḥādhiq, bāri'*
diabetes (n)	ديابيتس	*diyābīts*
diabetic (adj)	ديابيتي	*diyābītī*
diabolic-al (adj)	شيطاني، وحشي	*shayṭānī, waḥshī*
diagnose (v)	شخص المرض	*shakhkhaṣal maraḍ*
diagnosis (n)	تشخيص المرض	*tashkhīṣul maraḍ*
diagnostic (adj)	تشخيصي	*tashkhīṣī*
diagonal (adj/n)	قطري، خط قطري	*quṭrī, khaṭṭ quṭrī*
diagram (n)	رسم تخطيطي	*rasm takhṭīṭī*
dial (n)	ميناء الساعة، قرص	*mīnā'us sā'ah, qurṣ*
dial (v)	أدار	*adāra*
dialect (n)	لغة محلية	*lughah maḥalliyyah*
dialectal (adj)	لهجي، مختص بلهجة	*lahjī, mukhtaṣṣ bi lahjah*
dialectics (n)	منطق، تحليل منطقي	*manṭiq, taḥlīl manṭiqī*
dialogue (n)	محادثة، حوار	*muḥādathah, ḥiwār*

dialysis (n)	ديلزة	*dailazah*
diametre (n)	قطر الدائرة	*quṭrud dā'irah*
diametric (adj)	قطري، مستقيم	*quṭrī, mustaqīm*
diamond (n)	الماس، معين	*almās, mu'ayyan*
diarrhoea (diarrhea) (n)	إسهال	*ishāl*
diary (n)	يوميات	*yaumiyyāt*
dice (n)	نرد، لعبة النرد	*nard, lu'batun nard*
dictate (v)	أملى، أمر	*amlā, amara*
dictate (n)	أمر، حكم	*amr, ḥukm*
dictation (n)	إملاء، أمر جازم	*imlā', amr jāzim*
dictator (n)	حاكم مطلق	*ḥākim muṭlaq*
dictatorial (adj)	استبدادي، تحتيمي	*istibdādī, taḥtīmī*
dictatorship (n)	استبدادية	*istibdādiyyah*
diction (n)	أسلوب، إلقاء	*uslūb, ilqā'*
dictionary (n)	معجم، قاموس	*mu'jam, qāmūs*
dictum (n)	مثل سائر	*mathal sā'ir*
didactic (adj)	تعليمي، إرشادي	*ta'līmī, irshādī*
die (v)	مات، ارتحل	*māta, irtaḥala*
die (n)	قالب، نرد	*qālib, nard*
diesel (n)	ديزل	*dīzal*
diet (n)	غذاء، حمية	*ghidhā', ḥimyah*
differ (v)	اختلف، تنازع	*ikhtalafa, tanāza'a*
difference (n)	اختلاف، فرق	*ikhtilāf, farq*
different (adj)	مختلف، مغاير	*mukhtalif, mughāyir*
differential (adj)	تفاوتي، خلافي	*tafāwutī, khilāfī*
differentiate (v)	ميز، فرق	*mayyaza, farraqa*
differentiation (n)	تفريق، تمييز	*tafrīq, tamyīz*

difficult (adj)	صعب، عسير	*ṣa'b, 'asīr*
difficulty (n)	حرج، صعوبة، عسر	*ḥaraj, ṣu'ūbah, 'usr*
diffidence (n)	عدم الثقة	*'adamuth thiqah*
diffident (adj)	حيي، محجم، خفر	*ḥayiy, muḥjim, khafir*
diffuse (v)	صب، نشر	*ṣabba, nashara*
diffuse (adj)	منتشر، مسهب	*muntashir, mushib*
diffusion (n)	انتشار، إسهاب	*intishār, ishāb*
dig (v)	حفر، نقب، أقحم	*ḥafara, naqaba, aqḥama*
digest (v)	هضم، استوعب	*haḍama, istau'aba*
digestible (adj)	قابل للهضم	*qābil lil haḍm*
digestion (n)	هضم، تنسيق	*haḍm, tansīq*
digger (n)	حفار، حفارة	*ḥaffār, ḥaffārah*
digit (n)	رقم تحت العشرة	*raqm taḥtal 'asharah*
digital (adj)	إصبعي، رقمي	*iṣba'ī, raqmī*
dignified (adj)	جليل، مكرم	*jalīl, mukarram*
dignify (v)	بجل، كرم	*bajjala, karrama*
dignitary (n)	صاحب مقام رفيع	*ṣāḥibu maqām rafī'*
dignity (n)	جلال، شرف	*jalāl, sharaf*
digress (v)	استطرد، انحرف	*istaṭrada, inḥarafa*
digression (n)	استطراد، انحراف	*istiṭrād, inḥirāf*
dilapidate (v)	تخرب، تهدم	*takharraba, tahaddama*
dilapidated (adj)	خرب، متهدم	*kharib, mutahaddim*
dilate (v)	تمدد، اتسع	*tamaddada, ittasa'a*
dilation (n)	اتساع، تمديد	*ittisā', tamdīd*
dilemma (n)	مأزق، ورطة	*ma'ziq, warṭah*
diligence (n)	اجتهاد، كد	*ijtihād, kadd*

diligent (adj)	مجتهد، كاد، مثابر	*mujtahid, kādd, muthābir*
dilly-dally (v)	تلكأ، توانى	*talakk'a, tawānā*
dilute (v)	رقق، شعشع	*raqqaqa, sha'sha'a*
dim (adj)	معتم، ضعيف	*mu'tim, ḍa'īf*
dimension (n)	بعد، حجم	*bu'd, ḥajm*
dimensional (adj)	بعدي	*bu'dī*
diminish (v)	نقص، قلل	*naqqaṣa, qallala*
diminution (n)	نقص، تقليل	*naqṣ, taqlīl*
diminutive (adj)	تصغيري، مصغر	*taṣghīrī, muṣaghghar*
dimmer (n)	معتام	*mi'tām*
dimness (n)	إعتام، ظلمة	*i'tām, ẓulmah*
dimple (n)	هزمة، غمازة	*hazmah, ghammāzah*
din (n)	ضجيج، ضوضاء	*ḍajīj, ḍauḍā'*
dinar (n)	دينار	*dīnār*
dine (v)	تغدى، تعشى	*taghaddā, ta'ashshā*
diner (n)	حافلة الطعام	*ḥāfilatuṭ ṭa'ām*
ding-dong (n)	صوت الناقوس	*ṣautun nāqūs*
dining-car (n)	حافلة الطعام	*ḥāfilatuṭ ṭa'ām*
dining-room (n)	حجرة الطعام	*ḥujratuṭ ṭa'ām*
dinner (n)	وجبة الطعام	*wajbatuṭ ṭa'ām*
dinosaur (n)	دينوصور	*dīnūṣūr*
dioxide (n)	ثاني أكسيد	*thānī aksīd*
dip (v)	غمس، غط	*ghamasa, ghaṭṭa*
dip (n)	غمس، غط	*ghams, ghaṭṭ*
dipthong (n)	إدغام	*idghām*
diploma (n)	دبلوم	*diblūm*
diplomacy (n)	ديبلوماسية	*dīblūmāsiyah*

diplomat (n)	ديبلوماسي، لبق	*dīblūmāsī, labiq*
diplomatic (adj)	ديبلوماسي، سياسي	*dīblūmāsī, siyāsī*
diplomatist (n)	ديبلوماسي، سياسي	*dīblūmāsī, siyāsī*
dipper (n)	غطاس، طائر مائي	*ghaṭṭās, ṭā'ir mā'ī*
dipsomania (n)	كحال، إدمان الخمر	*kuḥāl, idmānul khamr*
dipsomaniac (adj)	مكحول	*makḥūl*
dire (adj)	رهيب، مريع	*rahīb, murī'*
direct (adj)	مباشر، صريح	*mubāshir, ṣarīḥ*
direct (v)	أدار، وجه	*adāra, wajjaha*
direct (adv)	مباشرةً	*mubāsharatan*
direction (n)	جهة، أمر، إرشاد	*jihah, amr, irshād*
directive (n)	تعليمات عسكرية	*ta'līmāt 'askariyyah*
directly (n)	مباشرةً، بلا واسطة	*mubāsharatan, bilā wāsiṭah*
director (n)	مدير، مخرج	*mudīr, mukhrij*
directorate (n)	مديرية	*mudīriyyah*
directory (n)	دليل، مرشد	*dalīl, murshid*
dirge (n)	ترنيمة جنائزية	*tarnīmah janā'iziyyah*
dirt (n)	وسخ، قذر	*wasakh, qadhar*
dirty (adj)	وسخ، قذر	*wasikh, qadhir*
disability (n)	عجز، وهن	*'ajz, wahn*
disable (v)	أعجز، أضعف	*a'jaza, aḍ'afa*
disabled (adj)	معاق، عاجز	*mu'āq, 'ājiz*
disadvantage (n)	ضرر، عائق	*ḍarar, 'ā'iq*
disadvantaged (adj)	محروم	*maḥrūm*
disadvantageous(adj)	مضر، مخسر	*muḍirr, mukhassir*
disagree (v)	خالف، عارض	*khālafa, 'āraḍa*
disagreeable (adj)	كريه، سيء الطبع	*karīh, sayyi'uṭ ṭab'*

disagreement (n) اختلاف، تعارض *ikhtilāf, ta'āruḍ*
disallow (v) رفض، أنكر *rafaḍa, ankara*
disappear (v) توارى، اختفى *tawāra, ikhtafā*
disappearance (n) اختفاء، توارٍ *ikhtifā', tawārin*
disappoint (v) خيب، أحبط *khayyaba, aḥbaṭa*
disappointed (adj) مخيب، قانط *mukhayyab, qāniṭ*
disappointment (n) خيبة أمل، فشل *khaibatu amal, fashal*
disapprobation =disapproval
disapproval (n) رفض، استنكار *rafḍ, istinkār*
disapprove (v) رفض، استنكر *rafaḍa, istankara*
disarm (v) نزع السلاح *naza'as silāḥ*
disarmament (n) نزع السلاح *naz'us silāḥ*
disarrange (v) بعثر، شوش *ba'thara, shawwasha*
disarray (n) تشوش، فوضى *tashawwush, fauḍā*
disaster (n) كارثة، نكبة *kārithah, nakbah*
disastrous (adj) مشؤوم، جالب للنوائب *mash'ūm, jālib lin nawā'ib*
disbar (v) شطب، أقصى *shaṭaba, aqṣā*
disbelief (n) جحود، كفر *juḥūd, kufr*
disbelieve (v) جحد، أنكر *jaḥada, ankara*
disburse (v) وزع، دفع *wazza'a, dafa'a*
disbursement (n) إنفاق، توزيع *infāq, tauzī'*
disc (n) قرص، أسطوانة فوتوغرافية *qurṣ, usṭuwānah fūtūgharāfiyyah*
discard (v) نبذ، رمى *nabadha, ramā*
discern (v) أدرك، رأى *adraka, ra'ā*
discerning (adj) فطن، ذكي *faṭin, dhakī*
discernment (n) فطنة، بصيرة *fiṭnah, baṣirah*

discharge (v)	فرغ، حرر	*farragha, ḥarrara*
discharge (n)	صرف من الخدمة	*ṣarf minal khidmah*
disciple (n)	حواري، تلميذ	*ḥawārī, tilmīdh*
disciplinarian (n)	نظامي، مؤدب	*niẓāmī, mu'addib*
disciplinary (adj)	انضباطي، تأديبي	*inḍibāṭī, ta'dībī*
discipline (v)	درب، أدب	*darraba, addaba*
discipline (n)	نظام، تأديب	*niẓām, ta'dīb*
disclaim (v)	تنازل عن الحق	*tanāzala 'anil ḥaqq*
disclose (v)	أفشى، كشف	*afshā, kashafa*
disclosure (n)	إفشاء، انكشاف	*ifshā', inkishāf*
discoloration (n)	تغير اللون	*taghayyauul laun*
discolour, discolor (v)	غير اللون	*ghayyaral laun*
discomfit (v)	أربك، أحبط	*arbaka, aḥbaṭa*
discomfiture (n)	ارتباك، خيبة	*irtibāk, khaibah*
discomfort (v/n)	أقلق، مشقة	*aqlaqa, mashaqqah*
disconcert (v)	أربك، أقلق	*arbaka, aqlaqa*
disconcerted (adj)	مرتبك، مضطرب	*murtabik, muḍṭarib*
disconcerting (adj)	مربك، مشوش	*murbik, mushawwish*
disconnect (v)	فصل، فرق	*faṣala, farraqa*
disconnected (adj)	منفصل، منفك	*munfaṣil, munfakk*
disconsolate (adj)	يائس، قانط	*yā'is, qāniṭ*
discontent (n)	استياء، سخط	*istiyā', sukhṭ*
discontented (adj)	مستاء، قلق البال	*mustā'in, qaliqul bāl*
discontinue (v)	أوقف، حجب	*auqafa, ḥajaba*
discontinuity (n)	انقطاع، توقف	*inqiṭā', tawaqquf*
discontinuous (adj)	منقطع، غير متواصل	*munqaṭi', ghair mutawāṣil*
discord (n)	خلاف، نزاع	*khilāf, nizā'*

discordant (adj)	متعارض، متنافر	*muta'āriḍ, mutanāfir*
discount (n)	تنــزيل، تخفيض	*tanzīl, takhfīḍ*
discount (v)	أسقط، رخص	*asqaṭa, rakhkhaṣa*
discourage (v)	ثبط العزم	*thabbaṭal 'azm*
discouragement (n)	تثبيط، تثبط	*tathbīṭ, tathabbuṭ*
discourse (n)	محادثة، محاضرة	*muḥādathah,muḥāḍarah*
discourteous (adj)	فظ، سمج	*faẓẓ, samij*
discourtesy (n)	فظاظة، جفاء	*faẓāẓah, jafā'*
discover (v)	كشف، اكتشف	*kashafa, iktashafa*
discovery (n)	كشف، اكتشاف	*kashf, iktishāf*
discredit (v)	أخزى، كذب	*akhzā, kadhdhaba*
discreditable (adj)	ضار للسمعة	*ḍārr lis sum'ah*
discreet (adj)	حكيم، حذر	*ḥakīm, ḥadhir*
discrepancy (n)	تعارض، تناقض	*ta'āruḍ, tanāquḍ*
discrete (adj)	مغاير، منفصل	*mughā'ir, munfaṣil*
discretion (n)	عقل، بصيرة	*'aql, baṣīrah*
discriminate (v)	ميز، أدرك الفرق	*mayyaza, adrakal farq*
discriminating (adj)	مميز، فارق	*mumayyiz, fāriq*
discrimination (n)	تمييز، إدراك الفرق	*tamyīz, idrākul farq*
discriminatory (adj)	مميز، تمييزي	*mumayyiz, tamyīzī*
discuss (v)	بحث، ناقش	*baḥatha, nāqasha*
discussion (n)	بحث، مناقشة	*baḥth, munāqashah*
disdain (n/v)	ازدراء، ازدرى	*izdirā', izdarā*
disdainful (adj)	ازدرائي، مزدرٍ	*izdirā'ī, muzdarin*
disease (n)	مرض، علة	*maraḍ, 'illah*
diseased (adj)	مريض، عليل	*marīḍ, 'alīl*
disembark (v)	أنزل، نزل	*anzala, nazala*
disembarkation (n)	إنزال من السفينة	*inzāl minas safīnah*

disengage (v)	حرر، خلص	*ḥarrara, khallaṣa*
disengagement (n)	تحرير، تحرر	*taḥrīr, taḥarrur*
disentangle (v)	فك، انحل	*fakka, inḥalla*
disfavour (n)	كره، ازدراء	*kurh, izdirā'*
disfigure (v)	شوه، مسخ	*shawwaha, masakha*
disgrace (n/v)	خزى، أخزى	*khizy, akhzā*
disgraceful (adj)	مخزٍ، شائن	*mukhzin, shā'in*
disgrantled (adj)	مستاءٍ، ناقم	*mustā'in, nāqim*
disguise (v)	تنكر، تقنع	*tanakkara, taqanna'a*
disguise (n)	تنكر، إخفاء	*tanakkur, ikhfā'*
disgust (v)	اشمئز، أعثى	*ishma'azza, a'thā*
disgust (n)	اشمئزاز، قرف	*ishmi'zāz, qaraf*
disgusted (adj)	مشمئز، مغثي	*mushma'izz, maghthī*
disgusting (adj)	مغثٍ، مقرف	*mughthin, muqrif*
dish (n)	طبق، صحن	*ṭabaq, ṣaḥn*
disharmony (n)	تنافر، عدم مواءمة	*tanāfur, adamu muwā'amah*
dishcloth (n)	قماشة الصحون	*qumāshatuṣ ṣuḥūn*
dishearten (v)	ثبط العزم	*thabbaṭal 'azm*
disheartening (adj)	مثبط القلب	*muthabbiṭul qalb*
dishonest (adj)	خائن، خادع	*khā'in, khādi'*
dishonesty (n)	خداع، خيانة	*khidā', khiyānah*
dishonour (n/v)	إهانة، أهان	*ihānah, ahāna*
dishonourable (adj)	شائن، مخزٍ	*shā'in, mukhzin*
disillusion (v)	حرر من الوهم	*ḥarrara minal wahm*
disincentive (n)	عقبة، عائق	*'aqabah, 'ā'iq*
disinclination (n)	نفور، كراهية	*nufūr, karāhiyyah*
disinclined (adj)	راغب عن	*rāghib 'an*

disinfect (v)	طهر من الجراثيم	*ṭahhara minal jarāthīm*
disinfectant (adj)	مبيد الجراثيم	*mubīdul jarāthīm*
disingenuous (adj)	مخادع، ماكر	*mukhādi', mākir*
disinherit (v)	حرم من الإرث	*ḥarama minal irth*
disintegrate (v)	فك، تحطم	*fakka, taḥaṭṭama*
disintegration (n)	تفسخ، تحطم	*tafassukh, taḥaṭṭum*
disinterest (n)	نزاهة	*nazāhah*
disinterested (adj)	نزيه	*nazīh*
disjointed (adj)	مفكك، مخلع	*mufakkak, mukhalla'*
disk=disc		
dislike (n/v)	كره، كره	*kurh, kariha*
dislocate (v)	خلع، نزع	*khala'a, naza'a*
dislodge (v)	أزاح، طرد	*azāḥa, ṭarada*
disloyal (adj)	خائن، غادر	*khā'in, ghādir*
disloyalty (n)	خيانة، غدر	*khiyānah, ghadr*
dismal (adj)	كئيب، موحش	*ka'īb, mūḥish*
dismantle (v)	عرى، جرد	*'arrā, jarrada*
dismay (n)	رعب، فزع	*ru'b, faza'*
dismay (v)	أرعب، أفزع	*ar'aba, afza'a*
dismember (v)	مزق، قطع	*mazzaqa, qaṭṭa'a*
dismiss (v)	صرف، طرد	*ṣarafa, ṭarada*
dismissal (n)	صرف، طرد	*ṣarf, ṭard*
dismount (v)	أنزل، ترجل	*anzala, tarajjala*
disobedience (n)	عصيان، مخالفة	*'iṣyān, mukhālafah*
disobedient (adj)	عاصٍ، متمرد	*'āṣin, mutamarrid*
disobey (v)	عصى، تمرد	*'aṣā, tamarrada*
disorder (n)	فوضى، اضطراب	*fauḍā, iḍṭirāb*
disordered (adj)	مضطرب، معتل	*muḍṭarib, mu'tall*

disorderely (adj)	مخل بالنظام	*mukhill bin niẓām*
disorganize,-ise (v)	أفسد، أخل	*afsada, akhalla*
disown (v)	أنكر، تبرأ من	*ankara, tabarra'a min*
disparage (v)	حط، انتقص	*ḥaṭṭa, intaqaṣa*
disparagingly (adv)	باستخفاف	*bistikhfāf*
disparate (adj)	متباين، متفاوت	*mutabāyin, mutafāwit*
disparity (n)	تباين، تفاوت	*tabāyun, tafāwut*
dispassionate (adj)	هادئ الطبع	*hādi'uṭ ṭab'*
dispatch (v/n)	أرسل، إرسال	*arsala, irsāl*
dispel (v)	بدد، طرد	*baddada, ṭarada*
dispensable (adj)	غير ضروري	*ghair ḍarūrī*
dispensary (n)	مستوصف	*mustauṣaf*
dispensation (n)	توزيع، تحلة	*tauzī', taḥillah*
dispense (v)	وزع، أحل	*wazza'a, aḥalla*
dispersal (n)	تشتيت، تبديد	*tashtīt, tabdīd*
disperse (v)	شتت، انتشر	*shattata, intashara*
dispersion (n)	تشتت، تبدد	*tashattut, tabaddud*
dispirit (v)	ثبط الهمة	*thabbaṭal himmah*
dispirited (adj)	مكتئب، متشائم	*mukta'ib, mutasha'im*
dispiriting (adj)	مثبط الهمة	*muthabbiṭul himmah*
displace (v)	أزاح، شرد	*azāḥa, sharrada*
displacement (n)	إزاحة، انزياح	*izāḥah, inziyāḥ*
display (v)	عرض، نشر	*'araḍa, nashara*
display (n)	عرض، إبراز	*'arḍ, ibrāz*
displease (v)	أغضب، أسخط	*aghḍaba, askhaṭa*
displeasure (n)	سخط، استياء	*sukhṭ, istiyā'*
disposable (adj)	متناول، في اليد	*mutanāwal, fil yad*
disposal (n)	تدبير، اطراح	*tadbīr, iṭṭirāḥ*

dispose (v)	قدر، نظم	*qaddara, naẓẓama*
disposed (adj)	ميال إلى	*mayyāl ilā*
disposition (n)	طبع، ميل	*ṭab', mail*
dispossess (v)	أفقد، سلب	*afqada, salaba*
dispossession (n)	طرد، سلب	*ṭard, salb*
disproportion (n)	تباين، عدم تناسب	*tabāyun, 'adamu tanāsub*
disproportionate (adj)	متباين، متفاوت	*mutabāyin, mutafāwit*
disprove (v)	دحض، رد على	*daḥaḍa, radda 'alā*
disputable (adj)	قابل للمناقشة	*qābil lil munāqashah*
disputation (n)	جدل، نزاع	*jadal, nizā'*
dispute (v)	تجادل، تنازع	*tajādala, tanāza'a*
dispute (n)	جدال، نزاع	*jidāl, nizā'*
disqualification (n)	تجرد من الأهلية	*tajarrud minal ahliyyah*
disqualify (v)	جرد من الأهلية	*jarrada minal ahliyyah*
disquiet (v/n)	أزعج، انزعاج	*az'aja, inzi'āj*
disquisition (n)	خطبة، بحث	*khuṭbah, baḥth*
disregard (v)	استخف، تجاهل عن	*istakhaffa, tajāhala 'an*
disregard (n)	استخفاف، إهمال	*istikhfāf, ihmāl*
disreputable (adj)	سيئ السمعة	*sayyi'us sum'ah*
disrepute (n)	فقدان السمعة	*fuqdānus sum'ah*
disrespect (n)	ازدراء، عدم احترام	*izdirā', 'adamu iḥtirām*
disrespectful (adj)	عديم الاحترام، شائن	*'adīmul iḥtirām, shā'in*
disrupt (v)	مزق، عطل	*mazaqa, 'aṭṭala*
disruption (n)	تمزيق، تعطل	*tamzīq, ta'aṭṭul*
disruptive (adj)	ممزق، مخل	*mumazziq, mukhill*
dissatisfaction (n)	استياء، عدم رضى	*istiyā', 'adamu riḍan*
dissatisfied (n)	مستاء، غير راضٍ	*mustā'in, ghair rāḍin*
dissatisfy (v)	أسخط، كدر	*askhaṭa, kaddara*

dissect (v)	فحص، حلل	*faḥaṣa, ḥallala*
dissection (n)	تشريح، تحليل	*tashrīḥ, taḥlīl*
disseminate (v)	بذر، نشر	*badhara, nashara*
dissemination (n)	نشر، بث	*nashr, baththth*
dissension (n)	نزاع، خصام	*nizā', khiṣām*
dissent (v/n)	عارض، معارضة	*'āraḍa, mu'āraḍah*
dissertation (n)	مقالة، رسالة	*maqālah, risālah*
dissidence (n)	خلاف، تباين	*khilāf, tabāyun*
dissident (adj)	متضارب، مختلف	*mutaḍārib, mukhtalif*
dissimilar (adj)	متباين، غير متشابه	*mutabāyin, ghair mutashābih*
dissimilarity (n)	تباين، اختلاف	*tabāyun, ikhtilāf*
dissimulate (v)	تظاهر بما ليس فيه	*taẓāhara bimā laisa fīh*
dissimulation (n)	رياء، تصنع	*riyā', taṣannu'*
dissipate (v)	بدد، انقشع	*baddada, inqasha'a*
dissipated (adj)	منغمس في الملذات	*munghamis fil maladhdhāt*
dissipation (n)	انغماس في الملذات	*inghimās fil maladhdhāt*
dissociate (v)	فصل، فرق	*faṣala, farraqa*
dissociation (n)	فصل، انفصال	*faṣl, infiṣāl*
dissolute (adj)	منغمس في الملذات	*munghamis fil maladhdhāt*
dissolution (n)	حل، انحلال	*ḥall, inḥilāl*
dissolve (v)	حل، ذاب	*ḥalla, dhāba*
dissonance (n)	تنافر الأصوات	*tanāfurul aṣwāt*
dissonant (adj)	متنافر، غير متناغم	*mutanāfir, ghair mutanāghim*
dissuade (v)	دعا بالعدول عن	*da'ā bil 'udūl 'an*
distance (n)	فترة، مسافة	*fatrah, masāfah*

distance (v)	أبعد، بز	*ab‘ada, bazza*
distant (adj)	بعيد، قصي	*ba‘īd, qaṣī*
distaste (n)	عيف، كره	*‘aif, kurh*
distasteful (adj)	كريه، بغيض	*karīh, baghīd*
distil (v)	استقطر، رشح	*istaqṭara, rashshaḥa*
distillation (n)	تقطير، ترشيح	*taqṭīr, tarshīḥ*
distillery (n)	معمل التقطير	*ma‘malut taqṭīr*
distinct (adj)	جلي، بين	*jalī, bayyin*
distinction (n)	امتياز، تفوق	*imtiyāz, tafawwuq*
distinctive (adj)	مميز، فارق	*mumayyiz, fāriq*
distinctly (adv)	بوضوح، بجلاء	*bi wuḍūḥ, bi jalā*
distinguish (v)	ميز، فرق	*mayyaza, farraqa*
distinguished (adj)	ممتاز، بارز	*mumtāz, bāriz*
distort (v)	شوه، حرف	*shawwaha, ḥarrafa*
distortion (n)	تشوه، تحرف	*tashawwuh, taḥarruf*
distract (v)	صرف، حول عن	*ṣarafa, ḥawwala ‘an*
distracted (adj)	متحير، ذاهل	*mutaḥayyir, dhāhil*
distracting (adj)	مربك، مذهل	*murbik, mudhhil*
distraction (n)	ارتباك، اضطراب	*irtibāk, iḍṭirāb*
distraught (adj)	شديد الاضطراب	*shadīdul iḍṭirāb*
distress (n)	أسىً، ألم، كرب	*asan, alam, karb*
distress (v)	أحزن، أوجع	*aḥzana, auja‘a*
distressing (adj)	مؤلم، موجع	*mu’lim, mūji‘*
distribute (v)	وزع، نثر	*wazza‘a, nathara*
distribution (n)	توزيع،تسويق السلع	*tauzī‘, taswīqus sila‘*
distributive (adj)	توزيعي، إفرادي	*tauzī‘ī, ifrādī*
distributor (n)	موزع، موزعة	*muwazzi‘, muwazzi‘ah*
district (n)	مقاطعة، منطقة	*muqāṭa‘ah, minṭaqah*

distrust (n/v)	ارتياب، ارتاب	*irtiyāb, irtāba*
distrustful (adj)	مرتاب، غير واثق	*murtāb, ghair wāthiq*
disturb (v)	بعثر، شوش	*ba'thara, shawwasha*
disturbance (n)	اضطراب، تشويش	*iḍṭirāb, tashwīsh*
disturbing (adj)	مزعج، مشوش	*muz'ij, mushawwish*
disunite (v)	فصل، فرق	*faṣala, farraqa*
disunity (n)	شقاق، عدم اتحاد	*shiqāq, 'adamu ittiḥād*
disuse (n)	هجر، إهمال	*hajr, ihmāl*
ditch (n)	مسال، خندق	*masāl, khandaq*
ditch (v)	نبذ، حط على الماء	*nabadha, ḥaṭṭa'alal mā'*
dither (v)	تردد، ارتجف	*taraddada, irtajafa*
dither (n)	تردد، توقف	*taraddud, tawaqquf*
ditto (n)	علامة التكرير	*'alāmatut takrīr*
dive (v)	غطس، غاص	*ghaṭasa, ghāṣa*
diver (n)	غطاس، غواص	*ghaṭṭās, ghawwāṣ*
diverge (v)	انحرف، انشعب	*inḥarafa, insha'aba*
divergence (n)	انشعاب، انفراج	*inshi'āb, infirāj*
divergent (adj)	مختلف، منفرج	*mukhtalif, munfarij*
divers (adj)	متعدد، مختلف	*muta'addid, mukhtalif*
diverse (adj)	مختلف، متنوع	*mukhtalif, mutanawwi'*
diversification (n)	تنويع، تشكيل	*tanwī', tashkīl*
diversify (v)	شكل، نوع	*shakkala, nawwa'a*
diversion (n)	تحويل،تحول	*taḥwīl, taḥawwul*
diversity (n)	تنوع، اختلاف	*tanawwu', ikhtilāf*
divert (v)	حول، سلى	*ḥawwala, sallā*
diverting (adj)	مسلٍ، ملهٍ	*musallin, mulhin*
divest (v)	جرد، سلب	*jarrada, salaba*
divide (v)	قسم، حصص	*qassama, ḥaṣṣaṣa*

divided (adj)	مقسوم، منقسم	*maqsūm, munqasim*
divident (n)	مقسوم، ربيحة	*maqsūm, rabīḥah*
divider (n)	قاسم، مقسم	*qāsim, muqassim*
divination (n)	عرافة، كهانة	*'irāfah, kihānah*
divine (adj)	إلهي، سماوي	*ilāhī, samāwī*
divine (v)	تنبأ، اكتشف	*tanabba'a, iktashafa*
divinity (n)	ألوهية، لاهوت	*ulūhiyyah, lāhūt*
divisible (adj)	قابل للانقسام	*qābil lil inqisām*
division (n)	قسم، مقاطعة	*qism, muqāṭa'ah*
divisional (adj)	قسمي، تقسيمي	*qismī, taqsīmī*
divisive (adj)	مسبب للشقاق	*musabbib lish shiqāq*
divisor (n)	قاسم، مقسوم عليه	*qāsim, maqsūm 'alaih*
divorce (n/v)	طلاق، طلق	*ṭalāq, ṭallaqa*
divorcee (n)	مطلقة	*muṭallaqah*
divulge (v)	أفشى سرًا، باح	*afshā sirran, bāḥa*
dizziness (n)	دوار، دوخة	*duwār, daukhah*
dizzy (adj)	مصاب بدوار	*muṣāb bi duwār*
do (v)	فعل، عمل، قام	*fa'ala, 'amila, qāma*
docile (adj)	سهل الانقياد	*sahlul inqiyād*
dock (n)	حوض، رصيف	*ḥauḍ, raṣīf*
docket (n)	قائمة، جدول	*qā'imah, jadwal*
dockyard (n)	مسفن	*masfan*
doctor (n)	دكتور، طبيب	*duktūr, ṭabīb*
doctor (v)	عدل، عالج	*'addala, 'ālaja*
doctorate (n)	درجة الدكتوراه	*darajatud duktūrāh*
doctorinal (adj)	عقدي، فقهي	*'aqadī, fiqhī*
doctorine (n)	عقيدة، مذهب	*'aqīdah, madhhab*
document (n)	وثيقة، مستند	*wathīqah, mustanad*

documentary (adj)	وثائقي، موضوعي	*wathā'iqī, mauḍū'ī*
documentation (n)	توثيق، بينة موثقة	*tauthīq, bayyinah muwaththaqah*
dodge (v)	راغ، تنقل	*rāgha, tanaqqala*
dodge (n)	مراوغة، حيلة	*murāwaghah, ḥīlah*
dodger (n)	مراوغ، محتال	*murāwigh, muḥtāl*
doe (n)	أنثى الظبي	*unthaẓ ẓaby*
doer (n)	فاعل، عامل	*fā'il, 'āmil*
doff (v)	نزع الثياب	*naza'ath thiyāb*
dog (n/v)	كلب، تعقب	*kalb, ta'aqqaba*
doge days	أيام ركود	*ayyāmu rukūd*
dogfish (n)	كلب البحر	*kalbul baḥr*
dogged (adj)	عنيد، فظ	*'anīd, faẓẓ*
dogma (n)	عقيدة، تعليم	*'aqīdah, ta'līm*
dogmatic (adj)	جازم، تعسفي	*jāzim, ta'assufī*
dogmatism (n)	دوغماتية، جزمية	*dughmātiyyah, jazmiyyah*
doings (n)	أعمال، نشاطات	*a'māl, nashāṭāt*
doldrums (n)	كآبة، ركود	*ka'ābah, rukūd*
dole (v)	أعطى، تصدق	*a'ṭā, taṣaddaqa*
dole (n)	إعانة، حصة	*i'ānah, ḥiṣṣah*
deleful (adj)	كئيب، حزين	*ka'īb, ḥazīn*
doll (n)	دمية، امرأة جميلة	*dumyah, imra'ah jamīlah*
dollar (n)	دولار	*dūlār*
dollar diplomacy (n)	ديبلوماسية الدولار	*dīblūmāsiyyatud dūlār*
dolly (n)	دمية	*dumyah*
dolorous (adj)	محزن، مكتئب	*muḥzin, mukta'ib*

dolphin (n)	دلفين	*dulfin*
domain (n)	ملكية، حقل	*milkiyyah, ḥaql*
dome (n)	قبة	*qubbah*
domestic (adj)	عائلي، أهلي، داخلي	*'ā'ilī, ahlī, dākhilī*
domesticate (v)	أهل، دجن، أنس	*ahhala, dajjana, annasa*
domesticity (n)	ألفة، حياة منـــزلية	*ulfah, ḥayāt manziliyyah*
domicile (n)	منـــزل، مقر	*manzil, maqarr*
dominance (n)	سيطرة، هيمنة	*saiṭarah, haimanah*
dominant (adj)	غالب، مسيطر	*ghālib, musaiṭir*
dominate (v)	سيطر، أطل	*saiṭara, aṭalla*
domination (n)	سيطرة، تسلط	*saiṭarah, tasalluṭ*
domineering (adj)	مستبد، مسيطر	*mustabidd, musaiṭir*
dominion (n)	ملكية، سيادة	*milkiyyah, siyādah*
don (n)	أستاذ جامعة	*ustādhu jāmi'ah*
donate (v)	منح، وهب	*manaḥa, wahaba*
donation (n)	تبرع، هبة	*tabarru', hibah*
donkey (n)	حمار، شخص غبي	*ḥimār, shakhṣ ghabī*
donor (n)	معط، واهب	*mu'ṭin, wāhib*
doom (n)	قضاء، قدر	*qaḍā', qadar*
doomsday (n)	يوم الحشر	*yaumul ḥashr*
door (n)	باب، مدخل	*bāb, madkhal*
doorman (n)	بواب	*bawwāb*
doormat (n)	ممسحة الأرجل	*mimsaḥatul arjul*
doorstep (n)	درجة الباب	*darajatul bāb*
doorway (n)	مدخل	*madkhal*
dormant (adj)	ساكن، نائم	*sākin, nā'im*

dormer (n)	روشن	*raushan*
dormitory (n)	مهجع في مدرسة	*mahja' fī madrasah*
dosage (n)	جرعة، تجريع	*jar'ah, tajrī'*
dose (n/v)	جرعة، جرع	*jar'ah, jarra'a*
dot (n/v)	نقطة، نقط	*nuqṭah, naqqaṭa*
dotage (n)	خرف، هتر	*kharaf, hatr*
dote (n)	خرف، شغف	*kharaf, shaghaf*
dotty (adj)	مغفل، مرقط	*mughaffal, muraqqaṭ*
double (n/adj)	ضعف، مضاعف	*ḍi'f, muḍā'af*
double (v)	ضاعف، حنى	*ḍā'afa, ḥanā*
doublet (n)	صدرة	*ṣudrah*
doubly (n)	مضاعفاً	*muḍā'afan*
doubt (n)	ريب، شك	*raib, shakk*
doubt (v)	ارتاب، شك	*irtāba, shakka*
doubtful (adj)	مبهم، مشكوك	*mubham, mashkūk*
doubtless (adj)	موثوق، غير مشكوك	*mauthūq, ghair mashkūk*
dough (n)	عجين، عجينة	*'ajīn, 'ajīnah*
doughty (adj)	باسل، جريء	*bāsil, jarī'*
dour (adj)	صارم، عنيد	*ṣārim, 'anīd*
dove (n)	يمامة، لطيف	*yamāmah, laṭīf*
dowager (n)	أرملة، سيدة مسنة	*armalah, sayyidah musinnah*
dowdy (adj)	عتيق الزي	*'atīquz ziyy*
down (adj)	منخفض، كئيب	*munkhafiḍ, ka'īb*
down (adv/prep)	إلى أدنى، نزولاً إلى	*alā adnā, nuzūlan ilā*
downbeat (adj)	متشائم، كئيب	*mutashā'im, ka'īb*
downcast (adj)	مكتئب، منكسر	*mukta'ib, munkasir*

downfall (n)	سقوط مفاجئ	*suqūṭ mufāji'*
downgrade (v)	أخفض المنـــزلة	*akhfaḍal manzilah*
downhearted (adj)	حزين، كئيب	*ḥazīn, ka'īb*
downhill (adj/adv)	منحدر، نحو سفح التل	*munḥadar, naḥwa safḥit tall*
downright (adj)	صريح، محض	*ṣarīḥ, maḥḍ*
downstairs (n/adj)	دور أسفل، سفلي	*daur asfal, suflī*
downstairs (adv)	في الدور الأسفل	*fīd dauril asfal*
downstream (adv)	نحو مجرى النهر	*naḥwa majran nahr*
downtrodden (adj)	مدوس بالأقدام	*madūs bil aqdām*
downward (adj)	منحدر، نازل	*munḥadir, nāzil*
downwards (adv)	إلى أسفل	*ilā asfal*
downwind (adj/adv)	باتجاه الريح	*bittijāhir rīḥ*
downy (adj)	ناعم، أملس	*nā'im, amlas*
dowry (n)	بائنة، مهر	*bā'inah, mahr*
doyen (n)	أقدم الأعضاء	*aqdamul a'ḍā'*
doze (n/v)	نعاس، نعس	*nu'ās, na'asa*
dozen (n)	دزينة، اثنا عشر	*dazīnah, ithnā 'ashara*
dozy (adj)	نعسان، وسنان	*na'sān, wasnān*
drab (adj)	كئيب، رتيب	*ka'īb, ratīb*
draft (n)	حوالة مالية، جرعة، مسودة	*ḥawālah māliyyah, jar'ah, musawwadah*
draft (v)	أعد، وضع المسودة	*a'adda, waḍa'al musawwadah*
draftsman (n)	رسام، مخطط	*rassām, mukhaṭṭiṭ*
drag (n)	عائق، حركة بطيئة	*'ā'iq, ḥarakah baṭī'ah*
drag (v)	جر، انسحب	*jarra, insaḥaba*
dragon (n)	تنين، شخص صارم	*tinnīn, shakhṣ ṣārim*

dragoon (n)	جندي في سلاح الفرسان	*jundī fī silāḥil fursān*
drain (n)	مصرف، مجرى	*maṣraf, majrā*
drain (v)	صرف، استنـــزف	*ṣarrafa, istanzafa*
drainage (n)	نظام المصارف	*niẓāmul maṣārif*
drainpipe (n)	أنبوب التصريف	*umbūbut taṣrīf*
dram (n)	مقدار ضئيل	*miqdār ḍa'īl*
drama (n)	دراما، رواية تمثيلية	*darāmā, riwāyah tamthīliyyah*
dramatic (adj)	تمثيلي، دراماتيكي	*tamthīlī, darāmātīkī*
dramatics (n)	فن التمثيل	*fannut tamthīl*
dramatist (n)	كاتب مسرحي	*kātib masraḥī*
dramatization (n)	مسرحة، تمثيل	*masraḥah, tamthīl*
dramatize,-ise (v)	مسرح، مثل	*masraḥa, maththala*
drape (v)	تدلى، ثنى	*tadallā, thannā*
draper (n)	تاجر الأجواخ	*tājirul ajwākh*
drapery (n)	تجارة الأجواخ	*tijāratul ajwākh*
drastic (adj)	عنيف، قاسٍ	*'anīf, qāsin*
draught (n)	جرعة، تنشق	*jar'ah, tanashshuq*
draughtsman (n)	رسام، مخطط	*rassām, mukhaṭṭiṭ*
draw (v)	جر، انتزع، رسم	*jarra, intaza'a, rasama*
draw (n)	سحب، رسم	*saḥb, rasm*
drawback (n)	عائق، نقيصة	*'ā'iq, naqīṣah*
drawbridge (n)	جسر متحرك	*jisr mutaḥarrik*
drawer (n)	درج، ساحب، رسام	*durj, sāḥib, rassām*
drawing (n)	سحب، رسم، صورة	*saḥb, rasm, ṣūrah*
drawing-room (n)	غرفة الاستقبال	*ghurfatul istiqbāl*
drawn (adj)	مسحوب، متعب	*masḥūb, mut'ab*

dray (n)	كراجة	*karrājah*
dread (n)	خوف، فزع	*khauf, faza'*
dread (v)	رهب، روع	*rahaba, rawwa'a*
dreadful (adj)	مفزع، كريه، فظيع	*mufzi', karīh, faẓī'*
dream (n/v)	حلم، حلم	*ḥulm, ḥalama*
dreamer (n)	حالم، شارد الفكر	*ḥālim, shāridul fikr*
dreamland (n)	أرض الأحلام	*arḍul aḥlām*
dreamlike (adj)	شبيه بالحلم	*shabīh bil ḥulm*
dream world (n)	عالم الأحلام	*'ālamul aḥlām*
dreamy (adj)	كثير الأحلام	*kathīrul aḥlām*
dreariness (n)	وحشة، كآبة	*waḥshah, ka'ābah*
dreary (adj)	موحش، كئيب	*mūḥish, ka'īb*
dredge (v)	رفع الوحل	*rafa'al waḥl*
dredge (n)	أداة لرفع الوحل	*adāt li ra'il waḥl*
dregs (n)	ثفل، حثالة	*thufl, ḥuthālah*
drench (v)	بل، بلل	*balla, ballala*
dress (n)	كسوة، ثوب، لباس	*kiswah, thaub; libās*
dress (v)	كسا، زين، ألبس	*kasā, zayyana, albasa*
dresser (n)	ملبس، خزانة لأدوات الطهو	*mulabbis, khizānah li adawātiṭ ṭahw*
dressing (n)	ضمادة، كسوة	*ḍimādah, kiswah*
dressing-gown (n)	جلباب	*jilbāb*
dressing-room (n)	حجرة اللبس	*ḥujratul labs*
dressing-table (n)	مزينة، خوان الزينة	*mizyanah, khiwānuz zīnah*
dressmaker (n)	خياطة	*khayyāṭah*
dressmaking (n)	خياطة	*khiyāṭah*
dressy (adj)	أنيق، متأنق	*anīq, muta'anniq*

dribble (v)	سال اللعاب، قطر	*sālal lu'āb, qaṭara*
drift (v)	جرى برفق، طاف	*jarā bi rifq, ṭāfa*
drift (n)	جرف، ركام، ثلج	*jarf, rukām, thalj*
driftwood (n)	خشب طافٍ	*khashab ṭāfin*
drill (v)	ثقب، دربَ	*thaqaba, darraba*
drill (n)	مثقاب، تدريب، نسيج قطني	*mithqāb, tadrīb, nasīj quṭnī□*
drink (v)	شرب، امتص	*shariba, imtaṣṣa*
drink (n)	شراب، مشروب	*sharāb, mashrūb*
drinkable (adj)	صالح للشرب	*ṣāliḥ lish shurb*
drinker (n)	شارب، سكير	*shārib, sikkīr*
drinking (n)	شرب، سكر	*shurb, sukr*
drip (v/n)	تقطر، تقطر	*taqaṭṭara, taqaṭṭur*
drive (v)	ساق، قاد	*sāqa, qāda*
drive (n)	نزهة في سيارة، طريق خاصة	*nuzhah fī sayyārah, ṭarīq khaṣṣah*
driver (n)	سائق، مضرب	*sā'iq, miḍrab*
driving (n)	قيادة، سوق	*qiyādah, sauq*
driving (adj)	محرك، عاتٍ	*muḥarrik, 'ātin*
drizzle (v/n)	رذ، رذاذ	*radhdha, radhādh*
drizzly (adj)	مرذ	*muridhdh*
droll (adj)	شاذ، مضحك	*shādhdh, muḍḥik*
drone (v)	أز، دندن	*azza, dandana*
drone (n)	أزيز، دندنة	*azīz, dandanah*
drool (v)	سال اللعاب	*sālal lu'āb*
droop (v)	ابتأس، انخفض	*ibta'asa, inkhafaḍa*
drop (n)	قطرة، جرعة	*qaṭrah, jar'ah*
drop (v)	قطر، سقط، هبط	*qaṭara, saqaṭa, habaṭa*

droplet (n)	قطيرة، نقيطة	*quṭairah, nuqaiṭah*
dropsy (n)	مرض الاستسقاء	*maraḍul istisqā'*
dross (n)	خبث، نفاية	*khabath, nufāyah*
drought (n)	جدب، قحط	*jadb, qaḥṭ*
drove (n)	حشد، قطيع	*ḥashd, qaṭī'*
drover (n)	سائق الماشية	*sā'iqul māshiyah*
drown (v)	غرق، أغرق	*gharaqa, aghraqa*
drowsiness (n)	نعاس، خمول	*nu'ās, khumūl*
drowsy (adj)	نعسان، وسنان	*na'sān, wasnān*
drudge (n)	كادح	*kādiḥ*
drudgery (n)	كدح، عمل شاق	*kadḥ, 'amal shāqq*
drug (n)	عقار، دواء	*'aqqār, dawā'*
druggist (n)	تاجر الأدوية	*tājirul adwiyah*
drugstore (n)	صيدلية	*ṣaidaliyah*
drum (n)	طبل، طبلة	*ṭabl, ṭablah*
drum (v)	قرع الطبل	*qara'aṭ ṭabl*
drumbeat (n)	نقرة على الطبل	*naqrah 'alaṭ ṭabl*
drumstick (n)	نقارة، زخمة	*naqqārah, zakhmah*
drunk (adj)	سكران، ثمل	*sakrān, thamil*
drunkard (n)	مدمن الخمر	*mudminul khamr*
drunker (adj)	سكران، مخمور	*sakrān, makhmūr*
dry (adj)	جاف، يابس	*jāff, yābis*
dry (v)	جف، جفف	*jaffa, jaffafa*
dry-clean (v)	نظجف	*naẓjafa*
dry-cleaning (n)	نظجفة	*naẓjafah*
dry dock (n)	حوض جاف	*ḥauḍ jāff*
dry ice (n)	جليد جاف	*jalīd jāff*
dual (adj)	مثنى، ثنائي	*mathannā, thunā'ī*

dualism (n)	ثنائية	*thunā'iyyah*
duality (n)	ثنائية، ازدواجية	*thunā'iyyah, izdiwājiyyah*
dual-purpose (n)	ثنائي الغرض	*thunā'iyyul gharaḍ*
dub (v)	لقب، سمى	*laqqaba, sammā*
dubious (adj)	مبهم، ملتبس	*mubham, multabis*
ducal (adj)	دوقي، أميري	*dūqī, amīrī*
duchess (n)	دوقة، أميرة	*dūqah, amīrah*
duck (n)	بط، بطة	*baṭṭ, baṭṭah*
duck (v)	غطس، تجنب	*ghaṭasa, tajannaba*
duct (n)	قناة، أنبوب	*qanāt, umbūb*
dud (adj)	باطل، عديم القيمة	*bāṭil, 'adīmul qīmah*
dude (n)	متأنق، مديني	*mat'anniq, madīnī*
due (n)	حق، دين	*ḥaqq, dain*
due (adj)	واجب، وافٍ	*wājib, wāfin*
due (adv)	مباشرةً، بسبب	*mubāsharatan, bi sababi*
duel (n)	مبارزة، نزاع	*mubārazah, nizā'*
duff (adj)	معطل، عديم القيمة	*mu'aṭṭal, 'adīmul qīmah*
duffer (n)	شخص متجول	*shakhṣ mutajawwil*
duke (n)	دوق، أمير	*dūq, amīr*
dukedom (n)	دوقية، إمارة	*dūqiyyah, imārah*
dulcet (adj)	مطرب، عذب	*muṭrib, 'adhb*
dulcimer (n)	آلة موسيقية	*ālah mausīqiyyah*
dull (adj)	غبي، بليد	*ghabī, balīd*
dullness (n)	بلادة، غباوة	*balādah, ghabāwah*
duly (adv)	في حينه، كما يجب	*fī ḥīnihi, kamā yajib*
dumb (adj)	أبكم، أخرس	*abkam, akhras*

dumbness (n)	خرس، صمت	*kharas, ṣamt*
dummy (n)	أحمق، تمثال لعرض الملابس	*aḥmaq, timthāl li 'arḍil malābis*
dump (n)	مقلب النفايات، ذخيرة	*maqlabun nufāyāt, dhakhīrah*
dump (v)	ألقى، أفرغ	*alqā, afragha*
dumpy (adj)	قصير و بدين	*qaṣīr wa badīn*
dune (adj)	غبي، مغفل	*ghabī, mughaffal*
dune (n)	كثيب	*kathīb*
dung (n)	روث، دمان	*rauth, damān*
dunk (v)	غمس، غمر	*ghamasa, ghamara*
duo (n)	زوج، اثنان	*zauj, ithnān*
dupe (v)	خدع، احتال	*khada'a, iḥtāla*
duplicate (n/adj)	مزدوج، مطابق	*muzdawij, muṭābiq*
duplicate (v)	ضاعف، نسخ	*ḍā'afa, nasakha*
duplication (n)	نسخة طبق الأصل	*nuskhah ṭibqal aṣl*
duplicity (n)	نفاق، خداع	*nifāq, khidā'*
durable (adj)	متين، متحمل	*matīn, mutaḥammil*
duration (n)	دوام، مدة، وقت	*dawām, muddah, waqt*
during (prep)	في غضون، خلال	*fī ghuḍūn, khilāla*
dusk (n)	غسق، ظلام	*ghasaq, ẓalām*
dusky (adj)	مظلم، معتم	*muẓlim, mu'tim*
dust (n)	غبار، رماد	*ghubār, ramād*
dust (v)	نفض الرماد	*nafaḍar ramād*
dustbin (n)	صندوق القمامة	*ṣundūqul qumāmah*
duster (n)	منفضة، مئزر	*minfaḍah, mi'zar*
dustman (n)	زبال	*zabbāl*
dustpan (n)	لقاطة الكناسة	*laqqāṭatul kunāsah*
dusty (adj)	مترب، كثير الغبار	*mutrib, kathīrul ghubār*
dutiful (adj)	مطيع، ممتثل	*muṭī', mumtathil*

duty (n)	واجب، فرض، شغل	*wājib, fard, shughl*
dwell (v)	أقام، سكن	*aqāma, sakana*
dweller (n)	مقيم، كامن	*muqīm, kāmin*
dwelling (n)	مسكن، دار	*maskan, dār*
dwindle (v)	تضاءل، انحط	*taḍā'ala, inḥaṭṭa*
dye (n/v)	صبغة، صبغ	*ṣibghah, ṣabagha*
dynamic (adj)	ديناميكي، فعال	*dainānīkī, fa''āl*
dynamical (adj)	ديناميكي، نشيط	*dainānīkī, nashīṭ*
dynamically (adv)	بالقوة والنشاط	*bil quwwah wan nashāṭ*
dynamics (n)	علم الديناميكا	*'ilmud dainānīkā*
dynamism (n)	دينامية، نشاطية	*dainānīyyah, nashāṭiyyah*
dynamite (n)	ديناميت، نساف	*dainānīt, nassāf*
dynamite (v)	نسف بالديناميت	*nasafa bid dainānīt*
dynamo (n)	دنام، مولد	*dinām, muwallid*
dynasty (n)	سلالة ملكية	*sulālah milkiyyah*
dysentery (n)	إسهال، زحار	*ishāl, zuḥār*

E

each (adj/pron)	كل، كل واحد	*kull, kullu wāḥid*
eager (adj)	مشتاق، تواق	*mushtāq, tawwāq*
eagerness (n)	اشتياق، رغبة	*ishtiyāq, raghbah*
eagle (n)	عقاب، نسر	*'uqāb, nasr*
eagle-eyed (adj)	حاد البصر	*ḥāddul baṣar*
eaglet (n)	عقيب	*'uqayyib*
ear (n)	أذن، حاسة السمع	*udhun, ḥāssatus sam'*
earache (n)	وجع الأذن	*waj'ul udhun*

cardrum (n)	طبلة الأذن	*ṭablatul udhun*
earl (n)	إيرل، لقب شرف	*īral, laqabu sharaf*
earliness (n)	بكور، تبكير	*bukūr, tabkīr*
early (adj/adv)	مبكر، مبكراً	*mubakkir, mubakkiran*
earn (v)	كسب، استحق	*kasaba, istaḥaqqa*
earnest (adj)	جاد، غير هازل	*jādd, ghair hāzil*
earnestly (adv)	بجد، بحماس	*bi jidd, bi ḥamās*
earnings (n)	مال مكسوب	*māl maksūb*
earring (n)	قرط، حلق	*qurṭ, ḥalaq*
earshort (n)	مرمى السمع	*marmas sam'*
ear-splitting (adj)	مصم للأذن	*muṣimm lil udhun*
earth (n)	أرض، تراب	*arḍ, turāb*
earth (v)	أرض، دفن	*arraḍa, dafana*
earthbound (adj)	راسخ، أرضي	*rāsikh, arḍī*
earthen (adj)	ترابي، أرضي	*turābī, arḍī*
earthenware (n)	آنية خزفية	*āniyah khazafiyyah*
earthiness (n)	أرضانية	*arḍāniyyah*
earthliness (n)	دنيوية	*dunyawiyyah*
earthly (adj)	أرضي، دنيوي	*arḍī, dunyawī*
earthquake (n)	زلزلة، زلزال	*zalzalah, zilzāl*
earth science	علم أرضي	*'ilm arḍī*
earthshaking (adj)	مزلزل	*muzalzil*
earthworm (n)	خرطوم، دودة الأرض	*khurṭūm, dūdatul arḍ*
earthy (adj)	ترابي، عملي	*turābī, 'amalī*
earwig (n)	أبو مقس	*abū miqaṣṣ*
earworm (n)	حشرة الذرة	*ḥasharatudh dharrah*
ease (n)	أراح، هدأ، سهل	*arāḥa, hadda'a, sahhala*
easily (adv)	بسهولة، براحة	*bi suhūlah, bi rāḥah*

east (n/adj)	شرق، شرقي	*sharq, sharqī*
easterly (adj)	مشرقي	*mashriqī*
eastern (adj)	شرقي	*sharqī*
eastwards (adv)	شرقاً، نحو الشرق	*sharqan, naḥwash sharq*
easy (adj)	سهل، هين، لين	*sahl, hayyin, layyin*
easygoing (adj)	متمهل، هادىء	*mutamahhil, hādi'*
eat (v)	أكل، تناول	*akala, tanāwala*
eatable (adj)	صالح للأكل	*ṣāliḥ lil akl*
eater (n)	آكل	*ākil*
eaves (n)	طنف، إفريز	*ṭunuf, ifrīz*
eavesdrop (v)	اختلس السمع	*ikhtalasas sam'*
ebb (n)	جزر، انحطاط	*jazr, inḥiṭāṭ*
ebb (v)	انحط، انحسر المد	*inḥaṭṭa, inḥasaral madd*
ebony (n/adj)	خشب الأبنوس، أبنوسي	*khashabul abnūs, abnūsī*
ebullence (n)	اهتياج، حماسة شديدة	*ihtiyāj, ḥamāsah shadīdah*
ebullent (adj)	متحمس، مهتاج	*mutaḥammis, muhtāj*
eccentric (n/adj)	غريب الأطوار، شاذ	*gharībul aṭwār, shādhdh*
eccentricity (n)	غرابة الأطوار، شذوذ	*gharābatul aṭwār, shudhūdh*
ecclesiastic (n)	كاهن، كنسي	*kāhin, kanasī*
ecclesiastical (adj)	كنسي، إكليريكي	*kanasī, iklīrīkī*
echo (n/v)	صدًى، أصدى	*ṣadan, aṣdā*
eclipse (n)	كسوف، خسوف	*kusūf, khusūf*
eclipse (v)	كسف، خسف	*kasafa, khasafa*
economic (adj)	اقتصادي، مادي	*iqtiṣādī, māddī*
economical (adj)	مقتصد، اقتصادي	*muqtaṣid, iqtiṣādī*

economically (adv)	اقتصاديًا، باقتصاد	*iqtiṣādiyyan, biqtiṣād*
economics (n)	علم الاقتصاد	*'ilmul iqtiṣād*
economist (n)	عالم اقتصادي	*'ālim iqtiṣādī*
economize,-ise (v)	وفر، اقتصد	*waffara, iqtaṣada*
economy (n)	اقتصاد، تدبير	*iqtiṣād, tadbīr*
ecstasy (n)	انجذاب، وجد، ذهول	*injidhāb, wajd, dhuhūl*
ecstatic (adj)	مفتن، مذهل	*muftin, mudhhil*
eczema (n)	اكزيما	*ikzīmā*
eden (n)	جنة عدن	*jannatu 'adn*
edge (n)	حافة، حد، طفن	*ḥāffah, ḥadd, ṭifn*
edge (v)	حرك، دفع، تقدم	*ḥarraka, dafa'a, taqaddama*
edible (adj)	صالح للأكل	*ṣāliḥ lil akl*
edict (n)	مرسوم، أمر عالٍ	*marsūm, amr 'ālin*
edification (n)	تثقيف، ترقية	*tathqīf, tarqiyah*
edifice (n)	صرح، مبنى ضخم	*ṣarḥ, mabnā ḍakhm*
edify (v)	ثقف، نور	*thaqqafa, nawwara*
edit (v)	حرر، أعد للطبع	*ḥarrara, a'adda liṭ ṭab'*
edition (n)	طبعة، نسخة	*ṭab'ah, nuskhah*
editor (n)	رئيس التحرير، محرر	*ra'īsut taḥrīr, muḥarrir*
editorial (adj)	خاص برئيس التحرير	*khāṣṣ bi ra'īsit taḥrīr*
editorial (n)	افتتاحية	*iftitāḥiyyah*
educate (v)	ربى، علم	*rabbā, 'allama*
educated (adj)	مثقف، مهذب	*muthaqqaf, muhadhdhab*
education (n)	تربية، تعليم	*tarbiyah, ta'līm*
educational (adj)	تربوي، تعليمي	*tarbawī, ta'līmī*
educationist (n)	عالم تربوي	*'ālim tarbawī*
efface (v)	طمس، محا	*ṭamasa, maḥā*

effect (n)	أثر، نتيجة، تأثير	*athar, natījah, ta'thīr*
effect (v)	أحدث، سبب	*aḥdatha, sabbaba*
effective (adj)	مؤثر، فعال	*mu'aththir, fa''āl*
effectiveness (n)	تأثير، فاعلية	*ta'thīr, fā'iliyyah*
effectual (adj)	مؤثر، فعلي	*mu'aththir, fi'lī*
effeminacy (n)	تأنث، تخنث	*ta'annus, takhannus*
effeminate (adj)	متأنث	*muta'annis*
effervescent (adj)	مهتاج، فائر	*muhtāj, fā'ir*
effete (adj)	واهن، عاقر	*wāhin, 'āqir*
efficacious (adj)	فعال، مؤثر	*fa''āl, mu'aththir*
efficacy (n)	تأثير، فعالية	*ta'thīr, fa''āliyyah*
efficiency (n)	فعالية، كفاية	*fa''āliyyah, kifāyah*
efficient (adj)	فعال، كفي	*fa''āl, kafī*
effigy (n)	صورة، تمثال	*ṣūrah, timthāl*
effluent (n)	دفق، فرع نهر	*dafq, far'u nahr*
effort (n)	جهد، اجتهاد، مسعى	*juhd, ijtihād, mas'ā*
effortless (adj)	هين، عفوي	*hayyin, 'afwī*
effrontery (n)	وقاحة، سلاطة	*waqāḥah, salāṭah*
effusion (n)	اندفاق، انسكاب	*indifāq, insikāb*
effusive (adj)	مسرف، فائض	*musrif, fā'iḍ*
eg (for example)	مثلاً	*mathalan*
egalitarian (n)	مساواتي	*musāwātī*
egalitarianism (n)	مساواتية	*musāwātiyyah*
egg (n)	بيضة، بيض	*baiḍah, baiḍ*
eggcup (n)	كأس البيضة	*ka'sul baiḍah*
eggshell (n)	قشرة البيضة	*qishratul baiḍah*
ego (n)	الأنا، غرور	*al anā, ghurūr*
egocentric (adj)	أنوي، أناني، فردي	*anawī, anānī, fardī*
egoism (n)	أنانية، غرور	*anāniyyah, ghurūr*

egoist (n)	أناني، أنوي، مغرور	*anānī, anawī, maghrūr*
egotism (n)	غرور، أنانية	*ghurūr, anāniyyah*
egotist (n)	أنانى، متبجح	*anānī, mutabajjiḥ*
egregious (adj)	فظيع، فاضح	*faẓī', fāḍiḥ*
eight (n)	ثمانية	*thamāniyah*
eighteen (n)	ثمانية عشر	*thamāniyata 'ashar*
eighteenth (adj)	الثامن عشر	*ath thāmin 'ashara*
eighth (adj/n)	ثامن، ثمن	*thāmin, thumn*
eightieth (adj)	ثمانون	*thamānūn*
eighty (n)	ثمانون	*thamānūn*
either (adv/conj)	أيضا، إما	*aiḍan, immā*
ejaculate (v)	هتف، قذف	*hatafa, qadhafa*
ejaculation (n)	هتاف، قذف	*hutāf, qadhf*
eject (v)	طرح، قذف	*ṭaraḥa, qadhafa*
ejection (n)	قذف، طرح	*qdhf, ṭarḥ*
elaborate (v)	اتقن، طور، وسع	*ittaqana, ṭawwara, wassa'a*
elaboration (n)	توسيع، تفصيل	*tausī', tafṣīl*
elapse (v)	انقضى، مضى	*inqaḍā, maḍā*
elastic (n/adj)	مطوط، متمغط	*maṭūṭ, mutamaghghiṭ*
elasticity (n)	تمغط، مرونة	*tamaghghuṭ, murūnah*
elated (adj)	مبتهج، تياه	*mubtahij, tayyāh*
elation (n)	ابتهاج، عجب	*ibtihāj, 'ujb*
elbow (n/v)	مرفق، دفع بالمرفق	*mirfaq, dafa'a bil mirfaq*
elder (n/adj)	أسن، أرشد	*asann, arshad*
elderly (adj)	متقدم في العمر	*mutaqaddim fil 'umr*
eldest (adj)	أكبر سنًا	*akbaru sinnan*
elect (v)	انتخب، اختار	*intakhaba, ikhtāra*

election (n)	انتخاب، اصطفاء	*intikhāb, iṣṭifā'*
electioneering (n)	فعالية للانتخاب	*fa''āliyyah lil intikhāb*
elective (adj/n)	انتخابي، موضوع	*intikhābī, mauḍū'*
	اختياري	*ikhtiyārī*
elector (n)	ناخب، مقترع	*nākhib, muqtari'*
electoral (adj)	انتخابي	*intikhābī*
electoral college	هيئة انتخابية	*hay'ah intikhābiyyah*
electorate (n)	جمهور الناخبين	*jumhūrun nākhibīn*
electric-al (adj)	كهربائي	*kahrabā'ī*
electrician (n)	مشتغل بالكهرباء	*mushtaghil bil kahrabā'*
electricity (n)	كهرباء	*kahrabā'*
electrification (n)	كهربة، تكهرب	*kahrabah, takahrub*
electrify (v)	كهرب	*kahraba*
electron (n)	الكترون، كهيرب	*iliktūrūn, kuhairib*
electronic (adj)	الكتروني	*iliktūrūnī*
electronics (n)	الكترونيات	*iliktūrūniyyāt*
elegance (n)	أناقة، كياسة	*anāqah, kiyāsah*
elegant (adj)	كيس، أنيق، رائع	*kayyis, anīq, rā'i'*
elegy (n)	رثاء، مرثاة	*rithā', marthāt*
element (n)	عنصر، جوهر، مبادئ	*'unṣur, jauhar, mabādi'*
elemental (adj)	عنصري، أساسي	*'unṣurī, asāsī*
elementary (adj)	ابتدائي، عنصري	*ibtidā'ī, 'unṣurī*
elephant (n)	فيل	*fīl*
elephantine (adj)	فيلي، ضخم	*fīlī, ḍakhm*
elevate (v)	رفع، أقام	*rafa'a, aqāma*
elevated (adj)	مرتفع، رفيع	*murtafi', rafī'*
elevating (adj)	منعش، رافع	*mun'ish, rāfi'*
elevation (n)	ارتفاع، تل، سمو	*irtifā', tall, sumuww*

elevator (n)	رافع، آلة رافعة	*rāfi', ālah rāfi'ah*
eleven (n)	أحد عشر	*aḥada 'ashara*
eleventh (adj)	حادي عشر	*ḥādī 'ashara*
eleventh hour	أخر لحظة	*ākhiru laḥẓah*
elicit (v)	استخرج، انتزع	*istakhraja, intaza'a*
elide (v)	رخم، حذف	*rakhkhama, ḥadhafa*
eligibility (n)	أهلية للانتخاب	*ahliyyah lil intikhāb*
eligible (adj)	مؤهل للانتخاب	*mu'ahhal lil intikhāb*
eliminate (v)	أزال، أخرج، حذف	*azāla, akhraja, ḥadhafa*
elimination (n)	إزالة، إقصاء	*izālah, iqṣā'*
elision (n)	ترخيم، حذف	*tarkhīm, ḥadhf*
elite (n)	نخبة، صفوة	*nukhbah, ṣafwah*
elixir (n)	الإكسير	*al iksīr*
elk (n)	الإلكة، أيل	*al ilkah, ayyil*
ellipsis (n)	حذف كلمة	*ḥazfu kalimah*
elm (n)	خشب الدردار	*khashabud dardār*
elocution (n)	حسن الإلقاء	*ḥusnul ilqā'*
elongate (v)	أطال، امتد	*aṭāla, imtadda*
elongated (adj)	ممدود، مطول	*mamdūd, muṭawwal*
elongation (n)	استطالة، تطويل	*istiṭālah, taṭwīl*
elope (v)	فر مع امرأة	*farra ma'a imra'ah*
elopement (n)	فرار مع الحبيب	*firār ma'al ḥabīb*
eloquence (n)	فصاحة، حسن البيان	*faṣāḥah, ḥusnul bayān*
eloquent (adj)	فصيح، بليغ	*faṣīḥ, balīgh*
else (adv)	أيضاً، وإلا	*aiḍan, wa illā*
elsewhere (adv)	في مكان آخر	*fi makān ākhar*
elucidate (v)	أوضح، شرح	*auḍaḥa, sharaḥa*
elucidation (n)	شرح، تفصيل	*sharḥ, tafṣīl*

elude (v)	راغ، تملص	*rāgha, tamallaṣa*
elusive (adj)	متملص، مراوغ	*mutamalliṣ, murāwigh*
emaciated (adj)	هزيل، سقيم	*hazīl, saqīm*
emaciation (n)	إهزال، إضعاف	*ihzāl, iḍ'āf*
email (n)	بريد الكتروني	*barīd illikturūnī*
emanate (v)	انبعث، خرج	*imba'atha, kharaja*
emanation (n)	انبثاق، انبعاث،خروج	*imbithāq, imbi'āth, khurūj*
emancipate (v)	أعتق، حرر	*a'taqa, ḥarrara*
emancipation (n)	إعتاق، تحرير	*i'tāq, taḥrīr*
emasculate (v)	خصى، أضعف	*khaṣā, aḍ'afa*
embalm (v)	ضمخ، صان من الفساد	*ḍammakha, ṣāna minal fasād*
embankment (n)	سد، جسر	*sadd, jisr*
embargo (n)	حظر، منع	*ḥaẓr, man'*
embark (v)	ركب السفينة، أنزل	*rakibas safīnah, anzala*
embarrass (v)	ورط، أربك	*warraṭa, arbaka*
embarrassed (adj)	مرتبك، حائر	*murtabik, ḥā'ir*
embarrassing (adj)	مربك، معقد	*murbik, mu'aqqad*
embarrassment (n)	ارتباك، حيرة	*irtibāk, ḥairah*
embassy (n)	سفارة	*sifārah*
embattled (adj)	محصن، معد للمعركة	*muḥaṣṣan, mu'add lil ma'rakah*
embed (v)	طمر، طوق بإحكام	*ṭamara, ṭawwaqa bi iḥkām*
embellish (v)	زين، زخرف	*zayyana, zakhrafa*
embellishment (n)	زينة، زخرفة	*zīnah, zakhrafah*
embezzle (v)	اختلس، سلب	*ikhtalasa, salaba*

embezzlement (n)	اختلاس، سرقة	*ikhtilās, sariqah*
embitter (v)	نغص، مرر	*naghghaṣa, marrara*
embitterment (n)	مرارة	*marārah*
emblazon (v)	زخرف، مجد	*zakhrafa, majjada*
emblazonment (n)	زخرفة بألوان زاهية	*zakhrafah bi alwān zāhiyah*
emblem (n)	شعار، رمز	*shi'ār, ramz*
emblematic (adj)	شعاري، رمزي	*shi'ārī, ramzī*
embodiment (n)	تجسيد، تجسد	*tajsīd, tajussud*
embody (v)	جسد، ضمن	*jassada, ḍammana*
embolden (v)	شجع، جرأ	*shajja'a, jarra'a*
embrace (v)	حضن، اعتنق	*ḥaḍana, i'tanaqa*
embrace (n)	اعتناق، قبول، حضن	*i'tināq, qabūl, ḥiḍn*
embrocation (n)	دلوك، مرهم	*dalūk, marham*
embroider (v)	طرز، زخرف	*ṭarraza, zakhrafa*
embroidery (n)	تطريز، شيء مطرز	*taṭrīz, shay' muṭarraz*
embroil (v)	شوش، ورط	*shawwasha, warraṭa*
embryo (n)	جنين	*janīn*
embryologist (n)	اختصاصي في علم الأجنة	*ikhtiṣāṣī fī 'ilmil ajinnah*
embryology (n)	علم الأجنة	*'ilmul ajinnah*
emend (v)	صحح، نقح	*ṣaḥḥaḥa, naqqaḥa*
emendation (n)	تصحيح، تنقيح	*taṣḥīḥ, tanqīḥ*
emerald (n/adj)	زمرد، زمردي	*zumurrud, zumurrudī*
emerge (v)	برز، بزغ	*baraza, bazagha*
emergence (n)	بزوغ، انبثاق	*buzūgh, imbithāq*
emergency (n)	طارىء، حاجة ملحة	*ṭāri', ḥājah muliḥḥah*
emergent (adj)	طارئ، بادٍ	*ṭāri', bādin*

emery (n)	صنفرة، صنباذج	*ṣanfarah, ṣumbādhaj*
emetic (adj)	مقيئ	*muqayyi'*
emigrant (n)	مهاجر، نازح	*muhājir, nāziḥ*
emigrate (v)	هاجر، نزح	*hājara, nazaḥa*
emigration (n)	هجرة، نزوح	*hijrah, nuzūḥ*
eminence (n)	سمو، رفعة	*sumuww, rif'ah*
eminent (adj)	بارز، ناتئ، سامٍ	*bāriz, nāti', sāmin*
emir (n)	أمير	*amīr*
emirate (n)	إمارة	*imārah*
emissary (n)	رسول، مبعوث	*rasūl, mab'ūth*
emission (n)	انبعاث، إصدار	*imbi'āth, iṣdār*
emit (v)	انبعث، قذف، صدر	*imba'atha, qadhafa, ṣadara*
emollient (adj)	مرطب، مهدئ	*muraṭṭib, muhaddi'*
emolument (n)	راتب، أجر	*rātib, ajr*
emotion (n)	عاطفة، إحساس	*'āṭifah, iḥsās*
emotional (adj)	مثير للعاطفة، عاطفي	*muthīr lil 'āṭifah, 'āṭifī*
emotionless (adj)	عديم العاطفة	*'adīmul 'āṭifah*
emotive (adj)	عاطفي، انفعالي	*'āṭifī, infi'ālī*
empathy (n)	اعتناق	*i'tināq*
emperor (n)	امبراطور، عاهل	*imbarāṭūr, 'āhil*
emphasis (n)	توكيد، تشديد	*taukīd, tashdīd*
emphasize,-ise (v)	أكد، شدد	*akkada, shaddada*
emphatic (adj)	مؤكد، مشدد، تاكيدي	*mu'akkad, mushaddad, ta'kīdī*
empire (n)	مملكة، امبراطورية	*mamlakah, imbarāṭūriyyah*
empirical (adj)	تجريبي، اختباري	*tajrībī, ikhtibārī*

empiricism (n)	تجريبية، تدجيل	*tajrībiyyah, tadjīl*
emplacement (n)	موضع المدفع	*mauḍi'ul midfa'*
employ (v)	وظف، استخدم	*wazzafa, istakhdama*
employ (n)	وظيفة، خدمة	*wazīfah, khidmah*
employee (n)	أجير، مستخدم، موظف	*ajīr, mustakhdam, muwazzaf*
employer (n)	مستخدم، مؤجر	*mustakhdim, mu'ajjir*
employment (n)	وظيفة، عمل، خدمة	*wazīfah, 'amal, khidmah*
emporium (n)	مركز تجاري	*markaz tijārī*
empower (v)	فوض، مكن	*fawwaḍa, makkana*
empowerment (n)	تفويض، سلطة	*tafwīḍ, sulṭah*
empress (n)	امبراطورة، عاهلة	*imbarāṭūrah, 'āhilah*
emptiness (n)	فراغ، خلاء، خلو	*farāgh, khalā', khuluww*
empty (adj)	فارغ، خالٍ	*fārigh, khālin*
empty (v)	جرد، أفرغ، صب	*jarrada, afragha, ṣabba*
empty-handed (adj)	صفر اليدين	*ṣifrul yadain*
empty-headed (adj)	أحمق، غبي	*aḥmaq, ghabī*
emulate (v)	نافس، باری	*nāfasa, bārā*
emulation (n)	منافسة، مباراة	*munāfasah, mubārāt*
emulator (n)	محاكي، مضاهي	*muḥākī, muḍāhī*
emulsion (n)	مستحلب، طبقة حساسة	*mustaḥlab, ṭabaqah ḥassāsah*
enable (v)	قدر، مكن	*qaddara, makkana*
enact (v)	أجرى، سن، مثل	*ajrā, sanna, maththala*
enactment (n)	تشريع، تمثيل	*tashrī', tamthīl*
en block (adv)	جملة	*jumlatan*
encamp (v)	خيم، عسكر	*khayyama, 'askara*
encampment (n)	مخيم، معسكر	*mukhayyam, mu'askar*

encapsulate (v)	كبسل، غلف	*kabsala, ghallafa*
encase (v)	غطى، وضع في صندوق	*ghaṭṭā, waḍa'a fi ṣundūq*
enchant (v)	سحر، فتن	*saḥara, fatana*
enchanter (n)	ساحر، فاتن	*sāḥir, fātin*
enchantment (n)	سحر، افتتان	*siḥr, iftinān*
enchantress (n)	ساحرة، امرأة فاتنة	*sāḥirah, imra'ah fātinah*
encircle (v)	طوق، أحاط	*ṭawwaqa, aḥāṭa*
enclave (n)	مقاطعة محاطة بأرض أجنبية	*muqāṭa'ah muḥāṭah bi arḍ ajnabiyyah*
enclose (v)	وضع في غلاف، سيج	*waḍa'a fi ghilāf, sayyaja*
enclosure (n)	سياج، مرفق	*siyāj, murfaq*
encode (v)	حول إلى رموز تلغرافية	*ḥawwala ilā rumūz tiligharāfiyyah*
encompass (v)	طوق، أحاط بـ	*ṭawwaqa, aḥāṭa bi*
encore (n/interj)	استعادة، مرةً ثانية	*isti'ādah, marratan thāniyah*
encounter (v)	صادم، واجه، قابل	*ṣādama, wājaha, qābala*
encounter (n)	مصادمة، مناوشة	*muṣādamah, munāwashah*
encourage (v)	شجع، استحث	*shajja'a, istaḥaththa*
encouragement (n)	تشجيع، تحريض	*tashjī', taḥrīḍ*
encouraging (adj)	مشجع، محرض	*mushajji', muḥarriḍ*
encroach (v)	تعدى، تجاوز	*ta'addā, tajāwaza*
encroachment (n)	اعتداء، تجاوز	*i'tidā', tajāwuz*
encumber (v)	عاق، ثقل على	*'āqa, thaqqala 'alā*
encumbrance (n)	عائق، ثقلة، حمل	*'ā'iq, thiqlah, ḥiml*
encyclopaedia,-pedia	دائرة معارف، موسوعة	*dā'iratu ma'ārif, mausū'ah*
encyclopaedic (adj)	معلمي، موسوعي	*ma'lamī, mausū'ī*

end (n)	نهاية، آخر، نتيجة	*nihāyah, ākhir, natījah*
end (v)	انتهى، أنهى، مات	*intahā, anhā, māta*
endanger (v)	عرض للخطر	*'arraḍa lil khaṭar*
endear (v)	حبب، كرم	*ḥabbaba, karrama*
endearment (n)	تحبب، تودد	*taḥabbub, tawaddud*
endeavour,-vor (v/n)	حاول، محاولة	*ḥāwala, muḥāwalah*
endemic (n/adj)	مستوطن، متوطن	*mustauṭin, mutawaṭṭin*
ending (n)	نهاية، انتهاء، موت	*nihāyah, intihā', maut*
endless (adj)	أبدي، متصل	*abadī, muttaṣil*
endorse (v)	ظهر، وافق	*ẓahhara, wāfaqa*
endorsement (n)	تظهير، موافقة	*taẓhīr, muwāfaqah*
endow (v)	وهب، وقف	*wahaba, waqafa*
endowment (n)	هبة، منح، وقف	*hibah, manḥ, waqf*
endurable (adj)	محتمل	*muḥtamal*
endurance (n)	تحمل، ثبات	*taḥammul, thabāt*
endure (v)	تحمل، ثبت، صبر	*taḥammala, thabata, ṣabara*
enduring (adj)	ثابت، حليم	*thābit, ḥalīm*
enema (n)	حقنة شرجية	*ḥuqnah sharajiyyah*
enemy (n)	عدو، خصم	*'aduww, khaṣm*
energetic (adj)	نشيط، فعال	*nashīṭ, fa''āl*
energetically (adv)	بنشاط، بهمة	*bi nashāṭ, bi himmah*
energyze,-yse (v)	نشط، استحث	*nashshaṭa, istaḥaththa*
energy (n)	نشاط، قوة	*nashāṭ, quwwah*
enervate (v)	أضعف، أوهن	*aḍ'afa, auhana*
enfeeble (v)	أضعف، ثبط	*aḍ'afa, thabbaṭa*
enfold (v)	لف، غلف	*laffa, ghallafa*
enforce (v)	قوى، نفذ	*qawwā, naffadha*

enforcement (n)	إلزام، تنفيذ	*ilzām, tanfīz*
enfranchise (v)	أعتق، منح حق الاقتراع	*a'taqa, manaḥa ḥaqqal iqtirā'*
engage (v)	جذب، وعد، خطب	*jadhaba, wa'ada, khaṭaba*
engaged (adj)	مشغول، مخطوبة	*mashghūl, makhṭūbah*
engagement (n)	خطبة، عهد، موعد	*khiṭbah, 'ahd, mau'id*
engaging (adj)	فاتن، جذاب	*fātin, jadhdhāb*
engender (v)	ولد، أحدث	*wallada, aḥdatha*
engine (v)	محرك، أداة ميكانيكية	*muḥarrik, adāt mīkānīkiyyah*
engineer (n)	مهندس	*muhandis*
engineer (v)	هندس، حرك، دبر	*handasa, ḥarraka, dabbara*
engineering (n)	هندسة	*handasah*
England (n)	إنجلترا	*injiltarā*
English (n/adj)	انكيزي، انكليزية	*inkilīzī, inkilīziyyah*
engrave (v)	نقش، طبع في الذهن	*naqasha, ṭaba'a fidh dhihn*
engraver (n)	نقاش، حفار	*naqqāsh, ḥaffār*
engraving (n)	نقش، صناعة الحفر	*naqsh, ṣinā'atul ḥafr*
engross (v)	استغرق، نسخ	*istaghraqa, nasakha*
engrossed (adj)	مستغرق، منهمك	*mustaghriq, munhamik*
engrossing (adj)	فاتن، مستحوذ	*fātin, mustaḥwidh*
engrossment (n)	انهماك، استغراق	*inhimāk, istighrāq*
engulf (v)	غمر، انغمس	*ghamara, inghamasa*
enhance (v)	غلى، زين، حسن	*ghallā, zayyana, ḥassana*

enhancment (n)	زينة، جمال	*zīnah, jamāl*
Enigma (n)	لغز، أحجية	*lughz, uḥjiyyah*
enigmatic (adj)	غامض، مبهم	*ghāmiḍ, mubham*
enjoin (v)	فرض، أمر	*faraḍa, amara*
enjoy (v)	استمتع، تلذذ	*istamta'a, taladhdhadha*
enjoyable (adj)	ممتع، سار	*mumti', sārr*
enjoyment (n)	استمتاع، هناء	*istimtā', hanā'*
enlarge (v)	كبر، وسع	*kabbara, wassa'a*
enlargement (n)	توسيع، تفصيل	*tausī', tafṣīl*
enlighten (v)	نور، ثقف	*nawwara, thaqqafa*
enlightened (adj)	مثقف، مطهر	*muthaqqaf, muṭahhar*
enlightenment (n)	تثقيف، تنوير	*tathqīf, tanwīr*
enlist (v)	جند، تجند	*jannada, tajannada*
enlistment (n)	تجنيد، تجند	*tajnīd, tajannud*
enliven (v)	أحيا، أنعش	*aḥyā, an'asha*
en masse (adv)	جملةً، ككل	*jumlatan, kakull*
enmity (n)	عداوة، خصومة	*'adāwah, khuṣūmah*
ennoble (v)	نبل، شرف	*nabbala, sharrafa*
enormity (n)	ضخامة، قباحة، شناعة	*ḍakhāmah, qabāḥah, shanā'ah*
enormous (adj)	ضخم، هائل، شنيع	*ḍakhm, hā'il, shanī'*
enough (n/adj)	مقدار كافٍ، كاف	*miqdār kāfin, kāfin*
enquire=inquire		
enquiry=inquiry		
enrage (v)	أغضب، أسخط	*aghḍaba, askhaṭa*
enrapture (v)	أفعم بالسرور، أبهج	*af'ama bis surūr, abhaja*
enrich (v)	أغنى، خصب	*aghnā, khaṣṣaba*

enrol (enroll) (v)	سجل، أدرج	*sajjala, adraja*
enrolment (n)	تسجيل، إدراج	*tasjīl, idrāj*
en route (adv)	في الطريق	*fiṭ ṭarīq*
enshrine (v)	ادخر، احتفظ	*iddakhara, iḥtafaẓa*
enshroud (v)	حجب، ستر	*ḥajaba, satara*
ensign (n)	راية، رمز	*rāyah, ramz*
enslave (v)	استعبد، استرق	*ista'bada, istaraqqa*
enslavement (n)	استعباد، استرقاق	*isti'bād, istirqāq*
ensue (v)	تلا، تبع	*talā, tabi'a*
ensuing (adj)	تال، آت	*tālin, ātin*
ensure (insure) (v)	ضمن، كفل	*ḍamina, kafala*
entail (v)	استلزم، وقف	*istalzama, waqafa*
entangle (v)	عقد، أربك	*'aqqada, arbaka,*
entanglement (n)	ارتباك، ورطة	*irtibāk, warṭah*
entente (n)	حلف، اتفاق ودي	*ḥilf, ittifāq wuddī*
enter (v)	دخل، أدخل	*dakhala, adkhala*
enterprise (n)	مشروع، مغامرة	*mashrū', mughāmarah*
enterprising (adj)	مغامر، مقدام	*mughāmir, miqdām*
entertain (v)	ضيف، سلى	*ḍayyafa, sallā*
entertainer (n)	مضيف، مغنٍ	*muḍayyif, mughannin*
entertaining (adj)	مسلٍّ، ممتع	*musallin, mumti'*
entertainment (n)	ضيافة، تسلية	*ḍiyāfah, tasliyah*
enthral (enthrall) (v)	فتن، أسر، استعبد	*fatana, asara, ista'bada*
enthralment,- allm-	استرقاق، استعباد	*istirqāq, isti'bād*
enthrone (v)	توج، عظم	*tawwaja, 'aẓẓama*
enthuse (v)	حمس، تحمس	*ḥammasa, taḥammasa*
enthusiasm (n)	حماسة، غيرة	*ḥamāsah, ghairah*
enthusiast (n)	متحمس، غيور	*mutaḥammis, ghayūr*

enthusiastic (adj)	متحمس	*mutaḥammis*
enthusiastically (adv)	بحماسة، بحمية	*bi ḥamāsah, bi ḥamiyyah*
entice (v)	أغرى، لفت	*aghrā, lafata*
enticement (n)	تحريض، إغراء	*taḥrīḍ, ighrā'*
enticing (adj)	محرض، مغري	*muḥarriḍ, mughrī*
entire (adj)	تام، كامل	*tāmm, kāmil*
entirely (adv)	تماماً، كليةً	*tamāman, kulliyyatan*
entitle (v)	لقب، خول	*laqqaba, khawwala*
entity (n)	وجود، كيان	*wujūd, kiyān*
entomb (v)	دفن، قبر	*dafana, qabara*
entomologist (n)	عالم بالحشرات	*'ālim bil ḥasharāt*
entomology (n)	علم الحشرات	*'ilmul ḥasharāt*
entourage (n)	حاشية، بطانة	*ḥāshiyah, biṭānah*
entrails (n)	أحشاء، أمعاء	*aḥshā', am'ā'*
entrance (n)	دخول، مدخل	*dukhūl, madkhal*
entrance (v)	أبهج، أذهل	*abhaja, adhhala*
entrant (n)	داخل، مشارك	*dākhil, mushārik*
entrap (v)	احتبل، صاد بفخ	*iḥtabala, ṣāda bi fakhkh*
entrapment (n)	احتبال	*iḥtibāl*
entreat (v)	تضرع، استعطف	*taḍarra'a, ista'ṭafa*
entreaty (n)	تضرع، التماس	*taḍarru', iltimās*
entrench (v)	رسخ، خندق	*rassakha, khandaqa*
entrenchment (n)	تحصين، ترسيخ	*taḥṣīn, tarsīkh*
entrepreneur (n)	مقاول، مغامر	*muqāwil, mughāmir*
entrust (v)	أودع، ائتمن	*auda'a, i'tamana*
entry (n)	دخول، مدخل، تدوين	*dukhūl, madkhal, tadwīn*

entwine (v)	شبك، ضفر	*shabbaka, ḍafara*
enumerate (v)	عدد، سرد	*'addada, sarada*
enumeration (n)	عد، سرد	*'add, sard*
enunciate (v)	أعلن، صرح	*a'lana, ṣarraḥa*
enunciation (n)	إعلان، بيان	*i'lān, bayān*
envelop (v)	لف، غلف	*laffa, ghallafa*
envelope (n)	ظرف، غلاف	*ẓarf, ghilāf*
enviable (adj)	مشتهى، مطموع	*mushtahā, maṭmū'*
envious (adj)	حسود، حاسد	*ḥasūd, ḥāsid*
environment (n)	بيئة، محيط	*bī'ah, muḥīṭ*
environmental (adj)	بيئي	*bī'ī*
environs (n)	ضواحي، نواحي	*ḍawāḥī, nawāḥī*
envisage (v)	تصور، تخيل	*taṣawwara, takhayyala*
envoy (n)	رسول، مندوب	*rasūl, mandūb*
envy (v)	غبط، حسد	*ghabaṭa, ḥasada*
envy (n)	حسد، غبط	*ḥasad, ghabṭ*
ephemera (n)	شيء سريع الزوال	*shay' sarī'uz zawāl*
ephemeral (adj)	سريع الزوال، زائل	*sarī'uz zawāl, zā'il*
epic (n)	شعر ملحمي	*shi'r malḥamī*
epicentre, -ter (n)	مركز سطحي	*markaz saṭḥī*
epicure (n)	أبيقوري، منغمس فى الملذات	*abīqūrī, munghamis fil maladhdhāt*
epicurean (adj)	أبيقوري، متنعم	*abīqūrī, mutana''im*
epidemic (n/adj)	وباء، وبائي	*wabā', wabā'ī*
epigram (n)	أبيغرام، قصيدة قصيرة	*abīgharām, qaṣīdah qaṣīrah*
epigrammatic (adj)	أبيغرامي، محكم	*abīgharāmī, muḥkam*
epigraph (n)	كتابة منقوشة	*kitābah manqūshah*

epilogue (epilog) (n)	خاتمة الكتاب	*khātimatul kitāb*
episcopal (adj)	أسقفي	*usqufī*
episode (n)	ايبيزود، حادثة عرضية	*ībīzūd, ḥādithah 'araḍiyyah*
episodic (adj)	ايبيزودي، عرضي	*ībīzūdī, 'araḍī*
epistle (n)	رسالة، رقعة	*risālah, ruq'ah*
epistolary (adj)	رسالي، رسائلي	*risālī, rasā'ilī*
epitaph (n)	عبارة مكتوبة على ضريح	*'ibārah maktūbah 'alā ḍarīḥ*
epithet (n)	لقب، نعت	*laqab, na't*
epitome (n)	مثال، ملخص	*mithāl, mulakhkhaṣ*
epitomize,-ise (v)	لخص، اختصر	*lakhkhaṣa, ikhtaṣara*
epoch (n)	عهد، فترة	*'ahd, fatrah*
epoch-making (adj)	صانع عهد جديد	*ṣāni'u 'ahd jadīd*
equable (adj)	مستوٍ، منتظم	*mustawin, muntaẓim*
equal (n)	ند، عدل، نظير	*nidd, 'adl, naẓīr*
equal (adj)	مساوٍ، متساوٍ	*musāwin, mutasāwin*
equal (v)	ضاهى، ساوى	*ḍāhā, sāwā*
equality (n)	استواء، مساواة	*istiwā', musāwāt*
equalization,-tion (n)	تسوية، تساوٍ	*taswiyah, tasāwin*
equalize,-ise (v)	سوى، عادل	*sawwā, 'ādala*
equally (adv)	على حد سواء، بالتساوي	*'alā ḥadd sawā', bit tasāwī*
equanimity (n)	ثبات الجأش، اتزان	*thabātul ja'sh, ittizān*
equate (v)	عدل، وازن	*'addala, wāzana*
equation (n)	معادلة، موازنة	*mu'ādalah, muwāzanah*
equator (n)	خط الاستواء	*khaṭṭul istiwā'*

equatorial (adj)	استوائي	*istiwā'ī*
equestrian (n/adj)	فارس، فروسي	*fāris, furūsī*
equidistant (adj)	متساوي الأبعاد	*mutasāwiyul ab'ād*
equilateral (adj)	متساوي الأضلاع	*mutasāwiyul aḍlā'*
equilibrium (n)	توازن، اتزان	*tawāzun, ittizān*
equine (adj)	فرسي، خيلي	*farasī, khailī*
equip (v)	زود، جهز	*zawwada, jahhaza*
equipment (n)	تجهيزات، معدات	*tajhīzāt, mu'addāt*
equitable (adj)	منصف، مقسط	*munṣif, muqsiṭ*
equity (n)	انصاف، عدل	*inṣāf, 'ȧdl*
equivalence (n)	تساوٍ، تكافؤ	*tasāwin, takāfu'*
equivalent (n/adj)	مساوٍ، متكافئ	*musāwin, mutakāfi'*
equivocal (adj)	ملتبس، غامض	*multabis, ghāmiḍ*
equivocate (v)	راوغ، وارب	*rāwagha, wāraba*
equivocation (n)	مراوغة، غموض	*murāwaghah, ghumūḍ*
era (n)	تاريخ، عصر، دهر	*tārīkh, 'aṣr, dahr*
eradicate (v)	أشع، أباد، استأصل	*asha''a, abāda, ista'ṣala*
eradication (n)	استئصال، إبادة	*isti'ṣāl, ibādah*
erase (v)	محا، كشط	*maḥā, kashaṭa*
eraser (n)	ممحاة، ماحي	*mimḥāt, māḥī*
erasure (n)	محو، انمحاء	*maḥw, inmiḥā'*
erect (adj)	منتصب، قائم	*muntaṣib, qā'im*
erect (v)	أقام، شيد، نصب	*aqāma, shayyada, naṣaba*
erectile (adj)	نعوظ، انتصابي	*na'ūẓ, intiṣābī*
erection (n)	انتصاب، انتشار	*intiṣāb, intishār*
erode (v)	تأكل، حت	*ta'akkala, ḥatta*
erosion (n)	تأكل، نخر	*ta'akkul, nakhr*
erotic (adj)	مثير للشهوة	*muthīr lish shahwah*

eroticism (n)	شهوة جنسية	*shahwah jinsiyyah*
err (v)	أخطأ، زل	*akhṭa'a, zalla*
errand (n)	رحلة قصيرة، مهمة	*riḥlah qaṣīrah, muhimmah*
errant (adj)	شارد، تائه، ضال	*shārid, tā'ih, ḍāll*
erratic (adj)	ضال، شارد	*ḍāll, shārid*
erratically (adv)	على نحو شاذ	*'alā naḥw shādhdh*
erratum (pl. errata)	جدول الخطأ	*jadwalul khaṭa'*
erroneous (adj)	غير صحيح	*ghair ṣaḥīḥ*
error (n)	غلطة، خطأ، زلة	*ghalṭah, khaṭa', zallah*
erstwhile (adj)	سابق	*sābiq*
erudite (adj)	واسع المعرفة	*wāsi'ul ma'rifah*
erudition (n)	سعة المعرفة	*sa'atul ma'rifah*
erupt (v)	ثار، انفجر، تنفط	*thāra, infajara, tanaffaṭa*
eruption (n)	ثوران، هيجان، تنفط	*thauran, hayajān, tanaffuṭ*
eruptive (adj)	ثائر، هائج، ثوراني	*thā'ir, hāyij, thaurānī*
escalate (v)	صعد، زاد في حدة	*ṣa''ada, zāda fi ḥiddah*
escalation (n)	تصعيد	*taṣ'īd*
escalator (n)	سلم دوار	*sullam dawwār*
escapade (n)	عمل طائش	*'amal ṭā'ish*
escape (v)	فر، نجا، أفلت	*farra, najā, aflata*
escape (n)	فرار، نجاة، ارتشاح	*firār, najāt, irtishāḥ*
escapee (n)	هارب، آبق	*hārib, ābiq*
escapism (n)	هربية	*taharrubiyyah*
eschew (v)	تجنب، تحاشى	*tajannaba, taḥāshā*
escort (n)	حرس، حامية	*ḥaras, ḥāmiyah*
especial (adj)	خصوصي، استثنائي	*khuṣūṣī, istithnā'ī*

especially (adv)	على الخصوص، خصوصاً	*'alal khuṣūṣ, khuṣūṣan*
espionage (n)	تجسس، استطلاع	*tajassus, istiṭlā'*
esplanade (n)	مستوية، ميدان	*Mustawiyah, maidan*
espousal (n)	مناصرة، خطبة	*munāṣarah, khiṭbah*
espouse (v)	ناصر، تزوج	*nāṣara, tazawwaja*
essay (n)	مقالة، تجربة	*maqālah, tajribah*
essayist (n)	منشي، كاتب المقالات	*munshī, kātibul maqālāt*
essence (n)	جوهر، روح، ماهية	*jauhar, rūḥ, māhiyyah*
essential (adj)	جوهري، أساسي	*jauharī, asāsī*
essentially (adv)	أساسيًا، ضروريًا	*asāsiyyan, ḍarūriyyan*
establish (v)	أسس، أنشأ، أقام	*assasa, ansha'a, aqāma*
establishment (n)	تأسيس، مؤسسة	*ta'sīs, mu'assasah*
estate (n)	ملكية، ممتلكات	*milkiyyah, mumtalakāt*
esteem (v)	أجل، احترم	*ajalla, iḥtarama*
esteem (n)	احترام، قيمة	*iḥtirām, qīmah*
esthete=aesthete		
esthetic=aesthetic		
estimable (adj)	جدير بالإجلال	*jadīr bil ijlāl*
estimate (v)	قدر، خمن	*qaddara, khammana*
estimate (n)	تقدير، تخمين	*taqdīr, takhmīn*
estimation (n)	رأي، تخمين	*ra'y, takhmīn*
estrange (v)	أقصى، نفر	*aqṣā, naffara*
estrangement (n)	إقصاء، نفور	*iqṣā', nufūr*
estuary (n)	مصب النهر	*maṣabbun nahr*
etcetera (etc)	إلى آخره	*ilā ākhirih*

etch (v)	حفر، رسم الخطوط	*ḥafara, rasamal khuṭūṭ*
etching (n)	حفر الكليشيهات	*ḥafrul kilīshīhāt*
eternal (adj)	أبدي، سرمدي	*abadī, sarmadī*
eternally (adj)	أبديًا، أزليًا	*abadiyyan, azaliyyan*
eternity (n)	أبدية، خلود	*abadiyyah, khulūd*
ether (n)	إتير، سماء	*itīr, samā'*
ethereal (adj)	إتيري، سماوي	*itīrī, samāwī*
ethic (n)	أخلاق	*akhlāq*
ethical (adj)	أخلاقي	*akhlāqī*
ethics (n)	علم الأخلاق	*'ilmul akhlāq*
ethnic-al (adj)	عرقي، سلالي	*'irqī, sulālī*
ethnocentric (adj)	مستعرق	*musta'riq*
ethnography (n)	اثنوغرافيا	*ithnūgharāfiyā*
ethnology (n)	علم الأعراق البشرية	*'ilmul a'rāq al bashariyyah*
ethos (n)	روح الشعب أوالمجتمع	*rūḥush sha'b awil mujtama'*
etiquette (n)	آداب المعاشرة	*ādābul mu'āsharah*
etymological (adj)	اشتقاقي، صرفي	*ishtiqāqī, ṣarfī*
etymology (n)	اتيمولوجيا، علم الاشتقاق	*itīmūlūjiyā, 'ilmul ishtiqāq*
eugenics (n)	يوجينيا، علم تحسين النسل	*yujīniyā, 'ilmu taḥsīnin nasl*
eulogize,-ise (v)	أثنى، أبن	*athnā, abbana*
eulogy (n)	ثناء، تأبين	*thanā', ta'bīn*
eunuch (n)	خصي، مخصي	*khaṣī, makhṣī*
euphemism (n)	لطف التعبير	*luṭfut ta'bīr*
euphemistic (adj)	لطيف، ملطف	*laṭīf, mulaṭṭaf*

euphoria (n)	شعور بالنشاط والابتهاج	*shu'ūr bin nashāṭ wal ibtihāj*
Europe (n)	أوروبة	*ūrūbah*
European (adj)	أوروبي	*ūrūbī*
evacuate (v)	أفرغ، نزح	*afragha, nazaḥa*
evacuation (n)	تفريغ، إخلاء، جلاء	*tafrīgh, ikhlā', jalā'*
evade (v)	تجنب، راغ	*tajannaba, rāgha*
evaluate (v)	قيم، قدر	*qayyama, qaddara*
evaluation (n)	تقدير، تثمين	*taqdīr, tathmīn*
evanescence (n)	زوال، اضمحلال	*zawāl, iḍmiḥlāl*
evanescent (adj)	سريع الزوال	*sarī'uz zawāl*
evangelical (adj)	انجيلي	*injīlī*
evangelism (n)	حماسة سليبية	*ḥamāsah salībiyyah*
evaporate (v)	تبخر، زال	*tabakhkhara, zāla*
evaporated milk (n)	حليب مكثف	*ḥalīb mukaththaf*
evaporation (n)	تبخير، تصعيد	*tabkhīr, taṣ'īd*
evasion (n)	تجنب، تملص	*tajannub, tamalluṣ*
evasive (adj)	مراوغ، تملصي	*murāwigh, tamalluṣī*
eve (n)	عشية، مساء	*'ashiyyah, masā'*
even (n)	مستوٍ، متكافئ، شفع	*mustawin, mutakāfi', shaf'*
even (adv)	حتى، أيضاً	*ḥattā, aiḍan*
even (v)	سوى، مهد، عادل	*sawwā, mahhada, 'ādala*
evening (n)	مساء، عشية	*masā', 'ashiyyah*
evenly (adv)	بالعدل، باستواء	*bil 'adl, bistiwā'*
evenness (n)	عدل، توازن، تكافؤ	*'adl, tawāzun, takāfu'*
event (n)	حادثة، واقعة	*ḥādithah, wāqi'ah*
eventful (adj)	كثيرالحوادث	*kathīrul ḥawādith*

eventual (adj)	نهائي، أخير	*nihā'ī, akhīr*
eventuality (n)	احتمال، نتيجة	*iḥtimāl, natījah*
eventually (adv)	أخيراً، في الأخر	*akhīran, fil ākhir*
ever (adv)	دائماً، أبداً	*dā'iman, adaban*
evergreen (adj)	دائم الخضرة	*dā'imul khuḍrah*
everlasting (adj)	دائم، أبدي	*dā'im, abadī*
evermore (adv)	دائماً، إلى الأبد	*dā'iman, ilal abad*
every (adj)	كل واحد	*kullu wāḥid*
everybody (pron)	كل شخص	*kullu shakhṣ*
everyday (adj)	كل يوم	*kullu yaum*
everyone (pron)	كل امرئ	*kullu imra'in*
everything (pron)	كل شيء	*kullu shay'*
everywhere (adv)	في كل مكان	*fī kulli makān*
evict (v)	أخرج، طرد	*akhraja, ṭarada*
eviction (n)	إخلاء، طرد	*ikhlā', ṭard*
evidence (n)	بينة، شهادة، شاهد	*bayyinah, shahādah, shāhid*
evidence (v)	برهن، شهد	*barhanȧ, shahida*
evident (adj)	واضح، بين	*wāḍiḥ, bayyin*
evidently (adv)	بجلاء، بوضوح	*bi jalā', bi wuḍūḥ*
evil (adj)	شرير، بغيض، مشؤوم	*sharīr, baghīḍ, mashū'ūm*
evil (n)	شر، إثم، كارثة	*sharr, ithm, kārithah*
evince (v)	أظهر، أثبت	*aẓhara, athbata*
evocation (n)	إثارة، استغاثة	*ithārah, istighāthah*
evocative (adj)	مثير للذكريات	*muthīr lidh dhikrayāt*
evoke (v)	أثار، استحضر	*athāra, istaḥḍara*
evolution (n)	نمو، تطور	*numuww, taṭawwur*

evolutionary (adj)	تطوري، نشوئي	*taṭawwurī, nushū'ī*
evolve (v)	نشأ، تطور، استخرج	*nasha'a, taṭawwara, istakhraja*
exacerbate (v)	فاقم، أثار	*fāqama, athāra*
exacerbation (n)	حدة، شدة	*ḥiddah, shiddah*
exact (adj)	مضبوط، محكم، دقيق	*maḍbūṭ, muḥkam, daqīq*
exactitude (n)	صحة، ضبط، دقة	*ṣiḥḥah, ḍabṭ, diqqah*
exactly (adv)	بالضبط، تماماً	*biḍ ḍabṭ, tamāman*
exactness (n)	ضبط، دقة	*ḍabṭ, diqqah*
exaggerate (v)	بالغ، غالى	*bālagha, ghālā*
exaggerated (adj)	مبالغ فيه	*mubālagh fīh*
exaggeration (n)	مبالغة، غلو	*mubālaghah, ghuluww*
exalt (v)	مجد، أعلى، رفع	*mujjada, a'lā, rafa'a*
exaltation (n)	تمجيد، إعلاء، إطراء	*tamjīd, i'lā', iṭrā'*
exalted (adj)	مجيد، أعلى	*majīd, a'lā*
examination (n)	امتحان، فحص	*imtiḥān, faḥṣ*
examine (v)	امتحن، فحص	*imtaḥana, faḥaṣa*
examiner (n)	ممتحن، مستنطق	*mumtaḥin, mustanṭiq*
example (n)	مثال، قدوة	*mithāl, qudwah*
exasperate (v)	أغضب، أسخط	*aghḍaba, askhaṭa*
exasperation (n)	غضب، سخط	*ghaḍab, sukhṭ*
excavate (v)	استخرج، كشف	*istakhraja, kashafa*
excavation (n)	حفر، كشف	*ḥafr, kashf*
excavator (n)	حفارة ميكانيكية	*ḥaffārah mīkānīkiyyah*
exceed (v)	تجاوز، زاد، فاق	*tajāwaza, zāda, fāqa*
exceedingly (adv)	إلى أبعد حد	*ilā ab'adi ḥadd*
excel (v)	تفوق، بز، فاق	*tafawwaqa, bazza, fāqa*

excellence (n)	تفوق، امتياز، فضيلة	*tafawwuq, imtiyāz, faḍīlah*
excellency (n)	سعادة، ميزة	*sa'ādah, mīzah*
excellent (adj)	ممتاز، متفوق	*mumtāz, mutafawwiq*
except (prep)	ماعدا، إلا	*mā 'adā, illā*
except (v)	استثنى، أخرج	*istathnā, akhraja*
exception (n)	استثناء، شذوذ	*istithnā', shudhūdh*
exceptional (adj)	استثنائي، نادر	*istithnā'ī, nādir*
exceptionally (adv)	على وجه الاستثناء	*'alā wajhil istithnā*
excerpt (n)	مقتطف، مقتبس	*muqtaṭaf, muqtabas*
excess (n)	فرط، زيادة، إسراف	*farṭ, ziyādah, isrāf*
excess (adj)	مفرط، زائد	*mufriṭ, zā'id*
excessive (adj)	مفرط، زائد	*mufriṭ, zā'id*
excessively (adv)	بإفراط، للغاية	*bi ifrāṭ, lil ghāyah*
exchange (n)	مبادلة، مقايضة، حوالة	*mubādalah, muqāyaḍah, ḥawālah*
exchange (v)	قايض، صرف	*qāyaḍa, ṣarafa*
exchangeable (adj)	قابل للمبادلة	*qābil lil mubādalah*
exchanger (n)	مقايض، صراف	*muqāyiḍ, ṣarrāf*
exchequer (n)	خزانة الدولة	*khizānatud daulah*
excise (n)	ضريبة، رسم	*ḍarībah, rasm*
excise (v)	استأصل، أزال، قطع	*ista'ṣala, azāla, qaṭa'a*
excision (n)	إزالة، استئصال	*izālah, isti'ṣāl*
excitability (n)	سرعة الاهتياج	*sur'atul ihtiyāj*
excitable (adj)	سريع الاهتياج	*sarī'ul ihtiyāj*
excitation (n)	إثارة، اهتياج	*ithārah, ihtiyāj*
excite (v)	هيج، أثار	*hayyaja, athāra*
excited (adj)	مثار، مهاج	*muthār, muhāj*

excitedly (adv)	باهتياج	*bihtiyāj*
excitement (n)	اهتياج، هَيج	*ihtiyāj, tahayyuj*
exciting (adj)	مهيج، مثير	*muhayyij, muthīr*
exclaim (v)	هتف، صاح	*hatafa, ṣāḥa*
exclamation (n)	هتاف، تعجب	*hutāf, ta'ajjub*
exclamatory (adj)	هتافي، تعجبي	*hutāfī, ta'ajjubī*
exclude (v)	استثنى، أخرج	*istathnā, akhraja*
exclusion (n)	استثناء، إخراج	*istithnā', ikhrāj*
exclusive (adj)	مانع، أنيق، غالٍ	*māni', anīq, ghālin*
exclusive (n)	مقالة مخصوصة	*maqālah makhṣūṣah*
exclusively (adv)	على وجه الحصر	*'alā wajhil ḥaṣr*
exclusiveness (n)	اقتصارية	*iqtiṣāriyyah*
exclusivity (n)	اقتصارية، مقصورية	*iqtiṣāriyyah, maqṣūriyyah*
excommunicate (v)	حرم من الكنيسة	*ḥarama minal kanīsah*
excommunication (n)	حرم كنسي	*ḥaram kanasī*
excoriate (v)	شجب، كشط	*shajaba, kashaṭa*
excrement (n)	غائط، براز	*ghā'iṭ, birāz*
excrescence (n)	نامية غريبة	*nāmiyah gharībah*
excreta (n)	مبرزات الجسم	*mubrazātul jism*
excrete (v)	أبرز، أفرز	*abraza, afraza*
excretion (n)	إبراز، إفراز، مبرز	*ibrāz, ifrāz, mubraz*
excruciating (adj)	موجع، مؤلم	*mūji', mu'lim*
exculpate (v)	برأ، برر	*barra'a, barrara*
exculpation (n)	تبرئة، تبرير	*tabri'ah, tabrīr*
excursion (n)	نزهة، رحلة قصيرة	*nuzhah, riḥlah qaṣīrah*
excusable (adj)	قابل المعذرة	*qābilul ma'dhirah*
excuse (n)	مقدرة، اعتذار	*maqdarah, i'tidhār*

excuse (v)	اعتذر، عفا، صفح	*i'tadhara, 'afā, ṣafaḥa*
execute (v)	أعدم، نفذ، أنجز	*a'dama, naffadha, anjaza*
execution (n)	إعدام، تنفيذ، إجراء	*i'dām, tanfīdh, ijrā'*
executioner (n)	جلاد	*jallād*
executive (adj/n)	تنفيذي، سطلة تنفيذية	*tanfīdhī, sulṭah tanfīdhiyyah*
executive council (n)	مجلس تنفيذي	*majlis tanfīdhī*
executor (n)	منفذ، وصي	*munaffidh, waṣī*
exegesis (n)	تفسير، تأويل	*tafsīr, ta'wīl*
exegete (n)	مفسر، مؤول	*mufassir, mu'awwil*
exemplar (n)	نموذج، مثال	*namūdhaj, mithāl*
exemplary (adj)	نموذجي، تمثيلي	*namūdhajī, tamthīlī*
exemplification (n)	تمثيل، مثل	*tamthīl, mathal*
exempli gratia (eg)	مثلاً	*mathalan*
exemplify (v)	مثل، ضرب مثلاً	*maththala, ḍaraba mathalan*
exempt (v)	استثنى، أعفى	*istathnā, a'fā*
exempt (n)	استثناء، مستثنى	*istithnā', mustathnā*
exemption (n)	استثناء، إعفاء	*istithnā', i'fā'*
exercise (n)	تمرين، ممارسة	*tamrīn, mumārasah*
exercise (v)	مارس، مرن	*mārasa, marrana*
exert (v)	بذل، مارس، استخدم	*badhala, mārasa, istakhdama*
exertion (n)	كد، جهد، اجتهاد	*kadd, jahd, ijtihād*
exhale (v)	أطلق رائحة، زفر	*aṭlaqa rā'iḥah, zafara*
exhaust (n)	عادم، استنفاد	*'ādim, istinfād*
exhaust (v)	أفرغ، أنهك	*afragha, anhaka*

exhausted (adj)	مستنفد، مضنىً	*mustanfad, muḍnan*
exhaustion (n)	تعب شديد، استنفاد	*ta'ab shadīd, istinfād*
exhaustive (adj)	مستنفد، مضنٍ	*mustanfid, muḍnin*
exhibit (v)	عرض، قدم، أظهر	*'araḍa, qaddama, aẓhara*
exhibit (n)	عرض، شيء معروض	*'arḍ, shay' ma'rūḍ*
exhibition (n)	معرض، عرض	*ma'riḍ, 'arḍ*
exhibitionism (n)	إظهارية	*iẓhāriyyah*
exhibitionist (n)	إظهاري، افتضاحي	*iẓhārī, iftiḍāḥī*
exhibitor (n)	عارض، مقدم	*'āriḍ, muqaddim*
exhilarate (v)	أبهج، أنعش	*abhaja, an'asha*
exhilarating (adj)	مبهج، مهيج	*mubhij, muhayyij*
exhilaration (n)	ابتهاج، انتعاش	*ibtihāj, inti'āsh*
exhort (v)	نصح، حث	*naṣaḥa, ḥaththa*
exhortation (n)	عظة، نصيحة	*'iẓah, naṣīḥah*
exhumation (n)	نبش، إخراج الجثث	*nabsh, ikhrājul juthath*
exhume (v)	نبش، أخرج	*nabasha, akhraja*
exigency (n)	ضرورة، اقتضاء	*ḍarūrah, iqtiḍā'*
exiguous (adj)	ضئيل، هزيل	*ḍa'īl, hazīl*
exile (n)	نفي، منفي	*nafy, manfī*
exile (v)	نفى، أبعد، اغترب	*nafā, ab'ada, ightaraba*
exist (v)	كان، بقى، وجد	*kāna, baqā, wujida*
existence (n)	كينونة، وجود	*kainūnah, wujūd*
existent (adj)	كائن، موجود	*kā'in, maujūd*
existential (adj)	وجودي	*wujūdī*
existing (adj)	حالي، حاضر	*ḥālī, ḥāḍir*
exit (n)	رحيل،خروج،مغادرة	*raḥīl, khurūj, mughādarah*
exit (v)	خرج، غادر	*kharaja, ghādara*

exodus (n)	هجرة، رحيل	*hijrah, raḥīl*
ex officio (adj/adv)	بحكم المنصب	*bi ḥukmil manṣib*
exonerate (v)	برأ، أعتق	*barra'a, a'taqa*
exorbitance (n)	فداحة، إفراط	*fadāḥah, ifrāṭ*
exorbitant (adj)	مفرط، فادح، باهظ	*mufriṭ, fādiḥ, bāhiẓ*
exorbitantly (adv)	بإفراط، بفداحة	*bi ifrāṭ, bi fadāḥah*
exorcise (v)	طرد الأرواح برقية	*ṭaradal arwāḥ bi ruqyah*
exorcism (n)	رقية، تعويذ	*ruqyah, ta'wīdh*
exorcist (n)	معالج بالرقى	*mu'ālij bir ruqā*
exotic (adj)	مجلوب، أجنبي	*majlūb, ajnabī*
expand (v)	وسع، بسط، مدد	*wassa'a, basaṭa, maddada*
expanse (n)	امتداد، رقعة منفسحة	*imtidād, ruq'ah munfasiḥah*
expansion (n)	توسيع، تمديد، بسط	*tausī', tamdīd, basṭ*
expansionism (n)	توسعية	*tawassu'iyyah*
expansive (adj)	متسع، ممتد	*muttasi', mumtadd*
expansively (adv)	بامتداد، باتساع	*bimtidād, bittisā'*
expansiveness (n)	توسع، تمدد	*tawassu', tamaddud*
expatiate (v)	أطنب، أسهب	*aṭnaba, ashaba*
expatriate (n)	منفي، مغترب	*manfī, mughtarib*
expect (v)	توقع، حسب، أمل	*tawaqqa'a, ḥasaba, amala*
expectance-cy (n)	توقع، ترقب	*tawwaqu', taraqqub*
expectant (adj)	متوقع، مرتقب	*mutawaqqi', murtaqib*
expectation (n)	توقع، ترقب، أمل	*tawaqqu', taraqqub, amal*
expediency (n)	ملاءمة، مناسبة	*mulā'amah, munāsabah*

expedient (adj/n)	ملائم، وسيلة	*mulā'im, wasīlah*
expedite (v)	عجل، سهل	*'ajjala, sahhala*
expedition (n)	بعثة، حملة	*ba'thah, ḥamlah*
expeditionary (adj)	حملي	*ḥamlī*
expeditious (adj)	سريع، ناشط	*sarī', nāshiṭ*
expel (v)	طرد، فصل	*ṭarada, faṣala*
expend (v)	أنفق، بذل	*anfaqa, badhala*
expenditure (n)	نفقة، إنفاق	*nafaqah, infāq*
expense (n)	نفقة، مصروف	*nafaqah, maṣrūf*
expensive (adj)	غالٍ، ثمين	*ghālin, thamīn*
experience (n)	تجربة، خبرة	*tajribah, khibrah*
experience (v)	اختبر، جرب، قاسى	*ikhtabara, jarraba, qāsā*
experienced (adj)	ذوخبرة، ذو تجربة	*dhū khibrah, dhū tajribah*
experiential (adj)	تجريبي، اختباري	*tajrībī, ikhtibārī*
experiment (n)	تجربة، اختبار	*tajribah, ikhtibār*
experiment (v)	جرب، اختبر	*jarraba, ikhtabara*
experimental (adj)	تجريبي، اختباري	*tajrībī, ikhtibārī*
experimentally (adv)	على وجه التجريب	*'alā wajhit tajrīb*
experimentation (n)	تجريب، اختبار	*tajrīb, ikhtibār*
expert (n/adj)	ذو خبرة، خبير	*dhū khibrah, khabīr*
expertise (n)	خبرة، معرفة واسعة	*khibrah, ma'rifah, wāsi'ah*
expiate (v)	كفر عن	*kaffara 'an*
expiation (n)	كفارة، تكفير	*kaffārah, takfīr*
expiration (n)	موت، انقضاء، زفير	*maut, inqiḍā', zafīr*
expiratory (adj)	زفيري	*zafīrī*
expire (v)	انتهى، انقضى، زفر	*intahā, inqaḍā, zafara*

expiry (n)	انقضاء، موت	*inqiḍā', maut*
explain (v)	شرح، فسر، وضح	*sharaḥa, fassara,waḍḍḥa*
explaination (n)	شرح، تفسير	*sharḥ, tafsīr*
explainatory (adj)	تفسيري، تعليلي	*tafsīrī, ta'līlī*
expletive (n)	كلمة تجديف	*kalimatu tajdīf*
explicable (adj)	قابل للشرح	*qābil lish sharḥ*
explicate (v)	فسر، وضح	*fassara, waḍḍaḥa*
explication (n)	تحليل، توضيح	*taḥlīl, tauḍīḥ*
explicit (adj)	واضح، صريح	*wāḍiḥ, ṣarīḥ*
explicitly (adv)	بوضوح، بصراحة	*bi wuḍūḥ, bi ṣarāḥah*
explode (v)	فجر، انفجر	*fajjara, infajara*
exploded (adj)	ممدد المنظر	*mumaddadul manẓar*
exploit (v)	استثمر، استغل	*istathmara, istaghalla*
exploitation (n)	استثمار، استغلال	*istithmār, istighlāl*
exploitative (adj)	استغلالي	*istighlālī*
exploiter (n)	مستغل	*mustaghill*
exploration (n)	استكشاف، فحص	*istikshāf, faḥṣ*
exploratory (adj)	استكشافي	*istikshāfī*
explore (v)	استكشف، تحرى	*istakshafa, taḥarrā*
explorer (n)	مستكشف، رائد	*mustakshif, rā'id*
explosion (n)	انفجار، فرقعة	*infijār, farqa'ah*
explosive (n/adj)	ماده متفجرة، انفجاري	*māddah mutafajjirah, infijārī*
exponent (n)	دليل، شارح	*dalīl, shāriḥ*
exponential (adj)	أسي، دليلي	*ussī, dalīlī*
export (v/n)	صدر السلع، تصدير	*ṣaddaras sila', taṣdīr*
exportation (n)	تصدير، سلعة مصدرة	*taṣdīr, sil'ah muṣaddarah*
exporter (n)	مصدر	*muṣaddir*

expose (v)	كشف، عرض، أفشى	*kashafa, 'arrada, afshā*
expose (n)	كشف، فضح، عرض	*kashf, fadh, 'ard*
exposed (adj)	مكشوف، معرض	*makshūf, mu'arrad*
exposition (n)	شرح، عرض	*sharh, 'ard*
expostulate (v)	جادل، اعترض على	*jādala, i'tarada 'alā*
exposure (n)	كشف، عرض، تعريض	*kashf, 'ard, ta'rīd*
expound (v)	وضح، فصل	*waddaha, fassala*
express (adj)	واضح، سريع	*wadīh, sarī'*
express (v)	أظهر، عبر	*azhara, 'abbara*
express (n)	اكسبريس، قطار سريع	*iksbres, qitār sarī'*
expression (n)	إظهار، تعبير، سيماء	*izhār, ta'bīr, sīmā'*
expressionism (n)	تعبيرية	*tà'bīriyyah*
expressionist (n)	تعبيري	*ta'bīrī*
expressionless (adj)	خلو من تعبير	*khilw min ta'bīr*
expressive (adj)	معبر، موضح	*mu'abbir, muwaddih*
expropriate (v)	جرد من الملكية	*jarrada minal milkiyyah*
expropriation (n)	تجريد من الملكية	*tajrīd minal milkiyyah*
expulsion (n)	طرد، إخراج	*tard, ikhrāj*
expunge (v)	شطب، حذف	*shataba, hadhafa*
expurgate (v)	حذف، هذب	*hadhafa, hadhdhaba*
exquisite (adj)	نفيس، رائع	*nafīs, rā'i'*
exquisitely (adv)	بنفاسة، بروعة	*bi nafāsah, bi rau'ah*
Ex-serviceman (n)	محارب قديم	*muhārib qadīm*
extant (adj)	موجود، باق	*maujūd, bāqin*
extempore (adj/adv)	مرتجل، ارتجالاً	*murtajal, irtijālan*
Extemporization (n)	ارتجال	*irtijāl*
extemporize,-ise (v)	ارتجل	*irtajala*
extend (v)	بسط، مد، قدم	*basata, madda, qaddama*

extended (adj)	مطول، ممدود	*muṭawwal, mamdūd*
extension (n)	بسط، توسيع، امتداد	*basṭ, tausī', imtidād*
extensive (adj)	واسع، فصيح، شامل	*wāsi', faṣīḥ, shāmil*
extent (n)	نطاق، امتداد	*niṭāq, imtidād*
extenuating (adj)	مخفف، ملطف	*mukhaffif, mulaṭṭif*
exterior (adj/n)	خارجي، مظهر خارجي	*khārijī, maẓhar khārijī*
exterminate (v)	أباد، استأصل	*abāda, ista'ṣala*
extermination (n)	إفناء، إبادة	*ifnā', ibādah*
external (adj)	خارجي، ظاهري	*khārijī, ẓāhirī*
externalize,-ise (v)	جسد، بين	*jassada, bayyana*
externally (adv)	خارجيًا، عرضيًا	*khārijiyyan, 'araḍiyyan*
extinct (adj)	هامد، مندرس	*hāmid, mundaris*
extinction (n)	انطفاء، اندراس، خمود	*inṭifā', indirās, khumūd*
extinguish (v)	أطفأ، حطم	*aṭfa'a, ḥaṭama*
extirpate (v)	اقتلع، استأصل	*iqtala'a, ista'sala*
extirpation (n)	إبادة، استئصال	*ibādah, isti'ṣāl*
extol (extoll) (v)	مجد، بجل	*majjada, bajjala*
extort (v)	ابتز، اغتصب	*ibtazaza, ightaṣaba*
extortion (n)	ابتزاز، اغتصاب	*ibtizāz, ightiṣāb*
extortionate (adj)	اغتصابي، ابتزازي	*ightiṣābī, ibtizāzī*
extra (n/adj)	إضافي، زائد	*iḍāfī, zā'id*
extract (v)	استخلص، اقتطف	*istakhlaṣa, iqtaṭafa*
extract (n)	مقتطف، عصارة، خلاصة	*muqtaṭaf, 'uṣārah, khulāṣah*
extraction (n)	استخلاص، عصارة	*istikhlāṣ, 'uṣārah*
extracurricular (n)	غير منهاجي	*ghair minhājī*

extradite (v)	سلم مجرما إلى حكومته	*sallama mujriman ilā ḥukūmatih*
extradition (n)	تسليم المتهم إلى حكومته	*taslīmul mattaham ilā hukūmatih*
extraneous (adj)	دخيل، غريب	*dakhīl, gharīb*
extraordinary (adj)	استثنائي، فوق العادة	*istithnā'ī, fauqal 'ādah*
extrapolate (v)	قدر استقرائياً	*qaddara istiqrā'iyyan*
extravagance (n)	إفراط، تبذير	*ifrāṭ, tabdhīr*
extravagant (adj)	مسرف، متطرف	*musrif, mutaṭarrif*
extravagantly (adv)	بغلو، بإسراف	*bi ghuluww, bi isrāf*
extravaganza (n)	فورة نشاط	*fauratu nashāṭ*
extreme (adj)	شديد، متطرف، أقصى	*shadīd, mutaṭarrif, aqṣā*
extreme (n)	طرف، حد أقصى	*ṭaraf, ḥadd aqṣā*
extremely (adv)	إلى أبعد حد، بإفراط	*ilā ab'adi ḥadd, bi ifrāṭ*
extremism (n)	تطرفية	*taṭarrufiyyah*
extremist (n)	متطرف	*mutaṭarrif*
extremity (n)	طرف، شدة	*ṭaraf, shiddah*
extricate (v)	خلص، حرر	*khallaṣa, ḥarrara*
extrovert (adj/n)	انبساطي، منبسط	*imbisāṭī, mumbasiṭ*
extrude (v)	بثق، قذف	*bathaqa, qadhafa*
extrusion (n)	بثق، نبط	*bathq, nabṭ*
exuberance (n)	غزارة، امتلاء بالحماسة	*ghazārah, imtilā' bil ḥamāsah*
exuberant (adj)	مليء بالحماسة	*malī' bil ḥamāsah*
exudation (n)	نضح، تحلب	*naḍḥ, taḥallub*
exude (v)	أفرز، نضح	*afraza, naḍaḥa*
exult (v)	طرب، هلل	*ṭaruba, tahallala*
exultant (adj)	متهلل، جذل	*mutahallil, jadhil*

exultantly (adv)	بابتهاج، بجذل	*biibtihāj, bi jadhal*
exultation (n)	جذل، ابتهاج	*jadhal, ibtihāj*
eye (n)	عين، بصر، نظرة	*'ain, baṣar, naẓrah*
eye (v)	حدق، راقب	*ḥaddaqa, rāqaba*
eyeball (n)	مقلة العين	*muqlatul 'ain*
eyebrow (n)	حاجب العين	*ḥājibul 'ain*
eyeful (n)	امرأة فاتنة	*imra'ah fātinah*
eyeglass (n)	نظارة	*naẓẓārah*
eyelash (n)	أهداب الجفن	*ahdābul jafn*
eyelet (n)	عيينة	*'uyaynah*
eyelid (n)	جفن العين	*jafnul 'ain*
eyepiece (n)	عينية	*'ainiyyah*
eyesight (n)	بصر	*baṣar*
eyesore (n)	قذًى للعين	*qadhan lil 'ain*
eyewash (n)	كلام مضلل	*kalām muḍallil*
eyewitness (n)	مشاهد، شاهد عين	*mushāhid, shāhidu 'ain*

F

fable (n)	خرافة، كذب	*khurāfah, kadhib*
fabled (adj)	خرافي، أسطوري	*khurāfī, usṭūrī*
fabric (n)	بنية، بناء، نسيج	*binyah, binā', nasīj*
fabricate (v)	اخترع، اختلق	*ikhtara'a, ikhtalaqa*
fabrication (n)	اختلاق، تلفيق	*ikhtilāq, talfīq*
fabulous (adj)	خرافي، بعيد التصديق	*khurāfī, ba'īdut taṣdīq*
fabulously (adv)	إلى أبعد حد	*ilā ab'adi ḥadd*
face (n)	وجه، سيماء، سطح	*wajh, sīmā', saṭḥ*
face (v)	واجه، قابل	*wājaha, qābala*
facet (n)	سطح صغير، مظهر	*saṭḥ ṣaghīr, maẓhar*

facetious (adj)	ظريف، فكه	*ẓarīf, fakih*
face value (n)	قيمة ظاهرية	*qīmah ẓāhiriyyah*
facial (adj)	وجهي، متعلق بالوجه	*wajhī, muta'alliq bil wajh*
facile (adj)	سطحي، سهل القياد	*saṭḥī, sahlul qiyād*
facilitate (v)	يسر، هون	*yassara, hawwana*
facility (n)	سهولة، هون	*suhūlah, haun*
facing (n)	سجاف، طلاء، دوران	*sijāf, ṭilā', daurān*
facsimile (n)	صورة طبق الأصل	*ṣūrah ṭibqal aṣl*
fact (n)	حقيقة، واقعة	*ḥaqīqah, wāqi'ah*
faction (n)	حزب، عصبة	*ḥizb, 'uṣbah*
factional (adj)	حزبي	*ḥizbī*
factitious (adj)	مصطنع، متكلف	*muṣṭana', mutakallaf*
factor (n)	عامل، أصل، باعث	*'āmil, aṣl, bā'ith*
factory (n)	مصنع، معمل	*maṣna', ma'mal*
factual (adj)	واقعي، حقيقي	*wāqi'ī, ḥaqīqī*
factually (adv)	في الحقيقة	*fil ḥaqīqah*
faculty (n)	قوة، مقدرة، شعبة	*quwwah, maqdirah, shu'bah*
fade (v)	اضمحل، خبا	*iḍmaḥalla, khabā*
faggot (n)	حزمة	*ḥuzmah*
fail (v)	فشل، سقط، وهن	*fashila, saqaṭa, wahana*
failing (n)	ضعف، نقص	*ḍa'f, naqṣ*
failing (prep)	في حال عدم حدوث	*fī ḥāli 'adami ḥudūth*
failure (n)	ضعف، تخلف، عجز	*ḍa'f, takhalluf, 'ajz*
faint (adj)	ضئيل، ضعيف	*ḍa'īl, ḍa'īf*
faint (v)	أغمي عليه	*ughmiya 'alaih*
fainthearted (adj)	مخلوع الفؤاد	*makhlū'ul fu'ād*
fair (adj)	جميل، صافٍ، واضح	*jamīl, ṣāfin, wāḍiḥ*

fair (adv)	بوضوح، بكياسة، بعدل	*bi wuḍūḥ, bi kiyāsah, bi ʻadl*
fair (n)	معرض، سوق موسمية	*maʻriḍ, sūq mausimiyyah*
fairground (n)	أرض للمعارض	*arḍ lil maʻāriḍ*
fairly (adv)	تماماً، بملاءمة، بعدل	*tamāman, bi mulā'amah, bi ʻadl*
fair-minded (adj)	عادل، مقسط	*ʻādil, muqsiṭ*
fair play (n)	عدل، إنصاف	*ʻadl, inṣāf*
fairway (n)	عرض البحر	*ʻurḍul bahr*
fairy (n)	جني، جنية	*jinnī, jinniyyah*
fairyland (n)	عبقر، موطن الجن	*ʻabqar, mauṭinul jinn*
faith (n)	إيمان، دين، ثقة	*īmān, dīn, thiqah*
faithful (adj)	أمين، مخلص، وفي	*amīn, mukhliṣ, wafī*
faithfully (adv)	بأمانة، بايمان	*bi amānah, bi īmān*
faithfulness (n)	إيمان، إخلاص	*īmān, ikhlāṣ*
faithless (adj)	خائن، كافر	*khā'in, kāfir*
fake (n/adj)	زائف، مزيف	*zā'if, muzayyaf*
fake (v)	زيف، لفق	*zayyafa, laffaqa*
fakir (n)	فقير	*faqīr*
falcon (n)	صقر	*ṣaqr*
fall (v)	سقط، وقع، هبط	*saqaṭa, waqaʻa, habaṭa*
fall (n)	سقوط، انحطاط	*suqūṭ, inḥiṭāṭ*
fallacious (adj)	خادع، وهمي	*khādiʻ, wahmī*
fallacy (n)	مغالطة، فكرة خاطئة	*mughālaṭah, fikrah khāṭi'ah*
fall back	تراجع	*tarājaʻa*
fall behind	تخلف	*takhallafa*
fall down	سقط، خر	*saqaṭa, kharra*

fall guy (n)	مغفل، ضحية الخداع	*mughaffal, ḍaḥiyyatul khidā'*
fallibility (n)	قابلية الخطأ	*qābiliyyatul khaṭa'*
fallible (adj)	معرض للخطأ	*mu'arraḍ lil khaṭa'*
fall in	انهار، انتهى	*inhāra, intahā*
fall into	وافق على	*wāfaqa 'alā*
fall off	انقص	*inqaṣṣa*
fall on	هاجم، انقض	*hājama, inqaḍḍa*
fallout (n)	سقط	*saqṭ*
fallow (n/adj)	أرض مراحة، هاجع	*arḍ murāḥah, hāji'*
fall short	انقص	*inqaṣṣa*
fall to	شرع، بدأ	*shara'a, bada'a*
false (adj)	كاذب، زائف، خاطئ	*kādhib, zā'if, khāṭi'*
falsehood (n)	كذب، بهتان	*kadhib, buhtān*
falsely (adv)	بزيف، بغدر	*bi zaif, bi ghadr*
falsification (n)	تزييف، تزوير	*tazyīf, tazwīr*
falsify (v)	شوه، زيف، كذب	*shawwaha, zayyafa, kadhaba*
falsity (n)	كذب، زيف، غدر	*kadhib, zaif, ghadr*
falter (v)	تلعثم، تردد	*tala'thama, taraddada*
faltering (adj)	متلعثم، مضطرب	*mutala'thim, muḍṭarib*
fame (n)	سمعة، شهرة	*sum'ah, shuhrah*
famed (adj)	مشهور، شهير	*mashhūr, shahīr*
familiar (adj)	عائلي، مألوف	*'ā'ilī, ma'lūf*
familiarity (n)	ألفة، اعتياد، وداد	*ulfah, i'tiyād, wadād*
familiarize,-ise (v)	عود، ألف	*'awwada, allafa*
familiarly (adv)	بطريقة حميمة	*bi ṭarīqah ḥamīmah*
family (n)	أسرة، عشيرة، نسب	*usrah, 'ashīrah, nasab*

family tree (n)	شجرة النسب	*shajaratun nasab*
famine (n)	جدب، مجاعة	*jadb, majā'ah*
famished (adj)	جوعان	*jau'ān*
famous (adj)	شهير، ذائع الصيت	*shahīr, dhā'i'uṣ ṣīt*
fan (n)	مروحة، هاوٍ، نصير	*mirwaḥah, hāwin, naṣīr*
fan (v)	ذرى، هوى، روح	*dharrā, hawwā, rawwaḥa*
fanatic (n)	شخص متعصب	*shakhṣ muta'aṣṣib*
fanatical (adj)	تعصبي، متعصب	*ta'aṣṣubī, muta'aṣṣib*
fanatically (adv)	تعصباً	*ta'aṣṣuban*
fanaticism (n)	تعصب، تحمس	*ta'aṣṣub, taḥammus*
fancier (n)	هاوٍ، غاوي	*hāwin, ghāwī*
fanciful (adj)	توهمي، خيالي	*tawahhumī, khayālī*
fancy (v)	أولع به، تخيل	*ūli'a bih, takhayyala*
fancy (adj)	فاخر، خيالي	*fākhir, khayālī*
fancy (n)	ولع، هوى، خيال	*wala', hawā, khayāl*
fanfare (n)	لحن قصير، نفخ بالبوق	*laḥn qaṣīr, nafkh bil būq*
fantastic (adj)	تصوري، وهمي، غريب	*taṣawwurī, wahmī, gharīb*
fantastically (adv)	بغرابة، في الوهم	*bi gharābah, fil wahm*
fantasy (n)	خيال، وهم، هوى	*khayāl, wahm, hawā*
far (adj)	بعيد، أقصى	*ba'īd, aqṣā*
far (adv)	بعيداً، جدًّا	*ba'īdan, jiddan*
far-away (adj)	بعيد، ناءٍ	*ba'īd, nā'in*
farce (n)	فرصة، مهزلة	*farṣah, mahzalah*
farcical (adj)	هزلي، مضحك	*hazlī, muḍḥik*
fare (n)	أجرة، نول، طعام	*ujrah, naul, ṭa'ām*

farewell (n/interj)	وداع، وداعاً	*wadā', wadā'an*
far-fetched (adj)	بعيد الاحتمال	*ba'īdul iḥtimāl*
farm (n/v)	مزرعة، زرع	*mazra'ah, zara'a*
farmer (n)	مزارع، فلاح	*muzāri', fallāḥ*
farm-hand (n)	عامل المزرعة	*'āmilul mazra'ah*
farm-house (n)	بيت المزرعة	*baitul mazra'ah*
farming (n)	زراعة، فلاحة	*zirā'ah, filāḥah*
farmland (n)	مزرعة	*mazra'ah*
farmstead (n)	مزرعة ومبانيها	*mazra'ah wa mabānīhā*
farmyard (n)	فناء المزرعة	*finā'ul mazra'ah*
far-off (adj)	بعيد، ناء	*ba'īd, nā'in*
far-reaching (adj)	بعيد المدى	*ba'īdul madā*
far-sighted (adj)	بصير بالعواقب	*baṣīr bil 'awāqib*
farther (adj)	أبعد، أقصى	*ab'ad, aqṣā*
farther (adv)	في مكان أبعد	*fī makān ab'ad*
farthest (adj/adv)	أبعد، أبعد ما يكون	*ab'ad, ab'ad mā yakūn*
fascinate (v)	فتن، سحر	*fatana, saḥara*
fascinating (adj)	آسر، فاتن	*āsir, fātin*
fascination (n)	فتنة، سحر	*fitnah, siḥr*
fascism (n)	فاشية	*fāshiyyah*
fascist (n)	مؤيد للفاشية	*mu'ayyid lil fāshiyyah*
fashion (n)	نمط، زي، طراز	*namaṭ, ziyy, ṭirāz*
fashion (v)	شكل، صاغ	*shakkala, ṣāgha*
fashionable (adj)	مطابق للزي الحديث	*muṭābiq liz ziyyil ḥadīth*
fashionably (adv)	مطابقا للزي الحديث	*muṭabīqan liz ziyyil ḥadīth*
fast (adj)	سريع، وفي، وثيق	*sarī', wafī, wathīq*
fast (adv)	بسرعة، بعجلة	*bi sur'ah, bi 'ajalah*

fast (n/v)	صوم، صام	*ṣaum, ṣāma*
fasten (v)	وثق، ركز	*waththaqa, rakkaza*
fastener (n)	مربطة	*mirbaṭah*
fastidious (adj)	نيق، متأنق	*nayyiq, muta'anniq*
fastidiously (adv)	بالتنوق	*bit tanawwuq*
fastidiousness (n)	نيقة	*nīqah*
fat (adj)	سمين، ضخم	*samīn, ḍakhm*
fat (n)	دهن، صفوة	*duhn, ṣafwah*
fatal (adj)	حاسم، مهلك	*ḥāsim, muhlik*
fatalism (n)	جبرية	*jabriyyah*
fatalist (n)	جبري	*jabrī*
fatality (n)	موت، نحس	*maut, naḥs*
fate (n)	قضاء، قدر، مصير	*qaḍā', qadar, maṣīr*
fated (adj)	مقدر، محتوم	*muqaddar, maḥtūm*
fateful (adj)	مشؤوم، محتوم	*mash'ūm, maḥtūm*
father (n)	أب، والد	*ab, wālid*
father (v)	ولد، ابتدع	*walada, ibtada'a*
fatherhood (n)	أبوة	*ubuwwah*
father-in-law (n)	أب الزوج أو الزوجة	*abuz zauj awiz zaujah*
fatherland (n)	وطن	*waṭan*
fatherless (adj)	يتيم	*yatīm*
fathom (v)	فهم جيداً، استقصى	*fahima jayyidan, istaqṣā*
fatigue (n)	تعب شديد، كدح	*ta'ab shadīd, kadḥ*
fatigued (adj)	تعبان، متعب	*ta'bān, mut'ab*
fatten (v)	سمن، سمن	*samina, sammana*
fattening (adj)	مسمن	*musammin*
fatty (n/adj)	بدين، دهني	*badīn, duhnī*
fatuity (n)	بلاهة، بلادة	*balāhah, balādah*

fatuous (adj)	أحمق، أبله	*aḥmaq, ablah*
fatuously (adv)	بحماقة، ببلادة	*bi ḥamāqah, bi balādah*
fault (n)	غلطة، زلة، عيب	*ghalṭah, zallah, 'aib*
fault (v)	عاب، زل	*'āba, zalla*
fault-finding (n)	تعييب	*ta'yīb*
faultless (adj)	بلا عيب، كامل	*bilā 'aib, kāmil*
faulty (adj)	ذو عيب	*dhū 'aib*
favour (favor) (n)	تأييد، فضل، رعاية	*ta'yīd, faḍl, ri'āyah*
favour (v)	حابى، من، دعم	*ḥābā, manna, da'ama*
favourable (adj)	مؤيد، إيجابي	*mu'ayyid, ījābī*
favoured (adj)	موهوب، تفضيلي	*mauhūb, tafḍīlī*
favourite (n/adj)	مفضل، محبوب	*mufaḍḍal, maḥbūb*
favouritism (n)	محاباة، تحيز	*muḥābāt, taḥayyuz*
fawn (v)	تملق، تزلف	*tamallaqa, tazallafa*
fawn (n)	خشف، ظبي صغير	*khishf, ẓaby ṣaghīr*
fax (n)	فاكس	*fāks*
fear (n)	خوف، خشية	*khauf, khashyah*
fear (v)	خاف، خشي	*khāfa, khashiya*
fearful (adj)	خائف، رهيب	*khā'if, rahīb*
fearfully (adv)	خوفاً، خائفاً	*khaufan, khā'ifan*
fearless (adj)	شجاع، جريء	*shujā', jarī'*
fearlessly (adv)	بشجاعة، بلا خوف	*bi shajā'ah, bilā khauf*
fearsome (adj)	مخيف، مهيب	*mukhīf, muhīb*
feasibility (n)	ملاءمة	*mulā'amah*
feasible (adj)	ممكن إجراؤه	*mumkin ijrā'uhu*
feast (n)	وليمة، مأدبة، عيد	*walīmah, ma'dubah, 'īd*
feast (v)	احتفل، أولم	*iḥtafala, aulama*
feat (n)	عمل بطولي، مأثرة	*'amal buṭūlī, ma'tharah*

feather (n)	ريش، نوع	*rīsh, nau'*
feather (v)	كسا بالريش	*kasā bir rīsh*
feather-brained (adj)	مغفل، أبله، طائش	*mughaffal, ablah, ṭā'ish*
featherly (adj)	خفيف، ريشي	*khafīf, rīshī*
feature (n)	هيئة، وصف، ميزة	*hai'ah, waṣf, mīzah*
feature (v)	ميز، أبرز	*mayyaza, abraza*
February (n)	فبراير، شباط	*fabrāyar, shubāṭ*
feckless (adj)	عاجز، غير بارع	*'ājiz, ghair bāri'*
fecklessness (n)	ضعف، عجز	*ḍa'f, 'ajz*
fecund (n)	منتج، كثير الثمر	*muntij, kathīruth thamar*
federal (adj)	فدرالي، اتحادي	*fidrālī, ittiḥādī*
federalism (n)	فدرالية، تحالف	*fidrāliyyah, taḥāluf*
federalist (n)	فدرالي، اقطاعي	*fidrālī, iqṭā'ī*
federate (v)	وحد في نظام فدرالي	*waḥḥada fī niẓām fidrālī*
federation (n)	اتحاد، حكومة فدرالية	*ittiḥād, ḥukūmah fidrāliyyah*
fed up (adj)	سئم، متخم	*sa'im, mutkham*
fee (n)	أجر، رسم، جعل	*ajr, rasm, ju'l*
feeble (adj)	واهن، ضئيل	*wāhin, ḍa'īl*
feeble-minded (adj)	أبله، ضعيف العقل	*ablah, ḍa'īful 'aql*
feebleness (n)	ضعف، وهن	*ḍa'f, wahan*
feed (v)	أطعم، أشبع	*aṭ'ama, ashba'a*
feed (n)	وجبة، علف	*wajbah, 'alaf*
feedback (n)	تغذية استرجاعية	*taghdhiyah istirjā'iyyah*
feeder (n)	زجاجة الإرضاع	*zujājatul irḍā'*
feel (v)	شعر، تلمس، أحس	*sha'ara, talammasa, aḥassa*
feel (n)	إحساس، حاسة اللمس	*iḥsās, ḥāssatul lams*

feeler (n)	مجس، لامس	*mijass, lāmis*
feeling (n)	عاطفة، إحساس، شعور	*'āṭifah, iḥsās, shu'ūr*
feign (v)	تظاهر، لفق	*taẓāhara, laffaqa*
feint (n/v)	خدعة، خدع	*khud'ah, khada'a*
felicitate (v)	هنأ، بارك لـه	*hanna'a, bāraka lahu*
felicitation (n)	تهنئة	*tahni'ah*
felicitous (adj)	لبق، مناسب، رائع	*labiq, munāsib, rā'i'*
felicity (n)	هناءة، سعادة	*hanā'ah, sa'ādah*
fell (v)	قطع، صرع	*qaṭa'a, ṣara'a*
fellow (n)	زميل، رفيق، ند	*zamīl, rafīq, nidd*
fellowship (n)	ألفة، مودة، رفقة	*ulfah, mawaddah, rifqah*
felt (n)	لباد	*libbād*
female (n/adj)	أنثى، نسوي	*unthā, niswī*
feminine (adj)	مؤنث، نسوي	*mu'annath, niswī*
feminity (n)	أنوثة	*unūthah*
feminism (n)	نظرية المساواة بين الجنسين	*naẓariyyatul musāwāt bainal jinsain*
feminist (n)	نسائي	*nisā'ī*
fence (n/v)	سياج، سيج	*siyāj, sayyaja*
fend (v)	صان، وقى	*ṣāna, waqā*
fender (n)	وقاء، حاجز الاصطدام	*wiqā', ḥājizul iṣṭidām*
fennel (n)	شمرة	*shumrah*
feral (adj)	ضار، آبد	*ḍārr, ābid*
ferment (v)	خمر، ثار	*khammara, thāra*
ferment (n)	اهتياج، قلق	*ihtiyāj, qalaq*
fermentation (n)	اختمار، تخمر	*ikhtimār, takhammur*
ferocious (adj)	ضار، شديد	*ḍārr, shadīd*
ferociously (adv)	بشدة، بضراوة	*bi shiddah, bi ḍarāwah*

ferocity (n)	وحشية، شدة	*waḥshiyyah, shiddah*
ferret (n)	ابن مقرض	*ibnu miqraḍ*
ferret (v)	صاد، بحث	*ṣāda, baḥatha*
ferrous (adj)	حديدي، حديدوز	*ḥadīdī, ḥadīdūz*
ferry (v/n)	نقل، معدية	*naqala, mu'addiyah*
ferryboat (n)	معدية	*mu'addiyah*
fertile (adj)	خصيب، مخصب	*khaṣīb, mukhṣib*
fertility (n)	خصب، كثرة الانتاج	*khiṣb, kathratul intāj*
fertilization,-isation	تخصيب، تلقيح	*takhṣīb, talqīḥ*
fertilize,-ise (v)	خصب، لقح	*khaṣṣaba, laqqaḥa*
fertilizer,-iser (n)	سماد	*samād*
fervent (adj)	متوهج، متحمس	*mutawahhij, mutaḥammis*
fervently (adv)	باهتياج، بحماسة	*bihtiyāj, bi ḥamāsah*
fervour (fervor)	اتقاد، حماسة	*ittiqād, ḥamāsah*
fester (n)	دمل، قرح	*dummal, qarḥ*
festival (n)	عيد، مهرجان	*'īd, mahrajān*
festive (adj)	بهيج، مرح	*bahīj, mariḥ*
festivity (n)	عيد، ابتهاج	*'īd, ibtihāj*
festoon (v/n)	فسطن، فسطون	*fasṭana, fasṭūn*
fetch (v)	أحضر، أتى به	*aḥḍara, atā bih*
fetching (adj)	ساحر، نشيط	*sāḥir, nashīṭ*
fete (n)	مهرجان، احتفال	*mahrajān, iḥtifāl*
fetish (n)	فتش، صنم، ولع	*fatash, ṣanam, wala'*
fetter (n)	قيد، غل	*qaid, ghull*
fetter (v)	قيد، غلل	*qayyada, ghallala*
feud (n)	ضغينة، عداء	*ḍaghīnah, 'idā'*

feudal (adj)	إقطاعي، ضغني	*iqṭā'ī, ḍaghanī*
feudalism (n)	نظام إقطاعي	*niẓām, iqṭā'ī*
fever (n)	حمى، اضطراب	*ḥummā, iḍṭirāb*
fevered (adj)	مصاب بحمى	*muṣāb bi ḥummā*
feverish (adj)	حمي، مضطرب	*ḥummī, muḍṭarib*
feverishly (adv)	باضطراب	*biḍṭirāb*
few (adj)	قليل، بعض	*qalīl, ba'ḍ*
fez (n)	طربوش	*ṭarbūsh*
fiance (n)	خاطب، مخطوب	*khāṭib, mukhṭūb*
fiancee (n)	خاطبة، مخطوبة	*khāṭibah, makhṭūbah*
fiasco (n)	إخفاق تام	*ikhfāq tāmm*
fibre (fiber) (n)	ليف، خيط	*līf, khaiṭ*
fibreglass=spun glass		
fibrous (adj)	ليفي، ذو ألياف	*līfi, dhū alyāf*
fickle (adj)	متقلب، متردد	*mutaqallib, mutaraddid*
fickleness (n)	تقلب، تردد	*taqallub, taraddud*
fiction (n)	قصة خيالية، تخيل	*qiṣṣah khayāliyyah, takhayyul*
fictional (adj)	قصصي، خيالي	*qaṣaṣī, khayālī*
fictionalize,-ise (v)	أفرغ في قالب روائي	*afragha fī qālib riwā'ī*
fictitious (adj)	خيالي، مفترض، ملفق	*khayālī, muftaraḍ, mulaffaq*
fiddle (n)	كمنجا، كمان	*kamanjā, kamān*
fidelity (n)	إخلاص، أمانة، صحة	*ikhlāṣ, amānah, ṣiḥḥah*
fidget (n/v)	متململ، تململ	*mutamalmil, tamalmala*
fidgety (adj)	متململ، قلق	*mutamalmil, qaliq*
field (n)	حقل، مجال، ميدان	*ḥaql, majāl, maidān*
field (v)	أوقف الكرة وردها	*auqafal kurah wa raddaha*
fiend (n)	شيطان، خبيث	*shayṭān, khabīth*

fiendish (adj)	شيطاني، وحشي	*shayṭānī, waḥshī*
fiendishly (adv)	بوحشية، بشدة	*bi waḥshiyyah, bi shiddah*
fierce (adj)	مفترس، عنيف، قاسٍ	*muftaris, 'anīf, qāsin*
fiery (adj)	متقد، ملتهب	*muttaqid, multahib*
fiesta (n)	مهرجان	*mahrajān*
fifteenth (n)	خامس عشر	*khāmis 'ashara*
fifth (adj)	خامس، خمسي	*khāmis, khumsī*
fifth column	طابور خامس	*ṭābūr khāmis*
fiftieth (adj)	خمسون	*khamsūn*
fifty (n)	خمسون	*khamsūn*
fifty-fifty (adv)	مناصفةً	*munāṣafatan*
fig (n)	ثمر التين	*thamarut tīn*
fight (v)	ناضل، قاتل، كافح	*nāḍala, qātala, kāfaḥa*
fight (n)	معركة، نضال، قتال	*ma'rakah, niḍāl, qitāl*
fighter (n)	محارب، مقاتل	*muḥārib, muqātil*
fighting (n)	شجار، قتال	*shijār, qitāl*
figment (n)	شيء ملفق	*shay' mulaffaq*
figurative (adj)	استعاري، مجازي	*isti'ārī, majāzī*
figure (n)	عدد، شكل، صورة	*'adad, shakl, ṣūrah*
figure (v)	ظهر، رسم، صور	*ẓahara, rasama, ṣawwara*
figurehead (n)	تمثال في مقدم السفينة	*timthāl fī muqaddamis safīnah*
figure of speech	تشبيه، استعارة	*tashbīh, isti'ārah*
filament (n)	خييط، سليك	*khuyait, sulaik*
filch (v)	سرق، سلب	*saraqa, salaba*
file (n)	ملف، مبرد، إضبارة	*milaff, mibrad, iḍbārah*

file (v)	أضبر، أبرد	*adbara, abrada*
filibuster (n)	تعطيل	*ta'ṭīl*
filigree (n)	تخريم تزييني	*takhrīm tazyīnī*
filings (n)	برادة	*burādah*
fill (v)	ملأ، حشا، سد	*mala'a, ḥashā, sadda*
fill (n)	شبع، حشوة	*shiba', ḥashwah*
filler (n)	حشوة	*ḥashwah*
fillet (n)	شريحة طرية	*sharīḥah ṭariyyah*
filling (n)	ملء، حشوة	*mal', ḥashwah*
filly (n)	مهرة، فلوة	*muhrah, filwah*
film (n)	فيلم، غطاء رقيق	*fīlm, ghiṭā' raqīq*
film (v)	صنع فيلما، غشى	*ṣana'a fīlman, ghashshā*
filmy (adj)	رقيق، شفاف	*raqīq, shaffāf*
filter (n)	مصفاة، مرشحة	*misfāt, mirshaḥah*
filter (v)	صفى، رشح	*ṣaffā, rashshaḥa*
filth (n)	قذر، وسخ	*wadhar, wasakh*
filthy (adj)	قذر، بذيء	*qadhir, badhī'*
filteration (n)	تصفية، ترشيح	*taṣfiyah, tarshīḥ*
fin (n)	زعنفة	*zi'nafah*
final (adj)	حاسم، نهائي	*ḥāsim, nihā'ī*
finale (n)	خاتمة، نهاية	*khātimah, nihāyah*
finalist (n)	مشترك في مباراة نهائية	*mushtarak fī mubārāt nihā'iyyah*
finality (n)	نهائية ، ختام	*nihā'iyyah, khitām*
finalize,-ise (v)	أنجز، بلور	*anjaza, balwara*
finally (adv)	أخيراً، في النهاية	*akhīran, fin nihāyah*
finance (n)	موارد مالية	*mawārid māliyyah*
finance (v)	مول، رسمل	*mawwala, rasmala*

financial (adj)	مالي	*mālī*
financier (n)	مالي، رأسمالي	*mālī, ra'asmālī*
finch (n)	عصفور	*'uṣfūr*
find (v)	علم، وجد، بلغ، تلقى	*'alima, wajada, balagha, talaqqā*
find (n)	لقية، اكتشاف	*luqyah, iktishāf*
finder (n)	معين	*ma'ayyin*
finding (n)	لقية، شيء مكتشف	*luqyah, shay' muktashaf*
fine (adj)	جميل، أنيق، ناعم، صاف	*jamīl, anīq, nā'im, ṣāfin*
fine (v/n)	غرم، غرامة	*gharrama, gharāmah*
fine arts	فنون جميلة	*funūn jamīlah*
finely (adv)	بأناقة، بخير	*bi anāqah, bi khair*
fineness (n)	أناقة، رقة، دقة	*anāqah, riqqah, diqqah*
finery (n)	أدوات الزينة	*adawātuz zīnah*
finger (n)	إصبع، مؤشر	*iṣba', mu'ashshir*
finger (v)	مس بالأصابع	*massa bil aṣābi'*
fingernail (n)	ظفر	*ẓufr*
fingerprint (n)	بصمة الإصبع	*baṣmatul iṣba'*
fingertrip (n)	بنانة، رأس الإصبع	*banānah, ra'sul iṣba'*
finicky (adj)	صعب الإرضاء	*ṣa'bul irḍā'*
finish (v)	أنهى، أنجز، أكمل	*anhā, anjaza, akmala*
finish (n)	نهاية، كمال	*nihāyah, kamāl*
finished (n)	مكمل، مصقول	*mukammal, maṣqūl*
finite (adj)	محدود، متناه	*maḥdūd, mutanāhin*
fir (n)	تنوب	*tannūb*
fire (n)	نار، حريق، وقود	*nār, ḥarīq, waqūd*
fire (v)	ألهب، أطلق، أثار	*alhaba, aṭlaqa, athāra*
fire-alarm (n)	نذير النار	*nadhīrun nār*

firearm (n)	سلاح ناري	*silāḥ, nārī*
fire-ball	كرة النار	*kuratun nār*
firebrand (n)	مهيج، جمرة	*muhayyij, jamrah*
fire-break (n)	حاجز النار	*ḥājizun nār*
firecracker (n)	مفرقعة نارية	*mufarqi'ah nāriyyah*
fire-drill (n)	تمرين على مكافحة الحرائق	*tamrīn 'alā makāfaḥatil ḥarā'iq*
fire-engine (n)	سيارة الإطفاء	*sayyāratul iṭfā'*
fire-escaper (n)	سلم النجاة	*sullamun najāt*
fire extinguisher (n)	مطفئة الحريق	*miṭfa'atul ḥarīq*
fire-fighter (n)	إطفائي	*iṭfā'ī*
fire-guard (n)	حاجزة النار	*ḥājizatun nār*
firelight (n)	ضوء النار	*ḍaw'un nār*
fireman (n)	إطفائي، وقاد	*iṭfā'ī, waqqād*
fireplace (n)	مصطلى، مستوقد	*muṣṭalā, mustauqad*
fireproof (adj)	صامد للنار	*ṣāmid lin nār*
fireside (n)	جانب المصطلى	*jānibul muṣṭalā*
firewood (n)	حطب الوقود	*ḥaṭabul waqūd*
fireworks (n)	ألعاب نارية	*al'āb nāriyah*
firing-line (n)	خط النار	*khaṭṭun nār*
firing-squad (n)	زمرة الإطلاق	*zumratul iṭlāq*
firm (adj)	راسخ، ثابت، متين	*rāsikh, thābit, matīn*
firm (v)	رسخ، وطد	*rassakha, waṭṭada*
firm (n)	شركة، بيت تجاري	*sharikah, bait tijārī*
firmament (n)	سماء	*samā'*
firmly (adv)	بثبات، برسوخ	*bi thabāt, bi rusūkh*
firmness (n)	ثبات، رسوخ	*thabāt, rusūkh*
first (n/adj)	أول، أولى	*awwal, ūlā*

first (adv)	أولاً	*awwalan*
first aid (n)	إسعاف أول	*is'āf awwal*
first class (n)	درجة أولى	*darajah ūlā*
first floor (n)	دور أول	*daur awwal*
first fruits (n)	نتائج أولى	*natā'ij ūlā*
first hand (adj)	مباشر	*mubāshir*
firstly (adv)	أولاً	*awwalan*
first-rate (adj)	ممتاز، جيد جدا	*mumtāz, jayyid jiddā*
fiscal (adj)	مالي، أميري	*mālī, amīrī*
fish (n)	سمك، لحم السمك	*samak, laḥmus samak*
fish (v)	حاول الصيد	*ḥāwalaṣ ṣaid*
fish cake	فطيرة السمك	*faṭīratus samak*
fisherman (n)	صياد السمك	*ṣayyādus samak*
fishery (n)	صيد السمك	*ṣaidus samak*
fishing (n)	صيد السمك	*ṣaidus samak*
fishmonger (n)	سماك	*sammāk*
fishy (adj)	سمكي	*samakī*
fission (n)	انفلاق، انشقاق	*infilāq, inshiqāq*
fissiparous (adj)	انقسامي	*inqisāmī*
fissure (n)	شق، فرجة	*shaqq, furjah*
fist (n)	قبضة، لكمة	*qabḍah, lakmah*
fit (adj)	ملائم، لائق، أهل	*mulā'im, lā'iq, ahl*
fit (v)	لاءم، لاق، هيأ	*lā'ama, lāqa, hayya'a,*
fit (n)	ملاءمة، نوبة مرض	*mulā'amah, naubatu maraḍ*
fitful (adj)	تشنجي، متقطع	*tashannujī, mutaqaṭṭi'*
fitness (n)	مناسبة، ملائمة	*munāsabah, mulā'amah*
fitter (n)	مركب، براد	*murakkib, barrād*

fitting (adj)	ملائم، مناسب	*mulā'im, munāsib*
fitting (n)	إحكام، تجهيزات	*iḥkām, tajhīzāt*
five (n)	خمس، خمسة	*khams, khamsah*
fives (n)	الفايفس	*alfāyifs*
fix (v)	ثبت، ركز، حدد	*thabbata, rakkaza, ḥaddada*
fix (n)	ورطة، رشوة	*warṭah, rishwah*
fixate (v)	ثبت، ركز، وجه	*thabbata, rakkaza, wajjaha*
fixation (n)	تعلق، تعود	*ta'alluq, ta'awwud*
fixed (adj)	ثابت، راسخ، مركز	*thābit, rāsikh, murakkaz*
fixture (n)	ثبات، رسوخ، تاريخ محدد	*thabāt, rusūkh, tārīkh muḥaddad*
fizz (v)	فار، أز، ثار	*fāra, azza, thāra*
fizz (n)	أزيز، فوران	*azīz, fawarān*
fizzle (v)	أخفق، فار	*akhfaqa, fāra*
flabbergast (v)	أذهل، أشده	*adhhala, ashdaha*
flabby (adj)	مترهل، ضعيف	*mutarahhil, ḍa'īf*
flaccid (adj)	مترهل، رخو	*mutarahhil, rikhw*
flaccidity (n)	رخاوة، ترهل	*rakhāwah, tarahhul*
flag (n)	راية، علم، سوسن	*rāyah, 'alam, sausan*
flag (v)	رفع الراية	*rafa'ar rāyah*
flagellant (adj)	متسوط	*mutasawwiṭ*
flagellate (v)	ضرب بالسوط	*ḍaraba bis sauṭ*
flagellation (n)	سوط، ضرب	*sauṭ, ḍarb*
flagon (n)	إبريق، قنينة كبيرة	*ibrīq, qinnīnah kabīrah*
flagrant (adj)	فاضح، فظيع	*fāḍiḥ, faẓī'*
flagship (n)	بارجة الأميرال	*bārijatul amīrāl*

flagstaff (n)	سارية العلم	*sāriyatul 'alam*
flagstone (n)	حجر لوحي	*ḥajar lauḥī*
flair (n)	ميل، نزعة	*mail, naz'ah*
flak (n)	مدفعية، مضادة للطائرات	*midfa'iyyah, muḍāddah liṭ ṭā'irāt*
flake (n/v)	قشارى، تقشر	*qushārā, taqashshara*
flaky (adj)	رقاقي، قشاري	*ruqāqī, qushārī*
flamboyance (n)	توهج، تموج	*tawahhuj, tamawwuj*
flamboyant (adj)	متوهج، متموج	*mutawahhij,mutamawwij*
flamboyantly (n)	متوهجاً، متموجاً	*mutawahhijan, mutamawwijan*
flame (n)	لهب، اضطرام، توهج	*lahab,iḍṭirām, tawahhuj*
flame (v)	التهب، تلظى، ثار	*iltahaba, talaẓẓā, thāra*
flaming (adj)	ملتهب، متقد	*multahib, muttaqid*
flamingo (n)	نحام	*nuḥām*
flammable (adj)	ملتهب، متوهج	*multahib, mutawahhij*
flange (n)	شفة، شفير	*shafah, shafīr*
flank (n)	خاصرة، كشح	*khāṣirah, kashḥ*
flank (v)	أحاط من جانبين	*aḥāṭa min jānibain*
flannel (n)	فلانيلة	*falānīlah*
flap (n)	خفقة، صفعة	*khafqah, ṣaf'ah*
flap (v)	أرخى، تحرك، ترفرف	*arkhā, taḥarraka, tarafrafa*
flapper (n)	امرأة شابة	*imra'ah shābbah*
flare (v)	أثار، توهج، اتسع	*athāra, tawahhaja, ittasa'a*
flare (n)	توهج،انفجار،اتساع	*tawahhuj, infijār, ittisā'*
flare-up (n)	انفجار الغضب	*infijārul ghaḍab*

flaring (adj)	باهر، مشتعل	*bāhir. mushta'il*
flash (n)	لمع، وميض، وهج	*lam', wamīḍ, wahj*
flash (v)	أومض، لمع، فجر	*aumaḍa, lama'a, fajjara*
flashback (n)	ارتجاع فني	*irtijā' fannī*
flash bulb = flash lamp		
flash-flood (n)	طوفان محلي	*ṭūfān maḥallī*
flashing (n)	حشوة معدنية	*ḥashwah ma'diniyah*
flash lamp (n)	مصباح ومضي	*miṣbāḥ wamḍī*
flash point (n)	نقطة الوميض	*nuqṭatul wamīḍ*
flashy (adj)	زاهٍ، خاطف للبصر	*zāhin, khāṭif lil baṣar*
flask (n)	قارورة، دورق	*qārūrah, dauraq*
flat (adj)	مسطح، مستوٍ، راكد	*musaṭṭaḥ, mustawin, rākid*
flat (n)	شقة، سطح، طابق	*shiqqah, saṭḥ, ṭābiq*
flat (adv)	انبطاحاً، تماماً، مباشرةً	*imbiṭāḥan, tamāman mubāshiratan*
flat fish	سمك مفلطح	*samak mufalṭaḥ*
flat-footed (adj)	أمسح	*amsaḥ*
flatten (v)	سطح، بسط، سوى	*saṭaḥa, basaṭa, sawwā*
flatter (v)	أطرى، مدح، تملق	*aṭrā, madaḥa, tamallaqa*
flatterer (n)	متملق، منافق	*mutamalliq, munāfiq*
flattery (n)	إطراء، مداهنة	*iṭrā', mudāhanah*
flatulence (n)	تطبل البطن	*taṭabbulul baṭn*
flatulent (adj)	متطبل البطن	*mutaṭabbilul baṭn*
flaunt (v)	تباهى، ازدهى	*tabāhā, izdahā*
flautist = flutist		
flavour (flavor) (v)	نكه، طيب	*nakkaha, ṭayyaba*
flavour (n)	نكهة، رائحة	*nakhah, rā'iḥah*
flavouring (n)	تتبيل، توابل	*tatbīl, tawābil*
flavourless (adj)	عديم النكهة	*'adīmun nakhah*

flaw (n)	عيب، نقص، شق	*'aib, naqṣ, shaqq*
flaw (v)	شق، خرق	*shaqqa, kharaqa*
flawless (adj)	بلا عيب، محكم	*bilā 'aib, muḥkam*
flax (n)	كتان، خيوط الكتان	*katān, khuyūṭul katān*
flaxen (adj)	مصنوع من الكتان	*maṣnū' minal katān*
flay (v)	سلب، سلخ، انتقد	*salaba, salakha, intaqada*
flea (n)	برغوث	*burghūth*
flea-bite (n)	ألم طفيف، قرصة برغوث	*alam ṭafīf, qurṣatu burghūth*
fleck (n)	نقطة، رقطة	*nuqṭah, ruqṭah*
fleck (v)	نقط، رقط	*naqqaṭa, raqqaṭa*
fledged (adj)	مكسو بريش	*maksū bi rīsh*
fledgling,-geling (n)	فرخ، غر	*farkh, ghirr*
flee (v)	فر، هرب	*farra, haraba*
fleece (n)	صوف الخراف، جزة	*ṣūful khirāf, jizzah*
fleece (v)	جز، سلب	*jazza, salaba*
fleecy (adj)	صوفي، ناعم	*ṣūfī, nā'im*
fleet (n)	أسطول، قافلة	*usṭūl, qāfilah*
fleet (adj)	رشيق، سريع	*rashīq, sarī'*
fleet admiral (n)	أميرال الأسطول	*amīrālul usṭūl*
fleeting (adj)	سريع الزوال	*sarī'uz zawāl*
flesh (n)	لحم، جسد	*laḥm, jasad*
fleshly (adj)	جسدى، شهوي	*jasadī, shahwī*
fleshy (adj)	بدين، سمين	*badīn, samīn*
flex (v)	ثنى، لوى	*thanā, lawā*
flexibility (n)	لدانة، مرونة	*ladānah, murūnah*
flexible (adj)	قابل للانثناء، مرن	*qābil lil inthinā', marin*
flick (n)	ضربة خفيفة، نقرة	*ḍarbah khafīfah, naqrah*
flick (v)	ضرب بالرفق	*ḍaraba bir rifq*

flicker (v)	ترجرج، خفق	*tarajraja. Khafaqa*
flicker (n)	ترجرج، خفق، بصيص	*tarajruj, khafq, baṣīṣ*
flight (n)	رحلة بالطائرة، طائرة، فرار	*riḥlah biṭ ṭā'irah, ṭā'irah, firār*
flight (v)	طار أسراباً	*ṭāra asrāban*
flightless (n)	عاجز عن الطيران	*'ājiz 'aniṭ ṭayarān*
flighty (adj)	سريع الزوال، متقلب	*sarī'uz zawāl, mutaqallib*
flimsy (adj)	سخيف، رقيق، رديء	*sakhīf, raqīq, radī'*
flinch (v)	أجفل، أحجم	*ajfala, aḥjama*
fling (v)	قذف، طرح، اندفع	*qadhafa, ṭaraḥa, indafa'a*
fling (n)	فترة انغماس في الملذات	*fatratu inghimās fil maladhdhāt*
flint (n)	صوان، ظر	*ṣawwān, ẓirr*
flinty (adj)	صواني، قاسٍ	*ṣawwānī, qāsin*
flip (v)	نقف، قلب	*naqafa, qalaba*
flip (n)	نقفة، نقرة	*naqfah, naqrah*
flippancy (n)	قحة، ذلاقة لسان	*qiḥah, dhalāqatu lisān*
flippant (adj)	ثرثار، وقح	*tharthār, waqiḥ*
flipper (n)	زعنفة	*zi'nifah*
flirt (v)	غنج، غازل	*ghanija, ghāzala*
flirtation (n)	غنج، مداعبة	*ghunj, mudā'abah*
flit (v)	طار، انتقل بسرعة	*ṭāra, intaqala bi sur'ah*
float (v)	طفا، جرى برفق	*ṭafā, jarā bi rifq*
float (n)	عوامة، طوف، كرة البرميل	*'awwāmah, ṭauf, kuratul barmīl*
floating (adj)	عائم، طافٍ، مترحل	*'ā'im, ṭāfin, mutaraḥḥil*
flock (n)	احتشد، اجتمع	*iḥtashada, ijtama'a*
flog (v)	ضرب بالسوط	*ḍaraba bis sauṭ*

flood (n)	طوفان، فيضان، مد	*ṭūfān, fayaḍān, madd*
flood (v)	غمر، أغرق	*ghamara, aghraqa*
floodgate (n)	مسرب الفيضان	*masrabul fayaḍān*
floodlight (n)	ضوء غامر	*ḍaw' ghāmir*
flood-plain (n)	رقة	*raqqah*
flood-tide (n)	مد، فيض غامر	*madd, faiḍ ghāmir*
floor (n)	دور، قاع، أرضية	*daur, qā', arḍiyyah*
floor (v)	هزم، أربك، أفحم	*hazama,arbaka,afḥama*
floorboard (n)	أرضية السيارة	*arḍiyyatus sayyārah*
flop (v)	ارتمى، تحول فجأةً	*irtamā, taḥawwala faj'atan*
flop (n)	ارتماء، هبوط مفاجئ	*irtimā', hubūṭ mufāji'*
floppy (adj)	متخبط، عريض لين	*mutakhabbiṭ, 'ariḍ layyin*
flora (n)	فلورا، حياة نباتية	*fulūrā, ḥayāt nabātiyyah*
floral (adj)	خاص بالإزهار	*khāṣṣ bil izhār*
florid (adj)	مزخرف، متورد	*muzakhraf, mutawarrid*
florist (n)	زهار	*zahhār*
floss (n)	مشاقة الحرير	*mushāqatul ḥarīr*
flotation (n)	تأسيس شركة	*ta'sīsu sharikah*
flotilla (n)	أسطول صغير	*usṭūl ṣaghīr*
flounce (v)	تخبط، انتفض	*takhabbaṭa, intafaḍa*
flounce (n)	هدب، حاشية	*hudb, ḥāshiyah*
flounder (v)	تخبط، تسكع	*takhabbaṭa, tasakka'a*
flour (n)	طحين، دقيق	*ṭaḥīn, daqīq*
flourish (v)	ازدهر، تبجح	*izdahara, tabajjaḥa*
flourish (n)	ازدهار، فترة الازدهار	*izdihār, fatratul izdihār*
flout (v)	أهان، هزأ	*ahāna, haza'a*
flow (v)	جرى، سال، فاض	*jarā, sāla, fāḍa*
flow (n)	تدفق، فيضان	*tadaffuq, fayaḍān*

flower (n)	زهرة، صفوة، نخبة	*zahrah, ṣafwah, nukhbah*
flower (v)	ازدهر، نما، أزهر	*izdahara, namā, azhara*
flowerpot (n)	أصيص	*aṣīṣ*
flu=influenza		
fluctuate (v)	تموج، تقلب	*tamawwaja, taqallaba*
fluctuation (n)	تموج، تقلب	*tamawwuj, taqallub*
flue (n)	مدخنة	*midkhanah*
fluency (n)	فصاحة، طلاقة	*faṣāḥah, ṭalāqah*
fluent (adj)	فصيح، سلس	*faṣīḥ, salis*
fluently (adv)	بطلاقة، بسلاسة	*bi ṭalāqah, bi salāsah*
fluff (n)	زغب، شيء زغب	*zaghab, shay' zaghib*
fluffy (adj)	زغب، كالزغب	*zaghib, kaz zaghib*
flude (n/adj)	سائل، مائع، سلس	*sā'il, mā'i', salis*
fludity (n)	سيولة، مرونة	*suyūlah, murūnah*
fluke (n)	حظ سعيد	*ḥaẓẓ sa'īd*
flummox (v)	أذهل، أخفق	*adhhala, akhfaqa*
flunk (v)	سقط في الامتحان	*saqaṭa fil imtiḥān*
flunky (n)	خادم، إمع	*khādim, imma'*
fluorescence (n)	استشعاع، تفلور	*istish'ā', tafalwur*
fluorescent (adj)	مستشعع، فلوي	*mustash'i', falwarī*
fluoride (n)	فلوريد	*fulūrīd*
fluorine (n)	فلورين	*fulūrīn*
flurry (n)	هبة ريح	*habbatu rīḥ*
flush (n)	تورد، فورة	*tawarrud, faurah*
flush (v)	تورد، شاع	*tawarrada, shā'a*
flush (adj)	فائض، غزير، مستوي السطح	*fā'iḍ, ghazīr, mustawiyus saṭḥ*
fluster (v)	خبل، ارتبك	*khabbala, irtabaka*
fluster (n)	اهتياج مرتبك	*ihtiyāj murtabik*

flute (n)	فلوت، مزمار	*fulūt, mizmār*
flutist (n)	عازف الفلوت	*'āziful fulūt*
flutter (v)	رفرف، صفق	*rafrafa, ṣafaqa*
flutter (n)	رفرفة، ارتعاش	*rafrafah, irti'āsh*
fluvial (adj)	نهري	*nahrī*
flux (n)	تقلب، جريان، تغير	*taqallub, jarayān, taghayyur*
fly (v)	طار، فر	*ṭāra, farra*
fly (n)	ذبابة	*dhubābah*
flyer = flier		
flying (adj/n)	طائر، طيران	*ṭā'ir, ṭayarān*
flyleaf (n)	ورقة الغفل	*waraqatul ghufl*
flyover = overpass		
fly paper (n)	ورق الذباب	*waraqudh dhubāb*
flysheet = handbill		
flyweight (n)	وزن الذبابة	*waznudh dhubābah*
flywheel (n)	حذافة	*ḥadhdhāfah*
foal (n/v)	فلو، ولدت فلواً	*filw, waladat filwan*
foam (n)	زبد، رغوة	*zabad, raghwah*
foam (v)	أرغى، أزبد	*arghā, azbada*
foamy (adj)	زبدي، رغوي	*zabadī, raghwī*
focal (adj)	بؤري، محرقي	*bu'rī, miḥraqī*
focalization,-isa- (n)	تبئير، تبؤر	*tab'īr, taba''ur*
focalize,-ise (v)	بؤر، تبأر	*ba''ara, taba''ara*
focus (n)	بؤرة، نقطة الاحتراق	*bu'rah, nuqṭatul iḥtirāq*
focus (v)	ركز، عدل البؤرة	*rakkaza,'addalal bu'rah*
focused (adj)	مركز	*murakkaz*
fodder (n)	علف	*'alaf*
foe (n)	عدو، خصم	*'aduww, khaṣm*
foetal (fetal) (adj)	خاص بالجنين	*khāṣṣ bil janīn*

foetus (fetus) (n)	جنين	*janīn*
fog (n/v)	ضباب، لف الضباب	*ḍabāb, laffaḍ ḍabāb*
foggy (adj)	ضبابي، غير واضح	*ḍabābī, ghair wāḍiḥ*
foggy (n)	محافظ، رجعي	*muḥāfiẓ, raj'ī*
foible (n)	نقطة ضعف	*nuqṭatu ḍa'f*
foil (n)	مغول، رقاقة معدنية	*mighwal, ruqāqah ma'diniyyah*
foil (v)	هزم، خيب	*hazama, khayyaba*
foist (v)	دس، أكره	*dassa, akraha*
fold (v)	طوى، ثنى، لف	*ṭawā, thanā, laffa*
fold (n)	حظيرة الخراف، جماعة	*ḥaẓīratul khirāf, jamā'ah*
foldaway (adj)	قابل للطي	*qābil liṭ ṭay*
folder (n)	ملف للأوراق	*milaff lil aurāq*
foliage (n)	أوراق النبتة	*aurāqun nabtah*
folio (n)	ورقة، حافظة أوراق	*waraqah, ḥāfiẓatu aurāq*
folk (n)	قوم، عشيرة	*qaum, 'ashīrah*
folk (adj)	شعبي	*sha'bī*
folklore (n)	تقاليد شعبية	*taqālīd sha'biyyah*
folk-song (n)	أغنية شعبية	*ughniyyah sha'biyyah*
folk-tale (n)	أسطورة شعبية	*usṭūrah sha'biyyah*
follow (v)	تبع، اتبع، تعقب	*tabi'a, ittaba'a, ta'aqqaba*
follower (n)	تابع، رادف	*tābi', rādif*
following (adj/n)	تالٍ، مجموعة أتباع	*tālin, majmū'atu atbā'*
folly (n)	حماقة، خرق	*ḥamāqah, khurq*
foment (v)	كمد، أثار	*kammada, athāra*
fond (adj)	مولع، محب	*mūla', muḥibb*
fondant (n)	فندان	*fundān*

fondle (v)	لاطف، ربت على	*lāṭafa, rabbata ʻalā*
fondling (adj)	مدلل، عزيز	*mudallil, ʻazīz*
fondly (adv)	بحنان، بإعزاز	*bi ḥanān, bi iʻzāz*
fondness (n)	حنان، إعزاز	*ḥanān, iʻzāz*
fonduce (n)	مذوبة	*mudhawwabah*
font (n)	حوض المعمودية	*ḥauḍul maʻmūdiyyah*
food (n)	طعام، قوت	*ṭaʻām, qūt*
foodstuff (n)	مادة غذائية	*māddah ghidhā'iyyah*
fool (n)	مجنون، مغفل، أحمق	*majnūn, mughaffal, aḥmaq*
fool (v)	لها، عبث	*lahā, ʻabatha*
foolhardy (adj)	متهور، طائش	*mutahawwir, ṭā'ish*
foolish (adj)	أحمق، سخيف	*aḥmaq, sakhīf*
foolishly (adv)	بحماقة، بسخافة	*bi ḥamāqah, bi sakhāfah*
foolishness (n)	حماقة، خرق	*ḥamāqah, khurq*
foolproof (adj)	غير خطر	*ghair khaṭir*
foolscap (n)	ورق ديواني	*waraq dīwānī*
fool's errand (n)	مغامرة سخيفة	*mughāmarah sakhīfah*
fool's paradise (n)	سعادة وهمية	*saʻādah wahmiyyah*
foot (n)	قدم، خطو	*qadam, khaṭw*
footage (n)	قدمية	*qadamiyyah*
football (n)	كرة القدم	*kuratul qadam*
footbridge (n)	جسر المشاة	*jisrul mushāt*
footed (adj)	ذو قدم	*dhū qadam*
footfall (n)	وقع أقدام	*waqʻu aqdām*
foothill (n)	تل سفحي	*tall safḥī*
foothold (n)	موقف، مركز	*mauqif, markaz*
footing (n)	رسوخ القدمين، أساس	*rusūkhul qadamain, asās*
footlights (n)	أضواء المسرح	*aḍwā'ul masraḥ*
footling (adj)	تافه، أحمق	*tāfih, aḥmaq*

footloose (adj)	حر، مترحل	*ḥurr, mutaraḥḥil*
footman (n)	خادم	*khādim*
footmark (n)	أثر القدم	*atharul qadam*
footnote (n)	حاشية، هامش	*ḥāshiyah, hāmish*
footpath (n)	ممر المشاة	*mamarrul mushāt*
footprint (n)	أثر القدم	*atharul qadam*
footrest (n)	مسند للقدمين	*misnad lil qadamain*
footsore (adj)	متقرح القدمين	*mutaqarriḥul qadamain*
footstep (n)	خطوة، أثر القدم	*khuṭwah, atharul qadam*
footstool (n)	مسند القدمين	*misnadul qadamain*
footwear (n)	لباس القدم	*libāsul qadam*
footwork (n)	حركة القدمين	*ḥarakatul qadamain*
for (prep)	لـ،لأجل، في سبيل	*li, li ajli, fī sabīli*
for (conj)	لأنه، نظراً لـ	*li annahu, naẓaran li*
forage (n)	علف للماشية	*'alaf lil māshiyah*
foray (n/v)	غزوة، غزا	*ghazwah, ghazā*
forbear (v)	امتنع، أمسك	*imtana'a, amsaka*
forbearance (n)	إمساك، صبر،رفق	*imsāk, ṣabr, rifq*
forbid (v)	حظر، منع	*ḥaẓẓara, mana'a*
forbidance (n)	منع، حظر	*man', ḥaẓr*
forbidden (adj)	محظور، ممنوع	*maḥẓūr, mamnū'*
force (n)	قوة، شدة، قسر	*quwwah, shiddah, qasr*
force (v)	أكره، دفع بالقوة	*akraha, dafa'a bil quwwah*
forced (adj)	قسري، اضطراري	*qasrī, iḍṭirārī*
force-feed (v)	علف الحيوان قسراً	*'alafal ḥaiwān qasran*
forceful (adj)	قوي، فعال	*qawī, fa''āl*
forcefully (adv)	بقوة، قسراً	*bi quwwah, qasran*
forcefulness (n)	قوة، قسر	*quwwah, qasr*

force majeure (n)	قوة قاهرة	*quwwah qāhirah*
forcemeat (n)	حشوة	*ḥashwah*
forceps (n)	كلاب الجراح	*kullābul jarrāḥ*
forcible (adj)	قسري، قوي	*qasrī, qawī*
ford (n)	مخاضة	*makhāḍah*
fore (adj)	أمامي، سابق	*amāmī, sābiq*
forearm (n/v)	ساعد، أعد	*sā'id, a'adda*
forebear (forbear) (n)	جد، سلف	*jadd, salaf*
foreboding (adj)	منذر بشر	*mundhir bi sharr*
forecast (v)	تكهن، تنبأ	*takahhana, tanabba'a*
forecast (n)	خطة، نبوءة	*kuṭṭah, nubū'ah*
forecaster (n)	منذر، متكهن	*mundhir, mutakahhin*
foreclose (v)	عاق، حبس الرهن	*'āqa, ḥabasar rahn*
foreclosure (n)	حبس الرهن	*ḥabsur rahn*
foredoomed (adj)	مقدر، مقضي عليه	*muqaddar, maqḍī 'alaih*
forefather (n)	جد، سلف	*jadd, salaf*
forefinger (n)	سبابة	*sabbābah*
forefeet (n)	قائمة أمامية	*qā'imah amāmiyyah*
forehead (n)	جبهة، مقدمة	*jabhah, muqaddamah*
foreign (adj)	أجنبي، غريب	*ajnabī, gharīb*
foreigner (n)	أجنبي، غريب	*ajnabī, gharīb*
foreign exchange	عملة أجنبية، مبادلة خارجية	*'umlah ajnabiyyah, mubādalah khārijiyyah*
foreign minister	وزير الخارجية	*wazīrul khārijiyyah*
foreign secretary	وزير الخارجية	*wazīrul khārijiyyah*
foreleg (n)	قائمة أمامية	*qā'imah amāmiyyah*
forelock (n)	ناصية، قصة	*nāṣiyah, quṣṣah*
foreman (n)	ملاحظ العمال	*mulāḥizul 'ummāl*
foremost (adj)	رئيسي، أول	*ra'īsī, awwal*
foremost (adv)	أولاً	*awwalan*

forename (n)	اسم أول	*ism awwal*
forensic (adj)	قضائي، جدلي	*qaḍā'ī, jadalī*
forerunner (n)	رائد، نذير	*rā'id, nadhīr*
foresee (v)	تنبأ، أدرك قبل الحدوث	*tanabba'a, adraka qablal ḥudūth*
foreshadow (v)	آذن، أنذر	*ādhana, andhara*
foreshore (n)	صدر الشاطئ	*ṣadrush shāṭi'*
foreshorten (v)	قصر	*qaṣṣara*
foresight (n)	بصيرة، حكمة	*baṣīrah, ḥikmah*
foreskin (n)	قلفة، غرلة	*qulfah, ghurlah*
forest (n)	غابة، حرج	*ghābah, ḥaraj*
forester (n)	مراقب الأحراج	*murāqibul aḥrāj*
forestry (n)	حرجة	*ḥarajah*
foretaste (n)	دلالة، توقع	*dalālah, tawaqqu'*
foretell (v)	تنبأ، تكهن	*tanabba'a, takahhana*
forethought (n)	تبصر، تدبر	*tabaṣṣur, tadabbur*
forever (adv)	إلى الأبد، أبداً	*ilal abad, abadan*
forewarn (v)	حذر مقدماً	*ḥadhdhara muqaddaman*
foreword (n)	مقدمة الكتاب، تمهيد	*muqaddamatul kitāb, tamhīd*
forefeit (v)	غرم، صادر	*gharama, ṣādara*
forefeit (n)	غرامة، مصادرة	*gharāmah, muṣādarah*
forefeiture (n)	خسران، مصادرة	*khusrān, muṣādarah*
forge (n)	كير الحداد، مسبك	*kīrul ḥaddād, misbak*
forge (v)	شكل، لفق	*shakkala, laffaqa*
forger (n)	مزور، مزيف	*muzawwir, muzayyif*
forgery (n)	تزييف، تزوير	*tazyīf, tazwīr*
forget (v)	نسي، سها	*nasiya, sahā*
forgetful (adj)	مهمل، كثير النسيان	*muhmil, kathīrun nisyān*
forgetfully (adv)	بإهمال	*bi ihmāl*

forgetfulness (n)	إهمال، نسيان	*ihmāl, nisyān*
forgettable (adj)	عرضة للنسيان	*'urḍah lin nisyān*
forgive (v)	عفا، غفر	*'afā, ghafara*
forgiveness (n)	مغفرة، عفو	*maghfirah, 'afw*
forgiving (adj)	غفور، صفوح	*ghafūr, ṣafūḥ*
forgo (v)	امتنع، أمسك	*imtana'a, amsaka*
fork (n)	شوكة، مذراة، مفرق طريق	*shaukah, midhrāt, mafraqu ṭarīq*
fork (v)	ذرى بمذراة، تفرع	*dharrā bi midhrāt, tafarra'a*
forked (adj)	متفرع، منشعب	*mutafarri', munsha'ib*
forlorn (adj)	مهجور، بائس	*mahjūr, bā'is*
form (n)	هيئة، استمارة، نمط	*hai'ah, istimārah, namaṭ*
form (v)	شكل، صاغ	*shakkala, ṣāgha*
formal (adj)	رسمي، عرفي، أصولي	*rasmī, 'urfī, uṣūlī*
formalism (n)	شكلية	*shakliyyah*
formalist (n)	شكلي	*shaklī*
formality (n)	تصرف شكلي، عادة رسمية	*taṣarruf shaklī, 'ādah rasmiyyah*
formalization,-isa- (n)	ترسيم، تشكيل	*tarsīm, tashkīl*
formalize,-ise (v)	شكل، رسم	*shakkala, rassama*
formally (adv)	حسب الرسوم، رسميًا	*ḥasbar rusūm, rasmiyyan*
format (n)	بنية، شكل	*binyah, shakl*
formation (n)	تشكيل، بينة	*tashkīl, binyah*
formative (adj)	توليدي،تصريفي،تقويمي	*taulīdī, taṣrīfī, taqwīmī*
former (adj)	سابق، آنف	*sābiq, ānif*
formerly (adv)	سابقاً، سالفاً	*sābiqan, sālifan*
formidable (adj)	مرعب، هائل	*mur'ib, hā'il*

formidably (adv)	مرعباً، بشكل هائل	*mur'iban, bi shakl hā'il*
formula (n)	صيغة، قاعدة	*ṣīghah, qā'idah*
formulate (v)	صيغ، استنبط	*ṣayyagha, istambaṭa*
formulation (n)	تصييغ، صيغة	*Taṣyīgh, ṣīghah*
fornicate (v)	زنا، فسق	*zanā, fasaqa*
fornication (n)	زنا، فسق	*zinā, fisq*
forsake (v)	هجر، تخلى	*hajara, takhallā*
forsaken (adj)	مهجور، منبوذ	*mahjūr, mambūdh*
forswear (v)	أنكر بقسم	*ankara bi qasam*
fort (n)	حصن، طابية	*ḥiṣn, ṭābiyah*
forte (adj/adv)	شديد، بشدة	*shadīd, bi shiddah*
forth (adv)	فصاعداً	*fa ṣā'idan*
forthcoming (adj)	وشيك، هال	*washīk, hāll*
forthright (adj)	مباشر، صريح	*mubāshir, ṣarīḥ*
forthwith (adv)	حالاً، توًّا	*ḥālan, tawwan*
fortieth (adj)	أربعون	*arba'ūn*
fortification (n)	تحصين، حصن	*taḥṣīn, ḥiṣn*
fortify (v)	حصن، قوى	*ḥaṣṣana, qawwā*
fortitude (n)	ثبات، جلد	*thabāt, jalad*
fortnight (n)	أسبوعان	*usbū'ān*
fortnightly (adv)	نصف شهري	*nisf shahrī*
fortress (n)	حصن، قلعة	*ḥiṣn, qal'ah*
fortuitous (adj)	سعيد، اتفاقي	*sa'īd, ittifāqī*
fortunate (adj)	سعيد، محظوظ	*sa'īd, maḥẓūẓ*
fortunately (adv)	لحسن الحظ	*li ḥusnil ḥaẓẓ*
fortune (n)	حظ، مصاير، بخت	*ḥaẓẓ, maṣāyir, bakht*
fortune-teller (n)	عراف، بصار	*'arrāf, baṣṣār*
fortune-telling (n)	عرافة، قراءة البخت	*'irāfah, qirā'atul bakht*
forty (n)	أربعون	*arba'ūn*
forum (n)	منتدى عام، اجتماع عام	*muntadā 'ām, ijtimā' 'ām*

forward (adj)	أمامي، تقدمي	*amāmī, taqaddumī*
forward (adv)	نحو الأمام، إلى الأمام	*naḥwal amām, ilal amām*
forward (v)	أرسل، عزز	*arsala, 'azzaza*
fossil (n)	مستحجر، مستحاث	*mustaḥjir, mustaḥāth*
fossilization,-isati (n)	تحجير، استحفار	*taḥjīr, istiḥfār*
fossilize,-ise (v)	حفر، تحجر	*ḥaffara, taḥajjara*
foster (v)	أرضع، رعا	*arḍa'a, ra'ā*
foul (adj)	قذر، شنيع، بذيء	*qadhir, shanī', badhī'*
foul (v)	أفسد، لوث	*afsada, lawwatha*
foul-mouthed (adj)	بذيء اللسان	*badhī'ul lisān*
foulness (n)	قذارة، بذاءة	*qadhārah, badhā'ah*
found (v)	أسس، أسبك	*assasa, asbaka*
foundation (n)	تأسيس، أساس	*ta'sīs, asās*
founder (n)	مؤسس، منشئ	*mu'assis, munshi'*
foundling (n)	طفل لقيط	*ṭifl laqīṭ*
foundry (n)	مسبك المعادن	*masbakul ma'ādin*
fount (n)	ينبوع، منبع	*yambū', mamba'*
fount (font) (n)	طقم حروف	*ṭaqmu ḥurūf*
fountain (n)	ينبوع، نافورة	*yambū', nāfūrah*
fountain-head (n)	منبع، مصدر رئيسي	*mamba', maṣdar ra'īsī*
fountain-pen (n)	قلم حبر	*qalamu ḥibr*
four (n)	أربع، أربعة	*arba', arba'ah*
fourteen (n)	أربعة عشر	*arba'ata 'ashara*
fourteenth (adj)	رابع عشر	*rābi' 'ashara*
fourth (adj)	رابع	*rābi'*
fourth dimension (n)	بعد رابع	*bu'd rābi'*
fourthly (adv)	رابعاً	*rābi'an*
fourth state (n)	طبقة رابعة، صحافة	*ṭabaqah rābi'ah, ṣiḥāfah*
fowl (n)	طير، ديك، دجاجة	*ṭair, dīk, dajājah*
fox (n)	ثعلب، شخص ماكر	*tha'lab, shakhṣ mākir*

fox (v)	أربك، خدع	*arbaka, khada'a*
foxglove (n)	قفاز الثعلب	*quffāzuth tha'lab*
foxhole (n)	حفرة المناوش	*ḥufratul munāwish*
foxhound (n)	صائد الثعالب	*ṣā'iduth tha'ālib*
foxtrot (n)	رقصة الفوكستروت	*raqṣatul fūksturūt*
foxy (adj)	ماكر	*mākir*
fracas (n)	شجار، قتال	*shijār, qitāl*
fraction (n)	كسر، كسرة	*kasr, kisrah*
fractional (adj)	كسري، جزئي	*kasrī, juz'ī*
fractious (adj)	شكس، غضوب	*shakis, ghaḍūb*
fracture (n)	كسر، شق	*kasr, shaqq*
fracture (v)	انكسر، مزق	*inkasara, mazzaqa*
fragile (adj)	قصم، سهل الانكسار	*qaṣim, sahlul inkisār*
fragility (n)	قصم، هشوشة	*qaṣm, hushūshah*
fragment (n)	شظية، كسرة	*shaẓiyyah, kisrah*
fragment (v)	شظى، تشظى	*shaẓẓā, tashaẓẓā*
fragmentary (adj)	شظوي، كسري	*shaẓawī, kisarī*
fragrance (n)	شذا، عرج، عبير	*shadhā, 'araj, 'abīr*
fragrant (adj)	عرج، ذو عبير	*'arij, dhū 'abīr*
frail (adj)	ضئيل، سهل الانقياد	*ḍa'īl, sahlul inqiyād*
frailty (n)	قصامة، ضعف	*qaṣāmah, ḍa'f*
frame (n)	إطار، هيكل، بناء	*iṭār, haikal, binā'*
frame (v)	ركب، شكل	*rakkaba, shakkala*
frame-up (n)	مكيدة	*makīdah*
framework (n)	إطار، نطاق، بنية	*iṭār, niṭāq, binyah*
franchise (n)	حق الانتخاب، امتياز	*ḥaqqul intikhāb, imtiyāz*
franchise (v)	منح حق الانتخاب	*manaḥa ḥaqqal intikhāb*
frank (adj)	صريح، واضح	*ṣarīḥ, wāḍiḥ*
frankly (adv)	بصراحة، بلا مواربة	*bi ṣarāḥah, bilā muwārabah*
frankness (n)	صراحة، وضاحة	*ṣarāḥah, waḍāḥah*

frantic (adj)	مسعور، شديد الاهتياج	*mas'ūr, shadīdul ihtiyāj*
frantically (adv)	بسعر، باهتياج شديد	*bi su'r, bihtiyāj shadīd*
fraternal (adj)	أخوي، ودي	*akhawī, wuddī*
fraternity (n)	إخاء، أخوة	*ikhā', ukhuwwah*
fraternization,-isa- (n)	تآخٍ، تصادق	*ta'ākhin, taṣāduq*
fraternize,-ise (v)	تآخى، تصادق	*ta'ākhā, taṣādaqa*
fratricide (n)	قتل الأخ	*qatlul akh*
fraud (n)	خداع،احتيال،محتال	*khidā', iḥtiyāl, muḥtāl*
fraudulence (n)	خداع، احتيال	*khidā', iḥtiyāl*
fraudulent (adj)	محتال، مخادع	*muḥtāl, mukhādi'*
fraudulently (adv)	باحتيال، بغدر	*biḥtiyāl, bi ghadr*
fraught (adj)	مملوء، مفعم	*mamlū', muf'am*
fray (n)	شجار، نزاع	*shijār, nizā'*
fray (v)	نسل الخيوط، أنهك	*nasalal khuyūṭ, anhaka*
freak (n)	فلتة، نزوة، هوىً	*faltah, nazwah, hawan*
freakish (adj)	عجيب، غريب	*'ajīb, gharīb*
freckle (v)	نمش، بقع	*nammasha, baqqa'a*
freckle (n)	نمش، كلف	*namash, kalaf*
free (adj)	حر، مستقل، طليق	*ḥurr, mustaqill, ṭalīq*
free (v)	أطلق، حرر	*aṭlaqa, ḥarrara*
free (adv)	بحرية، من غير قيد	*bi ḥurriyyah, min ghairi qaid*
freedom (n)	حرية، استقلال	*ḥurriyyah, istiqlāl*
free-for-all (n)	مناقشة عامة	*munāqashah 'āmmah*
freehand (n)	حرية التصرف	*ḥurriyyatut taṣarruf*
freehold (n)	امتلاك مطلق	*imtilāk muṭlaq*
freelance (n)	رمح طليق	*rumḥ ṭalīq*
free love (n)	حب طليق	*ḥubb ṭalīq*
freeman (n)	رجل حر	*rajul ḥurr*
freemanson (n)	بناء حر، ماسوني	*bannā' ḥurr, māsūnī*

freemansonry (n)	ماسونية	*māsūniyyah*
free port (n)	ميناء حر	*mīnā' ḥurr*
free trade (n)	تجارة حرة	*tijārah ḥurrah*
free verse (n)	شعر حر	*shi'r ḥurr*
freewheel (v)	انطلق بحرية	*inṭalqa bi ḥurriyyah*
free will (n)	حرية الإرادة	*ḥurriyyatul irādah*
freeze (v)	جمد، تجمد	*jammada, tajammada*
freeze (n)	تجميد، صقيع	*tajmīd, ṣaqī'*
freezer (n)	مجمد	*mujammid*
freezing-point (n)	نقطة التجمد	*nuqṭatut tajammud*
freight (n)	حمولة، شحنة	*ḥumūlaḥ, shaḥnah*
freight (v)	شحن، أثقل	*shaḥana, athqala*
freighter (n)	شاحن، شاحنة	*shāḥin, shāḥinah*
French (adj/n)	فرنسي، لغة فرنسية	*faransī, lughah faransiyyah*
frenetic (adj)	مسعور، شديد الاهتياج	*mas'ūr, shadīdul ihtiyāj*
frenzied (adj)	شديد الأهتياج	*shadīdul ihtiyāj*
frenzy (n)	سعر، نوبة، جنون	*su'r, naubah, junūn*
frequency (n)	تكرر، تواتر	*takarrur, tawātur*
frequent (v)	تردد، اختلف	*taraddada, ikhtalafa*
frequent (adj)	مألوف، متكرر	*ma'lūf, mutakarrir*
frequently (adv)	مراراً، تكراراً	*mirāran, takrāran*
fresco (n)	تصوير على حائط	*taṣwīr 'alā ḥā'iṭ*
fresh (adj)	طري، عذب، ناضر	*ṭarī, 'adhb, nāḍir*
fresh (adv)	حديثا، منذ لحظات	*ḥadīthan, mundhu laḥẓāt*
freshen (v)	نضر، عذب، جدد	*naḍḍara, 'adhdhaba, jaddada*
freshly (adv)	بنضارة، بانتعاش	*bi naḍārah, binti'āsh*
freshman (n)	تلميذ مبتدئ	*tilmīdh mubtadi'*
freshness (n)	نضارة، طراوة	*naḍārah, ṭarāwah*

freshwater (n)	نهري	*nahrī*
fret (v)	أغاظ، أبلى بالحك	*aghāẓa, ablā bil ḥakk*
fretful (adj)	نكد،شكس،مضطرب	*nakid, shakis, muḍṭarib*
fretfully (adv)	مضطرباً، بتبرم	*muḍṭariban, bi tabarrum*
fretsaw (n)	منشار الزخرفة	*minshāruz zakhrafah*
fretwork (n)	نقش شبكي	*naqsh shabakī*
friable (adj)	سهل الانسحاق،هش	*sahlul insiḥāq, hashsh*
friar (n)	راهب، أخ	*rāhib, akh*
friary (n)	دير، رهبنة	*dair, rahbanah*
fricassee (n)	لحم مفروم محمر	*laḥm mafrūm muḥammar*
fricative (n/adj)	احتكاكي	*iḥtikākī*
friction (n)	حك، فرك	*ḥakk, fark*
Friday (n)	يوم الجمعة	*yaumul jumu'ah*
fridge = refrigerator		
friend (n)	صديق، خل	*ṣadīq, khill*
friendless (adj)	عديم الأصدقاء	*'adīmul aṣdiqā'*
friendly (adj)	ودي، حبي	*wuddī, ḥubbī*
friendship (n)	صداقة، مودة	*ṣadāqah, mawaddah*
frieze (n)	فريز، إفريز	*farīz, ifrīz*
frigate (n)	حراقة، فرغاظة	*ḥarrāqah, firghāẓah*
fright (n)	رعب، شيء بشع	*ru'b, shay' bashi'*
frighten (v)	أرعب، ارتعب، أفزع	*ar'aba, irta'aba, afza'a*
frightening (adj)	مرعب، مخيف	*mur'ib, mukhīf*
frightful (adj)	مرعب، بغيض	*mur'ib, baghīḍ*
frightfully (adv)	بشكل مرعب	*bi shakl mur'ib*
frigid (adj)	قارس، بارد	*qāris, bārid*
frigidity (n)	برودة جنسية	*burūdah jinsiyyah*
frill (n)	هدب، ريش	*hudb, rīsh*
fringe (n)	هداب، حاشية	*huddāb, ḥāshiyah*

fringe (v)	هدب، زركش بالحواشي	*haddaba, zarkasha bil ḥawāshī*
fringe benefit	فائدة هدابية	*fā'idah huddābiyyah*
frippery (n)	ملابس متكلفة	*malābis mutakallafah*
frisk (v)	فتش، رقص مرحاً	*fattasha, raqaṣa maraḥan*
frisky (adj)	مرح، لعوب	*mariḥ, la'ūb*
fritter (n)	فطيرة مقلية	*faṭīrah maqliyyah*
frivolity (n)	عبث، سخافة	*'abath, sakhāfah*
frivolous (adj)	تافه، عابث	*tāfih, 'ābith*
frivolously (adv)	بتفاهة، بخفة	*bi tafāhah, bi khiffah*
frizz (n)	جعدة	*ja'dah*
frock (n)	عباءة، جلباب	*'abā'ah, jilbāb*
frog (n)	ضفدع	*ḍifda'*
frogman (n)	رجل ضفدع	*rajul ḍifda'*
frolic (adj/n)	مرح، مرح	*mariḥ, maraḥ*
frolicsome (adj)	مرح، مزوح	*mariḥ, mazūḥ*
from (prep)	من، عن، منذ	*min, 'an, mundhu*
frond (n)	ورقة، خوصة	*waraqah, khūṣah*
front (n)	صدر، مقدم	*ṣadr, muqaddam*
front (adj/v)	أمامي، واجه	*amāmī, wājaha*
frontage (n)	واجهة مبنى	*wājihatu mabnan*
frontal (adj)	أمامي، مباشر	*amāmī, mubāshir*
frontier (n)	حد، تخم	*ḥadd, takhm*
frontiersman (n)	تخومي	*tukhūmī*
frontispiece (n)	موجهة، مواجهة	*muwajjahah, muwājihah*
front man (n)	رئيس صوري	*ra'īs ṣuwarī*
front page (n)	خطير، مثير	*khaṭīr, muthīr*
frost (n)	درجة التجمد، صقيع، برودة	*darajatut tajammud, ṣaqī', burūdah*
frost (v)	غطى بالصقيع	*ghaṭṭā biṣ ṣaqī'*

frostbite (n)	قضمة الصقيع	*qaḍmatuṣ ṣaqīʻ*
frosty (adj)	بارد جدًا، مكسو بالصقيع	*bārid jiddan, maksū biṣ ṣaqīʻ*
froth (n)	زبد، رغوة	*zabad, raghwah*
froth (v)	أزبد، أرغى	*azbada, arghā*
frothy (adj)	مزبد، خفيف	*muzbid, khafīf*
frown (v)	عبس، قطب	*ʻabasa, qaṭṭaba*
frown (n)	عبوسة، جهومة	*ʻubūsah, juhūmah*
frozen (adj)	منجمد، مبرد	*munjamid, mubarrad*
frugal (adj)	مقتصد، اقتصادي	*muqtaṣid, iqtiṣādī*
frugality (n)	اقتصاد، تدبير المصروف	*iqtiṣād, tadbīrul maṣrūf*
frugally (adv)	باقتصاد، بتوفير	*biqtiṣād, bi taufīr*
fruit (n)	فاكهة، نتيجة ، فائدة	*fākihah, natījah, fāʼidah*
fruit (v)	أثمر	*athmara*
fruiterer (n)	فاكهاني	*fākihānī*
fruitful (adj)	مثمر، خصب	*muthmir, khaṣib*
fruitfully (adv)	بنوع مربح	*bi nauʻ murbiḥ*
fruitfulness (n)	إثمار، ثمرة	*ithmār, thamrah*
fruition (n)	إثمار، نيل المرام	*ithmār, nailul marām*
fruitless (adj)	عقيم، غير مثمر	*ʻaqīm, ghair muthmir*
fruity (adj)	فاكهي، ممتع جدًا	*fākihī, mumtiʻ jiddan*
frustrate (v)	أحبط، خيب	*aḥbaṭa, khayyaba*
frustrated (adj)	عديم الجدوى، مخيب	*ʻadīmul jadwā, mukhayyab*
frustrating (adj)	مخيب، محبط	*mukhayyib, muḥbiṭ*
frustration (n)	إحباط، تثبيط، خيبة	*iḥbāṭ, tathbīṭ, khaibah*
fry (v)	قلى، حمر	*qalā, ḥammara*
fry (n)	صغار السمك	*ṣighārus samak*
fryer (frier) (n)	مقلاة، طواية	*miqlāt, ṭawwāyah*
frying-pan =fryer		
fuddled (adj)	مرتبك، سكران	*murtabik, sakrān*

fudge (v)	راغ، غش	*rāgha, ghashsha*
fuel (n/v)	وقود، زود بالوقود	*waqūd, zawwada bil waqūd*
fugitive (adj/n)	لاجئ، آبق	*lāji', ābiq*
fulfil (fulfill) (v)	أتم، أنجز، وفى	*atamma, anjaza, wafā*
fulfilling (adj)	منجز، متم	*munjiz, mutimm*
fulfilment (n)	إنجاز، وفاء	*injāz, wafā'*
full (adj)	كامل، تام، مليء	*kāmil, tāmm, malī'*
full (adv)	تماماً، مباشرةً	*tamāman,mubāsharatan*
full-blooded (adj)	حقيقي، قوي	*ḥaqīqī, qawī*
full-blown (adj)	كامل، تام	*kāmil, tāmm*
full-bodied (adj)	ضخم الجسم، غني النكهة	*ḍakhmul jism, ghaniyyun nakhah*
full-dress (adj)	تام، كامل	*tāmm, kāmil*
full-fledged (adj)	كامل الرتبة، تام	*kāmilur rutbah, tāmm*
full house (n)	فول	*fūl*
full-length (n)	حجم طبيعي	*ḥajm ṭabī'ī*
full moon (n)	بدر	*badr*
full-scale (adj)	كلي، كامل	*kullī, kāmil*
full stop (n)	نقطة الوقف	*nuqṭatul waqf*
full-time (adj)	كامل	*kāmil*
fully (adv)	تماماً، كاملاً	*tamāman, kāmilan*
fulminate (v)	شجب بعنف	*shajaba bi 'unf*
fulmination (n)	شجب عنيف	*shajb 'anīf*
fulsome (adj)	سمج، ثقيل	*samij, thaqīl*
fume (n)	دخان، بخار، غضب	*dukhān,bukhār,ghaḍab*
fume (v)	دخن، استشاط غضبًا	*dakhkhana, istashāṭa ghaḍaban*
fumigate (v)	دخن، بخر	*dakhkhana, bakhkhara*
fumigation (n)	تدخين، تبخير	*tadkhīn, tabkhīr*

fun (n)	مزاح، لهو	*muzāḥ, lahw*
function (n)	عمل، حفلة رسمية	*'amal,ḥaflah rasmiyyah*
function (v)	عمل، أدى الوظيفة	*'amila, addal waẓīfah*
functional (adj)	وظيفي، عملي	*waẓīfī, 'amalī*
functionalism (n)	مذهب انتفاعي	*madhhab intifā'ī*
functionary (n)	موظف، مأمور	*muwaẓẓaf, ma'mūr*
fund (n)	مال، ذخيرة	*māl, dhakhīrah*
fund (v)	مول، ادخر	*mawwala, iddakhara*
fundamental (adj)	أساسي، رئيسي	*asāsī, ra'īsī*
fundamental (n)	أساس، جوهر	*asās, jauhar*
fundamentalism (n)	مذهب العصمة	*madhhabul 'iṣmah*
fundamentalist (n)	متعصب، متشدد	*muta'aṣṣib, mutashaddid*
funeral (n)	جنازة، حفلة جنائزية	*janāzah, ḥaflah janā'iziyyah*
funerary (adj)	خاص بالدفن	*khāṣṣ bid dafn*
funereal (adj)	جنائزي، مأتمي	*janā'izī, ma'tamī*
fungicide (n)	مبيد الفطر	*mubīdul fuṭr*
fungus (n)	فطر	*fuṭr*
funicular (adj)	حبلي، توتري	*ḥablī, tawatturī*
funnel (n)	مدخنة، قمع	*midkhanah, qam'*
funnel (v)	قمع	*qamma'a*
funny (adj)	مضحك، هزلي	*muḍḥik, hazlī*
fur (n)	فرو، وبر	*farw, wabar*
furious (adj)	ثائر، هائج، صاخب	*thā'ir, hā'ij, ṣākhib*
furiously (adv)	باهتياج، بغيظ	*bihtiyāj, bi ghaiẓ*
furiousness (n)	اهتياج، غيظ، احتدام	*ihtiyāj, ghaiẓ, iḥtidām*
furl (v)	لف، التف، طوى	*laffa, iltaffa, ṭawā*
furlong (n)	فرلنغ، مقياس طولي	*farlungh, miqyās ṭūlī*
furlough (n)	إجازة، رخصة	*ijāzah, rukhṣah*
furnace (n)	فرن، أتون	*furn, attūn*

furnish (v)	جهز، زود	*jahhaza, zawwada*
furnishings (n)	ملابس، قفافير	*malābis, qafāfīr*
furniture (n)	أثاث، مفروشات	*athāth, mafrūshāt*
furore (furor)	غضب، ضجة	*ghaḍab, ḍajjah*
furrier (n)	فراء	*farrā'*
furrow (n)	ثلم، أخدود	*thalm, ukhdūd*
furrow (v)	ثلم، تثلم	*thallama, tathallama*
furry (adj)	فروي، وبري	*farwī, wabarī*
further (adj)	إضافي، آخر، أبعد	*iḍāfī, ākhar, ab'ad*
further (v)	أيد، عزز	*ayyada, 'azzaza*
further (adv)	إلى حد أبعد، أيضاً	*ilā ḥadd ab'ad, aiḍan*
furtherance (n)	تعضيد، تأييد	*ta'ḍīd, ta'yīd*
furthermore (adj)	إلى هذا	*ilā hādha*
furthermost (adj)	أبعد، أقصى	*ab'ad, aqṣā*
furtive (adj)	مسروق، مختلس	*masrūq, mukhtalas*
furtiveness (n)	اختلاس، استراق	*ikhtilās, istirāq*
fury (n)	غضب شديد، هياج	*ghaḍab shadīd, hayāj*
fuse (n)	صمام كهربائي، فتيل المفرقعة	*ṣimām kahrabā'ī, fatīlul mufarqi'ah*
fuse (v)	صهر، دمج	*ṣahara, damaja*
fuselage (n)	جسم الطائرة	*jismuṭ ṭā'irah*
fusillade (n)	إطلاق الرصاص	*iṭlāqur raṣāṣ*
fusion (n)	صهر، اندماج، سبك	*ṣahr, indimāj, sabk*
fuss (n)	ضوضاء، اهتياج، جلبة	*ḍauḍā', ihtiyāj, jalabah*
fuss (v)	اهتاج، ضج	*ihtāja, ḍajja*
fussy (adj)	سريع الاهتياج، لجب	*sarī'ul ihtiyāj, lajib*
fusty (adj)	عفن، رجعي	*'afin, raj'ī*
futile (adj)	باطل، عقيم	*bāṭil, 'aqīm*
futility (n)	عبث، عقم	*'abath, 'uqm*
future (n/adj)	مستقبل، آتٍ	*mustaqbal, ātin*

futurism (n)	مستقبلية	*mustaqbaliyyah*
futurist (adj/n)	مستقبلي	*mustaqbalī*
futurity (n)	استقبالية	*istiqbāliyyah*
fuzz (n)	زغب، زئبر	*zaghab, zi'bar*
fuzzy (adj)	زغب، جعد، غائم	*zaghib, ja'd, ghā'im*

G

gabble (v)	هرف، بربر	*harafa, barbara*
gabble (n)	هذر، بربرة	*hadhar, barbarah*
gable (n)	جملون	*jamalūn*
gabled (adj)	ذو جملون	*dhū jamalūn*
Gad (v)	تسكع، أهام	*tasakka'a, ahāma*
gadfly (n)	نعرة، ذبابة الخيل	*nu'arah, dhubābatul khail*
gadget (n)	أداة، آلة	*adāt, ālah*
gaffe (n)	غلطة، زلة	*ghalṭah, zallah*
gaffer (n)	ناظر العمال	*nāẓirul 'ummāl*
gag (n)	كعام، مثير للضحك	*ki'ām, muthīr liḍ ḍaḥk*
gag (v)	كعم، سد، قيأ	*ka'ama, sadda, qayya'a*
gaggle (n)	جماعة، قطيع	*jamā'ah, qaṭī'*
gaiety (n)	مرح، مباهج، انبساط	*maraḥ, mabāhij, imbisāṭ*
gaily (adv)	بمرح، بحبور	*bi maraḥ, bi ḥubūr*
gain (n)	كسب، ربح	*kasb, ribḥ*
gain (v)	كسب، ربح، نال	*kasaba, rabiḥa, nāla*
gainful (adj)	مربح، نافع	*murbiḥ, nāfi'*
gainsay (v)	أنكر، خالف	*ankara, khālafa*
gait (n)	مشية، قامة	*mishyah, qāmah*
gaiter (n)	غيتر، جرموق	*ghaitar, jurmūq*
gala (n)	مهرجان، احتفال	*mahrajān, iḥtifāl*
galaxy (n)	كوكبة، مجرة	*kaukabah, majarrah*

gale (n)	عاصفة، ريح هوجاء	*'āṣifah, rīḥ haujā'*
gall (n)	صفراء، ضغينة، عفصة	*ṣafrā', ḍaghīnah, 'afṣah*
gall (v)	قرح، غاظ، تقرح	*qarraḥa, ghāẓa, taqarraḥa*
gallant (n/adj)	شجاع، أنيق	*shujā', anīq*
gallantly (adv)	بشجاعة، بمروءة	*bi shajā'ah, bi murū'ah*
gallantry (n)	بسالة، تودد للنساء	*basālah, tawaddud lin nisā'*
gall bladder (n)	مرارة	*marārah*
galleon (n)	غليون، قادوس	*ghalyūn, qādūs*
gallery (n)	رواق، شرفة خارجية	*riwāq, shurfah khārijiyyah*
galley (n)	قادس، لوح الطباعة	*qādis, lauḥuṭ ṭibā'ah*
galling (adj)	مثير، غائظ	*muthīr, ghā'iẓ*
gallivant (v)	سافر للتنــــزة	*sāfara lit tanazzuh*
gallon (n)	غالون	*ghālūn*
gallop (n)	عدو الفرس	*'adwul faras*
gallop (n)	جرى عدواً، عدا	*jarā 'adwan, 'adā*
gallows (n)	مشنقة، آلة الإعدام	*mishnaqah, ālatul i'dām*
gallstone (n)	حصاة صفرية	*ḥaṣāt ṣafrawiyyah*
galore (adv)	بوفرة، بكثرة	*bi wafrah, bi kathrah*
galosh (n)	كلوش، حذاء فوقي	*kalūsh, ḥidhā' fauqī*
galvanic (adj)	غلواني، عصبي	*ghalwānī, 'aṣabī*
galvanize,-ise (v)	غلون، نبه	*ghalwana, nabbaha*
gambit (n)	افتتاح، مناورة	*iftitāḥ, munāwarah*
gamble (n)	مقامرة، مغامرة	*muqāmarah, mughāmarah*
gamble (v)	قامر، غامر	*qāmara, ghāmara*

gambler(n)	مقامر، لاعب القمار	*muqāmir, lā'ibul qimār*
gambling (n)	قمار، مقامرة	*qimār, muqāmarah*
gambol (v)	طفر مرحاً	*ṭafara maraḥan*
game (n)	لعبة، مهنة، مباراة	*la'bah, mihnah, mubārāt*
game (adj)	مصمم، ثابت العزم	*muṣammam, thābitul 'azm*
gamekeeper (n)	حارس الطرائد	*ḥārisuṭ ṭarā'id*
gamely (adv)	ببسالة، بشجاعة	*bi basālah, bi shajā'ah*
gamut (n)	سلسلة كاملة	*silsilah kāmilah*
gamy (adj)	ذو طعم، نتن، فاسد	*dhū ṭa'm, natin, fāsid*
gander (n)	ذكر الإوز	*dhakarul 'iwazz*
gang (n)	جماعة، عصابة	*jamā'ah, 'iṣābah*
gang (v)	طقم	*ṭaqqama*
gangland (n)	عالم الإجرام المنظم	*'ālamul ijrām al munaẓẓam*
ganglion (n)	كتلة عصبية	*kutlah 'aṣabiyyah*
gangplank (n)	معبر	*mi'bar*
gangrene (n)	غنغرينا	*ghangharīnā*
gangster (n)	عضو في العصابة	*'uḍw fil 'iṣābah*
gangway (n)	ممر، ممر سالك	*mamarr, mamarr sālik*
gannet (n)	أطيش، غنيط	*aṭyash, ghanīṭ*
gantry (n)	جسر الإشارات	*jisrul ishārāt*
gap (n)	فجوة، فرجة، انقطاع	*fajwah, furjah, inqiṭā'*
gape (v)	فغر الفم	*fagharal fam*
garage (n)	مرأب	*mar'ab*
garage (v)	آوى في مرأب	*āwā fi mar'ab*
garb (n)	ملابس، زي	*malābis, ziyy*
garbage (n)	نفاية، كلام تافه	*nufāyah, kalām tāfih*
garbled (adj)	مشوش، مرتبك	*mushawwash, murtabik*

garcon (n)	نادل	*nādil*
garden (n)	حديقة، جنة، بستان	*ḥadīqah, jannah, bustān*
garden (v)	بستن، عمل في بستان	*bastana, ʻamila fī bustān*
garden city	مدينة جنائنية	*madīnah janā'iniyyah*
gardener (v)	بستاني، عامل في بستان	*bustānī, ʻāmil fī bustān*
gardenia (n)	غردينيا	*ghardīniyā*
gardening (n)	بستنة	*bastanah*
gargantuan (adj)	ضخم، هائل	*ḍakhm, hā'il*
gargle (v/n)	تغرغر، تغرغرة	*tagharghara, tagharghārah*
garish (adj)	مزخرف، مبهرج	*muzakhraf, mubahraj*
garland (n/v)	إكليل زهر، كلل	*iklīlu zahr, kallala*
garlic (n)	ثوم	*thūm*
garlicky	ثومي	*thūmī*
garment (n)	ثوب، كساء	*thaub, kisā'*
garner (v)	ادخر، كدس	*iddakhara, kaddasa*
garnet (n)	عقيق أحمر	*ʻaqīq aḥmar*
garnish (v)	زين، زود	*zayyana, zawwada*
garret (n)	علية، غرفة سطح	*ʻilliyyah, ghurfatu saṭḥ*
garrison (n)	حامية، حرس	*ḥāmiyah, ḥaras*
garrison (v)	أقام حامية	*aqāma ḥāmiyah*
garrotte (garotte) (n)	مخنق	*mikhnaq*
garrotte (v)	أعدم بالمخنق	*aʻdama bil mikhnaq*
garrulous (adj)	ثرثار، مهذار	*tharthār, mihdhār*
garter (n)	رباط للجورب	*ribāṭ lil jaurab*
gas (n)	غاز، كلام فارغ	*ghāz, kalām fārigh*
gas (v)	غوز، أطلق غازاً	*ghawwaza, aṭlaqa ghāzan*
gasbag (n)	ثرثار، مهذار	*tharthār, mihdhār*
gas chamber (n)	حجرة الغاز	*ḥujratul ghāz*

gaseous (adj)	غازي، بخاري	*ghāzī, bukhārī*
gash (n)	جرح بليغ	*jurḥ balīgh*
gasholder (n)	خزان الغاز	*khazzānul ghāz*
gasoline (n)	غازولين	*ghāzūlīn*
gasometre (n)	مغواز، خزان الغاز	*mighwāz, khazzānul ghāz*
gasp (n/v)	لهاث، لهث	*luhāth, lahatha*
gas station (n)	محطة بنـــزين	*maḥaṭṭatu binzīn*
gassy (adj)	غازي	*ghāzī*
gastric (adj)	معدي	*ma'idī*
gastrics (n)	التهاب المعدة	*iltihābul ma'idah*
gastronomy (n)	فن حسن الأكل	*fannu ḥuṣnil akl*
gasworks (n)	مصنع الغاز	*maṣna'ul ghāz*
gate (n)	باب، مدخل	*bāb, madkhal*
gatekeeper (n)	بواب، حارس الباب	*bawwāb, ḥārisul bāb*
gateway (n)	مدخل، بوابة	*madkhal, bawwābah*
gather (v)	جمع، لم، احتشد	*jama'a, lamma, iḥtashada*
gathering (n)	اجتماع، حشد	*ijtimā', ḥashd*
gauche (adj)	أخرق، غير لبق	*akhraq, ghair labiq*
gaudily (adv)	بزخرفة	*bi zakhrafah*
gaudiness (n)	بهرجة، زخرفة	*bahrajah, zakhrafah*
gaudy (adj)	مبهرج، مزوق	*mubahraj, muzawwaq*
gauge (gage) (n)	مقياس	*miqyās*
gauge (v)	قاس، قدر	*qāsa, qaddara*
gaunt (adj)	هزيل، نحيل	*hazīl, naḥīl*
gauntlet (n)	قفاز	*quffāz*
gauntness (n)	هزال، كآبة	*huzāl, ka'ābah*
gauze (n)	شاش، نسيج رقيق	*shāsh, nasīj raqīq*
gauzy (adj)	شفاف، هفاف	*shaffāf, haffāf*
gavotte (n)	غافوتية	*ghāfūtiyyah*
gawk (v)	حدق ببلاهة	*ḥaddaqa bi balāhah*

gawky (adj)	أخرق، غير لبق	*akhraq, ghair labiq*
gay (adj)	مرح، زاهٍ، خليع	*mariḥ, zāhin, khalī'*
gayness (n)	ابتهاج، مرح	*ibtihāj, maraḥ*
gaze (n)	نظرة محدقة	*naẓrah muḥaddiqa*
gaze (v)	حدق، شخص	*ḥaddaqa, shakhaṣa*
gazelle (n)	غزال، ظبي	*ghazāl, ẓaby*
gazette (n)	جريدة	*jarīdah*
gazetteer (n)	صحافي	*ṣiḥāfī*
gear (n)	ترس، جهاز، عدة	*turs, jihāz, 'uddah*
gear (v)	عدل، هيأ، جهز	*'addala, hayya'a, jahhaza*
gearbox (n)	علبة التروس	*'ulbatut turūs*
gearing (n)	تزويد بالتروس، جهاز	*tazwīd bit turūs, jihāz*
gear level (n)	ذراع التروس	*dhirā'ut turūs*
geazer (n)	رجل غريب	*rajul gharīb*
gel (n)	جل، مادة هلامية	*jall, māddah hulāmiyyah*
gelatine (n)	جيلاتين، هلام	*jīlātīn, hulām*
gelatinous (adj)	هلامي، لزج	*hulāmī, lazij*
geld (v)	خصى، أضعف	*khaṣā, aḍ'afa*
gelding (n)	فرس مخصي	*faras makhṣī*
gelignite (n)	جلجنيت	*jalijnīt*
gem (n)	جوهرة، حجر كريم	*jauharah, ḥajar karīm*
gender (n)	جنس	*jins*
gene (n)	جينة، مورثة	*jīnah, muwarrithah*
genealogical (adj)	نسبي، سلالي	*nasabī, sulālī*
genealogist (n)	اختصاصي بعلم الأنساب	*ikhtiṣāṣī bi 'ilmil ansāb*
genealogy (n)	علم الأنساب، سلسلة الأنساب	*'ilmul ansāb, silsilatul ansāb*
general (adj)	عام، شامل	*'āmm, shāmil*
general (n)	رئيس عام، جنرال	*ra'īs 'āmm, jinrāl*
general assembly (n)	مجلس أعلى	*majlis a'lā*

generalissimo (n)	القائد العام	*al qā'id al 'āmm*
generalist (n)	لااختصاصي	*lā ikhtiṣāṣī*
generality (n)	عمومية، أغلبية	*'umūmiyyah, aghlabiyyah*
generalization,-sat-	تعميم، عبارة عامة	*ta'mīm, 'ibārah 'āmmah*
generalize,-ise (v)	عمم، استقرى	*'ammama, istaqrā*
generally (adv)	عموماً، عادةً	*'umūman, 'ādatan*
general officer	ضابط كبير	*ḍābiṭ kabīr*
generalship (n)	منصب الجنرال	*manṣabul jinrāl*
generate (v)	ولد، ولد، أحدث	*walad, wallada, aḥdatha*
generation (n)	نسل، جيل، تولد	*nasl, jīl, tawallud*
generative (adj)	مولد، منتج	*muwallid, muntij*
generator (n)	مولد، مرجل	*muwallid, mirjal*
generic (adj)	عام، شامل، سائب	*'āmm, shāmil, sā'ib*
generosity (n)	سخاء، جود	*sakhā', jūd*
generous (adj)	كريم، سخي	*karīm, sakhī*
generously (adv)	بسخاء، بمروءة	*bi sakhā', bi murū'ah*
genesis (n)	سفر التكوين، أصل	*sifrut takwīn, aṣl*
genetic (adj)	أصلي، جيني، مورثي	*aṣlī, jīnī, muwarrithī*
geneticist (n)	اختصاصي في علم الوراثة	*ikhtiṣāṣī fī 'ilmil wirāthah*
genetics (n)	علم الوراثة، تركيب وراثي	*'ilmul wirāthah, tarkīb wirāthī*
genial (adj)	لطيف، أنيس	*laṭīf, anīs*
geniality (n)	لطافة، أنس	*laṭāfah, uns*
genially (adv)	بلطف، بانس	*bi luṭf, bi uns*
genie (n)	جني، عفريت	*jinnī, 'ifrīt*
genital (adj)	تناسلي، توالدي	*tanāsulī, tawāludī*
genitals (n)	أعضاء التناسل	*a'ḍā'ut tanāsul*
genitive (n)	حالة الإضافة، حالة الجر	*ḥālatul iḍāfah, ḥālatul jarı*
genitive (adj)	إضافي، جري	*iḍāfī, jarrī*

genius (n)	عبقرية، نبوغ، سجية	*'abqariyyah, nubūgh, sajiyyah*
genocide (n)	إبادة جماعية	*ibādah jamā'iyyah*
genre (n)	نوع، ضرب، أسلوب	*nau', ḍarb, uslūb*
genteel (adj)	أنيق، لطيف	*anīq, laṭif*
gentian (n)	جنطيانا	*janṭiyānā*
gentility (n)	نبالة، كياسة، رقة	*nabālah, kiyāsah, riqqah*
gentle (adj)	نبيل، لطيف، سهل الانقياد	*nabīl, laṭīf, sahlul inqiyād*
gentlefolk (n)	نبلاء، أشراف	*nubalā', ashrāf*
gentleman (n)	رجل نبيل، رجل كريم	*rajul nabīl, rajul karīm*
gentlemanly (adj)	جنتلماني، لطيف	*jïntilmānī, laṭīf*
gentleman's aggreement (n)	اتفاقية الجنتلمان	*ittifāqiyyatul jintilmān*
gentlewoman (n)	نبيلة المحتد	*nabīlatul maḥtid*
gently (adv)	بلطف، برقة	*bi luṭf, bi riqqah*
gentry (n)	طبقة عليا، أعيان	*ṭabaqah 'ulyā, a'yān*
genuflect (v)	حنى الركبة عبادةً	*ḥanar rukbah 'ibādatan*
genuflection,–lexi-	حني الركبة	*ḥanyur rukbah*
genuine (adj)	حقيقي، أصيل، صادق	*ḥaqīqī, aṣīl, ṣādiq*
genus (n)	جنس، نوع	*jins, nau'*
geographer (n)	عالم بالجغرافيا	*'ālim bil jughrāfiyā*
geographic-al (adj)	جغرافي	*jughrāfī*
geography (n)	علم الجغرافيا	*'ilmul jughrāfiyā*
geologic-al (adj)	جيولوجي	*jiwlūjī*
geologist (n)	اختصاصي في علم الجيولوجيا	*ikhtiṣāṣī fī 'ilmil jiwlūjiyā*
geology (n)	جيولوجيا	*jiwlūjiyā*
geometric-al (adj)	هندسي	*handasī*
geometry (n)	علم الهندسة	*'ilmul handasah*

geophysical (adj)	جيوفيزيائي	*jiwfīzyā'ī*
geophysics (n)	جيوفيزياء	*jiwfīzyā'*
geopolitics (n)	علم السياسة الطبيعية	*'ilmus siyāsah aṭ ṭabī'iyyah*
germ (n)	جرثومة، بزرة	*jurthūmah, bizrah*
German (adj/n)	ألماني، لغة ألمانية	*almānī, lughah almāniyyah*
germane (adj)	مناسب، موافق	*munāsib, muwāfiq*
germinate (v)	نبت، أنبت، أنشأ	*nabata, ambata, ansha'a*
germination (n)	إفراخ، نبت، نشوء	*ifrākh, nabt, nushū'*
gerund (n)	صيغة المصدر	*ṣīghatul maṣdar*
gestation (n)	حمل، حبل	*ḥaml, ḥabal*
gesticulate (v)	أومأ، شور	*auma'a, shawwara*
gesticulation (n)	إيماء، إيماءة	*īmā', īmā'ah*
get (v)	نال، فاز، كسب	*nāla, fāza, kasaba*
get across	عبر	*'abara*
get ahead	فاز، سبق	*fāza, sabaqa*
get around	خدع، تجنب	*khada'a, tajannaba*
get away	انصرف، فر	*inṣarafa, farra*
getaway (n)	فرار، انطلاق	*firār, inṭilāq*
get back	رجع، عاد	*raja'a, 'āda*
get down	نزل، ترجل	*nazala, tarajjala*
get in	دخل، أدخل	*dakhala, adkhala*
get into	ارتدى الملابس	*irtadal malābis*
get loose	تحرر، انفك	*taḥarrara, infakka*
get off	فر، انصرف	*farra, inṣarafa*
get on	نجح، تقدم	*najaḥa, taqaddama*
get out	خرج، استخرج	*kharaja, istakhraja*
get over	تغلب، اجتاز	*taghallaba, ijtāza*
get rid of	تخلص من	*takhallaṣa min*

get through	أنجز، اجتاز	*anjaza, ijtāza*
get to	بدأ، شرع	*bada'a, shara'a*
get together	اجتمع، كدس	*ijtama'a, kaddasa*
get-together (n)	اجتماع، حفلة	*ijtimā', ḥaflah*
get up	نهض، انتصب	*nahaḍa, intaṣaba*
get-up (n)	لباس، مظهر	*libās, maẓhar*
geyser (n)	سخانة، مسخن	*sakhkhānah, musakhkhin*
ghastly (adj)	مروع، شنيع	*murawwi', shanī'*
ghee (n)	جية	*jiyyah*
ghetto (n)	الغيت	*alghait*
ghost (n)	روح، شبح، ظل	*rūḥ, shabaḥ, ẓill*
ghostly (adj)	روحي، شبحي	*rūḥī, shabaḥī*
ghost town (n)	مدينة الأشباح	*madīnatul ashbāḥ*
ghost-writer (n)	شخص ألف لشخص أخر	*shakhṣ allafa li shakhṣ ākhar*
ghoul (n)	الغول	*alghūl*
giant (n)	مارد، عملاق	*mārid, 'imlāq*
giant (adj)	ضخم، عظيم الجسم	*ḍakhm, 'aẓīmul jism*
gibber (v)	ثرثر، هذر	*tharthara, hadhara*
gibberish (n)	ثرثرة، كلام غير واضح	*thartharah, kalām ghair wāḍiḥ*
gibbet (n)	مشنقة	*mishnaqah*
gibbon (n)	جبون	*jibbaun*
giddiness (n)	دوار، طيش	*duwār, ṭaish*
giddy (adj)	طائش، مصاب بدوار	*ṭā'ish, muṣāb bi duwār*
gift (n)	هبة، موهبة، نحلة	*hibah, mauhabah, niḥlah*
gifted (adj)	موهوب، ذكي	*mauhūb, dhakī*
gig (n)	جيغ	*jaigh*
gigantic (adj)	عملاقي، هائل	*'imlāqī, hā'il*
giggle (v/n)	قهقه، قهقهة	*qahqaha, qahqahah*

gild (v)	طلى بالذهب، موه	*ṭalā bidh dhahab, mawwaha*
gilded (adj)	مذهب	*mudhahhab*
gilt (n)	ذهب، شيء كالذهب	*dhahab, shay' kadh dhahab*
gilt-edged (adj)	مذهب الأطراف	*mudhahhabul aṭrāf*
gimcrack (n)	بهرج، سفساف	*bahraj, safsāf*
gimlet (n)	مثقاب، مخرز	*mithqāb, mikhraz*
gin (n)	جن، مسكر قوي	*jinn, muskir qawī*
ginger (n/v)	زنجبيل، نشط	*zanjabīl, nashshaṭa*
ginger beer (n)	جعة الزنجبيل	*ji'atuz zanjabīl*
gingerly (adj)	شديد الحذر	*shadīdul ḥadhr*
gingham (n)	جنهام	*jinhām*
giraffe (n)	زرافة	*zarāfah*
gird (v)	استعد للعمل	*ista'adda lil 'amal*
girder (n)	عارضة معدنية	*'āriḍah ma'diniyyah*
girdle (n)	حزام، طوق	*ḥizām, ṭauq*
girdle (v)	أحاط، طوق	*aḥāṭa, ṭawwaqa*
girl (n)	بنت، فتاة	*bint, fatāt*
girlfriend (n)	محبوبة، معشوقة	*maḥbūbah, ma'shūqah*
girlhood (n)	بنوتة	*bunūtah*
girlish (adj)	كالبنت	*kal bint*
girth (n)	حزام السرج	*ḥizāmus sarj*
gist (n)	لب، خلاصة، مخ	*lubb, khulāṣah, mukhkh*
give (v)	أعطى، منح، وهب	*a'ṭā, manaḥa, wahaba*
give away	وزع، أفشى	*wazza'a, afshā*
give in	قدم، استسلم	*qaddama, istaslama*
give into	سلم، انقاد	*sallama, inqāda*
given (adj)	محدد، معين	*muḥaddad, mu'ayyan*
give off	أخرج، أطلق	*akhraja, aṭlaqa*

give on	أشرف، أطل	*ashrafa, aṭalla*
give out	وزع، أخرج	*wazza'a, akhraja*
give over	كف، تخلى	*kaffa, takhallā*
giver (n)	معطي، مانح	*mu'ṭī, māniḥ*
give up	كف، تخلى	*kaffa, takhallā*
gizzard (n)	قانصة	*qāniṣah*
glacial (adj)	بارد جدًا، جليدي	*bārid jiddan, jalīdī*
glacier (n)	مجلدة	*majladah*
glad (adj)	مسرور، مبتهج	*masrūr, mubtahij*
gladden (v)	سر، أبهج	*sarra, abhaja*
glade (n)	فرجة في غابة	*furjah fī ghābah*
gladiator (n)	مجالد، مصارع	*mujālid, muṣāri'*
gladly (adv)	بسرور، بابتهاج	*bi surūr, bibtihāj*
gladness (n)	سرور، بهجة	*surūr, bahjah*
glamorous (adj)	فاتن، ساحر	*fātin, sāḥir*
glamour (glamor)	فتنة، سحر	*fitnah, siḥr*
glance (n)	لمحة، ومضة	*lamḥah, wamḍah*
glance (v)	أومض، لمح	*aumaḍa, lamaḥa*
glancing (adj)	غير مباشر، عرضي	*ghair mubāshir, 'araḍī*
gland (n)	غدة، سدادة	*ghuddah, sidādah*
glandular (adj)	غدي، فطري	*ghuddī, fiṭrī*
glare (n)	سطع، وهج، بهرجة	*saṭa', wahj, bahrajah*
glare (v)	سطع، لمع، توهج	*saṭa'a, lama'a, tawahhaja*
glaring (adj)	ساطع، زاهٍ	*sāṭi', zāhin*
glass (n)	زجاج، كأس	*zujāj, ka's*
glass-blowing (n)	نفخ الزجاج	*nafkhuz zujāj*
glassful (adj)	ملء كأس	*mil'u ka's*
glasshouse (n)	دفيئة	*dafī'ah*
glassware (n)	آنية زجاجية	*āniyah zujājiyyah*

glassy (adj)	زجاجي، جامد	*zujājī, jāmid*
glaze (v)	زجج، صقل	*zajjaja, ṣaqqala*
glazier (n)	زجاج	*zajjāj*
gleam (n)	وميض، شعة	*wamīḍ, shu''ah*
gleam (v)	ومض، لمح	*wamaḍa, lamaḥa*
glean (v)	جمع، التقط	*jama'a, iltaqaṭa*
glee (n)	طرب، مرح، جذل	*ṭarab, maraḥ, jadhal*
gleeful (adj)	مرح، طرب	*mariḥ, ṭarib*
gleefully (adv)	بمرح، بابتهاج	*bi maraḥ, bibtihāj*
glen (n)	وادٍ صغير، وهدة	*wādin ṣaghīr, wahdah*
glib (adj)	طبعي، غير متكلف، ذلق	*taba'ī, ghair mutakallaf, dhalq*
glide (v)	انزلق، انحدر	*inzalaqa, inḥadara*
glider (n)	منـــزلقة	*munzaliqah*
glimmer (n)	وميض، بصيص	*wamīḍ, baṣīṣ*
glimmer (v)	أومض، لاح	*aumaḍa, lāḥa*
glimmering (n)	وميض، بصيص	*wamīḍ, baṣīṣ*
glimpse (n)	نظرة خاطفة	*naẓrah khāṭifah*
glimpse (v)	ألقى نظرةً خاطفةً	*alqā naẓratan khāṭifah*
glint (v)	أومض، تلألأ	*aumaḍa, tala'la'a*
glint (n)	ومضة، إيماء	*wamḍah, īmā'*
glisten (v)	تلألأ، تألق	*tala'la'a, ta'allaqa*
glitter (v)	تألق، لمع	*ta'allaqa, lama'a*
glitter (n)	تألق، بهاء	*ta'alluq, bahā'*
glittering (adj)	متألق، لامع	*muta'alliq, lāmi'*
gloaming (n)	غسق، غبش	*ghasaq, ghabash*
gloat (v)	حدق بإعجاب	*ḥaddaqa bi i'jāb*
global (adj)	كروي، عالمي	*kurawī, 'ālamī*
globe (n)	كرة أرضية	*kurah arḍiyyah*
globular (adj)	كروي، كري	*kurawī, kurrī*

globule (n)	كرية	*kurayyah*
gloom (n)	كآبة، ظلام، غم	*ka'ābah, ẓalām, ghamm*
gloomy (adj)	متشائم، كئيب	*mutashā'im, ka'īb*
glorification (n)	تمجيد، تمجد	*tamjīd, tamajjud*
glorified (adj)	مجيد، جليل	*majīd, jalīl*
glorify (v)	مجد، بجل	*majjada, bajjala*
glorious (adj)	مجيد، رائع	*majīd, rā'i'*
glory (n)	شهرة، مجد، بهاء	*shuhrah, majd, bahā'*
gloss (n)	لمعان، بريق، تعليق	*lam'ān, barīq, ta'līq*
gloss (v)	صقل، علق	*ṣaqqala, 'allaqa*
glossary (n)	مسرد الكلمات العسيرة	*masradul kalimāt al 'asīrah*
glossy (adj)	صقيل، لامع	*ṣaqīl, lāmi'*
glove (n)	قفاز، كف	*quffāz, kaff*
glow (v)	اتقد، تورد	*ittaqada, tawarrada*
glow (n)	احتداد، توهج	*iḥtidād, tawahhuj*
glower (v)	حدق بانشداه	*ḥaddaqa binshidāh*
glowing (adj)	متوهج، متأجج	*mutawahhij, muta'ajjij*
glowworm (n)	سراج الليل	*sirājul lail*
glucose (n)	غلوكوز	*ghulūkūz*
glue (n)	غراء، مادة غروية	*ghirā', māddah gharawiyyah*
glum (adj)	كئيب، مكتئب	*ka'īb, mukta'ib*
glut (v)	أغرق، أتخم	*aghraqa, atkhama*
glut (n)	وفرة، إتخام، فيض	*wafrah, itkhām, faiḍ*
gluten (n)	غلوتين	*ghulūtīn*
glutton (n)	نهم، أكول	*nahim, akūl*
gluttonous (adj)	نهم، شره	*nahim, sharih*
glycerine (n)	غليسيرين	*ghilīsīrīn*
gnarled (adj)	كثير العقد	*kathīrul 'uqad*

gnash (v)	صر بالأسنان	*ṣarra bil asnān*
gnashing (n)	صرير الأسنان	*ṣarīrul asnān*
gnat (n)	جرجسة، بعوضة	*jirjisah, ba'ūḍah*
gnaw (v)	قضم، نخر، قرقض	*qaḍama, nakhara, qarqaḍa*
gnome (n)	قزم خرافي	*qazam khurāfi*
go (v)	ذهب، مضى، مرّ	*dhahaba, maḍā, marra*
go abroad	سافر إلى بلد أجنبي	*sāfara ilā balad ajnabī*
goad (v)	نخس بمهماز	*nakhasa bi mihmāz*
go against	عارض، خالف	*'āraḍa, khālafa*
go ahead	انطلق، تقدم	*inṭalaqa, taqaddama*
go-ahead (n)	إذن	*idhn*
go-ahead (adj)	ناشط، مغامر	*nāshiṭ, mughāmir*
goal (n)	أمد، هدف، مرمى	*amad, hadaf, marmā*
goalkeeper (n)	حارس المرمى	*ḥārisul marmā*
go along	رافق، تقدم	*rāfaqa, taqaddama*
go aside	تنحى، ابتعد	*tanaḥḥā, ibta'ada*
go stray	ضل، أخطأ	*ḍalla, akhṭa'a*
goat (n)	ماعز، خليع	*mā'iz, khalī'*
gob	كتلة	*kutlah*
gobbet (n)	قطعة لحم	*qiṭ'atu laḥm*
gooble (v)	التهم، اختطف	*iltahama, ikhtaṭafa*
go beyond	تجاوز، تخطى	*tajāwaza, takhaṭṭā*
god (n)	معبود، إله، حاكم	*ma'būd, ilāh, ḥākim*
godchild (n)	ابن بالمعبودية	*ibn bil ma'būdiyyah*
goddess (n)	معبودة، حاكمة	*ma'būdah, ḥākima*
godfather (n)	عراب، اشبين	*'ārrāb, ishbīn*
godhead (n)	ألوهية، ربوبية	*ulūhiyyah, rubūbiyyah*
godless (adj)	ملحد، كافر	*mulḥid, kāfir*
godlike (adj)	إلهي، شبيه بإله	*ilāhī, shabīh bi ilāh*

godmother (n)	عرابة، اشبينة	*'arrābah, ishbīnah*
godown (n)	مستودع بضائع	*mustauda'u baḍā'i'*
go down	سقط، غرق	*saqaṭa, gharaqa*
godparent (n)	عراب، عرابة	*'arrāb, 'arrābah*
godsend (n)	لقية، لقطة	*luqyah, luqṭah*
godson (n)	ابن بالمعبودية	*ibn bil ma'būdiyyah*
goer (n)	ذاهب	*dhāhib*
go for	هاجم، انحاز إلى	*hājama, inḥāza ilā*
go-getter (n)	شخص مغامر	*shakhṣ mughāmir*
goggle (v/n)	حملق، حملقة	*ḥamlaqa, ḥamlaqah*
goggles (n)	منظار الوقاية	*minẓārul wiqāyah*
go in	دخل، احتجب	*dakhala, iḥtajaba*
going (adj)	ذاهب، جارٍ	*dhāhib, jārin*
going (n)	ذهاب، سلوك	*dhahāb, sulūk*
goings-on (n)	أعمال، أحداث	*a'māl, aḥdāth*
goitre (goiter) (n)	جوتر	*jūtar*
gold (n)	ذهب، لون ذهبي	*dhahab, laun dhahabī*
golden (adj)	ذهبي، لامع	*dhahabī, lāmi'*
golden age (n)	عصر ذهبي	*'aṣr dhahabī*
golden rule (n)	قاعدة ذهبية	*qā'idah dhahabiyyah*
gold-field (n)	حقل الذهب	*ḥaqludh dhahab*
goldfish (n)	سمك ذهبي	*samak dhahabī*
goldsmith (n)	صائغ	*ṣā'igh*
golf (n)	لعبة الغولف	*lu'batul gūlf*
golfer (n)	لاعب الغولف	*lā'ibul gūlf*
golfing (n)	لعب الغولف	*la'bul gūlf*
gonad (n)	غدة تناسلية	*ghuddah tanāsuliyyah*
gondola (n)	غندول	*ghundūl*
gondolier (n)	غناديلي	*ghanādīlī*
gone (adj)	ماضٍ، ميت	*māḍin, mait*

goner (n)	هالك، ميؤوس	*hālik, mai'ūs*
gong (n)	جرس قرصي	*jaras qurṣī*
good (adj)	جيد، ملائم، صالح	*jayyid, mulā'im, ṣāliḥ*
good (adv)	جيداً، تماماً	*jayyidan, tamāman*
goodbye (interj)	وداعاً	*wadā'an*
good-for-nothing (adj	عديم القيمة	*'adīmul qīmah*
Good Friday (adj)	جمعة حزينة	*jumu'ah ḥazīnah*
good-hearted (adj)	سمح الطبع، كريم	*samḥuṭ ṭab', karīm*
good-humoured (adj)	بهيج، طلق المحيا	*bahīj, ṭalqul muḥayyā*
goodly (adj)	ضخم، كبير	*ḍakhm, kabīr*
good-natured (adj)	طلق المحيا، ودي، لطيف	*ṭalqul muḥayyā, wuddī, laṭīf*
goodness (n)	طيبة، جودة	*ṭībah, jūdah*
goods (n)	بضائع، سلع	*baḍā'i', sila'*
good-tempered (adj)	دمث الأخلاق، لطيف	*damithul akhlāq, laṭīf*
goodwill (n)	ارتياح، وداد	*irtiyāḥ, widād*
goody (n)	شيء لذيذ المذاق	*shay' ladhīdhul madhāq*
goody-goody (n)	شخص فاضل	*shakhṣ fāḍil*
goof (n)	أبله، أحمق	*ablah, aḥmaq*
go off	رحل، مات	*raḥila, māta*
goofy (adj)	أبله، أحمق	*ablah, aḥmaq*
go on	واصل، سلك	*wāṣala, salaka*
goon (n)	شخص أبله، معتوه	*shakhṣ ablah, ma'tūh*
goose (n)	وزة، أبله	*wazzah, ablah*
gooseberry (n)	كشمش	*kishmish*
goose-step (n)	خطوة الإوزة	*khuṭwatul iwazzah*
go out	غادر المنزل	*ghādaral manzil*
go over	فحص، أعاد	*faḥaṣa, a'āda*
gopher (n)	غوفرة	*ghaufarah*

gordian knot (n)	مشكلة عويصة	*mushkilah ʻawīṣah*
gore (n)	قطعة مثلثة، دم	*qiṭʻah muthallathah, dam*
gore (v)	جرح بقرن	*jaraḥa bi qarn*
gorge (v)	قم، أتخم	*tahama, atkhama*
gorgeous (adj)	بهي، فائق الجمال	*bahiyy, fā'iqul jamāl*
gorgon (n)	غرغونة، امرأة بشعة	*gharghūnah, imra'ah bashiʻah*
gorilla (n)	الغوريلا	*al ghūrīlā*
gorse (n)	جولق، رتم	*jaulaq, ratam*
gory (adj)	ملطخ بالدم	*mulaṭṭakh bid dam*
gosling (n)	فرخ الإوز	*farkhul iwazz*
gospel (n)	انجيل، بشارة	*injīl, bashārah*
gossip (n)	تحادث، مسامرة	*taḥāduth, musāmarah*
gossip (v)	تحدث، سامر	*taḥaddatha, sāmara*
Gothic (n/adj)	قوطي، لغة قوطية	*qūṭī, lughah qūṭiyyah*
go through	درس بدقة	*darasa bi diqqah*
gouache (n)	غواش، غواشية	*ghuwāsh, ghuwāshiyah*
gouge (n)	مظفار، حفر بالمظفار	*miẓfār, ḥafara bil miẓfār*
go up	صعد، ارتفع	*ṣaʻida, irtafaʻa*
gourd (n)	قرع، يقطين	*qarʻ, yaqṭīn*
gourmand (n)	نهم، شره	*nahim, sharih*
gout (n)	نقرس، داء المفاصل	*niqris, dā'ul mafāṣil*
govern (v)	حكم، تسلط	*ḥakama, tasallaṭa*
governance (n)	حكم، سيطرة	*ḥukm, saiṭarah*
governess (n)	حاكمة، معلمة	*ḥākimah, muʻallimah*
governing (adj)	حاكم، ذو سلطة	*ḥākim, dhū sulṭah*
government (n)	حكومة، دولة، سلطة	*ḥukūmah, daulah, sulṭah*
governmental (adj)	متعلق بالحكومة	*mutaʻalliq bil ḥukūmah*
governor (n)	حاكم، مدير	*ḥākim, mudīr*
gown (n)	ثوب نسائي، عباءة	*thaub nithā'ī, ʻabā'ah*

grab (v)	اختطف، أمسك	*ikhtaṭafa, amsaka*
grab (n)	اختطاف، انتزاع	*ikhtiṭāf, intizā'*
grace (n)	فضل، رحمة، حسن	*faḍl, raḥmah, ḥusn*
grace (v)	شرف، زين	*sharrafa, zayyana*
graceful (adj)	رشيق، لطيف الشمائل	*rashīq, laṭīfush shamā'il*
gracefully (adv)	برشاقة، بسماح	*bi rashāqah, bi samāḥ*
graceless (adj)	سمج، فاسد	*samij, fāsid*
gracious (adj)	رؤوف، كريم، لطيف	*ra'ūf, karīm, laṭīf*
graciously (adv)	بفضل، تكرماً	*bi faḍl, takarruman*
graciousness (n)	فضل، رحمة	*faḍl, raḥmah*
gradation (n)	درجة، تدرج	*darajah, tadarruj*
grade (v)	درج، بوب	*darraja, bawwaba*
grade (n)	طبقة، مرحلة، درجة	*ṭabaqah, marḥalah, darajah*
gradient (n)	درجة التحدر	*darajatut taḥaddur*
gradual (adj)	تدريجي، تدرجي	*tadrījī, tadarrujī*
gradually (adv)	تدريجاً، بالتدريج	*tadrījan, bit tadrīj*
graduate (n)	خريج جامعة	*khirrīju jāmi'ah*
graduate (v)	تخرج من جامعة	*takharraja min jāmi'ah*
graduation (n)	تخريج، تخرج	*takhrīj, takharruj*
graft (n)	نبتة مطعمة، اكتساب	*nabtah muṭa''amah, iktisāb*
graft (v)	طعم، ألحم	*ṭa''ama, alḥama*
grain (n)	حبة، ذرة، حنطة	*ḥabbah, dharrah, ḥinṭah*
grainy (adj)	محبب، مجزع	*muḥabbab, mujazza'*
gram (n)	الغرام	*al gharām*
grammar (n)	علم النحو والصرف	*'ilmun naḥw waṣ ṣarf*
grammarian (n)	نحوي، ماهر في النحو	*naḥwī, māhir fin naḥw*
grammar school	مدرسة ثانوية	*madrasah thānawiyyah*
grammatical (adj)	نحوي	*naḥwī*

gramophone (n)	فونوغراف، حاكي	*fūnūgharāf, ḥākī*
granary (n)	هري، مخزن الحبوب	*hury, makhzanul ḥubūb*
grand (adj)	رفيع، رائع، كبير	*rafi', rā'i', kabīr*
grandchild (n)	حفيد، حفيدة	*ḥafīd, ḥafīdah*
granddaughter (n)	حفيدة	*ḥafīdah*
grand duchess (n)	غراندوقة	*gharāndūqah*
grandee (n)	نبيل، شريف	*nabīl, sharīf*
grandeur (n)	جلال، فخامة، عظمة	*jalāl, fakhāmah, 'aẓmah*
grandfather (n)	جد، سلف	*jadd, salaf*
grandiloquence (n)	تفخيم الكلام	*tafkhīmul kalām*
grandiloquent (adj)	مفخم، متحذلق	*mufakhkham, mutaḥadhliq*
grandiose (adj)	فخيم، متكلف العظمة	*fakhīm, mutakallaful 'aẓmah*
grand jury (n)	هيئة المحلفين الكبرى	*hay'atul muḥallifīn al kubrā*
grandmother (n)	جدة	*jaddah*
grandparent (n)	جد، جدة	*jadd, jaddah*
grand piano (n)	بيان كبير	*bayān kabīr*
grand slam (n)	انتصار تام	*intiṣār tāmm*
grandson (n)	حفيد، سبط	*ḥafīd, sibṭ*
grandstand (n)	مدرج مسقوف	*mudarraj masqūf*
granite (n)	غرانيت	*gharānīt*
granny -nnie (n)	جدة	*jaddah*
grant (v)	منح، خول، سلم	*manaḥa, khawwala*
grant (n)	هبة، منحة	*hibah, minḥah*
granular (adj)	محبب، مبرغل	*muḥabbab, mubarghal*
granulated sugar	سكر محبب	*sukkar muḥabbab*
granule (n)	حبيبة، حبة صغيرة	*ḥubaibah, ḥabbah ṣaghīrah*
grape (n)	عنب، عنبة	*'inab, 'inabah*

grapefruit (n)	ليمون هندي	*laimūn hindī*
grapeshot (n)	قبنلة عنقودية	*qumbulah ʻunqūdiyyah*
grapevine (n)	كرمة، إشاعة	*karmah, ishāʻah*
graph (n)	رسم بياني	*rasm bayānī*
graphic (adj)	مرسوم، منقوش	*marsūm, manqūsh*
graphics (n)	فن الرسم البياني	*fannur rasm al bayānī*
graphite (n)	غرافيت	*gharāfīt*
grapple (n)	مرساة، كلاب	*mirsāt, kullāb*
grapple (v)	أمسك، أوثق	*amsaka, authaqa*
grasp (v)	أمسك، أدرك	*amsaka, adraka*
grasp (n)	إمساك، إدراك	*imsāk, idrāk*
grasping (adj)	جشع، طماع	*jashiʻ, ṭammāʻ*
grass (n)	عشب، مرعى	*ʻushb, marʻā*
grass (v)	كسا بالعشب	*kasā bil ʻushb*
grasshopper (n)	جندب	*jundub*
grass roots (n)	تربة سطحية	*turbah saṭḥiyyah*
grass widow (n)	مغيبة	*mughībah*
grassy (adj)	معشب، عشبي	*muʻshib, ʻushbī*
grate (n)	حاملة الوقود	*ḥāmilatul waqūd*
grate (v)	أثار، صر، أزعج	*athāra, ṣarra, azʻaja*
grateful (adj)	شاكر، مستحب	*shākir, mustaḥabb*
gratefully (adv)	شاكراً	*shākiran*
gratification (n)	شبع، إرضاء	*shibaʻ, irḍāʼ*
gratify (v)	أرضى، أشبع	*arḍā, ashbaʻa*
gratifying (adj)	مرضٍ، مشبع	*murḍin, mushbiʻ*
grating (n)	حاجز مشبك	*ḥājiz mushabbak*
gratis (adv)	مجانًا، بلا ثمن	*majjānan, bilā thaman*
gratitude (n)	شكر، إقرار بالفضل	*shukr, iqrār bil faḍl*
gratuitous (adj)	بدون مسوغ، اغتباطي	*bidūn musawwigh, ightibāṭī*
gratuity (n)	عطية، هبة	*ʻaṭiyyah, hibah*

grave (adj)	خطير، مهلك	*khaṭīr, muhlik*
grave (n)	قبر، ضريح	*qabr, ḍarīḥ*
gravel (n)	حصاة، حصباء	*ḥaṣāt, ḥaṣbā'*
gravestone (n)	شاهد، بلاطة الضريح	*shāhid, balāṭatuḍ ḍarīḥ*
graveyard (n)	مقبرة، جبانة	*maqbarah, jabbānah*
gravitate (v)	تحرك، انجذب	*taḥarraka, injadhaba*
gravitation (n)	انجذاب، نزعة	*ijidhāb, naz'ah*
gravity (n)	خطورة، جاذبية الأرض	*khuṭūrah, jādhibiyyatul arḍ*
gravy (n)	سلاء اللحم	*silā'ul laḥm*
gray (grey) (n)	رمادي، أشيب	*ramādī, ashyab*
grayish (adj)	ضارب إلى الرمادي	*ḍārib ilar ramādī*
graze (v)	رعى، سحج	*ra'ā, saḥaja*
grazier (n)	راعي الماشية	*rā'il māshiyah*
grease (n/v)	شحم، شحم	*shaḥm, shaḥḥama*
greasepaint (n)	ماكياج مسرحي	*mākiyāj masraḥī*
greasy (adj)	مشحم، زلق	*mushaḥḥam, zaliq*
great (adj)	كبير، عظيم، ضخم	*kabīr, 'aẓīm, ḍakhm*
greatly (adv)	كثيراً، عظيماً	*kathīran, 'aẓīman*
greatness (n)	عظمة، فخامة	*'aẓmah, fakhāmah*
greed (n)	جشع، طمع	*jasha', ṭama'*
greedily (adv)	بشراهة، بطمع	*bi sharāhah, bi ṭama'*
greedy (adj)	طماع، جشع	*ṭammā', jashi'*
Greek (adj)	يوناني	*yūnānī*
green (adj/n)	أخضر، لون أخضر	*akhḍar, laun akhḍar*
green (v)	خضر، خضر	*khaḍira, khaḍḍara*
green belt (n)	حزام أخضر	*ḥizām akhḍar*
greenery (n)	خضرة، خضار	*khuḍrah, khuḍār*
greengage (n)	برقوق أخضر	*barqūq akhḍar*
greengrocer (n)	خضرى	*khuḍarī*

greenhorn (n)	غر	*ghirr*
greenhouse (n)	دفيئة	*dafī'ah*
greenish (adj)	مخضر	*mukhḍar*
Green light (n)	ضوء أخضر	*ḍau' akhḍar*
greenness (n)	نضارة، اخضرار	*naḍārah, ikhḍirār*
greenroom (n)	حجرة خضراء	*ḥujrah khaḍrā'*
greet (v)	رحب، حيا	*raḥḥaba, ḥayyā*
greeting (n)	تهنئة، تحية	*tahni'ah, taḥiyyah*
gregarious (adj)	اجتماعي، قطيعي	*ijtimā'ī, qaṭī'ī*
grenade (n)	رمانة، قنبلة يدوية	*rummānah, qumbulah yadawiyyah*
grenadier (n)	رامي الرمانات	*rāmiyur rummānāt*
greyhound (n)	سلوقي	*salūqī*
grid (n)	مصبعة، لوح المركم	*muṣabba'ah, lauḥul mirkam*
griddle (n)	صينية	*ṣīniyyah*
gridiron (n)	مشواة	*mishwāt*
grief (n)	أسىً، بلية، كارثة	*asan, baliyyah, kārithah*
grievance (n)	شكوى، ضيم	*shakwā, ḍaim*
grieve (v)	أوسى، حزن	*ausā, ḥazina*
grievous (adj)	موجع، مؤلم	*mūji', mu'lim*
grievously (adv)	بحزن، بفظاعة	*bi ḥuzn, bi faẓā'ah*
griffin (n)	غرفين	*ghirfīn*
grill (n/v)	مشواة، شوى	*mishwāt, shawā*
grille (n)	مصبعة، مدرأة	*muṣabba'ah, mudarra'ah*
grim (adj)	ضار، كالح، شرس	*ḍārr, kāliḥ, sharis*
grimace (n/v)	كشرة، كشر	*kishrah, kashshara*
grime (n)	سخام، وسخ	*sukhām, wasakh*
grimy (adj)	وسخ، قذر	*wasikh, qadhir*

grin (n/v)	ابتسامة عريضة، كشر	*ibtisāmah ʻarīḍah, kashira*
grind (v)	طحن، جرش	*ṭaḥana, jarasha*
grind (n)	كدح، طحن	*kadḥ, ṭaḥn*
grinder (n)	مطحنة، طاحن	*miṭḥanah, ṭāḥin*
grinding (adj)	مضطهد	*muḍṭahid*
grindstone (n)	مسن، مجلخة	*misann, mijlakhah*
grip (v)	أمسك بإحكام	*amsaka bi iḥkām*
grip (n)	مسكة، قبضة	*maskah, qabḍah*
gripe (v)	شكا، أحزن	*shakā, aḥzana*
gripe (n)	شكوى، مظلمة	*shakwā, maẓlamah*
grisly (adj)	رهيب، مروع	*rahīb, murawwiʻ*
gristle (n)	غضروف	*ghuḍrūf*
gristly (adj)	غضروفي	*ghuḍrūfī*
grit (n)	حصىً، جريش	*ḥaṣan, jarīsh*
grit (v)	صقل الرخام	*ṣaqalar rukhām*
gritty (adj)	رملي، حازم	*ramlī, ḥāzim*
grizzled (adj)	أشيب	*ashyab*
groan (v)	أن، تأوه	*anna, ta'awwaha*
groan (n)	أنين، تأوه	*anīn, ta'awwuh*
grocer (n)	بقال، بدال	*baqqāl, baddāl*
grocery (n)	بقالة	*biqālah*
grog (n)	مشروب روحي	*mashrūb rūḥī*
groggy (adj)	مترنح، سكران	*mutaranniḥ, sakrān*
groin (n)	أربية، حنية	*arbiyyah, ḥaniyyah*
groom (n)	سائس الخيل، عريس	*sā'isul khail, ʻarīs*
groom (v)	ساس الخيل	*sāsal khail*
groove (n)	أخدود، ثلم	*ukhdūd, thalm*
grope (v)	تلمس الطريق	*talammasaṭ ṭarīq*

gross (adj)	فاضح، بذيء، مئة بالمئة	*fāḍiḥ, badhī', mi'ah bil mi'ah*
grotesque (n/adj)	بشع، غريب	*bashi', gharīb*
grotesquely (adv)	ببشاعة، بقباحة	*bi bashā'ah, bi qabāḥah*
grotto (n)	غار، كهف	*ghār, kahf*
ground (n)	سطح الأرض، أساس، قاع	*saṭḥul arḍ, asās, qā'*
ground (v)	أرض، اعتمد	*arraḍa, i'tamada*
ground crew (n)	ركب أرضي	*rakb arḍī*
ground floor	دور أرضي	*daur arḍī*
groundless (adj)	لا أساس لــه	*lā asās lahu*
groundlessly (adv)	بدون أساس	*bidūn asās*
groundnut (n)	فول سوداني	*fūl sūdānī*
ground rule (n)	قاعدة إجرائية	*qā'idah ijrā'iyyah*
groundsel (n)	زهرة الشيخ	*zahratush shaikh*
groundwork (n)	قاعدة، أساس	*qā'idhah, asās*
group (n)	جماعة، زمرة	*jamā'ah, zumrah*
group (v)	ضم، تجمع	*ḍamma, tajamma'a*
grouse (n)	طيهوج، شكوى	*ṭaihūj, shakwā*
grouse (v)	شكا، تذمر	*shakā, tadhammara*
grove (n)	أيكة، حديقة	*aikah, ḥadīqah*
grovel (v)	تذلل، دب	*tadhallala, dabba*
grovelling (adj)	متذلل، خسيس	*Mutadhallil, khasīs*
grow (v)	نبت، نشأ، برز	*nabata, nasha'a, baraza*
grower (n)	منبت	*mumbit*
growing (adj)	ناشئ	*nāshi'*
growl (v)	هدر، هر	*hadara, harra*
growl (n)	هدير، هرير	*hadīr, harīr*
grown (adj)	ناضج، تام	*nāḍij, tāmm*
grown-up (adj)	بالغ، راشد	*bāligh, rāshid*

growth (n)	نمو، تطور، نشوء	*numuww, taṭawwur, nushū'*
grub (v)	نكش، نبش	*nakasha, nabasha*
grubbiness (n)	قذارة، حقارة	*qadhārah, ḥaqārah*
grubby (adj)	قذر، وضيع	*qadhir, waḍī'*
grudge (v)	تذمر، حسد	*tadhammara, ḥasada*
grudge (n)	حقد، ضغينة	*ḥiqd, ḍaghīnah*
grudging (adj)	ضغن، حاقد	*ḍaghin, ḥāqid*
grudgingly (adv)	بحقد، بتذمر	*bi ḥiqd, bi tadhammur*
gruel (n)	ثريد، عصيدة	*tharīd, 'aṣīdah*
gruelling (adj)	مرهق، قاسٍ	*murhiq, qāsin*
gruesome (adj)	رهيب، مخيف	*rahīb, mukhīf*
gruff (adj)	فظ، غليظ الطبع	*faẓẓ, ghalīẓuṭ ṭab'*
gruffly (adv)	بفظاظة، بخشونة	*bi faẓāẓah, bi khushūnah*
grumble (v)	دمدم، هر	*damdama, harra*
grumble (n)	دمدمة، هرير	*damdamah, harīr*
grump (n)	نكد، رداءة الطبع	*nakad, radā'atuṭ ṭab'*
grumpy (adj)	رديء الطبع	*radī'uṭ ṭab'*
grunt (v/n)	قبع، قباع	*qaba'a, qubā'*
guarantee (n)	ضمانة، كفالة	*ḍamānah, kafālah*
guarantee (v)	ضمن، كفل	*ḍamina, kafala*
guarantor (n)	ضامن، كفيل	*ḍāmin, kafīl*
guard (n)	حماية، دفاع، حارس	*ḥimāyah, difā', ḥāris*
guard (v)	حرس، حمى، دافع	*ḥarasa, ḥamā, dāfa'a*
guarded (adj)	حذر	*ḥadhir*
guardedly (adv)	بحذر، بتيقظ	*bi ḥadhar, bi tayaqquẓ*
guardian (n)	حارس، وصي	*ḥāris, waṣī*
guardianship (n)	حراسة، قوامة	*ḥirāsah, qiwāmah*
guardsman (n)	حرسي	*ḥarasī*
guava (n)	جوافة، غوافة	*juwāfah, ghuwāfah*

gudgeon (n)	قوبيون نهري	*qūbyūn nahrī*
guerrilla (guerilla)	داغر، مدغرة	*dāghir, madgharah*
guess (v)	خمن، حسب	*khammana, ḥasiba*
guess (n)	حزر، ظن	*ḥazr, ẓann*
guesstimate (v)	خمن، حزر	*khammana, ḥazara*
guest (n)	ضيف، نزيل	*ḍaif, nazīl*
guest (v)	نزل ضيفاً	*nazala ḍaifan*
guffaw (n/v)	قهقهة، قهقه	*qahqahah, qahqaha*
guidance (n)	هداية، إرشاد	*hidāyah, irshād*
guide (v)	أرشد، هدى	*arshada, hadā*
guide (n)	مرشد، دليل، هادي	*murshid, dalīl, hādī*
guideline (n)	دليل، خط هادي	*dalīl, khaṭṭ hādī*
guild (n)	طائفة حرفية	*ṭā'ifah ḥirfiyyah*
guildhall (n)	دار البلدية	*dārul baladiyyah*
guile (n)	مكر، خداع، رياء	*makr, khidā', riyā'*
guileful (adj)	ماكر، خادع	*mākir, khādi'*
guileless (adj)	بريء، ساذج	*barī', sādhij*
guillemot (n)	غلموت، طائر مائي	*ghilmūt, ṭā'ir mā'ī*
guillotine (n)	مقصلة	*miqṣalah*
guilt (n)	إثم، جرم	*ithm, jurm*
guiltless (adj)	بريء، زكي	*barī', zakiyy*
guilty (adj)	مذنب، مجرم	*mudhnib, mujrim*
guinea (n)	جنيه انكليزي	*junaih inkilīzī*
guinea-fowl (n)	غرغر	*ghirghir*
guinea-pig (n)	خنزير غينيا	*khinzīr ghīniyā*
guise (n)	زي، هيئة	*ziyy, hai'ah*
guitar (n)	غيتار، قيثارة	*ghītār, qīthārah*
gulch (n)	عقيق، وادٍ متحدر	*'aqīq, wādin mutaḥaddir*
gulf (n)	خليج، دردور	*khalīj, durdūr*
gull (n/v)	نورس، خدع	*nauras, khada'a*

gullet (n)	حنجرة	*ḥanjarah*
gullible (adj)	ساذج، سهل الانخداع	*sādhij, sahlul inkhidā'*
gully (n)	أخدود، خندق	*ukhdūd, khandaq*
gulp (n)	بلعة، جرعة	*bal'ah, jar'ah*
gulp (v)	تجرع، أخمد	*tajarra'a, akhmada*
gum (n)	صمغ، لثة	*ṣamgh, lithah*
gum (v)	ألصق بالصمغ	*alṣaqa biṣ ṣamgh*
gun (n)	مدفع، بندقية	*midfa', bunduqiyyah*
gunboat (n)	سفينة مدفعية	*safīnah midfa'iyyah*
gunfire (n)	إطلاق المدافع	*iṭlāqul madāfi'*
gunman (n)	مسلح ببندقية	*musallaḥ bi bunduqiyyah*
gunner (n)	مدفعي	*midfa'ī*
gunnery (n)	رمي المدفعية	*ramyul midfa'iyyah*
gunpowder (n)	بارود	*bārūd*
gunrunner (n)	مهرب الأسلحة	*muharribul asliḥah*
gunrunning (n)	تهريب الأسلحة	*tahrībul asliḥah*
gunshot (n)	طلق ناري	*ṭalq nārī*
gunwale (n)	شفير، حرف المركب	*shafīr, ḥarful markab*
gurgle (v/n)	قرقر، قرقرة	*qarqara, qarqarah*
guru (n)	مرشد، غورو	*murshid, ghūrū*
gush (v)	تدفق، تفجر	*tadaffaqa, tafajjara*
gush (n)	تدفق، تفجر	*tadaffuq, tafajjur*
gushing (adj)	متدفق	*mutadaffiq*
gust (n)	ثورة نفس، عصفة ريح	*thauratu nafs, 'aṣfatu rīḥ*
gusto (n)	ذوق، ميل	*dhauq, mail*
gusty (adj)	عاصف، قاصف	*'āṣif, qāṣif*
gut (n)	أحشاء، قناة هضمية	*aḥshā', qanāt haḍmiyyah*
gut (v)	أتلف الجزء الداخلي	*atlafal juz' ad dākhilī*

gutless (adj)	جبان، عديم الحيوية	*jabān ʻadīmul ḥayawiyyah*
gutsy (adj)	باسل، مفعم بالحيوية	*bāsil, mufʻam bil ḥayawiyyah*
gutted (adj)	مكتئب، كئيب	*mukta'ib, ka'īb*
gutter (n)	قناة، بالوعة	*qanāt, bālūʻah*
guttural (adj)	حلقي، حنجري	*ḥalqī, ḥanjarī*
guy (n)	شخص، فتًى	*shakhṣ, fatan*
guy (v)	سخر من	*sakhira min*
guzzle (v)	أكل بسرعة	*akala bi surʻah*
gymkhana (n)	حفلة رياضية	*ḥaflah riyāḍiyyah*
gymnasium (n)	جمنازيوم، ملعب	*jimnāziyūm, malʻab*
gymnast (n)	جمنازي	*jimnāzī*
gymnastic (adj)	رياضي، جمنازي	*riyāḍī, jimnāzī*
gymnastics (n)	رياضة جمنازية	*riyāḍah jimnāziyyah*
gynaecologist (n)	طبيب نسائي	*ṭabīb nisā'ī*
gynaecology (n)	علم أمراض النساء	*ʻilmu amrāḍin nisā'*
gyp (v)	خدع، احتال	*khadaʻa, iḥtāla*
gypsum (n)	جص، جبص	*jiṣṣ, jibṣ*
gypsy (n/adj)	غجري	*ghajarī*
gyrate (v)	دوم، فتل	*dawwama, fatala*
gyration (n)	تدويم، دوران	*tadwīm, dawarān*
gyroscope (n)	جيروسكوب	*jīrūskūb*
gyroscopic (adj)	جيروسكوبي	*jīrūskūbī*

H

ha (interj)	ها	*hā*
haberdasher (n)	خردجي	*khurdajī*
haberdashery (n)	خردوات	*khurdawāt*
habit (n)	سلوك، خلق، عادة	*sulūk, khulq, ʻādah*

habitable (adj)	صالح للسكنى	*ṣāliḥ lis suknā*
habitant (n)	ساكن، مقيم	*sākin, muqīm*
habitation (n)	سكنى، مسكن	*suknā, maskan*
habitual (adj)	معتاد، اعتيادي	*mu'tād, i'tiyādī*
habitually (adv)	عادةً	*'ādatan*
habituate (v)	عود، روض	*'awwada, rawwaḍa*
hack (v)	قطع، كحكح	*qaṭṭa'a, kaḥkaḥa*
hack (n)	حسان الأجرة،	*ḥisānul ujrah,*
	معزقة، حزة	*mi'zaqah, ḥazzah*
hackle (n)	ريش، شعر	*rīsh, sha'r*
hackneyed (adj)	مبتذل، منتهك	*mubtadhal, muntahak*
hack-saw (n)	منشار المعادن	*minshārul ma'ādin*
hag (n)	عرافة، ساحرة	*'arrāfah, sāḥirah*
haggard (adj)	مضنىً، منهك	*muḍnan, munhak*
haggle (v)	ساوم، ماحك	*sāwama, māḥaka*
hail (n)	برد	*barad*
hail (v)	رحب، أمطرت	*raḥḥaba, amṭaratis*
	السماء برداً	*samā'u baradan*
hailstone (n)	بردة	*baradah*
hailstorm (n)	عاصفة البرد	*'āṣifatul barad*
hair (n)	شعر، وبر	*sha'r, wabar*
hair's breadth	عرض شعرة	*'arḍu sha'rah*
hairbrush (n)	فرشاة الشعر	*furshātush sha'r*
haircut (n)	حلاقة	*ḥilāqah*
hairdresser (n)	مزين، حلاق	*muzayyin, ḥallāq*
hairdressing (n)	حلاقة، قص الشعر	*ḥilāqah, qaṣṣush sha'r*
hairless (adj)	أمرد، عديم الشعر	*amrad, 'adīmush sha'r*
hairline (n)	خط شعري	*khaṭṭ sha'rī*
hairpin (n)	دبوس شعر	*dabbūsu sha'r*
hair-raising (adj)	مثير، مدهش	*muthīr, mudhish*

hair-splitting (n)	مماحكة، مكابرة	*mumāḥakah, mukābarah*
hairy (adj)	شعر، شعري	*sha'ir, sha'rī*
haj (jajj) (n)	حج	*ḥajj*
hake (n)	نازلي، سمك بحري	*nāzilī, samak baḥri*
halcyon (adj)	رائق، ذهبي	*rā'iq, dhahabī*
hale (adj)	سليم، صحيح	*salīm, ṣaḥīḥ*
half (n)	نصف، شطر	*niṣf, shaṭr*
half-and-half (adj)	متناصف	*mutanāṣif*
half-back (n)	ظهير مساعد	*ẓahīr musā'id*
half-baked (adj)	فطير، غر	*faṭīr, ghirr*
half-brother (n)	أخ غير شقيق	*akh ghair shaqīq*
half-caste (n/adj)	مولد، هجين	*muwallad, hajīn*
half-hearted (adj)	فاتر الهمة	*fātirul himmah*
half-hour (n)	نصف ساعة	*niṣfu sā'ah*
half-hourly (adv/adj)	خاص بنصف ساعة	*khāṣṣ bi niṣfi sā'ah*
half-life (n)	عمر نصفي	*'umr niṣfi*
half-light (n)	عتمة، قتمة	*'atamah, qatamah*
half moon (n)	هلال	*hilāl*
halfpenny (n)	نصف بنس	*niṣfu bins*
half-sister (n)	أخت غير شقيقة	*ukht ghair shaqīqah*
half-time (n)	فاصل انتصافي، عمل نصفي	*fāṣil intiṣāfi, 'amal niṣfi*
half-tone (n)	نصف نغمة، لون نصفي	*niṣfu naghmah, laun niṣfi*
half-truth (n)	نصف الحقيقة	*niṣful ḥaqīqah*
halfway (adj/adv)	جزئي، جزئياً	*juz'ī, juz'iyyan*
halfwit (n)	شخص أبله	*shakhṣ ablah*
halfwitted (adj)	أبله، أحمق	*ablah, aḥmaq*
halibut (n)	هلبوت	*halbūt*

halitosis (n)	بخر	*bakhar*
hall (n)	قاعة، ردهة	*qā'ah, radhah*
hallmark (n)	سمة مميزة، دمغة السلع	*simah mumayyizah, damghatus sila'*
hallowed (adj)	مقدس، مكرس	*muqaddas, mukarras*
hallucinate (v)	هلوس، هلج	*halwasa, halaja*
hallucination (n)	هلوسة، هذيان	*halwasah, hadhayān*
hallway (n)	مدخل، رواق	*madkhal, riwāq*
halo (n)	الهالة	*al hālah*
halogen (n)	الهالوجين	*al hālūjīn*
halt (n)	موقف، محطة	*mauqif, maḥaṭṭah*
halt (v)	أوقف، توقف	*auqafa, tawaqqafa*
halter (n)	رسن، حبل المشنقة	*rasan, ḥablul mishnaqah*
halting (adj)	أعرج	*a'raj*
haltingly (adv)	بعرج، بتردد	*bi 'araj, bi taraddud*
halve (v)	نصف، اقتسم	*naṣṣafa, iqtasama*
halyard, -alliy-(n)	الكر، حبل القلع	*alkarr, ḥablul qil'*
ham (n)	فخذ الخنزير، هاوٍ	*fakhidhul khinzīr, hāwin*
hamburger (n)	الهمبورغية	*al hambūrghiyyah*
hamlet (n)	قرية صغيرة	*qaryah ṣaghīrah*
hammer (n)	مطرقة	*miṭraqah*
hammer (v)	طرق، دق	*ṭaraqa, daqqa*
hammering (n)	طرقة، كدح	*ṭarqah, kadḥ*
hammoc (n)	أرجوحة شبكية	*urjūḥah shabakiyyah*
hamper (n)	سبت، عائق	*sabat, 'ā'iq*
hamper (v)	كبح، عاق	*kabaḥa, 'āqa*
hamster (n)	همستر	*hamastar*
hamstring (n)	أوتار المأبض	*autārul ma'biḍ*
hand (n)	يد، قبضة، عون	*yad, qabḍah, 'aun*

hand (v)	أعطى، سلم	*a'ṭā, sallama*
handbag (n)	حقيبة يد	*ḥaqībatu yad*
handball (n)	كرة اليد	*kuratul yad*
handbill (n)	إعلان يدوي	*i'lān yadawī*
handbook (n)	كتيب، دليل	*kutayyib, dalīl*
handbrake (n)	مكبح يدوي	*mikbaḥ yadawī*
handcart (n)	عربة اليد	*'arabatul yad*
handcuff (v)	قيد، صفد	*qayyada, ṣaffada*
handcuffs (n)	صفد، غل	*ṣafad, ghull*
handhold (n)	سند، دعامة	*sanad, di'āmah*
handicap (n)	عائق، عقبة	*'ā'iq, 'aqabah*
handicap (v)	عاق، عطل	*'āqa, 'aṭṭala*
handicapped (adj)	معاق، معطل	*mu'āq, mu'aṭṭal*
handicraft (n)	حرفة يدوية	*ḥirfah yadawiyyah*
handiwork (n)	عمل يدوي	*'amal yadawī*
handkerchief (n)	منديل، محرمة	*mindīl, maḥramah*
handle (n)	مقبض، مسكة	*miqbaḍ, maskah*
handle (v)	مس، عالج، دبر	*massa, 'ālaja, dabbara*
handlebar (n)	مقود الدراجة	*miqwadud darrājah*
handling (n)	تدبير، معالجة	*tadbīr, mu'ālajah*
handmade (adj)	يدوي، مصنوع باليد	*yadawī, maṣnū' bil yad*
handmaid (n)	وصيفة، خادمة	*waṣīfah, khādimah*
handrail (n)	درابزون	*darābazūn*
handsaw (n)	منشار يدوي	*minshār yadawī*
handset (n)	تلفون مركب	*tilifūn murakkab*
handshake (n/v)	مصافحة، صافح	*muṣāfaḥah, ṣāfaḥa*
handsome (adj)	وسيم، بارع، سخي	*wasīm, bāri', sakhī*
handsomely (adv)	ببراعة	*bi barā'ah*
handsomeness (n)	براعة، وسامة	*barā'ah, wasāmah*
handwriting (n)	كتابة، خط	*kitābah, khaṭṭ*

handwritten (adj)	مكتوب باليد	*maktūb bil yad*
handy (adj)	ملائم، بارع، قريب	*mulā'im, bāri', qarīb*
hang (v)	دلى، نكس، شنق	*dallā, nakkasa, shanaqa*
hang (n)	طريقة التدلي	*ṭarīqatut tadallī*
hangar (n)	حظيرة الطائرات	*ḥaẓīratuṭ ṭā'irāt*
hanger (n)	تعليقة الثياب	*ta'līqatuth thiyāb*
hanger-on (n)	العالة الطفيلي	*al 'ālah aṭ ṭufailī*
hanging (n)	شنق، ستارة	*shanq, sitārah*
hangman (n)	جلاد، شانق	*jallād, shāniq*
hangnail (n)	السأف	*as sa'af*
hangover (n)	أثر متخلف	*athar mutakhallif*
hank (n)	لفيفة، كبة	*lafīfah, kubbah*
hanker (v)	تاق، اشتهى	*tāqa, ishtahā*
hankering (n)	توق شديد	*tauq shadīd*
hanky-panky (n)	شعوذة، احتيال	*sha'ūdhah, iḥtiyāl*
hansom (n)	هنسومية	*hansūmiyyah*
haphazard (adj)	اتفاقي، عرضي	*ittifāqī, 'araḍī*
haphazardly (adv)	مصادفةً، اتفاقًا	*muṣādafatan, ittifāqan*
hapless (adj)	قليل الحظ	*qalīlul ḥaẓẓ*
happen (v)	حدث، وقع	*ḥadatha, waqa'a*
happening (n)	حادثة، حدث	*ḥādithah, ḥadath*
happily (adv)	بسعادة، بهناء	*bi sa'ādah, bi hanā'*
happiness (n)	سعادة، هناءة	*sa'ādah, hanā'ah*
happy (adj)	سعيد، محظوظ، مبتهج	*sa'īd, maḥẓūẓ, mubtahij*
happy-go-lucky (adj)	توكلي، مهمل	*tawakkulī, muhmil*
hara-kiri (n)	هراكيري	*harākīrī*
harangue (n)	خطاب رنان	*khiṭāb rannān*
harangue (v)	خطب، حاضر	*khaṭaba, ḥāḍara*
harass (v)	ضايق، أزعج	*ḍāyaqa, az'aja*

harassment (n)	انزعاج، مضايقة	*inzi'āj, muḍāyaqah*
harbinger (n)	رائد، نذير	*rā'id, nadhīr*
harbour (harbor) (n)	مرفأ، ملجأ	*marfa', malja'*
harbour (harbor) (v)	أوى، أخفى	*awā, akhfā*
harbourage (n)	إلجاء، ملجأ	*iljā', malja'*
harbour-master (n)	رئيس المرفأ	*ra'īsul marfa'*
hard (adj)	صلب، صعب، ثقيل	*ṣulb, ṣa'b, thaqīl*
hard (adv)	بكد، بقسوة، بإمعان	*bi kadd, bi qaswah, bi im'ān*
hard-boiled (adj)	مسلوق جيداً	*maslūq jayyidan*
harden (v)	قسا، قسى، صلب	*qasā, qassā, ṣallaba*
hardening (n)	تقسية، تصلب	*taqsiyah, taṣallub*
hard-headed (adj)	عنيد، عملي	*'anīd, 'amalī*
hard-hearted (adj)	متحجر الفؤاد	*mutaḥajjirul fu'ād*
hard labour (n)	أعمال شاقة	*a'māl shāqqah*
hard-liner (adj)	متشدد، متطرف	*mutashaddid, mataṭarrif*
hardly (adv)	بقسوة، بصعوبة	*bi qaswah, bi ṣu'ūbah*
hardship (n)	ضيق، مشقة	*ḍīq, mashaqqah*
hardware (n)	خردوات، بضائع حديدة	*khurdawāt, baḍā'i' ḥadīdiyyah*
hardy (adj)	جريء، شجاع	*jarī', shujā'*
hare (n)	أرنب وحشية	*arnab waḥshiyyah*
harebell (n)	جريس مستدير الورق	*jurais mustadīrul waraq*
harelip (n)	شفة أرنبية	*shafah arnabiyyah*
harem (n)	حريم	*ḥarīm*
haricot (n)	فاصوليا	*fāṣūliyā*
hark (v)	أصغى، أصاخ	*aṣghā, aṣākha*
harlequin (n)	مهرج، مضحك	*muharrij, muḍaḥḥik*

harlot (n)	مومس، بغي	*mūmis, baghī*
harm (n)	أذى، ضرر	*adhan, ḍarar*
harm (v)	آذى، أضر	*ādhā, aḍarra*
harmful (adj)	مؤذ، ضار	*mu'dhin, ḍārr*
harmless (adj)	غير مؤذٍ، أمين	*ghair mu'dhin, amīn*
harmlessly (adv)	بغير ضرر	*bighairi ḍarar*
harmlessness (n)	عدم ضرر	*'adamu ḍarar*
harmonic (adj)	تآلفي، توافقي	*ta'ālufī, tawāfuqī*
harmonica (n)	هرمونيكا	*harmūnīkā*
harmonious (adj)	متناغم، متناسق	*mutanāghim, mutanāsiq*
harmonium (n)	قدمية	*qadamiyyah*
harmonization (n)	انسجام، توافق	*insijām, tawāfuq*
Harmonize,-ise (v)	توافق، انسجم	*tawāfaqa, insajama*
harmony (n)	تآلف، تناسق، انسجام	*ta'āluf, tanāsuq, insijām*
harness (n)	طقم الفرس	*ṭaqmul faras*
harness (v)	طقم الفرس	*ṭaqqamal faras*
harp (n)	قيثار، معزف	*qīthār, mi'zaf*
harp (v)	عزف على القيثار	*'azafa 'alal qīthār*
harpoon (n)	حربون، صنارة	*ḥarbūn, ṣinnārah*
harpoon (v)	طعن بالحربون	*ṭa'ana bil ḥarbūn*
harpsichord (n)	بيان قيثاري	*biyān qīthārī*
harpy (n)	خطاف	*khaṭṭāf*
harridan (n)	عجوز شكسة	*'ajūz shakisah*
harrier (n)	هرار، جراء	*harrār, jarrā'*
harrow (n)	مسحاة، مسلفة	*misḥāt, mislafah*
harrow (v)	سلف، سحا	*salafa, saḥā*
harsh (adj)	خشن، قاسٍ	*khashin, qāsin*
harshly (adv)	بقسوة، بخشونة	*bi qaswah bi khushūnah*
harshness (n)	قسوة، خشونة	*qaswah, khushūnah*

hart (n)	ذكر الأيل	*dhakarul ayyil*
harvest (n)	حصاد، غلة	*ḥaṣād, ghallah*
harvest (v)	حصد، جنى	*ḥaṣada, janā*
harvester (n)	حصاد، حاصد	*ḥaṣṣād, ḥāṣid*
has-been (n)	آفل	*āfil*
hash (n)	لحم مفروم	*laḥm mafrūm*
hashish (n)	حشيش، قنب هندي	*ḥashīsh, qinnab hindī*
hasp (n)	مشبك	*mishbak*
hassle (n)	مشاحنة، مشاجرة	*mushāḥanah, mushājarah*
hassle (v)	تشاحن، تشاجر	*tashāḥana, tashājara*
haste (n)	عجلة، تهور	*'ajalah, tahawwur*
hasten (v)	استعجل، أسرع	*ista'jala, asra'a*
hastily (adv)	بسرعة، بعجلة	*bi sur'ah, bi 'ajalah*
hasty (adj)	مستعجل، متهور	*musta'jil, mutahawwir*
hat (n)	قبعة، منصب	*qubba'ah, manṣab*
hatch (n)	بويب، فتحة صغيرة	*buwaib, futḥah ṣaghīrah*
hatch (v)	فقس البيضة	*faqqasal baiḍah*
hatchery (n)	مفقس، مفرخ	*mafqas, mafrakh*
hatchet (n)	بليطة	*bulaiṭah*
hatchway (n)	باب أرضي	*bāb arḍī*
hate (n)	كره، بغض	*kurh, bughḍ*
hate (v)	كره، أبغض	*kariha, abghaḍa*
hateful (adj)	مكروه، بغيض	*makrūh, baghiḍ*
hatred (n)	بغض، حزازة	*bughḍ, ḥazāzah*
hatter (n)	قبعي، صانع القبعات	*qubba'ī, ṣāni'ul qubba'āt*
haughtily (adv)	بغطرسة، بكبرياء	*bi ghaṭrasah, bi kibriyā'*
haughtiness (n)	غطرسة، عجرفة	*ghaṭrasah, 'ajrafah*
haughty (adj)	متغطرس، متعجرف	*mutaghaṭris, muta'ajrif*
haul (v)	سحب، ساق	*saḥaba, sāqa*

haul (n)	سحب، صيد	*saḥb, ṣaid*
haulage (n)	نقل بالعربات	*naql bil 'arabāt*
haunch (n)	عجز، ورك	*'ajuz, warik*
haunt (v)	انتاب، أوى	*intāba, awā*
haunt (n)	مأوى، شبح	*ma'wā, shabaḥ*
haunted (adj)	كئيب، مكتئب	*ka'īb, mukta'ib*
haute couture (n)	أزياء مبتدعة	*azyā' mubtada'ah*
have (v)	ملك، أحرز، تناول	*malaka, aḥraza, tanāwala*
haven (n)	ملاذ، مأوى	*malādh, ma'wā*
have-nots (n)	فقير، معدم	*faqīr, mu'dim*
havoc (n)	دمار، فوضى شديدة	*dimār, fauḍā shadīdah*
hawk (n)	صقر، باز	*ṣaqr, bāz*
hawker (n)	بائع متجول	*bā'i' mutajawwil*
hawk-eyed (adj)	حاد البصر	*ḥāddul baṣar*
hawthorn (n)	زعرور بري	*zu'rūr barrī*
hay (n)	تبن، قش	*tibn, qashsh*
hay fever (n)	حمى الهشيم	*ḥummal hashīm*
haymaker (n)	تبان	*tabbān*
hazard (v)	خاطر، جازف	*khāṭara, jāzafa*
hazardous (adj)	خطر، مخطر	*khaṭir, mukhṭir*
haze (n)	سديم، ضباب رقيق	*sadīm, ḍabāb raqīq*
haze (v)	عاقب بشغل إضافي	*'āqaba bi shughl iḍāfī*
hazel (n)	بندق، لون البندق	*bunduq, launul bunduq*
hazel (adj)	بندقي اللون	*buduqiyyul laun*
hazelnut (n)	ثمرة البندق	*thamratul bunduq*
hazily (adv)	بإبهام، بغشاوة	*bi ibhām, bi ghashāwah*
haziness (n)	ضبابية، غشاوة	*ḍabābiyyah, ghashāwah*
hazy (adj)	ضبابي، غائم	*ḍabābī ghā'im*
he (pron)	هو	*huwa*

head (n)	رأس، عقل، رئيس	*ra's, 'aql, ra'īs*
head (v)	تقدم، اتجه	*taqaddama, ittajaha*
headache (n)	صداع، ورطة	*ṣudā', warṭah*
headband (n)	عصابة للرأس	*'iṣābah lir ra's*
headboard (n)	لوحة رأسية	*lauḥah ra'siyyah*
head cheese (n)	هدشيز	*hadshīz*
head-dress (n)	غطاء للرأس	*ghiṭā' lir ra's*
headed (adj)	ذو رأس	*dhū ra's*
headgear (n)	غطاء للرأس	*ghiṭā' lir ra's*
heading (n)	عنوان، رأسية	*'unwān, ra'siyyah*
headland (n)	أرض رأسية	*arḍ ra'siyyah*
headless (adj)	بلا رأس، بلا عقل	*bilā ra's, bilā 'aql*
headlight (n)	خط رأسي، عنوان	*khaṭṭ ra'sī, 'unwān*
headlong (adj)	بتهور، بغير توانٍ	*bi tahawwur, bighairi tawānin*
headman (n)	زعيم، رئيس	*za'īm, ra'īs*
headmaster (n)	مدير المدرسة	*mudīrul madrasah*
headphone (n)	سماعة الرأس	*sammā'atur ra's*
headquarters (n)	مركز رئيسي	*markaz ra'īsī*
headrest (n)	مسند للرأس	*misnad lir ra's*
headset (n)	سماعتا الرأس	*sammā'atar ra's*
headship (n)	رئاسة، زعامة	*ri'āsah, zi'āmah*
headstone (n)	شاهد الضريح	*shāhiduḍ ḍarīḥ*
headstrong (adj)	عنيد، جموح	*'anīd, jamūḥ*
headway (n)	تقدم، سير إلى الأمام	*taqaddum, sair ilal amām*
heady (adj)	متهور، مندفع	*mutahawwir, mundafi'*
heal (v)	شفى، اندمل	*shafā, indamala*
health (n)	صحة، عافية	*ṣiḥḥah, 'āfiyah*
healthful (adj)	صحي، نجيع	*ṣiḥḥī, najī'*

healthily (adv)	متمتعاً بالصحة	*mutamatti'an biṣ ṣiḥḥah*
healthy (adj)	سليم، متمتع بالصحة	*salīm, mutamatti' biṣ ṣiḥḥah*
heap (v)	كوم، أفعم	*kawwama, af'ama*
heap (n)	ركام، كومة	*rukām, kaumah*
hear (v)	سمع، أصغى	*sami'a, aṣghā*
hearing (n)	سمع، سماع	*sam', samā'*
hearing-aid (n)	مساعد سمعي	*musā'id sam'ī*
hearken (v)	أصغى، سمع	*aṣghā, sami'a*
hearsay (n)	رواية، إشاعة	*riwāyah, ishā'ah*
hearse (n)	عربة الموتى	*'arabatul mautā*
heart (n)	قلب، فؤاد، لب	*qalb, fu'ād, lubb*
heartache (n)	حزن، غم	*ḥuzn, ghamm*
heart attack (n)	نوبة القلب	*naubatul qalb*
heartbeat (n)	نبضة القلب	*nabḍatul qalb*
heartbreak (n)	أسىً، حسرة	*asan, ḥasrah*
heartbreaking (adj)	فاجع، مؤلم	*fāji', mu'lim*
heartbroken (adj)	منسحق القلب	*munsaḥiqul qalb*
heartburn (n)	حروة، حرقة	*ḥarwah, ḥarqah*
hearten (v)	شجع، قوى	*shajja'a, qawwā*
heartening (adj)	مشجع	*mushajji'*
heartfelt (adj)	قلبي، مخلص	*qalbī, mukhliṣ*
hearth (n)	موقد، مصطلى	*mauqid, muṣṭalā*
heartily (adv)	بحماسة، تماماً	*bi ḥamāsah, tamāman*
heartiness (n)	حماسة، قوة	*ḥamāsah, quwwah*
heartless (adj)	جبان، عديم الرحمة	*jabān, 'adīmur raḥmah*
heartlessly (adv)	بقسوة، بغير رغبة	*bi qaswah, bi ghairi raghbah*
heartstring (n)	أعمق المشاعر	*a'maqul mashā'ir*
heart-to-heart (adj)	صريح	*ṣarīḥ*

hearty (adj)	قلبي، ودي، كاف	*qalbī, wuddī, kāfin*
heat (n)	حر، حماوة، سخونة	*ḥarr, ḥamāwah, sukhūnah*
heat (v)	سخن، سخن	*sakhkhana, sakhana*
heater (n)	سخانة، مسخن	*sakhkhānah, musakhkhin*
heath (n)	مرج، أرض بور	*marj, arḍ būr*
heathen (adj/n)	وثني، همجي	*wathanī, hamajī*
heather (n)	خلنج	*khalanj*
heatstroke (n)	ضربة الحر	*ḍarbatul ḥarr*
heatwave (n)	موجة حرارية	*maujah ḥarāriyyah*
heave (v)	سحب، طرح، لهث	*saḥaba, ṭaraḥa, lahatha*
heave (n)	جيشان، سحب، غثيان	*jayashān, saḥb, ghathayān*
heaven (n)	جنة، سماء	*jannah, samā'*
heavenly (adj)	سماوي، مبهج	*samāwī, mubhij*
heavenward (adv)	نحو السماء	*naḥwas samā'*
heavily (adv)	بتثاقل، بشدة	*bi tathāqul, bi shiddah*
heavy (adj)	ثقيل، ضخم، كثيف	*thaqīl, ḍakhm, kathīf*
heavy-duty (adj)	متين	*matīn*
heavy-handed (adj)	أخرق، جائر	*akhraq, jā'ir*
heavy-hearted (adj)	محزون	*maḥzūn*
heavyweight (n)	شخص بدين	*shakhṣ badīn*
Hebraic (adj)	عبراني، عبري	*'ibrānī, 'ibrī*
Hebrew (adj)	يهودي، عبري	*yahūdī, 'ibrī*
Hebrew (n)	لغة عبرانية	*lughah 'ibrāniyyah*
heckle (v)	أحفا	*aḥfā*
hectare (n)	هكتار	*hiktār*
hectic (adj)	محموم، قلق	*maḥmūm, qaliq*
hector (v)	تغطرس، ناكد	*taghaṭrasa, nākada*

hedge (n)	وشيع، حاجز	*washī', ḥājiz*
hedge (v)	عاق، سيج	*'āqa, sayyaja*
hedgehog (n)	قنفذ	*qunfudh*
hedgerow (n)	وشيع	*washī'*
hedonism (n)	مذهب المتعة	*madhhabul mut'ah*
heed (n)	اهتمام، التفات	*ihtimām, iltifāt*
heed (v)	التفت، بالى، اعتنى	*iltafata, bālā, i'tanā*
heedful (adj)	منتبه، حذر	*muntabih, ḥadhir*
heedless (adj)	غافل، مهمل	*ghāfil, muhmil*
heedlessly (adv)	بغير اهتمام	*bighairi ihtimām*
heedlessness (n)	غفلة، عدم اكتراث	*ghaflah, 'adamu iktirāth*
heel (n)	عقب، شخص حقير	*'aqib, shakhṣ ḥaqīr*
heel (v)	مال، جنح	*māla, janaḥa*
hefty (adj)	ثقيل، ضخم	*thaqīl, ḍakhm*
hegemony (n)	سيطرة، سيادة	*saiṭarah, siyādah*
heifer (n)	عجلة	*'ijlah*
height (n)	ارتفاع، طول	*irtifā', ṭūl*
heighten (v)	رفع، أعلى	*rafa'a, a'lā*
heinous (adj)	شائن، شنيع	*shā'in, shanī'*
heir (n)	وارث، وريث	*wārith, warīth*
heir apparent	وارث شرعي	*wārith shar'ī*
heiress (n)	وريثة، وارثة	*warīthah, wārithah*
heirloom (n)	متاع، شيء ذو أهمية	*matā', shay' dhū ahammiyyah*
helicopter (n)	هليكوبتر	*halīkūbtar*
heliotrope (n)	رقيب الشمس	*raqībush shams*
heliport (n)	هلبرت	*halburt*
helium (n)	هليوم	*hiliyūm*
helix (n)	شيء لولبي	*shay' laulabī*
hell (n)	جهنم، جحيم	*jahannam, jaḥīm*

hellish (adj)	جهنمي، شيطاني	*jahannamī, shaiṭānī*
hello (interj)	هالو	*hālū*
helm (n)	مقبض دفة المركب	*miqbaḍu daffatil markab*
helmet (n)	خوذة	*khūdhah*
help (n)	مساعده، عون	*musā'adah, 'aun*
help (v)	ساعد، عاون	*sā'ada, 'āwana*
helper (n)	معاون، مساعد	*mu'āwin, musā'id*
helpful (adj)	معين، مفيد، مسعف	*mu'īn, mufīd, mus'if*
helpfully (adv)	بإسعاف، بنجدة	*bi is'āf, bi najdah*
helpfulness (n)	عون، مساعدة	*'aun, musā'adah*
helpless (adj)	عاجز، ضعيف	*'ājiz, ḍa'īf*
helplessly (adv)	عاجزاً	*'ājizan*
helplessness (n)	عجز، ضعف	*'ajz, ḍa'f*
helter-skelter (adv)	شذر مذر	*shadhar madhar*
hem (n)	هدب، حافة	*hudb, ḥāffah*
hem (v)	هدب، تنحنح	*haddaba, tanaḥnaḥa*
hemisphere (n)	نصف الكرة	*niṣful kurah*
hemispherical (adj)	مختص بنصف الكرة	*mukhtaṣṣ bi niṣfil kurah*
hemlock (n)	شوكران	*shaukrān*
hemp (n)	خيوط القنب	*khuyūṭul qinnab*
hen (n)	دجاجة، أنثى الطير	*dajājah, unthaṭ ṭair*
hence (adv)	من الآن، إذن	*minal ān, idhan*
henceforth (adv)	من الآن فصاعداً	*minal ān fa ṣā'idan*
henchman (n)	تابع موثوق	*tābi' mauthūq*
henna (n)	حناء	*ḥinnā'*
hepatitis (n)	التهاب الكبد	*iltihābul kabid*
heptagon (n)	مسبع	*musabba'*
heptagonal (adj)	سباعي الزوايا	*subā'iyyuz zawāyā*

her (pron)	لها، عندها	*lahā, 'indahā*
herald (n)	رسول، مناد، بشير	*rasūl, munādin, bashīr*
herald (v)	أعلن، أذاع	*a'lana, adhā'a*
herb (n)	عشب، عشبة عطرية	*'ushb, 'ushbah 'iṭriyyah*
herbaceous (adj)	عشبي، نباتي	*'ushbī, nabātī*
herbage (n)	عشب	*'ushb*
herbal (adj)	عشبي	*'ushbī*
herbalist (n)	عشاب، متاجر بالأعشاب	*'ashshāb, mutājir bil a'shāb*
herbivore (n)	حيوان عاشب	*ḥaiwān 'āshib*
herbivorous (adj)	عاشب، مقتات بالأعشاب	*'āshib, muqtāt bil a'shāb*
herculean (adj)	هرقلي	*hiraqlī*
Hercules (n)	هرقل	*hiraql*
herd (n)	جماعة، قطيع	*jamā'ah, qaṭī'*
herd (v)	ساق، جمع	*sāqa, jama'a*
herd instinct (n)	غريزة القطيع	*gharīzatul qaṭī'*
herdsman (n)	راعي القطيع	*rā'il qaṭī'*
here (adv)	هنا، الآن	*hunā, al ān*
hereabouts (adv)	في هذا الجوار	*fī hādhal jiwār*
hereafter (adv)	في ما بعد	*fī mā ba'd*
hereafter (n)	آخرة، حياة أخروية	*ākhirah, ḥayāt ukhrawiyyah*
hereby (adv)	بهذه الواسطة	*bi hādhihil wāsiṭah*
hereditary (adj)	وراثي، موروث	*wirāthī, maurūth*
heredity (n)	وراثة	*wirāthah*
herein (adv)	في هذا الموضع	*fī hādhal mauḍa'*
hereof (adv)	لكذا	*likadhā*
heresy (n)	بدعة، هرطقة	*bid'ah, harṭaqah*
heretic (n)	مهرطق	*muharṭiq*

heretical (adj)	ابتداعي، هرطقي	*ibtidā'ī, harṭaqī*
hereto (adv)	بهذه الوثيقة	*bi hādhihil wathīqah*
heretofore (adv)	حتى الآن	*ḥattal ān*
herewith (adv)	مرفقاً بهذا، بهذه الطريقة	*murfaqan bi hādhā, bi hādhihiṭ ṭarīqah*
heritage (n)	إرث، تراث	*irth, turāth*
hermaphrodite (n)	خنثى	*khunthā*
hermetic (adj)	كتيم، محكم السد	*katīm, muḥkamus sadd*
hermit (n)	ناسك، متعبد	*nāsik, muta'abbid*
hermitage (n)	صومعة، دير	*ṣauma'ah, dair*
hernia (n)	فتق	*fatq*
hero (n)	بطل، شجاع	*baṭal, shujā'*
heroic (adj)	بطولي، قوي	*buṭūlī, qawī*
heroic verse	وزن ملحمي	*wazn malḥamī*
heroin (n)	هيرويين	*hīrūyīn*
heroine (n)	بطلة، شجاعة	*baṭalah, shujā'ah*
heroism (n)	بطولة، بسالة	*buṭūlah, basālah*
heron (n)	بلشون	*balashūn*
herpes (n)	قوباء	*qūbā'*
herring (n)	رنكة	*rankah*
hers (pron)	لها، عندها	*lahā, 'indahā*
herself (pron)	نفسها	*nafsuhā*
hesitancy (n)	تردد، حيرة	*taraddud, ḥairah*
hesitant (adj)	متردد، متحير	*mutaraddid, mutaḥayyir*
hesitantly (adv)	بتوقف، بتردد	*bi tawaqquf, bi taraddud*
hesitate (v)	تردد، تأتأ	*taraddada, ta'ta'a*
hesitation (n)	تردد، تأتأة	*taraddud, ta'ta'ah*
heterodox (adj)	ابتداعي، هرطقي	*ibtidā'ī, harṭaqī*
heterodoxy (n)	ابتداع، هرطقة	*ibtidā', harṭaqah*

heterogeneous (adj)	متغاير العناصر	*mutaghāyirul 'anāṣir*
heterosexual (adj)	مشته للمغاير	*mushtahin lil mughāyir*
heterosexuality (n)	اشتهاء المغاير	*ishtihā'ul mughāyir*
heuristic (adj)	مشجع، مساعد	*mushajji', musā'id*
hew (v)	قطع بفأس	*qaṭa'a bi fa's*
hexagon (n)	مسدس الشكل	*musaddasush shakl*
hexagonal (adj)	مسدس	*musaddas*
hexametre (n)	سداسي التفاعيل	*sudāsiyyut tafā'īl*
hey (interj)	هاي	*hāi*
heyday (n)	ذروة، أوج	*dhirwah, auj*
hiatus (n)	ثغرة، فجوة	*thughrah, fajwah*
hibernate (v)	أسبت	*asbata*
hibernation (n)	إسبات، سبات الشتاء	*isbāt, subātush shitā'*
hiccough (n)	فواق، حازوقة	*fuwāq, ḥāzūqah*
hick (n)	شخص ريفي وأخرق	*shakhṣ rīfī wa akhraq*
hidden (adj)	مخبوء، مخفي	*makhbū', makhfī*
hide (v)	حجب، كتم، أخفى	*ḥajaba, katama, akhfā*
hide (n)	جلد الحيوان	*jildul ḥaiwān*
hide-and-seek (n)	غمضية	*ghamḍiyyah*
hideaway (n)	معتزل، مخبأ	*mu'tazal, makhba'*
hidebound (adj)	ضيق التفكير	*ḍayyiqut tafkīr*
hideous (adj)	بشع، شنيع	*bashi', shanī'*
hide-out (n)	مخبأ، ملجأ	*mukhba', malja'*
hiding (n)	اختباء، مخبأ	*ikhtibā', makhba'*
hierarchical (adj)	متعلق بالهرمية	*muta'alliq bil haramiyyah*
hierarchy (n)	حكومة الكهنة	*ḥukūmatul kahanah*
high (adj)	عالٍ، رفيع، سامٍ	*'ālin, rafī', sāmin*
high (n)	مكان مرتفع، قمة	*makān murtafi', qimmah*
high (adv)	عالياً، بترف	*'āliyan, bi taraf*

highborn (adj)	كريم المحتد	*karīmul maḥtid*
high chair	كرسي عالي	*kursī 'ālī*
High Commission	مندوب سامي	*mandūb sāmī*
highfalutin (n)	طنان، مدعٍ	*ṭannān, mudda'in*
high fidelity	أمانة بالغة	*amānah bālighah*
high flying	محلق، طنان	*muḥalliq, ṭannān*
high-handed (adj)	تحكمي، طاغٍ	*taḥakkumī, ṭāghin*
high jump (n)	قفز عالي	*qafz 'ālī*
highland (n/adj)	نجد، نجدي	*najd, najdī*
highlander (n)	نجدي، ساكن الهضاب	*najdī, sākinul hiḍāb*
high life (n)	بذخ، ترف	*badhakh, taraf*
highlight (n)	جزء ذو أهمية خاصة	*juz' dhū ahammiyyah khāṣṣah*
highlight (v)	ألقى ضوءً قويًا	*alqā ḍau'an qawiyyā*
high-minded (adj)	سامي المبادى	*sāmiyul mabādi'*
highness (n)	ارتفاع، سمو	*irtifā', sumuww*
high pressure	عالي الضغط	*'āliyuḍ ḍaghṭ*
high priest (n)	كاهن أكبر	*kāhin akbar*
high road (n)	طريق عام	*ṭarīq 'āmm*
high school (n)	مدرسة ثانوية	*madrasah thānawiyyah*
high sounding (adj)	طنان	*ṭannān*
high spirited (adj)	جريء، مقدام	*jarī', miqdām*
high-strung (adj)	عصبي المزاج	*'aṣabiyyul mizāj*
high tide (n)	ذروة المد	*dhirwatul madd*
high treason (n)	خيانة عظمى	*khiyānah 'uẓmā*
high water (n)	شديد القصر	*shadīdul qiṣar*
highway (n)	طريق عام	*ṭarīq 'āmm*
highwayman (n)	قاطع الطرق	*qāṭi'uṭ ṭuruq*
hijack (v)	اختطف، قسر	*ikhtaṭafa, qasara*
hike (v)	سافر، ارتفع	*sāfara, irtafa'a*

hike (n)	نزهة طويلة، ارتفاع	*nuzhah ṭawīlah, irtifā'*
hilarious (adj)	مرح، جذل	*mariḥ, jadhil*
hilariously (adv)	مرحاً، فرحاً	*maraḥan, faraḥan*
hilarity (n)	مرح صاخب	*maraḥ ṣākhib*
hill (n)	تل، هضبة	*tall, haḍabah*
hillock (n)	رابية، تل صغير	*rābiyah, tall ṣaghīr*
hillside (n)	منحدر التل	*munḥadarut tall*
hilly (adj)	كثير التلال	*kathīrut tilāl*
hilt (n)	مقبض السيف	*miqbaḍus saif*
him (pron)	ه	*hū*
himself (pron)	نفسه	*nafsuhu*
hind (n/adj)	أيلة، خلفي	*ayyilah, khalfī*
hinder (v)	منع، عاق	*mana'a, 'āqa*
Hindi (n)	لغة هندية	*lughah hindiyyah*
hindrance (n)	إعاقة، عائق، صد	*i'āqah, 'ā'iq, ṣadd*
hindsight (n)	إدراك مؤخر	*idrāk mu'akhkhar*
Hindu (n)	هندوسي	*hindūsī*
Hinduism (n)	هندوسية	*hindūsiyyah*
hinge (n/v)	مفصلة، مفصل	*mifṣalah, mafṣala*
hint (n/v)	إلماع، ألمع	*ilmā', alma'a*
hinterland (n)	منطقة خلفية	*minṭaqah khalfiyyah*
hip (n)	ورك	*warik*
hipped (adj)	ذو وركين	*dhū warikain*
hippie (n)	هبي، وجودي	*hibbī, wujūdī*
hippopotamus (n)	برنيق، جاموس البحر	*birnīq, jāmūsul baḥr*
hire (v)	استأجر، أجر	*ista'jara, ajjara*
hire (n)	أجرة، أجر	*ujrah, ajr*
hireling (n)	مأجور، خادم	*ma'jūr, khādim*
hire purchase (n)	شراء بالتقسيط	*shirā' bit taqsīṭ*
hirsute (adj)	قاسي الشعر	*qāsiyush sha'r*

his (pron)	لـه	*lahū*
Hispanic (adj)	أسباني	*asbānī*
hiss (v)	هس، هسهس	*hassa, hashasa*
hiss (n)	هسيس، هسهسة	*hasīs, hashasah*
histamine (n)	هستمين	*histamīn*
historian (n)	مؤرخ	*mu'arrikh*
historic-al (adj)	تاريخي، مختص بالتاريخ	*tārīkhī, mukhtaṣṣ bit tārīkh*
history (n)	تاريخ، علم التاريخ	*tārīkh, 'ilmut tārīkh*
histrionic (adj)	مسرحي، متكلف	*masraḥī, mutakallaf*
histrionics (n)	تمثيل مسرحي	*tamthīl masraḥī*
hit (v)	ضرب، عثر، صدم	*ḍaraba, 'athara, ṣadama*
hit (n)	ضربة، ارتطام	*ḍarbah, irtiṭām*
hitch (v)	ربط، عقد، حرك	*rabaṭa, 'aqqada, ḥarraka*
hitch (n)	عقدة، عقبة، ورطة	*'uqdah, 'aqabah, warṭah*
hitchhike (v)	سافر متطفلاً	*sāfara mutaṭaffilan*
hither (adv)	إلى هنا	*ilā hunā*
hitherto (adv)	حتى الآن	*ḥattal ān*
hive (n)	خلية نحل، قفير	*khaliyyatu naḥl, qafīr*
hive (v)	ادخر، احتل قفيراً	*iddakhara, iḥtalla qafīran*
hoard (n)	ذخيرة، مؤونة	*dhakhīrah, ma'ūnah*
hoard (v)	ادخر، اختزن	*iddakhara, ikhtazana*
hoarding (n)	لوحة إعلانات	*lauḥatu i'lānāt*
hoar-frost (n)	صقيع، سقيط	*ṣaqī', saqīṭ*
hoarse (adj)	أجش الصوت	*ajashshuṣ ṣaut*
hoarseness (n)	بحة في الصوت	*buḥḥah fiṣ ṣaut*
hoary (adj)	قديم، جليل	*qadīm, jalīl*
hoax (n/v)	خدع، خدعة	*khada'a, khud'ah*

hob (n)	حاجب حديدي	*ḥājib ḥadīdī*
hobble (v)	عرج، عاق	*'araja, 'āqa*
hobble (n)	عرج، ورطة	*'arāj, warṭah*
hobby (n)	هواية	*hiwāyah*
hobby-horse (n)	عصا فرسية	*'aṣā farasiyyah*
hobgoblin (n)	بعبع، غول	*bu'bu', ghūl*
hobnail (n)	مسمار النعل	*mismārun na'l*
hobnob (v)	خادن، عاشر	*khādana, 'āshara*
hobo (n)	عامل متجول	*'āmil mutajawwil*
hock (n)	عرقوب، رهن	*'urqūb, rahn*
hockey (n)	هوكي	*hūkī*
hocus-pocus (n)	هراء، تمويه	*hurā', tamwīh*
hod (n)	نقير	*naqīr*
hoe (n)	معزقة، مجرفة	*mi'zaqah, mijrafah*
hoe (v)	عزق الأرض	*'azaqal arḍ*
hog (n)	خنـــزير	*khinzīr*
hog (v)	قص، جز	*qaṣṣa, jazza*
hogwash (n)	كلام تافه	*kalām tāfih*
hoist (v/n)	رفع علماً، رفع	*rafa'a 'alaman, raf'*
hoity-toity (adj)	مستهتر، متشامخ	*mustahtir, mutashāmikh*
hold (v)	أمسك، قبض، حبس	*amsaka, qabaḍa, ḥabasa*
hold (n)	إمساك، سلطة، دعامة	*imsāk, sulṭah, di'āmah*
holdall (n)	حقيبة سفر، جراب	*ḥaqībatu safar, jirāb*
holdback (n)	عائق، إعاقة، مانع	*'ā'iq, i'āqah, māni'*
holder (n)	ممسك، حامل السند	*mimsak, ḥāmilus sanad*
holding (n)	ممتلكات	*mumtalakāt*
holding company (n)	شركة مهيمنة	*sharikah muhaiminah*
hole (n)	ثقب، جحر، ورطة	*thaqb, juḥr, warṭah*

hole (v)	ثقب، شق	*thaqaba, shaqqa*
holiday (n)	يوم العطلة	*yaumul 'uṭlah*
holiday (v)	قضى العطلة	*qaḍal 'uṭlah*
holiness (n)	قداسة، طهارة	*qadāsah, ṭahārah*
holler (v)	صاح، شكا	*ṣāḥa, shakā*
hollow (adj)	مجوف، غائر	*mujawwaf, ghā'ir*
hollow (n/v)	تجويف، جوف	*tajwīf, jawwafa*
hollowly (adv)	تماماً، كاملاً	*tamāman, kāmilan*
hollowness (n)	تجويف، تجوف	*tajwīf, tajawwuf*
holly (n)	بهشية	*bahshiyyah*
hollyhock (n)	خطمي وردي	*khiṭmī wardī*
hollywood (n)	صناعة السينما الأمريكية	*ṣinā'atus sīnma al amrīkiyyah*
holocaust (n)	محرقة، مجزرة	*maḥraqah, majzarah*
holster (n)	قراب المسدس	*qirābul musaddas*
holy (adj)	مقدس، طاهر	*muqaddas, ṭāhir*
Holy Communion	عشاء إلهي	*'ashā' ilāhī*
Holy Father	أب أقدس	*ab aqdas*
Holy Ghost (n)	الروح القدس	*ar rūḥul qudus*
Holy Week (n)	أسبوع الآلام	*usbū'ul ālām*
Holy Writ (n)	أسفار مقدسة	*asfār muqaddasah*
homage (n)	إجلال، ولاء، بيعة	*ijlāl, walā', bai'ah*
home (n)	بيت، منـــزل، دار	*bait, manzil, dār*
home (adj)	منـــزلي	*manzilī*
home (adv)	نحو البيت	*naḥwal bait*
home economics	تدبير منـــزلي	*tadbīr manzilī*
homeland (n)	الوطن	*al waṭan*
homeless (adj)	شريد، شارد	*sharīd, shārid*
homelessness (n)	شرود	*shurūd*
homelike (adj)	عائلي، بهيج	*'ā'ilī, bahīj*

homely (adj)	مألوف، عادي	*ma'lūf, 'ādī*
home-made (adj)	وطني الصنع	*waṭaniyyuṣ ṣun'*
homeopathy	معالجة مثلية	*mu'ālajah mithliyyah*
home rule (n)	حكم ذاتي	*ḥukm dhātī*
Home Secretary (n)	وزير الداخلية	*wazīrud dākhiliyyah*
homesick (adj)	مشوق للوطن	*mashūq lil waṭan*
homesickness (n)	شواق	*shuwāq*
homespun (adj)	بسيط، غير متكلف	*basīṭ, ghair mutakallaf*
homestead (n)	منــزل الأسرة	*manzilul usrah*
homework (n)	فرض منـــزلي	*farḍ manzilī*
homicidal (adj)	قتلي	*qatlī*
homicide (n)	قتل، قاتل	*qatl, qātil*
homily (n)	خطبة طويلة	*khuṭbah ṭawīlah*
homogeneity (n)	تجانس	*tajānus*
homogeneous (adj)	متجانس، متشابه	*mutajānis, mutashābih*
homogenize,-ise (v)	جانس، تجانس	*jānasa, tajānasa*
homograph (n)	لفظة مجانسة	*lafẓah mujānisah*
homonym (n)	لفظة مجانسة	*lafẓah mujānisah*
homophone = homonym		
homosexual (n/adj)	لوطي	*lūṭī*
homosexuality (n)	لواطة، اشتهاء المماثل	*liwāṭah, ishtihā'ul mumāthil*
hone (v)	شحذ، سن	*shaḥadha, sanna*
honest (adj)	صادق، مخلص	*ṣādiq, mukhliṣ*
honestly (adv)	بصدق، بأمانة	*bi ṣidq, bi amānah*
honesty (n)	صدق، أمانة	*ṣidq, amānah*
honey (n)	عسل، حبيب	*'asl, ḥabīb*
honeybee (n)	عسالة	*'assālah*
honeycomb (n)	قرص العسل	*qurṣul 'asl*
honeymoon (n)	شهر العسل	*shahrul 'asl*

honeymoon (v)	قضى شهر العسل	*qaḍā shahral ʻasl*
honeysuckle (n)	صريمة الجدي	*ṣarīmatul jady*
honorarium (n)	مكافأة شرفية	*mukāfa'ah sharafiyyah*
honorary (adj)	شرفي، إكرامي	*sharafī, ikrāmī*
honorific (adj)	تشريفي، تبجيلي	*tashrīfī, tabjīlī*
honour (honor) (n)	شرف، فخر، إجلال	*sharaf, fakhr, ijlāl*
honour (honor) (v)	أجل، شرف	*ajalla, sharrafa*
honourable (adj)	جدير بالاحترام	*jadīr bil iḥtirām*
hooch (n)	خمرة	*khamrah*
hood (n)	غطاء للرأس	*ghiṭā' lir ra's*
hooded (adj)	ذو غطاء، ذو غماء	*dhū ghiṭā', dhū ghimā'*
hoodlum (n)	سفاح	*saffāḥ*
hoodoo (n)	حظ عاثر	*ḥaẓẓ ʻāthir*
hoodwink (v)	خدع، غش	*khadaʻa, ghashsha*
hooey (n)	هراء	*hurā'*
hoof (n)	حف، حافر	*ḥuff, ḥāfir*
hook (n)	كلاب، خطاف، شرك	*kullāb, khuṭṭāf, sharak*
hook (v)	كلب، تكلب	*kallaba, takallaba*
hooked (adj)	مكلب، معقوف	*mukallab, maʻqūf*
hook-up (n)	مقرنة	*muqranah*
hookworm (n)	دودة الأنسيلوستوما	*dūdatul ansīlūstūmā*
hooligan (n)	سفاح	*saffāḥ*
hooliganism (n)	سفاحية	*saffāḥiyyah*
hoop (n)	طوق، طارة	*ṭauq, ṭārah*
hooray = hurrah		
hoot (n)	صياح استهجان	*ṣiyāḥu istihjān*
hoot (v)	صاح مستهجناً	*ṣāḥa mustahjinan*
hop (v)	وثب، حجل	*wathaba, ḥajala*
hop (n)	حشيشة الدينار	*ḥashīshatud dīnār*

hope (n)	أمل، رجاء	*amal, rajā'*
hopeful (adj)	مفعم بالأمل، راجٍ	*muf'am bil amal, rājin*
hopefully (adv)	مفعماً بالأمل	*muf'aman bil amal*
hopefulness (n)	رجاء، رجاة	*rajā', rajāh*
hopeless (adj)	يائس، عضال	*yā'is, 'uḍāl*
hopelessly (adv)	بقنوط، بيأس	*bi qunūṭ, bi ya's*
hopelessness (n)	يأس، قنوط	*ya's, qunūṭ*
hopper (n)	قادوس، واثب	*qādūs, wāthib*
hopscotch (n)	حجلة	*ḥajlah*
horde (n)	حشد، جماعة	*ḥashd, jamā'ah*
horizon (n)	الأفق	*al ufq*
horizontal (adj)	أفقي	*ufqī*
hormone (n)	هرمون	*harmūn*
hormonal (adj)	هرموني	*harmūnī*
horn (n)	قرن، بوق، نفير	*qarn, būq, nafīr*
horned (adj)	ذو قرون	*dhū qurūn*
hornet (n)	زنبور، دبور	*zambūr, dabūr*
hornpipe (n)	رقصة مزمارية	*raqṣah mizmāriyyah*
horny (adj)	قرني، صلب	*qarnī, ṣulb*
horoscope (n)	خريطة البروج	*kharīṭatul burūj*
horrendous (adj)	رهيب، مريع	*rahīb, murī'*
horrible (adj)	رهيب، مخيف	*rahīb, mukhīf*
horrid (adj)	بشع، بغيض	*bashi', baghīḍ*
horrific (adj)	مخيف، رهيب، مفزع	*mukhīf, rahīb, mufzi'*
horrify (v)	أرهب، روع	*arhaba, rawwa'a*
horrifying (adj)	مروع، رهيب	*murawwi', rahīb*
horror (n)	رعب، خوف	*ru'b, khauf*
horse (n)	فرس، حصان	*faras, ḥiṣān*
horseback (n)	صهوة الجواد	*ṣahwatul jawād*
horseflesh (n)	لحم الخيل	*laḥmul khail*

horsefly (n)	نعرة	*nu'arah*
horsehair (n)	سبيب	*sabīb*
horseman (n)	فارس، سائس الخيل	*fāris, sā'isul khail*
horsemanship (n)	فروسية	*furūsiyyah*
horseplay (n)	مزاح خشن	*muzāḥ khashin*
horsepower (n)	قدرة حصانية	*qudrah ḥiṣāniyyah*
horseradish (n)	جرجار	*jirjār*
horseshoe (n)	حدوة	*ḥadwah*
horsewhip (n/v)	سوط، جلد بالسوط	*sauṭ, jalada bis sauṭ*
horsy (adj)	فرسي، خيلي	*farasī, khailī*
horticultural (adj)	بستني، جناني	*bastanī, jinānī*
horticulture (n)	بستنة، جنانة	*bastanah, jinānah*
hose (n)	خرطوم، جورب	*khurṭūm, jaurab*
hose (v)	غسل بخرطوم	*ghasala bi khurṭūm*
hosier (n)	تاجر الملابس التحتانية	*tājirul malābis at taḥtāniyyah*
hosiery (n)	ملابس تحتانية	*malābis taḥtāniyyah*
hospice (n)	تكية	*takiyyah*
hospitable (adj)	مضياف، كريم	*miḍyāf, karīm*
hospital (n)	مستشفى، دار المعالجة	*mustashfā, dārul mu'ālajah*
hospitality (n)	حسن الضيافة، قرىً	*ḥusnuḍ ḍiyāfah, qiran*
hospitalization (n)	دخول في المستشفى	*dukhūl fil mustashfā*
hospitalize,-ise (v)	أدخل في المستشفى	*adkhala fil mustashfā*
host (n)	مضيف، جمهرة	*muḍīf, jamharah*
host (v)	أضاف	*aḍāfa*
hostage (n)	رهينة	*rahīnah*
hostel (n)	بيت الشباب، نزل	*baitush shabāb, nuzul*
hostess (n)	مضيفة	*muḍīfah*
hostile (adj)	معادٍ، عدائي	*mu'ādin, 'idā'ī*

hostility (n)	عداء، خصومة	*'idā', khuṣūmah*
hot (adj)	حار، حاد، ساخن	*ḥārr, ḥādd, sākhin*
hot air (n)	هذر، كلام فارغ	*hadhar, kalām fārigh*
hotbed (n)	مرتع	*marta'*
hot-blooded (adj)	سريع الاهتياج	*sarī'ul ihtiyāj*
hotchpotch (n)	خليط، مزيج	*khalīṭ, mazīj*
hotel (n)	فندق	*funduq*
hotfoot (adv)	بعجلة، حالاً	*bi 'ajalah, ḥālan*
hotfoot (v)	تعجل، استعجل	*ta'ajjala, ista'jala*
hothead (n)	شخص عجول	*shakhṣ 'ajūl*
hotheaded (adj)	متهور، حاد الطبع	*mutahawwir, ḥādduṭ ṭab'*
hothouse (n)	دفيئة	*dafī'ah*
hotplate (n)	لوح التسخين	*lauḥut taskhīn*
hotshot (n)	عامل بارع	*'āmil bāri'*
hot spring (n)	عينة حارة	*'ainah ḥārrah*
hot water (n)	مأزق، ورطة	*ma'ziq, warṭah*
hound (n)	كلب صيد، ضرو	*kalbu ṣaid, ḍirw*
hound (v)	تعقب، طارد، حرش	*ta'aqqaba, ṭārada, ḥarrasha*
hour (n)	ساعة، أوان	*sā'ah, awān*
hourglass (n)	ساعة رملية	*sā'ah ramliyyah*
houri (n)	حورية	*ḥūriyyah*
hourly (adj/adv)	ساعي، في كل ساعة	*sā'ī, fī kulli sā'ah*
house (n)	بيت، منـزل	*bait, manzil*
house (v)	أسكن، آوى	*askana, āwā*
house arrest (n)	إقامة جبرية	*iqāmah jabriyyah*
houseboat (n)	مركب البيت	*markabul bait*
housebreaking (n)	لصوصية	*luṣūṣiyyah*
housebroken (adj)	مروض، مدرب	*murawwaḍ, mudarrab*
houseful (adj)	ملء منـزل	*mil'u manzil*

household (n/adj)	أهل البيت، منـــزلي	*ahlul bait, manzilī*
householder (n)	رب البيت	*rabbul bait*
housekeeper (n)	مدبرة البيت	*mudabbiratul bait*
housekeeping (n)	تدبير شؤون المنـــزل	*tadbīru shu'ūnil manzil*
housemaid (n)	خادمة	*khādimah*
houseroom (n)	مبيت في منـــزل	*mabīt fī manzil*
housetop (n)	سطح البيت	*saṭḥul bait*
housewife (n)	ربة المنـــزل	*rabbatul manzil*
housing (n)	سكنى، مسكن	*suknā, maskan*
hovel (n)	عشة، كوخ	*'ushshah, kūkh*
hover (v)	حام، رفرف	*ḥāma, rafrafa*
how (adv/conj)	كيف، كيفما	*kaifa, kaifamā*
however (adv/conj)	ومع ذلك، مهما	*wa ma'a dhālik, mahmā*
howitzer (n)	قذاف	*qadhdhāf*
howl (n)	عواء، نباح	*'uwā', nubāḥ*
howl (v)	عوى، صرخ	*'awā, ṣarakha*
howler (n)	نابح، عواء	*nābiḥ, 'awwā'*
hub (n)	قب، محور	*qabb, miḥwar*
hubhub (n)	ضجيج، صخب	*ḍajīj, ṣakhab*
huckster (n)	بائع متجول	*bā'i' mutajawwil*
huddle (n)	حشد، جمهرة	*ḥashd, jamharah*
huddle (v)	اجتمع، احتشد	*ijtama'a, iḥtashada*
hue (n)	تدرج اللون، لون	*tadarrujul laun, laun*
huff (n)	نوبة غضب	*naubatu ghaḍab*
huffy (adj)	متعجرف، سريع الغضب	*muta'ajrif, sarī'ul ghaḍab*
hug (v)	عانق، حضن	*'ānaqa, ḥaḍana*
hug (n)	معانقة	*mu'ānaqah*
huge (adj)	ضخم، هائل	*ḍakhm, hā'il*

hullabaloo (n)	ضجة، ضوضاء	*ḍajjah, ḍauḍā'*
hum (v)	طن، دندن	*ṭanna, dandana*
hum (n)	طنين، ترنم	*ṭanīn, tarannum*
human (n)	إنسان، بشر	*insān, bashar*
human (adj)	إنساني، بشري	*insānī, basharī*
humane (adj)	شفوق، عطوف	*shafūq, 'aṭūf*
humanism (n)	فلسفة إنسانية، خيرية	*falsafah insāniyyah, khairiyyah*
humanitarian (adj)	خير، محسن	*khayyir, muḥsin*
humanity (n)	إنسانية، شفقة	*insāniyyah, shafaqah*
humanize,-ise (v)	لطف، هذب	*laṭṭafa, hadhdhaba*
humankind (n)	جنس بشري	*jins basharī*
humble (adj)	متواضع، وضيع	*mutawāḍi', waḍī'*
humble (v)	أذل، أخضع	*adhalla, akhḍa'a*
humbly (adv)	بتواضع، بتذلل	*bi tawāḍu', bi tadhallul*
humbug (n)	مخادعة، احتيال	*mukhāda'ah, iḥtiyāl*
humdinger (n)	شيء رائع جدا	*shay' rā'i' jiddan*
humdrum (adj)	رتيب، ممل	*ratīb, mumill*
humerus (n)	عظم العضد	*'aẓmul 'aḍud*
humid (adj)	رطب، ندي	*raṭb, nadiyy*
humidifier (n)	مرطبة	*muraṭṭibah*
humidity (n)	رطوبة، نداوة	*ruṭūbah, nadāwah*
humiliate (v)	أذل، أخزى	*adhalla, akhzā*
humiliation (n)	إخزاء، ذل	*ikhzā', dhull*
humiliating (adj)	مذل، مخز	*mudhill, mukhzin*
humility (n)	تواضع، ضعة	*tawāḍu', ḍa'ah*
hummingbird (n)	طائر طنان	*ṭā'ir ṭannān*
hummock (n)	رابية، أكمة	*rābiyah, akamah*
humorist (n)	مضحك، ظريف	*muḍḥik, ẓarīf*
humorous (adj)	ظريف، هزلي	*ẓarīf, hazlī*

humorously (adv)	بظرافة، بفكاهة	*bi ẓarāfah, bi fukāhah*
humour (humor) (n)	ظرف، فكاهة	*ẓarf, fukāhah*
hump (n)	حدبة، رابية	*ḥadabah, rābiyah*
hump (v)	حمل على ظهر	*ḥamala ʻalā ẓahr*
humped (adj)	محدب، مسنم	*muḥaddab, musannam*
humus (n)	دبال	*dubāl*
hunch (n)	حس باطني	*ḥiss bāṭinī*
hunch (v)	حنى، حدب	*ḥanā, ḥaddaba*
hunchback (n)	أحدب، ذو حدبة	*aḥdab, dhū ḥadabah*
hundred (n)	مأة	*mi'ah*
hundredth (adj)	المأة	*al mi'ah*
hunger (n)	جوع، سغب	*jūʻ, saghab*
hunger (v)	اشتهى، تاق	*ishtahā, tāqa*
hunger strike (n)	إضراب عن الطعام	*iḍrāb ʻaniṭ ṭaʻām*
hungrily (adv)	جائعاً، جوعاً	*jā'iʻan, jūʻan*
hungry (adj)	جائع، تواق	*jā'iʻ, tawwāq*
hunk (n)	قطعة ضخمة	*qiṭʻah ḍakhmah*
hunt (v)	صاد، فتش	*ṣāda, fattasha*
hunter (n)	صياد، قناص	*ṣayyād, qannāṣ*
hunting (n)	صيد، شطط	*ṣaid, shaṭaṭ*
huntsman (n)	صياد	*ṣayyād*
hurdle (n)	حاجز، عقبة	*ḥājiz, ʻaqabah*
hurdle (v)	وثب فوق حاجز	*wathaba fauqa ḥājiz*
hurl (v)	قذف، رشق	*qadhafa, rashaqa*
hurly-burly (n)	هرج ومرج	*harj wa marj*
hurrah (hurray) (interj)	هوراه	*hūrāh*
hurricane (n)	إعصار	*iʻṣār*
hurried (adj)	مسرع، مستعجل	*musriʻ, mustaʻjil*
hurriedly (adv)	بسرعة، بعجلة	*bi surʻah, bi ʻajalah*
hurry (n)	عجلة، سرعة	*ʻajalah, surʻah*

hurry (v)	أسرع، استعجل	*asra'a, ista'jala*
hurt (v)	آذى، ضر	*ādhā, ḍarra*
hurt (n)	جرح، ضرر	*jurḥ, ḍarar*
hurtle (v)	اندفع بعنف	*indafa'a bi 'unf*
husband (n)	زوج، بعل	*zauj, ba'l*
husbandman (n)	مزارع	*muzāri'*
husbandry (n)	زراعة، فلاحة	*zirā'ah, filāḥah*
hush (v)	هدأ، هدّأ	*hada'a, hadda'a*
hush (n)	سكوت بعد ضجة	*sukūt ba'da ḍajjah*
hush-hush (adj)	سري، مكتوم	*sirrī, maktūm*
hush money (n)	رشوة	*rishwah*
husk (n)	قشرة الثمرة	*qishratuth thamrah*
husk (v)	قشر	*qashara*
husky (adj)	قشري، قوي	*qishrī, qawī*
hussar (n)	هوصار	*hūṣār*
hussy (n)	فتاة فاجرة	*fatāt fājirah*
hustings (n)	إجراءات حملة	*ijrā'ātu ḥamlah*
	انتخابية	*intikhābiyyah*
hustle (n)	نشاط بالغ	*nashāṭ bāligh*
hustle (v)	دفع بسرعة	*dafa'a bi sur'ah*
hut (n)	كوخ، سقيفة	*kūkh, saqīfah*
hutch (n)	قفص، زريبة صغيرة	*qafaṣ, zarībah ṣaghīrah*
hybrid (adj/n)	هجين، نغل	*hajīn, naghl*
hybridize,-ise (v)	هجن، نغل	*hajjana, naghghala*
hydrant (n)	صنبور، حنفية	*ṣumbūr, ḥanafiyyah*
hydrate (v)	ميه، تميه	*mayyaha, tamayyaha*
hydration (n)	تمييه، تميه	*tamyīh, tamayyuh*
hydraulic (adj)	هيدروليكي	*haidurūlīkī*
hydraulics (n)	هيدروليات	*haidurūliyyāt*
hydrocarbon (n)	هيدروكربون	*haidurūkarbūn*

hydrocele (n)	أدرة، قيلة	*adrah, qailah*
hydrochloric acid	حمض الهيدروكلوريك	*ḥamḍul haidurūkulūrīk*
hydroelectric (n)	كهربيمائي	*kahrabīmā'ī*
hydrogen (n)	هيدروجين	*haidurūjīn*
hydrogen bomb	قنبلة هيدروجينية	*qumbulah haidurūjīniyyah*
hydroplane (n)	زلاقة مائية	*zallāqah mā'iyyah*
hydroponics (n)	زراعة بالماء	*zirā'ah bil mā'*
hydrotherapy (n)	معالجة مائية	*mu'ālajah mā'iyyah*
hygiene (n)	علم الصحة	*'ilmuṣ ṣiḥḥah*
hygienic (adj)	صحي، مختص بصحة	*ṣiḥḥī, mukhtaṣṣ biṣ ṣiḥḥah*
hymen (n)	غشاء البكارة	*ghishā'ul bukārah*
hymn (n)	ترتيلة، ترنيمة	*tartīlah, tarnīmah*
hymn (v)	سبح بالتراتيل	*sabbaḥa bit tarātīl*
hyperactive (adj)	ناشط بإفراط	*nāshiṭ bi ifrāṭ*
hyperbole (n)	غلو، إغراق	*ghuluww, ighrāq*
hyperbolic (adj)	متسم بالغلو	*muttasim bil ghuluww*
hypersensitive (adj)	مفرط الحساسية	*mufriṭul ḥassāsiyyah*
hypertension (n)	فرط ضغط الدم	*farṭu ḍaghṭid dam*
hyphen (n)	واصلة	*wāṣilah*
hyphenate (v)	وصل بواصلة	*waṣala bi wāṣilah*
hypnosis (n)	نوم مغنطيسي	*naum maghnaṭīsī*
hypnotic (n)	متعلق بنوم مغنطيسي	*muta'alliq bi naum maghnaṭīsī*
hypnotism (n)	تنويم مغنطيسي	*tanwīm maghnaṭīsī*
hypnotist (n)	منوم مغنطيسي	*munawwim maghnaṭīsī*
hypnotize,-ise (v)	نوم مغنطيسيًّا	*nawwama maghnaṭīsiyyan*
hypochondria (n)	وسواس المرض	*waswāsul maraḍ*

hypochondriac (adj)	مصاب بوسواس المرض	*muṣāb bi waswāsil maraḍ*
hypocrisy (n)	نفاق، رياء	*nifāq, riyā'*
hypocrite (n)	منافق، مراءٍ	*munāfiq, murā'in*
hypocritical (adj)	رياْئي، كاذب	*riyā'ī, kādhib*
hypodermic (n/adj)	تحجلدي	*taḥjildī*
hypotenuse (n)	وتر المثلث	*watarul muthallath*
hypothesis (n)	فرضية، ظنية	*farḍiyyah, ẓanniyyah*
hypothesize,-ise (v)	افترض	*iftaraḍa*
hypothetical (adj)	افتراضي، نظري	*iftirāḍī, naẓarī*
hysteria (n)	هستيريا، هرع	*histīriyā, hara'*
hysteric (adj)	هستيري، هرعي	*histīrī, hara'ī*
hysterics (n)	هستيريا	*histīriyā*

I

I (pron)	أنا	*anā*
iambic (adj)	عمبقي	*'ambaqī*
ibex (n)	وعل، بدن	*wa'l, badan*
ibid (ibidem)	في نفس المكان	*fī nafsil makān*
ice (n)	ثلج، جليد، برود	*thalj, jalīb, burūd*
ice (v)	برد، ثلج	*barrada, thallaja*
ice age (n)	عصر جليدي	*'aṣr jalīdī*
ice bag (n)	كيس الثلج	*kīsuth thalj*
iceberg (n)	جبل جليدي	*jabal jalīdī*
ice boat (n)	مركب الجمد	*markabul jamad*
icebox (n)	ثلاجة	*thallājah*
icebreaker (n)	كسارة الجمد، حاطم الجليد	*kassāratul jamad, ḥāṭimul jalīd*
ice-cap (n)	قلنسوة الجليد	*qalansuwatul jalīd*

ice-cold (adj)	مثلوج	*mathlūj*
ice-cream (n)	بوظة	*būẓah*
ice-field (n)	حقل الجليد	*ḥaqlul jalīd*
ice-floe (n)	طوف جليدي	*ṭauf jalīdī*
ice-pack (n)	جليد مترابط	*jalīd mutarābiṭ*
ice-pick (n)	معول الثلج	*mi'waluth thalj*
ice-skate (v)	تزلج على الجليد	*tazallaja 'alal jalīd*
ice-water (n)	ماء مبرد	*mā' mubarrad*
icon (n)	إيقونة، تمثال	*īqūnah, timthāl*
iconic (adj)	إيقوني	*īqūnī*
iconoclasm (n)	تحطيم التماثيل الدينية	*taḥṭīmut tamāthīl ad dīniyyah*
iconoclast (n)	محطم للتماثيل الدينية	*muḥaṭṭim lit tamāthīl ad dīniyyah*
iconoclastic (adj)	تحطيمي	*taḥṭīmī*
icy (adj)	جليدي، بارد جدا	*jalīdī, bārid jiddan*
idea (n)	فكرة، خطة، مثال	*fikrah, khuṭṭah, mithāl*
ideal (n)	مثل أعلى، هدف	*mathal a'lā, hadaf*
ideal (adj)	مثالي، تصوري	*mithālī, taṣawwurī*
idealism (n)	مثالية، مذهب مثالي	*mithāliyyah, madhhab mithālī*
idealist (n)	مثالي، خيالي	*mithālī, khayālī*
idealistic (adj)	مثالي	*mithālī*
ideality (n)	مثالية، شيء خيالي	*mithāliyyah, shay' khayālī*
idealize,-ise (v)	جعل مثاليًا	*ja'ala mithāliyyan*
ideally (adv)	مثاليًا، كلاسيكيًا	*mithāliyyan, kalāsīkiyyan*
identical (adj)	مماثل، مطابق	*mumāthil, muṭābiq*
identically (adv)	بالتماثل، بالتطابق	*bit tamāthul, bit taṭābuq*

identification (n)	مماثلة، مطابقة	*mumāthalah, muṭābaqah*
identify (v)	ماثل، طابق	*māthala, ṭābaqa*
identity (n)	هوية، تماثل، تطابق	*huwiyyah, tamāthul, taṭābuq*
identity card	بطاقة الهوية	*biṭāqatul huwiyyah*
ideogram (ideograph)	ايديوغرام	*īdiwgharām*
ideography (n)	ايديوغرافيا	*īdiwgharāfiyā*
ideologic-al (adj)	فكري، ايديولوجي	*fikrī, īdiwlūjī*
ideologically (adv)	ايديولوجيًّا	*īdiwlūjiyyan*
ideologist (n)	ايديولوجي، واضع النظريات	*īdiwlūjī, wāḍi'un naẓariyyāt*
ideology (n)	ايديولوجية، طريقة التفكير	*īdiwlūjiyyah, ṭarīqatut tafkīr*
idiocy (n)	حماقه، بلاهة	*ḥamāqah, balāhah*
idiom (n)	اصطلاح، تعبير خصوصي	*iṣṭilāḥ, ta'bīr khuṣūṣī*
idiomatic (adj)	اصطلاحي، فردي	*iṣṭilāḥī, fardī*
idiomatically (adv)	في الاصطلاح	*fil iṣṭilāḥ*
idiosyncrasy (n)	سجية، خاصة	*sajiyyah, khāṣṣah*
idiot (n)	أحمق، أبله	*aḥmaq, ablah*
idiotic (adj)	أحمق، معتوه	*aḥmaq, ma'tūh*
idiotically (adv)	بحماقة، ببلاهة	*bi ḥamāqah, bi balāhah*
idle (adj)	كسلان، مهمل	*kaslān, muhmil*
idle (v)	تكاسل، تبطل	*takāsala, tabaṭṭala*
idleness (n)	كسل، تعطل	*kasal, ta'aṭṭul*
idly (adv)	بتكاسل، عبثاً	*bi takāsul, 'abathan*
idol (n)	وثن، شبح، محبوب	*wathan, shabaḥ, maḥbūb*
idolater (n)	وثني، عابد الوثن	*wathanī, 'ābidul wathan*

idolatrous (adj)	وثني	*wathanī*
idolatry (n)	وثنية، حب أعمى	*wathaniyyah, ḥubb a'mā*
idolize,-ise (v)	أله، أحب حبًا جمًا	*allaha, aḥabba ḥubban jammā*
idyll (n)	قصيدة رعوية	*qaṣidah ra'wiyyah*
idyllic (adj)	رعوي	*ra'wī*
idyllically (adv)	على نحو رعوي	*alā naḥwin ra'wī*
if (conj)	إن، لو، إذا	*in, lau, idhā*
iffy (adj)	مشكوك	*mashkūk*
igloo (n)	كوخ قباني	*kūkh qubbānī*
igneous (adj)	ناري، بركاني	*nārī, burkānī*
ignite (v)	ألهب، أشعل	*alhaba, ash'ala*
ignition (n)	مشعلة، إشعال	*mush'ilah, ish'āl*
ignoble (adj)	حقير، دنيء، خسيس	*ḥaqīr, danī', khasīs*
ignominious (adj)	مذل، مخزٍ، فاضح	*mudhill, mukhzin, fāḍiḥ*
ignomity (n)	فضيحة، عار، خزى	*faḍīḥah, 'ār, khizy*
ignoramus (n)	جهول، غبي	*jahūl, ghabī*
ignorance (n)	جهل، غباوة	*jahl, ghabāwah*
ignorant (adj)	جاهل، غبي	*jāhil, ghabī*
ignore (v)	تجاهل، جهل	*tajāhala, jahila*
iguana (n)	إغوانة	*ighwānah*
ikon = icon		
ilk (n)	نوع، طبقة	*nau', ṭabaqah*
ill (adj)	سقيم، عليل	*saqīm, 'alīl*
ill (adv)	باستياء، بصعوبة	*bistiyā', bi ṣu'ūbah*
ill-advised (adj)	غير حكيم	*ghairu ḥakīm*
ill-bred (adj)	سيء التنشئة	*sayyi'ut tanshi'ah*
illegal (adj)	غير قانوني	*ghair qānūnī*

illegally (adv)	بطريقة غير قانونية	*bi ṭarīqah ghair qānūniyyah*
illegible (adj)	مستغلق، غير مقروء	*mustaghliq, ghair maqrū'*
illegitimacy (n)	نغولة، فساد النسب	*nughūlah, fasādun nasab*
illegitimate (adj)	نغل، غير شرعي	*naghil, ghair shar'ī*
ill-fated (adj)	سيء الطالع	*sayyi'uṭ ṭāli'*
ill-founded (adj)	واه	*wāhin*
ill-gotten (adj)	حرام، سحت	*ḥarām, suḥt*
illiberal (adj)	شحيح، متعصب، ضيق	*shaḥīḥ, muta'aṣṣib, ḍayyiq*
illicit (adj)	محظور، محرم	*maḥẓūr, muḥarram*
illiteracy (n)	أمية، جهالة	*ummiyyah, jahālah*
illiterate (adj)	أمي، غير متعلم	*ummī, ghair muta'allim*
ill-mannered (adj)	سيئ الأخلاق	*sayyi'ul akhlāq*
ill-natured (adj)	سيئ الطبع، شكس	*sayyi'uṭ ṭab', shakis*
illness (n)	سقم، مرض	*suqm, maraḍ*
illogic (adj)	غير معقول، غير منطقي	*ghair ma'qūl, ghair manṭiqī*
ill-starred (adj)	سيئ الطالع، مشؤوم	*sayyi'uṭ ṭāli', mash'ūm*
ill-treat (v)	أساء المعاملة	*asā'al mu'āmalah*
illuminate (v)	أضاع، أنار، زوق	*aḍā'a, anāra, zawwaqa*
illuminated (adj)	مزين بالرسوم	*muzayyan bir rusūm*
illuminating (adj)	مضيئ، موضح	*muḍī', muwaḍḍiḥ*
illumination (n)	إضاءة، إنارة	*iḍā'ah, inārah*
illusion (n)	وهم، أخدوعة	*wahm, ukhdū'ah*
illusory (adj)	خادع، موهم	*khādi', mūhim*
illustrate (v)	زين، زود بالرسوم، وضح	*zayyana, zawwada bir rusūm, waḍḍaḥa*
illustration (n)	تزيين، تزويد بالرسوم	*tazyīn, tazwīd bir rusūm*
illustrative (adj)	تزييني، توضيحي	*tazyīnī, tauḍīḥī*

illustrator (n)	مصور، رسام	*muṣawwir, rassām*
illustrious (adj)	شهير، جليل	*shahīr, jalīl*
image (n)	صورة، إيقونة، تمثال	*ṣūrah, īqūnah, timthāl*
imagery (n)	تخيلات، تصورات، تماثيل	*takhayyulāt, taṣawwurāt, tamāthīl*
imaginable (adj)	يمكن تخيله	*yumkin takhayyuluh*
imaginary (adj)	تخيلي، تصوري	*takhayyulī, taṣawwurī*
imagination (n)	تخيل، قدرة مبدعة	*takhayyul, qudrah mubdi'ah*
imaginative (adj)	تخيلي، مبدع الخيال	*takhayyulī, mubdi'ul khayāl*
imagine (v)	تصور، توهم، تخيل	*taṣawwara, takhayyala, tawahhama*
imam (n)	إمام، حاكم	*imām, ḥākim*
imbalance (n)	عدم التوازن	*'adamut tawāzun*
imbecile (n/adj)	معتوه، أبله	*ma'tūh, ablah*
imbecility (n)	حماقة، بلاهة	*ḥamāqah, balāhah*
imbibe (v)	امتص، تشرب	*imtaṣṣa, tasharraba*
imbroglio (n)	وضع مشوش، هرجلة	*waḍ' mushawwash, harjalah*
imbue (v)	صبغ، خضب	*ṣabagha, khaḍaba*
imitate (v)	حاكى، قلد	*ḥākā, qallada*
imitation (n)	محاكاة، تشبه	*muḥākāt, tashabbuh*
imitative (adj)	تقليدي، مقلد	*taqlīdī, muqallid*
imitator (n)	محاكي، مقلد	*muḥākī, muqallid*
immaculate (adj)	نقي، نظيف، طاهر	*naqī, naẓīf, ṭāhir*
immaculately (adv)	بنظافة، بنقاء	*bi naẓāfah, bi naqā'*
immaterial (adj)	روحي، غير مادي	*rūḥī, ghair māddī*
immature (adj)	خام، غير ناضج	*khām, ghair nāḍij*
immaturity (n)	عدم نضج	*'adamu nuḍj*

immeasurable (adj)	لا يمكن قياسه	*lā yumkin qiyāsuh*
immediacy (n)	فورية، عجلة	*fauriyyah, 'ajalah*
immediate (adj)	فوري، مباشر	*faurī, mubāshir*
immediately (adv)	على الفور، توًّا	*'alal faur, tawwan*
immemorial (adj)	سحيق	*saḥīq*
immense (adj)	واسع، ضخم	*wāsi', ḍakhm*
immensely (adv)	باتساع، بضخامة	*bittisā', bi ḍakhāmah*
immensity (n)	ضخامة، اتساع	*ḍakhāmah, ittisā'*
immerse (v)	غمر، غطس	*ghamara, ghaṭṭasa*
immersion (n)	غط، غمر	*ghaṭṭ, ghamr*
immigrant (n)	مهاجر	*muhājir*
immigration (n)	مهاجرة	*muhājarah*
imminence (adj)	وشك، قرب الوقوع	*washk, qurbul wuqū'*
imminent (adj)	وشيك، قريب الوقوع	*washīk, qarībul wuqū'*
imminently (adv)	على وشك	*'alā washk*
immobile (adj)	ثابت، جامد	*thābit, jāmid*
immobility (n)	ثبات، جمود	*thabāt, jumūd*
immobilize,-ise (v)	جمّد	*jammada*
immoderate (adj)	غير معتدل، مفرط	*ghair mu'tadil, mufriṭ*
immoderately (adv)	بغير اعتدال، بإفراط	*bighairi i'tidāl, bi ifrāṭ*
immodest (adj)	غير محتشم، وقح	*ghair muḥtashim, waqiḥ*
immoral (adj)	فاجر، خليع	*fājir, khalī'*
immorality (n)	فسوق، فساد الأخلاق	*fusūq, fasādul akhlāq*
immorally (adv)	بخلاعة، بفجور	*bi khalā'ah, bi fujūr*
immortal (adj/n)	خالد، شيء خالد	*khālid, shay' khālid*
immortality (n)	خلود، بقاء	*khulūd, baqā'*
immortalize,-ise (v)	خلد، أبد	*khallada, abbada*
immovable (adj)	راسخ، صامد	*rāsikh, ṣāmid*
immune (adj)	منيع، حصين	*manī', ḥaṣīn*
immunity (n)	حصانة، مناعة	*ḥaṣānah, manā'ah*

immunization (n)	تحصين، تمنيع	*taḥṣīn, tamnī'*
immunize,-ise (v)	حصن، منع	*ḥaṣṣana, manna'a*
immunology (n)	علم المناعة	*'ilmul manā'ah*
immure (v)	سور، سجن	*sawwara, sajana*
immutability (n)	ثبات، عدم تغير	*thabāt, 'adamu taghayyur*
immutable (adj)	ثابت، غير متغير	*thābit, ghair mutaghayyir*
imp (n)	عفريت، ولد مؤذ	*'ifrīt, walad mu'dhin*
impact (v)	أثر، رص، صدم	*aththara, raṣṣa, ṣadama*
impact (n)	أثر، صدمة	*athar, ṣadmah*
impair (v)	أتلف، أضر	*atlafa, aḍarra*
impale (v)	خوزق، سيج	*khauzaqa, sayyaja*
impalpable (adj)	غير محسوس، دقيق جدا	*ghair maḥsūs, daqīq jiddā*
impart (v)	بلغ، منح، أذاع	*ballagha, manaḥa, adhā'a*
impartial (adj)	غير متحيز، نزيه	*ghair mutaḥayyiz, nazīh*
impartiality (n)	إنصاف، تجرد	*inṣāf, tajarrud*
impartially (adv)	بغير تحيز، بقسط	*bighairi taḥayyuz, bi qisṭ*
impassable (adj)	لا يمكن عبوره	*lā yumkin 'ubūruh*
impasse (n)	ورطة، طريق مسدود	*warṭah, ṭarīq masdūd*
impassioned (adj)	متحمس، ملتهب	*mutaḥammis, multahib*
impassive (adj)	عديم العاطفة، هادئ	*'adīmul 'āṭifah, hādi'*
impatience (n)	ملل، نفاد صبر	*malal, nafadu ṣabr*
impatient (adj)	نافد الصبر، ملول	*nāfiduṣ ṣabr, malūl*
impatiently (adv)	بملل، بضجر	*bi malal, bi ḍajar*
impeach (v)	اتهم، ادعى على	*ittahama, idda'a 'alā*
impeachment (n)	اتهام، ادعاء	*ittihām, iddi'ā'*
impeccable (adj)	معصوم عن الخطأ	*ma'ṣūm 'anil khaṭa'*
impeccably (adv)	بدون خطأ	*bidūn khaṭa'*
impecunious (adj)	معدم، مفلس	*mu'dim, muflis*
impedance (n)	معاوقة، تعويق	*mu'āwaqah, ta'wīq*

impede (v)	أعاق، منع	*a'āqa, mana'a*
impediment (n)	عائق، مانع	*'ā'iq, māni'*
impedimenta (n)	معوقات	*mu'awwiqāt*
impel (v)	أكره، دفع	*akraha, dafa'a*
impending (adj)	وشيك، قريب	*washīk, qarīb*
impenetrability (n)	عدم التحايز، عدم التأثر	*'adamut taḥāyuz, 'adamut ta'aththur*
impenetrable (adj)	مستغلق، عديم التحايز	*mustaghliq, 'adīmut taḥāyuz*
imperative (n)	أمر، طلب، حاجة	*amr, ṭalab, ḥājah*
imperative (adj)	أمري، إلزامي	*amrī, ilzāmī*
imperceptible (adj)	غير محسوس	*ghair maḥsūs*
imperceptibly (adv)	على طريق غير محسوس	*'alā ṭarīq ghair maḥsūs*
imperfect (adj)	ناقص، غير تام	*nāqiṣ, ghair tāmm*
imperfection (n)	نقص، عيب	*naqṣ, 'aib*
imperfectly (adv)	بنقص، بعدم كمال	*bi naqṣ, bi 'adami kamāl*
imperial (adj)	امبراطوري، استبدادي	*imbarāṭūrī, istibdādī*
imperialism (n)	نظام امبراطوري، استعمار	*niẓām imbarāṭūrī, isti'mār*
imperialist (n)	مؤيد لامبراطورية	*mu'ayyid li imbarāṭūriyyah*
imperialistic (adj)	امبراطوري، استعماري	*imbarāṭūrī, isti'mārī*
imperil (v)	عرض للخطر	*'arraḍa lil khaṭar*
imperious (adj)	مستبد، عاتٍ	*mustabidd, 'ātin*
imperiously (adv)	باستبداد	*bistibdād*
imperishable (adj)	باقٍ، غير فانٍ	*bāqin, ghairu fānin*
impermanence (n)	زوال، عدم الدوام	*zawāl, 'adamud dawām*
impermanent (adj)	زائل، مؤقت	*zā'il, mu'aqqat*
impermeable (adj)	غير منفذ للسائل	*ghair munfidh lis sā'il*
impersonal (adj)	غير شخصي، مجهول	*ghair shakhṣī, majhūl*

impersonate (v)	شخص، مثل شخصًا	*shakhkhaṣa, maththala shakhṣan*
impersonation (n)	تشخيص، تمثيل شخص	*tashkhīṣ, tamthīlu shakhṣ*
impersonator (n)	مشخص	*mushakhkhiṣ*
impertinence (n)	وقاحة، عدم ارتباط	*waqāḥah, 'adamu irtibāṭ*
impertinent (adj)	وقح، سليط	*waqiḥ, salīṭ*
impertinently (adv)	بوقاحة، بسلاطة	*bi waqāḥah, bi salāṭah*
imperturbable (adj)	هادئ، ثابت الجأش	*hādi', thābitul ja'sh*
imperturbably (adv)	بهدوء، برزانة	*bi hudū', bi razānah*
impervious (adj)	منيع، كتيم	*manī', katīm*
impetigo (n)	داء جلدي، خصف	*dā' jildī, khaṣaf*
impetuosity (n)	تهور، طيش	*tahawwur, ṭaish*
impetuous (adj)	متهور، طائش	*mutahawwir, ṭā'ish*
impetuously (adv)	بتهور	*bi tahawwur*
impetus (n)	قوة دافعة	*quwwah dāfi'ah*
impiety (n)	عقوق، عدم تقوى	*'uqūq, 'adamu taqwā*
impinge (v)	ارتطم، اصطدم	*irtaṭama, iṣṭadama*
impious (adj)	عاق، غير ورع	*'āqq, ghair wari'*
impish (adj)	عفريتي، مؤذٍ	*'ifrītī, mu'dhin*
impishness (n)	عمل ضار	*'amal ḍārr*
implacable (adj)	غير قابل للتبدل، عنيد	*ghair qābil lit tabaddul, 'anīd*
implacably (adv)	بعنود	*bi 'unūd*
implant (n)	نسيج مزدرع	*nasīj muzdara'*
implant (v)	ازدرع، غرس، وطد	*izdara'a, gharasa, waṭṭada*
Implausible (adj)	غير محتمل	*ghair muḥtamal*
implement (v)	نفذ، زود بأدوات	*naffadha, zawwada bi adawāt*
implement (n)	أداة، آلة	*adāt, ālah*
implicate (v)	ورط، ضمن	*warraṭa, ḍammana*

implication (n)	تضمين، تورط	*taḍmīn, tawarruṭ*
implicit (n)	كامن، مضمر	*kāmin, muḍmar*
implicitly (adv)	بلا ريب، ضمنًا	*bilā raib, ḍimnan*
implode (v)	انفجر ضمناً	*infajara ḍimnan*
implore (v)	التمس، توسل	*iltamasa, tawassala*
imploring (adj)	متضرع، ملتمس	*Mutaḍarri', multamis*
implosion (n)	انفجار ضمني	*infijār ḍimnī*
imply (v)	تضمن، دل على	*taḍammana, dalla 'alā*
impolite (adj)	جلف، فظ	*jilf, faẓẓ*
impolitic (adj)	غير حكيم، أخرق	*ghair ḥakīm, akhraq*
imponderable (adj)	غير موزون	*ghair mauzūn*
import (v)	استورد، أدخل	*istaurada, adkhala*
importance (n)	أهمية، اعتبار	*ahammiyyah, i'tibār*
important (adj)	هام، ذو شأن	*hāmm, dhū sha'n*
importation (n)	استيراد، شيء مستورد	*istīrād, shay' mustaurad*
importer (n)	بلد مستورد	*balad mustaurid*
imports (n)	واردات	*wāridāt*
importunate (adj)	ملح، مزعج	*muliḥḥ, muz'ij*
importune (v)	أزعج، ألح	*az'aja, alaḥḥa*
impose (v)	فرض، استغل	*faraḍa, istaghalla*
imposing (adj)	جليل، مؤثر، مهيب	*jalīl, mu'aththir, muhīb*
imposition (n)	فرض، ضريبة	*farḍ, ḍarībah*
impossibility (n)	استحالة، عدم الإمكان	*istiḥālah, 'adamul imkān*
impossible (adj)	مستحيل، غير ممكن	*mustaḥīl, ghair mumkin*
impossibly (adv)	على نحو مستحيل	*'alā naḥw mustaḥīl*
impostor (imposter)	محتال، خادع	*muḥtāl, khādi'*
imposture (n)	خداع، احتيال	*khidā', iḥtiyāl*
impotence,-ncy (n)	عنة، عجز جنسى	*'unnah, 'ajz jinsī*
impotent (adj)	عنين، عقيم	*'innīn, 'aqīm*
impound (v)	زرب، جمع	*zaraba, jama'a*

impoverish (v)	أفقر، أجدب	*afqara, ajdaba*
impoverishment (n)	إفقار، سلب الخصب	*ifqār, salbul khiṣb*
impracticability (n)	غير عملية	*ghairu 'amaliyyah*
impracticable (adj)	غير عملي، متعذر التنفيذ	*ghair 'amalī, muta'adhdhirut tanfīdh*
impractical (adj)	غير عملي	*ghair 'amalī*
impracticality (n)	غير عملية	*ghair 'amaliyyah*
imprecation (n)	لعنة، شتم	*la'nah, shatm*
imprecise (adj)	مبهم، غامض	*mubham, ghāmiḍ*
imprecisely (adv)	على نحو غامض	*'alā naḥwin ghāmiḍ*
imprecision (n)	غموض، إبهام	*ghumūḍ, ibhām*
impregnable (adj)	حصين، منيع	*ḥaṣīn, manī'*
impregnate (v)	أخصب، أشبع	*akhṣaba, ashba'a*
impresario (n)	مدير الفرقة	*mudīrul firqah*
impress (v)	أثر، طبع	*aththara, ṭaba'a*
impression (n)	انطباع، تاثير، ختم	*inṭibā', ta'thīr, khatm*
impressionable (adj)	سريع التأثر	*sarī'ut ta'aththur*
impressionism (n)	انطباعية	*inṭibā'iyyah*
impressionist (n)	انطباعي	*inṭibā'ī*
impressionistic (adj)	انطباعي	*inṭibā'ī*
impressive (adj)	مؤثر، مثير	*mu'aththir, muthīr*
impressively (adv)	بطريق مؤثر	*bi ṭarīq mu'aththir*
imprint (v)	ختم، بصم	*khatama, baṣama*
imprint (n)	بصمة، ختم، دمغة	*baṣmah, khatm, damghah*
imprison (v)	سجن، حبس	*sajana, ḥabasa*
imprisonment (n)	سجن، حبس	*sajn, ḥabs*
improbability (n)	استحالة، عدم احتمال	*istiḥalah, 'adamu iḥtimāl*
improbable (adj)	بعيد الاحتمال	*ba'īdul iḥtimāl*
improbably (adv)	بطريق محال	*bi ṭarīq muḥāl*
improper (adj)	غير ملائم، بذيء	*ghair mulā'im, badhī'*

improperly (adv)	بطريق غير ملائم	*bi ṭarīq ghair mulā'im*
impropriety (n)	عدم احتشام، عدم ملاءمة	*'adamu iḥtishām, 'adamu mulā'amah*
improve (v)	أفاد، حسن	*afāda, ḥassana*
improvement (n)	تحسين، تحسن	*taḥsīn, taḥassun*
improvidence (n)	تبذير، إسراف	*tabdhīr, isrāf*
improvident (adj)	مسرف، مبذر	*musrif, mubadhdhir*
improvisation (n)	ارتجال	*irtijāl*
improvise (v)	ارتجل	*irtajala*
imprudence (n)	حماقة، عدم تبصر	*ḥamāqah, 'adamu tabaṣṣur*
imprudent (adj)	عديم البصيرة، أحمق	*'adīmul baṣīrah, aḥmaq*
imprudently (adv)	بحماقة، بغير بصيرة	*bi ḥamāqah, bi ghairi baṣīrah*
impudence (n)	وقاحة، صفاقة	*waqāḥah, ṣafāqah*
impudent (adj)	وقح، صفيق	*waqiḥ, ṣafīq*
impudently (adv)	بوقاحة، بسلاطة	*bi waqāḥah, bi salāṭah*
impulse (n)	دفع، دافع، محرك	*daf', dāfi', muḥarrik*
impulsive (adj)	دفعي، دافع	*daf'ī, dāfi'*
impulsiveness (n)	دفع، نزوة	*daf', nazwah*
impunity (n)	حصانة من عقاب	*ḥaṣānah min 'iqāb*
impure (adj)	قذر، دنس، نجس	*qadhir, danis, najis*
impurity (n)	نجس، بذاءة	*najas, badhā'ah*
impute (v)	اتهم، عزا	*ittahama, 'azā*
in (prep)	في، ب	*fī, ba*
in (adj)	داخلي، آتٍ، وافد	*dākhilī, ātin, wāfid*
inability (n)	عدم قدرة، عجز	*'adamu qudrah, 'ajz*
inaccessibility (n)	مناعة	*manā'ah*
inaccessible (adj)	منيع، حريز	*manī', ḥarīz*

inaccuracy (n)	عدم صحة، عدم دقة	*'adamu ṣiḥḥah, 'adamu diqqah*
inaccurate (adj)	غير مضبوط، غير دقيق	*ghair maḍbūṭ, ghair daqīq*
inaccurately (adv)	بطريق غير دقيق	*bi ṭarīq ghair daqīq*
inaction (n)	تبطل، تعطل	*tabaṭṭul, ta'aṭṭul*
inactive (adj)	كسلان، غيرناشط	*kaslān, ghair nāshiṭ*
inactivity (n)	سكون، عدم نشاط	*sukūn, 'adamu nashāṭ*
inadequacy (n)	عدم الوفاء، عدم ملائمة	*'adamul wafā', 'adamu mulā'amah*
inadequate (adj)	غير وافٍ، غير ملائم	*ghair wāfin, ghair mulā'im*
inadequately (adv)	بعدم ملائمة	*bi 'adami mulā'amah*
inadmissible (adj)	غير مقبول	*ghair maqbūl*
inadvertence (n)	إهمال، سهو	*ihmāl, sahw*
inadvertent (adj)	مهمل، غافل	*muhmil, ghāfil*
inadvisable (adj)	غير قابل للتحويل	*ghair qābil lit taḥwīl*
inane (adj)	فارغ، تافه	*fārigh, tāfih*
inanely (adv)	بتفاهة	*bi tafāhah*
inanimate (adj)	جماد، عديم الحياة	*jamād, 'adīmul ḥayāt*
inanity (n)	تفاهة، فراغ	*tafāhah, farāgh*
inapplicable (adj)	غير ملائم، غير قابل للتطبيق	*ghair mulā'im, ghair qābil lit taṭbīq*
inappropriate (adj)	غير ملائم، غير مناسب	*ghair mulā'im, ghair munāsib*
inappropriately (adv)	بعدم ملائمة	*bi 'adami mulā'amah*
inappropriateness (n)	عدم ملاءمة	*'adamu mulā'amah*
inapt (adj)	غير مناسب، غير ملائم	*ghair munāsib, ghair mulā'im*
inaptly (adv)	بعدم ملاءمة	*bi 'adami mulā'amah*

inaptness (n)	عدم ملائمة	*'adamu mulā'amah*
inarticulate (adj)	مجمجم، ممتنع عن التعبير	*mujamjam, mumtani' 'anit ta'bīr*
inarticulately (adv)	بطريق مجمجم	*bi ṭarīq mujamjam*
inasmuch as (conj)	لأن، بسبب	*li anna, bi sababi*
inattention (n)	غفلة، إهمال	*ghaflah, ihmāl*
inattentive (adj)	غافل، غير منتبه	*ghāfil, ghair muntabih*
inattentively (adv)	بدون انتباه، بغفلة	*bidūn intibāh, bi ghaflah*
inaudibility (n)	تعذر السماع	*ta'dhdhurus samā'*
inaudible (adj)	غير مسموع، خافت	*ghair masmū', khāfit*
inaudibly (adv)	بطريق غير مسموع	*bi ṭarīq ghair masmū'*
inaugural (adj)	افتتاحي، احتفالي	*iftitāḥī, iḥtifālī*
inaugurate (v)	دشن، افتتح	*dashshana, iftataḥa*
inauguration (n)	افتتاح، تدشين	*iftitāḥ, tadshīn*
inauspicious (adj)	منحوس، مشؤوم	*manḥūs, mash'ūm*
inauspiciously (adv)	على نحو مشؤوم	*'alā naḥwin mash'ūm*
inauthentic (adj)	غير موثوق به	*ghair mauthūq bih*
inauthenticity (n)	عدم موثوقية	*'adamu mauthūqiyyah*
inboard (adj/adv)	داخلي، في داخل السفينة	*dākhilī, fī dākhilis safīnah*
inborn (adj)	فطري، طبيعي	*fiṭrī, ṭabī'ī*
inbred (adj)	فطري، طبيعي	*fiṭrī, ṭabī'ī*
inbreeding (n)	استيلاد داخلي	*istīlād dākhilī*
incalculable (adj)	لا يعد، لا يحصى	*lā yu'add, lā yuḥṣā*
incalculably (adv)	بطريق لا يعد	*bi ṭarīq lā yu'add*
incandescence (n)	تأجج، اتقاد	*ta'ajjuj, ittiqād*
incandescent (adj)	متوهج، ساطع	*mutawahhij, sāṭi'*
incantation (n)	تعويذ، رقية	*ta'wīdh, ruqyah*
incapable (adj)	غير قادر، غير مؤهل	*ghair qādir, ghair mu'ahhal*
incapacitate (v)	أعجز، أضعف	*a'jaza, aḍ'afa*

incapacity (n)	عجز، عدم قدرة	*'ajz, 'adamu qudrah*
incarcerate (v)	سجن، حصر	*sajana, ḥaṣara*
incarceration (n)	حصر، سجن	*ḥaṣr, sajn*
incarnate (n)	مجسم، مجسد	*mujassam, mujassad*
incarnate (v)	جسد، جسم	*jassada, jassama*
incarnation (n)	تجسيد، تجسد	*tajsīd, tajassud*
incautious (adj)	غافل، عديم الحذر	*ghāfil, 'adīmul ḥidhr*
incautiously (adv)	بغفلة، بإهمال	*bi ghaflah, bi ihmāl*
incendiary (adj)	محرق، متسم بالإحراق	*muḥarriq, muttasim bil iḥrāq*
incense (v)	أثار السخط	*athāras sukhṭ*
incense (n)	عبق البخور، رائحة زكية	*'abaqul bakhūr, rā'iḥah zakiyyah*
incentive (adj)	مثير، محرض	*muthīr, muḥarriḍ*
inception (n)	بدء، ابتداء	*bad', ibtidā'*
incessant (adj)	متواصل، مستمر	*mutawāṣil, mustamirr*
incessantly (adv)	باستمرار، على الدوام	*bistimrār, 'alad dawām*
incest (n)	اتصال جنسي بين المحارم	*ittiṣāl jinsī bainal maḥārim*
incestuous (adj)	خاص بسفاح القربى	*khāṣṣ bi sifāḥil qurbā*
inch (n)	إنش، بوصة	*insh, būṣah*
inch (v)	سار ببطء	*sāra bi baṭ'*
inchoate (adj)	بدائي، خام	*bidā'ī, khām*
incidence (n)	حدوث، وقوع	*ḥudūth, wuqū'*
incident (n)	حادث، حدث	*ḥādith, ḥadath*
incidental (adj)	اتفاقي،عرضي،طارئ	*ittifāqī, 'araḍī, ṭāri'*
incinerate (v)	رمد	*rammada*
incineration (n)	ترميد	*tarmīd*
incinerator (n)	مرمد، محرق	*murammid, muḥarriq*

incipient (adj)	ابتدائي، أولي	*ibtidā'ī, awwalī*
incise (v)	نحت، حز	*naḥata, ḥazza*
incision (n)	حز، نقش	*ḥazz, naqsh*
incisive (adj)	قاطع، واضح	*qāṭi', waḍiḥ*
incisively (adv)	على نحو قاطع	*'alā naḥwin qāṭi'*
incisiveness (n)	وضوح، قاطعية	*wuḍūḥ, qāṭi'iyyah*
incisor (n)	القاطعة	*al qāṭi'ah*
incite (v)	حرض، حث	*ḥarraḍa, ḥaththa*
incitement (n)	تحريض، دافع	*taḥrīḍ, dāfi'*
incivility (n)	سماجة، فظاظة	*samājah, faẓāẓah*
inclement (adj)	صارم، عنيف	*ṣārim, 'anīf*
inclination (n)	رغبة، ميل، انحناء	*raghbah, mail, inḥinā'*
incline (v)	مال، انحنى، نزع	*māla, inḥanā, naza'a*
incline (n)	منحدر، حدور	*munḥadar, ḥudūr*
inclined (adj)	مائل، منحدر	*mā'il, munḥadir*
inclose = enclose		
inclosure = enclosure		
include (v)	شمل، تضمن	*shamila, taḍammana*
including (prep)	ضمن، شاملًا	*dimna, shāmilan*
inclusion (n)	تضمين، تضمن	*taḍmīn, taḍammun*
inclusive (adj)	شامل، متضمن	*shāmil, mutaḍammin*
inclusively (adv)	ضمناً، باشتمال	*ḍimnan, bishtimāl*
incognito (adj)	متخفٍّ، متستر	*mutakhaffin, mutasattir*
incoherence (n)	عدم تناسق، تفكك	*'adamu tanāsuq, tafakkuk*
incoherent (adj)	متنافر، منقطع	*mutanāfir, munqaṭi'*
incoherently (adv)	بتنافر، بعدم تناسق	*bi tanāfur, bi 'adami tanāsuq*
income (n)	دخل، إيراد	*dakhl, īrād*
incoming (adj)	وارد، مستهل	*wārid, mustahill*
incommensurability	عدم قياسية	*'adamu qiyāsiyyah*

incommensurable	لا يقاس	*lā yuqās*
incommensurate (adj)	غير ملائم، غير متكافئ	*ghair mulā'im, ghair mutakāfi'*
incomodate (v)	أزعج، ضايق	*az'aja, ḍāyaqa*
incomparable (adj)	لا يوازن	*lā yuwāzan*
incomparably (adv)	بطريق لا يوازن	*bi ṭarīq lā yuwāzan*
incompatibility (n)	تنافر، تضارب	*tanāfur, taḍārub*
incompatible (adj)	متنافر، متغاير	*mutanāfir, mutaghāyir*
incompetence (n)	عدم أهلية، عدم صلاحية	*'adamu ahliyyah, 'adamu ṣalāḥiyyah*
incompetent (adj)	غير مؤهل، عاجز	*ghair mu'ahhal, 'ājiz*
incompetently (adv)	على نحو عاجز	*'alā naḥwin 'ājiz*
incomplete (adj)	ناقص، غير تام	*nāqiṣ, ghair tāmm*
incompletely (adv)	بنقص	*bi naqṣ*
incompleteness (n)	نقص، عدم الكمال	*naqṣ, 'adamul kamāl*
incomprehensibility (n)	كون الشيء غير مفهوم	*kaunush shay' ghair mafhūm*
incomprehensible (adj)	غير مفهوم، مبهم	*ghair mafhūm, mubham*
incomprehensibly	على طريق مبهم	*'alā ṭarīq mubham*
incomprehension (n)	عجز عن الفهم	*'ajz 'anil fahm*
inconceivable (adj)	لا يتصور	*lā yutaṣawwar*
inconceivably (adv)	بطريق لا يتصور	*bi ṭarīq lā yutaṣawwar*
inconclusive (adj)	غير مقنع، غير قاطع	*ghair muqni', ghair qāṭi'*
inconclusively (adv)	على نحو غير مقنع	*'alā naḥw ghair muqni'*
incongruity (n)	عدم ملاءمة، تنافر	*'adamu mulā'amah, tanāfur*
incongruous (adj)	غير ملائم، متنافر	*ghair mulā'im, mutanāfir*
incongruously (adv)	بتنافر، بتضارب	*bi tanāfur, bi taḍārub*
inconsequential (adj)	غير هام	*ghair hāmm*

inconsequentially (adv)	بطريق غير هام	*bi ṭarīq ghair hāmm*
inconsiderable (adj)	تافه، طفيف	*tāfih, ṭafīf*
inconsiderate (adj)	قليل التبصر، طائش	*qalīlut tabaṣṣur, ṭā'ish*
inconsiderately (adv)	بعدم بصيرة، بتهور	*bi 'adami baṣīrah, bi tahawwur*
inconsistency (n)	عدم ترابط، تنافر	*'adamu tarābuṭ, tanāfur*
inconsistent (adj)	غير مترابط، متناقض	*ghair mutarābiṭ, mutanāqiḍ*
inconsistently (adv)	بعدم ترابط	*bi 'adami tarābuṭ*
inconsolable (adj)	غير متعزى	*ghair muta'azzā*
inconsolably (adv)	بطريق غير متعزى	*bi ṭarīq ghair muta'azzā*
inconspicuous (adj)	غير واضع	*ghair wāḍiḥ*
inconspicuously (adv)	على طريق غير واضح	*'alā ṭarīq ghair wāḍiḥ*
inconstancy (n)	تحول، تقلب	*taḥawwul, taqallub*
inconstant (adj)	عديم الثبات، متقلب	*'adīmuth thabāt, mutaqallib*
incontestable (adj)	لا يمكن نضاله	*lā yumkin niḍāluh*
incontinence (n)	عجز عن ضبط البول	*'ajz 'an ḍabṭil baul*
incontinent (adj)	عاجز عن ضبط البول	*'ājiz 'an ḍabṭil baul*
incontrovertible (adj)	بات، لا جدل فيه	*bātt, lā jadala fīh*
incontrovertibly (adv)	بغير جدل	*bi ghairi jadal*
inconvenience (n)	إزعاج، ضيق	*iz'āj, ḍīq*
inconvenience (v)	أزعج، ضايق	*az'aja, ḍāyaqa*
inconvenient (adj)	مزعج، غير ملائم	*muz'ij, ghair mulā'im*
inconveniently (adv)	بعدم راحة	*bi 'adami rāḥah*
incorporate (v)	دمج، أدخل	*damaja, adkhala*
incorporated (adj)	مندمج، محدودة	*mundamij, maḥdūdah*
incorporation (n)	دمج، اندماج	*damj, indimāj*

incorporeal (adj)	غير مادي، معنوي	*ghair māddī, ma'nawī*
incorrect (adj)	غير صحيح، غير دقيق	*ghair ṣaḥīḥ, ghair daqīq*
incorrectly (adv)	بعدم صحة، بخطأ	*bi'adami ṣiḥḥah, bi khaṭa'*
incorrectness (n)	عدم صحة، عدم دقة	*'adamu ṣiḥḥah, 'adamu diqqah*
incorrigible (adj)	لا يمكن إصلاحه	*lā yumkin iṣlāḥuh*
incorrigibly (adv)	بطريق لا يقوم	*bi ṭarīq lā yuqawwam*
incorruptible (adj)	غير قابل للفساد	*ghair qābil lil fasād*
increase (v)	زاد، ازداد	*zāda, izdāda*
increase (n)	زيادة، نمو، ازدياد	*ziyādah, numuww, izdiyād*
increasingly (adv)	أكثر فأكثر	*akthar fa akthar*
incredible (adj)	لا يمكن تصديقه	*lā yumkin taṣdīquh*
incredibly (adv)	بطريق غير مصدق	*bi ṭarīq ghair muṣaddaq*
incredulity (n)	شكوكية	*shukūkiyyah*
incredulous (adj)	شكوكي	*shukūkī*
incredulously (adv)	بريبة، بشك	*bi raibah, bi shakk*
increment (n)	إضافة، زيادة	*iḍāfah, ziyādah*
incremental (adj)	إضافي، متزائد	*iḍāfī, mutazā'id*
incrementally (adv)	إضافيًا	*iḍāfiyyan*
incriminate (v)	استذنب، جرم	*istadhnaba, jarrama*
incrimination (n)	تجريم، اتهام	*tajrīm, ittihām*
incubate (v)	حضنت البيض	*ḥaḍanatil baiḍ*
incubation (n)	حضانة، رخم	*ḥaḍānah, rakhm*
incubator (n)	حاضن، محضن	*ḥāḍin, miḥḍan*
inculcate (v)	طبع في الذهن	*ṭaba'a fidh dhihn*
incumbency (n)	واجب، مسؤولية	*wājib, mas'ūliyyah*
incumbent (adj)	ضروري، إجباري	*ḍarūrī, ijbārī*
incurable (n/adj)	معضول، عضال	*ma'ḍūl, 'uḍāl*
incurious (adj)	غافل، غير مبالٍ	*ghāfil, ghairu mubālin*

incursion (n)	غزوة، غارة	*ghazwah, ghārah*
indebted (adj)	مدين	*madīn*
indebtedness (n)	دين، مدينية	*dain, madīniyyah*
indecency (n)	عدم احتشام، فضاحة	*'adamu iḥtishām, faḍāḥah*
indecent (adj)	فاضح، شائن	*fāḍiḥ, shā'in*
indecently (adv)	بفضاحة، ببذاءة	*bi faḍāḥah, bi badhā'ah*
indecipherable (adj)	مطلسم	*muṭalsam*
indecision (n)	تردد، توقف	*taraddud, tawaqquf*
indecisive (adj)	غير حاسم، متردد	*ghair ḥāsim, mutaraddid*
indecisively (adj)	بتردد، بعدم حزم	*bi taraddud, bi 'adami ḥazm*
indecorous (adj)	غير محتشم	*ghair muḥtashim*
indeed (adv)	في الحقيقة، في الواقع	*fil ḥaqīqah, fil wāqi'*
indefatigable (adj)	لا يمل، لا يكل	*lā yamill, lā yakill*
indefensible (adj)	لا يمكن الدفاع عنه	*lā yumkinud difā' 'anh*
indefinable (adj)	لا يمكن تعريفه	*lā yumkin ta'rīfuh*
indefinably (adv)	على نحو لا يمكن تعريفه	*'alā nahw lā yumkin ta'rīfuh*
indefinite (adj)	غير محدد، مبهم	*ghair muḥaddad, mubham*
indefinitely (adv)	بدون تعيين	*bidūn ta'yīn*
indelible (adj)	متعذر محوه	*muta'adhdhir maḥwuh*
indelibly (adv)	بطريق لا يمكن محوه	*bi ṭarīq lā yumkin maḥwuh*
indelicacy (n)	عدم احتشام، سماجة	*'adamu iḥtishām, samājah*
indelicate (adj)	غير محتشم، سمج	*ghair muḥtashim, samij*
indent (v)	حز، سنن	*ḥazza, sannana*
indent (n)	وثيقة رسمية، طلب رسمي	*wathīqah rasmiyyah, ṭalab rasmī*
indentation (n)	ثلمة، بعجة	*thulmah, ba'jah*

independence (n)	استقلال، حرية	*istiqlāl, ḥurriyyah*
independency (n)	استقلال، دولة مستقلة	*istiqlāl, daulah mustaqillah*
independent (adj)	مستقل، استقلالي	*mustaqill, istiqlālī*
independently (adv)	باستقلال، بحرية	*bistiqlāl, bi ḥurriyyah*
indescribable (adj)	لا يمكن وصفه	*lā yumkin waṣfuh*
indescribably (adv)	بطريق لا يمكن وصفه	*bi ṭarīq lā yumkin waṣfuh*
indestructible (adj)	غير قابل للتخريب	*ghair qābil lit takhrīb*
indeterminable (adj)	لا يمكن تحديده	*lā yumkin taḥdīduh*
indeterminacy (n)	كون الشيء غير محدد	*kaunush shay' ghair muḥaddad*
indeterminate (adj)	غير محدد، عرجوني	*ghair muḥaddad, 'urjūnī*
index (n)	فهرس، أس، سبابة	*fihris, 'uss, sabbābah*
index (v)	فهرس	*fahrasa*
index finger (n)	السبابة	*as sabbābah*
Indian (n/adj)	هندي	*hindī*
Indian Summer (n)	صيف هندي	*ṣaif hindī*
indicate (v)	أشار، دل على	*ashāra, dalla 'alā*
indication (n)	إشارة، دلالة	*ishārah, dalālah*
indicative (adj)	دال على، مشير	*dāll 'alā, mushīr*
indicator (n)	دليل، مؤشر	*dalīl, mu'ashshir*
indices (pl of index)		
indict (v)	اتهم، ادعى على	*ittahama, idda'ā 'alā*
indictable (adj)	قابل للطعن، عرضة للاتهام	*qābil liṭ ṭa'n, 'urḍah lil ittihām*
indictment (n)	اتهام، شكوى	*ittihām, shakwā*
indifference (n)	عدم مبالاة، عدم تحيز	*'adamu mubālāt, 'adamu taḥayyuz*
indifferent (adj)	غير مبال، غير متحيز	*ghair mubālin, ghair mutaḥayyiz*
indifferently (adv)	بعدم مبالاة	*bi 'adami mubālāt*

indigenous (adj)	بلدي، وطني	*baladī, waṭanī*
indigent (adj)	معدم، فقير	*mu'dim, faqīr*
indigestible (adj)	عسر الهضم	*'asirul haḍm*
indigestion (n)	سوء الهضم	*sū'ul haḍm*
indignant (adj)	ساخط، ناقم	*sākhiṭ, nāqim*
indignantly (adv)	بسخط، بحنق	*bi sukhṭ, bi ḥanaq*
indignation (n)	سخط، نقمة	*sukhṭ, niqmah*
indignity (n)	تحقير، إهانة	*taḥqīr, ihānah*
indigo (n)	صبغ أزرق	*ṣibgh azraq*
indirect (adj)	غير مباشر، احتيالي	*ghair mubāshir, iḥtiyālī*
indirectly (adv)	بواسطة، مداورةً	*bi wāsiṭah, mudāwaratan*
indirect object	مفعول غير مباشر	*maf'ūl ghair mubāshir*
indirect tax	ضريبة غير مباشرة	*ḍarībah ghair mubāshirah*
indiscernible (adj)	لا يمكن إدراكه	*lā yumkin idrākuh*
indiscipline (n)	عدم انضباط	*'adamu inḍibāt*
indiscreet (adj)	طائش، مفشي	*ṭā'ish, mufshī*
indiscreetly (adv)	على نحو طائش	*'alā naḥw ṭā'ish*
indiscretion (n)	عدم تبصر، حماقة	*'adamu tabaṣṣur, ḥamāqah*
indiscriminate (adj)	غير مميز	*ghair mumayyiz*
indiscriminately (adv)	بدون تمييز	*bidūn tamyīz*
indispensible (adj)	لازم، ضروري	*lāzim, ḍarūrī*
indisposed (adj)	متوعك المزاج	*mutawa''ikul mizāj*
indisposition (n)	توعك، نفور	*tawa''uk, nufūr*
indisputable (adj)	لا نزاع فيه	*lā nizā' fīh*
indisputably (adv)	بدون نزاع	*bidūn nizā'*
indissoluble (adj)	غير قابل للانحلال	*ghair qābil lil inḥilāl*
indissolubly (adv)	بطريق لا ينحل	*bi ṭarīq lā yanḥall*
indistinct (adj)	غير واضح، غامض	*ghair wāḍiḥ, ghāmiḍ*

indistinctly (adv)	بغموض	*bi ghumūḍ*
indistinguishable (adj)	لا يمكن تمييزه، غامض	*lā yumkin tamyīzuh, ghāmiḍ*
individual (adj)	شخصي، فردي	*shakhṣī, fardī*
individual (n)	شخص، فرد	*shakhṣ, fard*
individualism (n)	فردانية، فردية	*fardāniyyah, fardiyyah*
individuality (n)	شخصية، فردية	*shakhṣiyyah, fardiyyah*
individualized (adj)	مميز، مخصص	*mumayyaz, mukhaṣṣaṣ*
individually (adv)	على الانفراد	*'alal infirād*
indivisible (adj)	غير قابل للانقسام	*ghair qābil lil inqisām*
indoctrinate (v)	لقن، علم	*laqqana, 'allama*
Indo-European (adj)	هندي أوروبي	*hindī ūrūbī*
indolence (n)	كسل، تراخٍ	*kasal, tarākhin*
indolent (adj)	كسول، متراخٍ	*kasūl, mutarākhin*
indomitable (adj)	لا يغلب، غير مغلوب	*lā yughlab, ghair maghlūb*
indomitably (adv)	على نحو لا يغلب	*'alā naḥw lā yughlab*
indoor (adj)	داخلي	*dākhilī*
indoors (adv)	نحو البيت	*naḥwal bait*
indrawn (adj)	مجذوب نحو الداخل	*majdhūb naḥwad dākhil*
indubitable (adj)	ثابت، محقق	*thābit, muḥaqqaq*
indubitably (adv)	بغير شك	*bighairi shakk*
induce (v)	أغرى، استحث	*aghrā, istaḥaththa*
inducement (n)	إغراء، حث	*ighrā', hathth*
induct (v)	جند، نصب	*jannada, naṣṣaba*
induction (n)	تجنيد، تنصيب	*tajnīd, tanṣīb*
inductive (adj)	حثي، تخليقي	*ḥaththī, takhlīqī*
indulge (v)	انغمس، أشبع	*inghamasa, ashba'a*
indulgence (n)	تسامح، إطلاق، انغماس	*tasāmuḥ, iṭlāq, inghimās*
indulgent (adj)	متسامح، متساهل	*mutasāmiḥ, mutasāhil*

indulgently (adv)	متساهلاً، بتسامح	*mutasāhilan, bi tasāmuḥ*
industrial (adj)	صناعي	*ṣinā'ī*
industrial arts (n)	فنون صناعية	*funūn ṣinā'iyyah*
industrialism (n)	صناعية	*ṣinā'iyyah*
industrialist (n)	صناعي	*ṣinā'ī*
industrialization(n)	تصنيع، تصنع	*taṣnī', taṣannu'*
industrialize,-ise (v)	صنع، تصنع	*ṣanna'a, taṣanna'a*
industrious (adj)	كاد، كادح	*kādd, kādiḥ*
industriously (adv)	بكد، باجتهاد	*bi kadd, bijtihād*
industry (n)	صناعة، حرفة	*ṣinā'ah, ḥirfah*
inebriated (adj)	سكران، ثمل	*sakrān, thamil*
inedible (adj)	غير صالح للأكل	*ghair ṣāliḥ lil akl*
ineffable (adj)	لا يمكن وصفه	*lā yumkin waṣfuh*
ineffably (adv)	بطريق لا يوصف	*bi ṭarīq lā yūṣaf*
ineffective (adj)	عديم التأثير، عاجز	*'adīmut ta'thīr, 'ājiz*
ineffectively (adv)	بلا تأثير	*bilā ta'thīr*
ineffectiveness (n)	عدم تأثير	*'adamu ta'thīr*
ineffectual (adj)	غير مجدٍ، غير مؤثر	*ghair mujdin, ghair mu'aththir*
ineffectually (adv)	بطريق غير فعال	*bi ṭarīq ghair fa''āl*
inefficiency (n)	عدم كفاءة، عدم أهلية	*'adamu kafā'ah, 'adamu ahliyyah*
inefficient (adj)	غير فعال، عاجز	*ghair fa''āl, 'ājiz*
inefficiently (adv)	على نحو غير كفء	*'alā naḥw ghair kuf'*
inelegant (adj)	سمج، غير أنيق	*samij, ghair anīq*
inelegantly (adv)	على نحو سمج	*'alā naḥwin samij*
ineligible (adj)	غير مؤهل للانتخاب	*ghair mu'ahhal lil intikhāb*
ineluctable (adj)	لا يمكن اجتنابه	*lā yumkin ijtinābuh*
inept (adj)	غير بارع، غير كفء	*ghair bāri', ghair kuf'*

ineptitude (n)	عدم ملاءمة، عدم براعة	*'adamu mulā'amah, 'adamu barā'ah*
ineptly (adj)	بدون براعة، بسخافة	*bidūn barā'ah, bi sakhāfah*
inequality (n)	تباين، عدم تساوٍ	*tabāyun, 'adamu tasāwin*
inequitable (adj)	جائر، غير منصف	*jā'ir, ghair munṣif*
inequity (n)	جور، حيف	*jaur, ḥaif*
ineradicable (adj)	لا يمكن استئصاله	*lā yumkin isti'ṣāluh*
inert (adj)	جامد، ساكن، عديم الحركة	*jāmid, sākin, 'adīmul ḥarakah*
inertia (n)	قصور ذاتي، جمود	*quṣūr dhātī, jumūd*
inertial (adj)	جامد، معطل	*jāmid, mu'aṭṭal*
inescapable (adj)	لا مفر منه	*lā mafarr minh*
inessential (adj)	غير جوهري، غير ضروري	*ghair jauhari, ghair ḍarūrī*
inestimable (adj)	لا يمكن إحصاؤه	*lā yumkin iḥṣā'uh*
inevitable (adj)	محتوم، متعذر اجتنابه	*maḥtūm, muta'adhdhir ijtinābuh*
inevitably (adv)	على نحو محتوم	*'alā naḥwin maḥtūm*
inexact (adj)	غير مضبوط، غير دقيق	*ghair maḍbūṭ, ghair daqīq*
inexcusable (adj)	متعذر إعذاره	*mata'adhdhir i'dhāruh*
inexcusably (adv)	بطريق لا يعذر	*bi ṭarīq lā yu'dhar*
inexhaustable (adj)	لا ينفد، لا يتعب	*lā yanfad, lā yat'ab*
inexhaustably (adv)	بطريق لا ينفد	*bi ṭarīq lā yanfad*
inexorable (adj)	لا يمكن استعطافه	*lā yumkin isti'ṭāfuh*
inexorably (adv)	بطريق متصلب	*bi ṭarīq mutaṣallib*
inexpensive (adj)	رخيص،معقول الثمن	*rakhīṣ, ma'qūluth thaman*
inexpensively (adv)	بثمن رخيص	*bi thaman rakhīṣ*

inexperience (n)	عدم خبرة	*'adamu khibrah*
inexperienced (adj)	عديم الخبرة، قليل التجربة	*'adīmul khibrah, qalīlut tajribah*
inexpert (adj)	غير حاذق، غير خبير	*ghair ḥādhiq, ghair khabīr*
inexpertly (adv)	بطريق غير حاذق	*bi ṭarīq ghair ḥādhiq*
inexplicable (adj)	غامض، لا يمكن توضيحه	*ghāmiḍ, lā yumkin tauḍīḥuh*
inexplicably (adv)	بطريق غامض	*bi ṭarīq ghāmiḍ*
inexpressible (adj)	لا يمكن تعبيره	*lā yumkin ta'bīruh*
inexpressibly (adv)	بطريق لا يعبر عنه	*bi ṭarīq lā yu'abbar 'anh*
inexpressive (adj)	خلو من المعنى	*khilw minal ma'nā*
inextinguishable (adj)	لا يمكن إطفاؤه	*lā yumkin iṭfā'uh*
inextremis (adj)	على عتبة الموت	*'alā 'atabatil maut*
inextricable (adj)	معقد، لا يمكن انفكاكه	*mu'aqqad, lā yumkin infikākuh*
inextricably (adv)	بطريق معقد	*bi ṭarīq mu'aqqad*
infallibility (n)	عصمة، تنزه عن الخطاء	*'iṣmah, tanazzuh 'anil khaṭa'*
infallible (adj)	متنزه عن الخطأ	*mutanazzih 'anil khaṭa'*
infallibly (adv)	بطريق معصوم	*bi ṭarīq ma'ṣūm*
infamous (adj)	سيئ السمعة	*sayyi'us sum'ah*
infamy (n)	سوء السمعة، خزي	*sū'us sum'ah, khizy*
infancy (n)	طفولة، بداءة	*ṭufūlah, badā'ah*
infant (n)	طفل، مبتدئ	*ṭifl, mubtadi'*
infanticide (n)	قتل الأطفال	*qatlul aṭfāl*
infantile (adj)	طفلي، طفولي	*ṭiflī, ṭufūlī*
infantilism (n)	قصاعة، طفالة	*qaṣā'ah, ṭafālah*
infantry (n)	كتيبة مشاة	*katībatu mushāt*

infantryman (n)	جندي من المشاة	*jundī minal mushāt*
infatuated (adj)	مفتون، متيم	*maftūn, mutayyam*
infatuation (n)	فتنة، تيم	*fitnah, taim*
infect (v)	أعدى، لوث بالجراثيم	*a'dā, lawwatha bil jarāthīm*
infection (n)	عدوى، إعداء، مرض معد	*'adwā, i'dā', maraḍ mu'din*
infectious (adj)	معدٍ، ملوث	*mu'din, mulawwith*
infectiously (adv)	بطريق معدٍ	*bi ṭarīq mu'din*
infer (v)	استنتج، استدل	*istantaja, istadalla*
inference (n)	استدلال، استنتاج	*istidlāl, istintāj*
inferior (adj/n)	أدنى، أسفل، سفلي	*adnā, asfal, suflī*
inferiority (n)	دناية، سفالة	*danāyah, safālah*
inferiority complex	مركب الدونية	*murakkabud dūniyyah*
inferno (n)	جحيم، جهنم	*jaḥīm, jahannam*
infertile (adj)	مجدب، غير مخصب	*mujdib, ghair mukhṣib*
infertility (n)	جدب، عدم خصب	*jadb, 'adamu khiṣb*
infest (v)	ضايق، أزعج	*ḍāyaqa, az'aja*
infestation (n)	انعجاج	*in'ijāj*
infidel (n)	كافر، ملحد	*kāfir, mulḥid*
infidelity (n)	خيانة زوجية	*khiyānah zaujiyyah*
infighting (n)	شجار تلاحمي	*shijār talāḥumī*
infiltrate (v)	تسلل، تسرب	*tasallala, tasarraba*
infiltration (n)	تسلل، ارتشاح	*tasallul, irtishāḥ*
infiltrator (n)	متسلل، مرتشح	*mutasallil, murtashiḥ*
infinite (adj)	غير متناهٍ، غير محدود	*ghair mutanāhin, ghair maḥdūd*
infinitive (n)	صيغة المصدر	*ṣighatul maṣdar*
infinity (n)	عدم تناهي	*'adamu tanāhī*
infirm (adj)	غير حازم، واهن	*ghair ḥāzim, wāhin*

infirmity (n)	عجز، عدم استقرار	*'ajz, 'adamu istiqrār*
inflamable (adj)	سريع الالتهاب، سريع الاهتياج	*sarī'ul iltihāb, sarī'ul ihtiyāj*
inflamation (n)	اشتعال، التهاب	*ishti'āl, iltihāb*
inflamatory (adj)	ملهب، مثير	*mulhib, muthīr*
inflame (v)	اشتعل، اهتاج	*ishta'ala, ihtāja*
inflatable (adj)	قابل للانتفاخ	*qābil lil intifākh*
inflate (v)	انتفخ، ازدهى	*intafakha, izdahā*
inflated (adj)	منتفخ، منفوخ	*muntafikh, manfūkh*
inflation (n)	نفخ، انتفاخ	*nafkh, intifākh*
inflationary (adj)	انتفاخي	*intifākhī*
inflect (v)	غير درجة الصوت	*ghayyara darajataṣ ṣaut*
inflection (n)	تغير في ارتفاع الصوت	*taghayyur fī irtifā'iṣ ṣaut*
inflexibility (n)	عدم التواء، صلابة	*'adamu iltiwā', ṣalābah*
inflexible (adj)	عنيد، لا يمكن تغييره	*'anīd, lā yumkin taghyīruh*
inflexibly (adv)	بطريق عنيد	*bi ṭarīq 'anīd*
inflict (v)	ابتلى، أصاب	*ibtalā, aṣāba*
infliction (n)	بلاء، عقوبة	*balā', 'uqūbah*
inflow (n)	مصب النهر، تدفق	*maṣabbun nahr, tadaffuq*
influence (n)	تأثير، نفوذ، سطوة	*ta'thīr, nufūdh, saṭwah*
influence (v)	أثر، استمال	*aththara, istamāla*
influential (adj)	مؤثر، ذو سطوة	*mu'ththir, dhū saṭwah*
influenza (n)	انفلونزا	*influwanzā*
influx = inflow		
inform (v)	أعلم، أخبر	*a'lama, akhbara*
informal (adj)	غير رسمي، عامي	*ghair rasmī, 'āmī*
informant (adj)	مخبر، مبلغ	*mukhbir, muballigh*
information (n)	إخبار، إعلام، اطلاع	*ikhbār, i'lām, iṭṭilā'*
informative (adj)	إعلامي، مثقف	*i'lāmī, muthaqqif*

informer (n)	معلم، مخبر	*mu'lim, mukhbir*
infraction (n)	خرق معاهدة	*kharqu mu'āhadah*
infra dig (adj)	حاط من قدر المرء	*ḥātt min qadril mar'*
infra-red (adj)	تحت الأحمر	*taḥtal aḥmar*
infrastructure (n)	بنية خفيضة	*binyah khafīḍah*
infrequency (n)	ندرة، قلة حدوث	*nadrah, qillatu ḥudūth*
infrequent (adj)	غير مواظب، قليل الحدوث	*ghair muwāẓib, qalīlul ḥudūth*
infrequently (adv)	نادراً، في الندرة	*nādiran, fin nadrah*
infringe (v)	نقض، خرق معاهدةً	*naqaḍa, kharaqa mu'āhadah*
infringement (n)	نقض، خرق	*naqḍ, kharq*
infuriate (v)	غاظ، أغضب	*ghāẓa, aghḍaba*
infuriating (adj)	مغضب، مهيج	*mughḍib, muhayyij*
infuriatingly (adv)	بأسلوب مهيج	*bi uslūb muhayyij*
infuse (v)	نقع، أشرب، نفخ	*naqa'a, ashraba, nafakha*
infusion (n)	نفخ، صب	*nafkh, ṣabb*
ingenious (adj)	مبدع، بارع	*mubdi', bāri'*
ingenuity (n)	إبداع، ذكاء	*ibdā', dhakā'*
ingenuous (adj)	ساذج، صريح	*sādhij, ṣarīḥ*
ingenuously (adv)	بأسلوب صريح	*bi uslūb ṣarīḥ*
inglorious (adj)	مخزٍ، شائن	*mukhzin, shā'in*
ingloriously (adv)	بطريق مخزٍ	*bi ṭarīq mukhzin*
ingot (n)	صبة	*ṣubbah*
ingrained (adj)	راسخ، متأصل	*rāsikh, muta'ṣṣil*
ingratiate (v)	استعطف، فاز بالحظوة	*ista'ṭafa, fāza bil ḥaẓwah*
ingratiating (adj)	مرضٍ، مداهن	*murḍin, mudāhin*
ingratitude (n)	جحود الفضل	*juḥūdul faḍl*
ingredient (n)	مقوم، عنصر	*muqawwim, 'unṣur*
ingress (n)	دخول، حق الدخول	*dukhūl, ḥaqqud dukhūl*

in-group (n)	جماعة تفضيلية	*jamā'ah tafḍīliyyah*
ingrowing (adj)	نامٍ في اللحم	*nāmin fil laḥm*
inhabit (v)	سكن، أقام	*sakana, aqāma*
inhabitant (adj)	مقيم، قاطن	*muqīm, qāṭin*
inhalation (n)	استنشاق	*istinshāq*
inhale (v)	استنشق الهواء	*istanshaqal hawā'*
inhaler (n)	منشاق	*minshāq*
inharmonious (adj)	متنافر، غير متناغم	*mutanāfir, ghair mutanāghim*
inherent (adj)	صلبي، فطري	*ṣulbī, fiṭrī*
inherit (v)	ورث	*waratha*
inheritance (n)	وراثة، ميراث	*wirāthah, mīrāth*
inheritor (n)	وارث	*wārith*
inhibit (v)	كبح، ثبط	*kabaḥa, thabbaṭa*
inhibition (n)	كبح، مانع	*kabḥ, māni'*
inhospitable (adj)	غير مضياف، غير كريم	*ghair miḍyāf, ghair karīm*
inhuman (adj)	غير انساني، قاسٍ	*ghair insānī, qāsin*
inhumane (adj)	قاسٍ، وحشي	*qāsin, waḥshī*
inhumanely (adv)	بطريق قاسٍ	*bi ṭarīq qāsin*
inimical (adj)	مؤذٍ، معادٍ	*mu'dhin, mu'ādin*
inimitable (adj)	لا نظير لـــه، فريد	*lā naẓīra lahu, farīd*
iniquitous (adj)	ظالم، جائر	*ẓālim, jā'ir*
iniquity (n)	جور، ظلم	*jaur, ẓulm*
initial (n/adj)	أول، ابتدائي	*awwal, ibtidā'ī*
initially (adv)	في البداية	*fil bidāyah*
initiate (v)	بدأ، استهل	*bada'a, istahalla*
initiation (n)	استهلال، بدء	*istihlāl, bad'*
initiative (adj)	ابتدائي، تمهيدي	*ibtidā'ī, tamhīdī*
inject (v)	حقن، أدخل	*ḥaqana, adkhala*

injection (n)	حقن، زرق، حقنة	*ḥaqn, zarq, ḥuqnah*
injudicious (adj)	غير حكيم، طائش	*ghair ḥakīm, ṭā'ish*
injure (v)	جرح، أضر	*jaraḥa, aḍarra*
injured (adj)	مجروح	*majrūḥ*
injurious (adj)	مؤذٍ، ضار	*mu'dhin, ḍārr*
injury (n)	ضرر، أذىً	*ḍarar, adhan*
injustice (n)	جور، ظلم	*jaur, ẓulm*
ink (n/v)	حبر، حبر	*ḥibr, ḥabbara*
inkling (n)	معرفة طفيفة	*ma'rifah ṭafīfah*
ink-pot=ink-well		
ink-well (n)	محبرة، دواة	*miḥbarah, dawāt*
inky (adj)	ملطخ بالحبر	*mulaṭṭakh bil ḥibr*
inlaid (adj)	مرصع، مطعم	*muraṣṣa', muṭa''am*
inland (adj/adv)	داخلي، في الداخل	*dākhilī, fid dākhil*
inlaws (n)	أقرباء الزوج أو الزوجة	*aqribā'uz zauj awiz zaujah*
inlay (v)	رصع، طعم	*raṣṣ'a, ṭa''ama*
inlay (n)	تطعيم، ترصيع	*taṭ'īm, tarṣi'*
inlet (n)	مدخل	*madkhal*
inmate (n)	ساكن، قاطن	*sākin, qāṭin*
in memorian (adv/prep)	إحياءً لذكرى	*iḥyā'an li dhikrā*
inmost (adj)	أعمق، أقصى	*a'maq, aqṣā*
inn (n)	حانة، فندق	*ḥānah, funduq*
innards (n)	أحشاء	*aḥshā'*
innate (adj)	فطري، جبلي	*fiṭrī, jibillī*
innately (adv)	على الفطرة	*'alal fiṭrah*
inner (adj)	داخلي، باطني	*dākhilī, bāṭinī*
innermost (adj)	أعمق، أوغل	*a'maq, aughal*
inner tube (n)	إطار داخلي	*iṭār dākhilī*

innings (n)	نوبة، دور	*naubah, daur*
innkeeper (n)	صاحب النــزل	*ṣāḥibun nuzul*
innocence (n)	براءة، سذاجة	*barā'ah, sadhājah*
innocent (adj)	بريء، بسيط	*barī', basīṭ*
innocuous (adj)	غير مؤذٍ	*ghair mu'dhin*
innovate (v)	ابتدع، ابتكر	*ibtada'a, ibtakara*
innovation (n)	ابتداع، ابتكار	*ibtidā', ibtikār*
innovative (adj)	مبتدع، مجدد	*mubtadi', mujaddid*
innovator (n)	مبتدع	*mubtadi'*
innuendo (n)	إلماع، تلميح	*ilmā', talmīḥ*
innumerable (adj)	لا يمكن إحصاه	*lā yumkin iḥṣā'uh*
inoculate (v)	أشرب، لقح	*ashraba, laqqaḥa*
inoculation (n)	تلقيح، تطعيم	*talqīḥ, taṭ'īm*
inoffensive (adj)	غير ضار	*ghair ḍārr*
inoperable (adj)	عصي الجراحة	*'aṣiyyul jirāḥah*
inoperative (adj)	غير فعال، عديم التأثير	*ghair fa''āl, 'adīmut ta'thīr*
inopportune (adj)	في غير محله	*fī ghairi maḥallihi*
inordinate (adj)	مغالٍ، مفرط	*mughālin, mufriṭ*
inordinately (adv)	بإفراط، بتطرف	*bi ifrāṭ, bi taṭarruf*
inorganic (adj)	غير عضوي، صنعي	*ghair 'uḍwī, ṣun'ī*
inorganic chemistry	كيمياء غير عضوية	*kīmiyā ghair 'uḍwiyyah*
in-patient (n)	مريض مقيم في مستشفى	*marīḍ muqīm fī mustashfā*
input (n)	الزاد	*az zād*
input (v)	زود	*zawwada*
inquest (n)	استجواب، فحص	*istijwāb, faḥṣ*
inquire (enq-) (v)	استعلم، بحث	*ista'lama, baḥatha*
inquirer (n)	باحث، مستعلم	*bāḥith, musta'lim*
inquiry (n)	استعلام، بحث	*isti'lām, baḥth*

inquisition (n)	تحقيق، محكمة التفتيش	*taḥqīq, maḥkamatut taftīsh*
inquisitive (adj)	محب للبحث، كثير السؤال	*muḥibb lil baḥth, kathīrus su'āl*
inquisitiveness (n)	حب للبحث والتفتيش	*ḥubb lil baḥth wat taftīsh*
inquisitor (n)	مفتش، باحث	*mufattisḥ, bāḥith*
inquisitorial (adj)	تفتيشي	*taftīshī*
inroad (n)	غزو، غارة	*ghazw, ghārah*
inrush (n)	دفق، تدفق	*dafq, tadaffuq*
insalivate (v)	رضب	*raḍḍaba*
insane (adj)	أحمق، مجنون	*aḥmaq, majnūn*
insanitary (adj)	غير صحي	*ghair siḥḥī*
insanity (n)	جنون، حماقة، عته	*junūn, ḥamāqah, 'uth*
insatiable (adj)	نهم، شره	*nahim, sharih*
inscribe (v)	أدرج، طبع، كتب	*adraja, ṭaba'a, kataba*
inscription (n)	كلام منقوش، إدراج	*kalām manqūsh, idrāj*
inscriptive (adj)	نقشي، كتابي	*naqshī, kitābī*
inscroll (v)	دون، سجل	*dawwana, sajjala*
inscrutability (n)	غموض، إبهام	*ghumūḍ, ibhām*
inscrutable (adj)	غامض، غير واضح	*ghāmiḍ, ghair wāḍiḥ*
inscrutably (adv)	بطريق غامض	*bi ṭarīq ghāmiḍ*
insect (n)	حشرة، دودة	*ḥasharah, dūdah*
insecticide (n)	مبيد الحشرات	*mubīdul ḥasharāt*
insecticidal (adj)	مبيد، قاتل	*mubīd, qātil*
insectivore (n)	آكل الحشرات	*ākilul ḥasharāt*
insectivorous (adj)	حشري	*ḥasharī*
insecure (adj)	خطر، غير آمن	*khaṭir, ghair āmin*
insecurely (adv)	بطريق خطر	*bi ṭarīq khaṭir*
insecurity (n)	خطر، عدم أمن	*khaṭar, 'adamu amn*
inseminate (v)	أحبل، أخصب	*aḥbala, akhṣaba*

insemination (n)	إحبال، إخصاب	*iḥbāl, ikhṣāb*
insensibility (n)	فقدان الحس، فقدان الشعور	*fuqdānul ḥiss, fuqdānush shu'ūr*
insensible (adj)	عديم الحس، فاقد الشعور	*'adīmul ḥiss, fāqidush shu'ūr*
insensibly (adv)	بدون شعور	*bidūn shu'ūr*
insensitive (adj)	متبلد الشعور	*mutaballidush shu'ūr*
insensitively (adj)	بدون إحساس	*bidūn iḥsās*
insensitivity (n)	تبلد، عدم مبالاة	*taballud, 'adamu mubālāt*
inseparability (n)	تلازم، عدم انفصال	*talāzum, 'adamu infiṣāl*
inseparable (adj)	غير منفصل، متلازم	*ghair munfaṣil, mutalāzim*
insert (v)	أقحم، أدرج	*aqḥama, adraja*
insert (n)	مقحمة	*muqḥamah*
insertion (n)	إقحام، إدراج، مندرج	*iqḥām, idrāj, mundaraj*
inset (v)	أدرج، أقحم	*adraja, aqḥama*
inset (n)	شيء مدرج	*shay' mudraj*
inshore (adj)	واقع قرب الشاطئ	*wāqi' qurbash shāṭi'*
inshore (adv)	نحو الشاطئ	*naḥwash shāṭi'*
inside (n/adj)	جزء داخلي، داخلي	*juz' dākhilī, dākhilī*
inside (adv/prep)	داخلاً، داخل	*dākhilan, dākhila*
insider (n)	مطلع	*muṭṭala'*
insidious (adj)	غادر، مغوٍ	*ghādir, mughwin*
insidiously (adv)	بطريق غادر	*bi ṭarīq ghādir*
insight (n)	تبصر، إدراك	*tabaṣṣur, idrāk*
insightful (adj)	بصير، ذو بصيرة	*baṣīr, dhū baṣirah*
insignificance (n)	تفاهة، عدم أهمية	*tafāhah, 'adamu ahammiyyah*
insignificant (adj)	تافه، قليل الأهمية	*tāfih, qalīlul ahammiyyah*
insincere (adj)	غير مخلص، مراءٍ	*ghair mukhliṣ, murā'in*

insincerely (adv)	بدون إخلاص	*bidūn ikhlāṣ*
insincerity (n)	رياء، نفاق	*riyā', nifāq*
insinuate (v)	لقن، دس	*laqqana, dassa*
insinuation (n)	تلقين، تلميح	*talqīn, talmiḥ*
insipid (adj)	تفه، غير ممتع	*tafih, ghair mumti'*
insist (v)	أصر، ألح	*aṣarra, alaḥḥa*
insistence (n)	إصرار، إلحاح	*iṣrār, ilḥāḥ*
insistent (adj)	ملح، مصر	*muliḥḥ, muṣirr*
insistently (adv)	بطريق مصر	*bi ṭarīq muṣirr*
in situ (adv)	في موضع أصلي	*fī mauḍa' aṣlī*
insole (n)	نعل باطن	*na'l bāṭin*
insolence (n)	وقاحة، عجرفة	*waqāḥah, 'ajrafah*
insolent (adj)	وقح، متعجرف	*waqiḥ, muta'ajrif*
insolently (adv)	بطريق متغطرس	*bi ṭarīq mutaghaṭris*
insoluble (adj)	غير قابل للذوبان	*ghair qābil lidh dhawabān*
insolvency (n)	عجز عن وفاء الدين	*'ajz 'an wafā'id dain*
insolvent (adj)	عاجز عن الدفع	*'ājiz 'anid daf'*
insomnia (n)	أرق	*araq*
insomniac (n/adj)	مصاب بالأرق	*muṣāb bil araq*
inspect (v)	فتش، عاين	*fattasha, 'āyana*
inspection (n)	تفتيش رسمي	*taftīsh rasmī*
inspector (n)	مفتش، مراقب	*mufattish, murāqib*
inspiration (n)	تأثير ملهم، إلهام	*ta'thīr mulhim, ilhām*
inspirational (adj)	إلهامي، روحي	*ilhāmī, rūḥī*
inspire (v)	نفخ روحاً، ألهم	*nafakha rūḥan, alhama*
inspired (adj)	موحًى به، ملهم	*mūḥan bih, mulham*
inspiring (adj)	مؤثر، مسبب	*mu'aththir, musabbib*
instability (n)	عدم ثبات، تقلب	*'adamu thabāt, taqallub*
install (instal) (v)	نصب، وظف	*naṣṣaba, waẓẓafa*

installation (n)	تنصيب، إقامة	*tanṣīb, iqāmah*
installment(instalment)	تنصيب، قسط	*tanṣīb, qisṭ*
instance (n)	مثال، اقتراح	*mithāl, iqtirāḥ*
instance (v)	مثل	*maththala*
instant (n)	شهر حالي	*shahr ḥālī*
instant (adj)	حالي، جارٍ، عاجل	*ḥālī, jārin, 'ājil*
instantaneous (adj)	فوري، توي	*faurī, tawwī*
instantaneously (adv)	بغير تأخير، توًا	*bighairi ta'khīr, tawwan*
instantly (adv)	توًا، على الفور	*tawwan, 'alal faur*
instead (adv)	عوضاً، بدلاً	*'iwaḍan, badalan*
instead of (prep)	عوضاً عن	*'iwaḍan 'an*
instep (n)	مشط القدم	*mushṭul qadam*
instigate (v)	أغرى، أثار	*aghrā, athāra*
instigation (n)	تحريض، إثارة	*taḥrīḍ, ithārah*
instigator (n)	محرض، مغرٍ	*muḥarriḍ, mughrin*
instill (instil) (v)	لقن، غرس	*laqqana, gharasa*
instinct (n)	فطرة، غريزة	*fiṭrah, gharīzah*
instinctive (adj)	فطري، غريزي	*fiṭrī, gharīzī*
institute (n)	معهد، مجمع	*ma'had, majma'*
institute (v)	أسس، أنشأ	*assasa, ansha'a*
institution (n)	مؤسسة، معهد	*mu'assasah, ma'had*
institutional (adj)	متعلق بمؤسسة	*muta'alliq bi mu'assasah*
instruct (v)	علم، أوصى	*'allama, auṣā*
instruction (n)	وصية، تعليم	*waṣiyyah, ta'līm*
instructional (adj)	تعليمي، تدريسي	*ta'līmī, tadrīsī*
instructive (adj)	منور، مثقف	*munawwir, muthaqqif*
instructor (n)	معلم، مدرس	*mu'allim, mudarris*
instrument (n)	أداة، آلة، واسطة	*adāt, ālah, wāsiṭah*
instrumental (adj)	ذرائعي، واسطي	*dharā'i'ī, wāsiṭī*

instrumentalist (n)	عازف على آلة موسيقية	*'āzif 'alā ālah mausīqiyyah*
instrumentality (n)	واسطة، فائدة	*wāsiṭah, fā'idah*
instrumentation (n)	استخدام الآلات	*istikhdāmul ālāt*
insubstantial (adj)	وهمي، واهٍ	*wahmī, wāhin*
insufferable (adj)	لا يمكن إطاقه	*lā yumkin iṭāquh*
insufferably (adv)	بطريق لا يطاق	*bi ṭarīq lā yuṭāq*
insufficiency (n)	عدم كفاية	*'adamu kifāyah*
insufficient (adj)	غير كافٍ، ناقص	*ghair kāfin, nāqiṣ*
insufficiently (adv)	بطريق لا يكفي	*bi ṭarīq lā yakfī*
insular (adj)	معزول، ضيق	*ma'zūl, ḍayyiq*
insularity (n)	عزل، انعزال	*'azl, in'izāl*
insulate (v)	عزل، فصل	*'azala, faṣala*
insulation (n)	عزل، فصل	*'azl, faṣl*
insulator (n)	عازل كهربائي	*'āzil kahrabā'ī*
insulin (n)	الانسولين	*al insūlīn*
insult (v)	حقر، أهان	*ḥaqqara, ahāna*
insult (n)	إهانة، حقارة	*ihānah, ḥaqārah*
insulting (adj)	مهين، مخزٍ	*muhīn, mukhzin*
insuperable (adj)	لا يغلب، لا يقهر	*lā yughlab, lā yuqhar*
insupportable (adj)	لا يمكن احتماله	*lā yumkin iḥtimāluh*
insurance (n)	تأمين، ضمان	*ta'mīn, ḍamān*
insure (v)	أمن، ضمن	*ammana, ḍamina*
insured (adj)	مؤمن عليه	*mu'amman 'alaih*
insurer (n)	مؤمن	*mu'ammin*
insurgency (n)	تمرد، عصيان	*tamarrud, 'iṣyān*
insurgent (adj)	متمرد، ثائر	*mutamarrid, thā'ir*
insurmountable (adj)	غير قابل للاحتمال	*ghair qābil lil iḥtimāl*
insurrection (n)	عصيان مسلح	*'iṣyān musallaḥ*
intact (adj)	سليم، محفوظ	*salīm, maḥfūẓ*

intake (n)	مسرب، امتصاص	*masrab, imtiṣāṣ*
intangible (adj)	غير ملموس، لا يدرك	*ghair malmūs, lā yudrak*
integral (adj)	متكامل، متتام	*mutakāmil, mutatāmm*
integrate (v)	اتحد، دمج	*ittaḥada, damaja*
integrated (adj)	موحد، مندمج	*muwaḥḥad, mundamij*
integration (n)	تكامل، توحيد	*takāmul, tauḥīd*
integrity (n)	تمامية، سلامة	*tamāmiyyah, salāmah*
intellect (n)	ذكاء، عقل	*dhakā', 'aql*
intellectual (adj)	فكري، عقلي	*fikrī, 'aqlī*
intellectual (n)	شخص مفكر	*shakhṣ mufakkir*
intellectually (adv)	بذكاء، بتبصر	*bi dhakā', bi tabaṣṣur*
intelligence (n)	ذكاء، إدراك، استخبارات	*dhakā', idrāk, istikhbārāt*
intelligent (adj)	ذكي، فطين	*dhakī, faṭīn*
intelligently (adv)	بذكاء	*bi dhakā'*
intelligentsia (n)	أهل الفكر	*ahlul fikr*
intelligibility (n)	وضوح، جلاء	*wuḍūḥ, jalā'*
intelligible (adj)	واضح، مفهوم	*wāḍiḥ, mafhūm*
intelligibly (adv)	بطريق واضح	*bi ṭarīq wāḍiḥ*
intemperance (n)	إفراط، إدمان السكر	*ifrāṭ, idmānus sukr*
intemperate (adj)	مفرط، مسرف	*mufriṭ, musrif*
intend (v)	نوى، أراد	*nawā, arāda*
intended (adj)	مطلوب، مراد	*maṭlūb, murād*
intense (adj)	شديد، كثيف	*shadīd, kathīf*
intensification (n)	تشديد	*tashdīd*
intensifier (n)	مقوي، مشدد	*muqawwī, mushaddid*
intensify (v)	شدد، كثف	*shaddada, kaththafa*
intensity (n)	شدة، قوة، حدة	*shiddah, quwwah, ḥiddah*
intensive (adj)	مقوٍّ، شديد	*muqawwin, shadīd*
intensly (adj)	بشدة، بقوة	*bi shiddah, bi quwwah*
intent (n)	قصد، نية، عزم	*qaṣd, niyyah, 'azm*

intent (adj)	مصمم، منكب	*muṣammim, munkabb*
intention (n)	عزم، قصد، هدف	*'azm, qaṣd, hadaf*
intentional (adj)	عمدي، قصدي	*'amadī, qaṣdī*
intentionally (adv)	عمداً، قصداً	*'amadan, qaṣdan*
inter (v)	دفن، قبر	*dafana, qabara*
interact (v)	تفاعل، تعامل	*tafā'ala, ta'āmala*
interaction (n)	تعامل، تفاعل	*ta'āmul, tafā'ul*
interactive (adj)	متفاعل	*mutafā'il*
interbreed (v)	هجن، تهاجن	*hajjana, tahājana*
intercede (v)	شفع، توسط	*shafa'a, tawassaṭa*
intercept (v)	حجز، أوقف	*ḥajaza, auqafa*
interception (n)	حجز، منع	*ḥajz, man'*
interceptor (n)	موقف، طائرة الاعتراض	*mūqif, ṭā'iratul i'tirāḍ*
intercession (n)	شفاعة، توسط	*shafā'ah, tawassuṭ*
interchange (v)	تبادل، تواضع	*tabādala, tawāḍa'a*
interchange (n)	تبادل، تقاطع	*tabādul, taqāṭu'*
interchangeable (adj)	قابل للتبادل	*qābil lit tabādul*
interchangeably (adv)	بطريق يمكن تبادله	*bi ṭarīq yumkin tabāduluh*
intercollegiate (adj)	جارٍ بين الكليات	*jārin bainal kulliyyāt*
intercom (n)	نظام الاتصال الداخلي	*niẓāmul ittiṣāl ad dākhilī*
intercommunication	تبادل الاتصال	*tabādulul ittiṣāl*
interconnect (v)	رابط، واصل	*rābaṭa, wāṣala*
interconnection (n)	مرابطة	*murābaṭah*
intercontinental (adj)	بيقاري	*baiqārrī*
intercourse (n)	جماع، تعامل	*jimā', ta'āmul*
interdenominational	بيطائفي	*baiṭā'ifī*
interdepartmental (adj)	بيدائري	*baidā'irī*
interdependence (n)	توافق، توقف	*tawāquf, tawaqquf*

interdependent (n)	متواقف	*mutawāqif*
interdict (n)	منع، نهي	*man', nahy*
interest (n)	منفعة، مصلحة، ربا	*manfa'ah, maṣlaḥah, ribā*
interest (v)	حث، رغب	*ḥaththa, raghghaba*
interested (adj)	راغب، مهتم	*rāghib, muhtamm*
interesting (adj)	ممتع، مشوق	*mumti', mushawwiq*
interface (n)	سطح بيني	*saṭḥ bainī*
interfere (v)	تدخل، تداخل	*tadakhkhala, tadākhala*
interference (n)	تدخل، تشوش، عقبة	*tadakhkhul, tashawwush, 'aqabah*
interfering (adj)	متعارض، متصادم	*muta'āriḍ, mutaṣādim*
interim (n)	فترة، غضون	*fatrah, ghuḍūn*
interim (adj)	مؤقت	*mu'aqqat*
interior (adj)	داخلي، باطني	*dākhilī, bāṭinī*
interior (n)	داخلية البلاد، داخل	*dākhiliyyatul bilād, dākhil*
interior decoration	فن الزخرفة الداخلية	*funnuz zakhrafah ad dākhiliyyah*
interject (v)	أقحم	*aqḥama*
interjection (n)	حرف تعجب	*ḥarfu ta'ajjub*
interlace (v)	شابك، تشابك	*shābaka, tashābaka*
interleave (v)	حشى الأوراق	*ḥashshal aurāq*
interline (v)	حشى بين السطور	*ḥashshā bainas suṭūr*
interlink (v)	حالق	*ḥālaqa*
interlock (v)	شابك، تشابك	*shābaka, tashābaka*
interlocutor (n)	محاور، محادث	*muḥāwir, muḥādith*
interlude (n)	فترة فاصلة	*fatrah fāṣilah*
intermarriage (n)	تزاوج، زواج لحمي	*tazāwuj, zawāj luḥmi*
intermarry (v)	تزاوج	*tazāwaja*
intermediary (adj)	وسيط، متوسط	*wasīṭ, mutawassiṭ*
intermediary (n)	وسيلة، واسطة	*wasīlah, wāsiṭah*

intermediate (adj/n)	متوسط، وسيط	*mutawassiṭ, wasīṭ*
interment (n)	دفن، قبر	*dafn, qabr*
interminable (adj)	غير متناه، مطول	*ghair mutanāhin, muṭawwal*
interminably (adv)	على نحو مطول	*'alā naḥw muṭawwal*
intermingle (v)	اختلط، امتزج	*ikhtalaṭa, imtazaja*
intermission (n)	فترة، توقف	*fatrah, tawaqquf*
intermittent (adj)	متقطع، متفتر	*mutaqaṭṭi', mutafattir*
intern (v)	اعتقل، حبس	*i'taqala, ḥabasa*
internal (adj)	داخلي، ذاتي	*dākhilī, dhātī*
internalization (n)	تذويت	*tadhwīt*
internalize,-ise (v)	ذوت	*dhawwata*
internally (adv)	داخليًا، باطنيًا	*dākhiliyyan, bāṭiniyyan*
international (adj)	دولي، أممي	*duwalī, umamī*
internationalism (n)	دولية	*duwaliyyah*
internationalization (n)	تدويل	*tadwīl*
internationalize,-ise (v)	دول	*dawwala*
internecine (n)	مميت، مهلك	*mumīt, muhlik*
internee (n)	معتقل، أسير حرب	*mu'taqal, asīru ḥarb*
internment (n)	اعتقال	*i'tiqāl*
interpenetrate (v)	تداخل	*tadākhala*
interpenetration (n)	تداخل	*tadākhul*
interpersonal (adj)	بيشخصي	*baishakhṣī*
interplanetary (adj)	بيكوكبي	*baikaukabī*
interplay (n)	تفاعل	*tafā'ul*
interpolate (v)	حشى في نص	*ḥashshā fī naṣṣ*
interpolation (n)	استكمال، استيفاء، تحشية	*istikmāl, istīfā', taḥshiyah*
interpose (v)	تداخل، وسط	*tadākhala, wassaṭa*
interpret (v)	فسر، شرح	*fassara, sharaḥa*

interpretation (n)	تفسير، تأويل	*tafsīr, ta'wīl*
interpreter (n)	مفسر، مترجم	*mufassir, mutarjim*
interpretive (adj)	تفسيري، تأويلي	*tafsīrī, ta'wīlī*
interracial (adj)	بيعرقي	*bai'irqī*
interrelate (v)	أقام علاقة متبادلة	*aqāma 'alāqah mutabādilah*
interrelation (n)	علاقة متبادلة	*'alāqah mutabādilah*
interrelationship (n)	علاقة متبادلة	*'alāqah mutabādilah*
interrogate (v)	سأل، استجوب	*sa'ala, istajwaba*
interrogation (n)	سؤال، استجواب	*su'āl, istijwāb*
interrogative (adj)	استفهامي	*istifhāmī*
interrogator (n)	مستجوب، مستنطق	*mustajwib, mustanṭiq*
interrupt (v)	قاطع، عاق	*qāṭa'a, 'āqa*
interrupter (n)	مقطع	*muqaṭṭi'*
interruption (n)	تطقع، مقاطعة	*taqaṭṭu', muqāṭa'ah*
intersect (v)	تقاطع، شطر	*taqāṭa'a, shaṭara*
intersection (n)	تقاطع، نقطة التقاطع	*taqāṭu', nuqṭatut taqāṭu'*
intersperse (v)	نثر، بعثر	*nathara, ba'thara*
interstate (adj)	متعلق بولايات	*muta'alliq bi wilāyāt*
interstellar (adj)	واقع بين النجوم	*wāqi' bainan nujūm*
interstice (n)	فرجة، فتحة	*furjah, futḥah*
intertwine (v)	جدل، شبك	*jadala, shabbaka*
interval (n)	فترة، فاصلة	*fatrah, fāṣilah*
intervene (v)	تدخل، تخلل	*tadakhkhala, takhallala*
intervention (n)	توسط، تخلل	*tawassuṭ, takhallul*
interventionism (n)	تدخلية	*tadakhkhuliyyah*
interventionist (n)	تدخلي	*tadakhkhulī*
interview (n)	مقابلة، مواجهة	*muqābalah, muwājahah*
interweave (v)	ناسج، حابك	*nāsaja, ḥābaka*

intestacy (n)	كونه غير موصٍ	*kaunuhu ghaira mūṣin*
intestate (adj)	غير موصٍ، بدون وصية	*ghair mūṣin, bidūn waṣiyyah*
intestinal (adj)	معوي	*mi'awī*
intestine (n)	معًى	*mi'an*
intimacy (n)	مودة، صداقة حميمة	*mawaddah, ṣadāqah ḥamīmah*
intimate (n)	صديق حميم	*ṣadīq ḥamīm*
intimate (adj)	حميم، عميق، صميمي	*ḥamīm, 'amīq, ṣamīmī*
intimate (v)	لمح، صرح	*lamaḥa, ṣarraḥa*
intimately (adj)	بطريق عميق	*bi ṭarīq 'amīq*
intimation (n)	إيعاز، تلميح	*ī'āz, talmīḥ*
intimidate (v)	أرعب، خوف	*ar'aba, khawwafa*
intimidating (adj)	مرعب، مرهب	*mur'ib, murhib*
intimidation (n)	تخويف، إرهاب	*takhwīf, irhāb*
into (prep)	نحو، في	*naḥwa, fī*
intolerable (adj)	غير محتمل، لايطاق	*ghair muḥtamal, lā yuṭāq*
intolerably (adv)	بطريق لا يحتمل	*bi ṭarīq lā yuḥtamal*
intolerance (n)	عدم تحمل، تعصب	*'adamu taḥammul, ta'aṣṣub*
intolerant (adj)	قليل التحمل، متعصب	*qalīlut taḥammul, muta'aṣṣib*
intonation (n)	تلحين، ترنيم	*talḥīn, tarnīm*
intone (v)	لحن، نغم	*laḥḥana, naghghama*
in toto (adv)	كليةً	*kulliyyatan*
intoxicant (n)	شيء مسكر	*shay' muskir*
intoxicate (v)	أسكر	*askara*
intoxicated (adj)	سكران، ثمل	*sakrān, thamil*

intoxicating (adj)	مسكر	*muskir*
intoxication (n)	سكر، ثمل، افتتان	*sukr, thamal, iftinān*
intractable (adj)	عنيد، غير طروق	*'anīd, ghair ṭarūq*
intransigence (n)	عناد، تصلب	*'inād, taṣallub*
intransigent (adj)	عنيد، متصلب	*'anīd, mutaṣallib*
intransitive (adj)	غير متعدٍّ، لازم	*ghair muta'addin, lāzim*
intrepid (adj)	جريء، مقدام	*jarī', miqdām*
intrepidity (n)	شجاعة، بسالة	*shajā'ah, basālah*
intricacy (n)	تعقيد	*ta'qīd*
intricate (adj)	معرقل، معقد	*mu'arqal, mu'aqqad*
intricately (adv)	بطريق معقد	*bi ṭarīq mu'aqqad*
intrigue (n)	مكيدة، خداع، دسيسة	*makīdah, khidā', dasīsah*
intrigue (v)	دبر مكيدةً، خدع	*dabbara makīdatan, khada'a*
intriguing (adj)	خادع، غامض	*khādi', ghāmiḍ*
intrinsic-al (adj)	حقيقي، أصلي	*ḥaqīqī, aṣlī*
intrinsically (adv)	في الحقيقة	*fil ḥaqīqah*
intro (n)	مقدمة	*muqaddimah*
introduce (v)	عرف، قدم	*'arrafa, qaddama*
introduction (n)	مقدمة، تعارف	*muqaddimah, ta'āruf*
introductory (adj)	تقديمي، تمهيدي	*taqdīmī, tamhīdī*
introspection (n)	تمعن، استبطان	*tama''un, istibṭān*
introspective (adj)	مستبطن	*mustabṭin*
introversion (n)	انطواء عن النفس	*inṭiwā' 'anin nafs*
introvert (n)	شخص منطوي	*shakhṣ munṭawī*
introverted (adj)	منطوٍ	*munṭawin*
intrude (v)	دخل عنوةً، وغل	*dakhala 'anwatan, waghala*
intruder (n)	معتدٍ، دخيل	*mu'tadin, dakhīl*

intrusion (n)	اعتداء، تطفل	*i'tidā', taṭafful*
intrusive (adj)	تطفلي، اقتحامي	*taṭaffulī, iqtiḥāmī*
intuit (v)	عرف بالحدس	*'arafa bil ḥads*
intuition (n)	حدس، بداهة	*ḥads, badāhah*
intuitive (adj)	بديهي، عقلي	*badīhī, 'aqlī*
intuitively (adv)	بالبديهة	*bil badīhah*
inundate (v)	أغرق، فاض	*aghraqa, fāḍa*
inundation (n)	إغراق، غمر	*ighrāq, ghamr*
inure (v)	عود، تعود	*'awwada, ta'awwada*
invade (v)	أغار، غزا	*aghāra, ghazā*
invader (n)	غاز، معتد	*ghāzin, mu'tadin*
invalid (adj)	باطل، غير قانوني	*bāṭil, ghair qanūnī*
invalidate (v)	أبطل، أفسد	*abṭala, afsada*
invalidation (n)	نسخ، بطلان	*naskh, buṭlān*
invaluable (adj)	لا يقدر بثمن	*lā yuqaddar bi thaman*
invariable (adj)	ثابت، غير متغير	*thābit, ghair mutaghayyir*
invariably (adv)	بلا تغير	*bilā taghayyur*
invasion (n)	غزو، غارة	*ghazw, ghārah*
invasive (adj)	اجتياحي، جائر	*ijtiyāḥī, jā'ir*
invective (n)	قدح، قذف	*qadḥ, qadhf*
invent (v)	اخترع، اختلق	*ikhtara'a, ikhtalaqa*
invention (n)	اختراع، شيء مخترع	*ikhtirā', shay' mukhtara'*
inventive (adj)	مبدع، إبداعي	*mubdi', ibdā'ī*
inventiveness (n)	إبداعية	*ibdā'iyyah*
inventor (n)	مبدع، مخترع	*mubdi', mukhtari'*
inventory (n)	قاعة الجرد	*qā'atul jard*
inverse (n/adj)	عكس، معكوس	*'aks, ma'kūs*
inversely (adv)	بالعكس، عكساً	*bil 'aks, 'aksan*
inversion (n)	عكس، قلب	*'aks, qalb*
invert (v)	عكس، حول	*'akasa, ḥawwala*

inverted commas	علامتا الاقتباس	*'alāmatal iqtibās*
invest (v)	ثمر، وظف	*thammara, waẓẓafa*
investigate (v)	استقصى، فحص	*istaqṣā, faḥaṣa*
investigation (n)	تحقيق، استقصاء	*taḥqīq, istiqṣā'*
investigative (adj)	استقصائي، تفتيشي	*istiqṣā'ī, taftīshī*
investigator (n)	فاحص، محقق	*fāḥiṣ, muḥaqqiq*
investiture (n)	تنصيب، تولية	*tanṣīb, tauliyah*
investment (n)	تشغيل، توظيف المال	*tashghīl, tauẓīful māl*
invidious (adj)	مثير للاستياء	*muthīr lil istiyā'*
invigilate (v)	راقب	*rāqaba*
invigilation (n)	مراقبة	*murāqabah*
invigilator (n)	مراقب، رقيب	*murāqib, raqīb*
invigorate (v)	نشط، شدد	*nashshaṭa, shaddada*
invincible (adj)	منيع، لا يغلب	*manī', lā yughlab*
inviolability (n)	مناعة، حرازة	*manā'ah, ḥarāzah*
inviolable (adj)	منيع، حرام	*manī', ḥarām*
inviolate (adj)	سليم، غير منتهك	*salīm, ghair muntahak*
invisibility (n)	اختفاء، توارٍ	*ikhtifā', tawārin*
invisible (adj)	غير مرئي، محجوب	*ghair mar'ī, maḥjūb*
invisibly (adv)	بطريق غير مرئي	*bi ṭarīq ghair mar'ī*
invitation (n)	دعوة، استدعاء	*da'wah, istid'ā'*
invite (v)	دعا، أغرى	*da'ā, aghrā*
invite (n)	دعوة	*da'wah*
inviting (adj)	مغرٍ، جاذب	*mughrin, jādhib*
invitingly (adv)	بطريق مغرٍ	*bi ṭarīq mughrin*
invocation (n)	تضرع، ابتهال	*taḍarru', ibtiḥāl*
invoice (n/v)	فاتورة، فوتر	*fātūrah, fautara*
invoke (v)	تضرع، استرحم	*taḍarra'a, istarḥama*
involve (v)	تلوث، ورط	*talawwatha, warraṭa*
involved (adj)	متورط، مستغرق	*mutawarriṭ, mustaghriq*

involvement (n)	تورط، تلوث	*tawarruṭ, talawwuth*
invulnerability (n)	مناعة، حصانة	*manā'ah, ḥaṣānah*
invulnerable (adj)	منيع، حصين	*manī', ḥaṣīn*
inward (adj/adv)	داخلي، نحو الداخل	*dākhilī, naḥwad dākhil*
inwardly (adv)	داخليًا، سرًا	*dākhiliyyan, sirran*
inwardness (n)	داخلية	*dākhiliyyah*
inwards (adv)	نحو الداخل	*naḥwad dākhil*
iodine (n)	اليود	*alyūd*
iodization,-isation	تأويد	*ta'wīd*
iodize,-ise (v)	يود	*yawwada*
Iran (n)	إيران	*īrān*
Iranian (adj/n)	ايراني	*īrānī*
Iraq (n)	العراق	*al 'irāq*
Iraqi (adj/n)	العراقي	*al 'irāqī*
irascible (adj)	سريع الغضب	*sarī'ul ghaḍab*
irate (adj)	غضوب، سريع الغضب	*ghaḍūb, sarī'ul ghaḍab*
ire (n)	غضب، حنق	*ghaḍab, ḥanaq*
iridium (n)	الايريديوم	*al īrīdiyūm*
Irish (n/adj)	ايرلنديون، ايرلندي	*iyarlandyūn, iyarlandī*
Irish coffee (n)	قهوة ايرلندية	*qahwah iyarlandiyyah*
Irish setter (n)	ساطر ايرلندي	*sāṭir iyarlandī*
irk (v)	ضايق، أزعج	*ḍāyaqa, az'aja*
irksome (adj)	مضايق، مضجر	*muḍāyiq, muḍjir*
iron (n)	حديد، مكواة	*ḥadīd, mikwāt*
iron (v)	كوى، قيد بالأصفاد	*kawā, qayyada bil aṣfād*
Iron Age	عصر الحديد	*'aṣrul ḥadīd*
Iron Curtain	ستار حديدي	*sitār ḥadīdī*
ironic-al (adj)	سخري، استهزائي	*sukhrī, istihzā'i*
ironically (adv)	استهزاء، تهكماً	*istihzā'an, tahakkuman*
ironing (n)	كي	*kayy*

ironing-board (n)	لوح الكي	*lauḥul kayy*
ironmonger (n)	تاجر الحديد	*tājirul ḥadīd*
ironmongery (n)	تجارة الحديد	*tijāratul ḥadīd*
ironstone (n)	حجر الحديد	*ḥajarul ḥadīd*
ironwork (n)	أدوات حديدية	*adawāt ḥadīdiyyah*
ironworks (n)	مصنع الحديد	*maṣna'ul ḥadīd*
irony (n)	سخرية، تعبير ساخر، تهكم	*sukhriyyah, ta'bīr sākhir, tahakkum*
irradiate (v)	أشع، أنار	*asha''a, anāra*
irradiation (n)	إشعاع، إنارة	*ish'ā', inārah*
irrational (adj)	غير معقول، غير عقلاني	*ghair ma'qūl, ghair 'aqlānī*
irrationality (n)	سخافة، عدم تعقل	*sakhāfah, 'adamu ta'aqqul*
irrationally (adv)	بدون فكر سليم	*bidūn fikr salīm*
irreconcilable (adj)	متضاد، متناقض	*mutaḍādd, mutanāqiḍ*
irrecoverable (adj)	لا يعوض	*lā yu'awwaḍ*
irredeemable (adj)	غير قابل للإصلاح	*ghair qābil lil iṣlāḥ*
irreducible (adj)	لا يمكن إنقاصه	*lā yumkin inqāṣuh*
irrefutable (adj)	لا جدل فيه	*lā jadala fīh*
irregular (n)	جندي غير نظامي	*jundī ghair niẓāmī*
irregular (adj)	شاذ، غير نظامي	*shādhdh, ghair niẓāmi*
irregularity (n)	شذوذ، شيء شاذ	*shudhūdh, shay' shādhdh*
irregularly (adv)	على نحو شاذ	*'alā naḥwin shādhdh*
irrelevance (n)	عدم ملاءمة	*'adamu mulā'amah*
irrelevant (adj)	في غير محله، غير متعلق	*fī ghairi maḥallih, ghair muta'alliq*
irrelevantly (adv)	بدون علاقة	*bidūn 'alāqah*
irreligious (adj)	غير ديني، لاديني	*ghair dīnī, lā dīnī*
irremediable (adj)	عضال، لا يداوى	*'uḍāl, lā yudāwā*

irremediably (adv)	بطريق لا يمكن علاجه	*bi ṭarīq lā yumkin 'ilājuh*
irremovable (adj)	لا يمكن نقله	*lā ymkin naqluh*
irreparable (adj)	لا يمكن ترميمه	*lā yumkin tarmīmuh*
irreparably (adv)	بطريق لا يمكن ترميمه	*bi ṭarīq lā yumkin tarmīmuh*
irreplaceable (adj)	لا يستبدل	*lā yustabdal*
irrepressible (adj)	لا يسيطر عليه	*lā yusaiṭar 'alaih*
irreproachable (adj)	لا يلام	*lā yulām*
irresistible (adj)	لا يقاوم	*lā yuqāwam*
irresistibly (adv)	بطريق لا يقاوم	*bi ṭarīq lā yuqāwam*
irresolute (adj)	متردد، متذبذب	*mutaraddid, mutadhabdhib*
irresolutely (adv)	بتردد	*bi taraddud*
irresolution (n)	تردد، توقف	*taraddud, tawaqquf*
irrespective of (prep)	بقطع النظر عن	*biqaṭ'in naẓar 'an*
irresponsibility (n)	عدم مسؤولية	*'adamu mas'ūliyyah*
irresponsible (adj)	غير مسؤول	*ghair mas'ūl*
irresponsibly (adv)	بدون الشعور بالمسؤولية	*bidūnish shu'ūr bil mas'ūliyyah*
irreverence (n)	عدم احترام، عدم توقير	*'adamu iḥtirām, 'adamu tauqīr*
irreverent (adj)	عديم الاحترام، وقح	*'adīmul iḥtirām, waqiḥ*
irreversible (adj)	لا يمكن قلبه	*lā yumkin qalbuh*
irreversibly (adv)	بطريق لا يقلب	*bi ṭarīq lā yuqlab*
irrevocable (adj)	لا يرد، لا ينسخ	*lā yuradd, lā yunsakh*
irrevocably (adv)	بطريق لا يرد	*bi ṭarīq lā yuradd*
irrigate (v)	أروى، سقى	*arwā, saqā*
irrigation (n)	إرواء، سقي	*irwā', saqy*
irritability (n)	نزق، حدة طبع	*nazaq, ḥiddatu ṭab'*
irritable (adj)	نزق، سريع التهيج	*naziq, sarī'ut tahayyuj*
irritably (adj)	بنـــزق	*bi nazaq*

irritant (adj)	مهيج، مثير	*muhayyij, muthīr*
irritate (v)	أسخط، هيج	*askhaṭa, hayyaja*
irritated (adj)	مهاج، مغضب	*muhāj, mughḍab*
irritating (adj)	مهيج، مسخط	*muhayyij, muskhiṭ*
irritatingly (adv)	بطريق مسخط	*bi ṭarīq muskhiṭ*
irritation (n)	سخط، هيج	*sukhṭ, tahayyuj*
irruption (n)	تفجر، ازدياد مفاجئ	*tafajjur, izdiyād mufāji'*
Islam (n)	الاسلام	*al islām*
Islamic (adj)	إسلامي، إسلامية	*islāmī, islāmiyyah*
island (n)	جزيرة	*jazīrah*
islander (n)	ساكن الجزيرة	*sākinul jazīrah*
islet (n)	جزيرة صغيرة	*jazīrah ṣaghīrah*
isolate (v)	عزل، فصل	*'azala, faṣala*
isolated (adj)	منفصل، منعزل	*munfaṣil, mun'azil*
isolation (n)	عزل، فصل	*'azl, faṣl*
isolationism (n)	انعزالية	*in'izāliyyah*
isolationist (n)	انعزالي	*in'izālī*
issue (n)	قضية، إصدار، ذرية	*qaḍiyyah, iṣdār, dhurriyyah*
issue (v)	أصدر، نشأ، انتهى	*aṣdara, nasha'a, intahā*
it (pron)	هو، هي، ه، ها	*huwa, hiya, hū, hā*
Italian (n/adj)	الايطالي	*al īṭālī*
italic (adj)	مائل	*mā'il*
italicize,-ise (v)	ميل	*mayyala*
italics (n)	حروف مائلة	*ḥurūf mā'ilah*
Italy (n)	إيطالية	*īṭāliyah*
itch (n)	حكة، أكال	*ḥikkah, ukāl*
item (n)	بند، موضوع، مفرد	*band, mauḍū', mufrad*
itemize,-ise (v)	فصل المفردات	*faṣṣalal mufradāt*
itinerant (adj)	متجول، متطوف	*mutajawwil, mutaṭwwif*

itinerant (n)	شخص متطوف	*shakhṣ mutaṭawwif*
itinerary (n)	دليل الرحالة	*dalīlur raḥḥālah*
itself (pron)	نفسه، نفسها	*nafsuhu, nafsuhā*
ivory (n)	عاج	*'āj*
ivory tower (n)	البرج العاجي	*al burj al 'ājī*

J

jab (n)	لطم، وخز	*laṭm, wakhz*
jab (v)	طعن، لطم	*ṭa'ana, laṭama*
jabber (v)	ثرثر، هذرم	*tharthara, hadhrama*
jack (n)	رافعة، مدوار	*rāfi'ah, midwār*
jack (v)	رفع، زاد	*rafa'a, zāda*
jackal (n)	ابن آوى	*ibn āwā*
jackass (n)	أحمق، غبي	*aḥmaq, ghabī*
jackboot (n)	جزمة عسكرية	*jazmah 'askariyyah*
jackdaw (n)	غراب الزيتون	*ghurābuz zaitūn*
jacket (n)	دثار، جاكيت، سترة	*dithār, jākīt, sitrah*
Jack Frost (n)	برد شديد	*bard shadīd*
jack-in-the-box	عفريت العلبة	*'ifrītul 'ulbah*
jacknife (n)	مطواة كبيرة	*miṭwāt kabīrah*
jacknife (v)	قطع بمطواة كبيرة	*qaṭa'a bi miṭwāt kabīrah*
jack of all trades	صاحب الصنائع السبع	*ṣāḥibuṣ ṣanā'i' as sab'*
jackpot (n)	كنـــز	*kanz*
Jacobian (adj)	جيمسي	*jaimisī*
jade (n)	يشب، يشم	*yashb, yashm*
jaded (adj)	منهك، متخم	*munhak, mutkham*
jagged (adj)	خشن، مفلول	*khashin, maflūl*
jaguar (n)	اليغور	*al yaghwar*
jail (n/v)	سجن، سجن	*sijn, sajana*
jailbird (n)	مجرم مزمن	*mujrim muzmin*

jailer (n)	سجان	*sajjān*
jam (n)	مربى، ازدحام، ورطة	*murabbā, izdiḥām, warṭah*
jam (v)	دفع بقوة، شوش	*dafa'a bi quwwah, shawwasha*
jamb (n)	عضادة الباب	*'iḍādatul bāb*
jamboree (n)	احتفال كبير	*iḥtifāl kabīr*
January (n)	يناير، قانون ثاني	*yanāyar, qānūn thānī*
jar (n)	جرة، صدمة	*jarrah, ṣadmah*
jar (v)	هز، تضارب، تنافر	*hazza, taḍāraba, tanāfara*
jargon (n)	جعجعة، رطانة	*ja'ja'ah, raṭānah*
jasmine (n)	ياسمين	*yāsmīn*
jaundice (n)	يرقان	*yaraqān*
jaundiced (adj)	مصاب بيرقان	*muṣāb bi yaraqān*
jaunt (n)	رحلة صغيرة للتنـــزة	*riḥlah ṣaghīrah lit tanazzuh*
jaunty (adj)	مرح، طروب	*mariḥ, ṭarūb*
javelin (n)	رمح صغير	*rumḥ ṣaghīr*
jaw (n)	فك، كلام سليط	*fakk, kalām salīṭ*
jawbone (n)	عظم الفك	*'aẓmul fakk*
jay (n)	ابو زريق	*abū zuraiq*
jaz (v)	نشط، أفعم بالحياة	*nashshaṭa, af'ama bil ḥayāt*
jaz (n)	موسيقي الجاز	*mausīqī al jāz*
jazzy (adj)	متعلق بالجاز، مزين	*muta'alliq bil jāz, muzayyan*
jealous (adj)	حسود، متحمس	*ḥasūd, mutaḥammis*
jealousy (n)	غيرة، حرص، حماس	*ghairah, ḥirṣ, ḥamās*
jeans (n)	جين	*jīn*
jeep (n)	جيب	*jīb*
jeer (v)	سخر، استهزأ	*sakhira, istahza'a*

jeer (n)	استهزاء، سخرية	*istihzā', sukhriyyah*
jelly (n)	هلام، شيء كالهلام	*hulām, shay' kal hulām*
jellyfish (n)	سمك هلامي	*samak hulāmī*
jeopardize,-ise (v)	أوقع في خطر	*auqa'a fī khaṭar*
jeopardy (n)	خطر، ورطة	*khaṭar, warṭah*
jerk (n)	نخعة، هزة	*nakh'ah, hazzah*
jerk (v)	نخع، هز	*nakha'a, hazza*
jerky (adj)	منتخع	*muntakhi'*
jersey (n)	جرسي، جرسية	*jursī, jursiyyah*
Jerusalem (n)	القدس	*al quds*
jest (n)	مزاح، سخرية	*muzāḥ, sukhriyyah*
jest (v)	مزح، سخر	*mazaḥa, sakhira*
Jesuit (n)	يسوعي	*yasū'ī*
Jesus (n)	مسيح	*masīḥ*
jet (n)	أنبوب، كهرمان أسود	*umbūb, kahramān aswad*
jet liner (n)	طائرة نفاثة	*ṭā'irah naffāthah*
Jew (n)	يهودي	*yahūdī*
jewel (n)	جوهرة، حلية	*jauharah, ḥilyah*
jewelled (adj)	مرصع بالجواهر	*muraṣṣa' bil jawāhir*
jeweller ((jeweler)	جوهري	*jauharī*
jewellery (n)	جواهر، حلىً	*jawāhir, ḥilan*
jig (n)	رقصة جيغ، جيغة	*raqṣatu jīgh, jīghah*
jiggered (adj)	في حيرة	*fī ḥairah*
jiggle (v)	تهزهز، هزهز	*tahazhaza, hazhaza*
jigsaw puzzle	أحجية الصور المقطوعة	*uḥjiyyatuṣ ṣuwar al maqṭū'ah*
jihad (n)	جهاد	*jihād*
jilt (v)	أعرضت المرأة عن محبها	*a'raḍatil mar'atu 'an muḥibbihā*
jimmy (jemmy)	مخل قصير	*mukhl qaṣīr*

jingle (n)	طنين، جلجلة	*ṭanīn, jaljalah*
jingle (v)	طن، جلجل	*ṭanna, jaljala*
jingoism (n)	الشوفينية	*ash shūfīniyyah*
jingoistic (adj)	شوفيني	*shūfīnī*
jink (v)	فر، راغ	*farra, rāgha*
jinx (n)	حظ عاثر	*ḥaẓẓ ʻāthir*
jitters (n)	نرفزة بالغة	*narfazah bālighah*
jittery (adj)	شديد النرفزة	*shadīdun narfazah*
job (n)	وظيفة، شغل، عمل	*waẓīfah, shughl, ʻamal*
jobless (adj)	لا وظيفة لـــه	*lā waẓīfah lahu*
jobless (n)	شخص عاطل من الوظيفة	*shakhṣ ʻāṭil minal waẓifah*
job lot	مجموعة سلع مختلفة	*majmūʻatu silaʻ mukhtalifah*
jockey (n)	جوكي، فارس	*jūkī, fāris*
jockey (v)	ناور لمنفعة شخصية	*nāwara li manfaʻah shakhṣiyyah*
jockstrap (n)	حمالة الأعضاء التوالدية	*ḥammālatul aʻḍāʼ at tawāludiyyah*
jocose (adj)	مرح، مزوح	*mariḥ, mazūḥ*
jocular (adj)	مازح، مضحك	*māziḥ, muḍḥik*
jocularity (n)	مزاح، هزل	*muzāḥ, hazl*
jog (v)	مشى، عدا، اهتز	*mashā, ʻadā, ihtazza*
jog (n)	عدو، هزة	*ʻadw, hazzah*
jogging (n)	مشي، عدو	*mashy, ʻadw*
join (v)	لحق، وصل، التحق	*laḥiqa, waṣala, iltaḥaqa*
joiner (n)	نجار بارع	*najjār bāriʻ*
joinery (n)	نجارة	*nijārah*
joint (n)	وصلة، مفصل	*wuṣlah, mafṣil*
joint (adj)	مشترك، متحد	*mushtarak, muttaḥid*

joint (v)	ضم، اتحد، وصل	*ḍamma, ittaḥada, waṣṣala*
joint account	حساب مشترك	*ḥisāb mushtarak*
jointly (adv)	باتحاد، باشتراك	*bittiḥād, bishtirāk*
joist (n)	جائز، دعامة	*jā'iz, di'āmah*
joke (n)	مزاح، هزل	*muzāḥ, hazl*
joke (v)	مزح، هزل	*mazaḥa, hazala*
joker (n)	مزاح، جوكر	*mazzāḥ, jūkar*
joking (n)	تنكيت، مزاح	*tankīt, muzāḥ*
jokingly (adv)	على سبيل المزاح	*'alā sabīlil muzāḥ*
jollification (n)	ابتهاج، مرح	*ibtihāj, maraḥ*
jolly (adj)	طروب، مبتهج	*ṭarūb, mubtahij*
jolly (adv)	إلى حد بعيد	*ilā ḥadd ba'īd*
jolly (v)	مزح، لاطف	*mazaḥa, lāṭafa*
jolt (n)	صدمة شديدة، ضيق	*ṣadmah shadīdah, ḍīq*
jolt (v)	ضايق، انتخع	*ḍāyaqa, intakha'a*
jostle (v)	صدم، رج، احتك	*ṣadama, rajja, iḥtakka*
jot (v)	سجل بسرعة	*sajjala bi sur'ah*
jottings (n)	مذكرة موجزة	*mudhakkirah mūjizah*
journal (n)	مجلة، جريدة، دفتر اليومية	*majallah, jarīdah, daftarul yaumiyyah*
journalese (n)	أسلوب صحفي	*uslūb ṣuḥufī*
journalism (n)	صحافة	*ṣiḥāfah*
journalist (n)	صحافي	*ṣiḥāfī*
journalistic (adj)	صحافي، صحفي	*ṣiḥāfī, ṣuḥufī*
journey (n)	رحلة، سفر، سياحة	*riḥlah, safar, siyāḥah*
journey (v)	سافر	*sāfara*
journeyman (n)	صانع بارع	*ṣāni' bāri'*
Jove (n)	جوبيتر	*jūbītar*
jovial (adj)	جذل، مبتهج	*jadhil, mubtahij*
jovially (adv)	مرحًا، جذلاً	*maraḥan, jadhalan*

jow (n)	خد، فك	*khadd, fakk*
joy (n)	سرور، فرح، جذل	*surūr, faraḥ, jadhal*
joyful (adj)	فرح، سار	*fariḥ, sārr*
joyfully (adv)	بسرور، بابتهاج	*bi surūr, bibtihāj*
joyless (adj)	مكتئب، حزين	*mukta'ib, ḥazīn*
joyous=joyful		
joyously=joyfully		
jubilant (adj)	مبتهج، متهلل	*mubtahij, mutahallil*
jubilantly (adv)	بابتهاج شديد	*bibtiḥāj shadīd*
jubilation (n)	ابتهاج شديد، مرح	*ibtihāj shadīd, maraḥ*
jubilee (n)	يوبيل	*yūbīl*
Judaism (n)	يهودية	*yahūdiyyah*
judge (n)	قاضي، حكم	*qāḍī, ḥakam*
judge (v)	حكم، قضى	*ḥakama, qaḍā*
judgement (n)	قضاء، حكم، رأي	*qaḍā', ḥukm, ra'y*
Judgement Day	يوم الحساب	*yaumul ḥisāb*
judicature (n)	نظام القضاء، قضاة	*niẓāmul qaḍā', quḍāt*
judicial (adj)	قضائي، محكمي	*qaḍā'ī, maḥkamī*
judiciary (n)	نظام قضائي	*niẓām qaḍā'ī*
judicious (adj)	حكيم، حازم	*ḥakīm, ḥāzim*
judo (n)	لعبة الجودو	*lu'batul jūdū*
jug (n)	إبريق، قارورة	*ibrīq, qārūrah*
jugful (adj)	ملء إبريق	*mil'u ibrīq*
juggernaut (n)	قوة ماحكة	*quwwah māḥikah*
juggle (v)	شعوذ، احتال	*sha'wadha, iḥtāla*
juggler (n)	مشعوذ، محتال	*musha'widh, muḥtāl*
jugular (adj)	وداجي	*widājī*
juice (n)	عصير، عصارة	*'aṣīr, 'uṣārah*
juicer (n)	عصارة	*'aṣṣārah*
juicy (adj)	كثير العصارة	*kathīrul 'uṣārah*

jukebox (n)	جكبكس	*jukbuks*
July (n)	يوليو، تموز	*yuliyū, tammūz*
jumble (v)	خلط، اختلط	*khallaṭa, ikhtalaṭa*
jumble (n)	خليط، خبطة	*khalīṭ, khabṭah*
jumbo (adj)	ضخم جدا	*ḍakhm jiddā*
jump (v)	وثب، نط، قفز	*wathaba, naṭṭa, qafaza*
jump (n)	وثبة، عقبة، ارتفاع مفاجئ	*wathbah, 'aqabah, irtifā' mufāji'*
jumper (n)	جوبية	*jūbiyyah*
jump-of (n)	انطلاق	*inṭilāq*
jumpy (adj)	قلق، عصبي	*qaliq, 'aṣabī*
junction (n)	اتصال، نقطة الاتصال	*ittiṣāl, nuqṭatul ittiṣāl*
juncture (n)	ظرف، وضع	*ẓarf, waḍ'*
June (n)	يونيو، حزيران	*yuniyū, ḥazīrān*
jungle (n)	غابة متلبدة، دغل	*ghābah mutalabbidah, daghal*
junior (adj)	أصغر سنًّا أو منــزلةً	*asgharu sinnan au manzilatan*
junior (n)	شخص أقل الأهمية	*shakhṣ aqallul ahammiyyah*
junk (n)	سلع بالية، ينك	*sila' bāliyah, yank*
junk (v)	طرح، نبذ	*ṭaraḥa, nabadha*
junket (n)	رحلة للمتعة	*riḥlah lil mut'ah*
Jupiter (n)	جوبيتر	*jūbītar*
juridical (adj)	قضائي، عدلي	*qaḍā'ī, 'adlī*
jurisdiction (n)	حق القضاء	*ḥaqqul qaḍā'*
jurisprudence (n)	قانون، تشريع، فقه	*qānūn, tashrī', fiqh*
jurisprudent (adj)	قاضي، محامي	*qāḍī, muḥāmī*
jurist (n)	قاضي، ماهر في القانون	*qāḍī, māhir fil qānūn*
juror (n)	عضو في هيئة المحلفين	*'uḍw fi hai'atil muḥallafin*
jury (n)	هيئة المحلفين	*hay'atul muḥallafin*

just (adj)	مقسط، عادل، مضبوط	*muqsiṭ, ‘ādil, maḍbūṭ*
just (adv)	تماماً، توًّا، مباشرةً	*tamāman, tawwan, mubāsharatan*
justice (n)	حق، عدل، قاضي	*ḥaqq, ‘adl, qāḍī*
Justice of the Peace	قاضي الصلح	*qāḍiṣ ṣulḥ*
justifiable (adj)	يبرر، يعذر	*yubarraru, yu‘dharu*
justification (n)	تبرئة، تبرير	*tabri’ah, tabrīr*
justified (adj)	مسوغ، معذور، مبرأ	*musawwagh, ma‘dhūr, mubarra’*
justify (v)	سوغ، برأ	*sawwagha, barra’a*
jute (n)	جوتة	*jūtah*
juvenile (n)	صبي، يافع، حدث	*ṣabiyy, yāfi‘, ḥadath*
juvenile (adj)	صبياني، أحداثي	*ṣibyānī, aḥdāthī*
juvenile court	محكمة الأحداث	*maḥkamatul aḥdāth*
juvenile delinquent	مجرم يافع	*mujrim yāfi‘*
juztapose (v)	جاور، وصل	*jāwara, waṣṣala*
juxtaposition (n)	تجاور، اتصال	*tajāwur, ittiṣāl*

K

kaleidoscope (n)	مشكال	*mishkāl*
kaleidoscopic (adj)	مشكالي	*mishkālī*
kangaroo (n)	كنغر	*kanghar*
kangaroo court	محكمة كنغرية	*maḥkamah kanghariyyah*
kaolin (kaoline) (n)	كاولين،صلصال صيني	*kāwlīn, ṣalṣāl ṣīnī*
karat=carat		
karate (n)	كاريت	*kārīt*
karma (n)	الكرما، قدر	*al karmā, qadar*
keel (n)	عارضة المركب	*‘āriḍatul markab*
keel (v)	انقلب، برد	*inqalaba, barada*
keen (adj)	شديد التوق، حاذق	*shadīdut tauq, ḥādhiq*

keen (v)	ندب، أعول	*nadaba, a'wala*
keep (v)	أخذ، حفظ، بقى	*akhadha, ḥafiẓa, baqā*
keep (n)	قوت، طعام	*qūt, ṭa'ām*
keep away	أبعد، منع	*ab'ada, mana'a*
keep back	منع، تجنب	*mana'a, tajannaba*
keep down	أقمع، ضبط	*aqma'a, ḍabaṭa*
keeper (n)	حارس، حافظ	*ḥāris, ḥāfiẓ*
keep in	كتم، حبس	*katama, ḥabasa*
keeping (n)	عناية، حفظ	*'ināyah, ḥifẓ*
keepsake (n)	هدية، تذكار	*hadiyyah, tidhkār*
keg (n)	كيغ، برميل صغير	*kaigh, barmīl ṣaghīr*
kelp (n)	نبتة البحر	*nabtatul baḥr*
ken (n)	مدى البصر	*madal baṣar*
ken (v)	عرف، علم	*'arafa, 'alima*
kennel (n)	وجار الكلب	*wijārul kalb*
kerb (n)	حاجز حجري	*ḥājiz ḥajarī*
kerchief (n)	وشاح، عصابة	*wishāḥ, 'iṣābah*
kernel (n)	نواة، لباب الشيء	*nawāt, lubābush shay'*
kerosene (kerosine)	كيروسين	*kīrūsīn*
ketchup (n)	كتشاب	*katshāb*
kettle (n)	ملاية الشاي	*mallāyatush shāy*
kettledrum (n)	نقارية	*naqqāriyah*
key (n)	مفتاح، مسمار خابوري	*miftāḥ, mismār khābūrī*
key (adj)	رئيسي، أساسي	*ra'īsī, asāsī*
keyboard (n)	لوحة المفاتيح في كمبيوتر	*lauḥatul mafātīḥ fi kambiutar*
keyhole (n)	ثقب المفتاح	*thaqbul miftāḥ*
keynote (n)	فكرة أساسية	*fikrah asāsiyyah*
keystone (n)	حجر العقد، مرتكز	*ḥajarul 'aqd, murtakiz*
khaki (n/adj)	كاكي	*kākī*

kick (v)	رفس، ضرب بالرجل	*rafasa, ḍaraba bir rijl*
kick (n)	رفسة، ابتهاج	*rafsah, ibtihāj*
kick-off (n)	رفسة أولى	*rafsah ūlā*
kid (n)	طفل، ولد صغير، صدي	*ṭifl, walad ṣaghīr, ṣady*
kid (v)	خدع	*khada'a*
kidnap (v)	خطف، اختطف	*khaṭafa, ikhtaṭafa*
kidnapping (n)	خطف الأشخاص	*khaṭful ashkhāṣ*
kidney (n)	كلية	*kulyah*
kidney bean	لوبياء	*lūbyā'*
kill (v)	قتل، ذبح، جزر	*qatala, dhabaḥa, jazara*
kill (n)	قتل، قتيل	*qatl, qatīl*
killer (n)	قاتل، سفاك	*qātil, saffāk*
killing (n)	قتل، جزر	*qatl, jazr*
killing (adj)	قاتل، مؤثر	*qātil, mu'aththir*
killjoy (n)	مفسد البهجة	*mufsidul bahjah*
kiln (n)	أتون	*attūn*
kilogram (n)	كيلوغرام	*kīlugharām*
kilometre (n)	كيلومتر	*kīlumitr*
kilowatt (n)	كيلوواط	*kīluwāṭ*
kilt (n)	كلتية	*kiltiyah*
kimono (n)	الكيمون	*alkaimūn*
kin (n)	قريب، نسيب	*qarīb, nasīb*
kind (n)	قسم، نوع	*qism, nau'*
kind (adj)	كريم، حنون	*karīm, ḥanūn*
kindergarten (n)	روضة الأطفال	*rauḍatul aṭfāl*
kind-hearted (adj)	رقيق القلب، حنون	*raqīqul qalb, ḥanūn*
kindle (v)	أثار، هيج، اضطرم	*athāra, hayyaja, iḍṭarama*
kindling (n)	ضرم، إضرام	*ḍaram, iḍrām*
kindly (adj)	عطوف، رقيق القلب	*'aṭūf, raqīqul qalb*
kindly (adv)	بكرم، بعطف	*bi karam, bi 'aṭf*

kindness (n)	كرم، فضل، لطف	*karam, faḍl, luṭf*
kindred (n)	أقرباء، أنسباء	*aqribā', ansibā'*
kindred (adj)	شقيق، مماثل	*shaqīq, mumāthil*
kinetic (adj)	حركي	*ḥarakī*
kinetic energy	طاقة حركية	*ṭāqah ḥarakiyyah*
king (n)	ملك، مليك	*malik, malīk*
kingdom (n)	ملك، مملكة	*mulk, mamlakah*
kingfisher (n)	سماك، رفراف	*sammāk, rafrāf*
kingly (adj)	ملوكي، ملكي	*mulūkī, malakī*
kingpin (n)	مقدم	*muqaddam*
kingship (n)	ملكية	*malakiyyah*
king-size (adj)	ضخم جدا	*ḍakhm jiddā*
kink (n)	فتلة في شعر أو حبل	*fatlah fī sha'r au ḥabl*
kink (v)	فتل، انفتل	*fatala, infatala*
kinship (n)	قرابة، نسب	*qarābah, nasab*
kinsman (n)	قريب، عزيز	*qarīb, 'azīz*
kinswoman (n)	قريبة، نسيبة	*qarībah, nasībah*
kiosk (n)	كشك	*kushk*
kiss (v)	قبل، لثم	*qabbala, lathama*
kiss (n)	قبلة، لثمة	*qublah, lathmah*
kit (n)	أمتعة، ملابس	*amti'ah, malābis*
kitchen (n)	مطبخ، مطهى	*maṭbakh, maṭhā*
kitchen cabinet	وزارة المطبخ	*wizāratul maṭbakh*
kitchenette (n)	مطبخ صغير	*maṭbakh ṣaghīr*
kitchen garden	بستان الخضر	*bustānul khuḍar*
kitchenware (n)	أواني المطبخ	*awānil maṭbakh*
kite (n)	طائرة ورقية، حدأة	*ṭā'irah waraqiyyah, ḥada'ah*
kith (n)	أقرباء، أنسباء	*aqribā', ansibā'*
kitten (n)	هريرة، قطيطة	*hurairah, quṭaiṭah*

kittenish (adj)	لعوب، جذل	*la'ūb, jadhil*
kittens (n)	قلق	*qalaq*
kitty (n)	هرة صغيرة، ولد صغير	*hirrah ṣaghīrah, walad ṣaghīr*
kleptomania (n)	دغر، هوس شديد للسرقة	*daghar, hawas shadīd lis sariqah*
knack (n)	براعة، مهارة	*barā'ah, mahārah*
knapsack (n)	حقيبة الظهر	*ḥaqībatuẓ ẓahr*
knave (n)	وضيع، خبيث، خائن	*waḍī', khabīth, khā'in*
knead (v)	دلك، جبل	*dalaka, jabala*
knee (n/v)	ركبة، ضرب بركبة	*rukbah, ḍaraba bi rukbah*
kneecap (n)	رضفة	*raḍfah*
knee-deep (adj)	مغمور إلى ركبتين، منهمك جدا	*maghmūr ilā rukbatain, munhamik jiddā*
knee-high (adj)	مرتفع إلى ركبتين	*murtafi' ilā rukbatain*
knee-jerk (n)	نبرة الركبة	*nabratur rukbah*
knee-length (adj)	بالغ الركبتين	*bālighur rukbatain*
kneel (v)	ركع، خضع	*raka'a, khaḍa'a*
knell (n)	قرعة الناقوس عند الموت	*qar'atun nāqūs 'indal maut*
knickers (n)	بنطلون قصير، نكرز	*banṭlūn qaṣīr, nakraz*
knick-knack (n)	حلية صغيرة	*ḥilyah ṣaghīrah*
knife (n/v)	سكين، قطع بسكين	*sikkīn, qaṭa'a bi sikkīn*
knife-edge (n)	حد السكين	*ḥaddus sikkīn*
knight (n)	فارس	*fāris*
knighthood (n)	فروسية، رتبة الفارس	*furūsiyyah, rutbatul fāris*
knightly (adj)	فرساني	*fursānī*
knit (v)	شابك، حبك، عقد	*shābaka, ḥabaka, 'aqqada*
knit (n)	ملابس محبوكة	*malābis maḥbūkah*
knitter (n)	حابك	*ḥābik*

knitting (n)	حبك، حياكة	*ḥabk, ḥiyākah*
knitwear (n)	ملابس محبوكة	*malābis maḥbūkah*
knob (n)	مسكة باب، عقدة	*maskatu bāb, ʻuqdah*
knock (v)	قرع، دق، ضرب	*qaraʻa, daqqa, ḍaraba*
knock (n)	قرعة، ضربة شديدة	*qarʻah, ḍarbah shadīdah*
knockabout (adj)	صخاب، عنيف	*ṣakhkhāb, ʻanīf*
knock-down (adj)	صارع، صارعة	*ṣāriʻ, ṣāriʻah*
knocker (n)	مقرعة الباب	*miqraʻatul bāb*
knock-kneed (adj)	أصك، أصدف	*aṣakk, aṣdaf*
knockout (n)	ضربة صارعة، شيء جذاب	*ḍarbah ṣāriʻah, shay' jadhdhāb*
knoll (n)	تل صغير ومدور	*tall ṣaghīr wa mudawwar*
knot (n)	عقدة، عجرة، مجموعة	*ʻuqdah, ʻujrah, majmūʻah*
knot (v)	عقد، تعقد	*ʻaqada, taʻaqqada*
knotty (adj)	معقد، معجرم	*muʻaqqad, muʻajram*
know (v)	علم، عرف، أدرك	*ʻalima, ʻarafa, adraka*
know-all (adj)	متعارف	*mutaʻārif*
know-how (n)	مهارة، براعة	*mahārah, barāʻah*
knowing (adj)	متعمد، عالم	*mutaʻammid, ʻālim*
knowingly (adv)	متعمداً، قصداً	*mutaʻammidan, qaṣdan*
knowledge (n)	علم، معرفة	*ʻilm, maʻrifah*
knowledgeable (adj)	ذو خبرة، كثير المعرفة	*dhū khibrah, kathīrul maʻrifah*
known (adj)	شهير، معروف	*shahīr, maʻrūf*
knuckle (n)	برجمة	*burjumah*
knuckleduster (n)	برجمية	*burjumiyah*
krona (n)	كرونا	*kurūnā*
Kurdish (adj/n)	كردي، كردية	*kurdī, kurdiyyah*

L

lable (n)	رقعة، لقب، طابع	*ruq'ah, laqab, ṭābi'*
label (v)	ألصق طابعاً	*alṣaqa ṭābi'an*
labia (n)	شفر،شفة	*shafr, shafah*
labial (adj)	شفوي، شفهي	*shafawī, shafahī*
laboratory (n)	مختبر، معمل	*mukhtabar, ma'mal*
laborious (adj)	كاد، شاق	*kādd, shāqq*
labour (labor) (n)	عمل، كد، طبقة العمال	*'amal, kadd, ṭabaqatul 'ummāl*
labour (labor) (v)	عمل، كد، كدح	*'amila, kadda, kadaḥa*
laboured (labored)	غير طبيعي	*ghair ṭabī'ī*
labourer (laborer) (n)	عامل، كادح	*'āmil, kādiḥ*
labouring (n)	كدح، جهد	*kadḥ, juhd*
labyrinth (n)	ورطة، مليء بالعقد	*warṭah, malī' bil 'uqad*
labyrinthine (adj)	معقد، مليء بالعقد	*mu'aqqad, malī' bil 'uqad*
lace (n/v)	رباط، شد برباط	*ribāṭ, shadda bi ribāṭ*
lacerate (v)	جرح، مزق	*jaraḥa, mazzaqa*
laceration (n)	جرح، تمزق	*jurḥ, tamazzuq*
lack (v)	أعوز، فقد	*a'waza, faqada*
lack (n)	فقدان، نقص، عوز	*fuqdān, naqṣ, 'awaz*
lackadaisical (adj)	واهن، ضعيف	*wāhin, ḍa'īf*
lackey (n)	مبزز، خادم	*mubazzaz, khādim*
lackluster (n)	باهت	*bāhit*
laconic (adj)	موجز، مختصر	*mūjaz, mukhtaṣar*
lacquer (n/v)	لك، طلى بلك	*lak, ṭalā bi lak*
lacrosse (n)	لعبة اللكروس	*lu'batul lakrūs*
lactic acid (n)	حامض لبني	*ḥāmiḍ labanī*
lactose (n)	سكر اللبن، لكتوز	*sukkarul laban, laktūz*
lacy (adj)	شريطي	*sharīṭī*

lad (n)	غلام، فتى، صبي	*ghulām, fatan, ṣaby*
ladder (n)	سلم، مرقاة	*sullam, mirqāt*
laddie (n)	ولد صغير، صبي	*walad ṣaghīr, ṣaby*
laden (adj)	محمل، موسوق	*muḥammal, mausūq*
ladle (v/n)	غرف، مغرفة	*gharafa, mighrafah*
lady (n)	سيدة، امرأة	*sayyidah, imra'ah*
ladybird (n)	دعسوقة	*du'sūqah*
lady-in-waiting (n)	وصيفة الملكة	*waṣīfatul malikah*
lady-killer (n)	فاتن النساء	*fātinun nisā'*
ladylike (adj)	ملائم للسيدة	*mulā'im lis sayyidah*
ladylove (n)	حبيبة، خليلة	*ḥabībah, khalīlah*
ladyship (n)	مقام السيدة	*maqāmus sayyidah*
lag (v)	تباطأ، غلف	*tabāṭa'a, ghallafa*
lag (n)	فترة، فاصلة	*fatrah, fāṣilah*
lager (n)	جعة، بيرة	*ji'ah, bīrah*
laggard (adj)	متمهل، متلكئ	*mutamahhil, mutalakki'*
lagoon (n)	لاغون، مستنقع	*lāghūn, mustanqa'*
lair (n)	مخبأ، وجار	*makhba', wijār*
laissez-faire (n)	سياسة عدم التدخل	*siyāsatu 'adamit tadakhkhul*
lake (n)	بحيرة، بركة	*buḥairah, birkah*
lamb (n)	حمل، عزيز	*ḥamal, 'azīz*
lambaste (v)	لام، نقد	*lāma, naqada*
lame (adj)	أعرج، واهن	*a'raj, wāhin*
lame duck	بطة عرجاء	*baṭṭah 'arjā'*
lamely (adv)	بعرج، بعجز	*bi 'araj, bi 'ajz*
lameness (n)	عرج، ركاكة	*'araj, rakākah*
lament (v)	ندب، ناح على	*nadaba, nāḥa 'alā*
lament (n)	نياحة، مرثاة	*niyāḥah, marthāt*
lamentation (n)	مرثاة، تفجع	*marthāt, tafajju'*

lamented (adj)	منتحب عليه	*muntaḥab ʻalaih*
laminate (v)	صفح، تصفح	*ṣaffaḥa, taṣaffaḥa*
laminated (adj)	مصفح	*muṣaffaḥ*
lamination (n)	تصفيح، تصفح	*taṣfīḥ, taṣaffuḥ*
lamp (n)	مصباح، مصباح كهربائي	*miṣbāḥ, miṣbāḥ kahrabāʼī*
lamplight (n)	نور المصباح	*nūrul miṣbāḥ*
lampoon (v/n)	هجا، هجاء	*hajā, hijāʼ*
lance (n/v)	رمح، طعن بالرمح	*rumḥ, ṭaʻana bir rumḥ*
lance-corporal (n)	وكيل عريف	*wakīl ʻarīf*
lancet (n)	مفصد، مشرط	*mifṣad, mishraṭ*
land (n)	أرض، قطعة أرض، بر	*arḍ, qiṭʻatu arḍ, barr*
land (v)	حط، هبط، رسا	*ḥaṭṭa, habaṭa, rasā*
landed (adj)	مالك أرض	*māliku arḍ*
landfall (n)	بدو اليابسة للمسافر	*buduwwul yābisah lil musāfir*
landholding (n)	ملك الأرض	*milkul arḍ*
landing (n)	هبوط، نزول إلى اليابسة	*hubūṭ, nuzūl ilal yābisah*
landing-craft (n)	صندل الإنزال	*ṣandalul inzāl*
landing-gear (n)	مهبطة	*mihbaṭah*
landlady (n)	مالكة الأرض	*mālikatul arḍ*
landlocked (adj)	مكتنف بالأرض	*muktanaf bil arḍ*
landlord (n)	مالك الأرض	*mālikul arḍ*
landmark (n)	معلم	*maʻlam*
landowner (n)	صاحب الأرض	*ṣāḥibul arḍ*
landscape (n)	مناظر طبيعية	*manāẓir ṭabīʻiyyah*
landscape (v)	زين، حسن	*zayyana, ḥassana*
landscape architect	مهندس المناظر	*muhandisul manāẓir*
land slide (n)	انهيال، أغلبية	*inhiyāl, aghlabiyyah*

landward (adj/adv)	واقع نحو اليابسة، نحو اليابسة	*wāqi' naḥwal yābisah, naḥwal yābisah*
lane (n)	زقاق، درب	*zuqāq, darb*
language (n)	لغة، أسلوب التكلم	*lughah, uslūbut takallum*
languid (adj)	بطيء، متكاسل	*baṭī', mutakāsil*
languidly (adv)	ببطوء، بتكاسل	*bi buṭū', bi takāsul*
languish (v)	فتر، ضعف	*fatura, ḍa'ufa*
languor (n)	ضعف، ضنىً، تراخٍ	*ḍa'f, ḍanan, tarākhin*
languorous (adj)	ضعيف، كسل، واهن	*ḍa'īf, kasil, wāhin*
languorously (adv)	بوهن، بترهل	*bi wahan, bi tarahhul*
lank (adj)	غير جعد	*ghair ja'd*
lantern (n)	مصباح، مشكاة، فانوس	*miṣbāḥ, mishkāt, fānūs*
lanyard (n)	حبل عنقي	*ḥabl 'unuqī*
lap (n)	حضن، مهد، ذيل، دورة مفردة	*ḥiḍn, mahd, dhail, daurah mufradah*
lap (v)	راكب، لعق، طوى	*rākaba, la'iqa, ṭawā*
lap-dog (n)	كلب الحضن	*kalbul ḥiḍn*
lapel (n)	طية صدر السترة	*ṭayyatu ṣadris sitrah*
lapidary (adj)	بالغ الأناقة، جوهري	*bālighul anāqah, jauharī*
lapse (v)	انقضى، انحدر، زال	*inqaḍā, inḥadara, zāla*
lapse (n)	زلة، انحطاط، فترة	*zallah, inḥiṭāṭ, fatrah*
larceny (n)	سرقة	*sariqah*
lard (n/v)	شحم الخنزير، شحم	*shaḥmul khinzīr, shaḥḥama*
larder (n)	موضع لحفظ المأكولات	*mauḍi' li ḥifẓil ma'kūlāt*
large (adj)	كبير، عظيم، عريض	*kabīr, 'aẓīm, 'arīḍ*
largely (adv)	بإسهاب، باتساع	*bi ishāb, bittisā'*
largeness (n)	إسهاب، سعة	*ishāb, sa'ah*
largess (largesse) (n)	هبة، عطية، سماحة	*hibah, 'aṭiyyah, samāḥah*
lark (n)	قنبرة، مزاح	*qumburah, muzāḥ*

lark (v)	مرح، مزح	*maraḥa, mazaḥa*
larva (n)	يرقة، دودة صغيرة	*yarqah, dūdah ṣaghīrah*
larval (adj)	يرقي	*yaraqī*
laryngitis (n)	التهاب الحنجرة	*iltihābul ḥanjarah*
larynx (n)	حنجرة	*ḥanjarah*
lascivious (adj)	شهواني، غليم	*shahwānī, ghillīm*
lasciviously (adv)	بشهوة	*bi shahwah*
lasciviousness (n)	شهوة، غلمة	*shahwah, ghulmah*
laser (n)	لازر	*lāzar*
lash (n)	ضربة، سوط، جلدة	*ḍarbah, sauṭ, jaldah*
lash (v)	ضرب بالسوط	*ḍaraba bis sauṭ*
lashing (n)	ضربة عنيفة، جلدة	*ḍarbah 'anīfah, jaldah*
lass (lassie) (n)	صبية، فتاة	*ṣabiyyah, fatāt*
lassitude (n)	تعب شديد	*ta'ab shadīd*
lasso (n/v)	وهق، وهق	*wahq, wahaqa*
last (v)	استمر، تحمل، بقى	*istamarra, taḥammala, baqā*
last (adj)	سابق، أخير، قاطع	*sābiq, akhīr, qāṭi'*
last (adv)	أخيراً، في النهاية	*akhīran, fin nihāyah*
last (n)	آخر، نهاية، ختام	*ākhir, nihāyah, khitām*
lasting (adj)	دائم، باقٍ	*dā'im, bāqin*
lastly (adv)	في النهاية، في الختام	*fin nihāyah, fil khitām*
latch (n/v)	مزلاج، ثبت بمزلاج	*mizlāj, thabbata bi mizlāj*
late (adj)	متأخر، راحل، حديث	*muta'khkhir, rāḥil, ḥadīth*
late (adv)	متأخراً، بتأخير	*muta'khkhiran, bi ta'khīr*
lately (adv)	أخيراً، حديثاً	*akhīran, ḥadīthan*
latent (adj)	كامن، خفي	*kāmin, khafiyy*
lateral (adj)	جانبي، جنبي	*jānibī, jambī*
latex (n)	لثى، ماء الشجر	*lathā, mā'ush shajar*
lathe (n)	مخرطة الخشب	*mikhraṭatul khashab*

lather (n/v)	زبد، زبد	*zabad, zabbada*
Latin (n/adj)	لاتيني، لغة لاتينية	*lātīnī, lughah lātīniyyah*
latitude (n)	خط العرض	*khaṭṭul 'arḍ*
latrine (n)	مرحاض	*mirḥāḍ*
latter (adj)	آخر، ثاني، أخير	*ākhir, thānī, akhīr*
latter-day (adj)	عصري	*'aṣrī*
latterly (adv)	حديثاً، حالياً	*ḥadīthan, ḥāliyan*
lattice (n)	شعرية	*sha'riyyah*
latticed (adj)	مزود بشعرية	*muzawwad bi sha'riyyah*
lattice-work (n)	شعرية	*sha'riyyah*
laud (v)	حمد، سبح	*ḥamida, sabbaḥa*
laudable (adj)	جدير بالثناء	*jadīr bith thanā'*
laudatory (adj)	مدحي، ثنائي	*madḥī, thanā'ī*
laugh (v)	ضحك، هزأ	*ḍaḥika, haza'a*
laugh (n)	ضحك، ضحكة	*ḍaḥk, ḍaḥkah*
laughable (adj)	مضحك، سخري	*muḍḥik, sukhrī*
laughing-gas (n)	غاز مضحك	*ghāz muḍaḥḥik*
laughing-stock (n)	أضحوكة	*uḍḥūkah*
laughter (n)	ضحك، قهقهة	*ḍaḥik, qahqahah*
launch (v)	استهل، روج، عوم	*istahalla, rawwaja, 'awwama*
launch (n)	زورق بخاري	*zauraq bukhārī*
launcher (n)	قاذفة الرمانات	*qādhifatur rummānāt*
launch pad (n)	منصة الإطلاق	*minaṣṣatul iṭlāq*
launder (v)	غسل وكوى الملابس	*ghasala wa kawal malābis*
launderette (n)	مغسلة	*maghsalah*
laundry (n)	غسل الملابس	*ghaslul malābis*
laureate (n)	شاعر البلاط الملكي	*shā'irul balāṭ al malakī*
laurel (n)	شجر الغار، غار	*shajarul ghār, ghār*
laurels (n)	مجد، شهرة	*majd, shuhrah*

lava (n)	حمم، سائل بركاني	*ḥumam, sā'il burkānī*
lavatory (adj)	مغسلة، مرحاض	*maghsalah, mirḥāḍ*
lavish (v)	أسرف، أنفق بسخاء	*asrafa, anfaqa bi sakhā'*
lavish (adj)	سخي، مسرف	*sakhī, musrif*
lavishly (adv)	بسخاء، بإسراف	*bi sakhā', bi isrāf*
law (n)	شرع، قانون، فقه	*shara', qānūn, fiqh*
law-abiding (adj)	مطيع للقانون	*muṭī' lii qānūn*
lawbreaker (n)	خارق للقانون	*khāriq lil qānūn*
lawful (adj)	حلال، قانوني، شرعي	*ḥalāl, qanūnī, shar'ī*
lawless (adj)	غير مطيع للقانون، عاصٍ	*ghair muṭī' lil qānūn, 'āṣin*
lawlessness (n)	عصيان، خرق القانون	*'iṣyān, kharqul qānūn*
lawmaker (n)	مشرع، شارع	*musharri', shāri'*
lawn (n)	مرجة، مخضرة	*marjah, makhḍarah*
lawn mower	جزارة العشب	*jazzāratul 'ushb*
lawn tennis	تنس المخضرة	*tanisul makhḍarah*
lawsuit (n)	دعوى، قضية	*da'wā, qaḍiyyah*
lawyer (n)	محامٍ، متشرع	*muḥāmin, mutasharri'*
lax (adj)	رخو، لين	*rikhw, layyin*
laxative (adj)	مسهل، ملين	*mushil, mulayyin*
laxity (n)	لين، رخاوة	*līn, rakhāwah*
lay (v)	وضع، بسط، نظم	*waḍa'a, basaṭa, naẓẓama*
lay (adj)	عادي، غير بارع	*'ādī, ghair bāri'*
lay (n)	قصة شعرية	*qiṣṣah shi'riyyah*
lay aside	ترك، أهمل	*taraka, ahmala*
lay down	خطط، وضع، أسس	*khaṭṭaṭa, waḍa'a, assasa*
layer (n)	طبقة، صف	*ṭabaqah, ṣaff*
layette (n)	كسوة المولود	*kuswatul maulūd*
lay in	ادخر للمستقبل	*iddakhara lil mustaqbal*

layman (n)	عادي، علماني	*'ādī, 'almānī*
lay off	ودع، تجنب، ترك	*wada'a, tajannaba, taraka*
lay-off (n)	تسريح موقت	*tasrīḥ muwaqqat*
lay on	أعد، زود	*a'adda, zawwada*
lay out	صرع، صرف، كد	*ṣara'a, ṣarafa, kadda*
layout (n)	نسق، تخطيط	*nasaq, takhṭīṭ*
lay over	أجل، أقام	*ajjala, aqāma*
lay up	أقعد، ادخر	*aq'ada, iddakhara*
laze (v)	تكاسل، تباطأ	*takāsala, tabāṭa'a*
tazily (adv)	بكسل، بتوانٍ	*bi kasal, bi tawānin*
laziness (n)	كسل، تراخٍ	*kasal, tarākhin*
lazy (adj)	كسول، متكاسل	*kasūl, mutakāsil*
lazybones (n)	كسول، متواني	*kasūl, mutawānī*
leach (v)	رشح، روق	*rashshaḥa, rawwaqa*
lead (v)	قاد، هدى، تقدم	*qāda, hadā, taqaddama*
lead (n)	رصاص، مركز أمامي، ورقة أولى	*raṣāṣ, markaz amāmī, waraqah ūlā*
lead astray	أضل، توه	*aḍalla, tawwaha*
leaden (adj)	بطيء، مكتئب	*baṭī', mukta'ib*
leader (n)	قائد، زعيم	*qā'id, za'īm*
leadership (n)	قيادة، زعامة	*qiyādah, zi'āmah*
leading (adj)	مقدم، رئيسي	*muqaddam, ra'īsī*
leading article	افتتاحية	*iftitāḥiyyah*
leading lady	ممثلة أولى	*mumaththilah ūlā*
leading man	ممثل أول	*mumaththil awwal*
leading question	سؤال إيحائي	*su'āl īḥā'ī*
leaf (n)	ورقة، صحيفة رقيقة	*waraqah, ṣaḥīfah raqīqah*
leaf (v)	قلب الصفحات	*qallabaṣ ṣafḥāt*
leafless (adj)	بغير أوراق	*bighairi aurāq*

leaflet (n)	وريقة	*wuraiqah*
leafy (adj)	ذو أوراق	*dhū aurāq*
league (n)	عصبة، فئة، فرسخ	*'uṣbah, fi'ah, farsakh*
leak (v)	نضح، رشح، تسرب	*naḍaḥa, rashshaḥa, tasarraba*
leak (n)	ثقب، ارتشاح	*thuqb, irtishāḥ*
leakage (n)	نضح، ارتشاح، تسرب	*naḍḥ, irtishāḥ, tasarrub*
leaky (adj)	واكف، راشح	*wākif, rāshiḥ*
lean (v)	انحنى، مال، اتكأ	*inḥanā, māla, ittaka'a*
lean (adj)	نحيف، هزيل، هبر	*naḥīf, hazīl, habr*
lean (n)	لحم هبر	*laḥmu habr*
leaning (n)	ميلان، نزعة	*mayalān, naz'ah*
leanness (n)	هزال، نحافة	*huzāl, naḥāfah*
lean-to (n)	مبنى منحدر السطح	*mabnā munḥadirus saṭḥ*
leap (v)	قفز، وثب	*qafaza, wathaba*
leap (n)	وثبة، قفزة	*wathbah, qafzah*
leap-frog (n)	قفزية	*qafziyyah*
leap year	سنة كبيسة	*sanah kabīsah*
learn (v)	حفظ، علم، عرف	*ḥafiẓa, 'alima, 'arafa*
learned (adj)	عالم، متبحر في العلم	*'ālim, mutabaḥḥir fil 'ilm*
learner (n)	طالب، تلميذ	*ṭālib, tilmīdh*
learning (n)	علم، معرفة، تعلم	*'ilm, ma'rifah, ta'allum*
lease (v)	أجر، استأجر	*ajjara, ista'jara*
lease (n)	إيجار، عقد الإيجار	*ījār, 'aqdul ījār*
leasehold (n)	أرض مستأجرة	*arḍ musta'jarah*
leaseholder (n)	مستأجر	*musta'jir*
leash (n)	رسن	*rasan*
least (n/adj)	أقل، أدنى	*aqall, adnā*
least (adv)	أقل ما يكون	*aqall mā yakūn*
leather (n)	جلد مدبوغ	*jild madbūgh*

leatherette (n)	قماش جلدي	*qumāsh jildī*
leathery (adj)	متين كالجلد	*matīn kal jild*
leave (v)	ترك، هاجر، غادر	*taraka, hājara, ghādara*
leave (n)	إذن، إجازة	*idhn, ijāzah*
leave behind	خلف وراءه	*khallafa warā'ahu*
leaved (adj)	ذو أوراق	*dhū aurāq*
leaven (n)	خميرة	*khamīrah*
leave off	كف، منع	*kaffa, mana'a*
leave out	أسقط، أهمل	*asqaṭa, ahmala*
Lebnan (n)	لبنان	*libnān*
Lebnese (adj/n)	لبناني، لغة لبنانية	*libnānī, lughah libnāniyyah*
lecher (n)	منغمس في الشهوات	*munghamis fish shahawāt*
lecherous (adj)	داعر، شهواني	*dā'ir, shahwānī*
lechery (n)	انغماس في الشهوات	*inghimās fish shahawāt*
lectern (n)	مقرأ، منضدة	*miqra', minḍadah*
lecture (n/v)	محاضرة، حاضر	*muḥāḍarah, ḥāḍara*
lecturer (n)	محاضر، مدرس	*muḥāḍir, mudarris*
lecturership (n)	منصب المحاضر	*manṣabul muḥāḍir*
ledger (n)	دفتر الحسابات	*daftarul ḥisābāt*
lee (n)	ملجأ، حمى	*malja', ḥiman*
leech (n)	دودوة علق، علقة	*dūdatu 'alaq, 'alaqah*
leek (n)	كراث	*kurāth*
leer (n)	نظرة شزراء	*naẓrah shazrā'*
leer (v)	نظر شزراً	*naẓara shazaran*
leery (adj)	ماكر، خادع، حذر	*mākir, khādi', ḥadhir*
leese (n)	تفل، راسب	*tufl, rāsib*
leeward (adj/adv)	متجه نحو الريح، نحو الريح	*muttajih naḥwar rīḥ, naḥwar rīḥ*
leeway (n)	مهلة	*muhlah*

left (n)	يسار، جهة يسرى	*yasār, jihah yusrā*
left (adj)	أيسر، يسرى	*aysar, yusrā*
left-hand (adj)	عامل بيد يسرى	*'āmil bi yad yusrā*
leftism (n)	يسارية	*yasāriyyah*
leftist (n)	يساري	*yasārī*
leftovers (n)	بقايا الطعام	*baqāyaṭ ṭa'ām*
left wing	جناح متطرف	*janāḥ mutaṭarrif*
left winger	عضو في الجناح المتطرف	*'uḍw fil janāḥ al mutaṭarrif*
leg (n)	رجل، قائمة	*rijl, qā'imah*
leg (v)	ركض، دفع	*rakaḍa, dafa'a*
legacy (n)	تراث، ميراث	*turāth, mīrāth*
legal (adj)	قانوني، شرعي	*qānūnī, shar'ī*
legality (n)	قانونية، صحة	*qānūniyyah, ṣiḥḥah*
legalization,-isation	تشريع، قانون	*tashrī', qānūn*
legalize,-ise (v)	أجاز، شرع	*ajāza, sharra'a*
legally (adv)	قانوناً، شرعاً	*qānūnan, shar'an*
legal tender	عملة قانونية	*'umlah qānūniyyah*
legate (n)	ممثل بابا الرسمي	*mumaththilu bābā ar rasmī*
legation (n)	وفد، مندوب	*wafd, mandūb*
legend (n)	أسطورة، قصة، خرافة	*usṭūrah, qiṣṣah, khurāfah*
legendary (adj)	خرافي، أسطوري	*khurāfī, usṭūrī*
leggings (n)	طماق	*ṭimāq*
leggy (adj)	طويل الساقين	*ṭawīlus sāqain*
legibility (n)	وضاحة، صراحة، جلاء	*waḍāḥah, ṣarāḥah, jalā'*
legible (adj)	جلي، صريح، مقروء	*jalī, ṣarīḥ, maqrū'*
legibly (adv)	بطريق واضح	*bi ṭarīq wāḍiḥ*
legion (n)	حشد، فيلق، ازدحام	*ḥashd, failaq, izdiḥām*

legionary (adj)	فيلقي	*failaqī*
legislate (v)	سن قانوناً، شرع	*sanna qānūnan, sharra'a*
legislation (n)	تشريع، سن القوانين	*tashrī', sannul qawānīn*
legislative (adj)	تشريعي	*tashrī'ī*
legislative assembly	جمعية تشريعية	*jam'iyyah tashrī'iyyah*
legislator (n)	شارع، مشرع	*shāri', musharri'*
legislature (n)	هيئة تشريعية	*hai'ah tashrī'iyyah*
legitimacy (n)	شرعية، قانونية	*shar'iyyah, qānūniyyah*
legitimate (adj)	قانوني، شرعي، حلال	*qānūnī, shar'ī, ḥalāl*
legitimately (adv)	قانوناً، شرعاً	*qānūnan, shar'an*
legitimize,-ise (v)	أجاز، حلل	*ajāza, ḥallala*
leisure (n)	وقت الفراغ، عطلة	*waqtul farāgh, 'uṭlah*
leisured (adj)	فارغ، مرفه	*fārigh, muraffah*
leisurely (adv)	على مهل، بغير عجل	*'alā mahal, bighairi 'ajal*
lemming (n)	لاموس	*lāmūs*
lemon (n)	ليمون، شجرة الليمون	*laimūn, shajaratul laimūn*
lemonade (n)	ليموناضة، عصير الليمون	*laimūnāḍah, 'aṣīrul laimūn*
lemony (adj)	ليموني	*laimūnī*
lemur (n)	ليمور، هوبر	*laimūr, haubar*
lend (v)	أقرض، أعار	*aqraḍa, a'āra*
lender (n)	مقرض، معير	*muqriḍ, mu'īr*
lending (n)	إعارة، إقراض	*i'ārah, iqrāḍ*
length (n)	طول، امتداد	*ṭūl, imtidād*
lengthen (n)	طول، مد	*ṭawwala, madda*
lengthways (adv)	طولاً، بالطول	*ṭūlan, biṭ ṭūl*
lengthwise (adv)	بالطول	*biṭ ṭūl*
lengthy (adj)	طويل، مفصل	*ṭawīl, mufaṣṣal*
leniency (n)	رفق، لين	*rifq, līn*

lenient (adj)	لين، رفيق	*layyin, rafīq*
leniently (adv)	برفق، بلين	*bi rifq, bi līn*
lens (n)	عدسة، عدسة العين	*'adasah, 'adasatul 'ain*
lentil (n)	حب العدس، نبات العدس	*ḥabbul 'adas, nabātul 'adas*
Leo (n)	برج الأسد	*burjul asad*
leonine (adj)	أسدي	*asadī*
leopard (n)	نمر	*namir*
leotard (n)	ثوب الراقصة	*thabur rāqiṣah*
leper (n)	مصاب بالجزام	*muṣāb bil juzām*
leprosy (n)	جزام	*juzām*
lesbian (n/adj)	مساحقة، سحاقي	*musāḥiqah, siḥāqī*
lesbianism (n)	مساحقة، سحاق	*musāḥaqah, siḥāq*
lesion (n)	أذى	*adhan*
less (adj)	أقل، أدنى	*aqall, adnā*
less (adv)	بدرجة أقل	*bi darajatin aqall*
lessee (n)	مستأجر، مؤاجر	*musta'jir, mu'ājir*
lessen (v)	أنقص، قل	*anqaṣa, qalla*
lesser (adj)	أقل، أهون	*aqall, ahwan*
lesson (n)	درس، عبرة	*dars, 'ibrah*
lessor (n)	مؤجر	*mu'ajjir*
lest (conj)	لئلا، مخافة أن	*li'allā, makhāfatan an*
let (v)	ترك، ودع، سمح	*taraka, wada'a, samaḥa*
let (n)	تأجير، عائق	*ta'jīr, 'ā'iq*
let-down (n)	خيبة	*khaibah*
lethal (adj)	مهلك، مميت	*muhlik, mumīt*
lethally (adv)	بطريق مهلك	*bi ṭarīq muhlik*
lethargic (adj)	سباتي، بليد، نعسان	*subātī, balīd, na'sān*
lethargy (n)	سبات، نعاس	*subāt, nu'ās*
letter (n)	حرف، خطاب، رسالة	*ḥarf, khiṭāb, risālah*

letter-box (n)	صندوق البريد	*ṣundūqul barīd*
letterhead (n)	رأسية الورقة	*ra'siyyatul waraqah*
lettering (n)	كتابة الحروف	*kitābatul ḥurūf*
letter of credit	كتاب الاعتماد	*kitābul i'timād*
lettuce (n)	الخس	*al khas*
leukaemia (leukemia)	لوكيميا	*lūkīmiyā*
levee (n)	سد، حاجز	*sadd, ḥājiz*
level (n)	مستوى، سطح، مخل	*mustawā, saṭḥ, mukhl*
level (adj)	مستوٍ، مسطح	*mustawin, musaṭṭaḥ*
level (v)	سوى، سطح، رفع بالمخل	*sawwā, saṭṭaḥa, rafa'a bil mukhl*
leverage (n)	فعل المخل، فائدة المخل	*fi'lul mukhl, fā'idatul mukhl*
leviathan (n)	لوياثان، شيء ضخيم	*liwiyāthān, shay' ḍakhīm*
levitate (v)	سبح في الهواء	*sabaḥa fil hawā'*
levity (n)	خفة، رعونة	*khiffah, ru'ūnah*
levy (v)	فرض ضريبة	*faraḍa ḍarībatan*
levy (n)	فرض الضرائب	*farḍuḍ ḍarā'ib*
lewd (adj)	فاسق، شهواني، فاجر	*fāsiq, shahwānī, fājir*
lewdness (n)	دعارة، فسق	*di'ārah, fisq*
lexical (adj)	معجمي، قاموسي، لغوي	*mu'jamī, qāmūsī, lughawī*
lexically (adv)	معجميًا، لغويًا	*mu'jamiyyan, lughawiyyan*
lexicographer (n)	معجمي، مؤلف القاموس	*mu'jamī, mu'alliful qāmūs*
lexicography (n)	تأليف المعاجم	*ta'līful ma'ājim*
lexicon (n)	قاموس، معجم	*qāmūs, mu'jam*
ley (n)	مرعى، مرج	*mar'ā, marj*
liability (n)	مسؤولية، دين	*mas'ūliyyah, dain*

liable (adj)	مسؤول، مطالب	*mas'ūl, muṭālab*
liase (v)	عمل معًا	*'amila ma'an*
liaison (n)	علاقة، صلة	*'alāqah, ṣilah*
liar (n)	كذاب، أفاك	*kadhdhāb, affāk*
libation (n)	إراقة، شراب	*irāqah, sharāb*
libel (n)	طعن، قذف	*ṭa'n, qadhf*
libel (v)	طعن بالنشر، اتهم	*ta'ana bin nashr, ittahama*
libellous (libelous)	قذفي، طعني	*qadhfī, ṭa'nī*
liberal (n/adj)	غير متعصب، متحرر، تحرري	*ghair muta'aṣṣib, mutaḥarrir, taḥarrurī*
liberalism (n)	تحررية، حرية الآراء	*taḥarruriyyah, ḥurriyyatul ārā'*
liberality (n)	حرية، سخاء، اتساع	*ḥurriyyah, sakhā', ittisā'*
liberalize,-ise (v)	وسع الأفكار	*wassa'al afkār*
liberate (v)	أعتق، حرر	*a'taqa, ḥarraa*
liberation (n)	تحرير، إطلاق	*taḥrīr, iṭlāq*
liberator (n)	محرر، معتق	*muḥarrir, mu'ṭiq*
libertine (adj)	خليع، بذيء	*khalī', badhī'*
liberty (n)	حرية، استقلال	*ḥurriyyah, istiqlāl*
libidinous (adj)	شهواني، لبيدي	*shahwānī, libīdī*
libido (n)	شهوة جنسية	*shahwah jinsiyyah*
Libra (n)	برج الميزان	*burjul mīzān*
librarian (n)	أمين المكتبة	*amīnul maktabah*
librarianship (n)	أمانة المكتبة	*amānatul maktaba*
library (n)	مكتبة، دار الكتب	*maktabah, dārul kutub*
libretto (n)	ألفاظ الأوبرا	*alfāẓul ūbrā*
licence (license) (n)	رخصة، إجازة رسمية	*rukhṣah, ijāzah rasmiyyah*
licence (v)	أجاز، منح رخصة رسمية	*ajāza, manaḥa rukhṣah rasmiyyah*
licensee (n)	حامل الرخصة	*ḥāmilur rukhṣah*

licentious (adj)	خليع، فاسق، داعر	*khalī', fāsiq, dā'ir*
licentiousness (n)	دعارة، فسق	*di'ārah, fisq*
lichen (n)	أسنة، حشيشة البحر	*usnah, ḥashīshatul baḥr*
lick (v)	لعق، هزم	*la'iqa, hazama*
lick (n)	لعق، مقدار ضئيل	*la'q, miqdār ḍa'īl*
licking (n)	ضربة عنيفة، هزيمة	*ḍarbah 'anīfah, hazīmah*
lid (n)	غطاء، جفن	*ghiṭā', jafn*
lidded (adj)	ذو غطاء، ذو جفن	*dhū ghiṭā', dhū jafn*
lie (v)	تمدد، تربص، استلقى	*tamaddada, tarabbaṣa, istalqā*
lie (n)	اضطجاع، كذب	*iḍṭijā', kadhib*
lied (n)	أغنية ليدة	*ughniyah līdah*
lie down	استلقى، اضطجع	*istalqā, iḍṭaja'a*
lieu	مكان، بدلاً	*makāna, badalan*
lieutenant (n)	نائب، قائم مقام	*nā'ib, qā'imu maqām*
lie with	توقف على، ضاجع	*tawaqqafa 'alā, ḍāja'a*
life (n)	حياة، روح، عيشة	*ḥayāt, rūḥ, 'īshah*
lifebelt (n)	حزام النجاة	*ḥizāmun najāt*
lifeblood (n)	دم الحياة	*damul ḥayāt*
lifeboat (n)	قارب النجاة	*qāribun najāt*
lifebuoy (n)	طافية النجاة	*ṭāfiyatun najāt*
life cycle (n)	دورة الحياة	*dauratul ḥayāt*
life expectancy	عمر متوقع	*'umr mutawaqqa'*
life-giving (adj)	منشط، محيي	*munashshiṭ, muḥyī*
lifeguard (n)	حرس	*ḥaras*
life history	تاريخ الحياة	*tārīkhul ḥayāt*
life insurance	تأمين على الحياة	*ta'mīn 'alal ḥayāt*
life-jacket (n)	صدار النجاة	*ṣidārun najāt*
lifeless (adj)	ميت، بدون حياة	*mait, bidūn ḥayāt*

lifelike (adj)	نابض بالحياة	*nābiḍ bil ḥayāt*
lifeline (n)	حبل الإنقاذ	*ḥablul inqādh*
lifelong (adj)	طول الحياة	*ṭūlul ḥayāt*
life preserver	صدار النجاة	*ṣidārun najāt*
life-saver (n)	نعمة، منقذ	*ni'mah, munqidh*
lifetime (n)	عمر، حياة	*'umr, ḥayāt*
life-work (n)	عمل العمر	*'amalul 'umr*
lift (v)	رفع، صعد	*rafa'a, ṣa''da*
lift (n)	رفعة، مصعد، قوة منشطة	*raf'ah, miṣ'ad, quwwah munashshiṭah*
ligament (n)	رباط	*ribāṭ*
ligature (n)	رابطة، رباط	*rābiṭah, ribāṭ*
light (n)	نور، ضوء، إشعال	*nūr, ḍau', ish'āl*
light (v)	أضاء، أشرق، حط	*aḍā'a, ashraqa, ḥaṭṭa*
light (adj)	خفيف، لطيف، يسير	*khafīf, laṭif, yasīr*
lighten (v)	خفف، أضاء	*khaffafa, aḍā'a*
lighter (n)	صندل، قداحة	*ṣandal, qaddāḥah*
light-fingered (adj)	ماهر في السرقة	*māhir fis sariqah*
light-headed (adj)	طائش، خفيف العقل	*ṭā'ish, khafīful 'aql*
light-hearted (adj)	جذل، مرح	*jadhil, mariḥ*
light-heartedly (adv)	بجذل، بمرح	*bi jadhal, bi maraḥ*
lighthouse (n)	منارة، منار	*manārah, manār*
lightly (adv)	باستخفاف، بمرح، بسهولة	*bistikhfāf, bi maraḥ, bi suhūlah*
lightning (n)	برق، وميض	*barq, wamīḍ*
lightning (adj)	سريع كالبرق	*sarī' kal barq*
lightship (n)	منارة عائمة	*manārah 'ā'imah*
lightweight (n/adj)	أخف، ضئيل، غيرهام	*akhaff, ḍa'īl, ghair hāmm*

light-year (n)	سنة ضوئية	*sanah ḍau'iyyah*
lignite (n)	فحم حجري، ليجنيت	*faḥm ḥajarī, lījnīt*
likable (likeable)	جدير بالحب	*jadīr bil ḥubb*
like (v)	ود، أحب، رغب	*wadda, aḥabba, raghiba*
like (n)	مثيل، نظير	*mathīl, naẓīr*
like (adj)	مماثل، مشابه	*mumāthil, mushābih*
like (adv)	تقريباً، إلى حدما	*taqrīban, ilā ḥaddim mā*
like (prep/conj)	مثل، مثلما	*mithl, mithlamā*
likely (adj)	محتمل، مرجو	*muḥtamal, marjuww*
liken (v)	شبه، ماثل	*shabbaha, māthala*
likeness (n)	مماثلة، شبه	*mumāthalah, shabah*
likewise (adv)	أيضاً، مثله	*aiḍan, mithlahu*
liking (n)	مودة، ولوع	*mawaddah, wulū'*
lilac (n)	زهرة الليلك	*zahratul lailak*
lilliputian (adj)	تافه، صغير	*tāfih, ṣaghīr*
lilt (n)	أغنية مرحة	*ughniyah mariḥah*
lilting (n)	أغنية قصيرة	*ughniyah qaṣīrah*
lily (n)	سوسن	*sausan*
lily-livered (adj)	جبان، مخلوع الفؤاد	*jabān, makhlū'ul fu'ād*
limb (n)	عضو، غصن كبير	*'uḍw, ghuṣn kabīr*
limber (v)	مرن، رشق	*marrana, rashshaqa*
limbo (n)	حالة انتقالية	*ḥālah intiqāliyyah*
lime (n)	كلس، دبق، ليم	*kils, dibq, laim*
lime (v)	كلس، جير	*kallasa, jayyara*
limelight (n)	ضوء، شهرة	*ḍau', shuhrah*
limeric (n)	لمريكية، قصيدة فكاهية	*limrīkiyyah, qaṣīdah fukāhiyyah*
limestone (n)	حجر الكلس	*ḥajarul kils*
limit (n)	تخم، حد، قيد	*takhm, ḥadd, qaid*
limit (v)	حصر، حدد، قيد	*ḥaṣara, ḥaddada, qayyada*

limitation (n)	تحديد، حد، حصر	*taḥdīd, ḥadd, ḥaṣr*
limited (adj)	محدود، محصور	*maḥdūd, maḥṣūr*
limiting (adj)	محدد، مقيد	*muḥaddid, muqayyid*
limitless (adj)	غير محدود	*ghair maḥdūd*
limousine (n)	ليموزين، سيارة مريحة	*līmūzīn, sayyārah murīḥah*
limp (adj)	أعرج، منهك، ضعيف	*a'raj, munhak, ḍa'īf*
limp (n)	عرج، ترنح	*'araj, tarannuḥ*
limp (v)	ترنح، عرج	*tarannaḥa, 'araja*
limpet (n)	بطلينوس	*baṭlīnūs*
limpid (adj)	صافٍ، شفاف، رائق	*ṣāfin, shaffāf, rā'iq*
limply (adv)	بعرج، باضطراب	*bi 'araj, biḍṭirāb*
linchpin (n)	شيء ذو أهمية	*shay' dhū ahammiyyah*
line (n	خط، سطر، صف	*khaṭṭ, saṭr, ṣaff*
line (v)	سطر، صف، رسم	*saṭṭara, ṣaffa, rasama*
lineage (n)	سلسلة نسب	*silsilatu nasab*
lineal (adj)	نسبي، وراثي، خطي	*nasabī, wirāthī, khaṭṭī*
lineaments (n)	ملامح، قسمات	*malāmiḥ, qasamāt*
linear (adj)	خطي، طولي	*khaṭṭī, ṭūlī*
linen (n)	ملابس كتانية	*malābis kattāniyyah*
liner (n)	باخرة خطية	*bākhirah khaṭṭiyyah*
linesman (n)	مساعد الحكم	*musā'idul ḥakam*
line-up (n)	صف من أشخاص	*ṣaff min ashkhāṣ*
linger (v)	تلبث، تمهل، تبطأ	*talabbatha, tamahhala, tabaṭṭa'a*
lingerie (n)	ملابس تحتية للنساء	*malābis taḥtiyyah lin nisā'*
lingo (n)	لغة أجنبية	*lughah ajnabiyyah*
lingua franca	لغة مشتركة	*lughah mushtarikah*
lingual (adj)	لساني، لغوي	*lisānī, lughawī*
liguist (n)	لغوي، عالم بلغات متعددة	*lughawī, 'ālim bi lughāt muta'addidah*
linguistic (adj)	لغوي	*lughawī*

linguistically (adv)	لغويًا	*lughawiyyan*
linguistics (n)	علم اللغة	*'ilmul lughah*
liniment (n)	مرهم، دهان، مروخ	*marham, dihān, marūkh*
lining (n)	بطانة، تبطين	*biṭānah, tabṭīn*
link (n)	ربط، صلة، حلقة	*rabṭ, ṣilah, ḥalqah*
link (v)	ارتبط، اتصل، ربط	*irtabaṭa, ittaṣala, rabaṭa*
linkage (n)	ارتباط، ترابط	*irtibāṭ, tarābuṭ*
linkman (n)	حامل المشعل	*ḥāmilul mish'al*
link-up (n)	اتصال، ارتباط	*ittiṣāl, irtibāṭ*
linnet (n)	زقيقية	*zuqaiqiyyah*
linseed (n)	بزر الكتان	*bazrul kattān*
lint (n)	نسالة الكتان	*nusālatul kattān*
lintel (n)	عتبة الباب	*'atabatul bāb*
lion (n)	أسد، رجل شجاع	*asad, rajul shujā'*
lioness (n)	لبوة، لبوءة	*labwah, labū'ah*
lionize,-ise (v)	بجل، كرم	*bajjala, karrama*
lip (n)	شفة، حافة	*shafah, ḥāffah*
lipped (adj)	ذو شفة	*dhū shafah*
lip-read (v)	استشفه	*istashfaha*
lip-reading (n)	استشفاه	*istishfāh*
lip-service (n)	تملق	*tamalluq*
lipstic (n)	أحمر الشفاه	*aḥmarush shifāh*
liquefy (v)	ذوب، سيل	*dhawwaba, sayyala*
lequeur (n)	مسكر معطر	*muskir mu'aṭṭar*
liquid (n/adj)	سائل، مائع، صافٍ	*sā'il, mā'i', ṣāfin*
liquidate (v)	سيل، صفى الحسابات	*sayyala, ṣaffal ḥisābāt*
liquidation (n)	تصفية، تحويل	*taṣfiyah, taḥwīl*
liquidator (n)	مصفي، مأمور التصفية	*muṣaffī, ma'mūrut taṣfiyah*
liquidity (n)	سيولة، ميوعة	*suyūlah, muyū'ah*

liquidize,-ise (v)	سيل، ميع	*sayyala, mayya'a*
liquidizer,-iser (n)	مميعة	*mumayyi'ah*
liquor (n)	مادة سائلة	*māddah sā'ilah*
lira (n)	ليرة	*līrah*
lisp (n/v)	لثغة، لثغ	*luthghah, lathigha*
lissom, lissome (adj)	رشيق، لدن	*rashīq, ladn*
list (v)	سجل، أدرج، مال	*sajjala, adraja, māla*
list (n)	قائمة، كشف، بيان	*qā'imah, kashf, bayān*
listen (v/n)	أصغى، إصغاء	*aṣghā, iṣghā'*
listener (n)	مستمع، سامع	*mustami', sāmi'*
listing (n)	جدول، قائمة	*jadwal, qā'imah*
listless (adj)	فاتر الهمة، متغافل	*fātirul himmah, mutaghāfil*
listlessly (adv)	بدون حماس	*bidūn ḥamās*
listlessness (n)	فتور الهمة، عدم حماس	*futūrul himmah, 'adamu ḥamās*
list price	سعر البيان	*si'rul bayān*
litancy (n)	ابتهال، سلسلة الصلوات	*ibtihāl, silsilatuṣ ṣalawāt*
literacy (n)	معرفة، قراءة وكتابة	*ma'rifah, qirā'ah wa kitābah*
literal (adj)	حرفي، لفظي، بسيط	*ḥarfī, lafẓī, basīṭ*
literally (adv)	حرفيًا، كلمة فكلمة	*ḥarfiyyan, kalimatan fa kalimah*
literary (adj)	أدبي، مختص بالأدب	*adabī, mukhtaṣṣ bil adab*
literate (adj)	متعلم، مثقف	*muta'allim, muthaqqaf*
literaty (n)	أديب، عالم	*adīb, 'ālim*
literature (n)	أدب، علوم الأدب	*adab, 'ulūmul adab*
lithe (adj)	رشيق، مرن	*rashīq, marin*
lithium (n)	ليثيوم	*lithiyūm*

lithography (n)	طباعة حجرية	*ṭibā'ah ḥajariyyah*
litigant (n)	خصم، مدعٍ	*khaṣm, mudda'in*
litigate (v)	داعى، قاضى	*dā'ā, qāḍā*
litigation (n)	مقاضاة، مداعاة	*muqāḍāt, mudā'āt*
litigious (adj)	مشاكس، متقاضٍ	*mushākis, mutaqāḍin*
litmus (n)	صبغة عباد الشمس	*ṣibghatu 'abbādish shams*
litre (liter) (n)	لتر	*litar*
litter (n)	ركام مبعثر، أوراق مبعثرة	*rukām muba'thar, aurāq muba'tharah*
litter (v)	بعثر، انتشر	*ba'thara, intashara*
little (adj)	قليل، يسير، صغير	*qalīl, yasīr, ṣaghīr*
little (adv)	قليلاً، نادراً	*qalīlan, nādiran*
little (n)	فترة قصيرة، مقدار قليل	*fatrah qaṣīrah, miqdār qalīl*
littoral (adj)	ساحلي	*sāḥilī*
liturgical (adj)	طقسي	*ṭaqsī*
liturgy (n)	طقس ديني	*ṭaqs dīnī*
livable, liveable (adj)	ملائم للعيش	*mulā'im lil 'aish*
live (adj)	حي، نشيط، مباشر	*ḥayy, nashīṭ, mubāshir*
live (v)	قطن، عاش، سكن	*qaṭana, 'āsha, sakana*
live (adv)	مباشرة، بغير أسطوانة	*mubāshiratan, bighairi usṭuwānah*
livelihood (n)	رزق، معاش	*rizq, ma'āsh*
liveliness (n)	نشاط، حيوية	*nashāṭ, ḥayawiyyah*
livelong (adj)	كل، بكامله	*kull, bi kāmilih*
lively (adj)	نشيط، رشيق، مفعم بالحياة	*nashīṭ, rashīq, muf'am bil ḥayāt*
liver (n)	كبد	*kabid*
liveried (adj)	مبزز	*mubazzaz*
livery (n)	بزة، كسوة مميزة	*bizzah, kiswah mumayyazah*
livery company	نقابة للصناع	*niqābah liṣ ṣannā'*

livery table	اسطبل للعربات	*asṭabal lil ʻarabāt*
livestock (n)	دواب، مواشٍ	*dawābb, mawāshin*
livid (adj)	شاحب، أدكن	*shāḥib, adkan*
living (n)	حياة، معيشة	*ḥayāt, maʻīshah*
living (adj)	حي، نشيط، قوي	*ḥayy, nashīṭ, qawī*
living death	حياة الموت	*ḥayātul maut*
living-room (n)	حجرة الجلوس	*ḥujratul julūs*
living wage	أجر كافٍ	*ajr kāfin*
lizard (n)	سحلية، سقاية	*siḥliyah, siqqāyah*
lo (interj)	انظر	*unẓur*
load (n)	حمولة، شحنة، ثقل	*ḥumūlah, shiḥnah, thiql*
load (v)	شحن، حمل، أثقل	*shaḥana, ḥammala, athqala*
loaded (adj)	محشو، محمل، مشحون	*maḥshū, muḥammal, mashḥūn*
loaf (n)	رغيف، قرص، كتلة	*raghīf, qurṣ, kutlah*
loaf (v)	عاش في العبث	*ʻāsha fil ʻabath*
loafer (n)	مضيع الوقت، متسكع	*muḍīʻul waqt, mutasakkiʻ*
loam (n)	تربة خصبة	*ṭurbah khaṣibah*
loamy (d)	طفالي	*ṭufālī*
loan (n)	قرض، إعارة	*qarḍ, iʻārah*
loan (v)	أقرض، أعار	*aqraḍa, aʻāra*
loath (adj)	كاره، غير راضٍ	*kārih, ghair rāḍin*
loathe (v)	اشمئز، كره	*ishmaʼazza, kariha*
loathing (n)	اشمئزاز، كره شديد	*ishmiʼzāz, kurh shadīd*
loathsome (adj)	كريه، بغيض	*karīh, baghīḍ*
lob (v)	قذف الكرة	*qadhafal kurah*
lobby (n)	رواق انتظار، ردهة المجلس	*riwāqu intiẓār, radhatul majlis*
lobby (v)	أثر على هيئة تشريعية	*aththara ʻalā hayʼah tashrīʻiyyah*
lobe (n)	شحمة الأذن	*shaḥmatul udhun*

lobotomy (n)	جراحة فصية	*jirāḥah faṣṣiyyah*
lobster (n)	جراد البحر، كركند	*jarādul baḥr, karkand*
lobster-pot (n)	شرك لصيد الكركند	*sharak li ṣaidil karkand*
local (adj)	محلي، موضعي	*maḥallī, mauḍi'ī*
local (n)	شخص محلي، نبأ محلي	*shakhṣ maḥallī, naba' maḥallī*
local authority	سلطة محلية	*sulṭah maḥalliyyah*
local call	مكالمة محلية	*mukālamah maḥalliyyah*
local colour	لون محلي	*laun maḥallī*
locale (n)	موقع، موضع	*mauqi', mauḍi'*
local government	حكومة محلية	*ḥukūmah maḥalliyyah*
locality (n)	محل، موضع	*maḥall, mauḍi'*
localization,-isation	مركزة، تمركز	*markazah, tamarkuz*
localize,-ise (v)	مركز، تمركز	*markaza, tamarkaza*
local time	وقت محلي	*waqt maḥallī*
locate (v)	وقع في مكان	*waqa'a fī makān*
location (n)	موقع، وضع، محل	*mauqi', waḍ', maḥall*
lock (n)	قفل، هويس، مكبح العربة	*qufl, hawīs, mikbaḥul 'arabah*
lock (v)	أقفل، أغلق	*aqfala, aghlaqa*
locker (n)	صندوق، درج	*ṣundūq, durj*
locker-room (n)	حجرة الأدراج المقفلة	*ḥujratul adrāj al muqaffala*
locket (n)	مدلاة	*mudallāt*
lockjaw (n)	كزاز	*kuzāz*
lockout (n)	إغلاق تعجيزي	*ighlāq ta'jīzī*
locksmith (n)	قفال، صانع الأقفال	*qaffāl, ṣāni'ul aqfāl*
lock-up (n)	سجن صغير	*sijn ṣaghīr*
locomotion (n)	تحرك، تنقل	*taḥarruk, tanaqqul*
locomotive (adj)	تنقلي، تحركي	*tanaqqulī, taḥarrukī*

locum (n)	مؤقت	*mu'aqqat*
locus (n)	موضع، محل، مقام	*mauḍi', maḥall, maqām*
locust (n)	جراد، جرادة	*jarād, jarādah*
locution (n)	أسلوب، تعبير	*uslūb, ta'bīr*
lode (n)	ممر مائي	*mamarr mā'ī*
lodestar (n)	نجم هادٍ	*najm hādin*
lodestone (n)	حجر المغنطيس	*ḥajarul mughanṭīs*
lodge (n)	مستجم، مأوى، كوخ	*Mustajamm, ma'wā, kūkh*
lodge (v)	أوى، سكن، قدم شكوى	*awā, sakana, qaddama shakwā*
lodger (n)	نزيل، مقيم	*nazīl, muqīm*
lodging (n)	منـــزل، مثوى	*manzil, mathwā*
lodging-house (n)	نزل	*nuzul*
loft (n)	علية، طبقة عليا	*'alliyyah, ṭabaqah 'ulyā*
loft (v)	ضرب الكرة إلى الارتفاع	*ḍarabal kurah ilal irtifā'*
lofty (adj)	مرتفع، عالٍ، شامخ	*murtafi', 'ālin, shāmikh*
log (n)	زند الخشب، سجل الأداء	*zandul khashab, sijillul adā'*
log (v)	قطع الأشجار، سجل	*qaṭa'al ashjār, sajjala*
loganberry (n)	توت لوغان	*tūt lūghān*
logarithm (n)	لوغارثم	*lūghārithm*
logarithmic (adj)	لوغارثمي	*lūghārithmī*
logbook (n)	سجل الأداء	*sijillul adā'*
loggerheads (n)	أبله، غبي، أحمق	*ablạh, ghabī, aḥmaq*
logic (n)	منطق، علم المنطق	*manṭiq, 'ilmul manṭiq*
logical (adj)	منطقي، معقول	*manṭiqī, ma'qūl*
logically (adv)	بطريقة منطقية	*bi ṭarīqah manṭiqiyyah*

logician (n)	منطقي، عالم بالمنطق	*manṭiqī, 'ālim bil manṭiq*
logistic-al (adj)	سوقي	*sauqī*
logistically (adv)	سوقيًا	*sauqiyyan*
logistics (n)	سوقيات	*sauqiyyāt*
log-jam (n)	ورطة، مأزق	*warṭah, ma'ziq*
loin (n)	حقو، صلب	*ḥaqw, ṣulb*
loincloth (n)	مئزر	*mi'zar*
loins (n)	أعضاء تناسلية	*a'ḍā' tanāsuliyyah*
loiter (v)	تسكع، تمهل	*tasakka'a, tamahhala*
loll (v)	ترهل، تدلى	*tarahhala, tadallā*
lollipop (n)	قطعة كراميل	*qiṭ'atu karāmīl*
lolly=lollipop		
lone (adj)	فريد، وحيد	*farīd, waḥīd*
loneliness (n)	انفراد، عزلة، وحدة	*infirād, 'uzlah, waḥdah*
lonely (adj)	منفرد، متوحد	*munfarid, mutawaḥḥid*
lonesome (adj)	متوحد، موحش	*mutawaḥḥid, mūḥish*
long (adj/n)	طويل، فترة طويلة	*ṭawīl, fatrah ṭawīlah*
long (v)	تاق، اشتاق	*tāqa, ishtāqa*
longbow (n)	قوس طويل	*qaus ṭawīl*
long-distance (adj)	قصي، بعيد المدى	*qaṣiyy, ba'īdul madā*
long division	قسمة طويلة	*qismah ṭawīlah*
longevity (n)	طول العمر	*ṭūlul 'umr*
longhand (n)	كتابة عادية	*kitābah 'ādiyah*
longitude (n)	خط الطول	*khaṭṭuṭ ṭūl*
longitudinal (adj)	طولي، طولاني	*ṭūlī, ṭūlānī*
long jump	قفز عريض	*qafz 'arīḍ*
long-life (n)	عمر طويل	*'umr ṭawīl*

long-lived (adj)	طويل العمر	*ṭawīlul 'umr*
long-sighted (adj)	بعيد النظر، طويل البصر	*ba'īdun naẓar, ṭawīlul baṣar*
long-suffering (adj)	صبور على الأذى	*ṣabūr 'alal 'adhā*
long-term (adj)	طويل الأجل	*ṭawīlul ajal*
long time	طويل المدة	*ṭawīlul muddah*
long-winded (adj)	طويل النفس	*ṭawīlun nafas*
look (v)	نظر، ظهر، بدا	*naẓara, ẓahara, badā*
look (n)	نظرة، طلعة، مظهر	*naẓrah, ṭal'ah, maẓhar*
look after	أعنى، اعتنى	*a'nā, I'tanā*
look ahead	نظر إلى الأمام	*naẓara ilal amām*
look back	التفت إلى الماضي	*iltafata ilal māḍī*
look down	ازدرى	*izdarā*
looker (n)	شخص جذاب	*shakhṣ jadhdhāb*
look for	بحث، تطلع	*baḥatha, taṭall'a*
look forward	تطلع بلهفة	*taṭalla'a bi lahfah*
look in	زار لمدة قصيرة	*zāra li muddah qaṣīrah*
looking-glass (n)	مرآة	*mir'āt*
look into	فحص، تصفح	*faḥaṣa, taṣaffaḥa*
look on	نظر بارتياب	*naẓara birtiyāb*
look out	تنبه، حذر	*tanabbaha, ḥadhira*
lookout (n)	حارس، مرقب	*ḥāris, marqab*
look up	بحث، تطلع	*baḥatha, taṭalla'a*
loom (n)	نول، منسج	*naul, minsaj*
loom (v)	تبلج، لاح	*taballaja, lāḥa*
loony (n/adj)	شخص معتوه، معتوه	*shakhṣ ma'tūh, ma'tūh*
loop (n)	عروة، حلقة، تحلق	*'urwah, ḥalaqah, taḥalluq*
loop (v)	تحلق، تقلب	*taḥallaqa, taqallaba*
loophole (n)	مهرب، مخلص	*mahrab, makhlaṣ*
loopy (adj)	معتوه، غير معقول	*ma'tūh, ghair ma'qūl*

loose (adj)	سائب، غير مشدود	*sā'ib, ghair mashdūd*
loose (v)	أرخى، حرر، حل	*arkhā, ḥarrara, ḥalla*
loose end	طرف سائب	*ṭaraf sā'ib*
loosen (v)	أرخى، حل، فك	*arkhā, ḥalla, fakka*
loot (n)	سلب، مال مسلوب، غنيمة	*salb, māl maslūb, ghanīmah*
loot (v)	غنم، سلب	*ghanima, salaba*
lop (v)	قطع الأغصان، قضب	*qaṭa'al aghṣān, qaḍḍaba*
lope (v/n)	تبختر، تبختر	*tabakhtara, tabakhtur*
lopsided (adj)	مائل إلى جانب	*mā'il ilā jānib*
loquacious (adj)	مهذار، ثرثار	*mihdhār, tharthār*
loquacity (n)	هذر، ثرثرة	*hadhar, thartharah*
lord (n)	مالك، ملك، مولى	*mālik, malik, maulā*
lordly (adj)	متكبر، فاخر، جليل	*mutakabbir, fākhir, jalīl*
lordship (n)	سيادة، حضرة، سلطان	*siyādah, ḥaḍrah, sultān*
lore (n)	معرفة، خبرة	*ma'rifah, khibrah*
lorgnette (n)	نظارات	*naẓẓārāt*
lorry (n)	لوري، شاحنة	*lūrī, shāḥinah*
lose (v)	خسر، ضاع، فقد	*khasira, ḍā'a, faqada*
loser (n)	خاسر، خسران	*khāsir, khasrān*
loss (n)	خسران، خسارة، ضياع	*khusrān, khasārah, ḍiyā'*
lost (adj)	مفقود، مستغرق	*mafqūd, mustaghriq*
lot (n)	جملة، نصيب، حصة	*jumlah, naṣīb, ḥiṣṣah*
lotion (n)	غسول	*ghasūl*
lottery (n)	حظ، قرعة	*ḥaẓẓ, qur'ah*
lotus (n)	لوطس، نيلوفر	*lūṭas, nīlūfar*
lotus eater	آكل اللوطس	*ākilul lūṭas*
loud (adj/adv)	عالٍ، بصوت عالٍ	*'ālin, bi ṣaut 'ālin*
loudly (adv)	بصوت عالٍ	*bi ṣaut 'ālin*

loud-mouth (n)	شخص صخاب	*shakhṣ ṣakhkhāb*
loud-mouthed (adj)	صخاب، كثير الكلام	*ṣakhkhāb, kathīrul kalām*
loudness (n)	ارتفاع، علو	*irtifā', 'uluww*
loudspeaker (n)	مجهاز	*mijhāz*
lough (n)	بحيرة	*buḥairah*
lounge (n)	قاعة للاستراحة	*qā'ah lil istirāḥah*
lounge (v)	تسكع، تبطأ، تكاسل	*taṣakka'a, tabaṭṭa'a, takāsala*
lounger (n)	متكاسل، متغافل	*mutakāsil, mutaghāfil*
louse (n/v)	قملة، خرب	*qamlah, kharraba*
lousy (adj)	قذر، خسيس، بذيء	*qadhir, khasīs, badhī'*
lout (n/adj)	فظ، جلف	*faẓẓ, jilf*
louvre (louver)	فتحة، شق التهوية	*futḥah, shiqqut tahwiyah*
louvred (adj)	ذو فتحات	*dhū futḥāt*
lovable (adj)	محبوب، محبب	*maḥbūb, muḥabbab*
love (n)	حب، مودة، ولوع	*ḥubb, mawaddah, wulū'*
love (v)	أحب، ود، أولع	*aḥabba, wadda, aula'a*
love affair	صلة غرامية	*ṣilah gharāmiyyah*
love-child (n)	ابن زنا	*ibnu zinā*
loveless (adj)	غير محبب	*ghair muḥabbab*
love-letter (n)	رسالة غرامية	*risālah gharāmiyyah*
loveliness (n)	جمال، فتنة	*jamāl, fitnah*
lovelorn (n)	خصلة الحب	*khuṣlatul ḥubb*
lovely (adv)	جميل، لطيف، بهيج	*jamīl, laṭīf, bahīj*
love-making (n)	مغازلة، معاشقة	*mughāzalah, mu'āshaqah*
love-match (n)	زواج الحب	*ziwājul ḥubb*

lover (n)	محب، مولع به	*muḥibb, mūla' bih*
lovesick (adj)	مريض الحب، ملوع	*marīḍul ḥubb, mulawwa'*
loving (adj)	حب، محبب	*ḥubb, muḥabbab*
low (adj)	منخفض، أسفل، وضيع	*munkhafiḍ, asfal, waḍī'*
lowbrow (n)	شيء دنيء	*shay' danī'*
low-down (adj)	وضيع، خسيس	*waḍī', khasīs*
lower (v)	خفض، انخفض، أذل	*khafaḍa, inkhafaḍa, adhalla*
lower (adj)	أسفل، أدنى	*asfal, adnā*
low land	أرض منخفضة	*arḍ munkhafiḍah*
low lander	ساكن الأرض المنخفضة	*sākinul arḍ al munkhafiḍah*
lowly (adj)	حقير، وضيع، دنيء	*ḥaqīr, waḍī', danī'*
loyal (adj)	أمين، مخلص، وفي	*amīn, mukhliṣ, wafī*
loyalist (n)	موالٍ	*muwālin*
loyally (adv)	مخلصاً، بإخلاص	*mukhliṣan, bi ikhlāṣ*
loyalty (n)	إخلاص، أمانة، ولاء	*ikhlāṣ, amānah, walā'*
lozenge (n)	معين، حلوى	*mu'ayyan, ḥalwā*
lubricant (n)	مزلق، مزيت	*muzalliq, muzayyit*
lubricate (v)	زلق، شحم	*zallaqa, shaḥḥama*
lubrication (n)	تزليق، تشحيم	*tazlīq, tashḥīm*
lubricious (adj)	أملس، زلق	*amlas, zaliq*
lucid (adj)	واضح، صافٍ، لامع	*wāḍiḥ, ṣāfin, lāmi'*
lucidity (n)	وضوح، جلاء، صفاء	*wuḍūḥ, jalā', ṣafā'*
lucidly (adv)	بوضوح، بجلاء	*bi wuḍūḥ, bi jalā'*
Lucifer (n)	إبليس، شيطان	*iblīs, shaiṭān*
luck (n)	حظ، نصيب	*ḥaẓẓ, naṣīb*
luckily (adv)	لحسن الحظ	*li ḥusnil ḥaẓẓ*
lucky (adj)	حسن الحظ، سعيد	*ḥasanul ḥaẓẓ, sa'īd*

lucrative (adj)	مربح، مكسب	*murbiḥ, muksib*
lucre (n)	مال، ربح	*māl, ribḥ*
ludicrous (adj)	مضحك، فكاهي	*muḍḥik, fukāhī*
ludicrously (adv)	بطريقة فكاهية	*bi ṭarīqah fukāhiyyah*
lug (v)	جر بجهد، جرجر	*jarra bi jahd, jarjara*
luggage (n)	عفش، أمتعة	*'afsh, amti'ah*
lugubrious (adj)	مكتئب، حزين	*mukta'ib, ḥazīn*
lugubriously (adv)	مكتئباً	*mukta'iban*
lugworm (n)	دودة حلقية	*dūdah ḥalaqiyyah*
lukewarm (adj)	بارد الهمة، فاتر	*bāridul himmah, fātir*
lull (v)	هدأ، هجع	*hadda'a, haja'a*
lull (n)	هجوع، هدوء	*hujū', hudū'*
lullaby (n)	تهويدة	*tahwīdah*
lumbago (n)	قطان، خزرة	*quṭān, khazrah*
lumbar (adj)	قطني	*qaṭanī*
lumber (n)	سقط المتاع، رديء المتاع	*saqaṭul matā', radī'ul matā'*
lumber (v)	تحرك بتثاقل	*taḥarraka bi tathāqul*
lumberjack (n)	خشاب	*khashshāb*
lumberyard (n)	فناء الأخشاب	*finā'ul akhshāb*
luminary (n)	نجم، شخص ماهر في حقله	*najm, shakhṣ māhir fī ḥaqlih*
luminous (adj)	منير، مضيء، واضح	*munīr, muḍī', wāḍiḥ*
luminousity (n)	إضاءة، وضوحة	*iḍā'ah, wuḍūḥah*
lump (n)	أغلبية، كتلة، جملة	*aghlabiyyah, kutlah, jumlah*
lump (v)	كتل، كوم	*kattala, kawwama*
lumpish (adj)	بليد، أحمق	*balīd, aḥmaq*
lumpy (adj)	كثير الكتل	*kathīrul kutal*
lunacy (n)	اختلال العقل، جنون	*ikhtilālul 'aql, junūn*

lunar (adj)	قمري، هلالي	*qamarī, hilālī*
lunatic (n)	أخرق، مجنون	*akhraq, majnūn*
lunatic fringe	جناح متطرف	*janāḥ mutaṭarrif*
lunch (n/v)	غداء، تناول الغداء	*ghadā', tanāwalal ghadā'*
luncheon (n)	غداء	*ghadā'*
lung (n)	رئة	*ri'ah*
lunge (n/v)	طعنة، طعن	*ṭa'nah, ṭa'ana*
lurch (n)	ميلان، ترنح، تمايل	*mayalān, tarannuḥ, tamāyul*
lurch (v)	تمايل، ترنح	*tamāyala, tarannaḥa*
lure (v)	أغرى، خدع	*aghrā, khada'a*
lure (n)	إغراء، خدعة	*ighrā', khud'ah*
lurid (adj)	متوهج، ممتقع	*mutawahhij, mumtaqi'*
luridly (adv)	بامتقاع، بتوهج	*bimtiqā', bi tawahhuj*
lurk (v)	ترصد، توارى	*taraṣṣada, tawārā*
luscious (adj)	حلو الذواق، مغرٍ	*ḥulwudh dhawāq, mughrin*
lush (adj)	خصب، مورق	*khaṣib, mūriq*
lust (n)	شهوة، رغبة جنسية	*shahwah, raghbah jinsiyyah*
lustful (adj)	شهواني، شبق	*shahwānī, shabiq*
lustre (luster)	بهاء، لمعان، مجد	*bahā', lam'ān, majd*
lustrous (adj)	لامع، صقيل	*lāmi', ṣaqīl*
lusty (adj)	ناشط، مفعم بالحيوية	*nāshiṭ, muf'am bil ḥayawiyyah*
lute (n/v)	عود، عزف على العود	*'ūd, 'azafa 'alal 'ūd*
lutenist (n)	عازف العود	*'āziful 'ūd*
luxuriance (n)	غزارة، ترف	*ghazārah, taraf*
luzuriant (adj)	مترف، منمق	*mutraf, munammaq*
luzuriate (v)	تمتع بحياة ترف	*tamatta'a bi ḥayāti taraf*

luxurious (adj)	مترف، منمق	*mutraf, munammaq*
luxuriously (adv)	بترف، بغزارة	*bi taraf, bi ghazārah*
luxury (n)	ترف، تنعم، رخاء	*taraf, tana''um, rakhā'*
lymph (n)	لنف	*limf*
lymphatic (adj)	لنفاوي	*limfāwī*
lynch (v)	لنش	*lanasha*
lyre (n)	قيثارة، عود	*qīthārah, 'ūd*
lyric (adj/n)	قيثاري، قصيدة	*qīthārī, qaṣīdah*
	غنائية	*ghinā'iyyah*
lyricism (n)	غنائية	*ghinā'iyyah*
lyricist (n)	شاعر غنائي	*shā'ir ghinā'ī*

M

ma (n)	أم، والده	*umm, wālidah*
macabre (adj)	رهيب، مروع	*rahīb, murawwi'*
macadam (n)	مكدام	*makadām*
macaroni (n)	معكرونة	*ma'karūnah*
macaroon (n)	معكرون	*ma'karūn*
macaw (n)	مقو، ببغاء أمريكي	*maqw, babghā' amrīkī*
mace (n)	صولجان، قضيب، تابل	*ṣaulajān, qaḍīb, tābil*
machete (n)	منجل كبير	*minjal kabīr*
machiavellian (adj)	مكيافلي	*makyāfilī*
machination (n)	دسيسة، مكيدة	*dasīsah, makīdah*
machine (n)	ماكينة، آلة، عدة	*mākinah, ālah, 'uddah*
machine (v)	صنع بماكينة	*ṣana'a bi mākīnah*
machine-gun (n)	رشاش	*rashshāsh*
machinery (n)	آلات، عدد، آلية	*ālāt, 'udad, āliyah*
machine tool	آلة مكنية	*ālah makaniyyah*
machinist (n)	ميكانيكي	*mīkānīkī*
mackerel (n)	سمك بحري	*samak baḥrī*

macrocosm (n)	الكون	*alkaun*
mad (adj)	أحمق، مجنون، معتوه	*aḥmaq, majnūn, ma'tūh*
madam (n)	سيدة، مديرة مأخور	*sayyidah, mudīratu ma'khūr*
madcap (adj)	متهور، مجازف	*mutahawwir, mujāzif*
madden (v)	جنن، خبل، أغضب	*jannana, khabbala, aghḍaba*
maddening (adj)	مجن، مغضب	*mujinn, mughḍib*
maddeningly (adv)	بطريقة مجنة	*bi ṭarīqah mujinnah*
made-up (n)	ممكيج، مختلق	*mumakyaj, mukhtalaq*
madhouse (n)	مستشفى المجانين	*mustashfal majānīn*
madly (adv)	بحماقة، بسعر	*bi ḥamāqah, bi su'r*
madman (n)	مجنون، معتوه	*majnūn, ma'tūh*
madness (n)	كلب، جنون، حماقة	*kalab, junūn, ḥamāqah*
Madonna (n)	مريم العذراء	*maryam al 'adhrā'*
madrigal (n)	قصيدة غزلية	*qaṣīdah ghazaliyyah*
maelstrom (n)	اضطراب شديد	*iḍṭirāb shadīd*
mafia (n)	مافية، منظمة سرية	*māfiyyah, munaẓẓamah sirriyyah*
magazine (n)	مجلة، مخزن الذخيرة	*majallah, makhzanudh dhakhīrah*
maggot (n)	دودة، يرقة	*dūdah, yaraqah*
magic (n/adj)	سحر، سحري	*siḥr, siḥrī*
magical (adj)	سحري، ساحر	*siḥrī, sāḥir*
magically (adv)	بطريقة ساحرة	*bi ṭarīqah sāḥirah*
magic circle	دائرة سحرية	*dā'irah siḥriyyah*
magician (n)	مشعوذ، ساحر، مجوسي	*masha'widh, sāḥir, majūsī*
magisterial (adj)	حاكمي، قضائي	*ḥākimī, qaḍā'ī*

magisterially (adv)	حاكميًا، قضائيًا	*ḥākimiyyan, qaḍā'iyyan*
magistracy (n)	حاكمية، هيئة القضاة، مأمورية	*ḥākimiyyah, hay'atul quḍāt, ma'mūriyyah*
magistrate (n)	حاكم، قاضي، مأمور	*ḥākim, qāḍī, ma'mūr*
magnanimity (n)	نخوة، شهامة	*nakhwah, shahāmah*
magnanimous (adj)	ذو نخوة، شهم	*dhū nakhwah, shahm*
magnate (n)	قطب، رجل متفوق	*quṭb, rajul mutafawwiq*
magnesia (n)	مغنيسيًا	*maghnīsiyā*
magnesium (n)	مغنسيوم	*maghnisiyūm*
magnet (n)	مغنطيس	*maghnaṭīs*
magnetic (adj)	مغنطيسي، جذاب	*maghnaṭīsī, jadhdhāb*
magnetically (adv)	مغنطيسيا	*maghnaṭīsiyyan*
magnetic field	حقل مغنطيسي	*ḥaql maghnaṭīsī*
magnetic north	شمال مغنطيسي	*shimāl maghnaṭīsī*
magnetic pole	قطب مغنطيسي	*quṭb maghnaṭīsī*
magnetic tape	شريط مغنطيسي	*sharīṭ maghnaṭīsī*
magnetism (n)	مغنطيسية، سحر	*maghnaṭīsiyyah, siḥr*
magnetize,-ise (v)	مغنط، فتن	*maghnaṭa, fatana*
magneto (n)	مغنيط	*maghnīṭ*
magnification (n)	تعظيم، تمجيد	*ta'ẓīm, tamjīd*
magnificence (n)	جلال، مجد، بهاء	*jalāl, majd, bahā'*
magnificent (adj)	فاخر، رفيع، عظيم	*fākhir, rafī', 'aẓīm*
magnificently (adv)	بجلال، ببهاء	*bi jalāl, bi bahā'*
magnify (v)	عظم، كبر، بجل	*'aẓẓama, kabbara, bajjala*
magnitude (n)	حجم، عظم، أهمية	*ḥajm, 'aẓm, ahammiyyah*
magnolia (n)	مغنولية	*maghnūliyah*
magpie (n)	عقعق	*'aq'aq*
mahogany (n)	ماهوغاني	*māhūghānī*
maid (n)	فتاة، خادمة، عذراء	*fatāt, khādimah, 'adhrā'*

maiden (n)	عذراء، فتاة، بكر	*'adhrā', fatāt, bikr*
maiden (adj)	أول، عانس، بتولي	*awwal, 'ānis, butūlī*
maidenhair (n)	كزبرة البئر	*kuzbaratul bi'r*
maidenhead (n)	بكارة، بتولة	*bakārah, butūlah*
maiden name (n)	اسم البتولة	*ismul butūlah*
maid of honour	وصيفة الشرف	*waṣīfatush sharaf*
maidservant (n)	خادمة	*khādimah*
mail (n)	بريد، نظام البريد، درع	*barīd, niẓāmul barīd, dir'*
mail (v)	أرسل بالبريد، درع	*arsala bil barīd, darra'a*
mailbag (n)	حقيبة البريد	*ḥaqībatul barīd*
mailbox (n)	صندوق البريد	*ṣundūqul barīd*
mailing (n)	إرسال البريد	*irsālul barīd*
mailman (n)	ساعي البريد	*sā'il barīd*
mail order (n)	طلب بريدي	*ṭalab barīdī*
maim (v)	أعجز، عطل، جدع	*a'jaza, 'aṭṭala, jada'a*
main (adj)	رئيسي، أساسي	*ra'īsī, asāsī*
main (n)	خط رئيسي، جزء رئيسي	*khaṭṭ ra'īsī, juz' ra'īsī*
mainland (n)	بر رئيسي	*barr ra'īsī*
mainly (adv)	على الأخص، في الأكثر	*'alal akhaṣṣ, fil akthar*
mainsail (n)	شراع رئيسي	*shirā' ra'īsī*
mainstay (n)	دعامة أساسية	*di'āmah asāsiyyah*
mainstreem (n)	اتجاه سائد	*ittijāh sā'id*
maintain (v)	عال، أيد، احتفظ، دافع	*'āla, ayyada, iḥtafaẓa, dāfa'a*
maintenance (n)	إعالة، محافظة، نفقة	*i'ālah, muḥāfaẓah, nafaqah*
maize (n)	ذرة	*dhurah*
majestic (adj)	جليل، فخم، ملوكي	*jalīl, fakhm, mulūkī*
majestically (adv)	بفخامة، بجلالة	*bi fakhāmah, bi jalālah*
majesty (n)	جلالة، فخامة	*jalālah, fakhāmah*

major (n/adj)	أكبر، أهم، رئيسي	*akbar, ahamm, ra'īsī*
major-general (n)	لواء	*liwā'*
majority (n)	أغلبية، أكثرية	*aghlabiyyah, akthariyyah*
make (v)	جعل، صنع، عمل	*ja'ala, ṣana'a, 'amila*
make-believe (n)	تخيل، تظاهر	*takhayyul, taẓāhur*
maker (n)	صانع، خالق، مبدع	*ṣāni', khāliq, mubdi'*
makeshift (n/adj)	بديل مؤقت	*badīl mu'aqqat*
make-up (n)	بنية، ماكياج	*binyah, mākyāj*
makeweight (n)	تتمة الوزن	*tatimmatul wazn*
making (n)	صنع، إحداث، إبداع	*ṣun', iḥdāth, ibdā'*
malachite (n)	ملكيت	*malakīt*
maladjusted (adj)	سيء التوافق	*sayyi'ut tawāfuq*
maladjustment (n)	سوء التوافق	*sū'ut tawāfuq*
maladministration	إساءة الإدارة	*isā'atul idārah*
maladroit (adj)	أخرق، غبي	*akhraq, ghabī*
malady (n)	داء، مرض	*dā', maraḍ*
malaise (n)	توعك المزاج	*tawa''akul mizāj*
malaria (n)	ملاريا، حمى متقطعة	*malāriyā, ḥummā mutaqaṭṭi'ah*
malcontent (n)	رجل ناقم	*rajul nāqim*
male (n/adj)	ذكر، مذكر	*dhakar, mudhakkar*
malefactor (n)	مجرم، مذنب	*mujrim, mudhnib*
malevolence (n)	حقد، ضغينة	*ḥiqd, ḍaghīnah*
malevolent (adj)	حاقد، مضطغن	*ḥāqid, muḍṭaghin*
malevolently (adv)	بغل، بحقد	*bi ghill, bi ḥiqd*
malformation (n)	تشوه	*tashawwuh*
malformed (adj)	مشوه	*mushawwah*
malfunction (n/v)	قصور، قصر	*quṣūr, qaṣar*
malice (n)	حقد، ضغينة، مكر	*ḥiqd, ḍaghīnah, makr*
malicious (adj)	حقود، حاسد، ماكر	*ḥaqūd, ḥāsid, mākir*

maliciously (adv)	بحقد، بخبث	*bi ḥiqd, bi khubth*
malign (v)	قذف، طعن، عاب	*qadhafa, ṭa'ana, 'āba*
malign (adj)	مؤذ، خبيث	*mu'dhin, khabīth*
malignancy (n)	خباثة، حقد	*khabāthah, ḥiqd*
malignant (adj)	مهلك، مؤذ	*muhlik, mu'dhin*
maligner (v)	تمارض، ادعى المرض	*tamāraḍa, idda'al maraḍ*
mall (n)	مال، مالة	*māl, mālah*
mallard (n)	بطة برية	*baṭṭah barriyyah*
malleability (n)	قابلية للطرق	*qābiliyyah liṭ ṭarq*
malleable (adj)	قابل للطرق، طريق	*qābil liṭ ṭarq, ṭarīq*
mallet (n)	مطرقة، مدقة	*miṭraqah, midaqqah*
mallow (n)	خبازة	*khubbāzah*
malnourished (adj)	سيء التغذية	*sayyi'ut taghdhiyah*
malnutrition (n)	سوء التغذية، سغل	*sū'ut taghdhiyah, saghal*
malodorous (adj)	كريه الرائحة	*karīhur rā'iḥah*
malpractice (n)	سوء التصرف	*sū'ut taṣarruf*
malt (n/v)	ملت، ملت	*malt, mallata*
malted milk	لبن مملت	*laban mumallat*
maltreat (v)	أساء إلى، آذى	*asā'a ilā, ādhā*
maltreatment (n)	إساءة، مخاشنة	*isā'ah, mukhāshanah*
mam (n)	والده، أم	*wālidah, umm*
mama (mamma)	أم، والدة	*umm, wālidah*
mamba (n)	ممبة، أفعى أفريقية	*mambah, af'ā afrīqiyyah*
mammal (n)	حيوان ثديي	*ḥaywān thadyī*
mammalian (adj)	ثديي، لبون	*thadyī, labūn*
mammary (adj)	ثديي	*thadyī*
mamoth (adj)	ضخم، هائل	*ḍakhm, hā'il*
mammy (n)	والده، أم	*wālidah, umm*
man (n)	رجل، إنسان، بشر	*rajul, insān, bashar*
man (v)	زود بالرجال	*zawwada bir rijāl*

manacle (n)	غل، صفاد	*ghull, ṣifād*
manacle (v)	صفد، غل	*ṣaffada, ghalla*
manage (v)	دبر، نظم، ساس	*dabbara, naẓẓama, sāsa*
manageable (adj)	سهل الانقياد	*sahlul inqiyād*
management (n)	إدارة، سياسة، تدبير	*idārah, siyāsah, tadbīr*
manager (n)	مدير، رئيس	*mudīr, ra'īs*
managerial (adj)	مديري، إداري	*mudīrī, idārī*
mandarin (n)	موظف كبير	*muwaẓẓaf kabīr*
mandate (n)	انتداب، تفويض	*intidāb, tafwīḍ*
mandate (v)	انتدب، فوض	*intadaba, fawwaḍa*
mandatory (adj)	انتدابي، مندوب	*intidābī, mandūb*
mandolin (n)	مندولين	*mandūlīn*
mandrake (n)	لفاح	*luffāḥ*
mane (n)	شعر، عرف	*sha'r, 'urf*
man-eater (n)	آكل البشر	*ākilul bashar*
maneuver (n)	مناورة، عرض	*munāwarah, 'arḍ*
manful (adj)	شجاع، باسل	*shujā', bāsil*
manganese (n)	منغنيز	*manghanīz*
mange (n)	مرض الجرب	*maraḍul jarab*
manger (n)	مذود، معلف	*midhwad, mi'laf*
mangle (v)	أتلف، شوه	*atlafa, shawwaha*
mangle (n)	مكواة أسطوانية	*mikwāt usṭuwāniyyah*
mango (n)	منجا، منجة	*manjā, manjah*
mangrove (n)	منغروف	*mangharūf*
mangy (adj)	جربي، أجرب	*jarabī, ajrab*
manhandle (v)	حرك بقوة، خاشن	*ḥarraka bi quwwah, khāshana*
manhole (n)	فتحة الدخول	*futḥatud dukhūl*
manhood (n)	رجولة، رجولية	*rujūlah, rujūliyyah*
man-hour (n)	عمل ساعي	*'amal sā'ī*

manhunt (n)	قنص بشري	*qanṣ basharī*
mania (n)	ولوع شديد، جنون، هوس	*wulū‘ shadīd, junūn, hawas*
maniac (n/adj)	مجنون، ممسوس	*majnūn, mamsūs*
maniacally (adv)	بجنون، بهوس	*bi junūn, bi hawas*
maniac-depressive	مسي انقباضي	*massī inqibāḍī*
manicure (n/v)	تدريم، درم	*tadrīm, darrama*
manicurist (n)	مدرم الأظافر	*mudarrimul aẓāfir*
manifest (adj)	واضح، ظاهر	*wāḍiḥ, ẓāhir*
manifest (v)	بين، أظهر	*bayyana, aẓhara*
manifestation (n)	إظهار، إبداء	*iẓhār, ibdā’*
manifesto (n)	بيان رسمي	*bayān rasmī*
manifold (adj)	متعدد، متنوع	*muta‘addid, mutanawwi‘*
manifold (n)	مشعب، وصلة	*mash‘ab, wuṣlah*
manila (n)	ورق مانيلا	*waraq mānīlā*
manipulate (v)	مارس، أعمل باليد	*mārasa, a‘mala bil yad*
manipulation (n)	معالجة باليد	*mu‘ālajah bil yad*
manipulative (adj)	يدوي	*yadawī*
mankind (n)	جنس بشري، إنسان	*jins basharī, insān*
manliness (n)	رجولة، شجاعة	*rujūlah, shujā‘ah*
manly (adj)	شجاع، رجلي	*shujā‘, rajulī*
manna (n)	من، غذاء سماوي	*mann, ghidhā’ samāwī*
mannequin (n)	منكين، قزم	*munkīn, qazam*
manner (n)	أسلوب، طريقة، سلوك	*uslūb, ṭarīqah, sulūk*
mannered (adj)	متكلف، متصنع	*mutakallaf, mutaṣanni‘*
mannerism (n)	تكلف، تأنق	*takalluf, ta’annuq*
mannish (adj)	كالرجل	*kar rajul*
manoeuvre=maneuver		
man of war	سفينة حربية	*safīnah ḥarbiyyah*

manor (n)	عزبة، إقليم	*'izbah, iqlīm*
monorial (adj)	عزبي، إقليمي	*'izbī, iqlīmī*
manpower (n)	طاقة بشرية	*ṭāqah bashariyyah*
manque (n)	فاشل، مخفق	*fāshil, mukhaffaq*
mansard (n)	سقف سندي	*saqf sanadī*
manse (n)	بيت القس	*baitul qiss*
manservant (n)	خادم	*khādim*
mansion (n)	قصر، منـــزل	*qaṣr, manzil*
manslaughter (n)	قتل غير عمدي	*qatl ghair 'amadī*
mantelpiece (n)	رف المصطلى	*rafful muṣṭalā*
mantle (n)	غطاء، غلاف، عباءة	*ghiṭā', ghilāf, 'abā'ah*
manual (adj/n)	يدوي، كتيب	*yadawī, kutayyib*
manually (adv)	باليد	*bil yad*
manufacture (v)	صنع، اصطنع	*ṣana'a, iṣṭana'a*
manufacture (n)	صنعة، صناعة	*ṣan'ah, ṣinā'ah*
manufacturer (n)	صاحب المصنع	*ṣāḥibul maṣna'*
manufacturing (n)	صناعة، صنعة	*ṣinā'ah, ṣun'ah*
manure (v/n)	سمد، سماد	*sammada, samād*
manuscript (n)	مخطوط، مخطوطة	*makhṭūṭ, makhṭūṭah*
many (adj)	كثير، متعدد	*kathīr, muta'addid*
maori (n/adj)	ماووري	*māwūrī*
map (n/v)	خريطة، رسم خريطةً	*kharīṭah, rasama kharīṭatan*
maple (n)	شجرة القيقب	*shajaratul qayqab*
maple syrup	شراب لقيقب	*sharābul qayqab*
mar (v)	أتلف، شوه	*atlafa, shawwaha*
marathon (n)	سباق المرثون	*sibāqul marathūn*
marauder (n)	نهاب، قاطع الطريق	*nahhāb, qāṭi'uṭ ṭarīq*
marauding (n)	ابتغاء النهب	*ibtighā'un nahb*
marble (n)	مرمر، رخام	*marmar, rukhām*

March (n)	مارس، آذار	*mārs, ādhār*
march (n)	زحف، سار	*zaḥafa, sāra*
march (n)	زحف، سير، تقدم	*zaḥf, sair, taqaddum*
marches (n)	تخم، حد	*takhm, ḥadd*
mare (n)	أنثى الخيل	*unthal khail*
margarine (n)	مرغرين	*margharīn*
margin (n)	هامش، حاشية	*hāmish, ḥāshiyah*
marginal (adj)	هامشي، حافي	*hāmishī, ḥāffī*
marguerite (n)	مرغريتا	*margharītā*
marigold (n)	آذريون	*ādharyūn*
marimba (n)	مرمبة، آلة موسيقية	*marimbah, ālah mausīqiyyah*
marina (n)	حوض لرسو السفن	*ḥauḍ li rusuwwis sufun*
marine (adj/n)	بحري، جندي بحري	*baḥrī, jundī baḥrī*
mariner (n)	ملاح، بحار	*mallāḥ, baḥḥār*
marionette (n)	دمية متحركة	*dumyah mutaḥarrikah*
marital (adj)	زوجي، مختص بالزواج	*zaujī, mukhtaṣṣ biz zawāj*
maritime (adj)	بحري، مختص بالبحر	*baḥrī, mukhtaṣṣ bil baḥr*
mark (n)	علامة، أثر، معلم	*'alāmah, athar, ma'lam*
mark (v)	وسم، عين	*wasama, 'ayyana*
marked (adj)	مميز، موسوم بعلامة	*mumayyaz, mausūm bi 'alāmah*
marker (n)	علامة، واسم بعلامة	*'alāmah, wāsim bi 'alāmah*
market (n/v)	سوق، اتجر في السوق	*sūq, ittajara fis sūq*
marketable (n)	صالح للبيع في السوق	*ṣāliḥ lil bai' fis sūq*
market garden	أرض الخضر	*arḍul khuḍar*
marketing (n)	تسويق	*taswīq*
market-place (n)	ساحة السوق	*sāḥatus sūq*
market price	سعر سوقي	*si'r sūqī*
market research	استطلاع سوقي	*istiṭlā' sūqī*

market value	قيمة سوقية	*qīmah sūqiyyah*
marking (n)	وسم، علامة	*wasm, 'alāmah*
marksman (n)	رامي، هداف	*rāmī, haddāf*
marksmanship (n)	رماية	*rimāyah*
mark-up (n)	رفع السعر	*raf'us si'r*
marlin (n)	مرلين، سمك بحري	*marlīn, samak baḥrī*
marmalade (n)	مرملاد، هلام الفاكهة	*marmalād, hulāmul fākihah*
marmoset (n)	قشة، قرد أمريكي	*qishshah, qird amrīkī*
maroon (adj)	أحمر داكن	*aḥmar dākin*
maroon (v)	هجر، ألقى على ساحل	*hajara, alqā 'alā sāḥil*
marquee (n)	خيمة، فسطاط	*khaimah, fusṭāṭ*
marquetry (n)	تطعيم الخشب	*taṭ'īmul khashab*
marriage (n)	زواج، تزوج	*zawāj, tazawwuj*
marriageable (adj)	صالح للزواج	*ṣāliḥ liz zawāj*
married (adj)	متزوج	*mutazawwij*
marrow (n)	مخ العظم، كوسا	*mukhkhul 'aẓm, kūsā*
marry (v)	زوج، تزوج	*zawwaja, tazawwaja*
Mars (n)	مريخ	*mirrīkh*
marsh (n)	مستنقع، سبخة	*mustanqa', sabakhah*
marshal (n)	مارشال، مدير الشرطة	*mārshāl, mudīrush shurṭah*
marshal (v)	نظم، صف	*naẓẓama, ṣaffa*
marshmallow (n)	حلوى خطمي	*ḥalwā khiṭmī*
marsupial (n/adj)	جرابي، كيسي	*jirābī, kīsī*
mart (n)	سوق	*sūq*
marten (n)	دلق، خز	*dalaq, khazz*
martial (adj)	عسكري، حربي	*'askarī, ḥarbī*
martial law	قانون عرفي	*qānūn 'urfī*

martin (n)	خطاف	*khuṭṭāf*
martinet (n)	رجل صارم	*rajul ṣārim*
martini (n)	مارتيني	*mārtīnī*
martyr (n/v)	شهيد، استشهد	*shahīd, istashhada*
martyrdom (n)	استشهاد	*istishhād*
marvel (n/v)	أعجوبة، أدهش	*u'jūbah, adhasha*
marvellous (marvelous) (adj)	مدهش، عجيب	*mudhish, 'ajīb*
marvellously (adv)	بطريق مذهل	*bi ṭarīq mudhhil*
Marxism (n)	ماركسية	*mārkisiyyah*
Marxist (n)	ماركسي	*mārkisī*
masculine (n/adj)	ذكر، مذكر	*dhakar, mudhakkar*
masculinity (n)	ذكورة، تذكير	*dhukūrah, tadhkīr*
mash (v/n)	هرس، هريس	*harasa, harīs*
mask (v/n)	تقنع، قناع	*taqanna'a, qinā'*
masochism (n)	ماسوشية	*māsūshiyyah*
masochist (n)	ماسوشي	*māsūshī*
masochistic (adj)	ماسوشي	*māsūshī*
mason (n)	بناء	*bannā'*
masonry (n)	صناعة البناء	*ṣinā'atul binā'*
masque (n)	نوع من المسرحية	*nau' minal masraḥiyyah*
masquerade (n/v)	تنكر، تنكر	*tanakkur, tanakkara*
mass (n)	ضخامة، عدد كبير	*ḍakhāmah, 'adad kabīr*
mass (v)	تكتل، تجمع	*takattala, tajamma'a*
massacre (v)	ذبح، قتل	*dhabaḥa, qatala*
massacre (n)	مذبحة، مجزرة	*madhbaḥah, majzarah*
massage (n/v)	دلك، دلك	*dalk, dallaka*
masseur (n)	مدلك	*mudallik*
massive (adj)	ضخم، كبير، واسع	*ḍakhm, kabīr, wāsi'*
massively (adv)	على نطاق واسع	*'alā niṭāq wāsi'*

massiveness (n)	عظم، ضخامة	*'iẓam, ḍakhāmah*
mass-produce (v)	أنتج على نطاق واسع	*antajja 'alā niṭāq wāsi'*
mass-production (n)	إنتاج جملي	*intāj jumalī*
mast (n)	دقل، سارية	*daqal, sāriyah*
master (n)	مدرس، سيد، حاكم، أستاذ	*mudarris, sayyid, ḥākim, ustādh*
master (v)	تضلع، برع	*taḍalla'a, bara'a*
masterful (adj)	مسيطر، بارع	*musaiṭir, bāri'*
masterfully (adv)	ببراعة، بتفوق	*bi barā'ah, bi tafawwuq*
master-key (n)	مفتاح عمومي	*miftāḥ 'umūmī*
masterly (adj)	بارع، ذو براعة	*bāri', dhū barā'ah*
mastermind (n)	عقل موجه	*'aql muwajjih*
mastermind (v)	خطط	*khaṭṭaṭa*
masterpiece (n)	قطعة ممتازة	*qiṭ'ah mumtāzah*
master-stroke (n)	عمل أستاذي	*'amal ustādhī*
mastery (n)	تفوق، تضلع، براعة	*tafawwuq, taḍallu', barā'ah*
masthead (n)	أعلى الصاري	*a'laṣ ṣārī*
mastic (n)	مصطكاء	*musṭakā'*
masticate (v)	مضغ، لاك	*maḍagha, lāka*
mastication (n)	مضغ الطعام، لوك	*maḍghuṭ ṭa'ām, lauk*
masturbate (v)	استمنى باليد	*istamnā bil yad*
masturbation (n)	استمناء باليد	*istimnā' bil yad*
mat (n)	حصير، ممسحة	*ḥaṣīr, mimsaḥah*
mat (v)	ضفر، جدل	*ḍafara, jadala*
match (n)	مباراة، نظير، كفء	*mubārāt, naẓīr, kuf'*
match (v)	كافأ، توافق، لاءم	*kāfa'a, tawāfaqa, lā'ama*
matchmaker (n)	صانع الزيجات	*ṣāni'uz zījāt*
matchmaking (n)	صنع الزيجات	*ṣun'uz zījāt*
matchless (adj)	لا يضاهي، فريد	*lā yuḍāhā, farīd*

matchwood (n)	شظايا خشبية	*shaẓāyā khashabiyyah*
mate (n)	رفيق، زميل	*rafīq, zamīl*
mate (v)	تزوج، تجامع	*tazawwaja, tajāma'a*
material (n/adj)	مادة، مادي	*māddah, māddi*
materialism (n)	مادية	*māddiyyah*
materialist (n)	مادي	*māddī*
materialistic (adj)	مادي، جسدي	*māddī, jasadī*
materiality (n)	مادية	*māddiyyah*
materialization	تجسيد، تجسد	*tajsīd, tajassud*
maternal (adj)	أمي، متعلق بالأم	*ummī, muta'alliq bil umm*
maternity (n)	أمومة	*umūmah*
mathematical (adj)	رياضي	*riyāḍī*
mathematically (adv)	بطريقة رياضية	*bi ṭarīqah riyāḍiyyah*
mathematician (n)	متخصص بالرياضيات	*mutakhaṣṣiṣ bir riyāḍiyyāt*
mathematics (n)	علم الرياضيات	*'ilmur riyāḍiyyāt*
matins (n)	صلاة الصباح	*ṣalātuṣ ṣabāḥ*
matriarch (n)	أم رئيسة	*umm ra'īsah*
matriarchal (adj)	متعلق بالأم الرئيسة	*muta'alliq bil umm ar ra'īsah*
matriarchy (n)	نظام أمومي	*niẓām umūmī*
matricide (n)	قتل الأم	*qatlul umm*
matriculate (v)	قبل طالب في كلية	*qubila ṭālibun fī kulliyyah*
matriculation (n)	قبول في كلية	*qabūl fī kulliyyah*
matrimonial (n)	زوجي، مختص بالزواج	*zaujī, mukhtaṣṣ biz zawāj*
matrimony (n)	زواج	*zawāj*
matrix (n)	قالب، رحم	*qālab, raḥim*
matron (n)	رئيسة، ربة منــزل، قيمة	*ra'īsah, rabbatu manzil, qayyimah*
matronly (adj)	قيمي	*qayyimī*

matt=mat		
matter (n)	شأن، مادة، قضية	*sha'n, māddah, qaḍiyyah*
matter (v)	هم	*hamma*
matter-of-fact (adj)	واقعي، في الواقع	*wāqi'ī, fil wāqi'*
mattins = matins		
mattock (n)	معول	*mi'wal*
mattress (n)	فرشة، حشية	*farshah, ḥashiyyah*
maturation (n)	نضج، انضجاج	*nuḍj, inḍijāj*
mature (v)	أنضج، نضج	*anḍaja, naḍaja*
mature (adj)	ناضج، بالغ، مدروس	*nāḍij, bāligh, madrūs*
maturely (adv)	برشد، بنضج	*bi rushd, bi nuḍj*
maturity (n)	رشد، نضج	*rushd, nuḍj*
maul (v)	خاشن، هرس	*khāshana, harasa*
maunder (v)	ثرثر، تسكع	*tharthara, tasakka'a*
mausoleum (n)	ضريح فخم البناء	*ḍarīḥ fakhmul binā'*
mauve (adj)	خبازي	*khubbāzī*
maveric (n)	شخص خارج	*shakhṣ khārij*
maw (n)	حوصلة الطائر	*ḥauṣalatuṭ ṭā'ir*
mawkish (adj)	مغث، كريه	*mughthin, karīh*
mawkishness (n)	كره، عطف صبياني	*kurh, 'aṭf ṣibyānī*
maxim (n)	مثل سائر، حكمة	*mathal sā'ir, ḥikmah*
maximal (adj)	أكبر، أعلى	*akbar, a'lā*
maximization (n)	زيادة إلى حد ممكن	*ziyādah ilā ḥadd mumkin*
maximize,-ise (v)	زاد إلى حد أكبر	*zāda ilā ḥadd akbar*
maximum (adj)	أقصى، أكبر	*aqṣā, akbar*
May (n)	مايو، نوار	*māyū, nawwār*
may (n)	زعرور بري	*za'rūr barrī*
may (v)	لعل، أمكن، ربما	*la'alla, amkana, rubbamā*
maybe (adj)	ربما	*rubbamā*

Mayday (n)	عيد نوار	*'īdu nawwār*
mayfly (n)	ذبابة نوار	*dhubābatu nawwār*
mayhem (n)	تشويه، تشوش	*tashwīh, tashawwush*
mayonnaise (n)	ميونيز	*mayūnīz*
mayor (n)	رئيس البلدية	*ra'īsul baladiyyah*
mayoral (adj)	متعلق برئيس البلدية	*muta'alliq bi ra'īsil baladiyyah*
mayoralty (n)	منصب رئيس البلدية	*manṣabu ra'īsil baladiyyah*
mayoress (n)	رئيسة البلدية	*ra'īsatul baladiyyah*
maypole (n)	سارية نوار	*sāriyatu nawwār*
maze (n)	متاهة، تيه	*matāhah, tīh*
me (pron)	ني، ي	*nī, yā*
mead (n)	ميد، ضرب من شراب مخمر	*mīd, ḍarb min sharāb mukhammar*
meadow (n)	مرج، مرجة، روضة	*marj, marjah, rauḍah*
meagre (meager) (n)	يسير، ضئيل، نحيل	*yasīr, ḍa'īl, naḥīl*
meal (n)	وجبة، أكلة	*wajbah, aklah*
mealtime (n)	وقت الطعام	*waqtuṭ ṭa'ām*
meal-mouthed (adj)	معسول اللسان	*ma'sūlul lisān*
mean (v)	أفاد، عنى، قصد	*afāda, 'anā, qaṣada*
mean (adj)	خسيس، دنيء، وضيع	*khasīs, danī', waḍī'*
meander (v)	تعرج، تسكع	*ta'arraja, tasakka'a*
meaning (n)	معنى، مراد	*ma'nā, murād*
meaningful (adj)	ذو معنى	*dhū ma'nā*
meaningfulness (n)	كونه ذو معنى	*kaunuhu dhū ma'nā*
meanly (adv)	بدناءة، بسفالة	*bi danā'ah, bi safālah*
meanness (n)	سفالة، دناءة، خسة	*safālah, danā'ah, khissah*
means (n)	موارد، وسائل	*mawārid, wasā'il*
meantime (n)	في غضون، خلال	*fī ghuḍūn, khilāla*

meanwhile (adv)	أثناء، في غضون	*athnā', fī ghuḍūn*
measles (n)	حصبة	*ḥaṣbah*
measly (adj)	تافه، ضئيل	*tāfih, ḍā'īl*
measurable (adj)	قابل للقياس	*qābil lil qiyās*
measurably (adv)	بطريق يقاس	*bi ṭarīq yuqās*
measure (v)	قاس، ضبط، وزن	*qāsa, ḍabaṭa, wazana*
measure (n)	قياس، مقياس، وزن	*qiyās, miqyās, wazn*
measured (adj)	مدروس، موزون	*madrūs, mauzūn*
measurement (n)	مقياس، قياس	*miqyās, qiyās*
meat (n)	لحم، لب الشيء	*laḥm, lubbush shay'*
meaty (adj)	لحيم، لحمي	*laḥīm, laḥmī*
Mecca (n)	مكة المكرمة	*makkah al mukarrama*
mechanic (n)	يدوي، ميكانيك	*yadawī, mīkānīk*
mechanical (adj)	ميكانيكي،حرفي،آلي	*mīkānīkī, ḥirafī, ālī*
mechanically (adv)	ميكانيكيًا	*mīkānīkiyyan*
mechanics (n)	علم الميكانيكا	*'ilmul mīkānīkā*
mechanism (n)	ميكانيكية، آلية	*mīkānīkiyyah, āliyyah*
mechanistic (adj)	ميكانيكي	*mīkānīkī*
mechanization (n)	مكننة	*maknanah*
mechanize,-ise (v)	مكنن، جعل ميكانيكيًا	*maknana, ja'ala mīkānīkiyyan*
medal (n)	وسام، مدالية	*wisām, madāliyah*
medallion (n)	مدالية كبيرة	*mādāliyah kabīrah*
medallist (n)	حائز وسام، موسم	*ḥā'izu wisām, muwassam*
meddle (v)	تدخل، تطفل	*tadakhkhala, taṭaffala*
meddler (n)	متطفل	*mutaṭaffil*
media (n)	وسائل، وسائط	*wasā'il, wasā'iṭ*
median (n/adj)	متوسط	*mutawassiṭ*
mediate (v)	توسط، تشفع	*tawassaṭa, tashaffa'a*
mediation (n)	توسط، وساطة	*tawassuṭ, wasāṭah*

mediator (n)	وسيط، مصلح	*wasīṭ, muṣliḥ*
medical (adj)	طبي، طبية	*ṭibbī, ṭibbiyyah*
medically (adv)	بطريقة طبية	*bi ṭarīqah ṭibbiyyah*
medicament (n)	عقار، دواء	*'aqqār, dawā'*
medicated (adj)	ممزوج بدواء	*mamzūj bi dawā'*
medicinal (adj)	طبي، دوائي	*ṭibbī, dawā'ī*
medicine (n)	دواء، طب	*dawā', ṭibb*
medico (n)	طبيب، طالب الطب	*ṭabīb, ṭālibuṭ ṭibb*
medieval (mediaeval)	مختص بالقرون الأولى	*mukhtaṣṣ bil qurūn al ūlā*
mediocre (adj)	متوسط، معتدل	*mutawassiṭ, mu'tadil*
mediocrity (n)	توسط، اعتدال	*tawassuṭ, i'tidāl*
meditate (v)	تفكر، تأمل	*tafakkara, ta'ammala*
meditation (n)	تأمل، تفكر	*ta'ammul, tafakkur*
meditative (adj)	تأملي، تفكيري	*ta'ammulī, tafkīrī*
Mediterranean (n)	متوسطي	*mutawassiṭī*
medium (adj/n)	وسيط، شيء وسيط	*wasīṭ, shay' wasīṭ*
medley (n)	لحن خليط، مزيج	*laḥn khalīṭ, mazīj*
meek (adj)	خاضع، حليم، وديع	*khāḍi', ḥalīm, wadī'*
meakly (adv)	بوداعة، بحلم	*bi wadā'ah, bi ḥilm*
meakness (n)	خضوع، رقة، وداعة	*khuḍū', riqqah, wadā'ah*
meet (v)	قابل، لقى، التقى	*qābala, laqiya, lāqā*
meeting (n)	اجتماع، حفلة	*ijtimā', ḥaflah*
meeting-house (n)	مبنى الاجتماع	*mabnal ijtimā'*
mega (adj)	ضخم، كبير جدًا	*ḍakhm, kabīr jiddā*
megalomania (n)	جنون العظمة	*junūnul 'aẓmah*
megalomaniac (adj)	مصاب بجنون العظمة	*muṣāb bi junūnil 'aẓmah*
megaphone (n)	بوق، صور	*būq, ṣūr*
megaton (n)	ميغاطن	*mīghāṭan*
melamine (n)	ميلامين	*mīlāmīn*

melancholia (n)	ملنخوليا	*malankhūliyā*
melancholiac (adj)	مصاب بملنخوليا	*muṣāb bi malankhūliyā*
melancholic (adj)	مكتئب، كئيب، محزن	*mukta'ib, ka'īb, muḥzin*
melancholy (n)	ملنخوليا، كآبة	*malankhūliyā, ka'ābah*
melange (n)	مزيج، خليط	*mazīj, khalīṭ*
meld (v)	مزج، صرح	*mazaja, ṣarraḥa*
melee (n)	عراك صاخب	*'irāk ṣākhib*
mellifluous (adj)	معسول، عذب	*ma'sūl, 'adhb*
mellow (adj)	ناضج، رخيم، يانع	*nāḍij, rakhīm, yāni'*
mellow (v)	لان، جعل يانعًا	*lāna, ja'ala yāni'an*
melodic (adj)	لحني	*laḥnī*
melodious (adj)	رخيم، مطرب	*rakhīm, muṭrib*
melodiously (adv)	بطريقة مطربة	*bi ṭarīqah muṭribah*
melodrama (n)	ميلودراما	*mīlūdarāmā*
melodramatically	ميلودراميًا	*mīlūdarāmiyyan*
melodramic (adj)	ميلودارمي	*mīlūdarāmī*
melody (n)	لحن، نغمة مطربة	*laḥn, naghmah muṭribah*
melon (n)	بطيخ أصفر	*biṭṭīkh aṣfar*
melt (v)	ذاب، ذوب، انصهر	*dhāba, dhawwaba, inṣahara*
melting-point (n)	نقطة الانصهار	*nuqṭatul inṣihār*
melting-pot (n)	بلد بوتقة	*balad būtaqah*
member (n)	عضو	*'uḍw*
membership (n)	عضوية	*'uḍwiyyah*
membrane (n)	غشاء	*ghishā'*
memento (n)	تذكرة، تذكار	*tadhkirah, tadhkār*
memo=memorandum		
memoir (n)	مذكرة، سيرة ذاتية	*mudhakkirah, sīrah dhātiyyah*
memorabilia (n)	حوادث جديرة بالتذكر	*ḥawādith jadīrah bit tadhakkur*
memorable (adj)	بارز، مشهور	*bāriz, mashhūr*

memorandum (n)	مذكرة، مفكرة	*mudhakkirah, mufakkirah*
memorial (adj/n)	تذكاري، نصب تذكاري	*tidhkārī, nuṣub tidhkarī*
memorial day	يوم الذكرى	*yaumudh dhikrā*
memorize,-ise (v)	حفظ، استظهر	*ḥafiẓa, istaẓhara*
memory (n)	ذاكرة، ذكرى	*dhākirah, dhikrā*
menace (n/v)	تهديد، هدد	*tahdīd, haddada*
menacing (adj)	مهدد، متوعد	*muhaddid, mutawa''id*
menacingly (adv)	مهدداً، بتهديد	*muhaddidan, bi tahdīd*
menage (n)	شؤون المنـــزل	*shu'ūnul manzil*
menagerie (n)	مجموعة الوحوش	*majmū'atul wuḥūsh*
mend (v)	رمم، أصلح	*rammama, aṣlaḥa*
mendacious (adj)	كاذب، أفاك	*kādhib, affāk*
mendacity (n)	كذب، إفك	*kadhib, ifk*
mendicant (n/adj)	متسول، شحاذ	*mutasawwil, shaḥḥādh*
mending (n)	ترميم، رتق	*tarmīm, ratq*
menial (adj/n)	دنيء، حقير	*danī', ḥaqīr*
meningitis (n)	التهاب السحايا	*iltihābus saḥāyā*
menopausal (adj)	إياسي	*iyāsī*
menopause (n)	سن اليأس	*sinnul ya's*
menses (n)	حيض، طمث	*ḥaiḍ, ṭamth*
menstrual (adj)	حيضي، طمثي	*ḥaiḍī, ṭamthī*
menstruate (v)	حاضت، طمثت	*ḥāḍat, ṭamathat*
menstruation (n)	حيض، طمث	*ḥaiḍ, ṭamth*
mental (adj)	ذهني، عقلي	*dhihnī, 'aqlī*
mental deficiency	نقص عقلي	*naqṣ 'aqlī*
mentality (n)	ذهنية، عقلية	*dhihniyyah, 'aqliyyah*
mentally (adv)	ذهنيًا، عقليًا	*dhihniyyan, 'aqliyyan*
menthol (n)	منثول	*manthūl*
mention (v/n)	ذكر، ذكر	*dhakara, dhikr*

mentor (n)	نصوح، مشير صادق	*naṣūḥ, mushīr ṣādiq*
menu (n)	قائمة الطعام	*qā'imatuṭ ṭa'ām*
mercantile (adj)	مركنتلي، تجاري	*markantalī, tijārī*
mercenary (n/adj)	جندي مرتزق، مرتزق	*jundī murtaziq, murtaziq*
merchandise (v/n)	تاجر، بضائع	*tājara, baḍā'i'*
merchandising (n)	ترويج السلع	*tarwījus sila'*
merchant (n/adj)	تاجر، تجاري	*tājir, tijārī*
merchantable (adj)	صالح للسوق	*ṣāliḥ lis sūq*
merchant marine	أسطول تجاري	*usṭūl tijārī*
merciful (adj)	رحيم، كريم، رؤوف	*raḥīm, karīm, ra'ūf*
mercifully (adv)	برحمة، بفضل	*bi raḥmah, bi faḍl*
merciless (adj)	عديم الرحمة، قاسٍ	*'adīmur raḥmah, qāsin*
mercilessly (adv)	بقسوة	*bi qaswah*
mercurial (adj)	عطاردي	*'uṭāridī*
Mercury (n)	عطارد	*'uṭārid*
mercy (n)	رحمة، فضل، رأفة	*raḥmah, faḍl, ra'fah*
mere (adj/n)	مجرد، بركة	*mujarrad, birkah*
merely (adv)	لا غير، ليس غير	*lā ghair, laisa ghair*
meretricious (adj)	مزوق، خادع	*muzawwaq, khādi'*
merge (v)	دمج، اندمج، انغمس	*damaja, indamaja, inghamasa*
merger (n)	اندماج، إدماج	*indimāj, idmāj*
meridian (n)	خط التنصيف	*khaṭṭut tanṣīf*
merit (n)	ميزة، أهلية، استحقاق	*mīzah, ahliyyah, istiḥqāq*
merit (v)	استحق، استأهل	*istaḥaqqa, ista'hala*
meritorious (adj)	مستأهل، ذو أهلية	*musta'hil, dhū ahliyyah*
mermaid (n)	بنت الماء	*bintul mā'*
merrily (adv)	بقصف، بمرح	*bi qaṣf, bi maraḥ*
merriment (n)	قصف، مرح	*qaṣf, maraḥ*

merry (adj)	مرح، جذل	*mariḥ, jadhil*
merry-go-round (n)	دوامة	*duwwāmah*
merrymaking (n)	قصف، مرح	*qaṣf, maraḥ*
mesa (n)	ميسة	*maisah*
mesh (n)	شبكة، شرك	*shabakah, sharak*
mesh (v)	تشابك، تناغم	*tashābaka, tanāghama*
meshed (adj)	مشبك، مشابك	*mushabbak, mushābak*
mesmeric (adj)	مسمري	*masmarī*
mesmerize,-ise (v)	مسمر	*masmara*
mess (n)	خبيصة، رفاق	*khabīṣah, rifāqul*
	المائدة، مأزق	*mā'idah, ma'ziq*
mess (v)	وسخ، أفسد	*wassakha, afsada*
message (n)	رسالة، خطاب	*risālah, khiṭāb*
messenger (n)	رسول، مبلغ	*rasūl, muballigh*
Messiah (n)	مسيح	*masīḥ*
messiah (n)	مخلص، منجي	*mukhalliṣ, munajjī*
messily (adv)	على نحو مختلط	*'alā naḥw mukhtaliṭ*
messiness (n)	اختلاط، فوضى	*ikhtilāṭ, fauḍā*
messy (adj)	غير مرتب، مختلط	*ghair murattab, mukhtaliṭ*
metabolic (adj)	أيضي	*aiḍī*
metabolism (n)	الأيض	*al aiḍ*
metabolize,-ise (v)	أيض، آض	*ayyaḍa, āḍa*
metal (n)	معدن، زلط	*ma'din, zalaṭ*
metallic (adj)	معدني، صلب	*ma'dinī, ṣulb*
metallurgical (adj)	متعلق بعلم المعادن	*muta'alliq bi 'ilmil*
		ma'ādin
metallurgist (n)	عالم بالمعادن	*'ālim bil ma'ādin*
metallurgy (n)	ميتالورجيا، علم	*mītālūrjiyā, 'ilmul*
	المعادن	*ma'ādin*
metalwork (n)	صنع الأدوات	*ṣun'ul adawāt al*
	المعدنية	*ma'diniyyah*
metamorphose (v)	غير، حول	*ghayyara, ḥawwala*

metamorphosis (n)	تحول، مسخ	*taḥawwul, maskh*
metaphor (n)	مجاز، استعارة	*majāz, isti'ārah*
metaphorical (adj)	مجازي، استعاري	*majāzī, isti'ārī*
metaphorically (adv)	بطريقة الاستعارة	*bi ṭarīqatil isti'ārah*
metaphysical (adj)	غيبي، ما ورائي	*ghaibī, mā warā'ī*
metaphysics (n)	مافوق الطبيعة	*mā fauqaṭ ṭabī'ah*
mete (v)	قاس، وزع	*qāsa, wazza'a*
meteor (n)	نيزك، شهاب	*naizak, shihāb*
meteoric (adj)	شهابي، جوي	*shihābī, jawwī*
meteorite (n)	حجر نيزكي	*ḥajar naizakī*
meteorological (adj)	أرصادي	*arṣādī*
meteorologist (n)	عالم بالأرصاد	*'ālim bil arṣād*
meteorology (n)	علم الأرصاد الجوية	*'ilmul arṣād al jawwiyyah*
methadone (n)	ميثادون، عقار مخدر	*mīthādūn, 'aqqār mukhaddir*
methane (n)	ميثان، غاز المناجم	*mīthān, ghāzul manājim*
method (n)	طريقة، أسلوب، منهج	*ṭarīqah, uslūb, manhaj*
methodical (adj)	منهجي، نظامي	*manhajī, niẓāmī*
methodically (adv)	بنظام، بنسق	*bi niẓām, bi nasaq*
methodology (n)	علم المناهج، ميثودولوجيا	*'ilmul manāhij, mīthūdūlūjiyā*
meticulous (adj)	موسوس، شديد التدقيق	*muwaswas, shadīdut tadqīq*
meticulously (adv)	بدقة شديدة	*bi diqqah shadīdah*
metier (n)	مهنة، شغل	*mihnah, shughl*
metre (meter) (n)	متر، عداد، وزن	*mitr, 'addād, wazn*
metre (meter) (v)	قاس، وزن	*qāsa, wazana*
metrical (adj)	عروضي، متري، قياسي	*'arūḍī, mitrī, qiyāsī*

metro (n)	قطار تحت الأرض، مترو	*qiṭār taḥtal arḍ, mitrū*
metropolis (n)	المدينة الأم	*al madīnah al umm*
metropolitan (adj)	متراني، عاصمي	*mitrānī, 'āṣimī*
mettle (n)	طبع، حمية	*ṭab', ḥamiyyah*
mew (v/n)	ماء، مواء	*mā'a, mawā'*
miasma (n)	جو عفن	*jaww 'afin*
mica (n)	ميكة	*maikah*
microbe (n)	ميكروب، جرثومة	*maikurūb, jurthūmah*
microbiologist (n)	عالم بالأحياء المجهري	*'ālim bil aḥyā' al mijharī*
microbiology (n)	علم الأحياء المجهري	*'ilmul aḥyā' al mijharī*
microcosm (n)	عالم صغير	*'ālam ṣaghīr*
microphone (n)	ميكروفون، مذياع	*maikurūfūn, midhyā'*
microscope (n)	ميكروسكوب، مجهر	*maikurūskūb, mijhar*
microscopic (adj)	مجهري، ميكروسكوبي	*mijharī, maikurūskūbī*
microwave (n)	موجة صغرى	*maujah ṣughrā*
mid (adj)	متوسط، منتصف	*mutawassiṭ, muntaṣif*
mid (n)	وسط، انتصاف	*wasaṭ, intiṣāf*
midday (n)	ظهر	*ẓuhr*
middle (n/adj)	وسط، متوسط	*wasaṭ, mutawassiṭ*
Middle Ages	القرون الوسطى	*al qurūn al wusṭā*
middle-brow (n/adj)	متوسط الثقافة	*mutawassiṭuth thaqāfah*
middle class	طبقة وسطى	*ṭabaqah wusṭā*
middle distance	سباق متوسط	*sibāq mutawassiṭ*
Middle East	شرق أوسط	*sharq ausaṭ*
middleman (n)	الوسيط	*al wasīṭ*
middleweight (n)	شخص متوسط الوزن	*shakhṣ mutawassiṭul wazn*
middling (adj)	متوسط، معتدل	*mutawassiṭ, mu'tadil*
midge (n)	ذبابة صغيرة	*dhubābah ṣaghīrah*
midget (n)	شخص صغير جدا	*shakhṣ ṣaghīr jiddā*

midland (adj)	داخلي	*dākhilī*
midnight (n)	منتصف الليل	*muntaṣaful lail*
midnight sun	شمس منتصف الليل	*shamsu muntaṣafil lail*
midriff (n)	جزء أوسط من جسم الإنسان	*juz' ausaṭ min jismil insān*
midshipman (n)	مرشح البحرية	*murashshaḥul baḥriyyah*
midst (n)	وسط، بين	*wasaṭ, baina*
midsummer (n)	منتصف الصيف	*muntaṣafuṣ ṣaif*
midway (adj/adv)	متوسط، في الوسط	*mutawassiṭ, fil wasaṭ*
midweek (n)	واقع في منتصف الأسبوع	*wāqi' fī muntaṣafil usbū'*
midweek (adv)	في وسط الأسبوع	*fī wasaṭil usbū'*
midwife (n)	مؤلدة، قابلة	*mu'allidah, qābilah*
midwifery (n)	قبالة، علم القبالة	*qibālah, 'ilmul qibālah*
midwinter (n)	منتصف الشتاء	*muntaṣafush shitā'*
mien (n)	مظهر، سيماء	*maẓhar, sīmā'*
miffed (adj)	مستاء، زعل	*mustā'in, za'il*
might (n)	مقدرة، قوة	*maqdurah, quwwah*
might (v)	أمكن، ربما	*amkana, rubbamā*
mightily (adv)	بقوة، بقدرة	*bi quwwah, bi qudrah*
mighty (adj)	قوي، قادر	*qawiyy, qādir*
migrant (n)	مهاجر، متنقل	*muhājir, mutanaqqil*
migrate (v)	هاجر، ارتحل	*hājara, irtaḥala*
migration (n)	هجرة، ارتحال	*hijrah, irtiḥāl*
migratory (adj)	ترحلي، ارتحالي	*taraḥḥulī, irtiḥālī*
mike=microphone		
mild (adj)	هادئ، لطيف	*hādi', laṭīf*
mildly (adv)	باعتدال، بلطف	*bi'tidāl, bi luṭf*
mildness (n)	لطف، لين	*luṭf, līn*

mile (n)	ميل	*mīl*
mileage (n)	مسافة بالميل	*masāfah bil mīl*
miler (n)	متسابق ميلي	*mutasābiq mīlī*
milestone (n)	معلم، صدة	*ma'lam, ṣuddah*
milieu (n)	بيئة	*bī'ah*
militancy (n)	قتال، كفاح، حربية	*qitāl, kifāḥ, ḥarbiyyah*
militant (adj/n)	محارب، مقاتل	*muḥārib, muqātil*
militarism (n)	عسكرية، حربية	*'askariyyah, ḥarbiyyah*
militarizaton,-isation (n)	تزويد بالقوات العسكرية	*tazwīd bil quwwāt al 'askariyyah*
military (adj)	عسكري، حربي	*'askarī, ḥarbi*
military (n)	قوات مسلحة	*quwwāt musallaḥah*
militate (v)	أثر، كافح	*aththara, kāfaḥa*
militia (n)	ميليشيا	*mīlīshiyā*
militiaman (n)	جندي من ميليشيا	*jundī min mīlīshiyā*
milk (n/v)	حليب، حلب	*ḥalīb, ḥalaba*
milkmaid (n)	حلابة، حالبة	*ḥallābah, ḥālibah*
milkman (n)	حلاب، لبان	*ḥallāb, labbān*
milk shake	مخفوق لبني	*makhfūq labanī*
milksop (n)	مخنث	*mukhannath*
milk tooth (n)	راضعة	*rāḍi'ah*
milky (adj)	لبني، كاللبن	*labanī, kal laban*
milky way	طريق لبنية	*ṭarīq labaniyyah*
mill (n/v)	طاحونة، طحن	*ṭāḥūnah, ṭaḥana*
millennium (n)	ألف عام	*alfu 'ām*
miller (n)	طحان، صاحب طاحونة	*ṭaḥḥān, ṣāḥibu ṭāḥūnah*
millet (n)	نبات دخن	*nabātu dukhn*
millibar (n)	مليبار	*millībār*
milligram (n)	مليغرام	*millīgharām*
millilitre (n)	مليليتر	*millīlītar*

millimetre (n)	مليمتر	*millīmitar*
milliner (n)	بائع القبعات النسائية	*bā'i'ul qubba'āt an nisā'iyyah*
million (n)	مليون	*malyūn*
millionaire (n)	مليونير	*malyūniyar*
millipede (n)	دودة صغيرة	*dūdah ṣaghīrah*
millisecond (n)	مليثانية	*millīthāniyah*
millpond (n)	بركة الطاحون	*birkatuṭ ṭāḥūn*
millstone (n)	حجر الرحى	*ḥajarur raḥā*
mime (n)	ميم، مقلد	*maim, muqallid*
mime (v)	ميم، قلد	*mayyama, qallada*
mimetic (adj)	تقليدي، ميمي	*taqlīdī, maimī*
mimic (v)	حاكى، قلد	*ḥākā, qallada*
mimic (n)	محاكي، مقلد	*muḥākī, muqallid*
mimicry (n)	فن المحاكاة	*fannul muḥākāt*
mimosa (n)	نبات السنط	*nabātus sanṭ*
minaret (n)	منار، مئذنة	*manār, mi'dhanah*
minatory (adj)	تهديدي، مهدد	*tahdīdī, muhaddid*
mince (v)	فرم، قطع	*farama, qaṭṭa'a*
mince (n)	قطع صغيرة	*qiṭa' ṣaghīrah*
mincemeat (n)	لحم مفروم	*laḥm mafrūm*
mincing (adj)	أنيق، رقيق	*anīq, raqīq*
mind (n)	عقل، ذاكرة	*'aql, dhākirah*
mind (v)	لاحظ، وعى، اهتم	*lāḥaẓa, wa'ā, ihtamma*
minded (adj)	مائل، نزاع، ميال	*mā'il, nazzā', mayyāl*
mindful (adj)	مهتم، واعٍ، منتبه	*muhtamm, wā'in, muntabih*
mindfully (adv)	باهتمام، باكتراث	*bihtimām, biktirāth*
mindless (adj)	غافل، غبي	*ghāfil, ghabī*
mindlessly (adv)	بغير مبالاة	*bighairi mubālāt*

mine (pron)	لي	*lī*
mine (n/v)	منجم، حفر منجمًا	*manjam, ḥafara manjaman*
miner (n)	مشتغل بالمعدن	*mushtaghil bil ma'din*
mineral (n)	معدن، فلز	*ma'din, filizz*
mineral water	مياه معدنية	*miyāh ma'diniyyah*
minestrone (n)	مينيسترون	*mīnīsturūn*
minesweeper (n)	كانسة الألغام	*kānisatul alghām*
mingle (v)	خلط، مزج، اختلط	*khalaṭa, mazaja, ikhtalaṭa*
miniature (adj/n)	مصغرة، صورة مصغرة	*muṣaghgharah, ṣūrah muṣaghgharah*
miniaturization (n)	نمنمة	*namnamah*
miniaturize,-ise (v)	نمنم، صغر	*namnama, ṣaghghara*
minicab (n)	سيارة منمنمة	*sayyārah munamnamah*
minim (n)	نصف نغمة	*niṣfu naghmah*
minimal (adj)	أدنى، أقل	*adnā, aqall*
minimize,-ise (v)	قلل، خفض	*qallala, khaffaḍa*
minimum (adj/n)	أقل، أدنى	*aqall, adnā*
minimum wage	أجر أدنى	*ajr adnā*
minion (n)	موظف أدنى	*muwaẓẓaf adnā*
miniskirt (n)	تنورة قصيرة	*tannūrah qaṣīrah*
minister (n)	وزير، كاهن، وكيل	*wazīr, kāhin, wakīl*
minister (v)	أعان، أسعف	*a'āna, as'afa*
ministerial (adj)	وزاري، تنفيذي	*wizārī, tanfīdhī*
ministration (n)	مساعدة، خدمة	*musā'adah, khidmah*
ministry (n)	وزارة، أعضاء الوزارة	*wizārah, a'ḍā'ul wizārah*
minor (adj/n)	قاصر، مراهق، غير هام	*qāṣir, murāhiq, ghair hāmm*
minority (n)	أقلية، سن القصور	*aqaliyyah, sinnul quṣūr*
minster (n)	كاتدرائية، كنيسة	*kātadrā'iyyah, kanīsah*

minstrel (n)	مغني، منشد	*mughannī, munshid*
mint (n/v)	دار الضرب، سك العملة	*dāruḍ ḍarb, sakkal 'umlah*
minuet (n)	رقصة المينويت	*raqṣatul mīnūyat*
minus (n/adj)	علامة ناقص، سلبي	*'alāmatu nāqiṣ, salbī*
minuscule (adj)	صغير جدا	*ṣaghīr jiddā*
minute (n)	دقيقة، لحظة	*daqīqah, laḥẓah*
minute (adj)	دقيق، صغير	*daqīq, ṣaghīr*
minute (v)	دون، سجل	*dawwana, sajjala*
minute-hand (n)	عقرب الدقائق	*'aqrabud daqā'iq*
minutely (adj)	بدقة، بالضبط	*bi diqqah, biḍ ḍabṭ*
miracle (n)	معجزة، أعجوبة	*mu'jizah, u'jūbah*
miracle play	تمثيلية أعاجيبية	*tamthīliyyah a'ājībiyyah*
miraculous (adj)	معجز، إعجازي	*mu'jiz, i'jāzī*
miraculously (adv)	بطريقة معجزة	*bi ṭarīqah mu'jizah*
mirage (n)	سراب، وهم، آل	*sarāb, wahm, āl*
mire (n/v)	وحل، وحل	*waḥl, waḥila*
mirror (n)	مرآة، منظار	*mir'āt, minẓār*
mirror (v)	عكس، انعكس	*'akasa, in'akasa*
mirth (n)	جذل، طرب	*jadhal, ṭarab*
misadventure (n)	كارثة، بلية، نازلة	*kārithah, baliyyah, nāzilah*
misanthrope (n)	مبغض البشر	*mubghiḍul bashar*
misanthropy (n)	بغض البشر	*bughḍul bashar*
misapplication (n)	إساءة الاستعمال	*isā'atul isti'māl*
misapprehend (v)	أخطأ الفهم	*akhṭa'al fahm*
misapprehension (n)	إخطاء الفهم	*ikhṭā'ul fahm*
misappropriate (v)	استعمل في غير محله	*ista'mala fī ghairi maḥallihi*
misbegotten (adj)	غير شرعي، غير صحيح	*ghair shar'ī, ghair ṣaḥīḥ*
misbehave (v)	أساء السلوك	*asā'as sulūk*

misbehaviour (n)	سوء السلوك	*sū'us sulūk*
miscalculate (v)	أخطأ الحساب	*akhṭa'al ḥisāb*
miscall (v)	أخطأ في التسمية	*akhṭa'a fit tasmiyah*
miscarriage (n)	إجهاض، خيبة	*ijhāḍ, khaibah*
miscarry (v)	أجهضت المرأة، خاب	*ajhaḍatil mar'ah, khāba*
miscegenation (n)	اختلاط الأجناس، تمازج الأجناس	*ikhtilāṭul ajnās, tamāzujul ajnās*
miscellaneous (adj)	متنوع، متعدد، شتى	*mutanawwi', muta'addid, shattā*
miscellany (n)	مجموع، مجموعة	*majmū', majmū'ah*
mischance (n)	سوء الحظ	*sū'ul ḥaẓẓ*
mischief (n)	أذى، سوء، ضرر	*adhā, sū', ḍarar*
mischievous (adj)	مزعج، مؤذ	*muz'ij, mu'dhin*
mischievously (adv)	بخبث، بسوء	*bi khubth, bi sū'*
misconceive (v)	أخطأ الفهم	*akhṭa'al fahm*
misconception (n)	خطأ، سوء الإدراك	*khaṭa', sū'ul idrāk*
misconduct (n)	سوء الإدارة، سوء السلوك	*sū'ul idārah, sū'us sulūk*
misconstruction (n)	سوء الفهم، سوء الإدراك	*sū'ul fahm, sū'ul idrāk*
misconstrue (v)	أساء التفسير، أساء التشريح	*asā'at tafsīr, asā'at tashrīḥ*
miscount (v)	أخطأ في العد	*akhṭa'a fil 'add*
miscreant (n)	جاحد، لئيم	*jāḥid, la'īm*
misdeed (n)	إثم، عمل شرير	*ithm, 'amal sharīr*
misdemeanour (n)	ذنب صغير، جنحة	*dhamb ṣaghīr, junḥah*
misdirect (v)	أضل، أساء الاستعمال	*aḍalla, asā'al isti'māl*
misdoing (n)	سيئة، ذنب	*sayyi'ah, dhamb*
miser (n)	شحيح، بخيل	*shaḥīḥ, bakhīl*
miserable (adj)	بائس، متعوس	*bā'is, mat'ūs*

miserably (adv)	بتعس، بشقاء	*bi ta'ṣ, bi shaqā'*
miserly (adj)	بخيل، شحيح	*bakhīl, shaḥīḥ*
misery (n)	بؤس، تعاسة	*bu's, ta'āsah*
misfire (v/n)	كبا، كبو	*kabā, kubuww*
misfit (n)	سيء التطابق، سيء التلاءم	*sayyi'ut taṭābuq, sayyi'ut talā'um*
misfortune (n)	سوء الحظ، بلية	*sū'ul ḥaẓẓ, baliyyah*
misgiving (n)	شك، ريب، ظن	*shakk, raib, ẓann*
misgovern (v)	أساء الحكم	*asā'al ḥukm*
misguided (adj)	مضلل، ضال	*muḍallil, ḍāll*
mishandle (v)	أساء التدبير	*asā'at tadbīr*
mishap (n)	بلية، حادث موجع	*baliyyah, ḥādith mūji'*
mishear (v)	أخطأ في السماع	*akhṭa'a fis samā'*
mishmash (n)	مزيج، خليط	*mazīj, khalīṭ*
misinform (v)	أساء الإعلام	*asā'al i'lām*
misinformation (n)	معلومات خاطئة	*ma'lūmāt khāṭi'ah*
misinterpret (v)	أساء التفسير، أساء التأويل	*asā'at tafsīr, asā'at ta'wīl*
misinterpretation (n)	إساءة التفسير	*isā'atut tafsīr*
misjudge (v)	أخطأ في الحكم	*akhṭa'a fil ḥukm*
misjudgement,-gment	خطأ في الحكم	*khaṭa' fil ḥukm*
mislay (v)	أضاع، فقد	*aḍā'a, faqada*
mislead (v)	أضل، تيه	*aḍalla, tayyaha*
misleading (adj)	مضل، خادع	*muḍill, khādi'*
misleadingly (adv)	بطريقة مضلة	*bi ṭarīqah muḍillah*
mismanage (v)	أساء الإدارة	*asā'al idārah*
mismanagement (n)	سوء التدبير	*sū'ut tadbīr*
mismatch (n)	زوج غير ملائم	*zauj ghair mulā'im*
misname (v)	أخطأ في التسمية	*akhṭa'a fit tasmiyah*
misnomer (n)	خطأ في تسمية	*khaṭa' fī tasmiyah*

misogamist (n)	كاره النساء	*kārihun nisā'*
misogamy (n)	كره للنساء	*kurh lin nisā'*
misplace (v)	وضع في غير محله	*waḍa'a fī ghairi maḥallihi*
misplaced (adj)	وضع في غير محله	*wuḍi'a fī ghairi maḥallihi*
misprint (n)	خطأ في الطبع	*khaṭa' fiṭ ṭab'*
mispronounce (v)	أخطأ في اللفظ	*akhṭa'a fil lafẓ*
misquotation (n)	خطأ في الاقتباس	*khaṭa' fil iqtibās*
misquote (v)	أخطأ في الاقتباس	*akhṭa'a fil iqtibās*
misread (v)	صحف، أخطأ في القراءة	*ṣaḥḥafa, akhṭa'a fil qirā'ah*
misrepresent (v)	صحف، حرف	*ṣaḥḥafa, ḥarrafa*
misrepresentation (n)	تصحيف، تحريف	*taṣḥif, taḥrīf*
misrule (n)	سوء الحكم	*sū'ul ḥukm*
miss (v)	فات، فقد، افتقد	*fātā, faqada, iftaqada*
miss (n)	خطأ، عدم الإصابة	*khaṭa', 'adamul iṣābah*
Miss (n)	آنسة، فتاة	*ānisah, fatāt*
missal (n)	كتاب القداس	*kitābul quddās*
misshapen (adj)	مشوه، ممسوخ	*mushawwah, mamsūkh*
missile (n)	صاروخ، قذيفة	*ṣārūkh, qadhīfah*
mission (n)	بعثة، رسالة دينية	*ba'thah, risālah dīniyyah*
missionary (n)	مرسل ديني	*mursal dīnī*
misspell (v)	أخطأ في التهجئة	*akhṭa'a fit tahji'ah*
misspend (v)	أساء الإنفاق، أسرف	*asā'al infāq, asrafa*
mist (n)	سديم، ضباب، طل	*sadīm, ḍabāb, ṭall*
mist (v)	أسدم، غشى	*asdama, ghashshā*
mistake (n/v)	خطأ، أخطأ	*khaṭa', akhṭa'a*
mistaken (adj)	مخطئ، غير صحيح	*mukhṭi', ghair ṣaḥīḥ*
mistakenly (adv)	خطأً، غلطاً	*khaṭa'an, ghalaṭan*
mister (Mr)	سيد، مستر	*sayyid, mistar*
mistime (v)	أساء استعمال الوقت	*asā'a isti'mālal waqt*

mistreat (v)	أساء المعاملة	*asā'al mu'āmalah*
mistreatment (n)	سوء المعاملة	*sū'ul mu'āmalah*
mistress (n)	سيدة، مديرة الأمور	*sayyidah, mudīratul umūr*
mistrial (n)	دعوة فاسدة	*da'wah fāsidah*
mistrust (v/n)	ارتاب، ارتياب	*irtāba, irtiyāb*
mistrustful (adj)	مرتاب، عديم الثقة	*murtāb, 'adīmuth thiqah*
mistrustfully (adv)	بارتياب	*birtiyāb*
misty (adj)	ضبابي، سديمي	*ḍabābī, sadīmī*
misunderstand (v)	أساء الفهم	*asā'al fahm*
misunderstanding	سوء الفهم	*sū'ul fahm*
misunderstood (adj)	مغلوط	*maghlūṭ*
misuse (v)	أساء الاستعمال	*asā'al isti'māl*
misuse (n)	سوء الاستعمال	*sū'ul isti'māl*
mite (n)	شيء صغير	*shay' ṣaghīr*
mitigate (v)	لطف، خفف	*laṭṭafa, khaffafa*
mitigating (adj)	ملطف، مسكن	*mulaṭṭif, musakkin*
mitigation (n)	تخفيف، تسكين	*takhfīf, taskīn*
mitre (miter)	تاج الأسقف	*tājul usquf*
mix (v)	خلط، مزج، اختلط	*khalaṭa, mazaja, ikhtalaṭa*
mix (n)	مزيج، خليط	*mazīj, khalīṭ*
mixed (adj)	مختلط، ممزوج	*mukhtalaṭ, mamzūj*
mixed farming	زراعة مختلطة	*zirā'ah mukhtalaṭah*
mixer (n)	مازج، خالط	*māzij, khāliṭ*
mixture (n)	مزيج، مزج	*mazīj, mazj*
moan (v)	ناح، أعول	*nāḥa, a'wala*
moan (n)	نواح، عويل، مناح	*nuwāḥ, 'awīl, manāḥ*
moat (n)	خندق	*khandaq*
mob (n/v)	سواد الناس، احتشد	*sawādun nās, iḥtashada*
mobile (n)	هاتف جوال	*hātif jawwāl*

mobile (adj)	متحرك، متنقل	*mutaḥarrik, mutanaqqil*
mobility (n)	قابلية التحرك، حركة	*qābiliyyatut taḥarruk*
mobilization,-isation	تحريك، تعبئة الجنود	*taḥrīk, ta'bi'atul junūd*
mobilize,-ise (v)	حرك، كيف	*ḥarraka, kayyafa*
mobster (n)	عضو في إصابة إجرامية	*'uḍw fī iṣābah ijrāmiyyah*
mock (v)	سخر، هزأ	*sakhira, haza'a*
mockery (n)	سخرية، تهكم	*sukhriyyah, tahakkum*
mockingbird (n)	طائر محاكي	*ṭā'ir muḥākī*
mockingly (adv)	باستهزاء، بازدراء	*bistihzā', bizdirā'*
modal (adj)	مشروط، شرطي	*mashrūṭ, sharṭī*
mode (n)	أسلوب، طريقة	*uslūb, ṭāriqah*
model (n)	نموذج، مثال،	*namūdhaj, mithāl,*
	عارضة الأزياء	*'āriḍatul azyā'*
moderate (adj)	معتدل، متوسط	*mu'tadil, mutawassiṭ*
moderate (n)	شخص ذو آراء	*shakhṣ dhū ārā'*
	معتدلة	*mu'tadilah*
moderate (v)	هدأ، خفف	*hada'a, khaffafa*
moderately (adv)	باعتدال، باقتصاد	*bi'tidāl, biqtiṣād*
moderation (n)	اعتدال، لطف، رفق	*i'tidāl, luṭf, rifq*
moderator (n)	وسيط، متوسط	*wasīṭ, mutawassiṭ*
modern (adj)	حديث، عصري	*ḥadīth, 'aṣrī*
modernism (n)	عصرانية، حب	*'aṣrāniyyah, ḥubbut*
	التجديد	*tajdīd*
modernist (n)	عصراني	*'aṣrānī*
modernistic (adj)	عصراني، تجديدي	*'aṣrānī, tajdīdī*
modernity (n)	عصرانية، حداثة	*'aṣrāniyyah, ḥadāthatu*
	عهد	*'ahd*
modernization (n)	تعصير، تعصر	*ta'ṣīr, ta'aṣṣur*
modernize,-ise (v)	عصر، جدد	*'aṣṣara, jaddada*
modest (adj)	محتشم، متواضع	*muḥtashim, mutawāḍi'*

modestly (adv)	باحتشام، بأدب	*biḥtishām, bi adab*
modesty (n)	حياء، احتشام	*ḥayā', iḥtishām*
modification (n)	تعديل، تكييف	*ta'dīl, takyīf*
modifier (n)	مقيد	*muqayyid*
modify (v)	عدل، حول، كيف	*'addala, ḥawwala, kayyafa*
modish (adj)	مطابق للزي الحديث	*muṭābiq liz ziyyil ḥadīth*
modulate (v)	غير، عدل	*ghayyara, 'addala*
modulation (n)	تغير، تعديل	*taghayyur, ta'dīl*
module (n)	مركبة	*markabah*
modus operandi	طريقة العمل	*ṭarīqatul 'amal*
modus vivendi	طريقة العيش	*ṭarīqatul 'aish*
mogul (n)	شخص بارز	*shakhṣ bāriz*
moist (adj)	رطب، مبتل	*raṭb, mubtall*
moisten (v)	بلل، رطب، خضل	*ballala, raṭṭaba, khaḍḍala*
moisture (n)	نداوة، بلل	*nadāwah, balal*
molar (n/adj)	ضرس، ضرسي	*ḍirs, ḍirisī*
mole (n)	خلد	*khuld*
molecular (adj)	جزيئي، ذري	*juzai'ī, dharrī*
molecule (n)	جزيء، ذرة	*juzai', dharrah*
molehill (n)	تل خلدي	*tall khuldī*
moleskin (n)	فرو الخلد	*farwul khuld*
molest (v)	تحرش، كدر	*taḥarrasha, kaddara*
molestation (n)	تحرش، ازعاج	*taḥarrush, iz'āj*
molester (n)	متحرش، مزعج	*mutaḥarrish, muz'ij*
moll (n)	قاطعة الطريق	*qāṭi'atuṭ ṭarīq*
mollify (v)	سكن، لين، لطف	*sakkana, layyana, laṭṭafa*
mollusc (mollusk)	رخوي	*rikhwī*
mollycoddle (v)	دلع، دلل	*dalla'a, dallala*
Molotov cocktail	كوكتيل مولوتوف	*kuktīl mūlūtūf*
molten (adj)	مذوب بالحرارة	*mudhawwab bil ḥarārah*

mom = mum		
moment (n)	فترة، لحظة، دقيقة	*fatrah, laḥẓah, daqīqah*
momentarily (adv)	لحظةً، برهةً	*laḥẓatan, burhatan*
momentary (adj)	سريع الانقضاء	*sarī'ul inqiḍā'*
momentous (adj)	مهم، خطير	*muhimm, khaṭīr*
momentum (n)	قوة دافعة	*quwwah dāfi'ah*
momma (mommy)	أم، والدة	*umm, wālidah*
monarch (n)	ملك، ملكة، سلطان	*malik, malikah, sulṭān*
monarchal (adj)	ملكي، سلطاني	*malakī, sulṭānī*
monarchism (n)	ملكية، سلطنة	*malakiyyah, salṭanah*
monarchist (n)	ملكي	*malakī*
monastery (n)	دير، صومعة	*dair, ṣauma'ah*
monastic (adj)	ديري، رهباني	*dairī, rahbānī*
monasticism (n)	رهبانية	*rahbāniyyah*
Monday (n)	يوم الاثنين	*yaumul ithnain*
monetarism (n)	سياسة العملة	*siyāsatul 'umlah*
monetary (adj)	مالي، عملي	*mālī, 'umlī*
money (n)	نقود، عملة، مال	*nuqūd, 'umlah, māl*
moneybags (n)	رجل غني	*rajul ghanī*
money-box (n)	حصالة	*ḥaṣṣālah*
moneyed (adj)	غني، مثرٍ	*ghanī, muthrin*
moneylender (n)	مقرض، مرابي	*muqriḍ, murābī*
money-maker (n)	جامع المال	*jāmi'ul māl*
money order	حوالة بريدية	*ḥawālah barīdiyyah*
mongol (n)	مغولي، منغولي	*mughūlī, munghūlī*
mongoose (n)	نمس	*nims*
mongrel (n)	هجين، هجينة	*hajīn, hajīnah*
monitor (v)	ضبط، راقب	*ḍabaṭa, rāqaba*
monitor (n)	مرقاب، محذر، عريف	*mirqāb, muḥadhdhir, 'arīf*

monkey (n)	قرد، ولد مزعج	*qird, walad muz'ij*
monkey (v)	عبث، لاعب	*'abatha, lā'aba*
monkey wrench	مفتاح انكليزي	*miftāḥ inkilīzī*
monkhood (n)	رهبانية	*rahbāniyyah*
monkish (adj)	رهباني، نسكي	*rahbānī, nuskī*
monochrome (n/adj)	أحادي اللون	*uḥādiyyul laun*
monocle (n)	نظارة لعين واحدة	*naẓẓārah li 'ain wāḥidah*
monogamous (adj)	خاص بالزواج الأحادي	*khāṣṣ biz zawāj al uḥādī*
monogamy (n)	زواج من شخص واحد	*zawāj min shakhṣ wāḥid*
monogram (n)	مونوغرام	*mūnūgharām*
monograph (n)	رسالة في موضوع واحد	*risālah fī mauḍū' wāḥid*
monolingual (adj)	خاص بلغة واحدة	*khāṣṣ bi lughah wāḥidah*
monologue (n)	مخاطبة المرء لنفسه، مونولوج	*mukhāṭabatul mar' li nafsih, mūnūlūj*
monoplane (n)	طيارة بسطح واحد	*ṭayyārah bi saṭḥ wāḥid*
monopolist (n)	محتكر	*muḥtakir*
monopolistic (adj)	احتكاري	*iḥtikārī*
monopolization (n)	احتكار، التزام	*iḥtikār, iltizām*
monopolize,-ise (v)	احتكر، التزم	*iḥtakara, iltazama*
monopoly (n)	احتكار، شركة محتكرة	*iḥtikār, sharikah muḥtakirah*
monosyllabic (adj)	ذو مقطع واحد	*dhū maqṭa' wāḥid*
monosyllable (n)	كلمة بمقطع واحد	*kalimah bi maqṭa' wāḥid*
monotheism (n)	توحيد، اعتقاد باله واحد	*tauḥīd, i'tiqād bi ilāh wāḥid*
nonotheist (n)	موحد، مؤمن	*muwaḥḥid, mu'min*
monotheistic (adj)	توحيدي	*tauḥīdī*
monotone (n)	اطراد رتيب	*iṭṭirād ratīb*
monotonous (adj)	ممل، رتيب	*mumill, ratīb*

monotony (n)	وتيرية، رتابة	*watīriyyah, ratābah*
Monsieur (n)	مسيو	*misyū*
Monsignor (n)	مونسينير، لقب الأساقفة	*mūnsīnyar, laqabul asāqifah*
monsoon (n)	ريح موسمية	*rīḥ mausimiyyah*
monster (n)	مخلوق غريب الشكل، هولة	*makhlūq gharībush shakl, hūlah*
monstrosity (n)	شيء هائل وبشع	*shay' hā'il wa bashi'*
monstrous (adj)	هائل، عجيب الخلقة	*hā'il, 'ajībul khilqah*
monstrously (adv)	بهول، بشاعة	*bi ṭarīqah ghair sawiyyah*
montage (n)	مونتاج، صورة مركبة	*mūntāj, ṣūrah murakkabah*
month (n)	شهر	*Shahr*
monthly (adj/adv)	شهري، شهريًا	*shahrī, shahriyyan*
monument (n)	معلم، أثر، مبنى تذكاري	*ma'lam, athar, mabnā tidhkārī*
monumental (adj)	تذكاري، نصبي	*tidhkārī, nuṣubī*
monumentally (adv)	بشدة	*bi shiddah*
moo (v/n)	خار، خوار	*khāra, khuwār*
mooch (v)	تسكع، تبطل	*tasakka'a, tabaṭṭala*
mood (n)	طبع، حالة، مزاج	*ṭab', ḥālah, mizāj*
moodily (adv)	بعبس، بكآبة	*bi 'abs, bi ka'ābah*
moodiness (n)	عبس، كآبة	*'abs, ka'ābah*
moody (adj)	متقلب المزاج، عابس	*mutaqallibul mizāj, 'ābis*
moon (n)	قمر، جرم سماوي	*qamar, jirm samāwī*
moon (v)	تسكع، أضاع الوقت	*tasakka'a, aḍā'al waqt*
moonbeam (n)	شعاع القمر	*shu'ā'ul qamar*
moonlight (n)	ضوء القمر	*ḍau'ul qamar*
moonlit (adj)	مقمر، مقمرة	*muqmir, muqmirah*

moonshine (n)	نور القمر، ضوء القمر	*nūrul qamar, ḍau'ul qamar*
moonstruck (adj)	مختلط العقل	*mukhtaliṭul 'aql*
moor (n/v)	مستنقع، أرسى السفينة	*mustanqa', arsas safīnah*
moorhen (n)	دجاجة الماء	*dajājatul mā'*
mooring (n)	مرساة، سلسلة الحبل	*marsāt, silsilatul ḥabl*
moorland (n)	أرض سبخة	*arḍ sabikhah*
moose (n)	موظ، ظبي أمريكي	*mūẓ, ẓaby amrīkī*
moot (v)	ناقش، باحث	*nāqasha, bāḥatha*
mop (n/v)	ممسحة، نظف بممسحة	*mimsaḥah, naẓẓafa bi mimsaḥah*
mope (v)	تسكع، استغرق في الهموم	*tasakka'a, istaghraqa fil humūm*
moral (n)	سلوك، أخلاق	*sulūk, akhlāq*
moral (adj)	أخلاقي، معنوي	*akhlāqī, ma'nawī*
morale (n)	معنوية	*ma'nawiyyah*
moralist (n)	كاتب أخلاقي	*kātib akhlāqī*
moralistic (adj)	أخلاقي	*akhlāqī*
morality (n)	صفات أخلاقية	*ṣifāt akhlāqiyyah*
morality play	تمثيلية أخلاقية	*tamthīliyyah akhlāqiyyah*
moralize,-ise (v)	رفع المستوى الأخلاقي	*rafa'al mustawā al akhlāqī*
morass (n)	ارتباك، تشوش	*irtibāk, tashawwush*
moratorium (n)	توقيف العمل	*tauqīful 'amal*
morbid (adj)	كئيب، حزين، مرضي	*ka'īb, ḥazīn, maraḍī*
morbidity (n)	كآبة، مرضية	*ka'ābah, maraḍiyyah*
morbidly (adv)	بكآبة، باعتلال	*bi ka'ābah, bi'tilāl*
mordant (adj)	لاذع، عضاض	*lādhi', 'aḍḍāḍ*
more (adj/adv)	أكثر، بدرجة أكثر	*akthar, bi darajah akthar*

moreover (adv)	فضلاً عن ذلك	*faḍlan 'an dhālik*
mores (n)	عرف، عادات	*'urf, 'ādāt*
morgue (n)	معرض الجثث	*ma'riḍul juthath*
moribund (adj)	هاجع، هالك، مشرف على الموت	*hāji', hālik, mushrif 'alal maut*
morn (n)	صبح، صباح	*ṣubḥ, ṣabāḥ*
morning (n)	صباح، ضحىً	*ṣabāḥ, ḍuḥan*
morning glory	مجد الصباح	*majduṣ ṣabāḥ*
morning sickness	غثيان الصباح	*ghathayānuṣ ṣabāḥ*
morning star	نجم الصباح	*najmuṣ ṣabāḥ*
morocco (n)	جلد الماعز	*jildul mā'iz*
moron (n)	أحمق، غبي، أبله	*aḥmaq, ghabī, ablah*
moronic (adj)	غبي، أبله	*ghabī, ablah*
morose (adj)	نكد، كئيب، حزين	*nakid, ka'īb, ḥazīn*
morosely (adv)	بنكد، بكآبة	*bi nakad, bi ka'ābah*
morphia=morphine		
morphine (n)	مورفين، مادة مخدرة	*mūrfīn, māddah mukhaddirah*
morphological (adj)	مورفولوجي، صرفي	*mūrfūlūjī, ṣarfī*
morphology (n)	مورفولوجيا، علم الصرف	*mūrfūlūjiyā, 'ilmuṣ ṣarf*
morris dance	رقصة المريسة	*raqṣatul murīsah*
morrow (n)	غد، يوم الغد	*ghad, yaumul ghad*
Morse code	نظام مورس	*niẓāmu mūrs*
morsel (n)	نقمة، هتامة، كسرة	*niqmah, hutāmah, kisrah*
mortal (adj/n)	فانٍ، هالك، مهلك	*fānin, hālik, muhlik*
mortality (n)	فناء، موت	*fanā', maut*
mortally (adj)	بطريقة مهلكة	*bi ṭarīqah muhlikah*
mortal sin	ذنب كبير	*dhamb kabīr*
mortar (n/v)	ملاط، ملط	*milāṭ, mallaṭa*

mortar board	لوح الملاط	*lauḥul milāṭ*
mortgage (n/v)	رهن، رهن	*rahn, rahana*
mortgagee (n)	مرتهن	*murtahin*
mortgagor,-ager (n)	راهن، مقدم الرهن	*rāhin, muqaddimur rahn*
mortician (n)	حانوتي	*ḥānūtī*
mortification (n)	إهانة، عار، شعور بالخزي	*ihānah, ʻār, shuʻūr bil khizy*
mortify (v)	أهان، أخزى، كبح	*ahāna, akhzā, kabaḥa*
mortifying (adj)	مخزٍ، مهين	*mukhzin, muhīn*
mortise (mortice) (n)	نقر	*naqr*
mortuary (n)	مستودع الجثث	*mustaudaʻul juthath*
mosaic (n)	فسيفساء	*fusaifasā'*
mosey (v)	ارتحل بغير هدف	*irtaḥala bighairi hadaf*
Moslem (n)	مسلم	*muslim*
mosque (n)	مسجد، معبد	*masjid, maʻbad*
mosquito (n)	بعوضة، بعوض	*baʻūḍah, baʻūḍ*
mosquito net	ناموسية، كلة	*nāmūsiyyah, killah*
moss (n)	طحلب، أشنة	*ṭuḥlub, ushnah*
mossy (adj)	مغطى بالطحلب	*mughaṭṭā biṭ ṭuḥlub*
most (adj/adv)	معظم، أغلب، أكثر	*muʻẓam, aghlab, akthar*
mostly (adv)	على الأغلب، بالأكثر	*ʻalal aghlab, bil akthar*
motel (n)	موتيل، فندق صغير	*mūtīl, funduq ṣaghīr*
moth (n)	عثة، بشارة	*ʻuththah, bashshārah*
mothball (n)	كرة العث	*kuratul ʻuthth*
moth-eaten (adj)	منقوب بالعث	*manqūb bil ʻuthth*
mother (n)	أم، والدة	*umm, wālidah*
mother (v)	اعتنى	*iʻtanā,*
motherhood (n)	أمومة	*umūmah*
mother-in-law (n)	أم الزوج، أم الزوجة	*ummuz zauj, ummuz zaujah*
motherland (n)	وطن الأم	*waṭanul umm*

motherless (adj)	يتيم الأم	*yatīmul umm*
motherliness (n)	حنان، رأفة	*ḥanān, ra'fah*
motherly (adj)	أمومي، كالأم	*umūmī, kal umm*
mother-of-pearl (n)	أم اللآلئ	*ummul la'āli'*
Mother's day (n)	عيد الأم	*'īdul umm*
mother tongue (n)	اللغة الأم	*al lughah al umm*
motif (n)	باعث، محرك	*bā'ith, muḥarrik*
motion (n)	تغوط، حركة	*taghawwuṭ, ḥarakah*
motion (v)	أومأ، أشار	*auma'a, ashāra*
motionless (adj)	غير متحرك، ساكن	*ghair mutaḥarrik, sākin*
motion picture	فيلم سينمائي	*film sīnmā'ī*
motion sickness	دوار الحركة	*duwārul ḥarakah*
motivate (v)	حرض، حث	*ḥarraḍa, ḥaththa*
motivation (n)	تحريض، حث	*taḥrīḍ, ḥathth*
motivational (adj)	تحريضي، محرض	*taḥrīḍī, muḥarriḍ*
motive (n/adj)	محرك، حافز	*muḥarrik, ḥāfiz*
motley (adj)	ملون، متنافر	*mulawwan, mutanāfir*
motor (adj/n)	محرك، سيارة	*muḥarrik, sayyārah*
motorbike (n)	موطوربيك	*mūṭūrbīk*
motor boat (n)	زورق موطوري	*zauraq mūṭūrī*
motorcade (n)	موكب سيارات	*maukibu sayyārāt*
motor car (n)	سيارة	*sayyārah*
motorcycle (n)	دراجة بخارية	*darrājah bukhāriyyah*
motorcyclist (n)	سائق الدراجة البخارية	*sā'iqud darrājah al bukhāriyyah*
motorist (n)	سائق السيارة	*sā'iqus sayyārah*
motorized (adj)	مزود بموطور	*muzawwad bi mūṭūr*
motted (adj)	مرقش، ملون	*muraqqash, mulawwan*
motto (n)	شعار	*shi'ār*

mould (mold) (n)	فطر، قالب	*fuṭr, qālib*
mould (v)	شكل، تعفن	*shakkala, ta'affana*
mound (n)	هضبة، رابية	*haḍbah, rābiyah*
mount (v)	ارتفع، ازداد، ركب	*irtafa'a, izdāda, rakiba*
mount (n)	جبل، مطية	*jabal, maṭiyyah*
mountain (n)	جبل، طود	*jabal, ṭaud*
mountain ash (n)	رماد الجبل	*ramādul jabal*
mountaineer (n)	متسلق الجبال	*mutasalliqul jibāl*
mountaineering (n)	رياضة تسلق الجبال	*riyāḍatu tasalluqil jibāl*
mountainous (adj)	هائل، ضخم، جبلي	*hā'il, ḍakhm, jabalī*
mountainside (n)	جانب الجبل، سند	*jānibul jabal, sanad*
mountaintop (n)	ذروة الجبل، قمة	*dhirwatul jabal, qimmah*
mounted (adj)	راكب الفرس	*rākibul faras*
mourn (v)	ناح، تفجع، ندب	*nāḥa, tafajja'a, nadaba*
mourner (n)	نداب، نائح	*naddāb, nā'iḥ*
mournful (adj)	محزن، مفجع	*muḥzin, mufji'*
mourning (n)	ندب، حداد	*nadb, ḥidād*
mouse (n)	فأر، فأرة	*fa'r, fa'rah*
moustache (n)	شارب، سبلة	*shārib, sabalah*
moustahed (adj)	ذو شارب	*dhū shārib*
mousy, mousey (adj)	جبان، هادئ	*jabān, hādi'*
mouth (n)	فم، مدخل، مصب	*fam, madkhal, maṣabb*
mouth (v)	تشدق، دمدم	*tashaddaqa, damdama*
mouthful (n)	ملء الفم، كلمة طويلة	*mil'ul fam, kalimah ṭawīlah*
mouth organ (n)	هرمونيكا، آلة موسيقية	*harmūnīkā, ālah mausīqiyyah*
mouthpiece (n)	جزء الفم، جزء من آلة موسيقية	*juz'ul fam, juz' min ālah mausīqiyyah*
mouthy (adj)	ثرثار، طنان	*tharthār, ṭannān*

movable (moveable)	قابل للتحرك	*qābil lit taḥarruk*
move (v)	حرك، تحرك، دار، انتقل	*ḥarraka, taḥarraka, dāra, intaqala*
move (n)	خطوة، حركة، نقل، دور	*khuṭwah, ḥarakah, naql, daur*
movement (n)	حركة، تغوط، نشاط	*ḥarakah, taghawwuṭ, nashāṭ*
movie (n)	فيلم، سينما	*film, sīnmā*
moving (adj)	محرك، مثير، محرض	*muḥarrik, muthīr, muḥarriḍ*
mow (v)	جز، حصد	*jazza, ḥaṣada*
mower (n)	جزازة، آلة الحصاد	*jazzāzah, ālatul ḥiṣād*
Mr	مستر، سيد	*mistar, sayyid*
Mrs	مسز، سيدة	*misiz, sayyidah*
much (adj/adv)	كثير، كثيراً	*kathīr, kathīran*
muck (n)	وسخ، قذر، روث	*wasakh, qadhar, rauth*
mucky (adj)	قذر، وحل	*qadhir, waḥil*
mud (n)	وحل، قذف	*waḥl, qadhf*
muddle (v)	اختلط، مزج، عكر	*ikhtalaṭa, mazaja, 'akkara*
muddle (n)	ارتباك، تشوش	*irtibāk, tashawwush*
muddled (adj)	مشوش، مرتبك	*mushawwash, murtabik*
muddling (adj)	مشوش، مخبل	*mushawwish, mukhabbil*
muddy (adj)	موحل، طيني	*mūḥil, ṭīnī*
muezzin (n)	مؤذن	*mu'adhdhin*
muff (n)	موفة، غطاء أنبوبي	*mūfah, ghiṭā' umbūbī*
muffin (n)	موفينية، نوع من الفطيرة	*mūfīniyyah, nau' minal faṭīrah*
muffle (v)	غطى، كتم، لفع	*ghaṭṭā, katama, laffa'a*
muffle (n)	لفاع	*lifā'*
mufti (n)	مفتي	*muftī*

mug (n)	كوز، طاس، شخص أبله	*kūz, ṭās, shakhṣ ablah*
mug (v)	هاجم، نهب	*hājama, nahaba*
mugger (n)	ناهب، مهاجم	*nāhib, muhājim*
muggy (adj)	رطب حار	*raṭb ḥārr*
mujahid (n)	مجاهد	*mujāhid*
mulberry (n)	شجرة التوت	*shajaratut tūt*
mule (n)	بغل، خف المرأة	*baghl, khufful mar'ah*
mull (v)	فكر، تدبر	*fakkara, tadabbara*
mullah (n)	فقيه، عالم بالشريعة	*faqīh, 'ālim bish sharī'ah*
mullet (n)	سمك بحري، بوري	*samak baḥrī, būrī*
mullion (n)	عماد	*'imād*
multi	كثير، متعدد	*kathīr, muta'addid*
multicellular (adj)	متعدد الخلايا	*muta'addidul khalāyā*
multicoloured (adj)	متعدد الألوان	*muta'addidul alwān*
multifarious (adj)	متعدد الأنواع	*muta'addidul anwā'*
multilateral (adj)	متعدد الجوانب	*muta'addidul jawānib*
multiple (adj/n)	مضاعف، مركب	*muḍā'af, murakkab*
multiplicable (adj)	قابل للضرب	*qābil liḍ ḍarb*
multiplication (n)	مضاعفة، عملية الضرب	*muḍā'afah, 'amaliyyatuḍ ḍarb*
multiplicity (n)	تكاثر، تعدد	*takāthur, ta'addud*
multiplier (n)	مضاعف، عدد مضروب فيه	*muḍā'if, 'adad maḍrūb fīh*
multiply (v)	ضرب، ضاعف، تكاثر	*ḍaraba, ḍā'afa, takāthara*
multipolar (adj)	متعدد الأقطاب	*muta'addidul aqṭāb*
multiracial (adj)	متعدد الأعراق	*muta'addidul a'rāq*
multitude (n)	عدد كبير، دهماء	*'adad kabīr, dahmā'*
multitudinous (adj)	متعدد، كثير، وافر	*muta'addid, kathīr, wāfir*
mum (mom) (n)	أم، والدة	*umm, wālidah*

mum (adj)	صامت، ساكت	*ṣāmit, sākit*
mumble (v)	دمدم، غمغم	*damdama, ghamghama*
mumble (n)	بربرة، دمدمة	*barbarah, damdamah*
mumbo-jumbo (n)	طقس معقد	*ṭaqs mu'aqqad*
mummify (v)	حنط	*ḥannaṭa*
mummy (n)	أم، مومياء	*umm, mūmyā'*
mumps (n)	نكاف، التهاب الغدة	*nukāf, iltihābul ghuddah*
mundane (adj)	ردئ، غير ممتع	*radi', ghair mumti'*
municipal (adj)	بلدي، مختص بالبلدية	*baladī, mukhtaṣṣ bil baladiyyah*
municipality (n)	بلدية، مجلس بلدي	*baladiyyah, majlis baladī*
munificence (n)	سخاء، جود	*sakhā', jūd*
munificent (adj)	كريم، سخي جدا	*karīm, sakhī jiddā*
munitions (n)	معدات عسكرية	*mu'addāt, 'askariyyah*
murder (n/v)	قتل، قتل	*qatl, qatala*
murderer (n)	قاتل، ذابح	*qātil, dhābiḥ*
murderess (n)	قاتلة، فاتكة	*qātilah, fātikah*
murderous (adj)	قاتل، مبيد، مهلك	*qātil, mubīd, muhlik*
murk (n)	ظلمة، ظلام	*ẓulmah, ẓalām*
murky (adj)	مظلم، معتم	*muẓlim, mu'tim*
murmur (v)	تذمر، هذر، خر	*tadhammara, hadhara, kharra*
murmur (n)	تذمر، طنين	*tadhammur, ṭanīn*
murmurous (adj)	مدمدم، متذمر	*mudamdim, mutadhammir*
muscat (n)	مسكات، نوع من العنب	*muskāt, nau' minal 'inab*
muscatel (n)	خمر المسكات	*khamrul muskāt*
muscle (n)	عضلة، قوة	*'aḍalah, quwwah*
muscle-bound (adj)	معتقل العضل، عديم المرونة	*mu'taqalul 'aḍal, 'adīmul murūnah*
muscular (adj)	قوي، عضلي	*qawiyy, 'aḍalī*

muse (v)	تأمل، تفكر	*ta'ammala, tafakkara*
Muses (n)	موزية	*mūziyyah*
museum (n)	متحف	*mutḥaf*
mush (n)	عصيدة، شيء طري	*'aṣīdah, shay' ṭariyy*
mushroom (n)	فطر	*fuṭr*
mushroom (v)	جمع الفطر، ازداد	*jama'al fuṭr, izdāda*
mushy (adj)	رقيق، طري	*raqīq, ṭariyy*
music (n)	موسيقي	*mausīqī*
musical (adj)	موسيقي، بارع في الموسيقي	*mausīqī, bāri' fil mausīqī*
musical (n)	مسرحية موسيقية	*masraḥiyyah mausīqiyyah*
music box (n)	صندوق موسيقي	*ṣundūq mausīqī*
music-hall (n)	مسرح المنوعات	*masraḥul munawwa'āt*
musician (n)	عازف الموسيقي	*'āziful mausīqī*
musicological (adj)	موسيقي	*mausīqī*
musicologist (n)	عالم بالموسيقي	*'ālim bil mausīqī*
musicology (n)	علم الموسيقي	*'ilmul mausīqī*
musk (n)	مسك	*misk*
musk deer (n)	أيل المسك	*ayyilul misk*
musket (n)	مسكيت، بندقية	*maskīt, bunduqiyyah*
musk-melon (n)	بطيخ أصفر	*biṭṭīkh aṣfar*
musk-rat (n)	فأر المسك	*fa'rul misk*
musk-rose (n)	ورد المسك	*wardul misk*
musky (adj)	مسكي، ممسك	*miskī, mumassak*
Muslim (Moslem)	مسلم	*muslim*
muslin (n)	موصلين	*mūṣlīn*
mussel (n)	بلح البحر	*balaḥul baḥr*

must (v)	ينبغي، يجب	*yambaghī, yajib*
must (n)	شيء ضروري، عصير العنب	*shay' ḍarūrī, 'aṣīrul 'inab*
mustard (n)	خردل	*khardal*
mustard gas (n)	غاز الخردل	*ghāzul khạrdal*
muster (n/v)	اجتماع، اجتمع	*ijtimā', ijtama'a*
mustiness (n)	تعفن، عتق	*ta'affun, 'itaq*
musty (adj)	عتيق، مخم	*'atīq, mukhimm*
mutability (n)	تقلب، تحول	*taqallub, taḥawwul*
mutable (adj)	متحول، متقلب	*mutaḥawwil, mutaqallib*
mutate (v)	تغير، تحول	*taghayyara, taḥawwala*
mutation (n)	تغير، تحول	*taghayyur, taḥawwul*
mute (adj)	صامت، أخرس	*ṣāmit, akhras*
mute (n)	مخفات	*mikhfāt*
mutely (adv)	في صمت	*fī ṣamt*
muteness (n)	صمت، صموت	*ṣamt, ṣumūt*
mutilate (v)	جدع، جذم	*jada'a, jadhama*
mutilate (n)	جدع، تشويه	*jad', tashbīh*
mutineer (n)	جندي متمرد	*jundī mutamarrid*
mutinous (adj)	متمرد، عاص	*mutamarrid, 'āṣin*
mutinously (adv)	تمرداً، عصيانا	*tamarrudan, 'iṣyānan*
mutiny (n)	تمرد، عصيان	*tamarrud, 'iṣyān*
mutt (n)	مغفل، أبله	*mughaffal, ablah*
mutter (n)	ثرثرة، بربرة	*thartharah, barbarah*
mutter (v)	بربر، ثرثر، دمدم	*barbara, tharthara, damdama*
mutton (n)	لحم الضأن	*laḥmuḍ ḍa'n*
mutton-head (n)	شخص أبله	*shakhṣ ablah*
mutual (adj)	مشترك، متبادل	*mushtarak, mutabādil*
muzzily (adv)	بارتباك، بشك	*birtibāk, bi shakk*

muzziness (n)	تشوش، ارتباك	*tashawwush, irtibāk*
muzzy (adj)	مشوش الذهن	*mushawwushudh dhihn*
my (pron)	لي، ي (مثلا قلمي)	*lī, yā (mathalan qalamī)*
mycology (n)	علم الفطريات	*'ilmul fuṭriyyāt*
myelitis (n)	التهاب النخاع الشوكي	*iltihābun nikhā' ash shaukī*

N

nab (v)	اعتقل، قبض	*i'taqala, qabaḍa*
nacelle (n)	كنة المحرك	*kinnatul muḥarrik*
nacre (n)	عرق اللؤلؤ	*'irqul lu' lu'*
nag (n)	فرس	*faras*
nag (v)	ناكد، تذمر	*nākada, tadhammara*
naiad (n)	نيادة، حورية الماء	*nayyādah, ḥūriyyatul mā'*
nail (n)	ظفر، مسمار	*ẓufr, mismār*
nail (v)	اعتقل، سمر	*i'taqala, sammara*
nail-brush (n)	فرشاة الأظافر	*furshātul aẓāfir*
naive (adj)	ساذج، سليم	*sādhij, salīm*
naively (adv)	بسذاجة، ببساطة	*bi sadhājah, bi basāṭah*
naivety (n)	سذاجة، بساطة	*sadhājah, basāṭah*
naked (adj)	عريان، معرى، مجرد	*'uryān, mu'arrā, mujarrad*
nakedly (adv)	بتجرد، بوضوح	*bi tajarrud, bi wuḍūḥ*
nakedness (n)	عراء، وضوح، تجرد	*'arā', wuḍūḥ, tajarrud*
namby-pamby (adj)	صبياني، عابث	*ṣibyānī, 'ābith*
name (n)	اسم، سمعة، شخص ذو سمعة	*ism, sum'ah, shakhṣ dhū sum'ah*
name (v)	سمى، عين	*sammā, 'ayyana*
name-day (n)	عيد الشفيع	*'īdush shafī'*
nameless (adj)	خامل الذكر، مجهول	*khāmiludh dhikr, majhūl*

namely (adv)	أي، أعني	*ay, a'nī*
nanny-goat (n)	معزاة	*mi'zāt*
nap (v/n)	قال، زئبر	*qāla, zi'bar*
napalm (n)	نيبم	*naibam*
nape(n)	مؤخر العنق	*mu'akhkharul 'unuq*
nàphthalene (n)	نفثالين	*nafthālīn*
napkin (n)	منديل، ممسحة الأيدي	*mindīl, mimsaḥatul 'aidī*
narcissism (n)	نرجسية، حب النفس	*narjisiyyah, ḥubbun nafs*
narcissitic (adj)	نرجسي	*narjisī*
narcissus (n)	نرجس، نرسيوس	*narjis, narsiyūs*
narcotic (n/adj)	شيء مخدر، مخدر	*shay' mukhaddir, mukhaddir*
nark (n)	عين، جاسوس	*'ain, jāsūs*
narrate (v)	روى، قص، أخبر	*rawā, qaṣṣa, akhbara*
narration (n)	رواية، حكاية	*riwāyah, ḥikāyah*
narrative (n/adj)	قصة، قصصي	*qiṣṣah, qiṣaṣī*
narrator (n)	راوٍ، قاصّ، حاكٍ	*rāwin, qāṣṣ, ḥākin*
narrow (adj)	ضيق، دقيق	*ḍayyiq, daqīq*
narrow (v)	ضاق، ضيق	*ḍāqa, ḍayyaqa*
narrowly (adv)	بضيق، بدقة	*bi ḍīq, bi diqqah*
narrow-minded (adj)	ضيق العقل	*ḍayyiqul 'aql*
narrow-mindedness	ضيق العقل، تعصب	*ḍīqul 'aql, ta'aṣṣub*
narrowness (n)	ضيق، تقلص	*ḍīq, taqalluṣ*
nasal (adj/n)	أنفي، صوت أنفي	*anfī, ṣaut anfī*
nasalize (v)	لفظ من الأنف	*lafaẓa minal anf*
nasally (adv)	بالأنف	*bil anf*
nascent (adj)	ناشيء، نابت، متولد	*nāshi', nābit, mutawallid*
nastily (adv)	بقذارة، بدناءة	*bi qadhārah, bi danā'ah*
nastiness (n)	قذارة، دناءة	*qadhārah, danā'ah*
nasty (adj)	بذيء، دنيء، قذر	*badhī', danī', qadhir*

nation (n)	شعب، دولة، أمة	*sha'b, daulah, ummah*
national (adj/n)	وطني، مواطن	*waṭanī, muwāṭin*
national bank (n)	بنك وطني	*bank waṭanī*
national debt (n)	دين قومي	*dain qaumī*
national guard (n)	حرس وطني	*ḥaras waṭanī*
nationalism (n)	قومية، وطنية	*qaumiyyah, waṭaniyyah*
nationalist (n)	قومي، مؤيد القومية	*qaumī, mu'ayyidul qaumiyyah*
nationalistic (adj)	قومي، وطني	*qaumī, waṭanī*
nationality (n)	قومية، جنسية	*qaumiyyah, jinsiyyah*
nationalization (n)	تأميم، تجنيس	*ta'mīm, tajnīs*
nationalize,-ise (v)	أمم، جنس	*ammama, jannasa*
national park	منتزة وطني	*muntazah waṭanī*
nation-wide (adj/adv)	قومي النطاق	*qaumiyyun niṭāq*
native (adj)	وطني، بلدي، طبيعي	*waṭanī, baladī, tabī'ī*
native (n)	ابن البلد، ساكن البلاد	*ibnul balad, sākinul balad*
Nativity (n)	ميلاد المسيح	*mīlādul masīḥ*
nattily (adv)	بأناقة، بنظافة	*bi anāqah, bi naẓāfah*
natty (adj)	أنيق، حاذق	*anīq, ḥādhiq*
natural (adj)	طبيعي، فطري، خلقي	*ṭabī'ī, fiṭrī, khilqī*
natural gas (n)	غاز طبيعي	*ghāz ṭabī'ī*
natural history (n)	تاريخ طبيعي	*tārīkh ṭabī'ī*
naturalism (n)	واقعية، طبيعية	*wāqi'iyyah, ṭabī'iyyah*
naturalist (n)	مؤيد للمذهب الطبيعي	*mu'ayyid lil madhhab aṭ ṭabī'ī*
naturalistic (adj)	طبيعي، واقعي	*ṭabī'ī, wāqi'ī*
naturalization,-isation (n)	تجنيس، تطبيع	*tajnīs, taṭbī'*
natural philosophy	فلسفة طبيعية	*falsafah ṭabī'iyyah*

natural resources	موارد طبيعية	*mawārid ṭabī'iyyah*
natural science	علوم طبيعية	*'ulūm ṭabī'iyyah*
natural selection	اصطفاء طبيعي	*iṣṭifā' ṭabī'ī*
nature (n)	طبيعة، فطرة، مزاج	*ṭabī'ah, fiṭrah, mizāj*
naught = nought		
naughtily (adv)	ببذاءة، بدعارة	*bi badhā'ah, bi da'ārah*
naughtiness (n)	خبث، دعارة	*khubth, da'ārah*
naughty (adj)	داعر، خبيث، بذيء	*dā'ir, khabīth, badhī'*
nausea (n)	غثيان، قرف	*ghathayān, qaraf*
nauseate (v)	أصيب بالغثيان	*uṣība bil ghathayān*
nauseous (adj)	مقرف، مغثٍ	*muqrif, mughthin*
nautical (adj)	بحري	*baḥrī*
nautical mile (n)	ميل بحري	*mīl baḥrī*
naval (adj)	بحري	*baḥrī*
navel (n)	سرة	*surrah*
navigable (adj)	صالح لسير السفن	*ṣāliḥ li sairis sufun*
navigate (v)	سافر بحراً، سير السفن	*sāfara baḥran, sayyaras sufun*
navigation (n)	سفر البحر، ملاحة	*safarul baḥr, milāḥah*
navigator (n)	ملاح، بحار	*mallāḥ, baḥḥār*
navvy (n)	عامل غير بارع	*'āmil ghair bāri'*
navy (n)	أسطول، سلاح بحري	*usṭūl, silāḥ baḥrī*
navy blue (n)	أزرق بحري	*azraq baḥrī*
nay (n)	لا، بل	*lā, bal*
near (adj)	قريب، مباشر	*qarīb, mubāshir*
near (v)	دنا، اقترب	*danā, iqtaraba*
near (prep)	قرب، على مقربة من	*qurba, 'alā maqrabati min*
nearby (adj)	على مقربة، قريب، مجاور	*'alā maqrabah, qarīb, mujāwir*
nearly (adv)	تقريباً، بالتقريب	*taqrīban, bit taqrīb*

nearness (n)	قرب، مقربة، دنو	*qurb, maqrabah, dunuww*
near-sighted (adj)	حسير البصر	*ḥasīrul baṣar*
near-sightedness (n)	حسر البصر	*ḥasarul baṣar*
neat (adj)	مرتب، نظيف، أنيق	*murattab, naẓīf, anīq*
neatness (n)	نظافة، طهارة	*naẓāfah, ṭahārah*
nebulous (adj)	غائم، سديمي، غامض	*ghā'im, sadīmī, ghāmiḍ*
necessaries (n)	أشياء ضرورية	*ashyā' ḍarūriyyah*
necessarily (adv)	ضرورةً، بالضرورة	*ḍarūratan, biḍ ḍarūrah*
necessary (adj)	ضروري، لازم	*ḍarūrī, lāzim*
necessitate (v)	أوجب، أحوج	*aujaba, aḥwaja*
necessitous (adj)	محتاج، معوز، ملح	*muḥtāj, mu'wiz, muliḥḥ*
necessity (n)	حاجة، ضرورة، عوز	*ḥājah, ḍarūrah, 'auz*
neck (n)	عنق، جزء ضيق من شيء	*'unuq, juz' ḍayyiq min shay'*
neck (v)	عانق	*'ānaqa*
neckerchief (n)	لفاع الرقبة	*lifā'ur raqabah*
necklace (n)	قلادة، عقد	*qilādah, 'iqd*
necktie (n)	ربطة العنق	*rabṭatul 'unuq*
necromancer (n)	عراف، ساحر	*'arrāf, sāḥir*
necromancy (n)	عرافة، سحر	*'irāfah, siḥr*
necropolis (n)	مقبرة قديمة	*maqbarah qadīmah*
nectar (n)	رحيق، سلافة، شراب الآلهة	*raḥīq, sulāfah, sharābul ālihah*
need (n/v)	حاجة، احتاج	*ḥājah, iḥtāja*
needful (adj)	ضروري، لازم	*ḍarūrī, lāzim*
needfully (adv)	بالضرورة، ضرورةً	*biḍ ḍarūrah, ḍarūratan*
needle (n)	إبرة، شيء كالإبرة	*ibrah, shay' kal ibrah*
needle (v)	استحث، حث	*istaḥaththa, ḥaththa*

needless (adj)	غير ضروري، غير لازم	*ghair ḍarūrī, ghair lāzim*
needlework (n)	شغل الإبرة	*shughlul ibrah*
needy (adj)	محتاج، معوز	*muḥtāj, mu'wiz*
nefarious (adj)	فظيع، شنيع	*faẓī', shanī'*
nefariously (adv)	بطريقة شائنة	*bi ṭarīqah shā'inah*
nefariousness (n)	شنعة، فظاعة	*shun'ah, faẓā'ah*
negate (v)	أنكر، رفض	*ankara, rafaḍa*
negation (n)	رفض، إنكار	*rafḍ, inkār*
negative (adj)	سلبي، نفي، منفي	*salbī, nafīy, manfīy*
negative (n)	جملة سلبية	*jumlah salbiyyah*
negative (v)	رفض، نفى، دحض	*rafaḍa, nafā, daḥaḍa*
negatively (adv)	سلبيًا، بطريق النفي	*salbiyyan, bi ṭarīqin nafy*
neglect (v/n)	أهمل، إهمال	*ahmala, ihmāl*
neglectful (adj)	مهمل، غفلان	*muhmil, ghaflān*
neglectfully (adv)	استخفافاً	*istikhfāfan*
neglectfulness (n)	إهمال، استخفاف، تهاون	*ihmāl, istikhfāf, tahāwun*
negligence (n)	إهمال، غفلة	*ihmāl, ghaflah*
negligent (adj)	متهاون، مهمل	*mutahāwin, muhmil*
negligently (adv)	إهمالاً	*ihmālan*
negligible (adj)	تافه، غير هام	*tāfih, ghair hāmm*
negotiable (adj)	يمكن تفاوضه	*yumkin tafāwuḍuh*
negotiate (v)	تداول، تفاوض	*tadāwala, tafāwaḍa*
negotiation (n)	مفاوضة، تداول	*mufāwaḍah, tadāwul*
negotiator (n)	مفاوض	*mufāwiḍ*
neigh (n/v)	صهيل، صهل	*ṣahīl, ṣahala*
neighbour (n/v)	جار، جاور	*jār, jāwara*
neighbourhood (n)	جوار، جيران	*jiwār, jīrān*
neighbouring (adj)	مجاور، متاخم	*mujāwir, mutākhim*
neighbourliness (n)	مودة، رأفة	*mawaddah, ra'fah*
neighbourly (adj)	ودي، ودادي	*wuddī, wadādī*
neither (adv/pron)	لا، لاهذا ولا ذاك	*lā, lā hādhā walā dhāka*

nemesis (n)	نقمة، عذاب	*niqmah, 'adhāb*
neologism (n)	تعبير جديد	*ta'bīr jadīd*
nephew (n)	ابن الأخ، ابن الأخت	*ibnul akh, ibnul ukht*
nephritis (n)	التهاب الكلية	*iltihābul kulyah*
nepotism (n)	محاباة الأقارب	*muḥābātul aqārib*
Neptune (n)	نبتون، اله البحر	*nibtūn, ilāhul baḥr*
nerve (n)	عصب، قوة	*'aṣab, quwwah*
nerve (v)	شجع، قوى	*shajja'a, qawwā*
nerveless (adj)	واهن، غير قوي	*wāhin, ghair qawī*
nervous (adj)	عصبي المزاج، منرفز	*'aṣabiyyul mizāj, munarfaz*
nervous breakdown	نهك عصبي	*nahak 'aṣabī*
nervous system (n)	جهاز عصبي	*jihāz 'aṣabī*
nervy (adj)	عصبي المزاج، سريع التأثر	*'aṣabiyyul mizāj, sarī'ut ta'aththur*
nest (n/v)	عش، بنى عشًا	*'ushsh, banā 'ushshan*
nest-egg (n)	مال مدخر	*māl muddakhar*
nestle (v)	استكن، استقر	*istakanna, istaqarra*
net (n/v)	شبكة، صاد بشبكة	*shabakah, ṣāda bi shabakah*
net (adj)	نهائي، خالص	*nihā'ī, khāliṣ*
nether (adj)	أسفل، سفلي	*asfal, suflī*
netting (n)	شبكة، شرك	*shabakah, sharak*
nettle (v)	أغضب، قرص	*aghḍaba, qaraṣa*
network (n)	شبكة	*shabakah*
neural (adj)	عصبي	*'aṣabī*
neuralgia (n)	ألم عصبي	*alam 'aṣabī*
neuritis (n)	التهاب الأعصاب	*iltihābul a'ṣāb*
neurologist (n)	طبيب الأمراض العصبية	*ṭabībul amrāḍ al 'aṣabiyyah*
neurology (n)	علم الأعصاب	*'ilmul a'ṣāb*

neurosis (n)	عصاب	*'uṣāb*
neurotic (adj/n)	عصابي	*'uṣābī*
neuter (adj/n)	محايد، شخص محايد	*muḥāyid, shakhṣ muḥāyid*
neuter (v)	خصى	*khaṣā*
neutral (adj/n)	حيادي، شخص محايد	*ḥiyādī, shakhṣ muḥāyid*
neutrality (n)	حياد	*ḥiyād*
neutralization,-isa-	تحايد، تعادل	*taḥāyud, ta'ādul*
neutralize,-ise (v)	حايد، تحايد	*ḥāyada, taḥāyada*
neutron (n)	نيوترون	*neutarūn*
never (adv)	أبدا، قط	*abadan, qaṭṭu*
nevermore (adv)	بعد اليوم أبدا	*ba'dal yaum abadan*
neverthless (adv)	مع أن، مع ذلك	*ma'a anna, ma'a dhālik*
new (adj)	جديد، حديث	*jadīd, ḥadīth*
newcomer (n)	قادم جديد	*qādim jadīd*
newel (n)	قائم الدربزين	*qā'imud darbazīn*
newfangled (adj)	مولع بالجديد	*mūlā' bil jadīd*
newly (adv)	من جديد	*min jadīd*
new moon (n)	هلال	*hilāl*
newness (n)	حداثة، جدة	*ḥadāthah, jiddah*
news (n)	خبر، نبأ	*khabar, naba'*
news agency	وكالة الأنباء	*wakālatul ambā'*
news agent	وكيل الأنباء	*wakīlul ambā'*
newscast (n)	نشرة الأخبار	*nashratul akhbār*
newscaster (n)	مذيع نشرة الأخبار	*mudhī'u nashratil akhbār*
news-letter (n)	رسالة أخبارية	*risālah akhbāriyyah*
newspaper (n)	صحيفة، جريدة	*ṣaḥīfah, jarīdah*
newsprint (n)	ورق الصحف	*waraquṣ ṣuḥuf*
news-vendor (n)	بائع الصحف	*bā'i'uṣ ṣuḥuf*
newsworthy (adj)	ذو أهمية أخبارية	*dhū ahammiyyah akhbāriyyah*
next (adj/adv)	تالٍ، بعد ذلك	*tālin, ba'da dhālik*

nexus (n)	رابطة	*rābiṭah*
nib (n)	طرف، رأس	*ṭaraf, ra's*
nibble (n)	طعام ضئيل المقدار	*ṭa'ām ḍa'īlul miqdār*
nice (adj)	متأنق، بارع، حسن	*muta'anniq, bāri', ḥasan*
nicely (adv)	بتأنق، ببراعة	*bi ta'annuq, bi barā'ah*
niceness (n)	براعة، أناقة	*barā'ah, anāqah*
nicety (n)	صحة، دقة	*ṣiḥḥah, diqqah*
nick (v)	حز، قبض	*ḥazza, qabaḍa*
nick (n)	حزة، ثلم، سجن	*ḥazzah, thalm, sijn*
nickel (n/v)	نكل، نكل	*nikl, nakkala*
nickname (n/v)	لقب، لقب	*laqab, laqqaba*
nicotine (n)	نيكوتين	*nīkūtīn*
niece (n)	ابنة الأخ، ابنة الأخت	*ibnatul akh, ibnatul ukht*
nifty (adj)	بارع، ممتاز	*bāri', mumtāz*
niggard (n)	شخص شحيح	*shakhṣ shaḥīḥ*
niggardliness (n)	شح، كزازة	*shuḥḥ, kazāzah*
niggardy (adj)	شحيح، كز	*shaḥīḥ, kazz*
niggle (v)	عبث، أضاع الوقت	*'abatha, aḍā'al waqt*
niggling (adj)	تافه، ثانوي	*tāfih, thānawī*
nigh (adv/prep)	قريباً، قرب	*qarīban, qurba*
night (n)	ليل، ليلة	*lail, lailah*
night-blindness (n)	عشا، عشاوة	*'ashā, 'ashāwah*
nightcap (n)	قلنسوة النوم	*qalansuwatun naum*
night-club (n)	ملهى ليلي	*malhā lailī*
night-dress (n)	منامة	*manāmah*
nightfall (n)	هبوط الليل، غسق	*hubūtul lail, ghasaq*
nightgown (n)	ثياب النوم	*thiyābun naum*
nightingale (n)	عندليب	*'andalīb*

night-long (adj)	جارٍ طول الليل	*jārin ṭūlal lail*
night-long (adv)	طوال الليل	*ṭiwālal lail*
nightly (adj/adv)	ليلي، ليلاً	*lailī, lailan*
nightmare (n)	كابوس، خبرة رهيبة	*kābūs, khibrah rahībah*
night-shirt (n)	قميص النوم	*qamīṣun naum*
night-watch (n)	حارس ليلي	*ḥāris lailī*
nihilism (n)	هلستية، عدمية	*nihlistiyyah, 'adamiyyah*
nihilist (n)	هلستي، مؤيد للعدمية	*nihlistī, mu'ayyid lil 'adamiyyah*
nihilistic (adj)	هلستي، عدمي	*nihlistī, 'adamī*
nil (n)	صفر	*ṣifr*
nimble (adj)	خفيف الحركة، رشيق	*khafīful ḥarakah, rashīq*
nincompoop (n)	أبله، مغفل	*ablah, mughaffal*
nine (n)	تسع، تسعة	*tis', tis'ah*
nineteen (n)	تسعة عشر	*tis'ah 'ashara*
nineteenth (adj)	تاسع عشر	*tāsi' 'ashara*
ninetieth (adj)	تسعون	*tis'ūn*
ninety (n)	تسعون	*tis'ūn*
ninny (adj)	أبله، ساذج	*ablah, sādhij*
ninth (adj)	تاسع	*tāsi'*
nip (v)	مص، قرص	*maṣṣa, qaraṣa*
nip (n)	قرصة، عض	*qarṣah, 'aḍḍ*
nippers (n)	كماشة، قصاج	*kammāshah, quṣāj*
nipple (n)	حلمة، حلم	*ḥalamah, ḥalam*
nippy (adj)	رشيق، سريع الحركة	*rashīq, sarī'ul ḥarakah*
nirvana (n)	نرفانا	*nirfānā*
nitrik (adj)	نتريك	*nitrīk*
nitrik acid (n)	حمض نتريك	*ḥamḍ nitrīk*
nitrogen (n)	نتروجين	*natrūjīn*
nitrogenous (adj)	نتروجيني	*natrūjīnī*

nitwit (n)	شخص أبله	*shakhṣ ablah*
no (adv/interj)	لا، ليس، كلا	*lā, laisa, kallā*
nob (n)	شخص رفيع المنـزلة	*shakhṣ rafī'ul manzilah*
nobility (n)	نبالة، شرف	*nabālah, sharaf*
noble (adj/n)	نبيل، كريم، جليل	*nabīl, karīm, jalīl*
nobleman (n)	نبيل، شريف	*nabīl, sharīf*
nobly (adv)	بشرف، بنبالة	*bi sharaf, bi nabālah*
nobody (pron)	لا أحد، ليس أحد	*lā aḥad, laisa aḥad*
nocturnal (adj)	متعلق بالليل، ليلي	*muta'alliq bil lail, lailī*
nocturnally (adv)	ليلاً	*lailan*
nocturne (n)	قطعة حالمة من موسيقي	*qiṭ'ah ḥālimah min mausīqī*
nod (v)	نكس، أومأ بالرأس	*nakkasa, auma'a bir ra's*
nod (n)	إيماء بالرأس	*īmā' bir ra's*
noddle (n)	رأس	*ra's*
node (n)	عجرة، عقدة	*'ujrah, 'uqdah*
nodular (adj)	عجيري، عقيدي	*'ujairī, 'uqaidī*
nodule (n)	عجرة صغيرة	*'ujrah ṣaghīrah*
nohow (adv)	بأية حالة، البتة	*bi ayyati ḥālah, albattah*
noise (n/v)	ضجيج، ضج	*ḍajīj, ḍajja*
noiseless (adj)	صامت، هادئ	*ṣāmit, hādi'*
noiselessly (adv)	بهدوء، بدون ضجة	*bi hudū', bidūn ḍajjah*
noiselessness (n)	هدوء، سكون	*hudū', sukūn*
noisily (adv)	بضجة، بصوت عالٍ	*bi ḍajjah, bi ṣaut 'ālin*
noisiness (n)	ضوضاء، ضجة	*ḍauḍā', ḍajjah*
noisome (adj)	بغيض، كريه	*baghīḍ, karīh*
noisy (adj)	كثير الضوضاء	*kathīruḍ ḍauḍā'*
nomad (n)	بدوي، متجول	*badawī, mutajawwil*
nomadic (adj)	بدوي، غير حضري	*badawī, ghair ḥaḍarī*
nomenclature (n)	وضع اسم، تسمية	*waḍ'u ism, tasmiyah*

nominal (adj)	اسمي، متعلق بالاسم	*ismī, muta'alliq bil ism*
nominate (v)	عين، رشح	*'ayyana, rashshaḥa*
nomination (n)	تعيين، ترشيح	*ta'yīn, tarshīḥ*
nominative (adj)	مرفوع، في حالة الرفع	*marfū', fī ḥālatir raf'*
nominee (n)	مرشح، معين	*murashshaḥ, mu'ayyan*
nonage (n)	عدم البلوغ، طفولة	*'adamul bulūgh, ṭufūlah*
nonagenarian (adj/n)	تسعوني	*tis'ūnī*
non-alignment (n)	عدم الانحياز	*'adamul inḥiyāz*
nonce (n)	مناسبة حاضرة فقط	*munāsabah ḥāḍirah faqaṭ*
nonchalant (adj)	عديم الاكتراث، غير مبال	*'adīmul iktirāth, ghair mubālin*
non-combatant (n)	شخص غير محارب	*shakhṣ ghair muḥārib*
non-commissioned	بدون رخصة	*bidūn rukhṣah*
non-committal (adj)	ملتبس، غير واضح	*multabis, ghair wāḍiḥ*
non-compliance (n)	امتناع، إنكار	*imtinā', inkār*
nonconformist (n)	منشق، مستقل	*munashshiq, mustaqill*
nonconformity (n)	عدم توافق، عدم تناغم	*'adamu tawāfuq, 'adamu tanāghum*
non-cooperation (n)	عدم تعاون	*'adamu ta'āwun*
none (pron)	لا أحد، ليس أحد	*lā aḥad, laisa aḥad*
nonentity (n)	شخص تافه	*shakhṣ tāfih*
nonesuch (n)	شخص فظ	*shakhṣ faẓẓ*
non-existent (adj)	عديم الوجود	*'adīmul wujūd*
non-interference (n)	عدم التدخل	*'adamut tadakhkhul*
non-observance (n)	إهمال، عدم اعتناء	*ihmāl, 'adamu i'tinā'*
nonpareil (n/adj)	شخص منقطع النظير	*shakhṣ munqaṭi'un naẓīr*
non-payment (n)	عدم دفع	*'adamu daf'*
nonplus (v)	حير، أربك	*ḥayyara, arbaka*
non-resident (n/adj)	لا إقامة لـه	*lā iqāmah lahu*

nonsense (n)	عبث، كلام فارغ	*'abath, kalām fārigh*
nonsensical (adj)	أحمق، فارغ	*aḥmaq, fārigh*
non-skid (adj)	غير منـــزلق	*ghair munzaliq*
non-stop (adj/adv)	بغير توقف	*bighairi tawaqquf*
non-union (adj)	غير نقابي	*ghair niqābī*
non-violence (n)	عدم عنف	*'adamu 'unf*
nook (n)	ركن، مخبأ، زاوية	*rukn, makhba', zāwiyah*
noon (n)	منتصف النهار	*muntaṣafun nahār*
noonday=noon		
noontide (n)	وقت الظهر	*waqtuẓ ẓuhr*
noose (n)	أحبولة، أنشوطة	*uḥbūlah, unshūṭah*
nor (conj)	ولا	*walā*
norm (n)	مبدأ، قاعدة، أصل	*mabda', qā'idah, aṣl*
normal (adj)	طبيعي، اعتيادي	*ṭabī'ī, i'tiyādī*
normality (n)	طبيعية، استواء	*ṭabī'iyyah, istiwā'*
normalization-isation (n)	تسوية، صورة طبيعية	*taswiyah, ṣūrah ṭabī'iyyah*
normalize,-ise (v)	طبع، سوى	*ṭabba'a, sawwā*
normative (adj)	معياري	*mi'yārī*
north (n/adj)	شمال، شمالي	*shimāl, shimālī*
northbound (adj)	مقود نحو الشمال	*maqūd naḥwash shimāl*
northeast (adj/adv)	نحو الشمال الشرقي	*naḥwash shimāl ash sharqī*
northerly (adj)	شمالي	*shimālī*
north pole (n)	قطب شمالي	*quṭb shimālī*
northwards (adv)	نحو الشمال	*naḥwash shimāl*
northwest (adj/adv)	نحو الشمال الغربي	*naḥwash shimāl al gharbī*
nose (n)	أنف، حاسة الشم	*anf, ḥāssatush shamm*
nose (v)	تقدم ببطاء	*taqaddama bi biṭā'*
nosebag (n)	مخلاة	*mikhlāt*

nosebleed (n)	رعاف	*ruʻāf*
nosegay (n)	باقة الأزهار	*bāqatul azhār*
nosily (adv)	بفضول	*bi fuḍūl*
nosiness (n)	فضول، بذاءة	*fuḍūl, badhā'ah*
nostalgia (n)	توق شديد إلى الماضي	*tauq shadīd ilal māḍī*
nostalgic (adj)	تواق إلى الماضي	*tawwāq ilal māḍī*
nostril (n)	منخر، حيشوم	*mankhir, ḥaishūm*
nosy (nosey) (adj)	فضولي	*fuḍūlī*
not (adv)	لا، ليس	*lā, laisa*
notability (n)	شهرة، وجاهة	*shuhrah, wajāhah*
notable (adj)	وجيه، ذو منزلة رفيعة	*wajīh, dhū manzilah rafīʻah*
notably (adv)	خصوصاً	*khuṣūṣan*
notary (n)	مسجل العقود	*musajjilul ʻuqūd*
notation (n)	ترقيم، تدوين	*tarqīm, tadwīn*
notch (v)	فل، ثلم	*falla, thalama*
notch (n)	فل، ثلم	*fall, thalm*
note (v)	لاحظ، دون	*lāḥaẓa, dawwana*
note (n)	مذكرة، تعليق، ملاحظة	*mudhakkirah, taʻlīq mulāḥaẓah*
notebook (n)	مذكرة	*mudhakkirah*
noted (adj)	مشهور، شهير	*mashhūr, shahīr*
notepaper (n)	ورق الرسائل	*waraqur rasā'il*
noteworthy (adj)	جدير بالذكر	*jadīr bidh dhikr*
nothing (n)	لا شيء	*lā shay'*
nothingness (n)	عدم، فراغ	*ʻadam, farāgh*
notice (n)	ملاحظة، انتباه، اعتناء	*mulāḥaẓah, intibāh, iʻtinā'*
notice (v)	لاحظ، أعلن، أعلم	*lāḥaẓa, aʻlana, aʻlama*

noticeable (adj)	قابل للملاحظة	*qābil lil mulāḥaẓah*
notice-board (n)	لوحة الإعلان	*lauḥatul i'lān*
notification (n)	إعلام، إنذار	*i'lām, indhār*
notify (v)	أعلن، أنذر	*a'lana, andhara*
notion (n)	تصور، رأي، ظن	*taṣawwur, ra'y, ẓann*
notional (adj)	نظري، تصوري	*naẓari, taṣawwurī*
notoriety (n)	سمعة سيئة	*sum'ah sayyi'ah*
notorious (adj)	سيء السمعة	*sayyi'us sum'ah*
notoriously (adv)	بطريقة سيئة	*bi ṭarīqah sayyi'ah*
notwithstanding (adv)	مع أن، مع ذلك	*ma'a anna, ma'a dhālik*
nought (n)	صفر، لا شيء	*ṣifr, lā shay'*
noun (n)	اسم	*ism*
nourish (v)	غذى، أقات	*ghadhdhā, aqāta*
nourishing (n)	مغذّ، مقوّ	*mughadhdhin, muqawwin*
nourishment (n)	تغذية، غذاء	*taghdhiyah, ghidhā'*
novel (adj)	جديد، حديث العهد	*jadīd, ḥadīthul 'ahd*
novel (n)	قصة، رواية	*qiṣṣah, riwāyah*
novelette (n)	رواية قصيرة	*riwāyah qaṣīrah*
novelist (n)	كاتب روائي	*kātib riwā'ī*
novelty (n)	جدة، بدعة	*jiddah, bid'ah*
November (n)	نوفمبر، تشرين الثاني	*nufimbar, tishrīn ath thānī*
novice (n)	مبتدئ، قليل الخبرة	*mubtadi', qalīlul khibrah*
now (adv)	الآن، حالاً	*al'ān, ḥālan*
nowadays (adv)	في الوقت الحاضر	*fil waqtil ḥāḍir*
nowhere (adv)	ليس في مكان ما	*laisa fī makānim mā*
noxious (adj)	ضار، سام	*ḍārr, sāmm*
noxiousness (n)	مضرة، أذية	*maḍarrah, adhiyyah*
nozzle (n)	فوهة، أنف	*fūhah, anf*
nuance (n)	فرق دقيق	*farq daqīq*

nubile (adj)	صالح للزواج	*ṣāliḥ liz zawāj*
nuclear (adj)	نووي	*nawawī*
nuclear energy (n)	طاقة نووية	*ṭāqah nawawiyyah*
nuclear war (n)	حرب نووية	*ḥarb nawawiyyah*
nucleic acid (n)	حامض نووي	*ḥāmiḍ nawawī*
nucleus (n)	نواة، قلب، مركز	*nawāt, qalb, markaz*
nude (adj/n)	عارٍ، عريان	*'ārin, 'uryān*
nudism (n)	مذهب العرى	*madhhabul 'urā*
nudist (n)	مؤيد لمذهب العرى	*mu'ayyid li madhhabil 'urā*
nudity (n)	عرية، عراء	*'uryah, 'arā'*
nugatory (adj)	باطل، زهيد	*bāṭil, zahīd*
nuisance (n)	مزعج، مقلق	*muz'ij, muqliq*
null (adj)	باطل، ملغى	*bāṭil, mulghan*
nullification (n)	إلغاء، إبطال	*ilghā', ibṭāl*
nullify (v)	أبطل، ألغى	*abṭala, alghā*
nullity (n)	بطلان، عدم جواز	*buṭlān, 'adamu jawāz*
numb (v/adj)	خدر، خدر	*khaddara, khadir*
number (n)	عدد، مجموعة	*'adad, majmū'ah*
numberless (adj)	لا يعد، لا يحصى	*lā yu'add, lā yuḥṣā*
numbness (n)	خدرة، فقدان الحس	*khudrah, fuqdānul ḥiss*
numeral (adj)	عددي	*'adadī*
numerate (v)	عد، عدد	*'adda, 'addada*
numeration (n)	عد، إحصاء	*'add, iḥṣā'*
numerator (n)	صورة الكسر، بسط	*ṣūratul kasr, basṭ*
numerical (adj)	عددي، رقمي	*'adadī, raqmī*
numerically (adv)	بترتيب عددي	*bi tartīb 'adadī*
numerous (adj)	متعدد، كثير	*muta'addid, kathīr*
numinous (adj)	روحي، روحاني	*rūḥī, rūḥānī*
numskull, numbskull	أحمق، أبله	*aḥmaq, ablah*
nun (n)	راهبة	*rāhibah*
nuncio (n)	سفير البابا	*safīrul bābā*
nunnery (n)	دير للراهبات	*dair lir rāhibāt*

nuptial (adj)	عرسي، زواجي	*'ursī, zawājī*
nuptials (n)	زواج، عرس	*zawāj, 'urs*
nurse (n)	ممرضة، مربية	*mumarriḍah, murabbiyah*
nurse (v)	مرض، ربى، أرضع	*marraḍa, rabbā, arḍa'a*
nursery (n)	دار الحضانة، مشتل	*dārul ḥaḍānah, mashtal*
nurseryman (n)	صاحب المشتل	*ṣāḥibul mashtal*
nursery rhyme	أغنية الأطفال	*ughniyatul aṭfāl*
nursery school	مدرسة الحضانة	*madrasatul ḥaḍānah*
nurture (v)	ربى، غذى، شجع	*rabbā, ghadhdhā, shajja'a*
nurture (n)	تربية، تنشئة، حضانة	*tarbiyah, tanshiyah, ḥaḍānah*
nut (n)	جوزة، حزقة، رأس	*jauzah, ḥazaqah, ra's*
nutrient (adj)	مغذي، مقوي	*mughadhdhī, muqawwī*
nutriment (n)	تغذية، غذاء	*taghdhiyah, ghidhā'*
nutrition (n)	غذاء، تغذية	*ghidhā', taghdhiyah*
nutritionist (n)	غذوي	*ghadhawī*
nutritious (adj)	مغذي، مقوي	*mughadhdhī, muqawwī*
nutritive (adj)	متعلق بالتغذية	*muta'alliq bit taghdhiyah*
nutshell (n)	قشرة الجوز	*qishratul jauz*
nylon (n)	نيلون	*nailūn*
nymph (n)	عروسة البحر، حورية البحر	*'arūsatul baḥr, ḥūriyyatul baḥr*
nymphomania (n)	غلمة نسوية	*ghulmah niswiyyah*
nymphomaniac (adj)	متعلق بالغلمة النسوية	*muta'alliq bil ghulmah an niswiyyah*

O

o (oh) (interj)	يا، أوه	*yā, ūh*
oaf (n)	أخرق، أبله	*akhraq, ablah*
oafish (adj)	ساذج، أبله	*sādhij, ablah*
oak (n)	بلوط	*ballūṭ*

oaken (adj)	بلوطي، سندياني	*ballūṭi, sindiyānī*
oar (n)	مجذاف	*mijdhāf*
oarsman (n)	مجذف	*mujadhdhif*
oasis (n)	واحة	*wāḥah*
oath (n)	يمين، قسم، حلف	*yamīn, qasam, ḥalf*
oats (n)	شوفان	*shūfān*
obbligato (adj)	ضروري، لازمي	*ḍarūrī, lāzimī*
obduracy (n)	قساوة القلب	*qasāwatul qalb*
obdurate (adj)	عنيد، متحجر القلب	*'anīd, mutaḥajjirul qalb*
obedience (n)	طاعة، إطاعة	*ṭā'ah, iṭā'ah*
obedient (adj)	مطيع، ممتثل	*muṭī', mumtathil*
obeisance (n)	انحناء، خضوع، احترام	*inḥinā', khuḍū', iḥtirām*
obese (adj)	سمين، شحيم، بدين	*samīn, shaḥīm, badīn*
obesity (n)	بدانة، سمنة	*badānah, simanah*
obey (v)	أطاع، أذعن	*aṭā'a, adh'ana*
obfuscate (v)	عتم، شوس	*'attama, shawwasa*
obituary (n)	نعي، تأبين	*na'y, ta'bīn*
object (n)	شيء، غرض، مفعول	*shay', gharaḍ, maf'ūl*
object (v)	اعترض، رفض	*i'taraḍa, rafaḍa*
objection (n)	اعتراض، معارضة	*i'tiraḍ, mu'āraḍah*
objectionable (adj)	غير مقبول، غير مرغوب	*ghair maqbūl, ghair marghūb*
objective (n)	هدف، قصد، غرض	*hadaf, qaṣd, gharaḍ*
objectivity (n)	تجرد عن الغرض	*tajarrud 'anil gharaḍ*
object lesson (n)	درس عملي	*dars 'amalī*
oblate (adj)	مفلطح	*mufalṭaḥ*
obligate (v)	ألزم، فرض	*alzama, faraḍa*
obligation (n)	واجب، فرض، التزام	*wājib, farḍ, iltizām*
obligatory (adj)	إجباري، إلزامي	*ijbārī, ilzāmī*
oblige (v)	أجبر، أكره	*ajbara, akraha*

obliged (adj)	شاكر، مقر بالجميل	*shākir, muqirr bil jamīl*
oblique (adj)	منحرف، زائغ، ملتوٍ	*munḥarif, zā'igh, multawin*
obliquity (n)	انحراف، ميلان	*inḥirāf, mayalān*
obliterate (v)	محا، أزال	*maḥā, azāla*
obliteration (n)	إزالة، طمس	*izālah, ṭams*
oblivion (n)	سهو، نسيان، سلوان	*sahw, nisyān, sulwān*
oblivious (adj)	كثير النسيان، غير واعٍ	*kathīrun nisyān, ghair wā'in*
oblong (n/adj)	مستطيل الشكل	*mustaṭīlush shakl*
obloquy (n)	خزي، قدح	*khizy, qadḥ*
obnoxious (adj)	بغيض، كريه جدا	*baghīḍ, karīh jiddā*
obnoxiousness (n)	كره شديد	*kurh shadīd*
obscene (adj)	قبيح، فاحش	*qabīḥ, fāḥish*
obscenity (n)	فحش، قذارة	*fuḥsh, qadhārah*
obscure (v)	عتم، أبهم	*'attama, abhama*
obscure (adj)	غامض، قاتم، غير واضح	*ghāmiḍ, qātim, ghair wāḍiḥ*
obscurely (adv)	بإبهام، بخفاء	*bi ibhām bi khafā'*
obscurity (n)	غموض، إبهام، ظلام	*ghumūḍ, ibhām, ẓalām*
obsequious (adj)	خاضع، متذلل	*khāḍi', mutadhallil*
obsequiousness (n)	تذلل، خضوع	*tadhallul, khuḍū'*
observable (adj)	جدير بالملاحظة	*jadīr bil mulāḥaẓah*
observance (n)	ملاحظة، مراقبة	*mulāḥaẓah, murāqabah*
observant (adj)	سريع الملاحظة، مراعٍ	*sarī'ul mulāḥaẓah, murā'in*
observation (n)	مراقبة، ملاحظة	*murāqabah, mulāḥaẓah*
observatory (n)	مرصد، مرقب	*marṣad, marqab*
observe (v)	لاحظ، راقب، تقيد	*lāḥaẓa, rāqaba, taqayyada*

observer (n)	مراقب، مراعٍ	*murāqib, murā'in*
obsessed (adj)	مصاب بالهجسات	*muṣāb bil hajasāt*
obsession (n)	هجسة، استحواذ	*hajsah, istiḥwādh*
obsessive (adj)	استحواذي	*istiḥwādhī*
obsolete (adj)	مهجور، مهمل	*mahjūr, muhmal*
obstacle (n)	عقبة، عائق، مانع	*'aqabah, 'ā'iq, māni'*
obstacle race (n)	سباق الحواجز	*sibāqul ḥawājiz*
obstetrician (n)	مولد	*muwallid*
obstetrics (n)	علم الولادة	*'ilmul wilādah*
obstinacy (n)	عناد، تشبث	*'inād, tashabbuth*
obstinate (adj)	عنيد، متشبث	*'anīd, mutashabbith*
obstinately (adv)	بتشبث، بعناد	*bi tashabbuth, bi 'inād*
obstruct (v)	سد، حجز	*sadda, ḥajaza*
obstruction (n)	سد، حاجز، عائق	*sadd, ḥājiz, 'ā'iq*
obstructive (adj)	عائق، حاجز	*'ā'iq, ḥājiz*
obtain (v)	نال، حصل، أحرز	*nāla, ḥaṣala, aḥraza*
obtainable (adj)	ممكن الحصول عليه	*mumkinul ḥuṣūl 'alaih*
obtrude (v)	تطفل، تعرض	*taṭaffala, ta'arraḍa*
obtrusion (n)	تطفل، تعرض	*taṭafful, ta'arruḍ*
obtrusive (adj)	متطفل، مضايق	*mutaṭaffil, muḍāyiq*
obtrusively (adv)	من طريق التطفل	*min ṭarīqit taṭafful*
obtrusiveness (n)	تطفل، فضول	*taṭafful, fuḍūl*
obtuse (adj)	أبلد، أحمق	*ablad, aḥmaq*
obtusely (adv)	بحمق، ببلادة	*bi ḥumq, bi balādah*
obtuseness (n)	حماقة، بلادة	*ḥamāqah, balādah*
obverse (n)	وجه الشيء، وجه العملة	*wajhush shay', wajhul 'umlah*
obviate (v)	أزال، تفادى	*azāla, tafādā*
obvious (adj)	واضح، بين، صريح	*wāḍiḥ, bayyin, ṣarīḥ*
obviously (adv)	بوضوح، بصراحة	*bi wuḍūḥ, bi ṣarāḥah*

obviousness (n)	وضوح، صراحة	*wuḍūḥ, ṣarāḥah*
occasion (n)	مناسبة، فرصة	*munāsabah, furṣah*
occasional (adj)	عرضي، حيني	*'araḍī, ḥīnī*
occasionally (adv)	أحيانًا، اتفاقًا	*aḥyānan, ittifāqan*
Occident (n)	بلاد غربية	*bilād gharbiyyah*
Occidental (adj)	غربي	*gharbī*
occult (adj)	خفي، غامض، سري	*khafī, ghāmiḍ, sirrī*
occupancy (n)	تملك، احتلال	*tamalluk, iḥtilāl*
occupant (n)	متملك، ساكن	*mutamallik, sākin*
occupation (n)	احتلال، شغل، مهنة	*iḥtilāl, shughl, mihnah*
occupational (adj)	احتلالي، مهني	*iḥtilālī, mihnī*
occupied (adj)	محتل، مشغول	*muḥtall, mashghūl*
occupier (n)	ساكن، واضع اليد	*sākin, wāḍi'ul yad*
occupy (v)	احتل، استولى	*iḥtalla, istaulā*
occur (v)	وقع، حدث، ظهر	*waqa'a, ḥadatha, ẓahara*
occurrence (n)	حدوث، وقوع	*ḥudūth, wuqū'*
ocean (n)	بحر، اوقيانوس	*baḥr, ūqyānūs*
oceanic (adj)	اوقيانوسي، بحري	*ūqyānūsī, baḥrī*
oceanographer (n)	اوقيانوغرافي	*ūqyānugharāfī*
oceanography (n)	علم الاوقيانوس	*'ilmul ūqyānūs*
o'clock (adv)	حسب الساعة	*ḥasabas sā'ah*
octagon (adj)	مثمن الزوايا	*muthammanuz zawāyā*
octane (n)	أوكتين	*ūktīn*
octave (n)	ثمانية	*thumāniyah*
octet (n)	لحن ثماني	*laḥn thumānī*
October (n)	اكتوبر، تشرين أول	*aktūbar, tishrīn awwal*
octogenarian (n)	شخص ثمانوني	*shakhṣ thumānūnī*
octopus (n)	أخطبوط	*ukhṭubūṭ*
ocular (adj)	عيني، بصري	*'ainī, baṣarī*
oculist (n)	طبيب العيون	*ṭabībul 'uyūn*

odd (adj)	شاذ، مفرد، وتري	*shādhdh, mufrad, watrī*
odd ball (n)	غريب الأطوار	*gharībul aṭwār*
oddity (n)	غرابة، شذوذ	*gharābah, shudhūdh*
oddly (adv)	بغرابة	*bi gharābah*
oddment (n)	بقية	*baqiyyah*
odds (n)	أرجحية، أغلبية	*arjaḥiyyah, aghlabiyyah*
ode (n)	أغنية، قصيدة	*ughniyyah, qaṣīdah*
odious (adj)	شنيع، قبيح، كريه	*shanī', qabīḥ, karīh*
odiousness (n)	قباحة، شناعة	*qabāḥah, shanā'ah*
odium (n)	بغض، كره	*bughḍ, kurh*
odorous (adj)	ذكي الرائحة، عطر	*dhakiyyur rā'iḥah, 'aṭir*
odour (odor) (n)	رائحة، شذا	*rā'iḥah, shadhā*
odourless (adj)	عديم الرائحة	*'adīmur rā'iḥah*
odyssey (n)	جولات طويلة	*jaulāt ṭawīlah*
of (prep)	من، عن، بسبب	*min, 'an, bi sababi*
off (adj)	معطل، مخبول، بعيد	*mu'aṭṭal, makhbūl, ba'īd*
off (prep)	من، عن، بحيث	*min, 'an, biḥaithu*
offal (n)	فضلات، زبالات	*faḍalāt, zubālāt*
off-beat (adj)	غريب الأطوار، شاذ	*gharībul aṭwār, shādhdh*
offence (offense)	إساءة، أذىً، جريمة	*isā'ah, adhan, jarīmah*
offend (v)	أساء، انتهك، أزعج	*asā'a, intahaka, az'aja*
offender (n)	مسيء، مجرم	*musī', muz'ij, mujrim*
offense (n)	هجوم، استياء	*hujūm, istiyā'*
offensive (adj)	مزعج، مغضب، كريه	*muz'ij, mughḍib, karīh*
offensive (n)	هجوم، إغاظة	*hujūm, ighāẓah*
offensively (adv)	بطريقة مزعجة	*bi ṭarīqah muz'ijah*
offensiveness (n)	إغاظة، إزعاج، هجومية	*ighāẓah, iz'āj, hujūmiyyah*
offer (v)	قدم، عرض، اقترح	*qaddama, 'araḍa, iqtaraḥa*
offering (n)	عرض، تقديم	*'arḍ, taqdīm*
offertory (n)	صدقات	*sadaqāt*

offhand (adj/adv)	مرتجل، ارتجالاً	*murtajal, irtijālan*
offhanded (adj)	مرتجل	*murtajal*
offhandedly (adv)	ارتجالاً، فوراً	*irtijālan, fauran*
office (n)	مكتب، منصب، خدمة	*maktab, manṣab, khidmah*
office boy (n)	ساعي المكتب	*sā'il maktab*
office holder (n)	موظف، ضابط	*muwaẓẓaf, ḍābiṭ*
office hours (n)	ساعات الدوام	*sā'ātud dawām*
officer (n)	ضابط، مسؤول، موظف	*ḍābiṭ, mas'ūl, muwaẓẓaf*
official (adj)	رسمي، قانوني	*rasmī, qānūnī*
official (n)	موظف، مأمور	*muwaẓẓaf, ma'mūr*
officialdom (n)	جماعة الموظفين	*jamā'atul muwaẓẓafīn*
officially (adv)	رسميًّا، قانونيًّا	*rasmiyyan, qānūniyyan*
officiate (v)	قام بخدمة	*qāma bi khidmah*
officious (adj)	متداخل، فضولي	*mutadākhil, fuḍūlī*
officiously (adv)	عبثًا، فضوليًّا	*'abathan, fuḍūliyyan*
officiousness (n)	فضول، لاغية	*fuḍūl, lāghiyah*
offing (n)	مقربة، وشك	*maqrabah, washak*
offprint (n)	مستخرج	*mustakhraj*
offset (n)	أوفسيت	*ūfsīt*
offset (v)	عادل، كافأ	*'ādala, kāfa'a*
offshoot (n)	فرع، شعبة	*far', shu'bah*
offshore (adj)	آتٍ من الشاطئ	*ātin miash shāṭi'*
offspring (n)	نسل، ذرية	*nasl, dhurriyyah*
off-stage (adj)	بعيد عن المسرح	*ba'īd 'anil masraḥ*
often (adv)	في أكثر الأحيان	*fī aktharil aḥyān*
ogle (v)	رمق بنظرة غرامية	*ramaqa bi naẓrah gharāmiyyah*
oh (interj)	يا، أوه	*yā, ūh*

oil (n)	زيت، دهن، نفط	*zait, duhn, nafiṭ*
oil (v)	زيت، دهن	*zayyata, dahana*
oilcake (n)	كسب	*kusb*
oilcloth (n)	قماش زيتي	*qumāsh zaitī*
oilfield (n)	حقل الزيت	*ḥaqluz zait*
oil-painting (n)	تصوير بالزيت	*taṣwīr biz zait*
oil-palm (n)	نخلة الزيت	*nakhlatuz zait*
oil-tanker (n)	ناقلة زيت	*nāqilatu zait*
oil well (n)	بئر زيت	*bi'ru zait*
oily (adj)	زيتي، دهني، زلق	*zaitī, duhnī, zaliq*
ointment (n)	مرهم	*marham*
okay (ok) (adj/adv)	حسن، حسناً	*ḥasan, ḥasanan*
okay (v)	وافق، صدق	*wāfaqa, ṣadaqa*
old (adj)	قديم، كبير السن	*qadīm, kabīrus sinn*
old-fashioned (adj)	قديم الطراز	*qadīmuṭ ṭirāz*
oldish (adj)	كالعتيق	*kal 'atīq*
oldman (n)	زوج، أب	*zauj, ab*
old-time (adj)	عتيق، قديم	*'atīq, qadīm*
old world (n)	عالم قديم	*'ālam qadīm*
olfactory (adj)	متعلق بحاسة الشم	*muta'alliq bi ḥāssatish shamm*
oligarch (n)	أوليغاركي	*ūlīghārkī*
oligarchy (n)	حكومة القلة، أوليغاركية	*ḥukūmatul qillah, ūlīghārkiyyah*
olive (n/adj)	زيتون، زيتوني	*zaitūn, zaitūnī*
olive-branch (n)	غصن الزيتون	*ghuṣnuz zaitūn*
Olympian (adj)	جليل، كريم	*jalīl, karīm*
Olympmic games (n)	مباريات أولمبية	*mubārayāt ūlambiyyah*
omlette (omlete) (n)	عجة البيض، أومليت	*'ujjatul baiḍ, ūmlīt*

omen (n)	فأل، طيرة	*fa'l, ṭiyarah*
omen (v)	تفاءل، تكهن	*tafā'ala, takahhana*
ominous (adj)	مشؤوم، نحس	*mash'ūm, naḥis*
omission (n)	إهمال، إغفال، حذف	*ihmāl, ighfāl, ḥadhf*
omit (v)	حذف، أغفل	*ḥadhafa, aghfala*
omnibus (n)	أومنيبوس، مجموع	*ūmnībūs, majmū'*
omnipotence (n)	قدرة كلية	*qudrah kulliyyah*
omnipotent (adj)	قدير، كلي القدرة	*qadīr, kulliyyul qudrah*
omnipresent (adj)	موجود في كل مكان	*maujūd fī kulli makān*
omniscience (n)	علم بكل شيء	*'ilm bi kulli shayy*
omniscient (adj)	عالم بكل شيء	*'ālim bi kulli shay'*
omnivorous (adj)	قارت	*qārit*
on (prep)	على، فوق	*'alā, fauqa*
once (adv)	ذات مرة، مرةً	*dhāta marrah, marratan*
oncoming (adj)	مقترب، دانٍ	*muqtarib, dānin*
oncoming (n)	دنو، اقتراب	*dunuww, iqtirāb*
one (pron/n)	أحد، واحد	*aḥad, wāḥid*
oneself (pron)	نفسه، نفسها	*nafsuh, nafsuhā*
one-sided (adj)	متحيز، وحيد الجانب	*mutaḥayyiz, waḥīdul jānib*
one-sidedness (n)	تحيز، تعصب	*taḥayyuz, ta'aṣṣub*
ongoing (adj)	مستمر، متطور	*mustamirr, mutaṭawwir*
onion (n)	بصلة، بصل	*baṣalah, baṣal*
onlooker (n)	متفرج، مشاهد	*mutafarrij, mushāhid*
only (adj/adv)	وحيد، فقط، فريد	*waḥīd, faqaṭ, farīd*
onomatopoea (n)	تسمية الأشياء بأصواتها	*tasmiyatul ashyā' bi aṣwātihā*
onrush (n)	تدفق، دفق	*tadaffuq, dafq*
onset (n)	هجوم، قدوم	*hujūm, qudūm*
onshore=ashore		

onside (adj/adv)	في الجانب الصحيح	*fil jānib, aṣ ṣaḥīḥ*
onslaught (n)	غزو، هجوم	*ghazw, hujūm*
onto (prep)	على، فوق	*'alā, fauqa*
ontology (n)	علم الوجود	*'ilmul wujūd*
onus (n)	مسؤولية، وجوب	*mas'ūliyyah, wujūb*
onward (adj)	موجه إلى الأمام	*muwajjah ilal amām*
onwards (adv)	إلى الأمام	*ilal amām*
oomph (n)	حماسة، حيوية	*ḥamāsah, ḥayawiyyah*
ooze (v)	نز، رشح	*nazza, rashaḥa*
ooze (n)	سبخة، ردغة	*sabkhah, radghah*
opacity (n)	غموض، إبهام	*ghumūḍ, ibhām*
opal (n)	أوبال، حجر كريم	*ūbāl, ḥajar karim*
opalscent (adj)	كالأوبال، متلألي	*kal ūbāl, mutala'lī*
opaque (adj)	غير شفاف، مبهم، معتم	*ghair shaffāf, mubham, mu'tim*
opaquely (adv)	بطريق معتم	*bi ṭarīq mu'tim*
opaqueness (n)	عتامة، غموض	*'atāmah, ghumūḍ*
open (adj)	مفتوح، مكشوف	*maftūḥ, makshūf*
open (n)	أرض مشكوفة، فتحة	*arḍ makshūfah, futḥah*
open (v)	فتح، انفتح، استهل	*fataḥa, infataḥa, istahalla*
open-air (adj)	حادث في الهواء الطلق	*ḥādith fil hawā'iṭ ṭalq*
open-and-shut (adj)	واضح، سهل جدا	*wāḍiḥ, sahl jiddā*
open-ended (adj)	غير محدد	*ghair muḥaddad*
open-eyed (adj)	يقظ، مفتوح العينين	*yaqiẓ, maftūḥul 'ainain*
open-handed (adj)	مبسوط اليد، سخي	*mabsūṭul yad, sakhiyy*
open-handedly (adv)	بسخاوة	*bi sakhāwah*
open-handedness (n)	سخاء، سخاوة	*sakhā', sakhāwah*
open-hearted (adj)	مخلص،وفي، كريم	*mukhliṣ, wafī, karīm*
opening (adj)	ابتداء، فتحة	*ibtidā', futḥah*
open letter	كتاب مفتوح	*kitāb maftūḥ*

openly (adv)	علانيةً، جهاراً	*'alāniyyatan, jihāran*
open-minded (adj)	منفتح العقل	*munfatiḥul 'aql*
ope-mouthed (adj)	فاغر الفم	*fāghirul fam*
opera (n)	أوبرا، مسرحية موسيقية	*ūbrā, masraḥiyyah mausīqiyyah*
opera glasses	منظار الأوبرا	*minẓārul ūbrā*
opera house	دار الأوبرا	*dārul ūbrā*
operate (v)	أجرى، أعمل، دبر	*ajrā, a'mala, dabbara*
operatic (adj)	أوبري، مسرحي	*ūbrī, masraḥī*
operating-theatre (n)	قاعة البضع	*qā'atul baḍ'*
operation (n)	عمل، فعل، عملية	*'amal, fi'l, 'amaliyyah*
operational (adj)	متعلق بالعمليات	*muta'alliq bil 'amaliyyāt*
operative (adj)	مؤثر، فعال، نافذ	*mu'aththir, fa''āl, nāfidh*
operator (n)	عامل، صانع، مدير شركة	*'āmil, ṣāni', mudīru sharikah*
operetta (n)	أوبريت، مسرحية قصيرة	*ūbrīt, masraḥiyyah qaṣīrah*
ophthalmic (adj)	مختص بالعيون، عيني	*mukhtaṣṣ bil 'uyūn, 'ainī*
ophthalmologist (n)	طبيب العيون	*ṭabībul 'uyūn*
ophthalmology (n)	طب العيون	*ṭibbul 'uyūn*
opinion (n)	رأي، فكر	*ra'y, fikr*
opinionated (adj)	عنيد، متعنت	*'anīd, muta'annit*
opium (n)	أفيون	*afyūn*
opponent (n)	خصم، مقاوم، مناوئ	*khaṣm, muqāwim, munāwi'*
opportune (adj)	مناسب، ملائم، موافق	*munāsib, mulā'im, muwāfiq*
opportunely (adv)	في الوقت المناسب	*fil waqtil munāsib*
opportunism (n)	انتهازية	*intihāziyyah*
opportunist (n)	انتهازي، نفعي	*intihāzī, naf'ī*

opportunity (n)	مناسبة، فرصة	*munāsabah, furṣah*
oppose (v)	عارض، قاوم، مانع	*ʻāraḍa, qāwama, mānaʻa*
opposed (adj)	معارض، مقاوم	*muʻāriḍ, muqāwim*
opposite (adj)	مقابل، مخالف، متضاد	*muqābil, mukhālif, mutaḍādd*
opposite (prep)	أمام، تجاه	*amāma, tujāha*
opposition (n)	تعارض، تقابل، معارضة	*taʻāruḍ, taqābul, muʻāraḍah*
oppress (v)	ضايق، ظلم، قمع	*ḍāyaqa, ẓalama, qamaʻa*
oppressed (adj)	مظلوم	*mazlūm*
oppression (n)	ظلم، جور، اضطهاد	*ẓulm, jaur, iḍṭihād*
oppressive (adj)	مضايق، جائر	*muḍāyiq, jā'ir*
oppressor (n)	ظالم، جائر	*ẓālim, jā'ir*
opprobrious (adj)	فاضح، مخزٍ، محقر	*fāḍiḥ, mukhzin, muḥaqqir*
opprobrium (n)	ازدراء، خزي، عيب	*izdirā', khizy, ʻaib*
opt (v)	اختار، انتقى	*ikhtāra, intaqā*
optical (adj)	عيني، بصري	*ʻainī, baṣari*
optician (n)	صانع النظارات	*ṣāniʻun naẓẓārāt*
optics (n)	علم البصريات	*ʻilmul baṣariyyāt*
optimism (n)	تفاءل بالخير	*tafā'ul bil khair*
optimist (n)	متفائل بالخير	*mutafā'il bil khair*
optimistic (adj)	تفاءلي، متفائل	*tafā'ulī, mutafā'il*
optimistically (adv)	متفائلاً بالخير	*mutafā'ilan bil khair*
option (n)	خيار، اختيار	*khiyār, ikhtiyār*
optional (adj)	اختياري	*ikhtiyārī*
opulence (n)	غنىً، غزارة	*ghinan, ghazārah*
opulent (adj)	غزير، غني	*ghazīr, ghanī*
or (conj)	أم، أو	*am, aw*
oracle (n)	مهبط الوحي	*mahbaṭul waḥy*

oracular (adj)	وحيي	*waḥyī*
oral (adj)	شفهي، لفظي	*shafahī, lafẓī*
oral (n)	اختبار شفهي	*ikhtibār shafahī*
orally (adv)	شفهيا	*shafahiyyan*
orange (n/adj)	برتقال، برتقالي	*burtaqāl, burtaqālī*
oration (n)	خطبة، خطابة	*khuṭbah, khiṭābah*
orator (n)	خطيب	*khaṭīb*
oratorical (adj)	خطابي	*khiṭābī*
oratory (n)	فن الخطابة، كنيسة صغيرة	*fannul khiṭābah, kanīsah ṣaghīrah*
orb (n)	كرة، مدار	*kurah, madār*
orbit (n)	مدار، حجاج العين	*madār, ḥajājul ʻain*
orbit (v)	دار، حوم	*dāra, ḥawwama*
orbital (adj)	مداري، حجاجي	*madārī, ḥajājī*
orchard (n)	بستان، حديقة	*bustān, ḥadīqah*
orchestra (n)	أركسترا، فرقة موسيقية	*urkistarā, firqah mausīqiyyah*
orchestral (adj)	متعلق بأركسترا	*mutaʻalliq bi urkistarā*
orchid (n)	سحلبية	*saḥlabiyyah*
ordain (v)	كرس، قدر، عين	*karrasa, qaddara, ʻayyana*
ordeal (n)	محنة، محاكمة بالتعذيب	*miḥnah, muḥākamah bit taʻdhīb*
order (n)	أمر، ترتيب، رتبة	*amr, tartīb, rutbah*
order (v)	أمر، رتب، نظم	*amara, rattaba, naẓẓama*
orderliness (n)	نظام، ترتيب	*niẓām, tartīb*
orderly (adj)	مرتب، منظم، طائع	*murattab, munaẓẓam, ṭā'iʻ*
ordinal (adj)	ترتيبي	*tartībī*
ordinal number	عدد ترتيبي	*ʻadad tartībī*

ordinance (n)	فرض، قانون، أمر	*farḍ, qūnūn, amr*
ordinarily (adv)	عادةً، اعتياديًّا	*'ādatan, i'tiyādiyyan*
ordinary (adj)	عادي، اعتيادي، معتاد	*'ādī, i'tiyādī, mu'tād*
ordnance (n)	ذخائر حربية	*dhakhā'ir ḥarbiyyah*
ordure (n)	روث، غائط	*rauth, ghā'iṭ*
ore (n)	معدن خام	*ma'din khām*
organ (n)	عضو، أرغن	*'uḍw, urghun*
organic (adj)	عضوي، أساسي	*'uḍwī, asāsī*
organism (n)	تركيب عضوي،متعضى	*tarkīb 'uḍwī, muta'aḍḍā*
organist (n)	عازف على الأرغن	*'āzif 'alal urghun*
organization,-isation	منظمة، تنظيم	*munaẓẓamah, tanẓīm*
organizational (adj)	نظامي، تنظيمي	*niẓāmī, tanẓīmī*
organize,-ise (v)	نظم، رتب، دبر	*naẓẓam, rattaba, dabbara*
organized,-ised (adj)	منظم، مرتب	*munaẓẓam, murattab*
organizer,-iser (n)	مرتب، مسؤول	*murattib, mas'ūl*
orgasm (n)	هزة الجماع	*hizzatul jimā'*
orgy (n)	طقس معربد	*ṭaqs mu'arbid*
orient (n)	شرق، بلاد شرقية	*sharq, bilād sharqiyyah*
oriental (adj)	شرقي، مشرقي	*sharqiyy, mashriqī*
orientalist (n)	مستشرق	*mustashriq*
orientate (v)	واجه الشرق	*wājahash sharq*
orientation (n)	اتجاه نحو الشرق	*ittijāh naḥwash sharq*
orifice (n)	فوهة، فتحة، نافذة	*fuwwahah, futḥah, nāfidhah*
origin (n)	أصل، مصدر	*aṣl, maṣdar*
original (adj)	أصيل، مبتكر	*aṣīl, mubtakir*
original (n)	نسخة أصلية	*nuskhah aṣliyyah*
originality (n)	أصالة، ابتكار	*aṣālah, ibtikār*
originally (adv)	أصلاً، في الأصل	*aṣlan, fil aṣl*
originate (v)	أبدع، أنشأ	*abda'a, ansha'a*

originator (n)	مبدع، منشئ	*mubdi', munshi'*
ornament (n)	حلية، زينة	*ḥilyah, zīnah*
ornamental (adj)	زخرفي، زيني	*zukhrufī, zīnī*
ornamentation (n)	زخرفة، تزيين	*zakhrafah, tazyīn*
ornate (adj)	منمق، مزين	*munammiq, muzayyin*
ornithology (n)	علم الطيور	*'ilmuṭ ṭuyūr*
orphan (n/v)	يتيم، يتم	*yatīm, yattama*
orphanage (n)	دار الأيتام	*dārul aitām*
orthodox (adj)	تقليدي، مستقيم الرأي	*taqlīdī, mustaqīmur ra'y*
orthodoxy (n)	تقليد، استقامة الرأي	*taqlīd, istiqāmatur ra'y*
orthography (n)	علم التجويد	*'ilmut tajwīd*
orthopaedic (adj)	تجبيري	*tajbīrī*
orthopaedics (n)	تجبير	*tajbīr*
orthopaedist (n)	مجبر	*mujabbir*
oryx (n)	مارية	*māriyah*
oscillate (v)	تقلب، ترجح	*taqallaba, tarajjaḥa*
oscillation (n)	تقلب، ترجح	*taqallub, tarajjuḥ*
osprey (n)	عقاب نسارية	*'uqāb nasāriyah*
osseous (adj)	عظمي	*'aẓmī*
ossification (n)	تحجر، تعظم	*taḥajjur, ta'aẓẓum*
ostensible (adj)	مزعوم، ظاهري	*maz'ūm, ẓāhirī*
ostensibly (adv)	ظاهراً، صوريًّا	*ẓāhiran, ṣuwariyyan*
ostentation (n)	تظاهر، تباهٍ	*taẓāhur, tabāhin*
ostentatious (adj)	تفاخري، متباهٍ	*tafākhurī, mutabāhin*
ostentatiously (adv)	بتباهٍ، بتفاخر	*bi tabāhin, bi tafākhur*
ostler (n)	سائس الخيل	*sā'isul khail*
ostracism (n)	نفي، طرد	*nafy, ṭard*
ostracize,-ise (v)	نفى، طرد	*nafā, ṭarada*
ostrich (n)	نعام، نعامة	*na'ām, na'āmah*
other (adj)	آخر، أخرى	*ākhar, ukhrā*

other (pron)	غير، مختلف	*ghair, mukhtalif*
otherwise (adv)	وإلا، خلافًا لذلك	*wā illā, khilāfan li dhālik*
otherwordly (adj)	أخروي، متعلق بعالم خيالي	*ukhrawī, muta'alliq bi 'ālam khayālī*
otiose (adj)	عديم النفع، متبطل	*'adīmun naf', mutabaṭṭil*
ottoman (n)	متكأ، مسند	*muttaka', masnad*
ouch (interj)	أوتش	*ūtsh*
ought (v)	يجب، يلزم	*yajib, yalzim*
ounce (n)	آونس	*āuns*
our (pron)	نا، لنا	*nā, lanā*
ourselves (pron)	أنفسنا	*anfusunā*
oust (v)	أخرج، أزاح، نبذ	*akhraja, azāḥa, nabadha*
out (adv)	إلى الخارج	*ilal khārij*
outbreak (n)	انفجار، انتشار، ثورة	*infijār, intishār, thaurah*
outbuilding (n)	مبنى إضافي	*mabnā iḍāfī*
outburst (n)	تفجر، ثوران	*tafajjur, thawarān*
outcast (adj/n)	منبوذ، مطرود	*mambūdh, maṭrūd*
outcaste=outcast		
outclass (v)	تفوق، امتاز	*tafawwaqa, imtāza*
outcome (n)	نتيجة، حاصل	*natījah, ḥāṣil*
outcry (n)	احتجاج شديد	*iḥtijāj shadīd*
outdated (adj)	مهجور، مهمل	*mahjūr, muhmal*
outdistance (v)	سبق، فاق	*sabaqa, fāqa*
outdo (v)	سبق، فاق، تغلب	*sabaqa, fāqa, taghallaba*
outdoor (adj)	خلوي	*khalawī*
outdoors (adv)	في الهواء، في الخلاء	*fil hawā', fil khalā'*
outer (adj)	خارجي	*khārijī*
outermost (adj)	أقصى، أبعد	*aqṣā, ab'ad*
outfall (n)	مصب نهر	*maṣabbu nahr*
outfight (v)	تغلب، هزم	*taghallaba, hazama*

outfit (n)	تجهيزات، معدات	*tajhīzāt, mu'addāt*
outflow (n)	تدفق، فيضان	*tadaffuq, fayaḍān*
outgoing (adj)	مرتحل، منسحب	*murtaḥil, munsaḥib*
outgrow (v)	فاق في النمو	*fāqa fin numuww*
outgrowth (n)	نمو	*numuww*
outhouse (n)	مبنى خارجي، مرحاض	*mabnā khārijiyy, mirḥāḍ*
outing (n)	نزهة، فسحة	*nuzhah, fusḥah*
outlandish (adj)	غير مألوف، مستهجن	*ghair ma'lūf, mustahjan*
outlandishness (n)	استهجان، غرابة	*istihjān, gharābah*
outlaw (n)	طريد القانون	*ṭarīdul qānūn*
outlaw (v)	حظر، طرد	*ḥaẓara, ṭarada*
outlay (n)	نفقة، إنفاق	*nafaqah, infāq*
outlet (n)	منفذ، مخرج	*manfadh, makhraj*
outline (n)	ملخص، مخطط	*mulakhkhaṣ, mukhaṭṭaṭ*
outline (v)	خطط، أوجز، رسم	*khaṭṭaṭa, aujaza, rasama*
outlive (v)	عاش أكثر من...	*'āsha akthara min*
outlook (n)	مظهر، وجهة نظر	*maẓhar, wijhatu naẓar*
outlying (adj)	قاصٍ، بعيد، ناءٍ	*qāṣin, ba'īd, nā'in*
outmoded (adj)	مهجور، قديم، عتيق	*mahjūr, qadīm, 'atīq*
outmost (adj)	أقصى، أبعد	*aqṣā, ab'ad*
out-patient (n)	مريض خارجي	*marīḍ khārijī*
outpost (n)	طليعة الجيش، مخفر أمامي	*ṭalī'atul jaish, makhfar amāmī*
outpouring (n)	تدفق، فيضان	*tadaffuq, fayaḍān*
output (n)	نتاج، حاصل	*nitāj, ḥāṣil*
outrage (n)	حنك، غضب، هتك	*ḥanak, ghaḍab, hatk*
outrage (v)	انهتك، ازدرى	*inhataka, izdarā*
outrageous (adj)	مسخط، فظيع	*muskhiṭ, faẓī'*
outrider (n)	المرافق الراكب	*almurāfiq ar rākib*
outright (adj)	صريح، واضح	*ṣarīḥ, wāḍiḥ*

outright (adv)	كلية، كافةً	*kulliyyatan, kāffatan*
outset (n)	بداية، مطلع	*bidāyah, maṭla'*
outshine (v)	بها، تألق أكثر من...	*bahā, ta'allaqa akthara min…*
outside (adj/adv)	خارجي، خارجاً	*khārijī, khārijan*
outside (prep)	خارج، إلى خارج	*khārija, ilā khāriji*
outsider (n)	خارجي، أجنبي، غريب	*khārijī, ajnabī, gharīb*
outsize (adj)	كبير إلى حد بعيد	*kabīr ilā ḥadd ba'īd*
outskirts (n)	ضواحي المدينة	*ḍawāḥil madīnah*
outspoken (adj)	صريح، واضح	*ṣarīḥ, wāḍiḥ*
outspokenly (adv)	بصراحة، بوضوح	*bi ṣarāḥah, bi wuḍūḥ*
outspokenness (n)	صراحة، وضوح	*sarāḥah, wuḍūḥ*
outspread (adj)	منتشر، ممدود	*muntashir, mamdūd*
outstanding (adj)	بارز، ممتاز	*bāriz, mumtāz*
outstation (n)	محطة نائية	*maḥaṭṭah nā'iyah*
outstreched (adj)	ممتد، ممدود	*mumtadd, mamdūd*
outstrip (v)	سبق، فاق	*sabaqa, fāqa*
outward (adj)	خارجي، ظاهري	*khārijī, ẓāhirī*
outwardly (adv)	ظاهراً، خارجياً	*ẓāhiran, khārijiyyan*
outweigh (v)	فاق في الوزن، رجح	*fāqa fil wazn, rajaḥa*
outwit (v)	فاق في الدهاء	*fāqa fid dahā'*
outwork (n)	تحصينات خارجية	*taḥṣīnāt khārijiyyah*
outworn (adj)	بالٍ، عتيق الزي	*bālin, 'atīquz ziyy*
oval (adj)	بيضوي	*baiḍawī*
ovarian (adj)	متعلق بالمبيض	*muta'alliq bil mabīḍ*
ovary (n)	مبيض	*mabīḍ*
ovation (n)	ترحيب بحماسة	*tarḥīb bi ḥamāsah*
oven (n)	تنور، فرن	*tannūr, furn*
over (prep)	فوق، على، أكثر من	*fauqa, 'alā, akthara min*
overall (adj/adv)	إجمالي، إجماليًا	*ijmālī, ijmāliyyan*

overall (n)	وزرة، معطف	*wizrah, mi'ṭaf*
overbalance (v)	رجح على	*rajaḥa 'alā*
overbearing (adj)	متغطرس، ظالم	*mutaghaṭris, ẓālim*
overbid (v)	زايد على	*zāyada 'alā*
overblown (adj)	متفتح، منتفخ	*mutafattiḥ, muntafikh*
overboard (adv)	عن ظهر السفينة	*'an ẓahris safīnah*
overburden (v)	حمل أكثر من...	*ḥammala akthara min…*
overcapitalize (v)	أسرف في التمويل	*asrafa fit tamwīl*
overcast (adj)	ملبد بالغيوم	*mulabbad bil ghuyūm*
overchange (v)	طلب الثمن أكثر من	*ṭalabath thamana akthara min…*
overcoat (n)	معطف، وزرة	*mi'ṭaf, wizrah*
overcome (v)	تغلب على، هزم	*taghallaba 'alā, hazama*
overcompensate (v)	أفرط في التعويض	*afraṭa fit ta'wīḍ*
overcrowded (adj)	مزدحم، مكتظ	*muzdaḥim, muktaẓẓ*
overcrowding (n)	ازدحام شديد	*izdiḥām shadīd*
overdo (v)	أفرط في العمل، بالغ	*afraṭa fil 'amal, bālagha*
overdose (n)	جرعة مفرطة	*jur'ah mufraṭah*
overdraft (n)	مبلغ مسحوب	*mablagh masḥūb*
overdraw (v)	سحب أكثر من...	*saḥaba akthara min…*
overdue (adj)	متأخر، غير مدفوع	*muta'akhkhir, ghair madfū'*
overeat (v)	أكل أكثر من...	*akala akthara min…*
overestimate (v)	قدر أكثر من...	*qaddara akthara min…*
overexpose (v)	بالغ في التعريض	*bālagha fit ta'rīḍ*
overflow (n)	فيضان، طفوح	*fayaḍān, ṭufūḥ*
overgrown (adj)	نامٍ بأسرع من...	*nāmin bi asra'a min…*
overgrowth (n)	سرعة في النمو	*sur'ah fin numuww*
overhang (v)	تدلى، أشرف على	*tadallā, ashrafa 'alā*
overhaul (v)	فحص بدقة، رمم	*faḥaṣa bi diqqah, rammama*

overhaul (n)	فحص دقيق	*faḥṣ daqīq*
overhead (adv)	فوق الرأس	*fauqar ra's*
overhead (adj)	كائن فوق الرأس	*kā'in fauqar ra's*
overhear (v)	سمع اتفاقاً	*sami'a ittifāqan*
overjoyed (adj)	مملوء بالابتهاج	*mamlū' bil ibtihāj*
overkill (n)	إسراف، إفراط	*isrāf, ifrāṭ*
overland (adj/adv)	بري، بالبر	*barrī, bil barr*
overlap (v)	طوى، تراكب	*ṭawā, tarākaba*
overlap (n)	تراكب، تداخل	*tarākub, tadākhul*
overlay (v)	غشى، طلى، موه	*ghashshā, ṭalā, mawwaha*
overlay (n)	طلاء، غطاء	*ṭilā', ghiṭā'*
overload (v)	حمل أكثر من...	*ḥammala akthara min…*
overlook (v)	أشرف على، طل	*ashrafa 'alā, ṭalla*
overly (adv)	. بإفراط، بإسراف	*bi ifrāṭ, bi isrāf*
overmanned (adj)	مزود بالعمال أكثر من...	*muzawwad bil 'ummāl akthara min…*
overmastering (adj)	لا يغلب، غامر	*lā yughlab, ghāmir*
overmuch (adj/adv)	مفرط، بإفراط	*mufriṭ, bi ifrāṭ*
overnight (adv/adj)	طول الليل، ليلي	*ṭūlal lail, lailī*
overpass (n)	جسر، معبر فوقي	*jisr, ma'bar fauqī*
overpay (v)	دفع أكثر من...	*dafa'a akthara min…*
overplay (v)	بالغ في الأهمية	*bālagha fil ahammiyyah*
overpower (v)	أخضع، قهر، هزم	*akhḍa'a, qahara, hazama*
overpowering (adj)	لا يقاوم، لا يغلب	*lā yuqāwam, lā yughlab*
overrate (v)	بالغ في التقدير	*bālagha fit taqdīr*
overreach (v)	احتال، خدع	*iḥtāla, khada'a*
override (v)	أهان، ألغى	*ahāna, alghā*
overrule (v)	فسخ، ألغى، تحكم	*fasakha, alghā, taḥakkama*
overrun (v)	غمر، اجتاح	*ghamara, ijtāḥa*

overseas (adj)	واقع عبر البحر	*wāqi‘ ‘abral bahr*
overseas (adv)	عبر البحر	*‘abral bahr*
oversee (v)	أشرف، راقب	*ashrafa, rāqaba*
overseer (n)	مشرف، مراقب	*mushrif, murāqib*
oversexed (adj)	شهواني	*shahwānī*
overshadow (v)	جعل معتماً	*ja‘ala mu‘timan*
overshoot (v)	تجاوز، اجتاز	*tajāwaza, ijtāza*
oversight (n)	خطأ غير عمدي	*khaṭa’ ghair ‘amadī*
oversimplification (n)	توضيح الشيء أكثر من...	*tauḍīḥush shay’ akthara min…*
oversleep (v)	نام أكثر من...	*nāma akthara min…*
overstate (v)	بالغ في التقرير	*bālagha fit taqrīr*
overstay (v)	أطال المكوث	*aṭālal mukūth*
overstep (v)	تخطى، تجاوز	*takhaṭṭā, tajāwaza*
overstock (v)	اختزن بإفراط	*ikhtazana bi ifrāṭ*
overstung (adj)	مفرط الحساسية	*mufriṭul ḥassāsiyyah*
overt (adj)	ظاهري، علني	*ẓāhirī, ‘alanī*
overtake (v)	باغت، تجاوز	*bāghata, tajāwaza*
overtax (v)	زاد الضرائب	*zādaḍ ḍarā’ib*
overthrow (v)	أسقط، قهر، قلب	*asqaṭa, qahara, qallaba*
overthrow (n)	هزيمة، سقوط	*hazīmah, suqūṭ*
overtime (n/adv)	وقت إضافي، إضافيًا	*waqt iḍāfī, iḍāfiyyan*
overture (n)	اقتراح، توشيح	*iqtirāḥ, taushīḥ*
overturn (v)	قلب، هدم	*qalaba, hadama*
overweening (adj)	متعجرف، مزهو	*muta‘ajrif, mazhuww*
overweight (adj)	أثقل من ...	*athqalu min…*
overweighted (adj)	أثقل	*athqal*
overwhelm (v)	قهر، اكتنف، غمر	*qahara, iktanafa, ghamara*
overwhelming (adj)	ساحق، غامر	*sāḥiq, ghāmir*
overwork (v)	أرهق بالعمل	*arhaqa bil ‘amal*

overwork (n)	عمل شاق، شغل إضافي	*'amal shāqq, shughl iḍāfī*
overwrought (adj)	منهوك بالعمل، في حالة عصبية	*manhūk bil 'amal, fī ḥālah 'aṣabiyyah*
oviparous (adj)	بيوض	*bayūḍ*
ovulate (v)	أباض	*abāḍa*
ovulation (n)	إباضة	*ibāḍah*
ovum (n)	بييضة	*buyaiḍah*
owe (v)	دان	*dāna*
owing (adj)	مستحق الدفع	*mustaḥiqqud daf'*
owing to (prep)	بسبب، ناشيء عن	*bisababi, nāshi' 'an*
owl (n)	بوم	*būm*
owlet (n)	بوم صغير	*būm ṣaghīr*
owlish (adj)	شبيه بالبوم	*shabīh bil būm*
own (v)	امتلك، اعترف	*imtalaka, i'tarafa*
own (prep)	خاصته	*khāṣṣatuh*
owner (n)	مالك، صاحب الشيء	*mālik, sāḥibush shay'*
ownership (n)	ملكية، حق الملك	*milkiyyah, ḥaqqul milk*
ox (n)	ثور، ذكر البقر	*thaur, dhakarul baqar*
oxeye (n)	عين الثور	*'ainuth thaur*
oxidation (n)	أكسدة	*aksadah*
oxidize,-ise (v)	أكسد، تأكسد	*aksada, ta'aksada*
oxigen (n)	أكسيجين	*aksījīn*
oxygenate=oxigenize		
oxygenize,-ise (v)	أكسج	*aksaja*
oyester (n)	محار، جندفلي	*maḥār, jandufli*
ozone (n)	الأوزون	*al ūzūn*

P

pace (n)	خطوة، مشية، عدو	*khuṭwah, mishyah, 'adw*
pace (v)	مشى بخطىً	*mashā bi khuṭan*
pace maker = pace setter		

pacesetter (n)	محدد الخطوة	*muḥaddidul khuṭwah*
pacific (adj)	سلمي، باسيفيكي	*silmī, bāsīfikī*
pacifically (adv)	بطريق سلمي	*bi ṭarīq silmī*
pacification (n)	تهدئة، معاهدة	*tahdi'ah, mu'āhadah*
pacifism (n)	سلامية	*salāmiyah*
pacifist (n)	مؤيد السلامة	*mu'ayyidus salāmah*
pacify (v)	هدأ، سكن	*hadda'a, sakkana*
pack (n)	حزمة، رزمة	*ḥuzmah, rizmah*
pack (v)	حزم، رزم	*ḥazama, razama*
package (n)	صرة، رزمة	*ṣurrah, rizmah*
package (v)	رزم، صر	*razama, ṣarra*
packer (n)	حازم، رازم	*ḥāzim, rāzim*
packet (n)	كتلة، حزمة صغيرة	*kutlah, ḥuzmah ṣaghīrah*
packing (n)	رزم، تعبئة	*razm, ta'bi'ah*
packing-case (n)	صندوق التعبئة	*ṣundūqut ta'bi'ah*
pact (n)	ميثاق، عهد	*mīthāq, 'ahd*
pad (n)	مخدة، حشية	*mikhaddah, ḥashiyyah*
pad (v)	حشا، مشى	*ḥashā, mashā*
padding (n)	حشوة، حشو	*ḥashwah, ḥashw*
paddle (n)	مجذاف، مغدف	*mijdhāf, mighdaf*
paddle (v)	جذف، غدف	*jadhdhafa, ghaddafa*
paddle steamer	مغدافية	*mighdāfiyyah*
paddock (n)	مستراد	*mustarād*
paddy (n)	أرز، حقل أرز	*aruzz, ḥaqlu aruzz*
padlock (n)	قفل، غال	*qufl, ghāl*
paediatric (adj)	متعلق بطب الأطفال	*muta'alliq bi ṭibbil aṭfāl*
paediatrician (n)	طبيب الأطفال	*ṭabībul aṭfāl*
paediatrics (n)	طب الأطفال	*ṭibbul aṭfāl*
pagan (n)	وثني، عابد الأوثان	*wathanī, 'ābidul authān*
paganism (n)	وثنية، عبادة الأوثان	*wathaniyyah, 'ibādatul authān*
page (n)	صفحة، خادم	*ṣafḥah, khādim*

page (v)	رقم الصفحات	*raqqamaṣ ṣafḥāt*
pageant (n)	مهرجان، أبهة	*mahrajān, ubbahah*
pageantry (n)	مواكب، أبهة	*mawākib, ubbahah*
paginate (v)	رقم الصفحات	*raqqamaṣ ṣafḥāt*
pail (n)	دلو، جردل	*dalw, jardal*
pailful (adj)	ملء دلو	*mil'u dalw*
pain (n)	وجع، ألم	*waj', alam*
pain (v)	أوجع، آلم	*auja'a, ālama*
painful (adj)	موجع، مؤلم	*mūji', mu'lim*
painfulness (n)	تألم، وجع	*ta'allum, waj'*
painless (adj)	غير موجع، غير مؤلم	*ghair mūji', ghair mu'lim*
paint (n)	صبغ، صبغ	*ṣabgh, ṣibgh*
paint (v)	صبغ، لون، رسم	*ṣabagha, lawwana, rasama*
painter (n)	مصور، رسام	*muṣawwir, rassām*
painting (n)	دهن، صورة ملونة	*dahn,ṣūrah mulawwanah*
pair (n/v)	زوج، زوج	*zauj, zawwaja*
pal (n)	خدين، زميل	*khadīn, zamīl*
palace (n)	قصر، بلاط	*qaṣr, balāṭ*
palatable (adj)	شهي، لذيذ المذاق	*shahiyy, ladhīdhul madhāq*
palatal (adj)	حلقي، مختص بالحلق	*ḥalaqī, mukhtaṣṣ bil ḥalaq*
palate (n)	حنك، سقف الحلق	*ḥanak, saqful ḥalaq*
palatial (adj)	صرحي، بلاطي	*ṣarḥī, balāṭī*
palaver (n)	هذر، ثرثرة	*hadhr, thartharah*
pale (adj)	شاحب، باهت، أصفر	*shāḥib, bāhit, aṣfar*
pale (v)	شحب، أشحب	*shaḥuba, ashḥaba*
paleness (n)	شحوب، اصفرار اللون	*shuḥūb, iṣfirārul laun*
palette (n)	لوحة الألوان، ملون	*lauḥatul alwān, malwan*

palette knife	مزاجة	*mazzājah*
palisade (n/v)	حسيكة، طوق بحسيكة	*ḥasīkah, ṭawwaqa bi ḥasīkah*
palish (adj)	شاحب، أصفر	*shāḥib, aṣfar*
pall (n)	غطاء النعش، بساط الرحمة	*ghiṭā'un na'sh, bisāṭur raḥmah*
pall (v)	مل، تفه	*malla, tafiha*
pallet (n)	حشية قش	*ḥashiyyatu qashsh*
palliasse (n)	فراش قش	*firāshu qashsh*
palliate (v)	لطف، سكن، خفف	*laṭṭafa, sakkana, khaffafa*
palliative (adj)	مخفف، مسكن	*mukhaffif, musakkin*
pallid (adj)	شاحب، مصفر	*shāḥib, muṣaffar*
pallidness (n)	شحوب اللون، اصفرار	*shuḥūbul laun, iṣfirār*
pallor (n)	شحوب، اصفرار اللون	*shuḥūb, iṣfirārul laun*
palm (n)	نخلة، راحة اليد	*nakhlah, rāḥatul yad*
palm (v)	مس براحة، خدع	*massa bi rāḥah, khada'a*
palmistry (n)	قراءة خطوط الكف	*qirā'atu khuṭūṭil kaff*
palm oil	زيت النخيل	*zaitun nakhīl*
palmy (adj)	كثير النخيل	*kathīrun nakhīl*
palpable (adj)	ملموس، جلي	*malmūs, jalī*
palpate (v)	فحص باللمس	*faḥaṣa bil lams*
palpation (n)	فحص باللمس	*faḥṣ bil lams*
palpitate (v)	ضرب، نبض، خفق	*ḍaraba, nabaḍa, khafaqa*
palpitation (n)	خفقان القلب	*khafaqānul qalb*
palsied (adj)	مشلول، أشل	*mashlūl, ashall*
palsy (n)	شلل	*shalal*
paltry (adj)	حقير، طفيف، تافه	*ḥaqīr, ṭafīf, tāfih*
pamper (v)	دلل، رفه، أفعم	*dallala, raffaha, af'ama*
pamphlet (n)	كتيب، رسالة	*kutayyib, risālah*
pamphleteer (n)	مؤلف رسائل	*mu'allifu rasā'il*
pan (n)	مقلاة، قدر، حلة	*miqlāt, qidr, ḥallah*
panacea (n)	دواء لكل داء	*dawā' li kulli dā'*

panama (n)	قبعة بناما	*qubba'atu banāmā*
pancake (n)	كعكة محلاة، فطيرة محلاة	*ka'kah muḥallāt, faṭīrah muḥallāt*
pancreas (n)	بنكرياس، معقد	*bankiryās, mi'qad*
panda (n)	بندة	*bandah*
pandemic (adj/n)	وبائي، وباء	*wabā'ī, wabā'*
pandemonium (n)	صخب، ارتباك	*ṣakhab, irtibāk*
pander (v)	عرص، قاد	*'arraṣa, qāda*
pander (n)	قواد، ديوث	*qawwād, dayyūth*
pane (n)	لوح زجاج	*lauḥu zujāj*
panegyric (n)	مديح، تقريظ، ثناء	*madīḥ, taqrīẓ, thanā'*
panel (n)	لوح، هيئة محلفين	*lauḥ, hay'atu muḥallafīn*
panel (v)	زود بألواح	*zawwada bi alwāḥ*
panelist (n)	عضو في هيئة المحلفين	*'uḍw fī hay'atil muḥallafīn*
pang (n)	كرب، غصة	*karb, ghuṣṣah*
panic (n)	ذعر، روع، هلع	*dhu'r, rau', hala'*
panic (v)	أرعب، روع	*ar'aba, rawwa'a*
panicky (adj)	مذعور، مرعوب	*madh'ūr, mar'ūb*
panic-stricken (adj)	مذعور، موهور	*madh'ūr, mauhūr*
pannier (n)	سلة، سبت	*sallah, sabat*
panoplied (adj)	ذو عدة كاملة	*dhū 'uddah kāmilah*
panoply (n)	عرض كامل، إبراز	*'arḍ kāmil, ibrāz*
panorama (n)	نظرة كاملة، منظر كامل	*naẓrah kāmilah, manẓar kāmil*
panoramic (adj)	شامل النظرة، بانورامي	*shāmilun naẓrah, bānūrāmī*
pansy (n)	زهرة الثالوث، مشتهي المماثل	*zahratuth thālūth, mushtahil mumāthil*
pant (v)	نفث، لهث	*nafatha, lahatha*
pant (n)	لهاث، نفث	*luhāth, nafth*
pantaloons (n)	بنطلون، سروال	*banṭlūn, sirwāl*

pantheism (n)	وحدة الوجود	*waḥdatul wujūd*
pantheist (n)	مؤمن بوحدة الوجود	*mu'min bi waḥdatil wujūd*
pantheistic (adj)	متعلق بوحدة الوجود	*muta'alliq bi waḥdatil wujūd*
panther (n)	نمر	*namir*
panties (n)	سروال تحتي للنساء	*sirwāl taḥtī lin nisā'*
pantomime (n)	مسرحية إيمائية	*masraḥiyyah īmā'iyyah*
pantry (n)	حجرة المؤنة	*ḥujratul mu'nah*
pants (n)	بنطلونات	*banṭlūnāt*
pap (n)	طعام ملائم للرضيع	*ṭa'ām mulā'im lir raḍī'*
papa (n)	أب، والد	*ab, wālid*
papacy (n)	باباوية	*bābāwiyyah*
papal (adj)	باباوي	*bābāwī*
paper (n)	جريدة، ورق	*jarīdah, waraq*
paper (v)	ورق	*warraqa*
paperback (n)	كتاب ورقي الغلاف	*kitāb waraqiyyul ghilāf*
paper-knife (n)	مقطع الورق	*miqṭa'ul waraq*
paper money	أوراق مالية	*aurāq māliyyah*
paperwork (n)	عمل ورقي	*'amal waraqī*
papery (adj)	ورقاني	*waraqānī*
paprika (n)	فلفل حلو	*filfil ḥulw*
par (n)	سعر التكافؤ	*si'rut takāfu'*
parable (n)	قصة أخلاقية، مثل	*qiṣṣah akhlāqiyyah, mathal*
parabolic (adj)	مثلي، تشبيهي	*mathalī, tashbīhī*
parachute (n)	مظلة هبوط	*miẓallatu hubūṭ*
parachutist (n)	مظلي، هابط بالمظلة	*miẓallī, ḥābiṭ bil miẓallah*
parade (v)	استعرض، احتفل	*ista'raḍa, iḥtafala*
parade (n)	استعراض عسكري	*isti'rāḍ 'askarī*

paradise (n)	فردوس، جنة	*firdaus, jannah*
paradisiacal (adj)	شبيه بالجنة	*shabīh bil jannah*
paradox (n)	تناقض ظاهري	*tanāquḍ ẓāhirī*
paradoxical (adj)	ظاهري التناقض	*ẓāhiriyyut tanāquḍ*
paraffin (n)	كيروسين، بارافين	*kīrūsīn, bārāfīn*
paragon (n)	نموذج، مثال	*namūdhaj, mithāl*
paragraph (n)	عبارة، فقرة	*'ibārah, fiqrah*
paragraph (v)	فقر	*faqqara*
parallel (adj)	متماثل، متوازن	*mutamāthil, mutawāzin*
parallel (n)	تشابه، تماثل	*tashābuh, tamāthul*
parallel (v)	تماثل، تشابه	*tamāthala, tashābaha*
parallelism (n)	توازٍ، محاذاة	*tawāzin, muḥādhāt*
paralysis (n)	شلل، فالج	*shalal, fālij*
paralytic (adj/n)	مشلول، شللي	*mashlūl, shalalī*
paralyze,-ise (v)	شل، فلج	*shalla, falaja*
paramount (adj)	أعظم، رئيسي	*a'ẓam, ra'īsī*
paramountcy (n)	علو، سمو	*'uluww, sumuww*
paranoia (n)	جنون الارتياب	*junūnul irtiyāb*
parapet (n)	جدار بارتفاع الشرفة	*jidār bi irtifā'ish shurfah*
paraphrase (v)	وضح، شرح	*waḍḍaḥa, sharaḥa*
paraphrase (n)	شرح، تفسير	*sharḥ, tafsīr*
parasite (n)	حيوان أونبات طفيلي	*ḥaywān aw nabāt ṭufailī*
parasitic-al (adj)	طفيلي	*ṭufailī*
parasol (n)	شمسية، مظلة خفيفة	*shamsiyyah, miẓallah khafīfah*
paratrooper (n)	جندي مظلي	*jundī miẓallī*
paratroops (n)	مظليون	*miẓalliyyūn*
parcel (n)	طرد، قطعة	*ṭard, qiṭ'ah*
parcel (v)	قسم، جزأ	*qassama, jazza'a*
parcel post	طرود بريدية	*ṭurūd barīdiyyah*

parch (v)	حمص، لفح، جفف	*ḥammaṣa, lafaḥa, jaffafa*
parchment (n)	رق، ورق رقي	*raqq, waraq raqiyy*
pardon (n)	عفو، صفح	*'afw, ṣafḥ*
pardon (v)	صفح، عفا	*ṣafaḥa, 'afā*
pardonable (adj)	قابل الصفح	*qābiluṣ ṣafḥ*
pardoner (n)	بائع الغفران	*bā'i'ul ghufrān*
pare (v)	قلم، قضب	*qallama, qaḍḍaba*
parent (n)	والد، والدة	*wālid, wālidah*
parentage (n)	أبوة، أصل، نسب	*ubuwwah, aṣl, nasab*
parental (adj)	أبوي	*abawiyy*
parenthesis (n)	جملة معترضة	*jumlah mu'tariḍah*
parenthetic-al (adj)	خاص بجملة معترضة	*khāṣṣ bi jumlah mu'tariḍah*
parenthood (n)	أبوة	*ubuwwah*
par excellence (adv)	غير منازع	*ghair munāza'*
pariah (n)	منبوذ، مطرود	*mambūdh, maṭrūd*
parings (n)	قشارة، قشرة	*qushārah, qishrah*
parish (n)	أبروشية	*abrūshiyah*
parishner (n)	أبروشي	*abrūshī*
parity (n)	تكافؤ، تساوٍ	*takāfu', tasāwin*
park (n)	منتزة، حديقة	*muntazah, ḥadīqah*
park (v)	أوقف السيارة	*auqafas sayyārah*
parking (n)	إيقاف السيارات لمدة	*īqāfus sayyārāt li muddah*
parlance (n)	لهجة، محادثة	*lahjah, muḥādathah*
parley (v)	فاوض العدو	*fāwaḍal 'aduww*
parley (n)	مفاوضة مع العدو	*mufāwaḍah ma'al 'aduww*
parliament (n)	مجلس النواب، برلمان	*majlisun nawwāb, barlamān*
parliamentarian (n)	برلماني	*barlamānī*

parliamentary (adj)	برلماني	*barlamānī*
parlour (parlor) (n)	قاعة الاستقبال، ردهة	*qā'atul istiqbāl, radhah*
parlous (adj)	خطر، محفوف بالمخاطر	*khaṭir, maḥfūf bil makhāṭir*
parochial (adj)	أبرشي	*abrashī*
parody (n)	محاكاة ساخرة	*muḥākāt sākhirah*
parole (n)	عهد للأسير	*'ahd lil asīr*
parricide (n)	قتل الأب أو الأم	*qatlul ab awil umm*
parrot (n)	ببغاء	*babghā'*
parry (v/n)	تجنب، تجنب	*tajannaba, tajannub*
parse (v)	حلل، أعرب	*ḥallala, a'raba*
parsimonious (adj)	شحيح، مقتر	*shaḥīḥ, muqtir*
parsimoniousness	شح، تقتير	*shuḥḥ, taqtīr*
parsimony (n)	شح، بخل شديد	*shuḥḥ, bukhl shadīd*
parsnip (n)	جزر أبيض	*jazar abyaḍ*
parson (n)	قسيس، كاهن	*qissīs, kāhin*
parsonage (n)	بيت القس	*baitul qiss*
part (n)	قسم، قطعة، جزء	*qism, qiṭ'ah, juz'*
part (v)	فصل، فرق، حصص	*faṣala, farraqa, ḥaṣṣaṣa*
partake (v)	شارك، اشترك	*shāraka, ishtaraka*
parterre (n)	روضة	*rauḍah*
partial (adj)	جزئي، متحيز	*juz'ī, mutaḥayyiz*
partiality (n)	محاباة، تحيز	*muḥābāt, taḥayyuz*
partially (adv)	بتحيز، جزئيًا	*bi taḥayyuz, juz'iyyan*
participant (n)	مشارك، شريك	*mushārik, sharīk*
participate (v)	شارك، اشترك	*shāraka, ishtaraka*
participation (n)	مشاركة، اشتراك	*mushārakah, ishtirāk*
participle (n)	اسم الفاعل، اسم المفعول	*ismul fā'il, ismul maf'ūl*
particle (n)	ذرة، دقيقة	*dharrah, daqīqah*
particoloured (adj)	متعدد الألوان	*muta'addidul alwān*

particular (adj)	خصوصي، مدقق	*khuṣūṣī, mudaqqiq*
particular (n)	تفصيل، مفردة	*tafṣīl, mufradah*
particularity (n)	خصوصية، تدقيق	*khuṣūṣiyyah, tadqīq*
particularization (n)	تخصيص، تعيين	*takhṣīṣ, ta'yīn*
particularize,-ise (v)	خصص، عين	*khaṣṣaṣa, 'ayyana*
particularly (adj)	خصوصاً، خاصة	*khuṣūṣan, khāṣṣatan*
parting (n)	فصل، تفريق	*faṣl, tafrīq*
partisan (n/adj)	موالٍ، مشايع	*muwālin, mushāyi'*
partisanship (n)	مشايعة، محازبة	*mushāya'ah, muḥāzabah*
partition (n)	تقسيم، تجزئة	*taqsīm, tajzi'ah*
partition (v)	فصل، قسم	*faṣala, qassama*
partitive (adj/n)	تبعيضي، لفظ تبعيضي	*tab'īḍī, lafẓ tab'īḍī*
partly (adv)	جزئياً	*juz'iyyan*
partner (n)	شريك، رفيق	*sharīk, rafiq*
partner (v)	شارك، صحب	*shāraka, ṣaḥiba*
partnership (n)	شركة، مشاركة	*shirkah, mushārakah*
partridge (n)	حجل	*ḥajal*
parturition (n)	ولادة، مخاض	*wilādah, makhāḍ*
party (n)	حزب، جماعة، حفلة	*ḥizb, jamā'ah, ḥaflah*
party line	خط جماعي	*khaṭṭ jamā'ī*
party-wall (n)	جدار مشترك	*jidār mushtarak*
pass (n)	بطاقة مجانية، اجتياز، مرور، ممر	*biṭāqah majjāniyyah, ijtiyāz, murūr, mamarr*
pass (v)	نجح، مر، انقضى، أصدر	*najaḥa, marra, inqaḍā, aṣdara*
passable (adj)	نافذ، مقبول، مطروق	*nāfidh, maqbūl, maṭrūq*
passage (n)	مرور، ممر، سفر	*murūr, mamarr, safar*
passage way	ممر، مسلك	*mamarr, maslak*
pass away (v)	انقضى، مات	*inqaḍā, māta*

passbook (n)	دفتر حساب	*daftaru ḥisāb*
pass by	مر، تغاضى	*marra, taghāḍā*
passenger (n)	مسافر، راكب	*musāfir, rākib*
passerby (n)	عابر سبيل	*'ābiru sabīl*
passing (adj/n)	مار، مرور	*mārr, murūr*
passion (n)	عاطفة، هيام، ولع	*'āṭifah, hiyām, wala'*
passionate (adj)	مشبوب بالعاطفة	*mashbūb bil 'āṭifah*
passionately (adv)	بعاطفة، بهيام	*bi 'āṭifah, bi hiyām*
passionflower (n)	زهرة الآلام	*zahratul ālām*
Passion Sunday	أحد الآلام	*aḥadul ālām*
Passion Week	أسبوع الآلام	*usbū'ul ālām*
passive (adj)	منفعل، مستسلم	*munfa'il, mustaslim*
passive (n)	فعل المجهول	*fi'lul majlūl*
passively (adv)	بدون نشاط، باستسلام	*bidūn nashāṭ, bistislām*
passiveness (n)	انفعال، عدم نشاط	*infi'āl, 'adamu nashāṭ*
passivity = passiveness		
passkey (n)	مفتاح خاص	*miftāḥ khāṣṣ*
pass on	انتقل، تنقل	*intaqala, tanaqqala*
Passover (n)	عيد الفصح	*'īdul faṣḥ*
passport (n)	جواز سفر	*jawāzu safar*
password (n)	كلمة السر	*kalimatus sirr*
past (adj/n)	ماضي، سابق	*māḍī, sābiq*
paste (n)	معجون، معكرون	*ma'jūn, ma'karūn*
pasteboard (n)	ورق مقوى	*waraq muqawwā*
pastel (n)	قلم بستلي	*qalam bastalī*
pastern (n)	رسغ الدابة	*rusghud dābbah*
pasteurization (n)	تعقيم، بسترة	*ta'qīm, bastarah*
pasteurize,-ise (v)	عقم، بستر	*'aqqama, bastara*
pastime (n)	لهو، تسلية	*lahw, tasliyah*

pastoral (adj)	ريفي، رعوي	*rīfī, ra'awī*
pastoral (n)	أنشودة رعوية	*unshūdah ra'awiyyah*
pastry (n)	فطيرة	*faṭīrah*
pasture (n/v)	مرعى، رعى	*mar'ā, ra'ā*
pasty (adj)	كالمعجون	*kal ma'jūn*
pat (v)	لمس، ربت	*lamasa, rabbata*
pat (n)	لمسة، ضربة خفيفة	*lamsah, ḍarbah khafīfah*
patch (v)	رمم، رقع	*rammama, raqa'a*
patch (n)	رقعة، قطعة صغيرة	*ruq'ah, qiṭ'ah ṣaghīrah*
patchiness (n)	رقع	*raq'*
patch pocket	جيب مثبت	*jaib muthabbat*
patchwork (n)	مرقعة، طصلقة	*muraqqa'ah, ṭaṣlaqah*
patchy (adj)	مرقع	*muraqqa'*
pate (n)	رأس	*ra's*
patent (n)	براءة الاختراع	*barā'atul ikhtirā'*
patent (adj)	واضح، برائي، مسجل	*wāḍiḥ, barā'ī, musajjal*
patent (v)	حصل على البراءة	*ḥaṣala 'alal barā'ah*
patentee (n)	صاحب البراءة	*ṣāḥibul barā'ah*
paternal (adj)	أبوي، والدي	*abawiyy, wālidī*
paternalism (n)	طريقة أبوية	*ṭarīqah abawiyyah*
paternally (adv)	من جهة الأب	*min jihatil ab*
paternity (n)	أبوة، والدية	*ubuwwah, wālidiyyah*
path (n)	طريق، سبيل، ممر	*ṭarīq, sabīl, mamarr*
pathetic (adj)	مثير للعواطف، مشجٍ	*muthīr lil 'awāṭif, mushajjin*
pathetically (adv)	بعاطفة، بشجون	*bi 'āṭifah, bi shujūn*
pathfinder (n)	مستكشف	*mustakshif*
pathless (adj)	غير مطروق	*ghair maṭrūq*
pathological (adj)	مرضي، باثولوجي	*maraḍī, bāthūlūjī*
pathologist (n)	اخصائي في علم الأمراض	*ikhṣā'ī fī 'lmil amrāḍ*

pathology (n)	علم الأمراض، باثولوجيا	*'ilmul amrāḍ, bāthūlūjiyā*
pathos (n)	إثارة العواطف، شفقة	*ithāratul 'awāṭif, shafaqah*
pathway (n)	طريق، ممر، مسلك	*ṭarīq, mamarr, maslak*
patience (n)	صبر	*ṣabr*
patient (adj/n)	صابر، مريض	*ṣābir, marīḍ*
patriarch (n)	أب، بطريك	*ab, baṭrīk*
patriarchal (adj)	أبوي، بطريكي	*abawī, baṭrīkī*
patriarchy (n)	نظام أبوي	*niẓām abawī*
patrician (adj)	نبيل، أصيل	*nabīl, aṣīl*
patricide (n)	قتل الأب	*qatlul ab*
patrimonial (adj)	إرثي، ميراثي	*irthī, mīrāthī*
patrimony (n)	ميراث	*mīrāth*
patriot (n)	محب الوطن، وطني	*muḥibbul waṭan, waṭanī*
patriotic (adj)	وطني	*waṭanī*
patriotism (n)	حب الوطن	*ḥubbul waṭan*
patrol (v/n)	عس، عسس	*'assa, 'asas*
patrolman (n)	شرطي خفير، عاس	*shurṭī khafīr, 'āss*
patrol wagon	سيارة الدورية	*sayyāratud dauriyyah*
patron (n)	حامي، ولي	*ḥāmī, walī*
patronage (n)	ولاية، رعاية، تعضيد	*wilāyah, ri'āyah, ta'ḍīd*
patronize, -nise (v)	عضد، ناصر	*'aḍḍada, nāṣara*
patronizing (adj)	معضد، مناصر	*mu'aḍḍid, munāṣir*
patter (n)	كلام مرغب	*kalām muraghghib*
pattern (n)	نموذج، مثال	*namūdhaj, mithāl*
pattern (v)	اقتدى، حاكى	*iqtadā, ḥākā*
paucity (n)	قلة، شذوذ	*qillah, shudhūdh*
paunchiness (n)	ضخامة البطن	*ḍakhāmatul baṭn*
paunchy (adj)	ضخم البطن	*ḍakhmul baṭn*
pauper (n)	فقير، عالة	*faqīr, 'ālah*

pause (n)	وقفة، ركزة	*waqfah, rakzah*
pause (v)	توقف، تأنى	*tawaqqafa, ta'annā*
pave (v)	رصف، مهد	*raṣafa, mahada*
pavement (n)	سطح مرصوف	*saṭḥ marṣūf*
pavilion (n)	جناح، سرادق	*janāḥ, surādiq*
paving (n)	رصيف، سطح مرصوف	*raṣīf, saṭḥ marṣūf*
paw (n)	مخلب	*mikhlab*
paw (v)	نبش بمخلب	*nabasha bi mikhlab*
pawn (n/v)	رهينة، رهن	*rahīnah, rahana*
pawnbroker (n)	مسترهن	*mustarhin*
pay (n)	دفع، جعل، أجر	*daf', ju'l, ajr*
pay (v)	أدى، دفع	*addā, dafa'a*
payable (adj)	واجب الدفع	*wājibud daf'*
payment (n)	دفع، أداء	*daf', adā'*
pea (n)	بسلة، حبة البسلة	*bisillah, ḥabbatul bisillah*
peace (n)	سلام، أمن	*salām, amn*
peaceable (adj)	سلمي، محب السلم	*silmī, muḥibbus silm*
peaceful (adj)	هادئ، سلمي	*hādi', silmī*
peacefully (adv)	بسلام، بهدوء	*bi salām, bi hudū'*
peacefulness (n)	سلمية، مسالمة	*silmiyyah, musālamah*
peacemaker (n)	صانع السلام	*ṣāni'us salām*
peacetime (n)	وقت السلم	*waqtus silm*
peach (n)	خوخ، خوخة	*khūkh, khūkhah*
peachy (adj)	خوخي	*khūkhī*
peacock (n)	طاؤوس	*ṭā'ūs*
peak (n)	ذورة، قمة	*dhirwah, qimmah*
peaky (adj)	شاحب، ضعيف	*shāḥib, ḍa'īf*
peal (v)	رن، قصف	*ranna, qaṣafa*
peal (n)	قصف، قرقعة	*qaṣf, qarqa'ah*

peanut (n)	فول سوداني	*fūl sūdānī*
pear (n)	إجاص	*ijjāṣ*
pearl (n)	لؤلؤ، شيء كاللؤلؤ	*lu'lu', shay' kal lu'lu'*
pearl barley	شعير محبب	*sha'īr muḥabbab*
pearl diver (n)	صائد اللؤلؤ	*ṣā'idul lu'lu'*
peasant (n)	فلاح، مزارع	*fallāḥ, muzāri'*
peasantry (n)	فلاحون، قرويون	*fallāḥūn, qarawiyyūn*
pebble (n)	حصاة، حصباء	*ḥaṣāt, ḥaṣbā'*
pebbly (adj)	مرصوف بالحصباء	*marṣūf bil ḥaṣbā'*
peck (v)	نقر، لقط	*naqara, laqaṭa*
peck (n)	نقرة، نقدة	*naqrah, naqdah*
pectic acid (n)	حامض بكتيكي	*ḥāmiḍ biktīkī*
pectoral (adj)	مختص بالصدر	*mukhtaṣṣ biṣ ṣadr*
peculate (v)	ابتز، اختلس	*ibtazza, ikhtalasa*
peculation (n)	اختلاس، ابتزاز	*ikhtilās, ibtizāz*
peculiar (adj)	غريب، فريد، خاص	*gharīb, farīd, khāṣṣ*
peculiarity (n)	غرابة، خصوصية	*gharābah, khuṣūṣiyyah*
peculiarly (adv)	بطريقة غريبة	*bi ṭarīqah gharībah*
pecuniary (adj)	مالي، نقدي	*mālī, naqdī*
pedal (n)	قدمية، دواسة	*qadamiyyah, dawwāsah*
pedal (adj)	قدمي، دواسي	*qadamī, dawwāsī*
pedal (v)	أعمل الدواسة	*a'malad dawwāsah*
pedant (n)	متحذلق	*mutaḥadhliq*
pedantic (adj)	تحذلقي	*taḥadhluqī*
pedantry (n)	حذلقة، ادعاء بالعلم	*ḥadhlaqah, iddi'ā bil 'ilm*
peddle (v)	باع البضائع متجولاً	*bā'al baḍā'i' mutajawwilan*
peddler (n)	بائع متجول	*bā'i' mutajawwil*
pederast (n)	لوطي، مشتهي المماثل	*lūṭī, mushtahil mumāthil*
pederasty (n)	لواطة	*liwāṭah*

pedestal (n)	قاعدة التمثال	*qā'idatut timthāl*
pedestrian (n)	ماشٍ، راجل	*māshin, rājil*
pedestrian (adj)	باهت، فاتر	*bāhit, fātir*
pedicure (n)	معالجة الأقدام	*mu'ālajatul aqdām*
pedigree (n)	شجرة النسب	*shajaratun nasab*
pediment (n)	قوصرة	*qauṣarah*
pedlar=peddler		
peek (v)	رمق، اختلس النظر	*ramaqa, ikhtalasan naẓar*
peek (n)	نظرة خاطفة	*naẓrah khāṭifah*
peel (v/n)	قشر، قشرة	*qashshara, qishrah*
peeler (n)	مقشرة	*miqsharah*
peelings (n)	قشارة	*qushārah*
peep (v)	رمق، بزغ	*ramaqa, bazagha*
peep (n)	نظرة خسلة، نظرة خاطفة	*naẓrah khuslah, naẓrah khāṭifah*
peer (v)	أمعن النظر	*am'anan naẓar*
peer (n)	ند، نبيل	*nidd, nabīl*
peerage (n)	رتبة الأمير	*rutbatul amīr*
peeress (n)	امرأة نبيلة	*imra'ah nabīlah*
peerless (adj)	لا نظير لـــه	*lā naẓīra lahu*
peeve (v)	أغضب، أزعج	*aghḍaba, az'aja*
peeved (adj)	غضب، غضبان	*ghaḍib, ghaḍbān*
peevish (adj)	غضوب، شكس	*ghaḍūb, shakis*
peg (n)	وتد، مشجب، كلاب	*watid, mishjab, kullāb*
peg (v)	ثبت بوتد	*thabbata bi watid*
pejorative (adj)	ازدرائي، تنقيدي	*izdirā'ī, tanqīdī*
pelican (n)	بجع	*baja'*
pellet (n)	كرة صغيرة من طعام	*kurah ṣaghīrah min ṭa'ām*
pellmell (adv)	شذر مذر	*shadhar madhar*

pellucid (adj)	شفاف، واضح جدًا	*shaffāf, wāḍiḥ jiddā*
pelt (v)	قذف، رشق	*qadhafa, rashaqa*
pelt (n)	فرو، جلد	*farw, jild*
pelvic (n)	حوضي	*ḥauḍī*
pelvis (n)	حوض، جوف	*ḥauḍ, jauf*
pen (n)	قلم، حظيرة	*qalam, ḥaẓīrah*
pen (v)	كتب، حبس في خطيرة	*kataba, ḥabasa fī ḥaẓīrah*
penal (adj)	قصاصي، جزائي	*qiṣāṣī, jazā'ī*
penal code	قانون العقوبات	*qānūnul 'uqūbāt*
penalization,-isation	معاقبة، جزاء	*mu'āqabah, jazā'*
penalize,-ise (v)	عاقب، جازى	*'āqaba, jāzā*
penalty (n)	غرامة، قصاص	*gharāmah, qiṣāṣ*
penance (n)	كفارة	*kaffārah*
pencil (n)	قلم رصاص	*qalamu raṣāṣ*
pencil (v)	رسم، كتب	*rasama, kataba*
pendant (n)	حلية متدلية	*ḥilyah mutadalliyah*
pendent (adj)	موقوف، متدلٍ	*mauqūf, mutadallin*
pending (adj)	متدلٍّ، معلقٍ	*mutadallin, mu'allaq*
pendulous (adj)	متدلٍّ، مترجح	*mutadallin, mutarajjiḥ*
pendulum (n)	رقاص، رقاص الساعة	*raqqāṣ, raqqāṣus sā'ah*
penetrable (adj)	قابل للتداخل	*qābil lit tadākhul*
penetrate (v)	تخلل، اخترق، اكتشف	*takhallala, ikhtaraqa, iktashafa*
penetrating (adj)	مخترق، حاد	*mukhtariq, ḥādd*
penetration (n)	دخول، إدراك، نفوذ	*dukhūl, idrāk, nufūdh*
penetrative (adj)	مخترق، مؤثر	*mukhtariq, mu'aththir*
penguin (n)	بطريق	*biṭrīq*
peninsula (n)	شبه جزيرة	*shibhu jazīrah*
peninsular (adj)	متعلق بشبه جزيرة	*muta'alliq bi shibhi jazīrah*
penis (n)	قضيب، آلة مخصوصة	*qaḍīb, ālah makhṣūṣah*
penitence (n)	توبة، ندامة	*taubah, nadāmah*

penitent (n)	تائب، نادم	*tā'ib, nādim*
penitential (adj)	متعلق بالتوبة	*muta'alliq bit taubah*
penitentiary (n/adj)	سجن، متعلق بالسجن	*sijn, muta'alliq bis sijn*
penmanship (n)	فن الخط	*fannul khaṭṭ*
pen name	اسم قلمي	*ism qalamī*
penniless (adj)	مفلس، معدم، فقير	*muflis, mu'dim, faqīr*
penny (n)	جنيه انكليزي، بنس	*junaih inkilīzī, bins*
pension (n)	معاش التقاعد، فندق صغير	*ma'āshut taqā'ud, funduq ṣaghīr*
pension (v)	أعطى معاش التقاعد	*a'ṭā ma'āshat taqā'ud*
pensionable (adj)	مؤهل للتقاعد	*mu'ahhal lit taqā'ud*
pensioner (n)	متقاعد	*mutaqā'id*
pensive (adj)	متأمل، حزين	*muta'ammil, ḥazīn*
pensiveness (n)	حزن، كآبة، تأمل	*ḥuzn, ka'ābah, ta'ammul*
pentagon (n)	مخمس	*mukhammas*
pentagonal (adj)	خماسي الزوايا	*khumāsiyyuz zawāyā*
penthouse (n)	سقيفة، مظلة	*saqīfah, miẓallah*
penultimate (adj)	واقع قبل الأخير	*wāqi' qablal akhīr*
penurious (adj)	مقتر، معدم، شحيح	*muqtir, mu'dim, shaḥīḥ*
penuriously (adv)	بشح، ببخل	*bi shuḥḥ, bi bukhl*
penuriousness (n)	شح، بخل، فقر	*shuḥḥ, bukhl, faqı*
penury (n)	فقر شديد	*faqr shadīd*
peon (n)	بيون، خادم	*bayyūn, khādim*
people (n/v)	ناس، عمر	*nās, 'ammara*
pepper (n/v)	فلفل، تبل بفلفل	*fulful, tabbala bi fulful*
peppercorn (n)	حب الفلفل	*ḥabbul fulful*
peppery (adj)	فلفلي، حاد الطبع	*fulfulī, ḥāddut ṭab'*
pepsin (n)	خميرة الهضم	*khamīratul haḍm*
per (prep)	لكل، عن كل	*li kulli, 'an kulli*
perambulate (v)	سار، تجول	*sāra, tajawwala*

perambulation (n)	تجول، سير على الأقدام	*tajawwul, sair ‘alal aqdām*
per annum	في السنة	*fis sanah*
per capita	لكل شخص	*li kulli shakhṣ*
perceivable (adj)	ممكن الإدراك	*mumkinul idrāk*
perceive (v)	أدرك، شعر	*adraka, sha‘ara*
per cent (adj/adv)	في المئة	*fil mi’ah*
per cent (n)	جزء من المئة	*juz’ minal mi’ah*
percentage (n)	نسبة مئوية	*nisbah mi’awiyyah*
perceptibility (n)	كون الشيء مدركاً	*kaunush shay’ mudrakan*
perceptible (adj)	يمكن إدراكه	*yumkin idrākuh*
perception (n)	إدراك، شعور، بصيرة	*idrāk, shu‘ūr, baṣīrah*
perceptive (adj)	حاد الطبع، فهيم	*ḥadduṭ ṭab‘, fahīm*
perceptiveness (n)	إدراك، إدراكية	*idrāk, idrākiyyah*
perceptivity=perceptiveness		
perch (n)	مجثم، مقعد عالي	*majtham, maq‘ad ‘ālī*
perch (v)	جثم، وقع على	*jathama, waqa‘a ‘alā*
perchance (adv)	من الممكن، ربما	*minal mumkin, rubbamā*
percipience (n)	إدراك، تمييز	*idrāk, tamyīz*
percipient (adj)	حاد الطبع، مميز	*ḥādduṭ ṭab‘, mumayyiz*
percolate (v)	قطر، ترشح	*qaṭṭara, tarashshaḥa*
percolation (n)	تقطير، ترشيح	*taqṭīr, tarshīḥ*
percussion (n)	قرع الصوت، دق	*qar‘uṣ ṣaut, daqq*
perdition (n)	هلاك النفس، خسران النفس	*halākun nafs, khusrānun nafs*
peregrination (n)	رحلة، سفر	*riḥlah, safar*
peremptory (adj)	آمري، قاطع	*āmirī, qāṭi‘*
perennial (adj)	دائم، طويل، خالد	*dā’im, ṭawīl, khālid*
perfect (adj)	تام، كامل	*tāmm, kāmil*
perfect (v)	أتم، أنجز	*atamma, anjaza*

perfection (n)	كمال، تمام	*kamāl, tamām*
perfectionalism (n)	كمالية	*kamāliyyah*
perfectionalist (n)	مؤيد الكمالية	*mu'ayyidul kamāliyyah*
perfectly (adv)	تماماً، بالتمام	*tamāman, bit tamām*
perfidious (adj)	غادر، خائن	*ghādir, khā'in*
perfidiously (adv)	بخيانة، بغدر	*bi khiyānah, bi ghadr*
perfidiousness (n)	خيانة، غدر	*khiyānah, ghadr*
perforate (v)	ثقب، خرم	*thaqaba, kharrama*
perforation (n)	تثقيب، تخريم	*tathqīb, takhrīm*
perforce (adv)	قهراً، جبراً	*qahran, jabran*
perform (v)	أدى، أنجز، مثل	*addā, anjaza, maththala*
performance (n)	عمل، إنجاز، تمثيل	*'amal, injāz, tamthīl*
performer (n)	ممثل، منجز، عامل	*mumaththil, munjiz, 'āmil*
perfume (n)	طيب، عطر	*ṭīb, 'iṭr*
perfume (v)	عطر، طيب	*'aṭṭara, ṭayyaba*
perfumer (n)	صانع العطور	*ṣāni'ul 'uṭūr*
perfumery (n)	صنع العطور	*ṣun'ul 'uṭūr*
perfunctoriness (n)	عدم اكتراث، عدم حماسة	*'adamu iktirāth, 'adamu ḥamāsah*
perfunctory (n)	بعدم اكتراث، بتهاون	*bi 'adami iktirāth, bi tahāwūn*
perhaps (adv)	لعل، ربما، عسى	*la'alla, rubbamā, 'asā*
peril (n)	خطر	*khaṭar*
perilous (adj)	محفوف بالمخاطر	*maḥfūf bil makhāṭir*
period (n)	مدة، عهد، حصة	*muddah, 'ahd, ḥiṣṣah*
periodic (adj)	دوري	*daurī*
periodical (n)	مجلة، نشرة دورية	*majallah, nashrah dauriyyah*
periodically (adv)	دوريًا، بالدور	*dauriyyan, bid daur*
peripheral (adj)	محيطي	*muḥīṭī*

periphery (n)	محيط	*muḥīṭ*
periphrasis (n)	حشو، إطناب	*ḥashw, iṭnāb*
perish (v)	هلك، تلف، فنى	*halaka, talifa, fanā*
perishable (adj)	فانٍ، بائد، تالف	*fānin, bā'id, tālif*
perisher (n)	ولد مزعج	*walad muz'ij*
perjure (v)	حلف زوراً	*ḥalafa zūran*
perjurer (n)	حانث بقسمه	*ḥānith bi qasmihi*
perk (v)	ابتهج، مرح	*ibtahaja, maraḥa*
perkiness (n)	مرح، ابتهاج	*maraḥ, ibtihāj*
perky (adj)	مبتهج، مرح	*mubtahij, mariḥ*
permanence (n)	دوام، بقاء	*dawām, baqā'*
permanency (n)	ثبات، دوام	*thabāt, dawām*
permanent (adj)	دائم، باقٍ، ثابت	*dā'im, bāqin, thābit*
permeate (v)	تخلل، تدخل	*takhallala, tadakhkhala*
permeation (n)	اختراق، تخلل	*ikhtirāq, takhallul*
permissible (adj)	مباح، مسموح	*mubāḥ, masmūḥ*
permission (n)	إذن، سماح، إجازة	*idhn, samāḥ, ijāzah*
permissive (adj)	مرخص، مخير	*murakhkhiṣ, mukhayyir*
permit (v)	رخص، سمح	*rakhkhaṣa, samaḥa*
permit (n)	إجازة، رخصة	*ijāzah, rukhṣah*
permutation (n)	تبديل، تغيير	*tabdīl, taghyīr*
permute (v)	غير الأحكام	*ghayyaral aḥkām*
pernicious (adj)	مؤذٍ، مهلك	*mu'dhin, muhlik*
peroration (n)	خاتمة الخطبة	*khātimatul khuṭbah*
peroxide (n)	بروكسيد	*burūksīd*
perpendicular (adj)	عمودي، رأسي	*'amūdī, ra'sī*
perpendicularity (n)	عمودية	*'amūdiyyah*
perpendicularly (adv)	عموديًا، تعامديًا	*'amūdiyyan, ta'āmudiyyan*
perpetrate (v)	ارتكب، اقترف	*irtakaba, iqtarafa*

perpetration (n)	ارتكاب، جريمة	*irtikāb, jarīmah*
perpetrator (n)	مقترف، مرتكب	*muqtarif, murtakib*
perpetual (adj)	دائم، مستمر	*dā'im, mustamirr*
perpetually (adv)	على الدوام	*'alad dawām*
perpetuate (v)	خلد، أبد	*khallada, abbada*
perpetuation (n)	تأبيد، تأديم	*ta'bīd, ta'dīm*
perpetuity (n)	أبدية، دوام	*abadiyyah, dawām*
perplex (v)	خبل، عقد، أربك	*khabala, 'aqqada, arbaka*
perplexed (adj)	معقد، مرتبك	*mu'aqqad, murtabik*
perplexity (n)	خبل، ارتباك، تعقيد	*khabl, irtibāk, ta'qīd*
perquisite (n)	أجرة إضافية	*ujrah iḍāfiyyah*
persecute (v)	اضطهد، ظلم، عذب	*iḍṭahada, ẓalama, 'adhdhaba*
persecution (n)	مضايقة، ظلم، تعذيب	*muḍāyaqah, ẓulm, ta'dhīb*
persecutor (n)	مضطهد، ظالم	*muḍṭahid, ẓālim*
perseverance (n)	مواظبة، مثابرة	*muwāẓabah, muthābarah*
persevere (v)	واظب، ثابر، داوم	*wāẓaba, thābara, dāwama*
persevering (adj)	مواظب، مثابر	*muwāẓib, muthābir*
Persian (n/adj)	فارسي	*farsī*
persimmon (n)	برسيمون	*barsīmūn*
persist (v)	ثابر، أصر على	*thābara, aṣarra 'alā*
persistence (n)	مثابرة، استقلال	*muthābarah, istiqlāl*
persistent (adj)	مثابر، مصر	*muthābir, muṣirr*
persistently (adv)	بمثابرة	*bi muthābarah*
person (n)	شخص	*shakhṣ*
persona (n)	شخص	*shakhṣ*
personable (adj)	حسن المظهر	*ḥasanul maẓhar*
personage (n)	شخصية بارزة	*shakhṣiyyah bārizah*

persona grata	شخص مقبول	*shakhṣ maqbūl*
personal (adj)	شخصي، ذاتي	*shakhṣī, dhātī*
personality (n)	شخصية بارزة	*shakhṣiyyah bārizah*
personalize,-ise (v)	جعل شخصيًا	*ja'ala shakhṣiyyan*
personally (adv)	شخصيًا، ذاتيًا	*shakhṣiyyan, dhātiyyan*
persona non grata	شخص غير مقبول	*shakhṣ ghair maqbūl*
personification (n)	تشخيص، تجسيم	*tashkhīṣ, tajsīm*
personify (v)	شخص، جسم	*shakhkhaṣa, jassama*
personnel (n)	ملاك، أفراد	*milāk, afrād*
perspective (n)	مشهد، منظر	*mashhad, manẓar*
perspicacious (adj)	فطين، حاد الذهن	*faṭīn, ḥāddudh dhihn*
perspicacity (n)	حدة النظر، فطانة	*ḥiddatun naẓar, faṭānah*
perspicuity (n)	وضوح، صراحة	*wuḍūḥ, ṣarāḥah*
perspicuous (adj)	واضح، جلي	*wāḍiḥ, jalī*
perspicuousness (n)	وضوح، سهولة	*wuḍūḥ, suhūlah*
perspiration (n)	عرق، رشح	*'araq, rashḥ*
perspire (v)	عرق، رشح	*'araqa, rashaḥa*
persuade (v)	استمال، أقنع	*istamāla, aqna'a*
persuasion (n)	استمالة، إقناع	*istimālah, iqnā'*
persuasive (adj)	مقنع، مستميل	*muqni', mustamīl*
persuasively (adv)	بإقناع، باقتناع	*bi iqnā', bi iqtinā'*
persuasiveness (n)	قدرة على الإقناع	*qudrah 'alal iqnā'*
pert (adj)	وقح، نشيط، سليط	*waqiḥ, nashīṭ, salīṭ*
pertain (v)	تعلق، اختص	*ta'allaqa, ikhtaṣṣa*
pertinacious (adj)	مصر، عنيد، متشبث	*muṣirr, 'anīd, mutashabbith*
pertinacity (n)	تشبث، إلحاح	*tashabbuth, ilḥāḥ*
pertinence (n)	ملاءمة، وثاقة الصلة	*mulā'amah, wathāqatuṣ ṣilah*
pertinent (adj)	ملائم، مطابق	*mulā'im, muṭābiq*

pertly (adv)	بوقاحة، بسلاطة	*bi waqāḥah, bi salāṭah*
pertness (n)	وقاحة، سلاطة	*waqāḥah, salāṭah*
perturb (v)	شوش، أقلق، أزعج	*shawwasha, aqlaqa, az'aja*
perturbation (n)	تشوش، إقلاق	*tashawwush, iqlāq*
perusal (n)	مطالعة بإمعان	*muṭāla'ah bi im'ān*
peruse (v)	طالع بإمعان	*ṭāla'a bi im'ān*
pervade (v)	شمل، تخلل	*shamila, takhallala*
pervasion (n)	تخلل، اختراق	*takhallul, ikhtirāq*
pervasive (adj)	شامل، عام، مخترق	*shāmil, 'āmm, mukhtariq*
pervasiveness (n)	تخلل، انتشار	*takhallul, intishār*
perverse (adj)	عنيد، متمرد، منحرف	*'anīd, mutamarrid, munḥarif*
perverseness (n)	شكاسة، عناد	*shakāsah, 'inād*
perversion (n)	انحراف، ضلال	*inḥirāf, ḍalāl*
perversity (n)	انحراف، عناد	*inḥirāf, 'inād*
pervert (v)	أفسد، أضل،حرف	*afsada, aḍalla, ḥarrafa*
pervert (n)	منحرف، ضال	*munḥarif, ḍāll*
pessimism (n)	تشاؤم، اعتقاد بالسوء	*tashā'um, i'tiqād bis sū'*
pessimist (n)	متشائم، تشاؤمي	*mutashā'im, tashā'umī*
pessimistically (adv)	متشائماً	*mutashā'iman*
pest (n)	شخص مزعج	*shakhṣ muz'ij*
pester (v)	أزعج، أبغض	*az'aja, abghaḍa*
pesticide (n)	مبيدة الحشرات	*mubīdatul ḥasharāt*
pestilence (n)	طاعون، وباء	*ṭā'ūn, wabā'*
pestilent (pestilential)	وبائي، مهلك	*wabā'ī, muhlik*
pestle (n)	مدقة	*midaqqah*
pet (n)	حيوان مدلل	*ḥaiwān mudallal*
pet (v)	دلل، قبل	*dallala, qabbala*

petal (n)	بتلة، ورقة الزهرة	*batalah, waraqatuz zahrah*
peter (v)	جنا، تلاشى	*janā, talāshā*
petite (adj)	أنيق، خفيف الجسم	*anīq, khafīful jism*
petition (n)	طلب، عريضة	*ṭalab, 'arīḍah*
petition (v)	قدم عريضةً	*qaddama 'arīḍatan*
petitioner (n)	مقدم العريضة	*muqaddimul 'arīḍah*
petrifaction (n)	تحجير، تحجر	*taḥjīr, taḥajjur*
petrify (v)	حجر، صلب	*ḥajjara, ṣallaba*
petrol (n)	بنـــزين	*binzīn*
petroleum (n)	بترول، نفط	*bitrūl, nifṭ*
petrologist (n)	متخصص بعلم الصخور	*mutakhaṣṣiṣ bi 'ilmiṣ ṣukhūr*
petrology (n)	علم الصخور	*'ilmuṣ ṣukhūr*
petticoat (n)	تنورة تحتانية	*tannūrah taḥtāniyyah*
pettily (adv)	بحقارة، بتفاهة	*bi ḥaqārah, bi tafāhah*
pettiness (n)	تفاهة، حقارة	*tafāhah, ḥaqārah*
pettish (adj)	شكس، نكد	*shakis, nakid*
pettishness (n)	شكاسة، نكد	*shakāsah, nakad*
petty (adj)	طفيف، زهيد، تافه	*ṭafīf, zahīd, tāfih*
petty cash	مبلغ صغير	*mablagh ṣaghīr*
petulance (n)	شكاسة، وقاحة	*shakāsah, waqāḥah*
petulant (adj)	شكس، سيء الطبع	*shakis, sayyi'uṭ ṭab'*
phallus (n)	قضيب، فالوس	*qaḍīb, fālūs*
phantasm (n)	طيف، خيال، وهم	*ṭaif, khayāl, wahm*
phantasy = phantasm		
phantom (n)	طيف، وهم، شبح	*ṭaif, wahm, shabaḥ*
Pharaoh (n)	فرعون مصر	*fir'aunu miṣr*
pharmaceutical (adj)	صيدلي	*ṣaidalī*

pharmaceutics (n)	صيدلة	*ṣaidalah*
pharmacist (n)	صيدلي	*ṣaidalī*
pharmacological (adj)	متعلق بعلم العقاقير	*muta'alliq bi 'ilmil 'aqāqīr*
pharmacology (n)	علم العقاقير	*'ilmul 'aqāqīr*
pharmacy (n)	صيدلية، صيدلة	*ṣaidaliyah, ṣaidalah*
pharynx (n)	بلعوم	*bul'ūm*
phase (n)	طور، دور، حالة	*ṭaur, daur, ḥālah*
phase (v)	نفد على مراحل	*naffada 'alā marāḥil*
phenomenal (adj)	شاذ، ظاهراتي	*shādhdh, ẓāhirātī*
phenomenally (adv)	بطريق غير اعتيادي	*bi ṭarīq ghair i'tiyādī*
phenomenon (n)	ظاهرة، مظهر	*ẓāhirah, maẓhar*
phial (n)	قنينة، قارورة	*qinnīnah, qārūrah*
philander (v)	داعب، غازل	*dā'aba, ghāzala*
philanderer (n)	مداعب، مغازل	*mudā'ib, mughāzil*
philanthropic (adj)	محب للبشر	*muḥibb lil bashar*
philanthropist (n)	محب البشر	*muḥibbul bashar*
philanthropy (n)	حب البشر	*ḥubbul bashar*
philately (n)	جمع الطوابع البريدية	*jam'uṭ ṭawābi' al barīdiyyah*
philippic (n)	كلام قارص، خطاب تقريعي	*kalām qāriṣ, khiṭāb taqrī'ī*
philological (adj)	متعلق بفلسفة اللغة	*muta'alliq bi falsafatil lughah*
philologist (n)	عالم بفلسفة اللغة	*'ālim bi falsafatil lughah*
philology (n)	علم اللغة، فيلولوجيا	*'ilmul lughah, fīlūlūjiyā*
philosopher (n)	فيلسوف، حكيم	*failasūf, ḥakīm*
philosophic-al (adj)	فلسفي، حكمي	*falsafī, ḥikamī*
philosophize,-ise (v)	تفلسف	*tāfalsafa*
philosophy (n)	فلسفة، علم الحكمة	*falsafah, 'ilmul ḥikmah*

phlegm (n)	بلغم، نخامة	*balgham, nukhāmah*
phlegmatic (adj)	بارد، فاتر	*bārid, fātir*
phobia (n)	رهاب، فوبيا	*ruhāb, fūbiyā*
phoenix (n)	عنقاء	*'anqā'*
phone (n)	تليفون، مسماع، صوت كلامي	*tilīfūn, mismā', ṣaut kalāmī*
phone (v)	تكلم بالتليفون	*takallama bit tilīfūn*
phonetic (adj)	لفظي، صوتي	*lafẓī, ṣautī*
phonetically (adv)	صوتيًا	*ṣautiyyan*
phonetician (n)	متخصص بالأصوات	*mutakhaṣṣiṣ bil aṣwāt*
phonetics (n)	علم الأصوات	*'ilmul aṣwāt*
phonic (adj)	متعلق بالأصوات	*muta'alliq bil aṣwāt*
phonograph (n)	حاكي، فونوغراف	*ḥākī, fūnūgharāf*
phonology (n)	علم الأصوات الكلامية	*'ilmul aṣwāt al kalāmiyyah*
phosphate (n)	فوسفات	*fūsfāt*
phosphorescence (n)	تألق، تفسفر	*ta'alluq, tafasfur*
phosphorescent (adj)	مضيء، مومض	*mūḍī', mūmiḍ*
phosphorous (adj)	فوسفوري	*fūsfūrī*
phosphorus (n)	فوسفور	*fūsfūr*
photocopy (n)	نسخة فوتوغرافية	*nuskha fūtūgharāfiyyah*
photograph (n)	صورة ضوئية	*ṣūrah ḍau'iyyah*
photograph (v)	صور فوتوغرافيًا	*ṣawwara fūtūgharāfiyyan*
photographer (n)	فوتوغرافي، ضوئي	*fūtūgharāfī, ḍau'ī*
photography (n)	فوتوغرافي	*fūtūgharāfī*
photosensitive (adj)	حساس للضوء	*ḥassās liḍ ḍau'*
photostat = photocopy		
photosynthesis (n)	تركيب ضوئي	*tarkīb ḍau'ī*
photosynthetic (adj)	متعلق بالتركيب الضوئي	*muta'alliq bit tarkīb aḍ ḍau'ī*
phrase (n)	عبارة، أسلوب	*'ibārah, uslūb*

phrase (v)	عبر بكلمات، سمى	*'abbara bi kalimāt, sammā*
phraseology (n)	أسلوب، تعبير	*uslūb, ta'bīr*
phrasing (n)	أسلوب التعبير	*uslūbut ta'bīr*
phrenology (n)	فراسة الدماغ	*firāsatud dimāgh*
physical (adj)	مادي، بدني، طبيعي	*māddī, badanī, ṭabī'ī*
physically (adv)	جسديًا، ماديًا	*jasadiyyan, māddiyyan*
physical science	علم طبيعي	*'ilm ṭabī'ī*
physician (n)	طبيب	*ṭabīb*
physicist (n)	عالم بالطبيعيات	*'ālim biṭ ṭabī'iyyāt*
physics (n)	علم الطبيعة، فيزياء	*'ilmuṭ ṭabī'ah, fīzyā'*
physiological (adj)	فيسيولوجي، وظائفي	*fisiulūjī, waẓā'ifī*
physiologist (n)	عالم بالفسلجة	*'ālim bil faslajah*
physiology (n)	فيسيولوجيا، علم الوظائف	*fisiulūjiyā, 'ilmul waẓā'if*
physique (n)	بنية الجسم	*binyatul jism*
pianist (n)	عازف البيان	*'āziful biyān*
piano (n)	بيان، بيانو	*biyān, bayānū*
piazza (n)	ساحة، قيسرية	*sāḥah, qaisariyyah*
pica (n)	بيكا	*baika*
picaresque (adj)	تشردي	*tasharrudī*
pick (n)	خيار، نخبة، معول	*khiyār, nukhbah, mi'wal*
pick (v)	التقط، انتخب، نقر	*iltaqaṭa, intakhaba, naqara*
picket (n)	خازوق، منخس	*khāzūq, minkhas*
picket (v)	وضع مفرزة	*waḍa'a mufrazah*
pickings (n)	لقاط، فتات	*luqāṭ, futāt*
pickle (n)	طرشي، ورطة	*ṭurshī, warṭah*
pick-me-up (n)	شراب منشط	*sharāb munashshiṭ*

pick out	اختار، انتخب	*ikhtāra, intakhaba*
pickpocket (n)	نشال	*nashshāl*
pick-up (n)	تسريع، التقاط الصوت	*tasrī', iltiqāṭuṣ ṣaut*
pick up	التقط، نهض	*iltaqaṭa, nahaḍa*
picnic (n/v)	نزهة، تنــزه	*nuzhah, tanazzaha*
pictorial (adj)	تصويري، مصور	*taṣwīrī, muṣawwir*
pictorial (n)	مجلة مصورة	*majallah muṣawwarah*
picture (n/v)	صورة، صور	*ṣūrah, ṣawwara*
picture book	كتاب مصور	*kitāb muṣawwar*
picture card	ورقة مصورة	*waraqah muṣawwarah*
picture gallery	معرض الصور	*ma'riḍuṣ ṣuwar*
picturesque (adj)	بهيج، رائع	*bahīj, rā'i'*
picturesqueness (n)	بهجة، روعة	*bahjah, rau'ah*
piddling (adj)	تافه، حقير	*tāfih, ḥaqīr*
pie (n)	فطيرة	*faṭīrah*
piebald (adj)	أرقط، أبلق	*arqaṭ, ablaq*
piece (n)	قطعة، نموذج	*qiṭ'ah, namūdhaj*
piece (v)	جمع، ضم	*jama'a, ḍamma*
piecemeal (adv)	تدريجيًا	*tadrījiyyan*
pied (adj)	متلون	*mutalawwin*
pierce (v)	وخز، خرق	*wakhaza, kharaqa*
piercing (adj)	ثاقب، خارق	*thāqib, khāriq*
piercingly (adv)	بطريق حاد	*bi ṭāriq ḥādd*
piety (n)	تقوى، ورع	*taqwā, wara'*
piffle (n)	عبث، هراء	*'abath, hurā'*
piffling (adj)	زهيد، تافه، حقير	*zahīd, tāfih, ḥaqīr*
pig (n)	خنــزير، شخص وقح	*khinzīr, shakhṣ waqiḥ*
pigeon (n)	حمامة، مسؤولية	*ḥamāmah, mas'ūliyyah*
pigeon breasted (adj)	حمامي الصدر	*ḥamāmiyyuṣ ṣadr*
pigeon-hole (n)	بيت الحمام	*baitul ḥamām*

pigeon-toed (adj)	حمامي الأصابع	*ḥamāmiyyul aṣābi'*
piggish (adj)	وقح، شره	*waqiḥ, sharih*
piggy (n)	خنزير صغير	*khinzīr ṣaghīr*
pigment (n)	صبغ، صبغة	*ṣabgh, ṣibghah*
pigmentation (n)	صبغ، خضب	*ṣabgh, khaḍb*
pike (n)	منخاس، رمح	*minkhās, rumḥ*
pikestaff (n)	عصا رامحة	*'aṣā rāmiḥah*
pilaster (n)	عمود مربع	*'amūd murabba'*
pile (n)	ركام، ركيزة	*rukām, rakīzah*
pile (v)	كوم، ركم	*kawwama, rakama*
pilfer (v)	سلب، سرق	*salaba, saraqa*
pilferage (n)	سرقة ، سلب	*sariqah, salb*
pilferer (n)	مختلس، سارق	*mukhtalis, sāriq*
pilgrim (n)	حاج، زائر	*ḥājj, zā'ir*
pilgrimage (n)	حج، رحلة مقدسة	*ḥajj, riḥlah muqaddasah*
pill (n)	حبة، بلبوعة	*ḥabbah, balbū'ah*
pillage (v/n)	نهب، نهب	*nahaba, nahb*
pillar (n)	عمود، قائمة	*'amūd, qā'imah*
pillbox (n)	علبة الحبوب	*'ulbatul ḥubūb*
pillion (n)	سرج، مقعد خلفي	*sarj, maq'ad khalfī*
pillory (n)	مشهرة	*mushahhirah*
pillow (n)	وسادة، مخدة	*wisādah, mikhaddah*
pillow (v)	وسد، توسد	*wassada, tawassada*
pillowcase (n)	غطاء الوسادة	*ghiṭā'ul wisādah*
pilot (n)	ربان الطائرة	*rubbānuṭ ṭā'irah*
pilot (v)	قاد، أرشد	*qāda, arshada*
pimp (n)	قواد، ديوث	*qawwād, dayyūth*
pimple (n)	بثرة، حبة	*bathrah, ḥabbah*
pimpled (adj)	منفط، مبثر	*munaffaṭ, mubaththar*
pimply (adj)	مبثر	*mubaththar*

pin (n)	دبوث، خابور	*dabbūth, khābūr*
pin (v)	شبك بدبوث	*shabaka bi dabbūth*
pincer (n)	كلاب، كماشة	*kullāb, kammāshah*
pinch (v)	قرص، ضيق	*qaraṣa, ḍayyaqa*
pinch (n)	قرصة، قبصة	*qarṣah, qabṣah*
pinched (adj)	بائس، تعس	*bā'is, ta'is*
pincushion (n)	وسادة الدبابيس	*wisādatud dabābīs*
pine (n)	شجرة الصنبور،	*shajaratuṣ ṣumbūr,*
	شجرة أناناس	*shajaratu anānās*
pine (v)	نحل، ذاب أسىً	*naḥula, dhāba asan*
pineapple (n)	أناناس، تفاح صنبوري	*anānās, tuffāḥ ṣumbūrī*
pine-needle (n)	إبرة الصنبور	*ibratuṣ ṣumbūr*
ping (v/n)	أز، أزيز	*azza, azīz*
ping-pong (n)	بنغبنغ	*binghbungh*
pin-head (n)	أبله، أحمق	*ablah, aḥmaq*
pinion (n)	ريشة	*rīshah*
pink (adj/n)	قرنفلي اللون	*qaranfuliyyul laun*
pink (v)	جرح، طعن	*jaraḥa, ṭa'ana*
pinkie (pinky)	خنصر	*khinṣar*
pinkish (adj)	قرنفلي	*qaranfulī*
pinnace (n)	سفينة صغيرة	*safīnah ṣaghīrah*
pinnacle (n)	برج، قمة	*burj, qimmah*
pinpoint (n)	شيء حاد، رأس	*shay' ḥādd, ra'sud*
	الدبوس	*dabbūs*
pint-sized (adj)	ضئيل، صغير	*ḍa'īl, ṣaghīr*
pioneer (n)	رائد، ممهد الطريق	*rā'id, mumahhiduṭ ṭarīq*
pioneer (v)	مهد الطريق، راد	*mahhadaṭ ṭarīq, rāda*
pious (adj)	متقى، ورع، زاهد	*muttaqī, wari', zāhid*
piously (adv)	اتقاءً، بتقوى	*ittiqā'an, bi taqwā*
piousness (n)	ورع، تقوى	*wara', taqwā*

pip (n)	بذرة، حبة	*badhrah, ḥabbah*
pipe (n)	أنبوب، مزمار، بيبة	*umbūb, mizmār, bībah*
pipe (v)	نقل بالأنابيب، زمر	*naqala bil anābīb, zammara*
pipe-dream (n)	أمل كاذب،حلم	*amal kādhib, ḥulm*
pipeline (n)	خط الأنابيب	*khaṭṭul anābīb*
piper (n)	عازف على مزمار	*'āzif 'alā mizmār*
piping (n)	مجموعة الأنابيب	*majmū'atul anābīb*
pip-squeak (n)	شخص قليل الأهمية	*shakhṣ qalīlul ahammiyyah*
piquancy (n)	حرافة، حدة	*ḥarāfah, ḥiddah*
piquant (adj)	حريف، لذاع	*ḥirrīf, ladhdhā'*
piracy (n)	انتحال، لص البحر	*intiḥāl, laṣṣul baḥr*
pirate (n)	منتحل، قرصان	*muntaḥil, qurṣān*
pirate (v)	انتحل، قرصن	*intaḥala, qarṣana*
piratical (adj)	انتحالي، قرصاني	*intiḥālī, qurṣānī*
piss (v/n)	بال، بول	*bāla, baul*
pistol (n)	طبنجة، مسدس	*ṭabanjah, musaddas*
piston (n)	بستون، مكبس	*bastūn, mikbas*
pit (n)	حفرة، نقرة، نواة	*ḥufrah, nuqrah, nawāt*
pit (v)	حفر، نقر	*ḥafara, naqqara*
pit-a-pat (adv)	بطقطقة	*bi ṭaqṭaqah*
pitch (n)	زفت، منحدر، رمية	*zift, munḥadar, ramyah*
pitch (v)	قير، زفت، انحدر	*qayyara, zaffata, inḥadara*
pitch-dark (adj)	أسود شديد	*aswad shadīd*
pitcher (n)	رامي، جرة	*rāmī, jarrah*
pitchfork (n)	مذراة	*midhrāt*
piteous (adj)	جدير بالشفقة	*jadīr bish shafaqah*
pitfall (n)	أحبولة، مأزق	*uḥbūlah, ma'ziq*
pith (n)	جوهر، لب	*jauhar, lubb*

pithy (adj)	بليغ، جوهري	*balīgh, jauharī*
pitiable (adj)	جدير بالشفقة	*jadīr bish shafaqah*
pitiful (adj)	يرثى لــه	*yurthā lahu*
pitifully (adv)	بشفقة، برثاء	*bi shafaqah, bi rithā'*
pitiless (adj)	عديم الشفقة	*'adīmush shafaqah*
pitilessly (adv)	بقساوة، بدون شفقة	*bi qasāwah, bi dūn shafaqah*
pitilessness (n)	عدم رحمة، عدم شفقة	*'adamu raḥmah, 'adamu shafaqah*
pittance (n)	مقدار ضئيل	*miqdār ḍa'īl*
pituitary (n)	غدة نخامية	*ghuddah nukhāmiyyah*
pity (n)	شفقة، رحمة	*shafaqah, raḥmah*
pity (v)	تحنن، رحم	*taḥannana, raḥima*
pivot (n)	محور، مدار	*miḥwar, madār*
pivot (v)	أدار على محور	*adāra 'alā miḥwar*
pivotal (adj)	محوري، مركزي	*miḥwarī, markazī*
pizza (n)	بتزه	*batzah*
placard (n/v)	إعلان، علق إعلانا	*i'lān, 'allaqa i'lānan*
placate (v)	سكن، هدأ	*sakkana, hadda'a*
placatory (adj)	مسترضي، مهدئ	*mustarḍī, muhaddi'*
place (n)	موضع، منــزلة، منصب	*mauḍa', manzilah, manṣab*
place (v)	وضع، عرض	*waḍa'a, 'araḍa*
placid (adj)	رابط الجأش، هادئ	*rābiṭul ja'sh, hādi'*
placidity (n)	هدوء، سكون	*hudū', sukūn*
placket (n)	فتحة الثوب	*futḥatuth thaub*
plagiarism (n)	انتحال، سرقة المؤلفات	*intiḥāl, sariqatul mu'allafāt*
plagiarize,-ise (v)	انتحل المؤلفات	*intaḥalal mu'allafāt*
plague (n)	طاعون، وباء، بلية	*ṭā'ūn, wabā', baliyyah*

plague (v)	أزعج، أهلك	*az'aja, ahlaka*
plain (adj)	بسيط، مستوٍ، واضح	*basīṭ, mustawin, wāḍiḥ*
plainly (adv)	بصراحة، ببساطة	*bi ṣarāḥah, bi basāṭah*
plainness (n)	بساطة، صراحة	*basāṭah, ṣarāḥah*
plaint (n)	شكوى، رثاء	*shakwā, rithā'*
plaintiff (n)	مدعٍ، شاكٍ	*mudda'in, shākin*
plaintive (adj)	شاكٍ، كئيب	*shākin, ka'īb*
plaintiveness (n)	شكوًى، رثاء	*shakwā, rithā'*
plan (n)	خطة، رسم	*khuṭṭah, rasm*
plan (v)	خطط، رسم	*khaṭṭaṭa, rasama*
plane (n)	طيارة، فأرة النجار	*ṭayyārah, fa'ratun najjār*
plane (adj)	مستوٍ، ممهد	*mustawin, mumahhad*
plane (v)	طار، ارتفع	*ṭāra, irtafa'a*
planet (n)	كوكب سيار	*kaukab sayyār*
planetary (adj)	سياري، مختص بالسيارات	*sayyārī, mukhtaṣṣ bis sayyārāt*
plank (n)	لوح خشب، بند رئيسي	*lauḥu khashab, band ra'īsī*
plank (v)	طرح، ألقى	*ṭaraḥa, alqā*
plant (n)	نبتة، غرسة، مصنع	*nabtah, gharsah, maṣna'*
plant (v)	غرس، رسخ	*gharasa, rassakha*
plantation (n)	زرع، مزرعة	*zar', mazra'ah*
planter (n)	مزارع	*muzāri'*
plaque (n)	صفيحة معدنية	*ṣafīḥah ma'diniyyah*
plasm (plasma)	مصل الدم، بلازما	*maṣlud dam, balāzmā*
plaster (n)	جص، ملاط	*jiṣṣ, milāṭ*
plaster (v)	جصص، ألصق	*jaṣṣaṣa, alṣaqa*
plasterboard (n)	لوح جصي	*lauḥ jiṣṣī*
plaster cast (n)	قالب جصي	*qālib jiṣṣī*
plastic (n)	لدن، بلاستيك	*ladn, balāstīk*

plastic (adj)	بلاستيكي، لين	*balāstīkī, layyin*
plasticine (n)	لدائنية	*ladā'iniyyah*
plastic surgery	جراحة تعويضية	*jirāḥah ta'wīḍiyyah*
plate (v)	طبق، صحن، صفيحة	*ṭabaq, ṣaḥn, ṣafīḥah*
plate (v)	طلى، صفح	*ṭalā, ṣaffaḥa*
plateau (n)	نجد، نشز	*najd, nashz*
plateful (adj)	ملء صحن	*mil'u ṣaḥn*
platelet (n)	صفيحة	*ṣafīḥah*
platform (n)	رصيف، منصة	*raṣīf, minaṣṣah*
plating (n)	تمويه، تصفيح	*tamwīh, taṣfīḥ*
platinum (n)	بلاتين، ذهب أبيض	*balātīn, dhahab abyaḍ*
platitude (n)	تفاهة، سخافة	*tafāhah, sakhāfah*
platiudinous (adj)	مبتذل، تافه	*mubtadhil, tāfih*
platonic (adj)	عذري، طاهر، افلاطوني	*'udhrī, ṭāhir, aflāṭūnī*
platoon (n)	عصبة، فصيلة	*'uṣbah, faṣīlah*
plaudit (n)	مدح، تصفيق استحساني	*madḥ, taṣfīq istiḥsānī*
plausibility (n)	استصواب، معقولية	*istiṣwāb, ma'qūliyyah*
plausible (adj)	مستصوب، معقول	*mustaṣwab, ma'qūl*
play (n)	ألعوبة، تمثيل، لعب	*ul'ūbah, tamthīl, la'ib*
play (v)	لعب، مثل، عزف	*la'iba, maththala, 'azafa*
playboy (n)	شخص مستهتر	*shakhṣ mustahtir*
player (n)	لاعب، ممثل	*lā'ib, mumaththil*
playfellow (n)	رفيق اللعب	*rafīqul la'ib*
playful (adj)	لعوب، ملاعب	*la'ūb, mulā'ib*
playfulness (n)	ملاعبة	*mulā'abah*
playground (n)	ملعب، ساحة	*mal'ab, sāḥah*
playhouse (n)	مسرح	*masraḥ*
playing-card (n)	ورقة اللعب	*waraqatul la'ib*
playing-field (n)	ملعب رياضي	*mal'ab riyāḍī*

playmate (n)	زميل اللعب	*zamīlul la'ib*
playroom (n)	حجرة اللعب	*ḥujratul la'ib*
plaything (n)	لعبة، ألعوبة	*lu'bah, ul'ūbah*
playtime (n)	وقت اللعب	*waqtul la'ib*
playwright (n)	كاتب مسرحي	*kātib masraḥī*
plea (n)	التماس، دعوى، حجة	*iltimās, da'wā, ḥujjah*
plead (v)	توسل، التمس	*tawassala, iltamasa*
pleadings (n)	مرافعة، مدافعة	*murāfa'ah, mudāfa'ah*
pleasant (adj)	لطيف، سار، بهيج	*laṭīf, sārr, bahīj*
pleasantly (adv)	بابتهاج، بسرور	*bibtihāj, bi surūr*
pleasantness (n)	سرور، ابتهاج، لطف	*surūr, ibtihāj, luṭf*
pleasantry (n)	مزاح، هزل	*muzāḥ, hazl*
please (v)	سر، أعجب	*sarra, a'jaba*
please (interj)	من فضلك	*min faḍlik*
pleased (adj)	راضٍ، مسرور	*rāḍin, masrūr*
pleasing (adj)	سار، مرضٍ	*sārr, murḍin*
pleasurable (adj)	مرضٍ، سار	*murḍin, sārr*
pleasure (n)	ابتهاج، سرور، ملذ	*ibtihāj, surūr, maladhdh*
pleat (n/v)	طية، طوى	*ṭayyah, ṭawā*
plebeian (adj/n)	عادي، عامي	*'ādī, 'āmī*
plebiscite (n)	استفتاء عام	*istiftā' 'āmm*
pledge (n)	عهد، رهن	*'ahd, rahn*
pledge (v)	وعد، رهن	*wa'ada, rahana*
plenary (adj)	تام، كامل	*tāmm, kāmil*
plenipotentiary (n)	سفير مفوض	*safīr mufawwaḍ*
plenteous (adj)	وافر، شبعان	*wāfir, shab'ān*
plenteously (adv)	بوفرة، بكثرة	*bi wafrah, bi kathrah*
plentiful (adj)	وافر، مثمر، غزير	*wāfir, muthmir, ghazīr*
plentifully (adv)	بوفرة، بغزارة	*bi wafrah, bi ghazārah*
plenty (pron)	وفرة، غزارة	*wafrah, ghazārah*

plenty (adv)	بوفرة، كثيراً	*bi wafrah, kathīran*
plethora (n)	زيادة، كثرة	*ziyādah, kathrah*
pleurisy (n)	ذات الجنب	*dhātul jamb*
pliability (n)	لدونة، مرونة	*ludūnah, murūnah*
pliable (adj)	مرن، لدن، سمج	*marin, ladn, samj*
pliancy (n)	مرانة، ملاءمة	*marānah, mulā'amah*
pliant (adj)	مرن، لين، طوي	*marin, layyin, ṭawī*
pliantly (adv)	بمرونة	*bi murūnah*
pliers (n)	زردية، كماشة صغيرة	*zaradiyyah, kammāshah ṣaghīrah*
plight (n)	ورطة، تعهد	*warṭah, ta'ahhud*
plight (v)	تعهد، خطب	*ta'ahhada, khaṭaba*
plod (v)	تهادى، سار ببطء	*tahādā, sāra bi baṭ'*
plosive (adj)	انفجاري	*infijārī*
plot (n)	مكيدة، قطعة أرض، رسم بياني	*makīdah, qiṭ'atụ arḍ, rasm bayānī*
plot (v)	تآمر، كاد، رسم	*ta'āmara, kāda, rasama*
plough (plow) (n)	محراث، جرافة	*miḥrāth, jarrāfah*
plough (plow) (v)	حرث، عزق	*ḥaratha, 'azaqa*
ploughman (n)	فلاح، حارث	*fallāḥ, ḥārith*
ploughshare (n)	شفرة المحراث	*shafratul miḥrāth*
ploy (n)	خداع، حيلة	*khidā', ḥīlah*
pluck (v)	قطف، نتف	*qaṭafa, natafa*
pluck (n)	شجاعة، جراءة	*shajā'ah, jarā'ah*
plucky (adj)	جسور، جريء	*jasūr, jarī'*
plug (n)	سدادة، قابس	*sidādah, qābis*
plug (v)	سد، أطلق	*sadda, aṭlaqa*
plum (n)	برقوق	*barqūq*
plumage (n)	ريش الطائر	*rīshuṭ ṭā'ir*
plumb (n)	فادن، رصاصة	*fādin, raṣāṣah*

plumb (v)	فحص، احتبر	*faḥaṣa, iḥtabara*
plumb (adv)	تماماً، كاملاً	*tamāman, kāmilan*
plumber (n)	سمكري، سباك	*samkarī, sabbāk*
plumbing (n)	رصاصة	*riṣāṣah*
plumb-line (n)	خط عمودي	*khaṭṭ 'amūdī*
plume (n)	ريش، شرف	*rīsh, sharaf*
plummet (n)	ثقل الفادن	*thiqalul fādin*
plump (adj)	بدين، ريان	*badīn, rayyān*
plump (v)	سمن، امتلأ	*samina, imtala'a*
plumpness (n)	سمنة، امتلاء الجسم	*simnah, imtilā'ul jism*
plunder (v)	نهب، سلب	*nahaba, salaba*
plunder (n)	سلب، نهب	*salb, nahb*
plunderer (n)	ناهب، قاطع الطريق	*nāhib, qāṭi'uṭ ṭarīq*
plunge (v)	غاص، أقحم	*ghāṣa, aqḥama*
plunge (n)	غوصة، اقتحام	*ghauṣah, iqtiḥām*
plunger (n)	غاطس، كباس	*ghāṭis, kabbās*
plunk (n)	نقرة، ضربة شديدة	*naqrah, ḍarbah shadīdah*
plural (n/adj)	جمع، جمعي	*jam', jam'ī*
pluralism (n)	تعددية	*ta'addudiyyah*
pluralist (n)	مؤيد التعددية	*mu'ayyidut ta'addudiyyah*
plurality (n)	تعدد، تجمع	*ta'addud, tajammu'*
plus (adj/n)	زائد، إضافي، إيجابي	*zā'id, iḍāfī, ījābī*
plus (prep)	أيضاً، بالإضافة	*aiḍan, bil iḍāfah*
plush (n)	بلش	*balsh*
plushiness (n)	فخامة، امتياز	*fakhāmah, imtiyāz*
plushy (adj)	مترف، فخم، بلشى	*mutrif, fakhm, balshī*
Pluto (n)	أفلوطن، بلوتو	*aflūṭun, bulūtū*
plutocracy (n)	حكومة الأغنياء	*ḥukūmatul aghniyā'*
plutocratic (adj)	متعلق بحكومة الأغنياء	*muta'alliq bi ḥukūmatil aghniyā'*
ply (n)	رقيقة، طية	*raqīqah, ṭayyah*

ply (v)	كد، ثابر	*kadda, thābara*
pneumatic (adj)	مملوء بالهواء	*mamlū' bil hawā'*
pneumonia (n)	ذات الرئة	*dhātur ri'ah*
poach (v)	سرق الصيد، انتهك	*saraqaṣ ṣaid, intahaka*
pock (n)	بثرة، جدرة	*bathrah, judrah*
pocked (adj)	مبثر	*mubaththar*
pocket (n)	جيب، كيس	*jaib, kīs*
pocket (v)	وضع في جيب	*waḍa'a fī jaib*
pocket-book (n)	محفظة الجيب	*mihfaẓatul jaib*
pocketful (adj)	ملء جيب	*mil'u jaib*
pocket-money (n)	مصروف الجيب	*maṣrūful jaib*
pod (n)	قرنة	*qurnah*
poem (n)	قصيدة، شعر	*qaṣīdah, shi'r*
poet (n)	شاعر	*shā'ir*
poetess (n)	شاعرة	*shā'irah*
poetic-al (adj)	شعري، تخيلي	*shi'rī, takhayyulī*
poetic justice	عدالة خيالية	*'adālah khayāliyyah*
poetic license	جواز شعري	*jawāz shi'rī*
poet laureate	شاعر البلاط	*shā'irul balāṭ*
poetry (n)	شعر، قصيدة	*shi'r, qaṣīdah*
pogrom (n)	قتل مخطط	*qatl mukhaṭṭaṭ*
poignancy (n)	حدة، صرامة	*ḥiddah, ṣarāmah*
poignant (adj)	أليم، شديد، حاد	*alīm, shadīd, ḥādd*
point (n)	نقطة، طرف، حافة	*nuqṭah, ṭaraf, ḥāffah*
point (v)	دل، أشار	*dalla, ashāra*
pointed (adj)	محدد، مدبب	*muḥaddad, mudabbab*
pointer (n)	مؤشرة	*mu'ashshirah*
pointless (adj)	مغفل، تافه	*mughaffal, tāfih*

pointlessness (n)	تفاهة، حماقة	*tafāhah, ḥamāqah*
poise (v)	وازن	*wāzana*
poise (n)	توازن، وزن	*tawāzun, wazn*
poison (n/v)	سم، سمم	*summ, sammama*
poisonous (adj)	سام، مهلك	*sāmm, muhlik*
poisonously (adv)	بطريق مهلك	*bi ṭarīq muhlik*
poke (v)	وخز، حرك، لكز	*wakhaza, ḥarraka, lakaza*
poke (n)	لكزة، وخزة	*lakzah, wakhzah*
poker (n)	مسعر، بوكر	*mis'ar, būkar*
pokiness (n)	ضيق	*ḍīq*
poky (adj)	ضيق، صغير	*ḍayyiq, ṣaghīr*
polar (adj)	قطبي	*quṭbī*
polarity (n)	قطبية، تناقض	*quṭbiyyah, tanāquḍ*
polarization (n)	استقطاب	*istiqṭāb*
polarize,-ise (v)	استقطب	*istaqṭaba*
polaroid (n)	مستقطبة	*mustaqṭabah*
pole (n)	قطب، قائمة، عمود	*quṭb, qā'imah, 'amūd*
pole-axe (n)	فأس الحرب	*fa'sul ḥarb*
polemic (adj/n)	جدلي، نقد عنيف	*jadalī, naqd 'anīf*
polemics (n)	فن المجادلة	*fannul mujādalah*
polemist (n)	مجادل، مناظر	*mujādil, munāẓir*
police (n)	رجال الشرطة	*rijālush shurṭah*
police (v)	حافظ، احترز	*ḥāfaẓa, iḥtaraza*
policeman (n)	شرطي	*shurṭī*
police station (n)	مخفر الشرطة	*mukhfarush shurṭah*
policy (n)	تدبير، حكمة، سياسة	*tadbīr, ḥikmah, siyāsah*
polish (v)	لمع، صقل	*lamma'a, ṣaqala*
polish (n)	صقل، جلاء	*ṣaql, jalā'*
Polish (adj)	بولندي	*būlandī*
Polish (n)	لغة بولندية	*lughah būlandiyyah*

polished (adj)	مصقول، مهذب	*maṣqūl, muhadhdhab*
polite (adj)	مهذب، مؤدب	*muhadhdhab, mu'addab*
politely (adv)	بكياسة، بلطف	*bi kiyāsah, bi luṭf*
politeness (n)	تهذيب، كياسة	*tahdhīb, kiyāsah*
politic (adj)	لبق، فطن	*labiq, faṭin*
political (adj)	سياسي	*siyāsī*
political science	علم السياسة	*'ilmus siyāsah*
politician (n)	رجل السياسة	*rajulus siyāsah*
politicize,-ise (v)	سيس	*sayyasa*
politics (n)	علم السياسة	*'ilmus siyāsah*
polity (n)	نظام الحكومة	*niẓāmul ḥukūmah*
poll (n)	اقتراع، جدول انتخاب	*iqtirā', jadwalu intikhāb*
poll (v)	اقترع، نال الأصوات	*iqtara'a, nālal aṣwāt*
pollard (v)	قطع غصون الشجرة	*qaṭa'a ghuṣūnash shajarah*
pollen (n)	لقح، طلع	*laqaḥ, ṭal'*
pollinate (v)	أبر، لقح	*abbara, laqqaḥa*
pollination (n)	تلقيح، تأبير	*talqīḥ, ta'bīr*
pollster (n)	مستفتي	*mustaftī*
poll-tax (n)	ضريبة الرؤوس	*ḍarībatur ru'ūs*
pollutant (adj)	ملوث، مجنس	*mulawwith, mujannis*
pollute (v)	دنس، نجس	*dannasa, najjasa*
pollution (n)	دنس، تجنس	*danas, tajnīs*
polo (n)	لعبة الكرة، بولو	*lu'batul kurah, būlū*
polonaise (n)	رقصة بولندية	*raqṣah būlandiyyah*
polyandrous (adj)	متعدد الأزواج	*muta'addidul azwāj*
polyandry (n)	تعدد الأزواج، تعدد الأسدية	*ta'addudul azwāj, ta'addudul asdiyah*
polygamist (n)	مؤيد تعدد الزوجات	*mu'ayyidu ta'addudiz zaujāt*
polygamous (adj)	متعدد الزوجات	*muta'addiduz zaujāt*

polygamy (n)	تعدد الزوجات	*ta'adduduz zaujāt*
polyglot (n)	متكلم بلغات متعددة	*mutakallim bi lughāt muta'addidah*
playglot (adj)	متعدد اللغات	*muta'addidul lughāt*
polygon (n)	متعدد الزوايا	*muta'addiduz zawāyā*
polyhedral (adj)	متعدد الجوانب	*muta'addidul jawānib*
polymorphous (adj)	متعدد الأشكال	*muta'addidul ashkāl*
polyphonic (adj)	متعدد الأصوات	*muta'addidul aṣwāt*
polysyllabic (adj)	متعدد المقاطع	*muta'addidul maqāṭi'*
polysyallable (n)	لفظ متعدد المقاطع	*kalimah muta'addidatul maqāṭi'*
polytechnic (n)	متعدد الفنون	*muta'addidul funūn*
polytheism (n)	شرك	*shirk*
polytheist (n)	مشرك	*mushrik*
polytheistic (adj)	متعلق بشرك	*muta'alliq bi shirk*
pomander (n)	كرة عطرية	*kurah 'iṭriyyah*
pomegranate (n)	رمان	*rummān*
pommel (n)	عجرة، رمانة	*'ujrah, rummānah*
pomp (n)	أبهة، عظمة	*ubbahah, 'aẓamah*
pomposity (n)	تباهٍ، غرور	*tabāhin, ghurūr*
pompous (adj)	متباهٍ، أبهي	*mutabāhin, ubbahī*
pompously (adv)	بتباهٍ، بغرور	*bi tabāhin, bi ghurūr*
pond (n)	بركة، فسقية	*birkah, fasqiyah*
ponder (v)	تأمل، تروى	*ta'ammala, tarawwā*
ponderous (adj)	ثقيل، ممل	*thaqīl, mumill*
ponderously (adv)	بتثاقل	*bi tathāqul*
ponderousness (n)	تثاقل، ثقالة	*thatāqul, thaqālah*
pontiff (n)	أسقف	*usquf*
pontifical (adj)	حبري، أسقفي	*ḥabrī, usqufī*

pontificate (n)	منصب الحبر	*manṣabul ḥabr*
pony (n)	حصان صغير	*ḥiṣān ṣaghīr*
poodle (n)	كلب جعد الشعر	*kalb ja'dush sha'r*
poof (poofter)	متخنث، لوطي	*mutakhannith, lūṭī*
pooh (interj)	أف	*uff*
pool (n)	غدير، بركة، مراهنة	*ghadīr, birkah, murāhanah*
poolroom (n)	مكتب المراهنة	*maktabul murāhanah*
poop (n)	مؤخر السفينة	*mu'akhkharus safīnah*
poor (n)	مسكين، فقير، ضعيف	*miskīn, faqīr, ḍa'īf*
poor-box (n)	صندوق الصدقات	*ṣundūquṣ ṣadaqāt*
poorly (adj)	ضعيف، هزيل	*ḍa'īf, hazīl*
poor-spirited (adj)	جبان، رديء	*jabān, radī'*
pop (n)	أنشودة شعبية، فرقعة	*unshūdah sha'biyyah, farqa'ah*
pop (v)	فرقع، فقع	*farqa'a, faqa'a*
popcorn (n)	فشار	*fushār*
Pope (n)	رأس الكنيسة، بابا	*ra'sul kanīsah, bābā*
pop eyed (adj)	جاحظ العينين	*jāḥiẓul 'ainain*
popgun (n)	بندقية الهواء	*bunduqiyyatul hawā'*
popish (adj)	باباوي، كاثوليكي	*bābāwī, kāthūlīkī*
poplar (n)	شجر الحور	*shajarul ḥaur*
poplin (n)	قماش قطني	*qumāsh quṭnī*
poppet (n)	دليل، عزيز	*dalīl, 'azīz*
poppy (adj)	خشخاش	*khashkhāsh*
poppycock (n)	هراء، لغو	*hurā', laghw*
populace (n)	عوام، جمهور	*'awām, jumhūr*
popular (adj)	محبوب، مألوف	*maḥbūb, ma'lūf*
popular front (n)	جبهة شعبية	*jabhah sha'biyyah*
popularity (n)	شهرة، شعبية	*shuhrah, sha'biyyah*

popularization (n)	تبسيط، إشهار	*tabsīṭ, ishhār*
popularize,-ise (v)	أشيع، أشهر	*ashya'a, ashhara*
populate (v)	سكن، أهل	*sakana, ahhala*
population (n)	عدد السكان، تعمير	*'adadus sukkān, ta'mīr*
populous (adj)	عامر، مزدحم	*'āmir, muzdaḥim*
porcelain (n)	خزف صيني	*khazaf ṣīnī*
porch (n)	سدة الباب، شرفة	*suddatul bāb, shurfah*
porcine (adj)	خنـــزيري	*khinzīrī*
pore (v)	تمعن، تأمل	*tama''ana, ta'ammala*
pore (n)	مسام	*masām*
pork (n)	لحم الخنـــزير	*laḥmul khinzīr*
porker (n)	خنوص مسمن	*khinnauṣ musamman*
pornographic (adj)	فاحش، إباحي	*fāḥish, ibāḥī*
pornography (n)	صورة داعرة	*ṣūrah dā'irah*
porosity (n)	مسامية	*masāmiyyah*
porosness = porosity		
porous (adj)	مسامي، نفيذ	*masāmī, nafīdh*
porphyry (n)	حجر سماقي	*ḥajar sumāqī*
porridge (n)	ثريد	*tharīd*
port (n)	ميناء، مرفأ، قيافة	*mīnā', marfa', qiyāfah*
portable (adj/n)	قابل للنقل	*qābil lin naql*
portage (n)	نقل، حمل	*naql, ḥaml*
portal (n)	مدخل، باب	*madkhal, bāb*
portend (v)	تنبأ، توعد	*tanabba'a, tawa''ada*
portent (n)	تنبؤ، إنذار	*tanabbu', indhār*
portentous (adj)	منذر بالسوء	*mundhir bis sū'*
porter (n)	حمال، بواب	*ḥammāl, bawwāb*
porterage (n)	عتالة، شيالة	*'itālah, shiyālah*
porterhouse (n)	حانة	*ḥānah*
portfolio (n)	محفظة أوراق، وزارة	*miḥfaẓatu aurāq, wizārah*

portico (n)	رواق معمد	*riwāq mu'ammad*
portion (n)	جزء، حصة	*juz', ḥiṣṣah*
portion (v)	وزع، قسم	*wazza'a, qassama*
portliness (n)	سمن، ضخامة	*siman, ḍakhāmah*
portly (adj)	جليل، صخيم	*jalīl, ḍakhīm*
portrait (n)	صورة، رسم، وصف	*ṣūrah, rasm, waṣf*
portraitist (n)	مصور	*muṣawwir*
portraiture (n)	فن التصوير	*fannut taṣwīr*
portray (v)	صور، وصف	*ṣawwara, waṣafa*
portrayal (n)	رسم، وصف	*rasm, waṣf*
pose (v)	استوضع، تصنع	*istauḍa'a, taṣanna'a*
pose (n)	مسئلة مربكة	*mas'alah murbikah*
poseur (n)	متكلف، مصطنع	*mutakallif, muṣṭani'*
posh (adj)	رائع، أنيق	*rā'i', anīq*
posit (v)	ادعى، افترض	*idda'ā, iftaraḍa*
position (n)	وضع، حالة	*waḍ', ḥālah*
positive (adj)	إيجابي، واقعي	*ījābī, wāqi'ī*
positively (adv)	في الحقيقة	*fil ḥaqīqah*
positivism (n)	وضعية	*waḍ'iyyah*
positivist (n)	مؤيد الوضعية	*mu'ayyidul waḍ'iyyah*
posse (n)	جماعة، عصابة	*jamā'ah, 'iṣābah*
possess (v)	امتلك، اقتنى	*imtalaka, iqtanā*
possession (n)	امتلاك، استيلاء	*imtilāk, istīlā'*
possessive (adj)	اقتنائي، امتلاكي	*iqtinā'ī, imtilākī*
possessive (n)	صيغة مضاف إليه	*ṣīghatu muḍāf ilaih*
possessor (n)	مالك، حائز	*mālik, ḥā'iz*
possibility (n)	امكانية، احتمال	*imkāniyyah, iḥtimāl*
possible (adj)	ممكن، محتمل	*mumkin, muḥtamal*
possibly (adv)	يمكن، يحتمل	*yumkin, yuḥtamal*
post (n)	دعامة، بريد، وظيفة	*di'āmah, barīd, waẓifah*

post (v)	أرسل بالبريد، نشر	*arsala bil barid, nashara*
postage (n)	أجرة البريد	*ujratul barīd*
postage stamp	طابع بريدي	*ṭāba' barīdī*
postal (adj)	بريدي	*barīdī*
postal card (n)	بطاقة بريدية	*biṭāqah barīdiyyah*
post-box (n)	صندوق البريد	*ṣundūqul barīd*
postcard (n)	بطاقة بريدية	*biṭāqah barīdiyyah*
post-date (v)	أخر التاريخ	*akhkharat tārīkh*
poster (n)	إعلان ملصق	*i'lān mulṣaq*
posterior (adj)	خلفي، متخلف	*khalfī, mutakhallif*
posterior (n)	كفل، عجيزة	*kafal, 'ajīzah*
posterity (n)	ذرية، خلف	*dhurriyyah, khalaf*
postern (n)	مدخل خلفي	*madkhal khalfī*
postgraduate (n)	ماجستير	*mājistīr*
posthumous (adj)	تالٍ لوفاة المرء	*tālin li wafātil mar'*
posthumously (adv)	بعد وفاة المرء	*ba'da wafātil mar'*
postman (n)	ساعي البريد	*sā'il barīd*
postmark (n)	ختم البريد	*khatmul barīd*
postmaster (n)	مدير مكتب البريد	*mudīru maktabil barīd*
postmistress (n)	مديرة مكتب البريد	*mudīratu maktabil barīd*
postmortem (adj)	تالٍ للحادثة	*tālin lil ḥādithah*
postmortem (n)	فحص جثة الميت	*faḥṣu juththatil mait*
postnatal (adj)	بعد الولادة	*ba'dal wilādah*
postnuptial (adj)	بعد الزواج	*ba'daz zawāj*
post office (n)	مكتب البريد	*maktabul barīd*
postpone (v)	أجل، أخر	*ajjala, akhkhara*
postponement (n)	تأجيل، إرجاء	*ta'jīl, irjā'*
postscript (n)	ملحق، ذيل	*mulḥaq, dhail*
postulant (n)	شخص مرشح	*shakhṣ murashshaḥ*
postulate (v/n)	سلم، شيء مسلم	*sallama, shay' musallam*

postulation (n)	تسليم، افتراض	*taslīm, iftirāḍ*
posture (n)	وضع، وضعة	*waḍ‘, waḍ‘ah*
posture (v)	توضع، اصطنع	*tawaḍḍa‘a, iṣṭana‘a*
post-war (adj)	بعد الحرب	*ba‘dal ḥarb*
posy (n)	باقة الأزهار	*bāqatul azhār*
pot (n)	قدر، علبة، أصيص	*qidr, ‘ulbah, aṣīṣ*
pot (v)	غرس في أصيص	*gharasa fī aṣīṣ*
potable (adj)	صالح للشرب	*ṣāliḥ lish shurb*
potassium (n)	بوتاسيوم	*būtāsiyūm*
potation (n)	شرب، شربة	*shurb, sharbah*
potato (n)	بطاطس	*baṭāṭis*
potato chip (n)	رقاقة بطاطسية	*ruqāqah baṭāṭisiyyah*
potency (n)	قوة، تأثير، نفوذ	*quwwah, ta’thīr, nufūdh*
potent (adj)	قوي، مؤثر	*qawī, mu’aththir*
potentate (n)	حاكم، مالك	*ḥākim, mālik*
potential (n)	إمكان، احتمال	*imkān, iḥtimāl*
potential (adj)	محتمل، إمكاني	*muḥtamal, imkānī*
potentially (adv)	بالقوة	*bil quwwah*
potently (adv)	بقوة	*bi quwwah*
potion (n)	جرعة، شربة	*jur‘ah, sharbah*
potter (n/v)	خزاف، تجول	*khazzāf, tajawwala*
pottery (n)	خزف، خزافة	*khazaf, khizāfah*
potty (adj)	حقير، ضئيل	*ḥaqīr, ḍa’īl*
pouch (n)	كيس، جيب، جراب	*kīs, jaib, jirāb*
poulterer (n)	بائع الدجاج	*bā’i‘ud dajāj*
poultry (n)	طيور داجنة	*ṭuyūr dājinah*
pounce (n)	هجوم مفاجئ	*hujūm mufāji’*
pounce (v)	انقض على، هجم	*inqaḍḍa ‘alā, hajama*
pound (n)	جنيه انكليزي، زريبة	*junaih inkilīzī, zarībah*
pound (v)	دق، سحق، قرع	*daqqa, saḥaqa, qara‘a*

poundage (n)	عمولة	*'umūlah*
pour (v)	سكب، صب	*sakaba, ṣabba*
pout (v)	بوز	*bawwaza*
pout (n)	تبويز، تجهم، عبس	*tabwīz, tajahhum, 'abas*
poverty (n)	فقر، فاقة	*faqr, fāqah*
poverty-stricken (adj)	فقير، مسكين	*faqīr, miskīn*
powder (n)	بارود، ذرور	*barūd, dharūr*
powder (v)	ذر، سحق	*dharra, saḥaqa*
powder-magazine (n)	مستودع البارود	*mustauda'ul bārūd*
power (n)	طاقة، سلطة، قوة	*ṭāqah, sulṭah, quwwah*
powerful (adj)	قوي، قدير	*qawiyy, qadīr*
powerfully (adv)	بقوة، بسلطة	*bi quwwah, bi sulṭah*
power house	محطة توليد الكهرباء	*maḥaṭṭatu taulīdil kahrabā'*
powerless (adj)	عديم القوة، ضعيف	*'adīmul quwwah, ḍa'īf*
power politics (n)	سياسة القوة	*siyāsatul quwwah*
power station = power house		
pox (n)	مرض نفاطي	*maraḍ nifāṭī*
practicability (n)	إمكانية الإجراء	*imkāniyyatul ijrā'*
practicable (adj)	ممكن إجراءه	*mumkin ijrā'uh*
practical (adj)	عملي، إجرائي	*'amalī, ijrā'ī*
practically (adv)	عمليًا	*'amaliyyan*
practice (n)	ممارسة، تمرين	*mumārasah, tamrīn*
practician = practitioner		
practise (v)	تدرب، مارس	*tadarraba, mārasa*
practitioner (n)	صاحب مهنة	*ṣāḥibu mihnah*
pragmatic (adj)	ذرائعي، عملي	*dharā'i'ī, 'amalī*
pragmatism (n)	ذرائعية، عملية	*dharā'i'iyyah, 'amaliyyah*
pragmatist (n)	عملي، ذرائعي	*'amalī, dharā'i'ī*
prairie (n)	مرج، ديسة	*marj, daisah*

praise (v)	أثنى، حمد	*athnā, ḥamida*
praise (n)	ثناء، حمد، مدح	*thanā', ḥamd, madḥ*
praiseworthy (adj)	جدير بالثناء	*jadīr bith thanā'*
pram (n)	عربة يد	*'arabatu yad*
prance (v)	وثب، طفر	*wathaba, ṭafara*
prance (n)	وثبة، طفرة	*wathbah, ṭafrah*
prank (n)	مزاح	*muzāḥ*
prate (v)	هذر، ثرثر	*hadhara, tharthara*
prattle (n)	ثرثرة الأطفال	*thartharatul aṭfāl*
pray (v)	صلى، ابتهل	*ṣallā, ibtahala*
prayer (n)	دعاء، صلاة	*du'ā', ṣalāt*
prayer-book (n)	كتاب الصلوات	*kitābuṣ ṣalawāt*
preach (v)	وعظ، نصح	*wa'aẓa, naṣaḥa*
preacher (n)	واعظ، ناصح	*wā'iẓ, nāṣiḥ*
preamble (n)	مقدمة، تمهيد	*muqaddamah, tamhīd*
prearrange (v)	رتب مقدماً	*rattaba muqaddaman*
prebend (n)	وقف كنسي	*waqf kanasī*
precarious (adj)	غير مستقر، متقلقل	*ghair mustaqirr, mutaqalqil*
precaution (n)	احتراس، احتياط	*iḥtirās, iḥtiyāṭ*
precautionary (adj)	وقائي، تحفظي	*wiqā'ī, taḥaffuẓī*
precautious (adj)	متحرس، متحوط	*mutaḥarris, mutaḥawwiṭ*
precede (v)	سبق، تقدم	*sabaqa, taqaddama*
precedence (n)	تقدم، أسبقية	*taqaddum, asbaqiyyah*
precedent (adj)	سابق، متقدم	*sābiq, mutaqaddim*
precept (n)	سنة، سلوك، أخلاق	*sunnah, sulūk, akhlāq*
preceptor (n)	معلم، مهذب	*mu'allim, muhadhdhib*
precession (n)	مبادرة، تقدم	*mubādarah, taqaddum*
precinct (n)	إقليم، منطقة	*iqlīm, minṭaqah*
preciosity (n)	حذلقة، تكلف	*ḥadhlaqah, takalluf*

precious (adj)	ثمين، كريم، نفيس	*thamīn, karīm, nafīs*
preciousness (n)	قيمة، نفاسة	*qīmah, nafāsah*
precipice (n)	هوة، جرف	*huwwah, juruf*
precipitate (n)	مترسب، متسرع	*mutarassib, mutasarri'*
precipitate (adj)	متهور، طائش	*mutahawwir, ṭā'ish*
precipitate (v)	عجل، طوح	*'ajjala, ṭawaḥa*
precipitately (adv)	بتهور، بعجلة	*bi tahawwur, bi 'ajalah*
precipitation (n)	تهور، تسرع	*tahawwur, tasarru'*
precipitous (adj)	شديد الانحدار	*shadīdul inḥidār*
precis (n)	خلاصة، ملخص	*khulāṣah, mulakhkhaṣ*
precise (adj)	محكم، دقيق، مضبوط	*muḥkam, daqīq, maḍbūṭ*
precisely (adv)	بدقة، بإحكام	*bi diqqah, bi iḥkām*
preciseness (n)	إحكام، ضبط	*iḥkām, ḍabṭ*
preclude (n)	عاق، حال	*'āqa, ḥāla*
preclusion (n)	عائق، منع	*'ā'iq, man'*
preclusive (adj)	مانع، عائق	*māni', 'ā'iq*
precocity (n)	نضج قبل الوقت	*naḍj qablal waqt*
precocious (adj)	مبكر النشوء	*mubakkirun nushū'*
precociousness (n)	نشوء قبل أوانه	*nushū' qabla awānihi*
precognition (n)	تبصر قبل الوقوع	*tabaṣṣur qablal wuqū'*
preconceived (adj)	متصور مقدماً	*mutaṣawwar muqaddaman*
preconception (n)	رأي مقدم	*ra'y muqaddam*
precondition (n)	شرط مسبق	*sharṭ musabbaq*
precurson (n)	نذير، طليعة	*nadhīr, ṭalī'ah*
predator (n)	حيوان مفترس	*ḥaiwān muftaris*
predatory (adj)	مفترس، جارح	*muftaris, jāriḥ*
predecease (v)	مات قبل الوقت	*māta qablal waqt*
predecessor (n)	جد، سلف	*jadd, salaf*
predestination (n)	قضاء، قدر	*qaḍā', qadr*
predestine (v)	قدر، قضى	*qaddara, qaḍā*

predeterminate (v)	حتم، قضى	*ḥattama, qaḍā*
predetermination (n)	قضاء وقدر	*qaḍā' wa qadr*
predicament (n)	ورطة، ارتباك	*warṭah, irtibāk*
predicate (n)	خبر، مسند	*khabar, musnad*
predicate (v)	أعلن، أظهر	*a'lana, aẓhara*
predicative (adj)	إسنادي، خبري	*isnādī, khabarī*
predict (v)	تنبأ، تكهن	*tanabba'a, takahhana*
predictable (adj)	قابل للتنبؤ	*qābil lit tanabbu'*
prediction (n)	تنبؤ، تكهن	*tanabbu', takahhun*
predictor (n)	متنبئ، كاهن	*mutanabbi', kāhin*
predigest (v)	هضم	*haḍḍama*
predilection (n)	ولوع، ميل	*walū', mail*
predispose (v)	هيأ، عرض	*hayya'a, 'arraḍa*
predisposition (n)	تهيؤ، ميل	*tahayyu', mail*
predominant (adj)	مسيطر، غالب	*musaiṭir, ghālib*
predominate (v)	غلب، استعلى	*ghalaba, ista'lā*
pre-eminence (n)	استعلاء، تفوق	*isti'lā', tafawwuq*
pre-eminent (adj)	فائق، متفوق	*fā'iq, mutafawwiq*
pre-empt (v)	احتل، امتلك قبل...	*iḥtalla, imtalaka qabla…*
pre-emption (n)	حق الشفعة	*ḥaqqush shuf'ah*
pre-emptive (adj)	شفعي، وقائي	*shuf'ī, wiqā'ī*
pre-exist (v)	وجد من قبل	*wujida min qabl*
pre-existence (n)	وجود من قبل	*wujūd min qabl*
pre-existent (adj)	كائن من قبل	*kā'in min qabl*
prefabricate (v)	صنع مقدمًا	*ṣana'a muqaddaman*
preface (n)	مقدمة، تمهيد	*muqaddamah, tamhīd*
prefatory (adj)	تمهيدي، افتتاحي	*tamhīdī, iftitāḥī*
prefect (n)	والي	*wālī*
prefecture (n)	ولاية، مقاطعة تحت والٍ	*wilāyah, muqāṭa'ah taḥta wālin*
prefer (v)	فضل، ميز، آثر	*faḍḍala, mayyaza, āthara*

preferable (adj)	أفضل، أحب	*afḍal, aḥabb*
preferably (adv)	على سبيل التفضيل	*'alā sabīlit tafḍīl*
preference (n)	تفضيل، خيار	*tafḍīl, khiyār*
preferential (adj)	تفضيلي، تمييزي	*tafḍīlī, tamyīzī*
preferment (n)	تفضيل، ترقية	*tafḍīl, tarqiyah*
prefigure (v)	تصور قبل الوقوع	*taṣawwara qablal wuqū'*
prefix (n)	بادئة، أداة تصدير	*bādi'ah, adātu taṣdīr*
prefix (v)	صدر كلمةً بوصلة	*ṣaddara kalimatan bi wuṣlah*
pregnancy (n)	حبل، حمل	*ḥabal, ḥaml*
pregnant (adj)	حبلى، مفعم	*ḥublā, muf'am*
prehensile (adj)	ممسك، إمساكي	*mumsik, imsākī*
prehension (n)	إمساك، قبض	*imsāk, qabḍ*
prehistoric (adj)	واقع قبل التاريخ	*wāqi' qablat tārīkh*
prehistory (n)	ما قبل التاريخ	*mā qablat tārīkh*
prejudge (v)	حكم مقدماً	*ḥakama muqaddaman*
prejudice (n)	تغرض، تحيز	*tagharruḍ, taḥayyuz*
prejudice (v)	غرض، أجحف	*gharraḍa, ajḥafa*
prejudiced (adj)	متحيز	*mutaḥayyīz*
prejudicial (adj)	مؤذٍ، مضر	*mu'dhin, muḍirr*
prelacy (n)	منصب الأسقف	*manṣabul usquf*
prelate (n)	أسقف، مدير الكنيسة	*usquf, mudīrul kanīsah*
preliminary (adj)	ابتدائي، تمهيدي	*ibtidā'ī, tamhīdī*
preliminary (n)	اختبار تمهيدي	*ikhtibār tamhīdī*
prelude (n)	استهلال، تمهيد	*istihlāl, tamhīd*
premarital (adj)	واقع قبل الزواج	*wāqi' qablaz zawāj*
premature (adj)	معجل، ناضج قبل الأوان	*mu'ajjal, nāḍij qablal awān*
premeditate (v)	تدبر، تعمد	*tadabbara, ta'ammada*

premeditation (n)	تروّ، تعمد	*tarawwin, ta'ammud*
premier (adj)	أول، أسبق	*awwal, asbaq*
premier (n)	رئيس الوزراء	*ra'īsul wuzarā'*
premiership (n)	رئاسة الوزارة	*ri'āsatul wizārah*
premise (n)	مقدمة منطقية	*muqaddamah manṭiqiyyah*
premises (n)	مباني تابعة لمنـــزل	*mabānī tābi'ah li manzil*
premium (n)	قسط، مكافأة	*qisṭ, mukāfa'ah*
premonition (n)	تحذير قبل الحدوث	*taḥdhīr qablal ḥudūth*
premonitory (adj)	تحذيري، تنبيهي	*taḥdhīrī, tambīhī*
pre-natal (adj)	حادث قبل الولادة	*ḥādith qablal wilādah*
preoccupation (n)	امتلاك مقدم	*imtilāk muqaddam*
preoccupied (adj)	مشغول، منهمك	*mashghūl, munhamik*
preoccupy (v)	شغل مقدماً	*shaghala muqaddaman*
pre-ordain (v)	قضى مقدماً	*qaḍā muqaddaman*
preparation (n)	إعداد، استعداد	*i'dād, isti'dād*
preparatory (adj)	إعدادي، تحضيري	*i'dādī, taḥḍīrī*
prepare (v)	هيأ، أعد	*hayya'a, a'adda*
prepared (adj)	مستعد، مهيأ	*musta'id, muhayya'*
preparedness (n)	استعداد، تهيؤ	*isti'dād, tahayyu'*
prepay (v)	دفع مقدماً	*dafa'a muqaddaman*
prepayment (n)	دفع مقدم	*daf' muqaddam*
preponderance (n)	تغلب، أكثرية	*taghallub, akthariyyah*
preponderant (adj)	وافر، غالب	*wāfir, ghālib*
preponderantly (adv)	بكثرة، بأرجحية	*bi kathrah, bi arjaḥiyyah*
preponderate (v)	رجح، ناف على	*rajaḥa, nāfa 'alā*
preposition (n)	حرف جر	*ḥarfu jarr*
prepositional (adj)	متعلق بحرف جر	*muta'alliq bi ḥarfi jarr*
prepossessing (adj)	جذاب، خلاب	*jadhdhāb, khallāb*
preposterous (adj)	مناف للعقل	*munāfin lil 'aql*

pre-record (v)	سجل مقدمًا	*sajjala muqaddaman*
prerequisite (adj/n)	لازم، شرط	*lāzim, sharṭ*
prerogative (n)	حق، امتياز	*ḥaqq, imtiyāz*
presage (n)	علامة، نذير	*'alāmah, nadhīr*
presage (v)	تنبأ	*tanabba'a*
pre-school (adj)	خاص بما قبل المدرسة	*khāṣṣ bimā qablal madrasah*
prescience (n)	علم بالغيب	*'ilm bil ghaib*
prescient (adj)	عالم بالغيب	*'ālim bil ghaib*
prescribe (v)	أمر، قضى	*amara, qaḍā*
prescription (n)	وصفة، أمر، قانون	*waṣfah, amr, qānūn*
prescriptive (adj)	مكتسب بطول المدة	*muktasab bi ṭūlil muddah*
presence (n)	حضور، وجود	*ḥuḍūr, wujūd*
presence of mind	حضور الذهن	*ḥuḍūrudh dhihn*
present (adj)	حاضر، موجود	*ḥāḍir, maujūd*
present (n)	وقت حاضر، هدية	*waqt ḥāḍir, hadiyyah*
present (v)	قدم، منح	*qaddama, manaḥa*
presentable (adj)	صالح للعرض	*ṣāliḥ lil 'arḍ*
presentation (n)	عرض، تقديم	*'arḍ, taqdīm*
presentiment (n)	شعور سابق	*shu'ūr sābiq*
presently (adj)	حالاً، توًّا	*ḥālan, tawwan*
preservation (n)	وقاية، صيانة	*wiqāyah, ṣiyānah*
preservative (adj)	صائن، واق	*ṣā'in, wāqin*
preserve (v)	صان، حفظ	*ṣāna, ḥafiẓa*
preserve (n)	شيء محفوظ	*shay' maḥfūẓ*
preside (v)	رأس، تصدر	*ra'asa, taṣaddara*
presidency (n)	رئاسة، مدة الرئاسة	*ri'āsah, muddatur ri'āsah*
president (n)	رئيس، مدير	*ra'īs, mudīr*
presidential (adj)	رئاسي	*ri'āsī*
press (n)	مكبسة، مطبعة، صحافة	*mikbasah, miṭba'ah, ṣiḥāfah*
press (v)	ضغط، عصر، كوى	*ḍaghaṭa, 'aṣara, kawā*

press agency	وكالة الإعلان	*wakālatul i'lān*
press agent	وكيل الإعلان	*wakīlul i'lān*
press-box (n)	مقصورة الصحافة	*maqṣūratuṣ ṣiḥāfah*
press conference	مؤتمر صحفي	*mu'tamar ṣuḥufī*
press gallery	مقصورة الصحفيين	*maqṣūratuṣ ṣuḥufiyyīn*
press release	مسبقة صحيفة	*musabbaqah ṣuḥufiyyah*
pressure (n)	ضغط، إلحاح، شدة	*ḍaghṭ, ilḥāḥ, shiddah*
pressure-cooker (n)	قدر ضغطية	*qidr ḍaghṭiyyah*
pressure group	جماعة الضغط	*jamā'atuḍ ḍaghṭ*
pressurization (n)	تكييف الضغط	*takyīfuḍ ḍaghṭ*
pressurize,-ise (v)	كيف الضغط	*kayyafaḍ ḍaghṭ*
prestige (n)	هيبة، كرامة، مقام	*haibah, karāmah, maqām*
prestigious (adj)	ذو مقام عال	*dhū maqām 'ālin*
presumable (adj)	ممكن تخمينه	*mumkin takhmīnuh*
presumably (adv)	على سبيل الافتراض	*'alā sabīlil iftirāḍ*
presume (v)	افترض، اجترأ	*iftaraḍa, ijtara'a*
presumption (n)	تحدس، تخمين	*taḥaddus, takhmīn*
presumptive (adj)	تخميني، افتراضي	*takhmīnī, iftirāḍī*
presumptuous (adj)	مجترئ، مدعٍ	*mujtari', mudda'in*
presumptuously (adv	بجراءة	*bi jarā'ah*
presuppose (v)	افترض مقدماً	*iftaraḍa muqaddaman*
presupposition (n)	افتراض مقدم	*iftirāḍ muqaddam*
pretend (v)	تظاهر، ادعى	*taẓāhara, idda'ā*
pretender (n)	متظاهر، مدعي	*mutaẓāhir, mudda'ī*
pretension (n)	دعوى، حجة	*da'wā, ḥujjah*
pretentious (adj)	مدعٍ، متعجرف	*mudda'in, muta'ajrif*
preterite (adj/n)	ماضي، سالف	*māḍī, sālif*
preternatural (adj)	غير طبيعي، شاذ	*ghair ṭabī'ī, shādhdh*
preternaturally (adv)	بطريق غير سوي	*bi ṭarīq ghair sawī*

pretext (n)	عذر، حجة	*'udhr, ḥujjah*
prettify (v)	جمل، زين	*jammala, zayyana*
prettily (adv)	بجمال، بحسن	*bi jamāl, bi ḥusn*
prettiness (n)	جمال، حسن، لطف	*jamāl, ḥusn, luṭf*
pretty (adj)	جميل، لطيف	*jamīl, laṭīf*
prevail (v)	تغلب، ساد	*taghallaba, sāda*
prevailing (adj)	سائد، متغلب	*sā'id, mutaghallib*
prevalence (n)	تفشٍّ، تغلب	*tafashshin, taghallub*
prevalent (adj)	غالب، عام	*ghālib, 'āmm*
prevaricate (v)	وارب، غبن	*wāraba, ghabana*
prevarication (n)	مواربة، غبن	*muwārabah, ghabn*
prevent (v)	منع، وقى	*mana'a, waqā*
preventable (adj)	يمكن منعه	*yumkin man'uh*
prevention (n)	منع، وقاية	*man', wiqāyah*
preventive (adj)	مانع، واقٍ	*māni', wāqin*
preview (n)	مشاهدة مسبقة	*mushāhadah musabbaqah*
previous (adj)	سابق، سالف	*sābiq, sālif*
previously (adv)	سابقاً، من قبل	*sābiqan, min qabl*
pre-war (adj)	واقع قبل الحرب	*wāqi' qablal ḥarb*
prey (v/n)	افترس، فريسة	*iftarasa, farīsah*
price (v)	سعر، حدد الثمن	*sa''ara, ḥaddadath thaman*
price (n)	ثمن، سعر	*thaman, si'r*
price-list (n)	قائمة الأسعار	*qā'imatul as'ār*
prick (v)	نخس، وخز	*nakhasa, wakhaza*
prick (n)	وخزة، ثقب	*wakhzah, thuqb*
prickle (n)	وخزة، شوكة	*wakhzah, shaukah*
prickly (adj)	شائك، كثير الشوك	*shā'ik, kathīrush shauk*
pride (n)	عجب، كبرياء	*'ujb, kibriyā'*
pride (v)	تكبر، افتخر	*takabbara, iftakhara*

priest (n)	قسيس، كاهن	*qissīs, kāhin*
priestess (n)	قسيسة، كاهنة	*qissīsah, kāhinah*
priesthood (n)	كهنوت، قسوسة	*kahanūt, qusūsah*
priestly (adj)	كهنوتي، اكليركي	*kahanūtī, iklīrikī*
prig (n)	مغتر بنفسه	*mughtarr bi nafsih*
prim (adj)	متأنق، متزمت	*muta'anniq, mutazammit*
primacy (n)	أولية	*awwaliyyah*
prima facie (adj)	بديهي	*badīhī*
primal (adj)	بدائي، أساسي	*bidā'ī, asāsī*
primarily (adv)	أولاً، في الأصل	*awwalan, fil aṣl*
primary (adj)	أولي، ابتدائي	*awwalī, ibtidā'ī*
primary school	مدرسة ابتدائية	*madrasah ibtidā'iyyah*
primate (n)	أسقف كبير	*usquf kabīr*
prime (adj)	رئيسي، أصلي	*ra'īsī, aṣlī*
prime (n)	شباب، صدر، شرخ	*shabāb, ṣadr, sharkh*
prime (v)	أعد، زود	*a'adda, zawwada*
prime cost	ثمن أصلي	*thaman aṣlī*
prime minister	رئيس الوزراء	*ra'īsul wuzarā'*
primer (n)	كتاب للمبتدئين	*kitāb lil mubtadi'īn*
primeval (adj)	بدائي، عتيق جدا	*bidā'ī, 'atīq jiddā*
primitive (adj)	بدائي، أصلي	*bidā'ī, aṣlī*
primordial (adj)	أساسي، بدائي	*asāsī, bidā'ī*
primordially (adv)	في البداية	*fil bidāyah*
primp (v)	بالغ في التزيين	*bālagha fit tazyīn*
primrose (n)	زهرة الربيع	*zahratur rabī'*
prince (n)	أمير، ابن الملك	*amīr, ibnul malik*
princely (adj)	نبيل، أميري	*nabīl, amīrī*
prince of wales	أمير ويلز	*amīru wīlz*
prince royal	ولي العهد	*waliyyul 'ahd*
princess (n)	أميرة	*amīrah*

principal (adj/n)	مدير، رئيس	*mudīr, ra'īs*
principality (n)	منصب المدير	*manṣabul mudīr*
principally (adv)	خصوصاً، ولا سيما	*khuṣūṣan, walā siyyamā*
principal parts	صيغ رئيسية	*ṣiyagh ra'īsiyyah*
principle (n)	قاعدة، منشأ	*qā'idah, mansha'*
principled (adj)	صاحب مبادئ	*ṣāḥibu mabādi'*
print (n)	طبعة، أثر	*ṭab'ah, athar*
print (v)	طبع، بصم	*ṭaba'a, baṣama*
printable (adj)	صالح للطبع	*ṣāliḥ liṭ ṭab'*
printer (n)	آلة طابعة	*ālah ṭābi'ah*
printing (n)	طباعة، طبعة	*ṭibā'ah, ṭab'ah*
printing-press (n)	آلة طابعة	*ālah ṭābi'ah*
printout (n)	نسخة مطبوعة	*nuskhah maṭbū'ah*
prior (adj)	سابق، متقدم	*sābiq, mutaqaddim*
prior (n)	رئيس دير	*ra'īsu dair*
priority (n)	أولية، تقدم	*awwaliyyah, taqaddum*
prison (n)	سجن، حبس	*sijn, ḥabs*
prisoner (n)	أسير، محبوس	*asīr, maḥbūs*
prison of war	أسير الحرب	*asīrul ḥarb*
pristine (adj)	بدائي، أولي	*bidā'ī, awwalī*
privacy (n)	خفاء، عزلة	*khafā', 'uzlah*
private (adj)	سري، شخصي، خاص	*sirrī, shakhṣī, khaṣṣ*
privateer (n)	مركب القرصنة	*markabul qarṣanah*
privately (adv)	سرًا، في الخفاء	*sirran, fil khafā'*
privation (n)	فاقة، عوز	*fāqah, 'auz*
privatize,-ise (v)	خصص	*khaṣṣaṣa*
privilege (n)	امتياز، حق ممتاز	*imtiyāz, ḥaqq mumtāz*
privileged (adj)	ممتاز، سري	*mumtāz, sirrī*
privily (adv)	سرًا، بصورة شخصية	*sirran, bi ṣūrah shakhṣiyyah*
privy (adj)	سري، خاص	*sirrī, khāṣṣ*

prize (n)	جائزة، منحة	*jā'izah, minḥah*
prize (adj)	جدير بجائزة	*jadīr bi jā'izah*
prize (v)	أعز، ثمن	*a'azza, thammana*
pro (n)	محترف	*muḥtarif*
probability (n)	احتمال، إمكانية	*iḥtimāl, imkāniyyah*
probable (adj)	محتمل، مرجح	*muḥtamal, murajjaḥ*
probably (adv)	من المحتمل	*minal muḥtamal*
probate (n)	إثبات، امتحان	*ithbāt, imtiḥān*
probation (n)	تدقيق، تحقيق	*tadqīq, taḥqīq*
probationer (n)	ممرضة تحت تجربة	*mumarriḍah taḥta tajribah*
probe (v)	جس، امتحن	*jassa, imtaḥana*
probe (n)	جس، تحقيق، مسبار	*jass, taḥqīq, misbār*
probing (adj)	جاس، ممتحن	*jāss, mumtaḥin*
probity (n)	نزاهة، أمانة	*nazāhah, amānah*
problem (n)	مسئلة مشكلة	*mas'alah mushkilah*
problematic-al (adj)	مشكل، شائك	*mushkil, shā'ik*
procedural (adj)	نهجي، إجرائي	*nahjī, ijrā'ī*
procedure (n)	نهج، إجراء	*nahj, ijrā'*
proceed (v)	تقدم، سار، واصل	*taqaddama, sāra, wāṣala*
proceedings (n)	إجراءات، حوادث	*ijrā'āt, ḥawādith*
proceeds (n)	عملية، منوال	*'amaliyyah, minwāl*
process (v)	عامل، سار في موكب	*'āmala, sāra fī maukib*
procession (n)	موكب، زفة	*maukib, zaffah*
processional (adj)	موكبي، احتفالي	*maukibī, iḥtifālī*
proclaim (v)	أعلن، أذاع	*a'lana, adhā'a*
proclamation (n)	إعلان، تصريح	*i'lān, taṣrīḥ*
proclivity (n)	ميل، انحدار	*mail, inḥidār*
procrastinate (v)	أجل، أمهل	*ajjala, amhala*
procreate (v)	أنتج، ولد	*antaja, walada*

procreation (n)	إنتاج، إنجاب	*intāj, injāb*
proctor (n)	مناظر، مراقب	*munāẓir, murāqib*
procure (v)	نال، حصل على	*nāla, ḥaṣala 'alā*
procurement (n)	حصول، نيل	*ḥuṣūl, nail*
procurer (n)	قواد، وقح	*qawwād, waqiḥ*
prod (v/n)	نخس، منخاس	*nakhasa, minkhās*
prodigal (adj/n)	مسرف، شخص مسرف	*musrif, shakhṣ musrif*
prodigality (n)	إسراف، تبذير	*isrāf, tabdhīr*
prodigious (adj)	ضخم، كبير جدا	*ḍakhm, kabīr jiddā*
prodigy (n)	ولد استثنائي	*walad istithnā'ī*
produce (v)	أنتج، أثمر	*antaja, athmara*
produce (n)	نتاج، محصول	*nitāj, maḥṣūl*
producer (n)	منتج، مبرز، مخرج	*muntij, mubriz, mukhrij*
product (n)	محصول، نتاج	*maḥṣūl, nitāj*
production (n)	إنتاج، محصول	*intāj, maḥṣūl*
productive (adj)	منتج، محدث	*muntij, muḥdith*
productivity (n)	إنتاجية	*intājiyyah*
profanation (n)	تجديف، انتهاك الحرمة	*tajdīf, intihākul ḥurmah*
profane (v)	جدف، انتهك	*jaddafa, intahaka*
profane (adj)	تجديفي، تدنيسي	*tajdīfī, tadnīsī*
profanity (n)	انتهاك الحرمة، تدنيس	*intihākul ḥurmah, tadnīs*
profess (n)	ادعى، اعترف	*idda'ā, i'tarafa*
professed (adj)	معترف، متظاهر به	*mu'taraf, mutaẓāhar bih*
professedly (adv)	صراحةً، علانيةً	*ṣarāḥatan, 'alāniyyatan*
profession (n)	مهنة، حرفة، إقرار	*mihnah, ḥirfah, iqrār*
professional (adj)	حرفي، فني	*ḥirafī, fannī*
professional (n)	محترف، صاحب المهنة	*muḥtarif, ṣāḥibul mihnah*
professionalism (n)	احترافية، حرفانية	*iḥtirāfiyyah, ḥirfāniyyah*
professionally (adv)	بطريق احترافي	*bi ṭarīq iḥtirāfī*
professor (n)	أستاذ كلية أو جامعة	*ustādhu kulliyyah au jāmi'ah*
professorial (adj)	مختص بأستاذ	*mukhtaṣṣ bi ustādh*

professorship (n)	منصب الأستاذ	*manṣabul ustādh*
proffer (v/n)	عرض، عرض	*'araḍa, 'arḍ*
proficiency (n)	براعة، تفوق	*barā'ah, tafawwuq*
proficient (adj)	بارع، حاذق	*bāri', ḥādhiq*
proficiently (adv)	ببراعة، بمهارة	*bi barā'ah, bi mahārah*
profile (n)	مظهر جانبي	*maẓhar jānibī*
profit (v)	انتفع، اكتسب	*intafa'a, iktasaba*
profit (n)	ربح، فائدة	*ribḥ, fā'idah*
profitable (adj)	مفيد، مكسب	*mufīd, muksib*
profiteer (v)	استغل	*istaghalla*
profligacy (n)	هتك، فجور	*tahattuk, fujūr*
profligate (adj)	فاجر، متهتك	*fājir, mutahattik*
pro forma (adj)	صوري	*ṣuwarī*
profound (adj)	عميق، متبحر	*'amīq, mutabaḥḥir*
profoundity (n)	عمق، غموض	*'umq, ghumūḍ*
profoundly (adv)	على نحو عميق	*'alā naḥwin 'amīq*
profuse (adj)	وافر، غزير، كثير	*wāfir, ghazīr, kathīr*
profusely (adv)	بغزارة، بكثرة	*bi ghazārah, bi kathrah*
profuseness (n)	غزارة، وفرة	*ghazārah, wafrah*
profusion=profuseness		
progenitor (n)	جد، سلف	*jadd, salaf*
progeny (n)	ذرية، خلف	*dhurriyah, khalaf*
prognosticate (v)	أنذر، تنبأ	*andhara, tanabba'a*
programme (program)	برنامج، لائحة	*barnāmaj, lā'iḥah*
programme (v)	خطط، برمج	*khaṭṭaṭa, barmaja*
progress (v)	ارتقى، تقدم	*irtaqā, taqaddama*
progress (n)	رقي، تقدم	*ruqiyy, taqaddum*
progression (n)	تقدم، تدرج	*taqaddum, tadarruj*
progressive (adj)	متصاعد، متقدم	*mutaṣā'id, mutaqaddim*

progressively (adv)	تقدميًا، تصاعديًا	*taqaddumiyyan, taṣā'udiyyan*
progressiveness (n)	تصاعدية، تقدمية	*taṣā'udiyyah, taqaddumiyyah*
prohibit (v)	حظر، منع	*ḥaẓara, mana'a*
prohibition (n)	حظر، تحريم	*ḥaẓr, taḥrīm*
prohibitive (adj)	تحريمي، تحظيري	*taḥrīmī, taḥẓīrī*
prohibitory (adj)	محرم، حظري	*muḥarrim, ḥaẓrī*
project (n)	مشروع، تدبير، خطة	*mashrū', tadbīr, khuṭṭah*
project (v)	اختط، دبر	*ikhṭaṭṭa, dabbara*
projection (n)	اختطاط، قذف، إسقاط	*ikhtiṭāṭ, qadhf, isqāṭ*
projector (n)	مسلاط	*mislāṭ*
proletariat (n)	طبقة العمال	*ṭabaqatul 'ummāl*
proliferate (v)	تكاثر، تضاعف	*takāthara, taḍā'afa*
proliferation (n)	توالد، تكاثر	*tawālud, takāthur*
prolific (adj)	كثير الأثمار، خصيب	*kathīrul athmār, khaṣīb*
prolix (adj)	مطول، مسهب	*muṭawwil, mushib*
prolixity (n)	إسهاب	*ishāb*
prolong (v)	أطال، أسهب	*aṭāla, ashaba*
prolongation (n)	تطويل، مد	*taṭwīl, madd*
promenade (v/n)	تنــزه، نزهة	*tanazzaha, nuzhah*
prominence (n)	بروز، تفوق	*burūz, tafawwuq*
prominent (adj)	بارز، ناتئ	*bāriz, nāti'*
prominently (adv)	بسمو، ببروز	*bi sumuww, bi burūz*
promiscuity (n)	اختلاط جنسي	*ikhtilāṭ jinsī*
promiscuous (adj)	مختلط، غير شرعي	*mukhtaliṭ, ghair shar'ī*
promiscuously (adj)	بطريق غير شرعي	*bi ṭarīq ghair shar'ī*
promise (v)	وعد، تعهد	*wa'ada, ta'ahhada*
promise (n)	عهد، وعد	*'ahd, wa'd*
promising (adj)	مرجو، مأمول	*marjuww, ma'mūl*

promissory (adj)	وعدي، ارتباطي	*waʻdī, irtibāṭī*
promote (v)	رقى، روج	*raqqā, rawwaja*
promoter (n)	مرقٍ، منشئ	*muraqqin, munshi'*
promotion (v)	ترقية، ترويج	*tarqiyah, tarwīj*
promotional (adj)	تشجيعي، مرقٍ	*tashjīʻī, muraqqin*
prompt (adj)	سريع، عاجل	*sarīʻ, ʻājil*
prompt (v)	حض، استفز	*ḥaḍḍa, istafazza*
promptitude (n)	سرعة، استعداد	*surʻah, istiʻdād*
promptly (adv)	على الفور، حالاً	*ʻalal faur, ḥālan*
promptness (n)	يقظة، حزم	*yaqẓah, ḥazm*
promulgate (v)	أذاع، نشر	*adhāʻa, nashara*
promulgation (n)	إذاعة، نشر	*idhāʻah, nashr*
prone (adj)	منكب، عرضة	*mankib, ʻurḍah*
prong (n)	شعبة، شوكة	*shuʻbah, shaukah*
pronominal (adj)	ضميري	*ḍamīrī*
pronoun (n)	ضمير	*ḍamīr*
pronounce (v)	لفظ، نطق، أعلن	*lafaẓa, naṭaqa, aʻlana*
pronounceable (adj)	قابل للنطق	*qābil lin nuṭq*
pronounced (adj)	صريح، بات	*ṣarīḥ, bātt*
pronouncement (n)	قرار، بيان	*qarār, bayān*
pronunciation (n)	تلفظ، نطق	*talaffuẓ, nuṭq*
proof (n)	دليل، برهان	*dalīl, burhān*
prop (v/n)	دعم، دعامة	*daʻama, diʻāmah*
propaganda (n)	دعاية، ترويج الدعوة	*diʻāyah, tarwījud daʻwah*
propagandist (n)	داعية، ناشر الدعوة	*dāʻiyah, nāshirud daʻwah*
propagandize,-ise (v)	روج، نشر	*rawwaja, nashara*
propagate (v)	أذاع، كثر	*adhāʻa, kaththara*
propagation (n)	توليد، نشر، إذاعة	*taulīd, nashr, idhāʻah*
propagator (n)	متكاثر، متوالد	*mutakāthir, mutawālid*

propel (v)	دسر، سير	*dasara, sayyara*
propellant (propellent)	داسر، وقود داسر	*dāsir, wuqūd dāsir*
propeller (n)	مدسرة، رفاس	*midsarah, raffās*
propensity (n)	نزعة، ميل	*naz'ah, mail*
proper (adj)	مناسب، لائق، صائب	*munāsib, lā'iq, ṣā'ib*
properly (adv)	بدقة، بصحة	*bi diqqah, bi ṣiḥḥah*
proper noun	اسم علم	*ismu 'alam*
propertied (adj)	صاحب أملاك	*ṣāḥibu amlāk*
property (n)	ملكية، خاصة	*milkiyyah, khāṣṣah*
prophecy (n)	تنبؤ، نبوة	*tanabbu', nubuwwah*
prophesy (v)	تنبأ، أنبأ	*tanabba'a, amba'a*
prophet (n)	نبي	*nabī*
prophetic-al (adj)	نبوي	*nabawī*
propitiate (v)	استعطف، استرضى	*ista'ṭafa, istarḍā*
propitiation (n)	استعطاف، كفارة	*isti'ṭāf, kaffārah*
propitiatory (adj)	استعطافي، استرضائي	*isti'ṭāfī, istirḍā'ī*
propitious (adj)	صفوح، موافق	*ṣafūḥ, muwāfiq*
propitiously (adv)	بتلاءم، بتوافق	*bi talā'um, bi tawāfuq*
proponent (adj)	مؤيد، نصير	*mu'ayyid, naṣīr*
proportion (n)	جزء، نسبة	*juz', nisbah*
proportional (adj)	تناسبي	*tanāsubī*
proportionally (adv)	بتناسب	*bi tanāsub*
proportionate (adj)	متناسب	*mutanāsib*
proportionately (adv	بتناسب	*bi tanāsub*
proportioned (adj)	متناسب، متناسق	*mutanāsib, mutanāsiq*
proposal (n)	عرض، اقتراح، مشروع	*'arḍ, iqtirāḥ, mashrū'*
propose (v)	اقترح، خطب	*iqtaraḥa, khaṭaba*
propsition (n)	بيان، اقتراح، مسألة	*bayān, iqtirāḥ, mas'alah*
proposition (v)	اقترح	*iqtaraḥa*

propound (v)	قدم، عرض	*qaddama, 'araḍa*
proprietary (adj)	امتلاكي، ملكي	*imtilākī, milkī*
proprietor (n)	صاحب الملك	*ṣāḥibul milk*
proprietorial (adj)	امتلاكي، تملكي	*imtilākī, tamallukī*
propriety (n)	ملاءمة، موافقة	*mulā'amah, muwāfaqah*
propulsion (n)	دسر، دفع إلى الأمام	*dasr, daf' ilal amām*
propulsive (adj)	دسري، داسر	*dasrī, dāsir*
prorogation (n)	تأجيل البرلمان	*ta'jīlul barlamān*
prosaic (adj)	نثري، ركيك	*nathrī, rakīk*
prosaically (adv)	نثراً، ركيكاً	*nathran, rakikan*
proscribe (v)	نفى، حرم	*nafā, ḥarama*
proscription (n)	نفي، تحريم	*nafy, taḥrīm*
prose (n)	نثر	*nathr*
prosecute (v)	حاكم، تابع، والى	*ḥākama, tāba'a, wālā*
prosecution (n)	موالاة، متابعة	*muwālāt, mutāba'ah*
prosecutor (n)	مدعٍ، مثابر	*mudda'in, muthābir*
prosily (adv)	بركاكة، بابتذال	*bi rakākah, bibtidhāl*
prosiness (n)	ركاكة، ابتذال	*rakākah, ibtidhāl*
prosodic (adj)	عروضي	*'arūḍī*
prosody (n)	علم العروض	*'ilmul 'arūḍ*
prospect (n)	منظر، مظهر	*manẓar, maẓhar*
prospect (v)	راد، نقب	*rāda, naqaba*
prospective (adj)	مرجو، متوقع	*marjuww, mutawaqqa'*
prospector (n)	منقب، رائد	*munaqqib, rā'id*
prospectus (n)	نشرة، منشور	*nashrah, manshūr*
prosper (v)	ازدهر، رخا	*izdahara, rakhā*
prosperity (n)	رخاء، ازدهار	*rakhā', izdihār*
prosperous (adj)	مزدهر، ناجح	*muzdahir, nājiḥ*
prosthesis (n)	جراحة ترقيعية	*jirāḥah tarqī'iyyah*
prostitute (n)	مومس، عاهرة	*mūmis, 'āhirah*

prostitute (v)	عرض لعهارة	*'araḍa li 'ahārah*
prostitution (n)	عهارة، بغاء	*'ahārah, baghā'*
prostrate (v)	سجد، كب	*sajada, kabba*
prostrate (adj)	متمدد، منبطح	*mutamaddid, mumbaṭiḥ*
prostration (n)	سجود، كب	*sujūd, kabb*
prosy (adj)	نثري، ركيك	*nathrī, rakīk*
protagonist (n)	بطل رواية	*baṭalu riwāyah*
protean (adj)	متقلب، متلون	*mutaqallib, mutalawwin*
protect (v)	حفظ، حمى	*ḥafiẓa, ḥamā*
protection (n)	حفظ، حماية	*ḥifẓ, ḥimāyah*
protective (adj)	حامٍ، واقٍ	*ḥāmin, wāqin*
protectionism (n)	حمائية	*ḥimā'iyyah*
protectionist (n)	مؤيد الحمائية	*mu'ayyidul ḥimā'iyyah*
protector (n)	مدافع، حامٍ	*mudāfi', ḥāmin*
protectorate (n)	دولة محمية	*daulah maḥmiyyah*
protein (n)	بروتين	*burūtīn*
protest (n)	احتجاج، شكوى	*iḥtijāj, shakwā*
protest (v)	احتج، شكا	*iḥtajja, shakā*
protestanism (n)	بروتستانية	*burūtistāniyyah*
protestant (n)	بروتستاني	*burūtistānī*
protestation (n)	إعلان، تصريح	*i'lān, taṣrīḥ*
protester (n)	محتج، معترض	*muḥtajj, mu'tariḍ*
protocol (n)	اتفاقية، بروتوكول	*ittifāqiyyah, burūtūkūl*
protoplasm (n)	جبلة أولى	*jiblah ūlā*
prototype (n)	نموذج أولي	*namūdhaj awwalī*
protozoan, -zoon	برزوي	*barzawī*
protract (v)	أطال، أخر	*aṭāla, akhkhara*
protraction (n)	تأخير، إطالة	*ta'khīr, iṭālah*
protractor (n)	منقلة	*minqalah*
protrude (v)	خرج، نتأ، أخرج	*kharaja, nata'a, akhraja*
protrusion (n)	نتوء، بروز	*nutū', burūz*
protrusive (adj)	ناتئ	*nāti'*

protuberance (n)	بروز، نتوء	*burūz, nutū'*
protuberant (adj)	بارز، ناتئ	*bāriz, nāti'*
proud (adj)	متكبر، متعجرف	*mutakabbir, muta'ajrif*
proudly (adv)	بكبر، بغرور	*bi kibr, bi ghurūr*
provable (adj)	ممكن إثباته	*mumkin ithbātuh*
prove (v)	أثبت، ثبت	*athbata, thabata*
proven (adj)	مثبت، مبرهن	*muthbat, mubarhan*
provenance (n)	أصل، مصدر	*aṣl, maṣdar*
provender (n)	علف	*'alaf*
proverb (n)	مثل، قول مأثور	*mathal, qaul ma'thūr*
proverbial (adj)	مثلي، مضروب به	*mathalī, maḍrūb bih*
provide (v)	زود، وفر	*zawwada, waffara*
provided (conj)	على شرط	*'alā sharṭ*
providence (n)	تدبير، عناية	*tadbīr, 'ināyah*
provident (n)	مدبر، متحوط	*mudabbir, mutaḥawwiṭ*
providential (adj)	حادث في وقت مناسب	*ḥādith fī waqt munāsib*
province (n)	إقليم، مقاطعة	*iqlīm, muqāṭa'ah*
provincial (adj)	إقليمي، عتيق الزي	*iqlīmī, 'atīquz ziyy*
provision (n)	مؤونة، إعداد	*ma'ūnah, i'dād*
provision (v)	مأن، زود بالمؤونة	*ma'ana, zawwada bil ma'ūnah*
provisional (adj)	موقت، وقتي	*muwaqqat, waqtī*
provisory (adj)	شرطي، وقتي	*sharṭī, waqtī*
provocation (n)	إثارة، إغضاب	*ithārah, ighḍāb*
provocative (adj)	محرض، مثير	*muḥarriḍ, muthīr*
provoke (v)	استفز، أغضب	*istafazza, aghḍaba*
provoking (adj)	مثير، مستفز	*muthīr, mustafizz*
provost (n)	رئيس الكلية أو الجامعة	*ra'īsul kulliyyah awil jāmi'ah*
prowess (n)	تفوق، براعة، امتياز	*tafawwuq, barā'ah, imtiyāz*
prowl (v)	تجسس، عس	*tajassasa, 'assa*

proximate (adj)	متقارب، مجاور	*mutaqārıb, :mujāwir*
proximately (adv)	تقريباً	*taqrīban*
proximity (n)	قرب، جوار	*qurb, jiwār*
proxy (n)	وكيل، وثيقة التفويض	*wakīl, wathīqatut tafwīḍ*
prude (n)	متحشمة	*mutaḥashshimah*
prudence (n)	حكمة، بصيرة، تدبر	*ḥikmah, baṣīrah, tadabbur*
prudency (n)	احتشام متكلف	*iḥtishām mutakallaf*
prudent (adj)	متحرس، متبصر	*mutaḥarris, mutabaṣṣir*
prudish (adj)	مفرط الاحتشام	*mufriṭul iḥtishām*
prune (n)	برقوق مجفف	*barqūq mujaffaf*
prune (v)	قلم الأشجار	*qallamal ashjār*
prurience (n)	شبق، تلهف	*shabaq, talahhuf*
prurient (adj)	شبق، شهواني	*shabiq, shahwānī*
pry (v)	تفحص، تفرس	*tafaḥḥaṣa, tafarrasa*
psam (n)	ترنيمة مقدسة	*tarnīmah muqaddasa*
pseud (n)	شخص كاذب	*shakhṣ kādhib*
pseudo (adj)	زائف، كاذب	*zā'if, kādhib*
pseudonym=pen name		
psyche (n)	نفس، روح	*nafs, rūḥ*
psychedelic (adj)	مخدر	*mukhaddir*
psychiatric (adj)	مختص بطب النفس	*mukhtaṣṣ bi ṭibbin nafs*
psychiatrist (n)	طبيب أمراض النفس	*ṭabību amrāḍin nafs*
psychiatry (n)	طب النفس	*ṭibbun nafs*
psychic (adj)	نفسي، مختص بالنفس	*nafsī, mukhtaṣṣ bin nafs*
psychological (adj)	نفسي، سيكولوجي	*nafsī, sīkūlūjī*
psychologist (n)	عالم بالنفس	*'ālim bin nafs*
psychology (n)	علم النفس، سيكولوجيا	*'ilmun nafs sīkūlūjiyā*
psychopath (n)	معتوه، مضطرب العقل	*ma'tūh, muḍṭaribul 'aql*
pub (n)	خمارة، حانة	*khammārah, ḥānah*
puberty (n)	سن البلوغ	*sinnul bulūgh*
pubic (adj)	عاني، خاص بالعانة	*'ānī, khaṣṣ bil 'ānah*

public (n)	جمهور، عموم	*jumhūr, 'umūm*
public (adj)	عام، عمومي	*'ām, 'umūmī*
publican (n)	صاحب حانة	*ṣāḥibu ḥānah*
publication (n)	طبع، نشر الكتب	*ṭab', nashrul kutub*
public house	حانة، خمارة	*ḥānah, khammārah*
publicist (n)	وكيل الدعاية	*wakīlud di'āyah*
publicity (n)	شيوع، إذاعة	*shuyū', idhā'ah*
publicize,-ise (v)	أعلن، أذاع	*a'lana, adhā'a*
publicly (adv)	علانيةً، جهاراً	*'alāniyatan, jihāran*
public opinion	رأي عام	*ra'y 'āmm*
public relations	علاقات عامة	*'alāqāt 'āmmah*
public school	مدرسة عامة	*madrasah 'āmmah*
publish (v)	نشر، أذاع	*nashara, adhā'a*
publisher (n)	ناشر الكتب	*nāshirul kutub*
puckish (adj)	مزعج، مؤذي	*muz'ij, mu'dhī*
pudding (n)	بودنغ، طبق من حلوى	*būdingh, ṭabaq min ḥalwā*
puddle (n)	موحلة الماء	*mauḥalatul mā'*
pudenda (n)	فرج المرأة	*farjul mar'ah*
pudgy (adj)	بدين وقصير	*badīn wa qaṣīr*
puerile (adj)	صبياني، سخيف	*ṣibyānī, sakhīf*
puff (n)	نفخة، نفس	*nafkhah, nafas*
puff (v)	لهث، نفث	*lahatha, nafatha*
puffin (n)	بفن	*bafan*
puffy (adj)	منتفخ، بدين	*muntafikh, badīn*
pug (n)	كلب صغير	*kalb ṣaghīr*
pugilism (n)	ملاكمة	*mulākamah*
pugilist (n)	ملاكم	*mulākim*
pugnacious (adj)	مخاصم، مولع بالخصام	*mukhāṣim, mūla' bil khiṣām*
pugnicity (n)	مشاكسة، حب القتال	*mushākasah, ḥubbul qitāl*
pug-nosed (adj)	أفطس الأنف	*afṭasul anf*

pull (v)	جر، انتزع	*jarra, intaza'a*
pull down	هدم، خرب	*hadama, kharraba*
pullet (n)	دجاجة صغيرة	*dajājah ṣaghīrah*
pulley (n)	بكرة، جرارة	*bakrah, jarrārah*
pull out	انتقل، انسحب	*intaqala, insaḥaba*
pull-over	بلوفر	*balaufar*
pull up	اقتلع، أوقف	*iqtala'a, auqafa*
pulmonary (adj)	رئوي	*ri'awī*
pulp (n)	لباب، لب	*lubāb, lubb*
pulpit (n)	منبر، منصة الخطابة	*mimbar, minaṣṣatul khiṭābah*
pulsate (v)	نبض، ضرب، خفق	*nabaḍa, ḍaraba, khafaqa*
pulsation (n)	نبضة، خفقة	*nabḍah, khafqah*
pulse (v)	نبض، خفق	*nabaḍa, khafaqa*
pulse (n)	حبة، ضربة، خفقة	*ḥabbah, ḍarbah, khafqah*
pulverization (n)	سحن، سحق	*saḥn, saḥq*
pulverize,-ise (v)	سحن، سحق	*saḥana, saḥaqa*
pummel (v)	لكم	*lakama*
pummelling (n)	ضربة عنيفة، لكمة	*ḍarbah 'anīfah, lakmah*
pump (n)	مضخة، طلمبة	*miḍakhkhah, ṭulumbah*
pump (v)	ضخ، انتـــزع، سحب	*ḍakhkha, intaza'a, saḥaba*
pumpkin (n)	يقطين	*yaqṭīn*
pun (v/n)	ورى، تورية	*warrā, tauriyah*
punch (n)	مثقب، لكمة عنيفة	*mithqab, lakmah 'anīfah*
punch (v)	ثقب، ضغط	*thaqaba, ḍaghaṭa*
punctilious (adj)	دقيق، محكم	*daqīq, muḥkam*
punctiliously (adv)	بدقة، بتدقيق	*bi diqqah, bi tadqīq*
punctiliousness (n)	دقة، إحكام	*diqqah, iḥkām*
punctual (adj)	مواظب، دقيق	*muwāẓib, daqīq*
punctuality (n)	مواظبة، دقة	*muwāẓabah, diqqah*
punctually (adv)	بمواظبة	*bi muwāẓabah*
punctuate (v)	وضع علامات الوقف	*waḍa'a 'alāmātil waqf*

punctuation (n)	وضع العلامات	*waḍ'ul 'alāmāt*
punctuation mark	علامة ترقيم	*'alāmatu tarqīm*
puncture (v)	خرق، خرز	*kharaqa, kharaza*
puncture (n)	ثقب، خرق	*thuqb, khurq*
pungency (n)	حدة، حرافة	*ḥiddah, ḥarāfah*
pungent (adj)	حاد، لاذع	*ḥādd, lādhi'*
punish (v)	عاقب، عذب	*'āqaba, 'adhdhaba*
punishable (adj)	مستحق للعقاب	*mustaḥiqq lil 'iqāb*
punishment (n)	عقوبة، قصاص	*'uqūbah, qiṣāṣ*
punitive (adj)	قصاصي، عقوبي	*qiṣāṣī, 'uqūbī*
punk (n)	وقح، بغي	*waqiḥ, baghiyy*
punt (n)	بنط، قارب	*banṭ, qārib*
puny (adj)	زهيد، ضعيف	*zahīd, ḍa'īf*
pupil (n)	تلميذ، بؤبؤ العين	*tilmīdh, bu'bu'u 'ain*
puppet (n)	ألعوبة، لعبة، دمية	*ul'ūbah, lu'bah, dumyah*
puppeteer (n)	محرك الدمى	*muḥarrikud dumā*
puppetry (n)	تحريك الدمى	*taḥrīkud dumā*
puppy (n)	جرء الكلب	*jar'ul kalb*
puppy-love (n)	غرام المراهقة	*gharāmul murāhaqah*
purchase (n/v)	شراء، اشترى	*shirā', ishtarā*
purchaser (n)	مشتري	*mushtarī*
purdah (n)	حجاب، ستارة	*ḥijāb, sitārah*
pure (adj)	نقي، صافٍ، خالص	*naqiyy, ṣāfin, khāliṣ*
pure-bred (adj)	صريح النسب	*ṣarīḥun nasab*
purely (adv)	بنقاء، بصفاء	*bi naqā', bi ṣafā'*
purgation (n)	تنظيف، تسهيل البطن	*tanẓīf, tashīlul baṭn*
purgative (adj/n)	مسهل	*mushil*
purge (v)	أسهل، طهر	*ashala, ṭahhara*
purge (n)	إسهال، تطهير	*ishāl, taṭhīr*
purification (n)	تنقية، تطهير	*tanqiyah, taṭhīr*
purify (v)	طهر، نقى	*ṭahhara, naqqā*
puritan (adj)	بيوريتاني، متزمت	*biurītānī, mutazammit*

puritanism (n)	تزمت، تطهرية	*tazammut, taṭahhuriyyah*
purity (n)	صفاء، نقاء، طهارة	*ṣafā', naqā', ṭahārah*
purl (n)	خيط ذهبي	*khaiṭ dhahabī*
purloin (v)	اختلس، سلب	*ikhtalasa, salaba*
purple (adj/n)	أرجواني، أرجوان	*urjuwānī, urjuwān*
purplish (adj)	ضارب إلى الأرجوان	*ḍārib ilal urjuwān*
purport (n)	مفهوم، مفاد	*mafhūm, mufād*
purpose (n)	قصد، غرض	*qaṣd, gharaḍ*
purpose (v)	قصد، نوى	*qaṣada, nawā*
purposeful (adj)	ذو عزم	*dhū 'azm*
purposefully (adv)	بقصد، بعزيمة	*bi qaṣd, bi 'azīmah*
purposeless (adj)	بلا معنىً، بلا هدف	*bilā ma'nan, bilā hadaf*
purposelessly (adv)	بدون غاية، عبثاً	*bidūn ghāyah, 'abathan*
purr (v/n)	خرخر، خرخرة	*kharkhara, kharkharah*
purse (n)	كيس، جزدان	*kīs, juzdān*
purser (n)	ضابط المحاسبة	*ḍābiṭul muḥāsabah*
pursuance (n)	تعاقب، تتابع	*ta'āqub, tatābu'*
pursue (v)	تتبع، تعقب	*tatabba'a, ta'aqqaba*
pursuer (n)	متابع، متعقب	*mutābi', muta'aqqib*
pursuit (n)	مواصلة، متابعة	*muwāṣalah, mutāba'ah*
purvey (v)	زوّد بمؤونة	*zawwada bi ma'ūnah*
purveyance (n)	مؤن، تموين	*mu'an, tamwīn*
purveyor (n)	ممون، ميار	*mumawwin, mayyār*
purview (n)	نطاق السلطة	*niṭāqus sulṭah*
pus (n)	صديد، مدة	*ṣadīd, middah*
push (v)	ضغط، دفع	*ḍaghaṭa, dafa'a*
push (n)	ضغط، دفع	*ḍaghṭ, daf'*
push-button (adj)	ضاغط	*ḍāghiṭ*
pusher (n)	شخص نهاز للفرص	*shakhṣ nahhāz lil furaṣ*
pushing (n)	دافع، ضاغط	*dāfi', ḍāghiṭ*
push-over (n)	مهمة سهلة	*muhimmah sahlah*
pushy (adj)	نهاز للفرص	*nahhāz lil furaṣ*

pussy (n)	قطة	*qiṭṭah*
pustule (n)	بثرة، قرحة	*bathrah, qarḥah*
put (v)	وضع، حط، عرض	*waḍa'a, ḥaṭṭa, 'araḍa*
putative (adj)	مزعوم، مفترض	*maz'ūm, muftaraḍ*
put away	طرح، حجز	*ṭarraḥa, ḥajaza*
put back	عاد، رجع	*'āda, raja'a*
put down	حط، أنزل	*ḥaṭṭa, anzala*
put forward	قدم، عرض	*qaddama, 'araḍa*
put off	صد، أجل	*ṣadda, ajjala*
put on	ارتدى	*irtadā*
put out	أصدر، أخرج	*aṣdara, akhraja*
putrefy (v)	فسد، تعفن	*fasada, ta'affana*
putrescent (adj)	آسن، متعفن	*āsin, muta'affin*
putrid (adj)	فاسد، متعفن	*fāsid, muta'affin*
putt (n)	ضربة غولف	*ḍarbatu ghūlf*
puttee (n)	مسماة	*mismāt*
putter (n)	صولجان	*ṣaulajān*
putty (n)	معجون، عجينة	*ma'jūn, 'ajīnah*
put up	وضع، أقام	*waḍa'a, aqāma*
puzzle (v)	حير، أربك	*ḥayyara, arbaka*
puzzle (n)	لغز، حيرة	*lughz, ḥairah*
pygmy (n/adj)	قزم، قزمي	*qazam, qazamī*
pyorrhea (n)	التهاب اللثة	*iltihābul lithah*
pyramid (n)	هرم	*haram*
pyramidal (adj)	هرمي	*haramī*
pyre (n)	محرقة	*maḥraqah*
pyrex (n)	زجاج مقاوم للحرارة	*zujāj muqāwim lil ḥarārah*
pyrite (n)	بيريت، معدن	*bairīt, ma'din*
pyromania (n)	هوس الإحراق	*hawasul iḥrāq*
python (n)	ثعبان، أصلة	*thu'bān, aṣalah*

Q

quack (n)	مشعوذ، بطبطة	*musha'widh, baṭbaṭah*
quack (v)	بطبط، صاح	*baṭbaṭa, ṣāḥa*
quadrangle (n)	مبنى رباعي الزوايا	*mabnā rubā'iyyuz zawāyā*
quadrangular (adj)	رباعي الزوايا	*rubā'iyyuz zawāyā*
quadrant (n)	ربع دائرة، ذات الربع	*rub' dā'irah, dhātur rub'*
quadratic equation	معادلة تربيعية	*mu'ādalah tarbī'iyyah*
quadrilateral (adj/n)	رباعي الأضلاع	*rubā'īyyul aḍlā'*
quadruped (n)	حيوان رباعي الأرجل	*ḥaiwān rubā'iyyul arjul*
quadruple (adj)	رباعي، رباعية	*rubā'ī, rubā'iyyah*
quadruple (v)	تضاعف أربع مرات	*taḍā'afa arba'a marrāt*
quagmire (n)	مستنقع	*mustanqa'*
quail (n)	سلوى	*salwā*
quail (v)	ذبل، وهن	*dhabula, wahana*
quaint (adj)	أنيق، ظريف، جذاب	*anīq, ẓarīf, jadhdhāb*
quake (v)	ارتجف، اهتز	*irtajafa, ihtazza*
qualification (n)	أهلية، لياقة	*ahliyyah, liyāqah*
qualified (adj)	مؤهل، لائق	*mu'ahhal, lā'iq*
qualifier (n)	مقيد، مؤهل	*muqayyid, mu'ahhil*
qualify (v)	أهل، نعت	*ahhala, na'ata*
qualitative (adj)	كيفي، نوعي	*kaifī, nau'ī*
quality (n)	كيفية، وصف، نوع	*kaifiyyah, waṣf, nau'*
qualm (n)	غثيان، شك، ارتياب	*ghathayān, shakk, irtiyāb*
quandary (n)	ورطة، ارتباك	*warṭah, irtibāk*
quantify (v)	قاس، قدر	*qāsa, qaddara*
quantitative (adj)	مقداري، كمي	*miqdārī, kammī*
quantity (n)	كمية، مقدار	*kammiyyah, miqdār*
quantum (n)	كم	*kamm*
quarantine (n)	كرنتينا، حجر صحي	*karantīnā, ḥajr ṣiḥḥī*

quarrel (n)	نزاع، خصام	*nizā', khiṣām*
quarrel (v)	تخاصم، تشاجر	*takhāṣama, tashājara*
quarrelsome (adj)	مشاكس، متشاجر	*mushākis, mutashājir*
quarry (n/v)	محتجر، احتجر	*muḥtajar, iḥtajara*
quart (n)	كوارت	*kawārt*
quarter (n)	ربع، جهة	*rub', jihah*
quarter (v)	قسم إلى أربعة أجزاء	*qassama ilā arba'ati ajzā'*
quarterly (adj/adv)	فصلي، فصليًا	*faṣlī, faṣliyyan*
quarter session	محكمة فصلية	*maḥkamah faṣliyyah*
quartz (n)	مرو، كوارتز	*marw, kawārtz*
quash (v)	ألغى، أخمد	*alghā, akhmada*
quatrain (n)	مقطوعة رباعية	*maqṭū'ah rubā'iyyah*
quaver (v)	اهتز، ارتعش	*ihtazza, irta'asha*
quaver (n)	تهدج، اهتزاز	*tahadduj, ihtizāz*
quavery (adj)	مرتجف، متهدج	*murtajif, mutahaddij*
quay (n)	رصيف الميناء	*raṣīful mīnā'*
quayside (n)	جانب الرصيف	*jānibur raṣīf*
queasy (adj)	مغثي، مضطرب	*maghthī, muḍṭarib*
queen (n)	ملكة، فرزان	*malikah, firzān*
queen bee	ملكة النحل	*malikatun naḥl*
queen consort	زوجة الملك	*zaujatul maḷik*
queen dowager	أرملة الملك	*armalatul malik*
queenly (adj)	لائق بملكة	*lā'iq bi malikaḥ*
queen mother	ملكة والدة	*malikah wālidah*
queer (adj)	غير مألوف، غريب الأطوار	*ghair ma'lūf, gharībul aṭwār*
queerly (adv)	خلافاً للعادة	*khilāfal lil 'ādah*
quell (v)	أخمد، قمع	*akhmada, qama'a*
quench (v)	روى، أخمد	*rawā, akhmada*
querulous (adj)	متذمر، دائم الشكوى	*mutadhammir, dā'imush shakwā*
querulousness (n)	تذمر، شكوى	*tadhammur, shakwā*

query (n)	سؤال، تساءل	*su'āl, tasā'ul*
query (v)	تساءل، شك	*tasā'ala, shakka*
quest (v)	بحث، طلب	*baḥatha, ṭalaba*
quest (n)	سؤل، بحث	*su'l, baḥth*
question (n)	سؤال، قضية	*su'āl, qaḍiyyah*
question (v)	سأل، استجوب	*sa'ala, istajwaba*
questionable (adj)	مشكوك، فيه نظر	*mashkūk, fīhi naẓar*
questioner (n)	سائل	*sā'il*
question mark	علامة استفهام	*'alāmatu istifhām*
questionnaire (n)	استبيان	*istibyān*
question time	فترة الأسئلة	*fatratul as'ilah*
queue (n)	صف، رتل، طابور	*ṣaff, ratal, ṭābūr*
queue (v)	وقف في رتل	*waqafa fī ratal*
quick (adj)	سريع، حاد، حي	*sarī', ḥādd, ḥayy*
quicken (v)	سرع، أثار	*sarra'a, athāra*
quickly (adj)	بسرعة	*bi sur'ah*
quickness (n)	عجلة، سرعة، حدة	*'ajala, sur'ah, ḥiddah*
quick-tempered (adj)	سريع الغضب	*sarī'ul ghaḍab*
quick-witted (adj)	حاد الذهن	*ḥāddudh dhihn*
quiescence (n)	هدوء، طمأنينة	*hudū', ṭuma'nīnah*
quiescent (adj)	هادئ، هامد	*hādi', hāmid*
quiet (adj)	هادئ، صامت	*hādi', ṣāmit*
quiet (n)	هدوء، سكون	*hudū', sukūn*
quiet (v)	أسكت، سكن	*askata, sakkana*
quieten (v)	هدأ، سكن	*hada'a, sakkana*
quietism (n)	طمأنينة، هدوء	*ṭuma'nīnah, hudū'*
quietly (adv)	بسكون، بهدوء	*bi sukūn, bi hudū'*
quietness (n)	سكوت، هدوء	*sukūt, hudū'*
quietude (n)	هدوء، سكون	*hudū', sukūn*
quill (n)	ريشة، لفة	*rīshah, laffah*
quilt (n)	لحاف	*liḥāf*
quilt (v)	ضرب اللحاف	*ḍarrabal liḥāf*

quintessence (n)	جوهر، لب	*jauhar, lubb*
quintessential (adj)	جوهري، مثالي	*jauharī, mithālī*
quip (n)	ملاحظة ظريفة	*mulāḥaẓah ẓarīfah*
quire (n)	رزمة	*ruzmah*
quirk (n)	صفة مميزة	*ṣifah mumayyizah*
quit (v)	ترك، هجر	*taraka, hajara*
quite (adv)	تماماً، كليةً	*tamāman, kulliyyatan*
quiver (n)	ارتجاف، كنانة	*irtijāf, kinānah*
quiver (v)	ارتجف، ارتعش	*irtajafa, irta'asha*
quiz (n)	أحجية، مزاحة	*uḥjiyyah, muzāḥah*
quizzical (adj)	مزاحي، هزلي	*muzāḥī, hazlī*
quod (n)	سجن	*sijn*
quorum (n)	نصاب، عدد كافي	*niṣāb, 'adad kāfi*
quota (n)	حصة، سهم	*ḥiṣṣah, sahm*
quotable (adj)	يستشهد به	*yustashhad bih*
quotation (n)	اقتباس، فقرة مقتبسة	*iqtibās, fiqrah muqtabasah*
quotation marks	علامتا الاقتباس	*'alāmatal iqtibās*
quote (v)	اقتبس، استشهد	*iqtabasa, istashhada*
quoth (v)	قال، نطق	*qāla, naṭaqa*
quotient (n)	حاصل، خارج القسمة	*ḥāṣil, khārijul qismah*

R

rabbi (n)	حبر، ربان	*ḥabr, rabbān*
rabbinical (adj)	حبري، رباني	*ḥabrī, rabbānī*
rabbit (n)	أرنب	*arnab*
rabbity (adj)	شبيه بالأرنب	*shabīh bil arnab*
rabble (n)	حشد، جمهور	*ḥashd, jumhūr*
rabid (adj)	مصاب بالكلب، كليب	*muṣāb bil kalb, kalīb*
rabies (n)	داء الكلب	*dā'ul kalb*
race (n)	مسابقة، عرق، أصل	*musābaqah, 'irq, aṣl*

race (v)	ركض، سابق	*rakaḍa, sābaqa*
racecard (n)	برنامج سباق الخيل	*barnāmaju sibāqil khail*
racecourse (n)	ميدان سباق الخيل	*maidānu sibāqil khail*
racehorse (n)	جواد السباق	*jawādus sibāq*
racer (n)	مسابق، مشارك	*musābiq, mushārik*
race-riot (n)	فتنة عرقية	*fitnah 'irqiyyah*
race-track (n)	حلبة السباق	*ḥalbatus sibāq*
racial (adj)	عرقي، جنسي	*'irqī, jinsī*
racialism (racism)	عرقية، سلالية	*'irqiyyah, sulāliyyah*
racially (adv)	سلاليًا، عرقيًا	*sulāliyyan, 'irqiyyan*
racily (adv)	بالحيوية	*bil ḥayawiyyah*
raciness (n)	حيوية، لذع	*ḥayawiyyah, ladh'*
rack (n)	رف، مخلعة	*raff, mikhla'ah*
racket (n)	مضرب التنس، ضوضاء، خدعة	*miḍrabut tinis, ḍauḍā', khud'ah*
racket (v)	انغمس في ملذات	*inghamasa fī maladhdhāt*
racketeer (n)	مبتز	*mubtazz*
racketeering (n)	ابتزاز	*ibtizāz*
rackety (adj)	مليء بالصخب	*malī' biṣ ṣakhab*
racy (adj)	مفعم بالحيوية، لاذع	*muf'am bil ḥayawiyyah, lādhi'*
radar (n)	رادار	*rādār*
radial (adj)	شعاعي	*shu'ā'ī*
radiance (n)	شعاع، تألق	*shu'ā', ta'alluq*
radiant (adj)	لامع، مشع	*lāmi', mushi''*
radiantly (adv)	بتوهج، ببهاء	*bi tawahhuj, bi bahā'*
radiate (v)	أشع، تشعع	*asha''a, tasha''a'a*
radiation (n)	شعاع، إشعاع	*shu'ā', ish'ā'*
radiator (n)	مشيع	*mushayyi'*
radical (adj)	أصلي، جذري	*aṣlī, jadhrī*
radical (n)	شخص متطرف، راديكالي	*shakhṣ mutaṭarrif, rādīkālī*
radicalism (n)	تطرفية	*taṭarrufiyyah*

radically (adv)	راديكاليًا، جذريًا	*rādīkāliyyan, jidhriyyan*
radio (n)	راديو	*rādiyū*
radioactive (adj)	إشعاعي النشاط	*ish'ā'iyyun nashāṭ*
radio astronomy	علم الفلك الإشعاعي	*'ilmul falak al ish'ā'ī*
radio car	سيارة لاسلكية	*sayyārah lāsilkiyyah*
radio frequency	تردد اللاسلكي	*taraddudul lāsilkī*
radiography (n)	صورة بالأشعة	*ṣūrah bil ashi''ah*
radiological (adj)	راديولوجي	*rādiulūjī*
radiology (n)	طب الأشعة، راديولوجيا	*ṭibbul ashi''ah, rādiulūjiyā*
radish (n)	فجل، فجلة	*fijl, fijlah*
radium (n)	راديوم	*rādiyūm*
raffish (adj)	خليع، دنيء	*khalī', danī'*
raffishly (adv)	بوضاعة، بدناءة	*bi waḍā'ah, bi danā'ah*
raffishness (n)	وضاعة، دناءة	*waḍā'ah, danā'ah*
raft (n/v)	رمث، نقل برمث	*ramath, naqala bi ramath*
rafter (n)	رافدة	*rāfidah*
rag (n)	خرقة، مزحة	*khirqah, mazḥah*
rag (v)	سخر، كايد	*sakhira, kāyada*
rage (n)	هياج، ثورة، غيظ	*hiyāj, thaurah, ghaiẓ*
rage (v)	هاج، أغاظ	*hāja, aghāẓa*
ragged (adj)	بالٍ، ممزق، أشعث	*bālin, mumazzaq, ash'ath*
raging (adj)	هائج، ثائر	*hā'ij, thā'ir*
ragtag (n)	رث الملابس	*raththul malābis*
raid (n)	غارة، هجوم	*ghārah, hujūm*
raid (v)	أغار، هاجم	*aghāra, hājama*
raider (n)	مغير	*mughīr*
rail (n)	قضيب، سكة حديدية	*qaḍīb, sikkah ḥadīdiyyah*
railhead (n)	نهاية الخط	*nihāyatul khaṭṭ*
railing (n)	درابزين	*darābazīn*
raillery (n)	مزحة، تهكم	*mazḥah, tahakkum*

railroad (railway)	سكة حديدية	*sikkah ḥadīdiyyah*
raiment (n)	ثياب، لباس	*thiyāb, libās*
rain (n)	مطر	*maṭar*
rain (v)	أمطر، صب	*amṭara, ṣabba*
rainbow (n)	قوس قزح	*qaus quzaḥ*
rain-check (n)	شيك المطر	*shīkul maṭar*
raincoat (n)	معطف المطر	*mi'ṭaful maṭar*
raindrop (n)	قطرة مطر	*qaṭratu maṭar*
rain fall (n)	نزول المطر، هطول المطر	*nuzūlul maṭar, huṭulul maṭar*
rain forest (n)	غابة المطر	*ghābatul maṭar*
rain-gauge (n)	مقياس المطر	*miqyāsul maṭar*
rainproof (adj)	صامد للمطر	*ṣāmid lil maṭar*
rain-water (n)	ماء المطر	*mā'ul maṭar*
rainy (adj)	كثير المطر	*kathīrul maṭar*
rainy day	يوم المطر	*yawmul maṭar*
raise (v)	رفع، بعث، نهض	*rafa'a, ba'atha, nahaḍa*
raisin (n)	زبيب	*zabīb*
rake (n/v)	مدمة، دم	*midammah, damma*
rakish (adj)	خليع، سافل	*khalī', sāfil*
rakishly (adv)	بخلاعة، بوضاعة	*bi khalā'ah, bi waḍā'ah*
rakishness (n)	دناءة، خلاعة	*danā'ah, khalā'ah*
rally (n)	اجتماع حاشد	*ijtimā' ḥāshid*
rally (v)	استجمع، حث	*istajma'a, haththa*
ram (n)	كبش، منجنيق الحرب	*kabsh, manjanīqul ḥarb*
ram (v)	دك، صدم	*dakka, ṣadama*
Ramadan (n)	رمضان	*ramaḍān*
ramble (v)	تجول، تنـــزه	*tajawwala, tanazzaha*
rambling (adj)	هائم، متعرش	*hā'im, muta'arrish*
ramification (n)	تشعب، شعبة	*tasha''ub, shu'bah*
ramify (v)	تشعب، تفرع	*tasha''aba, tafarra'a*
ramp (n)	انحدار، شبوب	*inḥidār, shubūb*

rampage (n)	اهتياج، ثورة	*ihtiyāj, thaurah*
rampage (v)	اهتاج، أثار	*ihtāja, athāra*
rampant (adj)	طافر، متفشٍّ	*ṭāfir, mutafashshin*
rampart (n)	سور، حاجز	*sūr, ḥājiz*
ranch (n)	مربى الماشية	*marbal māshiyah*
rancher (n)	صاحب المربى	*ṣāḥibul marbā*
racid (adj)	زنخ، عفن	*zanikh, 'afin*
racidness (n)	زنخ، عفونة	*zanakh, 'ufūnah*
rancorous (adj)	مغل، حقود	*mughill, ḥaqūd*
rancour (rancor) (n)	ضغينة، حقد	*ḍaghīnah, ḥiqd*
randily (adv)	بشبق	*bi shabaq*
randiness (n)	شبق، غلمة	*shabaq, ghulmah*
random (adj)	عشوائي، بلا قصد	*'ashwā'ī, bilā qaṣd*
randomly (adv)	بلا قصد، خبط عشواء	*bilā qaṣd, khabṭa 'ashwā'*
randy (adj)	شبق، شهواني	*shabiq, shahwānī*
range (n)	خط، صف، مجال	*khaṭṭ, ṣaff, majāl*
range (v)	صف، نسق	*ṣaffa, nassaqa*
range-finder (n)	مقدرة المدى	*muqaddiratul madā*
ranger (n)	حارث الغابة	*ḥārithul ghābah*
rank (n)	صف، درجة، رتبة	*ṣaff, darajah, rutbah*
rank (v)	رتب، صف	*rattaba, ṣaffa*
rank (adj)	نامٍ، زنخ، تام	*nāmin, zanikh, tāmm*
rankle (v)	التهب، اعتمل	*iltahaba, i'tamala*
ransack (v)	فتش، نهب	*fattasha, nahaba*
ransom (n)	فداء، فدية	*fidā', fidyah*
ransom (v)	افتدى، حرر	*iftadā, ḥarrara*
rap (n)	طرقة، طرق	*ṭarqah, ṭarq*
rapacious (adj)	طماع، حريص، نهاب	*ṭammā', ḥarīṣ, nahhāb*
rapacity (n)	حرص، طمع للسلب	*ḥirṣ, ṭama' lis salb*
rape (n)	اغتصاب امرأة، لفت	*ightiṣābu imra'ah, lift*
rape (v)	اغتصب المرأة	*ightaṣabal mar'ah*
rapid (adj)	مستعجل، سريع	*musta'jil, sarī'*

rapidity (n)	سرعة، عجلة	*sur'ah, 'ajalah*
rapid transit	نقل سريع	*naql sarī'*
rapier (n)	مغول	*mighwal*
rapine (n)	نهب، اغتصاب	*nahb, ightiṣāb*
rapport (n)	مواءمة، علاقة ودية	*muwā'amah, 'alāqah wuddiyyah*
rapprochement (n)	إعادة العلاقات الودية	*i'ādatul 'alāqāt al wuddiyyah*
rapt (adj)	ذاهل، مستغرق، منتشٍ	*dhāhil, mustaghriq, muntashin*
rapture (n)	هيام، طرب	*hiyām, ṭarab*
rapturous (adj)	جذل، طرب	*jadhil, ṭarib*
rapturously (adv)	بطرب، بجذل	*bi ṭarab, bi jadhal*
rare (adj)	نادر، شاذ	*nādir, shādhdh*
rarefied (adj)	قليل الكثافة	*qalīlul kathāfah*
rarely (adv)	قلما، نادراً	*qallamā, nādiran*
rareness (n)	ندرة، قلة وجود	*nudrah, qillatu wujūd*
raring (adj)	تواق، متلهف	*tawwāq, mutalahhif*
rarity (n)	شيء نادر	*shay' nādir*
rascal (n)	وغد، شخص خبيث	*waghd, shakhṣ khabīth*
rascality (n)	نذالة، سفالة	*nadhālah, safālah*
rascally (adj)	خبيث، نذيل	*khabīth, nadhīl*
rash (adj)	متهور، عجول	*mutahawwir, 'ajūl*
rash (n)	طفح جلدي	*ṭafḥ jildī*
rasp (n)	مبرد، برد	*mibrad, bard*
rasp (v)	برد بالمبرد	*barada bil mibrad*
raspberry (n)	توت العليق	*tūtul 'ullaiq*
rat (n)	جرز، فأر	*juraz, fa'r*
rate (n)	سعر، قيمة	*si'r, qīmah*
rate (v)	ثمن، سعر	*thammana, sa''ara*
ratepayer (n)	دافع الضرائب	*dāfi'uḍ ḍarā'ib*
rather (adv)	بالأحرى، بالأولى	*bil aḥrā, bil aulā*

ratification (n)	تصديق، إقرار	*taṣdīq, iqrār*
ratify (v)	صدق، أجاز	*ṣaddaqa, ajāza*
rating (n)	تخمين، تقدير	*takhmīn, taqdīr*
ratio (n)	نسبة	*nisbah*
ratiocination (n)	استدلال منطقي	*istidlāl manṭiqī*
ration (n)	مؤونة، جراية	*ma'ūnah, jarāyah*
ration (v)	زود بمؤن	*zawwada bi mu'an*
rational (adj)	معقول، عقلي	*ma'qūl,'aqlī*
rationale (n)	أساس منطقي	*asās manṭiqī*
rationalism (n)	مذهب عقلي	*madhhab 'aqlī*
rationalist (n)	مؤيد لمذهب عقلي	*mu'ayyid li madhhab 'aqlī*
rationalistic (adj)	عقلاني	*'aqlānī*
rationality (n)	عقل، معقولية	*'aql, ma'qūliyyah*
rationally (adv)	بطريق معقول	*bi ṭarīq ma'qūl*
rattle (n)	خشخشة، صليل	*khashkhashah, ṣalīl*
rattle (v)	صل، خشخش	*ṣalla, khashkhasha*
rattling (adj)	سريع	*sarī'*
raucous (adj)	خشن وصاخب	*khashin wa ṣākhib*
raucousness (n)	خشونة في الصوت	*khushūnah fiṣ ṣaut*
ravage (v)	خرب، أتلف	*kharraba, atlafa*
rave (v)	هذر، هذى	*hadhara, hadhā*
rave (n)	هذر، هذاء	*hadhar, hudhā'*
ravel (v)	انتسل، حل	*intasala, ḥalla*
raven (n)	غداف	*ghudāf*
ravening (adj)	مفترس، جارح	*muftaris, jāriḥ*
raverous (adj)	شديد الجوع، مفترس	*shadīdul jū', muftaris*
ravine (n)	وهد، وادي صغير	*wahd, wadī ṣaghīr*
ravish (v)	اختطف، اغتصب	*ikhtaṭafa, ightaṣaba*
ravishing (adj)	ساحر، فاتن	*sāḥir, fātin*
raw (adj)	خام، فج، ناقص	*khām, fijj, nāqis*
raw-boned (adj)	هزيل، نحيل	*hazīl, naḥīl*

rawhide (n)	جلد غير مذبوح	*jild ghair madhbūḥ*
raw materials	مواد خام	*mawādd khām*
ray (n)	شعاع، نور	*shu'ā', nūr*
raze (v)	هدم، محق	*hadama, maḥaqa*
razor (n)	محلاق	*miḥlāq*
razzle (n)	قصف	*qaṣf*
reach (v)	وصل، بلغ، امتد	*waṣala, balagha, imtadda*
reachable (adj)	متناول اليد	*mutanāwalul yad*
react (v)	فاعل، رد الفعل	*fā'ala, raddal fi'la*
reactant (n)	مفاعل	*mufā'il*
reaction (n)	رد فعل، مقاومة	*raddu fi'l, muqāwamah*
reactionary (adj)	رجعي، مقاوم	*raj'ī, muqāwim*
reactivate (v)	نشط مرة ثانية	*nashshaṭa marratan thāniyah*
reactor (n)	مفاعل، راد الفعل	*mufā'il, rāddul fi'l*
read (v)	قرأ، درس	*qara'a, darasa*
readable (adj)	سهل القراءة	*sahlul qirā'ah*
reader (n)	قارئ، أستاذ الجامعة	*qāri', ustādhul jāmi'ah*
readership (n)	كونه أستاذاً	*kaunuhu ustādhan*
readily (adv)	باستعداد، بسهولة	*bisti'dād, bi suhūlah*
readiness (n)	استعداد، سهولة	*isti'dād, suhūlah*
reading (n)	قراءة، دراسة	*qirā'ah, dirāsah*
reading-room (n)	غرفة القراءة	*ghurfatul qirā'ah*
ready (adj)	مستعد، حاضر	*musta'idd, ḥāḍir*
ready (v)	أعد، استعد	*a'adda, ista'adda*
ready-made (adj)	جاهز، حاضر	*jāhiz, ḥāḍir*
reaffirm (v)	أكد ثانيةً	*akkada thāniyatan*
real (adj)	أصلي، حقيقي	*aṣlī, ḥaqīqī*
real state	ملك ثابت، عقار	*milk thābit, 'aqār*
realign (v)	اصطف من جديد	*iṣṭaffa min jadīd*
realism (n)	واقعية	*wāqi'iyyah*
realistic (adj)	واقعي	*wāqi'ī*

realistically (adv)	واقعيةً	*wāqi'iyyatan*
reality (n)	حقيقة، واقعة	*ḥaqīqah, wāqi'ah*
realization,-isation	إدراك، فهم	*idrāk, fahm*
realize,-ise (v)	أدرك، تعقل	*adraka, ta'aqqala*
really (adv)	في الحقيقة، حقيقةً	*fil ḥaqīqah, ḥaqīqatan*
realm (n)	مملكة، دولة	*mamlakah, daulah*
real number	عدد حقيقي	*'adad ḥaqīqī*
reap (v)	حصد، جنى	*ḥaṣada, janā*
reaper (n)	حاصد، حصادة	*ḥāṣid, ḥaṣṣādah*
reappear (v)	ظهر ثانيةً	*ẓahara thāniyatan*
rear (v)	ربى، احتضن	*rabbā, iḥtaḍana*
rear (n)	مؤخرة، عجيزة	*mu'akhkharah, 'ajīzah*
rear-admiral (n)	عميد بحري	*'amīd baḥrī*
rearmost (adj)	أخير	*akhīr*
rearrange (v)	رتب ثانيةً	*rattaba thāniyatan*
rearwards (adv)	إلى الخلف	*ilal khalf*
reason (n)	سبب، عقل، إدراك	*sabab, 'aql, idrāk*
reason (v)	فكر، حاج	*fakkara, ḥājja*
reasonable (adj)	سديد، معقول	*sadīd, ma'qūl*
reasonableness (n)	معقولية	*ma'qūliyyah*
reasoned (adj)	مقنع بالحجة	*muqna' bil ḥujjah*
reasoning (n)	تفكر، حجة	*tafakkur, ḥujjah*
reassurance (n)	إعادة التأمين	*i'ādatut ta'mīn*
reassure (v)	أعاد التأمين	*a'ādat ta'mīn*
rebate (n)	إسقاط، تنــزيل	*isqāṭ, tanzīl*
rebel (n)	متمرد، ثائر	*mutamarrid, thā'ir*
rebel (v)	تمرد، عصى	*tamarrada, 'aṣā*
rebellion (n)	تمرد، ثورة	*tamarrud, thaurah*
rebellious (adj)	متمرد، ثائر	*mutamarrid, thā'ir*
rebirth (n)	ولادة جديدة	*wilādah jadīdah*
reborn (adj)	متجدد	*mutajaddid*
rebound (n)	رد، ارتد	*radda, irtadda*

rebound (v)	ارتداد، نط	*irtidād, naṭṭ*
rebuff (v)	رفض، رد	*rafaḍa, radda*
rebuff (n)	رفض، رد	*rafḍ, radd*
rebuild (v)	بنى ثانيةً	*banā thāniyatan*
rebuke (v)	زجر، وبخ	*zajara, wabbakha*
rebuke (n)	توبيخ، زجر	*taubīkh, zajr*
rebut (v)	رد التهمة	*raddat tuhmah*
rebuttal (n)	رد، إرجاع	*radd, irjā'*
recall (v/n)	استدعى، استدعاء	*istad'ā, istid'ā'*
recant (v)	جحد، أنكر	*jaḥada, ankara*
recantation (n)	ارتداد، جحد	*irtidād, jaḥd*
recapitulate (v)	لخص، اختصر	*lakhkhaṣa, ikhtaṣara*
recapitulation (n)	خلاصة، اختصار	*khulāṣah, ikhtiṣār*
recapture (v/n)	استرد، استرداد	*istaradda, istirdād*
recast (v)	جدد، أعاد الصياغة	*jaddada, a'ādaṣ ṣiyāghah*
recede (v)	تراجع، تنحى	*tarāja'a, tanaḥḥā*
receipt (n)	إيصال، استلام	*īṣāl, istilām*
receivable (adj)	مرتقب، مقبول	*murtaqab, maqbūl*
receive (v)	تلقى، استقبل	*talaqqā, istaqbala*
received (adj)	مقبول، مستلم	*maqbūl, mustalam*
receiver (n)	مستلم، سماعة التلفون	*mustalim, sammā'atut tilifūn*
recent (adj)	حديث، حالي	*ḥadīth, ḥālī*
recently (adv)	حديثاً، حالياً	*ḥadīthan, ḥāliyan*
receptacle (n)	وعاء، غلاف	*wi'ā', ghilāf*
reception (n)	استقبال، استلام	*istiqbāl, istilām*
receptionist (n)	مرحب، موظف الاستعلامات	*muraḥḥib, muwaẓẓaful isti'lāmāt*
reception room	حجرة الاستقبال	*ḥujratul istiqbāl*
receptive (adj)	واعٍ، متفتح	*wā'in, mutafattiḥ*
receptiveness (n)	تفتح، وعي	*tafattuḥ, wa'y*

receptivity=receptiveness

recess (n)	مدة العطلة، فجوة	*muddatul 'uṭlah, fajwah*
recession (n)	ركود، انحطاط	*rukūd, inḥiṭāṭ*
recessional (n)	ترنيمة الانسحاب	*tarnīmatul insiḥāb*
recessive (adj)	منحسر، مرتد	*munḥasir, murtadd*
recipe (n)	صيغة طهوية	*ṣīghah ṭahwiyyah*
recipient (n)	متلقي، متسلم	*mutalaqqī, mutasallim*
reciprocal (adj)	متبادل، تبادلي	*mutabādil, tabādulī*
reciprocate (v)	تبادل، تردد	*tabādala, taraddada*
reciprocation (n)	تبادل، معاوضة	*tabādul, mu'āwaḍah*
reciprocity (n)	أصول التبادل	*uṣūlut tabādul*
recital (n)	سرد، حفلة	*sard, ḥaflah*
recitation (n)	تلاوة، قراءة	*tilāwah, qirā'ah*
recitative (adj)	قصصي، سردي	*qaṣaṣī, sardī*
recite (v)	تلا، سرد	*talā, sarada*
reckless (adj)	عجول، طائش	*'ajūl, ṭā'ish*
recklessly (adv)	بتهور، بعجلة	*bi tahawwur, bi 'ajalah*
recklessness (n)	تهور، طيش	*tahawwur, ṭaish*
reckon (v)	اعتبر، حسب، عد	*i'tabara, ḥasaba, 'adda*
reckoner (n)	محاسب	*muḥāsib*
reckoning (n)	حساب، محاسبة	*ḥisāb, muḥāsabah*
reclaim (v)	استرد، استصلح	*istaradda, istaṣlaḥa*
recline (v)	اتكأ، انحنى	*ittaka'a, inḥanā*
recluse (n)	متنسك، منعزل	*mutanassik, mun'azil*
recognition (n)	اعتراف، قبول	*i'tirāf, qabūl*
recognizable,-isable	ممكن إدراكه	*mumkin idrākuh*
recognizance (n)	تعرف، تسليم	*ta'arruf, taslīm*
recognize,-ise (v)	سلم، قدر	*sallama, qaddara*
recoil (v)	ارتد، تراجع	*irtadda, tarāja'a*
recollect (v)	تذكر، استرد	*tadhakkara, istaradda*
recollection (n)	ذكرى، تذكر	*dhikrā, tadhakkur*
recommend (v)	مدح، أوصى، نصح	*madaḥa, auṣā, naṣaḥa*
recommendation (n)	توصية، نصيحة	*tauṣiyah, naṣīḥah*

recompense (v)	كافأ، جازى	*kāfa'a, jāzā*
recompense (n)	مكافأة، جزاء	*mukāfa'ah, jazā'*
reconcile (v)	صالح، وفق	*ṣālaḥa, waffaqa*
reconciliation (n)	صلح، توافق	*ṣulḥ, tawāfuq*
recondition (v)	أصلح، رمم	*aṣlaḥa, rammama*
reconsider (v)	راجع، أعاد النظر	*rāja'a, a'ādan naẓar*
reconstruct (v)	جدد البناء	*jaddadal binā'*
reconstruction (n)	بناء من جديد	*binā' min jadīd*
record (n)	محضر، تدوين	*maḥḍar, tadwīn*
record (v)	سجل، دون	*sajjala, dawwana*
recorder (n)	مسجلة	*musajjilah*
recording (n)	تسجيل، تدوين	*tasjīl, tadwīn*
record-player (n)	مستنقطة	*mustanqiṭah*
re-count (v)	عدد ثانيةً	*'addada thāniyatan*
recount (v)	فصل، عدد	*faṣṣala, 'addada*
recourse (n)	ملاذ، مأوى	*malādh, ma'wā*
recover (v)	أعاد، أخرج، استرد	*a'āda, akhraja, istaradda*
recovery (n)	استعادة، شفاء	*isti'ādah, shifā'*
recovery room	حجرة الطوارئ	*ḥujratuṭ ṭawāri'*
recreate (v)	أنعش، خلق من جديد	*an'asha, khalaqa min jadīd*
recreation (n)	تسلية، استجمام	*tasliyah, istijmām*
recreational (adj)	استجمامي، معد للتسلية	*istijmāmī, mu'add lit tasliyah*
recruit (v)	جند، قوى	*jannada, qawwā*
recruit (n)	جندي جديد	*jundiyy jadīd*
recruitment (n)	تطويع، تجنيد	*taṭwī', tajnīd*
rectangle (n)	شكل مستطيل	*shakl mustaṭīl*
rectangular (adj)	قائم الزوايا	*qā'imuz zawāyā*
rectifiable (adj)	ممكن تصحيحه	*mumkin taṣḥīḥuh*
rectification (n)	تصحيح، تقويم	*taṣḥīḥ, taqwīm*
rectifier (n)	مقوم	*muqawwim*

rectify (v)	صحح، قوم	*ṣaḥḥaḥa, qawwama*
rectitude (n)	صواب، استقامة	*ṣawāb, istiqāmah*
rector (n)	رئيس جامعة، قسيس	*ra'īsu jāmi'ah, qissīs*
rectum (n)	مستقيم	*mustaqīm*
recumbent (adj)	مستلقٍ، متكئ	*mustalqin, muttaki'*
recuperate (v)	تعافى، شفي	*ta'āfā, shufiya*
recuperation (n)	شفاء، تعافٍ	*shifā', ta'āfin*
recuperative (adj)	معافٍ، شافٍ	*mu'āfin, shāfin*
recur (v)	تكرر، عاد، دار	*takarrara, 'āda, dāra*
recurrence (n)	تكرار، عودة	*takrār, 'audah*
recurrent (adj)	متكرر الوقوع	*mutakarrirul wuqū'*
red (adj/n)	أحمر، لون أحمر	*aḥmar, laun aḥmar*
red alert (n)	إنذار أحمر	*indhār aḥmar*
red-blooded (adj)	شجيع، جرئ	*shajī', jari'*
redbreast (n)	أبو الحناء	*abul ḥinnā'*
Red Cross (n)	صليب أحمر	*ṣalīb aḥmar*
redden (v)	حمر	*ḥammara*
reddish (adj)	محمر	*muḥmarr*
redeem (v)	حرر، افتدى	*ḥarrara, iftadā*
redeemable (adj)	ممكن إعتاقه	*mumkin i'tāquh*
redemption (n)	فدية، إعتاق	*fidyah, i'tāq*
redemptive (adj)	إعتاقي، تخليصي	*i'tāqī, takhlīṣī*
red-handed (adj)	مضرج اليدين	*muḍarrajul yadayn*
red-letter (adj)	سعيد	*sa'īd*
red light	ضوء أحمر	*ḍau' aḥmar*
redolence (n)	عبير، شذا	*'abīr, shadhā*
redolent (adj)	عطر، عابق	*'aṭir, 'ābiq*
redouble (v)	ضاعف، بالغ	*ḍā'afa, bālagha*
redoubt (n)	معقل دفاعي	*ma'qil difā'ī*
redoubtable (adj)	مخيف، مروع	*mukhīf, murawwi'*
redound (v)	ارتد، تراجع	*irtadda, tarāja'a*
redress (v)	خلص، أنصف	*khallaṣa, anṣafa*

redress (n)	إنصاف، إصلاح	*inṣāf, iṣlāḥ*
red tape	شريط أحمر	*sharīṭ aḥmar*
reduce (v)	خفف، حول	*khaffafa, ḥawwala*
reduction (n)	تخفيض، تنقيص	*takhfīḍ, tanqīṣ*
redundancy (n)	زيادة، حشو	*ziyādah, ḥashw*
redundant (adj)	زائد، فاضل	*zā'id, fāḍil*
red wood (n)	خشب أحمر	*khashab aḥmar*
re-echo (v)	ردد الصدى	*raddadaṣ ṣadā*
reed (n)	قصبة	*qaṣabah*
reedy (adj)	كثير القصب	*kathīrul qaṣab*
reef (n)	صخور البحر، عقبة خطرة	*ṣukhūrul baḥr, 'aqabah khaṭirah*
reefer (n)	نوع من سترة	*nau' min sutrah*
reek (n)	رائحة كريهة	*rā'iḥah karīhah*
reel (n)	بكرة، ريل	*bakarah, rīl*
reel (v)	لف على بكرة	*laffa 'alā bakarah*
re-elect (v)	انتخب من جديد	*intakhaba min jadīd*
re-enter (v)	دخل ثانيةً	*dakhala thāniyatan*
re-entry (n)	دخول ثاني	*dukhūl thānī*
reeve (n)	رئيس مدينة أو منطقة	*ra'īsu madīnah aw minṭaqah*
re-examination (n)	اختبار ثان	*ikhtibār thānin*
re-examine (v)	اختبر ثانيةً	*ikhtabara thāniyatan*
refer (v)	أحال، استشهد به	*aḥāla, istashhada bih*
referee (n/v)	حكم، حكم	*ḥakam, ḥakama*
reference (n)	إحالة، مراجعة	*iḥālah, murāja'ah*
reference book	مرجع	*marja'*
reference library	مكتبة مرجعية	*maktabah marja'iyyah*
reference marks	علامة الإسناد	*'alāmatul isnād*
referendum (n)	مذكرة استعلامية	*mudhakkirah isti'lāmiyyah*
refill (v)	ملأ من جديد	*mala'a min jadīd*
refill (n)	عبوة جديدة	*'ubuwwah jadīdah*

refine (v)	نقح، نقى، صقل	*naqqaḥa, naqqā, ṣaqala*
refined (adj)	منقًى، مصقول	*munaqqan, maṣqūl*
refinement (n)	تنقية، تنقيح	*tanqiyah, tanqīḥ*
refiner (n)	مصفي، منقح	*muṣaffī, munaqqiḥ*
refinery (n)	معمل التصفية	*ma'malut taṣfiyah*
reflect (v)	عكس، انعكس	*'akasa, in'akasa*
reflection (n)	انعكاس، صورة منعكسة	*in'ikās, ṣūrah mun'akisah*
reflective (adj)	انعكاسي، عاكس	*in'ikāsī, 'ākis*
reflex (n)	فعل منعكس	*fi'l mun'akis*
reflex angle	زاوية منعكسة	*zāwiyah mun'akisah*
reflextion = reflection		
reflexive (adj)	انعكاسي	*in'ikāsī*
reform (v)	أصلح، قوم	*aṣlaḥa, qawwama*
reform (n)	إصلاح، تقويم	*iṣlāḥ, taqwīm*
reformation (n)	إصلاح، تهذيب	*iṣlāḥ, tahdhīb*
reformatory (adj)	إصلاحي	*iṣlāḥī*
reformer (n)	مصلح، مجدد	*muṣliḥ, mujaddid*
refract (v)	كسر الأشعة	*kasaral ashi''ah*
refraction (n)	انكسار الأشعة	*inkisārul ashi''ah*
refractory (adj)	جموح، شكس	*jamūḥ, shakis*
refrain (v)	أمسك عن، امتنع	*amsaka 'an, imtana'a*
refrain (n)	امتناع، قرار	*imtinā', qarār*
refresh (v)	أنعش، رطب	*an'asha, raṭṭaba*
refresher course	دورة تدريبية	*daurah tadrībiyyah*
refreshing (adj)	منعش، مرطب	*mun'ish, muraṭṭib*
refreshment (n)	انتعاش، مرطب	*inti'āsh, muraṭṭib*
refrigerant (adj)	مبرد، ملطف	*mubarrid, mulaṭṭif*
refrigerate (v)	برد، رطب	*barrada, raṭṭaba*
refrigeration (n)	تبريد، تثليج	*tabrīd, tathlīj*
refrigerator (n)	برادة، ثلاجة	*barrādah, thallājah*
refuge (n)	مأوى، ملجأ	*ma'wā, malja'*

refugee (n)	لاجئ، مهاجر	*lāji', muhājir*
refund (v)	رد، أعاد	*radda, a'āda*
refund (n)	إعادة النقود	*i'ādatun nuqūd*
refundable (adj)	يمكن إعادته	*yumkin i'ādatuh*
refusal (n)	رفض، امتناع	*rafḍ, imtinā'*
refuse (v)	رفض، منع	*rafaḍa, mana'a*
refuse (n)	نفاية، فضالة	*nufāyah, fuḍālah*
refutable (adj)	قابل للدحض	*qābil lid daḥḍ*
refutation (n)	نقض، دحض	*naqḍ, daḥḍ*
refute (v)	دحض، نقض	*daḥaḍa, naqaḍa*
regain (v)	استرجع، استرد	*istarja'a, istaradda*
regal (adj)	ملكي، مختص بالملوك	*malakī, mukhtaṣṣ bil mulūk*
regale (v)	أمتع	*amta'a*
regard (n)	احترام، مناسبة	*iḥtirām, munāsabah*
regard (v)	احترم، تعلق، عنى	*iḥtarama, ta'allaqa, 'anā*
regarding (prep)	في ما تعلق به	*fī mā ta'allaqa bih*
regardless (adj)	غافل، عديم الاهتمام	*ghāfil, 'adīmul ihtimām*
regards (n)	تحيات	*taḥiyyāt*
regency (n)	نيابة الملك	*niyābatul malik*
regenerate (v/adj)	جدد، متجدد	*jaddada, mutajaddid*
regeneration (n)	تجديد، تجدد	*tajdīd, tajaddud*
regenerative (adj)	تجديدي	*tajdīdī*
regent (n)	وصي، قائم بوصاية	*waṣī, qā'im bi waṣāyah*
regicide (n)	قتل الملك	*qatlul malik*
regime (n)	نظام الحكومة	*niẓāmul ḥukūmah*
regiment (n)	فرقة عسكرية	*firqah 'askariyyah*
regimental (adj)	متعلق بفوج	*muta'alliq bi fauj*
regimentals (n)	بزة الفوج	*bizzatul fauj*
region (n)	منطقة، إقليم	*minṭaqah, iqlīm*
regional (adj)	محلي، إقليمي	*maḥallī, iqlīmī*
regionalism (n)	إقليمية	*iqlīmiyyah*

register (v)	سجل، دون	*sajjala, dawwana*
register (n)	سجل	*sijill*
registered (adj)	مسجل	*musajjal*
registered post	بريد مسجل	*barīd musajjal*
registerer (n)	مسجل، كاتب	*musajjil, kātib*
registration (n)	تسجيل	*tasjīl*
registry (n)	مكتب تسجيل	*maktabu tasjīl*
registry office (n)	مكتب الزواج	*maktabuz zawāj*
regress (v)	انكفأ، ارتد	*inkafa'a, irtadda*
regression (n)	انكفاء، نكوص	*inkifā', nukūṣ*
regressive (adj)	انكفائي، ارتدادي	*inkifā'ī, irtidādī*
regret (v)	تأسف، ندم	*ta'assafa, nadima*
regret (n)	أسف، ندامة	*asaf, nadāmah*
regretful (adj)	نادم، متأسف	*nādim, muta'assif*
regretfully (adv)	متأسفاً، بندامة	*muta'assifan, bi nadāmah*
regrettable (adj)	يؤسف لـه	*yu'saf lahu*
regular (adj)	مواظب، منتظم	*muwāẓib, muntaẓim*
regular (n)	عضو في الجنود	*'uḍw fil junūd*
regularity (n)	نظام، تناسق	*niẓām, tanāsuq*
regularly (adv)	بانتظام، بترتيب	*bintiẓām, bi tartīb*
regulate (v)	ضبط، نظم	*ḍabaṭa, naẓẓama*
regulation (n)	انتظام، قانون	*intiẓām, qānūn*
regulator (n)	منظمة	*munaẓẓimah*
rehabilitate (v)	أهل من جديد	*ahhala min jadīd*
rehabilitation (n)	تأهيل جديد	*ta'hīl jadīd*
rehearing (n)	سماع ثاني	*simā' thānī*
rehearsal (n)	تدريب، تمرين	*tadrīb, tamrīn*
rehearse (v)	درب لأداء دور	*darraba li adā'i daur*
reign (v)	حكم، تسلط	*ḥakama, tasallaṭa*
reign (n)	سلطة، سلطان	*sulṭah, sulṭān*
reimburse (v)	عوض، أوفى	*'awwaḍa, aufā*
reimbursement (n)	تعويض	*ta'wīḍ*

rein (n)	عنان، زمام	*'inān, zimām*
reincarnate (v)	تجسد من جديد	*tajassada min jadīd*
reincarnation (n)	تناسخ، تجسد جديد	*tanāsukh, tajassud jadīd*
reinforce (v)	عزز، قوى	*'azzaza, qawwā*
reinforcement (n)	تعزيز، تقوية	*ta'zīz, taqwiyah*
reinstate (v)	أعاد إلى وضع سابق	*a'āda ilā waḍ' sābiq*
reissue (v)	أعاد الطبع	*a'ādaṭ ṭab'*
reissue (n)	طبعة جديدة	*ṭab'ah jadīdah*
reiterate (v)	ردد، كرر	*raddada, karrara*
reiteration (n)	تكرير، إعادة	*takrīr, i'ādah*
reject (v)	رفض، نبذ	*rafaḍa, nabadha*
rejection (n)	رفض، نبذ	*rafḍ, nabdh*
rejoice (v)	تمتع، طرب	*tamatta'a, ṭariba*
rejoicing (n)	ابتهاج، طرب	*ibtihāj, ṭarab*
rejoin (v)	انضم، لحق	*inḍamma, laḥiqa*
rejoinder (n)	رد، جواب	*radd, jawāb*
rejuvenate (v)	أعاد الشباب	*a'ādash shabāb*
rejuvenation (n)	إعادة الشباب	*i'ādatush shabāb*
rekindle (v)	أضرم من جديد	*aḍrama min jadīd*
relapse (v/n)	انتكس، انتكاس	*intakasa, intikās*
relate (v)	قص، تعلق به	*qaṣṣa, ta'allaqa bih*
related (adj)	متصل، متعلق	*muttaṣil, muta'alliq*
relation (n)	صلة، قرابة	*ṣilah, qarābah*
relationship (n)	قرابة، علاقة	*qarābah, 'alāqah*
relative (adj)	متعلق، متصل	*muta'alliq, muttaṣil*
relative (n)	شخص قريب	*shakhṣ qarīb*
relax (v)	استرخى، استجم	*istarkhā, istajamma*
relaxation (n)	تسلية، تراخٍ	*tasliyah, tarākhin*
relaxed (adj)	مسترخٍ، مستريح	*mustarkhin, mustarīḥ*
relay (n)	مرحلة، أبدال	*murḥilah, abdāl*
relay (v)	أرحل	*arḥala*
release (v)	حرر، أعتق	*ḥarrara, a'taqa*

release (n)	تحرير، إطلاق	*taḥrīr, iṭlāq*
relegate (v)	أخفض الرتبة	*akhfaḍar rutbah*
relegation (n)	إخفاض الرتبة	*ikhfāḍur rutbah*
relent (v)	رق، لان	*raqqa, lāna*
relentless (adj)	عديم الرحمة، قاسٍ	*'adīmur raḥmah, qāsin*
relentlessly (adv)	بقسوة	*bi qaswah*
relentlessness (n)	قسوة، عدم شفقة	*qaswah, 'adamu shafaqah*
relevance, –cy (n)	مطابقة، صلة	*muṭābaqah, ṣilah*
relevant (adj)	مناسب، موافق	*munāsib, muwāfiq*
reliability (n)	ثقة، عول	*thiqah, 'iwal*
reliable (adj)	موثوق، معول عليه	*mauthūq, mu'awwal 'alaih*
reliance (n)	اتكال، اعتماد	*ittikāl, i'timād*
reliant (adj)	متكل، معول	*muttakil, mu'awwil*
relics (n)	آثار، بقايا	*āthār, baqāyā*
relief (n)	راحة، إسعاف	*rāḥah, is'āf*
relieve (v)	أسعف، أراح	*as'afa, arāḥa*
relieved (adj)	مرتاح	*murtāḥ*
religion (n)	دين، مذهب	*dīn, madhhab*
religious (adj)	ديني، تقي	*dīnī, taqiyy*
religiousness (n)	تقوى، اتباع دين	*taqwā, ittibā'u dīn*
relinquish (v)	هجر، تنحى عن	*hajara, tanaḥḥā 'an*
relish (n)	تلذذ، استمتاع	*taladhdhudh, istimtā'*
relish (v)	استمتع، تلذذ	*istamta'a, taladhdhadha*
relocate (v)	نقل إلى مكان جديد	*naqala ilā makān jadīd*
relocation (n)	نقل إلى مكان جديد	*naql ilā makān jadīd*
reluctance (n)	إحجام، كره، اشمئزاز	*iḥjām, kurh, ishmi'zāz*
reluctant (adj)	مشمئز، كاره، محجم	*mushma'iz, kārih, muḥjim*
reluctantly (adv)	على كره، بعدم رغبة	*'alā kurh, bi 'adami raghbah*
rely (v)	اتكل، اعتمد	*ittakala, i'tamada*
remain (v)	بقي، فضل	*baqā, faḍala*
remainder (n)	بقية، فضلة	*baqiyyah, faḍla*

remains (n)	بقايا، فضلات	*baqāyā, faḍalāt*
remand (v)	رد، أرجع	*radda, arja'a*
remand (n)	محتجز، حبس احتياطي	*muḥtajaz, ḥabs iḥtiyāṭī*
remark (v/n)	لاحظ، ملاحظة	*lāḥaẓa, mulāḥaẓah*
remarkable (adj)	فائق، رائع	*fā'iq, rā'i'*
remarriage (n)	زواج ثانٍ	*zawāj thānin*
remarry (v)	تزوج مرة ثانية	*tazawwaja marratan thāniyah*
remediable (adj)	قابل للإعلاج	*qābil lil 'ilāj*
remedial (adj)	علاجي، إصلاحي	*'ilājī, iṣlāḥī*
remedy (v)	عالج، أصلح	*'ālaja, aṣlaḥa*
remedy (n)	معالجة، علاج	*mu'ālajah, 'ilāj*
remember (v)	تذكر، ذكر	*tadhakkara, dhakara*
rememberance (n)	تذكار، تذكر	*tadhkār, tadhakkur*
remind (v)	ذكر، نبه	*dhakkara, nabbaha*
reminder (n)	مذكر	*mudhakkir*
reminiscence (n)	تذكر ماضي، ذكرى ماضية	*tadhakkur māḍi, dhikrā māḍiyah*
reminiscent (adj)	متذكر، تذكري	*mutadhakkir, tadhakkurī*
remiss (adj)	متوان، مهمل	*mutawānin, muhmil*
remissness (n)	إهمال، تهاون	*ihmāl, tahāwun*
remit (v)	صفح عن، أرسل النقود	*ṣafaḥa 'an, arsalan nuqūd*
remittance (n)	تحويل النقود	*taḥwīlun nuqūd*
remittent (adj)	متقطع	*mutaqaṭṭi'*
remittent fever	حمى متقطعة	*ḥummā mutaqaṭṭi'ah*
remnant (n)	بقية، فضلة	*baqiyyah, faḍlah*
remonstrate (v)	احتج، اعترض	*iḥtajja, i'taraḍa*
remorse (n)	ندامة، مندم	*nadāmah, mandam*
remorseful (adj)	متسم بالندم، حي الضمير	*muttasim bin nadam, ḥayyuḍ ḍamīr*
remorseless (adj)	عديم الرحمة، حجري القلب	*'adīmur raḥmah, ḥajariyyul qalb*
remote (adj)	بعيد، قاصٍ	*ba'īd, qāṣin*

remote control	تحكم من بعد	*taḥakkum min bu'd*
remotely (adv)	بمقدار ضئيل	*bi miqdār ḍa'īl*
remoteness (n)	بعد، نأي	*bu'd, na'y*
remount (v)	ركب مرةً ثانيةً	*rakiba marratan thāniyah*
removable (adj)	يمكن نقله	*yumkinu naqluh*
removal (n)	نقل، إزالة	*naql, izālah*
remove (v)	أزال، نقل	*azāla, naqala*
removed (adj)	بعيد، قاص	*ba'īd, qāṣin*
remunerate (v)	عوض، كافأ	*'awwaḍa, kāfa'a*
remuneration (n)	أجرة، مكافأة	*ujrah, mukāfa'ah*
remunerative (adj)	مربح	*murbiḥ*
renaissance (n)	حركة جديدة، نهضة	*ḥarakah jadīdah, nahḍah*
renascent (adj)	منبعث، متجدد	*mumba'ith, mutajaddid*
render (v)	سلم، صير، عزف، شق	*sallama, ṣayyara, 'azafa, shaqqa*
rendering (n)	أداء، ترجمة	*adā', tarjamah*
rendezvous (n)	موعد، ملقى	*mau'id, malqā*
renew (v)	جدد، استأنف	*jaddada, ista'nafa*
renewable (adj)	ممكن تجديده	*mumkin tajdīduh*
renewal (n)	تجديد، تجدد	*tajdīd, tajaddud*
renounce (v)	رفض، أنكر	*rafaḍa, ankara*
renouncement (n)	تنسك، رفض	*tanassuk, rafḍ*
renovate (v)	جدد، رمم	*jaddada, rammama*
renovation (n)	تجديد، إصلاح	*tajdīd, iṣlāḥ*
renown (n)	صيت، شهرة	*ṣīt, shuhrah*
renowned (adj)	شهير، معروف	*shahīr, ma'rūf*
rent (v/n)	أجر، أجر	*ajjara, ajr*
rental (n)	إيجار، أجرة	*ījār, ujrah*
renunciation (n)	تنسك، تخلٍ	*tanassuk, takhallin*
reopen (v)	فتح ثانيةً	*fataḥa thāniyatan*
reorder (n)	طلب ثاني	*ṭalab thānī*

reorganization (n)	تنظيم من جديد	*tanẓīm min jadīd*
reorganize,-ise (v)	نظم من جديد	*naẓẓama min jadīd*
repair (n)	ترميم، إصلاح، حالة	*tarmīm, iṣlāḥ, ḥālah*
repair (v)	رمم، عالج	*rammama, ʻālaja*
repairable (adj)	ممكن ترميمه، يعوض	*mumkin tarmīmuh, yuʻawwaḍu*
reparation (n)	تعويض، إصلاح	*taʻwīḍ, iṣlāḥ*
reparations (n)	تعويضات	*taʻwīḍāt*
repartee (n)	براعة في الإجابة	*barāʻah fil ijābah*
repast (n)	وجبة، أكلة	*wajbah, aklah*
repatriate (v)	أعاد المرء إلى وطنه	*aʻādal mar'a ilā waṭanih*
repatriation (n)	إعادة إلى الوطن	*iʻādah ilal waṭan*
repay (v)	رد، وفى	*radda, wafā*
repayment (n)	رد، مكافأة	*radd, mukāfa'ah*
repeat (v)	كرر، ردد	*karrara, raddada*
repeat (n)	إعادة، تكرير	*iʻādah, takrīr*
repeated (adj)	مكرر، متكرر	*mukarrar, mutakarrir*
repeatedly (adv)	مراراً، تكراراً	*mirāran, takrāran*
repeating (n)	إعادة، تكرار	*iʻādah, takrār*
repel (v)	دافع، صد	*dāfaʻa, ṣadda*
repellent (adj)	راد، طارد	*rādd, ṭārid*
repent (v)	تاب، تأسف	*tāba, ta'assafa*
repentance (n)	توبة، ندامة	*taubah, nadāmah*
repentant (adj)	تائب، نادم	*tā'ib, nādim*
repercussion (n)	نتيجة غير مباشرة	*natījah ghairu mubāshirah*
repertory (n)	ذخيرة، ذخر	*dhakhīrah, dhukhr*
repertory theatre	مسرح الذخائر	*masraḥudh dhakhā'ir*
repetition (n)	إعادة، تكرر	*iʻādah, takarrur*
repetitious (adj)	حافل بالتكرار	*ḥāfil bit takrār*

repetitive = repetitious

replace (v)	استبدل، سد مسد	*istabdala, sadda masadda*
replacement (n)	استبدال، تعويض	*istibdāl, ta'wīḍ*
replenish (v)	أشبع، ملأ من جديد	*ashba'a, mala'a min jadīd*
replenishment (n)	امتلاء ثانية، سد النقص	*imtilā' thāniyah, saddun naqṣ*
replete (adj)	مفعم، ممتلئ	*muf'am, mumtali'*
repletion (n)	إشباع، اكتظاظ	*ishbā', iktiẓāẓ*
replica (n)	صورة منقولة	*ṣūrah manqūlah*
replicate (v)	استخرج نسخة مطابقة	*istakhraja nuskhah muṭābiqah*
replication (n)	نسخة مطابقة	*nuskhah muṭābiqah*
reply (v)	رد، أجاب	*radda, ajāba*
reply (n)	رد، جواب	*radd, jawāb*
report (v)	اختزل، روى	*ikhtazala, rawā*
report (n)	بيان، محضر	*bayān, maḥḍar*
reportage (n)	تحقيق صحفي	*taḥqīq ṣuḥufī*
report card (n)	تقرير مدرسي	*taqrīr madrasī*
reporter (n)	مراسل، مختزل، محرر	*murāsil, mukhtazil, muḥarrir*
repose (v)	اضطجع، استراح	*iḍṭaja'a, istarāḥa*
repose (n)	هدوء، اضطجاع، استراحة	*hudū', iḍṭijā', istirāḥah*
reposeful (adj)	هادئ	*hādi'*
repository (n)	مستودع، مخزن	*mustauda', makhzan*
repossess (v)	استرد الملكية	*istaraddal milkiyyah*
reprehend (v)	وبخ، انتهر	*wabbakha, intahara*
reprehensible (adj)	يستوجب التوبيخ	*yastaujibut taubīkh*
represent (v)	مثل، ناب عن	*maththala, nāba 'an*
representation (n)	نيابة، تمثيل، إظهار	*niyābah, tamthīl, iẓhār*
representative (n/adj)	ممثل، مندوب	*mumaththil, mandūb*
repress (v)	كبح، قمع	*kabaḥa, qama'a*
repression (n)	كبح، قمع، كبت	*kabḥ, qam', kabt*

repressive (adj)	كبحي، قمعي	*kabḥī, qam'ī*
reprieve (v)	أمهل، أرجأ التنفيذ	*amhala, arja'at tanfīdh*
reprieve (n)	إرجاء تنفيذ حكم	*irjā'u tanfīdhi ḥukm*
reprimand (v)	وبخ، أنب	*wabbakha, annaba*
reprint (n)	طبعة ثانية	*ṭab'ah thāniyah*
reprisal (n)	دحل، انتقام	*daḥl, intiqām*
reproach (v)	عير، لام	*'ayyara, lāma*
reproach (n)	لوم، تأنيب	*laum, ta'nīb*
reproachful (adj)	تعييري، تأنيبي	*ta'yīrī, ta'nībī*
reprobate (n)	شخص غير مؤدب	*shakhṣ ghair mu'addab*
reproduce (v)	أنتج، ولد	*antaja, wallada*
reproduction (n)	إنتاج، صورة منقولة	*intāj, ṣūrah manqūlah*
reproductive (adj)	توالدي، مولد	*tawāludī, mu'allid*
reproof (n)	تعنيف، توبيخ	*ta'nīf, taubīkh*
reprove (v)	وبخ، عنف	*wabbakha, 'annafa*
reproving (adj)	مستنكر، مؤنب	*mustankir, mu'annib*
reptile (n)	زاحف	*zāḥif*
reptilian (adj)	زاحفي	*zāḥifī*
republic (n)	دولة جمهورية	*daulah jumhūriyyah*
republican (adj)	جمهوري	*jumhūrī*
republican (n)	مؤيد للجمهورية	*mu'ayyid lil jumhūriyyah*
repudiate (v)	رفض، جحد	*rafaḍa, jaḥada*
repudiation (n)	رفض، إنكار	*rafḍ, inkār*
repugnance (n)	بغض، كره شديد	*bughḍ, kurh shadīd*
repugnant (adj)	مشمئز، بغيض	*mushma'izz, baghīḍ*
repulse (v)	صد، قاوم	*ṣadda, qāwama*
repulse (n)	صد، رد	*ṣadd, radd*
repulsion (n)	كره، اشمئزاز	*kurh, ishmi'zāz*
repulsive (adj)	منفر، مشمئز	*munaffir, mushma'izz*
reputable (adj)	محترم، حميد السمعة	*muḥtaram, ḥamīdus sum'ah*
reputation (n)	صيت، سمعة، شهرة	*ṣīt, sum'ah, shuhrah*

repute (v)	اعتبر، ظن	*i'tabara, ẓanna*
repute (n)	سمعة، صيت	*sum'ah, ṣīt*
reputed (adj)	حسن السمعة، شهير	*ḥasanus sum'ah, shahīr*
request (v)	طلب، التمس	*ṭalaba, iltamasa*
request (n)	طلب، سؤال	*ṭalab, su'āl*
requiem (n)	صلاة لراحة الموتى	*ṣalāt li rāḥatil mautā*
require (v)	تطلب، استلزم	*taṭallaba, istalzama*
requirement (n)	متطلب، حاجة	*mutaṭallib, ḥājah*
requisite (n/adj)	ضروري، لازم	*ḍarūrī, lāzim*
requisition (n)	طلب، استدعاء	*ṭalab, istid'ā*
requisition (v)	طلب، استدعى	*ṭalaba, istad'ā*
requital (n)	جزاء، عوض	*jazā', 'iwaḍ*
requite (v)	جازى، عوض	*jāzā, 'awwaḍa*
resale (n)	بيع ثاني	*bai' thānī*
rescind (v)	ألغى، أبطل	*alghā, abṭala*
rescue (v/n)	أنقذ، إنقاذ	*anqadha, inqādh*
research (v)	بحث، تقصى	*baḥatha, taqaṣṣā*
research (n)	بحث، تقميش	*baḥth, taqmīsh*
research work (n)	بحث علمي	*baḥth 'ilmī*
resemblance (n)	مشابهة، شبه	*mushābahah, shabah*
resemble (v)	شابه، ماثل	*shābaha, māthala*
resent (v)	استاء، استنكر	*istā'a, istankara*
resentful (adj)	مستاء، ممتعض	*mustā', mumta'iṣ*
resentfulness (n)	امتعاص، استياء	*imti'āṣ, istiyā'*
resentment (n)	غيظ، امتعاص	*ghaiẓ, imti'āṣ*
reservation (n)	حجز، تحفظ	*ḥajz, taḥaffuẓ*
reserve (v)	حجز، حفظ	*ḥajaza, ḥafiẓa*
reserve (n)	حفظ، شيء محفوظ، احتياط	*ḥifẓ, shay' maḥfūẓ, iḥtiyāṭ*
reserved (adj)	محجوز، متحفظ	*maḥjūz, mutaḥaffiẓ*
reservoir (n)	خزان الماء	*khazzānul mā'*
reset (v)	نضد من جديد	*naḍḍada min jadīd*

resettle (v)	أسكن من جديد	*askana min jadīd*
reshuffle (v)	عدل، خلط	*'addala, khalaṭa*
reshuffle (n)	تعديل مناصب الوزراء	*ta'dīlu manāṣibil wuzarā'*
reside (v)	سكن، استوطن	*sakana, istauṭana*
resident (n)	قاطن، مقيم	*qāṭin, muqīm*
residential (adj)	سكني، داخلي	*sakanī, dākhilī*
residual (adj)	فاضل، متبقي	*fāḍil, mutabaqqī*
residue (n)	بقية، فضلة	*baqiyyah, faḍlah*
resign (v)	استقال، تخلى عن	*istaqāla, takhallā 'an*
resignation (n)	استقالة، إذعان	*istiqālah, idh'ān*
resilience, -cy (n)	مرونة، ارتداد	*murūnah, irtidād*
resilient (adj)	مرن، رجوع	*marin, rajū'*
resist (v)	قاوم، عارض	*qāwama, 'āraḍa*
resistance (n)	مقاومة، تحمل	*muqāwamah, taḥammul*
resistant (adj)	مقاوم	*muqāwim*
resistable (adj)	يقاوم، يعارض	*yuqāwam, yu'āraḍ*
resistor (n)	مقاوم	*muqāwim*
resolute (adj)	عزم، ثابت العزم	*'āzim, thābitul 'azm*
resoluteness (n)	تصميم، ثبات في العزم	*taṣmīm, thabāt fil 'azm*
resolution (n)	تصميم، حل	*taṣmīm, ḥall*
resolve (v)	اعتزم، حل	*i'tazama, ḥalla*
resolved (adj)	عازم، موطد العزم	*'āzim, muwaṭṭadul 'azm*
resonance (n)	رنين، دوي	*ranīn, dawiyy*
resonant (adj)	داوٍ، رنان	*dāwin, rannān*
resonate (v)	رجع، رن	*raja'a, ranna*
resort (v)	التجأ، فزع إلى	*iltaja'a, faza'a ilā*
resort (n)	ملتجأ، ملاذ	*multaja', malādh*
resound (v)	دوى، رن	*dawwā, ranna*
resounding (adj)	مدوٍّ، مشتهر	*mudawwin, mushtahir*
resource (n)	مورد، وسيلة، دهاء	*maurid, wasīlah, dahā'*
resourceful (adj)	داهية، ذو براعة	*dāhiyah, dhū barā'ah*

resourcefulness (n)	دهاء، براعة	*dahā', barā'ah*
respect (v)	احترم، تعلق	*iḥtarama, ta'allaqa*
respect (n)	احترام، خصوص، ناحية	*iḥtirām, khuṣūṣ, nāḥiyah*
respectable (adj)	محترم، محتشم	*muḥtaram, muḥtashim*
respectful (adj)	متسم بالاحترام	*muttasim bil iḥtirām*
respecting (prep)	من جهة، بخصوص	*min jihah, bi khuṣūṣ*
respective (adj)	مختص، خصوصي	*mukhtaṣṣ, khuṣūṣī*
respectively (adv)	على التوالي	*'alat tawālī*
respiration (n)	تنفس	*tanaffus*
respirator (n)	منفسة	*manfasah*
respiratory (adj)	تنفسي	*tanaffusī*
respire (v)	تنفس	*tanaffasa*
respite (n)	إرجاء، مهلة	*irjā', muhlah*
resplendence (n)	بهاء، تألق	*bahā', ta'alluq*
resplendent (adj)	لامع، متألق	*lāmi', muta'alliq*
respond (v)	أجاب، طابق	*ajāba, ṭābaqa*
respondent (n)	مدعي، مجيب	*mudda'ī, mujīb*
response (n)	إجابة، رد	*ijābah, radd*
responsibility (n)	مسؤولية	*mas'ūliyyah*
responsible (adj)	مسؤول، مطالب	*mas'ūl, muṭālab*
responsive (adj)	إيجابي، مستجيب	*ījābī, mustajīb*
responsiveness (n)	استجابية	*istijābiyyah*
rest (v)	استراح، وقف	*istarāḥa, waqafa*
rest (n)	استراحة، بقية	*istirāḥah, baqiyyah*
restate (v)	صرح ثانيةً	*ṣarraḥa thāniyatan*
restatement (n)	تصريح جديد	*taṣrīḥ jadīd*
restaurant (n)	مطعم	*maṭ'am*
restaurateur (n)	صاحب المطعم	*ṣāḥibul maṭ'am*
restful (adj)	مريح، مطمئن	*murīḥ, muṭma'in*
rest-home (n)	مصحة	*maṣaḥḥah*
restitution (n)	رجوع، عودة	*rujū', 'audah*
restive (adj)	متململ، شامس	*mutamalmil, shāmis*

restless (adj)	قلق، مضطرب	*qaliq, muḍṭarib*
restlessly (adv)	باضطراب، بتململ	*biḍṭirāb, bi tamalmul*
restlessness (n)	قلق، تململ	*qalaq, tamalmul*
restoration (n)	استعادة، تجديد، إصلاح	*isti'ādah, tajdīd, iṣlāḥ*
restorative (adj)	محيي، مجدد	*muḥyī, mujaddid*
restorative (n)	شيء منعش	*shay' mun'ish*
restore (v)	أعاد، أحيا، أصلح	*a'āda, aḥyā, aṣlaḥa*
restrain (v)	كبح، حجز، قيد	*kabaḥa, ḥajaza, qayyada*
restrained (adj)	محجوز، مقيد	*maḥjūz, muqayyad*
restraint (n)	كبح، قيد، حجز	*kabḥ, qaid, ḥajz*
restrict (v)	حصر، حجز، قيد	*ḥaṣara, ḥajaza, qayyada*
restricted (adj)	محصور، مقيد	*maḥṣūr, muqayyad*
restriction (n)	حصر، ضبط، قيد	*ḥaṣr, ḍabṭ, qaid*
restrictive (adj)	حصري، تقييدي	*ḥaṣrī, taqyīdī*
restrictiveness (n)	حصرية، تقييدية	*ḥaṣriyyah, taqyīdiyyah*
rest-room (n)	حجرة التواليت	*ḥujratut tawālīt*
result (n)	نتيجة	*natījah*
result (v)	نتج، أدى	*nataja, addā*
resultant (adj)	ناشيء، ناتج	*nāshi', nātij*
resume (v)	استعاد، استأنف	*ista'āda, ista'nafa*
résumé (n)	خلاصة، سيرة ذاتية	*khulāṣah, sīrah dhātiyyah*
resumption (n)	استرجاع، عودة	*istirjā', 'audah*
resurgence (n)	انبثاق، انبعاث	*imbithāq, imbi'āth*
resurgent (adj)	منبعث، منبثق	*mumba'ith, mumbathiq*
resurrect (v)	بعث، أحيا	*ba'atha, aḥyā*
resurrection (n)	بعث الأموات	*ba'thul amwāt*
resuscitate (v)	أنعش، أحيا	*an'asha, aḥyā*
resuscitation (n)	إنعاش، انتعاش	*in'āsh, inti'āsh*
retail (n)	بيع بالتجزئة	*bai' bit tajzi'ah*
retain (v)	احتجز، احتفظ	*iḥtajaza, iḥtafaẓa*
retainer (n)	احتجاز، توكيل	*iḥtijāz, taukīl*

retaliate (v)	انتقم، ثأر	*intaqama, tha'ara*
retaliation (n)	ثأر، انتقام	*tha'r, intiqām*
retaliatory (adj)	انتقامي، ثأري	*intiqāmī, tha'rī*
retard (v)	أخر، أعاق	*akhkhara, a'āqa*
retardation (n)	تأخر، تعوق	*ta'akhkhur, ta'awwuq*
retarded (adj)	متأخر، متخلف	*muta'akhkhir, mutakhallif*
retention (n)	احتباس، احتجاز	*iḥtibās, iḥtijāz*
retentive (adj)	احتباسي، احتفاظي	*iḥtibāsī, iḥtifāẓī*
retentiveness (n)	احتفاظية، احتباسية	*iḥtifāẓiyyah, iḥtibāsiyyah*
reticence (n)	صموت، تكتم	*ṣumūt, takattum*
reticent (adj)	كتوم، كاظم	*katūm, kāẓim*
retinue (n)	بطانة، تبع	*biṭānah, tubba'*
retire (v)	تقاعد، اعتزل	*taqā'ada, i'tazala*
retired (adj)	متقاعد، منعزل	*mutaqā'id, mun'azil*
retirement (n)	تقاعد، انسحاب	*taqā'ud, insiḥāb*
retiring (adj)	خجول، منسحب	*khajūl, munsaḥib*
retort (n)	رد مفحم، معوجة	*radd mufḥim, mu'wajjah*
retort (v)	أفحم، جاوب	*afḥama, jāwaba*
retouch (v)	نمق، نقح	*nammaqa, naqqaḥa*
retrace (v)	تعقب، استعاد	*ta'aqqaba, ista'āda*
retract (v)	سحب، تقلص	*saḥaba, taqallaṣa*
retractile (adj)	قابل للانكماش	*qābil lil inkimāsh*
retraction (n)	انكماش، انسحاب	*inkimāsh, insiḥāb*
retreat (n)	ارتداد، انسحاب	*irtidād, insiḥāb*
retrench (v)	خفض، أنقص	*khaffaḍa, anqaṣa*
retrenchment (n)	تخفيض النفقات	*takhfīḍun nafaqāt*
retrial (n)	اختبار ثاني	*ikhtibār thānī*
retribution (n)	مجازاة، جزاء	*mujāzāt, jazā'*
retributive (adj)	جزائي	*jazā'ī*
retrievable (adj)	يسترد، يعوض	*yustaradd, yu'awwaḍ*
retrieval (n)	استرداد، عوض	*istirdād, 'iwaḍ*

retroactive (adj)	رجعي	*raj'ī*
retroactively (adv)	على نحو رجعي	*'alā naḥw raj'ī*
retrograde (adj)	انتكاسي، ارتجاعي	*intikāsī, irtijā'ī*
retrogress (v)	تردى، تراجع	*taraddā, tarāja'a*
retrogression (n)	تردٍّ، تراجع	*taraddin, tarāju'*
retrogressive (adj)	مترد، متقهقر	*mutaraddin, mutaqahqir*
retrospect (v)	استعاد الأحوال السابقة	*ista'ādal aḥwāl as sābiqah*
retrospection (n)	استعادة الأحوال السابقة	*isti'ādatul aḥwāl as sābiqah*
retrospective (adj)	استعادي	*isti'ādī*
return (v)	رجع، أعاد	*raja'a, a'āda*
return (n)	عودة، رد، إعادة	*'audah, radd, i'ādah*
return ticket	تذكرة إيابية	*tadhkirah iyābiyyah*
reunion (n)	اجتماع بعد افتراق	*itjimā' ba'da iftirāq*
reunite (v)	اجتمع بعد فترة	*ijtama'a ba'da fatrah*
reuse (n)	استعمال ثاني	*isti'māl thānī*
revaluation (n)	تحديد القيمة ثانيةً	*taḥdīdul qīmah thāniyatan*
revalue (v)	حدد القيمة من جديد	*ḥaddadal qīmah min jadīd*
revamp (v)	جدد، رمم	*jaddada, rammama*
reveal (v)	ألهم، أفشى	*alhama, afshā*
revealing (adj)	مكشف، ملهم	*mukshif, mulhim*
revel (n)	عربدة، طرب	*'arbadah, ṭarab*
revel (adj)	مرح، طرب	*mariḥ, ṭarib*
revelation (n)	وحي، إلهام	*waḥy, ilhām*
reveller (n)	مرح، معربد	*mariḥ, mu'arbid*
revelry (n)	مرح، قصف	*maraḥ, qaṣf*
revenge (v)	انتقم، ثأر	*intaqama, tha'ara*
revenge (n)	ثأر، انتقام	*tha'r, intiqām*
revengeful (adj)	منتقم، حقود	*muntaqīm, ḥaqūd*
revengefully (adv)	انتقاماً	*intiqāman*

revengefulness (n)	انتقامية، ثأرية	*intiqāmiyyah, tha'riyyah*
revenue (n)	دخل، مدخول	*dakhl, madkhūl*
revenue stamp (n)	طابع الدخل	*ṭāba'ud dakhl*
reverberant (adj)	داوٍ، متردد	*dāwin, mutaraddid*
reverberate (v)	تردد، دوى	*taraddada, dawwā*
reverberation (n)	ارتداد، صدىً	*irtidād, ṣadan*
revere (v)	كرم، بجل	*karrama, bajjala*
reverence (n)	تبجيل، احترام	*tabjīl, iḥtirām*
reverence (v)	بجل، وقر	*bajjala, waqqara*
reverend (adj)	موقر، محترم	*muwaqqar, muḥtaram*
reverent (adj)	موقر، توقيري	*muwaqqir, tauqīrī*
reverential (adj)	تبجيلي، احترامي	*tabjīlī, iḥtirāmī*
reverie (n)	تخيل، شرود الفكر	*takhayyul, shurūdul fikr*
reversal (n)	عكس، انعكاس، قلب	*'aks, in'ikās, qalb*
reverse (n)	عكس، ضد	*'aks, ḍidd*
reverse (adj)	معكوس، مضاد	*ma'kūs, muḍādd*
reverse (v)	عكس، ضاد	*'akasa, ḍādda*
reversible (adj)	قابل للكعس	*qābil lil 'aks*
reversion (n)	ارتداد، عكس	*irtidād, 'aks*
revert (v)	ارتد، عكس	*irtadda, 'akasa*
review (n)	معاينة، انتقاد	*mu'āyanah, intiqād*
review (v)	عاين، استعرض	*'āyana, ista'raḍa*
revile (v)	شتم، انتهر	*shatama, intahara*
revise (v)	نقح، أعاد النظر	*naqqaḥa, a'ādan naẓar*
revise (n)	إعادة نظر، تنقيح	*i'ādatu naẓar, tanqīḥ*
revision (n)	تنقيح، نسخة منقحة	*tanqīḥ nuskhah munaqqaḥah*
revitalization (n)	تجديد الحياة	*tajdīdul ḥayāt*
revitalize,-ise (v)	منح حياةً جديدة	*manaḥa ḥayātan jadīdah*
revival (n)	نهضة، ولادة جديدة	*nahḍah, wiladah jadīdah*
revivalism (n)	إحيائية	*iḥyā'iyyah*
revive (v)	أحيا، أنعش	*aḥyā, an'asha*

revivify (v)	نشط، منح الحياة	*nashshaṭa, manaḥal ḥayāt*
revocation (n)	إلغاء، امتناع	*ilghā', imtinā'*
revoke (v)	فسخ، ألغى	*fasakha, alghā*
revolt (v)	ثورة، عصيان	*thaurah, 'iṣyān*
revolt (v)	عصى، ثار	*'aṣā, thāra*
revolting (adj)	ثائر، مثير للسخط	*thā'ir, muthīr lis sukhṭ*
revolution (n)	ثورة، دورة، انقلاب	*thaurah, daurah, inqilāb*
revolutionary (adj)	ثوري، جذري	*thaurī, jadhrī*
revolutionize,-ise (v)	ثور، قلب	*thawwara, qalaba*
revolve (v)	دار، أدار	*dāra, adāra*
revolver (n)	مسدس	*musaddas*
revolving (adj)	دائر	*dā'ir*
revulsion (n)	اشمئزاز، تصريف	*ishmi'zāz, taṣrīf*
reward (v)	كافأ، جازى	*kāfa'a, jāzā*
reward (n)	مكافأة، جزاء، جائزة	*mukāfa'ah, jazā', jā'izah*
rewrite (v)	كتب مرةً ثانيةً	*kataba marratan thāniyah*
rhetoric (n)	علم البلاغة	*'ilmul balāghah*
rhetorical (adj)	بلاغي، منمق، بليغ	*balāghī, munammaq, balīgh*
rhetorical question	سؤال بلاغي	*su'āl balāghī*
rhinoceros (n)	كركدن	*karkadan*
rhyme (v)	قفى، سجع	*qaffā, sajja'a*
rhyme (n)	سجع، تقفية	*saj', taqfiyah*
rhythm (n)	اتزان، وزن شعري	*ittizān, wazn shi'rī*
rhythmic (adj)	متزن، متناغم	*muttazin, mutanāghim*
rib (n)	ضلع، دعامة	*ḍil', di'āmah*
rib (v)	سخر، ضحك	*sakhira, ḍaḥaka*
ribald (adj)	سفيه، وضيع	*safīh, waḍī'*
ribaldry (n)	سفاهة، بذاءة	*safāhah, badhā'ah*
ribbon (n)	شريط	*sharīṭ*
ribbons (n)	خرقة	*khirqah*

rice (n)	أرز، رز	*aruzz, ruzz*
rice-paper (n)	ورق الأرز	*waraqul aruzz*
rich (n)	غني، ثري، دسم	*ghaniyy, thariyy, dasim*
richly (adv)	بغنىً، بوفرة	*bi ghinan, bi wafrah*
richness (n)	غنىً، شرف، خصب	*ghinan, sharaf, khiṣb*
rickshaw (n)	ركشة، عربة يجرها رجل	*rikshah, 'arabah yajurruhā rajul*
rid (v)	أعتق، خلص	*a'taqa, khallaṣa*
riddance (n)	خلاص، انعتاق	*khalāṣ, in'itāq*
riddle (n)	أحجية، لغز	*uḥjiyyah, lughz*
riddle (v)	ألغز، عمى	*alghaza, 'ammā*
ride (n)	ركوب، رحلة	*rukūb, riḥlah*
ride (v)	ركب، امتطى	*rakiba, imtaṭā*
rider (n)	راكب	*rākib*
ridge (n)	حرف، قمة تلة	*ḥarf, qimmatu tallah*
ridge-pole (n)	رافدة	*rāfidah*
ridicule (v/n)	سخر، سخرية	*sakhira, sukhriyyah*
ridiculous (adj)	مضحك، سخري	*muḍḥik, sukhrī*
ridiculously (adv)	بهزء	*bi huz'*
riding (n)	ركوب الخيل	*rukūbul khail*
rife (adj)	شائع، سائد	*shā'i', sā'id*
riffle (v)	خلط أوراق اللعب	*khalaṭa aurāqal la'b*
rifle (n)	بندقية	*bunduqiyyah*
rifle (v)	نهب، سلب	*nahaba, salaba*
rift (n)	شق، فلع	*shaqq, fal'*
rig (n)	ترتيب الصواري	*tartībuṣ ṣawārī*
rigging (n)	حبال الصواري	*ḥibāluṣ ṣawārī*
right (adj)	صحيح، قويم، أيمن	*ṣaḥīḥ, qawīm, aiman*
right (n)	حق، صواب، يمين	*ḥaqq, ṣawāb, yamīn*
right (adv)	تواً، مباشرةً، تماماً	*tawwan, mubāsharatan, tamāman*
righteous (adj)	عادل، صالح، قويم	*'ādil, ṣāliḥ, qawīm*

righteously (adv)	بحق، بصواب	*bi ḥaqq, bi ṣawāb*
rightful (adj)	صحيح، ملائم، جائز	*ṣaḥīḥ, mulā'im, jā'iz*
right-hand (adj)	أيمن	*aiman*
right-handed (adj)	يميني	*yamīnī*
rightly (adv)	بحق، بصحة	*bi ḥaqq, bi ṣiḥḥah*
right-minded (adj)	قويم الرأي	*qawīmur ra'y*
right-mindedness (n)	قوام الرأي	*qawāmur ra'y*
right wing (n)	جناح أيمن	*janāḥ aiman*
rigid (adj)	صارم، صلب	*ṣārim, ṣulb*
rigidity (n)	صلابة، شدة	*ṣalābah, shiddah*
rigorous (adj)	عنيف، قاسٍ، صارم	*'anīf, qāsin, ṣārim*
rigorously (adv)	بصرامة، بشدة	*bi ṣarāmah, bi shiddah*
rigorousness (n)	قسوة، شدة، صرامة	*qaswah, shiddah, ṣarāmah*
rigour (rogor) (n)	صرامة، عنف، شدة	*ṣarāmah, 'unf, shiddah*
rim (n)	حافة، جرف	*ḥāffah, juruf*
rim (v)	حتر، وطر	*ḥattara, waṭṭara*
ring (n)	رنين، خاتم، حلقة، دائرة	*ranīn, khātam, ḥalqah, dā'irah*
ring (v)	رن، قرع، تحلق	*ranna, qara'a, taḥallaqa*
ring-finger (n)	إصبع الخاتم	*iṣba'ul khātim*
ringleader (n)	زعيم ثورة	*za'īmu thaurah*
ringmaster (n)	مدير الحلبة	*mudīrul ḥalbah*
rinse (v/n)	شطف، شطف	*shaṭafa, shaṭf*
riot (n)	شغب، هياج	*shaghab, hiyāj*
riot (v)	شاغب، عربد	*shāghaba, 'arbada*
riot act (n)	قانون الشغب	*qānūnush shaghab*
riotous (adj)	مشاغب، شغبي	*mushāghib, shaghabī*
riotousness (n)	مشاغبة	*mushāghabah*
rip (v)	شق، فلع	*shaqqa, fala'a*
rip (n)	شق، فلع	*shaqq, fal'*
rip-cord (n)	حبل التنفيس	*ḥablut tanfīs*

ripe (adj)	ناضج، كامل النمو	*nāḍij, kāmilun numuww*
ripen (v)	نضج، أنضج	*naḍaja, anḍaja*
ripeness (n)	نضج	*naḍj*
ripple (v/n)	تموج، تموج	*tamawwaja, tamawwuj*
rip-roaring (adj)	صاخب	*ṣākhib*
rip-saw (n)	منشار الشق	*minshārush shaqq*
rise (v)	طلع، نهض، قام، برز	*ṭala'a, nahaḍa, qāma, baraza*
rise (n)	نهضة، طلوع، صعود	*nahḍah, ṭulū', ṣu'ūd*
rising (adj)	طالع، مستقيظ	*ṭāli', mustaiqiẓ*
rising (n)	ثورة، نهضة	*thaurah, nahḍah*
risk (n)	مخاطرة، مجازفة	*mukhāṭarah, mujāzafah*
risk (v)	خاطر، غامر	*khāṭara, ghāmara*
riskily (adv)	بطريق خطر	*bi ṭarīq khaṭir*
riskiness (n)	مخاطرة، خطر	*mukhāṭarah, khaṭar*
risky (adj)	خطر، محفوف بالمخاطر	*khaṭir, maḥfūf bil makhāṭir*
rite (n)	شعيرة، طقس	*sha'īrah, ṭaqs*
ritual (adj)	طقسي، شعائري	*ṭaqsī, sha'ā'irī*
ritual (n)	كتاب الطقوس	*kitābuṭ ṭuqūs*
ritualism (n)	طقوسية	*ṭaqūsiyyah*
rival (n)	صنو، مزاحم	*ṣinw, muzāḥim*
rival (v)	نافس، زاحم	*nāfasa, zāḥama*
rivalry (n)	منافسة، مباراة	*munāfasah, mubārāt*
riven (adj)	متمزق	*mutamazziq*
river (n)	نهر	*nahr*
river-bed (n)	مجرى النهر	*majran nahr*
riverside (n)	ضفة النهر	*ḍiffatun nahr*
rivet (n)	برشام حديد	*burshām ḥadīd*
rivulet (n)	نهر صغير، جدول	*nahr ṣaghīr, jadwal*
Riyal (n)	ريال	*riyāl*
road (n)	طريق، درب	*ṭarīq, darb*

road-block (n)	عقبة في الطريق	*'aqabah fiṭ ṭarīq*
road-house (n)	نزل الطريق	*nuzuluṭ ṭarīq*
road-metal (n)	حصباء الطريق	*ḥaṣbā'uṭ ṭarīq*
road side	جانب الطريق	*jānibuṭ ṭarīq*
road test	اختبار الطريق	*ikhtibāruṭ ṭarīq*
roadway (n)	بدن الطريق	*badanuṭ ṭarīq*
roam (v)	طاف، جال	*ṭāfa, jāla*
roam (n)	جولان، تطواف	*jawalān, taṭwāf*
roamer (n)	جوال	*jawwāl*
roan (n/adj)	لون أسمر، كميت	*laun asmar, kumait*
roar (v/n)	زأر، زئير	*za'ara, za'īr*
roaring (adj)	عالٍ، صاخب	*'ālin, ṣākhib*
roast (v)	شوى، حمص	*shawā, ḥammaṣa*
roast (adj)	مشوي	*mashwī*
roaster (n)	مشواة، محمصة	*mishwāt, miḥmaṣah*
rob (v)	نهب، سلب	*nahaba, salaba*
robber (n)	لص، نهاب	*liṣṣ, nahhāb*
robbery (n)	سلب، سرقة	*salb, sariqah*
robe (n)	رداء، حلة	*ridā', ḥullah*
robe (v)	ألبس، ارتدى	*albasa, irtadā*
robin (n)	أبو الحن	*abul ḥinn*
robot (n)	ربوط، انسان آلي	*rabūṭ, insān 'ālī*
robust (adj)	قوي، عنيف	*qawī, 'anīf*
rock (n)	صخرة، صخر	*ṣakhrah, ṣakhr*
rock (v)	هز، ترجح	*hazza, tarajjaḥa*
rocket (n)	صاروخ، طائرة	*ṣārūkh, ṭā'irah*
	صاروخية	*ṣārūkhiyyah*
rocket (v)	ارتفع بسرعة	*irtafa'a bi sur'ah*
rock-salt (n)	ملح صخري	*milḥ ṣakhrī*
rocky (adj)	متحجر، راسخ، صخري	*mutaḥajjir, rāsikh, ṣakhrī*
rod (n)	صولجان، عصا	*ṣaulajān, 'aṣā*
rodomontade (n)	تباهٍ، تفاخر	*tabāhin, tafākhur*

roe (n)	ظبي، أيل، غزال	*ẓaby, ayyil, ghazāl*
rogation (n)	ابتهال	*ibtihāl*
rogation days	أيام الابتهال	*ayyāmul ibtihāl*
rogue (n)	مخادع، محتال	*mukhādi', muḥtāl*
roguery (n)	احتيال، خداع	*iḥtiyāl, khidā'*
rogues' gallery	سجل المجرمين	*sijillul mujrimīn*
roguish (adj)	احتيالي، متشرد	*iḥtiyālī, mutasharrid*
roguishly (adv)	بمكر، بتشرد	*bi makr, bi tasharrud*
roguishness (n)	تشرد، حيلة	*tasharrud, ḥīlah*
roistering (n)	عربيد، مرح صاخب	*'irbīd, maraḥ ṣākhib*
role (n)	دور، فصل	*daur, faṣl*
roll (n)	درج، لفة، قائمة	*darj, laffah, qā'imah*
roll (v)	دحرج، طوى، دار	*daḥraja, ṭawā, dāra*
roll-call (n)	نداء الحضور	*nidā'ul ḥuḍūr*
roller (n)	أسطوانة، محدلة	*usṭuwānah, miḥdalah*
roller-skate (n)	مزلجة معجلة	*mizlajah mu'ajjilah*
roller-towel (n)	منشفة دوارة	*minshafah dawwārah*
rolling-pin (n)	مرقاق	*mirqāq*
rolling-stock (n)	معدات دارجة	*mu'addāt dārijah*
roly-poly (n)	كعكة ملفوفة	*ka'kah malfūfah*
Roman (n/adj)	روماني، لاتيني	*rūmānī, lātīnī*
Roman Catholic	كاثوليكي	*kāthūlīkī*
romance (n)	رواية غرامية، قصة ملفقة	*riwāyah gharāmiyyah, qiṣṣah mulaffaqah*
romance (v)	لفق القصص	*laffaqal qiṣaṣ*
romantic (adj)	رومانتيكي، تخيلي	*rūmāntīkī, takhayyulī*
romanticism (n)	رومانتيكية	*rūmāntīkiyyah*
romp (n)	قصوف، مرح	*quṣūf, maraḥ*
romp (v)	قصف، مرح	*qaṣafa, maraḥa*
roof (n/v)	سقف، سقف	*saqf, saqafa*
roof-garden (n)	حديقة السطح	*ḥadīqatus saṭḥ*
roof-top (n)	سقف بيت	*saqfu bait*

roof-tree (n)	شرفة الجملون	*shurfatul jamalūn*
rook (n)	غداف، غشاش	*ghudāf, ghashshāsh*
rook (v)	احتال، خادع	*iḥtāla, khāda'a*
rookery (n)	مغدفة	*maghdafah*
room (n)	حجرة، غرفة، موضع	*ḥujrah, ghurfah, mauḍi'*
roomful (n)	ملء غرفة	*mil'u ghurfah*
room-mate (n)	رفيق الحجرة	*rafīqul ḥujrah*
room-service	خدمة الغرفة	*khidmatul ghurfah*
roomy (adj)	رحب، متسع، فسيح	*raḥb, muttasi', fasīḥ*
roost (n)	وقيعة، مجثم الطير	*waqī'ah, majthamuṭ ṭair*
roost (v)	استقر، جثم	*istaqarra, jathama*
rooster (v)	ديك	*dīk*
root (n)	جذر، أساس، أصل	*jidhr, asās, aṣl*
root (v)	جذر، رسخ، نقب	*jadhdhara, rasakha, naqqaba*
root beer (n)	جعد الجذور	*ja'dul judhūr*
rope (n)	حبل، مرسة	*ḥabl, marsah*
rope (v)	قيد بحبل	*qayyada bi ḥabl*
ropy (adj)	نحيل، متفتل	*naḥīl, mutafattil*
rosary (n)	مسبحة	*masbaḥah*
rose (n)	ورد، لون وردي	*ward, laun wardī*
rosette (n)	وردية	*wardiyyah*
rose-water (n)	ماء الورد	*mā'ul ward*
rose-window (n)	نافذة وردية	*nāfidhah wardiyyah*
rosewood (n)	خشب الورد	*khashabul ward*
roster (n)	جدول الخدمة	*jadwalul khidmah*
rostrum (n)	منبر الخطابة	*mimbarul khiṭābah*
rosy (adj)	وردي، متفائل	*wardī, mutafā'il*
rot (v)	بلي، تعطن	*baliya, ta'aṭṭana*
rot (n)	تعفن، فساد	*ta'affun, fasād*
rotary (adj)	رحوي، دوراني	*raḥawī, dawarānī*
rotate (v)	دار، أدار	*dāra, adāra*

rotation (n)	دوران، مناوبة	*dawarān, munāwabah*
rotational (adj)	دوراني	*dawarānī*
rotatory (adj)	دوراني، متناوب	*dawarānī, mutanāwib*
rote (v)	حفظ بتكرار الكلام	*ḥafiẓa bi takrāril kalam*
rotisserie (n)	مشواة	*mishwāt*
rotor (n)	دوار	*dawwār*
rotten (adj)	فاسد، متعفن	*fāsid, muta'affin*
rotter (n)	بغيض، كريه	*baghīḍ, karīh*
rough (adj)	رديء، خشن، قاسٍ	*radī', khashin, qāsin*
rough (n)	أرض وعرة	*arḍ wa'irah*
rough (v)	خشن، فظ، أشعث	*khashina, faẓẓa, ash'atha*
roughage (n)	طعام خشن	*ṭa'ām khashin*
roughen (v)	خشن، خشن	*khashuna, khashshana*
roughly (adv)	بوجه التقريب، بخشونة	*bi wajhit taqrīb, bi khushūnah*
roughneck (n)	شخص فظ	*shakhṣ faẓẓ*
roughness (n)	خشونة، رداءة	*khushūnah, radā'ah*
round (adj)	مدور، مستدير، مكمل	*mudawwar, mustadīr, mukammal*
round (n)	دائرة، حلقة، جولة	*dā'irah, ḥalqah, jaulah*
round (adv)	حول... ، حوالي	*ḥaula, ḥiwālai*
roundabout (adj)	غير مباشر	*ghair mubāshir*
roundish (adj)	شبيه بمستدير	*shabīh bi mustadīr*
roundly (adv)	صراحةً، تماماً	*ṣarāḥatan, tamāman*
round robin	عريضة حلقية	*'arīḍah ḥalaqiyyah*
round trip	رحلة انكفائية	*riḥlah inkifā'iyyah*
round-up (n)	جمع الأشخاص أو الماشية	*jam'ul ashkhāṣ awil māshiyah*
rouse (v)	أيقظ، هيج، نهض	*aiqaẓa, hayyaja, nahaḍa*
rousing (adj)	مثير، محرض	*muthīr, muḥarriḍ*
roustabout (n)	عمال في حقل بترول	*'ummāl fī ḥaqli bitrūl*
rout (v)	هزم، طرد	*hazama, ṭarada*

route (n)	طريق	*ṭarīq*
route march	سير طليق	*sair ṭalīq*
routine (n)	طريقة محددة، روتين	*ṭarīqah muḥaddadah, rūtīn*
routine (adj)	روتيني، نمطي	*rūtīnī, namaṭī*
rove (v)	جال، طاف	*jāla, ṭāfa*
rove (n)	تجوال، طواف	*tajwāl, ṭawāf*
rover (n)	متجول، هائم	*mutajawwil, hā'im*
row (n)	شغب، صف، تجذيف	*shaghab, ṣaff, tajdhīf*
row (v)	صف، جذف، شاغب	*ṣaffa, jadhdhafa, shāghaba*
rowdily (adv)	بشغب، بشكاسة	*bi shaghab, bi shakāsah*
rowdiness (n)	مشاغبة، شكاسة	*mushāghabah, shakāsah*
rowdy (adj)	مشاكس، مخاصم	*mushākis, mukhāṣim*
rowdyism (n)	حب للخصام	*ḥubb lil khiṣām*
rowing-boat (n)	زورق تجذيف	*zauraqu tajdhīf*
royal (adj)	ملكي	*malakī*
royal blue (n)	أزرق ملكي	*azraq malakī*
royalist (n)	مؤيد للملكية	*mu'ayyid lil malakiyyah*
royal jelly	عسل ملكي	*'asal malakī*
royally (adv)	ملكيًا	*malakiyyan*
royalty (n)	ملكية، نبل	*malakiyyah, nubl*
rub (v)	فرك، احتك، دلك	*faraka, iḥtakka, dalaka*
rub (n)	حك، فرك	*ḥakk, fark*
rubber (n)	ممحاة، مطاط	*mimḥāt, maṭṭāṭ*
rubber plant	شجرة المطاط	*shajaratul maṭṭaṭ*
rubber stamp	ختم مطاطي	*khatm maṭṭāṭī*
rubbery (adj)	مطاطي	*maṭṭāṭī*
rubbish (n)	نفاية، هراء	*nufāyah, hurā'*
rubble (n)	كسارة، نقاضة	*kusārah, nuqāḍah*
rubicund (adj)	ضارب إلى الحمرة	*ḍārib ilal ḥumrah*
ruby (n/adj)	ياقوت، ياقوتي	*yāqūt, yāqūtī*
rudder (n)	دفة السفينة	*daffatus safīnah*

ruddiness (n)	تورد، حمرة	*tawarrud, ḥumrah*
ruddy (adj)	أحمر، متورد	*aḥmar, mutawarrid*
rude (adj)	جلف، سمج، خشن	*jilf, samij, khashin*
rudely (adv)	بخشونة، بفظاظة	*bi khushūnah, bi faẓāẓah*
rudeness (n)	سماجة، خشونة	*samājah, khushūnah*
rudiment (n)	مبدأ، أصل	*mabda', aṣl*
rudimentary (adj)	مبدئي، أساسي، جرثومي	*mabda'ī, asāsī, jurthūmī*
rue (v)	تندم، تحسر	*tanaddama, taḥassara*
rueful (adj)	كئيب، آسف	*ka'īb, āsif*
ruff (v)	ألقى ورقة رابحة	*alqā waraqah rābiḥah*
ruffian (n)	شخص وحشي، وبش	*shakhṣ waḥshī, wabsh*
ruffle (v)	شوش، جعد	*shawwasha, ja''ada*
ruffle (n)	بساط غليظ	*bisāṭ ghalīẓ*
rugged (adj)	أشعث، وعر، عابس	*ash'ath, wa'ir, 'ābis*
ruggedly (adj)	بوعورة، بخشونة	*bi wu'ūrah, bi khushūnah*
ruggedness (n)	فظاظة، تجهم	*faẓāẓah, tajahhum*
ruin (n)	دمار، انهيار	*dimār, inhiyār*
ruin (v)	أهلك، دمر، خرب	*ahlaka, dammara, kharraba*
ruination (n)	تخريب، تدمير	*takhrīb, tadmīr*
ruinous (adj)	متهدم، مهلك	*mutahaddim, muhlik*
rule (n)	قانون، سلطة	*qānūn, sulṭah*
rule (v)	ساد، حكم	*sāda, ḥakama*
ruler (n)	مسطرة، حاكم	*misṭarah, ḥākim*
ruling (n)	حكم، سيطرة	*ḥukm, saiṭarah*
rumble (n)	لعلعة، قعقعة	*la'la'ah, qa'qa'ah*
rumble (v)	لعلع، كركر	*la'la'a, karkara*
ruminant (adj)	مشتر، متأمل	*mushtarr, muta'ammil*
ruminate (v)	اجتر، تأمل	*ijtarra, ta'ammala*
rumination (n)	تأمل، اجترار	*ta'ammul, ijtirār*
rummage (v)	فتش، نبش	*fattasha, nabbasha*
rummage (n)	تفتيش بدقة	*taftīsh bi diqqah*

rumour (rumor) (n)	شائعة، إشاعة	*shā'i'ah, ishā'ah*
rumour (rumor) (v)	شيع، روج	*shayya'a, rawwaja*
rump (n)	ردف، كفل	*ridf, kafal*
rumple (v)	غضن، تجعد	*ghaḍḍana, taja''ada*
rumpus (n)	ضجيج، جلبة	*ḍajīj, jalabah*
run (v)	جرى، عدا، أدار، هرب	*jarā, 'adā, adāra, haraba*
run (n)	عدو، جري، ركض	*'adw, jary, rakḍ*
run about	جال، طاف	*jāla, ṭāfa*
runaround (n)	تملص، مراوغة	*tamalluṣ, murāwaghah*
run away	فر، هرب	*farra, haraba*
runaway (n)	هروب، انطلاق بسرعة	*hurūb, inṭilāq bi sur'ah*
run down	كف عن العمل	*kaffa 'anil 'amal*
rung (n)	درجة سلم	*darajatu sullam*
run into	اصطدم، التقى	*iṣṭadama, iltaqā*
runner (n)	ركاض، ساعي	*rakkāḍ, sā'ī*
running (n)	ركض، إدارة	*rakḍ, idārah*
running (adj)	جارٍ، متواصل، متدفق	*jārin, mutawāṣil, mutadaffiq*
runny (adj)	كثير الارتشاح	*kathīrul irtishāḥ*
run out	انتهى، فرغ	*intahā, faragha*
run short	تناقص، نقص	*tanāqaṣa, naqaṣa*
rupee (n)	روبية	*rūbiyyah*
rupture (v)	فتق، فجر	*fataqa, fajjara*
rupture (n)	انفجار، فتق	*infijār, fatq*
rural (adj)	ريفي، قروي	*rīfī, qurawī*
ruse (n)	حيلة، خداع	*ḥīlah, khidā'*
rush (n)	تزاحم، اندفاع، هجوم	*tazāḥum, indifā', hujūm*
rush (v)	اندفع، أسرع، تزاحم	*indafa'a, asra'a, tazāḥama*
Russian (adj)	روسي	*rūsī*
Russian (n)	لغة روسية	*lughah rūsiyyah*
rust (v/n)	صدئ، صدأ	*ṣadi'a, ṣada'*
rustic (adj/n)	ريفي، ساذج	*rīfī, sādhij*

rusticate (v)	طرد، أخرج	*ṭarda, akhraja*
rustication (n)	طرد من كلية أو جامعة	*ṭard min kulliyyah au jāmi'ah*
rustle (v/n)	حف، حفيف	*ḥaffa, ḥafīf*
rustling (n)	خشخشة، حفيف	*khashkhashah, ḥafīf*
rusty (adj)	صدئ، مصاب بصدأ	*ṣadi', muṣāb bi ṣada'*
rut (n)	أخدود، ثلم	*ukhdūd, thalam*
ruthless (adj)	قاسٍ، عديم الرحمة	*qāsin, 'adīmur raḥmah*
ruthlessly (adv)	بقسوة	*bi qaswah*
ruthlessness (n)	قساوة القلب، عدم الرحمة	*qasāwatul qalb, 'adamur raḥmah*

S

sabbatical (adj)	إجازي، سبتي	*ijāzī, sabtī*
sabot (n)	قبقاب، سباط	*qabqāb, sabāṭ*
sabotage (n)	تخريب، تدمير	*takhrīb, tadmīr*
sabotage (v)	خرب، دمر	*kharraba, dammara*
saboteur (n)	مخرب، مدمر	*mukharrib, mudammir*
sabre (saber) (n)	سيف، حسام	*saif, ḥusām*
sachet (n)	كيس طيوب	*kīsu ṭuyūb*
sack (v)	صرف، طرد، نهب	*ṣarafa, ṭarada, nahaba*
sack (n)	جراب، سلب، صرف من الخدمة	*jirāb, salb, ṣarf minal khidmah*
sacking (n)	خيش، مسح	*khaish, misḥ*
sacrament (n)	سر مقدس	*sirr muqaddas*
sacramental (adj)	مختص بالسر المقدس	*mukhtaṣṣ bis sirr al muqaddas*
sacred (adj)	مقدس، مكرس	*muqaddas, mukarras*
sacredly (adv)	بطهارة، بقداسة	*bi ṭahārah, bi qadāsah*
sacredness (n)	تقدس، تكرس	*taqaddus, takarrus*
sacrifice (n)	ضحية، تضحية	*ḍaḥiyyah, taḍḥiyah*

sacrifice (v)	ضحى، قرب	*ḍaḥḥā, qarraba*
sacrificial (adj)	تقريبي	*taqrībī*
sacrificially (adv)	للتقرب	*lit taqarrub*
sacrilege (n)	تدنيس المقدسات	*tadnīsul muqaddasāt*
sacrilegous (adj)	مدنس، منتهك	*mudannis, muntahik*
sacrosanct (adj)	مقدس، لا يعدل	*muqaddas, lā yu'addal*
sad (adj)	حزين، محزن، مكتئب	*ḥazīn, muḥzin, mukta'ib*
sadden (v)	حزن، أحزن	*ḥazina, aḥzana*
saddle (n)	سرج، عتبة	*sarj, 'atabah*
saddle (v)	أسرج، أرهق	*asraja, arhaqa*
saddler (n)	صانع السروج	*ṣāni'us surūj*
saddlery (n)	سراجة	*sirājah*
sadism (n)	انحراف جنسي، سادية	*inḥirāf jinsī, sādiyyah*
sadist (n)	سادي	*sādī*
sadistic (adj)	خاص بسادية	*khaṣṣ bi sādiyyah*
sadness (n)	كآبة، حزن، هم	*ka'ābah, ḥuzn, hamm*
safari (n)	رحلة قنص	*riḥlatu qanṣ*
safe (adj)	مأمون، سالم	*ma'mūn, sālim*
safe (n)	خزينة حديد	*khazīnatu ḥadīd*
safebreaker (n)	محطم الخزائن	*muḥaṭṭimul khazā'in*
safe conduct	جواز المرور	*jawāzul murūr*
safe cracker = safebreaker		
safeguard (v)	حمى، وقى	*ḥamā, waqā*
safeguard (n)	وقاية، واقية	*wiqāyah, wāqiyah*
safety (n)	سلامة، أمان	*salāmah, amān*
safety-belt (n)	حزام الأمان	*ḥizāmul amān*
safety island (n)	جزيرة الأمان	*jazīratul amān*
safety lamp (n)	مصباح الأمان	*miṣbāḥul amān*
safety match (n)	ثقاب الأمان	*thiqābul amān*
safety razor (n)	موسى مأمونة	*mūsā ma'mūnah*
safety-value (n)	صمام الأمان	*ṣimāmul amān*
safety zone (n)	منطقة الأمان	*minṭaqatul amān*

saffron (n)	زعفران	*za'farān*
sag (n)	تدلّ، ارتخاء	*tadallin, irtikhā'*
sag (v)	انخفض، تدلى	*inkhafaḍa, tadallā*
saga (n)	قصة الأبطال	*qiṣṣatul abṭāl*
sagacious (adj)	حصف، فطن	*ḥaṣif, faṭin*
sagacity (n)	ذكاء، حصافة	*dhakā', ḥaṣafah*
sage (n/adj)	حكيم، عاقل	*ḥakīm, 'āqil*
sail (n)	قلع، شراع	*qil', shirā'*
sail (v)	أقلع، سافر بحراً	*aqla'a, sāfara baḥran*
sailboat (n)	مركب شراعي	*markab shirā'ī*
sailing (n)	إبحار، إقلاع	*ibḥār, iqlā'*
sailor (n)	ملاح، بحار	*mallāḥ, baḥḥār*
saint (n)	قديس، ولي	*qiddīs, walī*
sainted (adj)	مقدس، نقي	*muqaddas, naqī*
sainthood (n)	قداسة، قدسية	*qadāsah, qudsiyyah*
saintliness (n)	قداسة، ورع	*qadāsah, wara'*
saintly (adj)	قديس، ورع	*qiddīs, wari'*
sake (n)	غرض، سبيل	*gharaḍ, sabīl*
sake (saki)	خمر ياباني	*khamr yābānī*
salaam (n)	تحية، سلام	*taḥiyyah, salām*
salacious (adj)	شهواني، شبق	*shahwānī, shabiq*
salaciously (adv)	مثيراً للشهوة	*muthīran lish shahwah*
salaciousness (n)	شهوانية	*shahwāniyyah*
salacity (n)	غلمة، شبق	*ghulmah, shabaq*
salad (n)	سلطة، كامخ	*salaṭah, kāmakh*
salad-dressing (n)	صلصلة للسلطة	*ṣalṣalah lis salaṭah*
salaried (adj)	ذو راتب معين	*dhū rātib mu'ayyan*
salary (n)	راتب، مرتب	*rātib, murattab*
sale (n)	بيع، مبيع	*bai', mabī'*
salesclerk (n)	بائع	*bā'i'*
sales department	دائرة المبيعات	*dā'iratul mabī'āt*
salesman (n)	بائع	*bā'i'*

salesmanship (n)	فن البيع	*fannul bai'*
sales tax	ضريبة المبيعات	*ḍarībatul mabī'āt*
saleswoman (n)	بائعة	*bā'i'ah*
salient (adj/n)	بارز، زاوية بارزة	*bāriz, zāwiyah bārizah*
saline (adj)	ملحي	*milḥī*
salinity (n)	ملحية	*milḥiyyah*
saliva (n)	ريق، لعاب	*rīq, lu'āb*
sallow (adj)	شاحب اللون، أصفر	*shāḥibul laun, aṣfar*
sally (n)	هجوم مفاجئ، نزوة	*hujūm mufāji', nazwah*
sally (v)	هاجم، نزا	*hājama, nazā*
salon (n)	بهو، صالة	*bahw, ṣālah*
saloon (n)	صالون، بهو	*ṣālūn, bahw*
salt (n/adj)	ملح، مالح	*milḥ, māliḥ*
salt (v)	ملح، ملح	*mallaḥa, malaḥa*
salt-cellar (n)	مملحة، وعاء الملح	*mamlaḥah, wi'ā'ul milḥ*
salt-lick (n)	ملحة	*malḥah*
saltpetre (saltpeter)	ملح صخري	*milḥ ṣakhrī*
salt-shaker = salt-cellar		
salt-water	خاص بماء مالح	*khāṣṣ bi mā' māliḥ*
salubrious (adj)	نافع للصحة	*nāfi' liṣ ṣiḥḥah*
salubriousness (n)	صحية	*ṣiḥḥiyyah*
salutary (adj)	مفيد، نافع	*mufīd, nāfi'*
salutation (n)	تحية، تسليم	*taḥiyyah, taslīm*
salute (v)	سلم، حيا	*sallama, ḥayyā*
salute (n)	تحية عسكرية	*taḥiyyah 'askariyyah*
salvable (adj)	ممكن تخليصه	*mumkin takhlīṣuh*
salvage (v)	أنقذ، نجى	*anqadha, najjā*
salvage (n)	تعويض الإنقاذ	*ta'wīḍul inqādh*
salvation (n)	تخليص، إنقاذ	*takhlīṣ, inqādh*
salve (n)	مرهم، دهان	*marham, dihān*
salve (v)	أنقذ، أصلح	*anqadha, aṣlaḥa*
salver (n)	صينية	*ṣīniyyah*

same (adj)	نفس، عين	*nafs, ʻain*
sameness (n)	تماثل، تشابه	*tamāthul, tashābuh*
sample (n)	عينة، نموذج	*ʻayyinah, namūdhaj*
sample (v)	أخذ عينةً	*akhadha ʻayyinatan*
sampler (n)	قطعة من شغل الإبرة	*qiṭʻah min shughlil ibrah*
sanctification	تطهير، تقديس	*taṭhīr, taqdīs*
sanctify (v)	طهر، كرس	*ṭahhara, karrasa*
sanctimonious (adj)	منافق، زنديق	*munāfiq, zindīq*
sanctimoniousness	نفاق، تظاهر بالتقوى	*nifāq, taẓāhur bit taqwā*
sanction (n)	تصديق، إقرار	*taṣdīq, iqrār*
sanction (v)	صدق، أجاز	*ṣaddaqa, ajāza*
sanctity (n)	حرمة، قداسة	*ḥurmah, qadāsah*
sanctuary (n)	حرم، قدس، ملجأ	*ḥaram, quds, maljaʼ*
sanctum (n)	مكتب خاص	*maktab khāṣṣ*
sand (n/v)	رمل، رمل	*raml, rammala*
sandal (n)	صندل، نعل، خف	*ṣandal, naʻl, khuff*
sandalwood (n)	خشب الصندل	*khashabuṣ ṣandal*
sandbag (n)	كيس رمل	*kīsu raml*
sandbank (n)	قرارة رملية	*qarārah ramliyyah*
sand-bar (n)	مرتفع مرمل	*murtafaʻ murmil*
sand-blast (v)	سفع بالرمال	*safaʻa bir rimāl*
sandboy (n)	غلام الرمل	*ghulāmur raml*
sand-fly (n)	ذبابة الرمل	*dhubābatur raml*
sandman (n)	رمال	*rammāl*
sandpaper (n)	ورق الزجاج	*waraquz zujāj*
sandpiper (n)	زمار الرمل	*zammārur raml*
sandstone (n)	حجر رملي	*ḥajar ramlī*
sandstorm (n)	عاصفة رملية	*ʻāṣifah ramliyyah*
sandwich (n)	شطيرة، سندويتش	*shaṭīrah, sandwītsh*
sandwich (v)	شطر	*shaṭṭara*
sandy (adj)	رملي، مكسو بالرمل	*ramlī, maksuww bir raml*
sane (adj)	سليم العقل	*salīmul ʻaql*

sangfroid (n)	رباطة جأش، رزانة	*ribāṭatu ja'sh, razānah*
sanguinary (adj)	دموي، دامٍ	*damawī, dāmin*
sanguine (adj)	متحمس، واثق	*mutaḥammis, wāthiq*
sanitarian (adj)	اختصاصي في علم الصحة	*ikhtiṣāṣī fī 'ilmiṣ ṣiḥḥah*
sanitary (adj)	صحي، متعلق بالصحة	*ṣiḥḥī, muta'alliq biṣ ṣiḥḥah*
sanitary towel	منشفة صحية	*minshafah ṣiḥḥiyyah*
sanitation (n)	حفظ الصحة	*ḥifẓuṣ ṣiḥḥah*
sanity (n)	صحة العقل، سلامة العقل	*ṣiḥḥatul 'aql, salāmatul 'aql*
sap (n)	نسغ، خندق ضيق، أحمق	*nusgh, khandaq ḍayyiq, aḥmaq*
sap (v)	أضعف، قوض	*aḍ'afa, qawwaḍa*
sapience (n)	عقل، تعقل	*'aql, ta'aqqul*
sapient (adj)	عاقل، حكيم، ذكي	*'āqil, ḥakīm, dhakī*
sapling (n)	شجيرة	*shujairah*
sapper (n)	مهندس عسكري	*muhandis 'askarī*
sapphire (n/adj)	صفير، صفيري	*ṣaffir, ṣaffirī*
sarcasm (n)	هكم، استهزاء	*tahakkum, istihzā'*
sarcastic (adj)	هكمي، استهزائي	*tahakkumī, istihzā'ī*
sarcastically (adv)	على سبيل التهكم	*'alā sabīlit tahakkum*
sardonic (adj)	تكلفي، هكمي	*takallufī, tahakkumī*
sash (n)	زنار، إطار النافذة	*zinnār, iṭārun nāfidhah*
sashy (v)	انزلق، مشى خطىً	*inzalaqa, mashā khuṭan*
satan (n)	شيطان، إبليس	*shayṭān, iblīs*
satanic (adj)	شيطاني، إبليسي	*shayṭānī, iblīsī*
satchel (n)	حقيبة، قمطر	*ḥaqībah, qimṭar*
sated (adj)	مشبع، متخم	*mushba', mutkham*
satellite (n)	وصيف، قمر صناعي	*waṣīf, qamar ṣinā'ī*
satiate (v)	أتخم، أشبع	*atkhama, ashba'a*
satiety (n)	امتلاء، شبع	*imtilā', shiba'*
satin (adj/n)	أطلساني، أطلس	*aṭlasānī, aṭlas*

satiny (adj)	أطلساني، أملس	*aṭlasānī, amlas*
satire (n)	هجاء، قدح	*hijā', qadḥ*
satiric (adj)	هجائي، تنديدي	*hijā'ī, tandīdī*
satirist (n)	هاجٍ، شاعر هجاء	*hājin, shā'iru hijā'*
satirize,-ise (v)	هجا، ندد	*hajā, naddada*
satisfaction (n)	إشباع، اقتناع	*ishbā', iqtinā'*
satisfactorily (adv)	طبق المرام	*ṭibqal marām*
satisfactory (adj)	مرضٍ، مقنع، سار	*murḍin, muqni', sārr*
satisfied (adj)	مكتفٍ، قانع	*muktafin, qāni'*
satisfy (v)	أشبع، أقنع، كفى	*ashba'a, aqna'a, kafā*
satisfying (adj)	مقنع، مشبع	*muqni', mushbi'*
saturate (v)	أشرب، أتخم	*ashraba, atkhama*
saturated (adj)	منقوع، متخم	*manqū', mutkham*
saturation (n)	تشبع، تشرب	*tashabbu', tasharrub*
saturation point	نقطة التشبع	*nuqṭatut tashabbu'*
Saturday (n)	يوم السبت	*yaumus sabt*
Saturn (n)	زحل	*zuḥal*
saturnine (adj)	مكتئب، حزين	*mukta'ib, ḥazīn*
sauce (n)	صلصة	*ṣalṣah*
saucepan (n)	كفت	*kaft*
saucer (n)	صحيفة	*ṣuḥaifah*
saucy (adj)	وقح، سليط	*waqiḥ, salīṭ*
saunter (v)	تلكأ، تجول	*talakka'a, tajawwala*
saunter (n)	هوينى، تلكأ	*huwainā, talakku'*
sausage (n)	سجق	*sujuq*
savage (v)	هاجم بعنف	*hājama bi 'unf*
savage (adj)	متوحش، بربري	*mutawaḥḥish, barbarī*
savagely (adv)	بوحشية، بقساوة	*bi waḥshiyyah, bi qasāwah*
savageness (n)	توحش، همجية	*tawaḥḥush, hamajiyyah*
savagery (n)	همجية، وحشية	*hamajiyyah, waḥshiyyah*
save (v)	أنقذ، اقتصد	*anqadha, iqtaṣada*
save (prep)	إلا، ما عدا	*illā, mā 'adā*

saver (n)	منقذ، محافظ	*munqidh, muḥāfiẓ*
saving (n)	ادخار، مال موفر	*iddikhār, māl muwaffar*
savings account	حساب التوفير	*ḥisābut taufīr*
savings bank	بنك التوفير	*bankut taufīr*
saviour (savior) (n)	منقذ، مخلص	*munqidh, mukhalliṣ*
savour (savor) (v/n)	تذوق، مذاق	*tadhawwaqa, madhāq*
savoury (savory) (adj)	لذيذ الطعم، طعم	*ladhīdhuṭ ṭa'm, ṭa'im*
savvy (n)	معرفة، فهم	*ma'rifah, fahm*
savvy (v)	فهم، علم	*fahima, 'alima*
saw (n/v)	منشرة، نشر	*minsharah, nashara*
sawdust (n)	نشارة	*nushārah*
saw-horse (n)	حصان النشر	*ḥiṣānun nashr*
sawmill (n)	منشرة	*mansharah*
sawyer (n)	نشار	*nashshār*
Saxon (n)	سكسوني	*saksūnī*
saxophone (n)	سكسية	*saksiyyah*
say (v)	قال، لفظ	*qāla, lafaẓa*
say (n)	قول، خبر، رأي	*qawl, khabar, ra'y*
saying (n)	مثل، قول مأثور	*mathal, qaul ma'thūr*
say-so (n)	قول، رأي	*qawl, ra'y*
scab (n)	قرفة، قشرة الجرح	*qirfah, qishratul jurḥ*
scabbard (n)	قراب السيف	*qirābus saif*
scabies (n)	جرب	*jarab*
scaffold (n)	سقالة، محالة	*siqālah, maḥālah*
scaffoldings (n)	مواد لسقالات	*mawādd li siqālāt*
scalar (adj)	مدرج	*mudarraj*
scald (v)	سمط، سفع	*samaṭa, safa'a*
scald (n)	حرق، سمط	*ḥurq, samṭ*
scalding (adj)	غال، محرق	*ghālin, muḥriq*
scale (n)	مقياس، ميزان، صفيحة، درجة	*miqyās, mīzān, ṣafīḥah, darajah*
scale (v)	قاس، درج، تسلقى	*qāsa, darraja, tasallaqā*

scallop (n)	اسقلوب	*isqalūb*
scalp (n)	فروة الرأس	*farwatur ra's*
scamp (n)	ولد مؤذ	*walad mu'dhin*
scamper (v)	هرب، عداً	*haraba, 'adā*
scamper (n)	عدو، ركض	*'adw, rakḍ*
scan (v)	تفرس، فحص، قطع الشعر	*tafarrasa, faḥaṣa, qaṭṭa'ash shi'r*
scan (n)	فحص دقيق، تقطيع الأشعار	*faḥṣ daqīd, taqṭī'ul ash'ār*
scandal (n)	فضيحة، هتيكة، افتراء	*faḍīḥah, hatīkah, iftirā'*
scandalmonger (n)	أفاك	*affāk*
scandalmongering	افتراء، إفك	*iftirā', ifk*
scandalous (adj)	افترائي، قذفي، فاضح	*iftirā'ī, qadhfī, fāḍiḥ*
scandalously (adv)	بطريق فاضح	*bi ṭarīq fāḍiḥ*
scanner (n)	ماكينة فاحصة	*mākīnah fāḥiṣah*
scansion (n)	تقطيع الأشعار	*taqṭī'ul ash'ār*
scant (adj)	ناقص، قليل	*nāqiṣ, qalīl*
scanty (adj)	غير كاف، قليل	*ghair kāfin, qalīl*
scapegoat (n)	كبش الفداء	*kabashul fidā'*
scar (v/n)	ندب، ندبة	*nadiba, nadbah*
scarce (adj)	نادر، قليل الوجود	*nādir, qalīlul wujūd*
scarcely (adv)	نادراً، بصعوبة	*nādiran, bi ṣu'ūbah*
scarcity (n)	ندرة، قلة، فاقة	*nudrah, qillah, fāqah*
scare (v)	أفزع، أذعر	*afza'a, adh'ara*
scare (n)	ذعر، فزع	*dhu'r, faza'*
scarecrow (n)	فزاعة، خراعة	*fazzā'ah, kharrā'ah*
scared (adj)	فزع، مذعور	*fazi', madh'ūr*
scaremonger (n)	مروع	*murawwi'*
scarf (n)	وشاح، ربطة رقبة	*wishāḥ, rabṭatu raqabah*
scarf pin	دبوس الأربة	*dabbūsul urbah*
scarlet (adj/n)	قرمزي، ثوب قرمزي	*qirmizī, thaub qirmizī*

scathing (adj)	قاسٍ، مرير	*qāsin, marīr*
scatter (v)	بعثر، شتت	*ba'thara, shattata*
scatter-brained (adj)	مشتت الفكر، طائش	*mushattatul fikr, ṭā'ish*
scattered (adj)	مبعثر، مشتت	*muba'thar, mushattat*
scattering (n)	بعثرة، تشتت	*ba'tharah, tashattut*
scattiness (n)	تغافل، حماقة	*taghāful, ḥamāqah*
scatty (adj)	أحمق، مغفل	*aḥmaq, mughaffal*
scavenge (v)	بحث عن طعام	*baḥatha 'an ṭa'ām*
scenario (n)	نص سينمائي	*naṣṣ sīnmā'ī*
scene (n)	منظر، مشهد	*manẓar, mashhad*
scenery (n)	منظر المرسح، مشهد	*manẓarul marsaḥ, mashhad*
scenic (adj)	منظري، مسرحي	*manẓarī, masraḥī*
scent (n)	رائحة، شم، أريج	*rā'iḥah, shamm, arīj*
scent (v)	عطر، شم	*'aṭṭara, shamma*
sceptic (n)	مرتاب، شكوكي	*murtāb, shukūkī*
sceptical (adj)	شكي، مرتاب	*shakkī, murtāb*
scepticism (n)	شكوكية، شكية	*shukūkiyyah, shakkiyyah*
sceptre (scepter)	قضيب السلطة	*qaḍībus sulṭah*
schedule (n)	جدول، برنامج	*jadwal, barnāmaj*
schedule (v)	درج في جدول، سجل	*darraja fī jadwal, sajjala*
schema (n)	خطة	*khuṭṭah*
schematic (adj)	تخطيطي	*takhṭīṭī*
scheme (n)	خطة، مشروع	*khiṭṭah, mashrū'*
scheme (v)	اختط، رسم خطة	*ikhtaṭṭa, rasama khiṭṭah*
schism (n)	انشاق، اختلاف شديد	*inshiqāq, ikhtilāf shadīd*
scholar (n)	أديب، عالم	*'adīb, 'ālim*
scholarly (adj)	مثقف، مختص بدراسة	*muthaqqaf, mukhtaṣṣ bi dirāsah*
scholarship (n)	منحة دراسية	*minḥah dirāsiyyah*
scholastic (adj)	مدرسي، تعليمي	*madrasī, ta'līmī*

school (n)	مدرسة، مذهب	*madrasah, madhhab*
school (v)	درس، درب	*darrasa, darraba*
school age (n)	سن التلمذة	*sinnut talmadhah*
schoolboy (n)	تلميذ، طالب	*tilmīdh, ṭālib*
schoolfellow (n)	زميل المدرسة	*zamīlul madrasah*
school girl (n)	تلميذة، طالبة	*tilmīdhah, ṭālibah*
schoolhouse (n)	مبنى المدرسة	*mabnal madrasah*
schooling (n)	تعليم، تدريب	*ta'līm, tadrīb*
schoolman (n)	أستاذ الجامعة	*ustādhul jāmi'ah*
schoolmaster (n)	مدرس في مدرسة	*mudarris fī madrasah*
schoolmate (n)	رفيق المدرسة	*rafīqul madrasah*
schoolmistress (n)	مدرسة، معلمة	*mudarrisha, mu'allimah*
schoolteacher (n)	معلم، مدرس	*mu'allim, mudarris*
science (n)	علم، معرفة	*'ilm, ma'rifah*
scientific (adj)	علمي، فني	*'ilmī, fannī*
scientifically (adv)	بطريقة علمية	*bi ṭarīqah 'ilmiyyah*
scintillate (v)	تألق، تلألأ	*ta'allaqa, tala'la'a*
scintillation (n)	تألق، وميض	*ta'alluq, wamīḍ*
scissors (n)	مقص	*miqaṣṣ*
scoff (v)	هزأ، هكم	*haza'a, tahakkama*
scoff (n)	سخرية، هزء	*sukhriyyah, huz'*
scoffer (n)	مستهزئ	*mustahzi'*
scoffingly (adv)	باستهزاء، بتهكم	*bistihzā', bi tahakkum*
scold (v)	وبخ، زجر	*wabbakha, zajara*
scold (n)	سليقة، زجر	*salīqah, zajr*
scolding (n)	تعنيف، توبيخ	*ta'nīf, taubīkh*
scoop (n)	مغرفة، ملعقة	*mighrafah, mil'aqah*
scoop (v)	جرف، غرف	*jarafa, gharafa*
scoot (v)	انطلق بسرعة	*inṭalaqa bi sur'ah*
scooter (n)	دراجة الرجل	*darrājatur rijl*
scope (n)	مدى، مأرب، هدف	*madā, ma'rab, hadaf*
scorch (v)	حرق، لفح	*ḥaraqa, lafaḥa*

scorcher (n)	يوم حار جدا	*yawm ḥārr jiddā*
scorching (n)	محرق، لافح	*muḥriq, lāfiḥ*
score (v)	خدش، حز، أحرز، سجل	*khadasha, ḥazza, aḥraza, sajjala*
score (n)	علامة، حزازة، إحراز، خدش	*'alāmah, ḥazāzah, iḥrāz, khadsh*
score-board (n)	لوحة الإصابات	*lauḥatul iṣābāt*
scorer (n)	مسجل الإصابات	*musajjilul iṣābāt*
scorn (n)	استياء، احتقار	*istiyā', iḥtiqār*
scorn (v)	احتقر، ازدرى	*iḥtaqara, izdarā*
scornful (adj)	مزدرٍ، مستخف	*muzdarin, mustakhiff*
scorpion (n)	عقرب	*'aqrab*
Scot (n)	اسكتلندي	*iskatlandī*
scot-free (adv)	بدون أذىً، سالماً	*bidūn adhan, sāliman*
Scottish (adj)	اسكتلندي	*iskatlandī*
scoundrel (n)	محتال، وغد	*muḥtāl, waghd*
scour (v)	نظف، نقح، جال	*naẓẓafa, naqqaḥa, jāla*
scour (n)	تنظيف بالفرك	*tanẓīf bil fark*
scourge (n)	بلاء، كارثة	*balā', kārithah*
scout (n)	حارس، مستطلع	*ḥāris, mustaṭli'*
scout (v)	راقب، بحث	*rāqaba, baḥatha*
scowl (n/v)	عبوس، عبس	*'abūs, 'abasa*
scrabble (v/n)	خمش، خمش	*khamasha, khamsh*
scram (v)	انصرف بسرعة	*inṣarafa bi sur'ah*
scram (n)	تزاحم، تسلق	*tazāḥum, tasalluq*
scramble (n)	زحف، تسلق	*zaḥf, tasalluq*
scrap (n)	قصاصة، كسارة	*quṣāṣah, kusārah*
scrap (v)	كسر، تخاصم	*kasara, takhāṣama*
scrap-book (n)	سجل القصاصات	*sijillul quṣāṣāt*
scrape (v)	حك، صر، سحل	*ḥakka, ṣarra, saḥala*
scrape (n)	كشط، صرير، ورطة	*kashṭ, ṣarīr, warṭah*
scraper (n)	مكشطة	*mikshaṭah*

scrapy (adj)	كسري	*kisarī*
scratch (v)	خدش، هرش	*khadasha, harasha*
scratch (n)	خمش، خدش، خربشة	*khamsh, khadsh, kharbashah*
scratchiness (n)	خشونة، خدش	*khushūnah, khadsh*
scratch paper	ورق التسويد	*waraqut taswīd*
scratchy (adj)	صار، كثير الشوك، خشن	*ṣārr, kathīrush shauk, khashin*
scrawl (v/n)	ثبج، ثبج	*thabaja, thabaj*
scream (v)	صاح، زعق	*ṣāḥa, za'aqa*
scream (n)	صيحة، صرخة	*ṣaiḥah, ṣarkhah*
screamingly (adv)	صائحاً	*ṣā'iḥan*
screech (v)	صاح، صرخ، ذعر	*ṣāḥa, ṣarakha, dha'ara*
screen (n)	ستار، غربال، شاشة	*sitār, ghirbāl, shāshah*
screen (v)	ستر، غربل، فحص	*satara, gharbala, faḥaṣa*
screenplay = scenario		
screen test	اختبار الشاشة	*ikhtibārush shāshah*
screw (n)	برغي، لولب، برمة	*burghī, laulab, barmah*
screw (v)	برم، ربط بلولب	*barama, rabaṭa bi laulab*
screwdriver (n)	مفك البراغي	*mifakkul barāghī*
screwy (adj)	معتوه، غريب الأطوار	*ma'tūh, gharībul aṭwār*
scribble (v)	خربش، ثبج	*kharbasha, thabbaja*
scribbler (n)	مؤلف متعجل	*mu'allif muta'ajjil*
scribe (n)	ناسخ، مسجل	*nāsikh, musajjil*
scrimmage (n)	مناوشة، مشاجرة	*munāwashah, mushājarah*
scrimmage (v)	ناوش، هارش	*nāwasha, hārasha*
script (n)	مخطوطة، خط	*makhṭūṭah, khaṭṭ*
scriptual (adj)	كتابي	*kitābī*
scripture (n)	كتاب مقدس	*kitāb muqaddas*
script-writer (n)	كاتب النصوص	*kātibun nuṣūṣ*
scroll (n)	درج، طومار	*darj, ṭūmār*
scrounge (v)	اختلس	*ikhtalasa*

scrub (n)	أرض ذات أشجار غير نامية	*arḍ dhātu ashjār ghairu nāmiyah*
scrub (v)	نظف، فرك	*naẓẓafa, faraka*
scrubby (adj)	دنئ، سافل	*dani', sāfil*
scruffy (adj)	وضيع، رديء	*waḍī', radī'*
scrumptious (adj)	رائع، لذيذ	*rā'i', ladhīdh*
scrunch (v)	عصر، قضم	*'aṣara, qaḍama*
scruple (n)	تردد، وسواس	*taraddud, waswās*
scrupulous (adj)	متأنق، موسوس	*muta'anniq, muwaswas*
scrupulously (adv)	بوسوسة	*bi waswasah*
scrutinize,-ise (v)	دقق، تقصى	*daqqaqa, taqaṣṣā*
scrutiny (n)	تقصٍّ، تدقيق	*taqaṣṣin, tadqīq*
scud (v)	اندفع، انطلق	*indafa'a, inṭalaqa*
scuffle (v)	تخاصم، تشاجر	*takhāṣama, tashājara*
scuffle (n)	شجار، تعارك	*shijār, ta'āruk*
sculptor (n)	نحات، إزميل	*naḥḥāt, izmīl*
sculpture (v/n)	نحت، فن النحت	*naḥata, fannun naḥt*
scupper (n)	بالوعة السفينة	*bālū'atus safīnah*
scurf (n)	قشرة الرأس، هبرية	*qishratur ra's, hibriyyah*
scurfy (adj)	هبري	*hibrī*
scurrility (n)	بذاءة، دناءة	*badhā'ah, danā'ah*
scurrilous (adj)	بذيء، سفيه	*badhī', safīh*
scurrilousness (n)	بذاءة، سفاهة	*badhā'ah, safāhah*
scuttle (v)	عدا، مشى بخطىً	*'adā, mashā bi khuṭan*
scuttle (n)	فتحة ذات غطاء	*futḥah dhātu ghiṭā'*
scythe (n/v)	منجل، قطع بمنجل	*minjal, qaṭa'a bi minjal*
sea (n)	بحر، يم	*baḥr, yamm*
sea anemone (n)	شقيق البحر	*shaqīqul baḥr*
sea bed (n)	قاع البحر	*qā'ul baḥr*
seaboard (n)	ساحل، شاطئ	*sāḥil, shāṭi'*
sea-borne (adj)	بحري، أوقيانوسي	*baḥrī, ūqyānūsī*
sea-breeze (n)	نسيم البحر	*nasīmul baḥr*

sea-cow (n)	بقرة البحر	*baqaratul baḥr*
sea-dog (n)	ملاح ذو خبرة	*mallāḥ dhū khibrah*
seafarer (n)	ملال، نوتي	*mallāḥ, nūtī*
seafaring (n)	سفر بالبحر	*safar bil baḥr*
seafood (n)	سمكة بحرية	*samakah baḥriyyah*
sea-green (n)	أخضر بحري	*akhḍar baḥrī*
sea-horse (n)	فرس البحر	*farasul baḥr*
seal (v)	ختم، صدق	*khatama, ṣaddaqa*
seal (n)	ختم، عجل البحر	*khatm, 'ijlul baḥr*
sealed (adj)	مختوم	*makhtūm*
sea-legs (n)	ساق بحرية	*sāq baḥriyyah*
sea-lion (n)	أسد البحر	*asadul baḥr*
seam (n)	لفق، درزة	*lafq, darzah*
seaman (n)	نوتي، ملاح	*nūtī, mallāḥ*
seamanship (n)	ملاحة، نوتية	*milāḥah, nūtiyyah*
seamstress (n)	خياطة	*khayyāṭah*
seaplane (n)	طائرة مائية	*ṭā'irah mā'iyyah*
seaport (n)	ميناء، مرفأ	*mīnā', marfa'*
sea power (n)	قوة بحرية	*quwwah baḥriyyah*
search (v)	بحث، تقصى	*baḥatha, taqaṣṣā*
search (n)	بحث، تفتيش	*baḥth, taftīsh*
searchlight (n)	نور كشاف	*nūr kashshāf*
search-warrant	أمر التفتيش	*amrut taftīsh*
seascape (n)	مشهد البحر	*mushhadul baḥr*
sea-shore (n)	شاطئ البحر، جد	*shāṭi'ul baḥr, judd*
seaside (n)	ساحل، شاطئ البحر	*sāḥil, shāṭi'ul baḥr*
season (n)	فصل، موسم، زمن	*faṣl, mausim, zaman*
seasonable (adj)	ملائم، موافق	*mulā'im, muwāfiq*
seasonal (adj)	موسمي	*mausimī*
seasoning (n)	توابل، تتبيل	*tawābil, tatbīl*
seat (n)	مقعد، كرسي	*maq'ad, kursī*
seat (v)	أجلس، أركز	*ajlasa, arkaza*

seat-belt (n)	حزام التثبيت	*ḥizāmut tathbīt*
seating (n)	ترتيب المقاعد	*tartībul maqā'id*
sea-way (n)	طريق بحري	*ṭarīq baḥrī*
seaweed (n)	عشب بحري	*'ushb baḥrī*
seaworthy (adj)	صالح للأبحار	*ṣāliḥ lil abḥār*
secede (v)	انسحب، انفصل	*insaḥaba, infaṣala*
secession (n)	انسحاب، انعزال	*insiḥāb, in'izāl*
seclude (v)	عزل، فصل	*'azala, faṣala*
secluded (adj)	متوحد، منعزل	*mutawaḥḥid, mun'azil*
seclusion (n)	عزلة، خلوة	*'uzlah, khalwah*
second (n/adj)	ثاني، ثانية	*thānī, thāniyah*
second (v)	أيد، ثنى	*ayyada, thannā*
secondary (adj)	ثانوي، غير مهم	*thānawī, ghair muhimm*
secondary school	مدرسة ثانوية	*madrasah thānawiyyah*
second class	درجة ثانية	*darajah thāniyah*
secondly (adv)	ثانياً	*thāniyan*
secrecy (n)	كتمان، خفاء	*kitmān, khafā'*
secret (adj/n)	سري، سر	*sirrī, sirr*
secretarial (adj)	سكرتيري	*sikritīrī*
secretariat (n)	سكرتيرية	*sikritīriyyah*
secretary (n)	سكرتير، أمين	*sikritīr, amīn*
Secretary-General	أمين عام	*amīn 'ām*
Secretary of State	وزير الخارجية	*wazīrul khārijiyyah*
secrete (v)	أفرز، أخفى	*afraza, akhfā*
secretion (n)	إفراز، إخفاء	*ifrāz, ikhfā'*
secretive (adj)	متكتم، كتوم	*mutakattim, katūm*
secretiveness (n)	سرية، تكتم	*sirriyyah, takattum*
secretly (adv)	خفيةً، سرًّا	*khifyatan, sirran*
sectarian (adj)	طائفي، شيعي	*ṭā'ifī, shiya'ī*
sectarianism (n)	طائفية، تشيع	*ṭā'ifiyyah, tashayyu'*
section (n)	جزء، شعبة، قسم	*juz', shu'bah, qism*
section (v)	قطع، فصل، قسم	*qaṭa'a, faṣala, qassama*

sectional (adj)	قطاعي، محلي	*qiṭā'ī, maḥallī*
sector (n)	قطاع دائري	*qiṭā' dā'irī*
sectorial (adj)	قطاعي	*qiṭā'ī*
secular (adj)	علماني، دنيوي	*'almānī, dunyawī*
secularism (n)	علمانية، دنيوية	*'almāniyyah, dunyawiyyah*
secularist (n)	مؤيد لمذهب دنيوي	*mu'ayyid li madhhab dunyawī*
secularize,-ise (v)	حول إلى غرض دنيوي، علمن	*ḥawwala ilā gharaḍ dunyawī, 'almana*
secure (adj)	مأمون، متين	*ma'mūn, matīn*
secure (v)	صان، حاز، كفل	*ṣāna, ḥāza, kafala*
security (n)	أمن، ضمانة	*amn, ḍamānah*
Security Council (n)	مجلس الأمن	*majlisul amn*
sedate (adj)	رصين، هادئ	*raṣīn, hādi'*
sedation (n)	هدوء، سكون	*hudū', sukūn*
sedative (n)	عقار مسكن	*'aqqār musakkin*
sedentary (adj)	جلوسي، مطيل الجلوس	*julūsī, muṭīlul julūs*
sediment (n)	رسابة، ثفالة	*rusābah, thufālah*
sedimentary (adj)	رسابي، ثفالي	*rusābī, thufālī*
sedimentation (n)	رسوب، ترسب	*rusūb, tarassub*
sedition (n)	تحريض على التمرد، ثورة	*taḥrīḍ 'alat tamarrud, thaurah*
seditious (adj)	محرض، مثير	*muḥarriḍ, muthīr*
seduce (v)	أغرى، أغوى	*aghrā, aghwā*
seducer (n)	مغرٍ على الزنا	*mughrin 'alaz zinā*
seduction (n)	إغراء، إغواء	*ighrā', ighwā'*
seductive (adj)	مغرٍ، مضلل	*mughrin, muḍallil*
sedulous (adj)	مثابر، كدود	*muthābir, kadūd*
sedulously (adv)	بمثابرة، بجد	*bi muthābarah, bi jidd*
see (v)	رأى، فهم، شهد	*ra'ā, fahima, shahida*
seed (n)	بذرة، حبة	*badhrah, ḥabbah*

seed (v)	بذر، زرع	*badhara, zara'a*
seed-cake (n)	كعكة بذرية	*ka'kah badhriyyah*
seedling (n)	نبتة صغيرة	*nabtah ṣaghīrah*
seed-pearl (n)	لؤلؤة صغيرة	*lu'lu'ah ṣaghīrah*
seedy (adj)	موعوك، كثير البذور	*mau'ūk, kathīrul budhūr*
seek (v)	طلب، بحث، نشد	*ṭalaba, baḥatha, nashada*
seem (v)	لاح، بدا، ظهر	*lāḥa, badā, ẓahara*
seeming (adj)	ظاهري	*ẓāhirī*
seemingly (adv)	في ما يبدو، في الظاهر	*fī mā yabdū, fiẓ ẓāhir*
seemly (adj)	محتشم، ملائم	*muḥtashim, mulā'im*
seep (v)	تسيل، نز	*tasayyala, nazza*
seepage (n)	نز	*nazz*
see-saw (n)	نواسة	*nawwāsah*
seethe (v)	سلق، اهتاج	*salaqa, ihtāja*
segment (n)	قطعة دائرية	*qiṭ'ah dā'iriyyah*
segmentation (n)	تقطيع، تفلق	*taqṭī', tafalluq*
segregate (v)	فصل، عزل	*faṣala, 'azala*
segregation (n)	فصل، عزل	*faṣl, 'azl*
seismic (adj)	زلزالي	*zalzālī*
seismologist (n)	عالم بزلازل	*'ālim bi zalāzil*
seismology (n)	علم الزلازل	*'ilmuz zalāzil*
seize (v)	قبض، اغتصب، حجز	*qabaḍa, ightaṣaba, ḥajaza*
seizure (n)	قبض، حجز	*qabḍ, ḥajz*
seldom (adv)	نادراً، قلما	*nādiran, qallamā*
select (v)	اختار، انتخب	*ikhtāra, intakhaba*
select (adj)	مختار، مصطفى	*mukhtār, muṣṭafā*
selection (n)	انتقاء، نخبة	*intiqā', nukhbah*
selective (adj)	انتقائي، اختياري	*intiqā'ī, ikhtiyārī*
selectivity (n)	انتقائية، انتخابية	*intiqā'iyyah, intikhābiyyah*
selenium (n)	سلنيوم	*siliniyūm*
self (n)	نفس، عين	*nafs, 'ain*

self-abnegation (n)	نكران الذات	*nukrānudh dhāt*
self-absorbed (adj)	مستغرق في الذات	*mustaghriq fidh dhāt*
self-abuse (n)	انتقاص الذات	*intiqāṣudh dhāt*
self-addressed (adj)	معنون بعنوان المرسل	*mu'anwan bi 'unwānil mursil*
self-assertive (adj)	معتد بالذات	*mu'tadd bidh dhāt*
self-assured (adj)	واثق بنفسه	*wāthiq bi nafsih*
self-centred (adj)	معجب بذاته	*mu'jab bi dhātih*
self-centredness (n)	أنانية، تمتع بذاته	*anāniyyah, tamattu' bi dhātih*
self-confidence (n)	ثقة بالنفس	*thiqah bin nafs*
self-confident (adj)	واثق بنفسه	*wāthiq bi nafsih*
self-conscious (adj)	واعٍ ذاته، هيوب	*wā'in dhātahu, hayūb*
self-consciousness	وعي ذاته	*wa'yu dhātih*
self-contained (adj)	راضٍ بذاته	*rāḍin bi dhātih*
self-control (n)	ضبط النفس	*ḍabṭun nafs*
self-controlled (adj)	ضابط النفس	*ḍābiṭun nafs*
self-defence (n)	دفاع عن النفس	*difā' 'anin nafs*
self-denial (n)	نكران الذات	*nukrānudh dhāt*
self-determination	تقرير المصير، عزم	*taqrīrul maṣīr, 'azm*
self-discipline (n)	انضباط ذاتي	*inḍibāṭ dhātī*
self-drive (adj)	ذاتي الحركة	*dhātiyyul ḥarakah*
self-employed (adj)	ذو مهنة حرة	*dhū mihnah ḥurrah*
self-esteem (n)	احترام الذات	*iḥtirāmudh dhāt*
self-evident (adj)	بديهي، واضح بذاته	*badīhī, wāḍiḥ bi dhātih*
self-explanatory (adj)	مفسر بذاته	*mufassir bi dhātih*
self-important (adj)	معتد بنفسه	*mu'tadd bi nafsih*
self-imposed (adj)	مفروض ذاتيًا	*mafrūḍ dhātiyyan*
self-indulgence (n)	انغماس ذاتي	*inghimās dhātī*
self-indulgent (adj)	منغمس ذاتيًا	*munghamis dhātiyyan*
self-interest (n)	مصلحة شخصية	*maṣlaḥah shakhṣiyyah*
selfish (adj)	محب نفسه، أثر	*muḥibb nafsah, athir*

selfishly (adv)	باستئثار	*bisti'thār*
selfishness (n)	حب الذات، أنانية	*ḥubbudh dhāt, anāniyyah*
selfless (adj)	غير أناني، غيري	*ghair anānī, ghairī*
selflessly (adv)	بإيثار	*bi īthār*
selflessness (n)	إيثار	*īthār*
self-locking (adj)	ذاتي القفل	*dhātiyyul qafal*
self-made (adj)	عصامي	*'iṣāmī*
self-opinionated (adj)	مغرور	*maghrūr*
self-pity (n)	إشفاق على الذات	*ishfāq 'aladh dhāt*
self-portrait (n)	صورة ذاتية	*ṣūrah dhātiyyah*
self-possed (adj)	رابط الجأش	*rābiṭul ja'sh*
self-preservation (n)	حفظ الذات	*ḥifẓudh dhāt*
self-respect (n)	احترام النفس	*iḥtirāmun nafs*
self-sacrifice (n)	تضحية بالذات	*taḍḥiyah bidh dhāt*
self-satisfied (adj)	راضٍ عن نفسه	*rāḍin 'an nafsih*
self-service (n)	خدمة ذاتية	*khidmah dhātiyyah*
self-styled (adj)	مزيف	*muzayyaf*
self-sufficiency (n)	اكتفاء ذاتي	*iktifā' dhātī*
self-sufficient (adj)	متكل على نفسه	*muttakil 'alā nafsih*
self-supporting (adj)	قائم بنفقته، معيل بنفسه	*qā'im bi nafaqatih, mu'īl bi nafsih*
sell (v)	باع، روج، أسلم	*bā'a, rawwaja, aslama*
sell (n)	بيع، خداع، قنوت	*bai', khidā', qunūt*
seller (n)	بائع، كتاب رائج	*bā'i', kitāb rā'ij*
selvage (selvedge)	حاشية القماش	*ḥāshiyatul qumāsh*
semantics (n)	علم دلالات الألفاظ	*'ilmu dalālātil alfāẓ*
semblance (n)	شبه، مشابهة	*shibh, mushābahah*
semen (n)	مني	*manī*
semester (n)	فصل	*faṣl*
semi (n)	نصف	*niṣf*
semicircle (n)	نصف دائرة	*niṣfu dā'irah*
semicircular (adj)	نصف دائري	*niṣf dā'irī*

semicolon (n)	شولة منقوطة	*shaulah manqūṭah*
semi-conscious (adj)	نصف واعٍ	*niṣfu wā'in*
semi-detached (adj)	شبه منفصل	*shibhu munfaṣil*
semifinal (n)	شبه نهائي	*shibhu nihā'ī*
seminal (adj)	منوي، بزري، نطفي	*manawī, bizrī, nuṭfī*
seminar (n)	حلقة دراسية، مؤتمر، سمينار	*ḥalaqah dirāsiyyah, mu'tamar, samīnār*
semiprecious (adj)	شبه كريم	*shibhu karīm*
semi-skilled (adj)	متوسط المهارة	*mutawassiṭul mahārah*
Semite	سامي	*sāmī*
Semitic (adj)	سامي، سامية	*sāmī, sāmiyah*
semitone (n)	نصف نغمة	*niṣf naghmah*
semitropical (adj)	نصف استوائي	*niṣf istiwā'ī*
semivowel (n)	شبه صوت لين	*shibhu ṣaut līn*
senate (n)	مجلس الشيوخ	*majlisush shuyūkh*
senator (n)	سناتور، شيخ	*sinātūr, shaikh*
senatorial (adj)	سناتوري، مختص بالشيوخ	*sinātūrī, mukhtaṣṣ bish shuyūkh*
send (v)	أرسل، طرد	*arsala, ṭarada*
send-off (n)	توديع	*taudī'*
senior (adj/n)	أرشد، أكبر	*arshad, akbar*
seniority (n)	أولية، أسبقية	*awwaliyyah, asbaqiyyah*
sensation (n)	شعور، إحساس	*shu'ūr, iḥsās*
sensational (adj)	حسي، محرك العواطف	*ḥissī, muḥarrikul 'awāṭif*
sense (n)	حس، شعور، إدراك	*ḥiss, shu'ūr, idrāk*
sense (v)	شعر، أدرك، أحس	*sha'ara, adraka, aḥassa*
senseless (adj)	عديم الحس، فاقد الشعور	*'adīmul ḥiss, fāqidush shu'ūr*
sense-organ	عضو الحس	*'uḍwul ḥiss*
sensibility (n)	حساسية، دقة الإحساس	*ḥassāsiyyah, diqqatul iḥsās*
sensible (adj)	حساس، سريع التأثر	*ḥassās, sarī'ut ta'aththur*

sensitive (adj)	حسي، ذو حس	*ḥissī, dhū ḥiss*
sensitivity (n)	حساسية، إحساس	*ḥassāsiyyah, iḥsās*
sensor (n)	جهاز الإحساس	*jihāzul iḥsās*
sensory (adj)	متعلق بالحواس	*muta'alliq bil ḥawāss*
sensual (adj)	جسدي، حسي	*jasadī, ḥissī*
sensualist (n)	منغمس في الشهوات	*munghamis fish shahawāt*
sensuality (n)	انغماس في الشهوات	*inghimās fish shahawāt*
sensuous (adj)	حسي	*ḥissī*
sensuously (adv)	حسيًا	*ḥissiyyan*
sensuousness (n)	حسية	*ḥissiyyah*
sentence (n)	جملة، حكم	*jumlah, ḥukm*
sentence (v)	حكم على	*ḥakama 'alā*
sententious (adj)	مضجر، ممل	*muḍjir, mumill*
sentient (adj)	حساس، مدقق، واعٍ	*ḥassās, mudaqqiq, wā'in*
sentiment (n)	عاطفة، ميل	*'āṭifah, mail*
sentimental (adj)	عواطفي، تأثري	*'awāṭifī, ta'aththurī*
sentimentality (n)	عاطفية	*'āṭifiyyah*
sentinel (n)	خفير، حارس	*khafīr, ḥāris*
sentry (n)	حارس، ديدبان	*ḥāris, daidabān*
separable (adj)	قابل للفصل	*qābil lil faṣl*
separate (v)	فصل، فرق	*faṣala, farraqa*
separate (adj)	منفصل، مفكك	*munfaṣil, mufakkak*
separately (adv)	بانفصال، على انفراد	*binfiṣāl, 'alā infirād*
separation (n)	انفصال، عزل، فصل	*infiṣāl, 'azl, faṣl*
September (n)	سبتمبر، أيلول	*sibtimbar, ailūl*
septic (adj)	عفن، كرج	*'afin, karij*
sepulchral (adj)	ضريحي، مدفني	*ḍarīḥī, madfanī*
sepulchre (sepulcher)	ضريح، مدفن	*ḍarīḥ, madfan*
sequel (n)	ملحق، عاقبة، تكملة	*mulḥaq, 'āqibah, takmilah*
sequential (adj)	متعاقب، تالٍ	*muta'āqib, tālin*
sequentially (adv)	بسلسلة متعاقبة	*bi silsilah muta'āqibah*

sequestered (adj)	منعزل، متوحد	*mun'azil, mutawaḥḥid*
sequestrate (v)	حجز، نزع الملكية	*ḥajaza, naza'al milkiyyah*
sequestration (n)	نزع الملكية	*naz'ul milkiyyah*
seraglio (n)	حريم	*ḥarīm*
seraph (n)	ساروف	*sārūf*
seraphic (adj)	ساروفي، ملائكي	*sārūfī, malā'ikī*
serenade (n)	سريناد، عزف موسيقي	*sirīnād, 'azf mausīqī*
serene (adj)	هادئ، رصين	*hādi', raṣīn*
serenely (adv)	بهدوء، برصانة	*bi hudū', bi raṣānah*
serenity (n)	هدوء، رصانة	*hudū', raṣānah*
serf (n)	قن	*qinn*
serfdom (n)	قنانة، عبودية	*qinānah, 'ubūdiyyah*
sergeant (n)	رقيب، قائد	*raqīb, qā'id*
sergeant-major (n)	رقيب أول	*raqīb awwal*
serial (n/adj)	متسلسل، متتابع	*mutasalsil, mutatābi'*
serialize,-ise (v)	نشر بتسلسل	*nashara bi tasalsul*
serially (adv)	بتسلسل، بتتابع	*bi tasalsul, bi tatābu'*
series (n)	سلسلة، نسق	*silsilah, nasaq*
serif (n)	ذنابة	*dhinābah*
serious (adj)	خطير، رزين، وقور	*khaṭīr, razīn, waqūr*
seriously (adv)	باهتمام، برصانة، بجد	*bihtimām, bi raṣānah, bi jidd*
seriousness (n)	جدية، خطورة	*jiddiyyah, khuṭūrah*
sermon (n)	خطبة، موعظة	*khuṭbah, mau'iẓah*
serpent (n)	حية، ثعبان	*ḥayyah, thu'bān*
serpentive (adj)	متمعج، ملتف	*mutama''ij, multaff*
serum (n)	مصل، مصالة	*maṣl, muṣālah*
servant (n)	خادم، أجير	*khādim, ajīr*
serve (v)	خدم، نفع، كفى	*khadama, nafa'a, kafā*
server (n)	نادل، خادم	*nādil, khādim*
service (n)	خدمة، فضل	*khidmah, faḍl*

service (v)	أصلح، رمم	*aṣlaḥa, rammama*
service charge	رسم الخدمة	*rasmul khidmah*
serviceman (n)	جندي	*jundiyy*
service station (n)	محطة بنــزين	*maḥaṭṭatu binzīn*
serviette (n)	منديل المائدة	*mindīlul mā'idah*
servile (adj)	متذلل، خسيس	*mutadhallil, khasīs*
servility (n)	خضوع، ذل، رق	*khuḍū', dhull, riqq*
servitude (n)	عبودية، رق	*'ubūdiyyah, riqq*
sesame (n)	سمسم	*simsim*
session (n)	جلسة، دورة	*jalsah, daurah*
sessional (adj)	دوري، انعقادي	*daurī, in'iqādī*
set (v)	خصب، رتب، أحكم، غرب	*khaṣṣaba, rattaba, aḥkama, gharaba*
set (adj)	مرتب، معين	*murattab, mu'ayyan*
set (n)	مجموعة، غروب	*majmū'ah, ghurūb*
set bact	عاق، حجز	*'āqa, ḥajaza*
set-back (n)	عقبة، عائق	*'aqabah, 'ā'iq*
set down	أقعد، أنزل	*aq'ada, anzala*
set forth	بدأ الرحلة	*bada'ar riḥlah*
set free	حرر، أعتق	*ḥarrara, a'taqa*
set out	انطلق، سافر	*inṭalaqa, sāfara*
setting (n)	وضع، تركيب	*waḍ', tarkīb*
settle (v)	سوى، رتب، استوطن، قرر	*sawwā, rattaba, istauṭana qarrara*
settled (adj)	ثابت، راسخ	*thābit, rāsikh*
settlement (n)	استقرار، تسوية	*istiqrār, taswiyah*
settler (n)	مستوطن، مستعمر	*mustauṭin, musta'mir*
set up	أقام، نصب	*aqāma, naṣaba*
set-up (n)	بنية، تركيب	*binyah, tarkīb*
seven (n)	سبع، سبعة	*sab', sab'ah*
seventeen (n)	سبعة عشر	*sab'atu 'ashar*
seventeenth (adj)	سابع عشر	*sābi' 'ashar*

seventh (adj)	سابع	*sābi'*
seventieth (adj/n)	سبعون، جزء سبعون	*sab'ūn, juz' sab'ūn*
seventy (n)	سبعون	*sab'ūn*
sever (v)	قطع، فصل	*qaṭa'a, faṣala*
several (adj)	متعدد، منفصل	*muta'addid, munfaṣil*
severally (adv)	إفراديًّا، منفصلاً	*ifrādiyyan, munfaṣilan*
severance (n)	فصل، قطع	*faṣl, qaṭ'*
severe (adj)	عنيف، قاسٍ، صارم	*'anīf, qāsin, ṣārim*
severely (adv)	بصرامة، بعنف	*bi ṣarāmah, bi 'unf*
severity (n)	عنف، تجهم	*'unf, tajahhum*
sew (v)	خاط، خيط	*khāṭa, khayyaṭa*
sewage (n)	أقذار البواليع	*aqdhārul bawālī'*
sewer (n)	خائط، بالوعة	*khā'iṭ, bālū'ah*
sewing (n)	خياطة	*khiyāṭah*
sewing matchine	ماكينة الخياطة	*mākīnatul khiyāṭah*
sex (n)	جنس، اتصال جنسي	*jins, ittiṣāl jinsī*
sex act (n)	اتصال جنسي	*ittiṣāl jinsī*
sex appeal (n)	نداء جنسي	*nidā' jinsī*
sex chromosome	صبغية الجنس	*ṣibghiyyatul jins*
sex harmone	هرمون الجنس	*harmūnul jins*
sexless (adj)	عديم الجنسية	*'adīmul jinsiyyah*
sexologist (n)	طبيب أمراض جنسية	*ṭabību amrāḍ jinsiyyah*
sexology (n)	علم الجنس، سكسولوجيا	*'ilmul jins, siksūlūjiyā*
sexual (adj)	جنسي، توالدي	*jinsī, tawāludī*
sexual intercourse	جماع، مضاجعة	*jimā', muḍāja'ah*
sexuality (n)	نشاط جنسي	*nashāṭ jinsī*
sexy (adj)	جنسي، مثير للشهوة	*jinsī, muthīr lish shahwah*
shabbiness (n)	رثاثة، رداءة	*rathāthah, radā'ah*
shabby (adj)	رث، رديء، بالٍ	*rathth, radī', bālin*
shack (n)	كوخ	*kūkh*
shackle (n)	غل، صفاد	*ghull, ṣifād*

shackle (v)	صفد، غل	*ṣaffada, ghalla*
shade (n)	ظل، فيء، ستار	*ẓill, fai', sitār*
shade (v)	ظلل، قتم، ستر	*ẓallala, qattama, satara*
shades (n)	طيف، خيال	*ṭaif, khayāl*
shadow (n)	ظل، صورة، طيف، حزن	*ẓill, ṣūrah, ṭaif, ḥuzn*
shadow (v)	ظلل، أحزن، أظلم	*ẓallala, aḥzana, aẓlama*
shadowy (adj)	مظلم، مبهم	*muẓlim, mubham*
shady (adj)	ظليل، غامض	*ẓalīl, ghāmiḍ*
shaft (n)	قصبة رمح أو سهم	*qaṣabatu rumḥ aw sahm*
shaggy (adj)	خشن، أشعث	*khashin, ash'ath*
shake (v)	زعزع، رج، هز	*za'za'a, rajja, hazza*
shake (n)	هزة، ارتعاش، مصافحة	*hazzah, irti'āsh, muṣāfaḥah*
shaking (n)	اهتزاز، زلزال	*ihtizāz, zilzāl*
shake-up (n)	إصلاح عظيم	*iṣlāḥ 'aẓīm*
shakiness (n)	توعك، تزلزل	*tawa''uk, tazalzul*
shaky (adj)	متوعك، متقلقل	*mutawa''ik, mutaqalqil*
shall (v)	فعل معاون	*fi'l mu'āwin*
shallow (n)	ضحل، قليل الغور، سطحي	*ḍaḥl, qalīlul ghaur, saṭḥī*
shallowness (n)	سطحية	*saṭḥiyyah*
sham (n/adj)	كاذب، خادع، زائف	*kādhib, khādi', zā'if*
shame (n)	خزي، خجل	*khizy, khajal*
shame (v)	أخجل، أخزى	*akhjala, akhzā*
shameful (adj)	فاضح، مخزٍ	*fāḍiḥ, mukhzin*
shamefully (adv)	على نحو مخزٍ	*'alā naḥwin mukhzin*
shamefulness (n)	عار، خزي	*'ār, khizy*
shameless (n)	وقح، عديم الحياء	*waqiḥ, 'adīmul ḥayā'*
shamelessly (adv)	بدون حياء، بوقاحة	*bi dūn ḥayā', bi waqāḥah*
shamelessness (n)	وقاحة، عدم حياء	*waqāḥah, 'adamu ḥayā'*
shampoo (n)	شامبو	*shāmbū*
shank (n)	ساق، قصبة الرجل	*sāq, qaṣabatur rijl*

shape (n)	شكل، هيئة، شبح، قالب	*shakl, hay'ah, shabaḥ, qālab*
shape (v)	صاغ، شكل	*ṣāgha, shakkala*
shapeless (adj)	لا شكل لـه، مشوه	*lā shakla lahu, mushawwah*
share (v)	قاسم، حصص، شارك	*qāsama, ḥaṣṣaṣa, shāraka*
share (n)	حصة، سهم	*ḥiṣṣah, sahm*
shareholder (n)	مساهم	*musāhim*
shark (n)	قرش، سمك بحري	*qirsh, samak baḥrī*
shark-skin (n)	جلد القرش	*jildul qirsh*
sharp (adj)	حاد، قاسٍ، قاطع، حاذق	*ḥādd, qāsin, qāṭi‘, ḥādhiq*
sharpen (v)	شحذ، أبرى	*shaḥadha, abrā*
sharpener (n)	مبراة، مشحذ	*mibrāt, mishḥadh*
sharply (adv)	بحدة، بذكاء	*bi ḥiddah, bi dhakā'*
sharp-sighted (adj)	حاد البصر	*ḥāddul baṣar*
sharp-witted (adj)	ذكي، فطن	*dhakiyy, faṭin*
shatter (v)	حطم، كسر، تناثر	*ḥaṭṭama, kassara, tanāthara*
shattering (adj)	صارم، قاسٍ	*ṣārim, qāsin*
shatterproof (n)	صامد للكسر	*ṣāmid lil kasr*
shave (v)	حلق، سحج	*ḥalaqa, saḥaja*
shave (n)	حلاقة، سحج	*ḥilāqah, saḥj*
shaver (n)	محلاق كهربائي	*miḥlāq kahrabā'ī*
shaving (n)	حلاقة	*ḥilāqah*
shaving-brush (n)	فرشاة الحلاقة	*furshātul ḥilāqah*
shaving-cream (n)	معجون الحلاقة	*ma‘jūnul ḥilāqah*
shawl (n)	شال، رداء	*shāl, ridā'*
she (pron)	هى	*hiya*
sheaf (n)	حزمة، كدس	*ḥuzmah, kuds*
shear (v)	قص، جز	*qaṣṣa, jazza*
sheath (n)	غمد، قراب	*ghimd, qirāb*

sheathe (v)	غمد، غلف	*ghammada, ghallafa*
sheat-knife (n)	مدية غمدية	*mudyah ghimdiyyah*
shed (n)	سقيفة، مظلة	*saqīfah, miẓallah*
shed (v)	أراق، صب، سال	*arāqa, ṣabba, sāla*
sheen (n)	لمعان، بريق	*lam'ān, barīq*
sheep (n)	ضأن، نعجة، خروف	*ḍa'n, na'jah, kharūf*
sheep-dog (n)	كلب الراعي	*kalbur rā'ī*
sheep-fold (n)	حظيرة الغنم	*ḥaẓīratul ghanam*
sheepish (adj)	جبان، أخرق	*jabān, akhraq*
sheepskin (n)	جلد الغنم	*jildul ghanam*
sheer (adj)	صرف، خالص، محض	*ṣirf, khāliṣ, maḥḍ*
sheer (v)	صرف، حرف	*ṣarafa, ḥarafa*
sheet (n)	فرخ، صحيفة	*farkh, ṣaḥīfah*
shelf (n)	رف، صفة	*raff, ṣuffah*
shell (n)	قشرة، صدفة، قذيفة	*qishrah, ṣadafah, qadhīfah*
shell (v)	قشر، رمى بالقنابل	*qashshara, ramā bil qanābil*
shelfish (n)	محار	*maḥār*
shelter (n)	مأوى، ستر	*ma'wā, sitr*
shelter (v)	آوى، حمى، لجأ	*āwā, ḥamā, laja'a*
shelve (v)	وضع على رف	*waḍa'a 'alā raff*
shephered (v/n)	رعى، راعي	*ra'ā, rā'ī*
shepheredess (n)	راعية الغنم	*rā'iyatul ghanam*
sherbet (n)	شراب، مشروب	*sharāb, mashrūb*
shield (n)	ترس، مدرأ	*turs, midra'*
shield (v)	حمى، ستر	*ḥamā, satara*
shift (v)	نقل، بدل، انتقل	*naqala, baddala, intaqala*
shift (n)	تغير، مناوبة	*taghayyur, munāwabah*
shiftless (adj)	كسلان، غير نشيط	*kaslān, ghair nashīṭ*
shifty (adj)	داهية، ماكر	*dāhiyah, mākir*
shilling (n)	شلن، جنيه انكليزي	*shilin, junaih inkilīzī*

shimmer (n/v)	وميض، أومض	*wamīḍ, aumaḍa*
shin (n)	قصبة الرجل	*qaṣabatur rijl*
shine (n)	تألق، لمعة	*ta'alluq, lum'ah*
shine (v)	لمع، أضاء، أشرق	*lama'a, aḍā'a, ashraqa*
shiny (adj)	لامع، مضيء، مشرق	*lāmi', muḍī', mushriq*
ship (n)	مركب، سفينة	*markab, safīnah*
ship (v)	أرسل بسفينة، شحن	*arsala bi safīnah, shaḥana*
shipboard (n)	متن السفينة	*matanus safīnah*
shipment (n)	شحن في سفينة	*shaḥn fī safīnah*
shipper (n)	شاحن	*shāḥin*
shipping (n)	مجموعة السفن	*majmū'atus sufun*
shirt (n)	قميص	*qamīṣ*
shirting (n)	قماش لصنع القمصان	*qumāsh li ṣun'il qumṣān*
shritwaist (n)	بلوزة نسوية	*balūzah nisawiyyah*
shiver (v)	ارتعش، تشظى	*irta'asha, tashaẓẓā*
shiver (n)	رعشة، رجفة	*ra'shah, rajfah*
shoal (n)	سربة، قطيع	*surbah, qaṭī'*
shock (n)	صدمة، رجة	*ṣadamah, rajjah*
shock (v)	صدم، فجع	*ṣadama, faja'a*
shocking (adj)	مفجع، فظيع	*mufajji', faẓī'*
shockingly (adv)	بفظاعة، برداءة	*bi faẓā'ah, bi radā'ah*
shoddy (adj)	رديء	*radī'*
shoe (n)	حذاء، حدوة	*ḥidhā', ḥidwah*
shoe-lace (n)	شريط الحذاء	*sharīṭul ḥidhā'*
shoemaker (n)	صانع الأحذية	*ṣāni'ul aḥdhiyah*
shoot (v)	أطلق النار، انطلق بسرعة	*aṭlaqan nār, inṭalaqa bi sur'ah*
shoot (n)	برعم جديد	*bur'um jadīd*
shop (n)	دكان، محل	*dukkān, maḥall*
shop (v)	تسوق، تبضع	*tasawwaqa, tabaḍḍa'a*
shopkeeper (n)	صاحب الحانوت	*ṣāḥibul ḥānūt*
shopping (n)	تسوق	*tasawwuq*

shore (n)	شاطئ البحر	*shāṭi'ul baḥr*
shore (v)	دعم، سند	*da'ama, sanada*
short (adj)	قصير، صغير، مختصر	*qaṣīr, ṣaghīr, mukhtaṣar*
short (adv)	باختصار	*bikhtiṣār*
shortage (n)	نقص، عجز	*naqṣ, 'ajz*
short circuit (n)	دائرة قصر	*dā'iratu qiṣar*
shortcoming (n)	نقص، عيب	*naqṣ, 'aib*
shorten (v)	قصر، اختصر	*qaṣṣara, ikhtaṣara*
shorthand (n)	كتابة مختزلة	*kitābah mukhtazalah*
short-lived (adj)	قصير العمر	*qaṣīrul 'umr*
shortly (adj)	باختصار، عن قريب	*bikhtiṣār, 'an qarīb*
short-sighted (adj)	حسير، قصير البصر	*ḥasīr, qaṣīrul baṣar*
short-tempered (adj)	سريع الغضب	*sarī'ul ghaḍab*
short-term (adj)	قصير الأجل	*qaṣīrul ajal*
short-winded (adj)	ضيق النفس	*ḍayyiqun nafas*
shot (n)	طلقة نارية، محاولة، رش	*ṭalaqah nāriyyah, muḥāwalah, rashsh*
shot (adj)	متموج الألوان	*mutamawwijul alwān*
should (v)	يلزم، يجب	*yalzim, yajib*
shoulder (n)	كتف، منكب	*katif, mankib*
shoulder (v)	تنكب، رفع بالكتف	*tanakkaba, rafa'a bil katif*
shoulder-bag (n)	حقيبة الكتف	*ḥaqībatul katif*
shoulder-blade (n)	عظم كتفي	*'aẓm katifī*
shoulder-strap (n)	حمالة الكتف	*ḥimālatul katif*
shout (v)	صاح، هتف	*ṣāḥa, hatafa*
shout (n)	صياح، هتاف	*ṣiyāḥ, hutāf*
shove (v)	دسر، زق	*dasara, zaqqa*
shovel (v/n)	جرف، مجرفة	*jarafa, mijrafah*
shown (n)	عرض، مظهر، حفلة مسرحية	*'arḍ, maẓhar, ḥaflah masraḥiyyah*
show (v)	أظهر، عرض	*aẓhara, 'araḍa*
show-case (n)	خزانة العرض	*khizānatul 'arḍ*

show-down (n)	حسم لقضية	*ḥasm li qaḍiyyah*
shower (n)	دش، وابل	*dushsh, wābil*
shower (v)	رش، نفح	*rashsha, nafaḥa*
showgirl (n)	فتاة الاستعراض	*fatātul isti'rāḍ*
showing (n)	عرض، إظهار	*'arḍ, iẓhār*
showman (n)	مخرج المسرحية	*mukhrijul masraḥiyyah*
show-off (n)	شخص متباه	*shakhṣ mutabāhin*
show-piece (n)	تحفة، نموذج رائع	*tuḥfah, namūdhaj rā'i'*
show-place (n)	موطن رائع	*mauṭin rā'i'*
showroom (n)	صالة العرض	*ṣālatul 'arḍ*
shred (n)	خرقة، مزقة	*khirqah, mizqah*
shrewd (adj)	داه، مكار	*dāhin, makkār*
shrewdly (adv)	بدهاء، بمكر	*bi dahā', bi makr*
shrewdness (n)	دهاء، مكر	*dahā', makr*
shriek (v)	زعق، صرخ	*za'aqa, ṣarakha*
shriek (n)	صياح، زعيق	*ṣiyāḥ, za'īq*
shrill (adj)	حاد، شديد، صاخب	*ḥādd, shadīd, ṣākhib*
shrine (n)	حرم، مزار	*ḥaram, mazār*
shrink (v)	تقلص، انكمش	*taqallaṣa, inkamasha*
shrink (n)	انكماش، تقلص	*inkimāsh, taqalluṣ*
shrinkage (n)	تقلص، نقص	*taqalluṣ, naqṣ*
shroud (v)	غطى، حجب	*ghaṭṭā, ḥajaba*
shroud (n)	كفن، غطاء	*kafan, ghiṭā'*
shrub (n)	شجيرة	*shujairah*
shudder (v)	ارتعد بشدة	*irta'ada bi shiddah*
shudder (n)	ارتعاد، ارتجاف	*irti'ād, irtijāf*
shuffle (v)	دلف، خلط	*dalafa, khalaṭa*
shuffle (n)	دلوف، خلط	*dulūf, khalṭ*
shun (v)	تجنب، تنحى	*tajannaba, tanaḥḥā*
shunt (v)	حول، تحول	*ḥawwala, taḥawwala*
shut (v)	أغلق، أقفل	*aghlaqa, aqfala*
shut-down (n)	إغلاق، إيقاف	*ighlāq, īqāf*

shutter (n)	مصراع، شريحة	*miṣrā', sharīḥah*
shutter (v)	أغلق بمصراع	*aghlaqa bi miṣrā'*
shuttle (v)	توشع، تمور	*tawashsha'a, tamawwara*
shuttle (n)	مكوك	*makkūk*
shy (adj)	حيي، خجول	*ḥayī, khajūl*
shyly (adv)	بحياء، بنفور	*bi ḥayā', bi nufūr*
shyness (n)	حياء، جفول	*ḥayā', jufūl*
sick (adj)	مريض، عليل	*marīḍ, 'alīl*
sick-bed (n)	فراش المرض	*firāshul maraḍ*
sicken (v)	أمرض، أغثى	*amraḍa, aghthā*
sickening (adj)	ممرض، مغث	*mumriḍ, mughthin*
sickle (n)	منجل، مشول	*minjal, mishwal*
sick-leave (n)	إجازة مرضية	*ijāzah maraḍiyyah*
sickly (adj)	سقيم، عليل	*saqīm, 'alīl*
sickness (n)	مرض، غثيان	*maraḍ, ghathayān*
sick-room (n)	حجرة التمريض	*ḥujratut tamrīḍ*
side (n)	جانب، ضلع، جهة	*jānib, ḍil', jihah*
side-effect (n)	مفعول جانبي	*maf'ūl jānibī*
sidekick (n)	صديق، حميم	*ṣadīq, ḥamīm*
sidelight (n)	ضوء جانبي	*ḍaw' jānibī*
sideline (n)	خط جانبي	*khaṭṭ jānibī*
sideline (v)	أخرج	*akhraja*
sidereal (adj)	فلكي، نجمي	*falakī, najmī*
side-show (n)	مشهد جانبي	*mashhad jānibī*
side-step (n)	خطوة جانبية	*khuṭwah jānibiyyah*
side-track (n)	خط جانبي	*khaṭṭ jānibī*
sideways (adv)	على الجنب	*'alal jamb*
side-whiskers (n)	سبلة جانبية	*sabalah jānibiyyah*
siding =side-track		
siege (n)	محاصرة، حصار	*muḥāṣarah, ḥiṣār*
siesta (n)	قيلولة، استراحة الظهر	*qailūlah, istirāḥatuẓ ẓuhr*
sieve (n)	منخل	*munkhal*

sift (v)	نخل، تنخل	*nakhala, tanakhkhala*
sigh (v)	تنهد، تحسر	*tanahhada, taḥassara*
sigh (n)	تحسر، تنهد	*taḥassur, tanahhud*
sight (n)	منظر، بصر، رؤية	*manẓar, baṣar, ru'yah*
sighted (adj)	ذو نظر	*dhū naẓar*
sightless (adj)	أعمى	*a'mā*
sightseeing (n)	زيارة المآثر	*ziyāratul ma'āthir*
sightseer (n)	مشاهد، متفرج	*mushāhid, mutafarrij*
sign (n)	علامة، دليل، سمة	*'alāmah, dalīl, simah*
sign (v)	وقع، أومى	*waqqa'a, awmā*
signal (n)	إشارة، إيماءة	*ishārah, īmā'ah*
signal (adj)	مميز، رائع	*mumayyaz, rā'i'*
signalman (n)	ملوح	*mulawwiḥ*
signatory (n)	موقع، صاحب توقيع	*muwaqqi', ṣāḥibu tauqī'*
signature (n)	توقيع، إشارة	*tauqī', ishārah*
signboard (n)	لوحة الاسم، لافتة	*lauḥatul ism, lāfitah*
signet (n)	ختم	*khatm*
significance (n)	أهمية، مغزى	*ahammiyyah, maghzā*
significant (adj)	هام، ذو معنى	*hāmm, dhū ma'nā*
signification (n)	معنى، دلالة	*ma'nā, dalālah*
signify (v)	دل على، أفاد	*dalla 'alā, afāda*
silence (n/v)	سكوت، أسكت	*sukūt, askata*
silent (adj)	ساكت، ساكن	*sākit, sākin*
silently (adv)	بسكوت، بصمت	*bi sukūt, bi ṣamt*
silent partner	شريك صامت	*sharīk ṣāmit*
silicon (n)	سليكون	*silīkūn*
silk (n)	حرير، ثوب حريري	*ḥarīr, thaub ḥarīrī*
silken (adj)	حريري، ناعم كالحرير	*ḥarīrī, nā'im kal ḥarīr*
silkworm (n)	دودة الحرير	*dūdatul ḥarīr*
silky (adj)	حريري، ناعم	*ḥarīrī, nā'im*
sill (n)	جلسة الشباك، جدة موازية	*jalsatush shubbāk, juddah muwāziyah*
silliness (n)	سخف، حماقة	*sukhf, ḥamāqah*

silly (adj/n)	أحمق، سخيف	*aḥmaq, sakhīf*
silo (n)	سلوة، مخزن الغلال	*salwah, makhzanul ghilāl*
silt (v/n)	غرين، غرين	*gharyana, gharīn*
silver (n/adj)	فضة، فضي	*fiḍḍah, fiḍḍī*
silver (v)	طلى بالفضة	*ṭalā bil fiḍḍah*
silver-fish (n)	سمكة فضية	*samakah fiḍḍiyyah*
silver lining	حاشية فضية	*ḥāshiyah fiḍḍiyyah*
silver paper	ورق فضي	*waraq fiḍḍī*
silversmith (n)	صانع الفضة	*ṣāni'ul fiḍḍah*
silver-tongued (adj)	ذرب اللسان	*dharibul lisān*
silverware (n)	آنية المائدة الفضية	*āniyatul mā'idah al fiḍḍiyyah*
silvery (adj)	فضي، فضاني	*fiḍḍī, fiḍḍānī*
similar (adj)	شبيه، مماثل	*shabīh, mumāthil*
similarity (n)	مماثلة، مشابهة	*mumāthalah, mushābahah*
similarly (adj)	بالمثل، كذلك	*bil mithl, kadhālik*
simile (n)	تشبيه	*tashbīh*
similitude (n)	تشابه، شبه	*tashābuh, shabah*
simmer (v)	غطغط، جاش، أز	*ghaṭghaṭa, jāsha, azza*
simmer (n)	غليان، أزيز	*ghalayān, azīz*
simoom (n)	سموم، هبوب	*samūm, habūb*
simple (adj)	سهل، بسيط، هين	*sahl, basīṭ, hayyin*
simple fraction	كسر بسيط	*kasr basīṭ*
simple interest	فائدة بسيطة	*fā'idah basīṭah*
simple-minded (adj)	بسيط، أبله	*basīṭ, ablah*
simplicity (n)	سذاجة، بلاهة	*sadhājah, balāhah*
simplification (n)	تسهيل، تيسير	*tashīl, taisīr*
simplify (v)	يسر، سهل	*yassara, sahhala*
simply (adv)	ببساطة، بسذاجة	*bi basāṭah, bi sadhājah*
simulate (v)	تظاهر، تصنع	*taẓāhara, taṣanna'a*
simulated (adj)	زائف، متظاهر	*zā'if, mutaẓāhir*
simulation (n)	تظاهر، ادعاء، رياء	*taẓāhur, iddi'ā', riyā'*

simultaneity (n)	تزامن، تواقت	*tazāmun, tawāqut*
simultaneous (adj)	معاصر، حادث في وقت واحد	*mu'āṣir, ḥādith fī waqt wāḥid*
simultaneously (adv)	معاً، في آن واحد	*ma'an, fī ānin wāḥid*
simultaneousness = simultaneity		
sin (n)	إثم، ذنب، خطيئة	*ithm, dhamb, khaṭī'ah*
since (prep/conj)	منذ، بما أن، بسبب	*mundhu, bimā an, bi sababi*
sincere (adj)	صادق، مخلص	*ṣādiq, mukhliṣ*
sincerely (adv)	بصدق، بإخلاص	*bi ṣidq, bi ikhlāṣ*
sincerity (n)	إخلاص، وفاء	*ikhlāṣ, wafā'*
sinecure (n)	وظيفة عاطفة	*waẓīfah 'āṭifah*
sine die	إلى أجل غير مسمى	*ilā ajal ghair musammā*
sinew (n)	وتر العضلة، قوة	*watarul 'aḍalah, quwwah*
sinful (adj)	آثم، مذنب	*āthim, mudhnib*
sinfulness (n)	إثم، معصية	*ithm, ma'ṣiyah*
sing (v)	غنى، غرد، رتل	*ghannā, gharrada, rattala*
singe (v)	شوط، سفع	*shawwaṭa, safa'a*
singer (n)	مغنٍ، منشد	*mughannin, munshid*
single (adj)	وحيد، مفرد	*waḥīd, mufrad*
single (n)	مباراة فردية	*mubārāt fardiyyah*
single (v)	أفرد، ميز	*afrada, mayyaza*
single-handed (adj)	بمفرده، وحده	*bi mufradih, waḥdah*
single-minded (adj)	سليم النية، موطد العزم	*salīmun ṇiyyah, muwaṭṭidul 'azm*
singleness (n)	فردية، وحدانية	*fardiyyah, waḥdāniyyah*
singly (adv)	وحده، على انفراد	*waḥdah, 'alā infirād*
singular (adj/n)	مفرد، صيغة المفرد	*mufrad, ṣīghatul mufrad*
singularity (n)	تفرد، وحدة	*tafarrud, waḥdah*
sinister (adj)	نحس، مشؤوم	*naḥs, mash'ūm*
sink (v)	غرق، غاص، خسف	*ghariqa, ghāṣa, khasafa*
sink (n)	بالوعة، بلوعة	*bālū'ah, ballū'ah*

sinner (n)	آثم، مذنب	*āthim, mudhnib*
sinuosity (n)	تلوٍّ، تمعج	*talawwin, tama''uj*
sip (n)	رشفة، حسوة	*rashfah, ḥaswah*
sip (v)	رشف، مص	*rashafa, maṣṣa*
siphon (n)	سيفون، سحارة	*sīfūn, saḥḥārah*
sir (n)	سيد، مولى	*sayyid, mawlā*
sire (n)	والد، أب	*wālid, ab*
siren (n)	صفارة، غادة فتانة	*ṣaffārah, ghādah fattānah*
sister (n)	أخت، راهبة	*ukht, rāhibah*
sisterhood (n)	أختية، رهبنة	*ukhtiyyah, rahbanah*
sister-in-law	أخت الزوج، أخت الزوجة	*ukhtuz zauj, ukhtuz zaujah*
sisterly (adj)	أختي	*ukhtī*
sit (v)	جلس، قعد	*jalasa, qa'ada*
site (n)	موضع، مكان، محل	*mauḍi', makān, maḥall*
sitting (n)	جلوس، جلسة، مقعد	*julūs, jalsah, maq'ad*
sitting-room (n)	غرفة الجلوس	*ghurfatul julūs*
situate (v)	وقع، وضع	*qaqa'a, waḍa'a*
situated (adj)	واقع، كائن	*wāqi', kā'in*
situation (n)	وضع، موقع، منصب	*waḍ', mauqi', manṣab*
six (n)	ست، ستة	*sitt, sittah*
sixteen (n)	ستة عشر	*sittatu 'ashar*
sixteenth (adj)	سادس عشر	*sādis 'ashar*
sixth (adj/n)	سادس، سادسة	*sādis, sādisah*
sixtieth (adj/n)	ستون، جزء من ستين	*sittūn, juz' min sittīn*
sixty (n)	ستون	*sittūn*
size (n)	حجم، جرم، ضخامة	*ḥajm, jirm, ḍakhāmah*
sizeable (sizable)	ضخم، كبير الحجم	*ḍakhm, kabīrul ḥajm*
sizzle (v)	طش، أز	*ṭashsha, azza*
sizzle (n)	أزيز، طشطشة	*azīz, ṭashṭashah*
skate (n/v)	مزلج، تزلج	*mizlaj, tazallaja*
skeleton (n)	هيكل عظمي	*haikal 'aẓmī*

sketch (n)	رسم مسودة	*rasm musawwadah*
sketch (v)	رسم خطة	*rasama khuṭṭah*
sketch-book (n)	كراسة الرسم	*kurrāsatur rasm*
sketchy (adj)	ناقص، رديء	*nāqiṣ, radī'*
skew (adj)	منحرف، محرود	*munḥarif, maḥrūd*
skewer (n)	سفود، سيخ	*saffūd, sīkh*
ski (n)	زحلوفة، سكي	*zuḥlūfah, skī*
skid (n)	مزلقة، دحروجة	*mizlaqah, duḥrūjah*
skid (v)	انزلق، تزحلق	*inzalaqa, tazaḥlaqa*
skid row	شارع السقوط	*shāri'us suqūṭ*
ski jump	وثبة التزحلف	*wathbatut tazaḥluf*
skilful (skillful) (adj)	حاذق، ماهر	*ḥādhiq, māhir*
skilfully (adv)	بمهارة، بحذق	*bi mahārah,bi ḥidhq*
skill (n)	حذق، براعة	*ḥidhq, barā'ah*
skilled (adj)	حاذق، بارع	*ḥādhiq, bāri'*
skillet (n)	مقلاة، طواية	*miqlāt, ṭawwāyah*
skim (v)	نزع القشدة	*naza'al qishdah*
skimmer (n)	مقشدة، مرغاة	*miqshadah, mirghāt*
skim milk	حليب مقشود	*ḥālib maqshūd*
skin (n)	جلد، قشرة	*jild, qishrah*
skin-deep (adj)	طفيف، سطحي	*ṭafīf, saṭḥī*
skinny (adj)	نحيف، هزيل	*naḥīf, hazīl*
skin-tight (adj)	ضيق جدا	*ḍayyiq jiddā*
skip (v)	وثب، طفر، قفز	*wathaba, ṭafara, qafaza*
skip (n)	وثبة، طفرة، قفزة	*wathbah, ṭafrah, qafzah*
skipper (n)	ربان سفينة، قائد	*rubbānu safīnah, qā'idu*
	فريق رياضي	*farīq riyāḍī*
skirmish (v/n)	ناوش، مناوشة	*nāwasha, munāwashah*
skirt (n)	تنورة، حاشية	*tannūrah, ḥāshiyah*
ski suit	سترة التزلج	*sitratut tazalluj*
skittish (adj)	جفول، نفور	*jafūl, nafūr*
skulk (v)	هرب، اختفى	*taharraba, ikhtafā*

skull (n)	جمجمة، قحف، مخ	*jumjumah, qiḥf, mukhkh*
sky (n)	سماء، قبة زرقاء	*samā', qubbah zarqā'*
sky-blue (adj)	أزرق سماوي	*arzaq samāwī*
sky-high (adj)	مرتفع جدا	*murtafi' jiddā*
skylark (n)	قبرة	*qubbarah*
skylight (n)	منور	*manwar*
skyline (n)	صورة ظلية	*ṣūrah ẓilliyyah*
skywards (adv)	نحو السماء	*naḥwas samā'*
sky-writting (n)	كتابة سماية	*kitābah samāwiyyah*
slab (n)	لوحة، بلاطة	*lauḥah, balāṭah*
slack (adj)	متراخٍ، كاسد	*mutarākhin, kāsid*
slacken (v)	أرخى، توانى	*arkhā, tawānā*
slacker (n)	قعدي، متهرب	*qa'adī, mutaharrib*
slag (n)	حبث، جلخ	*ḥabath, jalakh*
slake (v)	نقع، خمد	*naqa'a, khamada*
slam (n)	ضربة عنيفة	*ḍarbah 'anīfah*
slam (v)	ضرب بعنف	*ḍaraba bi 'unf*
slander (n)	افتراء، وشاية	*iftirā', wishāyah*
slander (v)	قذف، افترى	*qadhafa, iftarā*
slanderer (n)	قاذف، مفتري، واشٍ	*qādhif, muftarī, wāshin*
slang (adj/n)	عامية، دارجة	*'āmiyah, dārijah*
slant (v)	انحدر، انحرف	*inḥadara, inḥarafa*
slant (n)	انحراف، ميل	*inḥirāf, mail*
slap (n)	طقطقة، لطمة	*ṭaqṭaqah, laṭmah*
slap (v)	صفع، لطم	*ṣafa'a, laṭama*
slash (v)	شرط، شطب	*sharaṭa, shaṭṭaba*
slash (n)	شرط، جرح، شطب	*sharṭ, jarḥ, shaṭb*
slat (n)	شريحة ضيقة	*sharīḥah ḍayyiqah*
slate (n)	لوحة، أردواز	*lauḥah, ardwāz*
slate (v)	بلط بأردواز	*ballaṭa bi ardwāz*
slattern (n)	امرأة متحشفة، مومس	*imra'ah mutaḥashshifah, mūmis*
slaughter (v)	ذبح، نحر	*dhabaḥa, naḥara*

slaughter (n)	ذبح، مذبحة	*dhabḥ, madhbaḥah*
slave (n)	رقيق، عبد، مملوك	*raqīq, 'abd, mamlūk*
slave (v)	كدح، كد	*kadaḥa, kadda*
slaver (n)	نخاس، لعاب، ريق	*nakhkhās, lu'āb, rīq*
slaver (v)	رال، سال اللعاب	*rāla, sālal lu'āb*
slavery (n)	عبودية، استرقاق	*'ubūdiyyah, istirqāq*
slave-trade (n)	نخاسة	*nikhāsah*
slavish (adj)	رقيقي، ذليل	*raqīqī, dhalīl*
slay (v)	ذبح، قتل	*dhabaḥa, qatala*
sledge (n)	مطرقة، مرزبة	*miṭraqah, mirzabah*
sleek (adj)	أملس، ناعم	*amlas, nā'im*
sleep (v)	نام، رقد	*nāma, raqada*
sleep (n)	نوم، هجوع	*naum, hujū'*
sleeper (n)	نائم، عربة النوم، رافدة	*nā'im, 'arabatun naum, rāfidah*
sleeping-car (n)	عربة النوم	*'arabatun naum*
sleeping partner	شريك موص	*sharī muwaṣṣin*
sleeping pill	حبة منومة	*ḥabbah munawwimah*
sleeping sickness	نوام	*nuwām*
sleepless (adj)	أرق، ساهد	*ariq, sāhid*
sleepy (adj)	ناعس، صامت	*nā'is, ṣāmit*
sleet (n)	قطقط، برد	*qiṭqiṭ, barad*
sleeve (n)	كم، ردن	*kumm, rudn*
sleeved (adj)	مردن	*muraddan*
sleeveless (adj)	غير مردن، بدون كم	*ghair muraddan, bi dūn kumm*
sleigh (n)	مركبة الجليد	*markabatul jalīd*
sleight (n)	حيلة، حذاقة	*ḥīlah, ḥadhāqah*
slender (adj)	طفيف، ضئيل	*ṭafīf, ḍa'īl*
sleuth (n)	بوليس سري	*būlīs sirrī*
slice (n)	شريحة، فلذة	*sharīḥah, fildhah*
slice (v)	قطع، شرح	*qaṭṭa'a, sharraḥa*

slide (v)	تزلق، تدفق	*tazallaqa, tadaffaqa*
slide (n)	تزلج، انزلاق	*tazalluj, inzilāq*
slide-rule (n)	مسطرة منــزلقة	*misṭarah munzaliqah*
sliding scale	مقياس انزلاقي	*miqyās inzilāqī*
slight (adj)	طفيف، خفيف، زهيد	*ṭafīf, khafīf, zahīd*
slight (v)	استخف، استهان	*istakhaffa, istahāna*
slightingly (adv)	ازدراءً، استخفافاً	*izdirā'an, istikhfāfan*
slightly (adv)	بخفة، قليلاً	*bi khiffah, qalīlan*
slim (adj)	هزيل، رقيق	*hazīl, raqīq*
slim (v)	أهزل، أنحل	*ahzala, anḥala*
slime (n)	وحل، رداغ	*waḥl, ridāgh*
slimy (adj)	لزج، دبق	*lazij, dabiq*
sling (n)	معلاق، مقلاع	*mi'lāq, miqlā'*
sling (v)	خذف، قذف بقوة	*khadhafa, qadhafa bi quwwah*
slink (v)	انسل، أفلت	*insalla, aflata*
slinky (adj)	انسلالي	*insilālī*
slip (v)	انزلق، انسل، زل	*inzalaqa, insalla, zalla*
slip (n)	زلة، انسلال، فرار	*zallah, insilāl, farār*
slipper (n)	شبشب، خف	*shibshib, khuff*
slippery (adj)	زلق، مراوغ	*zaliq, murāwigh*
slippy = slippery		
slipshod (adj)	مهمل، متحشف	*muhmil, mutaḥashshif*
slit (n)	شق، شدخ، كوة	*shaqq, shadkh, kuwwah*
slither (v)	انزلق، تزلق	*inzalaqa, tazallaqa*
slithery (adj)	زلق، منــزلق	*zaliq, munzaliq*
sliver (n)	شظية، شريحة	*shaẓiyyah, sharīḥah*
sliver (v)	شظى، شرح	*shaẓẓā, sharraḥa*
slobber (v)	رال، سال اللعاب	*rāla, sālal lu'āb*
slobber (n)	لعاب سائل	*lu'āb sā'il*
slobbery (adj)	ريالي، لعابي	*riyālī, lu'ābī*
slog (n)	ضربة عنيفة	*ḍarbah 'anīfah*

slog (v)	ضرب بقوة	*ḍaraba bi quwwah*
slogan (n)	نداء، هتاف عدائي	*nidā', hutāf 'idā'ī*
slogger (n)	شخص كادح	*shakhṣ kādiḥ*
slop (v)	دلق، اندلق	*dalaqa, indalaqa*
slop (n)	غسالة، فضلة	*ghusālah, fuḍlah*
slope (n)	منحدر، تحدر	*munḥadar, taḥaddur*
slope (v)	انحدر، انصرف	*inḥadara, inṣarafa*
slopy (adj)	موحل، معكر، قذر	*mūḥil, mu'akkar, qadhir*
slosh (v)	تدفق، تحرك بعنف	*tadaffaqa, taḥarraka bi 'unf*
slot (n)	ثقب، فتحة	*thaqb, futḥah*
sloth (n)	كسل، استرخاء	*kasal, istirkhā'*
sloven (n)	بذ، شخص قذر	*badhdh, shakhṣ qadhir*
slovenly (adj)	كسلان، قذر	*kaslān, qadhir*
slow (adj)	بطيء، متوانٍ	*baṭī', mutawānin*
slow (v)	أبطأ، تأخر	*abṭa'a, ta'khkhara*
slow-down (n)	تباطؤ	*tabāṭu'*
slowly (adv)	ببطء، بتأنٍّ	*bi baṭ', bi ta'annin*
slow-worm = blindworm		
slug (n)	رصاصة، سطر مسكوب	*raṣāṣah, saṭr maskūb*
sluggish (adj)	بطيء، بليد، كسلان	*baṭī', balīd, kaslān*
sluggishly (adv)	ببطء، ببلادة	*bi baṭ', bi balādah*
sluggishness (n)	بطء، بلادة، كسل	*baṭ', balādah, kasal*
sluice (n)	بوابة، سد	*bawwābah, sadd*
slum (n)	حي قذر، حي المساكين	*ḥayy qadhir, ḥayyul masākīn*
slumber (n)	هجوع، سبات	*hujū', subāt*
slumber (v)	هجع، نام	*haja'a, nāma*
slumberous (adj)	نائم، نعسان	*nā'im, na'sān*
slur (v)	لوث، ثلم السمعة	*lawwatha, thalamas sum'ah*
slur (n)	قذف، افتراء	*qadhf, iftirā'*

slush (n)	وحل، ردغة	*waḥl, radaghah*
slut (n)	امرأة قذرة	*imra'ah qadhirah*
sly (adj)	محتال، خبيث	*muḥtāl, khabīth*
slyly (adv)	بدهاء، بخبث	*bi dahā', bi khubth*
slyness (n)	دهاء، مكر	*dahā', makr*
smack (n)	صفعة عنيفة،نكهة	*ṣaf'ah 'anīfah, nakhah*
smack (v)	صفع، طقطق	*ṣafa'a, ṭaqṭaqa*
small (adj)	صغير، يسير، طفيف	*ṣaghīr, yasīr, ṭafif*
small arms	أسلحة خفيفة	*asliḥah khafīfah*
small-minded (adj)	ضيق التفكير	*ḍayyiqut tafkīr*
smallpox (n)	مرض الجدرى	*maraḍul judrā*
small talk	كلام سائر، قال وقيل	*kalām sā'ir, qāl wa qīl*
smart (adj)	متأنق، زاه، ناشط	*muta'anniq, zāhin, nāshiṭ*
smart (n)	وجع شديد، ألم	*waj' shadīd, alam*
smarten (v)	أنق، نشط	*annaqa, nashshaṭa*
smash (v)	حطم، هدم	*ḥaṭṭama, haddama*
smash (n)	تحطم، إخفاق	*taḥaṭṭum, ikhfāq*
smattering (n)	معرفة سطحية	*ma'rifah saṭḥiyyah*
smear (v)	لوث، لطخ	*lawwatha, laṭṭakha*
smear (n)	لطخة، مسحة	*laṭkhah, masḥah*
smeary (adj)	ملطخ، ملوث	*mulaṭṭakh, mulawwath*
smell (v)	شم، عبق	*shamma, 'abiqa*
smell (n)	رائحة، حاسة الشم	*rā'iḥah, ḥāssatush shamm*
smelly (adj)	كريه الرائحة	*karīhur rā'iḥah*
smelt (v)	صهر، سيح	*ṣahara, sayyaḥa*
smile (v)	تبسم، هش	*tabassama, hashsha*
smile (n)	ابتسام، تبسم	*ibtisām, tabassum*
smilingly (adv)	بابتسام، ببشاشة	*bibtisām, bi bashāshah*
smite (v)	ضرب بعنف	*ḍaraba bi 'unf*
smith (n)	صانع	*ṣāni'*
smitten (adj)	مصاب، مضروب	*muṣāb, maḍrūb*

smock (n)	ثوب فضفاض	*thaub faḍfāḍ*
smoke (v/n)	دخن، دخان	*dakhkhana, dukhān*
smokeless (adj)	بلا دخان، قليل الدخان	*bilā dukhān, qalīlud dukhān*
smoker (n)	مدخن	*mudakhkhin*
smoking (n)	تدخين	*tadkhīn*
smoking jacket	سترة التدخين	*sitratut tadkhīn*
smoking-room	حجرة التدخين	*ḥujratut tadkhīn*
smoky (adj)	دخاني، داخن	*dukhānī, dākhin*
smooch (n)	قبلة في الرقص	*qublah fir raqṣ*
smooth (adj)	مصقول، أملس، ناعم	*maṣqūl, amlas, nā'im*
smooth (v)	ملس، لطف	*mallasa, laṭṭafa*
smoothly (adv)	بملاسة، بلطافة	*bi malāsah, bi laṭāfah*
smoothness (n)	ملاسة، نعومة	*malāsah, nu'ūmah*
smother (v)	خنق، فطس	*khanaqa, faṭṭasa*
smuggle (v)	هرب البضائع	*harrabal baḍā'i'*
smuggling (n)	تهريب البضائع	*tahrībul baḍā'i'*
smut (n)	سخام، كتن	*sukhām, katan*
smut (v)	سنج، سخم	*sannaja, sakhkhama*
smutty (adj)	مسنج، قذر	*musannaj, qadhir*
snack (n)	لمجة، وجبة خفيفة	*lumjah, wajbah khafīfah*
snack-bar (n)	مطعم خفيف	*maṭ'am khafīf*
snag (n)	عقبة خفيفة، جذل	*'aqabah khafīfah, jidhl*
snake (n)	أفعى، حية	*af'ā, ḥayyah*
snaky (adj)	شبيه بالحية، ثعباني	*shabīh bil ḥayyah, thu'bānī*
snap (v)	فرقع، قصم، خطف	*farqa'a, qaṣama, khaṭafa*
snap (n)	عض، خطف، فرقعة	*'aḍḍ, khatf, farqa'ah*
snap (adj)	مفاجئ، في عجلة	*mufāji', fī 'ajalah*
snappish (adj)	نهاش، فظ	*nahhāsh, faẓẓ*
snappy (adj)	سريع الغضب، مفاجئ	*sarī'ul ghaḍab, mufāji'*
snapshot (n)	لقطة فوتوغرافية	*luqṭah fūtūgharāfiyyah*

snare (n)	شرك، أحبولة، مكيدة	*sharak, uḥbūlah, makīdah*
snare (v)	صاد بأحبولة	*ṣāda bi uḥbūlah*
snarl (v)	زمجر، همهم، عقد	*zamjara, hamhama, 'aqqada*
snarl (n)	عقدة، زمجرة	*'uqdah, zamjarah*
snatch (v)	اختطف، انتزع	*ikhtaṭafa, intaza'a*
snatch (n)	خطفة، انتزاع	*khaṭfah, intizā'*
snatcher (n)	مختطف، نتاش	*mukhtaṭif, nattāsh*
sneak (v)	تسلل، نم، اختلس	*tasallala, namma, ikhtalasa*
sneak (n)	غادر، سري	*ghādir, sirrī*
sneaking (adj)	خفي، خسيس	*khafiyy, khasīs*
sneer (v)	هزأ، تهكم	*haza'a, tahakkama*
sneer (n)	تهكم، استهزاء	*tahakkum, istihzā'*
sneeringly (adv)	سخريةً، ازدراءً	*sukhriyyatan, izdirā'an*
sneeze (n/v)	عطاس، عطس	*'uṭās, 'aṭasa*
sniff (n/v)	تنشق، تنشق	*tanashshuq, tanashshaqa*
snip (v)	قص، قصقص	*qaṣṣa, qaṣqaṣa*
snip (n)	قصاصة، قصقوصة	*quṣāṣah, quṣqūṣah*
snipper (n)	قصاصة، قطعة صغيرة	*quṣāṣah, qiṭ'ah ṣaghīrah*
snitch (v)	اختلس، أخذ خلسةً	*ikhtalasa, akhadha khilsatan*
snivel (v)	خن، عال	*khanna, 'āla*
snob (n)	متكبر، متعاظم، نفاج	*mutakabbir, muta'āẓim, naffāj*
snobbery (n)	تفنج	*tafannuj*
snobbish (adj)	متفنج	*mutafannij*
snobbishness (n)	تفنج	*tafannuj*
snow (n)	ثلج، جليد	*thalj, jalīd*
snow (v)	تساقط الثلج	*tasāqaṭath thalj*
snow ball	كرة الثلج	*kuratuth thalj*
snow-capped (adj)	مكلل بالثلوج	*mukallal bith thulūj*

snow-covered (adj)	مغطى بالثلج	*mughaṭṭā bith thalj*
snowfall (n)	تساقط الثلج	*tasāquṭuth thalj*
snow-field (n)	حقل الثلج	*ḥaqluth thalj*
snowstorm (n)	عاصفة ثلجية	*'āṣifah thaljiyyah*
snow-white (adj)	أبيض كالثلج	*abyaḍ kath thalj*
snowy (adj)	مكسو بالثلج، كثير الثلج	*maksuww bith thalj, kathīruth thalj*
snub (v)	زجر، انتهر	*zajara, intahara*
snub (n)	زجر، أفطس	*zajr, afṭas*
snuff (n)	نشوق، سعوط	*nushūq, su'ūṭ*
snuffle (v)	تنشق، تنفس	*tanashshaqa, tanaffasa*
snuffle (n)	خنة، تنشق	*khunnah, tanashshuq*
snug (adj)	دافئ، مريح	*dāfi', murīḥ*
so (adv)	هكذا، كذلك	*hākadhā, kadhālik*
so (conj)	لكي،وهكذا،حتى أن	*li kay, wa hākadhā, ḥattā an*
soak (v)	نقع، غمس	*naqa'a, ghamasa*
soak (n)	انتقاع، امتصاص	*intiqā', imtiṣāṣ*
soaking (adj)	منقوع، مبلل	*manqū', muballal*
so-and-so (n)	فلان، فلانة	*fulān, fulānah*
soap (n/v)	صابون، غسل بصابون	*ṣābūn, ghasala bi ṣābūn*
soap-box (n)	صندوق الصابون	*ṣundūquṣ ṣābūn*
soap opera	أوبرا صابونية	*ūbrā ṣābūniyyah*
soapy (adj)	أملس، زلق	*amlas, zaliq*
soar (v)	ارتفع، حام	*irtafa'a, ḥāma*
sob (v)	نشج، تنهد	*nashaja, tanahhada*
sob (n)	تنهد، نشيج	*tanahhud, nashīj*
sobbingly (adv)	برصانة، برزانة	*bi raṣānah, bi razānah*
sober (adj)	وقور، غير ثمل	*waqūr, ghair thamil*
soberiety (n)	رصانة، صحو، وقار	*raṣānah, saḥw, waqār*
sober-minded (adj)	وقور، رصين	*waqūr, raṣīn*
so-called (adj)	مزعوم، مسمى	*maz'ūm, musammā*

soccer (n)	لعبة كرة القدم	*lu'batu kuratil qadam*
sociability (n)	حسن المعاشرة، مؤانسة	*ḥusnul mu'āsharah, mu'ānasah*
sociable (adj)	ألوف، أنيس	*alūf, anīs*
social (adj)	اجتماعي، عمراني	*ijtimā'ī, 'umrānī*
socialism (n)	اشتراكية، اجتماعية	*ishtirākiyyah, ijtimā'iyyah*
socialist (n)	اشتراكي	*ishtirākī*
socialistic (adj)	اشتراكي	*ishtirākī*
socialite (n)	عضو بارز في المجتمع	*'uḍw bāriz fil mujtama'*
socialization,-isation	شتركة	*shatrakah*
socialize,-ise (v)	شترك	*shatraka*
socially (adv)	اجتماعيا، بألفة	*ijtimā'iyyan, bi ulfah*
social science	علم الاجتماع	*'ilmul ijtimā'*
social security	كفالة اجتماعية	*kafālah ijtimā'iyyah*
social service	خدمة اجتماعية	*khidmah ijtimā'iyyah*
social studies	دراسات اجتماعية	*dirāsāt ijtimā'iyyah*
social welfare	إنعاش اجتماعي	*in'āsh ijtimā'ī*
social work	عمل اجتماعي	*'amal ijtimā'ī*
social worker	عامل اجتماعي	*'āmil ijtimā'ī*
societal (adj)	مجتمعي، اجتماعي	*mujtama'ī, ijtimā'ī*
society (n)	مجتمع، معشر	*mujtama', ma'shar*
sociological (adj)	اجتماعي، عمراني	*ijtimā'ī, 'umrānī*
sociologist (n)	متخصص بعلم الاجتماع	*mutakhaṣṣiṣ bi 'ilmil ijtimā'*
sociology (n)	علم الاجتماع، علم العمران	*'ilmul ijtimā', 'ilmul 'umrān*
sock (n)	جورب قصير، ضربة قوية	*jaurab qaṣīr, ḍarbah qawiyyah*
socket (n)	محجر، ثغرة	*maḥjir, thughrah*
soda (n)	صودا	*ṣūdā*
soda-water (n)	ماء الصودا	*mā'uṣ ṣūdā*

sodium (n)	عنصر الصوديوم	*'unṣuruṣ ṣūdiyūm*
sodomite (n)	لوطي	*lūṭī*
sodomy (n)	لواطة	*liwāṭah*
sofa (n)	أريكة، ديوان	*arīkah, dīwān*
soft (adj)	لين، ناعم، رخو	*layyin, nā'im, rakhw*
softball (n)	كرة ناعمة	*kurah nā'imah*
soft currency	عملة سقيمة	*'umlah saqīmah*
soften (v)	لين، خفض	*layyana, khaffaḍa*
soft-hearted (adj)	رقيق القلب	*raqīqul qalb*
softly (adv)	بليونة، برقة	*bi luyūnah, bi riqqah*
softness (n)	نعومة، لين	*nu'ūmah, līn*
softwood (n)	خشب لين	*khashab layyin*
softy (n)	شخص ضعيف الجسم	*shakhṣ ḍa'īful jism*
soil (n)	أرض، تربة	*arḍ, turbah*
soil (v)	وسخ، لوث	*wassakha, lawwatha*
sojour (n)	إقامة مؤقتة	*iqāmah mu'aqqatah*
solace (v/n)	عزى، عزاء	*'azzā, 'azā'*
solar (adj)	شمسي	*shamsī*
solar plexus	ضفيرة شمسية	*ḍafīrah shamsiyyah*
solar system	نظام شمسي	*niẓām shamsī*
solder (n)	لحام المعادن	*liḥāmul ma'ādin*
soldier (n)	جندي، عسكري	*jundiyy, 'askariyy*
sole (n)	نعل حذاء	*na'lu ḥidhā'*
sole (adj)	وحيد، فريد	*waḥīd, farīd*
solely (adv)	بمفرده، فقط	*bi mufradih, faqaṭ*
solemn (adj)	وقور، مهيب، خطير	*waqūr, muhīb, khaṭīr*
solemness	هيبة، وقار	*haibah, waqār*
solemnity (n)	وقار، مهابة، جلال	*waqār, mahābah, jalāl*
solemnize,-ise (v)	احتفل، عيد	*iḥtafala, 'ayyada*
solemnly (adv)	بمهابة، بوقار	*bi mahābah, bi waqār*
solicit (v)	التمس، رجا	*iltamasa, rajā*
solicitor (n)	وكيل قضايا، محامٍ	*wakīlu qaḍāyā, muḥāmin*

solicitous (adj)	قلق، مضطرب البال	*qaliq, muḍṭaribul bāl*
solicitude (n)	قلق، اضطراب	*qalaq, iḍṭirāb*
solid (adj)	متين، راسخ، صلب	*matīn, rāsikh, ṣulb*
solidarity (n)	تضامن، تماسك	*taḍāmun, tamāsuk*
solidification (n)	ترسيخ، توطيد	*tarsīkh, tauṭīd*
solidify (v)	رسخ، جمد	*rassakha, jammada*
solidity (n)	صلابة، متانة، رسوخ	*ṣalābah, matānah, rusūkh*
solidly (adv)	بمتانة، بقوة	*bi matānah, bi quwwah*
soliloquy (n)	مناجاة في نفسه	*munājāt fī nafsih*
solitaire (n)	سلتير	*saltīr*
solitary (adj)	منعزل، مقفر	*mun'azil, muqfir*
solitary confinement	حبس انفرادي	*ḥabs infirādī*
solitude (n)	انفراد، عزلة	*infirād, 'uzlah*
solo (adj)	منفرد، متوحد	*munfarid, mutawaḥḥid*
solo (n)	رقص منفرد، طيران منفرد	*raqṣ munfarid, ṭayarān munfarid*
soloist (n)	عازف منفرد	*'āzif munfarid*
soluble (adj)	يمكن حله، يذوب	*yumkin ḥalluh, yadhūb*
solution (n)	حل، إذابة	*ḥall, idhābah*
solvable (adj)	قابل للحل	*qābil lil ḥall*
solve (v)	حل، أوضح	*ḥalla, auḍaḥa*
solvency (n)	مقدرة على الإذابة	*maqdurah 'alal idhābah*
solvent (adj)	قادر على الإيفاء	*qādir 'alal īfā'*
solvent (n)	مادة مذيبة	*māddah mudhībah*
sombre (somber)	كئيب، قاتم	*ka'īb, qātim*
sombrely (adv)	بكآبة، بقتوم	*bi ka'ābah, bi qutūm*
sombreness (n)	كآبة، هم	*ka'ābah, hamm*
some (adj/pron)	بعض، بضعة	*ba'ḍ, biḍ'ah*
somebody (n)	أحدما، شخص ما	*aḥdum mā, shakhṣum mā*
someday (n)	يوماً، يوما ما	*yauman, yaumam mā*
somehow (adv)	بكيفية ما، بطريقة ما	*bi kaifiyyatim mā, bi ṭarīqatim mā*
someone (pron)	شخص ما، واحد	*shakhṣum mā, wāḥid*

somersault (n)	انقلاب تام، شقلبة	*inqilāb tāmm, shaqlabah*
something (n)	شيء ما، أمر ما	*shay'um mā, amrum mā*
sometime (adv/adj)	سابقاً، سابق	*sābiqan, sābiq*
sometimes (adv)	أحياناً، تارةً	*aḥyānan, tāratan*
someway (adv)	بطريقة ما	*bi ṭarīqatim mā*
somewhat (adv)	بنوع ما، إلى حد ما	*bi nau'im mā, ilā ḥaddim mā*
somewhere (adv)	في مكان ما	*fī makānim mā*
son (n)	ابن، نجل	*ibn, najl*
song (n)	أغنية، غناء	*ughniyah, ghinā'*
songbird (n)	طائر مغرد	*ṭā'ir mugharrid*
songster (n)	مغني، شاعر	*mughannī, shā'ir*
songwriter (n)	ناظم الأغاني	*nāẓimul ughānī*
sonic (adj)	صوتي	*ṣautī*
son-in-law	صهر، زوج الابنة	*ṣahr, zaujul ibnah*
sonnet (n)	قصيدة من ١٤ بيت	*qaṣīdah min arba'a 'ashra bait*
sonneteer (n)	ناظم السونيتات	*nāẓimus sūnītāt*
sonorous (adj)	طنان، جهوري	*ṭannān, jahwarī*
soon (adv)	عاجلاً، قريباً	*'ājilan, qarīban*
soot (n)	سخام، هباب	*sukhām, hibāb*
soothe (v)	سكن، خفف	*sakkana, khaffafa*
soothing (adj)	مسكن، مهدئ	*musakkin, muhaddi'*
soothsayer (n)	عراف، منجم	*'arrāf, munajjim*
sop (v)	غمس، غمر	*ghamasa, ghamara*
sop (n)	عصيدة، غميسة	*'aṣīdah, ghamīsah*
sophisticate (n)	شخص متكلف	*shakhṣ mutakallaf*
sophisticated (adj)	متكلف، محنك	*mutakallaf, muḥannak*
sophistry (n)	مغالطة، سفسطة	*mughālaṭah, safsaṭah*
soppy (adj)	عاطفي جدا	*'āṭifi jiddā*
soprano (n)	ندي	*nadiyy*
sorcerer (n)	ساحر، عراف	*sāḥir, 'arrāf*

sorceress (n)	ساحرة، عرافة	*sāḥirah, 'arrāfah*
sordid (adj)	حقير، قذر، خسيس	*ḥaqīr, qadhir, khasīs*
sordidly (adv)	بخسة، بدناءة	*bi khissah, bi danā'ah*
sordidness (n)	خسة، قذارة	*khissah, qadhārah*
sore (adj)	متقرح، متألم	*mutaqarriḥ, muta'allim*
sore (n)	قرحة، حرقة	*qarḥah, ḥurqah*
sorely (adv)	بألم، بحرقة	*bi alam, bi ḥurqah*
soreness (n)	ألم، قرحة	*alam, qarḥah*
sorrow (n)	حزن، غم	*ḥuzn, ghamm*
sorrow (v)	حزن، كئب	*ḥazina, ka'iba*
sorrowful (adj)	محزن، كئيب	*muḥzin, ka'īb*
sorrowfulness (n)	حزن، اكتئاب	*ḥuzn, ikti'āb*
sorry (adj)	متأسف، آسف	*muta'assif, āsif*
sorry (interj)	أسفاً	*asafan*
sort (n)	نوع، قسم، طريقة	*nau', qism, ṭarīqah*
sort (v)	نسق، فرز	*nassaqa, faraza*
sorter (n)	فراز، فارز الرسائل	*farrāz, fārizur rasā'il*
sortie (n)	هجوم مفاجئ	*hujūm mufāji'*
sottish (adj)	سكران، أخرق	*sakrān, akhraq*
soul (n)	روح، جوهر، حياة	*rūḥ, jauhar, ḥayāt*
soulful (adj)	مفعم بالحيوية	*muf'am bil ḥayawiyyah*
soulless (adj)	فاقد الهمة	*fāqidul himmah*
soul-searching (n)	تحليل الذات	*taḥlīludh dhāt*
sound (n)	صوت، مجال السمع	*ṣauṭ, majālus sam'*
sound (v)	طن، قرع	*ṭanna, qara'a*
sound (adj)	مضبوط، متين، سليم	*maḍbūṭ, matīn, salīm*
soundly (adv)	بسلامة، بمتانة	*bi salāmah, bi matānah*
sound-proof (adj)	عازل للصوت	*'āzil liṣ ṣaut*
sound-track (n)	مدرج صوتي	*madraj ṣautī*
sound-wave (n)	موجة صوتية	*maujah ṣautiyyah*
soup (n)	صبة، حساء	*ṣubbah, ḥisā'*
soup-kitchen (n)	مطعم الفقراء	*maṭ'amul fuqarā'*

sour (adj)	حامض، مز، رائب	*ḥāmiḍ, muzz, rā'ib*
sour (v)	تحمض، تعفن	*taḥammaḍa, ta'affana*
source (n)	مصدر، منبع	*maṣdar, mamba'*
south (n/adj)	جنوب، جنوبي	*janūb, janūbī*
south (adv)	نحو الجنوب، جنوبا	*naḥwal janūb, janūban*
southbound (adj)	متوجه جنوبا	*mutawajjih janūban*
south-east (adj/adv)	جنوب شرقي، نحو الجنوب الشرقي	*janūb sharqī, naḥwal janūb ash sharqī*
southern (adj)	جنوبي	*janūbī*
southernmost (adj)	واقع في أقصى الجنوب	*wāqi' fī aqṣal janūb*
south pole	قطب جنوبي	*quṭb janūbī*
southwards (adv)	نحو الجنوب	*naḥwal janūb*
south-west (adj)	جنوبي غربي	*janūbī gharbī*
south-west (adv)	نحو الجنوب الغربي	*naḥwal janūb al gharbī*
south-western (adj)	جنوبي غربي	*janūbī gharbī*
souvenir (n)	تذكار، مفكرة	*tadhkār, mufakkirah*
sovereign (n)	ملك، سلطان	*malik, sulṭān*
sovereign (adj)	مطلق، غالب	*muṭlaq, ghālib*
sovereignty (n)	سلطة، مملكة	*sulṭah, mamlakah*
soviet (n)	مجلس السوفيات	*majlisus sūfyāt*
Soviet (adj)	سوفياتي	*sūfyātī*
sow (v)	بذر، نثر	*badhara, nathara*
sower (n)	باذر، زارع	*bādhir, zāri'*
soya bean (soy bean)	فول الصويا	*fūluṣ ṣūyā*
space (n)	فسحة، فترة، فراغ، فضاء	*fusḥah, fatrah, farāgh, faḍā'*
spacecraft (n)	سفينة الفضاء	*safīnatul faḍā'*
spaceman (n)	رائد الفضاء	*rā'idul faḍā'*
space station	محطة فضائية	*maḥaṭṭah faḍā'iyyah*
spacesuit (n)	بذلة فضائية	*badhlah faḍā'iyyah*
spacing (n)	توسيع، مباعدة	*tausī', mubā'adah*
spacious (adj)	فسيح، واسع	*fasīḥ, wāsi'*

spade (n)	معول، مجراف	*mi'wal, mijrāf*
span (n/v)	شبر، قاس بالشبر	*shibr, qāsa bish shibr*
Spanish (adj/n)	إسباني، لغة إسبانية	*isbānī, lughah isbāniyyah*
spank (v)	صفع، لطم	*ṣafa'a, laṭama*
spank (n)	صفعة، ضربة	*ṣaf'ah, ḍarbah*
spanner (n)	مفتاح ربط	*miftāḥu rabṭ*
spare (adj)	إضافي، زائد، يسير	*iḍāfī, zā'id, yasīr*
spare (v)	تجنب، استبقى	*tajannaba, istabqā*
sparingly (adv)	باقتصاد، بتدبير	*biqtiṣād, bi tadbīr*
spark (n)	شرارة، ومضة	*sharārah, wamḍah*
spark (v)	حث، التهب	*ḥaththa, iltahaba*
sparkle (v)	اشتعل، اتقد	*ishta'ala, ittaqada*
sparkle (n)	فوران، شرارة	*fawarān, sharārah*
sparkler (n)	ماسة، بوصاء	*māsah, būṣā'*
sparrow (n)	عصفور دوري	*'uṣfūr dūrī*
sparse (adj)	غير كث، متناثر	*ghair kathth, mutanāthir*
spat (n)	شجار غير عنيف	*shijār ghair 'anīf*
spate (n)	فيض، فيضان	*faiḍ, fayaḍān*
spatial (adj)	فضائي، حيزي	*faḍā'ī, ḥayyizī*
spatter (v)	طرطش، لطخ بالرش	*ṭarṭasha, laṭṭakha bir rash*
spatter (n)	لطخة، طشاش	*laṭkhah, ṭashāsh*
spatula (n)	مبسط، سكين الصيدلي	*mibsaṭ, sikkīnuṣ ṣaidalī*
spawn (v)	أفرخ، باض	*afrakha, bāḍa*
spawn (n)	بذرة، بيض	*badhrah, bīḍ*
speak (v)	تكلم، نطق، خطب	*takallama, naṭaqa, khaṭaba*
speaker (n)	خطيب، متكلم	*khaṭīb, mutakallim*
spear (n)	رمح، مزراق	*rumḥ, mizrāq*
spear (v)	طعن بالرمح	*ta'ana bir rumḥ*
special (adj)	خاص،مخصوص،خصوصي	*khāṣṣ, makhṣūṣ, khuṣūṣī*
special (n)	شخص أو شيء خاص	*shakhṣ aw shay' khāṣṣ*

special delivery	بريد مستعجل	*barīd musta'jal*
specialist (n)	إخصائي، متخصص	*ikhṣā'ī, mutakhaṣṣiṣ*
speciality (specialty)	صفة خاصة	*ṣifah khāṣṣah*
specialization (n)	تخصيص، تخصص	*takhṣīṣ, takhaṣṣuṣ*
specialize,-ise (v)	خصص، تخصص	*khaṣṣaṣa, takhaṣṣaṣa*
specially (adv)	خصوصاً، خاصة	*khuṣūṣan, khāṣṣatan*
species (n)	نوع، جنس، صنف	*nau', jins, ṣinf*
specific (adj)	خاص، محدد	*khāṣṣ, muḥaddad*
specifically (adv)	على وجه التخصيص	*'alā wajhit takhṣīṣ*
specification (n)	مواصفة، تخصيص	*muwāṣafah, takhṣīṣ*
specify (v)	واصف، خصص، عدد	*wāṣafa, khaṣṣaṣa, 'addada*
specimen (n)	عينة، نموذج	*'ayyinah, namūdhaj*
specious (adj)	حسن المنظر	*ḥasanul manẓar*
speck (n)	نكتة، لطخة	*nuktah, laṭkhah*
speckle (n)	رقطة، نقطة	*ruqṭah, nuqṭah*
spectacle (n)	منظر، مشهد	*manẓar, mashhad*
spectacles (n)	نظارات، عوينات	*naẓẓārāt, 'uwaināt*
spectacular (adj)	متعلق بالمناظر	*muta'alliq bil manāẓir*
spectacular (n)	شيء يستحق المشاهدة	*shay' yastaḥiqqul mushāhadah*
spectator (n)	متفرج، مشاهد	*mutafarrij, mushāhid*
spectral (adj)	طيفي، شبحي	*ṭaifī, shabaḥī*
spectre (specter)	شبح، طيف	*shabaḥ, ṭaif*
spectrum (n)	طيف النور	*ṭaifun nūr*
speculate (v)	تخمن، تحرز	*takhammana, taḥarraza*
speculation (n)	تخمين، تمعن	*takhmīn, tama''un*
speculative (adj)	تأملي، تخمني	*ta'ammulī, takhammunī*
speculator (n)	متبصر، متحرز	*mutabaṣṣir, mutaḥarriz*
speech (n)	كلام، خطاب	*kalām, khiṭāb*
speechless (adj)	أخرس، فاقد النطق	*akhras, fāqidun nuṭq*
speed (n)	سرعة، عجلة	*sur'ah, 'ajalah*

speedily (adv)	بسرعة، سريعاً	*bi sur'ah, sarī'an*
speedy (adj)	سريع، عجول	*sarī', 'ajūl*
spell (n)	رقية، سحر، دور	*ruqyah, siḥr, daur*
spell (v)	هجى، أفاد	*tahajjā, afāda*
spellbound (adj)	مسحور، منذهل	*masḥūr, mundhahil*
spelling (n)	هجاء، تهجئة	*hijā', tahji'ah*
spend (v)	أنفق، استعمل	*anfaqa, ista'mala*
spender (n)	منفق، مسرف	*munfiq, musrif*
spender thrift (n)	شخص مبذر	*shakhṣ mubadhdhir*
spent (adj)	متعب، مستهلك	*mut'ab, mustahlak*
sperm (n)	حيوان منوي	*ḥaiwān manawī*
spew (n)	قيء	*qay'*
sphere (n)	كرة، دائرة	*kurah, dā'irah*
spherical (adj)	كروي	*kurawī*
Sphinx (n)	أبو الهول المصري	*abul haul al miṣrī*
spice (n)	تابل، بهار	*tābil, bahār*
spiced (adj)	متبل	*mutabbal*
spicy (adj)	تابلي، عطري	*tābilī, 'iṭrī*
spider (n)	عنكبوت	*'ankabūt*
spider web	نسيج العنكبوت	*nasījul 'ankabūt*
spidery (adj)	عنكبوتي	*'ankabūtī*
spiel (n)	كلام مطول	*kalām muṭawwal*
spike (n)	مسمار كبير، رزة	*mismār kabīr, razzah*
spiked (adj)	شائك، مبرشم	*shā'il, mubarsham*
spill (v)	أهرق، أراق	*ahraqa, arāqa*
spill (n)	إراقة،كبوة	*irāqah, kabwah*
spillage (n)	إراقة، تدفق	*irāqah, tadaffuq*
spin (v)	نسج، أدار	*nasaja, adāra*
spin (n)	دوران، نسج	*dawarān, nasj*
spinach (n)	اسبانخ	*isbānakh*
spinal (adj)	شوكي، فقري	*shaukī, fiqrī*
spinal column	عمود فقري	*'amūd fiqrī*

spinal cord	حبل شوكي	*ḥabl shaukī*
spindle (n)	مغزل، وشيعة	*mighzal, washī'ah*
spine (n)	شوكة، عمود فقري	*shaukah, 'amūd fiqrī*
spineless (adj)	نحيل، لا فقري	*naḥīl, lā fiqrī*
spinner (n)	غزال	*ghazzāl*
spinneret (n)	مغزال	*mighzāl*
spinning (n)	برم، غزل، تدويم	*barm, ghazl, tadwīm*
spinning wheel	دولاب الغزل	*dūlābul ghazl*
spinster (n)	امرأة غير متزوجة	*imra'ah ghair mutazawwijah*
spiny (adj)	شائك، وعر	*shā'ik, wa'ir*
spiral (adj)	لولبي، حلزوني	*laulabī, ḥalazūnī*
spiral (v)	لولب، تلولب	*laulaba, talaulaba*
spire (n)	برج، ذورة	*burj, dhirwah*
spirit (n)	روح، حياة، شبح	*rūḥ, ḥayāt, shabaḥ*
spirited (adj)	نشيط، مفعم بالحيوية	*nashīṭ, muf'am bil ḥayawiyyah*
spiritless (adj)	مكتئب، عديم النشاط	*mukta'ib, 'adīmun nashāṭ*
spiritual (adj)	روحي، روحاني، شبحي	*rūḥī, rūḥānī, shabaḥī*
spiritualism (n)	روحانية	*rūḥāniyyah*
spirituality (n)	روحية، روحانية	*rūḥiyyah, rūḥāniyyah*
spiritualize,-ise (v)	طهر الروح، روحن	*ṭahharar rūḥ, rauḥana*
spirituous (adj)	كحولي	*kuḥūlī*
spiry (adj)	لولبي، حلزوني	*laulabi, ḥalazūnī*
spit (v)	بصق، بقبق	*baṣaqa, baqbaqa*
spit (n)	بصاق، سيخ	*buṣāq, sīkh*
spite (n)	حقد، إغاظة	*ḥiqd, ighāẓah*
spite (v)	غاظ، كاد	*ghāẓa, kāda*
spiteful (adj)	ضاغن، حقود	*ḍāghin, ḥaqūd*
spitefully (adv)	بضغينة، بحقد	*bi ḍaghīnah, bi ḥiqd*
spitefulness (n)	ضغينة، نكاية، غل	*ḍaghīnah, nikāyah, ghill*

spittle (n)	ريق، بصاق	*rīq, buṣāq*
spittoon (n)	مبصقة، متفلة	*mibṣaqah, mitfalah*
splash (v)	طرطش، رشش	*ṭarṭasha, rashshasha*
splash (n)	طرطشة، ترشاش	*ṭarṭashah, tarshāsh*
splay (v)	امتد، فلطح	*imtadda, falṭaḥa*
splay-footed (adj)	مفرطح القدم	*mufarṭaḥul qadam*
spleen (n)	طحال	*ṭiḥāl*
splendid (adj)	باهر، رائع	*bāhir, rā'i'*
splendiferous (adj)	فخم، سني	*fakhm, sannī*
splendour (splendor)	بهاء، روعة، سناء	*bahā', rau'ah, sanā'*
splenetic (adj)	شكس، غاضب	*shakis, ghāḍib*
splice (n)	وصلة، رباط	*wuṣlah, ribāṭ*
splint (n)	شظية، شريحة	*shaẓiyyah, sharīḥah*
splinter (n)	شريحة حادة	*sharīḥah ḥāddah*
split (v)	مزق، فلق، انشق	*mazzaqa, falaqa, inshaqqa*
split (n)	انفلاق، انشقاق	*infilāq, inshiqāq*
spoil (v)	أفسد، أتلف	*afsada, atlafa*
spoilage (n)	تلف، فساد	*talaf, fasād*
spoils (n)	غنيمة، سلب	*ghanīmah, salb*
spoke (n)	مكبح العربة	*mikbaḥul 'arabah*
spoken (adj)	منطوق به	*manṭūq bih*
spokesman (n)	ناطق بـ	*nātiq bi…*
spokeswoman (n)	ناطقة بـ	*nātiqah bi…*
spoliation (n)	إتلاف، اغتصاب	*itlāf, ightiṣāb*
sponge (n)	اسفنج	*isfanj*
sponge (v)	مسح بإسفنج	*masaḥa bi isfanj*
sponge-cake (n)	كعكة اسفنجية	*ka'kah isfanjiyyah*
spongy (adj)	اسفنجي، ممتص	*isfanjī, mumtaṣṣ*
sponsor (n)	كفيل، ضامن	*kafīl, ḍāmin*
sponsor (v)	كفل، رعى	*kafala, ra'ā*
sponsorship (n)	كفالة، ضمانة	*kafālah, ḍamānah*
spontaneity (n)	تلقائية، اختيارية	*tilqā'iyyah, ikhtiyāriyyah*

spontaneous (adj)	تلقائي، ذاتي	*tilqā'ī, dhātī*
spontaneously (adv)	تلقائيًا، عفويًا	*tilqā'iyyan, 'afwiyyan*
spontaneousness (n)	عفوية، تلقائية	*'afwiyyah, tilqā'iyyah*
spoon (n/v)	ملعقة، غرف بملعقة	*mil'aqah, gharafa bi mil'aqah*
spoonful (adj)	ملء ملعقة	*mil'u mil'aqah*
sporadic (adj)	متقطع، متفرق	*mutaqaṭṭi', mutafarriq*
sporadically (adv)	متباعداً عن بعضه	*mutabā'idan 'an ba'ḍih*
spore (n)	بذرة، بوغة	*badhrah, baughah*
sport (n)	ألعاب رياضية	*al'āb riyāḍiyyah*
sportive (adj)	لعوب، جذل	*la'ūb, jadhil*
sports-editor (n)	محرر الرياضة	*muḥarrirur riyāḍah*
sportsman (n)	رياضي، محب الألعاب الرياضية	*riyāḍī, muḥibbul al'āb ar riyāḍiyyah*
sportsmanship (n)	روح رياضية	*rūḥ riyāḍiyyah*
sports writer	محرر الرياضة	*muḥarrirur riyāḍah*
spot (n)	رقطة، بقعة، موضع	*ruqṭah, buq'ah, mauḍi'*
spot (v)	وسم، لطخ، رقط	*wasama, laṭṭakha, raqqaṭa*
spotless (adj)	نظيف، غير مبقع	*naẓīf, ghair mubaqqa'*
spotlight (n)	ضوء موضعي	*ḍau' mauḍi'ī*
spotted (adj)	ملطخ، منقط	*mulaṭṭakh, munaqqaṭ*
spouse (n)	زوج، زوجة	*zauj, zaujah*
spout (v)	انبثق، انبجس	*imbathaqa, imbajasa*
spout (n)	انبثاق، ميزاب، صنبور	*imbithāq, mīzāb, ṣumbūr*
sprain (v/n)	وثأ، وثء	*watha'a, wath'*
sprawl (v)	انبطح، استلقى	*imbaṭaḥa, istalqā*
sprawl (n)	تمدد، استلقاء	*tamaddud, istilqā'*
spray (v)	رش، رذ	*rashsha, radhdha*
spray (n)	مرشة، عسلوج	*mirashshah, 'uslūj*
spread (v)	بسط، مد، انتشر	*basaṭa, madda, intashara*
spread (n)	امتداد، انتشار	*imtidād, intishār*
spree (n)	مرح، بسط	*maraḥ, basṭ*

sprig (n)	غصن، فرع	*ghuṣn, far'*
spring (v)	طفر، ارتد، انبجس	*ṭafara, irtadda, imbajasa*
spring (n)	وثبة، نبع، ربيع	*wathbah, nab', rabī'*
sprinkle (v)	ذر، نضح، رش	*dharra, naḍaḥa, rashsha*
sprinkle (n)	رش، ذر، نثر	*rashsh, dharr, nathr*
sprinkling (n)	مقدار ضئيل، ذرة	*miqdār ḍa'īl, dharrah*
sprite (n)	شبح، جنية	*shabaḥ, jinniyyah*
sprout (n)	برعم، نبتة	*bur'um, nabtah*
sprout (v)	تبرعم، نبت	*tabar'ama, nabata*
spruce (adj)	متأنق، كيس	*muta'anniq, kayyis*
sprucely (adv)	بلباقة، بأناقة	*bi labāqah, bi anāqah*
spruceness (n)	لباقة، تأنق	*labāqah, ta'annuq*
spry (adj)	نشيط، خفيف الحركة	*nashīṭ, khafīful ḥarakah*
spur (v)	حث، همز	*ḥaththa, hamaza*
spur (n)	مهماز، منخس	*mihmāz, minkhas*
spurious (adj)	زائف، نغل	*zā'if, naghl*
spuriously (adv)	بنغولة، بزيف	*bi nughūlah, bi zaif*
spuriousness (n)	زيف، نغولة	*zaif, nughūlah*
spurn (v)	رفض بازدراء	*rafaḍa bizdirā'*
spurt (v)	تدفق، انفجر، بخ	*tadaffaqa, infajara, bakhkha*
spurt (n)	تدفق مفاجئ	*tadaffuq, mufāji'*
spy (n)	عين، جاسوس	*'ain, jāsūs*
spy (v)	تجسس، استطلع	*tajassasa, istaṭla'a*
squabble (v)	تشاجر، ناضل	*tashājara, nāḍala*
squabble (n)	نضال، شجار	*niḍāl, shijār*
squad (n)	شرذمة، حزب	*shirdhimah, ḥizb*
squadron (n)	أسطول، جمهرة	*usṭūl, jamharah*
squalid (adj)	حقير، خسيس	*ḥaqīr, khasīs*
squander (v)	أسرف، بدد	*asrafa, baddada*
square (adj)	مربع، أمين، محكم	*murabba', amīn, muḥkam*

square (n)	مساحة، مربع، تربيع	*masāḥah, murabba', tarbī'*
square (v)	ربع، عدل، قاس	*rabba'a, 'addala, qāsa*
squarely (adv)	بعدل، بأمانة	*bi 'adl, bi amānah*
squash (v)	سحق، هرس	*saḥaqa, harasa*
squash (n)	هريس، اسكواش	*harīs, iskwāsh*
squashy (adj)	سهل الهرس، لين	*sahlul hars, layyin*
squat (n)	قرفصا، جثوم	*qurfuṣā, juthūm*
squeak (n/v)	صرير، صر	*ṣarīr, ṣarra*
squeal (v)	صرخ، زعق	*ṣarakha, za'aqa*
squeal (n)	صرخة حادة، زعيق	*ṣarkhah ḥāddah, za'īq*
squeeze (v)	عصر، ضغط	*'aṣara, ḍaghaṭa*
squeeze (n)	عصر، عصارة	*'aṣr, 'uṣārah*
squeezer (n)	معصرة	*mi'ṣarah*
squint (n)	حول العين	*ḥawalul 'ain*
squinty (adj)	أحول العين	*aḥwalul 'ain*
squire (n)	سيد، قاضي	*sayyid, qāḍī*
squirrel (n)	سنجاب	*sinjāb*
squirt (v)	بخ، ضخ	*bakhkha, ḍakhkha*
squirt (n)	بخيخة، مضخة	*bukhkhīkhah, miḍakhkhah*
stab (v/n)	طعن، طعنة	*ṭa'ana, ta'nah*
stabbing (adj)	حاد جدًا	*ḥādd jiddan*
stability (n)	ثبات، استقرار	*thabāt, istiqrār*
stabilization,-isation	ترسيخ، تثبيت	*tarsīkh, tathbīt*
stabilize,-ise (v)	رسخ، مكن	*rassakha, makkana*
stable (adj)	ثابت، راسخ	*thābit, rāsikh*
stable (n)	اصطبل، مربط	*iṣtabl, marbaṭ*
stabling (n)	اصطبل الخيل	*iṣtablul khail*
stably (adv)	بثبات، برسوخ	*bi thabāt, bi rusūkh*
stack (n)	ركام، مدخنة	*rukām, midkhanah*
stack (v)	كدس، كوم	*kaddasa, kawwama*
stadium (n)	ملعب مدرج	*mal'ab mudarraj*

staff (n)	درجة، عكاز، عمال إدارة	*darajah, 'ukāz, 'ummālu idārah*
staff (v)	زود، وفر	*zawwada, waffara*
stag (n)	أيل، وعل	*ayyil, wa'l*
stage (n)	منصة، مرحلة	*minaṣṣah, marḥalah*
stage (v)	قدم على المسرح	*qaddama 'alal masraḥ*
stage direction	إرشادات مسرحية	*irshādāt masraḥiyyah*
stage door	باب المسرح الخلفي	*bābul masraḥ al khalfī*
stagger (v)	تمايل، صعق	*tamāyala, ṣa'aqa*
stagger (n)	تمايل، تردد	*tamāyul, taraddud*
staggering (adj)	صاعق، مذهل	*ṣā'iq, mudhhil*
staging (n)	سقالات في مبنى	*siqālāt fī mabnā*
stagnancy (n)	ركود، جمود	*rukūd, jumūd*
stagnant (adj)	راكد، ساكت	*rākid, sākit*
stagnate (v)	ركد، كسد	*rakada, kasada*
stagnation (n)	ركود، كساد	*rukūd, kasād*
stagy (adj)	مسرحي	*masraḥī*
staid (adj)	رصين، رزين	*raṣīn, razīn*
stain (n)	بقعة، لطخة	*buq'ah, laṭkhah*
stain (v)	لطخ، شان	*laṭṭakha, shāna*
stainless (adj)	نقي الذيل، غير ملطخ	*naqiyyudh dhail, ghair mulaṭṭakh*
stair (n)	درجة، سلم	*darajah, sullam*
staircase (n)	درج، سلالم	*daraj, salālim*
stairway (n)	سلم، درج	*sullam, daraj*
stake (n)	سنان، وتد	*sinān, watid*
state (adj)	مبتذل، بالٍ، تافه	*mubtadhil, bālin, tāfih*
stalk (n)	ساق النبات	*sāqun nabāt*
stalk (v)	تخطل في المشي	*takhaṭṭala fil mashy*
stall (n)	كشك، مربط، دكة	*kushk, marbiṭ, dikkah*
stall (v)	وضع في مربط	*waḍa'a fī marbiṭ*
stalwart (adj)	قوي الجسم، ضليع	*qawiyyul jism, ḍalī'*

stalwart (n)	قوة على الاحتمال	*quwwah 'alal iḥtimāl*
stammer (v)	تلجلج، تلعثم	*talajlaja, tala'thama*
stammer (n)	تلعثم، تمتمة	*tala'thum, tamtamah*
stammerer (n)	متلعثم، متلجلج	*mutala'thim, mutalajlij*
stammeringly (adv)	بتلعثم	*bi tala'thum*
stamp (n)	طابع، ختم، علامة	*ṭāba', khatm, 'alāmah*
stamp (v)	داس، رض، ختم	*dāsa, raḍḍa, khatama*
stampede (n)	فرار، جفول	*firār, jufūl*
stampede (v)	جفل، فر	*jafala, farra*
stamping ground	منتجع مألوف	*muntaja' ma'lūf*
stance (n)	وضعة، موقف	*wiḍ'ah, mauqif*
stanch (staunch) (v)	أرقأ، أوقف	*arqa'a, auqafa*
stanchion (n/v)	دعامة، دعم	*di'āmah, da'ama*
stand (n)	موقف، منصة، توقف	*mauqif, minaṣṣah, tawaqquf*
stand (v)	قام، وقف، احتمل	*qāma, waqafa, iḥtamala*
standard (n)	لواء، صف، معيار، قاعدة	*liwā', ṣaff, mi'yār, qā'idah*
standard (adj)	فصيح، سليم، معياري	*faṣīḥ, salīm, mi'yārī*
standard-bearer (n)	حامل اللواء	*ḥāmilul liwā'*
standardize,-ise (v)	قيس، عاير	*qayyasa, 'āyara*
standard time	وقت قياسي	*waqt qiyāsī*
stand aside	وقف جانباً	*waqafa jāniban*
stand by	ناصر، أيد	*nāṣara, ayyada*
standing (adj)	قائم، راكد	*qā'im, rākid*
standing (n)	وقوف، منـــزلة، حالة	*wuqūf, manzilah, ḥālah*
standing-room (n)	حيز الوقوف	*ḥayyizul wuqūf*
stand on	أصر، ألح	*aṣarra, alaḥḥa*
stand-pipe (n)	ماسورة قائمة	*māsūrah qā'imah*
standpoint (n)	وجهة نظر	*wijhatu naẓar*
standstill (n)	توقف تام	*tawaqquf tāmm*

stanza (n)	مقطع شعري	*maqṭa' shi'rī*
staple (n)	رزة، غرزة	*razzah, ghurzah*
staple (v)	ثبت برزة	*thabbata bi razzah*
staple (adj)	رئيسي، أساسي	*ra'īsī, asāsī*
stapler (n)	مشك سلكي	*mishakk silkī*
star (n)	نجم، كوكب	*najm, kaukab*
starboard (n)	ميمنة، يمين السفينة	*maimanah, yamīnus safīnah*
stardom (n)	نجمية	*najmiyyah*
stare (v)	حدق، تفرس	*ḥaddaqa, tafarrasa*
stare (n)	حملقة، تحديق	*ḥamlaqah, taḥdīq*
star-gazer (n)	مراقب النجوم، شارد الفكر	*murāqibun nujūm, shāridul fikr*
star-gazing (n)	مراقبة النجوم، شرود الفكر	*murāqabatun nujūm, shurūdul fikr*
stark (adj)	عار، مقفر	*'ār, muqfir*
starlight (n)	ضوء النجوم	*ḍau'un nujūm*
starling (n)	زرزور	*zurzūr*
start (n)	بداية، انطلاق، إجفال	*bidāyah, inṭilaq, ijfāl*
start (v)	بدأ، انطلق، استهل	*bada'a, inṭalaqa, istahalla*
starter (n)	مشترك، مبدئ	*mushtarik, mubdi'*
starting post	منطلق	*munṭalaq*
startle (v)	أجفل، أفزع	*ajfala, afza'a*
starvation (n)	مجاعة، سغابة	*majā'ah, saghābah*
starve (v)	سغب، مات جوعاً	*saghaba, māta jū'an*
stash (v/n)	أخبأ، مخبأ	*akhba'a, makhba'*
state (n)	حالة، ولاية، مقام	*ḥālah, wilāyah, maqām*
state (v)	صرح، قرر	*ṣarraḥa, qarrara*
statecraft (n)	فن الحكم	*fannul ḥukm*
stateliness (n)	فخامة، جلال	*fakhāmah, jalāl*
stately (adj)	فخم، جليل	*fakhm, jalīl*

statement (n)	تصريح، كشف الحساب	*taṣrīḥ, kashful ḥisāb*
statesman (n)	رجل دولة، سياسي	*rajulu daulah, siyāsī*
statesmanship (n)	تدبير أمور الدولة	*tadbīru umūrid daulah*
static (adj)	جامد، راكد، ساكت	*jāmid, rākid, sākit*
station (n)	محطة، موقف، مركز	*maḥaṭṭah, mauqif, markaz*
station (v)	ركز، أقام	*rakkaza, aqāma*
stationary (adj)	مستقر، غير متحرك	*mustaqirr, ghair mutaḥarrik*
stationer (n)	قرطاسي، وراق، أدوات الكتابة	*qirṭāsī, warrāq, adawātul kitābah*
statistic (n)	بند إحصائي	*band iḥṣā'ī*
statistical (adj)	إحصائي، تعدادي	*iḥṣā'ī, ta'dādī*
statistics (n)	علم الإحصاء	*'ilmul iḥṣā'*
statuary (n)	نحت التماثيل	*naḥtut tamāthīl*
statue (n)	تمثال، نصب	*timthāl, nuṣb*
statuesque (adj)	شبيه بالتماثيل	*shabīh bit tamāthīl*
statuette (n)	تمثال صغير	*timthāl ṣaghīr*
stature (n)	قامة، قد، مكانة	*qāmah, qadd, makānah*
status (n)	منـزلة، حالة، ظرف	*manzilah, ḥālah, ẓarf*
status quo	حالة راهنة	*ḥālah rāhinah*
statute (n)	قانون، سنة	*qānūn, sunnah*
statute-book (n)	سجل القوانين	*sijillul qawānīn*
statute law	قانون تشريعي	*qānūn tashrī'ī*
statutory (adj)	قانوني، نظامي	*qānūni, niẓāmī*
staunch (adj)	مخلص، معتمد، أمين	*mukhliṣ, mu'tamad, amīn*
stave (n)	ضلع البرميل	*ḍil'ul barmīl*
stay (n)	إقامة، مكوث، بقاء	*iqāmah, mukūth, baqā'*
stay (v)	أقام، بقى، وقف	*aqāma, baqā, waqafa*
staying power	قدرة على الاحتمال	*qudrah 'alal iḥtimāl*
stead (n)	عوض، بدل	*'iwaḍ, badal*
steadfast (adj)	راسخ، متين، مخلص	*rāsikh, matīn, mukhliṣ*

steadfastly (adv)	بمتانة، برسوخ	*bi matānah, bi rusūkh*
steadfastness (n)	ثبات، متانة، رسوخ	*thabāt, matānah, rusūkh*
steadily (adv)	بمثابرة، بثبات	*bi muthābarah, bi thabāt*
steadiness (n)	مثابرة، ثبات	*muthābarah, thabāt*
steady (adj)	مثابر، ثابت	*muthābir, thābit*
steady (v)	رسخ، ثبت	*rassakha, thabbata*
steady (n)	قرين، رفيق، زميل	*qarīn, rafīq, zamīl*
steak (n)	شريحة السمك أو اللحم	*sharīḥatus samak awil laḥm*
steal (v)	سرق، انتحل	*saraqa, intaḥala*
steal (n)	اختلاس، سرقة	*ikhtilās, sariqah*
stealth (n)	خسلة، سرقة	*khulsah, sariqah*
stealthily (adv)	خسلةً، سرًّا	*khulsatan, sirran*
stealthiness (n)	اختلاس، انتحال	*ikhtilās, intiḥāl*
stealthy (adj)	سري، مختلس	*sirrī, mukhtalas*
steam (v/n)	تبخر، بخار	*tabakhkhara, bukhār*
steamboat (n)	سفينة بخارية	*safīnah bukhāriyyah*
steam-engine (n)	محرك بخاري	*muḥarrik bukhārī*
steamer (n)	سفينة بخارية، باخرة	*safīnah bukhāriyyah, bākhirah*
steamy (adj)	بخاري	*bukhārī*
steed (n)	جواد، حصان جامع	*jawād, ḥiṣān jāmi'*
steel (n)	فولاذ	*fūlādh*
steel (v)	صلب، فولذ	*ṣallaba, fauladha*
steelworks (n)	مصنع الفولاذ	*maṣna'ul fūlādh*
steely (adj)	فولاذي، صلب	*fūlādhī, ṣulb*
steep (adj)	شديد الانحدار، باهظ	*shadīdul inḥidār, bāhiẓ*
steeple (n)	برج الكنيسة	*burjul kanīsah*
steeplechase (n)	سباق للخيل	*sibāq lil khail*
steer (v)	وجه، اتجه، أدار	*wajjaha, ittajaha, adār*
steer (n)	ثور مخصي	*thaur makhṣī*
steerage (n)	إدارة، اتجاه	*idārah, ittijāh*

steering-wheel (n)	عجلة القيادة	*'ajalatul qiyādah*
steersman (n)	مدير الدفة	*mudīrud daffah*
stellar (adj)	نجمي، كوكبي	*najmī, kaukabī*
stem (n)	ساق، جذل، أصل	*sāq, jidhl, aṣl*
stem (v)	كبح، أوقف، سد	*kabaḥa, auqafa, sadda*
stench (n)	رائحة كريهة	*rā'iḥah karīhah*
stencil (n)	صفيحة العلام، روسمة	*ṣafīḥatul 'alām, rausamah*
stenographer (n)	كاتب الاختزال	*kātibul ikhtizāl*
stenography (n)	كتابة مختزلة	*kitābah mukhtazalah*
step (n)	خطوة، درجة، أثر	*khuṭwah, darajah, athar*
step (v)	خطا، مشى	*khaṭā, mashā*
stepbrother (n)	أخ من أحد الوالدين	*akh min aḥadil wālidain*
step down	نزل	*nazala*
stepfather	زوج الأم	*zaujul umm*
step forward	خطا نحو الأمام	*khaṭā naḥwal amām*
step in	دخل	*dakhala*
stepmother (n)	رابة، زوجة الأب	*rābbah, zaujatul ab*
step-parent (n)	زوج الأم أو زوجة الأب	*zaujul umm au zaujatul ab*
stepsister (n)	أخت من أحد الوالدين	*ukht min aḥadil wālidain*
stereoscope (n)	مجسام، استريوسكوب	*mijsām, istiriyuskūb*
stereotype (n)	مصحف، مقولب	*muṣaḥḥaf, muqaulab*
stereotyped (adj)	مقولب، مقولبة	*muqaulab, muqaulabah*
stereotyping (n)	تصفيح، قولبة	*taṣfīḥ, qaulabah*
sterile (adj)	عقيم، عاقر، مجدب	*'aqīm, 'āqir, mujdib*
sterility (n)	عقم، قحل	*'uqm, qaḥl*
sterilization,-isation	تجديب، تعقيم	*tajdīb, ta'qīm*
sterilize,-ise (v)	عقم، جدب	*'aqqama, jaddaba*
sterling (adj)	نقي، صرف، خالص	*naqiyy, ṣirf, khāliṣ*
sterling (n)	عملة انجليزية	*'umlah injilīziyyah*

stern (adj)	كالح، قاسٍ	*kāliḥ, qāsin*
stern (n)	مؤخر السفينة	*mu'akhkharus safīnah*
stertorous (adj)	غطيطي، شخيري	*ghaṭīṭī, shakhīrī*
stethoscope (n)	مسماع صدري	*mismā' ṣadrī*
stew (n)	يخنة	*yakhnah*
stew (v)	سبك الطبخ	*sabbakaṭ ṭabkh*
steward (n)	مضيف، مدير، وكيل الخرج	*muḍīf, mudīr, wakīlul kharj*
stewardess (n)	مضيفة، مديرة	*muḍīfah, mudīrah*
stewardship (n)	وظيفة القهرمان	*waẓīfatul qahramān*
stick (n)	قضيب، شيء دبق	*qaḍīb, shay' dabiq*
stick (v)	ألصق، وضع، ثبت	*alṣaqa, waḍa'a, thabata*
sticker (n)	مادة دبقة، مثابر	*māddah dabiqah, muthābir*
stick-in-the-mud (n)	رجعي، غير مرتقٍ	*raj'ī, ghair murtaqin*
stickle (v)	ماحك، كابر	*māḥaka, kābara*
stickleback (n)	أبو شوكة	*abū shaukah*
stickler (n)	شديد التمسك	*shadīdut tamassuk*
sticky (adj)	لزج، دبق	*lazij, dabiq*
stiff (adj)	جامد، صلب، باهظ	*jāmid, ṣulb, bāhiẓ*
stiffen (v)	تصلب، تجمد	*taṣallaba, tajammada*
stiffly (n)	بيبوسة، بقسوة	*bi yabūsah, bi qaswah*
stiffness (n)	صلابة، يبوسة	*ṣalābah, yabūsah*
stifle (v)	خنق، كظم، أخمد	*khanaqa, kaẓama, akhmada*
stifling (adj)	خانق، كاتم	*khāniq, kātim*
stigma (n)	كي، وصمة عار	*kayy, waṣmatu 'ār*
stigmatize,-ise (v)	شان، وصم بالعار	*shāna, waṣama bil 'ār*
stiletto (n)	خنجر صغير	*khanjar ṣaghīr*
still (adj)	هادئ، ساكن	*hādi', sākin*
still (adv)	ومع ذلك، إلى الآن	*wa ma'a dhālik, ilal ān*
still (v)	هدأ، سكن	*hadda'a, sakkana*

still (n)	صورة فوتوغرافية	*ṣūrah fūtūgharāfiyyah*
still birth (n)	إجهاض جنين ميت	*ijhāḍu janīn mait*
stillborn (adj)	مولود ميتاً	*maulūd maitan*
stillness (n)	سكون، هدوء	*sukūn, hudū'*
stilt (n)	طول، أبوساق	*ṭuwwal, abū sāq*
stilted (adj)	متكلف، متضع	*mutakallaf, muttaḍi'*
stimulant (n)	شراب كحولي	*sharāb kuḥūlī*
stimulate (v)	نبه، حرك	*nabbaha, ḥarraka*
stimulating (adj)	منبه، منشط	*munabbih, munashshiṭ*
stimulation (n)	إثارة، تنبيه	*ithārah, tambīh*
stimulus (n)	حافز، مهيج	*ḥāfiz, muhayyij*
sting (n)	حمة، شوكة، لدغة	*humah, shaukah, ladghah*
sting (v)	قرص، لدغ	*qaraṣa, ladagha*
stinginess (n)	شح، قتر	*shuḥḥ, qatr*
stingy (adj)	شحيح، مقتر	*shaḥīḥ, muqattir*
stink (n)	رائحة كريهة، نتونة	*rā'iḥah karīhah, nutūnah*
stink (v)	نتن، تعفن	*natana, ta'affana*
stinker (n)	شيء نتن أو كريه	*shay' natin au karīh*
stinking (adj)	كريه، بغيض	*karīh, baghīḍ*
stint (v)	حصر، قيد	*ḥaṣara, qayyada*
stint (n)	قيد، حد	*qaid, ḥadd*
stipend (n)	راتب، معاش قسيس	*rātib, ma'āshu qissīs*
stipendary (adj)	ذو راتب معين	*dhū rātib mu'ayyan*
stipple (v)	رسم، رقط	*rasama, raqqaṭa*
stipulate (v)	اشترط، تعاقد	*ishtaraṭa, ta'āqada*
stipulation (n)	تعاقد، شرط	*ta'āqud, sharṭ*
stir (v)	أثار، حرك	*athāra, ḥarraka*
stir (n)	إثارة، حركة، اهتياج	*ithārah, ḥarakah, ihtiyāj*
stirrer (n)	شخص مزعج	*shakhṣ muz'ij*
stirring (adj)	مثير، محرك	*muthīr, muḥarrik*
stitch (n)	درزه، قطبة	*darzah, quṭbah*

stitch (v)	خاط، درز	*khāṭa, daraza*
stock (n)	مخزون، رأسمال، مصدر	*makhzūn, ra'sumāl, maṣdar*
stock (v)	اختزن، مون	*ikhtazana, mawwana*
stockade (n)	خط دفاعي	*khaṭṭ difā'ī*
stockbroker (n)	سمسار البورصة	*simsārul būrṣah*
stock-car (n)	عربة الماشية	*'arabatul māshiyah*
stock certificate	شهادة الأسهم	*shahādatul ashum*
stock company	شركة مساهمة	*sharikatu musāhamah*
stock exchange	بورصة	*būrṣah*
stockholder (n)	حامل الأسهم	*ḥāmilul ashum*
stockinet (n)	قماش قطني	*qumāsh quṭnī*
stocking (n)	جورب	*jaurab*
stockman (n)	مربي الماشية	*murabbil māshiyah*
stock-market (n)	بورصة، مصفق	*būrṣah, maṣfaq*
stockpile (n)	مخزون احتياطي	*makhzūn iḥtiyāṭī*
stockpot (n)	كشكول، حلة المرق	*kashkūl, ḥallatul maraq*
stocky (adj)	قوي الجسم	*qawiyyul jism*
stockyard (n)	فناء الماشية	*finā'ul māshiyah*
stoic (n/adj)	رزين، مثابر	*razīn, muthābir*
stoical (adj)	مثابر، متين	*muthābir, matīn*
stoicism (n)	مثابرة، رواقية	*muthābarah, riwāqiyyah*
stoke (v)	أتخم، ذكى	*atkhama, dhakkā*
stoker (n)	وقاد، مذكٍّ	*waqqād, mudhakkin*
stole (n)	بطرشين	*baṭrashīn*
stolid (adj)	سمج، متبلد	*samij, mutaballid*
stolidity (stolidness)	سماجة، بلاهة	*samājah, balāhah*
stomack (n)	معدة، رغبة في الطعام	*ma'idah, raghbah fiṭ ṭa'ām*
stomack-ache (n)	مغص، وجع المعدة	*maghṣ, waj'ul ma'idah*
stone (n)	حجارة، حجر، حصاة	*ḥijārah, ḥajar, ḥaṣāt*
stone (v)	رجم بالحجارة	*rajama bil ḥijārah*

stone-dead (adj)	أصم تماماً	*aṣamm tamāman*
stone-deaf (adj)	أصم تماما	*aṣamm tamāman*
stone-fruit (n)	فاكهة نواة	*fākihatu nawāt*
stoneless (adj)	غير ذي نواة	*ghair dhī nawāt*
stonemason (n)	معمار، بناء	*mi'mār, bannā'*
stoneware (n)	خزف حجري	*khazaf ḥajarī*
stonework (n)	مبنى حجري	*mabnā ḥajarī*
stony (adj)	حجري، متحجر	*ḥajarī, mutaḥajjir*
stool (n)	كرسي بلا ظهر	*kursī bilā ẓahr*
stoop (v)	انحط، انحنى	*inḥaṭṭa, inḥanā*
stoop (n)	انقضاض، انحناء	*inqiḍāḍ, inḥinā'*
stop (v)	وقف، منع، سد	*waqafa, mana'a, sadda*
stop (n)	وقوف، موقف، سد	*wuqūf, mauqif, sadd*
stoppage (n)	توقف، انسداد	*tawaqquf, insidād*
stop-press (n)	خبر أخير	*khabar akhīr*
stop-watch (n)	ساعة التوقف	*sā'atut tawaqquf*
storage (n)	خزن، مخزن	*khazn, makhzan*
store (v)	اختزن، ادخر	*ikhtazana, iddakhara*
store (n)	ذخيرة، مخزن	*dhakhīrah, makhzan*
storehouse (n)	مستودع، مخزن	*mustauda', makhzan*
storekeeper (n)	أمين المستودع	*amīnul mustauda'*
storey (n)	طابق، دور	*ṭābiq, daur*
storeyed (adj)	ذو طوابق	*dhū ṭawābiq*
stork (n)	لقلاق	*laqlāq*
storm (n)	عاصفة، زوبعة	*'āṣifah, zauba'ah*
storm-door (n)	باب العواصف	*bābul 'awāṣif*
stormproof (adj)	صامد للعواصف	*ṣāmid lil 'awāṣif*
stormy (adj)	عاصف، عجاج	*'āṣif, 'ajjāj*
story (n)	حكاية، قصة، رواية	*ḥikāyah, qiṣṣah, riwāyah*
story-book (n)	كتاب الحكايات	*kitābul ḥikāyāt*
story-teller (n)	قصاص، قاص	*qaṣṣāṣ, qāṣṣ*
stout (adj).	متين، صامد، عنيف	*matīn, ṣāmid, 'anīf*

stout-hearted (adj)	جريء، عنيد	*jarī', 'anīd*
stoutly (adv)	بمتانة، بقوة	*bi matānah, bi quwwah*
stoutness (n)	متانة، عنف	*matānah, 'unf*
stove (n)	موقد، فرن	*mauqid, furn*
stowage (n)	سعة الاختزان	*sa'atul ikhtizān*
stowaway (n)	شخص مستخفي	*shakhṣ mustakhfī*
straggle (v)	شرد، ضل	*sharada, ḍalla*
straight (adj)	قويم، متصل، مستقيم	*qawīm, muttaṣil, mustaqīm*
straight (adv)	مباشرةً، باستقامة	*mubāsharatan, bistiqāmah*
straighten (v)	قوم، سوى	*qawwama, sawwā*
straight fight	معركة ثنائية	*ma'rakah thunā'iyyah*
straightforward (adj)	صريح، مباشر	*ṣarīḥ, mubāshir*
straightforwardness	صراحة، وضاحة	*ṣarāḥah, waḍāḥah*
straightness (n)	استقامة، صراحة	*istiqāmah, ṣarāḥah*
straightway (adv)	مباشرةً، فوراً	*mubāsharatan, fauran*
strain (n)	صدع، ضغط، نزعة	*ṣad', ḍaghṭ, naz'ah*
strain (v)	جهد، وثأ، ضغط	*jahada, watha'a, ḍaghaṭa*
strait (n)	بوغاز، مضيق	*būghāz, maḍīq*
strand (n)	شاطئ، مهرقان، جديلة	*shāṭi', muhraqān, jadīlah*
strand (v)	جنح السفينة	*jannaḥas safīnah*
strange (adj)	غريب، مستهجن	*gharīb, mustahjan*
strangely (adv)	بغرابة، بشذوذ	*bi gharābah, bi shudhūdh*
strangeness (n)	غرابة، شذوذ	*gharābah, shudhūdh*
stranger (n)	أجنبي، غريب	*ajnabī, gharīb*
strangle (v)	خنق، جندل	*khanaqa, jandala*
stranglehold (n)	مسكة خانقة	*maskah khāniqah*
strangulate (v)	شنق، جندل	*shanaqa, jandala*
strangulation (n)	خنق، اختناق	*khanq, ikhtināq*
strap (n)	قشاط، سوط، شريط، طوق	*qushāṭ, sauṭ, sharīṭ, ṭauq*
strap (v)	شحذ، ساط	*shaḥadha, sāṭa*
strapless (adj)	بدون طوق	*bidūn ṭauq*

strapping (adj)	قوي الجسم	*qawiyyul jism*
stratagem (n)	خدعة، حيلة، مكيدة	*khud'ah, ḥīlah, makīdah*
strategic (adj)	استراتيجي	*istarātījī*
strategist (n)	ماهر في خطط حربية	*māhir fī khuṭaṭ ḥarbiyyah*
strategy (n)	استراتيجية، فن الحرب	*istarātījiyyah, fannul ḥarb*
stratify (v)	طابق، تراصف	*ṭābaqa, tarāṣafa*
stratum (n)	سافة، طبقة، رتبة	*sāfah, ṭabaqah, rutbah*
straw (n)	قش، تبن	*qashsh, tibn*
strawberry (n)	فراولة، شليك	*farāulah, shulaik*
stray (n/adj)	تائه، شارد	*tā'ih, shārid*
stray (v)	تاه، شرد	*tāha, sharada*
streak (n)	مسحة، خط، فترة	*masḥah, khaṭṭ, fatrah*
streak (v)	خطط، اندفع بسرعة	*khaṭṭaṭa, indafa'a bi sur'ah*
streaky (adj)	ذو خطوط ملونة، مزيح	*dhū khuṭūṭ mulawwanah, muzayyaḥ*
stream (n)	مجرى، جدول	*majrā, jadwal*
stream (v)	فاض، سال، جرى	*fāḍa, sāla, jarā*
streamlet (n)	نهير، جدول صغير	*nuhair, jadwal ṣaghīr*
streamline (v)	بسط، نظم	*basaṭa, naẓẓama*
streamlined (adj)	مبسط، منظم	*mubassaṭ, munaẓẓam*
street (n)	شارع	*shāri'*
street-girl (n)	بغي، مومس	*baghiyy, mūmis*
street-walker	مومس، بغي	*mūmis, baghī*
strength (n)	قدرة، قوة، متانة	*qudrah, quwwah, matānah*
strengthen (v)	قوى، عزز	*qawwā, 'azzaza*
strenuous (adj)	متحمس، شاق	*mutaḥammis, shāqq*
strenuously (adv)	بحماسة، بجراءة	*bi ḥamāsah, bi jarā'ah*
stress (n)	ضغط، توكيد، شدة	*ḍaghṭ, taukīd, shiddah*
stress (v)	أكد، أجهد	*akkada, ajhada*

streesful (adj)	مجهد، مؤكد	*mujhid, mu'akkid*
stretch (v)	بسط، مد	*basaṭa, madda*
stretch (n)	مدة، مدى، امتداد	*maddah, madā, imtidād*
stretcher (n)	نقالة، فارد	*naqqālah, fārid*
stretchy (adj)	مرن، لدن	*marin, ladin*
strew (v)	نثر، بذر، نشر	*nathara, badhara, nashara*
striated (adj)	محطط، مثلم	*muḥaṭṭaṭ, muthallam*
stricken (adj)	مبتلى، مضروب	*mubtalā, maḍrūb*
strict (adj)	صارم، دقيق	*ṣārim, daqīq*
strictly (adv)	بدقة، تماماً	*bi diqqah, tamāman*
stricture (n)	نقد قاسٍ	*naqd qāsin*
stride (n)	خطوة واسعة	*khuṭwah wāsi'ah*
strident (adj)	عالٍ، حاد	*'ālin, ḥādd*
strife (n)	كفاح، نزاع	*kifāḥ, nizā'*
strike (n)	إضراب عن العمل، اكتشاف مفاجئ	*iḍrāb 'anil 'amal, iktishāf mufāji'*
strike (v)	أضرب عن العمل، طعن، قرع	*aḍraba 'anil 'amal, ṭa'ana, qara'a*
strikebound (adj)	مخضع للإضراب	*mukhḍa' lil iḍrāb*
strike-breaker (n)	مفسد الإضراب	*mufsidul iḍrāb*
striker (n)	مضرب عن العمل	*muḍrib 'anil 'amal*
striking (adj)	لافت للنظر، جذاب	*lāfit lin naẓar, jadhdhāb*
string (v)	وتر، ركب وتراً	*wattara, rakkaba wataran*
string (n)	خيط، وتر، سلسلة	*khaiṭ, watar, silsilah*
stringency (n)	ضغط، صرامة	*ḍaghṭ, ṣarāmah*
stringent (adj)	صارم، اضطراري	*ṣārim, iḍṭirārī*
strip (v)	نزع، عرى، جرد	*naza'a, 'arrā, jarrada*
strip (n)	نزع، شقة، سلخة	*naz', shuqqah, salkhah*
stripe (n)	قلم، خط	*qalam, khaṭṭ*
striped (adj)	مخطط، مقلم	*mukhaṭṭaṭ, muqallam*
stripling (n)	مراهق، شارخ	*murāhiq, shārikh*

stripper (n)	متعرية، متجردة	*muta'arriyah, mutajarridah*
strip-tease (n)	تعري، تجرد	*ta'arrī, tajarrud*
stripy = striped		
strive (v)	جاهد، كدح	*jāhada, kadaḥa*
stroke (v)	مسد، ضرب برفق	*massada, ḍaraba bi rifq*
stroke (n)	قرعة، ضربة، صفقة	*qar'ah, ḍarbah, ṣafqah*
stroll (n)	تجول، تطواف	*tajawwul, taṭwāf*
strong (adj)	قوي، شديد، منيع	*qawī, shadīd, manī'*
strong-arm (adj)	صارم، عنيف	*ṣārim, 'anīf*
strong-box (n)	خزانة حديدية	*khizānah ḥadīdiyyah*
stronghold (n)	حصن، معقل	*ḥiṣn, ma'qil*
strong-minded (adj)	مستقل الرأي	*mustaqillur ra'y*
strong-room (n)	حجرة منيعة	*ḥujrah manī'ah*
strop (n)	مشحذة، قائش الأمواس	*mishḥadhah, qā'ishul amwās*
structural (adj)	بنائي، معماري	*binā'ī, mi'mārī*
structure (n)	مبنى، بناء، بنية	*mabnā, binā', binyah*
structure (v)	بنى، شيد	*banā, shayyada*
struggle (v)	كافح، جاهد، كد	*kāfaḥa, jāhada, kadda*
struggle (n)	كفاح، مجاهدة	*kifāḥ, mujāhadah*
strut (n)	اختيال، تفاخر	*ikhtiyāl, tafākhur*
stub (n)	عقب، جذل	*'aqib, jidhl*
stubble (n)	جذامة الحنطة وغيرها	*judhāmatul ḥinṭah wa ghairahā*
stubborn (adj)	عنيد، شديد الشكيمة	*'anīd, shadīdush shakīmah*
stubbornly (adv)	بشكاسة، بشكيمة	*bi shakāsah, bi shakīmah*
stubbornness (n)	عناد، شكاسة	*'inād, shakāsah*
stubby (adj)	كث، مكعبر	*kathth, muka'bar*
stucco (n/v)	جص، جصص	*jiṣṣ, jaṣṣaṣa*
stuccoed (adj)	مجصص	*mujaṣṣaṣ*

stuck-up (adj)	متكبر، أناني	*mutakabbir, anānī*
stud (n)	زر، جياد الاستيلاد	*zirr, jiyādul istīlād*
stud (v)	رصع، زين بخشبات	*raṣṣa'a, zayyana bi khashabāt*
student (n)	طالب، طالبة	*ṭālib, ṭālibah*
studied (adj)	مدروس، مبحوث فيه	*madrūs, mabḥūth fīh*
studio (n)	محترف، استوديو	*muḥtaraf, istūdiyū*
studious (adj)	جاهد، مجد	*jāhid, mujidd*
study (v)	بحث، طالع، درس	*baḥatha, ṭāla'a, darasa*
study (n)	دراسة، بحث	*dirāsah, baḥth*
stuff (v)	أمتعة، مواد	*amti'ah, mawādd*
stuff (n)	أتخم، حشا	*atkhama, ḥashā*
stuffing (n)	حشوة، تصبيرة	*ḥashwah, taṣbīrah*
stuffy (adj)	كتم، مسدود	*katim, masdūd*
stumble (v)	عثر، زل	*'athara, zalla*
stumble (n)	عثرة، زلة	*'athrah, zallah*
stump (n)	جدعة، جذمور	*jada'ah, judhmūr*
stump (v)	مشى بتثاقل، ارتبك	*mashā bi tathāqul, irtabaka*
stumpy (adj)	قصير وبدين	*qaṣīr wa badīn*
stun (v)	أدهش، أذهل	*adhasha, adhhala*
stunner (n)	امرأة جذابة	*imra'ah jadhdhābah*
stunning (adj)	جذاب، لافت للنظر	*jadhdhāb, lāfit lin naẓar*
stunt (v)	أعجز، أوقف النمو	*a'jaza, auqafan numuww*
stunt (n)	عمل مثير	*'amal muthīr*
stupendous (adj)	شاده، هائل	*shādih, hā'il*
stupid (adj)	أبله، أخرق، غبي	*ablah, akhraq, ghabī*
stupidity (n)	بلاهة، حماقة	*balāhah, ḥamāqah*
studidly (adv)	بغباوة، ببلاهة	*bi ghabāwah, bi balāhah*
stupor (n)	ذهول، خبل	*dhuhūl, khabal*
sturdy (adj)	قوي، متين، شديد	*qawī, matīn, shadīd*
stutter (v)	تلجلج، تمتم	*talajlaja, tamtama*

style (n)	أسلوب، طراز، زي	*uslūb, ṭirāz, ziyy*
style (v)	سمى، صمم الأزياء	*sammā, ṣammamal azyā'*
stylish (adj)	حديث الزي	*ḥadīthuz ziyy*
stylishly (adv)	بأناقة، بأسلوب فني	*bi anāqah, bi uslūb fannī*
stylishness (n)	أناقة، قيافة	*anāqah, qiyāfah*
stylist (n)	صاحب الأسلوب، مصمم الأزياء	*ṣāḥibul uslūb, muṣammimul azyā'*
stylistic (adj)	أسلوبي، تصميمي	*uslūbī, taṣmīmī*
suave (adj)	دمث، رقيق، لطيف	*damth, raqīq, laṭīf*
suavity (n)	دماثة، لطف	*damāthah, luṭf*
sub (v)	عمل بدل...	*'amila badla…*
subaltern (n)	ملازم أول	*mulāzim awwal*
subatomic (adj)	ذريري	*dhurairī*
subcommittee (n)	لجنة فرعية	*lajnah far'iyyah*
subconscious (adj)	دو وعي	*dū wa'y*
subcontinent (n)	شبه القارة	*shibhul qārrah*
subcontract (n)	عقد فرعي	*'aqd far'ī*
subdivide (v)	جزأ الجزء	*jazza'al juz'*
subdivision (n)	أجزاء مقسمة	*ajzā' muqassamah*
subdue (v)	أخضع، تغلب على	*akhḍa'a, taghallaba 'alā*
sub-editor (n)	محرر مساعد	*muḥarrir musā'id*
subheading (n)	عنوان فرعي	*'unwān far'ī*
subject (n)	موضوع، رعية	*mauḍū', ra'iyyah*
subject (v)	أخضع، عرض	*akhḍa'a, 'arraḍa*
subject (adj)	خاضع، تابع	*khāḍi', tābi'*
subjection (n)	خضوع، تذلل	*khuḍū', tadhallul*
subjective (adj)	فاعلي، شخصي	*fā'ilī, shakhṣī*
subjoin (v)	ألحق، أضاف	*alḥaqa, aḍāfa*
subjugate (v)	استعبد، قهر	*ista'bada, qahara*
subjugation (n)	إخضاع، استعباد	*ikhḍā', isti'bād*
subjunctive (adj/n)	شرطي، صيغة شرطية	*sharṭī, ṣīghah sharṭiyyah*
sublieutenant (n)	ملازم ثانٍ	*mulāzim thānin*

sublimate (v)	هذب، صعد	*hadhdhaba, ṣa''ada*
sublime (adj)	سامٍ، عالٍ، رفيع	*sāmin, 'ālin, rafī'*
sublimity (n)	سمو، جلال، رفعة	*sumuww, jalāl, rif'ah*
submarine (n/adj)	بحري، غائص	*baḥrī, ghā'iṣ*
submerge (v)	غمر، غاص	*ghamara, ghāṣa*
sumerged (adj)	غاطس، مغمور	*ghāṭis, maghmūr*
submergence (n)	غمر، غطس	*ghamr, ghaṭs*
submersion	غطس، غمر	*ghaṭs, ghamr*
submission (n)	إذعان، خضوع	*idh'ān, khuḍū'*
submissive (adj)	مذعن، مطيع	*mudh'in, muṭī'*
submissiveness (n)	طاعة، خضوع	*ṭā'ah, khuḍū'*
submit (v)	أسلم، استسلم، قدم	*aslama, istaslama, qaddama*
subordinate (n/adj)	تابع، ثانوي	*tābi', thānawī*
suborn (v)	أغرى، حرض	*aghrā, ḥarraḍa*
sub-plot (n)	حكة ثانوية	*ḥukkah thānawiyyah*
subscribe (v)	تبرع، رضي، اشترك	*tabarra'a, raḍiya, ishtaraka*
subscriber (n)	متبرع، مشترك في صحيفة	*mutabarri', mushtarik fī ṣaḥīfah*
subscription (n)	تبرع ، إمضاء، اشتراك	*tabarru', imḍā', ishtirāk*
subsequent (adj)	تابع، لاحق	*tābi', lāḥiq*
subsequently (adv)	بالتالي	*bit tālī*
subservience (n)	خشوع، تذلل، خنوع	*khushū', tadhallul, khunū'*
subservient (adj)	خانع، خاضع	*khāni', khāḍi'*
subside (v)	هدأ، غار، خمد	*hada'a, ghāra, khamada*
subsidence (n)	خمود، هدوء، هبوط	*khumūd, hudū', hubūṭ*
subsidiary (adj/n)	ثانوي، تابع	*thānawī, tābi'*
subsidize,-ise (v)	قدم إعانة مالية	*qaddama i'ānah māliyyah*
subsidy (n)	إعانة مالية	*i'ānah māliyyah*
subsist (v)	عاش، اقتات، بقى	*'āsha, iqtāta, baqā*

subsistence (n)	معاش، وجود، بقاء	*ma'āsh, wujūd, baqā'*
substance (n)	مادة، جوهر	*māddah, jauhar*
substantial (adj)	مادى، جوهري، واقعي	*māddī, jauharī, wāqi'ī*
substantially (adv)	بالفعل، بالقوة	*bil fi'l, bil quwwah*
substantiate (v)	برهن، أثبت	*barhana, athbata*
substantiation (n)	إثبات بالحجة	*ithbāt bil ḥujjah*
substantive (adj)	حقيقي، واقعي	*ḥaqīqī, wāqi'ī*
substantive (n)	اسم، كلمة	*ism, kalimah*
substitute (n)	بديل، نائب	*badīl, nā'ib*
substitute (v)	اعتاض، استبدل	*i'tāḍa, istabdala*
substitution (n)	بدل، استعاضة	*badal, isti'āḍah*
substratum (n)	قوام، أساس	*qiwām, asās*
subtenant (n)	مستأجر من الباطن	*musta'jir minal bāṭin*
subterranean (adj)	تحت سطح الأرض	*taḥta saṭḥil arḍ*
subtitle (n)	عنوان فرعي	*'unwān far'ī*
subtle (adj)	دقيق، محتال	*daqīq, muḥtāl*
subtlety (n)	رقة، دقة، حدة	*riqqah, diqqah, ḥiddah*
subtly (adv)	بدقة، بدهاء	*bi diqqah bi dahā'*
subtract (v)	طرح، أسقط	*ṭaraḥa, asqaṭa*
subtraction (n)	إسقاط، حبس	*isqāṭ, ḥabs*
subtropical (adj)	شبه استوائي	*shibhu istiwā'ī*
suburb (n)	ضاحية، ربض	*ḍāḥiyah, rabaḍ*
suburban (adj)	متعلق بضواحي المدينة	*muta'alliq bi ḍawāḥil madīnah*
suburbanite (n)	ساكن ضاحية	*sākinu ḍāḥiyah*
subvention (n)	إعانة مالية	*i'ānah māliyyah*
subversion (n)	تدمير، تخريب	*tadmīr, takhrīb*
subversive (adj/n)	مدمر، مخرب	*mudammir, mukharrib*
subvert (v)	هدم، دمر	*haddama, dammara*
subway (n)	ممر تحت الأرض، نفق	*mamarr taḥtal arḍ, nafaq*
succeed (v)	نجح، خلف	*najaḥa, khalafa*
succeeding (adj)	تالٍ، لاحق	*tālin, lāḥiq*

success (n)	نجاح، فلاح	*najāḥ, falāḥ*
successful (adj)	ناجح، مفلح	*nājiḥ, mufliḥ*
succession (n)	توالٍ، تتابع	*tawālin, tatābu'*
successive (adj)	متوالٍ، متتابع	*mutawālin, mutatābi'*
successively (adv)	على التوالي، بالتتابع	*'alat tawālī, bit tatābu'*
successor (n)	خلف، خليفة	*khalaf, khalīfah*
succinct (n)	موجز، بليغ	*mūjaz, balīgh*
succour (succor)	إعانة، إسعاف	*i'ānah, is'āf*
succour (v)	أعان، أسعف	*a'āna, as'afa*
succulent (adj)	غض، ريان	*ghaḍḍ, rayyān*
succumb (v)	استسلم، رزخ	*istaslama, razakha*
such (pron)	هكذا، هذا	*hākadhā, hādhā*
such (adj)	هائل، شديد	*hā'il, shadīd*
suchlike (pron)	وما إلى ذلك	*wamā ilā dhālik*
suck (v)	مص، امتص	*maṣṣa, imtaṣṣa*
sucker (n)	ممتص، ممص	*mumtaṣṣ, mimaṣṣ*
suckle (v)	أرضعت	*arḍa'at*
suction (n)	مص، امتصاص	*maṣṣ, imtiṣāṣ*
sudden (adj)	فجائي، بغتي	*fujā'ī, baghtī*
suddenly (adv)	فجأةً، بغتةً	*faj'atan, baghtatan*
suddenness (n)	بغتة، فجاءة	*baghtah, fujā'ah*
sue (v)	قاضى، داعى	*qāḍā, dā'ā*
suffer (v)	قاس، تحمل	*qāsa, taḥammala*
sufferance (n)	سماح، مقاساة	*samāḥ, muqāsāt*
sufferer (n)	مقاسٍ، متألم	*muqāsin, muta'allim*
suffering (n)	ألم، تكبد	*alam, takabbud*
suffice (v)	أغنى عن، كفى	*aghnā 'an, kafā*
sufficiency (n)	كفاية، مقدرة	*kifāyah, maqdirah*
sufficient (adj)	كافٍ، وافٍ	*kāfin, wāfin*
sufficiently (adv)	بمقدار كافٍ	*bi miqdār kāfin*
suffix (n)	لاحقة، إضافة	*lāḥīqah, iḍāfah*
suffocate (v)	خنق، فطس	*khanaqa, faṭṭasa*

suffocation (n)	تفطيس، اختناق	*taftīs, ikhtināq*
suffrage (n)	حق الاقتراع	*ḥaqqul iqtirā'*
suffuse (v)	نقع، خضب، نشر	*naqa'a, khaḍḍaba, nashara*
suffusion (n)	تشرب، انتشار	*tasharrub, intishār*
sufi	صوفي	*ṣūfī*
sufism (n)	تصوف	*taṣawwuf*
sugar (n)	سكر	*sukkar*
sugar-cane (n)	قصب السكر	*qaṣabus sukkar*
sugary (adj)	حلو، سكري	*ḥulw, sukkarī*
suggest (v)	اقترح، أوعز	*iqtaraḥa, au'aza*
suggestion (n)	اقتراح، إيعاز	*iqtirāḥ, ī'āz*
suggestive (adj)	إيعازي، موحٍ	*ī'āzī, mūḥin*
suicidal (adj)	انتحاري	*intiḥārī*
suicide (n)	انتحار، منتحر	*intiḥār, muntaḥir*
suit (n)	بذلة، طلب	*badhlah, ṭalab*
suit (v)	تلاءم، وافق	*talā'ama, wāfaqa*
suitable (adj)	مناسب، ملائم	*munāsib, mulā'im*
suitcase (n)	حقيبة سفر	*ḥaqibatu safar*
suite (n)	مجموعة، مجموعة غرف	*majmū'ah, majmū'atu ghuraf*
suitor (n)	مدعٍ، خاطب	*mudda'in, khāṭib*
sulk (v)	عبس، تجهم	*'abasa, tajahhama*
sulkness (n)	عبوس، تجهم	*'ubūs, tajahhum*
sulky (adj)	عابس، متجهم	*'ābis, mutajahhim*
sullen (adj)	مكتئب، عابس	*mukta'ib, 'ābis*
sully (v)	لوث، لطخ	*lawwatha, laṭṭakha*
sulphate (sulfate)	سلفات، كبريتات	*sulfāt, kibrītāt*
sulphur (sulfur)	كبريت	*kibrīt*
sulphuric (sulfuric)	كبريتي	*kibrītī*
sulphurous (sulfurous	مرير، قاسٍ	*marīr, qāsin*
sultan (n)	سلطان	*sulṭān*

sultanate (n)	سلطنة	*salṭanah*
sultriness (n)	زمتة، عكاكة	*zamtah, 'akākah*
sultry (adj)	عكيك، زمه	*'akīk, zamih*
sum (n)	مجموع، حاصل، مبلغ	*majmū', ḥāṣil, mablagh*
sum (v)	لخص، اختصر	*lakhkhaṣa, ikhtaṣara*
summarily (ad	باختصار، بسرعة	*bikhtiṣār, bi sur'ah*
summarize,-ise	لخص، أجمل	*lakhkhaṣa, ajmala*
summary (n)	خلاصة، اختصار	*khulāṣah, ikhtiṣār*
summary (adj)	مؤقت، معجل	*mu'aqqat, mu'ajjal*
summer (n)	فصل الصيف	*faṣluṣ ṣaif*
summer-house (n)	ظلة صيفية	*ẓullah ṣaifiyyah*
summer school	مدرسة صيفية	*madrasah ṣaifiyyah*
summer-time (n)	توقيت صيفي	*tauqīt ṣaifī*
summery (adj)	صيفي، قيظي	*ṣaifī, qaiẓī*
summit (n)	قمة، مؤتمر قمة	*qimmah, mu'tamaru qimmah*
summon (v)	دعا إلى الاجتماع	*da'ā ilal ijtimā'*
summons (n)	أمر، استدعاء	*amr, istid'ā'*
summons (v)	استدعى إلى المحكمة	*istad'ā ilal maḥkamah*
sump (n)	بالوعة، مجرى	*balū'ah, majrā*
sumptuous (adj)	سخي، فاخر	*sakhiyy, fākhir*
sumptuously (adv)	بسخاء، بترف	*bi sakhā', bi taraf*
sumptuousness (n)	سخاء، فخامة، بذخ	*sakhā', fakhāmah, badhkh*
sun (n)	شمس، حرارة	*shams, ḥarārah*
sunbeam (n)	شعاع الشمس	*shu'ā'ush shams*
sunburn (n)	سفعة، لفحة شمس	*saf'ah, lafḥatu shams*
Sunday (n)	يوم الأحد	*yaumul aḥad*
sunday school	مدرسة الأحد	*madrasatul aḥad*
sunder (v)	فصل، شطر	*faṣala, shaṭara*
sundial (n)	مزولة، ساعة شمسية	*mizwalah, sā'ah shamsiyyah*
sundries (n)	أشتات	*ashtāt*

sundry (adj)	مختلف، متعدد	*mukhtalif, muta'addid*
sunflower (n)	دوار الشمس	*dawwārush shams*
sun-glasses (n)	نظارات الشمس	*naẓẓārātush shams*
sun-god (n)	إله الشمس	*ilāhush shams*
sunken (adj)	مغمور، غاطس	*maghmūr, ghāṭis*
sun-lamp (n)	مصباح شمسي	*miṣbāḥ shamsī*
sunlight (n)	ضوء الشمس	*ḍau'ush shams*
sunlit (adj)	مضاء بنور الشمس	*muḍā' bi nūrish shams*
sunny (adj)	مشمش	*mushmish*
sunrise (n)	طلوع الشمس	*ṭulū'ush shams*
sunset (n)	غروب الشمس	*ghurūbush shams*
sunshade (n)	شمسية، ظلة	*shamsiyyah, ẓullah*
sunshine (n)	ضوء الشمس	*ḍau'ush shams*
sunspot (n)	كلفة الشمس	*kulfatush shams*
sup (v)	تجرع، شفط	*tajarra'a, shafaṭa*
sup (n)	شفطة، جرعة	*shafṭah, jur'ah*
super (adj)	ممتاز، رائع	*mumtāz, rā'i'*
superabundance (n)	غزارة، فيضان	*ghazārah, fayaḍān*
superabundant (adj)	غزير، وافر	*ghazīr, wāfir*
superannuate (v)	تقاعد، عجز	*taqā'ada, 'ajaza*
superannuated (adj)	متقاعد، عاجز	*mutaqā'id, 'ājiz*
superannuation (n)	تقاعد، إحالة إلى المعاش	*taqā'ud, iḥālah ilal ma'āsh*
superb (adj)	رائع، ممتاز، فائق	*rā'i', mumtāz, fā'iq*
superchanger (n)	شحان	*shaḥḥān*
supercilious (adj)	متكبر، متعجرف	*mutakabbir, muta'ajrif*
superciliousness (n)	تكبر، عجرفة	*takabbur, 'ajrafah*
super-duper (adj)	رائع، فائق	*rā'i', fā'iq*
superficial (adj)	ظاهري، سطحي	*ẓāhirī, saṭḥī*
superficiality (n)	سطحية	*saṭḥiyyah*
superficially (adv)	ظاهريًا، سطحيًا	*ẓāhiriyyan, saṭḥiyyan*
superfine (adj)	رائق جدا	*rā'iq jiddā*

superfluous (adj)	زائد، غير ضروري	*zā'id, ghair ḍarūrī*
superhuman (adj)	فوق الطبيعة البشرية	*fauqaṭ ṭabī'ah al bashariyyah*
superintend (v)	ناظر، أشرف	*nāẓara, ashrafa*
superintendence (n)	إشراف، مراقبة	*ishrāf, murāqabah*
superintendent (adj)	مدير، مشرف	*mudīr, mushrif*
superior (n/adj)	أفضل، أعلى	*afḍal, a'lā*
superiority (n)	تفوق، علو، سمو	*tafawwuq, 'uluww, sumuww*
superiority complex	مركب الأعلوية	*murakkabul a'lawiyyah*
superlative (adj/n)	أفضل، صيغة التفضيل	*afḍal, ṣīghatut tafḍīl*
supermarket (n)	سوق مركزية	*sūq markaziyyah*
supernatural (adj)	خارق الطبيعة	*khāriquṭ ṭabī'ah*
superpower (n)	دولة عظمى	*daulah 'uẓmā*
supersede (v)	حل محل...	*ḥalla maḥalla…*
supersonic (adj)	فوصوتي	*fauṣautī*
superstition (n)	خرافة، خزعبلة	*khurāfah, khuza'balah*
superstitious (adj)	خرافي، وهمي	*khurāfī, wahmī*
superstructure (n)	بنية فوقية	*binyah fauqiyyah*
supervene (v)	عرض، طرأ	*'araḍa, ṭara'a*
supervention (n)	عارض، طارئ	*'āriḍ, ṭāri'*
supervise (v)	أشرف، راقب	*ashrafa, rāqaba*
supervision (n)	إشراف، مراقبة	*ishrāf, murāqabah*
supervisor (n)	مشرف، مراقب	*mushrif, murāqib*
supervisory (adj)	إشرافي	*ishrāfī*
supine (adj)	مستلقٍ، مهمل	*mustalqin, muhmil*
supper (n)	عشاء	*'ashā'*
supplant (v)	حل محل...	*ḥalla maḥalla…*
supple (adj)	لين، لدن	*layyin, ladn*
supplement (n)	ملحق، تتمة	*mulḥaq, tatimmah*
supplement (v)	ألحق، أضاف	*alḥaqa, aḍāfa*
supplementary (adj)	إضافي، ملحق	*iḍāfī, mulḥaq*

supplicant (adj/n)	متضرع، مبتهل	*mutaḍarri', mubtahil*
supplicate (v)	تضرع، ابتهل	*taḍarra'a, ibtahala*
supplication (n)	تضرع، توسل	*taḍarru', tawassul*
supplier (n)	مزود، مورد	*muzawwid, muwarrid*
supply (v)	زود، ورد	*zawwada, warrada*
supply (n)	تزويد، مؤونة	*tazwīd, ma'ūnah*
support (v)	أيد، عضد، دعم	*ayyada, 'aḍḍada, da'ama*
support (n)	دعامة، تأييد	*di'āmah, ta'yīd*
supportable (adj)	محتمل	*muḥtamal*
supporter (n)	مؤيد، معضد	*mu'yyid, mu'aḍḍid*
supporting (adj)	ثانوي	*thānawī*
supportive (adj)	مساعد، مشجع	*musā'id, mushajji'*
suppose (v)	افترض، حسب	*iftaraḍa, ḥasiba*
supposed (adj)	مزعوم، مفترض	*maz'ūm, muftaraḍ*
supposing (conj)	على افتراض	*'alā iftirāḍ*
supposition (n)	افتراض، ظن	*iftirāḍ, ẓann*
suppository (n)	شيف، فتيلة	*shīf, fatīlah*
suppress (v)	قمع، كبت	*qama'a, kabata*
suppressor (n)	قامع، مكبح	*qāmi', mikbaḥ*
supremacy (n)	تفوق، سمو	*tafawwuq, sumuww*
supreme (adj)	أرفع، أسمى	*arfa', asmā*
supreme court	محكمة عليا	*maḥkamah 'ulyā*
surcharge (n)	ضريبة إضافية	*ḍarībah iḍāfiyyah*
sure (adj)	متيقن، محتوم	*mutayaqqin, maḥtūm*
sure-footed (adj)	راسخ القدم	*rāsikhul qadam*
surely (adv)	حقاً، بالتاكيد	*ḥaqqan, bit ta'kīd*
surety (n)	ضمانة، ضامن	*ḍamānah, ḍāmin*
surf (n)	أمواج متكسرة	*amwāj mutakassirah*
surface (n)	سطح، وجه	*saṭḥ, wajh*
surface (v)	سطح، ملس	*saṭṭaḥa, mallasa*
surface mail	بريد سطحي	*barīd, saṭḥī*
surface tension	توتر سطحي	*tawattur saṭḥī*

surface-to-air	من الأرض إلى الجو	*minal arḍ ilal jaww*
surfeit (n)	فرط، كثرة	*farṭ, kathrah*
surge (n)	طمو، موجة	*ṭumuww, maujah*
surge (v)	تدفق، تمور	*tadaffaqa, tamawwara*
surgeon (n)	جراح	*jarrāḥ*
surgery (n)	جراحة	*jirāḥah*
surgical (adj)	جراحي	*jirāḥī*
surly (adj)	جافي الطبع، فظ	*jāfiyuṭ ṭab', faẓẓ*
surmise (n)	حدس، ظن	*ḥads, ẓann*
surmount (v)	قهر، تغلب	*qahara, taghallaba*
surmountable (adj)	ممكن تحمله	*mumkin taḥammuluh*
surname (n)	كنية، لقب	*kunyah, laqab*
surpass (v)	تجاوز، تفوق	*tajāwaza, tafawwaqa*
surpassing (adj)	متفوق، استثنائي	*mutafawwiq, istithnā'ī*
surplas (n)	فضلة، زيادة	*faḍlah, ziyādah*
surplas (adj)	فاضل، زائد	*fāḍil, zā'id*
surprise (v)	أدهش، فاجأ	*adhasha, fāja'a*
surprise (n)	مفاجأة، دهش	*mufāja'ah, dahash*
surprising (adj)	مدهش، مذهل	*mudhish, mudhhil*
surprisingly (adv)	بدهشة	*bi dahshah*
surrender (v)	استسلم، تنازل	*istaslama, tanāzala*
surrender (n)	خضوع، تنازل	*khuḍū', tanāzul*
surreptitious (adj)	سري، بالغش	*sirrī, bil ghishsh*
surrogate (n)	نائب، وكيل	*nā'ib, wakīl*
surround (v)	أحاط، أحدق	*aḥāṭa, aḥdaqa*
surround (n)	طوق، حاشية	*ṭauq, ḥāshiyah*
surrounding (adj)	محيط، محدق	*muḥīṭ, muḥdiq*
surroundings (n)	بيئة	*bī'ah*
surtax (n)	رسم إضافي	*rasm iḍāfī*
surveillance (n)	إشراف، مراقبة	*ishrāf, murāqabah*
survey (v)	عاين، فحص، لاحظ	*'āyana, faḥaṣa, lāḥaẓa*
survey (n)	معاينة، فحص	*mu'āyanah, faḥṣ*

surveyor (n)	مساح الأراضي	*massāḥul arāḍī*
survival (n)	تخلف، بقاء	*takhalluf, baqā'*
survive (v)	بقي، نجا	*baqā, najā*
survivor (n)	خالف، ناجٍ	*khālif, nājin*
susceptible (adj)	سريع التأثر، حساس	*sarī'ut ta'aththur, ḥassās*
suspect (v)	شك، اتهم	*shakka, ittahama*
suspect (n)	ارتباك، شك	*irtibāk, shakk*
suspect (adj)	مشكوك، مشتبه	*mashkūk, mushtabah*
suspend (v)	علق، أرجأ، عطل	*'allaqa, arja'a, 'aṭṭala*
suspense (n)	قلق، تردد، حيرة	*qalaq, taraddud, ḥairah*
suspension (n)	تعطيل مؤقت، تعليق	*ta'ṭīl mu'aqqat, ta'līq*
suspension bridge	جسر معلق	*jisr mu'allaq*
suspicion (n)	شك، ريبة، اشتباه	*shakk, raibah, ishtibāh*
suspicious (adj)	مرتاب، مريب	*murtāb, murīb*
sustain (v)	عال، غذى، كايد	*'āla, ghadhdhā, kāyada*
sustenance (n)	معيشة، زرق، قوت	*ma'īshah, rizq, qūt*
swab (n)	ماسحة، ممسحة	*māsiḥah, mimsaḥah*
swagger (v)	اختال، تفاخر	*ikhtāla, tafākhara*
swallow (v)	ازدرد، ابتلع	*izdarada, ibtala'a*
swallow (n)	خطاف	*khaṭṭāf*
Swami (n)	سوامي، معلم هندوسي	*sawāmī, mu'allim hindūsī*
swamp (n)	أرض سبخة	*arḍ sabikhah*
swamp (v)	غرق، أغرق	*ghariqa, aghraqa*
swan (n)	إوز، تم	*iwazz, tamm*
swap (n/v)	مقايضة، قايض	*muqāyaḍah, qāyaḍa*
sward (n)	مرج، مخضرة	*marj, makhḍarah*
swarm (n)	خشرم، ثول	*khashram, thaul*
swarthy (adj)	داكن اللون	*dākinul laun*
swashbuckling (adj)	مغامر، مخاطر	*mughāmir, mukhāṭir*
swastika (n)	صليب، معكوس	*ṣalīb, ma'kūs*
swat (n)	ضربة عنيفة	*ḍarbah 'anīfah*
swathe (v/n)	لف، لفافة	*laffa, lifāfah*

sway (v)	ترنح، مال، هز	*tarannaḥa, māla, hazza*
sway (n)	ترنح، سيطرة	*tarannuḥ, saiṭarah*
swear (v)	حلف، أقسم، وعد	*ḥalafa, aqsama, wa'ada*
swear-word (n)	شتيمة، سباب	*shatīmah, sibāb*
sweat (n)	رشح، عرق	*rashḥ, 'araq*
sweat (v)	رشح، نز	*rashaḥa, nazza*
sweat-band (n)	عصابة العرق	*'iṣābatul 'araq*
sweat-gland (n)	غدة عرقية	*ghuddah 'araqiyyah*
sweaty (adj)	مبتل بالعرق	*mubtall bil 'araq*
sweater = jersey		
sweep (v)	كنس، جرف	*kanasa, jarafa*
sweep (n)	كنس، حركة	*kans, ḥarakah*
sweeper (n)	كناس	*kannās*
sweeping (adj)	شامل، جارف	*shāmil, jārif*
sweepings (n)	زبالة، كناسة	*zubālah, kunāsah*
sweet (n)	حلوى	*ḥalwā*
sweet (adj)	حلو، عذب	*ḥulw, 'adhb*
sweeten (v)	حلى، سكر	*ḥallā, sakkara*
sweetening (adj)	محلٍ	*muḥallin*
sweetheart (n)	حبيب، حبيبة	*ḥabīb, ḥabībah*
sweetie (n)	حبيب، فتىً	*ḥabīb, fatan*
sweetly (adv)	بعذوبة، بلطف	*bi 'udhūbah, bi luṭf*
swell (v)	ورم، انتفخ	*warima, intafakha*
swelling (n)	ورم، تورم	*waram, tawarrum*
swerve (v)	مال، انحرف	*māla, inḥarafa*
swift (adj)	رشيق، خفيف	*rashīq, khafīf*
swiftness (n)	خفة، رشاقة	*khiffah, rashāqah*
swig (v)	تجرع، شرب	*tajarra'a, shariba*
swill (v/n)	شطف، شطف	*shaṭafa, shaṭf*
swim (v)	سبح، عام	*sabaḥa, 'āma*
swim (n)	سباحة، عوم	*sibāḥah, 'aum*
swimmer (n)	عوام، سباح	*'awwām, sabbāḥ*

swimmingly (adv) بنجاح، بسهولة *bi najāḥ, bi suhūlah*
swimming pool بركة السباحة *birkatus sibāḥah*
swimming-suit (n) ثوب السباحة *thaubus sibāḥah*
swindle (v) غش، غبن *ghashsha, ghabana*
swindle (n) غش، اختلاس *ghishsh, ikhtilās*
swindler (n) مخادع، مختلس *mukhādi', mukhtalis*
swine (n) خنـــزير *khinzīr*
swing (v) تمرجح، تدلى، دار *tamarjaḥa, tadallā, dāra*
swing (n) أرجوحة، تأرجحة *urjūḥah, ta'arjaḥah*
swing bridge جسر دورا *jisr dawwār*
swingeing (adj) عنيف، حاد *'anīf, ḥādd*
swipe (n) ضربة عنيفة *ḍarbah 'anīfah*
swipe (v) صت، ضرب بعنف *ṣatta, ḍaraba bi 'unf*
swish (v) هسهس، حف *hashasa, ḥaffa*
Swiss (n/adj) سويسري *suwisrī*
switch (n) مفتاح، محولة، لبلوب *miftāḥ, muḥawwilah, lablūb*
switch (v) حول خط السير *ḥawwala khaṭṭas sair*
switchboard (n) لوحة المفاتيح *lauḥatul mafātīḥ*
swivel (n) وصلة متراوحة *wuṣlah mutarāwiḥah*
swollen (adj) متورم، منتفخ *mutawarrim, muntafikh*
swoon (v) أغمي عليه *ughmiya 'alaih*
swoop (v/n) انقض، انقضاض *inqaḍḍa, inqiḍāḍ*
sword (n) سيف، حسام *saif, ḥusām*
sword-dance (n) رقصة السيوف *raqṣatus suyūf*
swordsman (n) جندي مسلح بالسيف *jundiyy musallaḥ bis saif*
sycophancy (n) تملق، مداجاة *tamalluq, mudājāt*
sycophant (n) متملق، منافق *mutamalliq, munāfiq*
sycophantic (adj) متملق، ذليل *mutamalliq, dhalīl*
syllabic (adj) مقطعي، ذو مقاطع *maqṭa'ī, dhū maqāṭi'*
syllabify (v) قسم إلى أجزاء *qassama ilā ajzā'*
syllable (n) مقطع، جزء من كلمة *maqṭa', juz' min kalimah*

syllabus (n)	منهج دراسي	*manhaj dirāsī*
syllogism (n)	قياس	*qiyās*
syllogistic (adj)	قياسي	*qiyāsī*
sylph (n)	سلف، حورية	*silf, ḥūriyyah*
symbol (n)	رمز، تشبيه	*ramz, tashbīh*
symbolic (adj)	رمزي، تشبيهي	*ramzī, tashbīhī*
symbolism (n)	رمزية	*ramziyyah*
symbolist (n)	رمزي، شاعر رمزي	*ramzī, shā'ir ramzī*
symbolize,-ise (v)	رمز، شابه	*ramaza, shābaha*
symmetric-al (adj)	متناسق الأجزاء	*mutanāsiqul ajzā'*
symmetry (n)	تناسق، تناسب	*tanāsuq, tanāsub*
sympathetic (adj)	عاطف، ودي	*'āṭif, wuddī*
sympathetically (adv)	بتعطف، بوداد	*bi ta'aṭṭuf, bi wadād*
sympathize,-ise (v)	عطف، تعاطف	*'aṭafa, , ta'āṭafa*
sympathy (n)	عطف، حنو	*'aṭf, ḥunuww*
symphonic (adj)	سمفوني، متناغم	*simfūnī, mutanāghim*
symphony (n)	سمفونيا، تآلف	*simfūniyā, ta'āluf*
symposium (n)	مناقشة، حفلة المناقشة	*munāqashah, ḥaflatul munāqashah*
symptom (n)	علامة، عرض	*'alāmah, 'araḍ*
symptomatic (adj)	عرضي، دال	*'araḍī, dāll*
synagogue (n)	كنيس، مجمع اليهود	*kanīs, majma'ul yahūd*
synchronize,-ise (v)	زامن، تزامن	*zāmana, tazāmana*
syndicate (n)	نقابة، وكالة	*niqābah, wakālah*
syndicate (v)	نشر في صحف متعددة	*nashara fī ṣuḥuf muta'addidah*
syndrome (n)	مجموعة متزامنة	*majmū'ah mutazāminah*
synod (n)	سنودس، مجمع	*sinūdus, majma'*
synonym (n)	مرادف، مترادف	*murādif, mutarādif*
synonymous (adj)	مترادف، ترادفي	*mutarādif, tarādufī*
synopsis (n)	خلاصة، مختصر	*khulāṣah, mukhtaṣar*
syntax (n)	تركيب الكلام	*tarkībul kalām*

synthesis (n)	تأليف، تركيب	*ta'līf, tarkīb*
synthesize,-ise (v)	ركب، اصطنع	*rakkaba, iṣṭana'a*
synthetic (n)	مادة صنعية	*māddah ṣun'iyyah*
synthetic (adj)	تركيبي، صنعي	*tarkībī, ṣun'ī*
syphilis (n)	مرض السفلس	*maraḍus siflis*
syphilitic (n/adj)	سفلسي، مصاب بسفلس	*siflisī, muṣāb bi siflis*
syringe (n/v)	محقنة، حقن	*miḥqanah, ḥaqana*
syrup (n)	شراب	*sharāb*
syrupy (adj)	شرابي	*sharābī*
system (n)	نظام، طريقة، أسلوب	*niẓām, ṭarīqah, uslūb*
systematic (adj)	منسق، مرتب، منظم	*munassaq, murattab, munaẓẓam*
systematically (adv)	بنظام، بترتيب	*bi niẓām, bi tartīb*
systemize,-ise (v)	رتب، نظم	*rattaba, naẓẓama*

T

tab (n)	مقبض صغير، عروة	*miqbaḍ ṣaghīr, 'urwah*
taberancle (n)	مسكن مؤقت، خيمة	*maskan mu'aqqat, khaimah*
table (n)	طاولة، منضدة، لوحة	*ṭāwilah, minḍadah, lauḥah*
table (v)	وضع على الطاولة	*waḍa'a 'alaṭ ṭāwilah*
tebleau (n)	مشهد، لوحة رسم	*mashhad, lauḥatu rasm*
table-clothe (n)	سماط، غطاء المائدة	*simāṭ, ghiṭā'ul mā'idah*
tablespoonful (adj)	ملء ملعقة المائدة	*mil'u mil'aqatil mā'idah*
tablet (n)	لوحة، قرص	*lauḥah, qurṣ*
table-talk (n)	حديث المائدة	*ḥadīthul mā'idah*
table tennis	كرة الطاولة	*kuratuṭ ṭāwilah*
tableware (n)	أدوات المائدة	*adawātul mā'idah*
tabloid (n)	صحيفة مصغرة	*ṣaḥīfah muṣaghgharah*
taboo (n/adj)	حرام، محظور	*ḥarām, maḥẓūr*
tabular (adj)	منبسط، مسطح	*mumbasiṭ, musaṭṭaḥ*

tabulate (v)	سطح، جدول	*saṭṭaḥa, jadwala*
tabulator (n)	مجدولة	*mujadwilah*
tack (v)	سرج القماش	*sarrajal qumāsh*
tack (n)	حبل الشراع، مجرى السفينة	*ḥablush shirā', majras safīnah*
tackle (n)	بكرة، حبال السفينة	*bakrah, ḥibālus safīnah*
tackle (v)	تمكن، أمسك، تغلب	*tamakkana, amsaka, taghallaba*
tacky (adj)	لزج	*lazij*
tact (n)	حسافة، حذق	*ḥasāfah, ḥidhq*
tactful (adj)	لبق، بارع	*labiq, bāri'*
tactfully (adv)	ببراعة، بلباقة	*bi barā'ah, bi labāqah*
tactic (n)	وسيلة، طريقة	*wasīlah, ṭarīqah*
tactical (adj)	تكتيكي، مختص بالحركات الحربية	*taktīkī, mukhtaṣṣ bil ḥarakāt al ḥarbiyyah*
tactics (n)	فن الحركات الحربية	*fannul ḥarakāt al ḥarbiyyah*
tactile (adj)	لمسي، ملموس	*lamsī, malmūs*
tactless (adj)	غير لبق، غير بارع	*ghair labiq, ghair bāri'*
lactlessly (adv)	بدون لباقة	*bidūn labāqah*
tactlessness (n)	عدم لباقة	*'adamu labāqah*
taffeta (n)	نسيج حريري، تفتة	*nasīj ḥarīrī, tiftah*
tag (n)	عروة، خرقة، عبارة مؤكدة	*'urwah, khirqah, 'ibārah mu'akkadah*
tag (v)	زود بعروة أو خرقة	*zawwada bi 'urwah au khirqah*
tail (n)	ذنب، ذيل، مؤخر	*dhanab, dhail, mu'akhkhar*
tail (v)	تعقب، تبع	*ta'aqqaba, tabi'a*
tail-end (n)	نهاية، مؤخر	*nihāyah, mu'akhkhar*
tail-gate (n)	باب خلفي	*bāb khalfī*
tailless (adj)	أبتر الذنب	*abtarudh dhanab*
tail-light (n)	ضوء خلفي	*ḍau khalfī*

tailor (n/v)	خياط، خاط	*khayyāṭ, khāṭa*
tailoring (n)	خياطة	*khiyāṭah*
taint (n)	لطخة، شائبة	*laṭkhah, shā'ibah*
taint (v)	لوث، لطخ	*lawwatha, laṭṭakha*
taintless (adj)	غير ملطخ، نقي	*ghair mulaṭṭakh, naqī*
take (v)	أخذ، تناول،	*akhadha, tanāwala,*
	أمسك، فهم	*amsaka, fahima*
take away	أزال، أبعد	*azāla, ab'ada*
take back	استرد، استرجع	*istaradda, istarja'a*
take care	اعتنى، احترز	*i'tanā, iḥtaraza*
take hold	استولى، استحوذ	*istaulā, istaḥwadha*
take in	استوعب، واكب	*istau'aba, wākaba*
take off	خلع، نزع	*khala'a, naza'a*
take out	أخرج، حذف	*akhraja, ḥadhafa*
take over	ساد، استولى	*sāda, istaulā*
taker (n)	قابل الرهان	*qābilur rihān*
take up	شرع، رفع	*shara'a, rafa'a*
taking (adj)	ساحر، خلاب	*sāḥir, khallāb*
tale (n)	حكاية، أسطورة	*ḥikāyah, usṭūrah*
talebearer (n)	ناشر الإشاعات، نمام	*nāshirul ishā'āt, nammām*
talent (n)	ذكاء، موهبة	*dhakā', mauhibah*
talented (adj)	ذكي، موهوب	*dhakī, mauhūb*
talentless (adj)	بليد، غبي	*balīd, ghabī*
talent-scout (n)	كشاف المواهب	*kashshāful mawāhib*
taleteller = talebearer		
talisman (n)	طلسم، عوذة	*ṭillasm, 'audhah*
talk (v)	تكلم، تحدث	*takallama, taḥaddatha*
talk (n)	حديث، كلام	*ḥadīth, kalām*
talkative (adj)	كثير الكلام، مهذار	*kathīrul kalām, mihdhār*
talker (n)	متكلم في أسلوب خاص	*mutakallim fī uslūb khāṣṣ*
tall (adj)	طويل، ضخم	*ṭawīl, ḍakhm*
tallow (n)	شحم، ودك	*shaḥm, wadak*

tally (n)	انطباق، جريدة الحساب	*inṭibāq, jarīdatul ḥisāb*
tally (v)	انطبق، تناسب	*inṭabaqa, tanāsaba*
tambour (n)	منسج التطريز، طارة	*minsajut taṭrīz, ṭārah*
tambourine (n)	دف، طارة	*duff, ṭārah*
tame (adj)	أليف، وديع	*alīf, wadī'*
tame (v)	روض، دجن	*rawwaḍa, dajjana*
tameable (adj)	ممكن ترويضه	*mumkin tarwīḍuh*
tamp (v)	سد، رص	*sadda, raṣṣa*
tamper (v)	تحرش، عبث	*taḥarrasha, 'abitha*
tampon (n)	صمام	*ṣimām*
tan (n/v)	دباغ، دبغ	*dibāgh, dabagha*
tandem (n)	تندم، دراجة ترادفية	*tandam, darrājah tarādufiyyah*
tang (n)	نكهة حادة	*nakhah ḥāddah*
tangent (n)	مماس	*mumāss*
tangible (adj)	ملموس، محسوس	*malmūs, maḥsūs*
tangle (v)	تشابك، تحابك	*tashābaka, taḥābaka*
tangle (n)	عقدة، ورطة	*'uqdah, warṭah*
tank (n)	دبابة، صهريج، حوض	*dabbābah, ṣihrīj, ḥauḍ*
tanker (n)	طائرة لنقل البترول	*ṭā'irah li naqlil bitrūl*
tanner (n)	دباغ الجلود	*dabbāghul julūd*
tannery (n)	مدبغة	*midbaghah*
tantalize,-ise (v)	عذب، كابد	*'adhdhaba, kādaba*
tantrum (n)	نوبة غضب	*naubatu ghaḍab*
tap (n)	حنفية، نقطة التشعب، نقرة	*ḥanfiyyah, nuqṭatut tasha''ub, naqrah*
tap (v)	نزع، قرع	*naza'a, qara'a*
tap-dance (n)	رقص نقرى	*raqṣ naqrī*
tape (n/v)	شريط، شد بشريط	*sharīṭ, shadda bi sharīṭ*
taper (v)	تناقض، استدق	*tanāqaḍa, istadaqqa*
taper (n)	شمعة صغيرة	*sham'ah ṣaghīrah*
tape-recorder (n)	مسجلة شريطية	*musajjilah sharīṭiyyah*

tapestry (n)	قماش الفرش	*qumāshul farsh*
tapeworm (n)	دودة الشريط	*dūdatush sharīṭ*
tappet (n)	إصبع غماز	*iṣba' ghammāz*
tar (v/n)	قير، قار	*qayyara, qār*
tardily (adv)	ببطء، متأخراً	*bi baṭ', muta'akhkhiran*
tardiness (n)	بطء، تمهل	*baṭ', tamahhul*
tardy (adj)	بطيء، متأخر	*baṭī', muta'akhkhir*
tare (n)	فارغ في الوزن	*fārigh fil wazn*
target (n)	هدف، غرض، ترس	*hadaf, gharaḍ, turs*
target (v)	اتخذ هدفاً	*ittakhadha hadafan*
tariff (n)	تعريفة، بيان الأسعار	*ta'rīfah, bayānul as'ār*
tarnish (v)	قتم، عتم اللون	*qattama, 'attamal laun*
tarnish (n)	فقدان اللمعان	*fuqdānul lama'ān*
tarry (v)	تأخر، توانى	*ta'akhkhara, tawānā*
tarry (n)	قطراني، مقطرن	*qaṭrānī, muqaṭran*
tart (adj)	حامض، حاد	*ḥāmiḍ, ḥādd*
tart (n)	بغي، مومس	*baghī, mūmis*
task (n)	مهمة، واجب	*mahammah, wājib*
task (v)	كلف بعمل شاق	*kallafa bi 'amal shāqq*
task force	قوة عسكرية	*quwwah 'askariyyah*
taskmaster (n)	فارض المهام	*fāriḍul mahāmm*
tassel (n)	شرابة، شرشوبة	*shurrābah, sharshūbah*
tasseled (adj)	مزين بشرابات	*muzayyan bi shurrābāt*
taste (n)	ذوق، طعم	*ḍauq, ṭa'm*
taste (v)	تذوق، ذاق	*tadhawwaqa, dhāqa*
tasteful (adj)	حسن الذوق	*ḥasanudh dhauq*
tasteless (adj)	عديم الذوق، مسيخ	*'adīmudh dhauq, masīkh*
taster (n)	ذائق، ذواق	*dhā'iq, dhawwāq*
tasty (adj)	لذيذ المذاق، جذاب	*ladhīdhul madhāq, jadhdhāb*
ta-ta = goodbye		
tatters (n)	خرقة بالية	*khirqah bāliyah*

tattle (v)	هذر، بق	*hadhara, baqqa*
tattle (n)	هذر، ثرثرة	*hadhar, thartharah*
tattoo (n)	نوبة تمام، وشم	*naubatu tamām, washm*
tatty (adj)	خرق، ممزق	*khariq, mumazzaq*
taunt (v)	وبخ، عير	*wabbakha, 'ayyara*
taunt (n)	توبيخ مهين، قدح	*taubīkh muhīn, qadḥ*
tax (n)	ضريبة، رسم	*ḍarībah, rasm*
tax (v)	فرض ضريبة	*faraḍa ḍarībah*
taxation (n)	فرض الضرائب	*farḍuḍ ḍarā'ib*
taxi (n)	تاكسي، سيارة	*tāksī, sayyārah*
taximan (n)	سائق التاكسي	*sā'iqut tāksī*
taxpayer (n)	دافع الضرائب	*dāfi'uḍ ḍarā'ib*
tea (n)	شاي	*shāy*
teacake (n)	كعكة الشاي	*ka'katush shāy*
teach (v)	درس، علم	*darrasa, 'allama*
teachable (adj)	قابل للتعليم	*qābil lit ta'līm*
teacher (n)	معلم، مدرس	*mu'allim, mudarris*
teach-in (n)	حفلة دراسية	*ḥaflah dirāsiyyah*
teaching (n)	تعليم، تدريس	*ta'līm, tadrīs*
teacup (n)	فنجان الشاي	*finjānush shāy*
team (n)	فرقة، مجموعة، جماعة	*firqah, majmū'ah, jamā'ah*
team (v)	عمل في فريق	*'amila fī farīq*
teamester (n)	سائق الشاحنة	*sā'iqush shāḥinah*
team-work	عمل جماعي	*'amal jamā'ī*
tea-party (n)	حفلة الشاي	*ḥaflatush shāy*
teapot (n)	إبريق الشاي	*ibrīqush shāy*
tear (n)	قطرة، دمعة، خرق	*qaṭrah, dam'ah, kharq*
tear (v)	مزق، سفح الدم	*mazzaqa, safaḥad dam*
tear-drop (n)	دمعة	*dam'ah*
tearful (adj)	دامع، سريع البكاء	*dāmi', sarī'ul bukā'*
tear-gas (n)	غاز مسيل للدموع	*ghāz musīl lid dumū'*

tea-room (n)	صالة الشاي	*ṣālatush shāy*
tease (v)	ضايق، كابد	*ḍāyaqa, kābada*
tease (n)	مضايق، مبرم	*muḍāyiq, mubrim*
tea-service (n)	طقم للشاي	*ṭaqm lish shāy*
teaspoonful (adj)	ملء ملعقة شاي	*mil'u mil'aqati shāy*
teat (n)	حلمة الثدي	*ḥalamatuth thady*
technical (adj)	فني، تقني	*fannī, tiqnī*
technicality (n)	اصطلاح فني	*iṣṭilāḥ fannī*
technically (adv)	فنيًّا، اصطلاحيًّا	*fanniyyan, iṣṭilāḥiyyan*
technician (n)	فني، تقن	*fannī, tiqn*
technicolor (n)	تصوير بالألوان	*taṣwīr bil alwān*
technique (n)	تقنية، براعة فنية	*tiqniyyah, barā'ah fanniyyah*
technocracy (n)	حكومة الفنيين	*ḥukūmatul fanniyyīn*
technological (adj)	تكنولوجي	*tiknūlūjī*
technologist (n)	ماهر في تكنولوجيا	*māhir fī tiknūlūjiyā*
technology (n)	تكنولوجيا	*tiknūlūjiyā*
tedious (adj)	ممل، متعب	*mumill, mut'ib*
tediousness (n)	ملل، ضجر	*malal, ḍajr*
tedium =tediousness		
teem (v)	اكتظ، احتشد	*iktaẓẓa, iḥtashada*
teenage (teenaged)	مراهق	*murāhiq*
teenager (n)	ولد مراهق	*walad murāhiq*
teens (n)	عمر بين ١٣ و ١٩	*'umr bain 13 wa 19*
teeter (v)	ترنح، تمايل	*tarannaḥa, tamāyala*
teeth (pl. of tooth)	أسنان	*asnān*
telecommunication (n)	مواصلة بعيدة	*muwāṣalah ba'īdah*
telefilm (n)	فيلم تلفزيوني	*fīlm tilfizyūnī*
telegram (n)	برقية	*barqiyyah*
telegraph (n)	تلغراف، برقية	*tiligharāf, barqiyyah*
telegraph (v)	أرسل برقية	*arsala barqiyyah*
telegrapher (n)	عامل التلغراف	*'āmilut tiligharāf*

telegraphic (adj)	تلغرافي، برقي	*tiligharāfī, barqī*
telegraphy (n)	إرسال برقي	*irsāl barqī*
telephone (n)	هاتف، تلفون	*hātif, tilifūn*
telephone (v)	تكلم بالتلفون	*takallama bit tilifūn*
telephone book	دليل التلفون	*dalīlut tilifūn*
telephone exchange	مركز التلفون	*markazut tilifūn*
telephone line	خط تلفوني	*khaṭṭ tilifūnī*
telephone operator	عامل التلفون	*'āmilut tilifūn*
telephone set	جهاز التلفون	*jihāzut tilifūn*
teleprinter (n)	مبرقة كاتبة	*mubriqah kātibah*
telescope (n)	تلسكوب، مقراب	*tiliscūb, miqrāb*
telescopic (adj)	تلسكوبي	*tiliskūbī*
teletypewriter (n)	مبرقة كاتبة	*mubriqah kātibah*
televise (v)	نشر بالتلفزيون	*nashara bit tilfizyūn*
television (n)	تلفزيون	*tilfizyūn*
telex (n)	مبرقة مباشرة، تلكس	*mubriqah mubāshirah, tiliks*
tell (v)	قال، روى، أخبر	*qāla, rawā, akhbara*
teller (n)	محصي، مخبر	*muḥṣī, mukhbir*
telling (adj)	مؤثر، شديد	*mu'aththir, shadīd*
tell-tale (n)	واشٍ، نمام	*wāshin, nammām*
temper (n)	طبع، مزاج	*ṭab', mizāj*
temper (v)	عدل، لطف	*'addala, laṭṭafa*
temperament (n)	وسط، مزاج	*wasaṭ, mizāj*
temperamental (adj)	طبعي، مزاجي	*ṭab'ī, mizājī*
temperance (n)	اعتدال، عفة	*i'tidāl, 'iffah*
temperate (adj)	مقتصد، معتدل	*muqtaṣid, mu'tadil*
temperately (adv)	باعتدال، بضبط النفس	*bi'tidāl, bi ḍabṭin nafs*
temperature (n)	حرارة، درجة الحرارة	*ḥarārah, darajatul ḥarārah*
tempered (adj)	ذو مزاج معين	*dhū mizāj mu'ayyan*

tempest (n)	زوبعة، عاصفة	*zauba'ah, 'āṣifah*
tempestuous (adj)	عاصف، زوبعي	*'āṣif, zauba'ī*
template (n)	طبعة خراط	*ṭab'atu kharrāṭ*
temple (n)	هيكل، معبد، صدغ	*haikal, ma'bad, ṣudgh*
temporal (adj)	دنيوي، زمني	*dunyawī, zamanī*
temporarily (adv)	موقتاً،إلى حين	*muwaqqatan, ilā ḥīn*
temporary (adj)	موقت، وقتي	*muwaqqat, waqtī*
tempt (v)	أغرى، وسوس	*aghrā, waswasa*
temptation (n)	إغراء، وسوسة	*ighrā', waswasah*
tempter (n)	مغرٍ، مجرب	*mughrin, mujarrib*
tempting (adj)	مغوٍ، مغرٍ	*mughwin, mughrin*
ten (n)	عشر، عشرة	*'ashara, 'asharah*
tenable (adj)	حصين، منيع	*ḥaṣīn, manī'*
tenacious (adj)	متماسك، دبق	*mutamāsik, dabiq*
tenacity (n)	تشبث، لزوجة	*tashabbuth, luzūjah*
tenancy (n)	استئجار، حوز	*isti'jār, ḥauz*
tenant (n)	مستأجر، محتل	*musta'jir, muḥtall*
tenantry (n)	جماعة المستأجرين	*jamā'atul musta'jirīn*
tend (v)	اعتنى به، أفضى إلى	*i'tanā bih, afḍā ilā*
tendency (n)	ميل، انعطاف، اتجاه	*mail, in'iṭāf, ittijāh*
tendentious (adj)	ذو نزعة معينة	*dhū naz'ah mu'ayyanah*
tender (n)	سفينة ممونة	*safīnah mumawwinah*
tender (adj)	لين العريكة، سريع العطب	*layyinul 'arīkah, sarī'ul aṭb*
tender (v)	قدم طلباً، عرض سلعاً	*qaddama ṭalaban, 'araḍa sila'an*
tenderfoot (n)	قادم جديد	*qādim jadīd*
tender-hearted (adj)	رقيق الفؤاد	*raqīqul fu'ād*
tendon (n)	وتر، رباط	*watar, ribāṭ*
tenet (n)	عقيدة، اعتقاد	*'aqīdah, i'tiqād*

tenfold (adv/adj)	عشرة أضعاف، عشاري	*'asharatu aḍ'āf, 'ushārī*
tennis (n)	لعبة التنس	*lu'batut tanis*
tenor (n)	نزعة عامة	*naz'ah 'āmmah*
tense (adj)	متوتر، مشدود	*mutawattir, mashdūd*
tense (n)	زمن الفعل	*zamanul fi'l*
tense (v)	توتر، وتر	*tawattara, wattara*
tensely (adv)	بتوتر	*bi tawuttur*
tenseness (n)	توتر، مط	*tawattur, maṭṭ*
tensible (adj)	توتري	*tawatturī*
tension (n)	توتر، شد	*tawattur, shadd*
tent (n)	خيمة، فسطاط	*khaimah, fusṭāṭ*
tentacle (n)	مجس	*mijass*
tentative (adj)	تجريبي، غير حتمي	*tajrībī, ghair ḥatmī*
tenterhooks (n)	في توتر أو ارتباك	*fī tawattur aw irtibāk*
tenth (adj)	عاشر، عشري	*'āshir, 'ushrī*
tenuous (adj)	نحيف، نحيل	*naḥīf, naḥīl*
tenure (n)	تولٍّ، مدة الولاية	*tawallin, muddatul wilāyah*
tepid (adj)	لا حار ولا بارد	*lā ḥārr walā bārid*
tepidity (tepidness)	فتور، توسط درجة الحرارة	*futūr, tawassuṭu darajatil ḥarārah*
term (n)	مدة، اصطلاح، نهاية	*muddah, iṣṭilāḥ, nihāyah*
term (v)	سمى، وصف	*sammā, waṣafa*
terminal (n)	نهاية، آخر	*nihāyah, ākhir*
terminal (adj)	نهائي، فصلي	*nihā'ī, faṣlī*
terminate (v)	انتهى، حدد	*intahā, ḥaddada*
termination (n)	نهاية، لاحقة	*nihāyah, lāḥiqah*
terminology (n)	مصطلحات	*muṣṭalaḥāt*
terminus (n)	نهاية الخط أو الطريق	*nihāyatul khaṭṭ awiṭ ṭarīq*
terms (n)	شروط، حدود	*shurūṭ, ḥudūd*
terrace (n)	دكة، شرفة، سطيحة	*dakkah, shurfah, suṭaiḥah*
terrace (v)	زود بدكات	*zawwada bi dakkāt*

terrain (n)	قطعة أرض، منطقة	*qiṭ'atu arḍ, minṭaqah*
terrestrial (adj)	بري، أرضي	*barrī, arḍī*
terrible (adj)	مرعب، رهيب، فظيع	*mur'ib, rahīb, faẓī'*
terribly (adv)	بفظاعة، برداءة	*bi faẓā'ah, bi radā'ah*
terrific (adj)	رائع، هائل، ضخم	*rā'i', hā'il, ḍakhm*
terrified (adj)	مروع، مذعور	*murawwa', madh'ūr*
terrify (v)	أفزع، أرهب	*afza'a, arhaba*
territorial (adj)	إقليمي، مناطقي	*iqlīmī, manāṭiqī*
territory (n)	مقاطعة، قطر، إقليم	*muqāṭa'ah, quṭr, iqlīm*
terror (n)	رعب، هول، فزع	*ru'b, haul, faza'*
terrorism (n)	إرهاب، تهويل	*irhāb, tahwīl*
terrorist (n)	إرهابي	*irhābī*
terrorize,-ise (v)	روع، أفزع	*rawwa'a, afza'a*
terror-stricken (adj)	مذعور، مروع	*madh'ūr, murawwa'*
terry (n)	نسيج وبري	*nasīj wabarī*
terse (adj)	جامع، موجز	*jāmi', mūjaz*
tersely (adv)	بإحكام، بسداد	*bi iḥkām, bi sadād*
terseness (n)	حسن السبك	*ḥusnus sabk*
test (n)	اختبار، فحص	*ikhtibār, faḥṣ*
test (v)	اختبر، امتحن	*ikhtabara, imtaḥana*
testament (n)	وصية، ميثاق	*waṣiyyah, mīthāq*
testamentary (adj)	متعلق بوصية	*muta'alliq bi waṣiyyah*
testator (n)	موصي	*mūṣī*
testicle (n)	خصية	*khuṣyah*
testify (v)	شهد، قرر	*shahida, qarrara*
testimonial (n)	شهادة، ورقة الشهادة	*shahādah, waraqatush shahādah*
testimony (n)	شهادة، دليل	*shahādah, dalīl*
testiness (n)	نكادة، شكاسة	*nakādah, shakāsah*
testis (n)	خصية	*khuṣyah*
test paper	ورق الاختبار	*waraqul ikhtibār*
test tube	أنبوب الاختبار	*umbūbul ikhtibār*

testy (adj)	سريع الغضب	*sarī'ul ghaḍab*
tetanus (n)	مرض الكزاز	*maraḍul kuzāz*
tete-a-tete	حديث سري	*ḥadīth sirrī*
tether (n)	حبل، نطاق، قيد	*ḥabl, niṭāq, qaid*
text (n)	متن، نص	*matn, naṣṣ*
textbook (n)	كتاب مدرسي	*kitāb madrasī*
textile (n)	نسيج، منسوج	*nasīj, mansūj*
textual (adj)	متعلق بالنص	*muta'alliq bi naṣṣ*
texture (n)	بنية، نسيج	*binyah, nasīj*
than (conj/prep)	من، على أن	*min, 'alā an*
thank (v/n)	شكر، شكر	*shakara, shukr*
thankful (adj)	شاكر، شكور	*shākir, shakūr*
thankless (adj)	كنود، ناكر الجميل	*kanūd, nākirul jamīl*
thanks (n)	شكر، حمد	*shukr, ḥamd*
thanksgiving (n)	تقديم الشكر	*taqdīmush shukr*
thank-you (n)	شكر	*shukr*
that (pron)	ذلك، تلك	*dhālika, tilka*
that (adj)	الذي، التي	*alladhī, allatī*
that (conj)	لكي، أن	*likai, an*
thath (n)	سقف من قش، غماء	*saqf min qashsh, ghimā'*
thath (v)	غما، غمى	*ghamā, ghammā*
thaw (v)	ذاب، أذاب	*dhāba, adhāba*
the (artic)	لام التعريف	*lāmut ta'rīf*
theatre (theater)	مسرح، ملهى	*masraḥ, malhā*
theatre-goer (n)	إلف المسارح	*ilful masāriḥ*
theatre-in-the-round	مسرح مدور	*masraḥ mudawwar*
theatrical (adj)	مسرحي	*masraḥī*
theft (n)	سرقة، اختلاس	*sariqah, ikhtilās*
their (pron)	لهم، لهن	*lahum, lahunna*
theirs (pron)	لهم، لهن	*lahum, lahunna*
theism (n)	إيمان بالله	*īmān billāh*
them (pron)	هم، هن، ها	*hum, hunna, hā*

thematic (adj)	موضوعي، مبحثي	*mauḍū'ī, mabḥathī*
theme (n)	موضوع، مبحث	*mauḍū', mabḥath*
themselves (pron)	أنفسهم، أنفسهن	*anfusuhum, anfusuhunna*
then (adv)	حينئذ، إذن	*ḥīna'idhin, idhan*
thence (adv)	من هناك، من ثم	*min hunāk, min thamma*
theocracy (n)	حكومة دينية، ثيوقراطية	*ḥukūmah dīniyyah, thiuqarāṭiyyah*
theocratic (adj)	ثيوقراطي	*thiuqarāṭī*
theologian (n)	عالم باللاهوت	*'ālim bil lāhūt*
theological (adj)	لاهوتي	*lāhūtī*
theology (n)	علم اللاهوت	*'ilmul lāhūt*
theoretical (adj)	نظري، غير عملي	*naẓarī, ghair 'amalī*
theoretically (adv)	نظريًا	*naẓariyyan*
theorist (n)	واضع نظرية	*wāḍi'u naẓariyyah*
theory (n)	نظرية، رأي	*naẓariyyah, ra'y*
theosophy (n)	تصوف	*taṣawwuf*
therapist (n)	اختصاصي بالمعاجلة	*ikhtiṣāṣī bil mu'ālajah*
therapy (n)	معاجلة، مداواة	*mu'ālajah, mudāwāt*
there (adj)	هناك، حيث، ثم	*hunāk, ḥaithu, thamma*
thereabouts (adv)	قريب من ذلك	*qarīb min dhālik*
thereafter (adv)	بعد ذلك	*ba'da dhālik*
thereby (adv)	بذلك، لذلك	*bidhālik, lidhālik*
therefore (adv)	لذلك، لذلك الغرض	*lidhālik, lidhālikal gharaḍ*
therein (adv)	في ذلك المكان	*fī dhālikal makān*
thereof (adv)	من ذلك، منه	*min dhālik, minu*
thereto (adv)	إلى ذلك، إليه	*ilā dhālik, ilaih*
thereunder (adv)	تحت ذلك	*taḥta dhālik*
thereupon (adv)	على ذلك، عليه	*'alā dhālik, 'alaih*
thermal (adj)	حراري، مختص بالحرارة	*ḥarārī, mukhtaṣṣ bil ḥarārah*
thermal capacity	سعة حرارية	*sa'ah ḥarāriyya*
thermometer (n)	ثرمومتر، محر	*tharmūmitr, miḥarr*

thermonuclear (n)	نووي حراري	*nauwī ḥarārī*
thermoplastic (n)	لدن بالحرارة	*ladn bil ḥarārah*
thermos (n)	ترمس، كظيمة	*tarmus, kaẓīmah*
thesis (n)	أطروحة، مبحث	*uṭrūḥah, mabḥath*
thespian (n/adj)	ممثل مسرحي، مسرحي	*mumaththil masraḥī, masraḥī*
they (pron)	هم	*hum*
thick (adj)	كثيف، ثخين، غليظ	*kathīf, thakhīn, ghalīẓ*
thicken (v)	كثف، غلظ	*kaththafa, ghaluẓa*
thicket (n)	دغل، أجمة	*daghal, ajamah*
thick-headed (adj)	غبي، أحمق	*ghabī, aḥmaq*
thickness (n)	كثافة، سماكة	*kathāfah, samākah*
thickskinned (adj)	صفيق الجلد	*ṣafīqul jild*
thief (n)	لص	*liṣṣ*
thieve (v)	سرق، اختلس	*saraqa, ikhtalasa*
thievery (n)	سرقة، لصوصية	*sariqah, luṣūṣiyyah*
thievish (adj)	لصوصي	*luṣūṣī*
thigh (n)	فخذ، ورك	*fakhidh, wark*
thigh-bone (n)	عظم الفخذ	*'aẓmul fakhidh*
thimble (n)	قمع الخياطة، كشتبان	*qim'ul khiyāṭah, kushtubān*
thin (adj)	نحيف، ضئيل، رقيق	*naḥīf, ḍa'īl, raqīq*
thine (pron)	لك، لك	*laka, laki*
thing (n)	شيء، أمر، مسئلة	*shay', amr, mas'alah*
think (v)	حسب، تفكر، اعتقد	*ḥasiba, tafakkara, i'taqada*
think (n)	فكرة، رأي، ظن	*fikrah, ra'y, ẓann*
thinkable (adj)	ممكن تصوره	*mumkin taṣawwuruh*
thinker (n)	مفكر، فكير	*mufakkīr, fikkīr*
thinking (n)	فكر، تفكير	*fikr, tafkīr*
thinness (n)	رقة، نحافة	*riqqah, naḥāfah*
third (adj/n)	ثالث، ثلث	*thālith, thulth*

thirdly (adv)	ثالثاً	*thālithan*
third party	فريق ثالث	*farīq thālith*
third-rate (n)	رديء جدا	*radī' jiddā*
thirst (n)	عطش، ظمأ، هيام	*'aṭash, ẓama', hiyām*
thirsty (adj)	عطشان، ظمآن	*'aṭshān, ẓam'ān*
thirteen (n)	ثلاثة عشر	*thalāthatu 'ashara*
thirtieth (adj/n)	ثلاثون	*thalāthūn*
thirty (n)	ثلاثون	*thalāthūn*
this (pron)	هذا، هذه	*hādhā, hādhihi*
this (adv)	إلى هذا الحد	*ilā hādhal ḥadd*
thistle (n)	شوك	*shauk*
thither (adv)	إلى هناك	*ilā hunāk*
thong (n)	سير، شرعة	*sair, shar'ah*
thorax (n)	صدر، زور	*ṣadr, zaur*
thorn (n)	شوكة، حسكة	*shawkah, ḥasakah*
thorny (adj)	شائك، حسكي	*shā'ik, ḥasakī*
thorough (adj)	كامل، شامل	*kāmil, shāmil*
thoroughbred (adj)	أصيل، أنيق	*aṣīl, anīq*
thoroughfare (n)	طريق عام	*ṭarīq 'ām*
thoroughgoing (adj)	كامل، تام	*kāmil, tāmm*
thoroughly (adv)	تماماً، مئة بالمئة	*tamāman, mi'ah bil mi'ah*
thoroughness (n)	كل ما في الكلمة	*kullu mā fil kalimah*
thou (n)	أنت، أنت	*anta, anti*
though (conj)	برغم ذلك، مع أن	*bi raghmi dhālik, ma'a an*
thought (n)	فكرة، رأي، نية	*fikrah, ra'y, niyyah*
thoughtful (adj)	كثير التفكير، متأمل	*kathīrut tafkīr, muta'ammil*
thoughtfully (adv)	بعناية، بحسن الانتباه	*bi 'ināyah, bi ḥusnil intibāh*
thoughtless (adj)	طائش، غافل	*ṭā'ish, ghāfil*
thoughtlessly (adv)	بدون فكر أو تروٍّ	*bidūn fikr au tarawwin*
thoughtlessness (n)	عدم تفكير، طيش	*'adamu tafkīr, ṭaish*
thousand (n)	ألف	*alf*
thrash (v)	جلد، ضرب	*jalada, ḍaraba*

thrashing (n)	درس، ضرب	*dars, ḍarb*
thread (n)	خيط، سلك، عرق	*khaiṭ, silk, 'irq*
thread (v)	نظم، أسلك	*naẓama, aslaka*
threadbare (adj)	بال، رث	*bālin, raththth*
threat (n)	تهديد، وعيد	*tahdīd, wa'īd*
threaten (v)	هدد، توعد	*haddada, tawa''ada*
threateningly (adv)	بالتهديد	*bit tahdīd*
three (n)	ثلاث، ثلاثة	*thalāth, thalāthah*
threefold (adj/adv)	ثلاثي، ثلاثة أضعاف	*thulāthī, thalāthatu aḍ'āf*
thresh (v)	دق، درس	*daqqa, darasa*
thresher (n)	دراسة	*darrāsah*
threshold (n)	عتبة، مدخل	*'atabah, madkhal*
thrice (adv)	ثلاثاً، ثلاث مرات	*thalāthan, thalātha marrāt*
thrift (n)	اقتصاد، حسن التدبير	*iqtiṣād, ḥusnut tadbīr*
thrifty (adj)	مقتصد، مزدهر	*muqtaṣid, muzdahir*
thrill (n)	رجفة، هزة	*rajfah, hazzah*
thrill (v)	اهتز، هز	*ihtazza, hazza*
thrilled (adj)	مسرور، طرب	*masrūr, ṭarib*
thriller (n)	رواية مثيرة	*riwāyah muthīrah*
thrive (v)	نما، ازدهر	*namā, izdahara*
throat (n)	حلق، بلعوم	*ḥalq, bul'ūm*
throaty (adj)	حلقي	*ḥalqī*
throb (n/v)	خفقان، خفق	*khafaqān, khafaqa*
throne (n)	عرش، سرير الملك	*'arsh, sarīrul malik*
throng (v)	احتشد، تجمع	*iḥtashada, tajamma'a*
throng (n)	حشد، ازدحام	*ḥashd, izdiḥām*
throttle (v)	خنق، شنق	*khanaqa, shanaqa*
throttle (n)	حنجرة، حلق	*ḥanjarah, ḥalq*
through (adv)	تماماً، من أول إلى آخر	*tamāman, min awwal ilā ākhir*
through (prep)	خلال، عبر، بين	*khilāla, 'abra, baina*
throughout (adv)	طوال، في كل مكان	*ṭiwāla, fī kulli makān*

throw (v)	رمى، ألقى، طرح، نبذ	ramā, alqā, ṭaraḥa, nabadha
throw (n)	طرحة، رمية	ṭarḥah, ramyah
throw away	نبذ، طرح	nabadha, ṭaraḥa
throw back	عاق، رد	ʿāqa, radda
throw down	ألقى، طرح	alqā, ṭaraḥa
throw out	نبذ، رفض	nabadha, rafaḍa
thrush (n)	دج، مرض القلاع	dujj, maraḍul qulāʿ
thrust (v)	طعن، أقحم	taʿana, aqḥama
thrust (n)	طعنة، دفع	ṭaʿnah, dafʿ
thud (n)	صوت الخبط	ṣautul khabṭ
thug (n)	سفاح	saffāḥ
thumb (n)	إبهام	ibhām
thumb (v)	قلب، لوث	qallaba, lawwatha
thumb index (n)	دليل إبهامي	dalīl ibhāmī
thumb-nail (n)	ظفر الإبهام	ẓufrul ibhām
thumbscrew (n)	لولب إبهامي	laulab ibhāmī
thump (v)	جلد، ضرب، طرق	jalada, ḍaraba, ṭaraqa
thump (n)	طرقة، جلدة	ṭarqah, jaldah
thumping (adj)	كبير جدا، ضخم	kabīr jiddā, ḍakhm
thunder (v/n)	رعد، رعد	raʿada, raʿd
thunderbolt (n)	صاعقة	ṣāʿiqah
thunderclap (n)	هزيم الرعد	hazīmur raʿd
thundercloud (n)	سحابة رعادة	saḥābah raʿʿādah
thunderous (adj)	راعد، مدوٍ	rāʿid, mudawwin
thunderstorm (n)	عاصفة رعدية	ʿāṣifah raʿdiyyah
thunderstruck (adj)	مصعوق، مشدوه	maṣʿūq, mashdūh
Thursday (n)	يوم الخميس	yawmul khamīs
thus (adv)	هكذا، على هذا النمط	hākadhā, ʿalā hādhan namaṭ
thwart (v)	عاق، عارض، ضاد	ʿāqa, ʿāraḍa, ḍādda
thwart (n)	مقعد المجذف	maqʿadul mujadhdhif

thyroid (n)	غدة درقية	*ghuddah daraqiyyah*
tick (n)	نقطة صغيرة، تكة	*nuqṭah ṣaghīrah, tikkah*
tick (v)	وسم بنقطة، تك	*wasama bi nuqṭah, takka*
ticket (n)	تذكرة، بطاقة	*tadhkirah, biṭāqah*
ticking (n)	تيل الفرش	*tīlul farsh*
tickle (v)	دغدغ، أبهج	*daghdagha, abhaja*
tickle (n)	دغدغة، إبهاج	*daghdaghah, ibhāj*
tickler (n)	مسئلة مرتبكة	*mas'alah murtabikah*
ticklish (adj)	مضطرب، سريع الغضب	*mudṭarib, sarī'ul ghaḍab*
tidal (adj)	مختص بالمد والجزر	*mukhtaṣṣ bil madd wal jazr*
tidal wave	موجة مدية	*maujah maddiyyah*
tide (n)	مد وجزر، تيار	*madd wa jazr, tayyār*
tide (v)	عاون في وضع	*'āwana fī waḍ'*
tide-mark (n)	علامة المد والجزر	*'alāmatul madd wal jazr*
tideway (n)	مسلك المد	*maslakul madd*
tidily (adv)	بترتيب حسن	*bi tartīb ḥasan*
tidiness (n)	ترتيب، ملاءمة	*tartīb, mulā'amah*
tidings (n)	أنباء، أخبار	*ambā', akhbār*
tidy (adj)	أنيق، منظم، مرتب	*anīq, munaẓẓam, murattab*
tidy (v)	رتب، نظم	*rattaba, naẓẓama*
tie (v)	ربط، حزم	*rabaṭa, ḥazama*
tie (n)	رباط، أربة، صلة	*ribāṭ, urbah, ṣilah*
tie-pin = scarf pin		
tier (n)	صف، درجة، مئزر	*ṣaff, darajah, mi'zar*
tiff (n)	شجار بسيط، امتعاض	*shijār basīṭ, imti'āḍ*
tiger (n)	نمر، ببر	*namir, babar*
tight (adj)	محكم، مشدود	*muḥkam, mashdūd*
tighten (v)	شد، ضيق	*shadda, ḍayyaqa*
tight-fisted (adj)	مغلول اليد	*maghlūlul yad*
tightly (adv)	بضيق، بضبط	*bi ḍīq, bi ḍabṭ*
tightness (n)	ضيق، شدة	*ḍīq, shaddah*

tightrope (n)	حبل البهلوان	*ḥablul bahlawān*
tights (n)	رداء محكم	*ridā' muḥkam*
tigress (n)	نمرة	*namirah*
tile (n)	قرميدة، بلاطة	*qirmīdah, balāṭatu*
	اسمنت	*ismant*
till (n)	درج، صندوق النقود	*durj, ṣundūqun nuqūd*
till (v)	حرث، فلح	*ḥaratha, falaḥa*
till (conj/prep)	إلى، حتى	*ilā, ḥattā*
tillage (n)	حراثة، فلاحة	*ḥirāthah, filāḥah*
tiller (n)	فلاح، حارث	*fallāḥ, ḥārith*
tilt (v)	تمايل، تطاعن	*tamāyala, taṭā'ana*
tilt (n)	انحدار، إمالة	*inḥidār, imālah*
tilth (n)	حراثة، عزق	*ḥirāthah, 'azq*
timber (n)	خشب	*khashab*
timbered (adj)	مزود بالأخشاب	*muzawwad bil akhshāb*
timber-line (n)	نطاق شجري	*niṭāq shajarī*
timber-woolf (n)	ذئب الغابات	*dhi'bul ghābāt*
timbre (n)	جرس	*jars*
time (n)	وقت، زمن، أوان	*waqt, zaman, awān*
time (v)	وقت	*waqqatā*
time bomb	قنبلة موقوتة	*qumbulah mauqūtah*
time-card (n)	بطاقة للدوام	*biṭāqah lid dawām*
time-consuming (adj)	مستغرق وقتاً طويلاً	*mustaghriq waqtan ṭawīlan*
time exposure	تعريض زمني	*ta'rīḍ zamanī*
time-fuse (n)	صمامة زمنية	*ṣimāmah zamaniyyah*
timeless (adj)	خالد، دائم	*khālid, dā'im*
timely (adv)	في أوان، في وقت	*fī awān, fī waqt*
timepiece (n)	ساعة	*sā'ah*
timer (n)	ساعة السباق	*sā'atus sibāq*
time-server (n)	انتهازي	*intihāzī*
time-sheet (n)	صحيفة الدوام	*ṣaḥīfatud dawām*

timetable (n)	جدول المواعيد	*jadwalul mawāʻīd*
timid (adj)	جبان، فشل	*jabān, fashil*
timidity (timidness)	تهيب، جبانة	*tahayyub, jabānah*
timing (n)	توقيت	*tauqīt*
timorous (adj)	جبان، متخوف	*jabān, mutakhawwif*
timpani (n)	دفية	*daffiyyah*
tin (n)	صفيحة، قصدير	*ṣafīḥah, qaṣdīr*
tincture (n)	صبغة، لون	*ṣibghah, lawn*
tinder (n)	صوفان، حراق	*ṣūfān, ḥurāq*
tinder-box (n)	علبة القدح	*ʻulbatul qadḥ*
tine (n)	شوكة	*shaukah*
ting (v/n)	رن، رنين	*ranna, ranīn*
tinge (n/v)	لون خفيف، لون	*lawn khafīf, lawwana*
tingle (n)	وخز خفيف	*wakhz khafīf*
tinker (n)	سمكري، تنكاري	*samkarī, tinkārī*
tinkle (n)	رنين، صليل	*ranīn, ṣalīl*
tinman (n)	سمكري، صفاح	*samkarī, ṣaffāḥ*
tinny (adj)	صفيحي، غير متين	*ṣafīḥī, ghair matīn*
tinsel (n)	بهرجان	*bahrajān*
tinsmith (n)	صفاح، سمكري	*ṣaffāḥ, samkarī*
tint (n)	لون خفيف	*lawn khafīf*
tip (n)	رأس، نفحة، ضربة خفيفة	*ra's, nafḥah, ḍarbah khafīfah*
tip (v)	نفح، أمال، وهب	*nafaḥa, amāla, wahaba*
tip-off (n)	إلماع، تحذير	*ilmāʻ, taḥdhīr*
tipple (n)	خمر	*khamr*
tippler (n)	مدمن الخمر	*mudminul khamr*
tipster (n)	بائع المعلومات السرية	*bā'iʻul maʻlūmāt as sirriyyah*
tipsy (adj)	سكران قليلا	*sakrān qalīlā*
tiptoe (n)	طرف إصبع القدم	*ṭarafu iṣbaʻil qadam*
tiptop (adj)	رائع، ممتاز، بارع	*rā'iʻ, mumtāz, bāriʻ*

tire (v)	أتعب، أضجر	*at'aba, adjara*
tired (adj)	متعب، تعبان	*mut'ab, ta'bān*
tireless (adj)	لا يتعب، لا يمل	*lā yat'ab, lā yamill*
tiresome (adj)	ممل، متعب	*mumill, mut'ib*
tiring (adj)	متعب، شاق	*mut'ib, shāqq*
tissue (n)	نسيج، قماش	*nasīj, qumāsh*
tit (n)	حلمة، خبطة	*ḥalamah, khabṭah*
titan (n)	جبار، هائل القوة	*jabbār, hā'ilul quwwah*
titanic (adj)	هائل، ضخم	*hā'il, ḍakhm*
titillate (v)	دغدغ، لذذ	*daghdagha, ladhdhadha*
titivate (v)	تأنق، أنق	*ta'annaqa, annaqa*
title (n)	اسم كتاب، لقب، عنوان	*ismu kitāb, laqab, 'unwān*
titled (adj)	ذو لقب نبيل	*dhū laqab nabīl*
title-deed (n)	سند الملكية	*sanadul milkiyyah*
title-holder (n)	حامل اللقب	*ḥāmilul laqab*
title-page (n)	صفحة العنوان	*ṣafḥatul 'unwān*
title-role (n)	دور عنواني	*daur 'unwānī*
titmouse (n)	قرقف	*qurquf*
tittle-tattle (n)	قيل وقال	*qīl wa qāl*
titular (adj)	حامل لقب خاص	*ḥāmilu laqab khāṣṣ*
tizzy (n)	ارتباك، اهتياج	*irtibāk, ihtiyāj*
to (prep)	إلى، نحو، حتى	*ilā, naḥwa, ḥttā*
toad (n)	ضفدع البر	*ḍafda'ul barr*
toady (n/v)	متملق، تملق	*mutamalliq, tamallaqa*
toast (v)	دفأ، حمص	*dafa'a, ḥammaṣa*
toast (n)	خبز محمص	*khubz muḥammaṣ*
toaster (n)	محمصة	*miḥmaṣah*
toast-master	نخاب	*nakhkhāb*
tobacco (n)	تبغ، دخان	*tabgh, dukhān*
tobacconist (n)	بائع التبغ	*bā'i'ut tabgh*
tocsin (n)	ناقوس الخطر	*nāqūsul khaṭar*

today (n)	اليوم، الوقت الحاضر	*al yaum, al waqt al ḥāḍir*
toddle (v)	دلف، كرفس، درج	*dalafa, karfasa, daraja*
toddler (n)	طفل دارج	*ṭifl dārij*
toddy (n)	تودي	*tūdī*
to-do (n)	اهتياج، ضجة	*ihtiyāj, ḍajjah*
toe (n)	إصبع القدم، مقدم الحذاء	*iṣba'ul qadam, muqaddamul ḥidhā'*
toe-nail (n)	ظفر إصبع القدم	*ẓufru iṣba'il qadam*
toffee (n)	طوفي	*ṭūfī*
tog (v)	لبس، ارتدى	*labisa, irtadā*
together (adv)	معاً، متصلاً	*ma'an, muttaṣilan*
toggle (n)	مسمار العقدة	*mismārul 'uqdah*
togs (n)	ملابس	*malābis*
toil (v/n)	كدح، كدح	*kadaḥa, kadḥ*
toilet (n)	مرحاض، حمام	*mirḥāḍ, ḥammām*
toilet-paper (n)	ورق المرحاض	*waraqul mirḥāḍ*
toilet-soap (n)	صابون الزينة	*ṣābūnuz zīnah*
toilet-water (n)	ماء الزينة	*mā'uz zīnah*
token (n)	تذكار، رمز، علامة	*tadhkār, ramz, 'alāmah*
tolerable (adj)	محتمل، مطاق	*muḥtamal, muṭāq*
tolerably (adv)	باعتدال، بين بين	*bi'tidāl, bain bain*
tolerance (n)	احتمال، تسامح	*iḥtimāl, tasāmuḥ*
tolerant (adj)	صبور، متسامح	*ṣabūr, mutasāmiḥ*
tolerate (v)	احتمل، صبر على	*iḥtamala, ṣabara 'alā*
toleration (n)	احتمال، تسامح	*iḥtimāl, tasāmuḥ*
toll (n)	رسم، ضريبة، دق الجرس	*rasm, ḍarībah, daqqul jaras*
toll (v)	دق الجرس	*daqqal jaras*
toll-gate (n)	بوابة المكوس	*bawwābatul mukūs*
toll-house (n)	مكتب المكوس	*maktabul mukūs*
tomato (n)	طماطم	*ṭamāṭim*
tomb (n)	ضريح، قبر	*ḍarīḥ, qabr*

tomboy (n)	صبية ورشة	*ṣabiyyah warishah*
tombstone (n)	بلاطة الضريح	*balāṭatuḍ ḍarīḥ*
tome (n)	كتاب ضخم	*kitāb ḍakhm*
tommy-gun	رشيشة	*rushaishah*
tommy-rot (n)	سخافة، بلاهة	*sakhāfah, balāhah*
tomorrow (n/adv)	غد، غداً	*ghad, ghadan*
tom-tom (n)	طبلة صغيرة	*ṭablah ṣaghīrah*
ton (n)	طن، وسق	*ṭunn, wasq*
tone (n)	لهجة، نغمة، نبرة	*lahjah, naghmah, nabrah*
tone (v)	نغم، تناغم	*naghghama, tanāghama*
tongs (n)	ملقط، ملقطة	*milqaṭ, milqaṭah*
tongue (n)	لسان، لغة	*lisān, lughah*
tongueless (adj)	أخرس، بلا لسان	*akhras, bilā lisān*
tongue-tied (adj)	معقود اللسان	*ma'qūdul lisān*
tonic (n)	دواء مقوٍّ	*dawā' muqawwin*
tonight (n)	هذه الليلة	*hādhihil lailah*
tonight (adv)	في هذه الليلة	*fī hādhihil lailah*
tonnage (n)	وسق السفينة بالطن	*wasqus safīnah biṭ ṭunn*
tonsil (n)	لوزة الحلق	*lawzatul ḥalq*
too (adv)	أيضاً، كذلك	*aiḍan, kadhālik*
tool (n)	آلة، أداة	*ālah, adāt*
tool (v)	زود بالأدوات	*zawwada bil adawāt*
toot (n)	بواق، صفير	*buwāq, ṣafīr*
tooth (n)	سن، ضرس	*sinn, ḍirs*
toothache (n)	وجع السن	*waj'us sinn*
toothbrush (n)	فرشاة الأسنان	*furshātul asnān*
toothed (adj)	ذو أسنان، أسن	*dhū asnān, asann*
toothless (adj)	أدرد	*adrad*
toothpaste (n)	معجون الأسنان	*ma'jūnul asnān*
toothpick (n)	سلاكة الأسنان، خلالة	*sallākatul asnān, khilālah*
tooth powder	ذرور الأسنان	*dharūrul asnān*
toothsome (adj)	لذيذ المذاق	*ladhīdhul madhāq*

top (n)	قمة، ذروة، أعلى	*qimmah, dhirwah, a'lā*
top (v)	تفوق، اعتل، شذب	*tafawwaqa, i'talla, shadhdhaba*
topaz (n)	ياقوت، حجر كريم	*yaqūt, ḥajar karīm*
topcoat (n)	معطف خفيف	*mi'ṭaf khafīf*
top hat	قبعة رسمية	*qubba'ah rasmiyyah*
topic (n)	موضوع، مبحث	*mauḍū', mabḥath*
topical (adj)	موضعي، محلي	*mauḍi'ī, maḥallī*
topmost (adj)	أعلى، أرفع	*a'lā, arfa'*
top-notch (adj)	ممتاز، من الطراز الأول	*mumtāz, minaṭ ṭirāz al awwal*
topography (n)	طوبوغرافيا، رسم دقيق لموضع	*ṭūbūgharāfiyā, rasm daqīq li mauḍi'*
topple (v)	سقط، انقلب	*saqaṭa, inqalaba*
torch (n)	مشعل، مصباح	*mish'al, miṣbāḥ*
torment (n)	إيلام، عذاب	*īlām, 'adhāb*
torment (v)	عذب، ضايق	*'adhdhaba, ḍāyaqa*
tornado (n)	إعصار قمعي	*i'ṣār qam'ī*
torpedo (n)	طربيد	*ṭurbīd*
torpedo-boat (n)	زورق طربيد	*zauraqu ṭurbīd*
torpid (adj)	متبلد، خدر	*mutaballid, khadir*
torpidity (n)	خدر، سبات	*khadar, subāt*
torpor (n)	بلادة، خدر	*balādah, khadar*
torrent (n)	سيل، تيار	*sail, tayyār*
torrential (adj)	جارف، كالسيل	*jārif, kas sail*
torrid (n)	ملفوح بالحرارة، متلظّ	*malfūḥ bil ḥarārah, mutalaẓẓin*
torsion (n)	فتل، برم	*fatl, barm*
tortoise (n)	سلحفاة	*sulaḥfāt*
tortuosity (n)	التواء، تعرج	*iltiwā', ta'arruj*
tortuous (adj)	ملتوٍ، متمعج	*multawin, mutama''ij*
torture (v)	عذب، آلم	*'adhdhaba, ālama*

torture (n)	تعذيب، عذاب	*ta'dhīb, 'adhāb*
toss (v)	خلط، رمى، خفق	*khalaṭa, ramā, khafaqa*
toss (n)	رمي، طرح، إلقاء القرعة	*ramy, ṭarḥ, ilqāul qur'ah*
tot (n)	طفل صغير	*ṭifl ṣaghīr*
total (n)	مجموع، حاصل، كل	*majmū', ḥāṣil, kull*
total (adj)	إجمالي، كلي	*ijmālī, kullī*
totalitarian (n)	كلياتي، ديكتاتوري	*kulliyyātī, dīktātūrī*
totality (n)	مجموعية	*majmū'iyyah*
totally (adv)	تماماً، كليةً	*tamāman, kulliyyatan*
totter (v)	تمايل، ترنح	*tamāyala, tarannaḥa*
touch (v)	مس، لمس	*massa, lamasa*
touch (n)	لمسة، حاسة اللمس	*lamsah, ḥāssatul lams*
touched (adj).	متأثر	*muta'aththir*
touching (adj)	مؤثر، لامس	*mu'ththir, lāmis*
touchy (adj)	شديد الحساسية، وعق	*shadīdul ḥassāsiyyah, wa'iq*
tough (adj)	خشن، قاسٍ	*khashin, qāsin*
toughen (v)	خشن، متن	*khashshana, mattana*
toughness (n)	متانة، خشونة، صلابة	*matānah, khushūnah, ṣalābah*
tour (n)	رحلة، زيارة، سياحة	*riḥlah, ziyārah, siyāḥah*
tour (v)	ساح، جال	*sāḥa, jāla*
tourism (n)	سياحة	*siyāḥah*
tourist (n)	سائح، جوال	*sā'iḥ, jawwāl*
tourist class	درجة سياحية	*darajah siyāḥiyyah*
tournament (n)	مباراة، دورة	*mubārāt, daurah*
tousle (v)	شوث، لوث	*shawwatha, lawwatha*
tout (n)	باحث عن الزبائن	*bāḥith 'aniz zabā'in*
tow (v)	سحب، قطر	*saḥaba, qaṭara*
tow (n)	قطر، جر، نسالة	*qaṭr, jarr, nusālah*
towards (toward)	نحو، إلى جهة	*naḥwa, ilā jihati*
towel (n)	منشفة الوجه	*minshafatul wajh*

tower (v)	ارتفع، شمخ	*irtafa'a, shamakha*
tower (n)	برج، حصن	*burj, ḥiṣn*
towering (adj)	شامخ، عالٍ	*shāmikh, 'ālin*
tow-line (tow-rope)	حبل القطر	*ḥablul qaṭr*
town (n)	بلدة، قرية	*baldah, qaryah*
town council	مجلس بلدى	*majlis baladī*
town crier	منادي البلدة	*munādiyul baldah*
town hall	دار البلدية	*dārul baladiyyah*
town house	بيت في المدينة	*bait fil madīnah*
townsfolk (n)	سكان المدينة	*sukkānul madīnah*
township (n)	ناحية، منطقة	*nāḥiyah, minṭaqah*
townsman (n)	مواطن بلدي	*muwāṭin baladī*
toxaemia (toxemia)	تسمم الدم	*tasammumud dam*
toxic (adj)	سمي، سام	*summī, sāmm*
toxicity (n)	سمية	*summiyyah*
toxin (n)	تكسين، سمين	*tuksīn, summīn*
toy (n)	لعبة، ألعوبة	*lu'bah, ul'ūbah*
toy (v)	لها، لعب	*lahā, la'iba*
trace (n)	أثر، رسم، حبل العربة	*athar, rasm, ḥablul 'arabah*
trace (v)	تتبع، رسم	*tatabba'a, rasama*
tracer (n)	رسام، مرسمة	*rassām, mirsamah*
tracery (n)	زخرفة تشجيرية	*zakhrafah tashjīriyyah*
tracing (n)	رسم استشفافي	*rasm istishfāfī*
tracing-paper (n)	ورق الاستشفاف	*waraqul istishfāf*
track (n)	درب، مسلك، أثر القدم	*darb, maslak, atharul qadam*
track (v)	تعقب، تتبع	*ta'aqqaba, tatabba'a*
tract (n)	بقعة، جهاز، نبذة	*buq'ah, jihāz, nubdhah*
tractable (adj)	سهل الانقياد، طريق	*sahlul inqiyād, ṭarīq*
traction (n)	انسحاب، جر	*insiḥāb, jarr*
traction (v)	سحب، جر	*saḥaba, jarra*

traction-engine (n)	قاطرة الجر	*qāṭiratul jarr*
tractor (n)	جرارة، تراكتور	*jarrārah, tarāktūr*
trade (n)	تجارة، حرفة، مهنة	*tijārah, ḥirfah, mihnah*
trade (v)	تاجر، اتجر	*tājara, ittajara*
trade mark	علامة تجارية	*'alāmah tijāriyyah*
trade name	اسم تجاري	*ism tijārī*
trader (n)	تاجر، جلاب	*tājir, jallāb*
tradesman (n)	تاجر، صاحب المتجر	*tājir, ṣāḥibul matjar*
trades union	نقابة عمال	*niqābatu 'ummāl*
trade wind	ريح تجارية	*rīḥ tijāriyyah*
tradition (n)	حديث منقول، تقليد	*ḥadīth manqūl, taqlīd*
traditional (adj)	تقليدي، تواتري	*taqlīdī, tawāturī*
traditionally (adv)	تقليديًا	*taqlīdiyyan*
traditionalism (n)	تقليدية	*taqlīdiyyah*
traditionalist (n)	متمسك بالتقاليد	*mutamassik bit taqālīd*
traduce (v)	انتهك، وشى	*intahaka, washā*
traffic (n)	سير، نقل، حركة المرور	*sair, naql, ḥarakatul murūr*
traffic-light (n)	إشارة السير	*ishāratus sair*
tragedian (n)	مؤلف روايات محزنة	*mu'allifu riwāyāt muḥzinah*
tragedy (n)	رواية محزنة، مأساة	*riwāyah muḥzinah, ma'sāt*
tragic (adj)	مأساوي، مفجع	*ma'sāwī, mufji'*
trail (v)	تدلى، جر، زحف	*tadallā, jarra, zaḥafa*
trail (n)	أثر، ذيل، ممر	*athar, dhail, mamarr*
trailer (n)	عربة مقطورة، فيلم قصير	*'arabah maqṭūrah, fīlm qaṣīr*
train (n)	قطار، سلسلة، حشم	*qiṭār, silsilah, ḥasham*
train (v)	درب، تدرب	*darraba, tadarraba*
trainee (n)	مخضع للتدريب، تحت التمرين	*mukhḍa' lit tadrīb, taḥtat tamrīn*
trainer (n)	مدرب، مروض	*mudarrib, murawwiḍ*

training (n)	تدريب، تمرين	*tadrīb, tamrīn*
training-college	دار المعلمين	*dārul mu'allimīn*
trainman (n)	عامل في القطار	*'āmil fil qiṭār*
trait (n)	ميزة، خاصية	*mīzah, khaṣṣiyyah*
traitor (n)	خائن، غادر	*khā'in, ghādir*
traitorous (adj)	غادر، خائن	*ghādir, khā'in*
traitress (n)	خائنة، غادرة	*khā'inah, ghādirah*
tram (n)	ترام	*tarām*
tramcar (n)	مركبة ترام	*markabatu tarām*
trammels (n)	قيد، عائق	*qaid, 'ā'iq*
tramp (n)	متجول، عائر	*mutajawwil, 'ā'ir*
tramp (v)	سار على القدمين	*sāra 'alal qadamain*
trample (v)	داس، وطئ	*dāsa, waṭi'a*
trance (n)	غشية، سبات	*ghashyah, subāt*
tranquil (adj)	هادئ، مرتاح	*hādi', murtāḥ*
tranquillize,-ise (v)	هدأ، سكن	*hadda'a, sakkana*
tranquillizer,-iser (n)	عقار مسكن	*'aqqār musakkin*
tranquillity (tranquility)	هدوء، سكون	*hudū', sukūn*
transact (v)	أجرى، تعامل	*ajrā, ta'āmala*
transaction (n)	تعامل، إجراء	*ta'āmul, ijrā'*
transcend (v)	تفوق، تجاوز	*tafawwaqa, tajāwaza*
transcendence-cy (n	سمو، تجاوز	*summuww, tajāwuz*
transcendent (adj)	متعال، سامٍ	*muta'ālin, sāmin*
transcendental (adj)	متجاوز الحد	*mutajāwizul ḥadd*
transcribe (v)	نقل، نسخ، دون	*naqala, nasakha, dawwana*
transcript (n)	نسخة طبق الأصل	*nuskhah ṭibqal aṣl*
transfer (v)	حول، نقل، انتقل	*ḥawwala, naqala, intaqala*
transfer (n)	انتقال، تحويل، ترحيل	*intiqāl, taḥwīl, tarḥīl*
transferable (adj)	يمكن نقله	*yumkin naqluh*
transference (n)	نقل، تحويل	*naql, taḥwīl*

transfiguration (n)	تغيير المظهر	*taghyīrul maẓhar*
transfigure (v)	غير الهيئة	*ghayyaral hay'ah*
transfix (v)	رشق، طعن	*rashaqa, ṭa'ana*
transform (v)	حول، تحول	*ḥawwala, taḥawwala*
transformable (adj)	يمكن تحويله	*yumkin taḥwīluh*
transformation (n)	تحول، تغير	*taḥawwul, taghayyur*
transformer (n)	محول التيار	*muḥawwilut tayyār*
transfusion (n)	نقل الدم	*naqlud dam*
transgress (v)	تعدى، خالف	*ta'addā, khālafa*
transgression (n)	تعدّ، خطيئة	*ta'addin, khaṭī'ah*
transgressor (n)	متعدٍّ، منتهك	*muta'addin, muntahik*
transience-cy (n)	سرعة الزوال	*sur'atuz zawāl*
transient (adj)	عابر، وقتي	*'ābir, waqtī*
transistor (n)	راديو، ترانزيستور	*rādiu, tarānzīstūr*
transit (n)	نقل، عبور	*naql, 'ubūr*
transition (n)	انتقال، اجتياز	*intiqāl, ijtiyāz*
transitional (adj)	انتقالي، متحول	*intiqālī, mutaḥawwil*
transitive (adj)	انتقالي، متعدي	*intiqālī, muta'addī*
transitory (adj)	زائل، فانٍ	*zā'il, fānin*
translatable (adj)	ممكن ترجمته	*mumkin tarjamatuh*
translate (v)	ترجم، نقل	*tarjama, naqala*
translation (n)	ترجمة، تحويل	*tarjamah, taḥwīl*
translator (n)	مترجم، ناقل	*mutarjim, nāqil*
transliterate (v)	نقحر	*naqḥarah*
transliteration (n)	نقحرة	*naqḥarah*
transmission (n)	توصيل، نقل، انتقال	*tawṣīl, naql, intiqāl*
transmit (v)	أنفذ، أرسل، نقل	*anfadha, arsala, naqala*
transmitter (n)	مرسلة	*mursilah*
transmutation (n)	تحويل، تبديل	*taḥwīl, tabdīl*
transmute (v)	حول، غير	*ḥawwala, ghayyara*
transparency (n)	شفافية	*shaffāfiyyah*
transparent (adj)	شفاف، واضح	*shaffāf, wāḍiḥ*

transpiration (n)	رشح، عرق	*rashḥ, ʻaraq*
transpire (v)	رشح، شاع	*rashaḥa, shāʻa*
transplant (v)	نقل، ازدرع	*naqala, izdaraʻa*
tranplantation (n)	ازدراع	*izdirāʻ*
transport (n)	نقل، نظام نقل	*naql, niẓāmu naql*
transport (v)	نقل، نفى	*naqala, nafā*
transportation (n)	نقل، وسيلة نقل	*naql, wasīlatu naql*
transpose (v)	غير الوضع، نقل	*ghayyaral waḍʻ, naqqala*
transposition (n)	تغيير الوضع	*taghyīrul waḍʻ*
transverse (adj)	مستعرض	*mustaʻriḍ*
trap (n)	شرك، مكيدة	*sharak, makīdah*
trap (v)	أوقع في شرك	*awqaʻa fī sharak*
trap door	باب مسحور	*bāb masḥūr*
trapezium (n)	معين منحرف	*muʻayyan munḥarif*
trappings (n)	زخارف	*zakhārif*
trash (n)	عفاشة، سقاطة	*ʻufāshah, suqāṭah*
trashy (adj)	تافه، حقير	*tāfih, ḥaqīr*
trauma (n)	صدمة، جرح	*ṣadmah, jurḥ*
traumatic (adj)	رضي، جرحي	*raḍḍī, jurḥī*
travail (n)	كدح، مخاض	*kadḥ, makhāḍ*
travel (n)	سفر، رحلة	*safar, riḥlah*
travel agency	وكالة السفر	*wakālatus safar*
travel agent	وكيل السفر	*wakīlus safar*
traveller (traveler)	مسافر، سائح	*musāfir, sā'iḥ*
traveller's cheque	شيك السائح	*shīkus sā'iḥ*
traverse (v)	عارض، اعترض	*ʻāraḍa, iʻtaraḍa*
traverse (n)	مستعرض، معترض	*mustaʻriḍ, muʻtariḍ*
travesty (n)	محاكاة مضحكة	*muḥākāt muḍḥikah*
trawl (n)	شبكة صيد، مجزفة	*shabakatu ṣaid, mijzafah*
tray (n)	صينية، طبق	*ṣīniyyah, ṭabaq*
treacherous (adj)	خائن، غدار	*khā'in, ghaddār*
treacherously (adv)	خيانةً، غدراً	*khiyānatan, ghadran*

treachery (n)	غدر، خيانة	*ghadr, khiyānah*
treacle (n)	دبس السكر	*dibsus sukkar*
tread (v)	داس، مشى	*dāsa, mashā*
tread (n)	خطوة، دوس	*khuṭwah, daus*
treadle (n)	دواسة	*dawwāsah*
treadmill (n)	طاحون الدوس	*ṭāḥūnud daus*
treason (n)	غدر، ختر	*ghadr, khatr*
treasonable (adj)	خياني، خائن	*khiyānī, khā'in*
treasure (v)	كنــز، ادخر	*kanaza, iddakhara*
treasure (n)	كنــز، خزينة	*kanz, khazīnah*
treasurer (n)	خازن، أمين الصندوق	*khāzin, amīnuṣ ṣundūq*
treasure trove	لقية، لقطة	*luqyah, luqṭah*
treasury (n)	خزينة، بيت المال	*khazīnah, baitul māl*
treat (n)	مأدبة، دعوة	*ma'dubah, da'wah*
treat (v)	اعتبر، عامل، داوى	*i'tabara, 'āmala, dāwā*
treatise (n)	مقالة، رسالة	*maqālah, risālah*
treatment (n)	معالجة، معاملة	*mu'ālajah, mu'āmalah*
treaty (n)	معاهدة، معاثقة	*mu'āhadah, mu'āthaqah*
treble (n/adj)	ثلاثة أضعاف، عالٍ	*thalāthatu aḍ'āf, 'ālin*
tree (n)	شجر، عريشة	*shajar, 'arīshatul*
	العربة، صليب	*'arabah, ṣalīb*
trefoil (n)	برسيم	*birsīm*
trek (n)	رحلة بعربة ثيران	*riḥlah bi 'arabati thīrān*
trek (v)	رحل بعربة ثيران	*raḥala bi 'arabati thīrān*
trellis (n)	تكعيبة، تعريشة	*tak'ībah, ta'rīshah*
tremble (v)	ارتعد، ارتعش	*irta'ada, irta'asha*
tremble (n)	ارتعاش، رعشة	*irti'āsh, ra'shah*
trembly (adj)	مرتعد، مرتجف	*murta'id, murtajif*
tremendous (adj)	عظيم، هائل	*'aẓīm, hā'il*
tremor (n)	رعشة، رجفة	*ra'shah, rajfah*
tremulous (adj)	مرتج، مرتجف	*murtajj, murtajif*
trench (n/v)	خندق، حفر خندقاً	*khandaq, ḥafara khandaqan*

trenchant (adj)	قاطع، لاذع	*qāṭi', lādhi'*
trench coat	ممطرة	*mimṭarah*
trencher (n)	صحفة كبيرة	*ṣaḥfah kabīrah*
trend (n)	اتجاه، ميل	*ittijāh, mail*
trend (v)	مال، اتجه	*māla, ittajaha*
trepan (n)	منشار الجمجمة	*minshārul jamjamah*
trepidation (n)	ذعر، هلع، رجة	*dhu'r, hala', rajjah*
trespass (v)	تعدى، أخطأ	*ta'addā, akhṭa'a*
trespass (n)	تعدٍّ، إثم	*ta'addin, ithm*
trespasser (n)	متعدٍّ، منتهك الحرمة	*muta'addin, muntahikul ḥurmah*
tress (n)	ضفيرة شعر	*ḍafīratu sha'r*
trestle (n)	منصبة، تصليبة	*minṣabah, taṣlībah*
trestle-table (n)	طاولة منصبية	*ṭāwilah minṣabiyyah*
trial (n)	محنة، تجربة	*miḥnah, tajribah*
triangle (n)	شكل مثلث	*shakl muthallath*
triangular (adj)	مثلث الشكل	*muthallathush shakl*
tribal (adj)	قبلي، عشيري	*qabalī, 'ashīrī*
tribe (n)	قبيلة، عشيرة	*qabīlah, 'ashīrah*
tribesman (n)	رجل القبيلة	*rajulul qabīlah*
tribulation (n)	بلية، ضيق	*baliyyah, ḍīq*
tribunal (n)	محكمة، دار القضاء	*maḥkamah, dārul qaḍā'*
tributary (adj/n)	رافد، نهر صغير	*rāfid, nahr ṣaghīr*
tribute (n)	هدية، جزية، إتاوة	*hadiyyah, jizyah, itāwah*
trice (n)	لمحة، لحظة	*lamḥah, laḥẓah*
trick (n)	خدعة، حيلة	*khud'ah, ḥīlah*
trick (v)	احتال، خدع	*iḥtāla, khada'a*
trickery (n)	احتيال، خداع	*iḥtiyāl, khidā'*
trickle (v)	سال، نز	*sāla, nazza*
trickster (n)	مخادع، محتال	*mukhādi', muḥtāl*
tricky (adj)	دقيق، خادع، ماكر	*daqīq, khādi', mākir*
tricolour (tricolor)	علم مثلث الألوان	*'alam muthallathul alwān*

tricycle (n)	دراجة ثلاثية	*darrājah thulāthiyyah*
triennial (adj)	ثلاثي السنوات	*thulāthiyyus sanawāt*
trifle (n)	أمر زهيد، شيء تافه	*amr zahīd, shay' tāfih*
trifle (v)	عبث، ازدرى	*'abatha, izdarā*
trifling (adj)	طفيف، زري	*ṭafīf, zarī*
trigger (v)	قدح، أطلق، أحدث	*qadaḥa, aṭlaqa, aḥdatha*
trigger (n)	إطلاق، مقداح	*iṭlāq, miqdāḥ*
trilateral (adj)	ثلاثي الأضلاع	*thulāthiyyul aḍlā'*
trilingual (adj)	ثلاثي اللغات	*thulāthiyyul lughāt*
triliteral (adj)	ثلاثي الأحرف	*thulāthiyyul aḥruf*
trill (n)	رعشة الصوت	*ra'shatuṣ ṣaut*
trilogy (n)	ثلاثية	*thulāthiyyah*
trim (v)	هذب، رتب، شذب	*hadhdhaba, rattaba, shadhdhaba*
trim (n)	زينة، زركشة	*zīnah, zarkashah*
trimmer (n)	مزين، مهندم	*muzayyin, muhandim*
trimming (n)	ملابس الزينة	*malābisuz zīnah*
trinket (n)	حلية صغيرة	*ḥilyah ṣaghīrah*
trip (n)	رحلة قصيرة، عثرة	*riḥlah qaṣīrah, 'athrah*
trip (v)	عثر، أمسك	*'athara, amsaka*
tripartite (adj)	ثلاثي التشريم	*thulāthiyyut tashrīm*
triple (adj)	ثلاثي	*thulāthī*
triple (v)	تضاعف ثلاث مرات	*taḍā'afa thalātha marrāt*
triplicate (v)	طبع ثلاثيًا	*ṭaba'a thulāthiyyan*
trisect (v)	ثلث	*thallatha*
trite (adj)	رث، مبتذل	*rathth, mubtadhil*
triumph (v)	انتصر، ظفر	*intaṣara, ẓafara*
triumph (n)	انتصار، نجاح	*intiṣār, najāḥ*
triumphal (adj)	نصري، انتصاري	*naṣrī, intiṣārī*
triumphant (adj)	منتصر، مظفر	*muntaṣir, muẓaffar*
trivia (n)	أمور تافهة	*umūr tāfihah*
trivial (adj)	حقير، تافه	*ḥaqīr, tāfih*

triviality (n)	تفاهة، زهادة	*tafāhah, zahādah*
trivialize,-ise (v)	تفه	*taffaha*
trolley (n)	عربة مكسحة، ترولي	*'arabah mukassaḥah, tarūlī*
troop (n)	شرذمة، فرقة، جند	*shirdhimah, firqah, jund*
troop (v)	احتشد، مشى في جماعة	*iḥtashada, mashā fī jamā'ah*
trooper (n)	شرطي، فارس	*shurṭī, fāris*
troop-ship (n)	سفينة الجند	*safīnatul jund*
trope (n)	مجاز، استعارة	*majāz, isti'ārah*
trophy (n)	تذكار الانتصار، مدالية	*tadhkārul intiṣār, madāliyah*
tropic (n)	مدار استوائي	*madār istiwā'ī*
tropical (adj)	استوائي، استعاري	*istiwā'ī, isti'ārī*
trot (v)	هرول، خب	*harwala, khabba*
trot (n)	خبب، ركض	*khabab, rakḍ*
trotter (n)	جواد ممرن	*jawād mumarran*
trouble (n)	قلق، حرج، هم	*qalaq, ḥaraj, hamm*
trouble (v)	أقلق، ضايق	*aqlaqa, ḍāyaqa*
toruble-maker (n)	مضايق، مزعج	*muḍāyiq, muz'ij*
trouble-shooter (n)	حلال العقد	*ḥallālul 'uqad*
troublesome (adj)	مزعج، مضايق، شاق	*muz'ij, muḍāyiq, shāqq*
trough (n)	معلف، جرن	*ma'laf, jurn*
troupe (n)	جماعة الممثلين	*jamā'atul mumaththilīn*
trousers (n)	بنطلون، سراويل	*banṭlūn, sarāwīl*
trousseau (n)	جهاز العروس	*jihāzul 'arūs*
trowel (n)	مسطار، مالج	*misṭār, mālaj*
truant (n)	طالب متهرب	*ṭālib mutaharrib*
truce (n)	هدنة حربية	*hudnah ḥarbiyyah*
truck (n)	شاحنة، عربة خفيضة، خضر	*shāḥinah, 'arabah khafīḍah, khuḍar*
truck farm	مزرعة الخضار	*mazra'atul khaḍār*

trucking (n)	نقل بشاحنة	*naql bi shāḥinah*
truculence (n)	توحش، ضراوة	*tawaḥḥush, ḍarāwah*
truculent (adj)	متوحش، شرس	*mutawaḥḥish, sharis*
true (adj)	حقيقي، صحيح، صادق	*ḥaqīqī, ṣaḥīḥ, ṣādiq*
true-blue (n/adj)	صادق الولاء	*ṣādiqul walā'*
true-hearted (adj)	صادق، مخلص	*ṣādiq, mukhliṣ*
true-love (n)	محبوب	*maḥbūb*
truffle (n)	كمأة، طرطوفة	*kam'ah, ṭarṭūfah*
truism (n)	حقيقة ثابتة	*ḥaqīqah thābitah*
truly (adv)	في الواقع، حقاً	*fil wāqi', ḥaqqan*
trump (n)	ورقة رابحة، بواق	*waraqah rābiḥah, buwāq*
trumpet (n)	بوق، نفير	*būq, nafīr*
trumpet (v)	أعلن، أذاع	*a'lana, adhā'a*
truncate (v)	شذب، قرطم	*shdhdhaba, qarṭama*
truncheon (n)	صولجان، هراوة	*ṣaulajān, hirāwah*
trunk (n)	ساق، خرطوم	*sāq, khurṭūm*
truss (n)	حزام الفتق	*ḥizāmul fatq*
truss (v)	كتف، حزم	*kattafa, ḥazama*
trust (n)	اتكال، ائتمان، ثقة	*ittikāl, i'timān, thiqah*
trust (v)	اتكل، وثق، أمل	*ittakala, wathiqa, amala*
trustee (n)	أمين، وكيل	*amīn, wakīl*
trusteeship (n)	أمانة، وكالة	*amānah, wakālah*
trustful (adj)	واثق، آمن	*wāthiq, āmin*
trustfully (adv)	بثقة، باستئمان	*bi thiqah, bisti'mān*
trustworthiness (n)	أمانة، استمانة	*amānah, istimānah*
trustworthy (adj)	جدير بالثقة	*jadīr bith thiqah*
trusty (adj)	موثوق، أمين	*mauthūq, amīn*
truth (n)	حقيقة، صحة، صدق	*ḥaqīqah, ṣiḥḥah, ṣidq*
truthful (adj)	صادق، قويم	*ṣādiq, qawīm*
truthfully (adv)	بصدق، بأمانة	*bi ṣidq, bi amānah*
truthfulness (n)	صدق، صادقية	*ṣidq, ṣādiqiyyah*
try (v)	حاول، سعى، جرب	*ḥāwala, sa'ā, jarraba*

try (n)	محاولة، تجربة	*muḥāwalah, tajribah*
trying (adj)	متعب، شاق	*mut'ib, shāqq*
tub (n)	قصعة، بتية	*qaṣ'ah, bittiyyah*
tube (n)	ماسورة، قناة	*māsūrah, qanāt*
tuber (n)	حدبة، درنة	*ḥadabah, daranah*
tubercular (adj)	سلي، دربي	*sullī, daranī*
tuberculosis (n)	سل، تدرن	*sull, tadarrun*
tuberous (adj)	دربي، معقد	*daranī, mu'aqqad*
tuck (n)	ثنية، طية	*thanyah, ṭayyah*
tuck (v)	ثنى، شمر	*thannā, shammara*
Tuesday (n)	يوم الثلاثاء	*yaumuth thulāthā'*
tuft (n)	خصلة شعر، شوشة	*khuṣlatu sha'r, shūshah*
tufted (adj)	معنقد، ذو عنقود	*mu'anqad, dhū 'unqūd*
tug (v)	جر بشدة	*jarra bi shiddah*
tug (n)	شدة، جرة شديدة	*shaddah, jarrah shadīdah*
tug of war	صراع عنيف	*ṣirā' 'anīf*
tuition (n)	تعليم، أجرة التعليم	*ta'līm, ujratut ta'līm*
tumble (v)	طرح، ألقى، تقلب	*ṭaraḥa, alqā, taqallaba*
tumble (n)	تقلب، انهيار، سقوط	*taqallub, inhiyār, suqūṭ*
tumbrel (n)	عربة لنقل السجناء	*'arabah li naqlis sujanā'*
tumescence (n)	تورم، انتفاخ	*tawarrum, intifākh*
tumescent (adj)	منتفخ، متورم	*muntafikh, mutawarrim*
tumid (adj)	منتفخ، ناتئ	*muntafikh, nāti'*
tumidity (n)	تورم، نفنفة	*tawarrum, nafnafah*
tumorous (adj)	ورمي	*waramī*
tumour (tumor)	ورم، خراج	*waram, khurāj*
tumult (n)	فوضى، شغب، جلبة	*fawḍā, shaghab, jalabah*
tumultuous (adj)	متقلقل، مضطرب	*mutaqalqil, muḍṭarib*
tumulus (n)	ركام من تراب	*rukām min turāb*
tun (n)	تن، برميل للخمر	*tunn, birmīl lil khamr*
tune (n)	لحن، نغم	*laḥn, naghm*
tune (v)	دوزن، تناغم	*dawzana, tanāghama*

tuneful (adj)	مؤتلف الصوت، موزون النغم	*mu'talifuṣ ṣaut, mauzūnun naghm*
tuneless (adj)	غير متآلف، غير منسجم	*ghair muta'ālif, ghair munsajim*
tune-up (n)	شد الأوتار، دوزنة	*shaddul autār, dawzanah*
tunic (n)	سترة ضيقة	*sutrah ḍayyiqah*
tunnel (n)	نفق، سرداب	*nafaq, sirdāb*
turban (n)	تربان، عمامة	*turbān, 'imāmah*
turbaned (adj)	معمم	*mu'ammam*
turbid (adj)	كدر، مشوش	*kadir, mushawwash*
turbidity (turbidness)	كدورة، عكر	*kudūrah, 'akar*
turbulence (n)	شغب، ضوضاء	*shaghab, ḍauḍā'*
turbulent (adj)	مشاغب، هائج	*mushāghib, hā'ij*
turbulently (adv)	بشغب، باضطراب	*bi shaghab, biḍṭirāb*
turf (n)	مرج، خث	*marj, khuthth*
turgid (adj)	طنان، ممل	*ṭannān, mumill*
Turk (n)	شخص تركي	*shakhṣ turkī*
Turkey (n)	تركيا	*turkiyā*
Turkish (adj/n)	تركي، لغة تركية	*turkī, lughah turkiyyah*
turmeric (n)	كركم	*kurkum*
turmoil (n)	اضطراب، اهتياج	*iḍṭirāb, ihtiyāj*
turn (n)	قلب، دورة، تحول	*qalb, daurah, taḥawwul*
turn (v)	قلب، أدار، حول	*qallaba, adāra, ḥawwala*
turn aside	رد، أمال	*radda, amāla*
turn back	أعاد، رجع	*a'āda, raja'a*
turncoat (n)	مرتد	*murtadd*
turn down	رفض، رد	*rafaḍa, radda*
turner (n)	مشتغل في الخراطة	*mushtaghil fil khirāṭah*
turning (n)	تحول، انعطاف	*taḥawwul, in'iṭāf*
turning point	نقطة التحول	*nuqṭatut taḥawwul*
turn into	حول، تحول	*ḥawwala, taḥawwala*
turnip (n)	لفت، سلجم	*lift, saljam*

turnkey (n)	سجان	*sajjān*
turn off	صرف، طرد	*ṣarafa, ṭarada*
turnpike (n)	طريق رئيسية	*ṭarīq ra'īsiyyah*
turn over	قلب، انقلب	*qallaba, inqalaba*
turn out	طرد، أبعد	*ṭarada, ab'ada*
turnstile (n)	باب دوار	*bāb dawwār*
turntable (n)	مائدة دوارة	*mā'idah dawwārah*
turn up	ظهر، رجع	*ẓahara, raja'a*
turpitude (n)	شناعة، دناءة	*shanā'ah, danā'ah*
turret (n)	برج صغير، حصن صغير	*burj ṣaghīr, ḥiṣn ṣaghīr*
turtle (n)	سلحفاة	*sulaḥfāt*
turtle-dove	قمرية	*qumriyyah*
tusk (n)	ناب الفيل	*nābul fīl*
tussle (n)	صراع، شجار	*ṣirā', shijār*
tussle (v)	تصارع، تشاجر	*taṣāra'a, tashājara*
tut (interj)	صه، اسكت	*ṣah, uskut*
tutelage (n)	وصايا، حماية	*waṣāyā, ḥimāyah*
tutelary (adj)	وصائي، حامٍ	*waṣā'ī, ḥāmin*
tutor (n)	معلم خصوصي	*mu'allim khuṣūṣī*
tutor (v)	درس، علم	*darrasa, 'allama*
tutorial (n)	درس خصوصي	*dars khuṣūṣī*
tutorial (adj)	متعلق بمعلم خصوصي	*muta'alliq bi mu'allim khuṣūṣī*
twaddle (n)	هذيان، هذر	*hadhayān, hadhar*
twain (n)	زوج	*zawj*
twang (n)	رنين، غنة	*ranīn, ghunnah*
tweet (n)	سقسقة	*saqsaqah*
twelfth (adj)	ثاني عشر	*thānī 'ashara*
twelve (n)	اثنا عشر	*ithnā 'ashara*
twentieth (adj)	عشرون	*'ishrūn*
twenty (n)	عشرون	*'ishrūn*
twice (adv)	مرتين	*marratain*
twiddle (v)	فتل، عبث	*fatala, 'abatha*

twig (n)	عسلوج، غصن صغير	*'uslūj, ghuṣn ṣaghīr*
twig (v)	أدرك، لاحظ	*adraka, lāḥaẓa*
twiggy (adj)	كثير الغصينات	*kathīrul ghuṣaināt*
twilight (n)	شفق، نور الغسق	*shafaq, nūrul ghasaq*
twin (n)	توأمة، صنو	*tau'amah, ṣinw*
twin (v)	زاوج، ألحق	*zāwaja, alḥaqa*
twine (n)	خيط قنب	*khaiṭu qinnab*
twine (v)	فتل، جدل، لف	*fatala, jadala, laffa*
twinge (n)	وخز، ألم مفاجئ	*wakhz, alam mufāji'*
twinkle (n)	ومضة، تلألأ	*wamḍah, tala'lu'*
twinkle (v)	تلألأ، لمع	*tala'la'a, lama'a*
twinkling (n)	طرفة عين	*ṭarfatu 'ain*
twirl (v)	فتل، دار، انفتل	*fatala, dāra, infatala*
twist (n)	انفتال، التواء، فتلة	*infitāl, iltiwā', fatlah*
twist (v)	تلوى، انفتل، برم	*talawwā, infatala, barama*
twit (v)	سخر، هت	*sakhira, hatta*
twitch (n)	نتشة، ارتعاش	*natshah, irti'āsh*
twitch (v)	نتش، خطف	*natasha, khaṭafa*
twitchy (adj)	عصبي، متأثر	*'aṣabī, muta'aththir*
twitter (v)	زقزق، سقسق	*zaqzaqa, saqsaqa*
twitter (n)	تغريد، زقزقة	*taghrīd, zaqzaqah*
twittery (adj)	عصبي المزاج	*'aṣabiyyul mizāj*
two (n)	اثنان، اثنتان	*ithnān, ithnatān*
two-faced (adj)	ذو وجهين	*dhū wajhain*
twofold (adj/adv)	مضاعف، بصورة مضاعفة	*muḍā'af, bi ṣūrah muḍā'afah*
two-seater (n)	ذات المقعدين	*dhātul maq'adain*
twosome (n)	زوج	*zawj*
two-way (n)	ذو سكتين	*dhū sikkatain*
type (n)	نوع، طراز، حرف مطبعي	*nau', ṭirāz, ḥarf maṭba'ī*
type (v)	طبع على الآلة الكاتبة	*ṭaba'a 'alal ālah al kātibah*

typesetter (n)	منضد الحروف المطبعية	*munaḍḍidul ḥurūf al maṭba'iyyah*
typewriter (n)	آلة كاتبة	*ālah kātibah*
typhoid (n)	حمى تيفية	*ḥummā tīfiyyah*
typhoon (n)	تيفون، إعصار شديد	*tīfūn, i'ṣār shadīd*
typical (adj)	نموذجي، مثالي	*namūdhajī, mithālī*
typically (adv)	نموذجيًا	*namūdhajiyyan*
typify (v)	مثل، صور	*maththala, ṣawwara*
typist (n)	مشتغل على الآلة الكاتبة	*mushtaghil 'alal ālah al kātibah*
typographer (n)	منضد الحروف	*munaḍḍidul ḥurūf*
typographic (adj)	مطبعي	*maṭba'ī*
typography (n)	طباعة الحروف	*ṭibā'atul ḥurūf*
tyrannical (adj)	استبدادي	*istibdādī*
tyrannically (adv)	باستبداد، بجور	*bistibdād, bi jawr*
tyrannize,-ise (v)	طغى، استبد	*ṭaghā, istabadda*
tyrannous= tyrannical		
tyranny (n)	استبداد، طغيان، جور	*istibdād, ṭughyān, jawr*
tyrant (n)	مستبد، ظالم	*mustabidd, ẓālim*
tyre = tire		
tzar (n)	قيصر	*qaiṣar*

U

udder (n)	ضرع	*ḍar'*
ugliness (n)	بشاعة، شناعة	*bashā'ah, shanā'ah*
ugly (adj)	قبيح، شنيع	*qabīḥ, shanī'*
ulcer (n)	قرحة	*qarḥah*
ulcerate (v)	تقرح، قرح	*taqarraḥa, qarraḥa*
ulceration (n)	تقرح، قرحة	*taqarruḥ, qarḥah*
ulcerous (adj)	متقرح، تقرحي	*mutaqarriḥ, taqarruḥī*
ulterior (adj)	خفي، خلفي، أقصى	*khafī, khalfī, aqṣā*

ultimate (adj)	أخير، نهائي	*akhīr, nihā'ī*
ultimate (n)	نهاية، شيء نهائي	*nihāyah, shay' nihā'ī*
ultimately (adv)	في النهاية، أخيراً	*fin nihāyah, akhīran*
ultimatum (n)	قرار أخير، إنذار	*qarār akhīr, indhār*
ululate (v)	عال، نبح	*'āla, nabaḥa*
umber (n)	صباغ أحمر داكن	*ṣibāgh aḥmar dākin*
umbilical (adj)	سري	*surrī*
umbilical cord	حبل سري	*ḥabl surrī*
umbilicus (n)	سرة، وسط	*surrah, wasaṭ*
umbrella (n)	شمسية، مظلة	*shamsiyyah, miẓallah*
umpire (n)	حكم، فيصل	*ḥakam, faiṣal*
umpire (v)	حكم، فصل بين	*ḥakama, faṣala baina*
unabashed (adj)	غير خجلان	*ghair khajlān*
unabated (adj)	غير هامد	*ghair hāmid*
unable (adj)	عاجز، ضعيف	*'ājiz, ḍa'īf*
unabridged (adj)	غير مختصر	*ghair mukhtaṣar*
unacceptable (adj)	غير مقبول، مرفوض	*ghair maqbūl, marfūḍ*
unaccompanied (adj)	غير مستصحب، وحده	*ghair mustaṣḥab, waḥdah*
unaccountable (adj)	غير مسؤول	*ghair mas'ūl*
unaccustomed (adj)	غير معتاد	*ghair mu'tād*
unacknowledged	غير مسلم به	*ghair musallam bih*
unadulterated (adj)	خالص، غير مشوب	*khāliṣ, ghair mashūb*
unaffected (adj)	غير متأثر	*ghair muta'aththir*
unalloyed (adj)	خالص، محض	*khāliṣ, maḥḍ*
unanimity (n)	إجماع، اتحاد	*ijmā', ittiḥād*
unanimous (adj)	متفق عليه	*muttafaq 'alaih*
unanimously (adv)	بالإجماع، باتحاد الآراء	*bil ijmā', bittiḥādil ārā'*
unanswerable (adj)	قاطع، لا يجاب	*qāṭi', lā yujāb*
unarmed (adj)	أعزل، غير مدرع	*a'zal, ghair mudarra'*
unasked (adj)	غير مطلوب، اختياري	*ghair maṭlūb, ikhtiyārī*
unassuming (adj)	غير مدعٍ	*ghair mudda'in*

unattached (adj)	منفصل، غير متصل	*munfaṣil, ghair muttaṣil*
unavailing (adj)	غير مفيد، هدر	*ghair mufīd, hadr*
unavoidable (adj)	لا مناص منه	*lā manāṣ minh*
unaware (adj)	غافل، غير منتبه	*ghāfil, ghair muntabih*
unbalance (v)	خبل	*khabbala*
unbalanced (adj)	غير متوازن	*ghair mutawāzin*
unban (v)	رفع المغلاق	*rafa'al mighlāq*
unbearable (adj)	لا يحتمل	*lā yuḥtamal*
unbeatable (adj)	لا يهزم	*lā yuhzam*
unbeaten (adj)	غير مهزوم، غير مطروق	*ghair mahzūm, ghair maṭrūq*
unbecoming (adj)	لا يليق	*lā yalīq*
unbelief (n)	كفر، عدم إيمان	*kufr, 'adamu īmān*
unbelievable (adj)	لا يصدق	*lā yuṣaddaq*
unbeliever (n)	كافر، غير مؤمن	*kāfir, ghair mu'min*
unbelieving (adj)	غير مصدق	*ghair muṣaddiq*
unbend (v)	قوم، استقام	*qawwama, istaqāma*
unbending (adj)	عنيد، غير ميال	*'anīd, ghair mayyāl*
unbidden (adj)	غير مطلوب، غير مدعو	*ghair maṭlūb, ghair mad'ū*
unborn (adj)	لم يولد	*lam yūlad*
unbounded (adj)	غير محدود، غير متناهٍ	*ghair maḥdūd, ghair mutanāhin*
unbowed (adj)	غير مخضع	*ghair mukhḍa'*
unbridled (adj)	لا لجام لـــه	*lā lijāma lahu*
unbroken (adj)	غير منقطع، غير مكسور	*ghair munqaṭi', ghair maksūr*
unburden (v)	أراح، أنزل الحمل	*arāḥa, anzalal ḥiml*
uncalled-for (adj)	غير ضروري	*ghair ḍarūrī*
uncanny (adj)	غير طبيعي، غريب	*ghair ṭabī'ī, gharīb*
uncared-for (adj)	لم يعن به	*lam yu'na bih*
unceasing (adj)	متواصل، مستمر	*mutawāṣil, mustamirr*
unceasingly (adv)	باستمرار، بغير انقطاع	*bistimrār, bighairi inqiṭā'*

unceremonious (adj)	غير رسمي	*ghair rasmī*
uncertain (adj)	غير واثق، مشكوك	*ghair wāthiq, mashkūk*
uncertainty (n)	شك، تردد	*shakk, taraddud*
uncharitable (adj)	غير متسامح، جاف	*ghair mutasāmiḥ, jāfin*
uncharted (adj)	غير مدونً	*ghair mudawwan*
unchecked (adj)	لا يكبح	*lā yukbaḥ*
uncivil (adj)	غير متمدن، همجي	*ghair mutamaddin, hamajī*
uncle (n)	عم، خال	*'amm, khāl*
unclean (adj)	قذر، وسخ	*qadhir, wasikh*
uncomfortable (adj)	غير مريح، متعب	*ghair murīḥ, mut'ib*
uncomfortably (adv)	بضيق، بدون راحة	*bi ḍīq, bidūn rāḥah*
uncommitted (adj)	غير ملتزم	*ghair multazim*
uncommon (adj)	غير عادي، غير مألوف	*ghair 'ādī, ghair ma'lūf*
uncommonly (adv)	بغرابة، بطريق غير مألوف	*bi gharābah, bi ṭarīq ghair ma'lūf*
uncompromising	عنيد، لا يلين	*'anīd, lā yalīn*
unconcern (n)	عدم مبالاة	*'adamu mubālāt*
unconcerned (adj)	غير مبالٍ	*ghair mubālin*
unconditional (adj)	بلا شرط، مطلق	*bilā sharṭ, muṭlaq*
unconditioned (adj)	غير مشروط	*ghair mashrūṭ*
unconfirmed (adj)	غير مثبت	*ghair muthbat*
unconscious (adj)	فاقد الوعي، مغمىً عليه	*fādidul wa'y, mughman 'alaih*
unconsciously (adv)	بلا وعي	*bilā wa'y*
unconsciousness (n)	فقدان الوعي	*fuqdānul wa'y*
unconsidered (adj)	غير مروى فيه	*ghair murawwan fīh*
uncouth (n)	غريب، فظ، خشن	*gharīb, faẓẓ, khashin*
uncover (v)	كشف، عرى	*kashafa, 'arrā*
uncurl (v)	سدل	*sadala*
uncut (adj)	غير مقطوع	*ghair maqṭū'*
undaunted (adj)	باسل، مقدام	*bāsil, miqdām*

undecided (adj)	غير مجزوم	*ghair majzūm*
undeclared (adj)	غير مصرح	*ghair muṣarraḥ*
undeniable (n)	لا يجحد، محتوم	*lā yujḥad, maḥtūm*
under (prep)	تحت، أدنى	*taḥta, adnā*
underclothes (n)	ملابس تحتية	*malābis taḥtiyyah*
undercoat (n)	سترة تحتية	*sitrah taḥtiyyah*
undercurrent (n)	تيار تحتي	*tayyār taḥtī*
underdeveloped (adj)	ناقص النمو	*nāqiṣun numuww*
underdone (adj)	ناقص النضج	*nāqiṣun naḍj*
underestimate (n)	تقدير، بخس	*taqdīr, bakhs*
underexpose (v)	عرض تعريضاً ناقصاً	*'arraḍa ta'rīḍan nāqiṣan*
underexposure (n)	تعريض ناقص	*ta'rīḍ nāqiṣ*
undergarment (n)	ثوب تحتي	*thawb taḥtī*
undergo (v)	اجتاز، كابد	*ijtāza, kābada*
underground (n)	تحت سطح الأرض	*taḥta saṭḥil arḍ*
undergrowth (n)	فروة تحتية	*farwah taḥtiyyah*
underhand (adj)	سرى، محتال	*sirrī, muḥtāl*
underline (v)	رسم خطاً تحت العبارة	*rasama khaṭṭan taḥtal 'ibārah*
underlining (n)	شخص تافه	*shakhṣ tāfih*
undermentioned (adj)	مذكور أدناه	*madhkūr adnāhu*
undermine (v)	حفر، فوض	*ḥafara, fawwaḍa*
underneath (prep/adv)	تحت، في الأسفل	*taḥta, fil asfal*
undernourished (adj)	منقوص التغذية	*manqūṣut taghdhiyah*
undernourishment	نقص التغذية	*naqṣut taghdhiyah*
underpants (n)	سروال تحتي	*sirwāl taḥtī*
underpass (n)	مجاز سفلي	*majāz suflī*
underprivileged (adj	فقير، معدم	*faqīr, mu'dim*
underrate (v)	بخس التقدير	*bakhasat taqdīr*
underscore = underline		
underside (n)	جانب سفلي	*jānib suflī*

undersigned (adj)	موقع أدناه	*muwaqqa' adnāhu*
understand (v)	أدرك، فهم	*adraka, fahima*
understandable (adj)	سهل الفهم	*sahlul fahm*
understanding (n)	إدراك، فهم	*idrāk, fahm*
understood (adj)	مفهوم	*mafhūm*
undertake (v)	تولى، تكفل	*tawallā, takaffala*
undertaking (n)	مشروع، عمل	*mashrū', 'amal*
undertone (n)	صوت خفيض	*ṣaut khafīḍ*
undervalue (v)	بخس التقييم	*bakhasat taqyīm*
underwater (adj)	كائن تحت الماء	*kā'in taḥtal mā'*
underwear (n)	ثوب تحتي	*thaub taḥtī*
underweight (adj)	أخف من السوي	*akhaff minas sawī*
underworld (n)	أرض تحتي	*arḍ taḥtī*
underwriter (n)	ضامن التعهد	*ḍāminut ta'ahhud*
undeserved (adj)	غير مستأهل	*ghair musta'hil*
underservedly (adv)	بعدم استحقاق	*bi 'adami istiḥqāq*
undesirable (adj)	غير مرغوب فيه	*ghair marghūb fīh*
undignified (adj)	سافل، غير وجيه	*sāfil, ghair wajīh*
undivided (adj)	غير منقسم	*ghair munqasim*
undo (v)	أفسد، أبطل، حل	*afsada, abṭala, ḥalla*
undoing (n)	حل، خراب	*ḥall, kharāb*
undone (adj)	معطل، مفكوك	*mu'aṭṭal, mafkūk*
undoubted (adj)	لا شك فيه	*lā shakka fīh*
undoubtedly (adv)	دون شك، يقيناً	*dūna shakk, yaqīnan*
undress (v)	خلع الثياب، عرى	*khala'ath thiyāb, 'arrā*
undressed (adj)	مجرد من الملابس	*mujarrad minal malābis*
undue (adj)	غير لازم، غير مناسب	*ghair lāzim, ghair munāsib*
undulate (v)	تموج، تراوح	*tamawwaja, tarāwaḥa*
undulation (n)	تموج، ترجح	*tamawwuj, tarajjuḥ*
unduly (adv)	بإفراط	*bi ifrāṭ*
undying (adj)	سرمدي، خالد	*sarmadī, khālid*

unearth (v)	كشف، أخرج	*kashafa, akhraja*
unearthly (adj)	روحي، غير مادي	*rūḥī, ghair māddī*
uneasily (adv)	باضطراب، بقلق	*biḍṭirāb, bi qalaq*
uneasiness (n)	اضطراب، قلق	*iḍṭirāb, qalaq*
uneasy (adj)	قلق، مضطرب	*qaliq, muḍṭarib*
uneatable (adj)	لا يصلح للأكل	*lā yaṣluḥ lil akl*
uneducated (adj)	غير مثقف	*ghair muthaqqaf*
unemployed (adj)	عاطل عن العمل	*'āṭil 'anil 'amal*
unemployment (n)	بطالة	*baṭālah*
unending (adj)	لا نهاية لــه	*lā nihāyah lahu*
unequal (adj)	غير مستوٍ، غير كفؤ	*ghair mustawin, ghair kufu'*
unequivocal (adj)	جلي، صريح	*jalī, ṣarīḥ*
unerring (adj)	سديد، لا يخطئ	*sadīd, lā yukhṭi'*
uneven (adj)	غير مستوٍ، وعر	*ghair mustawin, wa'ir*
unexpected (adj)	غير متوقع	*ghair mutawaqqa'*
unexpectedly (adv)	فجأةً	*faj'atan*
unfailing (adj)	صائب، لا يكل	*ṣā'ib, lā yakill*
unfair (adj)	غير أمين، غير عادل	*ghair amīn, ghair 'ādil*
unfaithful (adj)	خائن، غير أمين	*khā'in, ghair amīn*
unfaithfulness (n)	خيانة، عدم أمانة	*khiyānah, 'adamu amānah*
unfamiliar (adj)	غير مألوف، غير معروف	*ghair ma'lūf, ghair ma'rūf*
unfamiliarity (n)	غرابة، عدم ألفة	*gharābah, 'adamu ulfah*
unfathomable (adj)	لا يسبر غوره	*lā yusbar ghauruh*
unfeigned (adj)	مخلص، صادق	*mukhliṣ, ṣādiq*
unfit (adj)	غير ملائم، غير مناسب	*ghair mulā'im, ghair munāsib*
unfold (v)	فض، نشر	*faḍḍa, nashara*
unforeseen (adj)	غير متوقع	*ghair mutawaqqa'*

unforgettable (adj)	لا ينسى	*lā yunsā*
unformed (adj)	غير مشكل	*ghair mushakkal*
unfortunate (adj)	تعيس، سيء الحظ	*ta'īs, sayyi'ul ḥaẓẓ*
unfortunately (adv)	لسوء الحظ	*li sū'il ḥaẓẓ*
unfounded (adj)	لا أساس لـــه	*lā asāsa lahu*
unfriendly (adj)	غير ودي، خصيم	*ghair wudddī, khaṣīm*
unfurl (v)	نشر، انتشر	*nashara, intashara*
ungainly (adj)	بشع، أخرق	*bashi', akhraq*
ungracious (adj)	فظ، غليظ	*faẓẓ, ghalīẓ*
ungrateful (adj)	ناكر المعروف	*nākirul ma'rūf*
unguarded (adj)	غير مصون	*ghair maṣūn*
unhappily (adv)	بتعاسة، باكتئاب	*bi ta'āsah, bikti'āb*
unhappiness (n)	تعاسة، هم	*ta'āsah, hamm*
unhappy (adj)	كئيب، حزين	*ka'īb, ḥazīn*
unhealthy (adj)	ضار، غير صحي	*ḍārr, ghair ṣiḥḥī*
unheard (adj)	غير مسموع	*ghair masmū'*
unheard-of (adj)	لم يسمع به	*lam yusma' bih*
unholy (adj)	غير مقدس، دنس	*ghair muqaddas, danis*
uniform (adj)	وحيد النسق، مستوٍ	*waḥīdun nasaq, mustawin*
uniform (n)	بزة رسمية	*bizzah rasmiyyah*
uniformed (adj)	مبزز	*mubazzaz*
uniformity (n)	اتساق، انتظام	*ittisāq, intiẓām*
unify (v)	وحد	*waḥḥada*
unilateral (adj)	أحادي الجانب	*uḥādiyyul jānib*
unimpeachable (adj)	بلا عيب، بريء	*bilā 'aib, barī'*
uninformed (adj)	جاهل، غير دارٍ	*jāhil, ghair dārin*
unintelligible (adj)	غامض، غير مفهوم	*ghāmiḍ, ghair mafhūm*
uninvited (adj)	غير مدعو	*ghair mad'ū*
uninviting (adj)	غير جذاب	*ghair jadhdhāb*
union (n)	اتحاد، وئام	*ittiḥād, wi'ām*
unionist (n)	اتحادي	*ittiḥādī*
unique (adj)	وحيد، فريد	*waḥīd, farīd*

unison (n)	انسجام، ائتلاف	*insijām, i'tilāf*
unit (n)	وحدة	*waḥdah*
unitarian (n)	موحد	*muwaḥḥid*
unite (v)	ربط، وحد	*rabaṭa, waḥḥada*
united (adj)	متحد، ملتئم	*muttaḥid, multa'im*
unity (n)	اتفاق، اتحاد	*ittifāq, ittiḥād*
universal (adj)	عالمي، عام، شامل	*'ālamī, 'ām, shāmil*
universality (n)	شمولية، عمومية	*shumūliyyah, 'umūmiyyah*
universally (adv)	بوجه العموم، عموماً	*bi wajhil 'umūm, 'umūman*
universe (n)	كون، عالم	*kaun, 'ālam*
university (n)	جامعة، مدرسة	*jāmi'ah, madrasah*
unjust (adj)	جائر، غير منصف	*jā'ir, ghair munṣif*
unjustifiable (adj)	لا عذر لـه	*lā 'udhra lahu*
unkind (adj)	قاسٍ، عديم الشفقة	*qāsin, 'adīmush shafaqah*
unkindly (adv)	بقسوة، بفظاظة	*bi qaswah, bi faẓāẓah*
unkindness (n)	قسوة، فظاظة	*qaswah, faẓāẓah*
unknowing (adj)	جاهل، غير مطلع	*jāhil, ghair muṭṭala'*
unknowingly (adv)	بغير علم، عن جهل	*bi ghairi 'ilm, 'an jahl*
unknown (adj)	مجهول، غير معروف	*majhūl, ghair ma'rūf*
unknown (n)	شخص أو شيء مجهول	*shakhṣ au shay' majhūl*
unlawful (adj)	غير شرعي، محظور	*ghair shar'ī, maḥẓūr*
unlawfully (adv)	بطريق غير شرعي	*bi ṭarīq ghair shar'ī*
unleash (v)	حرر	*ḥarrara*
unless (conj)	إلا، ما لم	*illā, mā lam*
unlettered (adj)	أمي، غير متعلم	*ummī, ghair muta'allim*
unlike (adj)	مغاير، مخالف	*mughāyir, mukhālif*
unlike (prep)	بخلاف	*bi khilāf*
unlikely (adj)	بعيد الوقوع، غير محتمل	*ba'īdul wuqū', ghair muḥtamal*
unlimited (adj)	غير محدود، مطلق	*ghair maḥdūd, muṭlaq*
unlisted (adj)	غير مدرج	*ghair mudraj*

unload (v)	فرغ الشحونة	*farraghash shuḥūnah*
unlock (v)	فض، فتح، صرر	*faḍḍa, fataḥa, ṣarrara*
unlocked-for (adj)	غير مرتقب	*ghair murtaqab*
unloose (v)	أرخى، استرخى	*arkhā, istarkhā*
unluckily (adv)	لسوء الحظ	*li sū'il ḥaẓẓ*
unlucky (adj)	مشؤوم، تعيس	*mash'ūm, ta'īs*
unman (v)	خصى، أضعف	*khaṣā, aḍ'afa*
unmanly (adj)	عديم الرجولة، جبان	*'adīmur rujūlah, jabān*
unmanned (adj)	مجرد عن الرجال	*mujarrad 'anir rijāl*
unmarried (adj)	أعزب، غير متزوج	*a'zab, ghair mutazawwij*
unmask (v)	خلع الأقنعة	*khala'al aqni'ah*
unmindful (adj)	متغافل، غير منتبه	*mutaghāfil, ghair muntabih*
unmistakable (adj)	واضح، صريح	*wāḍiḥ, ṣarīḥ*
unmitigated (adj)	تام، كامل	*tāmm, kāmil*
unmoved (adj)	رابط الجأش، ثابت	*rābiṭul ja'sh, thābit*
unnatural (adj)	غير طبيعي	*ghair ṭabī'ī*
unnaturally (adv)	بطريق غير طبيعي	*bi ṭarīq ghair ṭabī'ī*
unnecessarily (adv)	بطريق غير ضروري	*bi ṭarīq ghair ḍarūrī*
unnecessary (adj)	غير ضروري	*ghair ḍarūrī*
unnumbered (adj)	لا يعد	*lā yu'add*
unoccupied (adj)	شاغر، غير مشغول	*shāgir, ghair mashghūl*
unofficial (adj)	غير رسمي	*ghair rasmī*
unorthodox (adj)	غير تقليدي	*ghair taqlīdī*
unpack (v)	فك، أفرغ	*fakka, afragha*
unpaid (adj)	بلا أجرة، غير مدفوع	*bilā ujrah, ghair madfū'*
unpalatable (adj)	غير شهي، غير لذيذ	*ghair shahiyy, ghair ladhīdh*
unparalleled (adj)	لا مثيل لــه	*lā mathīla lahu*
unpleasant (adj)	بغيظ، كريه	*baghīẓ, karīh*
unpopular (adj)	غير شعبي، غير مقبول	*ghair sha'bī, ghair maqbūl*
unprecedented (adj)	لم يسبق مثله	*lam yusbaq mithluh*

unprejudiced (adj)	غير متحيز	*ghair mutaḥayyiz*
unpretentious (adj)	متواضع، بسيط	*mutawāḍi', basīṭ*
unprofessional (adj)	غير محترف	*ghair muḥtarif*
unprompted (adj)	تلقائي، عفوي	*tilqā'ī, 'afwī*
unpunished (adj)	غير معاقب	*ghair mu'āqab*
unqualified (adj)	عديم الأهلية، غير مؤهل	*'adīmul ahliyyah, ghair mu'ahhal*
unquestionable (adj)	لا نزاع فيه، أكيد	*lā nizā' fīh, akīd*
unquite (adj)	قلق، غير هادئ	*qaliq, ghair hādi'*
unravel (v)	حل، فك	*ḥalla, fakka*
unread (adj)	غير مقروء	*ghair maqrū'*
unreal (adj)	زائف، غير حقيقي	*zā'if, ghair ḥaqīqī*
unreasonable (adj)	بالغ، غير ضروري	*bāligh, ghair ḍarūrī*
unreel (v)	كر، انكر	*karra, inkarra*
unrelenting (adj)	غير منقطع، صارم	*ghair munqaṭi', ṣārim*
unreserved (adj)	غير متحفظ، مخلص	*ghair mutaḥaffiẓ, mukhliṣ*
unreservedly (adv)	بصراحة، بغير تحفظ	*bi ṣarāḥah, bi ghairi taḥaffuẓ*
unrest (n)	اضطراب، هياج	*iḍṭirāb, hiyāj*
unrestrained (adj)	غير مضبوط، مطلق	*ghair maḍbūṭ, muṭlaq*
unrestricted (adj)	غير محصور، غير مقيد	*ghair maḥṣūr, ghair muqayyad*
unripe (adj)	غير ناضج، فج	*ghair nāḍij, fajj*
unroll (v)	كشف، بسط	*kashafa, basaṭa*
unruffled (adj)	أملس، هادئ	*amlas, hādi'*
unruly (adj)	شديد الشكيمة، جامح	*shadīdush shakīmah, jāmiḥ*
unsaid (adj)	لم يذكر	*lam yudhkar*
unsaturated (adj)	غير مشبع	*ghair mushabba'*
unsavoury (unsavory	تفه، كريه	*tafih, karīh*
unscathed (adj)	غير مصاب بجرح	*ghair muṣāb bi jurḥ*
unscrew (v)	فك لولباً	*fakka laulaban*

unscrupulous (adj)	خليع، عديم الضمير	*khalī', 'adīmuḍ ḍamīr*
unseemliness (n)	عدم ملاءمة	*'adamu mulā'amah*
unseemly (adj)	غير ملائم، شائن	*ghair mulā'im, shā'in*
unseen (adj)	غير مرئي	*ghair mar'ī*
unsettle (v)	أزعج، شوش	*az'aja, shawwasha*
unsettled (adj)	غير مستقر، مضطرب	*ghair mustaqirr, muḍṭarib*
unsightly (adj)	قبيح المنظر، شنيع	*qabīḥul manẓar, shanī'*
unskilled (adj)	غير بارع	*ghair bāri'*
unsociable (adj)	غير أنيس، متوحد	*ghair anīs, mutawaḥḥid*
unsocial = antisocial		
unsolicited (adj)	بلا طلب، عفواً	*bilā ṭalab, 'afwan*
unsophisticated (adj	ساذج، طبيعي	*sādhij, ṭabī'ī*
unsound (adj)	غير راسخ، ركيك، فاسد	*ghair rāsikh, rakīk, fāsid*
unsparing (adj)	سخي، كريم، جزيل	*sakhī, karīm, jazīl*
unspeakable (adj)	لا يوصف	*lā yūṣaf*
unstable (adj)	غير مستقر، متقلب	*ghair mustaqirr, mutaqallib*
unsteady (adj)	متقلب، غير ثابت	*mutaqallib, ghair thābit*
unstuck (adj)	غير مثبت	*ghair muthabbat*
unstudied (adj)	غير متكلف، طبيعي	*ghair mutakallaf, ṭabī'ī*
unsuccessful (adj)	غير ناجح	*ghair nājiḥ*
unsure (adj)	غير متأكد	*ghair muta'akkid*
untangle (v)	فك، حل	*fakka, ḥalla*
unthinkable (adj)	لا يتصور	*lā yutaṣawwar*
untidy (adj)	وسخ، غير مرتب	*wasikh, ghair murattab*
until (conj/prep)	إلى أن، حتى، إلى	*ilā an, ḥattā, ilā*
untimely (adj)	قبل أوانه	*qabla awānih*
untold (adj)	لا يعبر عنه	*lā yu'abbar 'anhu*
untouchable (n)	منبوذ، مطروح	*mambūdh, maṭrūḥ*
untoward (adj)	سؤوم، نحس	*sa'ūm, naḥs*
untried (adj)	غير مجرب	*ghair mujarrab*

untrue (adj)	كاذب، غير حقيقي	*kādhib, ghair ḥaqīqī*
untruth (n)	كذب، عدم دقة	*kidhb, 'adamu diqqah*
untutored (adj)	ساذج، بسيط	*sādhij, basīṭ*
unused (adj)	غير مستعمل، غير معتاد	*ghair musta'mal, ghair mu'tād*
unusual (adj)	غير اعتيادي، نادر	*ghair i'tiyādī, nādir*
unusually (adv)	نادراً، شاذًّا	*nādiran, shādhdhan*
unutterable (adj)	لا ينطق به، لا يوصف	*lā yunṭaq bih, lā yūṣaf*
unvarnished (adj)	غير مصقول، بسيط	*ghair maṣqūl, basīṭ*
unveil (v)	كشف النقاب	*kashafan niqāb*
unwanted (adj)	غير مطلوب	*ghair maṭlūb*
unwarranted (adj)	غير مرخص	*ghair murakhkhaṣ*
unwary (adj)	متهور، مهمل	*mutahawwir, muhmil*
unwholesome (adj)	ضار، غير صحي	*ḍārr, ghair ṣiḥḥī*
unwilling (adj)	كاره، ممتنع	*kārih, mumtani'*
unwillingly (adv)	كرهاً، بلا رغبة	*kurhan, bilā raghbah*
unwise (adj)	غبي، غير بصير	*ghabī, ghair baṣīr*
unwisely (adv)	من غير بصيرة	*min ghairi baṣīrah*
unwitting (adj)	غير متعمد	*ghair muta'ammid*
unwittingly (adv)	بغير عمد أو قصد	*bighairi 'amad aw qaṣd*
unwonted (adj)	غير معتاد، غير مألوف	*ghair mu'tād, ghair ma'lūf*
unworldly (adj)	غير أرضي، روحي	*ghair arḍī, rūḥī*
unworthy (adj)	غير لائق، غير مستحق	*ghair lā'iq, ghair mustaḥiqq*
unwritten (adj)	غير مكتوب	*ghair maktūb*
unyielding (adj)	عنيد، لا يلين	*'anīd, lā yalīn*
up (adv/prep)	فوق، فما فوق	*fauqa, famā fauqa*
upbeat (adj)	مبتهج، متفائل	*mubtahij, mutafā'il*
upbraid (v)	وبخ، عنف	*wabbakha, 'annafa*
upbringing (n)	تربية، تنشئة	*tarbiyah, tanshi'ah*

update (v/n)	حدث، تحديث	*ḥaddatha, taḥdīth*
upgrade (v)	رفع إلى درجة أعلى	*rafa'a ilā darajah a'lā*
upheaval (n)	تعالٍ، جيشان	*ta'ālin, jayashān*
uphill (adj)	صاعد، شاق	*ṣā'id, shaqq*
uphill (adv)	صعداً	*ṣu'udan*
uphold (v)	عضد، دعم	*'aḍḍada, da'ama*
upholster (n)	نجد	*najjada*
uplift (v)	نهض، رفع	*nahaḍa, rafa'a*
uplift (n)	نهوض، ارتفاع	*nuhūḍ, irtifā'*
upon (prep)	فوق، على	*fauqa, 'alā*
upper (adj)	أعلى، فوقاني	*a'lā, fauqānī*
upper (n)	فرعة	*far'ah*
uppermost (adj)	أرفع، أعلى	*arfa', a'lā*
uppermost (adv)	نحو الأعلى	*naḥwal a'lā*
uppish (adj)	معتد بنفسه، مغرور	*mu'tad bi nafsih, maghrūr*
upright (adj)	عمودي، مستقيم	*'amūdī, mustaqīm*
uprising (n)	ثورة	*thaurah*
uproar (n)	ضوضاء، اضطراب	*ḍauḍā', iḍṭirāb*
uproarious (adj)	مضطرب، صاخب	*muḍṭarib, ṣākhib*
uproot (v)	استأصل، قلع	*ista'ṣala, qala'a*
upset (v)	أزعج، شوش، أفسد	*az'aja, shawwasha, afsada*
upset (n)	إفساد، قلق	*ifsād, qalaq*
upshot (n)	حاصل، نتيجة	*ḥāṣil, natījah*
upstage (adj)	في مؤخر المسرح	*fī mu'akhkharil masraḥ*
upstairs (adj)	أعلى، علوي	*a'lā, 'alawī*
upstairs (n)	دور أعلى	*daur a'lā*
upstairs (adv)	إلى دور أعلى	*ilā daur a'lā*
upstanding (adj)	صحيح، قويم، مستقيم	*ṣaḥīḥ, qawī, mustaqīm*
upstart (n)	محدث ثروة	*muḥdathu tharwah*
upstream (adj)	ضد التيار	*ḍiddat tayyār*
upsurge (n)	ارتفاع مفاجئ	*irtifā' mufāji'*

upswing (n)	حركة صاعدة	*ḥarakah ṣā'idah*
up-to-date (adj)	عصري، حديث	*'aṣrī, ḥadīth*
upward (adj)	أعلى، صاعد	*a'lā, ṣā'id*
upward,-ds (adv)	أكثر من، فصاعداً	*aktharu min, faṣā'idan*
uranium (n)	يورانيوم	*yūrāniyūm*
urban (adj)	مديني، حضري	*madīnī, ḥaḍarī*
urbane (adj)	لطيف، ظريف، مصقول	*laṭīf, ẓarīf, maṣqūl*
urbanity (n)	دماثة، لطف	*damāthah, luṭf*
urbanize,-ise (v)	مدن	*maddana*
Urdu (n)	لغة أردية	*lughah urdiyyah*
urea (n)	بولة، يوريا	*baulah, yūriyā*
ureter (n)	حالب	*ḥālib*
urethra (n)	إحليل، مجرى البول	*iḥlīl, majral baul*
urge (v)	استحث، حرض	*istaḥaththa, ḥarraḍa*
urge (n)	إلحاح، حث	*ilḥāḥ, ḥathth*
urgency (n)	إلحاح، اضطرار	*ilḥāḥ, iḍṭirār*
urgent (adj)	ضروري، لازب	*ḍarūrī, lāzib*
urgently (adv)	باستعجال، بسرعة	*bisti'jāl, bi sur'ah*
uric (adj)	بولي	*baulī*
uric acid	حامض بولي	*ḥāmiḍ baulī*
urinal (n)	مبولة	*mibwalah*
urinary (adj)	بولي، مختص بالبول	*baulī, mukhtaṣṣ bil baul*
urinate (v)	بال، شخ	*bāla, shakhkha*
urine (n)	بول	*baul*
urn (n)	ظرف، وعاء، جرة	*ẓarf, wi'ā', jarrah*
us (pron)	نا (ضمير المتكلم)	*nā*
usable (adj)	صالح للاستعمال	*ṣāliḥ lil isti'māl*
usage (n)	استعمال، عادة	*isti'māl, 'ādah*
use (v)	استعمل، عامل	*ista'mala, 'āmala*
use (n)	استعمال، فائدة	*isti'māl, fā'idah*
used (adj)	مستعمل، مستخدم	*musta'mal, mustakhdam*
useful (adj)	مفيد، نافع	*mufīd, nāfi'*

useless (adj)	غير مفيد، عقيم	*ghair mufīd, ʻaqīm*
user (n)	مستعمل	*mustaʻmil*
usher (n)	مرشد في مسرح	*murshid fī masraḥ*
usher (v)	أدخل، أرشد	*adkhala, arshada*
usual (adj)	معتاد، مألوف	*muʻtād, ma'lūf*
usually (adv)	اعتياداً، عادةً	*iʻtiyādan, ʻādatan*
usurer (n)	مراب	*murābin*
usurp (v)	اغتصب السلطة	*ightaṣabas sulṭah*
usury (n)	مراباة، ربا	*murābāt, ribā*
utensil (n)	إناء، أداة	*inā', adāt*
uterine (adj)	مختص بالرحم	*mukhtaṣṣ bir raḥim*
uterus (n)	رحم، محبل	*raḥim, maḥbil*
utilitarian (adj)	منفعي	*manfaʻī*
utility (n)	منفعة، فائدة	*manfaʻah, fā'idah*
utilize,-ise (v)	انتفع، استخدم	*intafaʻa, istakhdama*
utmost (adj)	أقصى، آخر	*aqṣā, ākhir*
utmost (n)	حد أقصى	*ḥadd aqṣā*
utter (v)	تفوه، نطق	*tafawwaha, naṭaqa*
utter (adj)	مطلق، كلي	*muṭlaq, kullī*
utterance (n)	تفوه، نطق	*tafawwuh, nuṭq*
utterly (adj)	تماماً، كليةً	*tamāman, kulliyyatan*
uttermost = utmost		

V

vacancy (n)	شغور، فراغ	*shughūr, farāgh*
vacant (adj)	شاغر، خالٍ	*shāghir, khālin*
vacate (v)	أفرغ، أبطل	*afragha, abṭala*
vacation (n)	عطلة، فراغ	*ʻuṭlah, farāgh*
vaccinate (v)	لقح ضد الجدري	*laqqaḥa ḍiddal judarī*
vaccination (n)	تلقيح، تطعيم	*talqīḥ, taṭʻīm*
vaccine (n)	لقاح، فكسين	*liqāḥ, faksīn*

vacillate (v)	تردد، تذبذب	*taraddada, tadhabdhaba*
vacillation (n)	تردد، تذبذب	*taraddud, tadhabdhub*
vacuity (n)	فراغ، فقدان	*farāgh, fuqdān*
vacuous (adj)	خلو، غبي	*khilw, ghabī*
vacuum (n)	فراغ، خلو، خواء	*farāgh, khuluww, khawā'*
vacuum cleaner	مكنسة كهربائية	*miknasah kahrabā'iyyah*
vacuum tube	صمام مفرغ	*ṣimām mufarragh*
vagary (n)	وهم، تخيل	*wahm, takhayyul*
vagina (n)	مهبل	*mahbil*
vaginal (adj)	مهبلي	*mahbilī*
vagrancy (n)	تشرد، ضلال	*tasharrud, ḍalāl*
vagrant (adj)	متشرد، متجول	*mutasharrid, mutajawwil*
vague (adj)	مبهم، غامض	*mubham, ghāmiḍ*
vagueness (n)	غموض، إبهام	*ghumūḍ, ibhām*
vain (adj)	مغتر، باطل	*mughtarr, bāṭil*
vainly (adv)	عبثاً، هدراً	*'abathan, hadran*
vainness (n)	عبث، سدًى	*'abath, sudan*
valance (n)	ستارة قصيرة	*sitārah qaṣīrah*
vale (n)	وهدة، وادٍ	*wahdah, wādin*
validiction (n)	توديع، وداع	*taudi', wadā'*
validictory (adj)	توديعي، وداعي	*taudī'ī, wadā'ī*
validictory (n)	خطبة الوداع	*khuṭbatul wadā'*
valentine (n)	بطاقة غرامية، محبوبة	*biṭāqah gharāmiyyah, maḥbūbah*
Valentine's Day	عيد القديس فالنتين	*'īdul qiddīs fālintīn*
valet (n)	وصيف،خادم خصوصي	*waṣīf, khādim khuṣūṣī*
valiant (adj)	باسل، شجيع	*bāsil, shajī'*
valid (adj)	شرعي، قانوني	*shar'ī, qānūnī*
validate (v)	جعل الشيء شرعيًا	*ja'alash shay' shar'iyyan*
validity (n)	شرعية، جواز	*shar'iyyah, jawāz*
valise (n)	حقيبة سفر، شنطة	*ḥaqībatu safar, shanṭah*
valley (n)	وادٍ	*wādin*

valour (valor)	بسالة، شجاعة	*basālah, shajā'ah*
valuable (adj)	ثمين، نفيس، قيم	*thamīn, nafīs, qayyim*
valuables (n)	أشياء ذات قيمة	*ashyā' dhāta qīmah*
valuation (n)	قيمة، تثمين	*qīmah, tathmīn*
value (v)	ثمن، قدر	*thammana, qaddara*
value (n)	قيمة، قدر، أهمية	*qīmah, qadr, ahammiyyah*
valueless (adj)	عديم القيمة، تافه	*'adīmul qīmah, tāfih*
valve (n)	مصراع، صمام	*miṣrā', ṣimām*
valvular (adj)	صمامي، مصراعي	*ṣimāmī, miṣrā'ī*
vamp (n)	وجه الحذاء	*wajhul ḥidhā'*
vampire (n)	هامة، مصاصة	*hāmah, maṣṣāṣah*
van (n)	عربة لنقل البضائع	*'arabah li naqlil baḍā'i'*
vandal (n)	مخرب الممتلكات	*mukharribul mumtalakāt*
vandalism (n)	تخريب الممتلكات	*takhrībul mumtalakāt*
vandalize,-ise (v)	خرب الممتلكات العامة	*kharrabal mumtalakāt al 'āmmah*
vane (n)	دوارة الهواء	*dawwāratul hawā'*
vanguard (n)	مقدمة، طليعة الجيش	*muqaddamah, ṭalī'atul jaish*
vanish (v)	زال، تلاشى	*zāla, talāshā*
vanishing-point (n)	نقطة التلاشي	*nuqṭatut talāshī*
vanity (n)	تفاهة، خيلاء	*tafāhah, khuyalā'*
vanquish (v)	تغلب على، قهر	*taghallaba 'alā, qahara*
vantage (n)	أفضلية، امتياز	*afḍaliyyah, imtiyāz*
vapid (adj)	مسيخ، تفه	*masīkh, tafih*
vapidity (n)	تفاهة، ابتذال	*tafāhah, ibtidhāl*
vaporization,-isation	تبخير، تبخر	*tabkhīr, tabakhkhur*
vaporize,-ise (v)	بخر، تبخر	*bakhkhara, tabakhkhara*
vaporizer,-iser (n)	مبخرة	*mubakhkhirah*
vaporous (adj)	بخاري، سريع الزوال	*bukhārī, sarī'uz zawāl*
vapour (vapor) (n)	بخار، وهم	*bukhār, wahm*
variability (n)	امكانية التحول	*imkāniyyatut taḥawwul*

variable (adj)	قابل التغيير، متحول	*qābitut taghyīr, mutaḥawwil*
variance (n)	تباين، مغايرة، اختلاف	*tabāyun, mughāyarah, ikhtilāf*
variant (adj)	متباين، مختلف	*mutabāyin, mukhtalif*
variation (n)	اختلاف، تغيير	*ikhtilāf, taghyīr*
varied (adj)	مختلف، متنوع	*mukhtalif, mutanawwi'*
variegated (adj)	ملون، منوع	*mulawwan, munawwa'*
variegation (n)	تلون، ترقش	*talawwun, taraqqush*
variety (n)	صنف، ضرب، تنوع	*ṣanf, ḍarb, tanawwu'*
various (adj)	متنوع، مختلف، متعدد	*mutanawwi', mukhtalif, muta'addid*
varnish (n)	ورنيش، برنيق	*warnīsh, barnīq*
varnish (v)	ورنش، زين	*warnasha, zayyana*
varsity (n)	جامعة	*jāmi'ah*
vary (v)	اختلف، تغير	*ikhtalafa, taghayyara*
vascular (adj)	وعائي، مختص بالأوعية الدموية	*wi'ā'ī, mukhtaṣṣ bil au'iyatid damawiyyah*
vase (n)	زهرية	*zuhriyyah*
vaseline (n)	مرهم الفازلين	*marhamul fāzlīn*
vassal (n)	مقطع	*muqṭa'*
vassalage (n)	مقطعية	*muqṭa'iyyah*
vast (adj)	فسيح، عظيم، ضخم	*fasīḥ, 'aẓīm, ḍakhm*
vastness (n)	انفساح، اتساع	*infisāḥ, ittisā'*
vat (n)	راقود، دن	*rāqūd, dann*
vault (n)	عقد، قبو، سرداب	*'aqd, qabw, sirdāb*
vault (v)	وثب، قفز	*wathaba, qafaza*
vaulted (adj)	مقنطر، مقبو	*muqanṭar, maqbuww*
vaunt (v)	تبجح، فاخر	*tabajjaḥa, fākhara*
veer (v)	أدار، غير إتجاه	*adāra, ghayyara ittijāh*
vegetable (n)	نبات من الخضر	*nabāt minal khuḍar*
vegetarian (n)	نباتي	*nabātī*

vegetate (v)	عاش خاملاً	*'āsha khāmilan*
vegetation (n)	نبات، خضار	*nabāt, khaḍār*
vehemence (n)	اتقاد، حدة	*ittiqād, ḥiddah*
vehement (adj)	حاد، متقد	*ḥādd, muttaqid*
vehemently (adv)	بشدة، بحدة	*bi shiddah, bi ḥiddah*
vehicle (n)	عربة، مركبة	*'arabah, markabah*
veil (n)	حجاب، ستار	*ḥijāb, sitār*
veil (v)	ستر، حجب	*satara, ḥajaba*
vein (n)	عرق، وريد	*'irq, warīd*
veined (adj)	معرق، كثير العروق	*mu'arraq, kathīrul 'urūq*
velar (adj/n)	حلقي، صوت حلقي	*ḥalqī, ṣaut ḥalqī*
velocity (n)	سرعة الضوء	*sur'atuḍ ḍaw*
velour (n)	مخمل، فيلور	*mukhmal, failūr*
velvet (n)	مخمل، قطيفة	*mukhmal, qaṭīfah*
venal (adj)	قابل للرشوة، يرتشى	*qābil lir rishwah, yurtashā*
venality (n)	ارتشاء، فساد	*irtishā', fasād*
vend (v)	باع، أشهر	*bā'a, ashhara*
vendetta (n)	ثأر	*tha'r*
vendor (n)	بائع	*bā'i'*
veneer (n)	قشرة خشبية	*qishrah khashabiyyah*
venerable (adj)	موقر، مكرم	*muwaqqar, mukarram*
venerate (v)	وقر، احترم	*waqqara, iḥtarama*
venereal disease	مرض تناسلي	*maraḍ tanāsulī*
vengeance (n)	أخذ الثأر، انتقام	*akhdhuth tha'r, intiqām*
vengeful (adj)	منتقم، حقود	*muntaqim, ḥaqūd*
venial (adj)	عرضي، صغير	*'araḍī, ṣaghīr*
venom (n)	سم، ضغينة	*summ, ḍaghīnah*
venomous (adj)	سام، حقود	*sāmm, ḥaqūd*
venous (adj)	وريدي، عرقي	*warīdī, 'irqī*
vent (n)	منفس، منفذ	*manfas, manfadh*
ventilate (v)	هوى، جدد الهواء	*hawwā, jaddadal hawā'*

ventilation (n)	تهوية، تجديد الهواء	*tahwiyah, tajdīdul hawā'*
ventilator (n)	مهواة، مروحة التهوية	*mihwāt, mirwaḥatut tahwiyah*
ventral (adj)	بطني	*baṭnī*
venture (v/n)	غامر، مغامرة	*ghāmara, mughāmarah*
venturesome (adj)	مغامر، مقدام	*mughāmir, miqdām*
venue (n)	مكان، موقع الحدوث	*makān, mauqi'ul ḥudūth*
Venus (n)	زهرة	*zuhrah*
veracious (adj)	صادق، صحيح	*ṣādiq, ṣaḥīḥ*
veracity (n)	صدق، صحة	*ṣidq, ṣiḥḥah*
veranda (verandah)	شرفة واسعة	*shurfah wāsi'ah*
verb (n)	فعل	*fi'l*
verbal (adj)	فعلي، شفهي	*fi'lī, shafahī*
verbalize,-ise (v)	عبر بألفاظ	*'abbara bi alfāẓ*
verbally (adv)	شفهيا، لفظيا	*shafahiyyan, lafẓiyyan*
verbal noun	اسم فعلي	*ism fi'lī*
verbosity (n)	إسهاب، إطناب	*ishāb, iṭnāb*
verdancy (n)	اخضرار، خضرة	*ikhḍirār, khuḍrah*
verdant (adj)	أخضر، ساذج	*akhḍar, sādhij*
verdict (n)	حكم، رأي، قرار	*ḥukm, ra'y, qarār*
verge (v)	أشرف، انحرف	*ashrafa, inḥarafa*
verge (n)	شفا، حافة	*shafā, ḥāffah*
verifiable (adj)	ممكن إثباته	*mumkin ithbātuh*
verification (n)	تحقيق، إثبات	*taḥqīq, ithbāt*
verify (v)	حقق، أثبت	*ḥaqqaqa, athbata*
verily (adv)	حقاً، حقيقةً	*ḥaqqan, ḥaqīqatan*
verisimilitude (n)	أرجحية الصحة	*arjaḥiyyatuṣ ṣiḥḥah*
veritable (adj)	حقيقي، واقعي	*ḥaqīqī, wāqi'ī*
verity (n)	صدق، صحة، حقيقة	*ṣidq, ṣiḥḥah, ḥaqīqah*
vermin (n)	حشرات، هوام	*ḥasharāt, hawāmm*
verminous (adj)	دودي، قذر	*dūdī, qadhir*
vernacular (n)	لغة عامية	*lughah 'āmiyah*

vernal (adj)	مختص بالربيع	*mukhtaṣṣ bir rabī‘*
versatile (adj)	طليق الحركة، متقلب	*ṭalīqul ḥarakha, mutaqallib*
verse (n)	مقطع شعري، شعر	*maqṭa‘ shi‘rī, shi‘r*
versed (adj)	متضلع، بارع	*mutaḍalli‘, bāri‘*
versification (n)	نظم الشعر	*naẓmush shi‘r*
versifier (n)	ناظم، شاعر	*nāẓim, shā‘ir*
versify (v)	نظم الأشعار	*naẓẓamal ash‘ār*
version (n)	نسخة، ترجمة	*nuskhah, tarjamah*
versus (n)	ضد، مقابل	*ḍidd, muqābil*
vertex (n)	قمة، رأس	*qimmah, ra’s*
vertical (adj/n)	عمودي، خط عمودي	*‘amūdī, khaṭṭ ‘amūdī*
vertically (adv)	رأسيًا، عموديًا	*ra’siyyan, ‘amūdiyyan*
vertigo (n)	دوخة، دوار	*daukhah, duwār*
verve (n)	حيوية، تحمس	*ḥayawiyyah, taḥammus*
very (adv)	جدًا، للغاية	*jiddan, lil ghāyah*
very (adj)	نفس، مجرد	*nafs, mujarrad*
vesicle (n)	حويصلة	*ḥuwaiṣalah*
vesicular (adj)	حويصلي	*ḥuwaiṣalī*
vespers (n)	صلاة المساء	*ṣalātul masā’*
vessel (n)	سفينة، مركب، وعاء	*safīnah, markab, wi‘ā’*
vest (n/v)	صدرة، ألبس	*ṣudrah, albasa*
vestibule (n)	ردهة، رواق	*radhah, riwāq*
vestige (n)	أثر، بقية	*athar, baqiyyah*
vestigial (adj)	أثري	*atharī*
vestment (n)	حلة، ثوب	*ḥullah, thaub*
vet (v/n)	فحص، بيطار	*faḥaṣa, baiṭār*
veteran (n)	شخص ممرس	*shakhṣ mumarras*
veterinary (adj)	بيطري	*baiṭarī*
veto (n)	فيتو، حق الرفض	*fītū, ḥaqqur rafḍ*
vex (v)	أثار، غاظ	*athāra, ghāẓa*
vexation (n)	إغاظة، إغضاب	*ighāẓah, ighḍāb*

vexatious (adj)	مغيظ، مكدر	*mughīẓ, mukaddir*
via (prep)	عن طريق، بواسطة	*'an ṭarīq, bi wāsiṭah*
viable (adj)	قابل للتطبيق	*qābil lit taṭbīq*
viaduct (n)	جسر طويل	*jisr ṭawīl*
vibrancy (n)	اهتزاز، نشاط	*ihtizāz, nashāṭ*
vibrant (adj)	مهتز، نابض بالحياة	*muhtazz, nābiḍ bil ḥayāt*
vibrate (v)	هز، ارتج	*hazza, irtajja*
vibration (n)	اهتزاز، خطران	*ihtizāz, khaṭarān*
vibrator (n)	هزازة	*hazzāzah*
vibratory	اهتزازي	*ihtizāzī*
vicar (n)	قس، كاهن	*qiss, kāhin*
vicarage (n)	بيت القس	*baitul qiss*
vicarous (adj)	بديلي	*badīlī*
vice (n)	عيب، رذيلة	*'aib, radhīlah*
viceregal (adj)	متعلق بنائب الملك	*muta'alliq bi nā'ibil malik*
viceroy (n)	نائب الملك، والٍ	*nā'ibul malik, wālin*
vice versa	والعكس بالعكس	*wal 'aks bil 'aks*
vicinity (n)	قرب، جوار	*qurb, jiwār*
vicious (adj)	رديء، فاسد، شرير	*radī', fāsid, shirrīr*
vicissitude (n)	تقلب، تغير	*taqallub, taghayyur*
victim (n)	ضحية، فريسة	*ḍaḥiyyah, farīsah*
victimize,-ise (v)	ضحى، غدر	*ḍaḥḥā, ghadara*
victor (n)	منتصر، غالب	*muntaṣir, ghālib*
victorious (adj)	منتصر، ظافر	*muntaṣir, ẓāfir*
victory (n)	نصر، غلبة	*naṣr, ghalabah*
victuals (n)	مؤن، أطعمة	*mu'an, aṭ'imah*
vide (v)	راجع، انظر	*rāji', unẓur*
video (n)	فيديو	*fīdyū*
videotape (n)	شريط تلفزيوني	*sharīṭ tilfizyūnī*
vie (v)	تنافس، سابق	*tanāfasa, sābaqa*
view (n)	رأي، منظر، معاينة	*ra'y, manẓar, mu'āyanah*

view (v)	عاين، فحص، رأى	*'āyana, faḥaṣa, ra'ā*
viewer (n)	معاين، مشاهد	*mu'āyin, mushāhid*
vigil (n)	مراقبة، سهر	*murāqabah, sahar*
vigilance (n)	احتراس، حذر	*iḥtirās, ḥadhar*
vigilant (adj)	حذر، منتبه	*ḥadhir, muntabih*
vignette (n)	نقش صغير	*naqsh ṣaghīr*
vigorous (adj)	شديد، قوي	*shadīd, qawī*
vigorously (adv)	بقوة، بشدة	*bi quwwah, bi shiddah*
vigour (vigor) (n)	قوة، نشاط، شدة	*quwwah, nashāṭ, shiddah*
vile (adj)	وضيع، رذيل، دنيء	*waḍī', radhīl, danī'*
vilification = defamation		
vilify (v)	ذم، سب	*dhamma, sabba*
villa (n)	فيلة، دارة	*fīllah, dārah*
village (n)	قرية، ضيعة	*qaryah, ḍai'ah*
villager (n)	قروي، فلاح	*qarawī, fallāḥ*
villain (n)	وغد، نذل	*waghd, nadhl*
villainous (adj)	رذيل، خسيس	*radhīl, khasīs*
villainy (n)	نذالة، خسة	*nadhālah, khissah*
vim (n)	قوة، نشاط	*quwwah, nashāṭ*
vindicate (v)	برر، برأ	*barrara, barra'a*
vindication (n)	تبرئة، تزكية	*tabri'ah, tazkiyah*
vindicative (adj)	انتقامي، حقود	*intiqāmī, ḥaqūd*
vine (n)	كرمة، كرم العنب	*karmah, karmul 'inab*
vinegar (n)	خل، حمض	*khall, ḥimḍ*
vineyard (n)	مزرعة الكرمة	*mazra'atul karmah*
vinous (adj)	خمري	*khamrī*
vintage (n)	غلة الكرمة	*ghallatul karmah*
violate (v)	انتهك الحرمة، اغتصب	*intahakal ḥurmah, ightaṣaba*
violation (n)	هتك العرض، اغتصاب	*hatkul 'irḍ, ightiṣāb*
violator (n)	منتهك، مغتصب	*muntahik, mughtaṣib*
violence (n)	شدة، عنف، قسوة	*shiddah, 'unf, qaswah*

violent (adj)	عنيف، قاسٍ، شديد	*'anīf, qāsin, shadīd*
violently (adv)	بشدة، بعنف	*bi shiddah, bi 'unf*
violet (n/adj)	بنفسج، بنفسجي	*banafsaj, banafsajī*
violin (n)	كمان	*kamān*
violinist (n)	عازف الكمان	*'āziful kamān*
viper (n)	أفعى سامة	*af'ā sāmmah*
viral (adj)	فيروسي	*fairūsī*
virgin (n/adj)	عذراء، بكر	*'adhrā', bikr*
virginal (adj)	عذري، بتولي	*'udhrī, batūlī*
virginity (n)	بكارة، عزوبة	*bakārah 'uzūbah*
virile (adj)	رجولي، قوي	*rajūlī, qawī*
virility (n)	رجولة، قوة	*rujūlah, quwwah*
virtual (adj)	عملي، حقيقي	*'amalī, ḥaqīqī*
virtually (adv)	عمليًا، في الواقع	*'amaliyyan, fil wāqi'*
virtue (n)	خاصية، فضل، تأثير	*khāṣṣiyyah, faḍl, ta'thīr*
virtuous (adj)	عفيف، بار، صالح	*'afīf, bārr, ṣāliḥ*
virtuousness (n)	فعالية، تأثير	*fa''āliyyah, ta'thīr*
virulence (n)	فوعة، تسمم، غل	*fau'ah, tasammum, ghill*
virulent (adj)	سام، مؤذٍ، قاسٍ	*sāmm, mu'dhin, qāsin*
virus (n)	فيروس، سم	*fīrūs, summ*
visa (n)	تاشيرة	*tāshīrah*
visage (n)	مظهر، سيماء	*maẓhar, sīmā'*
vis-à-vis (prep)	مقابل، مواجه	*muqābil, muwājih*
viscosity (n)	لزوجة، تدبق	*luzūjah, tadabbuq*
viscous (adj)	دبق، لزج	*dabiq, lazij*
visibility (n)	ظهور، رؤية	*ẓuhūr, ru'yah*
visible (adj)	مرئي، ظاهر	*mar'ī, ẓāhir*
visibly (adv)	بظهور، عياناً	*bi ẓuhūr, 'iyānan*
vision (n)	رؤية، تخيل، خيال	*ru'yah, takhayyul, khayāl*
visionary (adj)	خيالي، وهمي	*khayālī, wahmī*
visit (n)	زيارة، عيادة	*ziyārah, 'iyādah*
visit (v)	زار، عاد	*zāra, 'āda*

visitation (n)	تفتيش، معاينة	*taftīsh, mu'āyanah*
visiting card	بطاقة الزيارة	*biṭāqatuz ziyārah*
visiting professor	أستاذ زائر	*ustādh zā'ir*
visitor (n)	زائر، عائد	*zā'ir, 'ā'id*
visor (n)	مقدمة الخوذة	*muqaddamatul khūdhah*
vista (n)	مشهد، منظر	*mushhad, manẓar*
visual (adj)	بصري، مرئي، منظور	*baṣarī, mar'ī, manẓūr*
visualize,-ise (v)	تخيل، تصور	*takhayyala, taṣawwara*
vital (adj)	حيوي، نشيط، محيي	*ḥayawī, nashīṭ, muḥyī*
vitality (n)	حيوية، نشاط	*ḥayawiyyah, nashāṭ*
vitalize,-ise (v)	أحيى، نشط	*aḥyā, nashshaṭa*
vitals (n)	أعضاء حيوية	*a'ḍā' ḥayawiyyah*
vitamin (n)	حيمين، فيتامين	*ḥayamīn, fītāmīn*
vitiate (v)	أفسد، أتلف	*afsada, atlafa*
vitiation (n)	تلف، إتلاف، فساد	*talaf, itlāf, fasād*
vitreous (adj)	شبيه بالزجاج	*shabīh biz zujāj*
vituperate (v)	عاب، قدح	*'āba, qadaḥa*
vituperation (n)	قدح، توبيخ عنيف	*qadḥ, taubīkh 'anīf*
vituperative (adj)	قدحي، توبيخي	*qadḥī, taubīkhī*
vivacious (adj)	رشيق، نشيط، مرح	*rashīq, nashīṭ, mariḥ*
vivaciousness (n)	رشاقة، حيوية	*rashāqah, ḥayawiyyah*
vivacity (n)	مرح، نشاط، حيوية	*maraḥ, nashāṭ, ḥayawiyyah*
viva voce (n)	امتحان شفهي	*imtiḥān shafahī*
viva voce (adj/adv)	شفهي، شفهيًا	*shafahī, shafahiyyan*
vivid (adj)	زاه، بهي، جلي	*zāhin, bahī, jalī*
vividly (adv)	بحماسة، بجلاء	*bi ḥamāsah, bi jalā'*
vividness (n)	زهو، انتعاش	*zuhuww, inti'āsh*
viviparous (adj)	ولود	*walūd*
vivisection (n)	تشريح الأعضاء	*tashrīḥul a'ḍā'*
vixen (n)	أنثى الثعلب	*unthath tha'lab*
viz	أعني، أي	*a'nī, ay*

vocabulary (n)	مجموعة كلمات	*majmū'atu kalimāt*
vocal (adj)	صوتي، لفظي	*ṣautī, lafẓī*
vocal cords	أوتار صوتية	*autār ṣautiyyah*
vocalist (n)	مغني، مطرب	*mughnī, muṭrib*
vocalize,-ise (v)	لفظ، نطق	*lafaẓa, naṭaqa*
vocally (adv)	لفظيًا، نطقيًا	*lafẓiyyan, nuṭqiyyan*
vocation (n)	وظيفة، مهنة، نداء	*waẓīfah, mihnah, nidā'*
vocational (adj)	مهني، حرفي	*mihnī, ḥirfī*
vocative (adj/n)	ندائي، صيغة المنادى	*nidā'ī, ṣīghatul munādā*
vociferate (v)	صاح، هتف	*ṣāḥa, hatafa*
vociferous (adj)	صاخب، هاتف	*ṣākhib, hātif*
vogue (n)	زي شائع	*ziyy shā'i'*
voice (n)	صوت، تعبير	*ṣaut, ta'bīr*
voice (v)	لفظ، عبر	*lafaẓa, 'abbara*
voiceless (adj)	صامت، عديم الصوت	*ṣāmit, 'adīmuṣ ṣaut*
void (n)	فجوة، فراغ	*fajwah, farāgh*
void (adj)	خلو، شاغر، فارغ	*khilw, shāghir, fārigh*
volatile (adj)	متقلب، متبخر	*mutaqallib, mutabakhkhir*
volcanic (adj)	بركاني، متفجر	*burkānī, mutafajjir*
volcano (n)	بركان، جبل نار	*burkān, jabalu nār*
vole (n)	فول	*faul*
volition (n)	اختيار، خيار	*ikhtiyār, khiyār*
volley (n)	انطلاق الرصاصات في وقت واحد	*inṭilāqur raṣāṣāt fī waqt wāḥid*
volley-ball (n)	كرة طائرة	*kurah ṭā'irah*
volt (n)	فلط، وحدة كهربائية	*fulṭ, waḥdah kahrabā'iyyah*
voltage (n)	قوة التيار الكهربائي	*quwwatut tayyār al kahrabā'ī*
volte-face	تغيير المبدأ	*taghyīrul mabda'*
voluble (adj)	طلق اللسان، مهذار	*ṭalqul lisān, mihdhār*
volume (n)	حجم، مجلد	*ḥajm, mujallad*

voluminous (adj)	ضخم، عظيم الجرم	*ḍakhm, ʻaẓīmul jirm*
volantarily (adv)	طوعاً، عن طيب خاطر	*au'an, 'an ṭibi khāṭir*
volantary (adj)	طوعي، اختياري	*ṭau'ī, ikhtiyārī*
volantary (n)	قطعة من موسيقي أرغن	*qiṭ'ah min mausīqī urghun*
volanteer (v/n)	تطوع، متطوع	*taṭawwa'a, mutaṭawwi'*
voluptuary (adj)	حسي، شبق	*ḥissī, shabiq*
voluptuous (adj)	متنعم، شهواني	*mutana''im, shahwānī*
voluptuousness (n)	شهوانية، تنعم	*shahwāniyyah, tana''um*
volute (n)	شكل حلزوني	*shakl ḥalazūnī*
voluted (adj)	حلزوني، لولبي	*ḥalazūnī, laulabī*
vomit (v/n)	تقيأ، قيء	*taqayya'a, qay'*
voracious (adj)	شره، جشع	*sharih, jashi'*
voracity (n)	شراهة، جشع	*sharāhah, jasha'*
vortex (n)	دردور، دوامة	*durdūr, duwwāmah*
votary (n)	مريد، عابد مخلص	*murīd, 'ābid mukhliṣ*
vote (n)	صوت، انتخاب، رأي	*ṣaut, intikhāb, ra'y*
vote (v)	انتخب، اقترع	*intakhaba, iqtara'a*
voter (n)	ناخب، مقترع، مصوت	*nākhib, muqtari', muṣawwit*
vouch (v)	ضمن، استشهد	*ḍamina, istashhada*
voucher (n)	إيصال، رجعة	*īṣāl, raj'ah*
vouchsafe (v)	منح، وهب، تعطف	*manaḥa, wahaba, ta'aṭṭafa*
vow (v)	نذر، تعهد	*nadhara, ta'ahhada*
vow (n)	نذر، عهد	*nadhr, 'ahd*
vowel (n)	حرف علة، حرف لين	*ḥarfu 'illah, ḥarfu līn*
voyage (n)	رحلة بحرية	*riḥlah baḥriyyah*
voyage (v)	سافر، اجتاز	*sāfara, ijtāza*
voyager (n)	مسافر بحراً	*musāfir baḥran*
voyeur = peeper		
vulcanite (n)	مطاط صلد، فلكنيت	*maṭṭāṭ ṣald, fulkanīt*

vulgar (adj)	بذيء، سافل، دارج	*badhī', sāfil, dārij*
vulgarism (n)	تعبير سوقي	*ta'bīr sūqī*
vulgarity (n)	دناءة، سوقية	*danā'ah, sūqiyyah*
vulgarize,-ise (v)	أفسد، حط	*afsada, ḥaṭṭa*
vulnerability (n)	قابلية الانجراح	*qābiliyyatul injirāḥ*
vulnerable (adj)	غير حصين، عرضة للجرح	*ghair ḥaṣīn, 'urḍah lil jurh*
vulture (n)	نسر	*nasr*
vulva (n)	فرج	*farj*

W

wacky (adj)	غريب الأطوار، مضحك	*gharībul aṭwār, muḍḥik*
wad (v/n)	سطم، سطام	*saṭama, siṭām*
waddle (v)	تهادى، دلف	*tahādā, dalafa*
waddle (n)	تهادٍ، دلوف	*tahādin, dulūf*
waffle (n)	وفل	*wafl*
waft (n)	هبة ريح، موجة	*habbatu rīḥ, maujah*
wag (v)	اهتز، تهادى	*ihtazza, tahādā*
wag (n)	مضحك، مهذار	*muḍḥik, mihdhār*
wage (v)	شن حربا، خاطر	*shanna ḥarban, khāṭara*
wage (n)	أجرة، أجر	*ujrah, ajr*
waggle (v)	تهادى، اهتز	*tahādā, ihtazza*
waggle (n)	هزة، اهتزاز، تهادٍ	*hazzah, ihtizāz, tahādin*
wagon (waggon)	عربة لنقل البضائع	*'arabah li naqlil baḍā'i'*
waif (n)	شخص متشرد	*shakhṣ mutasharrid*
wail (v)	ناح، عال	*nāḥa, 'āla*
wail (n)	عويل، نواح	*'awīl, nawāḥ*
waist (n)	خصر، وسط	*khaṣr, wasaṭ*
waistcoat (n)	صدرة	*ṣudrah*
waistline (n)	خط الخصر	*khaṭṭul khaṣr*
wait (v)	انتظر، ترقب	*intaẓara, taraqqaba*

wait (n)	انتظار، ترقب	*intiẓār, taraqqub*
waiter (n)	نادل	*nādil*
waiting (n)	انتظار، توقف	*intiẓār, tawaqquf*
waiting-list (n)	قائمة الانتظار	*qā'imatul intiẓār*
waiting-room (n)	حجرة الانتظار	*ḥujratul intiẓār*
waitress (n)	نادلة، خادمة حانة	*nādilah, khādimatu ḥānah*
waive (v)	تنازل عن، تخلى عن	*tanāzala 'an, takhallā 'an*
waiver (n)	وثيقة التنازل	*wathīqatut tanāzul*
wake (v)	أيقظ، استيقظ، سهر	*ayqaẓa, istaiqaẓa, sahira*
wake (n)	سهر، يقظة	*sahar, yaqaẓah*
wakeful (adj)	منتبه، يقظ	*muntabih, yaqiẓ*
waken (v)	أيقظ، نبه	*aiqaẓa, nabbaha*
walk (n)	سير، نزهة	*sair, nuzhah*
walk (v)	مشى، سار	*mashā, sāra*
walker (n)	ماشٍ، راجل	*māshin, rājil*
waling-stick (n)	عصا	*'aṣā*
walk out (n)	إضراب عمالي	*iḍrāb 'ummālī*
wall (n)	جدار، حائط	*jidār, ḥā'iṭ*
wall (v)	سور، حوط	*sawwara, ḥawwaṭa*
wall-eyed (adj)	أبيض العينين	*abyaḍul 'ainain*
wallop (v/n)	لكم، لكمة	*lakama, lakmah*
walloping (adj)	ضخم، هائل	*ḍakhm, hā'il*
walloping (n)	ضربة عنيفة، هزيمة	*ḍarbah 'anīfah, hazīmah*
wallow (v)	تمرغ، انغمس	*tamarragha, inghamasa*
wallpaper (n)	ورق الجدران	*waraqul judrān*
walnut (n)	جوز، شجر الجوز	*jauz, shajarul jauz*
waltz (n)	رقصة الفالس	*raqṣatul fāls*
wan (adj)	باهت، شاحب	*bāhit, shāḥib*
wand (n)	صولجان، عصا الساحر	*ṣaulajān, 'aṣas sāḥir*
wander (v)	تاه، ضل، تجول	*tāha, ḍalla, tajawwala*
wander (n)	تجول، تيه	*tajawwul, tīh*
wanderer (n)	تائه، متجول	*tā'ih, mutajawwil*

wanderings (n)	تطوف، تجول	*taṭawwuf, tajawwul*
wanderlust (n)	شهوة التجوال	*shahwatut tajwāl*
wane (v)	تناقص، تضائل	*tanāqaṣa, taḍā'ala*
wanly (adv)	بشحوب، بتضاءل	*bi shuḥūb, bi taḍā'ul*
wanness (n)	شحوب، اصفرار اللون	*shuḥūb, iṣfirārul laun*
want (n)	اقتضاء، حاجة، قلة	*iqtiḍā', ḥājah, qillah*
want (v)	أراد، احتاج، أعوز	*arāda, iḥtāja, a'waza*
wanting (adj)	ناقص، مفقود	*nāqiṣ, mafqūd*
wanton (adj/n)	مستهتر، خليع، فاجر	*mustahtir, khalī', fājir*
wantonly (adv)	بخلاعة، ببطر	*bi khalā'ah, bi baṭar*
wantonness (n)	استهتار، خلاعة، تهور	*istihtār, khalā'ah, tahawwur*
war (n)	حرب، قتال	*ḥarb, qitāl*
war (v)	شن الحرب، حارب	*shannal ḥarb, hāraba*
warble (v)	غنى، غرد	*ghannā, gharrada*
war-cry (n)	هتاف الحرب	*hutāful ḥarb*
ward (n)	جناح، دائرة، قسم	*janāḥ, dā'irah, qism*
war-dance (n)	رقصة الحرب	*raqṣatul ḥarb*
warden (n)	مناظر، مراقب	*munāẓir, murāqib*
warder (n)	سجان، خفير	*sajjān, khafīr*
wardress (n)	سجانة	*sajjānah*
wardrobe (n)	صوان الملابس	*ṣiwānul malābis*
ware (n)	بضائع، سلع	*baḍā'i', sila'*
warehouse (n)	مخزن، مستودع	*makhzan, mustauda'*
warfare (n)	قتال، حرب	*qitāl, ḥarb*
warhead (n)	رأس النسيفة	*ra'sun nasīfah*
warily (adv)	بانتباه، بحذر	*bintibāh, bi ḥadhar*
wariness (n)	حذر، تحوط	*ḥadhar, taḥawwuṭ*
warlike (adj)	مولع بالحرب	*mūla' bil ḥarb*
warm (adj)	دافئ، حار، متقد	*dāfi', ḥārr, muttaqid*
warm (v)	دفّأ، دفأ، تحمس	*daffa'a, dafa'a, taḥammasa*
warm-blooded (adj)	حار الدم	*ḥārrud dam*

warm-hearted (adj)	عطوف، حنون	*'aṭūf, ḥanūn*
warm-heartedness (n)	حنان، محبة، شفقة	*ḥanān, maḥabbah, shafaqah*
warming-pan (n)	مدفأة السرر	*midfa'atus surur*
warmly (adv)	بحرارة، بحماسة	*bi ḥarārah, bi ḥamāsah*
warmonger (n)	مثير الحرب	*muthīrul ḥarb*
warmth (n)	حرارة، حماسة، دفء	*ḥarārah, ḥamāsah, dif'*
warn (v)	أنذر، نبه	*andhara, nabbaha*
warning (n)	تحذير، إنذار	*taḥdhīr, indhār*
wrap (v)	عوج، لوى، سدى	*'awija, lawā, saddā*
wrap (n)	سداة النسيج، عوج	*sadātun nasīj, 'iwaj*
warrant (v)	ضمن، فوض	*ḍamina, fawwaḍa*
warrant (n)	ضمانة، تفويض	*ḍamānah, tafwīḍ*
warrantable (adj)	ممكن تبريره، جائز	*mumkin tabrīruh, jā'iz*
warrantee (n)	ضمين	*ḍamīn*
warrant officer	ضابط صف	*ḍābiṭu ṣaff*
warrantor (n)	ضامن، كافل	*ḍāmin, kāfil*
warranty (n)	ضمانة، كفالة	*ḍamānah, kafālah*
warren (n)	مطردة	*maṭradah*
warrior (n)	جندي، محارب	*jundī, muḥārib*
warship (n)	سفينة حربية	*safīnah ḥarbiyyah*
wartime (n)	زمن الحرب	*zamanul ḥarb*
wary (adj)	حذر، متحوط	*ḥadhir, mutaḥawwiṭ*
wash (v)	غسل، غمر	*ghasala, ghamara*
wash (n)	غسل، اغتسال	*ghasl, ightisāl*
washable (adj)	قابل للغسل	*qābil lil ghasl*
wash-basin (n)	حوض الغسل	*ḥauḍul ghasl*
washboard (n)	لوح الغسل	*lauḥul ghasl*
washbowl = wahsbasin		
washerman (n)	غسال	*ghassāl*
washerwoman (n)	غسالة	*ghassālah*
washing matchine	غسالة، مغلسة	*ghassālah, mighsalah*

washing soda	صودا الغسيل	*ṣūdal ghasīl*
washroom (n)	مغسل	*maghsal*
wash-tub (n)	حوض الغسل	*ḥauḍul ghasl*
washy (adj)	شاحب، واهن	*shāḥib, wāhin*
wasp (n)	زنبور	*zumbūr*
waspish (adj)	نزق، نكد	*naziq, nakid*
wastage (n)	خسارة، نقصان	*khasārah, nuqṣān*
waste (v)	أضاع، أسرف	*aḍā'a, asrafa*
waste (n)	ضياع، نفاية، قفر	*ḍiyā', nufāyah, qafr*
waste (adj)	مبدد، مضياع	*mubaddid, miḍyā'*
wasteland (n)	أرض قاحلة	*arḍ qāḥilah*
waste product	منتجات مهملة	*muntajāt muhmalah*
watch (v)	راقب، حرس، ارتقب	*rāqaba, ḥarasa, irtaqaba*
watch (n)	مراقبة، حراسة	*murāqabah, ḥirāsah*
watch-dog (n)	كلب الحراسة	*kalbul ḥirāsah*
watcher (n)	حارس، مراقب	*ḥāris, murāqib*
watchful (adj)	منتبه، يقظ	*muntabih, yaqiẓ*
wathcmaker (n)	صانع الساعات	*ṣāni'us sā'āt*
wathcman (n)	خفير، مراقب	*khafīr, murāqib*
watch-tower (n)	برج المراقبة	*burjul murāqabah*
watchword (n)	كلمة السر	*kalimatus sirr*
water (n)	ماء، دمع	*mā', dam'*
water (v)	روى، نقع بالماء	*rawā, naqa'a bil mā'*
water-bird (n)	طير الماء	*ṭairul mā'*
water-biscuit (n)	بسكويت الماء	*biskuwītul mā'*
water-borne (adj)	منقول بالماء	*manqūl bil mā'*
water-bottle (n)	زجاجة ماء	*zujājatu mā'*
water-buffalo (n)	جاموس الماء	*jāmūsul mā'*
water-closet (n)	مرحاض	*mirḥāḍ*
water-colour (n)	لون مائي	*laun mā'ī*
water-cooled (adj)	مبرد بالماء	*mubarrad bil mā'*
waterfall (n)	شلال، هدار	*shallāl, haddār*

water-fowl (n)	طيور الماء	*ṭuyūrul mā'*
waterfront (n)	واجهة مائية	*wājihah mā'iyyah*
water-hammer (n)	طرق مائي	*ṭarq mā'ī*
water-hole (n)	ثقب مائي	*thaqb mā'ī*
water-ice (n)	مثلوجة مائية	*mathlūjah mā'iyyah*
watering-can (n)	مرشة	*mirashshah*
water-level (n)	ميزان مائي	*mīzān mā'ī*
water-lily (n)	نيلوفر	*nīlūfar*
water-line (n)	خط الماء	*khaṭṭul mā'*
water-logged (adj)	مثقل بالماء	*muthqal bil mā'*
waterman (n)	مجدف	*mujaddif*
watermark (n)	علامة مائية	*'alāmah mā'iyyah*
water-melon (n)	بطيخ أحمر	*biṭṭīkh aḥmar*
water-mill (n)	طاحونة مائية	*ṭāḥūnah mā'iyyah*
waterproof (n)	صامد للماء	*ṣāmid lil mā'*
water-ski (n)	زحلوفة مائية	*zuḥlūfah mā'iyyah*
waterspout (n)	فوهة، دردور	*fuwwahah, durdūr*
water-supply (n)	إمداد مائي	*imdād mā'ī*
water-tower (n)	برج الماء	*burjul mā'*
watery (adj)	مائي، رطب	*mā'ī, raṭb*
watt (n)	وحدة كهربائية، واط	*waḥdah kahrabā'iyyah, wāṭ*
wattage (n)	واطية	*wāṭiyyah*
wattle (n/v)	وتل، وتل	*watal, wattala*
wave (v)	تموج، موج	*tamawwaja, mawwaja*
wave (n)	موجة، تموج	*maujah, tamawwuj*
wavelet (n)	موجة صغيرة	*maujah ṣaghīrah*
waver (v)	ترنح، هدج	*tarannaḥa, tahaddaja*
waveringly (adv)	مضطرباً، مرتعشاً	*muḍṭariban, murta'ishan*
wavy (adj)	متموج، مضطرب	*mutamawwij, muḍṭarib*
wax (n/v)	شمع، شمع	*sham', shamma'a*
waxen (adj)	شمعي، أملس	*sham'ī, amlas*

wax work	تمثال من شمع	*timthāl min sham'*
waxy (adj)	ناعم، كالشمع	*nā'im, kash sham'*
way (n)	سبيل، طريقة، منوال	*sabīl, ṭarīqah, minwāl*
way (adv)	على سبيل	*'alā sabīl*
wayfarer (n)	عابر السبيل	*'ābirus sabīl*
waylay (v)	قطع الطريق	*qaṭa'aṭ ṭarīq*
wayward (adj)	متمرد، عنيد	*mutamarrid, 'anīd*
waywardness (n)	تمرد، عصيان	*tamarrud, 'iṣyān*
we (pron)	نحن	*naḥnu*
weak (adj)	ضعيف، ضئيل، واهن	*ḍa'īf, ḍa'īl, wāhin*
weaken (v)	أضعف، أوهن	*aḍ'afa, auhana*
weakling (n)	شخص ضعيف	*shakhṣ ḍa'īf*
weakly (adv)	بضعف، بوهن	*bi ḍa'f, bi wahan*
weak-minded (adj)	ضعيف العقل	*ḍa'īful 'aql*
weakness (n)	ضعف، وهن	*ḍa'f, wahan*
weal (n)	أثر الضرب، حبار	*atharuḍ ḍarb, ḥabār*
wealth (n)	ثروة، غنًى	*tharwah, ghinan*
wealthy (adj)	غني، ثري	*ghanī, tharī*
wean (n)	فطم، فصل	*faṭam, faṣl*
weapon (n)	سلاح، شوكة	*silāḥ, shaukah*
weaponery (n)	أسلحة	*asliḥah*
wear (v)	لبس، ارتدى	*labisa, irtadā*
wear (n)	ارتداء، لبس، ملابس	*irtidā', lubs, malābis*
wearily (adv)	بضجر، بسآمة	*bi ḍajar, bi sa'āmah*
weariness (n)	ملل، ضجر، تعب	*malal, ḍajar, ta'ab*
wearing (adj)	مرهق، شاق	*murhaq, shāqq*
wearisome (adj)	متعب، ممل	*mut'ib, mumill*
weary (adj)	سئم، ضجر	*sa'im, ḍajir*
weary (v)	أسئم، أتعب	*as'ama, at'aba*
weather (n)	جو، طقس	*jaww, ṭaqs*
weather (v)	تجوى، هوى	*tajawwā, hawwā*
weather-beaten (adj)	مسفوع	*masfū'*

weather-bound (adj)	موثق بحالة الجو	*mūthaq bi ḥālatil jaww*
weatherproof (adj)	صامد للجو	*ṣāmid lil jaww*
weave (v)	حبك، حاك، نسج	*ḥabaka, ḥāka, nasaja*
weave (n)	حياكة، طريقة النسج	*ḥiyākah, ṭarīqatun nasj*
weaver (n)	حائك، حباك	*ḥā'ik, ḥabbāk*
web (n)	نسج، وترة، شبكة	*nasj, watarah, shabakah*
web-footed (adj)	مكفف الأرجل	*mukaffaful arjul*
wed (v)	تزوج، ألف	*tazawwaja, allafa*
wedded (adj)	مشدود، متزوج	*mashdūd, mutazawwij*
wedding (n)	زواج، عرس، زفاف	*zawāj, 'urs, zifāf*
wedding-cake (n)	كعكة الزواج	*ka'katuz zawāj*
wedding-ring (n)	خاتم الزواج	*khātimuz zawāj*
wedge (n)	إسفين، خابور	*isfīn, khābūr*
wedlock (n)	زواج، قران	*zawāj, qirān*
Wednesday (n)	يوم الأربعاء	*yaumul arbi'ā'*
wee (adj)	صغير جدًا	*ṣaghīr jiddan*
weed (n)	عشب ضار	*'ushb ḍārr*
weedy (adj)	ملآن بالأعشاب الضارة	*mal'ān bil a'shāb aḍ ḍārrah*
week (n)	أسبوع	*usbū'*
weekday (n)	يوم الأسبوع	*yaumul usbū'*
week end	نهاية الأسبوع	*nihāyatul usbū'*
weekly (adj/adv)	أسبوعي، أسبوعيًا	*usbū'ī, usbū'iyyan*
weeny (adj)	صغير جدًا	*ṣaghīr jiddan*
weep (v)	بكى، ناح	*bakā, nāḥa*
weepy (adj)	كثير البكاء	*kathīrul bukā'*
weft (n)	لحمة النسيج	*luḥmatun nasīj*
weigh (v)	وزن، ثقل، أثقل	*wazana, thaqula, athqala*
weight (n)	وزن، ثقل، أهمية	*wazn, thiql, ahammiyyah*
weight (v)	ثقل، حمل	*thaqqala, ḥammala*
weightless (adj)	عديم الوزن، عديم الأهمية	*'adīmul wazn, 'adīmul ahammiyyah*
weight-lifting (n)	رفع الأثقال	*raf'ul athqāl*

weighty (adj)	ثقيل، شاق، خطير	*thaqīl, shāqq, khaṭīr*
weir (n)	سد، حبس	*sadd, ḥibs*
weird (adj)	عجيب، سحري، مروع	*'ajīb, siḥrī, murawwi'*
welcome (interj)	أهلاً وسهلاً	*ahlan wa sahlan*
welcome (adj/v)	مرحب به، رحب به	*murahḥab bih, raḥḥaba bih*
welcome (n)	ترحيب، ترحاب	*tarḥīb, tarḥāb*
weld (v)	ألحم، التحم	*alḥama, iltaḥama*
weld (n)	وصلة ملحومة	*wuṣlah malḥūmah*
welder (n)	لحام، آلة اللحم	*laḥḥām, ālatul laḥm*
welding (n)	لحام، لحم	*liḥām, laḥm*
welfare (n)	رفاهة، خير	*rafāhah, khair*
welfare state	دولة الرفاهة	*daulatur rafāhah*
well (n)	بئر، نبع	*bi'r, nab'*
well (adj)	جيد، حسن، بعافية	*jayyid, ḥasan, bi 'āfiyah*
well (adv)	حسناً، صواباً	*ḥasanan, ṣawāban*
well (interj)	عجباً، حسناً	*'ajaban, ḥasanan*
well-advised (adj)	صائب، حصيف	*ṣā'ib, ḥaṣīf*
well-appointed (adj)	كامل الأثاث	*kāmilul athāth*
well-being (n)	رفاهة، خير، عافية	*rafāhah, khair, 'āfiyah*
well-born (n)	كريم المحتد	*karīmul maḥtid*
well-bred (adj)	مربًى، مهذب	*murabban, muhadhdhab*
well-disposed (adj)	عاطف، ودي	*'āṭif,, wuddī*
well-done (adj)	مطهو جيداً	*maṭhuww jayyidan*
well-founded (adj)	راسخ الأثاث	*rāsikhul athāth*
well-heeled (adj)	غني، ذو ثروة	*ghanī, dhū tharwah*
well-informed (adj)	حسن الاطلاع	*ḥasanul iṭṭilā'*
well-known (adj)	معروف، شهير	*ma'rūf, shahīr*
well-nigh (adv)	تقريباً، على وشك	*taqrīban, 'alā washk*
well-spoken (adj)	فصيح، بليغ	*faṣīḥ, balīgh*
well-thought-of (adj)	حسن السمعة	*ḥasanus sum'ah*
well-timed (adj)	حسن التوقيت	*ḥasanut tauqīt*
well-wisher (n)	متمني الخير	*mutamanniyul khair*

well-worn (adj)	بالٍ، قديم	*bālin, qadīm*
Welsh (n)	لغة ويلزية	*lughah wīlziyyah*
welter (n)	اضطراب، تخبط،	*idṭirāb, takhabbuṭ,*
	اختلاط	*ikhtilāṭ*
west (n/adj)	غرب، غربي	*gharb, gharbī*
westbound (adj)	متجه نحو الغرب	*muttajih naḥwal gharb*
westerly (adj/n)	غربي، ريح غربية	*gharbī, rīḥ gharbiyyah*
western (n)	غربي، غربية	*gharbī, gharbiyyah*
westerner (n)	غربي، ساكن الغرب	*gharbī, sākinul gharb*
westernize,-ise (v)	غرب، تغرب	*gharraba, tagharraba*
westernmost (adj)	كائن في أقصى الغرب	*kā'in fī aqṣal gharb*
westward (adj)	غربي	*gharbī*
westwards (adv)	غرباً، نحو الغرب	*gharban, naḥwal gharb*
wet (adj)	مبتل، رطب	*mubtall, raṭb*
wet (v)	خضل، بلل	*khaḍḍala, ballala*
wet dock	حوض مائي	*ḥauḍ mā'ī*
wetness (n)	بلل، نداوة	*balal, nadāwah*
whacked (adj)	مضنًى، متعب	*muḍnan, mut'ab*
whacking (n)	ضربة شديدة	*ḍarbah shadīdah*
whale (n)	حوت، قيطس	*ḥūt, qaiṭas*
what (pron)	ماذا، ما، الذي	*mādhā, mā, alladhī*
what (interj)	ماذا، يا للعجب	*mādhā, yā lal 'ajab*
whatever (pron/adv)	ماذا، أي شي،	*mādhā, ayyu shay',*
	كل ما	*kullu mā*
whatsover (adv)	أيما، مهما	*ayyumā, mahmā*
wheat (n)	حنطة، قمح	*ḥinṭah, qamḥ*
wheedle (v)	كسب بالمداهنة	*kasaba bil mudāhanah*
wheel (n)	عجلة، دولاب	*'ajalah, dūlāb*
wheelchair (n)	كرسي مدولب	*kursī mudaulab*
wheeze (v)	أز، صفر	*azza, ṣafara*
wheezy (adj)	متنفس بصوت، صافر	*mutanaffis bi ṣaut, ṣāfir*
when (adv)	متى، ومن ثم	*matā, wa min thamma*

when (conj)	عندما، حينما	*'indamā, ḥīnamā*
whence (adv)	من أين	*min aina*
whenever (adv/conj)	متى	*matā*
whensoever = whenever		
where (adv)	أين، إلى أين	*aina, ilā aina*
where (conj)	حيث، حيثما	*ḥaithu, ḥaithumā*
whereabouts (adv)	أين، بقرب أين	*aina, bi qurbi aina*
whereas (conj)	حيث أن، مع أن	*ḥaithu an, ma'a an*
whereby (adv)	بأي شيء	*bi ayyi shay'*
wherein (adv)	في أي شيء، في ماذا	*fī ayyi shay', fī mādhā*
whereupon (conj)	عندئذ، ومن ثم	*'inda'idhin, wa min thamma*
wherever (conj)	أينما، حيثما	*ainamā, ḥaithumā*
wherewithal (n)	مال ضروري	*māl ḍarūrī*
whether (conj)	سواء، على أي حالة	*sawā', 'alā ayyi ḥālah*
whey (n)	مصل اللبن	*maṣlul laban*
which (adj/pron)	الذي، التي، أي، ما	*alladhī, allatī, ayy, mā*
whichever (adj/pron)	أيما، أي	*ayyumā, ayy*
whiff (n)	نشقة، نفحة	*nashqah, nafḥah*
while (n)	برهة، حين	*burhah, ḥīn*
while, whilst (conj)	بينما	*bainamā*
whim (n)	هوًى، ميل، وهم	*hawan, mail, wahm*
whimper (v)	نشج، بكى	*nashaja, bakā*
whimper (n)	أنين، نشيج	*anīn, nashīj*
whimsical (adj)	غريب الأطوار	*gharībul aṭwār*
whimsy (n)	نزوة، غرابة	*nazwah, gharābah*
wine (v)	أن، عوى	*anna, 'awā*
whine (n)	عواء، أنين	*'uwā', anīn*
whip (v)	خفق، ضرب، ساط	*khafaqa, ḍaraba, sāṭa*
whip (n)	سوط، حامل السوط، خفقان	*sauṭ, ḥāmilus sauṭ, khafaqān*
whipcord (n)	وتر	*watar*

whipping (n)	ضرب بالسياط	*ḍarb bis siyāṭ*
whippy (adj)	شبيه بالسوط	*shabīh bis sauṭ*
whirl (v)	لف، انعطف، دار	*laffa, in'aṭafa, dāra*
whirl (n)	دوامة، اندفاع، انعطاف	*duwwāmah, indifā', in'iṭāf*
whirlpool (n)	دوامة، دردور	*duwwāmah, durdūr*
whirlwind (n)	زوبعة، إعصار	*zauba'ah, i'ṣār*
whirr (whir) (v/n)	أز، أزيز	*azza, azīz*
whisk (n)	مخفقة، مقشة	*mikhfaqah, miqashshah*
whisk (v)	قش، حرك بسرعة	*qashsha, ḥarraka bi sur'ah*
whisker (n)	شارب	*shārib*
whisky (n)	وسكي، شراب مسكر	*wiskī, sharāb muskir*
whisper (v)	همس، وشوش	*hamasa, washwasha*
whisper (n)	همسة، وشوشة	*hamsah, washwashah*
whistle (v)	صفر، صفر	*ṣafara, ṣaffara*
whistle (n)	صفير، صفارة	*ṣafīr, ṣaffārah*
whit (n)	ذريرة	*dhurairah*
white (adj/n)	أبيض، لون أبيض	*abyaḍ, laun abyaḍ*
white flag	راية الاستسلام	*rāyatul istislām*
white house	بيت أبيض	*bait abyaḍ*
white line	خط أبيض	*khaṭṭ abyaḍ*
whiten (v)	بيض، ابيض	*bayyaḍa, ibyaḍḍa*
whiteness (n)	بياض، نقاء	*bayāḍ, naqā'*
white paper	بيان أبيض	*bayān abyaḍ*
whitewash (n)	ماء الكلس	*mā'ul kals*
whither (adv)	إلى أين، إلى حيث	*ilā aina, ilā ḥaithu*
whittle (v)	برى، نحت	*barā, naḥata*
whiz (whizz) (n)	أزيز، طنين	*azīz, ṭanīn*
whiz (v)	طن، أز	*ṭanna, azza*
who (pron)	من، الذي	*man, alladhī*
whoever (pron)	من، كل من	*man, kullu man*

whole (adj)	تام، كامل	*tāmm, kāmil*
whole (n)	كل، جميع	*kull, jamī'*
whole-hearted (adj)	قلبي، مخلص	*qalbī, mukhliṣ*
whole-heartedly (adv)	بإخلاص، قلبيًّا	*bi ikhlāṣ, qalbiyyan*
wholeness (n)	تمام، كمال	*tamām, kamāl*
whole number	عدد صحيح	*'adad ṣaḥīḥ*
wholesale (n)	بيع بالجملة	*bai' bil jumlah*
wholesaler (n)	بائع بالجملة	*bā'i' bil jumlah*
wholesome (adj)	مفيد، نافع للصحة	*mufīd, nāfi' liṣ ṣiḥḥah*
wholly (adv)	جملةً، كافةً، تماماً	*jumlatan, kāffatan, tamāman*
whom (pron)	من، الذي	*man, alladhī*
whoop (n)	هتاف، شهقة	*hutāf, shahqah*
whoop (v)	هتف، شهق	*hatafa, shahaqa*
whore (n)	مومس، زانية	*mūmis, zāniyah*
whore-house (n)	ماخور	*mākhūr*
whose (pron)	لمن، الذي	*liman, alladhī*
why (adv)	لماذا، بهذا السبب	*limādhā, bi hādhas sabab*
why (interj)	هتاف، تعجب	*hutāf, ta'ajjub*
wick (n)	ذبالة، فتيلة	*dhubālah, fatīlah*
wicked (adj)	مؤذٍ، شرير، ظالم	*mu'dhin, shirrīr, ẓālim*
widckedness (n)	شر، أذىً، خبث	*sharr, adhan, khubth*
wicker (n)	أملود	*umlūd*
wicket (n)	باب صغير، وكت	*bāb ṣaghīr, wakat*
wicket-keeper (n)	حارس الوكت	*ḥārisul wakat*
wide (adj)	عريض، واسع، فصيح	*'arīḍ, wāsi', faṣīḥ*
wide (adv)	إلى حد بعيد	*ilā ḥadd ba'īd*
wide-eyed (adj)	فاغر العينين	*fāghirul 'ainain*
widely (adv)	باتساع، بامتداد	*bittisā', bimtidād*
widen (v)	اتسع، عرض	*ittasa'a, 'arraḍa*
widespread (adj)	ممتد، شائع	*mumtadd, shā'i'*
widow (n)	أرملة	*armalah*

widower (n)	أرمل، أيم	*armal, ayyim*
widowhood (n)	ترمل، أيمة	*tarammul, aimah*
width (n)	سعة، عرض	*sa'ah, 'arḍ*
wield (v)	أدار، أحسن الاستعمال	*adāra, aḥsanal isti'māl*
wife (n)	زوجة، قرينة	*ẓaujah, qarīnah*
wifely (adj)	خاص بالزوجة	*khāṣṣ biz ẓaujah*
wig (n)	جمة، لمة	*jummah, limmah*
wigging (n)	توبيخ، تعنيف	*taubīkh, ta'nīf*
wild (adj)	وحشي، همجي، مفترس	*waḥshī, hamjī, muftaris*
wild (n)	حالة طبيعية	*ḥālah ṭabī'iyyah*
wilderness (n)	قفر، برية	*qafr, barriyyah*
wildfire (n)	حريق هائل	*ḥarīq hā'il*
wildfowl (n)	طريدة	*ṭarīdah*
wilful, willful (adj)	متعمد، تعمدي	*muta'ammid, ta'ammudī*
wilfully (adv)	تعمداً، قصداً	*ta'ammudan, qaṣdan*
wilfulness (n)	قصد، عمد	*qaṣd, 'amd*
will (n)	رغبة، فعل مساعد	*raghbah, fi'l musā'id*
will (v)	رغب، شاء	*raghiba, shā'a*
willing (adj)	راغب، راضٍ	*rāghib, rāḍin*
willingly (adv)	برغبة، اختياراً	*bi raghbah, ikhtiyāran*
willingness (n)	رضىً، رغبة	*riḍan, raghbah*
willow (n)	شجرة الصفصاف	*shajaratuṣ ṣafṣāf*
will-power (n)	قوة الإرادة	*quwwatul irādah*
wily (adj)	محتال، ماكر	*muḥtāl, mākir*
wimple (n)	خمار	*khimār*
win (v)	فاز، كسب، ظفر	*fāza, kasaba, ẓafara*
win (n)	ظفر، فوز	*ẓafar, fauz*
winch (n)	رافعة الأثقال، ونش	*rāfi'atul athqāl, winsh*
wind (n)	ريح، نفس	*rīḥ, nafas*
wind (v)	دس، لف، التف	*dassa, laffa, iltaffa*
windlass (n)	مرفاع	*mirfā'*
windmill (n)	طاحونة هوائية	*ṭāḥūnah hawā'iyyah*

window (n)	شباك، نافذة	*shubbāk, nāfidhah*
window-box (n)	أصيص النافذة	*aṣīṣun nāfidhah*
window-dressing (n)	فن الزخرفة	*fannuz zakhrafah*
window-pipe (n)	قصبة هوائية	*qaṣabah hawā'iyyah*
windshield (n)	حاجب الريح	*ḥājibur rīḥ*
windward (adv)	نحو الريح	*naḥwar rīḥ*
windy (adj)	عنيف، عاصف	*'anīf, 'āṣif*
wine (n)	نبيذ، خمر	*nabīdh, khamr*
wine-cellar (n)	قبو الخمر	*qabwul khamr*
wineglass (n)	كأس الخمر	*ka'sul khamr*
wing (n)	جناح، كنف	*janāḥ, kanaf*
wing (v)	طار، اجتاز	*ṭāra, ijtāza*
wink (v)	طرف، غمز	*ṭarafa, ghamaza*
wink (n)	طرفة عين، غمزة	*ṭarfatu 'ain, ghamzah*
winkle (v)	أخرج بعد جهد	*akhraja ba'da jahd*
winner (n)	فائز، ناجح	*fā'iz, nājiḥ*
winning (adj)	فائز، ناجح، ظافر	*fā'iz, nājiḥ, ẓāfir*
winnings (n)	مكاسب، أرباح	*makāsib, arbāḥ*
winsome (adj)	سار، جذاب، فاتر	*sārr, jadhdhāb, fātir*
winter (n/v)	شتاء، شتى	*shitā', shattā*
wipe (v)	مسح، أزال	*masaḥa, azāla*
wipe (n)	مسحة، مسح	*masḥah, masḥ*
wiper (n)	ممسحة	*mimsaḥah*
wire (n)	سلك، برقية، تلغراف	*silk, barqiyyah, tiligharāf*
wire (v)	ربط بسلك	*rabaṭa bi silk*
wire-haired (adj)	سلكي الشعر	*silkiyyush sha'r*
wireless (adj)	لا سلكي، راديو	*lāsilkī, rādiyū*
wire-worm (n)	دودة سلكية	*dūdah silkiyyah*
wisdom (n)	عقل، حكمة، معرفة	*'aql, ḥikmah, ma'rifah*
wise (adj)	حكيم، بصير	*ḥakīm, baṣīr*
wisely (adv)	بحكمة، ببصيرة	*bi ḥikmah, bi baṣīrah*
wish (v)	ابتغى، تمنى	*ibtaghā, tamannā*

wish (n)	أمنية، رغبة	*umniyyah, raghbah*
wishful (adj)	مشتاق، راغب، تائق	*mushtāq, rāghib, tā'iq*
wistful (adj)	مكتئب، حزين	*mukta'ib, ḥazīn*
wit (n)	ذكاء، فطنة، ظرف	*dhakā', fiṭnah, ẓarf*
witch (n)	ساحرة، عرافة	*sāḥirah, 'arrāfah*
witchcraft (n)	عرافة، سحر	*'irāfah, siḥr*
witchery (n)	عرافة	*'irāfah*
witching (adj)	ساحر، سحري، جذاب	*sāḥir, siḥrī, jadhdhāb*
with (prep)	مع، بـ، لدى	*ma'a, bi, ladā*
withdraw (v)	سحب، استرد	*saḥaba, istaradda*
withdrawal (n)	سحب، انسحاب	*saḥb, insiḥāb*
withdrawn (adj)	منعزل	*mun'azil*
wither (v)	يبس، ذبل، أذبل	*yabusa, dhabula, adhbala*
withering (adj)	مدمر، مزدرٍ	*mudammir, muzdarin*
withhold (v)	أمسك، كبح، منع	*amsaka, kabaḥa, mana'a*
within (prep)	داخل، ضمن، في	*dākhila, ḍimna, fī*
without (prep)	بدون، من غير	*bidūn, min ghair*
without (adv)	خارجاً، خارجيًّا	*khārijan, khārijiyyan*
withstand (v)	صبر، قاوم	*ṣabara, qāwama*
witless (adj)	غبي، مخبل	*ghabī, mukhabbal*
witness (n)	شاهد، شهادة	*shāhid, shahādah*
witness (v)	شهد	*shahida*
witness-box (n)	موقف الشاهد	*mauqifush shāhid*
wittingly (adv)	عمداً، قصداً	*'amdan, qaṣdan*
witty (adj)	ظريف، سريع الخاطر	*ẓarīf, sarī'ul khāṭir*
wizard (n)	ساحر، عراف	*sāḥir, 'arrāf*
wizardry (n)	قوة سحرية	*quwwah siḥriyyah*
woe (n)	ويل، بلية	*wail, baliyyah*
woeful (adj)	فاجع، مغموم، حزين	*fāji', maghmūm, ḥazīn*
wolf (n)	ذئب	*dhi'b*
wolfhound (n)	كلب ذئبي	*kalb dhi'bī*
woman (n)	امرأة، مرأة	*imra'ah, mar'ah*
womanhood (n)	نسوية، حالة المرأة	*niswiyyah, ḥālatul mar'ah*

womanish (adj)	نسوي، أنثوي	*niswī, unthawī*
womanliness (n)	أنوثة	*unūthah*
womanly (adj)	أنثوي، نسوي	*unthawī, niswī*
womb (n)	رحم	*raḥim*
womenfolk (n)	جماعة النساء	*jamā'atun nisā'*
wonder (n)	حيرة، تعجب، أعجوبة	*ḥairah, ta'ajjub, u'jūbah*
wonder (v)	تعجب، اندهش	*ta'ajjaba, indahasha*
wonderful (adj)	عجيب، بديع	*'ajīb, badī'*
wonderland (n)	أرض العجائب	*arḍul 'ajā'ib*
wonderment (n)	روعة، عجب	*rau'ah, 'ajab*
wonderous (adj)	عجيب، مدهش	*'ajīb, mudhish*
wont (n/adj)	عادة، متعود	*'ādah, muta'awwid*
woo (v)	تودد إلى، حاول الإقناع	*tawaddada ilā, ḥāwalal iqnā'*
wood (n)	خشب، حطب	*khashab, ḥaṭab*
woodcock (n)	دجاجة الأرض	*dajājatul arḍ*
woodcraft (n)	خشابة	*khishābah*
woodcutter (n)	حطاب، قطاع الخشب	*ḥaṭṭāb, qaṭṭā'ul khashab*
wooden (adj)	خشبي، من الخشب	*khashabī, minal khashab*
woodland (n)	غابة، حرج	*ghābah, ḥaraj*
woodman (n)	قاطع الأشجار	*qāṭi'ul ashjār*
woodpecker (n)	نقار الخشب	*naqqārul khashab*
woodwind (n)	آلة النفخ	*ālatun nafkh*
woodwork (n)	أشغال الخشب	*ashghālul khashab*
woodworm (n)	سوسة الخشب	*sūsatul khashab*
woody (adj)	ملتف الأشجار	*multafful ashjār*
wool (n)	صوف، وبر	*ṣūf, wabar*
woolen (adj)	صوفي، من الصوف	*ṣūfī, minaṣ ṣūf*
woolens (n)	ملابس صوفية	*malābis ṣūfiyyah*
woolly, wooly (adj)	مصنوع من الصوف	*maṣnū' minaṣ ṣūf*
woozy (adj)	مصاب بدوار، مشوش الذهن	*muṣāb bi duwār, mushawwashudh dhihn*
word (n)	لفظ، كلمة، رسالة	*lafẓ, kalimah, risālah*

wordiness (n)	كثرة الكلام، إطناب	*kathratul kalām, iṭnāb*
wording (n)	عبارة، تعبير	*'ibārah, ta'bīr*
work (n)	شغل، عمل، مؤلف	*shughl, 'amal, mu'allaf*
work (v)	عمل، أدار، اشتغل	*'amila, adāra, ishtaghala*
workable (adj)	ممكن إجراءه	*mumkin ijrā'uh*
workbook (n)	دفتر العمل	*daftarul 'amal*
workday (n)	يوم العمل	*yawmul 'amal*
worker (n)	عامل، صانع	*'āmil, ṣāni'*
work-force (n)	قوة عاملة	*quwwah 'āmilah*
workhorse (n)	حصان الشغل	*ḥiṣānush shughl*
working (adj/n)	عامل، عمل	*'āmil, 'amal*
working capital	رأس المال العامل	*ra'sul māl al 'āmil*
working class	طبقة عاملة	*ṭabaqah 'āmilah*
working day	يوم العمل	*yawmul 'amāl*
workman (n)	عامل، شغيل	*'āmil, shaghīl*
work-table (n)	طاولة الشغل	*ṭāwilatush shughl*
workshop (n)	معمل، ورشة	*ma'mal, warshah*
world (n)	دنيا، عالم	*dunyā, 'ālam*
worldliness (n)	دنيوية، محبة الدنيا	*dunyawiyyah, maḥabbatud dunyā*
worldly (adj)	دنيوي، أرضي	*dunyawī, arḍī*
world power	قوة عالمية	*quwwah 'ālamiyyah*
world war	حرب عالمية	*ḥarb 'ālamiyyah*
world-weary (adj)	ضجر من الدنيا	*ḍajir minad dunyā*
world-wide (adj)	عالمي النطاق	*'ālamiyyun niṭāq*
worm (n)	دودة، حشرة	*dūdah, ḥasharah*
wormeaten (adj)	بالٍ، مسوس	*bālin, musawwas*
worm-hole (n)	ثقب دودي	*thaqb dūdī*
wormy (adj)	كثير الديدان، دودي	*kathīrud dīdān, dūdī*
worn (adj)	منهوك القوى، بال	*manhūkul quwā, bālin*
worn-out (adj)	بال، رثّ	*bālin, rathth*
worried (adj)	مضطرب، قلق	*muḍṭarib, qaliq*

worrisome (adj)	مقلق، مضجر	*muqliq, mudjir*
worry (v)	أزعج، أقلق	*az'aja, aqlaqa*
worry (n)	قلق، اضطراب، هم	*qalaq, idṭirāb, hamm*
worse (adj)	أسوأ من	*aswa' min*
worsen (v)	أردأ، أساء	*arda'a, asā'a*
worship (n)	عبادة، إكرام	*'ibādah, ikrām*
worship (v)	عبد، سجد	*'abada, sajada*
worshipful (adj)	مبجل، مكرم	*mubajjal, mukarram*
worshipper (n)	عابد، مصلٍّ	*'ābid, muṣallin*
worst (adj)	أردأ، أسوأ	*arda', aswa'*
worst (v)	هزم، غلب	*hazama, ghalaba*
worth (n)	قيمة، ثروة، جدارة	*qīmah, tharwah, jadārah*
worth (adj)	ذو قيمة، لائق	*dhū qīmah, lā'iq*
worthily (adv)	بجدارة، بأهلية	*bi jadārah, bi ahliyyah*
worthiness (n)	استحقاق، أهلية	*istiḥqāq, ahliyyah*
worthless (adj)	عديم القيمة، تافه	*'adīmul qīmah, tāfih*
worthlessness (n)	رداءة، بطلان	*radā'ah, buṭlān*
worthwhile (adj)	جدير بالاهتمام	*jadīr bil ihtimām*
worthy (adj)	جدير، مستأهل	*jadīr, musta'hil*
would (v)	فعل مساعد	*fi'l musā'id*
would-be (adj)	مدعٍ، زاعم	*mudda'in, zā'im*
wound (v)	جرح، كلم	*jaraḥa, kalama*
wound (n)	جرح، كلم	*jurḥ, kalm*
wounded (adj)	جريح، كليم	*jarīḥ, kalīm*
wrangle (v)	تجادل، تشاحن	*tajādala, tashāḥanah*
wrangle (n)	مجادلة، مشاحنة	*mujādalah, mushāḥanah*
wrap (v)	لف، التف، غطى	*laffa, iltaffa, ghaṭṭā*
wrap (n)	غلاف، معطف	*ghilāf, mi'ṭaf*
wrapper (n)	غلاف، غطاء، دثار	*ghilāf, ghiṭā', dithār*
wrapping (n)	غطاء، غلاف	*ghiṭā', ghilāf*
wrath (n)	حنق، غيظ، سخط	*ḥanaq, ghaiẓ, sukhṭ*
wrathful (adj)	حانق، ساخط	*ḥāniq, sākhiṭ*

wreak (v)	انتقم، صب غضبه	*Intaqama, ṣabba ghaḍabahu*
wreath (n)	إكليل الأزهار، ضفيرة	*iklīlul azhār, ḍafīrah*
wreathe (v)	التف، جدل، ضفر	*iltaffa, jadala, ḍafara*
wreck (n)	سفينة أو طائرة متحطمة	*safīnah aw ṭā'irah mutaḥaṭṭimah*
wreck (v)	غرق، حطم	*gharaqa, ḥaṭṭama*
wreckage (n)	حطام السفينة	*ḥuṭāmus safīnah*
wrench (v)	حرف، لوى	*ḥarrafa, lawā*
wrench (n)	التواء، انقلاب مفاجئ	*iltiwā', inqilāb mufāji'*
wrest (v)	نزع بعنف، استخلص	*naza'a bi 'unf, istakhlaṣa*
wrestle (v)	صارع، تصارع	*ṣāra'a, taṣāra'a*
wrestler (n)	مصارع	*muṣāri'*
wrestling (n)	مصارعة، ملابطة	*muṣāra'ah, mulābaṭah*
wretch (n)	خسيس، حقير	*khasīs, ḥaqīr*
wretched (adj)	متعوس، دنيء	*mat'ūs, danī'*
wretchedly (adv)	بتعاسة، برداءة	*bi ta'āsah, bi radā'ah*
wretchedness (n)	تعاسة، شقاء	*ta'āsah, shaqā'*
wriggle (v)	تمعج، لوى	*tama''aja, lawwā*
wring (v)	استنزف، عصر	*istanzafa, 'aṣara*
wring (n)	استنزاف، عصر	*istinzāf, 'aṣr*
wrinkle (v)	جعد، تجعد	*ja''ada, taja''ada*
wrinkle (n)	جعدة، تجعد	*ja'dah, taja''ud*
wrist (n)	رسغ، معصم	*rusgh, mi'ṣam*
wristlet (n)	عصابة المعصم	*'iṣābatul mi'ṣam*
wrist-watch (n)	ساعة اليد	*sā'atul yad*
writ (n)	إعلام قضائي، وثيقة	*i'lām qaḍā'ī, wathīqah*
write (v)	كتب، ألف، سجل	*Kataba, allafa, sajjala*
writer (n)	كاتب، مؤلف	*kātib, mu'allif*
writhe (v)	جدل، لوى، تلوى	*Jadala, lawā, talawwā*
writing (n)	كتابة، خط	*kitābah, khaṭṭ*
writing-desk (n)	مكتب	*Maktab*

writing-paper (n)	ورق الكتابة	*waraqul kitābah*
written (adj)	مكتوب	*maktūb*
wrong (adj)	مخطئ، غير صحيح	*mukhṭI', ghair ṣaḥīḥ*
wrong (n)	خطأ، ظلم	*khaṭa', ẓulm*
wrong (v)	أخطأ، أساء إلى	*akhṭa'a, asā'a ilā*
wrongdoer (n)	آثم، ظالم	*āthim, ẓālim*
wrongdoing (n)	إثم، خطأ، ظلم	*ithm, khaṭa', ẓulm*
wrongful (adj)	ظالم، جائر	*ẓālim, jā'ir*
wrongfully (adv)	ظلماً، حيفاً، اعتداء	*ẓulman, ḥaifan, i'tidā'an*
wrongheaded (adj)	عنيد، متشبث	*'anīd, mutashabbith*
wrongly (adv)	ظلماً، خطأً	*ẓulman, khaṭa'an*
wrought (adj)	منمق، مزخرف	*munammaq, muzakhraf*

X

X chromosome (n)	صبغية سينية	*ṣibghiyyah sīniyyah*
xenon (n)	زينون	*zīnūn*
xenophobia (n)	رهاب الأجانب	*ruhābul ajānib*
xerox (n)	نسخة فوتوغرافية	*nuskhah fūtūgharāfiyyah*
xmas = christmas		
x-ray (n)	أشعة سينية	*ashi''ah sīniyyah*
x-ray (v)	صور بأشعة سينية	*ṣawwara bi ashi''ah sīniyyah*
xylophone (n)	خشبية	*khashabiyyah*

Y

yacht (n)	سفينة شراعية صغيرة، يخت	*Safīnah shirā'iyyah ṣaghīrah, yakht*
yack (v/n)	ثرثر، ثرثرة	*tharthara, tharthārah*
yahoo (n)	شخص جلف	*shakhṣ jilf*
yank (v)	خلع، نزع	*khala'a, naza'a*
yard (n)	ساحة، زريبة، ياردة	*sāḥah, zarībah, yārdah*

yard-stick (n)	عصا ياردية	*'aṣā yārdiyyah*
yarn (n)	غزل، حكاية	*ghazl, ḥikāyah*
yawl (n)	يول، مركب شراعي	*yūl, markab shirā'ī*
yawn (v)	تثاءب	*tathā'aba*
yawn (n)	تثاءب، فجوة	*tathā'ub, fajwah*
Y chromosome	صبغية صادية	*ṣibghiyyah ṣāddiyyah*
ye (pron)	أنتم، أنتن	*antum, antunna*
yea (adv)	أي نعم، بلى	*ay na'am, balā*
year (n)	سنة، عام، حول	*sanah, 'ām, ḥaul*
year-book (n)	حولية	*ḥauliyyah*
yearling (n)	حولي	*ḥawlī*
year-long (adj)	دائم سنة	*dā'im sanatan*
yearly (adv/adj)	سنويًا، سنوي	*sanawiyyan, sanawī*
yearn (v)	اشتاق، تاق	*ishtāqa, tāqa*
yearning (n)	توق شديد	*tauq shadīd*
yell (v)	صرخ، زعق، هتف	*ṣarakha, za'aqa, hatafa*
yell (n)	صرخة، زعقة	*ṣarkhah, za'qah*
yellow (adj/n)	أصفر، لون أصفر	*aṣfar, laun aṣfar*
yellow fever	حمى صفراء	*ḥummā ṣafrā'*
yellowish (adj)	ضارب إلى الصفرة	*ḍārib ilaṣ ṣufrah*
yellowishness (n)	صفرة	*ṣufrah*
yellowy (adj)	مصفر	*muṣaffar*
yelp (n/v)	عواء، عوى	*'uwā', 'awā*
yeoman (n)	فلاح صغير	*fallāḥ ṣaghīr*
yeoman's service	خدمة عظيمة	*khidmah 'aẓīmah*
yes (interj)	نعم، بلى	*na'am, balā*
yes-man (n)	إمعة، رجل الموافقة	*imma'ah, rajulul muwāfaqah*
yesterday (n/adv)	أمس	*Ams*
yeaster-year (n)	عام ماضي	*'ām māḍī*
yet (adv)	حتى الآن، أيضاً، حتى	*ḥattal ān, aiḍan, ḥattā*
yield (v)	أنتج، أذعن، خضع	*antaja, adh'ana, khaḍa'a*

yeilding (adj)	مطواع، لين	*miṭwā', layyin*
yoga (n)	يوغا	*yūghā*
yoke (n)	نير، ناف	*nīr, nāf*
yolk (n)	مح البيض	*muḥḥul baiḍ*
you (pron)	أنت، أنت، أنتم	*anta, anti, antum*
young (adj)	صغير السن، حديث	*ṣaghīrus sinn, ḥadīth*
young (n)	جرو، فرخ	*jarw, farkh*
younger (n/adj)	أصغر عمراً من...	*aṣgharu 'umran min*
youngest (adj)	أصغر	*aṣghar*
youngster (n)	طفل حديث السن	*ṭifl ḥadīthus sinn*
your (pron)	لك، لك، لكم	*laka, laki, lakum*
yours (pron)	لك، لك، لكم	*laka, laki, lakum*
yourself (pron)	نفسك، بنفسك	*Nafsak, bi nafsik*
youth (n)	شباب، زمن الصبا	*shabāb, zamanuṣ ṣibā*
youthful (adj)	شاب، فتًى	*shābb, fatan*
youthfulness (n)	شباب، فتاء	*shabāb, fatā'*
yule (n)	عيد الميلاد	*'īdul mīlād*

Z

zany (adj)	مضحك، هزلي	*muḍḥik, hazlī*
zeal (n)	حماسة، حمية	*ḥamāsah, ḥamiyyah*
zealot (n)	متحمس، غيور	*mutaḥammis, ghayyūr*
zealotry (n)	تحمس، تعصب	*taḥammus, ta'aṣṣub*
zealous (adj)	متحمس، غيور	*mutaḥammis, ghayyūr*
zealously (adv)	بحماسة	*bi ḥamāsah*
zebra (n)	حمار عتابي	*ḥimār 'atābī*
zenith (n)	ذروة، أوج، سمت	*dhirwah, auj, samt*
zephyr (n)	نسيم عليل	*nasīm 'alīl*
zero (n)	صفر	*ṣifr*
zero-hour (n)	ساعة الصفر	*sā'atuṣ ṣifr*

zest (n)	استمتاع، لذة شديدة	*istimtā‘, ladhdhah shadīdah*
zestful (adj)	متمتع	*mutamatti‘*
zigzag (n)	خط متعرج	*khaṭṭ muta‘arrij*
zigzag (v)	تعرج، تمعج	*ta‘arraja, tama‘‘aja*
Zionism (n)	صهيونية	*ṣahyūniyyah*
Zionist (n)	صهيوني	*ṣahyūnī*
zodiac (n)	دائرة البروج	*dā’iratul burūj*
zonal (adj)	منطقي، نطاقي	*minṭaqī, niṭāqī*
zone (n)	منطقة، دائرة	*minṭaqah, dā’irah*
zoo (n)	حديقة الحيوانات	*ḥadīqatul ḥaiwānāt*
zoological (adj)	حيواني	*ḥaiwānī*
zoological garden	حديقة الحيوانات	*ḥadīqatul ḥaiwānāt*
zoologist (n)	إخصائي في علم الحيوان	*ikhṣā’ī fī ‘ilmil ḥaiwān*
zoology (n)	علم الحيوان	*‘ilmul ḥaiwān*
zoom (v)	زوم، زام	*zawwama, zāma*
zoom lens (n)	عدسة التزويم	*‘adasatut tazwīm*